The cover for this textbook illustrates that retailing is a dynamic industry utilizing technologic innovation like this electronic shelf tag to provide a more rewarding shopping experience. Some examples of the technologies highlighted in this textbook are the use of the Internet for providing information and selling products and services to customers; use of social media and digital signage to communicate with customers; application of geographic information system (GIS) technology to determine store locations; integrated supply chain management systems, RFID, and CPFR (collaboration, planning, forecasting and replenishment) systems; analysis of customer databases to identify and tailor offerings to customers; and the use of profit optimization decision support systems for setting prices in different markets, taking markdowns, and allocating merchandise.

Through the use of these technologies, the United States remains the world's most sophisticated retail market. However, retail sales in the BRIC countries (Brazil, Russia, India, and China) are attractive markets with high potential growth. This edition highlights the growth of global retailers and the issues that they face when entering emerging markets.

Finally, this edition also highlights retailers' heightened concern for societal issues, the environment, and the people involved in making and transporting merchandise to markets. Retailers are buying merchandise with an eye toward its carbon footprint and other ecological factors. They have taken an active role in making sure that workers are treated humanely and can earn a living wage.

RETAILING MANAGEMENT

EIGHTH EDITION

Michael Levy, Ph.D.
Babson College

Barton A. Weitz, Ph.D.
University of Florida

Introducing Digital Co-Author:
Lauren Skinner Beitelspacher, Ph.D.
University of Alabama at Birmingham

McGraw-Hill Irwin

RETAILING MANAGEMENT
Published by McGraw-Hill/Irwin, a business unit of The McGraw-Hill Companies, Inc., 1221 Avenue of the
Americas, New York, NY, 10020. Copyright © 2012, 2009, 2007, 2004, 2001, 1998, 1995, 1992 by The McGraw-Hill

Some ancillaries, including electronic and print components, may not be available to customers outside the
United States.

This book is printed on acid-free paper.

1 2 3 4 5 6 7 8 9 0 DOW/DOW 1 0 9 8 7 6 5 4 3 2 1

ISBN   978-0-07-353002-4
MHID   0-07-353002-6

Vice president and editor-in-chief: *Brent Gordon*
Editorial director: *Paul Ducham*
Executive editor: *Sankha Basu*
Executive director of development: *Ann Torbert*
Editorial coordinator: *Gabriela Gonzalez*
Vice president and director of marketing: *Robin J. Zwettler*
Marketing director: *Amee Mosley*
Associate marketing manager: *Jaime Halteman*
Vice president of editing, design, and production: *Sesha Bolisetty*
Manager of photo, design & publishing tools: *Mary Conzachi*
Senior buyer: *Carol A. Bielski*
Senior designer: *Mary Kazak Sander*
Senior photo research coordinator: *Keri Johnson*
Senior media project manager: *Greg Bates*
Interior design: *Cara Hawthorne*
Cover design: *Pam Verros*
Cover images: © *Peter Lambert/ZBD Displays Ltd.; Liz Whitaker*
Typeface: *10.5/12 Janson*
Compositor: *Aptara®, Inc.*
Printer: *R. R. Donnelley*

Library of Congress Cataloging-in-Publication Data

Levy, Michael, 1950-
    Retailing management / Michael Levy, Barton A. Weitz. — 8th ed.
      p. cm.
    Includes index.
    ISBN-13: 978-0-07-353002-4 (alk. paper)
    ISBN-10: 0-07-353002-6 (alk. paper)
    1. Retail trade—Management.   I. Weitz, Barton A.   II. Title.
HF5429.L4828 2012
658.8'7—dc22

                              2010048858

ABOUT THE AUTHORS

Michael Levy, Ph.D.
Babson College
mlevy@babson.edu

Michael Levy, Ph.D., is the Charles Clarke Reynolds Professor of Marketing and Director of the Retail Supply Chain Institute at Babson College (www.babson.edu/retail). He received his Ph.D. in business administration from The Ohio State University and his undergraduate and MS degrees in business administration from the University of Colorado at Boulder. He taught at Southern Methodist University before joining the faculty as professor and chair of the marketing department at the University of Miami.

Professor Levy received the 2009 Lifetime Achievement Award by the American Marketing Association Retailing Special Interest Group. He has developed a strong stream of research in retailing, business logistics, financial retailing strategy, pricing, and sales management. He has published over 50 articles in leading marketing and logistics journals, including the *Journal of Retailing, Journal of Marketing, Journal of the Academy of Marketing Science,* and *Journal of Marketing Research.* He currently serves on the editorial review boards of the *Journal of Retailing, International Journal of Logistics Management, International Journal of Logistics and Materials Management,* and *European Business Review.* He is coauthor of *Marketing* (3e, 2012) *and M-Marketing* (2e, 2011), both with McGraw-Hill/Irwin. Professor Levy was co-editor of *Journal of Retailing* from 2001 to 2007. He co-chaired the 1993 Academy of Marketing Science conference and the 2006 Summer AMA conference.

Professor Levy has worked in retailing and related disciplines throughout his professional life. Prior to his academic career, he worked for several retailers and a housewares distributor in Colorado. He has performed research projects with many retailers and retail technology firms, including Accenture, Federated Department Stores, Khimetrics (SAP), Mervyn's, Neiman Marcus, ProfitLogic (Oracle), Zale Corporation, and numerous law firms.

Barton A. Weitz, Ph.D.
University of Florida
bart.weitz@cba.ufl.edu

Barton A. Weitz, Ph.D., received an undergraduate degree in electrical engineering from MIT and an MBA and a Ph.D. in business administration from Stanford University. He has been a member of the faculty at the UCLA Graduate School of Business and the Wharton School at the University of Pennsylvania and is presently the JCPenney Eminent Scholar Chair in Retail Management in the Warrington College of Business Administration at the University of Florida.

Professor Weitz is the founder of the David F. Miller Center for Retailing Education and Research at the University of Florida (www.cba.ufl.edu/mkt/retailcenter). The activities of the center are supported by contributions from 35 retailers and firms supporting the retail industry, including JCPenney, Macy's, Walmart, Office Depot, Walgreens, Target, Build-A-Bear, Brown Shoe, NPD, and the International Council of Shopping Centers. Each year, the center places more than 250 undergraduates in paid summer internships and management trainee positions with retail firms and funds research on retailing issues and problems.

Professor Weitz has won awards for teaching excellence and made numerous presentations to industry and academic groups. He has published over 50 articles in leading academic journals on channel relationships, electronic retailing, store design, salesperson effectiveness, and sales force and human resource management. His research has been recognized with two Louis Stern Awards for his contributions to channel management research and a Paul Root Award for the *Journal of Marketing* article that makes the greatest contribution to marketing practice. He serves on the editorial review boards of the *Journal of Retailing, Journal of Marketing, International Journal of Research in Marketing, Marketing Science,* and *Journal of Marketing Research.* He is a former editor of the *Journal of Marketing Research.*

Professor Weitz has been the chair of the American Marketing Association and a member of the board of directors of the National Retail Federation, the National Retail Foundation, and the American Marketing Association. In 1989, he was honored as the AMA/Irwin Distinguished Educator in recognition of his contributions to the marketing discipline. He was selected by the National Retail Federation as Retail Educator of the Year in 2005 and been recognized for lifetime achievements by American Marketing Association Retailing, Sales, and Inter-Organizational Special Interests Groups.

PREFACE

Retailing is a high-tech, global, growth industry that plays a vital economic role in society. Our objective in preparing the eighth edition is to stimulate student interest in retailing courses and careers by capturing the exciting, challenging, and rewarding opportunities facing both retailers and firms that sell their products and services to retailers, such as IBM and Procter & Gamble. The textbook focuses on the strategic issues facing the retail industry and provides a current, informative, "good read" for students.

As retailing continues to evolve and change, so do the ways in which we communicate to our students. We are very excited to introduce *Connect Marketing* for *Retailing Management*, 8e. While you may have seen *Connect Marketing* with other McGraw-Hill products, this is the first time it is offered for Retailing Management. Students will find lectures, practice materials, and eBook links for each chapter. A grade management system makes its use easy for the instructor. Lauren Skinner Beitelspacher, Ph.D., University of Alabama at Birmingham, is our digital coauthor, overseeing and leading the development of this exciting new addition to our package.

NEW FEATURES

In preparing the eight edition of *Retailing Management*, we have revised the textbook to address five important developments in retailing: (1) the increasing role of the Internet in retailing, (2) new ways to communicate with customers, (3) the greater emphasis on social responsibility by retailers, (4) the use of technology and analytical methods for decision making, and (5) globalization.

Evolving Role of the Internet Fifteen years ago, many experts thought that consumers would abandon the mall and shop for most products and services using the Internet. Traditional retailers would be replaced by a new breed of techno-savvy entrepreneurs. Now it is clear that the Internet is not replacing the traditional retail industry but rather enhancing the activities undertaken by traditional retailers—retailers that use multiple channels (Internet, catalog, stores, and mobile) to interact with their customers.

In the eighth edition, we go beyond Chapter 3, which is dedicated to multichannel retailing, to discuss Internet retailing applications throughout the textbook. For example,

- Use of the Internet for selection and training of employees (Chapters 9 and 16).
- Use of the Internet for communicating with vendors (Chapters 11, 12, and 13).
- Internet-based digital signage in stores (Chapter 17).
- Providing information and customer service through Web-enabled kiosks and POS terminals (Chapter 18).

New Ways to Communicate with Customers Retailers communicate with customers using a mix of methods, such as advertising, sales promotion, publicity, e-mail, blogs, and social media using Twitter, Facebook, YouTube, and blogs. Although many of these traditional methods, such as advertising, have been used for decades, Internet enabling technology has changed the way retailers utilize their promotional budgets and communicate with customers. For example,

- The impact of social networks on buying behavior (Chapter 4).
- The increased use of cell phones to allow customers to make price comparisons, locate merchandise, receive coupons, and buy merchandise (Chapter 15).

V

- The use of blogs, Twitter, Facebook, and YouTube to promote retailers and specific merchandise, as well as to collect customer attitudes about retailers and reviews of their product (Chapter 15).

- The use of the technology to customize and deliver coupons and other targeted promotions to customers. Customers also utilize Internet sites to find coupons to redeem at their favorite retailers (Chapter 15).

Social Responsibility of Retailers   Retail institutions are pervasive in our society and thus have a major impact on the welfare of their customers, suppliers, and employees. Given the importance of their societal role, both consumers and retailers are becoming more concerned about social issues facing the world, such as global warming, immigration, health care, and working conditions in less developed economies. Some of these social responsibility issues, identified with legal/ethical icons in the margins and discussed in the eighth edition, are:

- Consumer interest in green products (Chapter 4).

- Ethical issues in sourcing merchandise globally (Chapter 13).

- Considering sustainability issues in store operations (Chapter 16) and design (Chapter 17).

Use of Technology in Retailing   Retailing is a high-tech industry with retailers increasingly using communications and information systems technologies and analytical models to increase operating efficiencies and improve customer service. Some of these new technology applications, identified with technology icons in the margins and discussed in the eighth edition, are:

- Use of Web sites to sell products and services to customers (Chapter 3).

- Providing a seamless multichannel (stores, Web sites, and catalogs) interface so that customers can interact with retailers anytime, anywhere (Chapter 3).

- Stores of the future that use technology to provide a more rewarding shopping experience (Chapter 3).

- Application of geographic information system (GIS) technology for store location decisions (Chapter 8).

- Internet applications for effective human resource management (Chapter 9).

- Integrated supply chain management systems (Chapter 10).

- RFID (radio frequency identification) technology to improve supply chain efficiency (Chapter 10).

- CPFR (collaboration, planning, forecasting, and replenishment) systems for coordinating vendors and retailer activities (Chapter 10).

- Analysis of customer databases to determine customer lifetime value, target promotions toward a retailer's best customers, and undertake market basket analyses (Chapter 11).

- Implementation of marketing programs to increase customer share of wallet (Chapter 11).

- Sophisticated inventory management and assortment planning systems (Chapter 12).

- Reverse auctions for buying merchandise (Chapter 13).

- Use of profit-optimization decision support systems for setting prices in different markets and taking markdowns (Chapter 14).

- Developing targeted promotions using customer databases (Chapter 15).

- Internet-based training for store employees (Chapter 16).

- Decision support systems for scheduling sales associates (Chapter 16).

- EAS technology designed to reduce shoplifting (Chapter 16).

- Creating planograms to optimize sales and profits from merchandise categories (Chapter 17).
- Digital signage to reduce cost and increase message flexibility (Chapter 17 and a new case on Harrods Department Store).
- In-store kiosks, mobile devices, and the Internet to improve customer service (Chapter 18).
- Instant chat for servicing online customers (Chapter 18).

Globalization of the Retail Industry Retailing is a global industry. With a greater emphasis being placed on private-label merchandise, retailers are working with manufacturers located throughout the world to acquire merchandise. In addition, retailers are increasingly looking to international markets for growth opportunities. For instance, Sweden-based furniture retailer IKEA is successful because it is able to manufacture and sell relatively low priced stylish furniture to like-minded customers around the globe. Some of the global retailing issues, identified with icons in the margins, examined in this edition are:

- Retail efficiencies in different economies (Chapter 1).
- Illustrations of global expansion by retailers (Chapter 2).
- Cultural impacts on customer buying behavior (Chapter 4).
- Keys to successful entry into international markets (Chapter 5).
- Evaluation of international growth opportunities (Chapter 5).
- Differences in location opportunities in global markets (Chapter 7).
- Employee management issues in international markets (Chapters 9 and 16).
- Global sourcing of private-label merchandise (Chapter 13).
- Cultural differences in customer service needs (Chapter 18).

BASIC PHILOSOPHY

The eighth edition of *Retailing Management* maintains the basic philosophy of the previous seven editions. We continue to focus on key strategic issues with an emphasis on financial considerations and implementation through merchandise and store management. These strategic and tactical issues are examined for a broad spectrum of retailers, both large and small, domestic and international, selling merchandise and services.

Strategic Focus The entire textbook is organized around a model of strategic decision making outlined in Exhibit 1–4 in Chapter 1. Each section and chapter relates back to this overarching strategic framework. In addition, the second section of the book focuses exclusively on critical strategic decisions, such as selecting target markets, developing a sustainable competitive advantage, building an organizational structure and information and distribution systems to support the strategic direction, building customer loyalty, and managing customer relationships. The text explores in depth the resources that retailers use to develop sustainable competitive advantage, such as

- Selecting store location (Chapters 7, 8).
- Developing and maintaining human resources (Chapter 9).
- Managing information systems and supply chains (Chapter 10).
- Managing customer relationship management and loyalty programs (Chapter 11).

Financial Analysis The success of any retailer, like any other business, depends on its ability to make a profit, provide an adequate return to its owners, and be financially stable. The financial problems experienced by some well-known retail firms, like Circuit City, Sharper Image, and K-B Toys, highlight the need for a thorough understanding of the financial implications of strategic retail decisions. Financial analysis is emphasized in selected chapters, such as Chapter 6 on the overall strategy of the firm using the strategic profit model and the financial strength of retailers using cash flow and ratio analysis, Chapter 11 on the evaluation of customer lifetime value, and Chapter 12 on retail buying systems. Financial issues are also raised in the sections on negotiating leases, bargaining with suppliers, pricing merchandise, developing a communication budget, and compensating salespeople.

Implementing a Retail Strategy Although developing a retail strategy is critical to long-term financial performance, the execution of strategies is as important as the development of the strategy. Traditionally, retailers have exalted the merchant prince—the buyer who knew what the hot trends were going to be. While we provide a thorough review of merchandise management issues, the emphasis in retailing is shifting from merchandise management to the block and tackling of getting merchandise to the stores and customers and providing excellent customer service and an exciting shopping experience. Due to this shift toward store management, most students embarking on retail careers go into distribution and store management rather than merchandise buying. Thus, this text devotes an entire chapter to information systems and supply chain management and an entire section to store management.

Up-to-Date Information Retailing is a very dynamic industry, with new ideas and formats developing and traditional retailers constantly adapting to the changing environment or suffering financially. Most of the examples provided in the text have taken place in the last two years.

Balanced Approach The eighth edition continues to offer a balanced approach for teaching an introductory retailing course by including descriptive, how-to, and conceptual information in a highly readable format.

Descriptive Information Students can learn about the vocabulary and practice of retailing from the descriptive information throughout the text. Examples of this material are:

- Leading U.S. and international retailers (Chapter 1).
- Management decisions made by retailers (Chapter 1).
- Types of store-based and nonstore retailers (Chapter 2 and 3).
- Approaches for entering international markets (Chapter 5).
- Location options (Chapter 7).
- Lease terms (Chapter 8).
- Organization structure of typical retailers (Chapter 9).
- Flow of information and merchandise (Chapter 10).
- Branding strategies (Chapter 13).
- Methods for communicating with customers (Chapter 15).
- Store layout options and merchandise display techniques (Chapter 17).
- Career opportunities (Appendix 1A to Chapter 1).

How-to Information *Retailing Management* goes beyond this descriptive information to illustrate how and why retailers, large and small, make decisions. Procedures with examples are provided for making the following decisions:

- Managing a multichannel operation (Chapter 3).
- Scanning the environment and developing a retail strategy (Chapter 5).
- Analyzing the financial implications of retail strategy (Chapter 6).
- Evaluating location decisions (Chapter 8).
- Developing a merchandise assortment and budget plan (Chapters 12).

- Negotiating with vendors (Chapter 13).
- Pricing merchandise (Chapter 14).
- Recruiting, selecting, training, evaluating, and compensating sales associates (Chapter 16).
- Designing the layout for a store (Chapter 17).
- Providing superior customer service (Chapter 18).

Conceptual Information   *Retailing Management* also includes conceptual information that enables students to understand why decisions are made, as outlined in the text. As Mark Twain said, "There is nothing as practical as a good theory." Students need to know these basic concepts so they can make effective decisions in new situations. Examples of this conceptual information in the eighth edition are:

- Customers' decision-making process (Chapter 4).
- The strategic profit model and approach for evaluating financial performance (Chapter 6).
- Price theory and marginal analysis (Chapters 14 and 15).
- Motivation of employees (Chapter 16).
- In-store shopping behaviors (Chapter 17).
- The Service Gaps model for service quality management (Chapter 18).

Student-Friendly Textbook   This eighth edition creates interest and involves students in the course and the industry by making the textbook a "good read" for students. We use Refacts (retailing factoids), Retailing Views, and retail manager profiles at the beginning of each chapter to engage students.

Refacts   We have updated and added more interesting facts about retailing, called Refacts, in the margins of each chapter. Did you know that on average, Americans, with mobile phone Internet access, spend 2.7 hours a day connected to the Internet through their mobile phones? The primary usage of the mobile Internet connection is for socializing with others. Or that the teabag was developed by a Macy's buyer and pantyhose was developed by a JCPenney buyer?

Retailing Views   Each chapter contains either new or updated vignettes called Retailing Views to relate concepts to activities and decisions made by retailers. The vignettes look at major retailers, like Walmart, Walgreens, JCPenney, Target, Kohl's, Neiman Marcus, and Macy's, that interview students on campus for management training positions. They also discuss innovative retailers like REI, Starbucks, Zara, Mango, Top Shop, The Container Store, Sephora, Curves, Chico's, and Bass Pro Shops. Finally, a number of Retailing Views focus on entrepreneurial retailers competing effectively against national chains.

Profiles of Retail Managers   To illustrate the challenges and opportunities in retailing, each chapter in the eighth edition begins with a brief profile, in their own words, of a manager or industry expert whose job or expertise is related to the material in the chapter. These profiles range from Debbie Harvey, President of Ron Jon Surf Shop and Mike Odell, CEO of Pep Boys to Heather Graham, a Walgreen's store manager and Darius Jackson, a JCPenney buyer. They include people who have extensive experience in a specific aspect of retailing, like Krista Gibson, VP Marketing, at Chili's and Ramesh Murthy, VP Inventory Replenishment at CVS/Caremark.

The profiles illustrate how senior executives view the industry and suggest career opportunities for college students. They also provide students with firsthand information about what people in retailing do and the rewards and challenges of their jobs and careers.

SUPPLEMENTAL MATERIALS

To enhance the student learning experience, the eighth edition includes new cases and videos illustrating state-of-the-art retail practices, a Web-based computer exercise package for students, and a comprehensive online instructor's manual with additional cases and teaching suggestions.

Get Out and Do It! exercises are found at the end of each chapter. These exercises suggest projects that students can undertake by visiting local retail stores, surfing the Internet, or using the student Web site. A continuing assignment exercise is included so that students can engage in an exercise involving the same retailer throughout the course. The exercises are designed to provide a hands-on learning experience for students.

Monthly Newsletter with Short Cases based on recent retailing articles appearing in the business and trade press. Instructors can use these short cases to stimulate class discussions about current issues confronting retailers. The newsletter is e-mailed to instructors and archived on the text's Web page.

Ten New Cases including Walmart, Target Marketing with Google Adwords, Netflix Personalizes the Customer's Experience, Tiffany's and Blue Nile: Comparing Financial Performance, Attracting Gen-Y to a Retail Career, American Furniture Warehouse Sources Globally, Merchandise Exclusively for JCPenney, Active Endeavors Analyzes Its Customer Database, Generating Advertising Revenue From a Digital Screen Network and B-G Merchandise Budget Plan. All 38 cases in the textbook are either new or updated with current information. A number of the cases, such as Starbucks, Build-A-Bear, and Walmart, have videos that complement the written case.

Eight New Videos among the 35 video segments available to illustrate issues addressed in the text. The topics addressed by the new videos include using technology to enhance the shopping experience, Zappos' customer service, HR management at Hot Topics, Tesco's entry into the U.S., customer centricity at Best Buy, and Whole Foods' retail strategy.

Web Site for Students and Instructors (www.mhhe.com/levy8e) Just as retailers are using the Internet to help their customers, we have developed a Web site to help students and instructors use the eight edition of this textbook effectively. Some of the features on the Web site are:

- Multiple-choice questions on the student site.
- Experiential exercises for students.
- Chapter-by-chapter Instructor Manual coverage.
- Case and video notes.
- Retailing trade publications and professional associations.
- News articles about current events in retailing.
- PowerPoint slides summarizing key issues in each chapter.
- Hot links to retailing news sites and sites associated with the Internet exercises in the textbook.
- Additional cases about retailers.

ACKNOWLEDGMENTS

Throughout the development of this text, several outstanding individuals were integrally involved and made substantial contributions. First, Britt Hackmann (Babson College) for her important assistance in doing research for the book, writing examples, and preparing the manuscript for publication. We thank Lauren Skinner Beitelspacher of University of Alabama at Birmingham, for developing *Connect Marketing* for *Retailing Management*. We also recognize the invaluable contributions of Hope Bober Corrigan (Loyola College in Maryland) for editing the video package, and providing many useful teaching activities found in the Instructor's Manual. We also thank Kate Woodworth for helping us write and revise the Monthly Newsletter, several Retailing Views, and cases. We express our sincere appreciation to Dr. Nancy Murray (University of Wisconsin-Stout) for preparing the Test Bank and Chapter Quizzes and to Leroy Robinson, Jr., PhD (University of Houston-Clear Lake) for preparing the Instructor's Manual and PowerPoint slides. Special thanks go to Tracy Meyer (University of North Carolina Wilmington) for preparing the "Starting a Franchise Business." Appendix, to Christian Tassin (University of Florida) for preparing the appendix on "Starting Your Own Retail Business." We'd like especially to acknowledge the contribution of Kantar Retail. Their daily news briefing and research reports facilitated the research that has gone into this text.

We also appreciate the contributions of Margaret Jones, Cecilia Schulz and Betsy Trobaugh (David F. Miller Center for Retailing Education and Research, University of Florida), who provided invaluable assistance in preparing the manuscript.

The support, expertise, and occasional coercion from our Managing Developmental Editor, Gabriela Gonzalez, are greatly appreciated. The book would also never have come together without the editorial and production staff at McGraw-Hill/Irwin: Doug Hughes, Mary Conzachi, Harvey Yep, Carol Bielski, Mary Sander, Keri Johnson, and Gregory Bates.

Retailing Management has also benefited significantly from contributions by several leading executives and scholars in retailing and related fields. We would like to thank:

Tim Adams
Macy's

Mark Blakeley
Oracle

Cynthia Cohen
Strategic Mindshare

John Gremer
Walgreens

Dhruv Grewal
Babson College

Simon Hay
Dunnhumby

Linda Hyde
Retail Forward

Marlin Hutchins
Walgreens

Truman Hyde
Tires Plus

Steve Knopik
Beall's Inc.

Doug Koch
Famous Footwear

Bradley Macullum
ESRI

Rick Lawler
Hess

Bruce Mager
Macy's East

Kathy Mance
National Retail Federation

Richard A. McAllister
Florida Retail Federation

Mike MacDonald
DSW

Ramesh Murthy
CVS/Caremark

Steven Keith Platt
Platt Retail Institute

Susan Reda
Stores Magazine

Donna Rosenberg
Staples

Lori Schafer
SAS Retail

Bob Swan
JCPenney

John Thomas
Pinch-A-Penny

Suzanne Voorhees
The Grapevine Group

The eighth edition of *Retailing Management* has benefited from reviews by several leading scholars and many teachers of retailing and related disciplines. Together, these reviewers spent hundreds of hours reading and critiquing the manuscript. We gratefully acknowledge them and the following reviewers for their diligence and insight in helping us prepare previous editions:

Mark Abel
Kirkwood Community College

Stephen J. Anderson
Austin Peay State University

Jill Attaway
Illinois State University

Mary Barry
Auburn University

Lance A. Bettencourt
Indiana University

David Blanchette
Rhode Island College

Jeff Blodgett
University of Mississippi

George W. Boulware
Lipscomb University

Willard Broucek
Northern State University

Leroy M. Buckner
Florida Atlantic University

David J. Burns
Purdue University

Lon Camomile
Colorado State University

Donald W. Caudill
Bluefield State College

James Clark
Northeastern State University

Sylvia Clark
St. John's University

J. Joseph Cronin, Jr.
Florida State University

Angela D'Auria
Stanton Radford University

Irene J. Dickey
University of Dayton

Ann DuPont
University of Texas

Chloe I. Elmgren
Mankato State University

Richard L. Entrikin
George Mason University

David Erickson
Angelo University

Kenneth R. Evans
University of Missouri–Columbia

Richard Feinberg
Purdue University

Kevin Fertig
University of Illinois

Drew Ehrlich Fulton
Montgomery Community College

David M. Georgoff
Florida Atlantic University

Peter Gordon
Southeast Missouri State University

Larry Gresham
Texas A&M University

Tom Gross
University of Wisconsin

Sally Harmon
Purdue University

Susan Harmon
Middle Tennessee State University

Michael D. Hartline
Louisiana State University

Tony L. Henthorne
University of Southern Mississippi

Kae Hineline
McLennan Community College

David Horne
California State University–Long Beach

Joshua Holt
Brigham Young University

Michael Jones
Auburn University

Eugene J. Kangas
Winona State University

Herbert Katzenstein
St. John's University

Terrence Kroeten
North Dakota State University

Ann Lucht
Milwaukee Area Technical College

Elizabeth Mariotz
Philadelphia College of Textiles and Science

Tony Mayo
George Mason University

Harold McCoy
Virginia Commonwealth University

Michael McGinnis
University of South Alabama

Phyliss McGinnis
Boston University

Kim McKeage
University of Maine

Barbara Mihm
University of Wisconsin–Stevens Point

Robert Miller
Central Michigan University

Mary Anne Milward
University of Arizona

Cheryl O'Hara
Kings College

Dorothy M. Oppenheim
Bridgewater State University

Michael M. Pearson
Loyola University, New Orleans

Janis Petronis
Tarleton State University

Linda Pettijohn
Southern Missouri State University

John J. Porter
West Virginia University

Sue Riha
University of Texas–Austin

Nick Saratakes
Austin Community College

Laura Scroggins
California State University–Chico

Steve Solesbee
Aiken Technical College

Shirley M. Stretch
California State University–LA

William R. Swinyard
Brigham Young University

Amy Tomas
University of Vermont

Janet Wagner
University of Maryland

Gary Walk
Lima Technical College

Mary Weber
University of New Mexico

Sandy White
Greenville Tech College

Fred T. Whitman
Mary Washington College

Kathleen Debevic Witz
University of Massachusetts

Merv Yeagle
University of Maryland

Ron Zallocco
University of Toledo

We received cases from professors all over the world. Although we would like to have used more cases in the text and the Instructor's Manual, space was limited. We would like to thank all who contributed but are especially appreciative of the following authors whose cases were used in *Retailing Management* or in the Instructor's Manual:

Ronald Adams
University of North Florida

Laura Bliss
Stephens College

James Camerius
Northern Michigan University

Jeffrey M. Campbell
The University of Tennessee, Knoxville

Guy Cheston
Director of Advertising Sales & Sponsorship, Harrods

Daphne Comfort
University of Gloucestershire

Hope Bober Corrigan
Loyola College, Maryland

Tina Brienne Curley
Loyola College, Maryland

David Ehrlich
Marymount University

Sunil Erevelles
University of North Carolina, Charlotte

Ann Fairhurst
Indiana University

Linda F. Felicetti
Clarion University

GUIDED TOUR

For seven editions, Levy & Weitz's **Retailing Management** has been known for its strategic focus, decision-making emphasis, applications orientation, and readability. The authors and **McGraw-Hill/Irwin** are proud to introduce the eighth edition and invite you to see how this edition captures the exciting, dynamic nature of retailing.

STUDENT FEATURES

This edition continues the emphasis placed on creating interest and involving students in the course and the industry. Refacts, retailing views, and executive briefings at the beginning of each chapter make the textbook a "good read" for students.

Through real-world examples, students are given the opportunity to think about concepts in the text

Executive Briefings

To illustrate the opportunities and rewards from a career in retailing, each chapter begins with a profile of a retail manager, either a senior executive or recent college graduate, discussing their area of decision-making and their career path. This specific executive briefing from Chapter 3 portrays Al Callier, Vice President, Interactive Design & Web Production, of Universal Orlando Resort. In his profile, he states, "Today online electronic commerce is among our leading retail sales channels and a strategic pillar of our marketing efforts." Retailers are using the Internet and other technologies to provide more value to their customers, increase customer service, and improve operating efficiencies.

EXECUTIVE BRIEFING
Al Callier, Vice President, Interactive Design & Web Production, Universal Orlando® Resort

I am responsible for Universal Orlando Resort's digital content production including content strategy and Web site development, online advertising, and mobile content development for the United States and the United Kingdom. In 2002, when I joined Universal Orlando, the company was beginning to explore online e-commerce. Its Web site had online ticket purchase capability, but was more of an interactive print brochure describing the resort. Today online electronic commerce is among our leading retail sales channels and a strategic pillar of our marketing efforts.

Promoting the resort and selling tickets to the theme parks before people arrive in Orlando is critical. Visitors to Orlando may plan to visit a number of the attractions in the area during their vacation, but change plans once the vacation is underway. By making it more attractive to buy tickets online before visitors arrive in Florida, we achieve more advance purchases and commitment to visiting Universal Orlando.

At this point in the evolution of the Internet, most vacationers use online resources to research their trip as well as book and purchase specific products. We have designed our online channel to assist families as they plan their vacations. The process might begin with determining the type and location of a vacation, and conclude with choosing specific activities and then purchasing tickets for these activities. It is a highly involving process that typically engages the participation of multiple family members in different ways. We have designed our Web site and navigation to provide the information and assistance our guests will find useful at each phase of the process, and encourage them to include Universal Orlando in their vacation plans, buy tickets to our theme parks, and make reservations at our hotels.

Our Web site also plays an important role in building a compelling image of Universal Orlando Resort. Thus we consider the strategic brand communication objectives, as well as the different types of visitors and guest needs in the design of our Web site. Some visitors come to the resort more frequently and are more interested in specific offers and packages, while others are in the early phase of the vacation planning process and are seeking to get a basic understanding of the resort and theme parks. Our

QUESTIONS

What are the unique customer benefits offered by the three major retail channels: stores, catalogs, and the Internet?

Why are retailers moving toward using all three channels to interact with customers?

What are the key benefits and challenges in providing multichannel offerings?

How might technology affect the future multichannel shopping experience?

Chapter Questions

These critical thinking questions appear at the beginning of each chapter to give students the opportunity to prepare for what they will be required to understand in their reading.

Interesting and Readable Refacts

Refacts (retailing factoids) are interesting facts about retailing, related to the textual material, that are placed in the margins.

REFACT
More than 17 billion catalogs are mailed in the United States every year—about 56 for every American.[6]

Catalog Channel

The **catalog channel** is a nonstore retail channel in which the retail offering is communicated to customers through a catalog mailed to customers. About half of U.S. consumers shop through catalogs each year. The merchandise categories with the greatest catalog sales are drugs and beauty aids, computers and software, clothing and accessories, furniture and housewares, and books, music, and magazines.[5]

While sales growth through the direct selling channel is limited in the United States, companies like Avon and Mary Kay have effectively used this channel to sell products in less developed countries. Using the direct selling channel is particularly effective in less developed countries because an extensive infrastructure to supply stores is not required. Products are sent to hundreds of thousands of sales representatives in small villages. They pay for the products when they sell them.

REFACT

About 5.5 million sales representatives now sell Avon products around the world, be it lip gloss in Shanghai or face powder in Rio de Janeiro.[11]

The direct selling channel also is part of a movement around the world for women to have more economic independence. For example, Zhang Xiaoying, a 19-year-old woman from Guizhou, one of China's poorest regions, says, "I love the corporate culture of Mary Kay. This company teaches you to aspire to a higher level."

The direct selling channel is particularly effective in less developed areas that lack the infrastructure to support retail stores.

Before joining the company, many Mary Kay sales agents in China held low-paying jobs as secretaries, cashiers, and rural schoolteachers. Many were looking for a new focus in their lives. "Because my husband is a businessman, and he is busy, we talked less and less," says Lu Laidi, a Mary Kay sales director. "I felt my life was boring. I stayed home and barely dressed up."

The use of a direct selling channel has been controversial in China. Many direct sellers have been accused of operating sophisticated pyramid schemes and other swindles. In response to these concerns, China banned direct selling in 1998, saying that it was often a cover for "evil cults, secret societies and lawless and superstitious activities." In 2006, after heavy lobbying from American companies, China lifted its ban, and since then direct selling has grown into an $8 billion industry.

Sources: David Barboza, "Direct Selling Flourishes in China," *New York Times*, December 26, 2009; J. Alex Tarquinio, "Selling Beauty on a Global Scale," *New York Times*, November 1, 2008, p. B2

SUPPORT FOR STUDENT LEARNING

GET OUT AND DO IT! EXERCISES

Found at the end of each chapter, these exercises suggest projects that students can undertake by either visiting local retail stores, surfing the Internet, or using the student Web site. The exercises are designed to provide a hands-on learning experience for students. A continuing exercise is included in each chapter so that students can be involved in an experiential exercise involving the same retailer throughout the course.

GET OUT AND DO IT!

1. **CONTINUING CASE ASSIGNMENT: GO SHOPPING** Assume that you are shopping on the Internet for an item in the same merchandise category you analyzed for the Comparison Shopping exercise in Chapter 2. Go to the retailer's Web site, and compare the merchandise assortment offered, the prices, and the shopping experience in the store and on the store's Web site. How easy was it to locate what you were looking for? What were the assortment and pricing like? What was the checkout like? What features of the sites do you like and dislike, such as the look and feel of the site, navigation, and special features?

2. **INTERNET EXERCISE** Go to the Web sites of J. Crew (www.jcrew.com), JCPenney (www.jcpenney.com), and Lands' End (www.landsend.com), and shop for a pair of khaki pants. Evaluate your shopping experience at each site. Compare and contrast the sites and your experiences on the basis of characteristics you think are important to consumers.

3. **INTERNET EXERCISE** Assume that you are getting married and planning your wedding. Compare and contrast the usefulness of www.theknot.com and www.weddingchannel.com for planning your wedding. What features of the sites do you like and dislike? Indicate the specific services offered by these sites that you would use.

4. **INTERNET EXERCISE** Go to the Center for Democracy and Technology's home page at http://www.cdt.org/, and click on "Consumer Privacy" and then "Privacy Guide" (http://www.cdt.org/privacy/guide/basic/topten.html). Why is privacy a concern for Internet shoppers? What are the top-10 recommended ways for consumers to protect their privacy online? How many of these recommendations have you employed when using the Internet?

5. **INTERNET AND SHOPPING EXERCISE** Pick a merchandise category like microwave ovens, power drills, digital cameras, blenders, or coffee makers. Compare a retailer's offering in its local store and on its Internet site. What are the differences in the assortments offered through its store and Internet channel? Are the prices the same or different? What

Online Learning Center

The Online Learning Center provides students with exercises to evaluate international expansion opportunities, examine financial performance of retailers, analyze potential store locations, develop a merchandise budget plan, edit the assortment for a category, make pricing and markdown decisions, and determine break-even sales levels. Sample test questions and flash cards are provided for each chapter.

The student site provides:

- Chapter Quizzes
- Tutorials and Modules
- Flashcards

INSTRUCTOR RESOURCES

Online Learning Center

Through our convenient Online Learning Center, you can access everything you need in preparation for your course. A secured resource site provides your essential course materials to save you prep time before class.

www.mhhe.com/levy8e

The instructor site provides:

- Instructor's Manual
- PowerPoint Presentations
- Testbank/EZ Test
- Newsletters
- Tutorials and Modules for students
- Chapter Quizzes
- Flashcards for students

IRCD

The Instructor's Resource CD-ROM provides the resources an instructor needs to prepare for their course: includes the Instructor's Manual, PowerPoint slides, Test Bank, and Computerized Test Bank. ISBN: 0077325028

Video DVD

Over 30 video segments are available to illustrate issues addressed in the text. A number of the videos complement the cases located at the end of the text. These video segments are available on the Video DVD. ISBN: 007732501X

Retailing Newsletter

Each month, the authors prepare and distribute through email a Retailing Newsletter. The newsletters contain several videos and twelve abstracts of articles appearing in the business or trade press about current issues facing retailers specifically and the industry in general. These newsletters are also accessible on the Online Learning Center.

Cases

To stimulate class discussion about issues confronting retail managers, the authors provide current and thought-provoking cases. For this edition, included at the end of the text are a total of 38 cases with 10 brand new cases to use for your course.

Assurance of Learning Ready

Many educational institutions today are focused on the notion of *assurance of learning,* an important element of some accreditation standards. *Retailing Management* is designed specifically to support instructors' assurance of learning initiatives with a simple, yet powerful solution.

Each test bank question for *Retailing Management* maps to a specific chapter learning outcome/objective listed in the text. Instructors can use our test bank software, EZ Test and EZ Test Online, or *Connect Marketing* to easily query for learning outcomes/objectives that directly relate to the learning objectives for their course. Instructors can then use the reporting features of EZ Test to aggregate student results in similar fashion, making the collection and presentation of assurance of learning data simple and easy.

AACSB Statement

The McGraw-Hill Companies is a proud corporate member of AACSB International. Understanding the importance and value of AACSB accreditation, *Retailing Management,* Eighth Edition, recognizes the curricula guidelines detailed in the AACSB standards for business accreditation by connecting selected questions in the text and the test bank to the six general knowledge and skill guidelines in the AACSB standards.

The statements contained in *Retailing Management,* Eighth Edition, are provided only as a guide for the users of this textbook. The AACSB leaves content coverage and assessment within the purview of individual schools, the mission of the school, and the faculty. While *Retailing Management,* Eighth Edition, and the teaching package make no claim of any specific AACSB qualification or evaluation, we have within *Retailing Management,* Eighth Edition, labeled selected questions according to the six general knowledge and skills areas.

McGraw-Hill Customer Care Contact Information

At McGraw-Hill, we understand that getting the most from new technology can be challenging. That's why our services don't stop after you purchase our products. You can e-mail our Product Specialists 24 hours a day to get product-training online. Or you can search our knowledge bank of Frequently Asked Questions on our support website. **For Customer Support, call 800-331-5094, e-mail hmsupport@mcgraw-hill.com, or visit www.mhhe.com/support. One of our Technical Support Analysts will be able to assist you in a timely fashion.**

BRIEF CONTENTS

CONTENTS

CHAPTER 4   CUSTOMER BUYING BEHAVIOR 78

SECTION II   RETAILING STRATEGY

CHAPTER 5   RETAIL MARKET STRATEGY 110

CHAPTER 15 RETAIL COMMUNICATION MIX 398

SECTION IV STORE MANAGEMENT

CHAPTER 16 MANAGING THE STORE 432

CHAPTER 17 STORE LAYOUT, DESIGN, AND VISUAL MERCHANDISING 466

CHAPTER 18 CUSTOMER SERVICE 498

APPENDIX A STARTING YOUR OWN RETAIL BUSINESS 524

APPENDIX B STARTING A FRANCHISE BUSINESS 532

SECTION V   CASES

RETAILING
MANAGEMENT

The World of Retailing

The chapters in Section I provide background information about retail customers and competitors that is used to effectively develop and implement a retail strategy.

Chapter 1 describes the functions retailers perform and the variety of decisions they make to satisfy customers' needs.

Chapter 2 describes the different types of food, merchandise, and services retailers; the channels through which they offer products to their customers; and their ownership structures.

Chapter 3 examines how retailers use and coordinate multiple selling channels—stores, the Internet, catalogs—to interact with their customers.

Chapter 4 discusses the process that consumers go through when choosing retail outlets and buying merchandise and how retailers can affect this buying process.

The chapters in Section II focus on the strategic decisions retailers make.

The chapters in Sections III and IV explore tactical decisions involving merchandise and store management.

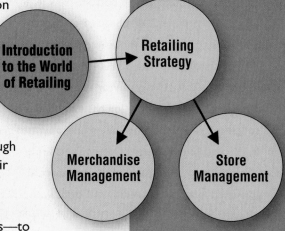

Introduction to the World of Retailing

EXECUTIVE BRIEFING
Debbie Harvey, President and Chief Operating Officer, Ron Jon Surf Shop

I am proud to be the president of Ron Jon Surf Shop, one of the most recognized names in surfing. Ron Jon started on the New Jersey Shore 50 years ago when the founder Ron DiMenna sold his first surfboard. A much larger "original store" is still located in Ship Bottom, New Jersey. Our flagship store located in Cocoa Beach, Florida, was started in 1963 and has grown over the years to be known as the world largest surf shop. The 52,000-square-foot store is open 24 hours a day 365 days a year and welcomes about 2 million visitors annually. Ron Jon has expanded over the last couple of years and now owns and operates nine stores. We also have licensees that operate airport locations, Caribbean locations, and a Ron Jon resort.

I graduated from the University of Florida with a BSBA in Marketing on a Friday, and started working for Maas Brothers (now part of Macy's) on the following Monday. I have been working in the retail industry ever since. My first position was as a manager of the women's department. After about a year of working in the stores I was promoted to a position in the buying office and eventually held senior merchandising leadership positions at Maas Brothers, Bealls Florida, HSN, and Goody's before joining Ron Jon.

I was attracted to retail because of family friends who were in the retail business. They both had worked for several large retailers, working their way up the ladder before starting their own business. After years in the business they still looked forward to the diversity and challenges that each new day presented. This has also been my experience. I truly look forward to coming to work each day. While each company I have worked for had a different culture and customer profile, the basics of retailing are the same: you have to serve your customer's needs.

Ron Jon's targets customers with active lifestyles who are looking for entertaining and fun experiences. Our customers typically visit us while on vacation or during a visit to the beach. We spend more than the average retailer in marketing dollars. Our marketing goal is to promote the Ron Jon brand and experience rather than a particular product or price. Our extensive billboard program has made us familiar to millions of visitors to our market areas. Every customer to our store receives a free sticker for his or her car. We promote the surfing lifestyle by sponsoring surf teams and contests. In addition we use the

CHAPTER 1

QUESTIONS

What is retailing?

What do retailers do?

Why is retailing important in our society?

What career and entrepreneurial opportunities does retailing offer?

What types of decisions do retail managers make?

Internet not only for a shopping site but also to promote our brand through social media.

Retailing is an industry that offers many daily challenges. Our business is not static and is constantly evolving and changing. For me that is what makes it fun and rewarding. We have to figure out what merchandise the customers want, manage the logistics of the merchandise flow, have efficient operations, provide outstanding customer service and provide an exciting shopping environment. I really feel a sense of accomplishment when we get all aspects of the business doing well at the same time.

Most consumers shopping in their local stores don't realize that retailing is a high-tech, global industry. For an example of the sophisticated technologies used by retailers, consider the following: If you are interested in buying an e-book reader, a number of retailers have Web sites at which you can learn about the features of the different models. You can buy the e-reader at one of these Web sites and have it delivered to your home or to a nearby store.

The retail buyer responsible for the e-reader product category has analyzed the marketplace and made decisions on which models and brands to stock in the retailer's stores. In addition to considering national brands such as Sony, the buyer might decide to work with e-reader manufacturers in China to develop a unique model that will be available only at the retailer's stores and its Web site.

When you decide to buy an e-reader in a store, the point-of-sale (POS) terminal used to make the transaction transmits data about the transaction to the retailer's distribution center and then on to the manufacturer. Data about your purchase are incorporated into a sophisticated inventory management system. When the in-store inventory level drops below a prespecified level, an electronic notice is automatically transmitted authorizing the shipment of more units to the retailer's distribution center and then to the store. The retail buyer analyzes the sales data to determine how many and which reader models will be stocked in the retailer's stores and what price will be charged. Finally, the retailer will store information about your e-reader purchase in its data warehouse and use this information to offer special promotions to you.

Historically, the retail landscape was dominated by local retailers that bought and resold merchandise from local suppliers. Forty years ago, some of the largest

Retailers use sophisticated technologies and information systems so that they can sell these e-readers to customers at low prices.

retailers in the United States—Walmart, Home Depot, and Best Buy—either were small start-ups or did not even exist. Yet today most retail sales are made by large national and international chains that buy merchandise all over the world. For example, Target Corporation has 27 full-service buying offices and 48 quality-control offices located throughout the world, employing over 1,200 people. Its engineers are responsible for evaluating the factories that do business with Target for quality, as well as labor rights and transshipment issues.[1]

Retailing is such a common part of our everyday lives that we often just take it for granted. Retail managers make complex decisions in selecting their target markets and retail locations; determining what merchandise and services to offer; negotiating with suppliers; distributing merchandise to stores; training and motivating sales associates; and deciding how to price, promote, and present merchandise. Considerable skill and knowledge are required to make these decisions effectively. Working in this highly competitive, rapidly changing environment is both challenging and exciting, and it offers significant financial rewards.

This book describes the world of retailing and offers key principles for effectively managing retail businesses. Knowledge of retailing principles and practices will help you develop management skills for many business contexts. For example, retailers are the customers for most business-to-consumer (B-to-C) companies such as Procter & Gamble and Hewlett-Packard. Thus brand managers in B-to-C companies need to have a thorough understanding of how retailers operate and make money so that they can get retailers to offer and promote their products. Financial and health care institutions use retail principles to develop their offerings, improve customer service, and provide convenient, easy access to their customers. Thus any students interested in professional B-to-C selling, marketing management, or finance will find this book useful.

WHAT IS RETAILING?

Retailing is the set of business activities that adds value to the products and services sold to consumers for their personal or family use. Often people think of retailing only as the sale of products in stores, but retailing also involves the sale of services such as overnight lodging in a motel, a doctor's exam, a haircut, a DVD rental, or a home-delivered pizza. Not all retailing is done in stores. Examples of nonstore retailing include Internet sales of hot sauces (www.firehotsauces.com), the direct sales of cosmetics by Avon, catalog sales by L.L. Bean and Patagonia, and DVD rentals through Redbox's kiosks.

The Retailer's Role in a Supply Chain

A **retailer** is a business that sells products and/or services to consumers for their personal or family use. Retailers are a key component in a supply chain that links manufacturers to consumers. A **supply chain** is a set of firms that make and deliver goods and services to consumers. Exhibit 1–1 shows the retailer's position within a supply chain.

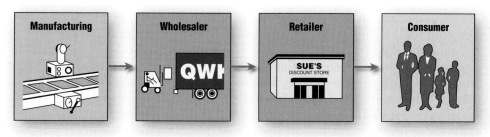

EXHIBIT 1–1
Example of a Supply Chain

Manufacturers typically design and make products and sell them to retailers or wholesalers. When manufacturers like Nike and Apple sell directly to consumers, they are performing both production and retail business activities. **Wholesalers** engage in buying, taking title to, often storing, and physically handling goods in large quantities and then reselling the goods (usually in smaller quantities) to retailers or other businesses. Wholesalers and retailers may perform many of the same functions described in the next section, but wholesalers focus on satisfying retailers' needs, while retailers direct their efforts to satisfying the needs of consumers. Some retailers, like Costco and Home Depot, function as both retailers and wholesalers: They perform retailing activities when they sell to consumers, but they engage in wholesaling activities when they sell to other businesses, such as restaurants or building contractors.

In some supply chains, the manufacturing, wholesaling, and retailing activities are performed by independent firms, but most supply chains feature some vertical integration. **Vertical integration** means that a firm performs more than one set of activities in the channel, as occurs when a retailer engages in wholesaling activities by operating its own distribution centers to supply its stores. **Backward integration** arises when a retailer performs some wholesaling and manufacturing activities, such as operating warehouses or designing private-label merchandise. **Forward integration** occurs when a manufacturer undertakes retailing and wholesaling activities, such as Ralph Lauren operating its own retail stores.

Most large retailers such as Safeway, Walmart, and Lowe's manage their own distribution centers and perform activities undertaken by wholesalers. They buy directly from manufacturers, have merchandise shipped to their warehouses, and then distribute the merchandise to their stores. Other retailers, such as J. Crew and Victoria's Secret, are even more vertically integrated. They design the merchandise they sell and then contract with manufacturers to produce it exclusively for them.

Retailers add value by providing an assortment of products that consumers can buy at one place.

Retailers Create Value

Why are retailers needed? Wouldn't it be easier and cheaper to buy directly from manufacturers? The answer, generally, is no because retailers are more efficient at performing the activities described below that increase the value of products and services for consumers. These value-creating activities include (1) providing an assortment of products and services, (2) breaking bulk, (3) holding inventory, and (4) providing services.

Providing Assortments   Supermarkets typically carry 20,000 to 30,000 different items made by more than 500 companies. Offering an assortment enables their customers to choose from a wide selection of products, brands, sizes, and prices at one location. Manufacturers specialize in producing specific types of products. For example, Frito-Lay makes snacks, Dannon makes dairy products, Skippy makes peanut butter, and Heinz makes ketchup. If each of these manufacturers had its own stores that sold only its own products, consumers would have to go to many different stores to buy the groceries needed to prepare a single meal.

Breaking Bulk   To reduce transportation costs, manufacturers and wholesalers typically ship cases of frozen dinners or cartons of blouses to retailers. Retailers then offer the products in smaller quantities tailored to individual consumers' and households' consumption patterns—an activity called **breaking bulk.** Breaking bulk is important to both manufacturers and consumers. It enables manufacturers to efficiently make and ship merchandise in larger quantities and enables consumers to purchase merchandise in smaller, more useful quantities.

Holding Inventory   A major value-providing activity performed by retailers is **holding inventory** so that the products will be available when consumers want them. Thus, consumers can keep a smaller inventory of products at home because they know local retailers will have the products available when they need more. This activity is particularly important to consumers with limited storage space.

Providing Services   Retailers provide services that make it easier for customers to buy and use products. For example, retailers offer credit so that consumers can have a product now and pay for it later. They display products so that consumers can see and test them before buying. Some retailers employ salespeople in stores or maintain Web sites to answer questions and provide additional information about products.

Increasing the Value of Products and Services   By providing assortments, breaking bulk, holding inventory, and providing services, retailers increase the value that consumers receive from their products and services. Consider a door in a shipping crate in an Iowa manufacturer's warehouse. The door cannot satisfy the needs of a do-it-yourselfer (DIYer) who wants to replace a closet door today. The DIYer finds this door more valuable and will pay more if it is available from a nearby home improvement center that also sells the brackets and tools needed to hang the door and provides sales associates who can explain which door is best for closets and how the door should be hung. In addition, many retailers are involved in designing innovative products and services. For example, a Macy's buyer designed the first tea bag, and a JCPenney buyer invented panty hose.

SOCIAL AND ECONOMIC SIGNIFICANCE OF RETAILING

Social Responsibility

Most retailers try to be socially responsible. **Corporate social responsibility (CSR)** involves an organization voluntarily taking responsibility for the impact of its activities on its employees, its customers, the community, and the environment. Firms typically go through several stages before they fully integrate corporate social responsibility into their strategy. Companies in the first stage engage only in CSR activities required by law. In this stage, companies are not actually convinced of the importance of CSR actions. In the second stage, companies go beyond activities required by law to engage in CSR activities that provide a short-term financial benefit to the company. For example, a retailer might reduce the energy consumption of its stores just because doing so costs less. In the third stage, companies operate responsibly because they believe this is the "right thing" to do. Companies in the fourth and final stage engage in socially and environmentally responsible actions because they believe these activities must be done for the "well-being" of everyone. These companies have truly incorporated the concept of CSR into their business strategy.[2] Retailing View 1.1 illustrates how retailers provide value to their communities and society, as well as to their customers.

Retail Sales

U.S. retail sales in 2007 were $4.5 trillion, but this sales level underestimates the impact of retailing on the U.S. economy because it does not include the sales of

---

RETAILING VIEW   Socially Responsible Retailers   1.1

CSR activities are associated with retailers' internal operations and the design and manufacturing of the products they sell. For example, many retailers are building LEED-certified stores. The Leadership in Energy and Environmental Design (LEED) certification is based on an assessment of the store's impact on human and environmental health, sustainable site de-

Retailers were among the first responders to help the victims of Hurricane Katrina.

velopment, water savings, energy efficiency, materials selection, and indoor environmental quality. Some features in a prototype LEED-certified McDonald's restaurant are its permeable pavement that cleans rainwater; a cistern buried behind the restaurant that collects rainwater, which is used to water the landscaping; a roof garden that insulates the restaurant; the use of less-toxic cleaners and of paints and resins that do not emit chemical odors; and the installation of low-flow toilets and urinals that use less water than standard low-flow toilets.

Other firms take a more hands-on approach to helping the communities in which they reside. For example, Home Depot's 300,000 associates contribute thousands of hours of service a year through Team Depot, the retailer's volunteer corps. In addition, the Home Depot Foundation, the company's philanthropic arm, has donated $190 million (cash and in-kind) to nonprofit organizations, supported the development of more than 95,000 homes, planted more than 1.2 million trees, and built or refurbished more than 1,875 playgrounds, parks and greenspaces.

Tiffany was the first big jewelry retailer to respond to the Dirty Metals report by Earthworks. The report revealed that

REFACT

The average 18-carat gold wedding ring leaves in its wake 20 tons of mine waste.[3]

in countries as diverse as Ghana, Indonesia, the United States, and Peru, gold mining harmed people and the environment. The report detailed problems such as arsenic emissions, cyanide and mercury poisoning, excessive water and energy consumption, child labor, the spread of HIV, and the displacement of people from their homes. Tiffany decided to take a stance and purchase gold only from suppliers that abide by "the golden rules" set forth by the No Dirty Gold campaign. The rules outline appropriate practices related to human rights, safe working conditions, and the protection of local communities and ecosystems.

Walmart is working with its suppliers, retailers, nongovernment organizations (NGOs), and the government to develop a global product sustainability rating index that measures the carbon footprint—the aggregate of all carbon dioxide and other greenhouse gases (GHGs) emitted during manufacture and distribution—of every product sold in its stores. Walmart feels that when its customers can assess a product's carbon footprint as easily as they can its price, they will be more sensitive to protecting the environment.

REFACT

One plastic bag can take up to 500 years to decay in a landfill.[4]

Sources: Susan Reda, "Retailers Make Small Advances into the World of Carbon Footprinting," *Stores,* October 2009; Alan Wolf, "Chains Embrace Eco Strategies," *TWICE,* March 30, 2009; Andrew Martin, "Green Plans in Blueprints of Retailers," *New York Times,* November 8, 2008; Claire Adler, "Clean Campaign Gathers Traction," *Financial Times,* November 8, 2008, p. 14.

many consumer services such as entertainment, home repairs, and health care. Approximately 8.1 percent of the total gross domestic product comes from retailing. Although large retail chains account for the majority of retail sales, most retailers are small businesses. Of the 1.9 million retail firms in the United States, 95 percent of them operate only one store; less than 1 percent of U.S. retail firms have more than 100 stores; and only 10 percent of U.S. retailers have sales greater than $2.5 million.[5]

Employment

Retailing is one of the nation's largest industries in terms of employment. More than 29 million people were employed in retailing in 2007—approximately 21 percent of the nonagricultural U.S. workforce. From 1997 to 2007, retailing added over 1.1 million jobs to the U.S. economy, significantly contributing to U.S. job growth. Even though the period included a recession, retailing still accounted for 6 percent of all new jobs created from 1997 to 2007. Finally, retailing is expected to add another 687,000 jobs by 2016, making it an important source of future job growth.[6]

STRUCTURE OF RETAILING AND DISTRIBUTION CHANNELS AROUND THE WORLD

Global Retailers

Retailing is a global industry. Many retailers are pursuing growth by expanding their operations to other countries. Exhibit 1–2 lists the 20 largest retailers in the world. Walmart remains the undisputed leader in the retail industry, with sales that are more than three times greater than those of Carrefour, the second-largest retailer.

EXHIBIT 1–2   World's Largest Retailers

	Name of Company	Country of Origin	2007 Retail Sales ($ billions)	Countries of Operation	2002–2007 Retail Sales CAGR (%)*
1	Walmart Stores, Inc.	U.S.	374,526	15	10.3
2	Carrefour S.A.	France	112,604	34	3.6
3	Tesco plc	U.K.	94,740	13	12.4
4	Metro AG	Germany	87,586	32	4.6
5	The Home Depot, Inc.	U.S.	77,349	6	5.8
6	The Kroger Co.	U.S.	70,235	1	6.3
7	Schwarz Unternehmens Treuhand KG	Germany	69,346	24	12.6
8	Target Corp.	U.S.	63,367	1	7.6
9	Costco Wholesale Corp.	U.S.	63,088	8	10.7
10	Aldi GmbH & Co. oHG	Germany	58,487	15	4.3
11	Walgreen Co.	U.S.	53,762	2	13.4
12	Rewe-Zentral AG	Germany	51,929	14	2.8
13	Sears Holdings Corp.	U.S.	50,703	5	10.5
14	Groupe Auchan SA	France	49,295	10	5.5
15	Lowe's Companies, Inc.	U.S.	48,283	2	12.8
16	Seven & I Holdings	Japan	47,891	4	n/a
17	CVS Caremark Corp.	U.S.	45,087	1	14.4
18	E. Leclerc	France	44,686	6	4.5
19	Edeka Zentrale AG & Co. KG	Germany	44,609	3	n/a
20	Safeway, Inc.	U.S.	42,286	2	5.6

Source: *2009 Global Powers in Retailing* (New York: Deloitte Touche Tohmatsu, January 2010).

*Compound annual growth in sales over the last five years.

The largest 250 retailers operated in 6.8 countries on average, with 21.3 percent of their sales coming from outside the retailers' home countries. Retailers headquartered in Europe are more international than U.S.-based retailers. The average European retailer in the top 250 had a presence in 11.1 countries, with over one-third of their total retail sales coming from foreign countries. In contrast, the 87 U.S.-based companies among the top 250 had 88.3 percent of their sales from domestic operations.[7]

Retailers offering food and other fast-moving consumer goods (FMCG) dominate the top-250 list; however, retailers in this sector tend to be the least international. On average, FMCG retailers operated in 4.9 countries, generating 23.4 percent of sales from foreign operations.[8]

Retailers that focus on hard lines such as consumer electronics, appliances, and furniture experience better financial performance than FMCG and apparel retailers. However, the large retailers with the best financial performance are well known for their strong brands, such as Hennes & Mauritz (H&M), Fast Retailing (better known for the Uniqlo chain in Japan), and Inditex (best known for Zara), as well as Apple and Amazon.[9]

Differences in Distribution Channels

The nature of retailing and distribution channels around the world differs. Some critical differences among the retailing and distribution systems in the United States, European Union, China, and India are summarized in Exhibit 1–3. For example, the U.S. retail industry has the greatest retail density and concentration of large retail firms. Many U.S. retailers operate stores with over 20,00 square feet and operate their own warehouses, eliminating the need for wholesalers. This combination of large stores and large firms in the United States results in a very efficient distribution system.

The Chinese and Indian distribution systems are characterized by small stores operated by relatively small firms and a large independent wholesale industry. To make the daily deliveries to these small retailers efficient, the merchandise often passes through several levels of distributors. In addition, the infrastructure to support retailing, especially the transportation and communication systems, is not as well developed as it is in Western countries. These efficiency differences mean that a much larger percentage of the Indian and Chinese labor force is employed in distribution and retailing than is the case in the United States.

Comparison of Retailing and Distribution across the World   **EXHIBIT 1–3**

	United States	European Union	India	China
Concentration (% of retail sales made by large retailers)	High	High	Low	Low
Retail density	High	Medium	Low	Low
Average store size	High	Medium	Low	Low
Role of wholesalers	Limited	Moderate	Extensive	Extensive
Infrastructure supporting efficient supply chains	Extensive	Extensive	Limited	Limited
Restriction on retail locations, store size, and ownership	Few	Considerable	Considerable	Few

Sources: Based on data from World Bank Indicators, http://web.worldbank.org/WBSITE/EXTERNAL/DATASTATISTICS/0,,menuPK:232599~pagePK:64133170~piPK:6413 3498~theSitePK:239419,00.html (August 23, 2007); *CIA World Fact Book,* https://www.cia.gov/library/publications/the-world-factbook/ (January 13, 2010); University of Missouri Archive, http://www.umsl.edu/services/govdocs/wofact92/index.html (January 13, 2010); Retail Analysis, www.igd.com/analysis/ (January 12, 2010).

Government policies in India and Europe restrict the growth of large retail chains and large stores.

The European distribution system falls between the American and the Chinese and Indian systems on this continuum of efficiency and scale. In northern Europe, retailing is similar to that in the United States, with high concentration levels in some national markets. For example, 80 percent or more of sales in sectors such as food and home improvements are made by five or fewer firms. Southern European retailing is more fragmented across all sectors. For example, traditional farmers' market retailing remains important in some sectors, operating alongside large "big-box" formats.

Social and political objectives are important factors that have created these differences in distribution systems in the major markets. An important priority of the Indian and European economic policies is to reduce unemployment by protecting small businesses such as neighborhood retailers.[10] Some countries have passed laws protecting small retailers, as well as strict zoning laws to preserve green spaces, protect town centers, and inhibit the development of large-scale retailing in the suburbs. The population density in the United States is much lower than that in India, China, or Europe. Thus, there is less low-cost real estate available for building large stores in these countries compared with the United States. Finally, retail productivity is reduced when countries restrict the hours that stores can operate. For example, in France, many stores close at 7 p.m. on weeknights. Labor unions in France and elsewhere in Europe are opposed to U.S.-style 24/7 shopping because of the strains it could put on store employees.[11]

OPPORTUNITIES IN RETAILING

Management Opportunities

To cope with a highly competitive and challenging environment, retailers hire and promote people with a wide range of skills and interests. Students often view retailing as part of marketing, because managing distribution (place) is one of the 4P's of marketing. But retailers are businesses and, like manufacturers, undertake all the traditional business activities. Retailers raise capital from financial institutions; purchase goods and services; use accounting and management information systems to control their operations; manage warehouses and distribution systems; design and develop new products; and undertake marketing activities such as advertising, promotion, sales force management, and market research. Thus, retailers employ people with expertise and interests in finance, accounting, human resource management, supply chain management, and computer systems, as well as marketing.

Retail managers are often given considerable responsibility early in their careers. Retail management is also financially rewarding. Starting salaries are typically between $35,000 and $55,000 for college graduates entering management trainee positions. After completing a management trainee program, retail managers can double their starting salary in three to five years if they perform well. Senior buyers and others in higher managerial positions and store managers make between $120,000 and $160,000.[12] (See Appendix 1A at the end of this chapter.)

Entrepreneurial Opportunities

Retailing also provides opportunities for people who wish to start their own business. Some of the world's richest people are retailing entrepreneurs. Many are well known because their names appear over stores' doors; others you may not recognize. Retailing View 1.2 examines the life of one of the world's greatest entrepreneurs, Sam Walton. Some other innovative retail entrepreneurs include Jeff Bezos, Anita Roddick, and Ingvar Kamprad.

Jeff Bezos (Amazon.com)   After his research uncovered that Internet usage was growing at a 2,300 percent annual rate in 1994, Jeffrey Bezos, the 30-year-old son of a Cuban refugee, quit his job on Wall Street and left behind a hefty bonus to start an Internet business. While his wife MacKenzie was driving their car across country, Jeff pecked out his business plan on a laptop computer. By the time they reached Seattle, he had rounded up the investment capital to launch the first Internet book retailer. The company, Amazon.com, is named after the river that carries the greatest amount of water, symbolizing Bezos's objective of achieving

---

RETAILING VIEW   Sam Walton, Founder of Walmart (1918–1992)   1.2

Like Henry Ford with his Model T, Sam Walton revolutionized the retail industry. After graduating from the University of Missouri in 1940, Walton began working at a JCPenney store in Des Moines, Iowa. He served in the army during World War II and then purchased a Ben Franklin variety store franchise in Newport, Arkansas. He boosted sales by finding suppliers that would sell him merchandise at lower prices than his cost to buy from Ben Franklin.

Walton lost his store, however, in 1950 when the landlord refused to renew his lease. He then moved to Bentonville, Arkansas, where he and a younger brother franchised another Ben Franklin store. Walton employed a new self-service system that he had discovered at two Ben Franklin stores in Minnesota. He placed the checkout registers and clerks at the front of the store rather than scattering them throughout. By 1960, Walton had 15 stores in Arkansas and Missouri that laid the foundation for Walmart.

By the early 1960s, some retailers in large, urban, eastern cities had developed the discount store concept incorporating self-service, shallow but broad assortments, low overhead costs, and large parking lots. In 1962, Walton brought this format to small southern towns, opening his first Walmart Discount City in Rogers, Arkansas.

Walton often visited his stores, dropping in unannounced to check the merchandise presentation or financial performance and talk to his "associates." He prided himself on a profit-sharing program and a friendly, open, supportive atmosphere—business practices he had learned when working for JCPenney. He often led his workers in the Walmart cheer: "Give me a W! Give me an A! Give me an L! Give me a Squiggly! (Here, everybody sort of does the twist.) Give me an M! Give me an A! Give me an R! Give me a T! What's that spell? Walmart! What's that spell? Walmart! Who's number one? THE CUSTOMER!"

He offered his own formula for how a large company should operate: "Think one store at a time. That sounds easy enough,

Sam Walton believed in "Management by Walking Around."

but it's something we've constantly had to stay on top of. Communicate, communicate, communicate: What good is figuring out a better way to sell beach towels if you aren't going to tell everybody in your company about it? Keep your ear to the ground: A computer is not—and will never be—a substitute for getting out in your stores and learning what's going on."

In 1991, due to the success of his concept and management practices, Walton became America's wealthiest person; however, he maintained his simple, unassuming lifestyle. Whenever he traveled on business, he rented the same compact economy cars and stayed in the same inexpensive hotels as his employees did. He died of leukemia in 1992. Walmart is now the world's largest corporation.

Sources: Michael Bergdahl, *The Retail Revolution: How Wal-Mart Created a Brave New World of Business* (New York: Metropolitan Books, 2009); Michael Bergdahl, *The 10 Rules of Sam Walton: Success Secrets for Remarkable Results* (Hoboken, NJ: Wiley, 2006).

REFACT

Jeff Bezos chose the domain name "Amazon.com" because at the time, Yahoo.com listed its search results in alphabetical order; therefore, Amazon would be at or near the top of the search results.[14]

the greatest volume of Internet sales. He was one of the few dot-com leaders to recognize that sweating the details was critical to success. Under his leadership, Amazon developed technologies to make shopping on the Internet faster, easier, and more personal than shopping in stores by offering personalized recommendations and home pages. Amazon.com has become more than a bookstore. It is now the largest online retailer, with annual sales over $20 billion—three times more sales than the second-largest online retailer. Amazon also provides virtual stores and fulfillment services for many other retailers.[13]

Anita Roddick (The Body Shop)   Anita Roddick, who passed away in 2007, opened the first Body Shop in Brighton, England, to make some extra income for her family. She did not have any business background but had traveled widely and understood the body rituals of women. She expanded the small store that initially sold 15 products into a 2,000-store chain offering more than 300 products throughout the world. From the start, Roddick recycled bottles to save money, but such actions also became the foundation for The Body Shop's core values. It endorses only environmentally friendly products and stands against animal testing. Roddick used her business as a means to communicate about human rights and environmental issues. Many of the products in The Body Shop contain materials from farming communities in South America and thereby help those communities maintain their way of life. Today the L'Oreal-owned chain operates in 55 countries. Deeply involved in charitable causes, Roddick was an early proponent of AIDS research and campaigned for the environment and human rights and against animal testing and violence toward women.[15]

Ingvar Kamprad, IKEA's founder, started in business as a child by selling matches to neighbors from his bicycle.

Ingvar Kamprad (IKEA)   Ingvar Kamprad, the founder of the Swedish-based home furnishing retailer chain IKEA, was always an entrepreneur. His first business was selling matches to neighbors from his bicycle. He discovered he could make a good profit by buying matches in bulk and selling them individually at a low price. He then expanded to selling fish, Christmas tree decorations, seeds, ballpoint pens, and pencils. By the time he was 17 years of age, he had earned a reward for succeeding in school. His father gave him the money to establish what is now IKEA. Like Sam Walton, the founder of Walmart, Kamprad is known for his frugality. He drives an old Volvo, flies economy class, and encourages IKEA employees to write on both sides of a sheet of paper. This thriftiness has translated into a corporate philosophy of cost cutting throughout IKEA so that the chain can offer quality furniture with innovative designs at low prices. According to *Forbes* magazine, Kamprad is the richest person in Europe and the fourth-richest person in the world, with an estimated net worth of around $33 billion.[16]

REFACT

The acronym IKEA is made up of the initials of the founder's name (Ingvar Kamprad) plus those of Elmtaryd, his family farm, and the nearby village Agunnaryd.[17]

THE RETAIL MANAGEMENT DECISION PROCESS

This book is organized around the management decisions that retailers must make to provide value to their customers and develop an advantage over their competitors. Exhibit 1–4 identifies the chapters in this book associated with each type of decision.

Understanding the World of Retailing—Section I

The first step in the retail management decision process, as Exhibit 1–4 shows, is understanding the world of retailing. Retail managers need to know the environment in which they operate before they can develop and implement effective strategies.

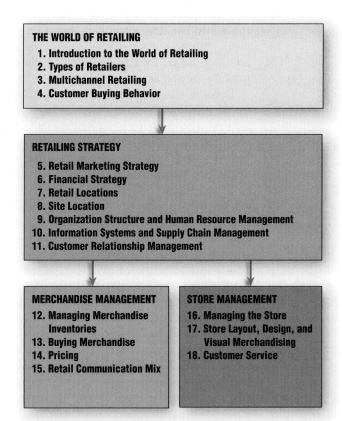

EXHIBIT 1–4
Retail Management
Decision Process

The first section of this book therefore provides a general overview of the retailing industry and its customers.

The critical environmental factors in the world of retailing are (1) the macroenvironment and (2) the microenvironment. The impacts of the macroenvironment—including technological, social, and ethical/legal/political factors—on retailing are discussed throughout this book. For example, the influence of technology on the rise of multichannel retailing is reviewed in Chapter 3; the use of new information and supply chain technologies is examined in Chapters 10 and 11; and new communication technologies are discussed in Chapter 15.

The retailer's microenvironment focuses specifically on its competitors and customers.

Competitors   At first glance, identifying competitors appears easy: A retailer's primary competitors are other retailers that use the same type of store. Thus, department stores compete against other department stores, and supermarkets compete with other supermarkets. This competition between the same type of retailers is called **intratype competition.**

Yet to appeal to a broader group of consumers, many retailers are increasing the variety of merchandise they offer. By offering greater variety in a store, retailers satisfy the needs of customers seeking a one-stop shopping experience. For example, clothing and food are now available in grocery, department, and discount stores and even drugstores. Walgreens has added jewelry, accessories, and apparel to its already extensive health and beauty categories to meet the lifestyle needs of its customers. When retailers offer merchandise not typically associated with their type of store, such as clothing in a drugstore, the result is **scrambled merchandising.** Scrambled merchandising increases **intertype competition,** or competition between retailers that sell similar merchandise using different types of stores, such as discount and department stores.

Increasing intertype competition has made it harder for retailers to identify and monitor their competition. In one sense, all retailers compete against one another

REFACT

Fred Lazarus Jr., founder of Lazarus Department Stores, which is now part of Macy's, promoted the idea of fixing Thanksgiving Day during the fourth week of November to expand the Christmas shopping season. Congress adopted his proposal in 1941.[18]

When a drugstore offers the same merchandise as a discount store, it is engaging in intertype competition.

for the dollars that consumers spend on goods and services. But the intensity of competition is greatest among retailers located near one another whose offerings are viewed as very similar.

Because the convenience of a location is the most important consideration in store choice, a store's proximity to competitors is a critical factor in identifying competition. Consider two DVD rental stores, Blockbuster and Harry's Video, in two suburbs 10 miles apart. The stores are the only specialty DVD rental retailers within 50 miles, but a grocery store also rents a limited selection of DVDs in the same strip center as Blockbuster. Due to the distance between Blockbuster and Harry's Video, they probably don't compete against each other intensely. Customers who live near Harry's Video will rent DVDs there, whereas customers close to Blockbuster will rent DVDs at Blockbuster or the grocery store. In this case, Harry's major competition may be movie theaters, cable television, Netflix, or a Redbox kiosk inside a nearby drugstore. It is too inconvenient for customers who live close to Harry's to rent DVDs elsewhere. In contrast, Blockbuster might compete most intensely with the grocery store.

Management's view of competition also may differ depending on the manager's position within the retail firm. For example, the manager of the Saks Fifth Avenue women's sportswear department in Bergen County, New Jersey, views the other women's sportswear specialty stores in the Riverside Square mall as her major competitors. But the Saks store manager views the Bloomingdale's store in a nearby mall as her strongest competitor. These differences in perspective arise because the department sales manager is primarily concerned with customers for a specific category of merchandise, whereas the store manager is concerned with customers seeking the entire selection of all merchandise and services offered by a department store.

The CEO of a retail chain, in contrast, views competition from a much broader geographic perspective. For example, Nordstrom might identify its strongest competitor as Macy's in the Northwest, Saks in northern California, and Bloomingdale's in northern Virginia. The CEO may also take a broader strategic perspective and recognize that other activities compete for consumers' disposable income. For example, Safeway's CEO adopts the consumer's perspective and recognizes that grocery stores are competing with drugstores, convenience stores, and restaurants for customers' food dollars.

Retailing is an intensely competitive industry. Thus understanding the different types of retailers and how they compete with one another is critical to developing and implementing a retail strategy. Chapter 2 discusses various types of retailers and their competitive strategies, and Chapter 3 concentrates on how retailers adopt multichannel strategies to give themselves a competitive edge.

Customers   The second factor in the microenvironment is customers. Retailers must respond to broad demographic and lifestyle trends in our society, such as the growth in the senior and minority segments of the U.S. population or the importance of shopping convenience to the increasing number of two-income families. To develop and implement an effective strategy, retailers must understand why customers shop, how they select a store, and how they select among that store's merchandise—the information found in Chapter 4.

Developing a Retail Strategy—Section II

The next stages in the retail management decision-making process, formulating and implementing a retail strategy, are based on an understanding of the macro- and microenvironments developed in the first section of this book. Section II focuses on decisions related to developing a retail strategy, whereas Sections III and IV pertain to decisions surrounding the implementation of the strategy.

The **retail strategy** indicates how the retailer plans to focus its resources to accomplish its objectives. It identifies (1) the target market, or markets, toward which the retailer will direct its efforts; (2) the nature of the merchandise and services the retailer will offer to satisfy the needs of the target market; and (3) how the retailer will build a long-term advantage over its competitors.

The nature of a retail strategy can be illustrated by comparing the strategies of Walmart and Best Buy. Initially, Walmart identified its target market as small towns (fewer than 35,000 in population) in Arkansas, Texas, and Oklahoma. It offered name-brand merchandise at low prices in a broad array of categories, ranging from laundry detergent to girls' dresses, but offerings in each category were limited. Today, even as Walmart stores have expanded across the world, the selection in each category remains limited. A Walmart store might have only three models of high-definition television sets, while an electronic category specialist like Best Buy might carry 30 models.

In contrast to Walmart, Best Buy defines its primary target as consumers living in suburban areas of large cities. Rather than carrying many merchandise categories, Best Buy stores specialize in consumer electronics and carry most types and brands currently available in the market. Walmart emphasizes self-service: Customers select their merchandise, bring it to the checkout line, and then carry it to their cars. But Best Buy provides more customer service. It has knowledgeable, trained salespeople to assist customers with certain types of merchandise, such as home entertainment centers, and provides delivery and installation of these systems.

Because Walmart and Best Buy both emphasize competitive prices, they have made strategic decisions to sustain their low prices by developing a cost advantage over their competitors. Both firms have sophisticated distribution and management information systems to manage inventory. Their strong relationships with their suppliers enable them to buy merchandise at low prices.

Strategic Decision Areas   The key strategic decision areas for a firm involve the definition of its market, financial status, location, organizational and human resource structure, information systems, supply chain organization, and customer relationships.

Chapter 5 discusses how the selection of a retail market strategy requires analyzing the environment and the firm's strengths and weaknesses. When major environmental changes occur, the current strategy and the reasoning behind it must be reexamined. The retailer then decides what, if any, strategy changes are needed to take advantage of new opportunities or avoid new threats in the environment.

The retailer's market strategy must be consistent with the firm's financial objectives. Chapter 6 reviews how financial variables, such as return on investment, inventory turnover, and profit margin, can be used to evaluate the market strategy and its implementation.

Decisions regarding location (reviewed in Chapters 7 and 8) are important for both consumer and competitive reasons. First, location is typically consumers' top consideration when selecting a store. Generally consumers buy gas at the closest service station and patronize the shopping mall that's most convenient to their home or office. Second, location offers an opportunity to gain a long-term advantage over the competition. When a retailer has the best location, a competing retailer must settle for the second-best location.

A retailer's organization design and human resource management strategies are intimately related to its market strategy. For example, retailers that attempt to serve national or regional markets must make trade-offs between the efficiency of centralized buying and their need to tailor merchandise and services to local demands. Retailers that focus on customer segments seeking high-quality customer service need to motivate and enable sales associates to provide the expected levels of service. The organization structure and human resource policies discussed in Chapter 9 coordinate the activities of buyers, store managers, and sales associates in the implementation of the retailing strategy.

Retail information and supply chain management systems also offer a significant opportunity for retailers to gain strategic advantage. Chapter 10 reviews how retailers are developing sophisticated computer and distribution technologies to monitor flows of information and merchandise from vendors to retail distribution centers to retail stores. These technologies are part of an overall inventory management system that enables retailers to (1) make sure desired merchandise is available when customers want it and (2) minimize the retailer's inventory investment.

Retailers, like most businesses, want to develop repeat purchases and loyalty in their best customers. Chapter 11 examines customer relationship management—the process that retailers use to identify, design programs for, increase the share of wallet of, provide more value to, and build loyalty among their best customers. The role of these strategic retail decisions, covered in Section III, is illustrated below by the strategic changes JCPenney has undertaken to cope with changes in its environment.

JCPenney Moves from Main Street to Multichannel Retailing

Sixty years ago, JCPenney's target market was middle-income consumers living in small towns. In its Main Street locations, Penney sold high-quality, staple soft goods—underwear, socks, basic clothing, sheets, tablecloths, and so forth—at low prices with friendly service. To reduce costs, all sales were cash; the company didn't offer credit to its customers. Penney had considerable expertise in the design and purchase of private-label soft goods—brands developed by Penney and sold exclusively at its stores.

To tailor its offerings to local communities, its organization structure was decentralized. Each store manager determined the type of merchandise sold, the pricing of merchandise, and the management of store employees. Merchandise was shipped directly to each store from the suppliers. Promotional efforts were limited and also controlled by store managers. Penney's store managers were active participants in their community's social and political activities.

Penney's long-term financial performance was threatened because of changes in its macro- and microenvironment. First, rising education and disposable income created a growing interest in fashionable merchandise rather than the more staple goods Penney was offering. Second, the development of the interstate highway system stimulated the decline of inner cities, the growth of suburbs, and the development of regional malls. Small-town residents were attracted to these conveniently located, large, regional shopping malls. Third, Sears (the nation's largest retailer at the time) and regional department store chains were abandoning their inner-city locations and opening stores in regional malls.

In the early 1960s, Penney changed its strategy in response to these changes in its environment. It shifted its strategy to target suburban families; open larger stores in regional malls; and add new merchandise lines: appliances, auto supplies, paint, hardware, sporting goods, consumer electronics, and moderately priced fashionable clothing. The firm began to offer credit, sales through direct mail catalogs, and other services to this more discerning, time-pressured, middle-income, suburban market segment. (It is interesting to note that as JCPenney was moving from small towns to suburban malls, Walmart began opening discount stores in small towns.)

To effectively control its mall-based department stores, Penney installed a national communication network. Store managers could monitor daily sales of each type of merchandise in their store and every other store in the chain. Buyers at corporate headquarters in New York and then Dallas communicated daily with merchandise managers in each store over a satellite TV link, but store managers continued to make merchandise decisions for their stores and merchandise continued to be shipped directly to each store.

Penney's strategy targeting middle-income suburban families was successful until another major change in its microenvironment in the 90s forced Penney to alter its strategy again. The success of discount stores posed a growing threat for JCPenney. Department stores targeting middle-income families, such as JCPenney and Sears, were caught in the middle between higher-priced, fashion-oriented department store chains like Macy's and discount stores offering more fashionable apparel, such as Target. In addition, Kohl's launched a department store concept that was appealing to Penney's target market. Kohl's off-the-mall locations were more convenient for customers, and its centralized buying and more sophisticated supply management systems enabled Kohl's to get a cost advantage over Penney.

To compete effectively in this new environment, Penney made some strategic changes that affect how it operates, its organizational structure, where it locates its stores, its store atmosphere, and its merchandise/service offerings. Some specific changes are:

- Penney reorganized its store, catalog, and Internet channels to provide a seamless, multichannel offering for its customers so that they can shop at Penney anywhere, anytime. Now JCPenney is one of the largest retailers selling merchandise through its catalog and Internet channels.

- It reduced its distribution costs by shipping merchandise through distribution centers rather than using direct delivery from suppliers to stores.

- It centralized merchandise management. Buyers at corporate headquarters, rather than store managers, make the merchandise decisions. This centralization of merchandise decisions enables JCPenney to use its size to buy merchandise at a lower cost and respond more quickly to changing fashions.

- To increase customer convenience, JCPenney is building new stores away from malls in stand-alone locations and designing the stores with centralized checkout counters rather than checkout counters in each area of the store.

- It offers more fashionable merchandise with exclusive designer brands including MNG by Mango, American Living by Ralph Lauren, C7P by Chip and Pepper Foster, Liz Claiborne, Nicole by Nicole Miller, and Allen B. by Allen B. Schwartz. It has also added France's Sephora cosmetics as a "store-in-stores" concept.

JCPenney has evolved its strategy to changes in the retail environment. It now offers more fashion-forward merchandise in mall and off-mall stores plus its catalog and Internet channels.

EXHIBIT 1–5
Elements in the Retail Mix

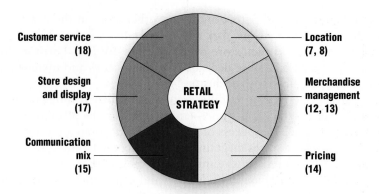

Implementing the Retail Strategy—Sections III and IV

To implement a retail strategy, retailers develop a retail mix that satisfies the needs of its target market better than that of its competitors. The **retail mix** is a set of decisions retailers make to satisfy customer needs and influence their purchase decisions. Elements in the retail mix (Exhibit 1–5) include the types of merchandise and services offered, merchandise pricing, advertising and promotional programs, store design, merchandise display, assistance to customers provided by salespeople, and convenience of the store's location. Section III reviews the implementation decisions made by buyers, and Section IV focuses on decisions made by store managers.

Managers in the buying organization must decide how much and what types of merchandise to buy (Chapter 12), what vendors to use and how to interact with them (Chapter 13), the retail prices to set (Chapter 14), and how to advertise and promote merchandise (Chapter 15). Store managers must determine how to recruit, select, and motivate sales associates (Chapter 16), where and how merchandise will be displayed (Chapter 17), and the nature of services to provide for customers (Chapter 18). In the next section, we use Whole Foods Market, one of the fastest-growing supermarket chains, to illustrate the merchandise and store management decisions supporting a retailer's strategy.

Whole Foods Market: An Organic and Natural Food Supermarket Chain

In the 1960s, natural, organic foods were available only in farmers' markets or small specialty stores catering to counterculture consumers. Consumers who patronized these health food stores felt that eating organic food would liberate them from the grasp of big agribusiness and food processors that were destroying the land with chemical pesticides, mistreating migrant farmworkers, and hooking people on unhealthy processed foods.

Whole Foods' strategy is to target a broader market of health-conscious and environmentally conscious consumers by using a more traditional supermarket format, rather than small, specialty health food stores.

Merchandise Management   In terms of merchandise, Whole Foods stores offer the array of food categories typically found in a supermarket. However, the assortment emphasizes organic and natural products that are fresh, nutritious, and safe to eat. Products are free of artificial preservatives, colors, flavors, and sweeteners, as well as hydrogenated fats and other unacceptable ingredients. In addition, Whole Foods seeks out and supports local producers whose fruits and vegetables meet its standards, particularly those who farm organically and are dedicated to environmentally friendly, sustainable agriculture.

Whole Foods offers seven lines of private-label products. Buyers work with artisan food producers and organic farmers to attain products sold under the superpremium Authentic Food Artisan brand. Its core private brands are called Whole

Brands (department-specific products), Whole Foods (premium products), and Whole Kids Organic (organic products for children). The 365 Day Everyday Value and 365 Day Organic Everyday Value lines provide natural products at value prices.

Store Management   All Whole Foods employees are organized into self-managed teams that meet regularly to discuss issues and solve problems. Almost all team members have stock options in the firm. Other company benefits include a 20 percent team member store discount, health care coverage for domestic partners, and a personal wellness account to help cover health care expenses. Every three years team members select their benefits package through a companywide vote. To ensure that employees are compensated equitably, the company has a cap on salaries so that no employee's total compensation can be greater than 19 times the compensation of the lowest-level employee. Whole Foods has been on *Fortune* magazine's "100 Best Companies to Work For" list for 13 consecutive years.

Whole Foods' decisions on visual merchandising and store design reinforce its strategy.[20] Its stores are designed to make grocery shopping fun—to transform a supermarket into an interactive theater with corporate staff serving as the producer and store management as the director. Sections of its newer stores are designed with self-contained architecture that curves inward, creating a feeling of intimacy that encourages shoppers to linger. The warm feeling of the store is enhanced by signs made of an eco-friendly woodlike material rather than plastic. Art gallery–type lighting focuses attention on produce.

Finally, Whole Foods' store management provides excellent customer service. Curious about the life of a chicken in the display case? It comes with a 16-page booklet and an invitation to visit the live chickens at the company's Pennsylvania farm. Ask about a farmer, and you get a name and personal details. Inquire about a cut of fish while at the free seafood filleting station, and you get the name of the captain on one of Whole Foods' own fishing boats.

Whole Foods' Web site has extensive information about natural and organic foods. Looking for the nearest Whole Foods store? Want a recipe for a creative chicken dish? Whole Foods Market has an iPhone application that allows customers to search for stores by zip code (with hours, address, maps, and specials on each store page) and access the more than 2,000 recipes Whole Foods has online. The recipes can be searched by ingredient, special diets, and other elements such as "budget"

Whole Foods has a retail mix that implements its strategy targeting health-conscious consumers.

and "family friendly." Each recipe contains detailed preparation instructions and nutritional information. The application also includes an "On Hand" feature by which customers can enter ingredients and get back meal recommendations.

Ethical and Legal Considerations

When making the decisions discussed previously, managers need to consider the ethical and legal implications of their decisions, in addition to the effects that those decisions have on the profitability of their firms and the satisfaction of their customers. **Ethics** are the principles governing individuals and companies that establish appropriate behavior and indicate what is right and wrong. Defining the term is easy, but determining what the principles are is difficult. What one person thinks is ethical, another may consider unethical.

What is ethical can vary from country to country and from industry to industry. For example, offering bribes to overcome bureaucratic roadblocks is an accepted practice in Middle Eastern countries but is considered unethical, and even illegal, in the United States. Ethical principles also can change over time. For example, some years ago, doctors and lawyers who advertised their services were considered unethical. Today such advertising is accepted as common practice.

Examples of difficult situations that retail managers face include the following:

- Should a retailer sell merchandise that it suspects was made using child labor?
- Should a retailer advertise that its prices are the lowest available in the market, even though some are not?
- Should a retail buyer accept an expensive gift from a vendor?
- Should a retailer charge a supplier a fee for getting a new item in its store?
- Should retail salespeople use a high-pressure sales approach when they know the product is not the best for the customer's needs?
- Should a retailer disclose product information that may affect whether or not it is purchased?
- Should a retailer promote a product as being "on sale" if it never sold at a higher, nonsale price?
- Should a retailer offer credit at a higher interest rate or sell products at higher prices in stores patronized mostly by low-income customers?

Laws dictate which activities society has deemed to be clearly wrong, those activities for which retailers and their employees will be punished through the federal or state legal systems. However, most business decisions are not regulated by laws. Often retail managers have to rely on their firms' and industries' codes of ethics and/or their own codes of ethics to determine the right thing to do.

Many companies have codes of ethics to provide guidelines for their employees in making their ethical decisions. These ethical policies provide a clear sense of right and wrong so that companies and their customers can depend on their employees when questionable situations arise. However, in many situations, retail managers need to rely on their personal code of ethics—their personal sense of what is right or wrong.

Exhibit 1–6 lists some questions you can ask yourself to determine whether a behavior or activity is unethical. The questions emphasize that ethical behavior is determined by widely accepted views of what is right and wrong. Thus, you should engage only in activities about which you would be proud to tell your family, friends, employer, and customers. If the answer to any of these questions is yes, the behavior or activity is probably unethical, and you should not do it.

Your firm can strongly affect the ethical choices you will have to make. When you view your firm's policies or requests as improper, you have three choices:

1. *Ignore your personal values, and do what your company asks you to do.* Self-respect suffers when you have to compromise your principles to please an employer. If

1. Would I be embarrassed if a customer found out about this behavior?
2. Would my supervisor disapprove of this behavior?
3. Would most coworkers feel that this behavior is unusual?
4. Am I about to do this because I think I can get away with it?
5. Would I be upset if a company did this to me?
6. Would my family or friends think less of me if I told them about engaging in this activity?
7. Am I concerned about the possible consequences of this behavior?
8. Would I be upset if this behavior or activity was publicized in a newspaper article?
9. Would society be worse off if everyone engaged in this behavior or activity?

EXHIBIT 1–6
Checklist for Making
Ethical Decisions

you take this path, you will probably feel guilty and be dissatisfied with your job in the long run.

2. *Take a stand, and tell your employer what you think.* Try to influence the decisions and policies of your company and supervisors.

3. *Refuse to compromise your principles.* Taking this path may mean you will get fired or be forced to quit.

You should not take a job with a company whose products, policies, and conduct conflict with your standards. Before taking a job, investigate the company's procedures and selling approach to see whether they conflict with your personal ethical standards. Throughout this text, we will highlight the legal and ethical issues associated with the retail decisions made by managers.

SUMMARY

Retailing is a global, high-tech industry that plays a major role in the global economy. About one in five U.S. workers is employed by retailers. Increasingly, retailers are selling their products and services through more than one channel—such as stores, Internet, and catalogs. Firms selling services to consumers, such as dry cleaning and automobile repairs, are also retailers.

Retailing is defined as a set of business activities that add value to the products and services sold to consumers for their personal or family use. These value-added activities include providing assortments, breaking bulk, holding inventory, and providing services.

Retailing offers opportunities for exciting, challenging careers, either by working for a retail firm or starting your own business. Aspects of retail careers are discussed in Appendix 1A. Suggestions about starting your own business and franchising appear in Appendix 1 and Appendix 2 at the end of the book.

The retail management decision process involves developing a strategy for creating a competitive advantage in the marketplace and then developing a retail mix to implement that strategy. The strategic decisions, discussed in the first section of this textbook, involve selecting a target market, defining the nature of the retailer's offering, and building a competitive advantage through locations, human resource management, information and supply chain management systems, and customer relationship management programs.

The merchandise and store management decisions for implementing the strategy, discussed in the second half of this textbook, involve selecting a merchandise assortment, buying merchandise, setting prices, communicating with customers, managing the store, presenting merchandise in stores, and providing customer service. Large retail chains use sophisticated information systems to analyze business opportunities and make these decisions about how to operate their businesses in multiple countries.

KEY TERMS

backward integration, *7*

breaking bulk, *8*

corporate social responsibility (CSR), *8*

ethics, *22*

forward integration, *7*

holding inventory, *8*

intertype competition, *15*

intratype competition, *15*

retailer, *6*

retailing, *6*

retail mix, *20*

retail strategy, *17*

scrambled merchandising, *15*

supply chain, *6*

vertical integration, *7*

wholesalers, *7*

GET OUT AND DO IT!

1. **CONTINUING CASE ASSIGNMENT** In most chapters of this textbook, there will be a GET OUT AND DO IT! assignment that will give you an opportunity to examine the strategy and tactics of one retailer. Your first assignment is to select a retailer and prepare a report on the retailer's history, including when it was founded and how it has evolved over time. To ensure that you can get information about the retailer for subsequent Continuing Case Assignments, the retailer you select should:

   - *Be a publicly held company so that you can access its financial statements and annual reports.* Do not select a retailer that is owned by another company. For example, since Bath & Body Works is owned by Limited Brands, you can get financial information about only the holding company and not the individual companies it owns, such as Victoria's Secret and White Barn Candle.
   - *Focus on one type of retailing.* For example, Abercrombie & Fitch operates just one type of specialty stores and thus would be a good choice. However, Walmart operates discount stores, warehouse club stores, and supercenters and thus would not be a good choice.
   - *Be easy to visit and collect information about.* Some retailers and store managers may not allow you to interview them about the store, take pictures of the store, talk with sales associates, or analyze the merchandise assortment in the store. Try to pick a retailer with a local store manager who can help you complete the assignments.

   Some examples of retailers that meet the first two criteria are Whole Foods Market, Dress Barn, Burlington Coat Factory, Ross Stores, Ann Taylor, Cato, Finish Line, Foot Locker, Brookstone, Claire's, Walgreens, Staples, Office Depot, Borders, American Eagle Outfitter, Pacific Sunwear, Abercrombie & Fitch, Tiffany & Co., Zales, Autozone, Pep Boys, Hot Topic, Wet Seal, Best Buy, Family Dollar, Dollar General, Michaels, PetSmart, Dillard's, Pier 1 Imports, Home Depot, Lowe's, Bed Bath & Beyond, Men's Warehouse, Kroger, Kohl's, Radio Shack, Safeway, and Target.

2. **GO SHOPPING** Visit a local retail store, and describe each of the elements in its retail mix.

3. **INTERNET EXERCISE** Data on U.S. retail sales are available at the U.S. Bureau of the Census Internet site at http://www.census.gov/retail/#ecommerce. Look at "Estimates of Monthly Retail and Food Services Sales by Kind of Business" for the most recent year. In which months are sales the highest? Which kinds of businesses experience the greatest fluctuations in monthly sales? List reasons that help explain your findings.

4. **INTERNET EXERCISE** Go to the home pages of Macy's Careers After College (http://www.macysjobs.com/college/), Sears Holdings Corporation College Programs (http://www.searsholdings.com/careers/college), and National Retail Federation Retail Careers Center (http://www.nrf.com/RetailCareers/) to find information about retail careers with these organizations. Review the information about the different positions described. In which positions would you be interested? Which positions are not of interest to you? Which employer would interest you? Why?

5. **INTERNET EXERCISE** Choose one of the top-20 retailers (Exhibit 1–2). Go to the company's Web site, and find out how the company started and how it has changed over time.

6. **INTERNET EXERCISE** Go online and find an example of a retailer involved in corporate social responsibility. In a brief paragraph describe how this retailer is taking steps to contribute to a social or ethical cause.

DISCUSSION QUESTIONS AND PROBLEMS

1. What is your favorite retailer? Why do you like this retailer? What would a competitive retailer have to do to get your patronage?

2. From your perspective, what are the benefits and limitations of purchasing a home entertainment system directly from a number of component manufacturers rather than from a retailer?

3. What retailers would be considered intratype competitors for a convenience store chain such as 7-Eleven? What firms would be intertype competitors?

4. How does Walmart contribute and detract from the communities in which it operates stores?

5. Choose a U.S.-based retailer that wants to open a new store outside the United States for the first time. Which country should it pursue? Why?

6. Think of your top-five favorite retailers. Are they regional, national, or global companies? Could any of the regional or national companies have success in the future in a global market? Explain your response. What countries were the original homes for the global retailers? What contributed to the success of the expansion from the home country to an international market?

7. Why do retail managers need to consider ethical issues when making decisions?

8. From a personal perspective, how does retailing rate as a potential career compared with others you are considering?

9. How might managers at different levels of a retail organization define their competition?

10. Retailing View 1.1 describes how some retailers are acting socially responsibly. Take the perspective of a stockholder in one of these companies. What effect will these activities have on the value of its stock? Why might they have a positive or negative effect?

SUGGESTED READINGS

Cao, L. L., and M. Dupuis. "Core Competencies, Strategy and Performance: The Case of International Retailers in China." *International Review of Retail, Distribution and Consumer Research* 19 (September 2009), pp. 349–358.

Etgar, Michael, and Dalia Rachman-Moore. "Determinant Factors of Failures of International Retailers in Foreign Markets." *International Review of Retail, Distribution and Consumer Research* 17 (February 2007), pp. 79–81.

Krafft, Manfred, and Murali K. Mantrala. *Retailing in the 21st Century: Current and Future Trends*, 2nd ed. New York: Springer, 2010.

Kumar, Sameer, Mathew J. Anselmo, and Kathryn J. Berndt. "Transforming the Retail Industry: Potential and Challenges with RFID Technology." *Transportation Journal* 48 (Fall 2009), pp. 61–72.

Lee, Min-young, Ann Fairhurst, and Scarlett Wesley. "Corporate Social Responsibility: A Review of the Top 100 US Retailers." *Corporate Reputation Review* (London) 12 (Summer 2009), pp. 140–159.

Lichtenstein, Nelson. *The Retail Revolution: How Wal-Mart Created a Brave New World of Business*, 2nd ed. New York: Metropolitan Books, 2010.

Plunkett, Jack (ed.) *Plunkett's Retail Industry Almanac 2010*. Houston: Plunkett Research, 2009.

Reynolds, Jonathan, and Latchezar Hristov. "Are There Barriers to Innovation in Retailing?" *International Review of Retail, Distribution and Consumer Research* 19 (September 2009), pp. 317–333.

Sharp Paine, Lynn. "Ethics: A Basic Framework." *Harvard Business Review*, May 14, 2007, pp. 35–50.

2009 Global Powers in Retailing. New York: Deloitte Touche Tohmatsu, January 2010.

APPENDIX 1A   Careers in Retailing

Retailing offers exciting and challenging career opportunities. Few other industries grant as many responsibilities to young managers. When students asked Dave Fuente, former CEO of Office Depot, what they needed to become a CEO someday, he responded, "You need to have profit and loss responsibility and the experience of managing people early in your career." Entry-level retail jobs for college graduates offer both these opportunities. Most college graduates begin their retail careers as assistant buyers, merchandise planners, or department managers in stores. In these positions, they are responsible for the profitability of a line of merchandise or an area of the store, and they manage people who work for them.

Even if you work for a large company, retailing provides an opportunity for you to do your own thing and be rewarded. You can come with an idea, execute it almost immediately, and see how well it is doing by reviewing the sales data at the end of the day.

Retailing offers a variety of career paths, such as buying, store management, sales promotion and advertising, personnel, operations/distribution, loss prevention, and finance. In addition, retailing offers almost immediate accountability for talented people, so they can reach key management positions fairly quickly. Starting salaries are competitive, and the compensation of top management ranks among the highest in any industry.

CAREER OPPORTUNITIES

In retail firms, career opportunities are in merchandising/buying, store management, and corporate staff functions. Corporate positions are in accounting, finance, real estate, promotions and advertising, computer and distribution systems, and human resources.

The primary entry-level opportunities for a retailing career are in the areas of buying and store management. Buying positions are more numbers-oriented, whereas store management positions are more people-oriented. Entry-level positions on the corporate staff are limited. Retailers typically want all of their employees to understand their customers and their merchandise. Therefore, most executives and corporate staff managers begin their careers in merchandise or store management.

Store Management

Successful store managers must have the ability to lead and motivate employees. They also need to be sensitive to customers' needs by making sure that merchandise is available and neatly displayed.

Store management involves all the discipline necessary to run a successful business: sales planning and goal setting, overall store image and merchandise presentation, budgets and expense control, customer service and sales supervision, personnel administration and development, and community relations.

Since store managers work in stores, they are often at quite a distance from the home office, which means they have limited direct supervision. Their hours generally mirror those of their store and can therefore include some weekends and evenings. In addition, they spend time during nonoperating hours tending to administrative responsibilities.

The typical entry-level store management position is a department manager with responsibility for merchandise presentation, customer service, and inventory control for an area of the store. The next level is an area or group manager with responsibility for executing merchandising plans and achieving sales goals for several areas, as well as supervising, training, and developing department managers. Beyond these positions, you might be promoted to store manager, then to district manager responsible for a group of stores, and then to regional manager responsible for a group of districts.

Merchandise Management

Merchandise management attracts people with strong analytical capabilities, an ability to predict what merchandise will appeal to their target markets, and a skill for negotiating with vendors as well as store management to get things done. Many retailers have broken the merchandising management activities into two different yet parallel career paths: buying and merchandise planning.

Retail merchandise buyers are similar to financial portfolio managers. They invest in a portfolio of merchandise, monitor the performance (sales) of the merchandise, and on the basis of the sales, either decide to buy more merchandise that is selling well or get rid of (discount) merchandise that is selling poorly. Buyers are responsible for selecting the type and amount of merchandise to buy, negotiating the wholesale price and payment terms with suppliers, setting the initial retail price for the merchandise, monitoring merchandise sales, and making appropriate retail price adjustments. Thus buyers need to have good financial planning skills, knowledge of their customers' needs and wants and competitive activities, and the ability to develop good working relationships with vendors. To develop a better understanding of their customers, buyers typically stay in contact with their stores by visiting them, talking to sales associates and managers, and monitoring the sales data available through their merchandise management systems.

Planners have an even more analytical role than buyers. Their primary responsibility is to determine the assortment of merchandise sent to each store—how many styles, colors, sizes, and individual items. Once the merchandise is in the stores, planners closely monitor sales and work with buyers on decisions such as how much additional merchandise to purchase if the merchandise is doing well or when to mark down the merchandise if sales are below expectations.

The typical entry-level position of college graduates interested in merchandise management is either assistant buyer or assistant planner in a merchandise category such as men's athletic shoes or consumer electronics. In these positions, you will do the sales analysis needed to support the decisions eventually made by the planner or buyer for whom you work. From this entry-level position, you could be promoted to buyer and then divisional merchandise manager, responsible for a number of merchandise categories. Most retailers believe that merchandise management skills are not category-specific. Thus, as you are promoted in the buying organization, you will probably work in various merchandise categories.

Corporate Staff

The corporate staff positions in retail firms involve activities and require knowledge, skills, and abilities similar to those in comparable positions in nonretail firms. Thus many managers in these positions identify with their profession rather than the retail industry. For example, accountants in retail firms view themselves as accountant, not retailers.

Management Information Systems (MISs)   Employees in this area are involved with applications for capturing data and developing and maintaining inventory, as well as the design of store systems such as POS terminals, self-checkout systems, and in-store kiosks.

Operations/Distribution   Operations employees are responsible for operating and maintaining the store's physical plant; providing various customer services; overseeing the receipt, ticketing, warehousing, and distribution of a store's inventory; and buying and maintaining store supplies and operating equipment. Students in operations and MIS typically major in production, operations, or computer information systems.

Promotions/Advertising   Promotion's many aspects include public relations, advertising, visual merchandising, and special events. This department attempts to build the retail firm's brand image and encourage customers to visit the retailer's stores and/or Web site. Managers in this area typically major in marketing or mass communications.

Loss Prevention   Loss prevention employees are responsible for protecting the retailer's assets. They develop systems and procedures to minimize employee theft and shoplifting. Managers in this area often major in sociology or criminology, although, as we discuss in Chapters 9 and 16, loss prevention is beginning to be viewed as a human resource management issue.

Finance/Accounting   Many retailers are large businesses involved in complicated corporate structures. Most retailers also operate with a tight net profit margin. With such a fine line between success and failure, retailers continue to require financial experts. The finance/accounting division is responsible for the financial health of the company. Employees in this division prepare financial reports for all aspects of the business, including long-range forecasting and planning, economic trend analysis and budgeting, shortage control and internal audits, gross and net profit, accounts payable to vendors, and accounts receivable from charge customers. In addition, they manage the retailer's relationship with the financial community. Students interested in this area often major in finance or accounting.

Real Estate   Employees in the real estate division are responsible for selecting locations for stores, negotiating leases and land purchases, and managing the leasehold costs. Students entering this area typically major in real estate or finance.

Store Design   Employees working in this area are responsible for designing the store and presenting merchandise and fixtures in the store. Talented, creative students in business, architecture, art, and other related fields will have innumerable opportunities for growth in the area of retail store design.

Human Resource Management   Human resource management is responsible for the effective selection, training, placement, advancement, and welfare of employees. Because there are seasonal peaks in retailing (such as Christmas, when many extra people must be hired), human resource personnel must be flexible and highly efficient.

MYTHS ABOUT RETAILING

Sales Clerk Is the Entry-Level Job in Retailing

Many students and their parents think that people working in retailing have jobs as sales clerks and cashiers. They hold this view because, as customers in retail stores, they typically interact only with sales associates, not their managers. But as we have discussed in this chapter, retail firms are large, sophisticated corporations that employ managers with a wide variety of knowledge, skills, and abilities. Entry-level positions for college are typically management trainees in the buying or store organization, not sales associates.

Management trainees in retailing are given more responsibility more quickly than their counterparts in other industries. Buyers are responsible for choosing, promoting, pricing, distributing, and selling millions of dollars' worth of merchandise each season. The department manager, generally the first position after a training program, is often responsible for merchandising one or more departments, as well as managing 20 or more full- and part-time sales associates.

College and University Degrees Are Not Needed to Succeed in Retailing

While some employees are promoted on the basis of their retail experience, a college degree is needed for most retail management positions, ranging from store manager to CEO. More than 150 colleges and universities in the United States offer programs of study and degrees or majors in retailing.

Retail Jobs Are Low-Paying

Starting salaries for management trainees with a college degree range from $30,000 to $65,000 a year, and the compensation of top management ranks with the highest in industry. For example, store managers with only a few years of experience can earn up to $100,000 or more, depending on their performance bonuses. A senior buyer for a department store earns from $50,000 to $90,000 or

more. A big box store manager can earn from $50,000 to $150,000; a discount store manager makes from $70,000 to $100,000 or more; and a specialty store manager earns from $35,000 to $60,000 or more.

Compensation varies according to the amount of responsibility. Specialty store managers are generally paid less than department store managers because their annual sales volume is lower. But advancements in this area can be faster. Aggressive specialty store managers often are promoted to district managers and run 8 to 15 units after a few years, so they quickly move into higher pay brackets.

Because information systems enable retailers to assess the sales and profit performance of each manager, and even each sales associate, the compensation of retail managers is closely linked to objective measures of their performance. As a result, in addition to their salaries, retail managers are generally given strong monetary incentives based on the sales they create.

A compensation package consists of more than salary alone. In retailing, the benefits package is often substantial and may include a profit-sharing plan, savings plan, stock options, medical and dental insurance, life insurance, long-term disability protection and income protection plans, and paid vacations and holidays. Two additional benefits of retailing careers are that most retailers offer employees valuable discounts on the merchandise they sell, and some buying positions include extensive foreign travel.

Retailing Is a Low-Growth Industry with Little Opportunity for Advancement

While the growth rate of retail parallels the growth rate of the overall economy, many opportunities for rapid advancement exist simply because of the sheer size of the retail industry. With so many retail firms, there is always a large number of firms that are experiencing a high growth rate, opening many new stores, and needing store managers and support staff positions.

Working in Retailing Requires Long Hours and Frequent Relocation

Retailing has an often exaggerated reputation of demanding long and unusual hours. Superficially, this reputation is true. Store managers do work some evenings and weekends. But progressive retailers realize that if the unusual hours aren't offset by time off at other periods during the week, many managers become inefficient, angry, and resentful—in other words, burned out. It's also important to put the concept of long hours into perspective. Most professional careers require more than 40 hours a week for the person to succeed. In a new job with new tasks and responsibilities, the time commitment is even greater.

Depending on the type of retailer and the specific firm, retailing enables executives to change locations often or not at all. In general, a career path in store management has more opportunity for relocation than paths in buying/merchandising or corporate. Because buying and corporate offices are usually centrally located, these positions generally are not subject to frequent moves. In addition, employees in corporate positions and merchandise management tend to work during normal business hours.

Types of Retailers

EXECUTIVE BRIEFING
Michael MacDonald, President and CEO,
DSW Shoe Warehouse

After receiving a BBA, I started my career as a CPA in public accounting. Three years later, I took a financial position with a Detroit-based retail department store chain, J.L. Hudson Company. While working full-time at Hudson, I earned an MBA by attending evening classes over a three-year period.

A synopsis of my career illustrates the range of skills needed by a CEO and also demonstrates the ever-changing nature of retail: Many of the department store chains I have worked for have merged or been acquired, with name changes along the way. Today these companies are known as Target Corporation, Macy's, and Saks Incorporated.

By the time I was 29 years old, I had risen to CFO; and then, after nine years with what was then known as the Dayton-Hudson Corporation, I accepted a position at Marshall Field's. There I added IT responsibilities to my portfolio. From Marshall Field's, I went to Carson Pirie Scott (CPS) as chief administrative officer, adding legal, real estate, and supply chain responsibilities. In 1997, I was appointed CEO of CPS. My responsibilities broadened again to include merchandising, marketing, and stores. Two other chains were merged into CPS, and the resulting company was subsequently sold. In 2006, I joined Shopko Stores as CEO; and, three years later, I became CEO of DSW Shoe Warehouse.

DSW is a $1.6 billion footwear retailer—the number-two branded adult footwear retailer in the United States. We operate 306 stores in 39 states and 350 leased shoe departments as well as an e-commerce site, DSW.com. Our retail strategy combines a breathtaking assortment of wanted brands; 20,000 to 30,000 pairs of shoes per store; an everyday discount pricing model; a convenient, assisted self-select service model; and a no-frills shopping environment.

CHAPTER 2

QUESTIONS

What are the different types of retailers?

How do retailers differ in terms of how they meet the needs of their customers?

What trends are shaping today's retailers?

How do services retailers differ from merchandise retailers?

What are the types of ownership for retail firms?

It's my responsibility to lead strategy development, create operational alignment within the company, oversee talent selection and development, and serve as the primary communicator within the company. My days are spent communicating with functional heads to assess progress on initiatives, discuss opportunities and risks, and solve problems. I also track business trends, visit stores, monitor progress on strategic initiatives, meet with investors and suppliers, and communicate regularly with the board of directors. In short, I attend or oversee a lot of meetings.

I derive great satisfaction from leading a team of motivated individuals who are working together for a common purpose and getting results. I love dealing with a product with which customers have an emotional attachment, and I enjoy the immediate customer feedback I get via daily sales reports. I also enjoy developing people's talents, leading, communicating, creating an environment where people have fun, and creating an alignment of teams, and I enjoy competing . . . and winning!

You want to have a good cup of coffee in the morning, not instant, but you don't want to bother with grinding coffee beans, boiling water, pouring it through ground coffee in a filter, and waiting. Think of all the different retailers that could help you satisfy this need. You could get your cup of brewed coffee from the drive-through window at the local Starbucks, or you could decide to buy an automatic coffeemaker with a timer so that your coffee will be ready when you wake up. You could purchase the coffeemaker at a discount store like Walmart or Target, a department store like Macy's, a drugstore like CVS, or a category specialist like Best Buy. If you want to buy the coffeemaker without taking the time to visit a store, you could order it from the JCPenney catalog or go to www.thefind.com, search for "coffee and espresso maker," and review the information on 167,124 products sold by 13,794 retailers from Kohl's to Cooking.com.

All these retailers are competing against one another to satisfy your need for a hassle-free, good cup of coffee. Many are selling the same brands, but they offer different services, prices, environments, and convenience. For example, if you want to buy a low-price, basic coffeemaker, you can go to a discount store. But if you are interested in a coffeemaker with more features and want to have someone explain the different features, you can visit a department store or a category specialist.

To develop and implement a retail strategy, retailers need to understand the nature of competition in the retail marketplace. This chapter describes the different types of retailers and how they compete against one another by offering different benefits to consumers. These benefits are reflected in the nature of the retail mixes used by the retailers to satisfy customer needs: the types of merchandise and services offered, the degree to which their offerings emphasize services versus merchandise, and the prices charged.

RETAILER CHARACTERISTICS

The 1.9 million[1] U.S. retailers range from street vendors selling hot dogs to multichannel retailers such as Staples that offer products in their stores and through catalog and Internet channels. The different types of retailers offer unique benefits. The type of retailer a consumer chooses to patronize depends on the benefits the consumer is seeking. For example, you might value the convenience of buying a gift shirt from a catalog retailer that will ship it to a friend in another city. Alternatively, you might prefer to buy a shirt from a local store when making a purchase for yourself so that you can try it on. You might go to a discount store to buy an inexpensive shirt for a camping trip or a sporting goods specialty store to buy a shirt with the insignia of your favorite football team.

These retailers survive and prosper because they satisfy a group of consumers' needs more effectively than their competitors, and thus consumers patronize different retail types when they have different needs. As consumer needs and competition change, new retail formats are created and existing formats evolve. The initial category specialists in toys, consumer electronics, and home improvement supplies have been joined by a host of new specialists, including Zappos.com (shoes), Ulta (cosmetics), and Crate & Barrel (housewares). Rental companies represent an interesting retail format that has evolved from simple car or equipment rental companies to Netflix and Redbox movie rental firms. Bag Borrow or Steal, described in Retailing View 2.1, rents luxury.

At eBay Motors consumers can buy cars and motorcycles from thousands of individuals as well as established dealers. This Internet retailer competes with traditional automobile dealers that sell new and used cars using more conventional retailing methods. Many retailers are broadening their assortment so that their offerings overlap and competition increases. For example, office supply stores compete with warehouse clubs, supercenters, supermarkets, and convenience stores because they sell many of the same products.

The Internet channel has fundamentally changed the way many people shop. OpenTable, for instance, lets you make online restaurant reservations in many U.S. cities. Consumers are able to order food, locate retail stores, or find product information on their mobile phones. The Internet has also provided shoppers with multiple shopping channels. (See Chapter 3.) For instance, you may browse and buy products on walmart.com but pick up your purchases at the store. While in the store, you may see a giant trampoline that you would rather order online and have it delivered to your door.

The most basic characteristic used to describe the different types of retailers is their retail mix, or the elements retailers use to satisfy their customers' needs. Four elements of the retail mix are particularly useful for classifying retailers: the type of merchandise and/or services offered, the variety and assortment of merchandise offered, the level of customer service, and the price of the merchandise.

Type of Merchandise

The United States, Canada, and Mexico have developed a classification scheme, called the **North American Industry Classification System (NAICS),** to collect data on business activity in each country. Every business is assigned a hierarchical,

REFACT

The NAICS replaces the Standard Industrial Classification (SIC) system that had been used by the U.S. Census Bureau since the 1930s.

six-digit code based on the type of products and services it sells. The first two digits identify the firm's business sector, and the remaining four digits identify various subsectors.

The classifications for retailers selling merchandise, based largely on the type of merchandise sold, are illustrated in Exhibit 2–1. Merchandise retailers are in sectors 44 and 45. The next three digits provide a finer classification of merchandise retailers. For example, retailers selling clothing and clothing accessories are classified as 448, clothing stores as 4481, and men's clothing stores as 44811. The sixth digit, not illustrated in Exhibit 2–1, captures differences between the North American countries using the classification scheme.

RETAILING VIEW   Rent Some Luxury   2.1

Can't afford this purse? Just rent it from Bag Borrow or Steal.

Bag Borrow or Steal, founded in 2004 (www.BagBorrowOrSteal.com) rents luxury products such as handbags, jewelry, watches, and sunglasses to more than 1 million members. Customers have the option of becoming members by paying a monthly subscription fee that allows them to rent items for 20 percent off the listed prices and provides additional perks such as priority access to certain merchandise and reward points. For example, a BCBG clutch is available for about $9 a week or $25 a month for nonmembers, but members get 20 percent off. On the higher end, a Chloe Small Paddington Satchel bag that retails for about $1,300 rents for about $100 a week or $250 a month for nonmembers and about $65 a week and $200 a month for members. If a customer "falls in love" with an item, she has the option of paying a reduced price for it, based on its condition and age. The Web site also offers an outlet store that sells items at 40 to 85 percent off the suggested retail price, depending on their condition.

When it was just getting started, 70 percent of Bag Borrow or Steal's sales were from its opening price point bags, those under $500, and included many well-known brands such as Kate Spade and Coach. Now about 80 percent of its sales are

from the bags that retail for $1,500 and up from well-known designers like Gucci and Prada. The business has grown considerably; a typical wholesale buy from a vendor is from $500,000 to $750,000, an amount even rare for the biggest luxury retailers like Bergdorf Goodman.

Many of their customers already have designer bags or other high-end accessories but cannot afford to buy the selection that is available to them through Bag Borrow or Steal. A bag, for instance, is an accessory item for which many consumers are willing to spend up to their limit, or above, because of its "noticeability" compared with other articles of clothing. "Fashionistas" especially value the ability to carry many designer bags throughout the year rather than just one or two.

Sources: http://fora.tv/2009/02/13/Weathering_the_Storm_Retail_Solutions_for_All_Seasons#Bag_Borrow_or_Steal_Fashion_Meets_Online_Innovation (accessed October 6, 2009); Paul Demery, "New Capital Wave," *InternetRetailer.com,* September 2008; Sarah Lacy, "The Tech Beat," *BusinessWeek,* March 7, 2006; Kate M. Jackson, "Renting a Handful of Luxury," *Boston Globe,* October 13, 2005; www.bagborrow-orsteal.com (accessed October 6, 2009).

EXHIBIT 2–1
NAICS Codes for
Retailers

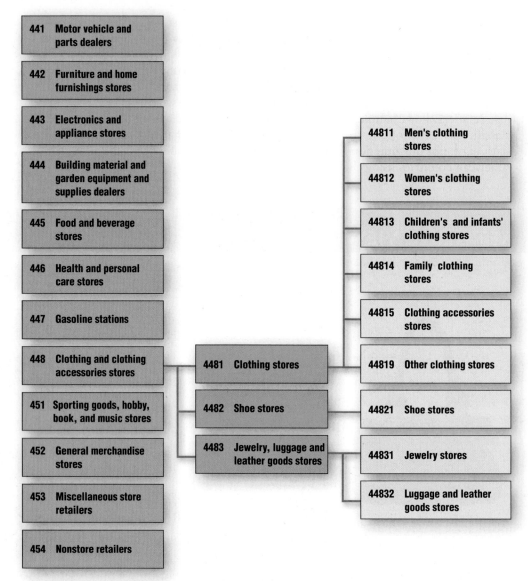

SOURCE: "North American Industry Classification System (NAICS)," U.S. Census Bureau, http://www.census.gov/epcd/www/naics.html.

Most services retailers are classified in sectors 71 (arts, entertainment, and recreation) and 72 (accommodation and food services). For example, food services and drinking places are in category 722, which is subdivided into full-service restaurants (7221) and limited-service eating places like fast-food restaurants (7222).

Variety and Assortment

Retailers can offer the same merchandise but differ in the variety and assortment of merchandise offered. **Variety** is the number of merchandise categories a retailer offers. **Assortment** is the number of different items offered in a merchandise category. Variety is often referred to as the **breadth of merchandise,** and assortment is referred to as the **depth of merchandise.** Each different item of merchandise is called a **stock-keeping unit (SKU).** Some examples of SKUs include an original scent, 33-ounce box of Tide laundry detergent with bleach or a blue, long-sleeve, button-down-collar Ralph Lauren shirt, size medium.

Warehouse clubs, discount stores, and toy stores all sell toys, but warehouse clubs and full-line discount stores sell many other categories of merchandise in addition to toys (i.e., they have greater variety). Stores specializing in toys stock

Variety and Assortment of Kayaks in Different Retail Outlets **EXHIBIT 2–2**

Retailer	Brand	White-Water	Recreational	Sea Touring	Fishing
EMS (Eastern Mountain Sports)	Necky		X	X	
	Wilderness Systems		X	X	X
	Hurricane			X	
	Perception		X		
	Old Town		X		
	Airis				X
			7 SKUs $489–$1,209	14 SKUs $1,259–$1,695	3 SKUs $975–$1,365
Outdoorplay.com	Axiom	X			
	Axis	X			
	WaveSport	X			
	Dagger	X	X	X	
	Airis	X	X		
	NRS	X			
	Wilderness Systems		X	X	X
	Perception		X	X	
	Necky		X	X	
	Advanced Elements		X		
	Ocean Kayak				X
	Freedom Hawk				X
		27 SKUs $649–$1,538	23 SKUs $449–$1,299	20 SKUs $794–$1,699	12 SKUs $849–$1,999
Walmart	K2			X	
	Waterquest		X		
	Airhead		X		
	Coleman		X		
			4 SKUs $299.98–$377.99	1 SKU $349.99	

more types of toys (more SKUs) and thus offer a greater assortment (i.e., greater depth in the form of more models, sizes, and brands) than the full-line discount stores or warehouse clubs.

Variety and assortment can also be applied to a specific merchandise category rather than an entire store. Exhibit 2–2 shows the breadth and depth of kayaks carried by EMS (Eastern Mountain Sports), an outdoor gear and equipment category specialist; Outdoorplay.com, an Internet kayak specialty retailer; and Walmart, a full-line discount store. Although EMS carries many of the same brands as Outdoorplay.com, EMS offers a narrower assortment—only four of the five categories—than Outdoorplay.com. Outdoorplay.com carries a deeper assortment of kayaks. Walmart has the least variety (only two categories) and the shallowest assortment, offering only 5 SKUs compared with 24 at EMS and 82 at Outdoorplay.com.

Services Offered

Retailers also differ in the services they offer customers. Customers expect almost all retailers to provide certain services: displaying merchandise, accepting credit cards, providing parking, and being open at convenient hours. Some retailers charge customers for other services, such as home delivery and gift wrapping. However, retailers may differ on other services. For example, EMS offers assistance in selecting the appropriate kayak, as well as repairs. Outdoorplay.com and Walmart do not provide these services.

Prices and the Cost of Offering Breadth and Depth of Merchandise and Services

Stocking a deep and broad assortment, like the one EMS offers in kayaks, is appealing to customers but costly for retailers. When a retailer offers many SKUs,

Rate EMS's variety and assortment of kayaks compared to Outdoorplay.com and Walmart.

its inventory investment increases, because the retailer must have backup stock for each and every SKU.

Similarly, services attract customers to the retailer, but they also are costly. More staff must be paid to provide information and assist customers, alter products to meet customers' needs, and demonstrate merchandise. Child care facilities, restrooms, dressing rooms, and check rooms take up valuable store space that could be used to stock and display merchandise. Offering delayed billing, credit, or installment payments requires a financial investment that could be used to buy more merchandise.

To make a profit, retailers that offer broader variety, deeper assortments, and/or additional services need to charge higher prices. For example, department stores have higher prices than discount stores because of their higher costs. Department stores stock more fashionable merchandise and have to reduce prices when they make a mistake in guessing what the popular styles will be. They also provide more personal sales service and have more expensive mall locations. In contrast, discount stores appeal to customers who are looking for lower prices. These consumers are less interested in the costly services provided by department stores. Thus, a critical retail decision involves the trade-off between the costs and benefits of maintaining additional inventory or providing additional services. Chapters 6 and 12 address the considerations required in making this trade-off.

In the next sections, we discuss the different types of food retailers and then general merchandise and services retailers. Exhibit 2–3 contains information about the size and growth rates for each of these retail sectors.

EXHIBIT 2–3
Sales and Growth Rate for Retail Sectors

	Estimated Sales, 2013 ($ millions)	Estimated Sales Growth 2008–2013 (%)
Food Retailers		
Conventional supermarkets	$622,896	3.3
Supercenters	354,905	7.1
Warehouse clubs	159,075	6.7
Convenience stores	748,186	3.0
General Merchandise Retailers		
Department stores	73,291	−0.9
Apparel and accessory specialty stores	210,236	4.5
Jewelry stores	36,848	3.4
Shoe stores	29,606	1.8
Furniture stores	66,262	2.2
Home furnishing stores	59,465	2.8
Office supply stores	26,404	2.2
Sporting goods stores	49,717	5.3
Bookstores	19,101	2.1
Building material, hardware, and garden supply stores	393,254	3.6
Consumer electronics and appliance stores	141,800	4.4
Drugstores	250,172	4.2
Full-line discount stores	126,385	0.0
Extreme-value stores	52,454	3.1
Nonstore Retailers		
Nonstore retailing	340,421	9.0
E-commerce	282,055	15.0

Sources: *Economic Forecast: Outlook to 2013 Food, Drug, Mass* (Columbus, OH: Retail Forward, November 2008); *Economic Forecast: Outlook to 2013 Homegoods* (Columbus, OH.: Retail Forward, November 2008); *Economic Forecast: Outlook to 2013 Softgoods* (Columbus, OH: Retail Forward, November 2008).

FOOD RETAILERS

The food retailing landscape is changing dramatically. Twenty years ago, consumers purchased food primarily at conventional supermarkets. Now conventional supermarkets account for slightly more than half of food sales (not including restaurants). The fastest-growing sectors of the food retail market are supercenters, warehouse clubs, convenience stores, and extreme-value food retailers.[3] While full-line discount stores like Walmart and warehouse clubs like Costco are offering more food items, traditional supermarkets are carrying more nonfood items. Many supermarkets offer pharmacies, health care clinics, photo processing centers, banks, and cafés.

The world's largest food retailer, Walmart, has more than $165 billion in sales of supermarket-type merchandise, followed by Carrefour (France), Tesco (United Kingdom), Metro Group (Germany), Schwartz Group (Germany), and Kroger (United States).[4] The largest supermarket chains in the United States are Kroger, Safeway, Supervalu, Publix, and Ahold US.[5]

Most of Walmart's food sales are generated from its supercenter format, whereas Carrefour garners most of its sales using the hypermarket format that it developed. The remaining larger food retailers primarily sell through conventional supermarkets. Exhibit 2–4 shows the retail mixes for different types of food retailers.

Supermarkets

A **conventional supermarket** is a large, self-service retail food store offering groceries, meat, and produce, as well as some nonfood items, such as health and beauty aids and general merchandise.[6] Perishables including meat, produce, baked goods, and dairy products account for 44 percent of supermarket sales and typically have higher margins than packaged goods.[7]

Whereas conventional supermarkets carry about 30,000 SKUs, **limited-assortment supermarkets,** or **extreme-value food retailers,** only stock about 2,000 SKUs.[8] The two largest limited-assortment supermarket chains in the United States are Save-A-Lot and ALDI. Retailing View 2.2 describes ALDI, a firm that makes Walmart seem luxurious.

Rather than carrying twenty brands of laundry detergent, limited-assortment supermarkets offer one or two brands and sizes, one of which is a store brand. Stores are designed to maximize efficiency and reduce costs. For example, merchandise is shipped in cartons on crates that can serve as displays so that no unloading is needed. Some costly services that consumers take for granted, such as free bags and paying with credit cards, are not provided. Stores are typically

	Conventional Supermarket	Limited-Assortment Supermarket	Supercenter	Warehouse Club	Convenience Store
Percentage food	70–80	80–90	30–40	60	90
Size (000 sq. ft.)	35–40	7–10	160–200	100–150	3–5
SKUs (000)	30–40	1–1.5	100–150	20	2–3
Variety	Average	Narrow	Broad	Broad	Narrow
Assortment	Average	Shallow	Deep	Shallow	Shallow
Ambience	Pleasant	Minimal	Average	Minimal	Average
Service	Modest	Limited	Limited	Limited	Limited
Prices	Average	Lowest	Low	Low	High
Gross margin (%)	20–22	10–12	15–18	12–15	25–30

EXHIBIT 2–4
Characteristics of Food Retailers

located in second- or third-tier shopping centers with low rents. By trimming costs, limited-assortment supermarkets can offer merchandise at prices 40 percent lower than those at conventional supermarkets.[10]

Trends in Supermarket Retailing   Although conventional supermarkets still sell a majority of food merchandise, they are under substantial competitive pressure. Everyone wants a piece of the food retail pie. Supercenters are rapidly attracting conventional supermarket customers with their broader assortments of food and general merchandise at attractive prices. General merchandise discount chains like Target and Walmart and extreme-value retailers like Dollar General and Family Dollar are increasing the amount of space they devote to consumables. Convenience stores are also selling more fresh merchandise.

Supercenters and warehouse clubs are particularly troublesome for supermarkets because their superior operating efficiencies enable them to have low costs and prices. These stores have tremendous bargaining power in the market because they can buy such large quantities. They also have invested heavily in state-of-the-art supply chains, assortment planning, and pricing systems that reduce their inventories while increasing their sales and margins. These activities are discussed in more detail in Chapters 10 and 12. Warehouse club stores concentrate on buying

2.2   RETAILING VIEW   ALDI: Provides Excellent Value in the United States

At ALDI in Germany and in the United States, customers bag their own groceries and rent grocery carts for a refundable fee of 25 cents. As a result, the company does not have to hire staff to bag groceries or recover carts from parking lots. Products are displayed in the same boxes in which they arrived, again minimizing the amount of needed labor. ALDI takes only cash, thus avoiding processing fees or bad checks. Stores are open only during peak shopping hours to minimize energy costs. ALDI limits its labor cost to 6 percent of sales, compared to 12 to 16 percent for the typical supermarket, by keeping limited store staff.

ALDI, short for "Albrecht Discount," after its founder Karl Albrecht, operates 8,500 stores worldwide and 1,000 in the United States. In Germany, 90 percent of the population shops at ALDI. With a saturated market, ALDI is looking for more growth in the United States.

ALDI achieves huge cost savings by offering around 1,300 SKUs compared to 45,000 at an average grocery store; this means higher inventory turnover and less spoilage. Ninety-five percent of sales are from its private-label brands, which provide

ALDI provides quality merchandise at low prices by reducing its assortment to control store operating expenses.

a higher profit margin than national brands. ALDI's products are priced 16 to 24 percent below retail prices at discount stores and 40 percent below retail prices at traditional supermarkets.

When ALDI first entered the United States in 1976, and the United Kingdom in 1990, it opened in low-income areas. But these sites were generally unsuccessful because poorer consumers could not afford fresh products, so much of the store's perishable merchandise went to waste. Now ALDI puts its stores in locations that attract middle-class shoppers who have higher disposable income and education but still want to save money.

ALDI also owns Trader Joe's. In keeping with its low-cost model, Trader Joe's features mainly private-label products and a limited selection, but its environment is more upscale and it specializes in fresh and gourmet products.

Source: Cecilie Rohwedder and David Kesmodel, "ALDI Looks to U.S. for Growth," *Wall Street Journal,* January 13, 2009; Andrew Martin, "The Allure of Plain Vanilla," *New York Times,* September 7, 2008.

special deals because they do not carry the consistent and deep assortment found in supermarkets.

To compete successfully against intrusions by other food retailing formats, conventional supermarkets are differentiating their offerings by (1) emphasizing fresh perishables, (2) targeting health-conscious and ethnic consumers, (3) providing better value with private-label merchandise, and (4) providing a better shopping experience.

Fresh Merchandise   Fresh-merchandise categories are the areas around the outer walls of a supermarket, known as the **"power perimeter,"** that include the dairy, bakery, meat, florist, produce, deli, and coffee bar. These departments attract consumers and are very profitable. Conventional supermarkets are building on their strength in these categories and devoting more space and attention to them. They are promoting fresh merchandise with cooking exhibitions and "action" stations, such as store-made sushi and freshly grilled meat.

Another example of the emphasis on "fresh" is the meal solutions offered to time-pressured consumers. Supervalu Inc., for instance, has introduced a line of more than 150 items that aim to rival restaurant-quality food, including items such as pork carnitas enchilada casserole and pineapple upside-down cake. Cincinnati-based Kroger Co. recently expanded its options to include items such as lobster bisque, baked ziti, and dinner packages that feed a family of four for $10.[11]

In response to this consumer desire for more and better fresh merchandise, food retailers such as Tesco (Fresh and Easy), Fresh Faire (Kroger), and Fresh Market are opening food stores focusing on the power perimeter merchandise. These **fresh supermarkets** are smaller (30,000 versus 40,000 square feet) and more convenient than traditional supermarkets and have less space devoted to packaged goods.

Health/Organic Merchandise
Conventional supermarkets are offering more natural, organic, and fair-trade foods for the growing segment of consumers who are health-conscious and environmentally conscious. **Fair trade** is the practice of purchasing from factories that pay workers a living wage, considerably more than the prevailing minimum wage, and offer other benefits such as onsite medical treatment. In addition, traditional supermarket chains are opening smaller-format stores such as GreenWise Market (Publix) targeting health-conscious consumers who patronize Whole Foods.

A related food retailing trend is offering locally grown products, a trend brought about in response to

Health-conscious and environmentally conscious consumers are demanding natural, organic, and fair-trade foods from food retailers.

environmental concerns and the increasing financial costs (e.g., fuel) of transporting food long distances. The **locavore movement** focuses on reducing the carbon footprint caused by the transportation of food throughout the world. Food miles are calculated using the distance that foods travel from the farm to the plate. Many Americans appreciate the idea of supporting local businesses, but they also want the variety of products they can find everyday in their grocery store. It is difficult to maintain a balance between buying locally and maintaining such variety.

Ethnic Merchandise   Hispanics, who now constitute 15 percent of the U.S. population, have significantly different shopping and eating patterns from those of the general population.[13] They are more likely to prepare meals from scratch, spend more on groceries, prefer stores with bilingual staff and signage, and place importance on fresh food. In addition to adding more ethnic merchandise in conventional supermarkets, retailers are opening supermarkets targeting Hispanic consumers.

For example, Northgate markets are a 30-store chain in California that caters to just Hispanic consumers. The stores are about 50,000 square feet in size, allowing them to offer shoppers a large service meat department, bakery, tortillería, and prepared foods, in addition to a sizable selection of domestic and imported Latin American grocery goods.[14]

Walmart has initiated its Supermercado concept, using the Sam's Club warehouse business model. The first Supermarcado de Walmart is in a 40,000-square-foot converted Neighborhood Market. Its opening day featured food and beverage samples overseen by a mariachi band belting out Spanish-language ballads. The Supermarcados will include no ethnic aisles, a smaller frozen-food section, and fewer brands of peanut butter, a generally unpopular product among Hispanic consumers. But the bakery will be larger, and an additional kitchen will serve an assortment of traditional Hispanic foods. All the signage is in both English and Spanish.[15]

Private-Label Merchandise   Conventional supermarket chains are leveraging their quality reputation to offer more private-label merchandise. Private-label brands (discussed in Chapter 13) benefit both customers and retailers. The benefits to customers include having more choices and finding the same ingredients and quality as in national brands at a lower price. The benefits of private-label brands to retailers include increased store loyalty, the ability to differentiate themselves from the competition, lower promotional costs, and higher gross margins compared with national brands.

Improving the Shopping Experience   Creating an enjoyable shopping experience through better store ambience and customer service is another approach that supermarket chains use to differentiate themselves from low-cost, low-price competitors. Supermarkets are increasingly incorporating "food as theater" concepts, such as open-air market designs, cooking and nutrition classes, demonstrations, baby-sitting services, and food tasting.

Supercenters

Supercenters are large stores (185,000 square feet) that combine a supermarket with a full-line discount store. Walmart operates 2,700 supercenters in the United States, accounting for 81 percent of total supercenter sales and leading its competitors Meijer, SuperTarget (Target), Fred Meyer (Kroger), and Super Kmart Center (Sears Holding).[17] By offering broad assortments of grocery and general merchandise products under one roof, supercenters provide a one-stop shopping experience.

General merchandise (nonfood) items are often purchased on impulse when customers' primary reason for coming to the supercenter is to buy groceries. General merchandise has higher margins, enabling the supercenters to price food items more aggressively. However, supercenters are very large, so some customers find them inconvenient because it can take a long time to find the items they want.

Hypermarkets are also large (100,000 to 300,000 square feet), combination food (60 to 70 percent) and general merchandise (30 to 40 percent) stores. The world's second-largest retailer, Carrefour, operates hypermarkets. Hypermarkets typically stock fewer SKUs than do supercenters—between 40,000 and 60,000 items, ranging from groceries, hardware, and sports equipment to furniture and appliances to computers and electronics.

Hypermarkets were created in France after World War II. By building large stores on the outskirts of metropolitan areas, French retailers could attract customers and not violate strict land-use laws. They have spread throughout Europe and become popular in some South American countries such as Argentina and Brazil.

Hypermarkets are not common in the United States, although hypermarkets and supercenters are similar. Both hypermarkets and supercenters are large, carry grocery and general merchandise categories, offer self-service, and are located in warehouse-type structures with large parking facilities. However, hypermarkets carry a larger proportion of food items than do supercenters and have a greater emphasis on perishables—produce, meat, fish, and bakery items. Supercenters, in contrast, have a larger percentage of nonfood items and focus more on dry groceries, such as breakfast cereal and canned goods, instead of fresh items.

Supercenters and hypermarkets face challenges in finding locations for new **big-box** (large, limited-service) stores. In Europe and Japan, land for building large stores is limited and expensive. New supercenters and hypermarkets in these areas often have to be multistory, which increases operating costs and reduces shopper convenience. Furthermore, some countries place restrictions on the size of new retail outlets. In the United States, there has been a backlash against large retail stores, particularly Walmart outlets. These opposing sentiments are based on local views that big-box stores drive local retailers out of business, offer low wages, provide nonunion jobs, have unfair labor practices, threaten U.S. workers through their purchase of imported merchandise, and cause excessive automobile and delivery truck traffic.

Warehouse Clubs

Warehouse clubs are retailers that offer a limited and irregular assortment of food and general merchandise with little service at low prices for ultimate consumers and small businesses. The largest warehouse club chains are Costco, Sam's Club (Walmart), and BJ's Wholesale Club (operating only on the East Coast of the United States). Customers are attracted to these stores because they can stock up on large packs of basics like paper towels, large-size packaged groceries like a quart of ketchup, best-selling books and CDs, fresh meat and produce, and an unpredictable assortment of upscale merchandise and services at low prices. For example, at Costco you can buy a 5-carat diamond ring for $99,999.99 with an appraised value of $153,450. Sam's Club focuses more on small businesses, providing services such as group health insurance as well as products. BJ's has beefed up its assortment of fresh meat and produce in recent years. Although package sizes are large compared to those in conventional grocery stores, BJ's provides convenient individual packaging—an attribute that is particularly appealing to its more upscale customers.

Warehouse clubs are large (100,000 to 150,000 square feet) and typically located in low-rent districts. They have simple interiors and concrete floors. Aisles are wide so that forklifts can pick up pallets of merchandise and arrange them on the selling floor. Little service is offered. Warehouse clubs can offer low prices because they use low-cost locations, have inexpensive store designs, and offer little customer service; they further keep inventory holding costs low by carrying a limited assortment of fast-selling items. In addition, they buy merchandise

People go to warehouse clubs such as Costco to search for treasures like computers at prices lower than those of competitors.

opportunistically. For example, if Hewlett-Packard is introducing new models of its printers, warehouse clubs will buy the inventory of the older models at a significant discount and then offer them for sale until the inventory is depleted.

Most warehouse clubs have two types of members: wholesale members who own small businesses and individual members who purchase for their own use. For example, many small restaurants are wholesale customers that buy their supplies, food ingredients, and desserts from a warehouse club rather than from food distributors. To cater to their business customers, warehouse clubs sell food items in very large containers and packages—sizes that also appeal to larger families. Typically, members pay an annual fee of around $50, which amounts to significant additional income for the chains.

Convenience Stores

Convenience stores provide a limited variety and assortment of merchandise at a convenient location in 3,000- to 5,000-square-foot stores with speedy checkout. Convenience stores enable consumers to make purchases quickly, without having to search through a large store and wait in a long checkout line. Over half the items bought are consumed within 30 minutes of purchase.

Convenience stores offer only limited assortments and variety, and they charge higher prices than supermarkets. Milk, eggs, and bread once represented the majority of their sales, but now the majority of sales come from gasoline and cigarettes.

Convenience stores face increased competition from other formats. Supercenter and supermarket chains are attempting to increase customer store visits by offering gasoline and tying gasoline sales to their frequent-shopper programs. For example, at Giant Eagle's GetGo locations shoppers get a 1 percent discount on groceries for every 10 gallons of gasoline purchased using their fuelperks card.[19] Drugstores and full-line discount stores also have easily accessible areas of their stores filled with convenience store merchandise.

In response to these competitive pressures, convenience stores are taking steps to decrease their dependency on gasoline sales, tailor assortments to local markets, and make their stores even more convenient to shop in. To get gasoline customers to spend more on other merchandise and services, convenience stores are offering more fresh food and healthy fast food that appeal to today's on-the-go consumers, especially women and young adults. Some convenience stores are adding fast casual restaurants, like BP's Wild Bean Café; 7-Eleven offers hot food cooked in its stores, including chicken wings and pizza. Wawa, a mid-Atlantic chain, is offering hot to-go meals such as soups, hoagies, and ciabatta melts. The chain is also introducing a drive-in store.[20] Finally, convenience stores are adding new services, such as financial service kiosks that give customers the opportunity to cash checks, pay bills, and buy prepaid telephone minutes, theater tickets, and gift cards.

To increase convenience, convenience stores are opening smaller stores close to where consumers shop and work. For example, 7-Eleven has stores in airports, office buildings, and schools. Easy access, storefront parking, and quick in-and-out access are key benefits offered by convenience stores. They also are exploring the use of technology to increase shopping convenience. For example, Sheetz, a Pennsylvania-based convenience store chain, has touch-screen "Made-to-Order" kiosks at which customers can order customized deli sandwiches, wraps, salads, subs, and nachos while pumping gasoline.[21]

GENERAL MERCHANDISE RETAILERS

The major types of general merchandise retailers are department stores, full-line discount stores, specialty stores, category specialists, home improvement centers, off-price retailers, and extreme-value stores. Exhibit 2–5 summarizes the characteristics of general merchandise retailers that sell through stores.

Characteristics of General Merchandise Retailers   **EXHIBIT 2–5**

Type	Variety	Assortment	Service	Prices	Size (000 sq. ft.)	SKUs (000)	Location
Department stores	Broad	Deep to average	Average to high	Average to high	100–200	100	Regional malls
Discount stores	Broad	Average to shallow	Low	Low	60–80	30	Stand alone, power strip centers
Specialty stores	Narrow	Deep	High	High	4–12	5	Regional malls
Category specialists	Narrow	Very deep	Low to high	Low	50–100	20–40	Stand alone, power strip centers
Home improvement centers	Narrow	Very deep	Low to high	Low	80–120	20–40	Stand alone, power strip centers
Drugstores	Narrow	Very deep	Average	Average to high	3–15	10–20	Stand alone, strip centers
Off-price stores	Average	Deep but varying	Low	Low	20–30	50	Outlet malls
Extreme-value retailers	Average	Average and varying	Low	Low	7–15	3–4	Urban, strip

Department Stores

Department stores are retailers that carry a broad variety and deep assortment, offer customer services, and organize their stores into distinct departments for displaying merchandise. The largest department store chains in the United States are Macy's, JCPenney, Sears, Kohl's, Nordstrom, Dillards, and Neiman Marcus.[23]

Traditionally, department stores attracted customers by offering a pleasing ambience, attentive service, and a wide variety of merchandise under one roof. They sold both soft goods (apparel and bedding) and hard goods (appliances, furniture, and consumer electronics). But now most department stores focus almost exclusively on soft goods. The major departments are women's, men's, and children's apparel, home furnishings, cosmetics, kitchenware, and small appliances. Each department within the store has a specific selling space allocated to it, as well as salespeople to assist customers. The department store often resembles a collection of specialty shops.

Department store chains can be categorized into three tiers. The first tier includes upscale, high-fashion chains with exclusive designer merchandise and excellent customer service, such as Neiman Marcus, Bloomingdale's (part of Macy's Inc.), Nordstrom, and Saks Fifth Avenue (part of Saks Inc.). Macy's and Dillards are in the second tier of traditional department stores, in which retailers sell more modestly priced merchandise with less customer service. The value-oriented third tier—Sears, JCPenney, and Kohl's—caters to more price-conscious consumers.

Department stores still account for some of retailing's traditions—special events and parades (Macy's Thanksgiving parade in New York City), Santa Claus lands, and holiday decorations. But many consumers are questioning the benefits and costs of shopping at department stores. Department stores are not as convenient as discount stores, such as Target, because they are located in large regional malls rather than local neighborhoods. However, JCPenney and Sears are following Kohl's by opening stores in nonmall locations. Customer service has diminished in the second- and third-tier stores because of the retailers' desire to increase profits by reducing labor costs. In addition, department stores, because of the large number of fashionable SKUs, have not been as successful as discount stores and food retailers in reducing costs by working with their vendors to establish just-in-time inventory systems.[26]

To deal with their eroding market share, department stores are (1) attempting to increase the amount of exclusive merchandise they sell, (2) undertaking marketing campaigns to develop strong images for their stores and brands, and (3) expanding their online presence.

REFACT

T. Stewart was the first U.S. department store, opening in 1847 in New York.[24]

REFACT

There are only 10 department store chains with sales of at least $3 billion: upscale Neiman Marcus, Saks Fifth Avenue, and Nordstrom; midtier Macy's and Dillard's; value chains JCPenney, Kohl's, and Sears; and regional chains Bon-Ton and Belk.

Department stores' share of total retail sales has been shrinking since the 1980s. Together, the top-10 chains have sales of about $110 billion, about one-fourth of Walmart's.[25]

To differentiate their merchandise offerings and strengthen their image, department stores are aggressively seeking exclusive arrangements with nationally recognized brands. For example, Macy's has introduced exclusive apparel and home lines from celebrities Donald Trump, Jessica Simpson, and Martha Stewart.[27] It is also the exclusive department store retailer for the Tommy Hilfiger and Ellen Tracy brands; Kohl's is now the exclusive licensee for the designer brand Dana Buchman (formerly a high-end brand) and the lifestyle brand Mudd, and it is also exclusively selling the celebrity's lifestyle apparel line LC Lauren Conrad.[28] Ralph Lauren designed a line of casual apparel exclusively for JCPenney called American Living.

In addition, department stores are placing more emphasis on developing their own private-label brands. Macy's has been very successful in developing a strong image for its brands, such as I.N.C. (young women's fashion) and Tools of the Trade (housewares). At the same time, however, some lines that have been heretofore available exclusively at department stores are now competing with them. For example, watch and accessories maker Fossil Inc. has its own stores, and cosmetics manufacturer Estée Lauder is available directly to consumers online.[29]

In recent years, discount sales events at some department stores have increased dramatically. These sales have trained some consumers to wait for items to be placed on sale rather than buy them at full price. In response, department stores are shifting their marketing activities from promotional sales to brand-building activities involving television advertising and specialty fashion publications.

Finally, most department stores are becoming active participants in multichannel retailing. At Macy's and Nordstrom, for instance, customers can buy or reserve products online and then pick them up at the store. Customers can also return online purchases to stores. At Macy's and JCPenney, sales associates can order out-of-stock merchandise online via their point-of-sale (POS) terminals. JCPenney has online sales of over $1.5 billion and is one of the largest catalog retailers in the United States.

Full-Line Discount Stores

Full-line discount stores are retailers that offer a broad variety of merchandise, limited service, and low prices. Discount stores offer both private labels and national brands. The largest full-line discount store chains are Walmart, Target, and Kmart (Sears Holding). Walmart alone accounts for 67 percent of discount store retail sales. Full-line discount stores confront intense competition from category specialists that focus on a single category of merchandise, such as Staples, Best Buy, Bed Bath & Beyond, Sports Authority, and Lowe's. In response to this competitive threat, Walmart is converting its discount stores into supercenters. Walmart is expected to reach 3,000 supercenters by 2013, while its discount stores should decrease to around two-thirds of their current level.[31] Supercenters are more efficient because of the economies of scale that result from the high traffic generated by the food offering.

Target has experienced considerable growth in the last decade because its stores offer fashionable merchandise at low prices in a pleasant shopping environment. It has developed an image of "cheap chic," continuously offering limited-edition exclusive apparel and cosmetic lines through its GO International campaign by teaming with new designers such as Alexander McQueen, Anna Sui, Jemma Kidd, and Petra Strand.[32]

Specialty Stores

Specialty stores concentrate on a limited number of complementary merchandise categories and provide a high level of service. Exhibit 2–6 lists some of the largest specialty store chains.

Specialty stores tailor their retail strategy toward very specific market segments by offering deep but narrow assortments and sales associate expertise. For example,

EXHIBIT 2–6
Specialty Store Retailers

Accessories/Cosmetics	Electronics/Software	Optical
Claire's	Apple	LensCrafters
Coach	Blockbuster	Sunglass Hut
Hot Topic	Brookstone	**Health/Beauty**
Apparel	GameStop	The Body Shop
Abercrombie & Fitch	Radio Shack	GNC
Ann Taylor		Sephora
Brooks Brothers	**Housewares**	Teavana
The Buckle	Crate & Barrel	**Shoes**
Forever 21	Pottery Barn	ALDO
The Gap	Restoration Hardware	FootLocker
H&M	Williams Sonoma	Nine West
J.Crew	**Jewelry**	Steve Madden
Victoria's Secret	Tiffany & Co.	The Walking Company
Zara	Zale	

Victoria's Secret is the leading specialty retailer of lingerie and beauty products in the United States. Using a multipronged location strategy that includes malls, lifestyle centers, and central business districts, Victoria's Secret offers fashion-oriented lingerie collections, fragrances, and cosmetics. Its message is conveyed using supermodels and world-famous runway shows.[34]

Sephora, France's leading perfume and cosmetic chain—a division of luxury-goods conglomerate LVMH (Louis Vuitton-Moet Hennessy)—is another example of an innovative specialty store concept. In the United States, prestige cosmetics are typically sold in department stores. Each brand has a separate counter with salespeople available to help customers. Sephora is a cosmetic and perfume specialty store offering a deep assortment in a self-service, 6,000- to 9,000-square-foot format. Its stores offer over 15,000 SKUs and more than 200 brands, including its own private-label brand. Merchandise is grouped by product category, with the brands displayed alphabetically so that customers can locate them easily. Customers are free to shop and experiment on their own. Sampling is encouraged. Knowledgeable salespeople are available to assist customers. The low-key, open-sell environment results in customers' spending more time shopping.

Sephora is an innovative specialty store selling perfume and cosmetics.

Some of the fastest-growing specialty store concepts were developed by European retailers. The Spain-based Zara chain and Sweden's H&M have introduced cheap and chic "fast fashion" to the United States.[35] Fast-fashion companies introduce new products two to three times a week, compared with 10 to 12 times a year at traditional specialty stores, to ensure that they offer the most trendy and up-to-date fashions. Because of the constantly fresh atmosphere, customers develop a "buy it now" shopping behavior; next week, the store will have different merchandise. As a result, fast-fashion retailers actually sell 85 percent of their merchandise at full price compared with only 60 percent at traditional stores.

Many manufacturers have opened their own specialty stores in recent years. Consider, for instance, Levi's (jeans and casual apparel), Godiva (chocolate), Apple (computers, phones), Cole Haan (shoes and accessories), Lacoste (apparel), Coach (purses and leather accessories), Tumi (luggage), Wolford (intimate apparel), Lucky brand (jeans and casual apparel), Samsonite (luggage), Polo/Ralph Lauren (apparel and home), and Sur La Table (housewares). Tired of being at the mercy of retailers to purchase and merchandise their products, these manufacturers and specialty retailers can control their own destiny by operating their own stores. Retailing View 2.3 describes an interesting retailer that specializes in video games.

Drugstores

Drugstores are specialty stores that concentrate on health and personal grooming merchandise. Prescription pharmaceuticals often represent almost 70 percent of drugstore sales. The largest drugstore chains in the United States are Walgreens, CVS, and Rite Aid—three chains that account for about 66 percent of U.S. drugstore sales, up from 45 percent in 2002.[36] Much of this increased concentration has occurred through mergers and acquisitions. For instance, CVS acquired Longs, Sav-On, and Osco; Rite Aid acquired Brooks and Eckerd.

2.3   RETAILING VIEW   Specializing in Everything Video Games . . . Buy, Play, Sell

Through online interactions, which enhance the GameStop Web site presence, as well as in-store experiences, GameStop has become a one-stop shop for products and knowledge related to video gaming. Gaming enthusiasts hang out at the stores and online, chat with other gamers, discover the codes and tricks of a game, and find passwords that help them achieve higher levels of play.

Video gaming is the fastest-growing entertainment category. GameStop, with over 6,200 stores in 17 countries, enjoyed a 24 percent sales increase in 2008, including a 12 percent increase in same-store sales, through its GameStop, EB Games, Electronics Boutique, EBgames.com, and GameStop.com brands. Although the typical video gamer is a 35-year-old man, 65 percent of U.S. households actively participate in gaming.

A typical video game is used for approximately 80 hours, making it a great value on a cost-per-hour basis, especially compared with other forms of entertainment. The introduction of *Guitar Hero* and *RockBand,* games that encourage groups of people to participate in musical renditions, has extended GameStop's customer base to a new and different market. The success of Nintendo Wii has also helped GameStop. For instance, the game *Gold's Gym Cardio Workout* is used with Nintendo, so workout enthusiasts and even senior citizens are taking up gaming.

Despite their value, new video games are relatively expensive, costing about $60. So GameStop sells used games and equipment and grants customers credit for used games they trade in to the store. Since it sells used games for about twice the trade-in price, it achieves gross margins on used-game sales that contribute 48 percent more to its bottom line than the new games do.

GameStop also engages customers through in-store events such as the "Halo 3: ODST Melee in Manhattan" competition, which is designed to find the best gamer in the United States. Gamers go to their nearest GameStop store on a specific day to compete in the first round of the tournament. This is followed by several elimination rounds culminating with the top 16 playing off in New York City for a $5,000 cash prize.

Sources: Dylan Duarte, "GameStop Holding $5000 ODST Tournament," *Gamepro.com,* October 1, 2009; Craig Guillot, "Masters of the Game," *Stores,* July 2009; http://www.gamestop.com/gs/tournaments/h3o/default.aspx (accessed October 5, 2009).

EXHIBIT 2–7
Category Specialists

Apparel/Shoe/Accessories	Furniture	Sporting Goods	Office Supply
Mens Warehouse	IKEA	Bass Pro Shops Outdoor World	Office Depot
DSW	Pier 1	Cabela's	Staples
Books	Sofa Express	Dick's Sporting Goods	Office Max
Barnes & Noble	**Home**	L.L. Bean	**Pet Supplies**
Borders	Bed Bath & Beyond	Golfsmith	PetSmart
Consumer Electronics	The Great Indoors	REI	PETCO
Best Buy	World Market	Sports Authority	**Musical Instruments**
Crafts	The Container Store	**Toys**	Guitar Center
Michaels	**Home Improvement**	Toys "R" Us	
Entertainment	Home Depot		
Chuck E. Cheese	Lowe's		
Dave & Busters	Menards		

Drugstores face competition from pharmacies in discount stores and from pressure to reduce health care costs. The major drugstore chains are offering a wider assortment of merchandise, including more frequently purchased food items, the convenience of drive-through windows for picking up prescriptions, and in-store medical clinics. To build customer loyalty, the chains are changing the role of their pharmacists from simply dispensing pills (referred to as "count, pour, lick, and stick") to providing health care assistance, such as explaining how to use a nebulizer. Drugstores are expanding their role as a fill-in trip destination by carrying products typically found in convenience stores, such as beverages, and making them easily accessible at the front of the store.

REFACT

Due to increased competition, the drugstore industry's share of retail pharmacy sales was 45 percent in 2008, down from 59.2 percent in 2005 and 64.1 percent in 2000.[37]

Category Specialists

Category specialists are big-box stores that offer a narrow but deep assortment of merchandise. Exhibit 2–7 lists some of the largest category specialists in the United States.

Most category specialists predominantly use a self-service approach, but they offer assistance to customers in some areas of the stores. For example, Staples stores have a warehouse atmosphere, with cartons of copy paper stacked on pallets, plus equipment in boxes on shelves. But in some departments, such as computers and other high-tech products, it provides salespeople in the display area to answer questions and make suggestions. Bass Pro Shops Outdoor World is a category specialist offering merchandise for outdoor recreational activities. The stores offer everything a person needs for hunting and fishing—from 27-cent plastic bait to boats and recreational vehicles costing $45,000. Sales associates are knowledgeable outdoors people. Each is hired for a particular department that matches that person's expertise. All private-branded products are field-tested by Bass Pro Shops' professional teams: the Redhead Pro Hunting Team and Tracker Pro Fishing Team.

By offering a complete assortment in a category, category specialists can "kill" a category of merchandise for other retailers and

Category specialists, like Staples, offer a deep assortment of merchandise at low prices.

thus are frequently called **category killers.** Using their category dominance and buying power, they buy products at low prices and are ensured of supply when items are scarce. Department stores and full-line discount stores located near category specialists often have to reduce their offerings in the category because consumers are drawn to the deep assortment and relatively low prices at the category killer.

Although category specialists compete with other types of retailers, competition between them is intense. Competing category specialists such as Lowe's and Home Depot, or Staples and Office Depot, have difficulty differentiating themselves on most of the elements of their retail mixes. They all provide similar assortments, because they have similar access to national brands, and they all provide the same level of service. Primarily then, they compete on price and location. Some category specialists are also experiencing intense competition from warehouse clubs like Sam's Club and Costco.[38]

Some category specialists are attempting to differentiate themselves with customer service. For example, Home Depot and Lowe's hire licensed contractors as sales associates to help customers with electrical and plumbing repairs. They also provide classes to train home owners in tiling, painting, and other tasks to give shoppers the confidence to tackle their do-it-yourself (DIY) projects on their own. Besides beefing up its sales associates' training to help customers purchase high-tech products like computers and printers, Staples has implemented "Easy Tech" in its stores to help people with computer and related problems and has installed Staples Copy and Print shops to compete with Fedex Kinkos.

Extreme-Value Retailers

Extreme-value retailers are small discount stores that offer a limited merchandise assortment at very low prices. They offer a broad variety but shallow assortment of household goods, health and beauty aids, and groceries. Some extreme-value retailers, such as Dollar General, are adding refrigerated coolers and expanding their food offerings so that they can be known as the best destination store for a greater variety of household necessities.[40] The extreme-value retailers are Dollar General and Family Dollar.[41]

Extreme-value retailers primarily target low-income consumers. These customers want well-known brands but cannot afford to buy the large-size packages offered by full-line discount stores or warehouse clubs. Vendors such as Procter & Gamble often create special, smaller packages for extreme-value retailers. Higher-income consumers are increasingly patronizing these stores for the thrill of the hunt. Some shoppers see extreme-value retailers as an opportunity to find some hidden treasure among the household staples.

Despite some of these chains' names, few just sell merchandise for a dollar. The two largest—Dollar General and Family Dollar—do not employ a strict dollar limit and sell merchandise for up to $20. The names imply a *good value* but do not limit customers to the arbitrary dollar price point. Dollar Tree experimented with selling merchandise for more than a dollar, but it is back to being a dollar purist.[43]

Off-Price Retailers

Off-price retailers, also known as **closeout retailers,** offer an inconsistent assortment of brand-name merchandise at a significant discount off the manufacturers' suggested retail price (MSRP). America's largest off-price retail chains are TJX Companies (which operates T.J.Maxx and Marshalls, Winners, HomeGoods, TK-Maxx, AJWright, and HomeSense), Ross Stores, Burlington Coat Factory, and Big Lots. Overstock.com and Bluefly.com are the largest Internet off-price retailers.

Off-price retailers are able to sell brand-name and even designer-label merchandise at 20 to 60 percent lower than the MSRP because of their unique buying and merchandising practices.[45] Most merchandise is bought opportunistically from manufacturers that have overruns, canceled orders, forecasting mistakes

Off-price retailers like T.J.Maxx sell designer handbags for much less than department and specialty stores do.

causing excess inventory, close-outs, and irregulars. They also buy excess inventory from other retailers. **Closeouts** are end-of-season merchandise that will not be used in following seasons. **Irregulars** are merchandise that has minor mistakes in construction. Typically, merchandise is purchased at one-fifth to one-fourth of the original wholesale price. Off-price retailers can buy at low prices because they do not ask suppliers for advertising allowances, return privileges, markdown adjustments, or delayed payments. (Terms and conditions associated with buying merchandise are detailed in Chapter 13.)

Due to this opportunistic buying, customers cannot be confident that the same type of merchandise will be in stock each time they visit the store. Different bargains will be available on each visit. For many off-price shoppers, however, inconsistency is exactly why they like to go there. They enjoy hunting for hidden treasures. To improve their offerings' consistency, some off-price retailers complement their opportunistically bought merchandise with merchandise purchased at regular wholesale prices.

A special type of off-price retailer is the outlet store. **Outlet stores** are off-price retailers owned by manufacturers or retailers. Those owned by manufacturers are also referred to as **factory outlets.** Manufacturers view outlet stores as an opportunity to improve their revenues from irregulars, production overruns, and merchandise returned by retailers. Others view it as simply another channel in which to sell their merchandise. For instance, Coach and Brooks Brothers manufacture lines exclusively for their outlet stores. North Face, on the other hand, sells the same merchandise that it creates for its regular retail stores and wholesale business. Outlet stores also allow manufacturers some control over where their branded merchandise may be sold at discount prices.[46]

Retailers with strong brand names such as Saks Fifth Avenue (Saks Fifth Avenue's Off 5th) and Williams-Sonoma operate outlet stores too. By selling excess merchandise in outlet stores rather than at markdown prices in their primary stores, these department and specialty store chains can maintain an image of offering desirable merchandise at full price.[47]

Outlet stores can have an adverse effect on profits, however, because they shift sales from full-price retailers to the lower-priced outlets. Additionally, outlet stores are becoming more promotional to compete with increased activity at other outlet stores within the same mall and with traditional off-price stores.[48]

SERVICES RETAILING

The retail firms discussed in the previous sections sell products to consumers. However, **services retailers,** or firms that primarily sell services rather than merchandise, are a large and growing part of the retail industry. Consider a typical Saturday: After a bagel and cup of coffee at a nearby Einstein Bros. Bagels, you go to the laundromat to wash and dry your clothes, drop a suit off at a dry cleaner, leave film to be developed at a Walgreens drugstore, and make your way to Jiffy Lube to have your car's oil changed. In a hurry, you drive through a Taco Bell so that you can eat lunch quickly and not be late for your haircut at 1 p.m. By midafternoon, you're ready for a workout at your health club. After stopping at home for a change of clothes, you're off to dinner, a movie, and dancing with a friend. Finally, you end your day with a café latte at Starbucks, having interacted with 10 different services retailers during the day.

Several trends suggest considerable future growth in services retailing. For example, the aging population will increase demand for health care services. Younger people are also spending more time and money on health and fitness. Busy parents in two-income families are willing to pay to have their homes cleaned, lawns maintained, clothes washed and pressed, and meals prepared so that they can spend more time with their families.

Exhibit 2–8 shows the wide variety of services, along with some national companies that provide these services. These companies are retailers

Service providers, like this automobile oil change service, are retailers too.

EXHIBIT 2–8
Services Retailers

Type of Service	Service Retail Firms
Airlines	American, Southwest, British Airways, JetBlue
Automobile maintenance and repair	Jiffy Lube, Midas, AAMCO
Automobile rental	Hertz, Avis, Budget, Enterprise
Banks	Citi, Wachovia, Bank of America
Child care centers	Kindercare, Gymboree
Dry cleaners	Zoots
Education	Babson College, University of Florida, Princeton Review
Entertainment	Disney World, Six Flags, Chuck E. Cheese, Dave & Busters
Express package delivery	FedEx, UPS, U.S. Postal Service
Fast food	Wendy's, McDonald's, Starbucks
Financial services	Merrill Lynch, Morgan Stanley, American Express, VISA
Fitness	Jazzercise, Bally's, Gold's Gym
Health care	Humana, HCA, Kaiser
Home maintenance	Chemlawn, Mini Maid, Roto-Rooter
Hotels and motels	Hyatt, Sheraton, Marriott, Days Inn
Income tax preparation	H&R Block
Insurance	Allstate, State Farm, Geico
Internet access/electronic information	Google, Internet Explorer, Mozilla Firefox, Safari
Movie theaters	AMC, Odeon/Cineplex
QSR	Panera Bread, Red Mango, Pinkberry
Real estate	Century 21, Coldwell Banker
Restaurants	Applebees's, Cheesecake Factory
Truck rentals	U-Haul, Ryder
Weight loss	Weight Watchers, Jenny Craig, Curves
Video rental	Blockbuster
Vision centers	LensCrafters, Pearle

because they sell goods and services to consumers. However, some are not just retailers. For example, airlines, banks, hotels, and insurance and express mail companies sell their services to businesses as well as consumers. Also, many services retailers, such as lawyers and doctors, do not appear in the exhibit because they focus on local markets and do not have a national presence.

Organizations such as banks, hospitals, health spas, legal clinics, entertainment firms, and universities that offer services to consumers traditionally have not considered themselves retailers. Yet due to increased competition, these organizations are adopting retailing principles to attract customers and satisfy their needs. For example, Zoots is a dry-cleaning chain in the Boston area.[49] Founded by a former Staples executive, Zoots has adopted many retailing best practices: It has convenient locations, and it offers pickup and delivery service. Zoots stores also provide extended hours, are open on weekends, and offer a drop-off option for those who cannot get to the store during operating hours. The stores are bright and clean. Customers can check their order status, schedule a pickup, and provide special instructions using the online MY ZOOTS service. Clerks are taught to welcome customers and acknowledge their presence, especially if there is a line.

Going to Zoots to pick up laundry and dry cleaning is as easy as going to an ATM machine.

All retailers provide goods and services for their customers. However, the emphasis placed on the merchandise versus the service differs across retail formats, as Exhibit 2–9 shows. On the left side of the exhibit are supermarkets and warehouse clubs. These retail formats consist of self-service stores that offer very few services, except perhaps displaying merchandise, cashing checks, and assisting customers at checkout. Moving along the continuum from left to right, department and specialty stores provide higher levels of service. In addition to providing assistance from sales associates, they offer services such as gift wrapping, bridal registries, and alterations. Optical centers and restaurants lie somewhere in the middle of the merchandise-service continuum. In addition to selling frames, eyeglasses, and contact lenses, optical centers provide important services like eye examinations and eyeglass fittings. Similarly, restaurants offer food plus a place to eat, music in the background, a pleasant ambience, and table service. As we move to the right end of the continuum, we encounter retailers whose offerings are

Continuum of Merchandise and Services Retailers   **EXHIBIT 2–9**

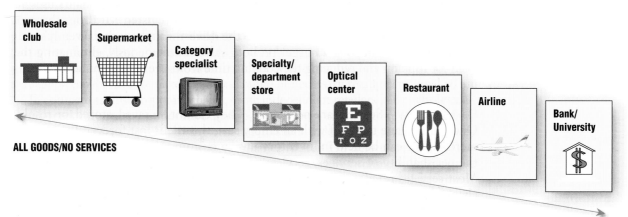

Corporate Retail Chains

A **retail chain** is a company that operates multiple retail units under common ownership and usually has centralized decision making for defining and implementing its strategy. Retail chains can range in size from a drugstore with two stores to retailers with thousands of stores, such as Safeway, Walmart, Target, and JCPenney. Some retail chains are divisions of larger corporations or holding companies. For example, The Gap has four divisions, The Gap, Banana Republic, Old Navy, and Piperlime. It has many more brands within these divisions, including Baby Gap, GapKids, GapBody, GapMaternity, Athleta, and Editions. Royal Ahold owns 14 retail chains, including Stop and Shop, Giant, and Peapod in the United States and ICA and Albert Heijh in Europe.

Franchising

Franchising is a contractual agreement between a franchisor and a franchisee that allows the franchisee to operate a retail outlet using a name and format developed and supported by the franchisor. More than 40 percent of all U.S. retail sales are made by franchisees.[52] Exhibit 2–10 lists some retailers governed by franchise agreements.

In a franchise contract, the franchisee pays a lump sum plus a royalty on all sales for the right to operate a store in a specific location. The franchisee also agrees to operate the outlet in accordance with procedures prescribed by the franchisor. The franchisor provides assistance in locating and building the store, developing

2.4 RETAILING VIEW   Tart Frozen Yogurt—the Sweet Franchise

Pinkberry opened in 2005 in West Hollywood. Its popularity has spurred competition by Red Mango, another franchise, which is growing faster than Pinkberry, old standby TCBY, and some smaller regional chains. Pinkberry offers two tart flavors, vanilla and green tea, while Red Mango features Pomegranate by POM Wonderful and Tangomonium flavor (the company's invention). These 70-calorie-a-serving treats can run $5 to $8 with toppings like almonds, coconuts, mangos, and raspberries.

The appeal of these franchises to customers is not just the low fat of frozen yogurt but also its ability to boost people's immune system and improve calcium absorption. The tart frozen yogurt is dense with active cultures and probiotics. These health benefits, along with the great taste, has changed the way consumers think about frozen yogurt. Consumers are making multiple yogurt purchases each week, instead of buying it as an occasional nonroutine indulgence.

Howard Schultz, the chair of Starbucks, invested $27.5 million in Pinkberry through his venture capital firm and appears to be trying to make it the Starbucks of frozen-yogurt chains. Expectations are high, including a growth plan to have one Pinkberry for every 10 Starbucks in the country. Red Mango would like to have 500 units in the United States but is controlling its growth by carefully selecting its franchisees and monitoring their performance. Many franchises become very popular and ultimately fail within five years as a result of growing too large, too fast. An interesting incentive to attract franchisees by reducing their risk is Red Mango's Store Buy Back program, in which the corporate franchise will buy back a store in the first six months if the franchisee is not satisfied.

New franchises like Red Mango appeal to customers because its frozen yogurt is low-fat, boosts people's immune systems, and improves calcium absorption.

If the frozen-yogurt market becomes as competitive as the premium coffee market, then TCBY may become the Dunkin' Donuts of yogurt franchises, while Red Mango and Pinkberry will be the Starbucks.

Sources: Blair Chancey, "Red Mango Revolution," *QSR Magazine,* October 1, 2009; Kelly Bayliss, "Free Fro-Yo Today," *NBC Philadelphia,* September 23, 2009; Molly Knight, "Cold Competition," *Shopping Centers Today,* February 2008.

EXHIBIT 2–10
Retailers Using Franchise
Business Model

Food Retailers
7-Eleven
Arby's
Ben & Jerry's
Cold Stone Creamery
Denny's
Domino's Pizza
Dunkin' Donuts
Johnny Rockets
McDonald's
Olive Garden
Panera Bread
Subway
KFC
Taco Bell

Services Retailers
1-800-GOT-JUNK?
AAMCO
Cash Now
Century 21 Real Estate
Coldwell Banker
Curves
Hampton Inn

UPS stores
InterContinental hotels
Jackson Hewitt Tax Service
Jani-King
Jazzercise
Jiffy Lube
LA Weight Loss
Lawn Doctor
Liberty Tax Service
Mail Boxes
Midas
Payless Car Rental
RE/MAX
Rent-a-Wreck

Merchandise Retailers
Ace Hardware
Culligan
GNC
Matco Tools
Merle Norman
Pearle Vision
Sign-A-Rama

the products or services sold, training managers, and advertising. To maintain each franchisee's reputation, the franchisor also makes sure that all outlets provide the same quality of services and products.

The franchise ownership format attempts to combine the advantages of owner-managed businesses with the efficiencies of centralized decision making in chain store operations. Franchisees are motivated to make their stores successful because they receive the profits (after the royalty is paid). The franchisor is motivated to develop new products and systems and to promote the franchise because it receives a royalty on all sales. Advertising, product development, and system development are efficiently performed by the franchisor, with costs shared by all franchisees. Retailing View 2.4 describes the sweet and tart world of frozen-yogurt franchises. Appendix B at the end of the book provides a more detailed description of franchising.

SUMMARY

This chapter has explained the different types of retailers and how they compete with different retail mixes to sell merchandise and services to customers. To collect statistics about retailing, the federal government classifies retailers by the type of merchandise and services they sell. But this classification method may not be useful to determine a retailer's major competitors. A more useful approach for understanding the retail marketplace is to classify retailers on the basis of the retail mix, merchandise variety and assortment, services, location, pricing, and promotion decisions they make to attract customers.

During the past 30 years, U.S. retail markets have been characterized by the emergence of many new retail institutions. Traditional institutions (supermarkets, convenience stores, drugstores, and department, discount, and specialty stores) have been joined by category specialists, supercenters, hypermarkets, extreme-value retailers, warehouse clubs, and off-price retailers. In addition, there has been substantial growth in services retailing.

The inherent differences between services and merchandise result in services retailers' emphasizing training of employees, whereas merchandise retailers emphasize inventory management issues. Traditional retail institutions have changed in response to the new types of retailers. For example, drugstores carry merchandise associated with convenience stores. Supermarkets are focusing more attention on meal solutions and perishables.

KEY TERMS

assortment, *32*

big box, *39*

breadth of merchandise, *32*

category killer, *46*

category specialist, *45*

closeout retailer, *46*

closeouts, *47*

convenience store, *40*

conventional supermarket, *35*

department store, *41*

depth of merchandise, *32*

drugstore, *44*

extreme-value food retailer, *35*

extreme-value retailer, *46*

factory outlet, *47*

fair trade, *37*

franchising, *52*

fresh supermarket, *37*

full-line discount store, *42*

hypermarket, *38*

irregulars, *47*

limited-assortment supermarket, *35*

locavore movement, *37*

North American Industry Classification System (NAICS), *30*

off-price retailer, *46*

outlet store, *47*

power perimeter, *37*

retail chain, *52*

services retailer, *48*

specialty store, *42*

stock-keeping unit (SKU), *32*

supercenter, *38*

variety, *32*

warehouse club, *39*

wholesale-sponsored voluntary cooperative group, *51*

GET OUT AND DO IT!

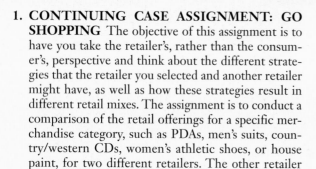

1. **CONTINUING CASE ASSIGNMENT: GO SHOPPING** The objective of this assignment is to have you take the retailer's, rather than the consumer's, perspective and think about the different strategies that the retailer you selected and another retailer might have, as well as how these strategies result in different retail mixes. The assignment is to conduct a comparison of the retail offerings for a specific merchandise category, such as PDAs, men's suits, country/western CDs, women's athletic shoes, or house paint, for two different retailers. The other retailer selected might be a direct competitor using the same format or a retailer selling similar merchandise to a different target market with a different format.

   Your comparison should include the following:
   - The strategy pursued by the two retailers—each retailer's target market and general approach to satisfying the needs of that target market.
   - The retail mixes (store location, merchandise, pricing, advertising and promotion, location of merchandise category in store, store design, customer service) used by each of the retailers.
   - With respect to the merchandise category, a detailed comparison of the variety and depth of assortment. In comparing the merchandise offerings, use a table similar to that in Exhibit 2–2.

   To prepare this comparison, you need to visit the stores, observe the retail mixes in the stores, and play the role of a customer to observe the service.

2. **GO SHOPPING** Go to an athletic footwear specialty store such as Foot Locker, a department store, and a discount store. Analyze their variety and assortment of athletic footwear by creating a table similar to that in Exhibit 2–2.

3. **GO SHOPPING** Keep a diary for two weeks of where you shop, what you buy, and how much you spend. Get your parents to do the same thing. Tabu-

late your results by type of retailer. Are your shopping habits significantly different from or are they similar to those of your parents? Do your and your parents' shopping habits coincide with the trends discussed in this chapter? Why or why not?

4. **GO SHOPPING** Describe how the supermarket where you shop is implementing organic, locally grown, ethnic, and private-label merchandise. If any of these categories of merchandise are missing, explain whether you believe it could be a potential opportunity for growth for this supermarket.

5. **INTERNET EXERCISE** Data on U.S. retail sales are available from the U.S. Bureau of the Census Internet site at www.census.gov/mrts/www/mrts.html. Look at the unadjusted monthly sales by NAICS. Which categories of retailers have the largest percentage of sales in the fourth quarter (the holiday season)? Do your findings make sense to you? Why or why not?

6. **INTERNET EXERCISE** Four large associations of retailers are the National Retail Federation (www.nrf.com), the Food Marketing Institute (www.fmi.org), the National Association of Chain Drug Stores (www.nacds.org), and the National Association of Convenience and Petroleum Stores (www.nacsonline.com). Visit these sites, and report on the latest retail developments and issues confronting the industry.

7. **INTERNET EXERCISE** Go to *Entrepreneur Magazine's* Franchise Zone Web page at http://www.entrepreneur.com/franchises/rankings/franchise500-115608/2009,.html, and view the top-500 franchises for the past year. How many of the retailers in the top 10 have you patronized as a customer? Did you know that they were operated as a franchise? Look at the lists from previous years to see changes in the rankings. Click on the link "About the Franchise 500," and describe which factors were used to develop

the list. Finally, what is the nature of the businesses that seem to lend themselves to franchising?

8. Bed Bath & Beyond is a category specialist with about 930 stores throughout the United States and Ontario, Canada. It sells domestics (bed linens, bathroom and kitchen items) and home furnishings (cookware and cutlery, small household appliances, picture frames, and organizing supplies). What are the SIC and NAICS codes used by this retailer? What other retailers compete against Bed Bath & Beyond, and which store format is implemented by each competitor?

DISCUSSION QUESTIONS AND PROBLEMS

1. Distinguish between variety and assortment. Why are these important elements of the retail market structure?

2. Choose a small, independent retailer, and explain how it can compete against a large national chain.

3. What do off-price retailers need to do to compete against other formats in the future?

4. Compare and contrast the retail mixes of convenience stores, traditional supermarkets, supercenters, and warehouse stores. Can all of these food retail institutions be successful over the long run? How? Why?

5. Could a full-line discount store, such as Target or Walmart, be successful opening stores using another retail format, such as convenience stores or department stores? Explain why or why not.

6. Why are retailers in the limited-assortment supermarket and extreme-value discount store sectors growing so rapidly?

7. The same brand and model of personal computer is sold by specialty computer stores, discount stores, category specialists, online retailers, and warehouse stores. Why would a customer choose one retail format over the others?

8. Choose a product category that both you and your parents purchase (e.g., business clothing, casual clothing, music, electronic equipment, shampoo). In which type of store do you typically purchase this merchandise? What about your parents? Explain why there is, or is not, a difference in your store choices.

9. At many optical stores, you can get your eyes checked *and* purchase glasses or contact lenses. How is the shopping experience different for the service as compared to the product? Design a strategy to get customers to purchase both the service and the product. In so doing, delineate specific actions that should be taken to acquire and retain optical customers.

10. Many experts believe that customer service is one of retailing's most important issues. How can retailers that emphasize price (e.g., discount stores, category specialists, off-price retailers) improve customer service without increasing costs and, thus, prices?

SUGGESTED READINGS

Borghini, Stefania, Nina Diamond, Roberts Kozinets, Mary Ann McGrath, Albert M. Muñiz Jr., and John F. Sherry Jr. "Why Are Themed Brandstores So Powerful? Retail Brand Ideology at *American Girl Place*." *Journal of Retailing* 85, no. 3 (2009).

Enrique, Badia. *Zara and Her Sisters: The Story of the World's Largest Clothing Retailer*. New York: Palgrave Macmillan, 2009.

Fishman, Charles. *The Wal-Mart Effect*. New York: Penguin, 2007.

Kim, Sang-Hoon, and S. Chan Choi. "The Role of Warehouse Club Membership Fees in Retail Competition." *Journal of Retailing* 83, no. 2 (2007), pp. 171–181.

Mitchell, Stacy. *Big-Box Swindle: The True Cost of Mega-Retailers and the Fight for America's Independent Businesses*. Boston: Beacon Press, 2006.

Raju, Jagmohan Z., and John Zhang. "Channel Coordination in the Presence of a Dominant Retailer." *Marketing Science* 24, no. 2 (2009), pp. 254–262.

Rivkin, Jan W., and Troy Smith. "Organic Growth at Wal-Mart." *Harvard Business Review*, January 23, 2007, pp. 1–4.

Spector, Robert. *Category Killers: The Retail Revolution and Its Impact on Consumer Culture*. Boston: Harvard Business School, 2005.

Weitz, Barton A., and Mary Brett Whitfield. "Trends in U.S. Retailing," in *Retailing in the 21st Century—Current and Future Trends*, eds. Manfred Kraft and Murali Mantrala. Berlin: Springer, 2006, pp. 59–75.

Whitaker, Jan. *Service and Style: How the American Department Store Fashioned the Middle Class*. New York: St. Martin's Press, 2006.

Windsperger, Josef, and Rajiv P. Dant. "Contractibility and Ownership Redirection in Franchising: A Property Rights View." *Journal of Retailing* 82, no. 3 (2006), pp. 259–272.

Multichannel Retailing

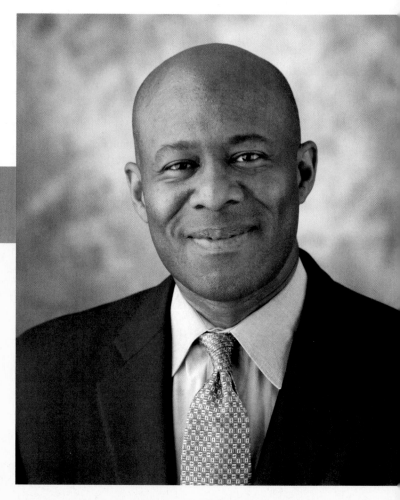

EXECUTIVE BRIEFING

Al Callier, Vice President, Interactive Design &
Web Production, Universal Orlando® Resort

I am responsible for Universal Orlando Resort's digital content production including content strategy and Web site development, online advertising, and mobile content development for the United States and the United Kingdom. In 2002, when I joined Universal Orlando, the company was beginning to explore online e-commerce. Its Web site had online ticket purchase capability, but was more of an interactive print brochure describing the resort. Today online electronic commerce is among our leading retail sales channels and a strategic pillar of our marketing efforts.

Promoting the resort and selling tickets to the theme parks before people arrive in Orlando is critical. Visitors to Orlando may plan to visit a number of the attractions in the area during their vacation, but change plans once the vacation is underway. By making it more attractive to buy tickets online before visitors arrive in Florida, we achieve more advance purchases and commitment to visiting Universal Orlando.

At this point in the evolution of the Internet, most vacationers use online resources to research their trip as well as book and purchase specific products. We have designed our online channel to assist families as they plan their vacations. The process might begin with determining the type and location of a vacation, and conclude with choosing specific activities and then purchasing tickets for these activities. It is a highly involving process that typically engages the participation of multiple family members in different ways. We have designed our Web site and navigation to provide the information and assistance our guests will find useful at each phase of the process, and encourage them to include Universal Orlando in their vacation plans, buy tickets to our theme parks, and make reservations at our hotels.

Our Web site also plays an important role in building a compelling image of Universal Orlando Resort. Thus we consider the strategic brand communication objectives, as well as the different types of visitors and guest needs in the design of our Web site. Some visitors come to the resort more frequently and are more interested in specific offers and packages, while others are in the early phase of the vacation planning process and are seeking to get a basic understanding of the resort and theme parks. Our

Really smart business strategy

goal is to smoothly facilitate the online process—to *inform, persuade,* and ultimately achieve *conversion* to online sales transaction.

After I graduated with a BSBA majoring in Marketing from the University of Florida and earned an MBA at Clark Atlanta University, I started my business career in product brand management at Oscar Mayer Foods Corp., a division of Kraft Foods. Subsequently, I worked in senior product management positions at The Pillsbury Company and The Coca-Cola Company, and later was responsible for marketing at GoTo.com/Overture Services Inc., a pioneer of the Web search marketing industry—acquired by Yahoo.com. Universal Orando gives me the opportunity to leverage my knowledge and experience to create an effective online multichannel offering that enhances the overall experience for our guests.

Widespread access to and use of the Internet has significantly changed shopping behaviors and the retailing industry. More than 80 percent of a broad cross section of U.S. retailers sell merchandise through multiple channels. All the large retailers and 94 percent of the U.S. retailers with the best financial performance are multichannel operators.[1] **Multichannel retailers** are retailers that sell merchandise or services through more than one channel.

Many small, store-based retailers also use an Internet channel as well as a store channel. For example, New Yorkers can visit one of Little Pie's two Manhattan locations and enjoy an assortment of flavors, from Old-Fashioned Apple Pie to the company's most famous taste, Sour Cream Apple Walnut. With annual sales of less than $5 million, Little Pie still receives orders for over 100 pies a week from its Web site (www.littlepiecompany.com). Mary Jo Slatter, an independent casting director who lives in California and describes herself as a "Little Pie groupie," says, "I order early in the morning, and I get it the next day. It tasted like you got it right out of the oven."[2]

In this chapter, we take a strategic perspective to examine the three primary channels through which retailers can communicate with and sell merchandise and services to their customers. We first briefly describe all retail channels and then review the unique benefits that each of the three major channels offers to consumers. Then we outline the reasons for retailers to provide a multichannel offering— the benefits to retailers of providing a multichannel offering. Next we describe the challenges multichannel retailers face in using these channels synergistically and providing a seamless multichannel offering for their customers. At the end of the chapter, we illustrate how integrating these channels and using new technologies will create a compelling shopping experience in the future.

The role of the Internet in retailing is discussed throughout the rest of the text-book. Some specific applications are managing employees, buying merchandise, managing customer relationships, advertising and promoting merchandise, and providing customer service.

RETAIL CHANNELS

A **retail channel** is the way a retailer sells and delivers merchandise and services to its customers. The most common channel used by retailers is a store. Retailers also use a variety of nonstore channels including the Internet, catalogs and direct mail, direct selling, television home shopping, and automated retailing. The estimated percentage of annual retail sales (excluding motor vehicles and food services annual sales) made through each channel is shown in Exhibit 3–1. The vast majority of sales are made through the store channel, but the catalog and Internet channels also account for significant sales.

Internet Channel

Internet retailing, also called **online retailing, electronic retailing,** and **e-tailing,** is a retail channel in which the offering of products and services for sale is communicated to customers over the Internet. A decade ago retail experts predicted that a new breed of high-tech, Web-savvy entrepreneurs would dominate the retail industry. Everyone would be doing their shopping over the Internet. Stores would close due to lack of traffic, and paper catalogs would become obsolete.

Even though sales through the Internet channel are forecasted to grow at about 10 percent annually, more than three times faster than sales through the store or catalog channel, Internet sales are expected to represent less than 10 percent of retail sales (excluding automotive and food services) by 2013.[3] More than one-quarter of apparel shoppers look up basic information about stores—such as location, hours, or special events—on retailer sites; 22 percent research merchandise; 21 percent compare prices; and 21 percent download coupons for use in stores.[4] Thus the Internet facilitates rather then revolutionizes retailing.

Catalog Channel

The **catalog channel** is a nonstore retail channel in which the retail offering is communicated to customers through a catalog mailed to customers. About half of U.S. consumers shop through catalogs each year. The merchandise categories with the greatest catalog sales are drugs and beauty aids, computers and software, clothing and accessories, furniture and housewares, and books, music, and magazines.[5]

EXHIBIT 3–1
Estimated Annual U.S. Retail Sales by Channel, 2009*

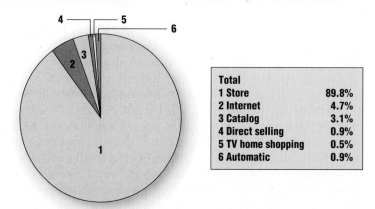

Total	
1 Store	89.8%
2 Internet	4.7%
3 Catalog	3.1%
4 Direct selling	0.9%
5 TV home shopping	0.5%
6 Automatic	0.9%

SOURCES: U.S. Census Bureau, "Estimates of Monthly Retail and Food Services Sales by Kind of Business: 2009" (http://www.census.gov/retail/mrts/www/data/excel/mrtssales92-09.xls); personal communication with the Direct Selling Association, Direct Marketing Association, and National Automatic Merchandising Association.

*Excluding sales of motor vehicles, food services, and travel.

Although firms spend millions of dollars mailing catalogs, only about 1.3 percent of the catalogs mailed generate a direct sale.[7] The use of catalogs is coming under attack from consumer groups that believe that catalogs are an unnecessary waste of natural resources. In the United States, catalogs account for 3 percent of the roughly 80 million tons of paper products used annually. That is more than either magazines or books.[8] Further, catalogs' share of sales is declining relative to the Internet. But catalogs are not going away. Their role is shifting from primarily generating sales to driving traffic to the Internet and physical stores.

Direct Selling

Direct selling is a retail channel in which salespeople interact with customers face-to-face in a convenient location, either at the customer's home or at work. Direct salespeople demonstrate merchandise benefits and/or explain a service; take an order; and deliver the merchandise. Direct selling is a highly interactive retail channel in which considerable information is conveyed to customers through face-to-face discussions. However, providing this high level of information, including extensive demonstrations, is costly.

Annual U.S. sales through direct selling are over $30 billion; worldwide, they are more than $100 billion.[9] The largest categories of merchandise sold through direct selling are personal care (e.g., cosmetics, fragrances), home and family care (e.g., cooking and kitchenware), wellness (e.g., weight loss products, vitamins), and leisure and educational items (e.g., books, videos, toys).

Almost all the 14 million salespeople who work in direct sales are independent agents.[10] They are not employed by the direct sales firm but, rather, act as independent distributors, buying merchandise from the firms and then reselling it to consumers. In most cases, direct salespeople may sell their merchandise to anyone, but some companies, such as Avon, assign territories to salespeople who regularly contact households in their territory. Retailing View 3.1 describes how the direct selling channel is particularly effective in less developed countries.

RETAILING VIEW   Direct Selling in China   3.1

While sales growth through the direct selling channel is limited in the United States, companies like Avon and Mary Kay have effectively used this channel to sell products in less developed countries. Using the direct selling channel is particularly effective in less developed countries because an extensive infrastructure to supply stores is not required. Products are sent to hundreds of thousands of sales representatives in small villages. They pay for the products when they sell them.

REFACT

About 5.5 million sales representatives now sell Avon products around the world, be it lip gloss in Shanghai or face powder in Rio de Janeiro.[11]

The direct selling channel also is part of a movement around the world for women to have more economic independence. For example, Zhang Xiaoying, a 19-year-old woman from Guizhou, one of China's poorest regions, says, "I love the corporate culture of Mary Kay. This company teaches you to aspire to a higher level."

The direct selling channel is particularly effective in less developed areas that lack the infrastructure to support retail stores.

Before joining the company, many Mary Kay sales agents in China held low-paying jobs as secretaries, cashiers, and rural schoolteachers. Many were looking for a new focus in their lives. "Because my husband is a businessman, and he is busy, we talked less and less," says Lu Laidi, a Mary Kay sales director. "I felt my life was boring. I stayed home and barely dressed up."

The use of a direct selling channel has been controversial in China. Many direct sellers have been accused of operating sophisticated pyramid schemes and other sales swindles. In response to these concerns, China banned direct selling in 1998, saying that it was often a cover for "evil cults, secret societies and lawless and superstitious activities." In 2006, after heavy lobbying from American companies, China lifted its ban, and since then direct selling has grown into an $8 billion industry.

Sources: David Barboza, "Direct Selling Flourishes in China," *New York Times*, December 26, 2009; J. Alex Tarquinio, "Selling Beauty on a Global Scale," *New York Times*, November 1, 2008, p. B2

Two special types of direct selling are the party plan and multilevel systems. About one-quarter of all direct sales are made using a **party plan system.** Salespeople encourage customers to act as hosts and invite friends or coworkers to a "party." The host or hostess receives a gift or commission for arranging the party. At the party the merchandise is demonstrated and attendees place orders. A party plan system can be, but does not have to be, used in a multilevel network.

In a **multilevel system,** independent businesspeople serve as master distributors, recruiting other people to become distributors in their network. The master distributors either buy merchandise from the firm and resell it to their distributors or receive a commission on all merchandise purchased by the distributors in their network. In addition to selling merchandise themselves, the master distributors are involved in recruiting and training other distributors.

Some multilevel direct selling firms are illegal pyramid schemes. A **pyramid scheme** develops when the firm and its program are designed to sell merchandise and services to other distributors rather than to end users. The founders and initial distributors in pyramid schemes profit from the inventory bought by later participants, but little merchandise is sold to consumers who use it.

Television Home Shopping

Television home shopping is a retail channel in which customers watch a television program that demonstrates merchandise and then place orders for that merchandise, usually by telephone, via the Internet, or via the TV remote.[14] The three forms of TV home shopping retailing are (1) cable channels dedicated to television shopping, (2) infomercials, and (3) direct-response advertising. **Infomercials** are programs, typically 30 to 60 minutes long, that mix entertainment with product demonstrations and then solicit orders placed by telephone. **Direct-response advertising** consists of one- to two-minute advertisements on television and radio that describe products and provide an opportunity for consumers to order them.

The two largest retailers using this channel are HSN and QVC, followed by ShopNBC and Jewelry Television. Although most consumers with cable or satellite television access can patronize a television shopping channel, relatively few watch on a regular basis. Furthermore, most of the purchases are made by a relatively small proportion of viewers. Like catalogs, TV home shopping networks are embracing the Internet; the major home shopping networks all have online operations.

The major advantage of TV home shopping is that customers can see the merchandise demonstrated either on their television screens or through streaming videos on the Internet. In response to the increase in cooking, decorating, do-it-yourself, and other lifestyle programming, home shopping retailers have incorporated more demonstrations into their programming in an attempt to educate their potential customers and create more drama.

Redbox, with its automated distribution channel, competes against Netflix's Internet channel and Blockbuster's multichannel offering.

Automated Retailing

Automated retailing is a retail channel in which merchandise or services are stored in a machine and dispensed to customers when they deposit cash or use a credit card. Automated retailing machines, also known as **vending machines,** are typically placed at convenient, high-traffic locations, such as in workplaces or on university campuses. The vast majority of automated retailing sales are from cold beverages, candy, and snacks.

Automated retailing isn't just for soda and candy bars anymore. ZoomShops, for instance, are automated, self-service stores that offer customers the convenience of purchasing merchandise using touch-screen technology. At the stores, located in over 800 airports, malls, and retail stores, customers can purchase iPods, Sony products, Proactiv acne products, Rosetta Stone language learning software, Mark cosmetics, and even a select line of merchandise from Macy's.

Another interesting automated retailing application is taking the DVD rental business by storm. Redbox rents DVDs for $1 a day in over 22,000 locations, including McDonald's, Walmart, Walgreens, Albertsons, and 7-Eleven Circle-K. The retailer rents over 7.5 million movies weekly, close to the sales reported by its mail-order rival Netflix. Redbox's success, as well as its challenge, is keeping its inventory of DVDs fresh and available when customers want to rent them. It attempts to have 40 percent of its titles be movies released on DVD within the previous two weeks. Customers can check the inventory of a particular machine and reserve a copy of any title at Redbox's Internet site.

REFACT

The Greek mathematician Hero invented the first vending machine in 215 BC to vend holy water in Egyptian temples. The first commercial coin-operated vending machines were introduced in London, England, in the early 1880s to dispense postcards.[15]

REFACT

Redbox has great locations; 150 million people every week walk within 10 feet of one of its vending machines.[16]

BENEFITS OFFERED BY THE RETAIL CHANNELS

In this section, we discuss the benefits offered to customers by the three major channels. By using a combination of channels, multichannel retailers can leverage these benefits and overcome the limitations of each channel to attract and satisfy more customers. Exhibit 3–2 lists the unique benefits of the three channels. In the following section, we discuss the benefits to retailers that integrate the use of these channels.

Store Channel

Stores offer several benefits to customers that they cannot get when they shop through nonstore channels such as catalogs or the Internet.

Touching and Feeling Products   Perhaps the greatest benefit offered by stores is the opportunity for customers to use all five senses—touching, smelling, tasting, seeing, and hearing—when examining and evaluating products. Although new technologies such as 3-D can enhance representations of products on a computer screen, these visual improvements do not provide the same level of information customers get when they actually try on a swimsuit or smell the fragrance of a candle.

Stores	Catalogs	Internet
Touching and feeling merchandise	Safety	Safety
Personal service	Convenience	Convenience
Risk reduction	Ease of use	Broad and deep assortments
Immediate gratification		Extensive and timely information
Entertainment and social interaction		Personalization
Browsing		
Cash payment		

EXHIBIT 3–2
Benefits Provided by Different Channels

Personal Service   Although consumers are often critical of the personal service they get in stores, sales associates still have the unique ability to provide meaningful, personalized information. They can tell customers if a suit looks good on them, suggest a tie to go with a dress shirt, or answer questions customers might have about what is appropriate to wear at a business-casual event.

Risk Reduction   The opportunity to use all five senses when evaluating products and to get personalized information increases the likelihood that consumers will be satisfied with their purchases. In addition, the physical presence of the store reduces perceived risk and increases customers' confidence that any problems with a purchase will be corrected. Customers can easily access people in the store to resolve issues concerning defective or unsuitable merchandise or to get additional information on how to use a product.

Immediate Gratification   Customers can get the merchandise immediately after they buy it from stores. Thus, when customers have a fever or need a last-minute gift, for example, they do not have to wait a day or two for the delivery of a prescription from Drugstore.com or of a gift from Amazon.com.

Entertainment and Social Experience   In-store shopping can be a stimulating experience for some people, providing a break in their daily routine and enabling them to interact with friends. All nonstore retail formats are limited in the degree to which they can satisfy these entertainment and social needs. Retailing View 3.2 describes how Bass Pro Shops stores offer an exciting and rewarding shopping experience for their customers.

3.2   RETAILING VIEW   Bass Pro Shops Makes Shopping Fun

People drive for hours and even stay overnight to visit one of Bass Pro Shops' 56 stores. In addition to providing a deep assortment of outdoors merchandise, the stores offer a wide range of free activities ranging from laser arcades to rock climbing. Most of the stores offer pistol and archery ranges inside sound-isolated rooms sealed by protective glass. Golfers can practice at an indoor driving range. These ranges are staffed by experts who can talk about sighting a gun or explain the fine points of a shoulder turn. All stores have fly-tying demonstrations, and some even have an outdoor pond for testing fly-fishing equipment.

The typical customer at Bass Pro is male and averse to crowds and shopping. "I'll do just about anything to avoid shopping," says John Brown, a small-business owner in Cheyenne, Wyoming. His wife says that in 35 years of marriage she's persuaded him to go shopping only twice. Yet one day last month he invited her to drive 100 miles with him for a day of shopping. "I'm like a kid in a candy store here," he said, dropping a new tackle box into his cart.

The stores are typically designed to be compatible with the local environment. For example, the store in Leeds (north central Alabama) is built on 120 acres, with a mile-long entrance that winds through a

The excitement generated in a Bass Pro Shops store cannot be equaled by other channels.

nature park over three bridges and around a 4-acre lake. The store has an 18,500-gallon aquarium filled with fish native to Alabama, a 3,500-gallon trout pond, an archery range, and a NASCAR ride simulator emulating the nearby Talladega Speedway.

Sources: Jayne O'Donnell, "Bass Pro CEO Hooked Dream Job," *USA Today*, September 30, 2009; Roy Williams, "Bass Pro Shops Offers Sneak Peek before Opening," *Birmingham News*, October 5, 2008.

REFACT

Over 100 million people annually visit Bass Pro Shops, compared with 60 million visitors to Disney World in Orlando.

Browsing   Shoppers often have only a general sense of what they want (e.g., a sweater, something for dinner, a gift) but don't know the specific item they want. So they go to a store to see what is available before they decide what to buy. Although some consumers surf the Web and look through catalogs for ideas, most consumers still find it easier to browse in stores.

Cash Payment   Stores are the only channel through which consumers can make cash payments. Some customers prefer to pay with cash because it is quicker, resolves the transaction immediately, and does not result in potential interest payments or excessive debt. Other customers are concerned about security and identity theft and thus prefer to use their credit card or debit card in person rather than electronically sending the payment information via the Internet.

Catalog Channel

The catalog channel provides some benefits to customers like safety and convenience that are associated with all nonstore channels. However, catalogs also have some unique convenience advantage over other nonstore formats.

Safety   Security in malls and shopping areas is becoming an important concern for many shoppers, particularly the elderly. Nonstore retail channels enable customers to review merchandise and place orders from a safe environment—their home.[18]

Convenience   Catalogs offer the convenience of looking at merchandise and placing an order from almost anywhere 24/7. However, catalogs are easier to browse through than Web sites. Consumers can refer to the information in a catalog anytime by simply picking it up from the coffee table. They can take a catalog to the beach and browse through it without an Internet connection. Finally the information in a catalog is easily accessible for a long period of time.

Internet Channel

Shopping over the Internet provides the safety and convenience of catalogs and other nonstore formats. However, the Internet, compared with store and catalog channels, also has the potential to offer a greater selection of products and more personalized information about products and services.

Broader and Deeper Assortments   One benefit of the Internet channel, compared with the other two channels, is the vast number of alternatives that consumers can consider. The number of SKUs available in a store is limited by the store's size. The number of pages in a catalog limits the number of SKUs that can be viewed in a catalog channel.

More Timely Information for Evaluating Merchandise   An important service offered to customers is providing information that helps them make better buying decisions. The retail channels differ in terms of how much information customers can access. The amount of information available through the store channel is limited by the number of sales associates and the space for signage. Similarly, the information available through a catalog channel is limited by the number of pages in the catalog. In contrast, the information provided through the Internet channel is unlimited. The vast amount of information available through the Internet channel enables customers using this channel to solve problems rather than just get information about specific products.

   In addition to providing more information, the Internet channel offers customers more current information whenever they want it. Retailing View 3.3 describes an Internet site that offers products plus information, some of which is generated by customers, which can help couples solve the problems associated with planning their wedding.

Finally, consumers can access information from other consumers through the Internet channel—information that may be viewed as less biased than information provided by a retailer or manufacturer. Many retailers provide an opportunity for customers to post reviews of products or services they have bought.

Personalization   Due to the Web's interactive nature, the most significant potential benefit of the Internet channel is its ability to personalize merchandise offerings and information for each customer economically. Customers control some of this personalization. Customers shopping on an Internet channel can drill down through Web pages until they have enough information to make a purchase decision. In addition, when using the Internet channel, customers can format the information so that it can be effectively used when they are comparing alternatives. For example, Office Depot provides information about alternatives selected by the customer in a side-by-side comparison format. In contrast, customers in stores usually have to inspect each brand, one item at a time, and then remember the different attributes to make a comparison.

The retailer can play a more proactive role in personalizing merchandise and information through the Internet channel. For example, many retailers offer

3.3   RETAILING VIEW   Helping Couples Get Ready for the Big Day

The typical engagement and wedding planning process lasts 14 months, costs almost $25,000, and involves many emotionally charged decisions, such as how many and which people to invite, what print style to use on the invitations, where to hold the reception, what music to play during the ceremony, and what gifts to list in the bridal registry. Traditionally, the bride's family managed the wedding planning process. With more couples getting married when they are older, both working, and living farther from their parents, planning a wedding has become much more challenging.

Internet wedding sites, such as The Knot (www.theknot.com) and the Wedding Channel (www.weddingchannel.com), offer couples and their families planning guides and advice. A budgeting tool allows the couple to enter a dollar amount (say, $9,000) and the number of guests (30), and it calculates, on the basis of national averages, how much they can spend on elements such as the bride's dress ($540) and bouquet ($68). With the tool, couples can also enter what they have actually spent, and it recalculates the sums that can be spent elsewhere. A planning tool is available to make sure arrangements are made, and reminders are e-mailed to the couple when key dates loom.

Couples can chat with experts and other couples on issues such as dealing with a micromanaging mother-in-law or divorced parents. Gift registries can be created at different retailers and broadcast to guests through e-mail. Couples can collect information from home rather than having to make visits to different

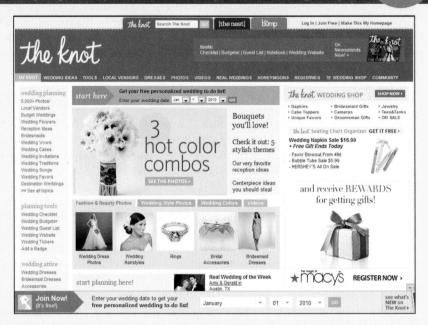

TheKnot.com offers information and merchandise to help couples prepare for their weddings.

suppliers. They can narrow the list of potential places for the reception by looking at photos on the Web, and they can download bands' audio clips from the Web instead of going to hear different bands play. Hotel reservations for out-of-town guests can be made over the Internet, and maps can be created to show those guests how to get to the hotel and reception. Finally, couples can have their own personal site on which they post their wedding pictures.

Sources: www.weddingchannel.com; www.theknot.com (accessed January 10, 2010).

Office Depot offers a personalized shopping experience on its Web site by providing information about alternatives selected by the customer in a side-by-side comparison format.

live chats: Customers can click a button at any time and have an instant messaging e-mail or voice conversation with a customer service representative. This technology also enables retailers to send a proactive chat invitation automatically to customers on the site. The timing of these invitations can be based on the time the visitor has spent on the site, the specific page the customer is viewing, or a product on which the customer has clicked. At Bluefly.com, for example, if a visitor searches for more than three items in five minutes, thereby demonstrating more than a passing interest, Bluefly will display a pop-up window with a friendly face offering help.

The interactive nature of the Internet also provides an opportunity for retailers to personalize their offerings for each of their customers. For example, Amazon.com serves customers a personalized landing page with information about books and other products of interest based on the customer's past purchases and search behavior on the Web site. Amazon also sends interested customers customized e-mail messages that notify them that their favorite author or recording artist has published a new book or released a new CD. Another personalization opportunity is presenting customers with recommendations of complementary merchandise. Just as a well-trained salesperson would make recommendations to customers before checkout, an interactive Web page can make suggestions to shoppers about additional items that they might like to consider.

For example, a shopper at the retail site FigLeaves.com takes a close look at a silky pair of women's slippers. Next, a recommendation appears for a man's bathrobe. This type of surprising connection is the result of sophisticated software, run on powerful computers, that analyzes extensive behavioral data, from mouse clicks to search queries. Why the bathrobe? ATG, the company that crunches data for FigLeaves, found that certain types of female shoppers at certain times of the week are likely to be shopping for men.[20]

The Internet channel is particularly effective at making personalized recommendations to customers.

Sears Holdings has gone one step further by developing a "personal shopper" application for the iPhone mobile digital device. With this application, customers can photograph the desired product anywhere and have the picture sent immediately to a team of "expert shoppers." The expert shoppers then work to find the item and contact the customer via phone or e-mail. But retailers also risk losing sales through the latest generation of comparison-shopping applications, some of which will search for the lowest-priced product in a given area on the basis of a bar code photo taken in a store by a consumer with his mobile phone.[21]

Perceived Risks in Electronic Shopping Some consumers are concerned about buying products through an electronic channel. The two critical perceived risks are (1) the security of credit card transactions on the Internet and (2) potential privacy violations. Although many consumers remain concerned about credit card security, extensive security problems have been rare. Almost all retailers use sophisticated technologies to encrypt communications.

All major credit card companies provide the same consumer protection for transactions through store and Internet channels. Typically, a consumer is liable for no more than $50 as long as she reports the unauthorized use in a timely manner. The consequences of security breaches can be far worse for the retailer from which the number was stolen. Security breaches can ruin a retailer's reputation and possibly expose it to legal liability.[22]

Consumers also are concerned about the ability of retailers to collect information about their purchase history, personal information, and search behavior on the Internet.[23] Consumers may be worried about how this information will be used in the future. Will it be sold to other retailers, or will the consumer receive unwanted promotional materials online or in the mail? Issues related to privacy, and the steps that retailers are taking to allay these concerns, are discussed in more detail in Chapter 11.

BENEFITS OF MULTICHANNEL RETAILING

In the previous section, we outlined the benefits offered by the different retail channels. In this section, we describe how retailers, typically store-based retailers, are using multiple channels to improve their offerings to their customers and build a competitive advantage.

Traditional store-based and catalog retailers are using multiple channels, typically adding and placing more emphasis on their electronic channels, for five reasons. First, the electronic channel gives retailers an opportunity to overcome the limitations of their primary existing channel. Second, providing a multichannel offering increases customer satisfaction and loyalty. Third, an electronic channel enables retailers to gain valuable insights into their customers' shopping behavior. Fourth, by using an electronic or catalog channel, retailers can economically enter new markets. Fifth, a multichannel offering provides the bases for building a strategic advantage. The benefits to retailers of operating multiple channels are discussed below.

Overcoming the Limitations of an Existing Format

Increased Assortments   By using a combination of channels, retailers can better satisfy their consumers' needs by exploiting the benefits and overcoming the deficiencies of each channel. For example, one of the greatest constraints facing store-based retailers is the size of their stores. However, due to the low cost of computer memory, the number of SKUs presented through an Internet channel is virtually unlimited. In addition, the inventory needed to support each SKU offered is lower in an Internet channel compared to a store channel because the inventory supporting an Internet channel is consolidated in a small number of distribution centers rather than a large number of stores.

By complementing their store channel with an Internet channel accessed from Internet-enabled kiosks, POS terminals, or mobile devices, retailers can dramatically expand the assortment offered to their customers. For example, Home Depot and Sears have a limited number of major appliance models in their stores, but customers can use a Web-enabled kiosk to look at an expanded selection of appliances, get more detailed information, and place orders. Thus an Internet channel enables retailers to keep their overall inventory costs low and still satisfy the demand for less popular styles, colors, or sizes.

Low-Cost, Consistent Execution   Another limitation of the store channel is its costly but inconsistent execution. Customers can get personalized information from sales associates in stores. Over time, sales associates can learn what customers like and want. They can select a few outfits and make an appointment to show these outfits to customers or even take the outfits to the customer's office or home. However, customers can get this benefit only when the sales associates are present. Also, providing it consistently is costly. Training and retaining knowledgeable sales associates are expensive, and even the best sales associates have bad days.

This inconsistency is most problematic for retailers selling new, complex merchandise. For example, consumer electronic retailers such as Best Buy find it difficult to communicate the features and benefits of the newest products to all of their sales associates. To address this problem, Best Buy installed kiosks designed to be used by sales associates and customers to obtain product information. Thus, adding an Internet channel offers an opportunity to provide "personal" service at a low cost.

Multichannel retailers use Internet-enabled kiosks in their stores to offer customers a greater merchandise assortment.

Current Information   Catalog retailers also use electronic channels to overcome the limitations of their catalogs. Once a catalog is printed, it cannot be updated economically with the latest price changes and new merchandise. Therefore, Lands' End uses its Internet site to provide customers with real-time information about stock availability and price reductions on clearance merchandise.

Increasing Customer Satisfaction and Loyalty

Introducing an electronic channel may lead to some cannibalization. The customers who formerly made purchases in a retailer's store now make the same purchases through the retailer's Internet channel.[25] However, there is a growing segment of multichannel shoppers—consumers for whom a multichannel offering is particularly appealing.

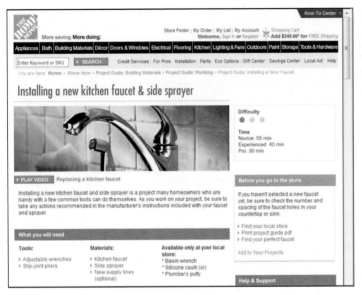

By providing information to help customers complete do-it-yourself projects, Home Depot continues to increase customer satisfaction.

For example, by focusing on the purpose for which a set of products will be used, store-based retailers can offer solution Web sites that stimulate customers to view more products than they otherwise would have considered. Customers can go to Williams-Sonoma's Web site to get information for planning a margarita party or a picnic. Its Web site describes everything they need for the occasion. Home Depot's Web site walks customers through the steps of installation and repair projects, thereby giving do-it-yourselfers confidence to tackle home improvement tasks. The directions include the level of difficulty and a list of the tools and materials needed to complete the project successfully.

By providing a greater array of benefits through multichannel offerings, retailers can increase their **share of customers' wallets**—the percentage of purchases made from the specific retailer. For example, Neiman Marcus' multichannel customers spend 3.6 times more than their single-channel customers do.[26]

Gaining Insights into Consumer Shopping Behavior

An electronic channel provides valuable insights into how and why customers shop and are dissatisfied or satisfied with their experiences.[27] This information on how customers shop a store or merchandise category is useful for designing stores or Web sites. For example, after a customer purchases a book, Amazon.com recommends additional books that might be of interest to the customer based on purchases made by other customers who have bought that book.

Collecting data on how customers navigate through a Web site is quite easy. By placing a cookie (a small computer program that collects information about computer usage) on a customer's hard drive, the retailer can monitor each mouse click. The click-stream data can provide insights into what characteristics of products customers considered and what products customers looked at but did not buy.[28] To collect this information from store or catalog shoppers would be quite difficult; someone would have to follow them around the store or observe them going through catalog pages. The search data are useful for determining whether a store or Web site should be laid out by brands, size, color, or price point.

Expanding Market Presence

The market for store-based retailers is typically limited to consumers living in close proximity to the retailer's stores. By adding the Internet channel, retailers can expand their market without having to build new stores. Adding an electronic channel is particularly attractive to retailers with strong brand names but limited locations and distribution. For example, retailers such as Harrod's, REI, IKEA, and Neiman Marcus are widely known for offering unique, high-quality merchandise. If these retailers had only a store channel, customers would have to travel to England or major U.S. cities to buy merchandise they carry.

Building a Strategic Advantage

Multichannel retailers have the opportunity to develop a strategic advantage over single-channel competitors. Two strategic resources that multichannel retailers have and that are not easily detected or duplicated by store-based, single-channel competitors are (1) propriety information about customer purchase history and shopping behavior and (2) unique "how-to" knowledge about coordinating operational activities across channels.

It is difficult for most store-based retailers to develop extensive purchase histories of their customers because the retailers are unable to link transactions to customers who pay cash or use third-party credit cards. In contrast, all transactions through the Internet and catalog channels have the customer identification information needed to send the product to the customer. In addition, the Internet channel offers the opportunity to collect search-behavior as well as transaction data. Therefore, multichannel retailers have a greater opportunity to develop extensive, proprietary information about their customers and can use this information to more effectively target their offerings and marketing activities.

Another strategic resource possessed by effective multichannel retailers is the knowledge associated with integrating multiple channels. Customers want the retailers they patronize to recognize them no matter which channel they use. Knowing how to synergistically coordinate these different channels provides retailers with a strategic advantage.

OTHER MULTICHANNEL RETAILING ISSUES

This section discusses two important issues that need to be considered when providing a multichannel offering—the cost of selling products through the different channels and the potential for disintermediation.

Which Channel Has the Lowest Costs?

Many people think that retailers incur less cost when selling merchandise through an electronic channel compared to a store channel. When selling merchandise through the Internet channel, retailers do not incur the costs of building and operating stores and compensating employees working in those stores. Since customers think the costs associated with the Internet channel are lower, they expect the prices to be lower for merchandise sold through that channel. However, Internet retailers incur significant costs to design, maintain, and refresh a Web site; attract customers to the site; maintain distribution systems and warehouses dedicated to fulfilling orders from individual customers; and deal with a high level of returns. These overhead costs associated with operating an electronic channel may even be greater than the costs of operating physical stores.

Will Manufacturers Bypass Retailers and Sell Directly to Consumers?

Disintermediation occurs when a manufacturer sells directly to consumers, bypassing retailers. Retailers are concerned about disintermediation because manufacturers can get direct access to their consumers by establishing a retail site on the Internet.[29] Hewlett-Packard printers and accessories are sold both directly to consumers through its Web site (www.hewlettpackard.com) and, at the same time, indirectly through retailers such as Office Depot's stores and its Web site (www.officedepot.com). However most manufacturers lack the skills to sell directly to consumers. They are not as efficient as retailers at performing the retailing functions.

Retailers have considerably more expertise than manufacturers in distributing merchandise directly to customers, providing complementary assortments, and collecting and using information about customers. Retailers also have an advantage over manufacturers because they can provide a broader array of products and services, such as various brands or special offerings, to solve customer problems. For example, if consumers want to buy the components for a home entertainment center from a variety of manufacturers, they must go to several different Internet sites and still cannot be sure that the components will work together or arrive at the same time.

Manufacturers that sell directly to consumers risk losing the support of the retailers they bypass. Therefore, many manufacturers, such as Energizer (www.energizer.com), the world's largest producer of batteries and flashlights, use their Web sites only as a marketing tool to show customers which products are available and then direct them to nearby stores at which they can purchase the products.

CHALLENGES OF EFFECTIVE MULTICHANNEL RETAILING

Consumers desire a seamless experience when interacting with multichannel retailers. They want to be recognized by a retailer whether they interact with a sales associate or kiosk in a store, log on to the retailer's Web site, or contact the retailer's call center by telephone. Customers may want to buy a product through the retailer's Internet or catalog channel and pick it up or return it to a local store; find out if a product offered on the Internet channel is available at a local store; and, when unable to find a product in a store, determine whether it is available for home delivery through the retailer's Internet channel.

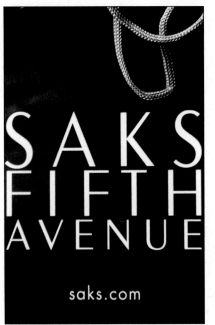

Saks promotes its Internet channel by displaying the URL on its shopping bags.

Retailers also benefit by using multiple channels synergistically. Multichannel retailers can use one channel to promote the services offered by other channels. For example, the URL of a store's Web site can be advertised on in-store signs, shopping bags, credit card billing statements, POS receipts, and the print or broadcast advertising used to promote the store. The physical stores and catalogs are also advertisements for a retailer's other channels. The retailer's electronic channel can be used to stimulate store visits by announcing special store events and promotions. Multichannel retailers can leverage their stores to lower the cost of fulfilling orders and processing returned merchandise. They can use their stores as "warehouses" for gathering merchandise for delivery to customers. Customers also can be offered the opportunity to pick up and return merchandise at the retailer's stores rather than pay shipping charges. Many retailers will waive shipping charges when orders are placed online or through the catalog if the customer physically comes into the store.

However, providing this seamless experience for customers and exploiting the synergies between channels is challenging. These challenges, and trade-off decisions confronting multichannel retailers, are discussed in the following sections.

Providing an Integrated Shopping Experience

Multichannel retailers are still struggling to provide an integrated shopping experience across all their channels because unique skills and resources are needed to manage each channel.[30] For example, retail distribution centers (DCs) supporting a store channel are designed to move merchandise in cartons from suppliers' inbound trucks to outbound trucks going to the retailer's stores. Retailers are so efficient at moving these cartons that they often remain in the DC for less than a day. In contrast, the DCs supporting a catalog and Internet channel are designed to receive merchandise in cartons and then break the cartons down to individual items for picking, repacking, and shipment to individual customers. The differences in handling and shipping individual items versus cartons means that unique packaging is needed for the same items sold through the different channels.

Even the marketing activities may be different because the objective of store or Internet channel marketing is to attract consumers to the store or Web site, while a catalog channel involves pushing the offering to targeted consumers.

REFACT

A study of large national retailers found that 96 percent could not access online customer profiles in-store or at call centers.[31]

The information systems for managing store and nonstore channels also differ. Store channel information systems are typically product-centric, while nonstore channels are customer-centric. Information systems for stores are designed to record product transactions and manage product inventory. The information system keeps track of how much merchandise was shipped into a store and how much was sold, and then it determines how much needs to be reordered.

On the other hand, information systems for nonstore channels are more customer-centric because, in addition to managing inventory, these systems provide a record of each customer's purchase history and even search behavior. This additional information can be used to target promotions to specific customers. Integrating store-based systems to be more customer-centric is difficult.

Because of these operational differences, many multichannel retailers have separate organizations for each channel. However, the trend is for multichannel retailers to integrate their operations across channels rather than have separate organizations. For example, when Walmart launched its electronic channel, www. walmart.com, it created an autonomous subsidiary located near Silicon Valley and staffed with managers who had no previous connection with Walmart or even retailing but had considerable expertise in network design. JCPenney had separate divisions for its store and nonstore channels, with separate merchandise management, distribution, advertising, and promotion management. Both Walmart and JCPenney have subsequently integrated the management of their store and nonstore channels at their corporate headquarters.

Other retailers outsource the management of their electronic channels, an approach that further increases the challenges in providing a seamless customer interface and building a competitive advantage. For example, GSI Commerce manages the Internet channel, the Web site and fulfillment, for several competing sporting goods retailers—Dick's, Sports Authority, and Modell's. It's hard to differentiate a retail offering and build a competitive advantage when the same supplier is managing a business activity for competing retailers.

Supporting M-Commerce

Customers can access a retailer's Internet channel using a variety of devices ranging from a desktop computer to a mobile phone. Due to the rapid growth of domestic and international broadband access through mobile devices, retailers are very interested in developing **m-commerce**—the purchase of products and services through mobile devices. However, the typical retailer's Web site is not currently designed to accommodate the mobile device's small screen and slower download speeds. A number of firms such as ESPN have developed special Web sites for access through mobile devices. In addition, retailers have developed apps, small computer programs, that enable mobile device users to engage in an activity such as shopping.

However, many retailer mobile apps are simply minor updates of the retailer's existing Web site to accommodate the mobile device's smaller screen. Macy's iShop, on the other hand, is an example of a mobile device app that is designed to take advantage of the unique navigational tools in the iPhone's user interface. On the home page, customers can choose to browse from a menu of 12 departments. After selecting the department, customers are given the "slot machine interface" that is familiar to iPhone users—three scrolling wheels let the user fine-tune the search by category, brand, and price, and a click of the "Go" button retrieves all products that are a match (second image). From there, it's just two more clicks to either purchase the product online or have it sent to a nearby store.

This Macy's iPhone app facilitates m-commerce by effectively using the mobile device's navigation.

Users can browse for products in several ways. Men's shirts, for example, can be found through the men's department, and they can also be found by clicking "Top Rated" and then navigating to the men's department. Sale and clearance departments are also broken down for browsing. Hitting the "Offers" button generates a page of current promotional offers. Promotional offers can also be accessed on the basis of store location—hitting the "More" button and then selecting "Store information" employs the iPhone's location awareness to find the nearest store and then shows promotional offers valid at that store. Once in the store, customers simply show the on-screen bar-coded coupon at checkout to have the discount applied. While this application offers are a great service for mobile shopping customers, it works only with the iPhone device.[34]

Organizing for Multichannel Retailing

Since each of the channels offers a unique set of benefits, the profiles of a retailer's customers who use the different channels are not the same. Thus a critical decision facing multichannel retailers is the degree to which they should integrate the operations of the channels or have different organizations for each channel. At one extreme of this continuum is complete integration—selling the same products at the same prices through the same distribution system for all channels. At the other extreme is having different organizations manage each channel so that the channels are tailored to different target markets. There are very few retailers that pursue a strategy at either end of this continuum. To determine where they should fall on the continuum, retailers have to address several issues, such as the use of a centralized, common customer database and consistency in brand image, pricing, and assortments across channels.[36]

Centralized Customer Database   While there are differences of opinion about whether to integrate or separately manage many key multichannel activities, there is a general consensus on the need to establish a centralized customer data warehouse with a complete history of each customer's interaction with the retailer.[37] The centralized customer data warehouse is crucial for exploiting the ability to collect detailed customer data through the Internet channel and provide a seamless experience for customers when they interact with the retailer through multiple channels.

Brand Image   Retailers need to provide a consistent brand image of themselves and their private-label merchandise across all channels. For example, Patagonia reinforces its image of selling high-quality, environmentally friendly sports equipment in its stores, catalogs, and Web site. Each of these channels emphasizes function, not fashion, in the descriptions of Patagonia's products. Patagonia's concerns about the environment are communicated by carefully lighting its stores and using recycled polyester in many of its clothes, as well as only organic, rather than pesticide-intensive, cotton. Its Web blog, www.thecleanestline.com, is dedicated to essays and other features on environmental activism, innovative design, and sports. Retailing View 3.4 describes how Build-A-Bear Workshop uses multiple channels to build and reinforce its brand image.

Merchandise Assortment   Typically, different assortments are appropriate for each of the channels. For example, multichannel retailers offer a broader and deeper merchandise assortment through their Internet channel than through their store channel. The Internet channel is more efficient for selling merchandise that does not have broad appeal.

The channels also differ in terms of their effectiveness in generating sales for types of merchandise. For example, the store channel is better suited for selling products with important "touch-and-feel" attributes such as the fit of a shirt, the taste of an ice cream flavor, or the smell of a perfume. On the other hand, an Internet channel might be just as effective as a store channel for selling products with important "look-and-see" attributes such as price, color, and grams of fat. Evaluating these products does not require senses beyond sight. Because of the problems of providing touch-and-feel information, apparel retailers experience return rates of more than 20 percent on purchases made through an electronic channel but only 10 percent on purchases made in stores.

Pricing Pricing represents another difficult decision for a multichannel retailer. Customers expect pricing consistency across channels (excluding shipping charges and sales tax). However, in some cases, retailers need to adjust their pricing strategy because of the competition they face in different channels. For example, BarnesandNoble.com offers lower prices through its electronic channel than through its stores to compete effectively against Amazon.com.

Retailers with stores in multiple markets often set different prices for the same merchandise to deal with differences in local competition. Typical customers do not realize these price differences because they are exposed only to the prices in their local markets. However, multichannel retailers may have difficulties sustaining regional price differences when customers can easily check prices on the Internet.

RETAILING VIEW The Build-A-Bear Workshop Uses Multiple Channels to Enhance Its Image

3.4

The Build-A-Bearville Web site (left) reinforces its brand image generated by its stores (right).

The Build-A-Bear Workshop creates a memorable experience for children that contributes to its strong brand image. Children enter the store, choose the type of animal, stuff and dress the animal, and then bring the stuffed animal to life by inserting a heart, giving it a name, and registering it. The child leaves the store with a new furry friend and its birth certificate. "Kids today move seamlessly between online and real-world play," says Dave Finnegan, Build-A-Bear Workshop's chief information and logistics bear. "We're already an interactive brand and a place where kids use their imagination, creativity and self-expression to have fun. All of this interactive customization makes things come to life in a new way."

The Build-A-Bear Internet channel (www.buildabearville.com) reinforces and extends its brand image. At the Web site, children can create an avatar for themselves and choose a gender, hairstyle, eye color, skin tone, and clothing style. When the code on the birth certificate of the animal bought in the store is entered, the animal springs to life on the Web site, appearing in a backpack carried by the avatar. Together, the child and the animal can play games, learn, and interact with other avatars and their furry friends.

Each Build-A-Bear animal has a unique virtual item that comes with it. Children can trade or collect the items in Bearville. Bearville residents receive a Cub Condo, which they can paint, decorate, and to which they can invite guests. They also can purchase virtual items for their Cub Condo or outfits for themselves or their animal. The virtual avatar earns points when a "real" child makes a purchase in a Build-A-Bear store. The receipt from the purchase has a code that the child redeems online for Bear Bucks.

Build-A-Bear also tries to make sure the site is safe. When a child signs up, parents receive an e-mail inviting them to select and control communication options based on age and comfort level. Build-A-Bear also monitors the site for safe socialization. Thus Build-A-Bear uses its Internet channel to enhance its image and encourage children to continue their interaction with the retailer and visit its stores multiple times.

Sources: Sandy Smith, "Beary Interactive: Build-A-Bear Is Hands-On in Kids' Real and Virtual Worlds," *Stores,* June 2009; Samantha Murphy, "New to the Neighborhood," *Chain Store Age,* February 2008, p. 51.

Reduction of Channel Migration   The availability of an Internet channel enables customers to easily search for information about products and their prices during a shopping episode. Browsing on the Internet channel and purchasing the merchandise at a store is the most common use of multiple channels during a shopping episode. This pattern was used by over 78 percent of U.S. consumers surveyed, while only 8 percent used the second most widely used pattern, browsing in a store and making the purchase over the Internet.[38]

However, multichannel retailers want to prevent **channel migration**—consumers' collecting information about products on their channels and then buying the product from a competitor.[40] Retailers want customers to both search for information and complete the transaction through their channels, but the low cost of searching on the Internet increases the opportunity for channel migration. Thus customer retention during shopping episodes is a challenge for multichannel retailers. Note that before the Internet, customers typically researched and purchased products during a trip to one store because it was too "costly" to visit multiple stores. Two approaches that multichannel retailers can use to reduce channel migration are (1) to offer uniquely relevant information based on proprietary data the retailer has collected about the customers and (2) promote private-label merchandise that can be purchased only from the retailer.

MULTICHANNEL SHOPPING IN THE FUTURE

The following hypothetical scenario illustrates the seamless interface across channels that customers in the future may experience.

Shopping Experience Scenario

It's Tuesday morning, and Judy Jamison is eating breakfast thinking about buying a new dress for the party she'll be attending this Friday night at the new club downtown. She sends a tweet to her friends about her plans to go shopping after work today and asks for suggestions of retailers she might visit. She gets some suggestions from friends and then decides to do some research on the Internet. She logs on to her laptop, accesses her personal shopper program called FRED, and has the following interactive dialog:

Fred: Do you wish to browse, go to a specific store, or buy a specific item?

Judy: Specific item.

Fred: Occasion? [Menu appears and Judy selects.]

Judy: Dress.

Fred: Type of dress? [Menu appears.]

Judy: Cocktail dress.

Fred: Price range? [Menu appears.]

Judy: $175–$200.

[Now FRED goes out and literally shops the world electronically, visiting the servers for companies selling cocktail dresses in Europe, Asia, Africa, Australia, and North and South America.]

Fred: 1,231 items have been identified. How many do you want to review? [Menu appears.]

Judy: Just 5.

[FRED selects the five best alternatives on the basis of information it has about Judy's style preferences. The five cocktail dresses appear on the screen with the price, brand name, and retailer listed beneath each one. Judy clicks on each dress to get more information about it. With another click, she sees a full-motion video of a woman who looks similar to Judy modeling the dress. She selects the dress she finds most appealing.]

However, Judy decides not to buy the dress because she is not sure the dress will fit right when it arrives and she will not have time to return it and get another size. She likes the Robert Rodriguez styles FRED found, so she goes to Brand-Habit.com, types in the designer's name and her zip code, and finds the closest store that carries his designs. The site directs her to the store's Web site to look at more dresses. She decides to visit the store after work.

Shortly after Judy walks into the store, a chip in her credit card signals her presence and status as a frequent shopper to a mobile device held by the store sales associate responsible for preferred clients. Information about items in which Judy might be interested, including the items she viewed on the Web site through FRED, is downloaded from the store server to Judy's and the sales associate's devices.

A sales associate approaches Judy and says, "Hello, Ms. Jamison. My name is Joan Bradford. How can I help you?" Judy tells the associate she needs to buy a dress for a party. She has seen some dresses on the store's Web site and would like to look at them in the store. The sales associate takes Judy to a virtual dressing room.

In the dressing room, Judy sits in a comfortable chair and views the dresses displayed on her image, which has been drawn from a body scan stored in Judy's customer file. Information about Judy's recent visit to the retailer's Web site and her past purchases is used to select the dresses displayed.

Using her mobile phone, Judy shares this personalized viewing with her friend, who is still at work in California. They discuss which dress looks best on Judy. Then, using her mobile phone again, Judy drills down to find more information about the dress—the fabric, cleaning instructions, and so forth. Finally, she selects a dress and purchases it with one click.

Using information displayed on her mobile device, the sales associate Joan suggests a handbag and scarf that would complement the dress. These accessories are added to the image of Judy in the dress. Judy decides to buy the scarf but not the handbag. Finally, Judy is told about the minor alterations needed to make the dress a perfect fit. She can check the retailer's Web site to find out when the alterations are completed and then indicate whether she wants the dress delivered to her home or she will pick it up at the store.

As Judy passes through the cosmetics department on her way to her car, she sees an appealing new lipstick shade. She decides to purchase the lipstick and a 3-ounce bottle of her favorite perfume and walks out of the store. The store systems sense her departure, and the merchandise she has selected is automatically charged to her account through signals from radio frequency identification (RFID) chips.

Supporting the Shopping Experience

This scenario illustrates the advantages of having a customer database shared by all channels and integrated across all systems. The sales associate and the store systems are able to offer superior customer service based on this database, which contains information about Judy's body scan image, her interaction with the retailer's Web site, and her past purchases and preferences. The technology also supports the retailer's business model, which determines to offer customers the products and services that will provide the best shopping experience.

Before Judy went into the store, she interacted with a search engine to find where the particular brand and product she was looking for could be found. She then interacted with the retailer's Web site to review the available merchandise before she went to the store, check the status of her alterations, and decide about having the merchandise delivered to her home. The scenario also includes some new technologies that will exist in the store of the future, such as RFID, self-checkout, and personalized virtual reality displays.

SUMMARY

Traditional store-based and catalog retailers are adding electronic channels and evolving into integrated, customer-centric, multichannel retailers. This evolution toward multichannel retailing has been driven by the increasing desire of customers to communicate with retailers anytime, anywhere, anyplace.

Each of the major channels (stores, catalogs, and Web sites) offers unique benefits to customers. The store channel enables customers to touch and feel merchandise and use the products immediately after they are purchased. Catalogs enable customers to browse through a retailer's offerings anytime and anyplace without an Internet connection. A unique benefit offered by the electronic channel is the opportunity for consumers to search across a broad range of alternatives, develop a smaller set of alternatives based on their needs, get specific information about the alternatives they want, and make an order with a few clicks.

By offering multiple channels, retailers overcome the limitations of each channel. Thus, Web sites can be used to extend the geographic presence and assortment offered by the store channel, market promotions, educate consumers, and provide an intimate link between the retailer and the customer. Stores can be used to provide a multiple sensory experience and an economical method of getting merchandise to both stores and Internet customers.

Providing a seamless interface across channels is challenging for multichannel retailers. Meeting the shopper's expectations requires the development and use of common customer databases and integrated systems. In addition, multichannel retailers will have to make decisions about how to use the different channels to support the retailer's brand image, as well as how to present consistent merchandise assortments and pricing across channels.

KEY TERMS

automated retailing, *60*

catalog channel, *58*

channel migration, *74*

direct-response advertising, *60*

direct selling, *59*

disintermediation, *69*

electronic retailing, *58*

e-tailing, *58*

infomercials, *60*

Internet retailing, *58*

live chat, *65*

m-commerce, *71*

multichannel retailer, *57*

multilevel system, *60*

online retailing, *58*

party plan system, *60*

pyramid scheme, *60*

retail channel, *58*

share of customers' wallets, *68*

television home shopping, *60*

vending machines, *60*

GET OUT AND DO IT!

1. **CONTINUING CASE ASSIGNMENT: GO SHOPPING** Assume that you are shopping on the Internet for an item in the same merchandise category you analyzed for the Comparison Shopping exercise in Chapter 2. Go to the retailer's Web site, and compare the merchandise assortment offered, the prices, and the shopping experience in the store and on the store's Web site. How easy was it to locate what you were looking for? What were the assortment and pricing like? What was the checkout like? What features of the sites do you like and dislike, such as the look and feel of the site, navigation, and special features?

2. **INTERNET EXERCISE** Go to the Web sites of J. Crew (www.jcrew.com), JCPenney (www.jcpenney.com), and Lands' End (www.landsend.com), and shop for a pair of khaki pants. Evaluate your shopping experience at each site. Compare and contrast the sites and your experiences on the basis of characteristics you think are important to consumers.

3. **INTERNET EXERCISE** Assume that you are getting married and planning your wedding. Compare

and contrast the usefulness of www.theknot.com and www.weddingchannel.com for planning your wedding. What features of the sites do you like and dislike? Indicate the specific services offered by these sites that you would use.

4. **INTERNET EXERCISE** Go to the Center for Democracy and Technology's home page at http://www.cdt.org/, and click on "Consumer Privacy" and then "Privacy Guide" (http://www.cdt.org/privacy/guide/basic/topten.html). Why is privacy a concern for Internet shoppers? What are the top-10 recommended ways for consumers to protect their privacy online? How many of these recommendations have you employed when using the Internet?

5. **INTERNET AND SHOPPING EXERCISE** Pick a merchandise category like microwave ovens, power drills, digital cameras, blenders, or coffee makers. Compare a retailer's offering in its local store and on its Internet site. What are the differences in the assortments offered through its store and Internet channel? Are the prices the same or different? What

has the retailer done to exploit the synergies between the channels?

6. **INTERNET EXERCISE:** Look up "Estimated Quarterly U.S. Retail Sales: Total and E-Commerce," tabulated by the Retail Indicators Branch of the U.S. Census Bureau, at http://www.census.gov/mrts/www/data/html/07Q1table3.html. First, using Excel, create a bar graph of the e-commerce retail sales in millions of dollars for the past five years. How would you describe the growth trend? Project the e-commerce retail sales for the second quarter of next year. How did you make this forecast? Second, again using Excel, create a bar graph of the e-commerce retail sales as a percentage of total retail sales for the past five years. How would you describe the growth trend? Project the e-commerce retail sales as a percentage of total retail sales for the second quarter of next year. How did you make this forecast?

DISCUSSION QUESTIONS AND PROBLEMS

1. Why are store-based retailers aggressively pursuing sales through electronic channels?

2. What capabilities are needed to be an effective multichannel retailer?

3. From a customer's perspective, what are the benefits and limitations of stores? Catalogs? Retail Web sites?

4. Would you buy clothes on the basis of the way they look on a customized virtual model? Why or why not?

5. Why are the electronic and catalog channels so popular for gift giving?

6. Should a multichannel retailer offer the same assortment of merchandise for sale, at the same price, on its Web site and in its stores? Why or why not?

7. Which of the following categories of merchandise do you think could be sold effectively through an electronic channel: jewelry, TV sets, computer software, high-fashion apparel, pharmaceuticals, and health care products such as toothpaste, shampoo, and cold remedies? Why?

8. Assume you are interested in investing in a Web site targeting people who enjoy active outdoor recreation, such as hiking, rock climbing, and kayaking. What merchandise and information would you offer on the site? What type of entity do you think would be most effective in running the site: a well-known outdoors person, a magazine targeting outdoor activity, or a retailer selling outdoor merchandise, such as Patagonia or REI? Why?

9. Outline a strategy for a local, independent store-based retailer to add an Internet channel. How would you design its Web site? What information and merchandise would you have on the Web site?

10. When you shop online for merchandise, how much time do you spend browsing versus buying? When you shop in a store for merchandise, how much time do you spend browsing versus buying? Explain your responses.

SUGGESTED READINGS

Ansari, Asim, Carl F. Mela, and Scott A. Neslin. "Customer Channel Migration." *Journal of Marketing Research* 45, no. 1 (2008), pp. 60–76.

Frambach, Ruud T., Henk C. A. Roest, and Trichy V. Krishnan. "The Impact of Consumer Internet Experience on Channel Preference and Usage Intentions across the Different Stages of the Buying Process." *Journal of Interactive Marketing* 21, no. 2 (2007), pp. 26–41.

Konus, Umut, Peter C. Verhoef, and Scott A. Neslin. "Multichannel Shopper Segments and Their Covariates." *Journal of Retailing* 84, no. 4 (2008), pp. 398–413.

Mendelsohn, Tamara, Brian Tesch, and Carrie A. Johnson. *Trends 2007: Multichannel Retail*. Cambridge: Forrester, 2007.

Neslin, S. A., and V. Shankar. "Key Issues in Multichannel Management: Current Knowledge and Future Directions." *Journal of Interactive Marketing* 23, no. 1 (2009), pp. 35–48.

Ratchford, Brian T. "Online Pricing: Review and Directions for Research." *Journal of Interactive Marketing*, February 2009, pp. 82–90.

Venkatesan, Rajkumar, V. Kumar, and Nalini Ravishanker. "Multichannel Shopping: Causes and Consequences." *Journal of Marketing* 71, no. 2 (2007), pp. 114–132.

Verhoef, Peter C., Scott A. Neslin, and Björn Vroomen. "Multichannel Customer Management: Understanding the Research-Shopper Phenomenon." *International Journal of Research in Marketing* 24, no. 2 (2007), pp. 129–148.

Weitz, Barton A. "Electronic Retailing," in *Retailing in the 21st Century—Current and Future Trends*, 2nd ed., eds. Manfred Kraft and Murali Mantrala. Berlin: Springer, 2010, pp. 309–323.

Zhang Jie, Paul Farris, John Irvin, Tarun Kushwaha, Thomas Steenburgh, and Barton Weitz. "Crafting Integrated Multichannel Retailing Strategies." *Journal of Interactive Marketing*, forthcoming.

Customer Buying Behavior

EXECUTIVE BRIEFING

Don Unser, Group President, Retail Business Group, The NPD Group, Inc.

The NPD Group provides information about consumer buying behavior that helps our clients, both retailers and vendors, make better, fact-based decisions. The reports provided by our system are derived from two databases—POS sales data and consumer panel data.

The point of sale (POS) data are supplied by over 800 retail clients around the world, detailing sales in over 125,000 stores. The database provides sales for discreet products and their prices across four general merchandise categories offered by a broad cross-section of retailers including department, discount, and specialty stores. Retailers share this sales data in exchange for the knowledge we provide from our analyses.

The online consumer panel consists of 2.5 million people who have agreed to participate in surveys and provide information on their purchase behavior. In addition to sales by product and retailer, the database includes demographic and other information about the panel members including customer satisfaction evaluations following specific purchase occasions. This database allows sales tracking across all industry segments, by demographic segments. We use statistical techniques to ensure that the consumer sample is representative of the population.

Our systems are designed to make it easy for retailers to get the data that help them analyze market performance and make fact-based decisions. A variety of reports are available drawing on both databases. For example, an automotive parts retailer reviewed a fair share report that compared their market share in each merchandise category to their overall market share and discovered some areas in which they were not getting their fair share—they had a market share of 8 percent in the category compared to their overall market share of 11 percent. By drilling down into the data, the buyer for the category adjusted its assortment plan, changing the emphasis placed on specific brands and SKUs. The result was an increase in annual sales of $3 million and a promotion.

Due to the breadth and depth of data we collect and analyze, we are able to track broad changes in shopping behaviors. The choice of food and meals by consumers in their 20s, referred to as Gen Y or Millennials, defers

CHAPTER 4

QUESTIONS

How do customers make decisions about what retailer to patronize, what channel to use, and what merchandise to buy?

What social and personal factors affect customer purchase decisions?

How can retailers get customers to visit their stores more frequently and buy more merchandise during each visit?

Why and how do retailers group customers into market segments?

from other generations. We find that they have a high degree of confidence in their judgments and heed cravings at the moment and place high value on minimal preparation time. They are more likely than consumers in other age groups to use frozen entrées and other quick-prep items. These young adults have been among the hardest-hit by the recession and are heavy patrons of low-priced retailers. One-third of Millennials shop at Walmart and other mass merchants. Food retailers and restaurants have a major opportunity—and challenge—in learning how to communicate effectively with this "connected" generation, as well as offering products and meal/snack solutions that fit their spontaneous, budget-conscious lifestyles.

As discussed in Chapter 1, an effective retail strategy satisfies customer needs better than do competitors' strategies. Thus, understanding customer needs and buying behavior is critical to formulating and implementing an effective retail strategy. Successful retailers are customer-centric—their strategic and tactical decisions revolve around their present and potential customers.

This chapter focuses on how customers process information and make decisions about what stores to patronize, what channels to use, and what products and services to buy.[1] It describes the stages customers go through when making purchase decisions and the factors that influence their buying process. Since it typically is not cost-efficient for retailers to develop unique offerings for individual customers, retailers target their offerings to groups of customers (market segments) with similar needs and buying processes. The chapter concludes with a discussion of how these market segments are formed. We then use information about the buying process to discuss how retailers can identify the market segments that will be the target of their retail strategy. The appendix to this chapter examines special aspects of consumer behavior that concern retailers selling fashion merchandise.

THE BUYING PROCESS

The following scenario illustrates the steps consumers go through when purchasing merchandise. Eva Mendoza, a student at the University of Washington, is beginning to interview for jobs. Eva planned to wear the blue suit her parents gave her several years ago to the interviews. But looking at her suit, she realizes that it's

While the Internet enables consumers shopping online to collect price information with little effort, they can also get information about the quality and performance of products at a low search cost. The additional information about product quality might lead customers to pay more for high-quality products, thus decreasing the importance of price.[15] In addition, retailers using an Internet channel can differentiate their offerings by providing better services and information. Even with the low search cost, research shows significant price dispersions for retailers offering the same branded products through an Internet channel. The price differences for branded products persist even though economic theory suggests that prices should be the same for all retailers as search costs for branded products diminish.[16]

Evaluation of Alternatives: The Multiattribute Model

The multiattribute attitude model provides a useful way to summarize how customers use the information they have collected to evaluate and select retailers, channels, and products. We discuss this model in detail because it offers a framework for developing a retailing strategy.[17]

The **multiattribute attitude model** is based on the notion that customers see a retailer, a product, or a channel as a collection of attributes or characteristics. The model is designed to predict a customer's evaluation of a product, retailer, or channel on the basis of (1) its performance on relevant attributes and (2) the importance of those attributes to the customer.

Beliefs about Performance   To illustrate this model, consider the store choice decision confronting a young, single, professional Milwaukee woman who needs groceries. She considers three alternatives: (1) a supercenter store in the next suburb, (2) her local supermarket store, or (3) a grocer that operates only an Internet channel, such as Peapod. Her perception of the offerings provided by these retailers is shown in Exhibit 4–2.

The customer mentally processes the "objective" information about each grocery retailer in part A of Exhibit 4–2 and forms an impression of the benefits each one provides. Part B of Exhibit 4–2 shows her beliefs about these benefits. Notice

EXHIBIT 4–2
Characteristics of Food Retailers

A. INFORMATION ABOUT STORES SELLING GROCERIES			
Store Characteristics	Supercenter	Supermarket	Internet Grocer
Grocery prices	20% below average	Average	10% above average
Delivery cost ($)	0	0	10
Total travel time (minutes)	30	15	0
Typical checkout time (minutes)	10	5	2
Number of products, brands, and sizes	40,000	30,000	40,000
Fresh produce	Yes	Yes	Yes
Fresh fish	Yes	Yes	No
Ease of finding products	Difficult	Easy	Easy
Ease of collecting nutritional information about products	Difficult	Difficult	Easy

B. BELIEFS ABOUT STORES' PERFORMANCE BENEFITS*			
Performance Benefits	Supercenter	Supermarket	Internet Grocer
Economy	10	8	6
Convenience	3	5	10
Assortment	9	7	5
Availability of product Information	4	4	8

*10 = excellent, 1 = poor.

that some benefits combine several objective characteristics. For example, the convenience benefit combines travel time, checkout time, and ease of finding products. Grocery prices and delivery cost affect her beliefs about the economy of shopping at the various retail outlets.

The degree to which each retailer provides each benefit is represented on a 10-point scale: 10 means the retailer performs very well in providing the benefit; 1 means it performs very poorly. In this example, no retailer has superior performance on all benefits. The supercenter performs well on economy and assortment but is low on convenience. The Internet grocer offers the best convenience but is weak on economy and assortment.

Importance Weights   The young woman in the preceding example forms an overall evaluation of each alternative on the basis of the importance she places on each benefit the retailers provide. The importance she places on a benefit can also be represented using a 10-point rating scale, with 10 indicating the benefit is very important to her and 1 indicating it's very unimportant. Using this rating scale, the importance of the retailers' benefits for the young woman and for a parent with four children is shown in Exhibit 4–3, along with the performance beliefs previously discussed. Notice that the single woman values convenience and the availability of product information much more than economy and assortment. But to the parent, economy is very importance and assortment is moderately important, whereas convenience and product information aren't very important.

The importance of a retailer's benefits differs for each customer and also may differ for each shopping trip. For example, the parent with four children may stress economy for major shopping trips but place more importance on convenience for a fill-in trip.

In Exhibit 4–3, the single woman and parent have the same beliefs about each retailer's performance, but they differ in the importance they place on the benefits the retailers offer. In general, customers can differ in their beliefs about retailers' performances as well as in their importance weights.

Evaluating Retailers   Research has shown that a customer's overall evaluation of an alternative (in this situation, three retailers) is related to the sum of the performance beliefs multiplied by the importance weights. Thus, we calculate the young, single woman's overall evaluation or score for the supercenter as follows:

$$
\begin{aligned}
4 \times 10 &= 40 \\
10 \times 3 &= 30 \\
5 \times 9 &= 45 \\
9 \times 4 &= \underline{36} \\
&\ 151
\end{aligned}
$$

EXHIBIT 4–3
Evaluation of Retailers

Characteristic	IMPORTANCE WEIGHTS*		PERFORMANCE BELIEFS		
	Young Single Woman	Parent with Four Children	Supercenter	Supermarket	Internet Grocer
Economy	4	10	10	8	6
Convenience	10	4	3	5	10
Assortment	5	8	9	7	5
Availability of product information	9	2	4	4	8
OVERALL EVALUATION					
Young single woman			151	153	221
Parent with four children			192	164	156

*10 = very important, 1 = very unimportant.

Exhibit 4–3 shows the overall evaluations of the three retailers using the importance weights of the single woman and the parent. For the single woman, the Internet grocer has the highest score, 221, and thus has the most favorable evaluation. She would probably select this retailer for most of her grocery shopping. On the other hand, the supercenter has the highest score, 192, for the parent, who'd probably buy the family's weekly groceries there.

When customers are about to select a retailer, they don't actually go through the process of listing store characteristics, evaluating retailers' performances on these characteristics, determining each characteristic's importance, calculating each store's overall score, and then patronizing the retailer with the highest score. The multiattribute attitude model does not reflect customers' actual decision process, but it does predict their evaluation of alternatives and their choice. In addition, the model provides useful information for designing a retail offering. For example, if the supermarket could increase its performance rating on assortment from 7 to 10 (perhaps by adding a bakery and a wide selection of prepared meals), customers like the parent might shop at the supermarket more often than at the supercenter.

The application of the multiattribute attitude model in Exhibit 4–3 deals with a customer who is evaluating and selecting a retailer. The same model can also be used to describe how a customer evaluates and selects which channel to use (store, Internet, or catalog) or what merchandise to buy from a retailer. For example, the model could be used to describe Eva Mendoza's choice of the three suits she was considering.

Implications for Retailers   In this section, we describe how a retailer can use the multiattribute attitude model to encourage customers to shop at the retailer more frequently. First, the model indicates what information customers use to decide which retailer to patronize or which channel to use. Second, it suggests tactics that retailers can undertake to influence customers' store, channel, and merchandise choices.

To develop a program for attracting customers, retailers need to do market research to collect the following information:

1. Alternative retailers that customers consider.
2. Characteristics or benefits that customers consider when evaluating and choosing a retailer.
3. Customers' ratings of each retailer's performance on the characteristics.
4. The importance weights that customers attach to the characteristics.

Armed with this information, the retailer can use several approaches to influence customers to patronize its store or Internet site.

Getting into the Consideration Set   Retailers need to be included in the customer's **consideration set,** or the set of alternatives the customer evaluates when making a choice of a retailer to patronize. To be included in the consideration set, retailers develop programs to increase the likelihood that customers will remember them when they're about to go shopping. Retailers can increase customer awareness through communication and location decisions. For example, retailers can get placement at the top of the screen when consumers are using a search engine term for products they sell. They can develop communication programs that link categories they sell with their name. Starbucks locates several stores in the same area so that customers are exposed more frequently to the store name as they drive through the area.

After ensuring that it is in consumers' consideration set, a retailer can use four methods to increase the chances that customers will select it for a visit:

1. Increase beliefs about the store's performance.
2. Decrease the performance beliefs for competing stores in the consideration set.
3. Increase customers' importance weights.
4. Add a new benefit.

Changing Performance Beliefs   The first approach involves altering customers' beliefs about the retailer's performance by increasing the retailer's performance rating on a characteristic. For example, the supermarket in Exhibit 4–3 would want to increase its overall rating by improving its rating on all four benefits. The supermarket could improve its rating on economy by lowering prices and its assortment rating by stocking more gourmet and ethnic foods. Retailing View 4.2 illustrates how Lowe's altered the performance beliefs of women about its stores.

Because it can get costly for a retailer to improve its performance on all benefits, retailers must focus on improving their performance on those benefits that are important to customers in their target market. For example, Best Buy knows that an important benefit for its customers is not to be without their computers for lengthy amounts of time when repairs are needed. So it has a 165,000-square-foot "Geek Squad City" warehouse designed to cut the time it takes to repair and return a PC to one to three days. Geek Squad "agents" fix more than 2,000 laptops a day.[18]

A change in a performance belief about an important benefit results in a large change in customers' overall evaluations. In Exhibit 4–3, the supermarket should attempt to improve its convenience ratings if it wants to attract more young, single women who presently prefer shopping on the Internet. If its convenience rating

RETAILING VIEW   Do It Herself at Lowe's

4.2

You might think that home improvement centers are a retail recreation destination mostly for men. Men visit the stores on the weekends to check out the new tools and buy material for do-it-yourself (DIY) projects. But more than 50 percent of the sales at home improvement centers actually are made to women. Women not only make the decisions about what materials to use for home improvement projects but also end up doing much of the work themselves.

Lowe's was early to recognize the importance of female customers. It redesigned its stores to be brighter, lose the warehouse look, and feature departments more appealing to women. Aisles were widened to help eliminate "butt brush," the uncomfortable contact that can occur as customers navigate narrow, crowded aisles.

To make the store feel less intimidating, Lowe's made the shelves shorter and used lower aisle markers like those in grocery stores, with maps to help customers find products. However, Lowe's needed to balance the performance beliefs and importance weights that women have about their stores with those of men. Its male customers might shun stores if they find them too feminine. However Lowe's also found that women held the same negative view of overly feminine home improvement stores, so it decided to

Lowe's changed its store design to change women's beliefs about the pleasantness of its store environment.

teach women about tools rather than carrying tools specifically designed for women. One section of its Web site, www.lowes.com/howto, provides online clinics and videos to help customers successfully implement their own DIY projects at home.

Sources: Tony Bingham and Pat Galagan, "Training at Lowe's: Let's Learn Something Together," *T + D*, November 2009, pp. 35–41; Amanda Junk, "Women Wield the Tools: Lowe's, Habitat for Humanity Teaches Them How," *McClatchy-Tribune Business News*, July 18, 2009; and Cecile B. Corral, "Lowe's Outlines Expansion Plans," *Home Textiles Today*, October 5, 2009, p. 6.

REFACT

Women make more than 85 percent of all consumer purchases and purchase 50 percent or more in categories typically considered male—banking and financial services, electronics, automobiles, PCs, and many other big-ticket items.[19]

rose from 5 to 8, its overall evaluation among young, single women would increase from 153 to 183 and thus be much higher than their evaluation of supercenters. Note that an increase in the rating from 8 to 10 for a less important benefit, such as economy, would have less effect on the store's overall evaluation. The supermarket might try to improve its rating on convenience by increasing the number of check-out stations, using customer scanning to reduce checkout time, or providing more in-store information so that customers could locate merchandise more easily.

Research further suggests that consumers in Germany, France, and the United Kingdom place different weights on three important attributes—price/value, service/quality, and relationships—when selecting a retailer to patronize. German consumers tend to place more weight on price/value, whereas customer service and product quality are more important for French consumers, and affinity benefits such as loyalty cards and preferred customer programs are more important for English consumers. Thus, in general, retailers that emphasize price and good value will be more successful in Germany than in France or the United Kingdom.[20]

Another approach for altering evaluations is to decrease customers' performance ratings of a competing store. This approach may be illegal and usually isn't very effective, because bad-mouthing competitors generally backfires and customers typically don't believe a firm's negative comments about its competitors anyway.

Changing Importance Weights   Altering customers' importance weights is another approach to influencing store choice. A retailer wants to increase the importance customers place on benefits for which its performance is superior and decrease the importance of benefits for which it has inferior performance.

For example, if the supermarket in Exhibit 4–3 tried to attract families who shop at supercenters, it could increase the importance of convenience for them. Typically, changing importance weights is harder than changing performance beliefs, because importance weights reflect customers' personal values.

Adding a New Benefit   Finally, retailers might try to add a new benefit to the set of benefits customers consider when selecting a retailer. For example, Baksheesh (www.baksheeshfairtrade.com) sells handcrafted gifts from around the world at its two northern California stores. It attempts to add new benefit by emphasizing that its merchandise is **fair trade**—its merchandise is made by workers who are paid a fair wage, not just a minimum wage.[21] A fair wage means that workers are able to live relatively comfortably within the context of their local area. The workers make enough money for housing, food, health care, education for their children, and some disposable income. Offering fair-trade merchandise is a benefit that is important to consumers who are concerned about the welfare of people in less developed countries. To get a high evaluation on this new benefit, Baksheesh sells only certified gifts. The approach of adding a new benefit is often effective, because it's easier to change customer evaluations of new than of old benefits.

Purchasing the Merchandise or Service

Customers don't always patronize a store or purchase a brand or item of merchandise with the highest overall evaluation. The product or service offering the greatest benefits (having the highest evaluation) may not be available from the retailer, or the customer may feel that its risks outweigh the potential benefits. One measure of retailers' success at converting positive evaluations to purchases is the number of real or virtual abandoned carts in the retailer's store or Web site.

Retailers use various tactics to increase the chances that customers will convert their positive evaluations into purchases. Retailers can reduce the number of abandoned carts by making it easier to purchase merchandise. They can reduce the actual wait time for buying merchandise by having more checkout lanes open and placing them conveniently in the store. To reduce perceived wait times, they can install digital displays to entertain customers waiting in line.[22]

Customers' perceived risk in making a purchase decision can be reduced by providing sufficient information that reinforces the customer's positive evaluation. For example, Eva's friend Britt, the salesperson, and another potential customer provided Eva with positive feedback to support her purchase decision. Finally, risks are reduced when retailers offer liberal return policies, money-back guarantees, and refunds if customers find the same merchandise available at lower prices from another retailer.

Conversion rates are particularly low for consumers using an Internet channel because consumers are able to easily keep track of things they like. They can look at products, throw them in their cart, and delay a purchase decision. Retailers do a few things to encourage customers to make a purchase decision. For example, Zappos.com and Overstock.com create urgency by alerting customers when an item they have put in their shopping cart is almost sold out. Other sites, such as Gilt Groupe, offer items for a specified 36-hour period,

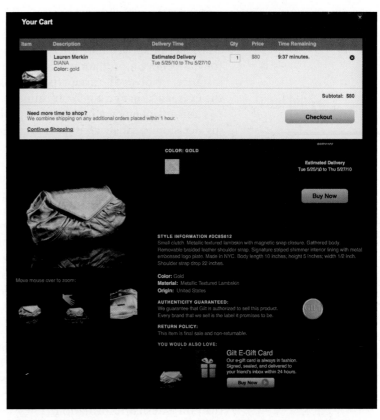

Gilt.com encourages customers to buy now by offering a limited number of items for a short time period. Once items are placed in a shopping cart members have 10 minutes to check out without losing the items.

and Neiman Marcus runs two-hour, online-only sales. While the Internet channel makes it easier for shoppers to delay purchase decisions, it also makes it easier to identify potential customers and encourage them to buy. Many retailers send reminder e-mails to visitors about items in carts they have abandoned.[23]

Postpurchase Evaluation

The buying process doesn't end when a customer purchases a product. After making a purchase, the customer uses the product and then evaluates the experience to determine whether it was satisfactory or unsatisfactory. **Satisfaction** is a postconsumption evaluation of how well a store or product meets or exceeds customer expectations. This **postpurchase evaluation** then becomes part of the customer's internal information and affects store and product evaluations and purchase decisions. Unsatisfactory experiences can motivate customers to complain to the retailer, patronize other stores, and select different brands in the future. Consistently high levels of satisfaction build store and brand loyalty, important sources of competitive advantage for retailers.[24]

TYPES OF BUYING DECISIONS

In some situations, customers like Eva Mendoza spend considerable time and effort selecting a retailer and evaluating alternative products—going through all the steps in the buying process described in the preceding section. In other situations, buying decisions are made automatically with little thought. Three types of customer decision-making processes are extended problem solving, limited problem solving, and habitual decision making.

Extended Problem Solving

Extended problem solving is a purchase decision process in which customers devote considerable time and effort to analyzing their alternatives. Customers typically engage in extended problem solving when the purchase decision involves a lot of risk and uncertainty. Financial risks arise when customers purchase an expensive product or service. Physical risks are important when customers feel that a product or service may affect their health or safety. Social risks arise when customers believe a product will affect how others view them. Lasik eye surgery, for instance, involves all three types of risks: It can be expensive, potentially damage the eyes, and change a person's appearance.

Consumers engage in extended problem solving when they are making a buying decision to satisfy an important need or when they have little knowledge about the product or service. Due to the high risk in such situations, customers go beyond their internal knowledge to consult with friends, family members, or experts. They may visit several retailers before making a purchase decision.

Retailers stimulate sales from customers engaged in extended problem solving by providing the necessary information in a readily available and easily understood manner and by offering money-back guarantees. For example, retailers that sell merchandise involving extended problem solving provide information on their Web sites describing the merchandise and its specifications, have informational displays in their stores (such as a sofa cut in half to show its construction), and use salespeople to demonstrate features and answer questions.

Limited Problem Solving

Limited problem solving is a purchase decision process involving a moderate amount of effort and time. Customers engage in this type of buying process when they have had some prior experience with the product or service and their risk is moderate. In such situations, customers tend to rely more on personal knowledge than on external information. They usually choose a retailer they have shopped at before and select merchandise they have bought in the past. The majority of customer purchase decisions involve limited problem solving.

Retailers attempt to reinforce this buying pattern and make it habitual when customers are buying merchandise from them. If customers are shopping elsewhere, however, retailers need to break this buying pattern by introducing new information or offering different merchandise or services.

Eva Mendoza's buying process illustrates both limited and extended problem solving. Her store choice decision was based on her knowledge of the merchandise in various stores she had shopped in and her search on Brandhabit.com. Considering this information, she felt the store choice decision was not very risky; thus, she engaged in limited problem solving when deciding to visit Macy's. But her buying process for the suit was extended. This decision was important to her; thus, she spent time acquiring information from a friend, the salesperson, and another shopper to evaluate and select a suit.

One common type of limited problem solving is **impulse buying,** or **unplanned purchasing,** which is a buying decision made by customers on the spot after seeing the merchandise.[26] Retailers encourage impulse-buying behavior by using prominent point-of-purchase (POP) or point-of-sale (POS) displays to attract customers' attention. Retailers have long recognized that the most valuable real estate in the store is at the point of purchase. An increasing number of nonfood retailers are looking to increase impulse buys from customers by offering candy, gum, and mints at their cash registers. Electronic shoppers are also stimulated to purchase impulsively when Internet retailers put special merchandise on their home pages and suggest complementary merchandise just before checkout.

Habitual Decision Making

Habitual decision making is a purchase decision process involving little or no conscious effort. Today's customers have many demands on their time. One way they cope with these time pressures is by simplifying their decision-making process. When a need arises, customers may automatically respond with, "I'll buy the same thing I bought last time from the same store." Typically, this habitual decision-making process occurs when decisions aren't very important to customers and involve familiar merchandise they have bought in the past. When customers are loyal to a brand or a store, they engage in habitual decision making.

Brand loyalty means that customers like and consistently buy a specific brand in a product category. They are reluctant to switch to other brands if their favorite brand isn't available. For example, loyal Coca-Cola drinkers won't buy Pepsi, no matter what. Thus, retailers can satisfy these customers' needs only if they offer the specific brands desired.

Brand loyalty creates both opportunities and problems for retailers. Customers are attracted to stores that carry popular brands, but because retailers must carry these high-loyalty brands, they may not be able to negotiate favorable terms with the suppliers of the popular national brands. If, however, the high-loyalty brands are private-label brands (i.e., brands owned by the retailer), retailer loyalty is heightened. Chapter 13 covers buying and stocking branded and private-label merchandise.

Retailer loyalty means that customers like and habitually visit the same retailer to purchase a type of merchandise. Retailing View 4.3 describes the habitual decision making engaged in by some of Aroma Espresso's customers and how the cafés use digital signage at the point of purchase to stimulate impulse purchases.

All retailers would like to increase their customers' loyalty, and they can do so by selecting a convenient location (see Chapters 7 and 8), offering complete assortments of national and private-label brands (Chapter 13), reducing the number of stockouts (Chapter 13), rewarding customers for frequent purchases (Chapter 11), or providing good customer service (Chapter 18).

RETAILING VIEW   Using Digital Displays to Stimulate Unplanned Purchases

4.3

The store choice decision for many of Aroma Espresso's customers is habitual. Every morning they stop by the café for an espresso before work. They make this decision with little thought. When customers order their morning coffee at Aroma Espresso Bars, an image of a croissant or muffin appears on a digital display next to the cash register. The point-of-purchase displays show a beverage or cookie when customers order a sandwich or salad for lunch. These displays are very effective at stimulating unplanned purchases. Sales of displayed items have increased by as much as 68 percent in outlets where the systems are installed.

The system determines the specific item displayed on the basis of typical buying behaviors of customers and the inventory levels in the café. For example, a croissant is programmed to appear on the display when a customer orders an espresso since it is the most common pastry purchased with an espresso at an outlet. In addition, the inventories in the store are used to determine the appropriate item to display. Customers are encouraged to buy Danish sweet rolls when muffins are running low.

Retailers are starting to use even more advanced technologies to stimulate impulse purchases. They are installing tiny cameras that scan shoppers' faces to determine their sex, race,

Aroma Espresso Bar uses digital displays at the point of sale to stimulate impulse purchases.

and approximate age, and then display particularly appropriate merchandise.

Sources: www.aroma.us (accessed March 13, 2010); Jennifer L. Schenker, "Point-of-Sale Advertising Goes High Tech," *BusinessWeek*, September 22, 2008.

SOCIAL FACTORS INFLUENCING THE BUYING PROCESS

Exhibit 4–4 illustrates how customer buying decisions are influenced by the customer's social environment: family, reference groups, and culture.

Family

Many purchase decisions involve products that the entire family will consume or use. The previous discussion of the buying process focused on how one person makes a decision. When families make purchase decisions, they often consider the needs of all family members.[27] When choosing a vacation site, for example, all family members may participate in the decision making. In other situations, one member of the family may assume the decision-making role. For example, the husband might buy the groceries, which the wife then uses to prepare their child's lunch, which the child consumes in school. In this situation, the store choice decision might be made by the husband, but the brand choice decision might be made by the mother, although it likely is greatly influenced by the child.

Children play an important role in family buying decisions. Resort hotels now realize they must satisfy children's needs as well as those of adults. For example, Hyatt hotels greet families by offering books and games tailored to the children's ages. Parents checking in with infants receive a first-day supply of baby food or formula and diapers at no charge. Baby-sitting and escort services to attractions for children also are offered.

Retailers can attract consumers who shop with other family members by satisfying the needs of all those family members. For example, Nordstrom provides sitting areas in its store where men may watch a football game while their wives shop. By accommodating the needs of men and children who might not be interested in shopping, the retailer keeps the family in the stores longer and thereby encourages them to buy more merchandise.

Reference Groups

A **reference group** includes one or more people whom a person uses as a basis of comparison for beliefs, feelings, and behaviors. A consumer might have a number of different reference groups, although the most important is the family, as we discussed in the previous section. These reference groups affect buying decisions by (1) offering information, (2) providing rewards for specific purchasing behaviors, and (3) enhancing a consumer's self-image. Retailing View 4.4 describes the role of reference groups for tween shoppers

EXHIBIT 4–4
Social Factors Affecting
Buying Decisions

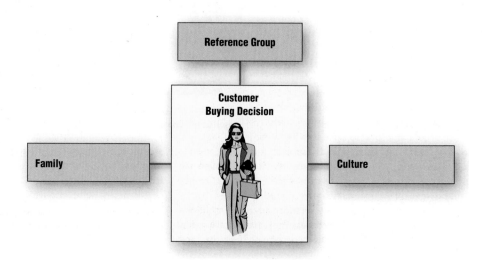

Reference groups provide information to consumers directly through conversation or indirectly through observation. For example, Eva received valuable information from her friend about the suits she was considering. On other occasions, Eva might look to women like skier Lindsey Vonn and tennis player Maria Sharapova to guide her selection of athletic apparel or Taylor Swift or Beyoncé for casual fashion advice. The role of reference groups in creating fashion is discussed in the appendix to this chapter.

By identifying and affiliating with reference groups, consumers create, enhance, and maintain their self-image. Customers who want to be seen as members of an elite social class may shop at prestige retailers, whereas others who want to create the image of an outdoor enthusiast might buy merchandise from the L.L. Bean Web site.

Retailers are particularly interested in identifying and reaching out to those in a reference group who act as store advocates and actively influence others in the group. **Store advocates** are customers who like a store so much that they actively share their positive experiences with friends and family. Consumers see so much advertising that they have become suspicious of the claims being made. Thus, they are relying more on their own social networks for information about stores to patronize and merchandise to buy.

REFACT

Victoria's Secret has the highest percentage of advocates among its customers. Twenty-three percent of its customers are store advocates, compared with an average of 13 percent for other retailers.[28]

RETAILING VIEW   Retailing to Tweens   4.4

Tween shoppers, between the ages of 5 and 12, are a large and growing market for retailers. The U.S. census estimates that by 2020 there will be 23 million tweens in the United States. With President Obama's daughters, Malia and Sasha, in the White House, attention will focus even more on this emerging group and the "first tweens" will likely be representatives of their generation.

Tweens are a hot market for clothes, music, and entertainment, but retailing to tweens is complicated. They are still forming their personalities and are torn between family and BFFs (best friends forever) and between fitting in and learning how to be an individual. Friends and status are important to tweens. For boys, friendships revolve around technology and sports. Girls like to talk, either about other girls or about boys, but the boys are not really into girls yet.

The purchase decisions of tweens are influenced by family members and friends.

REFACT

In a recent survey of tweens, responses showed that, during the last week, 42 percent of the girls surveyed shopped at a mall, 39 percent played a video game, and 29 percent gave product advice to parents. Only 24 percent of the boys shopped at a mall, but 83 percent played a video game, and 31 percent gave product advice to parents.[29]

Tween girls may want to emulate their older sister, but they are still little girls at heart. They like fun, frilly, glittery, sensory environments that tap into the kid in them. They want to be treated as young, but not babyish. Tween girls might want to look like their 16-year-old sister but the apparel assortments need to be fine-tuned to their younger body type and be more modest and sensible. Retailers need to create a mood of power and excitement for tween girls—colorful storefront windows and Web sites, light displays, photographic sticker booths, ear-piercing stations, and gumball machines. Special fixtures should be placed at eye level for younger girls, even though the girls will be visiting the store with mom, because the tweens choose and the parents pay.

Sources: Sharon Jayson, "It's Cooler than Ever to Be a Tween," *USA Today*, September 2, 2009; Jane O'Donnell, "Marketers Keep Pace with 'Tweens,'" *USA Today*, April 11, 2007.

Culture

Culture is the meaning, beliefs, morals, and values shared by most members of a society. For example, an important value in most Western cultures is individualism—people should look out only for themselves. Thus, consumers in individualistic cultures rely on their own inner standards and beliefs when making decisions. However, Eastern cultures value collectivism, emphasizing that consideration of others, particularly family, should guide behavior. Thus, social relationships are more important and material goods are less important to consumers in collectivist cultures.

Research has found that collectivists are more price-sensitive than individualistic consumers about private goods—products and services consumed privately such as personal hygiene products—but less price-sensitive about goods consumed in public, such as apparel. In addition, consumers in collectivist cultures are more prone to shop in groups than are individualistic consumers.[30]

Chinese shoppers have even started shopping in teams to bargain for bigger discounts. The practice, called *tuangou*, or team purchase, begins on Internet chat rooms, where like-minded consumers develop plans to buy appliances, furnishings, food, and even cars in bulk. Then they go together to stores and demand discounts. In an increasingly competitive marketplace, retailers in China are bending to the demands of these groups.[31]

Subcultures are distinctive groups of people within a culture. Members of a subculture share some customs and norms with the overall society but also have some unique perspectives. Subcultures can be based on geography (southerners), age (Gen Y), ethnicity (Asian-Americans), lifestyle (preppies), or a college. For instance, the culture at your college may evoke an "intellectual," "athletic," or "party" reputation among potential students. This subcultural environment influences, to some extent, the way students spend their leisure time and select the stores, brands, and merchandise they purchase.

Many retailers and shopping center managers have recognized the importance of appealing to different cultures and subcultures.[33] For instance, the U.S. Hispanic population is growing faster than any other market segment, and Hispanics' purchasing power is rising faster than that of the general population. Many retailers, particularly supermarkets in areas with large Hispanic populations, have dedicated significant space to products that are indigenous to particular Spanish-speaking countries. The product mix will, however, differ depending on the region of the country. Merchandise should reflect that, for instance, Miami has a large Cuban and Latin American population, whereas Los Angeles and Texas have more people from Mexico. Bilingual employees are a critical success factor for stores catering to the Hispanic population. Recent research found that Hispanic families tend to shop together, particularly on Sunday. To appeal to this group, shopping centers are adding Mexican restaurants to their food courts and Hispanic entertainment.

Many retailers and shopping center managers have adjusted their strategies to appeal to different cultures and subcultures.

MARKET SEGMENTATION

The preceding discussion focused on (1) how individual customers evaluate and select stores, channels, and merchandise and (2) the factors affecting their decision making. To be cost-effective, retailers identify groups of these customers (market segments) and target their offerings to meet the needs of typical customers in a segment rather than the needs of a specific customer. At one time, Walmart used a "one-size-fits-all" strategy. The merchandise selection was very similar across the United States, without much regard to geographic or demographic variations.

This approach worked well when most of its stores were located in rural areas in the Southeast. But as it opened stores in more diverse locations, it realized it had to develop different retail mixes for different market segments. It now targets and provides different offerings in stores that serve African-Americans, Hispanics, affluent customers, empty nesters, suburbanites, and rural residents.[34]

A **retail market segment** is a group of customers whose needs are satisfied by the same retail mix because they have similar needs. For example, families traveling on a vacation have different needs than executives on business trips. Thus, Marriott offers hotel chains with different retail mixes for each of these segments—Marriott Hotels and Resort for vacationers and business conferences and Marriott Residence Inns for families traveling by car.

The Internet enables retailers to target individual customers efficiently and market products to them on a one-to-one basis. This one-to-one marketing concept is discussed in Chapter 11, as it pertains to customer relationship management.

Criteria for Evaluating Market Segments

Customers can be grouped into segments in many different ways. Exhibit 4–5 shows some different methods for segmenting retail markets. There's no simple way to determine which method is best, although four criteria useful for evaluating whether a retail segment is a viable target market are as follows: actionable, identifiable, substantial, and reachable.

EXHIBIT 4–5
Methods for Segmenting Retail Markets

Segmentation Descriptor	Example of Categories
GEOGRAPHIC	
Region	Pacific, Mountain, Central, South, Mid-Atlantic, Northeast
Population density	Rural, suburban, urban
Climate	Cold, warm
DEMOGRAPHIC	
Age	Under 6, 6–12, 13–19, 20–29, 30–49, 50–65, over 65
Gender	Male, female
Family life cycle	Single, married with no children, married with youngest child under 6, married with youngest child over 6, married with children no longer living at home, widowed
Family income	Under $19,999, $20,000–29,999, $30,000–49,999, $50,000–$74,999, over $75,000
Occupation	Professional, clerical, sales, craftsperson, retired, student, homemaker
Education	Some high school, high school graduate, some college, college graduate, graduate degree
Religion	Catholic, Protestant, Jewish, Muslim
Race	Caucasian, African-American, Hispanic, Asian
Nationality	American, Japanese, British, French, German, Italian, Chinese
PSYCHOSOCIAL	
Social class	Lower, middle, upper
Lifestyle	Striver, driver, devoted, intimate, altruist, fun seeker, creative
Personality	Aggressive, shy, emotional
FEELINGS AND BEHAVIORS	
Attitudes	Positive, neutral, negative
Benefit sought	Convenience, economy, prestige
Stage in decision process	Unaware, aware, informed, interested, intend to buy, bought previously
Perceived risk	High, medium, low
Innovativeness	Innovator, early adopter, early majority, late majority, laggard
Loyalty	None, some, completely
Usage rate	None, light, medium, heavy
Usage situation	Home, work, vacation, leisure
User status	Nonuser, ex-user, potential user, current user

Actionable   The fundamental criteria for evaluating a retail market segment are that (1) customers in the segment must have similar needs, seek similar benefits, and be satisfied by a similar retail offering and (2) those customers' needs must differ from the needs of customers in other segments. **Actionable** means that the retailer should know what to do to satisfy needs for the consumers in the segment. According to this criterion, it makes sense for Lane Bryant to segment the apparel market on the basis of the demographic characteristic of physical size. Customers who wear large sizes have different needs than those who wear small sizes, so they are attracted to a store offering a unique merchandise mix. In the context of the multiattribute attitude model discussed earlier, women who wear large sizes place more importance on fit and fashion because it's relatively hard for them to satisfy these needs.

In contrast, it wouldn't make sense for a supermarket to segment its market on the basis of customer size. Large and small men and women probably have the same needs, seek the same benefits, and go through the same buying process for groceries. This segmentation approach wouldn't be actionable for a supermarket retailer because the retailer couldn't develop unique mixes for large and small customers. However, a segmentation scheme based on demographics such as household income and ethnicity would be actionable.

Identifiable   **Identifiable** means that the retailer is able to determine which customers are in the market segment. When customers are identifiable, the retailer can determine (1) the segment's size and (2) the consumers to whom the retailer needs to target its communications and promotions. For example, supermarket retailers use customer demographics to identify where they should put their stores and the merchandise that they should carry. More prepared foods, gourmet foods, fancy produce, and expensive cuts of meat would go into stores in neighborhoods with higher average incomes. It is equally important to ensure that the segments are distinct from one another, because too much overlap between segments means that distinct marketing strategies aren't needed. If, for example, a regional grocery store chain had stores located in neighborhoods containing people with similar demographics, there would be no need to vary its merchandise selection.

Substantial   If a market is too small or its buying power insignificant (i.e., not **substantial**), it cannot generate sufficient profits to support the retailing mix activities. For example, the market for pet pharmaceuticals is probably not large enough in one local area to serve as a target market segment, but a national market could be served through the Internet channel.

Reachable   **Reachable** means that the retailer can target promotions and other elements of the retail mix to consumers in the segment. For example, AutoZone targets men who repair their own automobiles themselves. Potential customers in this segment are reachable because they read car magazines, watch NASCAR on TV, and have distinct television viewing habits.

Approaches for Segmenting Markets

Exhibit 4–5 illustrates the wide variety of approaches for segmenting retail markets. No one approach is best for all retailers. Instead, they must explore various factors that affect customer buying behavior and determine which factors are most important for them.

Geographic Segmentation   **Geographic segmentation** groups customers according to where they live. A retail market can be segmented by countries (Japan, Mexico) or by areas within a country, such as states, cities, and neighborhoods.

Because customers typically shop at stores convenient to where they live and work, individual retail outlets usually focus on the customer segment reasonably close to the outlet.

Segments based on geography can be identifiable, substantial, and reachable. It's easy to determine who lives in a geographic segment, such as the Paris metropolitan area, and then determine how many potential customers are in that area. It is also relatively simple to target communications and locate retail outlets for customers in Paris and then determine if customers are being responsive to those communications. However, when customers in different geographic segments have similar needs, it is inefficient to develop unique retail offerings by geographic markets. For example, a fast-food customer in Detroit probably seeks the same benefits as a fast-food customer in Los Angeles. Thus, it wouldn't be useful to segment the U.S. fast-food market geographically.

Demographic Segmentation   **Demographic segmentation** groups consumers on the basis of easily measured, objective characteristics such as age, gender, income, and education. Demographic variables are the most common means of defining segments, because consumers in these segments can be easily identified, their size can be determined, and the degree to which they can be reached by and are responsive to media can be easily assessed.

However, demographics may not be useful for defining segments for some retailers because the motivations for purchasing transcend simple demographics. For example, demographics are poor predictors of users of activewear, such as jogging suits and running shoes. At one time, retailers assumed that activewear would be purchased exclusively by young people, but the health and fitness trend has led people of all ages to buy this merchandise. Relatively inactive consumers also find activewear to be comfortable.

Geodemographic Segmentation   **Geodemographic segmentation** uses both geographic and demographic characteristics to classify consumers. This segmentation scheme is based on the principle that "birds of a feather flock together." Consumers in the same neighborhoods tend to buy the same types of cars, appliances, and apparel and shop at the same types of retailers.[35]

One widely used tool for geodemographic market segmentation is the Tapestry™ Segmentation system developed and marketed by Esri.[36] Tapestry Segmentation classifies all U.S. residential neighborhoods into 65 distinctive segments based on socioeconomic and demographic characteristics. The information in Exhibit 4–6 describes three Tapestry segments. These neighborhoods, with their similar demographics and buying behaviors, can be any place in the United States.

Geodemographic segmentation is particularly appealing to store-based retailers, because customers typically patronize stores close to their neighborhood. Thus, retailers can use geodemographic segmentation to select locations for their stores and tailor the assortment in the stores to the preferences of the local community. In Chapter 8, we illustrate how geodemographic segmentation is used to make store location decisions.

Lifestyle Segmentation   Of the various methods of segmenting, lifestyle is the one that delves the most into how consumers describe themselves. **Lifestyle,** or **psychographics,** refers to how people live, how they spend their time and money, what activities they pursue, and their attitudes and opinions about the world in which they live. For example, a person may have a strong need for adventure. This need then motivates the person to buy products compatible with that lifestyle. For instance, Harley-Davidson motorcycle owners share a slice of the American Dream—the freedom to conquer the open road.

EXHIBIT 4–6
Examples of Tapestry

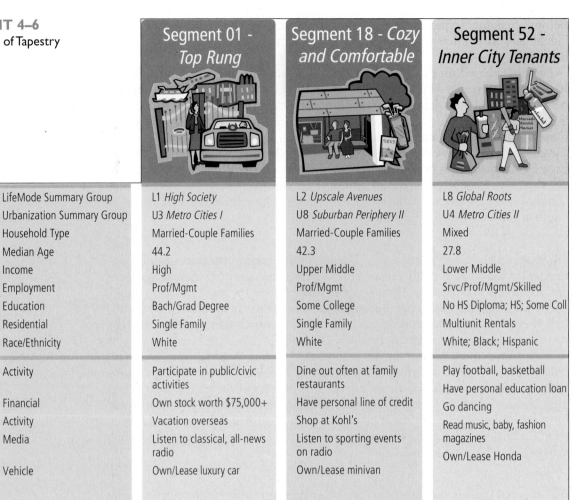

	Segment 01 - *Top Rung*	Segment 18 - *Cozy and Comfortable*	Segment 52 - *Inner City Tenants*
LifeMode Summary Group	L1 *High Society*	L2 *Upscale Avenues*	L8 *Global Roots*
Urbanization Summary Group	U3 *Metro Cities I*	U8 *Suburban Periphery II*	U4 *Metro Cities II*
Household Type	Married-Couple Families	Married-Couple Families	Mixed
Median Age	44.2	42.3	27.8
Income	High	Upper Middle	Lower Middle
Employment	Prof/Mgmt	Prof/Mgmt	Srvc/Prof/Mgmt/Skilled
Education	Bach/Grad Degree	Some College	No HS Diploma; HS; Some Coll
Residential	Single Family	Single Family	Multiunit Rentals
Race/Ethnicity	White	White	White; Black; Hispanic
Activity	Participate in public/civic activities	Dine out often at family restaurants	Play football, basketball
Financial	Own stock worth $75,000+	Have personal line of credit	Have personal education loan
Activity	Vacation overseas	Shop at Kohl's	Go dancing
Media	Listen to classical, all-news radio	Listen to sporting events on radio	Read music, baby, fashion magazines
Vehicle	Own/Lease luxury car	Own/Lease minivan	Own/Lease Honda

SOURCE: Esri, "Tapestry Segmentation: The Fabric of America's Neighborhoods," www.esri.com/library/fliers/pdfs/tapestry_segmentation.pdf.

Lifestyle segments can be identified through consumer surveys that ask respondents to indicate whether they agree or disagree with statements such as, "My idea of fun in a national park would be to stay in an expensive lodge and dress up for dinner," "I often crave excitement," or "I could not stand to skin a dead animal." Retailers today are placing more emphasis on lifestyles than on demographics to define a target segment.

One of the most widely used tools for **lifestyle segmentation** is **VALS™**, developed by Strategic Business Insights. On the basis of responses to the VALS survey, consumers are classified into the eight segments shown in Exhibit 4–7. On the horizontal dimension, the segments are described by their resources, including their income, education, health, and energy level, as well as their degree of innovativeness. The segments on top have more resources and are more innovative; those on the bottom have fewer resources and are less innovative. The segments are also grouped vertically on the basis of their primary psychological motivation. The demographics of each group are provided. GeoVALS™ estimates the percent of each VALS type by zip code.

Firms are finding that lifestyles are often more useful for predicting consumer behavior than are demographics. For instance, some college students and some day laborers may have similar demographics such as age and income, but they spend that income quite differently because of their very different values and lifestyles. There are limitations to using lifestyle segmentation, however. Lifestyles

EXHIBIT 4–7
VALS American Lifestyle

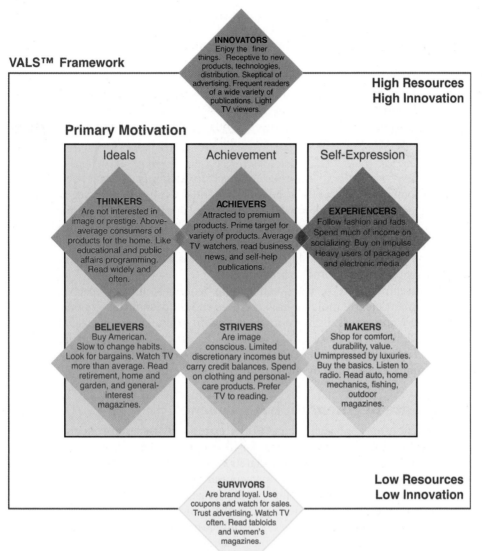

SOURCE: Strategic Business Insights (SBI) (www.strategicbusinessinsights.com/).

are not as objective as demographics, and it is harder to identify potential customers. With demographics, a firm like Nike can easily identify its customers as men or women and direct its marketing strategies to each group differently. For these reasons, lifestyle segmentation is often used in conjunction with other segmentation methods.

Buying-Situation Segmentation   The buying behavior of customers with the same demographics or lifestyle can differ depending on their buying situation. Thus, retailers may use **buying situations,** such as fill-in versus weekly shopping, to segment a market. For example, in Exhibit 4–3, the parent with four children evaluated the supercenter more positively than the Internet grocer or supermarket for weekly grocery purchases. But if the parent ran out of milk during the week, he or she would probably go to the convenience store rather than the wholesale club for this fill-in shopping. In terms of Exhibit 4–3's multiattribute attitude model, convenience would be more important than assortment in the fill-in shopping situation. Similarly, an executive might stay at a convention hotel on a business trip and a resort during a family vacation.

Buying-situation segmentation rates high among the criteria for evaluating market segments. The segments are actionable, because it is relatively easy to determine what a marketer should do to satisfy the needs of a particular segment. They are identifiable and accessible, because retailers or service providers can determine who the customers are on the basis of who has purchased the product or service and under what circumstances. Once they have identified the customer segment, they can assess its size.

Benefit Segmentation   Another approach for defining a target segment is to group customers seeking similar benefits; this method is called **benefit segmentation**. In the multiattribute attitude model, customers in the same benefit segment would have a similar set of importance weights for the attributes of a store or product. For example, customers who place high importance on fashion and style and low importance on price might form a fashion segment, whereas customers who place more importance on price would form a price segment.

Benefit segments are very actionable. The benefits sought by customers in the target segment clearly indicate how retailers should design their offerings to appeal to those customers. But customers in benefit segments aren't easily identified or accessed; it's hard to look at a person and determine what benefits he or she is seeking. Typically, the audience for the media used by retailers is described by demographics rather than by the benefits they seek.

Composite Segmentation Approaches

No segmentation approach meets all the criteria. For example, segmenting by demographics and geography is ideal for identifying and accessing customers, but these characteristics often are unrelated to customers' needs. Thus these approaches may not indicate the actions necessary to attract customers in these segments. In contrast, knowing what benefits customers are seeking is useful for designing an effective retail offering; the problem is identifying which customers are seeking these benefits. For these reasons, **composite segmentation** uses multiple variables to identify customers in the target segment according to their benefits sought, lifestyles, and demographics.

Best Buy has introduced its "Customer Centricity" program to target five composite segments.[37] Each of these segments, referred to by a first name, has a manager responsible for developing a retail strategy for the market segment. "Barrys" are the best customers. They are affluent professional men, 30 to 60 years of age, who make a minimum of $150,000 a year and drive luxury cars. Barry is the kind of guy who walks in to Best Buy, sees a $30,000 home theater system, and says, "I'll take it." In contrast, "Jills" are the busy suburban moms, "Buzzes" are focused, active younger men, and "Rays" are family men who like their technology practical. The fifth segment consists of small businesses buying their consumer electronics at Best Buy.

A group of stores has been redesigned to focus on a specific segment or two with significant representation in the local area. For example, Jill stores have personal shoppers and areas for children to play while mom shops. The soundtrack playing in the background is often children's music. Stores catering to Barrys have special areas for displaying high-end entertainment systems and also have experts in mobile technology. Stores for Jills dedicate more inventory to items like learning software and feature softer colors and a children's technology department. The Buzz-oriented stores, by contrast, feature the very latest technologies and video games. They have comfortable places in which customers can sample technologies, complete with sofas and flat-screen televisions for testing video games and consoles. Ray stores focus more on low price.

SUMMARY

To satisfy customer needs, retailers must thoroughly understand how customers choose retailers to patronize, channels to use, and merchandise to buy. This chapter describes the stages in the decision-making process (need recognition, information search, evaluation of alternatives, choice of alternatives, purchase, and postpurchase evaluations) and how retailers can influence their customers at each stage.

The importance of the stages depends on the nature of the customer's decision. When decisions are important and risky, the buying process is longer because customers spend more time and effort on the information search and evaluation of alternatives. When buying decisions are less important to customers, they spend little time in the buy-

ing process and their buying behavior may become habitual.

The buying process of consumers is influenced by their personal beliefs, attitudes, and values and by their social environment. The primary social influences are provided by the consumers' families, reference groups, and culture.

To develop cost-effective retail programs, retailers group customers into segments. Some approaches for segmenting markets are based on geography, demographics, geodemographics, lifestyles, usage situations, and benefits sought. Because each approach has its advantages and disadvantages, retailers typically define their target segment by several characteristics.

KEY TERMS

actionable, *98*

benefit segmentation, *102*

brand loyalty, *93*

buying process, *80*

buying situation, *101*

compatibility, *107*

complexity, *107*

composite segmentation, *102*

consideration set, *88*

conversion rate, *85*

cross-shopping, *82*

culture, *96*

demographic segmentation, *99*

everyday-low-pricing policy, *85*

extended problem solving, *91*

external sources, *83*

fair trade, *90*

fashion, *105*

geodemographic segmentation, *99*

geographic segmentation, *98*

habitual decision making, *92*

hedonic needs, *81*

identifiable, *98*

impulse buying, *92*

information search, *83*

internal sources, *83*

knockoff, *106*

lifestyle, *99*

lifestyle segmentation, *100*

limited problem solving, *92*

mass-market theory, *106*

multiattribute attitude model, *86*

observability, *107*

postpurchase evaluation, *91*

psychographics, *99*

reachable, *98*

reference group, *94*

retailer loyalty, *93*

retail market segment, *97*

satisfaction, *91*

store advocate, *95*

subculture, *96*

subculture theory, *106*

substantial, *98*

trialability, *107*

trickle-down theory, *106*

unplanned purchasing, *92*

utilitarian needs, *81*

VALS, *100*

GET OUT AND DO IT!

1. **CONTINUING CASE ASSIGNMENT: GO SHOPPING** Visit the retail store operated by the target firm for your continuing assignment, and pose as a shopper. Write down all the things that the store does to try to stimulate customers to buy merchandise.

2. **GO SHOPPING** Go to a supermarket, and watch people selecting products to put in their shopping carts. How much time do they spend selecting products? Do some people spend more time than others? Why is this the case? Does consumer behavior vary in the store perimeter versus in the aisles? Explain your observations.

3. **WEB OLC EXERCISE** Go to the student side of the book's Web site to develop a multiattribute attitude model describing your evaluation of and decision about some relatively expensive product you bought recently, such as a car or a consumer electronics product. Open the multiattribute model exercise. List the attributes you considered in the left-hand column. List the alternatives you considered in the top row. Fill in the importance weights for each attribute in the second column (10 = very important, 1 = very unimportant); then fill in your evaluation of each product on each attribute (10 = excellent performance, 1 = poor performance). Based on your

importance weights and performance beliefs, the evaluation of each product appears in the bottom row. Did you buy the product with the highest evaluation?

4. **INTERNET EXERCISE**   To better understand the segmentation classification of consumers, Strategic Business Insights has developed the VALS tool, which uses psychology to segment people according to their distinct personality traits. Go to the firm's home page at www.strategicbusinessinsights.com/vals/presurvey.shtml, and take the survey to identify your VALS profile according to your values, attitudes, and lifestyle. According to the results, what is your VALS profile type? Do you agree with your consumer profile? Why or why not? How can retailers effectively use the results of this survey when planning and implementing their business strategies?

5. **INTERNET EXERCISE**   Retailers want to segment the market on the basis of the geographic

classification of customers to select the best sites for their businesses. Go to the ESRI Business Information Solutions home page at www.esri.com/data/community_data/community-tapestry/index.html, type in the zip code for your hometown or your campus, and read the results. How would a retailer, such as a local restaurant, use the information in this report when making a decision about whether to open a location in this zip code?

6. **INTERNET EXERCISE**   Go to the following Internet sites offering information about the latest fashions: www.style.com (*Vogue, W*), www.fashioninformation.com (U.K.), and www.telegraph.co.uk/fashion/index.jhtml (U.K.). Write a brief report describing the latest apparel fashions that are being shown by designers. Which of these fashion trends do you think will be popular with college students? Why?

DISCUSSION QUESTIONS AND PROBLEMS

1. Does the customer buying process end when a customer buys some merchandise? Explain your answer.

2. Describe how service retailers, such as hotels, provide information to potential customers to answer questions about rates, services offered, and other amenities. How is this similar to and different from the information provided by product manufacturers?

3. Considering the steps in the consumer buying process (Exhibit 4–1), describe how you (and your family) used this process to select your college or university. How many schools did you consider? How much time did you invest in this purchase decision? When you were deciding on which college to attend, what objective and subjective criteria did you use in the alternative evaluation portion of the consumer buying process?

4. In Exhibit 4–6, The Inner City Tenant is described. How should banks, restaurants, drugstores, and car dealers alter their retail mixes to meet the needs of this segment compared to the Top Rung segment?

5. Any retailer's goal is to get customers in its store so that they can find the merchandise that they are looking for and make a purchase at this location. How could a

sporting goods retailer ensure that the customer buys athletic equipment at its outlet?

6. A family-owned used-book store across the street from a major university campus wants to identify the various segments in its market. What approaches might the store owner use to segment its market? List two potential target market segments based on this segmentation approach. Then contrast the retail mix that would be most appropriate for the two potential target segments.

7. How does the buying decision process differ when consumers are shopping on the Internet compared with shopping in a store in terms of locations or sites visited, time spent, and brands?

8. Using the multiattribute attitude model, identify the probable choice of a local car dealer for a young, single woman and for a retired couple with limited income (see the table below). What can the national retail chain do to increase the chances of the retired couple patronizing its dealership? You can use the multiattribute model template on the student side of the book's Web site to analyze this information.

	IMPORTANCE WEIGHTS		PERFORMANCE BELIEFS		
Performance Attributres	Young, Single Woman	Retired Couple	Local Gas Station	National Service Chain	Local Car Dealer
Price	2	10	9	10	3
Time to complete repair	8	5	5	9	7
Reliability	2	9	2	7	10
Convenience	8	3	3	6	5

9. Think of a recent purchase that you made, and describe how social environmental factors, including reference group, family, and culture, influenced your buying decision. How are retailers using social media to impact your buying decisions?

10. Think about the merchandise sold at Office Depot, Staples, and Office Max, and list three to four types of merchandise that fall into extended problem solving, limited problem solving and habitual decision making for college students. Explain how the categories of merchandise would change for each type of buying decision if the customer was the owner of a medium-size business.

SUGGESTED READINGS

Arnold, Mark J., and Kristy Reynolds. "Affect and Retail Shopping Behavior: Understanding the Role of Mood Regulation and Regulatory Focus." *Journal of Retailing* 85 (September 2009), pp. 308–320.

Hawkins, Delbert, David L. Mothersbaugh, and Roger J. Best. *Consumer Behavior*, 11th ed. New York: McGraw-Hill/Irwin, 2009.

Hui, Sam K., Eric T. Bradlow, and Peter S. Fader. "Testing Behavioral Hypotheses Using an Integrated Model of Grocery Store Shopping Path and Purchase Behavior." *Journal of Consumer Research* 36 (October 2009), pp. 478–495.

Iverson, Annemarie. *In Fashion: From Retail to the Runway, Everything You Need to Know to Break into the Fashion Industry*. New York: Clarkson Potter, 2010.

Peter, J. Paul, and Jerry Olson. *Consumer Behavior*, 9th ed. New York: McGraw-Hill, 2009.

Schmitz, Gertrud. "The Effects of Acquisition and Transaction Shopping Value Perceptions on Retail Format Usage Intentions: An Illustration from Discount Stores." *International Review of Retail Distribution and Consumer Research* 19 (May 2009), pp. 81–101.

Solomon, Michael. *Consumer Behavior*, 9th ed. Englewood Cliffs, NJ: Prentice Hall, 2008.

Sorensen, Herb. *Inside the Mind of the Shopper*. Philadelphia: Wharton School, 2009

Underhill, Paco. *Why We Buy: The Science of Shopping*, updated and revised. New York: Simon & Schuster, 2008.

APPENDIX 4A   Customer Buying Behavior and Fashion

Many retailers sell fashionable merchandise. To sell this type of merchandise profitably, retailers need to (1) understand how fashions develop and diffuse throughout the marketplace and (2) use operating systems that enable them to match supply and demand for this seasonal merchandise. This appendix reviews the consumer behavior aspects of fashion; the operating systems for matching supply of and demand for fashion merchandise are discussed in Chapter 12.

Fashion is a type of product or a way of behaving that is temporarily adopted by a large number of consumers because the product, service, or behavior is considered socially appropriate for the time and place.[38] For example, in some social groups, it is or has been fashionable to have brightly colored hair or tattoos, wear a coat made from animal fur, or have a beard. Even though a wide range of activities and products go in and out of fashion, in many retail environments the term *fashion* is associated with apparel and accessories.

CUSTOMER NEEDS SATISFIED BY FASHION

Fashion gives people an opportunity to satisfy many emotional and practical needs. Through fashions, people develop their own identity. They also can use fashions to manage their appearance, express their self-image and feelings, enhance their egos, and make an impression on others. Through the years, fashions have become associated with specific lifestyles or the roles people play. You wear different clothing styles when you are attending class, going out on a date, or interviewing for a job.

People use fashions to both develop their own identity and gain acceptance from others. These two benefits of fashion can be opposing forces. If you choose to wear something radically different, you will achieve recognition for your individuality but might not be accepted by your peers. To satisfy these conflicting needs, manufacturers and retailers offer customers designs that are fashionable and still enable consumers to express their individuality.

Consumers also adopt fashions to overcome boredom. People get tired of wearing the same clothing and seeing the same furniture in their living rooms. They seek changes in their lifestyles by buying new clothes or redecorating their houses to meet their changing tastes, preferences, and income.

HOW DO FASHIONS DEVELOP AND SPREAD?

Fashions are not universal. A fashion might be accepted in one geographic region, country, or age group and not in another. Consider how your idea of "fashionable" differs from that of your parents. Many of you might have a hard time imagining them dressed in distressed, hip-hugging jeans and a tight t-shirt. Well, they might have just as much trouble picturing you in a double-breasted business suit. One interesting sports fashion trend has been the uniforms for college

EXHIBIT 4–8
Stages in the Fashion
Life Cycle

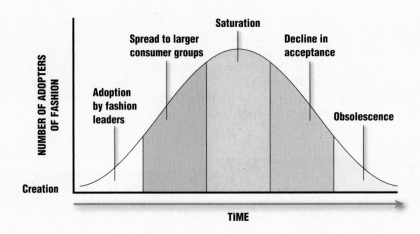

and NBA basketball players. Thirty years ago, they sported long hair and wore tight, short shorts and Converse shoes. Now they have short hair and wear baggy shorts and Nike shoes (see www.nba.com/photostore/).

The stages in the fashion life cycle are shown in Exhibit 4–8. The cycle begins with the creation of a new design or style. Then some consumers recognized as fashion leaders or innovators adopt the fashion and start a trend in their social group. The fashion spreads from the leaders to others and is accepted widely as a fashion. Eventually, the fashion is accepted by most people in the social group and can become overused. Saturation and overuse set the stage for that fashion's decline in popularity and the creation of new fashions. The time span of a fashion life cycle varies depending on the type of product and the market. The cycle for apparel fashions for young teenagers is measured in months or even weeks, whereas the fashion cycle for home furnishings may last several years.

Creation

New fashions arise from a number of sources. Fashion designers are one source of creative inspirations, but fashions are also developed by creative consumers, celebrities, and even retailers. When high-profile actors, performers, and athletes wear the latest styles in television shows and movies, on stage, or on the red carpet, consumers interested in fashion often adopt and follow these trends.

REFACT

The bikini was designed by a former civil engineer, Louis Reard, in 1947.[39]

Adoption by Fashion Leaders

The fashion life cycle really starts when the fashion is adopted by leading consumers. These initial adopters of a new fashion are called *fashion leaders, innovators,* or *trendsetters,* and they are the first people to display the new fashion in their social group. If the fashion is too innovative or very different from currently accepted fashion, it might not be accepted by the social group, thereby prematurely ending its life cycle.

Three theories have been proposed to explain how fashion spreads within a society. The **trickle-down theory** suggests that fashion leaders are consumers with the highest social status—wealthy, well-educated consumers.

After they adopt a fashion, the fashion trickles down to consumers in lower social classes. When the fashion is accepted in the lowest social class, it is no longer acceptable to the fashion leaders in the highest social class.

Manufacturers and retailers stimulate this trickle-down process by copying the latest styles displayed at designer fashion shows and sold in exclusive specialty stores. These copies, referred to as **knockoffs,** are sold at lower prices through retailers targeting a broader market. For example, designers at JCPenney view fashion shows on their computers in Plano, Texas, and interpret the designs for their market.[40] If the designers in Paris and Milan are showing turtlenecks, the JCPenney designers determine what aspects of that fashion will appeal to their broader market and then have their designs manufactured in Asia. It is likely that the knockoff turtlenecks will be on the shelves at JCPenney well before the higher-priced originals get to the high-end specialty and department stores.

The second theory, the **mass-market theory,** suggests that fashions spread across different peer groups. Each group has its own fashion leaders who play key roles in their own social networks. Fashion information trickles across groups rather than down from the upper classes to the lower classes. For instance, motorcycle jackets and other gear have become fashion for many who have never been on a motorcycle, thanks to designers' interpretations of traditional garments and fashion leaders' desire to try something different.

The third theory, the **subculture theory,** is based on the development of recent fashions. Subcultures of mostly young and less affluent consumers, such as urban youth, started fashions for such things as colorful fabrics, t-shirts, sneakers, jeans, black leather jackets, and surplus military clothing. Many times, fashions are started unintentionally by people in lower-income consumer groups and trickle up to mainstream consumer classes. For example, workers wear blue jeans that have holes in them and are distressed from manual labor, their t-shirts are faded from working in the sun, and people who paint houses are covered in splashes of paint. These looks have been adapted by manufacturers and sold to many different consumer groups. The more distress, the more people are willing to pay.

These theories of fashion development indicate that fashion leaders can come from many different places and social groups. In our diverse society, many types of consumers have the opportunity to be the leaders in setting fashion trends.

Spread to Large Consumer Groups

During this stage, the fashion is accepted by a wider group of consumers referred to as *early adopters*. The fashion becomes increasingly visible, receives greater publicity and media attention, and is readily available in retail stores. The relative advantage, compatibility, complexity, trialability, and observability of a fashion affect the time it takes for that fashion to spread through a social group. New fashions that provide more benefits have a higher relative advantage compared with existing fashions, and these new fashions spread faster. Fashions are often adopted by consumers because they make people feel special. Thus, more exclusive fashions like expensive clothing are adopted more quickly in an affluent target market. On a more utilitarian level, clothing that is easy to maintain, such as wrinkle-free pants, will diffuse quickly in the general population.

Compatibility is the degree to which the fashion is consistent with existing norms, values, and behaviors. When new fashions aren't consistent with existing norms, the number of adopters and the speed of adoption are lower. Skinny jeans are only compatible with a relatively small percentage of the public that wears jeans. Although they may be moderately successful for a few seasons, they will never achieve widespread acceptance.

Complexity refers to how easy it is to understand and use the new fashion. Consumers have to learn how to incorporate a new fashion into their lifestyles. For example, a platform, 6-inch, stiletto-heeled pump is difficult to walk in unless you are only taking a quick strut down the runway.

Trialability refers to the costs and commitment required to adopt the fashion initially. For example, designers that have trunk shows to preview and presell the new season's fashions often bring only a sample of each piece. The consumer has to make a guess as to her or his size and hope that the garment will have a good fit and style. Consumers have to spend a lot of money buying a new type of expensive apparel to be in fashion, so the rate of adoption is faster if consumers can see how the clothing looks on them without having to buy it.

Observability is the degree to which the new fashion is visible and easily communicated to others in the social group. Clothing fashions are very observable compared with fashions for the home, such as sheets and towels. It is therefore likely that a fashion in clothing will spread more quickly than a new color scheme or style for the bedroom.

Fashion retailers engage in many activities to increase the adoption and spread of a new fashion throughout their target market. Compatibility is increased and complexity is decreased by showing consumers how to coordinate a new article of fashion clothing with other items the consumer already owns. Trialability is increased by providing dressing rooms so that customers can try on clothing and see how it looks on them. Providing opportunities for customers to return merchandise also increases trialability. Retailers increase observability by displaying fashion merchandise in their stores and advertising it in the media.

Saturation

In this stage, the fashion achieves its highest level of social acceptance. Almost all consumers in the target market are aware of the fashion and have decided to either accept or reject it. At this point, the fashion has become old and boring to many people.

Decline in Acceptance and Obsolescence

When fashions reach saturation, they have become less appealing to consumers. Because most people have already adopted the fashion, it no longer provides an opportunity for people to express their individuality. Fashion creators and leaders thus are beginning to experiment with new fashions. The introduction of a new fashion speeds the decline of the preceding fashion.

Retailing Strategy

Section I described the decisions retail managers make in formulating and implementing their strategy; the different types of retailers; the multiple channels—stores, the Internet, and catalogs—that retailers use to interact with and sell merchandise to their customers; and factors that affect consumers' choices of retailers, channels, and merchandise. This broad overview of retailing provides the background information needed to develop and implement an effective retail strategy.

The chapters in Section II discuss specific strategic decisions made by retailers:

Chapter 5 describes the development of a retail market strategy.

Chapter 6 examines the financial strategy associated with the market strategy.

Chapters 7 and 8 discuss the location strategy for retail outlets.

Chapter 9 looks at the firm's organization and human resource strategies.

Chapter 10 examines systems used to control the flow of information and merchandise.

Chapter 11 details approaches that retailers take to manage relationships with their customers.

As outlined in Chapter 1, the decisions discussed in Section II are more strategic than tactical because they involve committing significant resources to developing long-term advantages over the competition in a target market segment.

Sections III and IV review the more tactical decisions regarding merchandise and store management that are involved in implementing the retail strategy. These implementation decisions affect a retailer's efficiency, but their impact is shorter-term than that of the strategic decisions reviewed in Section II.

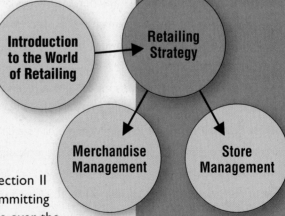

Retail Market Strategy

EXECUTIVE BRIEFING
Michael R. Odell, Chief Executive Officer
Pep Boys

After 4 years in the red, Pep Boys turned a profit in 2009, and in fact we made more money than during the previous 12 years combined. We are also on track to continue to improve that performance over the coming years.

So how did we start? We started by looking at the landscape—the industry and the macro-environment, customers, competition, and internal factors. We then developed our SWOT—strengths, weaknesses, opportunities, threats. From that we developed our vision, strategies, and tactics; including turning weaknesses, like larger than necessary stores spread across a wider than necessary geography, into competitive advantages. Our vision is to be the automotive solutions provider of choice for the value-oriented customer.

Pep Boys has a unique business model, in that it serves both the DIFM (Do It for Me) and the DIY (Do It Yourself) markets. The DIFM market is four times larger than the DIY market. It is also growing a little faster due to the increasing complexity of vehicle designs. And, 6 players account for over 40 percent of the DIY market, while 10 players account for only 10 percent of the DIFM market. For these reasons, Pep Boys' strategy leads with its service business, with the objective of becoming the market leader.

Pep Boys has several competitive advantages over other automotive service providers. Pep Boys "does everything." We are a full service provider for maintenance, tires, and repairs. "When the light comes on, just come in," is not just our advertising slogan. It's what we do. Our repair capabilities are more extensive than other shops because of our advanced technicians, equipment and training. Pep Boys also does everything "for less" because of our DIY business. It allows us to buy quality parts directly from the manufacturers and to pass those savings onto our customers. Pep Boys also provides national warranty coverage.

Pep Boys has a competitive advantage over other automotive retailers too. Pep Boys' larger stores are a weakness for a pure DIY player—they cost more. But we are using that asset for a competitive advantage to provide a wider assortment of appearance and performance products and accessories. We think of ourselves as the candy store for the automotive enthusiast, which makes our shopping experience more fun. And that assortment serves both DIFM and DIY customers.

Our turnaround started by focusing on our customers—what they want as compared to what we were providing. But our turnaround is grounded in our people, and making it easier for them to provide our customers with what they want. The key to any business model is making sure that all of the pieces to the puzzle fit together. They have to be pointed in the same direction and mutually reinforcing.

Retailers need to devote more attention to long-term strategic planning to cope effectively with the growing intensity of retail competition as well as shifts in customer needs. These changes in the retail environment are the result of the emergence of new competitors, formats, technologies, and globalization. The retail strategy indicates how retailers will deal effectively with their environment, customers, and competitors.[1] As the retail management decision-making process (discussed in Chapter 1) indicates, retailing strategy (Section II) is the bridge between understanding the world of retailing (Section I) and the more tactical merchandise management and store operation activities (Sections III and IV) undertaken to implement the retail strategy.

The first part of this chapter defines the term *retail strategy* and discusses three important elements of retail strategy: (1) the target market segment, (2) the retail format, and (3) the retailer's bases of sustainable competitive advantage. Then we outline approaches retailers use to build a sustainable competitive advantage. After reviewing the various growth opportunities, specifically international expansion, that retailers can pursue, the chapter concludes with a discussion of the strategic retail planning process.

WHAT IS A RETAIL STRATEGY?

The term *strategy* is frequently used in retailing. For example, retailers talk about their merchandise strategy, promotion strategy, location strategy, or branding strategy. The term is used so commonly that it might appear that all retailing decisions are strategic decisions, but *retail strategy* isn't just another expression for *retail management.*

Definition of Retail Market Strategy

A **retail strategy** is a statement identifying (1) the retailer's target market, (2) the format the retailer plans to use to satisfy the target market's needs, and (3) the bases on which the retailer plans to build a sustainable competitive advantage.[3] The **target market** is the market segment(s) toward which the retailer plans to focus its resources and retail mix. A **retail format** describes the nature of the retailer's operations—its retail mix (type of merchandise and services offered, pricing policy, advertising and promotion programs, store design and visual merchandising, typical locations, and customer services)—that it will use to satisfy the needs of its target market. A **sustainable competitive advantage** is an advantage the retailer has over its competition that is not easily copied by competitors and thus can be maintained over a long period of time. The following are a few examples of retail strategies:

- *Lululemon Athletica.* Lululemon is a Canadian specialty store chain selling apparel and accessories supporting the practice of yoga. The products it sells include headbands, bamboo blocks, and yoga mats printed with encouraging healthy-living slogans like "Drink fresh water." The signature Lulu item is the Groove Pant, cut with special gussets and flat seams to create a feeling of a drop of water free from gravity. Lululemon's apparel is made with special materials, Silverescent and Luon, enabling customers to engage in vigorous yoga exercises and still look attractive. Lululemon stores are a community hub where people can learn about and discuss the physical aspects of healthy living, from yoga and diet to running and cycling, as well as the spiritual aspects of life. To create this community, the company recruits local ambassadors before opening a store. These ambassadors, usually popular yoga teachers but also triathletes or runners, are given Lulus and featured on bulletin boards in the stores.[4]

- *Magazine Luiza.* One of Brazil's largest nonfood retailers, Magazine Luiza targets low-income consumers by selling consumer electronics and appliances on installment payment plans and offering affordable credit in a country with a significant number of people living in poverty. Customers buying merchandise on credit return to the store each month to make payments in person. Frequently they are enticed to purchase more merchandise during these visits. In a country where almost half the population does not have a checking account, the retailer also provides services—including personal loans and insurance policies—that would otherwise be out of reach to most customers. Even though 80 percent of its sales are paid for in installments, its default rate is 50 percent lower than that of other Brazilian retailers.[5]

- *Curves.* With over 10,000 locations, Curves is the largest fitness franchise in the world. Curves Clubs can be found in more than 70 countries. While most fitness centers target an 18- to 34-year-old demographic segment, Curves' customers are female baby boomers, typically living in small towns. Curves' fitness centers don't have treadmills, saunas, locker rooms, mirrors, aerobics classes, or free weights. Members work out on 8 to 12 hydraulic resistance machines, stopping between stations to walk or jog in place. The clubs' standard routine is finished in 30 minutes and is designed to burn 500 calories. Club members usually pay a monthly fee that is considerably less than what they would pay in conventional fitness centers. Rather than attracting customers from other clubs, Curves draws consumers who haven't considered joining a fitness club before.[6]

• *Save-A-Lot.* From a single store in 1977, Save-A-Lot, a wholly owned subsidiary of SuperValu, has grown to more than 1,000 stores, making it the nation's 13th-largest U.S. supermarket chain. Save-A-Lot stores offer an edited assortment of only 1,250 SKUs compared to 20,000 to 30,000 SKUs in a conventional supermarket. By offering only the most popular items, most of which are private-label merchandise, Save-A-Lot reduces its costs and is able to price its merchandise 40 percent lower than prices at conventional supermarkets. Due to its buying power, Save-A-Lot is able to develop customized product specifications that provide high-quality, private-label merchandise at low prices. Finally, most stores lack grocery store–style shelving

Lululemon's strategy focuses on selling products that appeal to consumers seeking spiritual enrichment through yoga. The chain builds a competitive advantage through its network of local yoga teachers who promote its offering.

and, instead, have the items in specially printed cut-out cardboard shipping cases on industrial-style shelving. Customers typically bring their own bags and bag their own groceries, and stores typically charge customers for bags.[7]

Each of these retail strategies involves (1) the selection of target market segment(s), (2) the selection of a retail format (the elements in the retail mix), and (3) the development of a sustainable competitive advantage that enables the retailer to reduce the level of competition it faces. Now let's examine these central concepts of a retail strategy.

TARGET MARKET AND RETAIL FORMAT

The **retailing concept** is a retail management orientation that focuses on determining the needs of the retailer's target market and satisfying those needs more effectively and efficiently than competitors do. Successful retailers are customer-centric. They focus on the needs of their customers and satisfy those needs better than their competitors do.

A **retail market** is a group of consumers with similar needs (a market segment) and a group of retailers that satisfy those needs using a similar retail format.[8] Exhibit 5–1 illustrates a set of retail markets for women's clothing. It lists various retail formats in the left-hand column. Each format offers a different retail mix to its customers. Market segments are listed in the exhibit's top row. As mentioned in Chapter 4, these segments could be defined in terms of the customers' geographic location, demographics, lifestyle, buying situation, or benefits sought. In this exhibit, we divide the market into three fashion-related segments: (1) conservative—consumers who place little importance on fashion; (2) traditional—those who want classic styles; and (3) fashion-forward—those who want the latest fashions.

Each square of the matrix in Exhibit 5–1 describes a potential retail market in which retailers compete for consumers with similar needs. For example, Walmart and Kmart stores in the same geographic area compete with each other using a discount store format to target conservative customers. Bloomingdale's and Neiman Marcus compete against each other using a department store format targeting the fashion-forward segment.

The women's clothing market in Exhibit 5–1 is just one of several representations that we could have used. Retail formats might be expanded to include off-price stores and category specialists. Rather than being segmented by fashion

EXHIBIT 5–1   Retail Markets for Women's Apparel

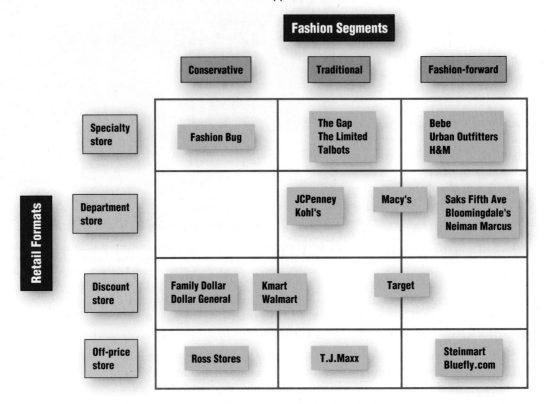

orientation, the market could be segmented using the other approaches described in Chapter 4. Although Exhibit 5–1 isn't the only way to describe the women's retail clothing market, it does illustrate how retail markets can be defined in terms of retail format and customer market segments.

Exhibit 5–1's matrix describes the battlefields on which women's apparel retailers compete. The position in each battlefield (cell in the matrix) indicates the first two elements of a retailer's strategy: the fashion segment (the *x* axis) and the retail format (the *y* axis).

Consider the situation confronting Target as it refines its retail strategy for the women's clothing market. Should Target compete in all 15 retail markets shown in Exhibit 5–1, or should it focus on a limited set of markets? If Target decides to focus on a limited set of markets, which should it pursue? Target's answers to these questions define its retail strategy and indicate how it will focus its resources.[9]

BUILDING A SUSTAINABLE COMPETITIVE ADVANTAGE

The final element in a retail strategy is the retailer's approach to building a sustainable competitive advantage. Establishing a competitive advantage means that the retailer, in effect, builds a wall around its position in a retail market, that is, around its present and potential customers and its competitors. When the wall is high, it will be hard for competitors outside the wall (i.e., retailers operating in other markets or entrepreneurs) to enter the market and compete for the retailer's target customers.

Any business activity that a retailer engages in can be the basis for a competitive advantage. But some advantages are sustainable over a long period of time, while others can be duplicated by competitors almost immediately. For example, it would

EXHIBIT 5–2
Methods of Developing
Sustainable Competitive
Advantage

Sources of Advantage	SUSTAINABILITY OF ADVANTAGE	
	Less Sustainable	More Sustainable
Customer loyalty (Chapters 11 and 16)	Habitual repeat purchasing because of limited competition in the local area	Building a brand image with an emotional connection with customers; using databases to develop and utilize a deeper understanding of customers
Location (Chapters 7 and 8)		Convenient locations
Human resource management (Chapter 9)	More employees	Committed, knowledgeable employees
Distribution and information systems (Chapter 10)	Bigger warehouses; automated warehouses	Shared systems with vendors
Unique merchandise (Chapters 12 and 13)	More merchandise; greater assortment; lower price; higher advertising budgets; more sales promotions	Exclusive merchandise
Vendor relations (Chapter 13)	Repeat purchases from vendor due to limited alternatives	Coordination of procurement efforts; ability to get scarce merchandise
Customer service (Chapter 18)	Hours of operation	Knowledgeable and helpful salespeople

be hard for Peets Coffee & Tea to establish a long-term advantage over Starbucks by simply offering the same coffee specialties at lower prices. If Peets' lower prices were successful in attracting customers, Starbucks would soon realize that Peets had lowered its prices and would quickly match the price reduction. This might lead to a price war that Starbucks is likely to win because it has lower costs due to its larger size. Similarly, it's hard for retailers to develop a long-term advantage by offering broader or deeper assortments of national brands. If the broader and deeper assortment attracts a lot of customers, competitors will simply go out and buy the same branded merchandise for their stores. Exhibit 5–2 indicates which aspects of these potential sources of advantage are more and less sustainable.

Over time, all advantages erode due to competitive forces, but by building high walls, retailers can sustain their advantage for a longer time. Thus, establishing a sustainable competitive advantage is the key to positive long-term financial performance.

Three approaches for developing a sustainable competitive advantage are (1) building strong relationships with customers, (2) building strong relationships with suppliers, and (3) achieving efficient internal operations. Each of these approaches involves developing an asset—loyal customers, strong vendor relationships, committed effective human resources and efficient systems, and attractive locations—that is not easily duplicated by competitors.[10] Let's look at each of these approaches.

Relationships with Customers—Customer Loyalty

Customer loyalty means that customers are committed to buying merchandise and services from a particular retailer. Loyalty is more than simply liking one retailer over another. Loyalty means that customers will be reluctant to patronize competitive retailers. For example, loyal customers will continue to have their car serviced at Jiffy Lube, even if a competitor opens a store nearby and charges slightly lower prices.

Some activities that retailers engage in to build loyalty are (1) developing a strong brand image, (2) having a clear and consistent positioning, (3) providing outstanding customer service, and (4) undertaking customer relationship management (CRM) programs. In addition, other activities discussed in this section also contribute to developing customer loyalty. For example, providing convenient locations encourages patronage, which can develop into loyalty. Engaging in

REFACT

A survey of 3,500 consumers indicates that, among food retailers in the United States, Walmart has the highest loyalty in the Northeast and Northwest but Publix has the highest loyalty in the Southeast, Kroger in the Midwest, and HEB in the Southwest.[11]

human resource management practices develops competent, committed sales associates, leading to better customer service and subsequent customer loyalty.

Brand Image   Retailers build customer loyalty by developing a well-known, attractive image of their brand, their name. For example, when most consumers think about fast food or hamburgers or french fries, they immediately think of McDonald's. Their image of McDonald's includes many favorable beliefs such as fast service, consistent quality, and clean restrooms.

Strong brand images facilitate customer loyalty because they reduce the risks associated with purchases. They assure customers that they will receive a consistent level of quality and satisfaction from the retailer. The retailer's image can also create an emotional tie with a customer that leads the customer to trust the retailer. Consumers know, for instance, that when they purchase products from L.L.Bean, the retailer guarantees that its customers will be pleased with their purchases. L.L.Bean "guarantees to give 100% satisfaction in every way. Return anything purchased from us at any time if it proves otherwise. We do not want you to have anything from L.L.Bean that is not completely satisfactory. [We] do not consider a sale complete until goods are worn out and [the] customer [is] still satisfied."[13] The steps retailers take to develop a strong brand image are discussed in Chapter 15.

Positioning   A retailer's brand image reflects its positioning strategy. **Positioning** is the design and implementation of a retail mix to create an image of the retailer in the customer's mind relative to its competitors. A perceptual map is frequently used to represent the customer's image and preferences for retailers.

Exhibit 5–3 offers a hypothetical perceptual map of retailers selling women's clothing in the Washington, D.C., area. The two dimensions in this map, fashion and service, represent the two primary characteristics that consumers in this example use in forming their images of retailers.

Perceptual maps are developed so that the distance between two retailers' positions on the map indicates how similar the stores appear to consumers. For example, Neiman Marcus and Saks Fifth Avenue are very close to each other on the map because consumers in this illustration see them as offering similar services and fashion. In contrast, Nordstrom and Marshalls are far apart, indicating consumers think they're quite different. Note that stores close to each other compete vigorously because consumers feel they provide similar benefits and have similar images.

In this example, Macy's has an image of offering moderately priced, fashionable women's clothing with good service. T.J.Maxx offers slightly less fashionable clothing with considerably less service. Sears is viewed as a retailer offering women's clothing that is not very fashionable with moderate customer service.

The ideal points (marked by red dots on the map) indicate the characteristics of an ideal retailer for consumers in different market segments. For example, consumers in segment 3 prefer a retailer that offers high-fashion merchandise with low service, while consumers in segment 1 want more traditional apparel and aren't concerned about service. The ideal points are located so that the distance between a retailer's position, or image (marked with a blue "x"), and the ideal point indicates how consumers in the segment evaluate that retailer.

Retailers that are closer to an ideal point are evaluated more favorably by the consumers in the segment than are retailers located farther away. Thus, consumers in segment 6 prefer Forever 21 and Bebe to Neiman Marcus because these retailers are more fashion-forward and their target customers do not require such high service levels. Retailers strive to develop an image desired by customers in their target segment and thus develop loyalty with those customers.

Unique Merchandise   It is difficult for a retailer to develop customer loyalty through its merchandise offerings because most competitors can purchase and sell the same popular national brands. But many retailers build customer loyalty

Hypothetical Perceptual Map of Women's Apparel Market in Washington, D.C. **EXHIBIT 5–3**

FASHION FORWARD

X Zara
X Forever 21 ⑥
Bebe **X**

Neiman Marcus **X**
Sak's Fifth Ave **X** ④
X Bloomingdale's
Nordstrom **X**

X Bluefly.com

Marshalls **X** ③
T.J.Maxx **X**

X Macy's
Banana Republic **X**

The Limited **X** ⑤
X JCPenney

Target **X**

② **X** Abercrombie and Fitch
The Gap **X**
X American Eagle Outfitters
X Old Navy

X Talbots
X Chico's
⑦

X Sears

①
X Walmart

X Kmart

LIMITED SERVICE   **EXTENSIVE SERVICE**

TRADITIONAL

by developing **private-label brands** (also called **store brands** or **own brands**)—products developed and marketed by a retailer and available only from that retailer.[15] For example, Costco's powerful private-label brand, Kirkland Signature, engenders strong brand loyalty among a significant group of consumers and consequently generates considerable loyalty toward Costco. The quality image of its private-label products makes a significant contribution to the image of Costco. Retailing View 5.1 describes how IKEA builds customer loyalty through its unique merchandise. Issues pertaining to the development of store-brand merchandise are discussed in Chapter 13.

Customer Service Retailers also can develop customer loyalty by offering excellent customer service.[16] Consistently offering good service is difficult because customer service is provided by retail employees who are less consistent than machines. Machines can be programmed to make every box of

Costco has developed a strong private label, Kirkland, which creates customer loyalty toward the products and Costco. If you want to buy Kirkland products, you have to purchase them from Costco.

Cheerios identical. But employees do not provide a consistent level of service because they vary in their training, motivation, and mood.

It takes considerable time and effort to build a tradition and reputation for customer service. But once a retailer has earned a service reputation, it can sustain this advantage for a long time because it's hard for a competitor to develop a comparable reputation. For example, Ritz-Carlton hotels are world-renowned for providing outstanding customer service. Every day, its employees gather for a 15-minute staff meeting and share "WOW stories"—true stories of employees who have gone above and beyond conventional customer service expectations. In one story, a hotel chef in Bali found special eggs and milk for a guest with food allergies in a small grocery store in another country and had them flown to the hotel. In another WOW story, a hotel's laundry service failed to remove a stain on a guest's suit before the guest left, and the manager flew to the guest's house to personally deliver a reimbursement of the cost of the suit. Telling these WOW stories focuses employees on customer service and gives them recognitions for the efforts they make.[17] Chapter 18 discusses how retailers develop a customer service advantage.

Customer Relationship Management Programs   Customer relationship management (CRM) programs, also called **loyalty** or **frequent shopper programs,** are activities that focus on identifying and building loyalty with a retailer's most valued customers.[19] These programs typically involve offering customers rewards

REFACT

The Ritz-Carlton is the only hotel chain and the first service company to win the annual Malcolm Baldrige National Quality Award. It has won the award twice.[18]

5.1   RETAILING VIEW   The IKEA Way

IKEA, a global retailer headquartered in Sweden, offers a wide range of well-designed, functional home furnishing products at low prices. It's easy to make high-quality products and sell them at a high price or make low-quality products to sell at a low price. But IKEA has to be cost-effective and innovative to sell quality products at low prices.

Creating IKEA's unique merchandise starts on the factory floor. IKEA product developers and designers work closely with suppliers to efficiently use production equipment and raw materials and keep waste to a minimum. For example, an IKEA product developer learned about board-on-frame construction touring a door factory. This technique is cost-effective and environmentally friendly because sheets of wood are layered over a honeycomb core to provide a strong, lightweight structure with a minimal wood content. This type of construction is used in many IKEA products, such as its LACK tables.

IKEA's designers go beyond the factory floor to consider transportation costs. Many items IKEA sells are shipped and sold disassembled in flat packs to reduce transportation costs and make it easier for customers to take them home. However, some products like lamps take up a lot of space even when disassembled. The LAMPAN illustrates the IKEA way of offering extremely low price with beautiful design and high quality. This was achieved by developing a new packing method in which the lamp shade could be used as a bucket for the lamp base.

IKEA reduces labor costs in its stores by providing signage with extensive information about its products and their quality, presenting its products in room settings, and prominently displaying price tags. These features enable customers to serve themselves and reduce IKEA's labor costs.

IKEA considers all costs when designing its unique, low-cost, fashionable merchandise. The LACK table and LAMPAN lamp are classic IKEA designs.

Sources: www.IKEA.com (accessed March 30, 2010); "The Man Who Named the Furniture," *Financial Times,* January 16, 2010, p. 30; Yongquan Hu and Huifang Jiang, "Innovation Strategy of Retailers: From the View of Global Value Chains," *6th International Conference on Service Systems and Service Management,* 2009, pp. 340–345.

based on the amount of services or merchandise they purchase. For example, airlines offer free tickets to travelers who have flown a prescribed number of miles, and Subway gives customers a free sandwich for each 10 they purchase.

The discounts offered by these programs may not create loyalty. Customers may join loyalty progams of competing retailers and continue to patronize multiple retailers. However, the data collected about customer shopping behavior by these programs can provide insights that enable retailers to build and maintain loyalty. For instance, Harry Rosen, a Canadian specialty retailer selling designer menswear, has a system for collecting and saving customer data. Every Harry Rosen salesperson can access the

Salespeople use the information in Harry Rosen's customer database to improve the customer service they offer, target promotions to specific customers, and build customer loyalty.

firm's customer database from any POS terminal in any store. The database indicates what the customer has bought in the past and also provides personal information. All sales associates are urged to contribute to the database. If a wife buys a birthday gift for her husband, salespeople are encouraged to find out when his birthday is and how old he is and include this information in the system rather than in their personal notebooks.

The information system improves Harry Rosen's customer service and the targeting of retail promotions. For example, when garments are left in the store for alterations, the system tracks their progress and electronically notifies the salesperson of any delay so that the salesperson can relay this information to the customer. Heavy spenders are identified and invited to special promotional events. When new merchandise arrives, the salesperson can identify customers who have bought that type of merchandise in the past and inform them of the new merchandise.[20] Thus the data developed through the loyalty program enables a retailer to develop a personal relationship with customers that builds loyalty. CRM programs are discussed in detail in Chapter 11.

Relationships with Suppliers

A second approach for developing competitive advantage is developing strong relationships with companies that provide merchandise and services to the retailer, such as real estate developers, advertising agencies, and transportation companies. Of these relationships with suppliers, the most important are relationships with vendors.

Vendor Relations By strengthening relationships with each other, both retailers and vendors can develop mutually beneficial assets and programs that will give the retailer-vendor pair an advantage over competing pairs. For example, Ralph Lauren and JCPenney collaborated to develop the American Living apparel merchandise sold exclusively at JCPenney. Similarly, Estée Lauder and Kohl's worked together to develop the American Beauty cosmetics sold exclusively at Kohl's. These collaborations are win-win situations. By working together, both parties develop a sustainable competitive advantage and increase their sales and profits.

The relationship between Procter & Gamble and Walmart initially focused on improving supply chain efficiencies. Today, the partners in this relationship share sensitive information with each other so that Walmart is better able to plan for the introduction of new P&G products and even develop some unique packaging for P&G's national brands exclusively available at Walmart. Walmart shares its sales data with P&G so that P&G can better plan its production and use a just-in-time inventory management system to reduce the level of inventory in the system. From their initial focus on improving supply chain efficiency, P&G and Walmart now work together on other initiatives such as Family Moments to produce family-friendly TV programming.

Relationships with vendors, like relationships with customers, are developed over a long time and may not be easily offset by a competitor.[21] Chapter 13 examines how retailers work with their vendors to build mutually beneficial, long-term relationships.

Efficiency of Internal Operations

In addition to strong relationships with external parties, customers and suppliers, retailers can develop competitive advantages by having more efficient internal operations. Efficient internal operations enable retailers to have a cost advantage over competitors or offer customers more benefits than do competitors at the same cost.

Larger company size typically produces more efficient internal operations. Larger retailers have more bargaining power with vendors and thus can buy merchandise at lower costs. Larger retailers can also invest in developing sophisticated systems and spread the fixed cost of these systems over more sales. In addition to size, other approaches for improving internal operating efficiencies are human resource management and information and supply chain management systems.

Human Resource Management   Retailing is a labor-intensive business, in which employees play a major role providing services for customers and building customer loyalty.[22] Knowledgeable and skilled employees committed to the retailer's objectives are critical assets that support the success of many retailers.

JCPenney chairman and CEO Mike Ullman emphasizes the power of employees to build a sustainable competitive advantage.[23] He notes, "The associates are the first customers we sell. If it doesn't ring true to them, it's impossible to communicate and inspire the customer." To build involvement and commitment among its employees, Penney has dropped many of the traditional pretenses that define an old-style hierarchical organization. For instance, at the Plano, Texas, corporate headquarters, all employees are on a first-name basis, workweeks are flexible, and leadership workshops help build the executive team for the future.

Recruiting, training, and retaining great employees are challenging. Chapter 9 examines how retailers build their human resource assets by developing programs to motivate and coordinate employee efforts, providing appropriate incentives, fostering a strong and positive organizational culture and environment, and managing diversity. Programs for developing a human resource competitive advantage are discussed in Chapter 9.

Distribution and Information Systems   All retailers strive to reduce operating costs—the costs associated with running the business—and make sure that the right merchandise is available at the right time and place. The use of sophisticated distribution and information systems offers an opportunity for retailers to achieve these efficiencies.[24] Through its data sharing about merchandise sales, information flows seamlessly from Walmart to its vendors to facilitate quick and efficient merchandise replenishment that avoids costly stockouts. Walmart's distribution and information systems have enabled it to have a cost advantage that its competitors cannot overcome. This component of competitive advantage is discussed in Chapter 10.

In addition to using information systems to improve supply chain efficiency, the customer purchase data collected by information systems provide an opportunity for retailers to tailor store merchandise assortments to the market served by each of its stores and to tailor promotion to the specific needs of individual customers. These data about its customer buying behavior are a valuable asset offering an advantage that is not easily duplicated by competitors. These applications of information systems are discussed in more detail in Chapter 11.

Location

While committed relationships with external parties and efficient internal operations are important sources of advantage, location is a pervasive source of advantage in retailing. The classic response to the question, "What are the three most important things in retailing?" is "Location, location, location." Location is a critical opportunity for developing competitive advantage for two reasons. First, location is the most important factor determining which store a consumer patronizes. For example, most people shop at the supermarket closest to where they live. Second, location is a sustainable competitive advantage because it is not easily duplicated. Once Walgreens has put a store at the best location at an intersection, CVS is relegated to the second-best location.

Starbucks has developed a strong competitive advantage with its locations. As it expanded across the United States, it saturated each market before entering a new market. For example, there were more than 100 Starbucks outlets in the Seattle area before the company expanded to a new region. Starbucks frequently opens several stores close to one another. It has two stores on two corners of the intersection of Robson and Thurlow in Vancouver. By having such a high density of stores, Starbucks makes it very difficult for a competitor to enter a market and find good locations. Approaches for evaluating and selecting locations are discussed in Chapters 7 and 8.

Starbucks creates a competitive advantage by picking multiple good locations that saturate an area.

Multiple Sources of Advantage

To build an advantage that is sustainable for a long period of time, retailers typically cannot rely on a single approach, such as good locations or excellent customer service. Instead, they use multiple approaches to build as high a wall around their position as possible.[25] For example, McDonald's long-term success is based on providing customers with a good value that meets their expectations, having good customer service, possessing a strong brand name, and offering convenient locations. By pursuing all these strategies effectively, McDonald's has developed a strong competitive position in the quick-service restaurant market.

In addition to its unique products and associated customer loyalty, IKEA has a large group of loyal customers due to its strong brand image and the pleasant shopping experience it provides its customers. Walmart complements its size advantage with strong vendor relationships and clear positioning of a retailer that offers superior value. Starbucks combines its location advantage with unique products, committed employees, a strong brand name, and strong relationships with coffee growers to build an overall advantage that is very difficult for competitors to erode. Retailing View 5.2 describes The Container Store, a retailer that has also built multiple bases of sustainable competitive advantages through unique merchandise, excellent customer service, and strong customer and vendor relationships.

In the preceding sections, we have discussed the focus of a retailer's strategy, its target market and retail format, and the approaches that retailers take to build a sustainable competitive advantage and defend their position from competitive attacks. When retailers develop these competitive advantages, they have valuable assets such as strong relationships with customers and/or vendors, great locations, and effective and efficient systems. In the next section, we discuss how retailers leverage these assets to expand their businesses. By expanding their businesses, they create a cost advantage from the larger size.

GROWTH STRATEGIES

Four types of growth opportunities that retailers may pursue—market penetration, market expansion, retail format development, and diversification—are shown in Exhibit 5–4.[26] The vertical axis indicates the synergies between the retailer's present markets and the growth opportunity—whether the opportunity involves markets the retailer is presently pursuing or new markets. The horizontal axis indicates the synergies between the retailer's present retail mix and the retail mix of the growth opportunity—whether the opportunity exploits the retailer's skills and knowledge in operating its present format or requires new capabilities to operate a new format.

Market Penetration

A **market penetration growth opportunity** is a growth opportunity directed toward existing customers using the retailer's present retailing format. Such opportunities involve either attracting new consumers from the retailer's current target market who don't patronize the retailer currently or devising approaches that get current customers to visit the retailer more often or buy more merchandise on each visit.

Market penetration approaches include opening more stores in the target market and/or keeping existing stores open for longer hours. Other approaches involve displaying merchandise to increase impulse purchases and training salespeople to cross-sell. **Cross-selling** means that sales associates in one department

5.2 RETAILING VIEW   The Container Store—Building a Competitive Advantage by Selling Products That Make Life Simpler

The Container Store sells products to help customers solve problems, or challenges, as the company likes to call them, in organizing their lives. It offers more than 10,000 innovative products including multipurpose shelving and garment bags to organize closets; portable file cabinets and magazine holders to create order in home offices; backpacks, modular shelving, and CD holders to make dorm rooms less cluttered; and recipe holders, bottles, jars, and recycling bins to bring harmony to kitchens. Over 1,500 new products are added to its assortment every year.

Over the years, the company has developed strong vendor relationships. Most of its vendors' primary focus was to manufacture products for industrial use. Yet, over time, the company has worked closely with its vendors to develop products that are appropriate for the home.

The Container Store's sales associates provide outstanding customer service. The company actively recruits customers who are intrigued with helping people organize. It spends considerable time educating sales associates about the merchandise (240 hours versus the typical 12 hours for new retail employees) and then empowering them to use their own intuition and creativity to solve customer challenges.

Employees are very committed to the company; as a result, its turnover rate is among the lowest in the retail industry. The Container Store also has appeared on *Fortune*'s list of the "100 Best Companies to Work For" in each of the last 11 years.

One of several bases of competitive advantage The Container Store has is the quality and commitment of its employees—a human resource asset.

and "Three Good Hires? He'll Pay More for One Who's Great," *New York Times*, March 14, 2010; Paul Keegan, "CEO Maxine Clark, of Build-A-Bear, Traded in Her Kid-Filled Existence for a Day in the Orderly Aisles of the Container Store, Doing the "Closet Dance" ... While Kip Tindell, CEO of the Container Store, Stuffed Monkeys, Lions, and Bears," *Fortune*, February 8, 2010, pp. 68–72.

Sources: Bianna Golodryga and Angela Ellis, "Inside the Container Store: Secrets of America's Favorite Stores," *ABC News*, March 30, 2010,

EXHIBIT 5–4
Growth Opportunities

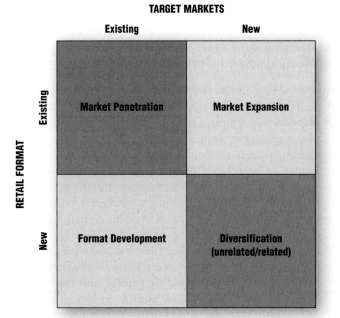

attempt to sell complementary merchandise from other departments to their customers. For example, a sales associate who has just sold a Blu-Ray player to a customer will take the customer to the accessories department to sell special cables to improve the performance of the player.

Market Expansion

A **market expansion growth opportunity** involves using the retailer's existing retail format in new market segments. For example, Dunkin' Donuts has been opening new stores outside its traditional target market in the northeastern United States.[27]

When Chico's acquired White House Black Market, it engaged in a market penetration growth opportunity. Chico's and White House Black Market have similar retail formats. They are both mall-based specialty apparel stores. But Chico's targets women between the ages of 35 and 55, while White House Black Market targets a younger age segment. In contrast, Chico's acquisition of Soma, a mall-based specialty store chain offering lingerie for women between 35 and 55, was a market penetration opportunity—same market and similar operations; however, Chico's and Soma offered different products.

Retail Format Development

A **retail format development growth opportunity** is an opportunity in which a retailer develops a new retail format—a format with a different retail mix—for the same target market. The U.K.-based retailer Tesco has employed a retail format development growth strategy by operating several different food store formats that all cater to essentially the same target market. The smallest is Tesco Express, up to 3,000 square feet. These stores are located close to where customers live and work. Tesco Metro stores are 7,000 to 15,000 square feet, bring convenience to city center locations, and specialize in offering a wide range of ready-to-eat-meals. Tesco Superstores, up to 50,000 square feet, are the oldest format. In recent years, the company has added nonfood products, such as DVDs and books, to improve customer satisfaction. Finally, Tesco Extra stores, more than 60,000 square feet, are designed to be a one-stop destination, with the widest range of food and nonfood products, from housewares and clothing to garden furniture.[28]

Diversification

A **diversification growth opportunity** is one in which a retailer introduces a new retail format directed toward a market segment that's not currently served by the retailer. Diversification opportunities are either related or unrelated.

Related versus Unrelated Diversification

In a **related diversification growth opportunity,** the retailer's present target market or retail format shares something in common with the new opportunity. This commonality might entail purchasing from the same vendors, operating in similar locations, using the same distribution or management information system, or advertising in the same newspapers to similar target markets. In contrast, an **unrelated diversification growth opportunity** has little commonality between the retailer's present business and the new growth opportunity.

Through acquisition, Home Depot built a wholesale building supply business, called HD Supply, which generated over $3 billion annual sales. Management felt that this growth opportunity would be synergistic with the firm's retail business, because its stores were already selling similar merchandise to contractors. Thus, Home Depot viewed this growth opportunity as a related diversification, because the targeted customers (i.e., contractors) would be similar, and the new large contractor market could be served using warehouses similar to Home Depot's present retail stores. In addition, Home Depot would realize cost savings by placing larger orders with vendors because it would be selling to both retail and wholesale customers.

In hindsight, though, the HD Supply actually was an unrelated diversification. The large contractor market served by HD Supply sold primarily pipes, lumber, and concrete—products with limited sales in Home Depot's retail stores. Selling these supplies to large contractors involved competitive bidding and transporting large, bulky orders to job sites—skills that Home Depot lacked. So Home Depot sold this unrelated diversification to concentrate on its core retail small-contractor business.[29]

Vertical Integration

Vertical integration describes diversification by retailers into wholesaling or manufacturing. For example, some retailers go beyond designing their private-label merchandise to owning factories that manufacture the merchandise. When retailers integrate backward and manufacture products, they are making risky investments because the requisite skills to make products are different from those associated with retailing them. In addition, retailers and manufacturers have different customers. The immediate customers for a manufacturer's products are retailers, while a retailer's customers are consumers. Thus, a manufacturer's marketing activities are very different from those of a retailer. Note that designing private-label merchandise is a related diversification because it builds on the retailer's knowledge of its customers, but actually making the merchandise is an unrelated diversification.

Growth Opportunities and Competitive Advantage

Typically, retailers have the greatest competitive advantage and most success when they engage in opportunities that are similar to their present retail operations and markets. Thus, market penetration growth opportunities have the greatest chances of succeeding because they build on the retailer's present bases of advantage and don't involve entering new, unfamiliar markets or operating new, unfamiliar retail formats.

When retailers pursue market expansion opportunities, they build on their advantages in operating a retail format and apply this competitive advantage in a new market. A retail format development opportunity builds on the retailer's relationships and loyalty of present customers. Even if a retailer doesn't have experience and skills in operating the new format, it hopes to attract its loyal customers to it. Retailers have the least opportunity to exploit a competitive advantage when they pursue diversification opportunities.

In the next section, we provide a more detailed discussion of one growth opportunity—expanding operations to international markets. This growth opportunity is particularly attractive to large retailers that have saturated their domestic market.

GLOBAL GROWTH OPPORTUNITIES

As retailers saturate their domestic markets, many find international expansion to be an attractive growth opportunity. Of the 50 largest retailers in the world, only 12 operate in one country.[30] By expanding internationally, retailers can increase their sales, leverage their knowledge and systems across a greater sales base, and gain more bargaining power with vendors. But international expansion is risky, because retailers must deal with different government regulations, cultural traditions, consumer preferences, supply chains, and languages. Retailing View 5.3 describes the substantial differences in apparel preferences for men and women in India compared to those in Western countries.

We first discuss the attractiveness of different opportunities for global expansion and then the keys to success for expanding globally. Finally we review the approaches that retailers can take to enter international markets.

Attractiveness of International Markets

Two factors that are often used to determine the attractiveness of different international opportunities are (1) the potential size of the retail market in the country and (2) the degree to which the country does and can support the entry of foreign retailers.[31] Some indicators of these factors are shown in Exhibit 5–5. The (+) or (−) indicates whether the indicator is positively or negatively related to the factor.

RETAILING VIEW   The Fashion Mavens Are Men in India   **5.3**

Most Indian women prefer to wear traditional garments at work and in social contexts.

The steady growth of the Indian economy has provided an increased propensity to spend among a growing middle class of 25- to 35-year-olds. This has stimulated growth of the Indian retail industry. For a number of years, India has been among the two or three most attractive nations for international retail market expansion. However, there are significant cultural challenges for Western apparel retailers contemplating entry into the Indian market.

In India, men's ready-made apparel generates about two to three times more sales than women's apparel—just the opposites of the sales pattern in Western countries. For the affluent male consumer, clothing is reflective of lifestyle and social status. Awareness of preference for luxury brands is very high. International luxury brands carry symbolic meanings and enhance emotional rewards for male consumers.

While brands play an important role in Indian male consumers' apparel selection, international brands are not important to Indian females in general. Indian ethnic garments and garments mixing ethnic and Western styling are desired by Indian women. International retail firms in this sector face competition from numerous local designers because most Indian women patronize designer boutiques. They have confidence in their personal assessments of product quality and are willing to buy from small and less well known brands. In addition, body shapes differ significantly between Western and Indian women. To be successful, retailers entering the women's apparel market need to offer culturally relevant products that are connected with Indian tradition.

Sources: V. Chattaraman, "The Indian Consumer," *Journal of the International Fashion and Apparel Industry* 4 (July 2009); Dale Anne Reiss and Ranjan Biswas, "The Evolving Retail Market in India," *ICSC Research Review* 14, no. 1 (2007), pp. 26–37.

EXHIBIT 5–5
Indicators of the
Attractiveness of
International Markets

Country Potential	Country Support
• Population (+)	• Market share of modern retailing (+)
• Population growth rate (+)	• Quality of infrastructure, transportation, and communications (+)
• Gross domestic product (GDP) (+)	• Urban population (+)
• GDP per capita (+)	• Market share of leading domestic retailers (−)
• Retail sales (+)	• Ease of doing business (+)
• Growth rate in retail sales (+)	• Business-friendly laws and regulations (+)
• Retail sales per capita (+)	• Political stability (+)
• Income distribution (+) or (−)	
• Age distribution (+) or (−)	

The most attractive countries are those with large and growing potential sales as indicated by the level and growth rate of present retail sales and the amount of money people have in the country to spend on services and merchandise as indicated by GDP, GDP growth rate, and GDP per capita. Income and age distribution can be either positively or negatively related to market attractiveness, depending on the type of retailer evaluating the country for entry. For example, a retailer of video games, such as Gamestop, would find a country with a large percentage of people under 19 to be more attractive than a country with a large percentage of people over 65. High-fashion retailers that sell expensive merchandise, such as Neiman Marcus and Cartier, would find a country that has a significant percentage of the population with high incomes to be more attractive than a country that has a large percentage of people in poverty.

With respect to company support, most retailers considering entry into foreign markets are successful retailers that use sophisticated management practices. Thus they would find countries that support modern retailing, have more advanced infrastructures, and have significant urban populations to be more attractive. In addition, countries lacking strong domestic retailers but having a stable economy and political environment would be more attractive.

The factors outlined in Exhibit 5–5 are weighted to develop an attractiveness index. One index ranking the 20 most attractive international retail markets, along with some demographic information about the countries, is shown in Exhibit 5–6. Of the top 20 counties in this ranking, 10 are emerging economies. The emerging international markets that receive the most attention from global retailers are India, China, Russia, and Brazil, collectively referred to as "the BRIC" (Brazil, Russia, India, China) countries.

China and India are by far the largest retail markets in emerging economies. However, these two countries offer different opportunities and challenges for retailers contemplating entry.

REFACT

Organized retailing such as multiunit, self-service supermarkets accounts for just 4 percent of retail sales in India.[32]

India In India, the retail industry is divided into organized and unorganized sectors. The unorganized retailing includes the small independent retailers—the local *kirana* shops, owner-operated general stores, *paan/beedi* shops, convenience stores, and handcart and street vendors. Most Indians shop in open markets and millions of independent grocery shops called *kirana*. However, India's growing, well-educated, aspirational middle class wants a more sophisticated retail environment and global brands.

While the demand for modern (organized) retailing exists in India, entering the Indian market is challenging. As the world's largest pluralistic democracy, with myriad cultures and 22 official languages, India actually is a conglomeration of discrete markets. In addition, government regulations impede foreign investment in retailing. Non-Indian firms cannot have a controlling interest in retail firms and thus must partner with an Indian firm. Retailers must comply with a myriad of regulations before opening stores and shipping merchandise. For example, there

Global Retail Opportunity Rankings   **EXHIBIT 5–6**

Rank	Country	Index	Retail Sales* (2008)	Retail Sales Growth Rate** (2008–2013)	GDP per Capita (2008)	% of Population under 20 (2008)	% of Income Made by Highest Quintile
1	China	83	$1,004	7.0%	3,315	28.7	51.9
2	Russia	71	478	6.6	11,807	21.5	46.6
3	United States	69	3,686	2.8	45,859	27.5	45.6
4	India	62	435	5.7	1,016	40.9	45.3
5	Malaysia	58	59	4.6	8,141	41.5	54.3
6	South Africa	54	95	5.0	5,693	40.5	62.2
7	United Kingdom	52	851	1.6	43,785	23.5	44.0
8	Australia	51	229	2.9	47,400	25.5	41.3
9	Canada	50	384	2.1	45,426	23.1	39.9
10	Brazil	50	467	4.2	8,197	35.4	61.1
11	France	49	828	1.0	46,016	24.8	40.2
12	Vietnam	49	43	5.5	1,040	36.0	44.3
13	Philippines	48	79	5.2	1,866	45.7	50.6
14	Sweden	47	109	2.0	52,790	23.1	36.6
15	Argentina	46	102	5.0	8,214	34.2	55.4
16	Japan	45	1,278	0.0	38,559	18.5	35.7
17	Spain	45	484	2.0	35,331	19.4	42.0
18	Nigeria	44	94	4.0	1,451	52.4	49.2
19	Turkey	43	341	3.3	10,472	36.6	49.7
20	Thailand	42	120	3.0	4,115	28.9	49.0

* Billions of U.S. dollars.

** Estimated compound annual growth rate.

SOURCE: Frank Badillo, "Global Retail Outlook," *Retail Forward,* May 2009.

are taxes for moving goods to different states and even within states. Walmart's entry into India is a partnership with Bharti Enterprises to open wholesale outlets called Best Price Modern Wholesale. The outlets are allowed to sell only to firms that register by showing tax documents that prove they own retail outlets. The development of organized retailing is being undertaken by industrial conglomerates that have limited expertise in running retail chains.[33]

In India, as in most emerging markets, most people shop at small, independent retailers.

China   Government regulations of retailing are much less onerous in China than in India and direct foreign investment in encouraged. Since the lifting of most operational restrictions on international retailers, six global food retailers (Auchan, Carrefour, Ito-Yokado, Metro, Tesco, and Walmart) have entered China. Although much of this retail development has been in the large eastern cities of Shanghai, Beijing, Guangzhou, and Shenzhen, these Tier 1 markets are approaching saturation for hypermarkets; the interior Tier 2 and Tier 3 markets are very attractive.

China is rapidly developing the infrastructure to support modern retailing. Highway density in China is already approaching that in the United States. China has a number of high-quality airports and a rapidly developing sophisticated railroad network.[34]

However, doing business in China is still challenging. Operating costs are increasing, managerial talent is becoming more difficult to find and retain, and an underdeveloped and inefficient supply chain predominates.

Russia   In Russia, the impediments to market entry are less visible but more problematic. Corruption is rampant, with various administrative authorities capable of impeding operations if payments are not made. Retailers encounter severe logistical challenges in supporting operations in Russia. There are long delays at borders and ports and a scarcity of containers. Over 70 percent of international container shipments come through the Saint Petersburg port, which is very congested. Retailers often cannot rely on domestic products because the quality of products made in Russia is poor. Finally, much of the purchasing power is concentrated in Moscow, where salaries are about double those in other regions. But Moscow is already saturated with shopping centers.

Brazil   Brazil has the largest population and strongest economy in Latin America. It is a country of many poor people and a few very wealthy families. Brazilian retailers have developed some very innovative practices for retailing to low-income families, including offering credit and installment purchases. Many low-income customers go from week to week paying their credit card commitments. Most major retailers offer their own credit card facility, with "signing up" booths at the entrances to their stores.

The very wealthy Brazilians provide a significant market for luxury goods and retailers. Even though they are approximately 1 percent of the population, this equates to approximately 19 million people, a market just a little smaller than all of Australia.

Keys to Success

Four characteristics of retailers that have successfully exploited international growth opportunities are (1) a globally sustainable competitive advantage, (2) adaptability, (3) a global culture, and (4) financial resources.

Globally Sustainable Competitive Advantage   Entry into nondomestic markets is most successful when the expansion opportunity builds on the retailer's core bases of competitive advantage. For example, Walmart and ALDI have a significant cost advantage and thus are most successful in international markets in which price plays an important role in consumer decision making and a distribution infrastructure is available to enable these firms to exploit their logistical capabilities. In contrast, H&M and Zara are more successful in international markets that value lower-priced, fashionable merchandise.

Some U.S. retailers have a competitive advantage in global markets because American culture is emulated in many countries, particularly by young people. Due to rising prosperity and the rapidly increasing access to networks such as MTV that feature American programming, fashion trends in the United States are spreading to young people in emerging countries. The global MTV generation prefers Coke to tea, athletic shoes to sandals, Chicken McNuggets to rice, and credit cards to cash. In the last few years, China's major cities have sprouted American stores and restaurants, including KFC, Pizza Hut, and McDonald's. Shanghai and Beijing have over 100 Starbucks stores even though coffee had never been the drink of choice before Starbucks came to town. But Chinese urban dwellers go to Starbucks to impress a friend or because it's a symbol of a new kind of lifestyle. Although Western products and stores have gained a reputation for high quality and good service in China, in some ways it is the American culture that many Chinese consumers want.

Adaptability   Although successful global retailers build on their core competencies, they also recognize cultural differences and adapt their core strategy to the needs of local markets.[37] Color preferences, the preferred cut of apparel, and sizes differ across cultures. For example, in China, white is the color of mourning, and brides wear red dresses. Food probably has the greatest diversity of tastes around the world.

Carrefour is an expert at understanding and integrating itself into local regions. For example, it realized early on that the merchandising of fish differs for each local market. In San Francisco, fish is sold dead and filleted; in France, fish is sold dead but whole on ice with the head still intact; and in China, fish is sold live. However, consumers in the middle and western parts of China have more confidence in frozen fish, because they are so far from the ocean.[38] Carrefour and Tesco make sure that more than 90 percent of the merchandise they sell is produced in the country in which it is sold.[39]

Peak selling seasons also vary across countries. In the United States, many stores experience a sales increase in August, when families stock up on back-to-school supplies and apparel. However, this month is one of the slowest sales periods in Europe, because most people are on vacation. Back-to-school season in Japan occurs in April.

Store designs and layouts often need to be adjusted in different parts of the world. In the United States, for instance, discount stores are usually quite large and on one level. In other parts of the world, such as Europe and parts of Asia, where space is at a premium, stores must be designed to fit smaller footprints and are often housed in multiple levels. In some cultures, social norms dictate that men's and women's clothing cannot be displayed next to each other.

Government regulations and cultural values can also affect store operations. Some differences, such as holidays, hours of operation, and regulations governing part-time employees and terminations, are easy to identify. Other factors require a deeper understanding. For example, Latin American culture is very family oriented, so traditional U.S. work schedules would need to be adjusted so that Latin American employees could have more time with their families. Boots, a U.K. drugstore chain, has the checkout clerks in its Japanese stores standing up because it discovered that Japanese shoppers found it offensive to pay money to a seated clerk, but retailers have to provide seating for checkout clerks in Germany. Retailers in Germany also must recycle packaging materials sold in their stores. Also in Germany, seasonal sales can be held only during specific weeks and apply only to specific product categories, and the amount of the discounts are limited. Spanish and French retailers work under government-controlled operating hours and must mind policies prohibiting midseason sales.

Global Culture   To be global, retailers must think globally. It is not sufficient to transplant a home-country culture and infrastructure to another country. In this regard, Carrefour is truly global. In the early years of its international expansion, it started in each country slowly, an approach that reduced the company's ethnocentrism. Further enriching its global perspective, Carrefour has always encouraged the rapid development of local management and retains few expatriates in its overseas operations. Carrefour's management ranks are truly international. One is just as likely to run across a Portuguese regional manager in Hong Kong as a French or Chinese one. Finally, Carrefour discourages the classic overseas "tour of duty" mentality often found in U.S. firms. International assignments are important in themselves, not just as stepping stones to ultimate career advancement back in France. The globalization of Carrefour's culture is perhaps most evident in the speed with which ideas flow throughout the organization. A global management structure of regional committees, which meet regularly, advances the awareness and implementation of global best practices. The proof of Carrefour's global commitment lies in the numbers: It has had more than 30 years of international experience in 30 countries, both developed and developing.[40]

Financial Resources   Expansion into international markets requires a long-term commitment and considerable up-front planning. Retailers find it very difficult to generate short-term profits when they make the transition to global retailing.

Although firms such as Walmart, Carrefour, Office Depot, and Costco often initially have difficulty achieving success in new global markets, these large firms generally are in a strong financial position and therefore have the ability to keep investing in projects long enough to become successful.

Entry Strategies

Four approaches that retailers can take when entering nondomestic markets are direct investment, joint venture, strategic alliance, and franchising.[41]

Direct Investment   **Direct investment** occurs when a retail firm invests in and owns a retail operation in a foreign country. This entry strategy requires the highest level of investment and exposes the retailer to the greatest risks, but it also has the highest potential returns. A key advantage of direct investment is that the retailer has complete control of the operations. For example, McDonald's chose this entry strategy for the U.K. market, building a plant to produce buns when local suppliers could not meet its specifications.

Joint Venture   A **joint venture** is formed when the entering retailer pools its resources with a local retailer to form a new company in which ownership, control, and profits are shared. A joint-venture entry strategy reduces the entrant's risks. In addition to sharing the financial burden, the local partner provides an understanding of the market and has access to local resources, such as vendors and real estate. Many foreign countries, such as India, require that foreign entrants partner with domestic firms. Problems with this entry approach can arise if the partners disagree or the government places restrictions on the repatriation of profits.

Strategic Alliance   A **strategic alliance** is a collaborative relationship between independent firms. For example, a retailer might enter an international market through direct investment but use independent firms to facilitate its local logistical and warehousing activities.

Franchising   **Franchising** offers the lowest risk and requires the least investment. However, the retailer has limited control over the retail operations in the foreign country, its potential profit is reduced, and the risk of assisting in the creation of a local domestic competitor increases. The U.K.-based Marks & Spencer, for example, has franchised stores in 30 countries.[42] The franchising appendix at the end of the text provides a thorough discussion of this method of entering global markets.

THE STRATEGIC RETAIL PLANNING PROCESS

In the previous sections, we reviewed the elements in a strategy statement, the potential approaches for building a sustainable competitive advantage, and the potential growth opportunities that retailers can consider. In this section, we outline the process retailers use to review their present situation and decide on a strategy to pursue.

The **strategic retail planning process** is the set of steps a retailer goes through to develop a strategy and plan[43] (see Exhibit 5–7). It describes how retailers select target market segments, determine the appropriate retail format, and build sustainable competitive advantages. As indicated in Exhibit 5–7, it is not always necessary to go through the entire process each time a strategy and plan are developed (step 7). For instance, a retailer could evaluate its performance and go directly to step 2 to conduct a situation audit.

The planning process can be used to formulate strategic plans at different levels within a retail corporation. For example, the corporate strategic plan of Tesco indicates how to allocate resources across the corporation's various divisions, such as

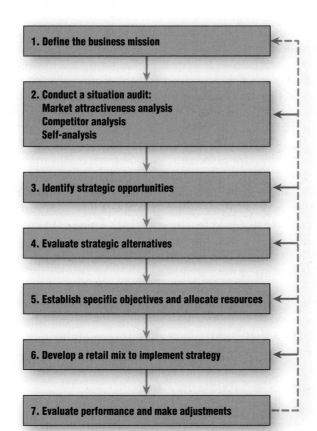

EXHIBIT 5–7
Stages in the Strategic
Retail Planning Process

Tesco, Tesco Extra, Tesco Express, Tesco Metro, Tesco Homeplus, and One Stop. Each division, in turn, develops its own strategic plan.

As we discuss the steps in the retail planning process, we will apply each step to the planning process Kelly Bradford is undertaking. Kelly owns Gifts To Go, a small, two-store chain in the Chicago area. One of her 1,000-square-foot stores is located in the downtown area; the other is in an upscale suburban mall. The target market for Gifts To Go is upper-income men and women looking for gifts in the $50 to $500 price range. The stores have an eclectic selection of merchandise, including handmade jewelry and crafts, fine china and glassware, perfume, watches, writing instruments, and a variety of one-of-a-kind items. Gifts To Go also has developed a number of loyal customers who are contacted by sales associates when family anniversaries and birthdays come up. In many cases, customers have a close relationship with a sales associate and enough confidence in the associate's judgment that they tell the associate to pick out an appropriate gift. The turnover of Gifts To Go sales associates is low for the industry, because Kelly treats associates as part of the family. The company pays for medical insurance for all associates, and they share in the profits of the firm.

Step 1: Define the Business Mission

The first step in the strategic retail planning process is to define the business mission. The **mission statement** is a broad description of a retailer's objectives and the scope of activities it plans to undertake.[44] While the principle objective of a publicly held firm is to maximize its stockholders' wealth, firms are concerned about their impact on society.

For example, Maxine Clark, founder and chief executive bear at Build-A-Bear Workshop, in discussing her goals for the company, says, "We also believe strongly that we need to give back to the communities in which we have stores. For example, as part of our on-going commitment to children's health and wellness, we introduced a series of Nicki Bears to honor Nicki Giampolo, a young girl who lost her life to cancer. A portion of the sales of each Nicki is donated to support programs that help children maintain normal lives while they struggle with difficult health issues."[45] Owners of small, privately held firms frequently have other objectives, such as achieving a specific level of income and avoiding risks rather than maximizing income.

The mission statement defines the general nature of the target segments and retail formats on which the firm will focus. For example, the mission statement of an office supply category specialist, "Serve the customer, build value for shareholders, and create opportunities for associates," is too broad. It fails to provide a sense of strategic direction.

In developing the mission statement, managers need to answer five questions: (1) What business are we in? (2) What should our business be in the future? (3) Who are our customers? (4) What are our capabilities? (5) What do we want to accomplish? Gifts To Go's mission statement is "The mission of Gifts To Go is to be the leading retailer of higher-priced gifts in Chicago and provide a stable income of $100,000 per year for the owner."

Because the mission statement defines the retailer's objectives and the scope of activities it plans to undertake, Gifts To Go's mission statement clarifies that its management won't consider retail opportunities outside the Chicago area, selling low-priced gifts, or activities that might jeopardize its ability to generate $100,000 in annual income.

Step 2: Conduct a Situation Audit

After developing a mission statement and setting objectives, the next step in the strategic planning process is to conduct a **situation audit,** an analysis of the opportunities and threats in the retail environment and the strengths and weaknesses of the retail business relative to its competitors. The elements in the situation analysis are shown in Exhibit 5–8.

Market Factors   Some critical factors related to consumers and their buying patterns are the target market size and growth, sales cyclicality, and seasonality. Market size, typically measured in retail sales dollars, is important because it indicates a retailer's opportunity to generate revenues to cover its investment.

Growing markets are typically more attractive than mature or declining markets. For example, retail markets for limited-assortment, extreme-value retailers are growing faster than are those for department stores. Typically, the return on investment may be higher in growing markets because competition is less intense than in mature markets. Because new customers are just beginning to patronize stores in growing markets, they may not have developed strong store loyalties and thus might be easier to attract to new retail offerings.

EXHIBIT 5–8
Elements in a Situation Audit

MARKET FACTORS

Size
Growth
Seasonality
Business cycles

COMPETITIVE FACTORS

Barriers to entry
Bargaining power of vendors
Competitive rivalry

ENVIRONMENTAL FACTORS

Technology
Economic
Regulatory
Social

ANALYSIS OF STRENGTHS AND WEAKNESSES

Management capabilities
Financial resources
Locations
Operations
Merchandise
Store management
Customer loyalty

Firms are often interested in minimizing the business cycle's impact on their sales. Thus, retail markets for merchandise that is affected by economic conditions (such as cars and major appliances) are less attractive than retail markets that are less affected by economic conditions (such as food).

In general, markets with highly seasonal sales are unattractive because a lot of resources are needed to accommodate the peak season and then the resources go underutilized the rest of the year. Retailers can take steps to reduce seasonality; for instance, ski resorts can promote summer vacations.

To conduct an analysis of the market factors for Gifts To Go, Kelly Bradford went on the Internet to get information about the size, growth, and cyclical and seasonal nature of the gift market in general and, more specifically, in Chicago. On the basis of her analysis, she concluded that the market factors were attractive. The market for more expensive gifts was large, growing, and not vulnerable to business cycles. The only negative aspect was the high seasonality of gifts, with peaks at Valentine's Day, June (due to weddings), Christmas, and other holidays.

Competitive Factors   The nature of the competition in retail markets is affected by barriers to entry, the bargaining power of vendors, and competitive rivalry.[46] Retail markets are more attractive when competitive entry is costly. **Barriers to entry** are conditions in a retail market that make it difficult for other firms to enter the market. Some of these conditions are (1) scale economies, (2) customer loyalty, and (3) the availability of great locations.

Scale economies are cost advantages due to a retailer's size. Markets dominated by large competitors with scale economies are typically unattractive because the dominant firms have sustainable cost advantages. For example, an entrepreneur would view the drugstore market as unattractive because it is dominated by three large firms, Walgreens, CVS, and Rite Aid. These firms have considerable cost advantages over an entrepreneur because they have significant bargaining power over suppliers and can buy merchandise at lower prices. They have the resources to invest in the latest technology and can spread the fixed costs of such investments across more outlets.

Retail markets dominated by a well-established retailer that has developed a loyal group of customers also are unattractive. For example, Home Depot's high customer loyalty in Atlanta, where it has its corporate offices, makes it hard for a competing home improvement center to enter the Atlanta market.

Finally, the availability of locations may impede competitive entry. Staples, for instance, attributes part of its success over its rivals in the northeastern United States to its first-mover advantage. The Northeast has a preponderance of mature but stable retail markets, so finding new locations is more difficult there than it is in most of the rest of the United States. Because Staples started in the Northeast, it was able to open stores in the best available locations.

Entry barriers are a double-edged sword. A retail market with high entry barriers is very attractive for retailers presently competing in that market, because those barriers limit competition. However, markets with high entry barriers are unattractive for retailers not already in the market.

Another competitive factor is the **bargaining power of vendors.** Markets are less attractive when only a few vendors control the merchandise sold in the market. In such situations, vendors have the opportunity to dictate prices and other terms (like delivery dates), reducing the retailer's profits. For example, the market for retailing fashionable cosmetics is less attractive because two suppliers, Estée Lauder (Estée Lauder, Clinique, Prescriptives, Aveda, Jo Malone, Bumble and Bumble, Tommy Hilfiger, MAC, and Origins) and L'Oréal (Maybelline, Giorgio Armani, RedKen, Lancôme, Garnier, and Ralph Lauren) provide most of the desirable premium brands. Because department stores need these brands to support a fashion image, the suppliers have the power to sell their products to retailers at high prices.

The final competitive factor is the level of competitive rivalry in the retail market. **Competitive rivalry** is the frequency and intensity of reactions to actions undertaken by competitors. When rivalry is high, price wars erupt, employee raids occur, advertising and promotion expenses increase, and profit potential falls. Conditions that may lead to intense rivalry include (1) a large number of competitors that are all about the same size, (2) slow growth, (3) high fixed costs, and (4) a lack of perceived differences between competing retailers. For example, Home Depot and Lowe's have an intense rivalry in many markets.

When Kelly Bradford started to analyze the competitive factors for Gifts To Go, she realized that identifying her competitors wasn't easy. Although there were no gift stores carrying similar merchandise at the same price points in the Chicago area, there were various other retailers from which a customer could buy gifts. She identified her primary competitors as department stores, craft galleries, catalogs, and Internet retailers. Kelly felt there were some scale economies in developing customer databases to support gift retailing. The lack of large suppliers meant that vendors' bargaining power wasn't a problem, and competitive rivalry was minimal because the gift business was not a critical part of a department store's overall business. In addition, merchandise carried by the various retailers offered considerable differentiation opportunities.

Environmental Factors   Environmental factors that can affect market attractiveness include technological, economic, regulatory, and social changes. When a retail market is going through significant changes in technology, existing competitors are vulnerable to new entrants that are skilled at using the new technology. Many traditional store-based retailers were slow to develop their multichannel Internet strategies fully. For instance, in the 1990s, few retailers offered the ability for customers to purchase over the Internet and return merchandise to a store. Today, however, the larger multichannel retailers set the standards for services provided through technology.

Some retailers may be more affected by economic conditions than others. During tough economic times, retailers that offer a perceived high-value offering, such as discount, off-price, warehouse clubs, and extreme-value retailers, are in a much better position than retailers specializing in luxury goods, such as jewelry stores, designer apparel specialty stores, and gourmet and organic grocers.

Government regulations can reduce the attractiveness of a retail market. For example, until recently, government regulations made it difficult for foreign-owned retailers to open stores in India.[47] Also, many local governments within the United States have tried to stop Walmart from entering their markets in an attempt to protect locally owned retailers.

Finally, trends in demographics, lifestyles, attitudes, and personal values affect retail markets' attractiveness. Apple specializes in developing aesthetically designed products in areas of popular technology. Its stores also mimic the high-tech design of its products and are known to have "Apple Style." The products are appealing to aficionados of technology, as well as to nontechnological consumers. Apple Stores are simple to navigate and friendly, and the architecture is similar to that of a fashion or luxury store.[48]

Retailers need to answer three questions about each environmental factor:

1. What new developments or changes might occur, such as new technologies and regulations or different social factors and economic conditions?

2. What is the likelihood that these environmental changes will occur? What key factors affect whether these changes will occur?

3. How will these changes affect each retail market, the firm, and its competitors?

Kelly Bradford's primary concern when she did an environmental analysis was the potential growth of Internet gift retailers such as RedEnvelope. Gifts seem ideal for an electronic channel, because customers can order the item over the

In performing a self-analysis, the retailer considers the potential areas for developing a competitive advantage listed below and answers the following questions:

At what is our company good?

In which of these areas is our company better than our competitors?

In which of these areas does our company's unique capabilities provide a sustainable competitive advantage or a basis for developing one?

EXHIBIT 5–9
Elements in a Strengths and Weaknesses Analysis

 MANAGEMENT CAPABILITY
Capabilities and experience of top management
Depth of management—capabilities of middle management
Management's commitment to firm

 MERCHANDISING CAPABILITIES
Knowledge and skills of buyers
Relationships with vendors
Capabilities in developing private brands
Advertising and promotion capabilities

 FINANCIAL RESOURCES
Cash flow from existing business
Ability to raise debt or equity financing

 STORE MANAGEMENT CAPABILITIES
Management capabilities
Quality of sales associates
Commitment of sales associates to firm

 OPERATIONS
Overhead cost structure
Quality of operating systems
Distribution capabilities
Management information systems
Loss prevention systems
Inventory control systems

 LOCATIONS

 CUSTOMERS
Loyalty of customers

Internet and have it shipped directly to the gift recipient. Kelly also recognized that the electronic channel could effectively collect information about customers and then target promotions and suggestions to them when future gift-giving occasions arose.

Strengths and Weaknesses Analysis   The most critical aspect of the situation audit is for a retailer to determine its unique capabilities in terms of its strengths and weaknesses relative to the competition. A **strengths and weaknesses analysis** indicates how well the business can seize opportunities and avoid harm from threats in the environment. Exhibit 5–9 outlines some issues to consider in performing a strengths and weaknesses analysis.

Here is Kelly Bradford's analysis of Gifts To Go's strengths and weaknesses:

Management capability	Limited—Two excellent store managers and a relatively inexperienced person helped Kelly buy merchandise. An accounting firm kept the financial records for the business but had no skills in developing and utilizing customer databases.
Financial resources	Good—Gifts To Go had no debt and a good relationship with a bank. Kelly had saved $255,000 that she had in liquid securities.
Operations	Poor—While Kelly felt Gifts To Go had relatively low overhead, the company did not have a computer-based inventory control system or management and customer information systems. Her competitors (local department stores, catalog, and Internet retailers) certainly had superior systems.
Merchandising capabilities	Good—Kelly had a flair for selecting unique gifts, and she had excellent relationships with vendors providing one-of-a-kind merchandise.
Store management capabilities	Excellent—The store managers and sales associates were excellent. They were very attentive to customers and loyal to the firm. Employee and customer theft were kept to a minimum.
Locations	Excellent—Both of Gifts To Go's locations were excellent. The downtown location was convenient for office workers. The suburban mall location was at a heavily trafficked juncture.
Customers	Good—While Gifts To Go did not achieve the sales volume in gifts done in department stores, the company had a loyal base of customers.

Step 3: Identify Strategic Opportunities

After completing the situation audit, the next step is to identify opportunities for increasing retail sales. Kelly Bradford presently competes in gift retailing using a specialty store format. The strategic alternatives she is considering are defined in terms of the growth opportunities in Exhibit 5–4. Note that some of these growth strategies involve a redefinition of her mission.

Step 4: Evaluate Strategic Opportunities

The fourth step in the strategic planning process is to evaluate opportunities that have been identified in the situation audit. The evaluation determines the retailer's potential to establish a sustainable competitive advantage and reap long-term profits from the opportunities being evaluated. Thus, a retailer must focus on opportunities that utilize its strengths and its competitive advantage.

Both the market attractiveness and the strengths and weaknesses of the retailer need to be considered in evaluating strategic opportunities. The greatest investments should be made in market opportunities for which the retailer has a strong competitive position. Here's Kelly's informal analysis:

Growth Opportunity	Market Attractiveness	Competitive Position
Increase size of present stores and amount of merchandise in stores	Low	High
Open additional gift stores in Chicago area	Medium	Medium
Open gift stores outside the Chicago area (new geographic segment)	Medium	Low
Sell lower-priced gifts in present stores or open new stores selling low-priced gifts (new benefit segment)	Medium	Low
Sell apparel and other nongift merchandise to same customers in same or new stores	High	Medium
Sell similar gift merchandise to same market segment using the Internet	High	Low
Open apparel stores targeted at teenagers	High	Low
Open a category specialist selling low-priced gifts	High	Low

Step 5: Establish Specific Objectives and Allocate Resources

After evaluating the strategic investment opportunities, the next step in the strategic planning process is to establish a specific objective for each opportunity. The retailer's overall objective is included in the mission statement; the specific objectives are goals against which progress toward the overall objective can be measured. Thus, these specific objectives have three components: (1) the performance sought, including a numerical index against which progress may be measured; (2) a time frame within which the goal is to be achieved; and (3) the level of investment needed to achieve the objective. Typically, the performance levels are financial criteria such as return on investment, sales, or profits. Kelly's objective is to increase profits by 20 percent in each of the next five years. She expects she will need to invest an additional $25,000 in her apparel and other nongift merchandise inventory.

Step 6: Develop a Retail Mix to Implement the Strategy

The sixth step in the planning process is to develop a retail mix for each opportunity in which an investment will be made and control and evaluate performance. Decisions related to the elements in the retail mix are discussed in Sections III and IV.

Step 7: Evaluate Performance and Make Adjustments

The final step in the planning process is to evaluate the results of the strategy and implementation program. If the retailer is meeting or exceeding its objectives, changes aren't needed. But if the retailer fails to meet its objectives, reanalysis is required. Typically, this reanalysis starts with reviewing the implementation programs, but it may indicate that the strategy (or even the mission statement) needs to be reconsidered. This conclusion would result in starting a new planning process, including a new situation audit. Retailing View 5.4 illustrates how changes in the competitive environment forced Hot Topic to reevaluate its entire retail format.

Strategic Planning in the Real World

The planning process in Exhibit 5–7 suggests that strategic decisions are made in a sequential manner. After the business mission is defined, the situation audit is performed, strategic opportunities are identified, alternatives are evaluated, objectives are set, resources are allocated, the implementation plan is developed, and, finally, performance is evaluated and adjustments are made. But actual planning processes have interactions among the steps. For example, the situation audit may uncover a logical alternative for the firm to consider, even though this alternative isn't included in the mission statement. Thus, the mission statement may need to be reformulated. The development of the implementation plan might reveal that the resources allocated to a particular opportunity are insufficient to achieve the objective. In that case, the objective would need to be changed, the resources would need to be increased, or the retailer might consider not investing in the opportunity at all.

RETAILING VIEW   Hot Topic Emphasizes Its Strength in Indie Music   **5.4**

Hot Topic, which started in the late 1980s, differentiated itself from other mall-based retailers targeting the Generation Y segment by offering an edgier alternative. It offered goth merchandise in its stores, which were frequented by customers and sales associates with tattoos, multiple piercings, spiked hair, and all-black clothing. Over time, Hot Topic looked like an also-ran in the crowded teen-retailer market. The taste of fickle teens had changed. Its sales were stagnant. Mall foot traffic was down.

Hot Topic analyzed its situation and discovered that its basis of advantage among teens wasn't its goth image but its connection to the indie music scene—the small avant-garde bands it promoted with its private-label t-shirts. So it repositioned itself, reducing its emphasis on goth-look apparel and placing more emphasis on merchandise linked to cutting-edge music and entertainment.

Today, its stores feel more like campus student centers with loud music, dark walls, and bulletin boards crammed with concert flyers and staff music picks. Hot Topic began hosting free acoustic shows, called Local Static, featuring bands chosen by salespeople in its local stores. The company stresses its connection with music through its music download site, ShockHound.

It also licensed exclusively *Twilight*'s four-book-and-film franchise about teen vampire love. The movie's stars did a national tour of Hot Topic stores, and the retailer supplied hot chocolate and pizza to thousands of fans.

Hot Topic's store design reflects alterations in its retail strategy in response to changes in its environment.

Sources: Kate Rockwood, "How Hot Topic's Culture-Heavy Strategy Helped It Sizzle during the Downturn," *Fast Company*, September 1, 2009; Jayne O'Donnell, "Hot Topic CEO Betsy McLaughin Lives in Two Worlds," *USA Today*, March 23, 2010.

SUMMARY

Strategic planning is an ongoing process. Every day, retailers audit their situations, examine consumer trends, study new technologies, and monitor competitive activities. But the retail strategy statement does not change every year or every six months; the strategy statement is reviewed and altered only when major changes in the retailer's environment or capabilities occur.

When a retailer undertakes a major reexamination of its strategy, the process for developing a new strategy statement may take a year or two. Potential strategic directions are generated by people at all levels of the organization and then evaluated by senior executives and operating personnel to ensure that the eventual strategic direction is profitable in the long run and can be implemented.

A retailer's long-term performance is largely determined by its strategy. A strategy coordinates employees' activities and communicates the direction the retailer plans to take. Thus, the retail market strategy describes both the strategic direction and the process by which the strategy is to be developed.

The retail strategy statement includes the identification of a target market and the retail format (its offering) to be directed toward that target market. The statement also needs to indicate the retailer's approaches for building a sustainable competitive advantage. Five important opportunities for retailers to develop sustainable competitive advantages are (1) customer loyalty, (2) location, (3) human resource management, (4) distribution and information systems, and (5) vendor relations,

The strategic planning process consists of a sequence of steps: (1) defining the business mission, (2) conducting a situation audit, (3) identifying strategic opportunities, (4) evaluating the alternatives, (5) establishing specific objectives and allocating resources, (6) developing a retail mix to implement the strategy, and (7) evaluating performance and making adjustments.

KEY TERMS

bargaining power of vendors, *133*

barriers to entry, *133*

competitive rivalry, *134*

cross-selling, *122*

customer loyalty, *115*

direct investment, *130*

diversification growth opportunity, *124*

franchising, *130*

frequent shopper program, *118*

joint venture, *130*

loyalty program, *118*

market expansion growth opportunity, *123*

market penetration growth opportunity, *122*

mission statement, *131*

own brand, *117*

positioning, *116*

private-label brand, *117*

related diversification growth opportunity, *124*

retail format, *112*

retail format development growth opportunity, *123*

retailing concept, *113*

retail market, *113*

retail strategy, *112*

scale economies, *133*

situation audit, *132*

store brand, *117*

strategic alliance, *130*

strategic retail planning process, *130*

strengths and weaknesses analysis, *135*

sustainable competitive advantage, *112*

target market, *112*

unrelated diversification growth opportunity, *124*

vertical integration, *124*

GET OUT AND DO IT!

1. **CONTINUING CASE ASSIGNMENT** Prepare an analysis of the company you selected for the continuing assignment. Identify its direct competitors, its target market and positioning, its strategy with respect to its competitors, its retail format (the elements in its retail mix—merchandise variety and assortment, pricing, locations), and its bases for developing a competitive advantage relative to its competitors. Outline the retailer's strengths, weaknesses, opportunities, and threats relative to its competitors. Pick a specific country in which the firm does not operate, and make a recommendation about whether the retailer should enter the country and, if so, how it should do so.

2. **INTERNET EXERCISE** Visit the Web sites for IKEA (www.ikea.com) and Starbucks (www.starbucks.

com). Are the look and feel of these Internet sites consistent with the in-store experience of these retailers?

3. **INTERNET EXERCISE** Go to the Web sites for Walmart (www.walmartstores.com), Carrefour (www.carrefour.fr), Royal Ahold (www.ahold.com), and Metro AG (www.metro.de). Which chain has the most global strategy? Justify your answer.

4. **GO SHOPPING** Visit two stores that sell similar merchandise categories and cater to the same target segment(s). How are their retail formats (the elements in their retail mixes) similar? Dissimilar? On what bases do they have a sustainable competitive advantage? Explain which you believe has a stronger position.

5. **WEB OLC EXERCISE** Go to the student side of the book's Web site, and click on "Market Position

Matrix."*Exercise 1:* This spreadsheet describes an analysis of international growth opportunities. What numbers in the matrices would have to change to make China and France more attractive opportunities? To make Brazil and Mexico less attractive opportunities? Change the numbers in the matrices, and see what effect this has on the overall position of the opportunity in the grid. *Exercise 2:* The market attractiveness/competitive position matrix can also be used by a department store to evaluate its merchandise categories and determine how much it should invest in each category. Fill in the

importance weights (10 = very important, 1 = not very important) and the evaluations of the merchandise categories (10 = excellent, 1 = poor), and then see what is recommended by the plot on the opportunity matrix. *Exercise 3:* Think of another investment decision that a retailer might make, and analyze it using the strategic analysis matrix. List the alternatives and the characteristics of the alternatives, and then put in the importance weights for the characteristics (10 = very important, 1 = not very important) and the evaluation of each alternative on each characteristic (10 = excellent, 1 = poor).

DISCUSSION QUESTIONS AND PROBLEMS

1. For each of the four retailers discussed at the beginning of the chapter (Lululemon, Curves, Magazine Luiza, Save-A-Lot), describe its strategy and the basis of its competitive advantage.

2. Choose a retailer, and describe how it has developed a competitive strategic advantage.

3. Give an example of a market penetration, a retail format development, a market expansion, and a diversification growth strategy that Best Buy might use.

4. Choose your favorite retailer. Draw and explain a positioning map, like that shown in Exhibit 5–3, that includes your retailer, retailers that sell the same types of merchandise, and the target customer segments (ideal points).

5. Do a situation analysis for McDonald's. What is its mission? What are its strengths and weaknesses? What environmental threats might it face over the next 10 years? How could it prepare for these threats?

6. What are Neiman Marcus's and PetSmart's bases for sustainable competitive advantage? Are they really sustainable, or are they easily copied?

7. Assume you are interested in opening a restaurant in your town. Go through the steps in the strategic planning process shown in Exhibit 5–7. Focus on conducting a situation audit of the local restaurant market, identifying and evaluating alternatives, and selecting a target market and a retail mix for the restaurant.

8. The Gap owns several chains, Old Navy and Banana Republic. What type of growth opportunity was The Gap pursuing when it opened each of these retail concepts? Which is most synergistic with the original Gap chain?

9. Identify a store or service provider that you believe has an effective loyalty program. Explain why it is effective.

10. Choose a retailer that you believe could be, but is not yet, successful in other countries. Explain why you think it could be successful.

11. Amazon.com started as an Internet retailer selling books. Then it pursued a variety of growth opportunities including expanding to groceries, DVDs, apparel, software, and travel services; introducing e-readers (Kindle); operating the Internet channel for other retailers; and hosting virtual stores for small, independent retailers. Evaluate these growth opportunities in terms of the probability that they will be profitable businesses for Amazon.com. What competitive advantages does Amazon.com bring to each of these businesses?

SUGGESTED READINGS

Aaker, David. *Strategic Market Management*, 6th ed. New York: Wiley, 2009.

Batra, Mansi, and Linda Niehm. "Social and Cultural Considerations for International Retail Firms: An Opportunity Analysis Framework for Apparel Retailing in India." *Clothing and Textiles Research Journal* 27 (2009), pp. 287–303.

Brennan, David P., and Lorman L. Lundsten. "An Assessment of Walmart's Global Expansion Strategy in Light of Its Domestic Strategy." *European Retail Research* 23, no. 1 (2009), pp. 183–214.

Burt, Steve, Keri Davies, John Dawson, and Leigh Sparks. "Categorizing Patterns and Processes in Retail Grocery Internationalization." *Journal of Retailing and Consumer Services* 15 (March 2008), pp. 78–92.

Cao, Lanlan, and Marc Dupuis. "Strategy and Sustainable Competitive Advantage of International Retailers in China." *Journal of Asia-Pacific Business* 11, no. 1 (2010), pp. 6–27.

Etgar, Michael, and Dalia Rachman-Moore. "Determinant Factors of Failures in Foreign Markets." *International Review of Retail, Distribution and Consumer Research* 17, no. 1 (2007), pp. 79–100.

Fox, Edward J., and Raj Sethuraman. "Retail Competition," in *Retailing in the 21st Century—Current and Future Trends*, 2nd ed., eds. Manfred Kraft and Murali Mantrala. Berlin: Springer, 2010, pp. 239–256.

Gauri, Dinesh Kumar, Minakshi Trivedi, and Dhruv Grewal. "Understanding the Determinants of Retail Strategy: An Empirical Analysis." *Journal of Retailing* 84 (September 2008), pp. 256–267.

"Global Retail Outlook." *Retail Forward*, March 2009.

Grewal, Dhruv, Ram Krishnan, Michael Levy, and Jeanne Mungar. "Retail Success and Key Drivers," in *Retailing in the 21st Century—Current and Future Trends*, 2nd ed., eds. Manfred Kraft and Murali Mantrala. Berlin: Springer, 2010, pp. 15–30.

Lehmann, Donald, and Russell Winer. *Analysis for Marketing Planning*, 7th ed. Burr Ridge, IL: McGraw-Hill/Irwin, 2007.

Financial Strategy

EXECUTIVE BRIEFING

Lary Sinewitz, Executive Vice-President,
BrandsMart USA

BrandsMart is the No. 1 retailer in South Florida and Atlanta of consumer appliances, electronics, and housewares. Our mission is to deliver the best name-brand products to our customers at the lowest prices possible. Each of our stores has thousands of products in stock including televisions, all types of appliances, audio, video, home theater, large flat screen TVs, car stereos, small appliances, computers, cellular and satellite phones, entertainment furniture, and thousands of accessories. This means our customers can take most products with them or choose to let our professional delivery and installation department deliver the products to their homes.

We can offer the lowest prices in our markets because of our buying power with vendors; our scale with over $125 million sales in each location; and our low margins. But to provide a good return for our investors, we need to couple the low margins with high inventory turnover. Our goal is to have 10 to 12 inventory turns a year. Most people think that the key to financial performance is profit margin, but with us it's inventory turnover.

We don't want any merchandise in our stores for over 60 days. So when our buyers have dated merchandise—merchandise that has been in the stores over 60 days—they need to explore ways of getting rid of the merchandise without impacting profits. They often negotiate to get the vendor to take back the slow selling merchandise in exchange for merchandise that is more appealing to our customers. Vendors may also elect to have us reduce the price of the slow moving inventory and then compensate us for the loss margin.

In addition to exploring approaches for increasing inventory turnover, we are very aggressive at keeping our overhead costs lost. Several times a year we take a close look at our SG&A expenses to see if there are ways we can reduce labor, energy, and advertising costs and still attract customers to our stores and provide a rewarding shopping experience for them. Our salespeople are commissioned so that labor costs only increase if sales go up. We leverage our advertising budget with contributions from our vendors through their co-op advertising programs. However, some vendors require us to advertise their products at the manufacturer suggested retail price even though we might

CHAPTER 6

QUESTIONS

How is a retail strategy reflected in a retailer's financial objectives?

What are the two paths to improving financial performance?

What is the strategic profit model, and how is it used to evaluate performance and investment decisions?

What measures do retailers use to assess their performance?

be selling it at a lower price in our stores. So we tell our customers in our advertising and on our Web site that they may find even lower prices when they visit our stores.

The two keys to the success of our business are keeping a close watch on the financial drivers of our business model and developing a deep understanding of the financial implications of decisions we make from buying office supplies to choosing the merchandise we sell to customers.

Financial objectives and goals are an integral part of a retailer's market strategy. In Chapter 5, we examined how retailers develop their strategy and build a sustainable competitive advantage to generate a continuing stream of profits. In this chapter, we look at how financial analysis is used to assess the retailer's market strategy—to monitor the retailer's performance, assess the reasons its performance is above or below expectations, and provide insights into appropriate actions that can be taken if performance falls short of expectations.

For example, Kelly Bradford, the owner of Gifts To Go, whom we described in Chapter 5, needs to know how well she is doing because she wants to stay in business, be successful, increase the profitability of her company, and realize her goal of generating an annual income over $100,000. To assess her performance, she can add up the receipts at the end of each day. But this simple measure, sales, doesn't provide a complete assessment of how she is doing financially, and it may even be misleading. For instance, she might find that sales meet expectations and her accountant tells her business is profitable, but she doesn't have the cash to buy new merchandise or pay her employees. When this happens, Kelly needs to analyze her business to determine the cause of the problem and what can be done to overcome it.

In this chapter, we first review the types of objectives that retailers have. Then we introduce the strategic profit model and use it to analyze the factors affecting the financial performance of a firm and approaches for improving performance. To illustrate the use of this model, we examine and compare the factors affecting the performance of Family Dollar Stores and Nordstrom, two successful retailers targeting customers at the opposite ends of the income distribution. Then we demonstrate how the model can be used to evaluate one of the growth opportunities Kelly Bradford is considering. In the last part of this chapter, we examine productivity measures that assess the performance of retailing activities, merchandise management, and store operations.

OBJECTIVES AND GOALS

As we discussed in Chapter 5, the first step in the strategic planning process involves articulating the retailer's objectives and the scope of activities it plans to undertake. These objectives guide the development of the retailer's strategy and the specific performance goals that determine whether the retailer's objectives are being achieved.[1] When the goals are not being achieved, the retailer knows that it must take corrective actions. Three types of objectives that a retailer might have are (1) financial, (2) societal, and (3) personal.

Financial Objectives

When assessing the financial performance of a firm, most people focus on profits: What were the retailer's profits or profit as a percentage of sales last year, and what will they be this year and into the future? But the appropriate financial performance measure is not profits but return on assets. **Return on assets (ROA)** is the profit generated by the assets possessed by the firm. Kelly Bradford set a financial objective of making a profit of at least $100,000 a year, but she really needs to consider the assets she needs to employ to make the desired $100,000. Kelly Bradford would be delighted if she made $100,000 and only needed $500,000 in assets (a 20 percent ROA) but would be disappointed if she had to use $4,000,000 in assets to make $100,000 profit (a 2.5 percent ROA).

Societal Objectives

Societal objectives are related to broader issues that provide benefits to society—that is, making the world a better place to live. For example, retailers might be concerned about providing employment opportunities for people in a particular area or for minorities or people with disabilities. Other societal objectives might

---

6.1   RETAILING VIEW   Teeing Up Kids

Meri Zeiff, a first grade teacher in California, launched an entrepreneurial retail venture because she was upset that her students were coming to school in T-shirts with negative messages on them. She saw kids wearing T-shirts with slogans like "Spoiled Brat" or "I'm with Stupid" and thought they were not "how happy kids think. That's how a jaded adult tells a kid to think." Her research supported her contention. Kids preferred T-shirts with "First grade rocks!" "Go green!" and "I love Mommy!" She created a business, Verymeri. In her retail business, children under 18 submit designs for T-shirts, and customers vote on their favorites. The winners are added to her product line and receive 3 percent of the profits from their designs.

But Zeiff wanted to do more than just create a happy T-shirt retail outlet. From the beginning, her company has had a charitable component. It donates part of its profits to a program called Free Arts for Abused Children. As the company grew, she decided to let the children support the charities of their choice. Winning designers choose their favorite charity, and another 3 percent of the profits from the sales of the $24 shirts are donated to that organization. Zeiff estimates that about $50,000 has been donated to various charities. She says this component of her business allows children to voice their concerns and act on the issues that matter to them in the world. As a first-grade teacher, she says, "I always stressed to my kids the idea of giving, the idea of sharing, the idea of

One of Meri Zeiff's objectives when she started her retail business was to make kids happy.

always being kind. . . . That's how I ran my classroom. It's how I run my business."

Sources: www.verymeri.com; Gwen Moran, "Teed Up," *Entrepreneur Magazine*, April 2010.

include offering people unique merchandise, such as environmentally friendly products; providing an innovative service to improve personal health, such as weight reduction programs; or sponsoring community events. Retailing View 6.1 describes a retail entrepreneur offering a happy message for children.

Compared to financial objectives, societal performance objectives are more difficult to measure. But explicit societal goals can be set, such as specific reductions in energy usage and excess packaging, increased use of renewable resources, and support for nonprofit organizations such as United Way and Habitat for Humanity.

Personal Objectives

Many retailers, particularly owners of small, independent businesses, have important personal objectives, including self-gratification, status, and respect. For example, the owner/operator of a bookstore may find it rewarding to interact with others who like reading and authors who visit the store for book-signing promotions. By operating a popular store, a retailer might become recognized as a well-respected business leader in the community.

While societal and personal objectives are important to some retailers, all retailers need to be concerned about financial objectives or they will fail. Therefore, the remaining sections of this chapter focus on financial objectives and the factors affecting a retailer's ability to achieve financial goals.

REFACT

In 1946, George Nelson Dayton, the son of Target Corporation's founder, established a standard of contributing 5 percent of the corporation's income to programs that serve the communities in which it has stores.[2]

STRATEGIC PROFIT MODEL

The **strategic profit model,** illustrated in Exhibit 6–1, is a method for summarizing the factors that affect a firm's financial performance, as measured by return on assets. Return on assets is an important performance measure for a firm and its stockholders because it measures the profits that a firm makes relative to the assets it possesses. Two retailers that each generate profits of $1 million, at first glance, might look like they have comparable performance. But the performance of the retailers looks quite different if one has $10 million in assets and the other has $25 million. The performance of the first would be higher because it needs fewer assets to earn its profit than does the other. Thus, a retailer cannot only concern itself with making a profit. It must make a profit efficiently by balancing both profit and assets needed to make the profit.

The **operating profit margin,** also called **earnings before interest and taxes (EBIT),** is a measure of the profitability from continuing operations of a retailer and is a useful predictor of the retailer's profitability in the future. **Asset turnover** is the retailer's net sales divided by its assets. This financial measure assesses the

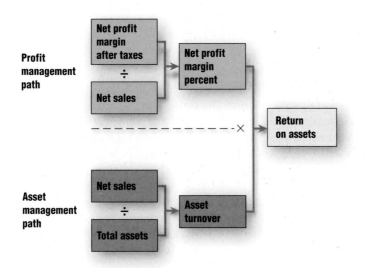

EXHIBIT 6–1

Components in the Strategic Profit Model

	Net Profit Margin	×	Asset Turnover	=	Return on Assets
La Chatelaine Bakery	1%		10 times		10%
Lehring Jewelry	10%		1 time		10%

productivity of a firm's investment in its assets and indicates how many dollars are generated for each dollar of assets—the firm's sales with regard to the assets needed to generate the sales. Thus, if a retailer's asset turnover is 3.0, it generates $3 in sales for each dollar invested in the firm's assets.

The retailer's ROA is determined by multiplying the two components together:

$$\text{Net profit margin} \times \text{Asset turnover} = \text{Return on assets (ROA)}$$

$$\frac{\text{Net profit}}{\text{Net sales}} \times \frac{\text{Net sales}}{\text{Total assets}} = \frac{\text{Net profit}}{\text{Total assets}}$$

The strategic profit model decomposes ROA into two components: (1) operating profit margin percentage and (2) asset turnover. These two components illustrate that ROA is determined by two sets of activities—profit margin management and asset turnover management—and that a high ROA can be achieved by various combinations of operating profit margins and asset turnover levels.

To illustrate the different approaches for achieving a high ROA, consider the financial performance of two very different hypothetical retailers, as shown in Exhibit 6–2. La Chatelaine Bakery has a net operating profit margin of only 1 percent and an asset turnover of 10, resulting in an ROA of 10 percent. Its operating profit margin percentage is low because it is in a highly competitive market with little opportunity to differentiate its offering. Consumers can buy basically the same baked goods from a wide variety of retailers, as well as from the other bakeries in the area. However, its asset turnover is relatively high because the firm has a very low level of inventory assets—it sells everything the same day it is baked.

On the other hand, Lehring Jewelry Store has a net operating profit margin of 10 percent—10 times higher than that of the bakery. Even though it has a much higher operating profit margin percentage, the jewelry store has the same ROA because it has a very low asset turnover of 1. Lehring's asset turnover is low compared with the bakery's because Lehring has a high level of inventory and stocks a lot of items that take many months to sell.

In the next sections, we take a closer look at these two components of ROA. We examine the relationship between these ratios and a firm's retail strategy and describe how these financial measures can be used to assess performance with traditional accounting information. To illustrate the financial implications of different retail strategies, we compare the financial performance of Family Dollar and Nordstrom. The retail strategies of these two retailers is reviewed in Retailing View 6.2.

Profit Margin Management Path

The information used to examine the profit margin management path comes from the retailer's income statement, also called the *statement of operations*. The income statement summarizes a firm's financial performance over a period of time, typically a quarter or year. To capture all the sales, gift card purchases, and returns from the holiday season, many retailers set their fiscal year as beginning on February 1 and ending on January 31 of the following year.

Exhibit 6–3 shows income statements adapted from the annual reports of Family Dollar Stores and Nordstrom. The components in the profit margin management path portion of the strategic profit model are summarized for both retailers in Exhibit 6–4.

RETAILING VIEW   Family Dollar and Nordstrom—Retailers Targeting
Customers at the Opposite Ends of the Income Distribution

Family Dollar (left) and Nordstrom (right) have radically different retail strategies and financial performance ratios. Family Dollar emphasizes the asset management performance path, while Nordstrom emphasizes the margin management path.

Family Dollar Stores and Nordstrom both have a high ROA but they achieve this high level of financial performance with significantly different retail strategies. Family Dollar is an extreme-value, general merchandise retail chain with over 6,700 stores in 44 states. It is one of the fastest-growing retail chains in the United States. The firm continues to pursue its original vision of operating relatively small (7,500- to 9,000-square-foot), self-service stores located in neighborhoods convenient to low- and middle-income consumers. Its merchandise assortment features basic goods for family and home needs. Its no-frills, low-overhead, limited-assortment, and cash-and-carry offering provides its customers with good value at very low prices. Its merchandise is sold at everyday low prices, with most items priced under $10.

REFACT

The first Family Dollar store was opened in Charlotte, North Carolina, in 1959 by a 21-year-old entrepreneur, Leonard Levine.[3]

In 2005, Family Dollar started to add more refrigerated and frozen-food options and other perishables to its food assortment of snacks and beverages. It now offers meal solution alternatives for its busy, cost-conscious shoppers. While initially its stores accepted only cash, it now accepts credit cards, as well as benefits from federal and state food-stamp programs.

The three pillars of Family Dollar's efforts to maintain its high sales growth rate are (1) open more stores in urban markets; (2) expand its assortment in food categories, including more fresh products and meal solutions; and (3) put more emphasis on the apparel category. Expansion into urban markets is attractive because of the limited competition. Perishables and apparel are attractive because of their higher margins.

Nordstrom, Inc., is an upscale department store chain in the United States. It operates over 115 department stores and

70 Nordstrom Rack clearance stores in 28 states. John W. Nordstrom opened the first Nordstrom store in 1887 in Seattle, which continues to be Nordstrom's headquarters and the site of its flagship store. While the initial store was a shoe retailer, today the stores also sell clothing, accessories, handbags, jewelry, cosmetics, fragrances, and, in some locations, home furnishings. However, Nordstrom continues to carry an extraordinarily deep and broad assortment of shoes, about 15,000 SKUs in a typical department store.

Nordstrom is known for its outstanding customer service. Its customer-centric organizational culture is epitomized by its "handbook" that is given to new employees. The original handbook was a single 5- by 8-inch gray card containing 75 words:

Welcome to Nordstrom

We're glad to have you with our Company. Our number one goal is to provide outstanding customer service. Set both your personal and professional goals high. We have great confidence in your ability to achieve them.

Nordstrom Rules: Rule #1: Use good judgment in all situations. There will be no additional rules.

Please feel free to ask your department manager, store manager, or division general manager any question at any time.

Now, in addition to this card, a full handbook of other more specific rules and legal regulations is given to new employees.

Sources: www.familydollar.com (accessed April 15, 2010); www.neimanmarcus.com (accessed April 15, 2010); Susan Reda, "Quick-Trip Strategy, Long-Term Plan," *Stores*, July 2008, p. 26; Deena M. Amato-McCoy, "A Dollar for Their Innovative Thoughts," *Chain Store Age*, January 2008, p. 29; www.nordstrom.com (accessed April 1, 2010); Robert Spector and Patrick McCarthy, *The Nordstrom Way to Customer Service Excellence* (Hoboken, NJ: Wiley, 2005).

EXHIBIT 6–3

Fiscal Annual Income Statement for Family Dollar and Nordstrom ($ millions)

	Family Dollar 8/29/2009	Nordstrom 1/30/2010
Net sales	$7,401	$8,276
COGS	4,822	5,328
Gross margin	2,579	2,948
SG&A	2,121	2,109*
Operating profit margin	458	839
Interest	63	138
Taxes	160	255
Net profit	235	446
Gross margin (%)	34.8	35.6
SG&A as % of sales	28.7	25.5
Operating profit margin (%)	6.2	10.1
Profit margin (%)	3.2	5.4

*Includes buying and occupancy costs.

SOURCES: Family Dollar Stores 10-K report submitted to SEC October 27, 2009; Nordstrom 10-K report submitted to SEC March 20, 2010.

Components in the Profit Management Path   The four components in the profit margin management path are net sales, cost of goods sold (COGS), gross margin, and operating profit margin. **Net sales** are the total revenues received by a retailer that are related to selling merchandise during a given time period. The sources of revenue are sales to customers minus the credit and cash refunds customers received for returned merchandise.

Sources of revenue that are not considered part of net sales are special charges to customers and credit card interest. For example, warehouse clubs generate revenue from annual membership fees, and retailers with frequent shopper programs may charge customers for enrolling in the program. Nordstrom has its own credit card on which it receives revenues from late payments. We do not consider these

EXHIBIT 6–4

Profit Management Path for Family Dollar Stores and Nordstrom

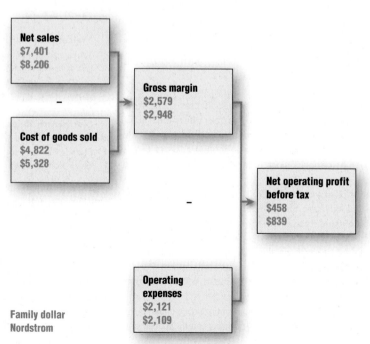

SOURCES: Family Dollar Stores 10-K report submitted to SEC October 27, 2009; Nordstrom 10-K report submitted to SEC March 20, 2010.

other sources of revenue as part of net sales because they reflect business activities unrelated to the merchandise sold.

Some retailers have additional revenue sources related to merchandise sales, such as payments from vendors. For example, supermarket retailers often charge consumer packaged goods manufacturers a fee to stock a new product. Retailers may also require that vendors pay a penalty when the merchandise bought from the vendor does not meet all the terms of the purchase agreement, such as those regarding delivery. Such payments from vendors are typically incorporated into the income statement as a reduction in the COGS.

Cost of goods sold (COGS) is the amount a retailer pays to vendors for the merchandise the retailer sells. **Gross margin,** also called **gross profit,** is the net sales minus the cost of the goods sold. It is an important measure in retailing because it indicates how much profit the retailer is making on merchandise sold, without considering the expenses associated with operating the store and corporate overhead expenses.

$$\text{Gross margin} = \text{Net sales} - \text{Cost of goods sold}$$

Operating expenses include **selling, general, and administrative (SG&A) expenses** plus the depreciation of the retailer's assets. The SG&A includes overhead costs associated with normal business operations, such as salaries for sales associates and managers, advertising, utilities, office supplies, transportation from the retailer's warehouses to its stores, and rent.

Some retailers will include other expenses, such as the cost of opening or closing stores and/or the cost of integrating an acquisition in their operations, in addition to depreciation and SG&A as operating expenses. When estimating a retailer's operating expenses, one needs to decide whether these other expenses are related to the normal operations of the retailer or are **extraordinary nonrecurring expenses** that arise only during the year in which they are incurred. For example, the expenses for store openings might occur each year as a growing retailer opens new stores, while expenses related to an acquisition probably occur only in the specific year of the acquisition and may not reflect the operating income the retailer will realize in the future.

Operating profit margin, also called *earnings before interest and taxes (EBIT),* is the gross margin minus operating and extraordinary recurring expenses. Finally, **net profit margin** is the operating profit minus interest and taxes. We focus on the operating profit margin because it reflects the performance of retailers' fundamental operations, not the financial decisions retailers make concerning taxes and capital structure (borrowing money versus selling stock).

$$\text{Operating profit margin} = \text{Gross margin} - \text{Operating expenses} - \text{Extraordinary (recurring) operating expenses}$$

$$\text{Net profit margin} = \text{Operating profit margin} - \text{Taxes} - \text{Interest} - \text{Extraordinary nonrecurring expenses}$$

Analyzing Performance on the Profit Margin Management Path   The level of sales, gross margin, and operating profit in Exhibit 6–4 provide some useful information about the financial performance of the two retailers. However, it is difficult to compare the performance of the retailers when they differ in size. If Family Dollar was interested in comparing its performance with Walmart, it would expect that Walmart would have a much greater gross margin and operating profit because it has 50 times greater sales than Family Dollar. Thus, some of the differences in the income statement numbers will be due to differences in size, not in the performance of the retailers. It is useful to consider ratios with net sales in the denominator when evaluating a retailer's performance and comparing it to other retailers. Three useful ratios in the profit management path are gross margin percentage, operating profit margin percentage, and SG&A as a percentage of sales.

As she expects, Gifts-To-Go.com's projected asset turnover is higher than that of Gifts To Go's stores, because Kelly estimates that Gifts-To-Go.com will have a higher inventory turnover, and its other assets are lower.

$$\frac{\text{Net sales}}{\text{Total assets}} = \text{Asset turnover}$$

Stores: $\quad \dfrac{700,000}{\$380,000} = 1.84$

Gifts-To-Go.com: $\quad \dfrac{440,000}{\$211,000} = 2.09$

Because Kelly's estimates for the net profit margin and asset turnover for Gifts-To-Go.com are higher than those for her stores, Gifts-To-Go.com achieves a higher ROA. Thus, this strategic profit model analysis indicates that Gifts-To-Go.com is a financially viable growth opportunity for Kelly.

	Net profit margin	×	Asset turnover	=	Return on assets
Stores:	8.54%	×	1.84	=	15.7%
Gifts-To-Go.com:	10.3%	×	2.09	=	21.5%

Using the Strategic Profit Model to Analyze Other Decisions   Kelly might consider an investment in a computerized inventory control system that would help her make better decisions about which merchandise to order, when to reorder merchandise, and when to lower prices on merchandise that is not being bought.

If she buys the system, her sales will increase because she will have a greater percentage of merchandise that is selling well and fewer stockouts. Her gross margin percentage will also increase because she won't have to mark down as much slow-selling merchandise.

Looking at the asset turnover management path, the purchase of the computer system will increase her fixed assets by the amount of the system, but her inventory turnover will increase and the level of inventory assets will decrease, because she is able to buy more efficiently. Thus, her asset turnover will probably increase, because sales will increase at a greater percentage than will total assets. Total assets may actually decrease if the additional cost of the inventory system is less than the reduction in inventory.

ANALYSIS OF FINANCIAL STRENGTH

The previous sections have illustrated how the strategic profit model can be used to analyze the factors affecting some key retail performance ratios—operating profit margin percentage and asset turnover. The model provides insights into how retailers can improve their performance. However, retailing is a highly competitive industry, and thus major bankruptcies are common. Exhibit 6–10 lists some retailers of significant size that have filed for bankruptcy protection since 2008. Retailers, vendors, and investors need to assess the financial strength of a firm. Specifically, what are the chances that the retailer will continue to operate or will go bankrupt? In this section we discuss measures used to assess the financial strength of retailers—the probability that they will go bankrupt. These measures include cash flow, debt-to-equity ratio, quick ratio, and current ratio.

Cash-Flow Analysis

You might think that a retailer's profits determine its financial strength. If a retailer is profitable, there is little chance it will go bankrupt; but if it incurs losses for an extended period of time, the chances of its going bankrupt are significant. However, retailers can be forced to declare bankruptcy even when they show a profit on their income statements. Retailers become insolvent and declare bankruptcy when they do not have the cash needed to meet their obligations—when they cannot pay their employees, their landlords (rent), and/or their vendors.

Basha's	Goody's
Bi-Lo	K-B Toys
Boscov's	Linens 'n Things
Bruno's	Mervyns
Circuit City	Mrs. Fields Famous Brands
Crabtree & Evelyn	Ritz Camera
Eddie Bauer	Sharper Image
Filene's Basement	S&K Warehouse
Golfer's Warehouse	Steve & Berry's
Gottschalks	

EXHIBIT 6–10
Major Retail Bankruptcies since 2008

Profits are not the same as cash flow. For example, a retailer might borrow money from a bank. The loan appears as a liability on its balance sheet. The interest on the loan, a relatively small percentage of the loan value, appears as an interest expense on the retailer's income statement and reduces the retailer's profits slightly. However, when the retailer is required to pay back the loan to the bank, the retailer must have a significant amount of cash available to pay for the entire amount of the loan.

Retailers have cash coming in from the sales of merchandise, and they use this cash to pay vendors, employees, developers, utilities, and the like. The amount of cash coming into the business, and when it comes into the business, is crucial because the availability of cash allows retailers to continue operating in the longer term.

The cash receipts and expenditures tend to be fairly stable. Employee salaries, vendor invoices, and rent, for example, are paid monthly or weekly. Sometimes, however, retailers face radical changes in the flow of cash. During the holiday season, for instance, retailers have to buy and pay for more merchandise to support the higher-than-normal level of sales.

One measure of financial strength is cash flow. In addition to providing a balance sheet and income statement, firms also provide a cash-flow statement as another indicator of the financial strength of the firm. Cash flow is calculated by making certain adjustments to net profit. These adjustments involve adding or subtracting differences in revenue and expenses that occur from one period to the next. For example, if inventories increase from one time period to another, cash flow decreases because cash was spent to buy more inventory. If SG&A decreases, cash flow decreases—less cash was required to pay for the overhead expenses. In addition, some income statement entries that affect net profits, such as depreciation, do not involve cash. Depreciation is not really a cash expense; it is an amount that is deducted from the total value of an asset that was previously paid for.

Debt-Equity Ratio

The **debt-to-equity ratio** is the retailer's short- and long-term debt divided by the value of the owners' or stockholders' equity in the firm. Owners' equity is the difference after subtracting all liabilities from assets. It is the owners' (or stockholders') investment in the business. The debt-to-equity ratio measures how much money a company can safely borrow over long periods of time. A high ratio means the retailer faces greater risk and more potential for bankruptcy. Generally, when retailers that have a debt-to-equity ratio of over 40 to 50 percent, they face significant risk of financial problems.

Current Ratio

The **current ratio** is probably the best-known and most often used measure of financial strength. The current ratio is short-term assets divided by short-term liabilities. It evaluates the retailer's ability to pay its short-term debt obligations, such as accounts payable (payments to suppliers) and short-term loans payable to a bank, with short-term assets such as cash, accounts receivable, and inventory.

EXHIBIT 6–11
Financial Strength
Measures for Family
Dollar and Nordstrom

	Family Dollar 8/29/2009	Nordstrom 1/30/2010	Average for General Merchandise Retailers*
Net profit margin (%)	16.1	12.8	5.4
Cash flow ($ millions)	530	1,251	—
Debt to equity	1.04	5.99	1.39
Current ratio	1.51	2.01	1.06
Quick ratio	0.25	0.60	0.24

SOURCE: Calculations from financial statements in 10-K reports filed with SEC.

Quick Ratio

The **quick ratio,** sometimes called the **acid-test ratio,** is a more stringent test of financial strength than the current ratio because it removes inventory from the short-term assets. Inventory is the short-term asset that takes the longest to convert into cash. Thus, if a retailer needs cash to pay its short-term liabilities, it cannot rely on inventory to provide an immediate source for cash.

The financial strength measures for Family Dollar and Nordstrom are shown in Exhibit 6–11. These measures of financial strength indicate that Family Dollar and Nordstrom are in relatively strong financial positions. Both have a significant positive cash flow. Nordstrom has a high debt-to-equity ratio but strong current and quick ratios.

While ROA and its components and assessments of cash flow are important indicators of a retailer's performance, Retailing View 6.4 discusses some other considerations that private equity firms consider when making investments in retailers.

6.4   RETAILING VIEW   Private Equity Firms Invest in Retailers

Private equity firms have been making significant investments in retail firms. For example, Blackstone Group and Bain Capital teamed up to buy the craft store chain Michaels for $6 billion, and KKR and several other firms bought Toys "R" Us for $6.6 billion; Texas Pacific, with its partners, bought Neiman Marcus for $5.1 billion, and Leonard Green & Partner bought The Container Store.

Private equity firms are firms that invest their money and the money of others, such as union pension funds and university endowments. Rather than buying stock in companies, private equity investors buy the entire company from its stockholders, improve the efficiency of the firm (often by hiring new senior managers), and then sell the acquired company several years later. Because shares for the acquired company after the acquisition are not traded on the stock exchange, the company can take a long-term perspective toward improving the firm's operations since it does not have to issue the quarterly reports required by the Securities and Exchange Commission (SEC). The managers of the acquired firms thus can reengineer a business to move away from Wall Street's ceaseless scrutiny of monthly comparable store sales and quarterly growth in earnings.

Private equity firms find retailers attractive investments because many of them have strong cash flows and undervalued assets and respond quickly to efficiency improvements and changes in strategic direction. Whereas the typical small investor focuses on profits and return on assets, private equity firms are interested in cash flow—the money that the retailer generates from its operations. A company with a higher cash flow

reduces the risk of bankruptcy and provides money to invest in improving efficiencies, such as installing information systems or remodeling stores.

Retailers frequently have undervalued assets, such as well-known private-label brands, leases for space in attractive locations, or the land on which their stores are located. A private equity company can sell these assets after it acquires a retailer or use the assets as collateral to get loans. For example, a private equity firm might sell the rights to use a well-known private-label brand to a company that would license the brand to other firms. Thus, the whole of the retailer is often less than the sum of its parts.

The recession and the accompanying credit crisis have dampened private equity firms' interest in retail acquisitions. The decline in consumer spending has made it difficult to make money on core operating businesses. In the past, many of these acquisitions were financed with short-term acquisition loans, which were meant to be eventually replaced with permanent financing. But private equity firms have had trouble getting permanent loans since late 2007. Finally, the dramatic drop in real estate values and increasing vacancies in the retail sector have taken away the safety net created by the undervalued real estate.

Sources: Elaine Misonzhnik, "Private Equity Racks Up Checkered Record in Retail Buyouts," *Retail Traffic,* June 29, 2009; Marcus Leroux, "Private Equity Shrugs Off Its Image as a Big Bad Wolf Stalking the High Street," *The Times,* November 2, 2009; Dan Freed, "Stocking Up: Why Buyout Firms Love Retail," *Investment Dealers' Digest,* July 23, 2007, pp. 16–20.

SETTING AND MEASURING PERFORMANCE OBJECTIVES

In the previous sections, we have discussed the measures used to evaluate the overall financial performance of a retailer—ROA and its components. In this section we review some measures used to assess the performance of specific assets possessed by a retailer—its employees, real estate, and merchandise inventory. Retailers use these measures to evaluate the firm's performance and set objectives.

Setting performance objectives is a necessary component of any firm's strategic management process. Performance objectives should include (1) a numerical index of the performance desired against which progress may be measured, (2) a time frame within which the objective is to be achieved, and (3) the resources needed to achieve the objective. For example, "earning reasonable profits" isn't a good objective. It doesn't provide specific goals that can be used to evaluate performance. What's reasonable? When do you want to realize the profits? A better objective would be "earning $100,000 in profit during calendar year 2010 on a $500,000 investment in inventory and building."

Top-Down versus Bottom-Up Process

Setting objectives in large retail organizations entails a combination of the top-down and bottom-up approaches to planning.

Top-down planning means that goals get set at the top of the organization and passed down to the lower operating levels. In a retailing organization, top-down planning involves corporate officers developing an overall retail strategy and assessing broad economic, competitive, and consumer trends. With this information, they develop performance objectives for the corporation. These overall objectives are then broken down into specific objectives for each buyer and merchandise category and for each region, store, and even department within stores and the sales associates working in those departments.

The overall strategy determines the merchandise variety, assortment, and product availability, plus the store size, location, and level of customer service. Then the merchandise vice presidents decide which types of merchandise are expected to grow, stay the same, or shrink. Next, performance goals are established for each buyer and merchandise manager. This process is reviewed in Chapter 12.

Similarly, regional store vice presidents translate the company's performance objectives into objectives for each district manager, who then develops objectives with the store managers. The process then trickles down to department managers in the stores and individual sales associates. The process of setting objectives for sales associates in stores is discussed in Chapter 16.

This top-down planning is complemented by a bottom-up planning approach. **Bottom-up planning** involves lower levels in the company developing performance objectives that are aggregated up to develop overall company objectives. Buyers and store managers estimate what they can achieve, and their estimates are transmitted up the organization to the corporate executives.

Frequently there are disagreements between the goals that have trickled down from the top and those set by lower-level employees of the organization. For example, a store manager may not be able to achieve the 10 percent sales growth set for his or her region because a major employer in the area has announced plans to lay off 2,000 employees. The differences between bottom-up and top-down plans are resolved through a negotiation process involving corporate executives and operating managers. If the operating managers aren't involved in the objective-setting process, they won't accept the objectives and thus will be less motivated to achieve them.

Who Is Accountable for Performance?

At each level of the retail organization, the business unit and its manager should be held accountable only for the revenues, expenses, cash flow, and contribution to ROA that they can control. Thus, expenses that affect several levels of the organization (e.g., labor and capital expenses associated with operating a corporate headquarters) shouldn't be arbitrarily assigned to lower levels. In the case of a store, for example, it may be appropriate to set performance objectives based on sales, sales associate productivity, store inventory shrinkage due to employee theft and shoplifting, and energy costs. If the buyer lowers prices to get rid of merchandise and therefore profits suffer, it is not fair to assess a store manager's performance on the basis of the resulting decline in store profit.

Performance objectives and measures can be used to pinpoint problem areas. The reasons that performance may be above or below planned levels must be examined. Perhaps the managers involved in setting the objectives aren't very good at making estimates. If so, they may need to be trained in forecasting. Also, buyers may misrepresent their business unit's ability to contribute to the firm's financial goals to get a larger inventory budget than is warranted and consequently earn a higher bonus. In either case, investment funds would be misallocated.

Actual performance may differ from what the plan predicts due to circumstances beyond the manager's control. For example, there may have been a recession. Assuming the recession wasn't predicted, or was more severe or lasted longer than anticipated, there are several relevant questions: How quickly were plans adjusted? How rapidly and appropriately were pricing and promotional policies modified? In short, did the manager react to salvage an adverse situation, or did the reaction worsen the situation?

Performance Objectives and Measures

Many factors contribute to a retailer's overall performance, and this makes it hard to find a single measure to evaluate performance. For instance, sales are a global measure of a retail store's activity level. However, a store manager could easily increase sales by lowering prices, but the profit realized on that merchandise (gross margin) would suffer as a result. Clearly, an attempt to maximize one measure may lower another. Managers must therefore understand how their actions affect multiple performance measures. It's usually unwise to use only one measure, because it rarely tells the whole story.

The measures used to evaluate retail operations vary depending on (1) the level of the organization at which the decision is made and (2) the resources the manager controls. For example, the principal resources controlled by store managers are space and money for operating expenses (such as wages for sales associates and utility payments to light and heat the store). Thus, store managers focus on performance measures like sales per square foot and employee costs.

Types of Measures

Exhibit 6–12 breaks down a variety of retailers' performance measures into three types: input measures, output measures, and productivity measures. **Input measures** are the resources or money allocated by a retailer to achieve outputs, or results. For example, the amount and selection of merchandise inventory, the number of stores, the size of the stores, the employees, advertising, markdowns, store hours, and promotions all require managerial decisions to allocate resources.

Output measures assess the results of a retailer's investment decisions. For example, sales revenue, gross margin, and net profit margin are all output measures and ways to evaluate a retailer's input or resource allocation decisions. A **productivity measure** (the ratio of an output to an input) determines how effectively retailers use their resources—what return they get on their investments.

In general, because productivity measures are ratios of outputs to inputs, they are very useful for comparing the performance of different business units. Suppose Kelly Bradford's two stores are different sizes: One has 5,000 square feet, and the other has 10,000 square feet. It's hard to compare the stores' performances using just output or input measures, because the larger store will probably generate

Performance Objectives and Measures Used by Retailers   **EXHIBIT 6–12**

Level of Organization	Output	Input	Productivity (output/input)
Corporate (measures for entire corporation)	Net sales Net profits Growth in sales, profits, comparable store sales	Square feet of store space Number of employees Inventory Advertising expenditures	Return on assets Asset turnover Sales per employee Sales per square foot
Merchandise management (measures for a merchandise category)	Net sales Gross margin Growth in sales	Inventory level Markdowns Advertising expenses Cost of merchandise	Gross margin return on investment (GMROI) Inventory turnover Advertising as a percentage of sales* Markdown as a percentage of sales*
Store operations (measures for a store or department within a store)	Net sales Gross margin Growth in sales	Square feet of selling areas Expenses for utilities Number of sales associates	Net sales per square foot Net sales per sales associate or per selling hour Utility expenses as a percentage of sales* Inventory shrinkage*

*These productivity measures are commonly expressed as an input-output ratio.

more sales and have higher expenses. But if the larger store has lower space productivity because it generates $210 net sales per square foot and the smaller store generates $350 per square foot, Kelly knows that the smaller store is operating more efficiently, even though it's generating lower sales.

Corporate Performance   At a corporate level, retail executives have three critical resources (inputs)—merchandise inventory, store space, and employees—that they can manage to generate sales and profits (outputs). Thus, effective productivity measures of the utilization of these assets include asset and inventory turnover, sales per square foot of selling space, and sales per employee.

As we have discussed, ROA is an overall productivity measure combining the profit margin percentage and asset turnover management. Another commonly used measure of overall performance is **comparable store sales growth** (also called **same-store sales growth**), which considers growth in stores that have been open for at least one year. Growth in sales can result from increasing the sales generated per store or the number of stores. Growth in same-store sales assesses the first component in sales growth and thus indicates how well the retailer is doing with its core business concept. New stores do not represent growth from last year's sales but, rather, new sales created where no other sales existed the year before. Thus, a decrease in same-store sales indicates that the retailer's fundamental business approach is not being well received by its customers, even if overall sales are growing because the retailer is opening more new stores.

Merchandise Management Measures   The critical resource (input) controlled by merchandise managers is merchandise inventory. Merchandise managers also have the authority to set initial prices and lower prices when merchandise is not selling (i.e., take a markdown). Finally, they negotiate with vendors over the price paid for merchandise.

Inventory turnover is a productivity measure of the management of inventory; higher turnover means greater inventory management productivity. Gross margin percentage indicates the performance of merchandise managers in negotiating with vendors and buying merchandise that can generate a profit. Discounts (markdowns) as a percentage of sales are also a measure of the quality of the merchandise buying decisions. If merchandise managers have a high percentage of markdowns, they may not be buying the right merchandise or the right quantities, because they weren't able to sell some of it at its original retail price. Note that gross margin and discount percentages are productivity measures, but they are typically expressed as an input divided by an output as opposed to the typical productivity measures that are outputs divided by inputs.

Store Operations Measures   The critical assets controlled by store managers are the use of the store space and the management of the store's employees. Thus, measures of store operations productivity include sales per square foot of selling space and sales per employee (or sales per employee per working hour, to take into account that some employees work part-time). Store management is also responsible for controlling theft by employees and customers (referred to as inventory shrinkage), store maintenance, and energy costs (lighting, heating, and air conditioning). Thus, some other productivity measures used to assess the performance of store managers are inventory shrinkage and energy costs as a percentage of sales.

Assessing Performance: The Role of Benchmarks

As we have discussed, the financial measures used to assess performance reflect the retailer's market strategy. For example, because Family Dollar has a different business strategy than Nordstrom, it has a lower profit margin. But it earns an acceptable ROA because it increases its inventory and asset turnovers by stocking a more limited merchandise assortment of less fashionable, staple items. In contrast, Nordstrom specializes in apparel and accessories, and this requires a broad and deep merchandise assortment. Thus, it has lower inventory and asset turnover but achieves an acceptable ROA through its higher profit margins. In other words, the performance of a retailer cannot be assessed accurately simply by looking at isolated measures, because they are affected by the retailer's strategy. To get a better assessment of a retailer's performance, we need to compare it to a benchmark. Two commonly used benchmarks are (1) the performance of the retailer over time and (2) the performance of the retailer compared with that of its competitors.

Performance over Time   One useful approach for assessing a retailer's performance compares its recent performance with its performance in the preceding months, quarters, or years. Exhibit 6–13 shows the performance measures for Family Dollar and Nordstrom over a three-year period.

Over the three years from 2007 to 2009, Family Dollar's sales have been increasing while Nordstrom's sales have decreased. Its gross margin has improved while Nordstrom's percentage has decreased. Almost all of Family Dollar's

EXHIBIT 6–13   Performance Measures for Family Dollar and Nordstrom

Fiscal Year:	FAMILY DOLLAR			NORDSTROM		
	2009	2008	2007	2009	2008	2007
Net sales ($ millions)	7,401	6,984	6,834	8,276	8,272	8,828
Gross margin (%)	34.8	33.6	34.0	35.6	34.5	37.4
SG&A as % of sales	28.7	28.4	28.3	25.5	25.4	24.0
Operating profit margin (%)	6.1	5.3	5.7	10.1	9.1	13.4
Asset turnover	2.60	2.62	2.6	1.26	2.62	2.6
Inventory turnover	4.85	4.49	4.23	5.93	6.02	5.78
ROA (%)	16.1	13.8	14.8	12.8	23.8	34.9
Sales per employee	200	202	198	172	162	161
Sales per square foot	157	152	152	368	388	435
Comparable store sales (%)	4.0	1.0	2.0	−7.2	−12.4	3.9
Sales per store ($ thousands)	1,120	1,063	1,061	45,000	48,950	56,980

SOURCE: Calculations from financial statements in 10-K reports filed with the SEC.

	Nordstrom	Macy's	Kohl's
Net sales ($ millions)	8,276	23,489	17,178
Gross margin (%)	35.6	40.5	37.8
SG&A as % of sales	25.5	34.3	24.1
Operating profit margin (%)	10.1	6.2	13.7
Asset turnover	1.26	1.10	1.31
Inventory turnover	5.93	3.03	3.66
ROA (%)	12.80	6.80	17.90
Sales per employee	172	146	129
Sales per square foot	368	152	217
Comparable store sales (%)	−7.2	−5.3	0.4
Sales per store ($ thousands)	44,978	27,732	16,236

EXHIBIT 6–14
Financial Performance of Nordstrom and Other National Department Store Chains (fiscal year 2009)

SOURCE: Calculations from financial statements in 10-K reports filed with the SEC.

productivity measures are either staying the same or improving. Specifically, comparable store sales, inventory turnover, and ROA are all improving. On the other hand, Nordstrom's productivity is degenerating. Gross margin percentage, ROA, and sales per square foot are all decreasing, while its SG&A percentage is increasing and comparable store sales are negative. Sales per employee is improving, but this might be because the number of employees is down, which could lead to a decrease in customer service and a long-term decrease in sales.

Note that Nordstrom's decline in performance relative to Family Dollar during this time period might be due primarily to the bad economy. Upscale department stores have been adversely affected by the economic recession, while extreme-value retailers have picked up new customers looking for good deals.

Performance Compared to Competitors   A second approach for assessing a retailer's performance involves comparing its performance with that of its competitors. Exhibit 6–14 compares the performance of Nordstrom with two other national department store chains, Macy's and Kohl's. Kohl's has considerably better comparable store sales. Macy's has a higher gross margin percentage than the other two department store chains, but this benefit is offset by Macy's higher SG&A expenses as a percentage of sales. Nordstrom, on the other hand, has greater labor and space productivity.

SUMMARY

This chapter explains some basic elements of the retailing financial strategy and examines how retailing strategy affects the financial performance of a firm. We use the strategic profit model as a vehicle for understanding the complex interrelations between financial ratios and retailing strategy. We also note that different types of retailers have different financial operating characteristics. Specifically, department store chains like Nordstrom generally have higher profit margins and lower turnover ratios than extreme-value retailers like Family Dollar. Yet when margin and turnover are combined into return on assets, it is possible to achieve similar financial performance.

In addition to assessing the performance of a retail operation, the chapter also examines measures used to assess the financial strength of a retailer—the probability of the business declaring bankruptcy. Four measures of financial strength are cash flow, debt-to-equity ratio, current ratio, and quick ratio.

We also describe some financial performance measures used to evaluate different aspects of a retailing organization. Although the return-on-assets ratio in the strategic profit model is appropriate for evaluating the performance of the retail executives responsible for managing the firm, other measures are more appropriate for more specific activities. For instance, inventory turnover and gross margin are appropriate for buyers, whereas store managers should be concerned with sales or gross margin per square foot or per employee.

KEY TERMS

accounts receivable, *150*

assets, *149*

asset turnover, *143*

bottom-up planning, *159*

comparable store sales
  growth, *161*

cost of goods sold (COGS), *147*

current assets, *149*

current ratio, *157*

debt-to-equity ratio, *157*

earnings before interest and taxes
  (EBIT), *143*

extraordinary nonrecurring
  expenses, *147*

fixed assets, *151*

gross margin, *147*

gross margin percentage, *148*

gross profit, *147*

in-house credit card, *150*

input measures, *160*

inventory turnover, *151*

liabilities, *150*

net profit margin, *147*

net sales, *146*

operating expenses, *147*

operating profit margin, *143*

output measures, *160*

productivity measures, *160*

proprietary store credit card, *150*

quick ratio, *129*

return on assets (ROA), *142*

same-store sales growth, *161*

selling, general, and administrative
  (SG&A) expenses, *147*

strategic profit model, *143*

top-down planning, *159*

GET OUT AND DO IT!

1. **CONTINUING CASE ASSIGNMENT** Evaluate the financial performance of the retailer you have selected for the Continuing Case Assignment and of another store that sells similar merchandise categories but to a very different target market. If yours is a high-margin–low-turnover store, compare it with a low-margin–high-turnover store. You can get this information from your chosen store's latest annual report, available in the "investor relations" area of its Web site, at Hoovers Online, or in the Edgar files at www.sec.gov. Explain, from a marketing perspective, why you would expect the return on assets, gross margin percentage, net profit margin percentage, inventory turnover, asset turnover, cash flow, debt-to-equity ratio, quick ratio, and current ratio to differ between the two stores. Which retailer achieves better overall financial performance?

2. **INTERNET EXERCISE** Go to the latest annual reports, and use the financial information to update the numbers in the net profit margin management model and the asset turnover management model for Family Dollar and Nordstrom. Have there been any significant

changes in their financial performance? Why are the key financial ratios for these two retailers so different?

3. **GO SHOPPING** Go to your favorite store, and interview the manager. Determine how the retailer sets its performance objectives. Evaluate its procedures relative to the procedures presented in the text.

4. **WEB OLC EXERCISE** Go to the strategic profit model (SPM) on the student side of the book's Web site. The SPM tutorial was designed to provide a refresher course on the basic financial ratios leading to return on assets and walks you through the process step-by-step. A calculation page is also included that will calculate all the ratios. You can type in the numbers from a firm's balance sheet and income statement to see the financial results produced with the current financial figures. You can also access an Excel spreadsheet for SPM calculations. The calculation page or the Excel spreadsheet can be used for Case 12, "Tiffany's and Blue Nile: Comparing Financial Performance," page 552.

DISCUSSION QUESTIONS AND PROBLEMS

1. Why does a retailer need to use multiple performance measures to thoroughly evaluate its performance?

2. Describe how a multiple-store retailer might set its annual performance objectives.

3. Buyers' performance is often measured by the gross margin percentage. Why is this measure more appropriate than net profit percentage?

4. How does the strategic profit model assist retailers in planning and evaluating the performance of their marketing and financial strategies?

5. Neiman Marcus (a chain of high-service department stores) and Walmart target different customer segments. Which retailer would you expect to have a higher gross margin? Higher expense-to-sales ratio?

Higher inventory turnover? Higher asset turnover? Higher net profit margin percentage? Why?

6. What elements in the strategic model are affected if a retailer decides to build and open 10 new stores?

7. What differences would you expect to see when comparing Gifts To Go's specialty store strategic profit model with that of two dry-cleaning service businesses?

8. Using the following information from Lowe's 2010 income statement and balance sheet, taken from Hoovers, determine its asset turnover, net profit margin percentage, and ROA. (Figures are in millions of dollars.)

Net sales	$47,220
Total assets	$33,005
Net profit	$ 1,783

9. Using the following information taken from the 2010 balance sheet and income statement for Urban Outfitters, develop a strategic profit model. (Figures are in millions of dollars.) You can access an Excel spread-sheet for SPM calculations on the student side of the book's Web site.

Net sales	$1,937.8
Cost of goods sold	$1,151.7
Operating expenses	$ 447.2
Inventory	$ 186.1
Accounts receivable	$ 78.0
Other current assets	$ 422.7
Fixed assets	$ 540.0

10. Examine Walgreens', CVS Caremark's, and Rite Aid's 2009 financial performance in the table below. Evaluate Walgreens' performance against direct external competition using the financial data and ratios. Is Walgreens' performance the same as, better than, or worse than that of CVS and Rite Aid? Why is this the case? If your university library has access to hoovers.com (or a similar database), look up these financial ratios for the current year. Has the financial performance improved or worsened for these three retailers?

Key Numbers	Walgreen	CVS Caremark	Rite Aid
Annual sales ($ millions)	63,335.0	98,729.0	25,669.1
Employees	238,000	295,000	97,500
Gross profit margin (%)	27.95	20.64	26.58
Pretax profit margin (%)	5.12	5.99	(1.87)
Net profit margin (%)	3.24	3.74	(2.01)
Return on assets (%)	8.30	6.00	(6.30)
Inventory turnover	6.4	8.0	5.6
Asset turnover	2.6	1.6	3.1

Source: http://premium.hoovers.com > Walgreen Co. > Competitive Landscape.

SUGGESTED READINGS

Anderson, Torben Juul, and Peter Winther Schrøder. *Strategic Risk Management Practice: How to Deal Effectively with Major Corporate Exposures*. Cambridge: Cambridge University Press, 2010.

Berlin, Brett, Robert LeHane, Richard NeJame, and Todd Meyers. "Symposium: Business Bankruptcy Panel: Hot Topics in Retail Bankruptcy." *Emory Bankruptcy Developments Journal* 25 (2009).

Brealey, Richard, Stewart C. Myers, and Franklin Allen. *Principles of Corporate Finance*, 9th ed. New York: McGraw-Hill, 2008.

Ehrhardt, Michael C., and Eugene F. Brigham. *Corporate Finance*, 4th ed. Florence, KY: South-Western, 2010.

Garrison, Ray H., Eric Noreen, and Peter C. Brewer. *Managerial Accounting*, 13th ed. New York: McGraw-Hill, 2009.

Lehmann, Donald R., and David J. Reibstein. *Marketing Metrics and Financial Performance*. Cambridge, MA: Marketing Science Institute, 2006.

O'Sullivan, Don, and Andrew V. Abela. "Marketing Performance Measurement Ability and Firm Performance." *Journal of Marketing* 71, no. 2 (2007), pp. 79–93.

Wild, John. *Financial and Managerial Accounting*, 4th ed. New York: McGraw-Hill, 2010.

Wood, Steve, and Neil Wrigley. "Last Great US Department Store Consolidation?" *International Journal of Retail & Distribution Management* 35, no. 1 (2007), pp. 20–37.

Young professionals and retired empty-nesters are moving into these areas to enjoy the convenience of shopping, restaurants, and entertainment near where they live.

Central Business District   The **central business district (CBD)** is the traditional downtown business area in a city or town. Due to its daily activity, it draws many people and employees into the area during business hours. The CBD is also the hub for public transportation, and there is a high level of pedestrian traffic. Finally, many CBDs have a large number of residents living in the area.

Although CBD locations in the United States declined in popularity among retailers and their customers for years, many are experiencing a revival as they become gentrified, drawing in new retailers and residents that crave an urban experience and want to be able to walk to do errands and shopping. Retailing View 7.1 examines the gentrification of an old neighborhood in Cleveland's CBD.

However, limited parking and longer driving times can discourage suburban shoppers from patronizing stores in a CBD. Shopping flow in the evening and on weekends is also slow in many CBDs. Shoplifting is also a concern, requiring increased security costs and/or inventory losses. Finally, unlike shopping centers, CBDs tend to suffer from a lack of planning. One block may contain upscale boutiques, and the next may be populated with low-income housing, and this means consumers may not have access to enough interesting retailers that they can visit in one shopping trip.

REFACT

The most expensive retail locations are Fifth Avenue in New York City, which costs $1,500 to $2,000 per square foot annually; Causeway Bay in Hong Kong, which costs about $1,200; Avenue des Champs-Elysées in Paris, renting for $922; New Bond Street in London, at $814; and Ginza in Tokyo, at $683 per square foot annually.[4]

7.1   RETAILING VIEW   Gentrified Cleveland

Parts of Cleveland's central business district, as with so many CBDs in the United States, are struggling to retain their business, social, cultural, and retail vitality. Business parks and malls in the suburbs have all but suffocated these once vital urban centers. But dedicated, persevering, and risk-taking entrepreneurial developers working with forward-thinking urban planners and city leaders are slowly turning some of these areas around.

Take, for instance, Cleveland's East Fourth Street, the site of a 600,000-square-foot, $110 million, historic redevelopment project. About one-third is retail space, and the rest is housing. It has 14 restaurants, 8 bars, a 16-lane bowling alley, a coffee shop, a theater, a nightclub, and a concert stage that attracts national talent. Above the restaurants are 322 rental apartments. The area is spectacularly appointed with art, flowers, decorative paving, planters, outdoor seating, and special overhead lighting. East Fourth Street represents about 14 percent of the $800 million in new housing, hotels, and retail stores in Cleveland's CBD.

Since coal and steel were no longer going to be the backbone of Cleveland's economy, city leaders and local developers reinvented the CBD using an entertainment-focused strategy. In the mid-1990s they built two new stadiums for the city's football and baseball teams, a new arena for its basketball team, and the Rock and Roll Hall of Fame. To provide incentives for the East Fourth Street project, the city provided $10 million in tax breaks and other incentives for street improvements to

Cleveland's East Fourth Street is a gentrification project that includes retail stores, restaurants, bars, a bowling alley, a theater, and more. Two-thirds of the space is for apartments.

lure Pickwick & Frolic, a restaurant and nightclub, and the House of Blues, a concert producer, to the area. Today residents and suburbanites flock to East Fourth Street before and after sports and entertainment events, as well as for an interesting afternoon or evening "on the town."

Sources: Keith Schneider, "An Enclave of Entertainment in Cleveland," *New York Times,* July 8, 2009; Wendy McManamon, "Tastemakers: Pickwick & Frolic's Nick Kostis: the 'Mayor of East 4th,'" *Cleveland.com,* March 14, 2009.

Main Street   **Main Street** refers to the traditional shopping area in smaller towns or to a secondary business district in a suburb or within a larger city. Streets in some of these areas have been converted into pedestrian walkways.

Main Streets share most of the characteristics of a primary CBD, but their occupancy costs are generally lower. Main Street locations do not draw as many people as the primary CBD because fewer people work in the area and the fewer stores generally mean a smaller overall selection. In addition, Main Streets typically don't offer the range of entertainment and recreational activities available in the more successful primary CBDs. Finally, the planning organization for the town or redevelopment often imposes some restrictions on Main Street store operations.

In the European Union, Main Street locations (called High Streets in the United Kingdom) are threatened by large big-box retailers located outside the city limits. The EU is trying to restrain superstores' growth by limiting their size and subsidizing the redevelopment of Main Street areas to help local retailers compete. Europe has greater population density and less space, and strict planning and greenbelt laws provide a sharp division between town and country. Suburbs are few, thus minimizing urban sprawl. But preserving the environment comes at a cost for Europe. The limits on out-of-town, big-box retailing reduce competition and retailing efficiency, causing higher prices.[5]

Inner City   The term **inner city** in the United States refers to a high density urban area that has higher unemployment and lower median income than the surrounding metropolitan area. Some retailers have avoided opening stores in the inner city because they believe it is riskier and achieves lower returns than other areas. As a result, inner-city consumers often have to travel to the suburbs to shop, even for food items. Conservatively, inner-city consumers constitute $120 billion in annual retail spending power.[7] Although income levels are lower in inner cities than in other neighborhoods, inner-city retailers often achieve a higher sales volume and higher margins, resulting in higher profits.

Retailing can play an important role in inner-city redevelopment activities by providing needed services and jobs for inner-city residents, as well as property taxes to support the redevelopment. Because of the potential of this untapped market and incentives from local governments, developers are increasing their focus on opportunities in the inner city. Often local governments will use the right

REFACT

Baby boomers and echo boomers are moving to downtown areas to have easy access to everything and to save on transportation costs.[6]

In the United Kingdom, small retailers with inner-city, High Street locations remain popular but face competition from larger retailers such as supermarkets and hypermarkets.

of eminent domain to buy buildings and land and then sell it to developers at an attractive price. However, inner-city redevelopments can be controversial. For instance, people are concerned about the residents displaced by the development, increased traffic, and parking difficulties.

The offerings at inner-city grocery stores have traditionally been particularly unattractive. Instead of offering fresh meat and produce, they tend to feature lower-priced packaged foods that have longer shelf lives. The limited number of supermarkets in the inner city means that residents have to take buses to do their shopping. But government programs, in partnership with nonprofit organizations, are working to change the inner-city supermarket landscape. For instance, in an inner-city Philadelphia neighborhood, a new supermarket, stocked with fresh produce, a pharmacy, and various ethnic products, has opened within walking distance of most of the neighborhood. Nonprofit organizations such as Philadelphia's Food Trust lobby for loans and government subsidies that will support supermarkets in lower-income areas.[8] Retailing View 7.2 describes how Magic Johnson has brought retailing to the inner city. Although we have discussed these urban developments in terms of unplanned locations, they also may be managed shopping centers, as discussed in the following section.

7.2 RETAILING VIEW Magic Johnson Brings Retailing to the Inner City

In 13 unparalleled years in the National Basketball Association, Earvin "Magic" Johnson rewrote the record books and dazzled fans with his no-look passes and clutch jump shots. He led the Los Angeles Lakers to five championships. After he announced to the world in 1991 that he had contracted HIV, many thought he would retire from public life. Instead, for Johnson, basketball was just the beginning. He makes over 100 public appearances every year, exceeding those he made in his basketball career.

After basketball, he took his game to a different arena, one in which the obstacles are higher and the challenges greater. His new career began with a relatively modest partnership with Loews Cineplex Entertainment, formerly Sony Retail Entertainment. After doing some research, Magic and his partners realized that minorities make up approximately 32 to 35 percent of the nationwide movie audience but there were few theaters in minority neighborhoods. Minorities living in the inner city were driving 30 to 40 minutes to get to a theater. So it seemed natural to build movie theaters in urban neighborhoods across the country.

With the theaters in place, the next step was finding other businesses that would complement these theaters. What they found was most casual sit-down restaurants targeted similar demographics and market conditions. Because of either the franchise holders or the companies in charge, eateries weren't willing to commit to urban locations. Magic and his partners had customers coming in saying they loved the theaters, but they had to go all the way across town if they wanted to get something to eat. So, next, Magic collaborated with Starbucks, to be its only joint-venture partner in the United States, and with T.G.I. Fridays.

Magic Johnson Enterprises is dedicated to urban business development; it partners with Burger King, 24 Hour Fitness, Starbucks, and many more businesses to facilitate their operations in inner-city locations. His Burger King locations outperform others in the same market by 10 percent.

No longer a presence on the basketball court, Magic Johnson has become a leader in urban retail developments.

The Magic Johnson Foundation is a nonprofit organization that educates and creates innovative programs for the advancement of minority groups. Magic Johnson actively promotes HIV/AIDS awareness education to prevent the spread of the disease.

Not all of his projects are successful, however. In October 2009, a 13-year-old underperforming 12-screen complex at Greenbriar Mall in Atlanta closed. In 1996, Johnson had invested $8 million to build the complex.

Sources: Rachel Tobin Ramos, "Magic Johnson Cinema at Greenbriar Mall to Close," *Atlanta Business News,* October 5, 2009; www.magicjohnson.com (accessed October 8, 2009); Jill Lerner, "999 Peachtree Aims for Slot in 'Midtown Mile,'" *Atlanta Business Chronicle,* February 9, 2007; Claire Heininger, "Magic Johnson Tells Newark to Get Smart on HIV/AIDS," www.nj.com, July 17, 2007.

SHOPPING CENTERS

A **shopping center** is a group of retail and other commercial establishments that are planned, developed, owned, and managed as a single property. By combining many stores at one location, the development attracts more consumers to the shopping center than would be the case if the stores were at separate locations. The developer and shopping center management carefully select a set of retailers that are complementary to provide consumers with a comprehensive shopping experience, including a well-thought-out assortment of retailers. However, surprisingly, it's not uncommon, for instance, for a store's sales to increase when a competing store enters the shopping center.

The shopping center management maintains the common facilities such as the parking area—an arrangement referred to as **common area maintenance (CAM)**—and is responsible for providing security, parking lot lighting, outdoor signage for the center, advertising and special events to attract consumers, and so on. Lease agreements typically require that retailers in the center pay a portion of the CAM costs for the center according to the size of their store's space and/or sales volume. The shopping center management can also place restrictions on the operating hours, signage, and even the type of merchandise sold in the stores.

Most shopping centers have at least one or two major retailers, referred to as **anchors,** such as Macy's, Walmart, or Kroger. These retailers are courted by the center's developer because they attract a significant number of consumers and consequently make the center more appealing for other retailers. To get these anchor retailers to locate in a center, developers frequently give them special deals, such as reduced lease costs.

In strip shopping centers, supermarkets are typically anchors, whereas department stores traditionally anchor enclosed shopping malls. However, a lifestyle center may not have anchors, whereas power centers consist primarily of multiple "anchor" stores.

The number and gross leasable area (GLA) for the different types of shopping centers are shown in Exhibit 7–2. Each of these location types is discussed next.

Neighborhood and Community Shopping Centers

Neighborhood and **community strip shopping centers** (also called simply **strip shopping centers**) are attached rows of nonenclosed stores, with on-site parking usually located in front of the stores. The most common layouts are linear,

REFACT

The largest U.S. shopping center owner is Simon Property Group, headquartered in Indianapolis, which has interest in 387 properties, comprising 263 million square feet of gross leaseable space.[9]

EXHIBIT 7–2
U.S. Shopping Centers

Type	Number	Share of Total Shopping Center Gross Leasable Area (%)
Enclosed Malls (total)	1,385	16.1
Regional	773	5.9
Super-regional	612	10.1
Open-Air Centers (total)	102,066	83.7
Strip/convenience	63,254	16.8
Neighborhood	26,447	28.5
Community	9,040	23.5
Lifestyle	410	1.9
Power center	2,049	11.4
Theme/festival	457	0.6
Outlet	373	1.2

SOURCE: International Council of Shopping Centers data resources, Table 11, http://edata.icsc.org/tables/ (accessed February 25, 2010).

Neighborhood shopping centers are attached rows of nonenclosed stores, with on-site parking usually located in front of the stores.

L-shaped, and inverted U-shaped. Historically, the term "strip center" has applied to the linear configuration.

Smaller centers (neighborhood centers) are typically anchored by a supermarket or a drugstore and designed for day-to-day convenience shopping. The larger centers (community centers) are typically anchored by at least one big-box store such as a discount department store, an off-price retailer, or a category specialist. The anchors are supported by smaller specialty stores offering hardware, flowers, and a variety of personal services, such as barber shops and dry cleaners.

The primary advantages of these centers are that they offer customers convenient locations and easy parking and they have relatively low occupancy costs. The primary disadvantage is that smaller centers have a limited trade area due to their size, and they lack entertainment and restaurants. In addition, there is no protection from the weather. As a result, neighborhood and community centers do not attract as many customers as larger, enclosed malls do.

Current neighborhood and community centers have fewer local, independent stores than they did in the past. National chains such as The Children's Place, Borders, Kohl's, Radio Shack, and Marshalls compete effectively against their rival mall-based stores by offering the convenience of a neighborhood or community center. In these locations, they can offer lower prices, partly because of the lower occupancy cost, and their customers can drive right up to the door.

Power Centers

Power centers are shopping centers that consist primarily of collections of big-box retail stores, such as full-line discount stores (Target), off-price stores (Marshalls), warehouse clubs (Costco), and category specialists (Lowe's, Staples, Michaels, Barnes & Noble, Best Buy, Sports Authority, Toys "R" Us). Although these centers are "open-air," unlike traditional strip centers, power centers often include several freestanding (unconnected) anchors and only a minimum number of small specialty store tenants. Many power centers are located near an enclosed shopping mall.

Exhibit 7–3 illustrates that power centers have experienced the greatest growth over the last 10 years. This growth in power centers reflects the growth of category specialists. Many power centers are now larger than some regional malls and have

REFACT

One of the first strip shopping centers, Silver Springs Shopping Center in Maryland, opened in 1938 with a 1,000-seat movie theater, 19 stores, and a grocery store as an anchor.[10]

REFACT

The first power center, featuring a general merchandise discount store, category specialists, off-price retailers, and warehouse clubs, opened in Coloma, California, in 1986.

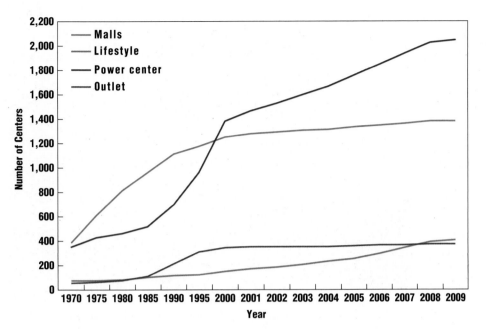

EXHIBIT 7–3
Growth of Different Types of Planned Shopping Centers

SOURCE: Data based on International Council of Shopping Centers, data resources, Table 11, http://edata.icsc.org/tables/ (accessed February 25, 2010).

trade areas as large as regional malls. Power centers offer low occupancy costs and modest levels of consumer convenience and vehicular and pedestrian traffic.

Shopping Malls

Shopping malls are enclosed, climate-controlled, lighted shopping centers with retail stores on one or both sides of an enclosed walkway. Parking is usually provided around the perimeter of the mall. Shopping malls are classified as either **regional malls** (less than 800,000 square feet) or **superregional malls** (more than 800,000 square feet). Super-regional centers are similar to regional centers, but because of their larger size, they have more anchors, specialty stores, and recreational opportunities and draw from a larger geographic area. They often are considered tourist attractions. Retailing View 7.3 describes some of Asia's mega malls.

Shopping malls have several advantages over alternative locations. First, shopping malls attract many shoppers and have a large trade area because of the number of stores and the opportunity to combine shopping with entertainment. They provide an inexpensive form of entertainment. Older citizens get their exercise by walking the malls, and teenagers hang out and meet their friends, though some malls are restricting their admittance in the evenings. Thus malls generate significant pedestrian traffic inside the mall. Second, customers don't have to worry about the weather, and thus malls are appealing places to shop during cold winters and hot summers. Third, mall management ensures a level of consistency that benefits all the tenants. For instance, most major malls enforce uniform hours of operation.

However, malls also have some disadvantages. First, mall occupancy costs are higher than those of strip centers, freestanding sites, and most central business districts. For example, the occupancy cost (rent, common area maintenance, and taxes) for an enclosed mall is almost 140 percent greater than that for an open-air shopping center ($35.42 compared to $14.55 per square foot).[12] Second, some retailers may not like mall management's control of their operations, such as strict rules governing window displays and signage. Third, competition within shopping centers can be intense. Several specialty and department stores might sell very similar merchandise and be located in close proximity. Fourth, freestanding

7.3   RETAILING VIEW   Mega Malls in Asia

Eight of the ten largest malls in the world are located in Asia, and of these, seven were built since 2004. (See Exhibit 7–4.) The West Edmonton Mall is the largest mega mall in North America; the King of Prussia Mall is the largest mega mall in the United States but the 11th-largest in the world. The largest mall in the world, the New South China Mall in Dongguan, China, was built in 2005 and has 7.1 million gross leasable square feet. Unfortunately, its poor location was unable to attract retail tenants, and it is currently 99 percent vacant.[14] The Dubai Mall is currently the seventh-largest mega mall in the world, but when completed, it will be the largest in the world.

Mall development is rapidly growing to keep up with the lifestyle and income changes in Asia. Mega malls are mixed-use centers with retail, dining, entertainment, and residential living. They house many familiar, global, luxury brands, including Gucci, Hermes, Versace, and Cartier. The malls, located in places like Singapore, Hong Kong, and Kuala Lumpur, are impressive because of their large size and the entertainment choices they offer (cinemas, bowling alleys, windmills, children's theme parks, skating rinks, and an abundance of restaurants).

When customers get tired of shopping at the Dubai Mall in the United Arab Emirates, they can go skiing inside!

EXHIBIT 7–4   The Largest Mega Malls

Shopping Mall	Year Opened	GLA* (million sq. ft.)	Total Area (million sq. ft.)	Stores	Comments
1 Jin Yuan (Golden Resources Shopping Mall) Beijing, China	2004	6.0	7.3	1,000+	Also known as the "Great Mall of China," this mega mall has six floors and is located near the Fourth Ring Road, west of Beijing.
2 SM City North EDSA Philippines	1985	5.0		1,100+	
3 Central World Plaza Bangkok, Thailand	2006	4.6	11	500+	21-screen cinemas, bowling lanes, and restaurants; also a convention center (not included in the GLA).
4 SM Mall of Asia Philippines	2006	4.2	4.4	600	
5 West Edmonton Mall Edmonton, Alberta, Canada	1981	3.8	6.0	800	Largest shopping mall in North America; includes indoor wave pool, amusement areas, hotel, restaurants, and 20,000 parking spaces.
6 Cevahir Istanbul Istanbul, Turkey	2005	3.8	4.5	280	The largest shopping mall in Europe; has six floors, cinemas, a roller coaster, and a theater.
7 The Dubai Mall Dubai, United Arab Emirates	2008	3.77	5.9	600	
8 Berjaya Times Square Kuala Lumpur, Malaysia	2003	3.5	7.5	1,000+	Includes 45 restaurants, a theme park, and a 3D Digi-IMAX theater.
9 Beijing Mall Beijing, China	2005	3.4	4.7	600	Four levels of shopping with interior residences; located near Fifth Ring Road, southeast of Beijing.
10 Zhengjia Plaza (Grandview Mall) Guangzhou, China	2005	3.0	4.5		Enclosed in a complex that includes a 48-story hotel and 30-story office building.
11 King of Prussia Mall Philadelphia, Pennsylvania, USA	1962	2.8		327	Created by connecting together three adjacent malls, managed by a single company.
12 South Coast Plaza Costa Mesa, California, USA	1967	2.7		280	The highest revenue volume mall in the United States. It also is home to the Orange Lounge, a branch of the Orange County Museum of Art.

* Gross leasable area—the total usable, rental space in a building.

Sources: Stan Sesser, "The New Spot for Giant Malls: Asia," *Wall Street Journal,* September, 16, 2006; Tom Van Riper, "World's Largest Malls," *Forbes,* January 9, 2007; http://www.easternct.edu/depts/amerst/MallsWorld.htm (accessed July 25, 2007).

locations, strip centers, lifestyle centers, and power centers are more convenient because customers can park in front of a store, go in and buy what they want, and go about their other errands. Fifth, some malls were built more than 40 years ago and have not been subject to any significant remodeling, so they appear run-down and unappealing to shoppers. Furthermore, these older malls are often located in areas with unfavorable demographics, because the population has shifted from the near suburbs to outer suburbs. Finally, the consolidation in the department store sector has decreased the number of potential anchor tenants and diminished the drawing power of enclosed malls.

For these reasons, mall traffic and sales have been declining, and limited resources are being spent on new mall development. Very few new malls have been developed over the last five years. To address this decline, mall managers and developers are trying to enhance the mall shopping experience and redevelop failing malls.

One approach shopping mall developers are employing to deal with the aging malls and the changing demographics in their mall's trade area is to more closely tailor their offerings to cater to their markets. For instance, older shopping centers are being repositioned to appeal to Hispanic and Asian markets. These centers typically have both national and Hispanic- or Asian-focused retailers. Because these centers are often situated in dense urban areas where parks are scarce, the malls substitute for the town square. These malls tend to be more recession-proof than other malls because they sell more necessities and are anchored by supermarkets and low-cost eateries.

Another approach for enhancing the mall experience is to renovate or redevelop existing malls. Some redevelopment projects convert enclosed regional malls to include open-air components, becoming a lifestyle center. For example, Santa Monica Place in Thousand Oaks, California, has a new open-air walkway, outdoor public plaza, and rooftop dining deck.[16]

> ### REFACT
> Hispanics are forecasted to spend $1.4 trillion annually in the United States by 2013. The combined buying power of African-Americans, Asians, and Native Americans is over $1.5 trillion, almost 14 percent of the nation's total buying power.[15]

Lifestyle Centers

Lifestyle centers are shopping centers that have an open-air configuration of specialty stores, entertainment, and restaurants, with design ambience and amenities such as fountains and street furniture. Lifestyle centers resemble the main streets in small towns, where people stroll from store to store, have lunch, and sit for a while on a park bench talking to friends. Thus, they cater to the "lifestyles" of consumers in their trade areas. Lifestyle centers are particularly attractive to specialty retailers. Some lifestyle centers are anchored by department stores, such as Macy's and Dillard's, and category specialists.

People are attracted to lifestyle centers not only because of their shops and restaurants but also because of their outdoor attractions such as a pop-up fountain, ice cream carts, stilt walkers, balloon artists, magicians, face painters, concerts, and other events. Since lifestyle centers have some limited auto access, customers can be dropped off right in front of a store.

Since lifestyle centers are not enclosed, bad weather can be an impediment to traffic. But some centers, like the Easton Town Center in Columbus, Ohio, thrive despite the climate.[17] When the weather is bad, tough Ohioans simply bundle up and take a stroll.

Due to the ease of parking, lifestyle centers are very convenient for shoppers, and the occupancy costs, like

Lifestyle centers are even popular in colder climates, like the Easton Town Center in Columbus, Ohio.

those of all open-air developments, are considerably lower than those for enclosed malls. But they typically have less retail space than enclosed malls and thus may attract fewer customers than enclosed malls. Many lifestyle centers are located near higher-income areas, so the higher purchases per visit compensate for the fewer number of shoppers. Finally, many lifestyle centers are part of larger, mixed-use developments, which are described in the next section.

Mixed-Use Developments

Mixed-use developments (MXDs) combine several different uses into one complex including retail, office, residential, hotel, recreation, or other functions. They are pedestrian-oriented and therefore facilitate a live, work, play environment.[18] They appeal to people who have had enough of long commutes to work and the social fragmentation of their neighborhoods and are looking for a lifestyle that gives them more time for the things they enjoy and an opportunity to live in a genuine community. In addition, MXDs are popular with retailers because they bring additional shoppers to their stores. They are also popular with governments, urban planners, and environmentalists because they provide a pleasant, pedestrian environment and are an efficient use of space. Developers also like MXDs because they use space productively. For instance, land costs the same whether a developer builds a shopping mall by itself or an office tower on top of the mall or parking structure.

The Boca Mall, a 430,000-square-foot regional shopping mall in Boca Raton, Florida, opened in 1974. Decades later, the mall was plagued by two trends: population growth occurring elsewhere and competing malls that were attracting most of its patrons. The original anchors and many of the specialty stores departed. The Boca Mall was demolished and replaced with a mixed-use development called Mizner Park. Mizner Park has commercial office space located above the ground-floor retail space on one side of the street, and residential units sit above the retail space on the opposite side of the street.[19]

Minzer Park in Boca Raton combines retail, residential, and entertainment offerings in one location with unique boutiques, eateries, music, movies, and art galleries conveniently located close to ocean-front apartments and condos.

Outlet Centers

Outlet centers are shopping centers that contain mostly manufacturers' and retailers' outlet stores. On average, outlet center rent rates are lower than those at shopping malls, and their sales per square foot are comparable.[20]

Chelsea Premium Outlet (owned by Simon Property), Tanger Outlets, and Prime Outlets are the largest outlet center operators in the United States. VF Corp. (which includes 7 for All Mankind, Vans, Wrangler, Lee, Nautica, North Face, and others) and Phillips Van-Heusen (including Calvin Klein, Van Heusen, Izod, Bass, and Arros) are the largest retailers in the outlet sector.[21]

Some outlet centers have a strong entertainment component, including movie theaters and restaurants to keep customers on the premises longer. For example, Tanger outlets at the Arches on Long Island, New York, holds a multiplex theater, with an IMAX movie theater; a health club; a courtyard with outdoor seating; and a fountain area that is converted into an ice skating rink in the winter.[22]

Outlet center tenant mix has changed significantly, with many new leases signed by retailers that have never had outlet stores before, such as Victoria's Secret, QVC, Bally, and Dooney and Bourke. Luxury retailers, such as Chanel, Gucci, Prada, Salvatore Ferragamo, Burberry, and Coach, have opened stores in outlet shopping centers.[23]

Tourism represents 50 percent of the traffic generated for many outlet centers. Thus, many are located with convenient interstate access and close to popular tourist attractions. Some center developers actually organize bus tours to bring people hundreds of miles to their malls. As a result, the primary trade area for some outlet centers is 50 miles or more.

Outlet centers are also very popular outside the United States, with about 150 centers in Europe, Turkey, and Dubai. The largest outlet center in Europe is the Freeport Lisbon Designer Outlet in Portugal.[24] Outlet malls are also particularly attractive in Japan, given its large population, interest in American brands, and growing consumer enthusiasm for value retailing concepts.

Theme/Festival Centers

Theme/festival centers are shopping centers that typically employ a unifying theme carried by the individual shops in their architectural design and, to an extent, in their merchandise. The biggest appeal of these centers is to tourists. The centers typically contain tenants similar to those in specialty centers, except that there are usually no large specialty stores or department stores. Theme/festival centers can be anchored by restaurants and entertainment facilities.

A theme/festival center might be located in a place of historical interest, such as Quincy Market and Faneuil Hall in Boston or Ghirardelli Square in San Francisco. Alternatively, it may attempt to replicate a historical place, like the Grand Canal Shops at the Venetian in Las Vegas, or create a unique shopping environment, like Universal CityWalk in Los Angeles.

Larger, Multiformat Developments—Omnicenters

New shopping center developments are combining enclosed malls, lifestyle centers, and power centers. Although centers of this type do not have an official name, they may be referred to as **omnicenters.**

Omnicenters represent a response to several trends in retailing, including the desire of tenants to lower common area maintenance charges by spreading the

Ghirardelli Square in San Francisco is a theme center because of its historical architectural interest.

costs among more tenants and to function inside larger developments that generate more pedestrian traffic and longer shopping trips. In addition, they reflect the growing tendency of consumers to cross-shop, as occurs when a Walmart customer also patronizes the Cheesecake Factory and Nordstrom's, as well as the desire of time-scarce consumers to go to one place that offers everything. For example, the 1.3 million-square-foot St. John's Town Center in Jacksonville, Florida, is divided into three components: a lifestyle center with a Dillard's department store anchor, a community center anchored by Dick's Sporting Goods and a Barnes & Noble bookstore, and a Main Street with Cheesecake Factory and P.F. Chang's restaurants as anchors.[25]

OTHER LOCATION OPPORTUNITIES

Pop-up stores, stores within a store, kiosks, and airports are other location alternatives for many retailers. Retailing View 7.4 describes some of Subway's nontraditional locations and the accommodations it needed to make to secure those locations.

7.4   RETAILING VIEW   Subway Goes to Church

Subway Restaurants, with 32,000 outlets in 87 countries, is finding it increasingly difficult to maintain its growth by opening new stores in traditional locations. It is in competition with other fast-food restaurants for spots in strip malls and alongside highways, so it is now more creative about locating new stores. The chain has over 4,000 nontraditional locations including convenience stores, college campuses, athletic clubs, hospitals, airports, department stores, car dealerships, laundromats, and churches. In the past several years, Subway has opened restaurants inside a church in upstate New York, a laundromat in California, a Goodwill Industries store in South Carolina, a car dealership in Germany, and 110 hospitals throughout the United States.

With its menu of sandwiches, Subway has an easier time opening in unusual venues because it has a simpler kitchen than traditional fast-food restaurants, which require frying and grilling equipment. Hospitals and religious facilities have a favorable attitude toward Subway because it promotes its sandwiches as a fresher, healthier alternative to traditional fast food.

Subway often has to make special accommodations when opening stores in nontraditional locations though. For example, the first of many kosher Subway stores opened in the Jewish Community Center of Cleveland in 2006, and Subway is now the largest kosher chain in the United States. The kosher stores still have Steak and Cheese subs, except the cheese is a soy-based product. In observance of the Jewish Sabbath, these restaurants are closed on Friday afternoon and all day Saturday.

When a Subway opened in the True Bethel Baptist Church of Buffalo, New York, in a low-income area of town, the franchisee worked closely with church leaders. To support the congre-

To maintain growth, Subway has opened outlets in nontraditional locations like this one in a Goodwill Industries store.

gation and create jobs, church leaders had approached several fast-food franchisors about opening a franchise in a corner of the church. Subway was the only chain that was flexible enough toward the space available and the operating hours to accommodate the church. The chain agreed to waive its requirement of a Subway sign on the outside of the building and created a parking pattern to keep restaurant traffic from displacing churchgoers during services.

Sources: Stewart Ain, "The Chain-ing of Kosher Food," *Thejewishweek.com*, September, 22, 2009; "The Subway Restaurant Chain Again Named Number One Franchise," Subway press release, February 2, 2005; Howard Riell, "When Only a QSR Will Do," *Food Service Director*, February 15, 2007, pp. 46–47; Janet Adamy, "For Subway, Every Nook and Cranny on the Planet Is Possible Site for a Franchise," *Wall Street Journal*, September 1, 2006, p. A1.

Pop-Up Stores and Other Temporary Locations

Retailers and manufacturers sometimes open **pop-up stores,** which are stores in temporary locations that focus on new products or a limited group of products. A few years ago pop-up stores were a major investment for retailers because of the high start-up costs amortized over a very short lease and relatively high lease costs.[26] Now, with retail space more plentiful and less expensive, these stores have become more popular. Retailers and manufacturers are using these spaces to create buzz, test new concepts, or even evaluate a new neighborhood or city. Pop-up stores are even popping-up on college campuses. For instance, Victoria's Secret's Pink (a young women's clothing brand of Limited Brands Inc.),

Temporary stores, like this Kiehl's pop-up store at the University of Colorado, are fashion brands' latest attempt at developing brand loyalty among college students.

sustainable-clothing brand RVL7, and Kiehl's Since 1851 (a skin and hair-care company owned by L'Oréal SA), have opened pop-up stores on college campuses.[27]

Other retailers, often one-person operations, open temporary stores to take advantage of the holiday season in December or to get visibility and additional sales at festivals or concerts, such as the Newport Jazz Festival, weekend crafts fairs, or farmers' markets. For instance, in New York's Columbus Circle, 100 vendors sell a variety of gifts from Yogawear to handmade glass jewelry.[28] Cities around the United States generally welcome these temporary retailers because they bring in people, and therefore excitement and money, to the area. Local retailers, who pay high rents, aren't necessarily so enthusiastic, because some of the temporary retailers use the same suppliers.

Store within a Store

Another nontraditional location for retailers is within other, larger stores. Retailers, particularly department stores, have traditionally leased space to other retailers, such as sellers of fine jewelry, furs, or high-end designer brands. Grocery stores have been experimenting with the store-within-a-store concept for years with service providers like coffee bars, banks, film processors, and medical clinics. JCPenney has over 150 Sephora cosmetics shops within its new stores.

Merchandise Kiosks

Merchandise kiosks are small selling spaces, typically located in the walkways of enclosed malls, airports, college campuses, or office building lobbies. Some are staffed and resemble a miniature store or cart that could be easily moved. Others are 21st century versions of vending machines, such as the Apple kiosks that sell iPods and other high-volume Apple products.

For mall operators, kiosks are an opportunity to generate rental income in otherwise vacant space and offer a broad assortment of merchandise for visitors. They also can generate excitement from retailers like national cell phone provider Sprint to smaller niche products like Israeli Dead Sea cosmetics, leading to additional sales for the entire mall. Moreover, mall kiosks can be changed quickly to match seasonal demand.

When planning the location of kiosks in a mall, operators are sensitive to their regular mall tenants' needs. They are careful to avoid kiosks that block any storefronts, create an incompatible image, or actually compete directly with permanent tenants by selling similar merchandise.

Airports

A high-pedestrian area that has become popular with national retail chains is airports. Passengers arrive earlier for their flights than they did in the past, leaving them more time to shop. In addition, a cutback in airline food service has more people seeking sustenance in the airport.[29] As a result, sales per square foot at airport malls are often much higher than at regular mall stores. However, rents are higher too. Also, costs can be higher—hours are longer, and because the location is often inconvenient for workers, the businesses have to pay higher wages. The best airport locations tend to be ones where there are many connecting flights (Atlanta and Frankfurt) and international flights (New York's Kennedy and London's Heathrow), because customers have downtime to browse through stores. The best-selling products are those that make good gifts, necessities, and easy-to-pack items.

LOCATION AND RETAIL STRATEGY

The selection of a location type must reinforce the retailer's strategy. Thus, the location-type decision needs to be consistent with the shopping behavior and size of the target market and the retailer's positioning in its target market. Each of these factors is discussed next. Retailing View 7.5 summarizes how Bealls, a value-oriented, off-price retailer, selects locations based on its overall retail strategy.

Shopping Behavior of Consumers in Retailer's Target Market

A critical factor affecting the type of location that consumers select to visit is the shopping situation in which they are involved. Three types of shopping situations are convenience shopping, comparison shopping, and specialty shopping.

7.5 RETAILING VIEW   Bealls's Locations Support Its Strategy

In addition to its Florida-based department stores, Bealls operates more than 500 Bealls department stores and Bealls Outlet and Burke's Outlet stores in Sunbelt states from South and North Carolina to California. Its strategy is to sell, to price-sensitive customers, value-priced apparel in 15,000- to 25,000-square-foot stores. To serve these customers, Bealls needs to keep its prices and costs down. Its no-advertising strategy makes it very important to locate stores in heavily trafficked intersections or strip shopping centers to attract customers

Bealls uses a geodemographic service to identify and evaluate potential markets. It knows the geodemographic profiles of its customers and tries to locate its stores where a lot of those customers live. Once it identifies a community that meets its criteria, the next step is to find a specific location in the area. Its best locations are in strip shopping centers with an anchor like Walmart, Target, or a grocery store that attracts a lot of shoppers.

Sometimes it finds an appealing site that is 30,000 to 40,000 square feet, bigger than it would prefer. To take advantage of such opportunities, it sometimes will partner with a complementary retailer, like Big Lots, an off-price retailer focusing on hard goods, and both retailers approach the property owner together.

Bealls Outlet attracts customers by locating stores in heavily trafficked strip shopping centers with trade areas that match the profile of its target market.

Convenience Shopping   When consumers are engaged in **convenience shopping situations,** they are primarily concerned with minimizing their effort to get the product or service they want. They are relatively insensitive to price and indifferent about which brands to buy. Thus, they don't spend much time evaluating different brands or retailers; they simply want to make the purchase as quickly and easily as possible. Examples of convenience shopping situations are getting a cup of coffee during a work break, buying gas for a car, or buying milk for breakfast in the morning.

Retailers targeting customers involved in convenience shopping, such as convenience stores and gas stations, usually locate their stores close to where their customers are and make it easy for them to access the location, park, and find what they want. Thus, convenience stores are generally located in neighborhood strip centers and freestanding locations. Drugstores and fast-food restaurants also cater to convenience shoppers and thus select locations with easy access, parking, and the added convenience of a drive-through window. Convenience also plays an important role for supermarkets and full-line discount stores. Generally, shoppers at these stores are not particularly brand- or store-loyal and do not find shopping in these stores enjoyable. Thus, these stores typically are also located in neighborhood strip centers and freestanding locations.

Comparison Shopping   Consumers involved in **comparison shopping situations** have a general idea about the type of product or service they want but they do not have a well-developed preference for a brand or model. However, the purchase decisions are more important to them, so they seek information and are willing to expend effort to compare alternatives. Consumers typically engage in this type of shopping behavior when buying furniture, appliances, apparel, consumer electronics, hand tools, and cameras.

Furniture retailers, for instance, often locate next to one another to create a "furniture row." In New York City, a number of retailers selling houseplants and flowers are all located in Chelsea between 27th and 30th Streets on 6th Avenue, and diamond dealers are located on West 47th Street between 5th and 6th Avenues. These competing retailers locate near one another because doing so facilitates comparison shopping and thus attracts customers to the locations.

Enclosed malls offer the same benefits to consumers interested in comparison shopping for fashionable apparel. Thus, department stores and specialty apparel retailers locate in enclosed malls for the same reason that houseplant retailers locate together on 6th Avenue in New York City. By colocating in the same mall, they attract more potential customers interested in comparison shopping for fashionable apparel. Even though the enclosed mall might be inconvenient compared with a freestanding location, comparison shopping is easier after the customers have arrived.

Category specialists offer the same benefit of comparison shopping as a collection of colocated specialty stores like those described previously. Rather than going to a set of small hardware stores when comparison shopping for an electric drill, consumers know they can get almost anything they need to fix or build a house in either Home Depot or Lowe's. Thus, category specialists are **destination stores,** places where consumers will go even if it is inconvenient, just like enclosed malls are destination locations for fashionable-apparel comparison shopping. Category specialists locate in power centers, primarily to reduce their costs and create awareness of their location and secondarily to benefit from multiple retailers that attract more consumers and the resulting potential for cross-shopping. Basically, power centers are a collection of destination stores.

Specialty Shopping   When consumers go **specialty shopping,** they know what they want and will not accept a substitute. They are brand and/or retailer loyal and will pay a premium or expend extra effort, if necessary, to get exactly what they want. Examples of these shopping occasions include buying organic vegetables, adopting a dog from the animal shelter, or buying a new, high-quality stovetop and oven. The retailers they patronize when specialty shopping also are destination stores. Thus, consumers engaged in specialty shopping are willing to travel to an inconvenient location. Having a convenient location is not as important for retailers selling unique merchandise or services.

Density of Target Market

A second, but closely related, factor that affects the choice of location type is the density of the retailer's target market in relation to the location. A good location has many people in the target market who are drawn to it. So a convenience store located in a CBD can be sustained by customers living or working in fairly close proximity to the store. Similarly, a comparison shopping store located next to a Walmart is a potentially good location because Walmart draws lots of customers from a very large area. It is not as important to have high customer density near a store that sells specialty merchandise, because people are willing to search out this type of merchandise. A Porsche dealer, for instance, need not be near other car dealers or in close proximity to its target market, because those seeking this luxury car will drive to wherever the dealer may be.

Uniqueness of Retail Offering

Finally, the convenience of their locations is less important for retailers with unique, differentiated offerings than for retailers with an offering similar to other retailers. For example, Bass Pro Shops provides a unique merchandise assortment and store atmosphere. Customers will travel to wherever the store is located, and its location will become a destination.

LEGAL CONSIDERATIONS

 Legal considerations need to be examined when evaluating different location types. Laws regarding how land may be used have become so important that they often are a retailer's first consideration in a site search. Legal issues that affect the location decision include environmental and sustainability issues, zoning, building codes, signs, and licensing requirements.

Environmental and Sustainability Issues

The Environmental Protection Agency, as well as state and local agencies, has become increasingly involved with issues that could affect retail stores. Two environmental issues have received particular attention in recent years. The first is above-ground risks, such as asbestos-containing materials or lead pipes used in construction. These materials can be removed relatively easily.

The second issue is hazardous materials that have been stored in the ground. This consideration can be particularly important for a dry cleaner because of the chemicals it uses or for an auto repair shop because of its need to dispose of used motor oil and battery fluid. The costs of cleaning up hazardous materials can range from several thousand to many millions of dollars per site.

Real estate transactions almost always require an environmental impact statement on the property. Relying on past public filings of buried tanks and other potential hazards can be unreliable and does not provide protection in court. Retailers have two remedies to protect themselves from these environmental hazards. The best option at their disposal is to stipulate in the lease that the lessor is responsible for the removal and disposal of any such material if it is found. Alternatively, the retailer can buy insurance that specifically protects it from these risks.

Although laws related to the environment restrict the nature of retail developments, many new developments go beyond these legal requirements to address sustainability and energy-efficiency issues. New retail developments are using energy-efficient building materials, heating and cooling systems, water-efficient landscaping, and natural lighting. Santa Monica Place in California, for instance, added a solar roof, increased natural air ventilation, and changed the lighting to fluorescent.[31]

Walmart is taking a lead in the sustainability arena. It has experienced energy savings of 15 percent in its buildings and trucks since 2005. It also uses solar energy at 22 of its sites and conserves an acre of wildlife habitat for every acre that it occupies.[32] Also, Walmart is opening energy-efficient stores called HE (high efficiency) that are 25 to 30 percent more efficient than stores opened in 2005. These stores include LED lighting in refrigerator and freezer cases that are 50 percent more efficient than fluorescent lighting, a reflective white roof, sensor-activated low-flow bathroom faucets, recycled construction materials, and daylight harvesting technology that dims indoor lights when it is bright outside.[33]

Zoning and Building Codes

Zoning determines how a particular site can be used. For instance, some parts of a city are zoned for residential use only; others are zoned for light industrial and retail uses. **Building codes** are similar legal restrictions that specify the type of building, signs, size and type of parking lot, and so forth, that can be used at a particular location. Some building codes require a certain-size parking lot or a particular architectural design. In Santa Fe, New Mexico, for instance, building codes require that buildings keep a traditional mud stucco (adobe) style.

The building code in Santa Fe, New Mexico, requires that buildings keep a traditional mud stucco (adobe) style.

Signs   Restrictions on the use of signs can affect a particular site's desirability. Sign sizes and styles may be restricted by building codes, zoning ordinances, or even the shopping center management. At the Bal Harbour Shops in North Miami Beach, for example, all signs (even sale signs) must be approved by the shopping center management before implementation by each individual retailer.

Licensing Requirements   Licensing requirements may vary in different parts of a region. For instance, some Dallas neighborhoods are dry, meaning no alcoholic beverages can be sold; in other areas, only wine and beer can be sold. Such restrictions can affect retailers other than restaurants and bars. For instance, a theme/festival shopping center that restricts the use of alcoholic beverages may find its clientele limited at night.

Legal issues such as those mentioned here can discourage a retailer from pursuing a particular site. These restrictions aren't always permanent, however. Although difficult, time consuming, and possibly expensive, lobbying efforts and court battles can change these legal restrictions.

SUMMARY

Decisions about where to locate a store are critical to any retailer's success. Location decisions are particularly important because of the high-cost, long-term commitment and the impact on customer patronage. Choosing a particular location type involves evaluating a series of trade-offs. These trade-offs generally include the occupancy cost of the location, the pedestrian and vehicle customer traffic associated with the location, the restrictions placed on store operations by the property managers, and the convenience of the location for customers. In addition, legal issues need to be considered when selecting a site.

Retailers have a plethora of types of sites from which to choose. Each type of location has advantages and disadvantages. Many central business districts, inner-city, and Main Street locations have become more viable options than they were in the past because of gentrification of the areas, tax incentives, and lack of competition. There also are a wide variety of shopping center types for retailers. They can locate in a strip or power center, or they can go into an enclosed mall or a lifestyle, theme/festival, or outlet center. Other nontraditional sites are mixed-use developments, pop-up stores and other temporary locations, stores within a store, and airports.

KEY TERMS

anchor, *173*

building codes, *185*

central business district (CBD), *170*

common area maintenance (CAM), *173*

community strip shopping center, *173*

comparison shopping situation, *183*

convenience shopping situation, *183*

destination store, *183*

freestanding site, *169*

gentrification, *169*

inner city, *171*

lifestyle center, *177*

Main Street, *171*

merchandise kiosk, *181*

mixed-use development (MXD), *178*

neighborhood strip shopping center, *173*

omnicenter, *179*

outlet center, *178*

outparcel, *169*

pop-up store, *181*

power center, *174*

regional mall, *175*

shopping center, *173*

shopping mall, *175*

specialty shopping, *183*

strip shopping center, *173*

superregional mall, *175*

theme/festival center, *179*

trade area, *168*

zoning, *185*

GET OUT AND DO IT!

1. **CONTINUING CASE ASSIGNMENT** Interview the manager of the shopping center that contains the retailer you selected for the Continuing Assignment. Write a report summarizing which retailers the shopping center manager thinks are his or her best tenants and why they are valued. How does the manager rate the retailer you have selected? What criteria does he or she use?

2. **INTERNET EXERCISE** Go to the Web page for Faneuil Hall Marketplace at www.faneuilhallmarketplace.com and the online site for CocoWalk at http://www.cocowalk.net. What kinds of centers are these? List their similarities and differences. Who is the target market for each of these retail locations?

3. **GO SHOPPING** Go to your favorite shopping center, and analyze the tenant mix. Do the tenants appear to complement one another? What changes would you make in the tenant mix to increase the overall health of the center?

4. **GO SHOPPING** Visit a lifestyle center. What tenants are found in this location? Describe the population characteristics around this center. How far would

people drive to shop at this lifestyle center? What other types of retail locations does this lifestyle center compete with?

5. **INTERNET EXERCISE** Go to the home page for Simon Property Group, http://www.simon.com/about_simon/our_business/default.aspx, and read about the types of shopping centers that this developer manages. What is the difference between their businesses?

6. **INTERNET EXERCISE** Go to the home page of your favorite enclosed mall, and describe the mall in terms of the following characteristics: number of anchor stores, number and categories of specialty stores, number of sit-down and quick-service restaurants, and types of entertainment offered. What are the strengths and weaknesses of this assortment of retailers? What are the unique features of this particular mall?

7. **GO SHOPPING** Visit a power center that contains a Target, Staples, Sports Authority, Home Depot, or other category specialists. What other retailers are in the same location? How is this mix of stores beneficial to both shoppers and retailers?

DISCUSSION QUESTIONS AND PROBLEMS

1. Why is store location such an important decision for retailers?

2. Pick your favorite store. Describe the advantages and disadvantages of its current location, given its target market.

3. Home Depot typically locates in either a power center or a freestanding site. What are the strengths of each location for this home improvement retailer?

4. As a consultant to 7-Eleven convenience stores, American Eagle Outfitters, and Porsche of America, what would you say is the single most important factor in choosing a site for these three very different types of stores?

5. Retailers are developing shopping centers and freestanding locations in central business districts that have suffered decay. Some people have questioned the ethical and social ramifications of this process, which is known as gentrification. What are the benefits and problems associated with gentrification?

6. Staples, Office Max, and Office Depot all have strong multichannel strategies. How do competition and the Internet affect their strategies for locating stores?

7. In many malls, quick-service food retailers are located together in an area known as a food court. What are the advantages and disadvantages of this location for the food retailers? What is the new trend for food retailers in the shopping environment?

8. Why would a Payless ShoeSource store locate in a neighborhood shopping center instead of a regional shopping mall?

9. How does the mall near your home or university combine the shopping and entertainment experiences?

10. Consider a big city that has invested in an urban renaissance. What components of the gentrification project attract both local residents and visiting tourists to spend time shopping, eating, and sightseeing in this location?

SUGGESTED READINGS

Brooks, Charles, Patrick J. Kaufmann, and Donald R. Lichtenstein. "Trip Chaining Behavior in Multi-Destination Shopping Trips: A Field Experiment and Laboratory Replication." *Journal of Retailing* 84, no. 1 (2008), pp. 29–38.

ICSC. *21st Century Retail Centers: Context, Culture and Community.* New York: ICSC, 2009.

ICSC. *Winning Shopping Center Designs*, 32nd ed. New York: ICSC, 2009.

Jerath, Kinshuk, and Z. John Zhang. "Store-Within-a-Store." *Journal of Marketing Research*, forthcoming.

Kramer, Anita. *Dollars & Cents of Shopping Centers/The SCORE 2010.* Washington, DC: Urban Land Institute, 2010.

Ruoh-Nan, Yan, and Molly Eckman. "Are Lifestyle Centres Unique? Consumers' Perceptions across Locations." *International Journal of Retail & Distribution Management* 37, no. 1 (2009), pp. 24–42.

Teller, Christoph. "Shopping Streets versus Shopping Malls— Determinants of Agglomeration Format Attractiveness from the Consumers' Point of View." *International Review of Retail, Distribution and Consumer Research* 18, no. 4 (2008), pp. 381–403.

Teller, Christoph, and Thomas Reutterera. "The Evolving Concept of Retail Attractiveness: What Makes Retail Agglomerations Attractive When Customers Shop at Them?" *Journal of Retailing and Consumer Services* 15, no. 3 (2008), pp. 127–143.

Van Uffelen, Chris. *Malls & Department Stores.* Berlin: Braun, 2008.

Yudelson, Jerry. *Sustainable Retail Development: New Success Strategies.* New York: ICSC, 2009.

Retail Site Location

EXECUTIVE BRIEFING
Rick Lawlor, Vice President Retail Marketing
Hess Corporation

When I was in high school, my goal was to become a Major League Baseball player. I attended La Salle University in Philadelphia where I played baseball. Unfortunately, injuries and a couple of knee surgeries ended my baseball career ambitions. After a stint at Allstate, I entered the management training program at Mobil. I rose through the ranks to eventually be in charge of Mobil's North American retail franchise operations. My group at Mobil developed the "On the Run" convenience store concept and the *speedpass*, a keychain RFID device enabling customers to pay for gasoline purchases electronically.

In 1996, I joined the management team at Hess Corporation. Hess is a vertically integrated energy company involved in oil exploration, refining, and retail sales. While Hess is the 55th largest U.S. corporation, it is considered a small company by oil industry standards. When I first joined Hess, the company had only 100 retail outlets. Shortly thereafter, the company decided to put more emphasis on its retail business, and through a combination of acquisitions and new build projects, we are now the leading independent gasoline/convenience store retailer on the U.S. East Coast. We own and operate over 1,400 stores, serving customers in 16 states from Rhode Island to Florida, generating over $6 billion in annual sales. Every day, more than 1.3 million customers are served at a Hess branded location.

Leon Hess started the company in 1933 driving a truck door-to-door delivering heating oil. Over the years we have continued his emphasis on providing value to our customers, saving them time and money. Our Hess Express stores are designed to offer customers an answer to today's fast-paced lifestyle by providing the convenience of 'one-stop shopping.' Our gasoline is priced two to four cents under the price of the major oil companies. In five minutes, we'll fill up both your car and your stomach so you can get in and out of our locations quickly.

The location of our stores is critical to providing value to our customers and is paramount to our success. We have a staff that evaluates the location of stores we are considering to build or acquire. When evaluating

CHAPTER 8

QUESTIONS

What factors do retailers consider when determining where to locate their stores?

What is a trade area for a store, and how do retailers determine the trade area?

What factors do retailers consider when deciding on a particular site?

How do retailers forecast sales for new store locations?

Where can retailers get information to evaluate potential store locations?

What issues are involved in negotiating leases?

---

locations, we look at all the numbers—the size and characteristics of the store's trading area, the demographics and geodemographics of the customers that drive by the location and live in the area. However, the most important factors for us are visibility and access—that is, can customers see the signage for our stores and easily make a right turn into the location on their way home? While the data on a location are useful, we never open a location without looking at it in person to assess its visibility and access.

Chapter 5 emphasized the strategic importance of location decisions. Although location decisions can create strategic advantage, like all strategic decisions, they are also risky because they involve a significant commitment of resources. Opening a store at a site often involves committing to a lease of five years or more or purchasing land and building a store. If the store's performance is below expectations, the retailer may not be able to recover its investment easily by having another party move in and assume the lease or buy the building.

Chapter 7 reviewed the different types of locations available to retailers and why certain types of retailers gravitate toward particular locations. This chapter takes a closer look at how retailers choose specific sites to locate their stores.

Selecting retail locations involves the analysis of a lot of data and the use of sophisticated statistical models. Because most retailers make these decisions infrequently, it is not economical for them to employ full-time real estate analysts with state-of-the-art skills. Thus, small retailers often use firms that provide the geographic and demographic data and consulting services needed to evaluate specific sites. However, there continues to be an element of art in making these location decisions.

This chapter reviews the steps retailers go through in selecting their store locations and negotiating leases. The first part of the chapter examines the factors retailers consider in selecting a general area for locating stores and determining the number of stores to operate in an area. Then this chapter reviews different approaches used to evaluate specific sites and estimate the expected sales if and when a store is located at that site. Finally, the chapter looks at the various terms that are negotiated when a retailer commits to leasing space for its store.

EVALUATING SPECIFIC AREAS FOR LOCATIONS

Areas that retailers consider for locating stores might be countries, areas within a country such as a province in France or a state in the United States, particular cities, or areas within cities. In the United States, retailers often focus their analysis on a **metropolitan statistical area (MSA)** because consumers tend to shop within an MSA and media coverage and demographic data for analyzing location opportunities often are organized by MSA.

An MSA is a core urban area containing a population of more than 50,000 inhabitants, together with adjacent communities that have a high degree of economic and social integration with the core community. For example, many people in an MSA commute to work in the urban core but live in the surrounding areas. An MSA can consist of one or several counties and usually is named after the major urban area in the MSA. For example, the Cincinnati-Middleton MSA consists of 15 counties (3 in Indiana, 7 in Kentucky, and 5 in Ohio) with a population of 2,155,137; the Missoula, Montana, MSA consists of one county with a population of 107,320. A **micropolitan statistical area (MiSA)** is a smaller unit of analysis, with only about 10,000 inhabitants in its core urban area.[2]

The best areas for locating stores are those that generate the highest long-term profits for a retailer. Some factors affecting the long-term profit generated by stores that should be considered when evaluating an area include (1) the economic conditions, (2) competition, (3) the strategic fit of the area's population with the retailer's target market, and (4) the costs of operating stores (see Exhibit 8–1). Note that these factors are similar to those that retailers consider when evaluating an investment in a new business growth opportunity or entry into a foreign market, as discussed in Chapter 5.

Economic Conditions

Because locations involve a commitment of resources over a long time horizon, it is important to examine an area's level and growth of population and employment. A large, fully employed population means high purchasing power and high levels of retail sales. Exhibit 8–2 shows the population growth for MSAs in the United States.

But population and employment growth alone aren't enough to ensure a strong retail environment in the future. Retail location analysts must determine how long such growth will continue and how it will affect demand for merchandise sold in

EXHIBIT 8–1

Factors Affecting the Demand for a Retail or Trade Area

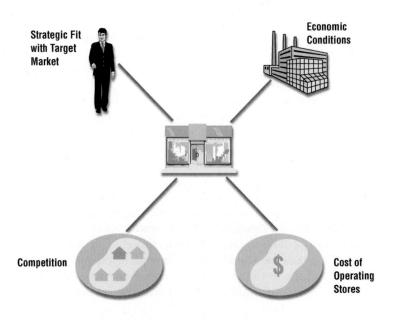

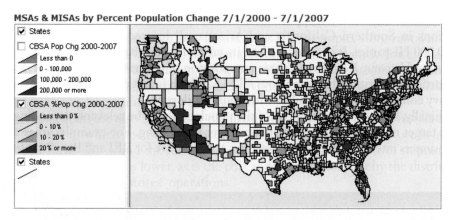

MSAs & MISAs by Percent Population Change 7/1/2000 - 7/1/2007

☑ States
☐ CBSA Pop Chg 2000-2007
   Less than 0
   0 - 100,000
   100,000 - 200,000
   200,000 or more
☑ CBSA %Pop Chg 2000-2007
   Less than 0%
   0 - 10%
   10 - 20%
   20% or more
☑ States

EXHIBIT 8–2
Population Growth of Metropolitan Statistical Areas

SOURCE: http://www.proximityone.com/msa0007.htm#maps, (accessed August 1, 2010).

the stores. For instance, the economies of some Rust Belt cities like Flint, Michigan, experience greater peaks and valleys because of their dependence on specific industries such as automobiles. If growth is not diversified in various industries, the area may be unattractive because of extreme cyclical trends. However, many areas that have been traditionally dependent on agriculture, a declining industry, have attempted to bring in new industries, such as manufacturing and high tech, to help diversify their economies.

Also, it is useful to determine which areas are growing quickly and why. For instance, the east side of Seattle, Washington, has become a desirable retail location because of its proximity to Microsoft's corporate headquarters. But the performance of these retail locations is inextricably linked to the financial performance of Microsoft.

In most cases, areas where the population is large and growing are preferable to those with declining populations. However, some retailers, such as Subway, often go into new strip shopping centers with few nearby households with the anticipation that the surrounding suburban area will eventually be built up enough to support the stores.

Competition

The level of competition in an area clearly affects the demand for a retailer's merchandise. Walmart's early success was based on a location strategy of opening stores in small towns with little competition. It offered consumers in small towns quality merchandise at low prices. Previously, rural consumers either shopped in small stores with limited assortments or drove to larger towns.

Although they once were viewed as undesirable areas, inner-city neighborhoods today host many full-service restaurant chains. Restaurants like IHOP, T.G.I. Friday's, Chili's, and Denny's are moving into urban areas from Oakland, California, to New York. They are discovering that these previously underserved markets are attractive because of the lack of competition, the relatively high level of disposable income of the residents, and the large, untapped labor force. Retailing View 8.1 describes how Whole Foods and Trader Joe's cater to an urban market segment, another area that tends to experience little competition in certain retail segments.

Strategic Fit

Population level, growth, and competition alone don't tell the whole story. The area needs to have consumers who are in the retailer's target market—who are attracted to the retailer's offerings and interested in patronizing its stores. Thus, the area must have the right demographic and lifestyle profile. The size and composition of households in an area can be an important determinant of success.

REFACT

The first Walmart Discount City opened in Rogers, Arkansas, in 1962.[3]

Location Characteristics

Some factors associated with specific locations that retailers consider when evaluating a site are (1) parking, (2) store visibility, and (3) adjacent retailers.

Parking The amount and quality of parking facilities are critical for evaluating a shopping center and specific site within the center. On the one hand, if there aren't enough spaces or the spaces are too far from the store, customers will be discouraged from patronizing the site and the store. On the other hand, if there are too many open spaces, the shopping center may be perceived as having unpopular stores. A standard rule of thumb is 5.5:1,000 (five and one-half spaces per thousand square feet of retail store space) for a shopping center and 10 to 15 spaces per 1,000 square feet for a supermarket.

Retailers need to observe the shopping center at various times of the day, week, and season. They also must consider the availability of employee parking, the proportion of shoppers using cars, parking by nonshoppers, and the typical length of a shopping trip.

An issue closely related to the amount of available parking facilities but extended into the shopping center itself is the relative congestion of the area. **Congestion** is an excess level of traffic that results in customer delays. There is an optimal level of congestion for customers. Too much congestion can make shopping slow, irritate customers, and generally discourage sales. However, a relatively high level of activity in a shopping center creates excitement and can stimulate sales.

Visibility **Visibility** refers to customers' ability to see the store from the street. Good visibility is less important for stores with a well-established and loyal customer base, but most retailers still want a direct, unimpeded view of their store. In

---

8.2 RETAILING VIEW The Importance of a Right Turn

One retailer's demise can be another retailer's opportunity. Jones Hardware & Building Supply in Wake Forest, North Carolina, survived the Great Depression and the relocation of the town's largest employer, so it believed it could survive Home Depot coming to town. However, the traffic pattern near the store was changed to accommodate new Home Depot and Target stores. The hardware store's once-accessible, prized corner-lot location was crippled by a new intersection that prevented a left turn into the store's parking lot. Customers needing to turn left to the store were forced to make a U-turn and access Jones Hardware through an adjoining Winn-Dixie parking lot. Whether it was this inconvenience or the arrival of Lowe's Home Improvement across from Home Depot, the fate of the smaller retailer was sealed and within two years Jones Hardware closed.

That same corner lot soon became the site of the town's or area's first Walgreens, because the location satisfies Walgreens' fundamental real estate strategy: to be easily accessible for residents as they return home from work. Walgreens positions its stores so that evening commuter traffic can make an easy right turn into the store's parking lot. The former Jones Hardware store fronts a key artery for afternoon commuter traffic, and the CVS store in the shopping center across from the Walgreens has to rely on customer loyalty to motivate those same commuters to make the less convenient left-hand turn into its parking area.

Walgreens selects locations that enable it to offer drive-through prescription pickup—a value-added customer service.

Sources: http://www.northbrook.il.us/Government/BoardsCommissions/Passouts/2008/072208RBM/documents/5.Walgreens-Traffic-Reviews.pdf (accessed December 2, 2009); Jim Frederick, "The Hedgehog vs. the Elephant: Winning the Walgreen Way," *Drug Store News,* March 19, 2007; Connie Gentry, "Science Validates Art," reprinted by permission from *Chain Store Age,* April 2005, pp. 83–84. Copyright Lebhar-Friedman, Inc., 425 Park Avenue, New York, NY 10022.

an area with a highly transient population, such as a tourist center or large city, good visibility from the road is particularly important.

Adjacent Tenants   Locations with complementary, as well as competing, adjacent retailers have the potential to build traffic. Complementary retailers target the same market segment but have a different, noncompeting merchandise offering. For example, Save-A-Lot, a limited-assortment supermarket targeting price-sensitive consumers, prefers to be colocated with other retailers targeting price-sensitive consumers, such as Big Lots, Family Dollar, or even Walmart.

Have you ever noticed that competing fast-food restaurants, automobile dealerships, antique dealers, or even shoe and apparel stores in a mall are located next to one another? Consumers looking for these types of merchandise are involved in convenience or comparison shopping situations, as we described in Chapter 7. They want to be able to make their choice easily in the case of convenience shopping, or they want to have a good assortment so that they can "shop around." This grouped location approach is based on the principle of **cumulative attraction,** which states that a cluster of similar and complementary retailing activities will generally have greater drawing power than isolated stores that engage in the same retailing activities.

Store visibility is an important consideration when evaluating a site. The Banana Republic store (left) is clearly visible, whereas the stores going up the stairs (right) are not.

REFACT

Microsoft is opening its stores in close proximity to its rival Apple so that it can attract potential customers interested in technology.[8]

Restrictions and Costs

As we will learn later in this chapter, retailers may place restrictions on the type of tenants that are allowed in a shopping center in their lease agreement. Some of these restrictions can make the shopping center more attractive for a retailer. For example, a specialty men's apparel retailer may prefer a lease agreement that precludes other men's specialty apparel retailers from locating in the same center. A florist in a strip center may specify that if the grocery anchor tenant vacates the center, it can be released from its lease. Retailers would look unfavorably on a shopping center with a sign size restriction that prevented easy visibility of the store's name from the street. At the end of the chapter, we discuss some other restrictions and cost issues involved in negotiating a lease.

Locations within a Shopping Center

Locating within a shopping center affects both sales and occupancy costs, in that the better locations have higher occupancy costs. In a strip shopping center, the locations closest to the supermarket are more expensive because they attract greater foot traffic. So a flower shop or sandwich shop that may attract impulse buyers should be close to the supermarket. But a shoe repair store, which does not cater to customers shopping on impulse, could be in a lower-traffic location farther away from the supermarket because customers in need of this service will seek out the store. In other words, it is a destination store.

The same issues apply to evaluating locations within a multilevel, enclosed shopping mall. Stores that cater to consumers engaging in comparison shopping, such as shoppers buying fashionable apparel, benefit from being in more expensive locations near the department store anchors, which are destinations for comparison apparel shoppers. As apparel shoppers enter and leave the department store, they walk by and may be attracted to neighboring specialty store retailers. In contrast, a retailer such as Foot Locker, another destination store, need not be in the most expensive location, because many of its customers know they're in the market for its type of product before they even go shopping.

Another consideration is how to locate stores that appeal to similar target markets. In essence, customers want to shop where they'll find a good assortment of merchandise. The principle of cumulative attraction applies to both stores that sell complementary merchandise and those that compete directly with one another. Consider Exhibit 8–4, a map of the Columbia Mall, the centerpiece of the planned community of Columbia, Maryland. The mall's trade area includes about three-quarters of a million people, located in wealthy Howard County, which is positioned halfway between Baltimore, Maryland, and Washington, D.C. Some of the mall's tenants are restaurants P.F. Chang's, Uno Chicago Grill, and Champs; a 14-screen, state-of-the-art, stadium-seating cinema; and L.L.Bean, Domain, Restoration Hardware, Banana Republic, bebe, Build-A-Bear Workshop, Abercrombie & Fitch, Starbucks, J.Crew, and GUESS stores.

Many of the tenants are positioned within the mall into category zones to better match their target audience. A good example of this positioning is the location of retailers selling children's apparel and related merchandise. Looking at the map

EXHIBIT 8–4   Grouping Retailers in an Enclosed Mall

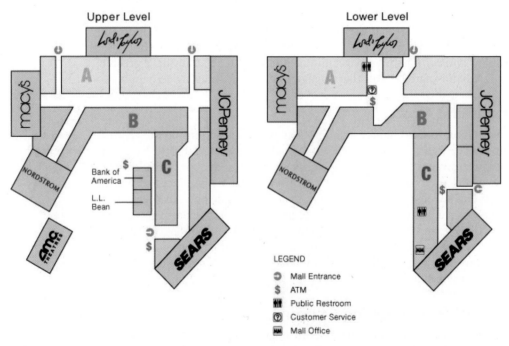

These three shoe stores are positioned next to each other because they appeal to the same target markets and therefore draw more customers.

in Exhibit 8–4, note that Gymboree and Abercrombie Kids are located side by side in Section B on the lower level. A short escalator ride to the upper level takes busy parents and their children to the Build-A-Bear Workshop and the Disney Store, all located in Section B. Directly across the walkway in Section A, shoppers can visit GapKids and Justice for more children's clothing and accessories.

TRADE AREA CHARACTERISTICS

After identifying several sites that have acceptable traffic flow, accessibility, and other location characteristics, the next step is to collect information about the trade area that can be used to forecast sales for a store located at the site. The retailer first needs to define the trade area for the site. Once the trade area is defined, the retailer can use several different information sources to develop a detailed understanding of the nature of consumers in the site's trade area.

Trade Area Definition

A **trade area** is a contiguous geographic area that accounts for the majority of a store's sales and customers. Trade areas can be divided into three zones, as shown in Exhibit 8–5. The exhibit shows the trade area zones for a shopping center located at the red square: the 5-minute drive-time zone (light brown), the 10-minute zone (blue), and the 15-minute zone (green).

The trade area zones shown in Exhibit 8–5 are not concentric circles based on distance from the store but, rather, are irregular polygons based on the location of roads, highways, and natural barriers, like rivers and valleys, that affect the driving time to the store. The location of competitive stores can also affect the actual trade area configuration.

The **primary trading area** is the geographic area from which the shopping center or store site derives 50 to 70 percent of its customers. The **secondary trading area** is the geographic area of secondary importance in terms of customer sales, generating about 20 to 30 percent of the site's customers. The **tertiary trading area** or **fringe** (the outermost area) includes the remaining customers who shop at

EXHIBIT 8–5
Zones in a Trade Area

the site but come from widely dispersed areas. These customers might travel an unusually long distance because they do not have comparable retail facilities closer to home, or they may drive near the store or center on their way to or from work.

The best way to define the three zones is based on driving time rather than distance. Thus, the primary trading area might be defined as customers within 5 minutes' driving time of the site; the secondary trading area, as customers with a 10-minute drive; and the tertiary zone, as customers more than 15 minutes away from the site by car. In bigger cities where driving times are lengthy, such as Los Angeles, the primary trading area may be 15 minutes; the secondary trading area, 40 minutes; and the tertiary trading area, more than 1 hour. However, it is much easier to collect information about the number of people and their characteristics in the different zones by geographic distance than by driving time. Thus, retailers often define the zones by distance—such as 3, 5, and 10 miles from the site—rather than driving time.

Factors Affecting the Size of the Trade Area

The actual boundaries of a trade area are determined by the store's accessibility, natural and physical barriers, and level of competition, which we discussed previously in this chapter. The boundaries are also affected by the type of shopping area and type of store.

Trade area size is influenced by the type of store or shopping area. A Starbucks in a central business district, for example, may have a trade area of only two or three blocks; a category specialist like Best Buy may draw customers from 10 miles away; and The Container Store, which is the only store of its kind in a city, might draw customers from 30 miles away. The size of the trading area is determined by the nature of the merchandise sold, the assortment offered, and the location of alternative sources for the merchandise. People go to convenience stores because they can buy products like milk and bread quickly and easily; thus, their trade areas are relatively small. Category specialists, in contrast, offer a large choice of brands and products for which customers are engaged in comparison shopping. Thus, customers generally drive some distance to shop at these stores.

Recall from Chapter 7 that a destination store is a place where consumers will go even if it is inconvenient. In general, destination stores have a large trade area—people are willing to drive farther to shop there. Examples of destination stores are shopping mall anchor stores such as department stores, certain specialty stores such as IKEA, category specialists such as Staples and Office Depot, and some service providers such as IMAX theaters.

A **parasite store** is one that does not create its own traffic and whose trade area is determined by the dominant retailer in the shopping center or retail area. A colocated dry cleaner would be a parasite store to a Walmart store because people tend to stop at the dry cleaner on the way to or from Walmart and other stores. Its business is thus derived from Walmart and other businesses in the area. Some retail experts have noted that Walmart can be a destructive force to competition in a trade area because it is so dominant. Yet some parasite stores and stores that have learned to provide product or service offerings that complement, rather than compete with, those of Walmart actually benefit from its presence.

For example, Party City, the world's largest party supply retailer, has over 600 company-owned franchised stores. They offer a wide selection of merchandise for celebratory occasions, such as birthdays and anniversaries, as well as for seasonal events, such as Halloween and Thanksgiving. Party City looks for regional power centers with nationally recognized cotenants such as Walmart, Target, or Kohl's because of the traffic these stores bring to the center. It chooses locations that have a high density of solid middle-income shoppers, a growing population, and a high percentage of children. Party City carries a broader assortment and deeper variety of party supplies than Walmart or Target.[9] Other examples of parasite stores are food court restaurants and kiosks in a mall.

Measuring the Trade Area for a Retail Site

Retailers can determine the trade area for their existing stores by customer spotting. **Customer spotting** is the process of locating the residences of customers for a store on a map and displaying their positions relative to the store location. The addresses for locating the customers' residences usually are obtained by asking the customers, recording the information from a check or Internet channel purchase, or collecting the information from customer loyalty programs. The data collected

This Party City store picks up customers from Kohl's. It is therefore a parasite store.

from customer spotting can be processed in two ways: manually plotting the location of each customer on a map or using a geographic information system like those described later in this chapter. Retailing View 8.3 describes how multichannel retailers use their catalog and Internet sales data to spot customers and use that information to identify potential store locations.

It is more challenging to estimate the trade area for a new store location than for existing locations. However, retailers typically use information about the trade areas for existing stores to estimate the trade areas for new stores. For example, a sporting goods retail chain with 7,000-square-foot stores located in neighborhood shopping centers might find that the primary trading area for its stores is a drive of less than 10 minutes, the secondary trading area is a drive of 10 to 20 minutes, and the tertiary trading zone is more than a 20-minute drive. Assuming the site under consideration is located in an area that has similar demographic and lifestyle characteristics, the retailer assumes the trade areas for the new site will be defined by the same 10- and 20-minute drive times.

Sources of Information about the Trade Area

To further analyze the attractiveness of a potential store site, a retailer needs information about both the consumers and the competitors in the site's trade area. Two widely used sources of information about the nature of consumers in a trade area are (1) data published by the U.S. Census Bureau, based on the *Decennial*

8.3 RETAILING VIEW Customer Spotting for Multichannel Retailers

Multichannel retailers that sell merchandise using catalogs and the Internet have an advantage over store-based retailers in locating and evaluating potential store sites because they can apply their customer data to help them determine which locations are more likely to be profitable. For example, Talbots, a specialty apparel multichannel retailer, relies primarily on catalog and Internet sales data when determining whether and where to open a store. It has developed and validated a formula for analyzing its catalog and Internet sales data to tell where its customers are and what they're buying. Hypothetically, if Talbots did $150,000 in catalog sales in a particular area last year, it knows it can put a store there and do $1 million to $1.5 million in retail sales.

Using these nonstore sales data, Talbots opens successful stores in locales that other retailers overlook. At one time, Talbots thought its classic styles appealed only to women in the Northeast and Midwest, but strong catalog sales in the Sun Belt states encouraged the company to open stores in warmer climates. Nonstore sales data also identified some locations it would not normally consider. For instance, although Fishkill, New York—some 75 miles north of New

Talbots, L.L.Bean, and Orvis use the addresses of their catalog and Internet customers to determine promising locations for their future stores.

York City—has a population of fewer than 20,000 people, it is the site of a profitable Talbots store. Some of the company's best-performing stores are in similar, overlooked areas. Talbots is often a destination location, and it knows it has established customer bases in these towns and surrounding areas.

Although outdoor and apparel Internet and catalog retailers L.L.Bean and Orvis have a much smaller physical store presence, they both utilize similar customer-spotting procedures for locating new stores. In particular, Bean noticed a high number of catalog and online purchases coming from southeastern Massachusetts. So it opened a store in Dedham, just south of Boston. Orvis examines its customer database by zip code, looking for areas with high concentrations of customers. After narrowing the potential markets, Orvis matches the geodemographics in the areas with those of its target customers to isolate the best potential locations.

Sources: Tziperman Lotan, "Legacy Place L.L. Bean Opens in Dedham," *Wicked Local Easton*, July 27, 2009; Bruce Soderholm, Senior Vice President, Operations, Talbots, personal communication, April 2006.

Census of the United States, and (2) data from geographic information systems, provided by several commercial firms.

Demographic Data from U.S. Census Bureau

A **census** is a count of the population of a country as of a specified date. The first U.S. decennial census was undertaken in 1790 as part of a constitutional mandate to periodically reapportion state representation in the House of Representatives on the basis of states' population.

Every 10 years, census takers attempt to gather demographic information (sex, age, ethnicity, education, marital status, etc.) from every household in the United States. The census questionnaire also asks about such things as foster children and stepchildren, the presence of solar heat in the home, and grandparents as primary caregivers of children. The decennial census is more than just a head count; it provides a snapshot of the country's demographic, social, and economic characteristics.

The U.S. Census Bureau prepares periodic reports summarizing the data from two sources: the census demographics for each person and additional data collected from a sample of the population. The smallest geographic entity for which census data are available is the **census block,** an area bounded on all sides by visible (roads, rivers, etc.) and/or invisible (county or state boundaries) features. There are 8 million census blocks in the United States, each containing the residences of about 40 people. The smallest unit for the sample data is the **block group,** a collection of adjacent blocks that contain between 300 and 4,000 people. Data are also available at higher levels of aggregation, including zip code, census tract (collections of adjacent block groups), county, state, and region.[12]

Although the data from the U.S. Census Bureau can be used to develop a better understanding of the nature of consumers in a region or trade area, these data have several limitations. First, because they are based on information collected every 10 years, they are not very current, although the projections are reasonably accurate. Second, the data are not particularly user-friendly. It is difficult to utilize census data to examine the trade areas for various locations for specific products or services. Thus, most retailers rely on the geographic information system data offered by a number of companies to examine trade areas for potential stores.

Geographic Information System Suppliers

A **geographic information system (GIS)** is a system of hardware and software used to store, retrieve, map, and analyze geographic data; a GIS also includes the operating personnel and the data that go into the system. The key feature of GIS data is that they are identified with a coordinate system (latitude and longitude) that references a particular place on Earth. The data in the systems include spatial features such as rivers and roads, as well as descriptive information associated with the spatial features, such as the street address and the characteristics of the household at the address.

Firms such as Esri (www.esri.com), Claritas (www.claritas.com), and Map-Info (www.mapinfo.com) that construct and offer services involving GIS combine updated demographic census data with data from other sources that describe consumer spending patterns and lifestyles in a geographic area. In addition, they provide a user-friendly interface so that the data can be accessed and analyzed easily. Frequently, the outputs from the system are maps that enable retailers to visualize the implications of the data quickly. For example, the map in Exhibit 8–6 shows the trading areas for three branch banks that a retailer has in an MSA and a fourth branch it is considering, as well as the residences of its customers relative to the branch at which they bank. This map suggests that people bank near their work and, thus, that the new location might cannibalize from the other branches.

EXHIBIT 8–6
GIS Map for Bank Trade
Areas in an MSA

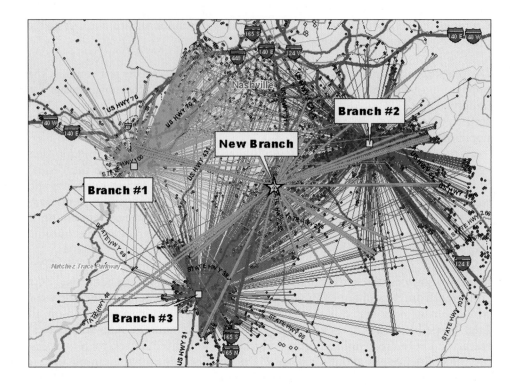

For example, a retailer interested in developing a deeper understanding of the trade areas for several sites can provide Esri with the street addresses for the sites under consideration. The system then provides the projected data shown in the table below current year estimates and five-year projections pertaining to people living within a 3-, 5-, and 10-mile radius of the sites.

Gender	Occupation
Income	Travel time to work
Disposible income	Transportation mode to work
Net worth	Household composition
Education	Household expenditures by NAICS categories
Age	Geodemographic market segment
Race/ethnicity	Market potential index
Employment status	Spending potential index

An example of a report on the retail goods and services purchased by residents in a trade area is shown in Exhibit 8–7. In addition to presenting the demographic data, this sample report contains some special data—the lifestyle segments represented in the trade area and the spending power index for various retail categories—that are discussed next. But first consider how the hamburger chain Wendy's utilizes GIS information.

Not too long ago, Wendy's used demographic data like household income to make site selection decisions. Now it uses a model based on GIS data that help it decide on which markets to focus, such as whether to concentrate on Miami or Salt Lake City. On a micro level, the GIS tools help Wendy's select a site within the market. Working with a Web-based tool from Nielsen Claritas, which we described in Chapter 4, the GIS team accesses data about Wendy's existing stores to create projected sales forecasts for new sites. The analysis takes less than a minute and provides maps with great detail, such as traffic counts, shopping center locations, competitors, and surrounding neighborhoods. Also, the information is updated whenever the market changes.

Retail Goods and Services Expenditures
Sample Report

Proposed Location
100 S Wacker Dr, Chicago, IL 60606-4006
Ring: 1 mile radius

Latitude: 41.8805
Longitude: -87.63715

Top Tapestry Segments:		Demographic Summary	2010	2015
Metro Renters	68.4%	Population	45,534	50,151
Laptops and Lattes	23.4%	Households	24,338	26,808
City Strivers	2.7%	Families	7,223	7,843
Main Street, USA	1.8%	Median Age	35.7	35.8
Metropolitans	1.6%	Median Household Income	$81,441	$100,632

	Spending Potential Index	Average Amount Spent	Total
Apparel and Services	120	$2,873.94	$69,945,928
Men's	112	$512.65	$12,476,953
Women's	104	$861.55	$20,968,522
Children's	121	$485.96	$11,827,277
Footwear	84	$349.13	$8,497,153
Watches & Jewelry	173	$335.43	$8,163,589
Apparel Products and Services[1]	352	$329.21	$8,012,434
Computer			
Computers and Hardware for Home Use	169	$324.62	$7,900,647
Software and Accessories for Home Use	169	$48.15	$1,171,788
Entertainment & Recreation	155	$4,996.06	$121,594,105
Fees and Admissions	155	$960.54	$23,377,534
Membership Fees for Clubs[2]	155	$253.65	$6,173,216
Fees for Participant Sports, excl. Trips	145	$154.42	$3,758,358
Admission to Movie/Theatre/Opera/Ballet	172	$260.56	$6,341,578
Admission to Sporting Events, excl. Trips	149	$88.77	$2,160,410
Fees for Recreational Lessons	147	$201.16	$4,895,736
Dating Services	257	$1.98	$48,236
TV/Video/Audio	161	$2,003.60	$48,763,617
Community Antenna or Cable TV	157	$1,130.81	$27,521,629

Tapestry™ Segmentation Esri and other GIS suppliers have developed schemes for classifying geographic areas in the United States by combining census and survey data about people's lifestyles and purchasing behavior with the mapping capabilities of GIS. The analysis is based on the premise that "birds of a feather flock together." Specifically, people who live in the same neighborhoods tend to have similar lifestyles and consumer behavior patterns.

The Esri Tapestry Segmentation system classifies all U.S. residential neighborhoods into 65 distinctive segments, based on demographic and socioeconomic characteristics. Exhibit 8–7 is a hypothetical report for the area within a 1.5-mile radius of 100 S. Wacker Drive in Chicago. Each segment provides a description of the typical person in that segment. The largest segment in the trade area report in Exhibit 8–7 is Metro Renters.[13] According to Esri, residents of Metro Renters neighborhoods are young (approximately 30 percent are in their 20s) well-educated singles beginning their professional careers in some of the largest U.S. cities such as New York City, Los Angeles, and Chicago. The median age is 33.6 years; the median household income is $56,311. Most rent apartments in high-rise buildings, living alone or with a roommate. They travel, read two or more daily newspapers, listen to classical music and public radio, and go online. To stay fit, they work out regularly at clubs, play tennis and volleyball, practice yoga, ski, and jog. They go dancing and to the movies, attend rock concerts, visit museums, and throw frisbees. Painting and drawing are favorite hobbies. They are politically liberal.

EXHIBIT 8–8
Location of Target
Customers in Shopping
Center Trade Area

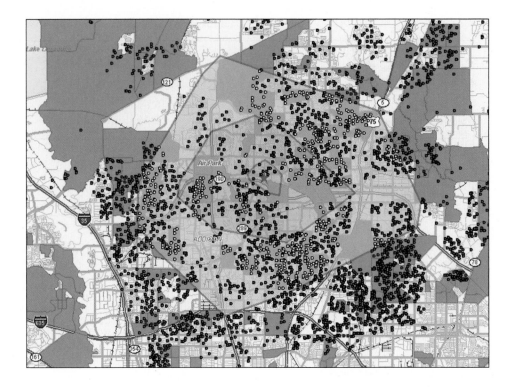

Several similar, competing segmentation systems are currently commercially available, including PRIZM (Potential Rating Index for Zip Markets), which was developed by Nielsen Claritas and is described in Chapter 4.

Exhibit 8–8 shows the location of customers who have the desired geodemographic profile on a trade area map for a shopping center. Note that most of the retailer's desirable customers are not even in the tertiary trade area; thus, this shopping center would not be a desirable location. (The shopping center is designated by the red star. The primary trade area is green; the secondary trade area is lavender; and the tertiary trade area is turquoise.)

Nonmarried, young adults with college educations tend to live in large metropolitan areas.

Spending Potential Index   Data in Esri's Consumer Spending database is reported by product or service; variables include total expenditures, average amount spent per household, and a **Spending Potential Index (SPI).** The SPI compares the local average expenditure by product to the national average amount spent. An index of 100 is average. For example, an SPI of 120 shows that average spending by local consumers is 20 percent above the national average; an SPI of 80 means that average local spending is 20 percent below the national average. (See Exhibit 8–7.)

Competition in the Trade Area

In addition to needing information about the residents in a trade area, retailers need to know about the amount and type of competition in the trade area. Although GIS vendors provide data on the location of competitive retailers, there are also other sources for this information. For example, most retailer Web sites list not only all current store locations but future sites as well. A more traditional method of accessing competitive information is to look through the Yellow Pages of the telephone book. Other sources of competitive information include directories published by trade associations, chambers of commerce, *Chain Store Guide* (published by CSG Information Services, www.csgis.com), and municipal and county governments.

ESTIMATING POTENTIAL SALES FOR A STORE SITE

Three approaches for using information about the trade area to estimate the potential sales for a store at the location are (1) the Huff gravity model, (2) regression analysis, and (3) the analog method.

Huff Gravity Model

The **Huff gravity model**[14] for estimating the sales of a retail store is based on the concept of gravity: Consumers are attracted to a store location, just like Newton's falling apple was attracted to the Earth. In this model, the force of the attraction is based on two factors: the size of the store (larger stores have more pulling power) and the time it takes to travel to the store (stores that take more time to get to have less pulling power). The mathematical formula for predicting the probability of a customer's going to a specific store location is

$$P_{ij} = \frac{S_j / T_{ij}^{\lambda}}{\Sigma S_j / T_{ij}^{\lambda}}$$

where

P_{ij} = probability that customer i shops at location j

S_j = size of the store at location j

T_{ij} = travel time for customer i to get to location j

The formula indicates that the larger the size (S_j) of the store compared with competing stores' sizes, the greater the probability that a customer will shop at the location. A larger size is generally more attractive in consumers' eyes because it means more merchandise assortment and variety. Travel time or distance (T_{ij}) has the opposite effect on the probability that a consumer will shop at a location. The greater the travel time or distance from the consumer, compared with that of competing locations, the lower the probability that the consumer will shop at the location. Generally, customers would rather shop at a close store than a distant one.

The exponent λ reflects the relative effect of travel time versus store size. When λ is equal to 1, store size and travel time have an equal but opposite effect on the

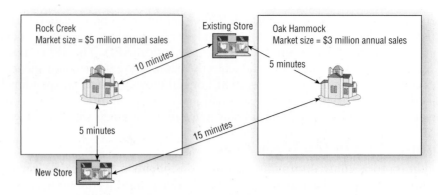

probability of a consumer's shopping at a store location. When λ is greater than 1, travel time has a greater effect, and when λ is less than 1, store size has a greater effect. The value of λ is affected by the nature of the shopping trips consumers generally take when visiting the specific type of store. For instance, travel time or distance is generally more important for convenience goods than for shopping goods because people are less willing to travel a great distance for a quart of milk than they are for a new pair of shoes. Thus, a larger value for λ is assigned if the store being studied specializes in convenience shopping trips rather than comparison shopping trips. The value of λ is usually estimated statistically using data that describe shopping patterns at existing stores.

To illustrate the use of the Huff model, consider the situations shown in Exhibit 8–9. A small town has two communities, Rock Creek and Oak Hammock. The town currently has one 5,000-square-foot drugstore with annual sales of $8 million, $3 million of which come from Oak Hammock residents and $5 million from Rock Creek residents. A competitive chain is considering opening a 10,000-square-foot store. As the exhibit illustrates, the driving time for the average Rock Creek resident to the existing store is 10 minutes, but it would be only five minutes to the new store. In contrast, the driving time for the typical Oak Hammock resident to the existing drugstore is 5 minutes and would be 15 minutes to the new store. Based on its past experience, the drugstore chain has found that λ equals 2 for its store locations. Using the Huff formula, the probability of a Rock Creek resident's shopping at the new location, P_{RC}, is

$$P_{RC} = \frac{10,000/5^2}{10,000/5^2 + 5,000/10^2} = .889$$

The probability of Oak Hammock residents' shopping at the new location, P_{OH}, is

$$P_{OH} = \frac{10,000/15^2}{10,000/15^2 + 5,000/5^2} = .182$$

The expected sales (probability of patronage times market size) for the new location thus would be

.889 × $3 million + .182 × $5 million = $4,910,000

This simple application assumes that the market size for drugstores in the community will remain the same at $8 million with the addition of the new store. We also could have considered that two drugstores would increase the total size of the market. In addition, rather than do the calculations for the average customer located in the middle of each community, we could have calculated the probabilities that each customer in the two communities would go to the new location.

Even though the Huff gravity model considers only two factors affecting store sales—travel time and store size—its predictions are quite accurate because these two factors typically have the greatest effect on store choice.[15] The regression approach discussed in the next section provides a way to incorporate additional factors into the sales forecast for a store under consideration.

Regression Analysis

The **regression analysis** approach is based on the assumption that factors that affect the sales of existing stores in a chain will have the same impact on stores located at new sites being considered. When using this approach, the retailer employs a technique called *multiple regression* to estimate a statistical model that predicts sales at existing store locations. The technique can consider the effects of the wide range of factors discussed in this chapter, including site characteristics, such as visibility and access, and characteristics of the trade area, such as demographics and lifestyle segments represented.

Consider the following example: A chain of sporting goods stores has analyzed the factors affecting sales in its existing stores and found that the following model is the best predictor of store sales (the weights for the factors, such as 275 for the number of households, are estimated using multiple regression):

Stores sales = 275 × number of households in trade area (15-minute drive time)
+ 1,800,000 × percentage of households in trade area with
    children under 15 years of age
+ 2,000,000 × percentage of households in trade area in
    Aspiring young segment
+ 8 × shopping center square feet
+ 250,000 if visible from street
+ 300,000 if Walmart in center

The sporting goods chain is considering the following two locations:

Variable	Location A	Location B
Households within 15 minute drive time	11,000	15,000
% of households with children under 15 years old	70%	20%
% of households in *Aspiring young* segment	60%	10%
Sq ft of shopping center	200,000	250,000
Visible from street	yes	no
Walmart in shopping center	yes	no

Using the statistical model, the forecasted sales for location A are

Stores sales at location A = $7,635,000 = 275 × 11,000
+ 1,800,000 × 0.7
+ 2,000,000 × 0.6
+ 8 × 200,000
+ 250,000
+ 300,000

and forecasted sales for location B are:

Store sales at location B = $6,685,000 = 275 × 15,000
+ 1,800,000 × 0.2
+ 2,000,000 × 0.1
+ 8 × 250,000

Note that location A has greater forecasted sales, even though it has a smaller trading area population and shopping center size, because the profile of its target market fits the profile of the trade area better.

Analog Approach

To develop a regression model, a retailer needs data about the trade area and site characteristics from a large number of stores. Because small chains cannot use the regression approach, they use the similar but more subjective analog approach. When using the **analog approach,** the retailer simply describes the site and trade area characteristics for its most successful stores and attempts to find a site with similar characteristics. The use of this approach is described in the following illustration.

ILLUSTRATION OF SITE SELECTION: EDWARD BEINER PURVEYOR OF FINE EYEWEAR

Edward Beiner Purveyor of Fine Eyewear is a nine-store Florida retailer specializing in upper-end, high-fashion eyewear. Its store in South Miami is in a Main Street location. Although a Main Street location does not draw from a trade area as large as a central business district or a shopping center, it serves the people working and living in the area.

The retailers in this Main Street location recognize that their location lacks the entertainment and recreation found in shopping centers, so they sponsor art and music festivals to bring people to the area. On Halloween, each store provides candy to its future customers and their parents.

Edward Beiner Purveyor of Fine Eyewear recognizes other issues that make its South Miami Main Street location less than perfect. There's no protection against the heavy rains that characterize the area's subtropical climate. Security also could be an issue, although most stores are closed at night. Finally, parking is often a problem.

In general, though, Edward Beiner finds its Main Street location attractive. The rent is much less than it would be in a shopping mall. There is usually good pedestrian traffic. Because the properties in the Main Street location are owned by several individuals, the landlords have less control over the tenants than they would in a planned shopping center. Finally, there are other optical stores in the area, although the competition is not intense due to the exclusive lines Edward Beiner carries.

Edward Beiner Purveyor of Fine Eyewear wants to open a new location. Because the South Miami site is its best store, it would like to find a location whose trade area has similar characteristics. It has identified several potential locations that it is evaluating.

Using the analog approach, Edward Beiner undertakes the following steps:

1. Do a competitive analysis.
2. Define present trade area.
3. Analyze trade area characteristics.
4. Match characteristics of present trade area with potential sites.

Edward Beiner Purveyor of Fine Eyewear specializes in high-fashion eyewear and targets affluent consumers.

Competitive Analysis of Potential Locations   **EXHIBIT 8–10**

(1) Trade Area	(2) Eyeglasses/ Year/ Person	(3) Trade Area Population	(4) Total Eyeglasses Potential	(5) Estimated Eyeglasses Sold	(6) Trade Area Potential Units	(7) Trade Area Potential Percentage	(8) Relative Level of Competition
South Miami	0.2	85,979	17,196	7,550	9,646	56.09%	Low
Site A	0.2	91,683	18,337	15,800	2,537	13.83	Medium
Site B	0.2	101,972	20,394	12,580	7,814	38.32	Low
Site C	0.2	60,200	12,040	11,300	740	6.15	High
Site D	0.2	81,390	16,278	13,300	2,978	18.29	Medium

Conduct Competitive Analysis

The competitive analysis of the four potential sites being considered by Edward Beiner is shown in Exhibit 8–10. To perform the analysis, Edward Beiner first estimated the number of eyeglasses sold per year per person (column 2), obtained from industry sources. Then the area population was taken from U.S. Census data (column 3). Column 4 is an estimate of the trade area potential reached by multiplying column 2 by column 3.

The estimates of the number of eyeglasses sold in the trade areas, column 5, are based on visits to competitive stores. Column 6 represents the unit sales potential for eyeglasses in the trade areas, or column 4 minus column 5. Then the trade area potential penetration is calculated by dividing column 6 by column 4. For instance, because the total eyeglass potential for the South Miami store trade area is 17,196 pairs and an additional 9,646 pairs could be sold in that trade area, 56.09 percent of the eyeglass market in this area remains untapped. The bigger the number, the lower the competition.

Column 8, the relative level of competition, is subjectively estimated on the basis of column 7. Unlike other optical stores in the trade area, Edward Beiner Optical carries a very exclusive merchandise selection. In general, however, the higher the trade area potential, the lower the relative competition will be.

On the basis of the information in Exhibit 8–10, Edward Beiner Optical should locate its new store at site B. The trade area potential is high, and competition is relatively low. Of course, relative competition is only one issue to consider. Later in this section, we'll consider competition along with other issues to determine which is the best new location for Edward Beiner Optical.

Define Present Trade Area

On the basis of customer spotting data gathered from Beiner's data warehouse of current customers, the trade area map in Exhibit 8–11 was generated using Esri's GIS software. The zones are based on drive times: 5 minutes for the primary trade area (red), 10 minutes for the secondary trade area (purple), and 20 minutes for the tertiary trade area (green). Note that the trade area boundaries are oblong because the major highways, especially U.S. 1, run north and south. Not only do the north-south highways bring traffic to the area, but heavy traffic often makes them difficult to cross. Biscayne Bay also limits the trade area on the east.

Because Edward Beiner Optical has a Main Street location, its trade area is smaller than it would be if the store were located in a regional shopping mall. However, Edward Beiner Optical is one of several optical shops in this business district. Having similar shopping goods stores in the same vicinity expands its trade area boundaries; more people are drawn to the area to shop because of its expanded selection. In addition, Edward Beiner Optical's trade area is limited on the south by a large regional shopping center that has several stores carrying similar merchandise.

EXHIBIT 8–11   Trade Area for Edward Beiner Optical

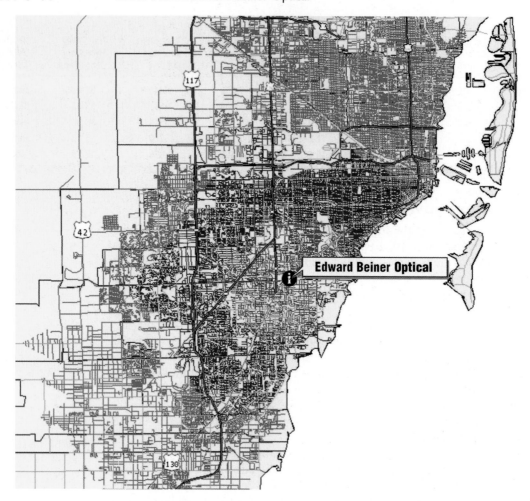

Identify Trade Area Characteristics

Having defined its trade area, Edward Beiner Optical reviewed a number of reports describing the characteristics of its trade area. Some of interesting findings from these reports were:

* The average household income is $92,653. In addition, 27.6 percent of the households have incomes between $75,000 and $149,000, and 13.7 percent have incomes over $150,000. The 3-mile ring surrounding Edward Beiner Optical is very affluent.

* The area surrounding Edward Beiner Optical has a population that is 53.1 percent Hispanic.

Match Characteristics of Present Trade Area with Potential Sites

Edward Beiner Optical believes that the profile of its current trade area is high income, predominantly white-collar occupations, a relatively large percentage of older residents, upscale geodemographic segments, and relatively low competition for expensive, high-fashion eyewear. Exhibit 8–12 compares Edward Beiner's current location with four potential locations on these five factors.

Four Potential Locations for a New Edward Beiner Optical Store   **EXHIBIT 8–12**

Store Location	Average Household Income	White-Collar Occupations	Percentage Residents Age 45 and Over	Predominant Geodemographic Segments	Level of Competition
Edward Beiner					
Optical	$100,000	High	37%	Top One Percent	Low
Site A	60,000	High	25	Young Immigrant Families	Medium
Site B	70,000	Low	80	Gray Power	Low
Site C	100,000	High	30	Young Literati	High
Site D	120,000	High	50	Upper-Income Empty-Nesters	Medium

Although the potential customers of site A typically have white-collar occupations, they also have relatively low incomes and are comparatively young. Young Immigrant Families also tend to have young families, so expensive eyewear may not be a priority purchase. Finally, there's a medium level of competition in the area.

The Gray Power residents surrounding site B have moderate incomes and are mostly retired. Even though competition would be low and most residents need glasses, these customers are more interested in value than in fashion.

Site C has strong potential because the Young Literati residents in the area are young and have a strong interest in fashion. Although working, they are busy furnishing their first homes and apartments and paying off college loans. They probably would appreciate Edward Beiner's fashionable assortment, but they won't appreciate the high prices. Also, other high-end optical stores are entrenched in the area.

Site D is the best location for Edward Beiner. The residents are older professionals or early retirees with high incomes. Upper-Income Empty-Nesters are sophisticated consumers of adult luxuries like high-fashion eyewear. Importantly, this geodemographic segment is similar to a large segment in Edward Beiner's current location.

Unfortunately, finding analogous situations isn't always as easy as in this example. The weaker the analogy, the more difficult the location decision will be. When a retailer has a relatively small number of outlets (say, 20 or fewer), the analog approach is often best. As the number of stores increases, it becomes more difficult for the analyst to organize the data in a meaningful way. More analytical approaches, such as regression analysis, then are necessary.

NEGOTIATING A LEASE

Once a particular site is chosen, retailers still face a multitude of decisions, including the types and terms of the lease.

Types of Leases

Most retailers lease store sites. Although there are advantages to owning a store site (such as stable mortgage payments and freedom from lease covenants), most retailers don't wish to tie up their capital by owning real estate. Also, most of the best locations—such as in shopping malls—are available only by leasing. There are two basic types of leases: percentage and fixed-rate.

Percentage Leases   Although there are many combinations within each type of lease, the most common form is a **percentage lease**, in which the rent is based on a percentage of sales. In addition to the percentage of sales, retailers typically pay a maintenance fee based on a percentage of their square footage of leased space. Most malls use some form of percentage lease. Because retail leases typically run for 5 to 10 years, they appear equitable to both parties if rents go up (or down) with sales and inflation.

A **percentage lease with a specified maximum** is a lease that pays the lessor, or landlord, a percentage of sales up to a maximum amount. This type of lease rewards good retailer performance by allowing the retailer to hold rent constant above a certain level of sales. A similar variation, the **percentage lease with a specified minimum**, specifies that the retailer must pay a minimum rent, no matter how low sales are.

Another type of percentage lease is a **sliding scale lease,** in which the percentage of sales paid as rent decreases as the sales go up. For instance, a retailer may pay 4 percent on the first $200,000 in sales and then 3 percent on sales greater than $200,000. Similar to the percentage lease with a specified maximum, the sliding scale rewards high-performing retailers.

Fixed-Rate Leases   The second basic type of lease is a **fixed-rate lease,** most commonly used by community and neighborhood centers. A retailer pays a fixed amount per month over the life of the lease. With a fixed-rate lease, the retailer and landlord know exactly how much will be paid in rent, but as noted previously, this type of lease does not appear as popular as the various forms of percentage leases.

A variation of the fixed-rate lease is the **graduated lease,** in which rent increases by a fixed amount over a specified period of time. For instance, rent may be $1,000 per month for the first three years and $1,250 for the next five years.

A **maintenance-increase-recoupment lease** can be used with either a percentage or fixed-rate lease. This type of lease allows the landlord to increase the rent if insurance, property taxes, or utility bills increase beyond a certain point.

Terms of the Lease

Although leases are formal contracts, they can be changed to reflect the relative power and specific needs of the retailer. Because the basic format of most leases is developed by the lessor (the property owner), the lease's terms may be slanted in favor of the lessor. It is therefore up to the lessee (the party signing the lease, in this case, the retailer) to be certain that the lease reflects the lessee's needs. Let's look at some clauses retailers may wish to include in a lease.

Cotenancy Clause   Some retail leases contain a **cotenancy clause.** Taking many forms, some cotenancy clauses require that a certain percentage of a shopping center be leased, while others name specific retailers or types of retailers that are to remain open. If these terms are not met, the retailers with the cotenancy clauses may demand rent reductions or leave altogether. If a retailer has not yet moved in, it can back out of the center if the tenants specified in the cotenancy clause either leave the center or fail to move in. Cotenancy clauses have become particularly important in the last few years as many retailers, including several large chains like Circuit City and Linens 'N Things, have created vacancies as a result of their bankruptcies.

Prohibited-Use Clause   A **prohibited-use clause** limits the landlord from leasing to certain kinds of tenants. Many retailers don't want the landlord to lease space to establishments that take up parking spaces but do not bring in shoppers, such as a bowling alley, skating rink, meeting hall, dentist, or real estate office. Retailers may also wish to restrict the use of space from those establishments that could harm the shopping center's wholesome image. Prohibited-use clauses often specify that bars, pool halls, game parlors, off-track betting establishments, massage parlors, and pornography retailers are unacceptable.

Tiffany & Co., the famous high-end jeweler, is employing its lease's prohibited-use clause in a lawsuit against the Westfield Century City shopping center in Los Angeles. It alleges that a new H&M store in this mall would tarnish its high-end image. Although H&M is a fashion-forward retailer, it also carries relatively low-priced merchandise. Tiffany's lease with Westfield forbids retailers "whose merchandise and/or price points are not considered to be luxury, upscale or better by conventional retail industry standards" to use or lease certain spaces within, fronting, or adjacent to the Tiffany store.[16]

Exclusive-Use Clause   An **exclusive-use clause** prohibits the landlord from leasing to retailers that sell competing products. For example, a discount store's lease may specify that the landlord cannot lease to other discount stores, variety stores, or limited-assortment value retailers.

Some retailers also are particular about how the storefront appears. For instance, a women's specialty store may specify that the storefront must have floor-to-ceiling glass to maximize window displays and improve customers' ability to see into the store. Other retailers believe it is important that nothing blocks the view of the store from the street, so they specify that the landlord cannot place any outparcels in the parking lot. An **outparcel** is a building (such as a bank or McDonald's) or kiosk (such as an automatic teller machine) that sits in the parking lot of a shopping center but is not physically attached to the center.

SUMMARY

Location decisions have great strategic importance because they have significant effects on store choice and are difficult advantages for competitors to duplicate. Picking good sites for locating stores is part science and part art.

Some factors retailers consider when evaluating an area to locate stores are (1) the economic conditions, (2) competition, (3) the strategic fit of the area's population with the retailer's target market, and (4) the costs of operating stores. Having selected an area to locate stores, the next decision is how many stores to operate in that area.

When making the decision about how many stores to open in an area, retailers have to consider the trade-offs between lower operating costs and potential cannibalization from multiple stores in an area. Most retail chains open multiple stores in an area because promotion and distribution economies of scale can be achieved. However, locating too many additional stores in an area can result in diminishing returns due to cannibalization.

The next step for a retailer is to evaluate and select a specific site. In making this decision, retailers consider three factors: (1) the characteristics of the site, (2) the characteristics of the trading area for a store at the site, and (3) the estimated potential sales that can be generated by a store at the site.

Trade areas are typically divided into primary, secondary, and tertiary zones. The boundaries of a trade area are determined by how accessible it is to customers, the natural and physical barriers that exist in the area, the type of shopping area in which the store is located, the type of store, and the level of competition.

Once retailers have the data that describe their trade areas, they use several analytical techniques to estimate demand. The Huff gravity model predicts the probability that a customer will choose a particular store in a trade area; the model is based on the premise that customers are more likely to shop at a given store or shopping center if it is conveniently located and offers a large selection. Regression analysis is a statistically based model that estimates the effects of a variety of factors on existing store sales and uses that information to predict sales for a new site. The analog approach—one of the easiest to use—can be particularly useful for smaller retailers. Using the same logic as regression analysis, the retailer can make predictions about sales by a new store on the basis of sales in stores in similar areas.

Finally, retailers need to negotiate the terms of a lease. These lease terms affect the cost of the location and may restrict retailing activities.

KEY TERMS

accessibility, *195*

analog approach, *210*

artificial barrier, *195*

block group, *203*

census, *203*

census block, *203*

congestion, *196*

cotenancy clause, *214*

cumulative attraction, *197*

customer spotting, *201*

exclusive-use clause, *215*

fixed-rate lease, *214*

fringe, *199*

geographic information system (GIS), *203*

GET OUT AND DO IT!

1. **CONTINUING CASE ASSIGNMENT** Evaluate the location of a store operated by the retailer you have selected for the Continuing Case Assignment. What is the size and shape of the retailer's trade area? Describe the positive and negative aspects of its location. Compare the store's location with the locations of its competitors.

2. **INTERNET EXERCISE** Go to http://www.esri.com/library/fliers/pdfs/tapestry_segmentation.pdf, and identify five segments that you would expect to find in your zip code. Then go to www.gis.com/index.html, and type in your zip code. Compare the segments that are found in your zip code with your initial prediction. Are they similar or different?

3. **INTERNET EXERCISE** Go to www.gis.com/index.html, the home page for Esri Geographical Information Systems, and click on "Demo: What is GIS?" After watching the three-minute video, explain how retailers can make better decisions with GIS.

4. **INTERNET EXERCISE** The U.S. Census Bureau tracks key population characteristics, such as age, gender, disability, employment, income, language, poverty, and race. Go to the U.S. Census Bureau home page at factfinder.census.gov/home/saff/main.html?_lang=en, and, using the Population Finder, look up key demographic data for your state. Explain which factors would be most important for retailers considering this location to evaluate.

5. **GO SHOPPING** Go to a shopping mall. Get or draw a map of the stores. Analyze whether the stores are clustered in some logical manner. For instance, are all the high-end stores together? Is there a good mix of retailers catering to comparison shoppers near one another?

6. **GO SHOPPING** Visit a jewelry store in an enclosed mall and one in a neighborhood strip shopping center. List the pros and cons for each location. Which location is the most desirable? Why is this the case?

7. **WEB OLC EXERCISE** Go to the student side of the book's Web site, and click on "Location." You will see an Excel spreadsheet that contains the sales for 45 retail locations of a sporting goods retail chain, plus the characteristics of each location: number of households in trading area, percentage of households with children under 15 years old, percentage of households in appropriate Tapestry segments that the retailer is targeting, distance from a Walmart store, and distance from a Sports Authority store. Estimate a multiple regression model that predicts sales as a function of the site characteristics, and use the estimate weights to evaluate the two sites at the bottom of the spreadsheet.

DISCUSSION QUESTIONS AND PROBLEMS

1. Which factors do retailers consider when evaluating an area of the country to locate stores? How do retailers determine the trade area for a store?

2. True Value Hardware plans to open a new store. Two sites are available, both in middle-income neighborhood centers. One neighborhood is 20 years old and has been well maintained. The other was recently built in a newly planned community. Which site is preferable for True Value? Why?

3. Trade areas are often described as concentric circles emanating from the store or shopping center. Why is this practice used? Suggest an alternative method. Which would you use if you owned a store in need of a trade area analysis?

4. Under what circumstances might a retailer use the analog approach for estimating demand for a new store? What about regression analysis?

5. Retailers have a choice of locating on a mall's main floor or second or third level. Typically, the main floor offers the best, but most expensive, locations. Why would specialty stores such as Radio Shack and Foot Locker choose the second or third floor?

6. What retail locations are best for department stores, consumer electronics category killers, specialty apparel stores, and warehouse stores? Discuss your rationale.

7. If you were considering the ownership of a Taco Bell franchise, what would you want to know about the location in terms of traffic, population, income, employment, and competition? What else would you need to research about a potential location?

8. A drugstore is considering opening a new location at shopping center A, with hopes of capturing sales from a new neighborhood under construction. Two nearby shopping centers, B and C, will provide competition. Using the following information and the Huff gravity model, determine the probability that residents of the new neighborhood will shop at shopping center A:

Shopping center	Size (000's sq. ft.)	Distance from new neighborhood (miles)
A	3,500	4
B	1,500	5
C	300	3

Assume that $\lambda = 2$.

SUGGESTED READINGS

Chen, Rachel J. C. "Significance and Variety of Geographic Information System (GIS) Applications in Retail, Hospitality, Tourism, and Consumer Services." *Journal of Retailing and Consumer Services* 14, no. 4 (2007), pp. 247–248.

Cliquet, Gerard. *Geomarketing Methods and Strategies in Spatial Marketing*. Washington, DC: ISTE Special Priced Titles, 2007.

Duggal, Niti. *Use of GIS in Retail Location Analysis*. Saarbrucken: VDM Verlag, 2008.

González-Benito, Óscar, César Bustos-Reyes, and Pablo Muñoz-Gallego. "Isolating the Geodemographic Characterisation of Retail Format Choice from the Effects of Spatial Convenience." *Marketing Letters* 18, no. 1/2 (2007), pp. 45–59.

Hernandez, Tony. "Enhancing Retail Location Decision Support: The Development and Application of Geovisualization." *Journal of Retailing and Consumer Services* 14, no. 4 (2007), pp. 249–258.

Ozuduru, Burcu. *Trade Area Modeling in Retail Location Analysis*. Saarbrucken: VDM Verlag, 2009.

Scott, Peter. *Geography and Retailing*. Edison, NJ: Aldine Transaction, 2007.

Teller, Christoph, and Thomas Reutterer. "The Evolving Concept of Retail Attractiveness: What Makes Retail Agglomerations Attractive When Customers Shop at Them?" *Journal of Retailing and Consumer Services* 15, no. 3 (2008), pp. 127–143.

Wood, Steve, and Sue Browne. "Convenience Store Location Planning and Forecasting—a Practical Research." *International Journal of Retail and Distribution Management* 35, no. 4 (2007), pp. 233–255.

Yudelson, Jerry. *Sustainable Retail Development: New Success Strategies*. New York: Springer, 2009.

Human Resource Management

EXECUTIVE BRIEFING
Teresa Orth, Vice President, Human Resources
Toys"R"Us, Inc.

After graduating from Fairfield University with a degree in sociology, I began the executive training program at Abraham & Strauss (A&S), a regional department store chain, which later became part of the Macy's organization. My primary interest has always been in human resources management, but I started my retail career as a department manager in an A&S store. This invaluable experience provided me a great foundation for my career and a keen sensitivity that the decisions made in the corporate office impact thousands of employees working in stores every day. Later, I worked in corporate training and college recruiting for A&S.

Today, I serve as Vice President, Human Resources at Toys"R"Us, Inc., where I am responsible for employee relations at the company's Corporate Headquarters in Wayne, NJ, and for its Distribution Centers. In this role, I lead the organization's talent acquisition and learning teams, and direct many of the company's strategic human resources initiatives, including college recruitment, talent assessment, and succession planning.

Toys"R"Us was one of the first big box category killers, but later struggled due to intense competition from the discount stores. In 2005, the company was acquired by an investment group consisting of affiliates of Bain Capital Partners LLC, Kohlberg Kravis Roberts & Co., and Vornado Realty Trust, and became a private company. In February 2006, Jerry Storch was named the new Chairman and CEO of Toys"R"Us, Inc.

Jerry has significantly changed the culture at Toys"R"Us, Inc. Under his leadership, the company has embraced a "Playing to Win" philosophy and a commitment to solidifying its position as the toy and baby products authority. We have again become a growth company by creating a unique and rewarding shopping experience for our customers, and have begun to integrate the company's toy and baby businesses to provide one-stop shopping convenience.

Over the past several years, the company has also worked to develop an integrated company structure,

CHAPTER 9

QUESTIONS

What are the objectives of human resource management?

What major issues face human resource managers?

What activities do retail employees undertake, and how are they typically organized?

How does a retailer coordinate employees' activities and motivate employees to work toward the retailer's goals?

What human resource management programs are used for building a committed workforce?

With what legal issues are human resource managers concerned?

creating cross-functional learning opportunities for employees, and operating as "One Company"—with two great brands—on a global basis. This structure allows us to further align the synergies of the toy and baby businesses.

The most rewarding aspect of my job is helping our employees reach their full potential. Sometimes employees are not able to perform well because we have not placed the right person in the right job. In other situations, an employee just may not be a good fit for our company. It is really gratifying to me when we are able to provide solutions that enable both the employee and the company to grow.

Retailers achieve their financial objectives by effectively managing their five critical assets: locations, merchandise inventory, stores, employees, and customers. This chapter focuses on the organization and management of employees—the retailer's human resources. As Howard Schultz, chairman and chief global strategist of Starbucks, emphasizes, "The relationship that we have with our people and the culture of our company is our most sustainable competitive advantage."[1]

Sherry Hollock, vice president of talent and organization development at Macy's, emphasizes the importance of human resources in retailing:

One of the biggest challenges facing Macy's, and most other retail chains, is hiring and retaining managers to lead our company in the coming years. The changing demographics are working against our hiring and retention objectives. Over the next ten years, a lot of our senior managers, members of the Baby Boomer generation, will be retiring. So we are going to be competing with other retailers and firms in other industries for a smaller pool of available managers in the generations behind the Boomers. In addition, retailing is becoming a much more sophisticated business. Our managers need to be comfortable with new technologies, information and supply chain management systems, and international business as well as managing a diverse workforce and buying merchandise.[2]

Human resource management is particularly important in retailing because employees play a major role in performing its critical business functions. In manufacturing firms, capital equipment (machinery, computer systems, robotics) often is used to perform the jobs employees once did. But retailing and other service businesses remain labor-intensive. Retailers still rely on people to perform the basic retailing activities, such as buying, displaying merchandise, and providing service to customers.

Two chapters in this text are devoted to human resource management because it is such an important issue for the performance of retail firms. This chapter focuses on the broad strategic issues involving organization structure; the general approaches used for motivating and coordinating employee activities; and the management practices for building an effective, committed workforce and reducing turnover.

The activities undertaken to implement the retailer's human resource strategy, including recruiting, selecting, training, supervising, evaluating, and compensating sales associates, are typically undertaken by store management. Such operational issues will be discussed in more detail in Chapter 16, in the Store Management section of this textbook.

OBJECTIVES OF HUMAN RESOURCE MANAGEMENT

A primary objective of human resource (HR) management is to build a basis for a sustainable competitive advantage. This advantage is attainable since labor costs account for a significant percentage of a retailer's total expenses. Therefore, the effective management of employees can produce a cost advantage. Also, the experience that most customers have with a retailer is determined by the activities of employees who select merchandise, provide information and assistance, and stock displays and shelves. Thus, employees can play a major role in differentiating a retailer's offering from its competitor's. Finally, these potential advantages are difficult for competitors to duplicate. For example, Nordstrom employees are known to provide outstanding customer service. However, most retailers are not able to develop the same customer-oriented culture in their firms. Retailing View 9.1 describes how Men's Wearhouse built a competitive advantage through effective human resource management.

Another strategic objective of human resource management is to align the capabilities and behaviors of employees with the short- and long-term goals of the retail firm. Retailers use several standard metrics to measure how they are doing. One human resource metric is **employee productivity**—the retailer's sales or profit divided by the number of employees. Employee productivity can be improved by increasing the sales generated by employees, reducing the number of employees, or both.

Whereas employee productivity is directly related to the retailer's short-term profits, other measures of employee attitudes, such as job satisfaction and commitment, have important effects on the long-term performance of the retailer. Committed employees are more motivated to assist the retailer in achieving its goals, such as improving the satisfaction of customers and building customer loyalty. They also are less likely to leave the company. In addition to using surveys to

REFACT

Retail employee turnover is almost 60 percent for full-time associates and almost 115 percent for part-time employees.[3]

EXHIBIT 9–1
Downward Performance Spiral

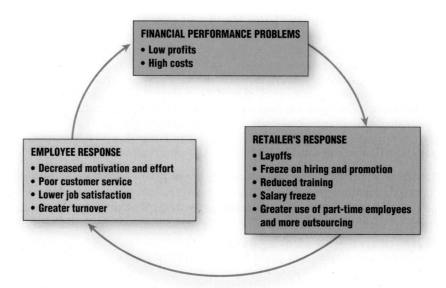

FINANCIAL PERFORMANCE PROBLEMS
- Low profits
- High costs

RETAILER'S RESPONSE
- Layoffs
- Freeze on hiring and promotion
- Reduced training
- Salary freeze
- Greater use of part-time employees and more outsourcing

EMPLOYEE RESPONSE
- Decreased motivation and effort
- Poor customer service
- Lower job satisfaction
- Greater turnover

measure these employee attitudes, retailers also consider employee turnover as a behavioral measure of employee commitment. **Employee turnover** equals

$$\frac{\text{Number of employees leaving their job during the year}}{\text{Number of positions}}$$

If a store owner had five sales associate positions but three employees left and were replaced during the year, the turnover would be 3 ÷ 5 = 60 percent. Note that turnover can be greater than 100 percent if a substantial number of people are replaced more than once during the year. In our example, if the replacements for the three employees that left also left during the year, the turnover would be 6 ÷ 5 = 120 percent.

A failure to consider both long- and short-term objectives can result in the mismanagement of human resources and a downward performance spiral, as shown in Exhibit 9–1. Sometimes, when retailers' sales and profits decline due to increased competition, retailers respond by decreasing labor costs. They reduce the number of sales associates in stores, hire more part-timers, and spend less on training. Although these actions may increase short-term productivity and profits, they have an adverse effect on long-term performance because employee morale and customer service decline.[4]

RETAILING VIEW   Men's Wearhouse: Using Human Resources to Build a Competitive Advantage   9.1

While the sale of men's tailored clothing has declined during the past 30 years, Men's Wearhouse, founded by George Zimmer when he was only 24 years of age, has continued to gain market share, becoming one of the largest specialty retailers of men's apparel in North America. Men's Wearhouse sales have grown to over $1.9 billion through more than 805 retail store locations in the United States and Canada.

The core of the company's strategy is to offer superior customer service delivered by knowledgeable, caring salespeople, called *wardrobe consultants*. The term *wardrobe consultant* was chosen intentionally to emphasize that sales associates are professionals, like physicians or attorneys.

George Zimmer believes in a win-win-win philosophy, in which the customer, the wardrobe consultant, and the company all do well. Because the company believes that its job is to develop the untapped human potential in its employees, it devotes considerable attention to training. Some of Men's Wearhouse's core philosophies include the following:

Fulfillment at work. Job satisfaction—everyone wants to have it. So how does Men's Wearhouse help its employees find it? It all starts with trust and respect.

Don't be afraid of mistakes. You can tell a lot about a company by observing the way it handles mistakes. Men's Wearhouse focuses on the learning opportunities that mistakes provide. It likes to say that it celebrates its successes and its failures.

Balancing work and family life. Men's Wearhouse encourages employees to balance the worlds inside and outside the workplace.

Having fun at work with friends. A workplace filled with fun among friends is *good* for business.

Celebrate individual and team success. Men's Wearhouse recognizes that individual excellence and team excellence are interrelated—they support each other. That's why it celebrates both individual and team achievements.

Extensive training and teamwork enable Men's Wearhouse sales personnel to provide excellent customer service and build a competitive advantage for the firm.

Promote from within. Skills and experience at a job are only part of the picture. When picking its leaders, Men's Wearhouse looks for people who care about others, take the time to listen, and show enthusiasm when working toward team and individual goals. That's why it promotes people it already knows.

Source: Eric Hagen, "Men's Warehouse CEO Offers Advice for Good and Bad Economic Times," *ABCnewspapers.com,* November 12, 2009; Sharon Edelson, "The Training Advantage," *WWD,* April 2, 2007, p. 14; "Give People a Second Chance," *Business 2.0,* May 2007, p. 67; Men's Wearhouse 2008 Annual Report, www.menswearhouse.com (accessed November 16, 2009).

ISSUES IN RETAIL HUMAN RESOURCE MANAGEMENT

Human resource management in retailing is very challenging for several reasons. First, it is difficult to achieve a delicate balance between the ability to satisfy the needs of employees, the ability of HR professionals at the corporate offices to set policies, and the capabilities of store managers to implement those policies. Second, retailers have increased their proportion of part-time employees in an effort to reduce expenses. Third, as the U.S. population has become more diverse, so has retailers' labor pool, making managing diversity an important objective for HR professionals in retailing. Finally, retailers that have expanded beyond their home country's borders modify and adjust their HR perspectives, policies, and procedures.

Balancing the Human Resource Triad

Retailers such as Home Depot, Wegmans, Men's Wearhouse, and The Container Store believe that human resources are too important to be left to the human resource department. The full potential of a retailer's human resources is realized when three elements of the HR triad work together—HR professionals, store managers, and employees (see Exhibit 9–2).

Human resource professionals, who typically work out of the corporate office, have specialized knowledge of HR practices and labor laws. They are responsible for establishing HR policies that enforce the retailer's strategy and provide the tools and training used by store managers and employees to implement those policies. Store managers are responsible for bringing the policies to life through their daily management of the employees who work for them. The issues confronting HR professionals are discussed in this chapter. Chapter 16, in the Store Management section of this book, reviews the responsibilities of store managers. Finally, the employees also share in the management of human resources. They can play an active role by providing feedback on the policies, managing their own careers, defining their job functions, and evaluating the performance of their managers and coworkers.

Expense Control

Retailers must control their expenses if they are to be profitable. Thus, they are cautious about paying high wages to hourly employees who perform low-skill jobs. To control costs, retailers often hire people with little or no experience to work as sales associates, bank tellers, and waiters. High turnover, absenteeism, and poor performance often result from this use of inexperienced, low-wage employees.

The lack of experience and motivation among many retail employees is particularly troublesome because these employees are often in direct contact with customers. Poor appearance, manners, and attitudes can have a negative effect on sales and customer loyalty. Research has shown that in some types of retail

EXHIBIT 9–2
Human Resource Triad

operations, a modest investment in hiring more staff will result in a significant increase in sales.[5] If customers can't find a particular product on their own, or if they can't get an explanation of how it works or how it is used, the product probably won't sell. One method of controlling expenses is to utilize part-time employees, an issue discussed in the next section.

Part-Time Employees

Retailers' needs for store employees vary depending on the time of day, day of week, time of year, and promotion schedule. Retailers use computerized scheduling systems that are designed to boost service and trim costs by matching staff size to customer traffic, hour by hour. These systems can factor the effects of store promotions, sporting events, graduations, and even the weather to determine the right staffing for different hours and days. To minimize costs, the systems suggest that retailers complement their full-time (40-hours-per-week) store employees with part-time workers. Part-time employees are less expensive than comparable full-time employees. Further, they are usually offered no health or retirement benefits and little job security. The growth of part-time staff in retailing has been slightly outpacing that of full-time staff since 2000.[6]

Utilizing Diverse Employee Groups

The changing demographic pattern will result in a chronic shortage of qualified sales associates. So, besides utilizing less expensive part-time labor, retailers are increasing their efforts to recruit, train, manage, and retain mature, minority, and handicapped workers

Although young employees have traditionally made up the majority of the retail labor force, retailers have realized that what these employees want out of their jobs and work environments is quite different from what their older supervisors want and, therefore, that different approaches need to be used to manage them. They want more flexibility, meaningful jobs, professional freedom, and a better work-life balance than older employees do. Younger employees readily switch jobs if their expectations aren't met, making employee turnover high.[8]

To help ease the overall labor shortage and the perceived deficiencies of younger workers, retailers are increasingly turning to older employees because they are more reliable, have lower turnover rates, and often have better work performance.[11] Training costs are also lower for older people since they generally have had strong work experience. These advantages of hiring older employees counterbalance any increased costs in missed days for medical problems. Home Depot even offers winter work in Florida and summer work in Maine. By building relationships with groups such as the American Association of Retired Persons (AARP), Home Depot helps people like military retirees find jobs.

International Human Resource Issues

The management of employees working for international retailers is especially challenging. Differences in work values, economic systems, and labor laws mean that HR practices that are effective in one country might not be effective in another. For example, U.S. retailers rely heavily on individual performance appraisals and rewards tied to individual performance—a practice consistent with the individualistic U.S. culture. However, in countries with a collectivist culture, such as China and Japan, employees downplay individual desires and focus on the needs of the group. Thus, group-based evaluations and incentives are more effective in those countries.[12]

The legal/political system in countries often dictates the human resource management practices that retailers can use. For example, in Spain, a company must pay 45 days' salary for every year worked if it fires someone.[13] In the Netherlands, employers must get approval from the government to lay off employees. Governments in Colombia, Venezuela, Japan, Korea, and China can also block layoffs.[14]

REFACT

The average supermarket worker has lost three hours of employment a week since 2003, from 32.3 hours to 29.5 in 2007, reversing a previous upward trend. Retail workers overall have lost 0.7 hour a week over the same period.[7]

REFACT

Approximately one-third of retail employees are 24 years old or younger.[9]

REFACT

Women account for nearly two-thirds of the retail industry's part-time workforce.[10]

The staffing of management positions in foreign countries raises a wide set of issues. Should management be local, or should expatriates be used? How should the local managers or expatriates be selected, trained, and compensated? For example, at the France-based hypermarket chain Carrefour, it is likely for a Brazilian to be managing a store in China. In fact, Carrefour prides itself on grooming managers for global experiences.

The following sections of this chapter examine three important strategic issues facing retail HR professionals:

1. The design of the organization structure for assigning responsibility and authority for tasks to people and business units.

2. The approaches used to coordinate the activities of the firm's departments and employees and motivate employees to work toward achieving company goals.

3. The programs used to build employee commitment and retain valuable human resources.

DESIGNING THE ORGANIZATION STRUCTURE FOR A RETAIL FIRM

The **organization structure** identifies the activities to be performed by specific employees and determines the lines of authority and responsibility in the firm. The first step in developing an organization structure is to determine the tasks that must be performed. Exhibit 9–3 shows tasks that are typically performed in a retail firm.

These tasks are divided into four major categories in retail firms: strategic management, administrative management (operations), merchandise management, and store management. The organization of this textbook is based on these tasks and the managers who perform them.

Section II of this text focuses on strategic and administrative tasks. Strategic marketing and finance decisions (discussed in Chapters 5 and 6) are undertaken primarily by senior management: the CEO, chief operating officer, vice presidents, and the board of directors that represents shareholders in publicly held firms. Administrative tasks (discussed in Chapters 7–11) are performed by corporate employees who have specialized skills in human resource management, finance, accounting, real estate, distribution, management information systems, marketing, operations, visual merchandising, and general counsel (legal).

In retail firms, category managers, buyers, and merchandise planners are involved in merchandise management (Section III), and store managers and the regional managers above them are involved in the management of the stores (Section IV). These managers are responsible for implementing the strategic plans and making the day-to-day decisions that directly affect the retailer's performance.

To illustrate the connection between the tasks performed in Exhibit 9–3 and the organization structure presented in the following sections, the tasks are color-coded. Red ■ is used for the strategic tasks, green ■ for the administrative tasks, blue ■ for the merchandising tasks, and yellow ▢ for the store management tasks.

Organization of a Single-Store Retailer

Initially, the owner-manager of a single store may be the entire organization. When he or she goes to lunch or heads home, the store closes. As sales grow, the owner-manager hires employees. Coordinating and controlling employee activities is easier in a small store than in a large chain of stores; the owner-manager simply assigns tasks to each employee and watches to see that these tasks are performed properly. Because the number of employees is limited, single-store retailers have little **specialization.** Each employee must perform a wide range of activities, and the owner-manager is responsible for all management tasks.

Tasks Performed by a Typical Retail Firm   **EXHIBIT 9–3**

STRATEGIC MANAGEMENT
- **Develop overall retail strategy**
- **Identify the target market**
- **Determine the retail format**
- **Design organizational structure**
- **Develop private-label merchandise**
- **Develop Internet/catalog strategy**
- **Develop global strategy**

MERCHANDISE MANAGEMENT
- **Buy merchandise**
  - **Select, negotiate with, and evaluate vendors**
  - **Select merchandise**
  - **Place orders**
- **Control merchandise inventory**
  - **Develop merchandise budget plans**
  - **Allocate merchandise to stores**
  - **Review open-to-buy and stock positions**
- **Price merchandise**
  - **Set initial prices**
  - **Adjust prices**

STORE MANAGEMENT
- **Recruit, hire, and train store personnel**
- **Plan labor schedules**
- **Evaluate store and personnel performance**
- **Maintain store facilities**
- **Locate and display merchandise**
- **Sell merchandise to customers**
- **Repair and alter merchandise**
- **Provide services such as gift wrapping and delivery**
- **Handle customer complaints**
- **Take physical inventory**
- **Prevent inventory shrinkage**

ADMINISTRATIVE MANAGEMENT
- **Marketing**
  - **Promote the firm, its merchandise, and its services**
  - **Plan communication programs including advertising**
  - **Plan special promotions and events**
  - **Manage public relations**
- **Manage human resources**
  - **Develop policies for managing store personnel**
  - **Recruit, hire, and train managers**
  - **Keep employee records**
- **Manage supply chain**
  - **Receive merchandise**
  - **Store merchandise**
  - **Ship merchandise to stores**
  - **Return merchandise to vendors**
- **Manage financial performance**
  - **Provide timely information on financial performance**
  - **Forecast sales, cash flow, and profits**
  - **Raise capital from investors**
  - **Select and manage locations (real estate)**
- **Visual Merchandising**
  - **Develop and coordinate displays in stores and windows**
- **Management Information Systems**
  - **Work with all functional areas to develop and operate information systems for merchandising, marketing, accounting, finance, etc.**
- **General counsel (legal)**
  - **Work with all functional areas to be in compliance with laws and regulations**

Strategic management	**Store management**
Merchandise management	**Administrative management**

As sales continue to increase, specialization in management may occur when the owner-manager hires additional management employees. Exhibit 9–4 illustrates the common division of management responsibilities into merchandise and store management. The owner-manager continues to perform strategic management tasks. The store manager may be responsible for administrative tasks associated with receiving and shipping merchandise and managing the employees.

REFACT
Mellerio dits Meller, the French jeweler founded in 1613, is one of the oldest family-owned retail chains still operating.[16]

EXHIBIT 9–4   Organization Structure for a Small Retailer

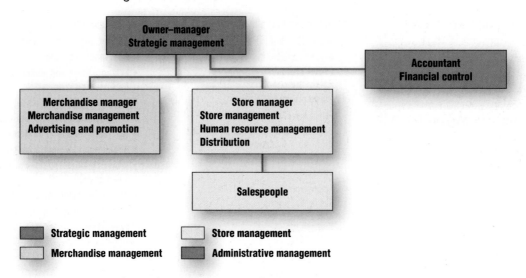

The merchandise manager or **buyer** may handle the advertising and promotion tasks, as well as merchandise selection and inventory management tasks. Often the owner-manager contracts with an accounting firm to perform financial control tasks for a fee.

Organization of a National Retail Chain

In contrast to the management of a single store, the management of a retail chain is complex. Managers must supervise units that are geographically distant from one another. In the following sections, we discuss the organization structure of a typical retail chain.

Exhibit 9–5 shows the organization chart of a typical department store. Overseeing and responsible for the entire organization is the chief executive officer (CEO). Reporting directly to the CEO is the president of global operations, president of direct channels, and president of private-label operations. Also reporting to the CEO is the senior vice president of merchandising, senior vice president of stores, and senior vice president of operations, plus the chief marketing and financial officers.

Merchandising   Looking at the merchandising division, the **senior vice president (SVP) of merchandising** works with buyers and planners to develop and coordinate the management of the retailer's merchandise offering and ensure that it is consistent with the firm's strategy. The organization and responsibilities of the merchandising division are detailed in Chapters 12 to 14.

The buyers in the merchandise division are responsible for determining the merchandise assortment, pricing, and managing relationships and negotiating with vendors. Most retail chains have a set of planning positions parallel to the buying positions supervised by a senior vice president of planning who is at the same level as the merchandise managers in the buying organization. The **merchandising planners** are responsible for allocating merchandise and tailoring the assortment of several categories for specific stores in a geographic area.

As shown in Exhibit 9–5, there are several levels of management in the merchandise division—general merchandise managers (GMMs), divisional merchandise managers (DMMs), and buyers. Most large retailers have several GMMs who are responsible for several merchandise classifications. Similarly, several DMMs report to each GMM and a number of buyers report to each DMM.

Organization of a Typical Department Store   **EXHIBIT 9–5**

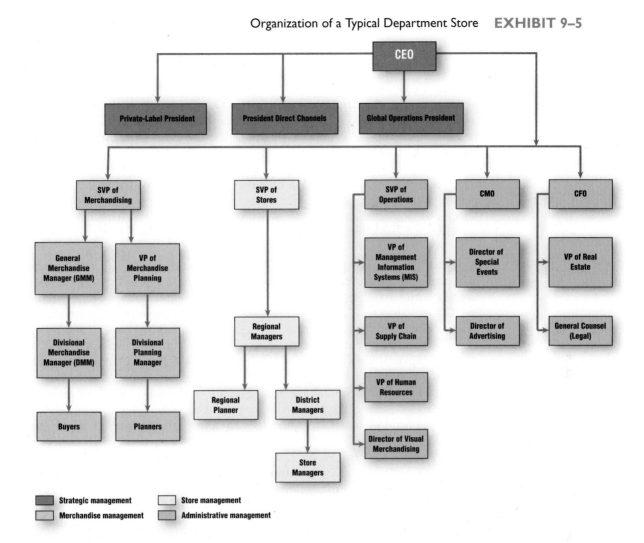

Strategic management   Store management
Merchandise management   Administrative management

Stores   The **senior vice president (SVP) of stores** supervises all activities related to stores, including working with the regional managers, who supervise district managers, who supervise the individual store managers. Store managers in large stores have several assistant store managers who report to them (not depicted in Exhibit 9–5). One assistant manager is responsible for administration and manages the receiving, restocking, and presentation of the merchandise in the store. Another is responsible for human resources, including selecting, training, and evaluating employees. A third is responsible for operations such as store maintenance and store security.

Each region has regional planners who work as liaisons between stores in their region and the corporate planners to ensure that the stores have the right merchandise, at the right time, in the right quantities. The stores division also works closely with the real estate division (under the chief financial officer) to plan new stores and with those in charge of visual merchandising, layout, and store design.

Operations   The **chief operations officer (COO)** oversees managers in charge of management information systems (MISs), supply chain, human resources, and visual merchandising. The COO is also in charge of shrinkage and loss prevention and the operation and maintenance of the physical assets of the firm, such as stores, offices, distribution and fulfillment centers, and trucks (these functions are not reflected in Exhibit 9–5).

Marketing   The **chief marketing officer (CMO)** works with staff to develop advertising and promotion programs. Managers in charge of public relations, annual events, credit marketing, and cause-related marketing initiatives also report to the CMO.

Finance   The **chief financial officer (CFO)** works with the CEO on financial issues such as equity-debt structure and credit card operations. In addition, the real estate division and general counsel (legal) divisions, headed by vice presidents, report to the CFO.

Retailers vary considerably on how they organize their private-label development activities, international operations, and catalog and/or electronic channel. Exhibit 9–5 shows these activities as being performed by wholly owned subsidiaries with the presidents of three subsidiaries reporting to the CEO.

Private Label   The **private-label president** is responsible for the conceptualization, design, sourcing, quality control, and marketing of private-label and exclusive merchandise. When the private-label organization is a separate division, as in Exhibit 9–5, buyers in the merchandising division often evaluate the private-label merchandise offering as they would any other vendor, and they are therefore free to accept or reject the merchandise offered. In some retail organizations, decisions on what private-label merchandise is included in the retailer's assortment are made by the merchandising divisions and its buyers, and the sourcing and quality control are done by a VP of private-label development. In either case, the managers involved with private-label merchandise work closely with buyers and planners to ensure that the merchandise offered in each category is coherent.

Direct Channels   The **president of direct channels** is responsible for the selection and pricing of the merchandise assortment offered through the catalog and Internet channels, the maintenance and design of the retailer's Web site, customer call centers, and the fulfillment centers that fill orders for individual customers. However, a number of multichannel retailers are integrating the operation of the Internet and catalog channels into their store channel. At these retailers, the selection and management of the merchandise offered in all three channels for a category is made by the same buyers, rather than separate buyers for each channel.

Global   The **global operations president** oversees retailing operations outside the home country. The size and complexity of this operation is determined by the number of countries served and the number of stores within each country. Regardless of size, many of the functions performed by the home-country operation are duplicated in the global operations. For instance, the global organization typically has merchandising, stores, and operations divisions. It would also have vice presidents or directors in charge of marketing and finance.

RETAIL ORGANIZATION DESIGN ISSUES

Two important issues in the design of a retail organization are (1) the degree to which decision making is centralized or decentralized and (2) the approaches used to coordinate merchandise and store management. The first issue translates into whether the decisions about activities such as merchandise management, information and distribution systems, and human resource management are made by regional, district, or store managers or by managers in the corporate headquarters. The second issue arises because retailers divide merchandise and store management activities into different organizations within the firm. Thus, they need to develop ways to coordinate these interdependent activities.

Centralization versus Decentralization

Centralization occurs when the authority for retailing decisions is delegated to corporate managers rather than to geographically dispersed managers; **decentralization** occurs when the authority for retail decisions is assigned to lower levels in the organization. Macy's is an example of a retail corporation that has migrated from geographically decentralized decision making to centralized decision making. Yet, at the same time, its My Macy's program is designed to provide important merchandising information to the central buying organization so that Macy's can offer its geographically dispersed customers customized assortments. See Retailing View 9.2.

Retailers reduce costs when decision making is centralized in corporate management. First, overhead falls because fewer managers are required to make the merchandise, human resource, marketing, real estate, information system, and financial decisions.

Second, by coordinating buying across geographically dispersed stores, the company can achieve lower prices from suppliers. The retailer can negotiate better purchasing terms by placing one large order rather than a number of smaller orders.

RETAILING VIEW   My Macy's: Centralize Expenses and Decentralize Merchandising Decisions   **9.2**

Macy's Inc. acquired May Department Stores at the end of 2005, expanding the department store giant from 450 stores to 808, overnight. After the acquisition, Macy's focused on centralizing its decision making to decrease its companywide costs. The 808 stores were divided into 7 regional offices, each controlling 60 to 200 stores in up to 10 states, with corporate offices in Cincinnati and New York City. The seven regions were then reduced to three regions to further consolidate corporate expenses. In September 2006, all the regional names acquired through the acquisition, including Marshall Field's, Meier & Frank, Burdine's, and Foley's, were converted to the name Macy's to further consolidate corporate expenses and enable the retailer to roll out national ad campaigns with a consistent brand image.

Formerly, each of the seven regional offices operated as an independent business with its own buying organization. Thus, seven Macy's buyers would approach one vendor. The My Macy's initiative, implemented in 2009, consolidated the regional buyers into one office in New York City. It also created a new position, district planner, which is responsible for keeping the pulse on what customers are looking for in about 10 stores. Each planner is responsible for one category, such as women's, men's, accessories, or home. The planners spend time in the stores, talking to customers, employees, and store managers, and the information they gather is consolidated at the regional level and then communicated to the central buying office in New York City.

Although the My Macy's initiative streamlined its expense structure, Macy's realized that it was not able to adequately serve the regionalized tastes of its customers. When department

store chains had fewer stores, buyers knew what their customers' needs were and could tailor their assortments accordingly. For Macy's, this was impossible to do with so many stores.

The local input has changed how buying decisions are made. For example, in Columbus, Ohio, there is a tremendous demand for golf apparel because people wear it on the golf course, to parties, and even to church. There is also a significant market for licensed products of The Ohio State University, based in Columbus. So Columbus stores now carry more golf and Ohio State apparel. In Chicago, buyers increased the number of size-11 women's shoes because of the unusually high demand in that area.

Macy's is having its cake and eating it too. The partial decentralization of the merchandising function enables Macy's store employees, store managers, and even customers to directly affect the merchandise and services offered. Yet the centralization of much of the rest of the organization enables Macy's to keep better control of its expenses.

Sources: www.macysinc.com/Macys/mymacys.aspx (accessed December 7, 2009); www.macysinc.com/Macys/maps.aspx (accessed December 7, 2009); "CEO Terry Lundgren: A Focus on Turning 'My Macy's' into Your Macy's," *Knowledge@Wharton*, November 11, 2009; Tim Feran, "Macy's Trying a Local Approach," *Columbus Dispatch*, September 21, 2009; Michael Barbaro, "Given Fewer Coupons, Shoppers Snub Macy's," *New York Times*, September 29, 2007; Michael Barbaro, "After Smooth Sales Talk, Stores Take Macy's Name," *New York Times*, August 26, 2006; Constance L. Hays and Andrew Ross Sorkin, "Retailing Shake-Up: The New Chief; A Soloist Holds Forth on Retailing," *New York Times*, March 1, 2005.

Third, centralization provides an opportunity to have the best people make decisions for the entire corporation. For example, in a centralized organization, people with the greatest expertise in areas such as management information systems (MISs), buying, store design, or visual merchandise can offer all stores the benefit of their skills.

Fourth, centralization increases efficiency. Standard operating policies developed at the corporate headquarters are applied to the stores, allowing store managers to focus on their core responsibilities. For example, corporate merchandisers perform considerable research to determine the best method of presenting merchandise. They provide detailed guides for displaying merchandise to each store manager so that all stores have a consistent brand image throughout the country. Because they offer the same core merchandise in all stores, centralized retailers can achieve economies of scale by advertising through national media rather than more costly local media.

Although centralization has advantages in reducing costs, its disadvantage is that it makes it more difficult for a retailer to adapt to local market conditions. For example, Gainesville is located in central Florida, and thus the manager in charge of the fishing category at the Sports Authority corporate office might think that the Gainesville store's customers primarily engage in freshwater fishing. But the local store manager knows that most of his customers drive 90 miles to go saltwater fishing in either the Gulf of Mexico or the Atlantic Ocean.

In addition to problems with tailoring its merchandise to local needs, a centralized retailer may have difficulty responding to local competition and labor markets. Because pricing is established centrally, individual stores may not be able to respond quickly to competition in their market. Finally, centralized personnel policies may make it hard for local managers to pay competitive wages in their area or hire appropriate types of salespeople.

However, centralized retailers are relying more on their information systems to react to local market conditions. For example, many retailers are now using merchandise and pricing optimization techniques. With specialized software packages, buyers can determine optimal pricing, markdowns, and size and quantity allocations on a store-by-store or region-by-region basis. These techniques are discussed in detail in Chapters 12 and 14.

Coordinating Merchandise and Store Management

Small, independent retailers have little difficulty coordinating their stores' buying and selling activities. Owner-managers typically buy the merchandise and work with their salespeople to sell it. In close contact with customers, the owner-managers know what their customers want.

In contrast, large retail firms organize the buying and selling functions into separate divisions. Buyers specialize in buying merchandise and have limited contact with the store management responsible for selling it. While this specialization increases buyers' skills and expertise, it makes it harder for them to understand customers' needs. Three approaches large retailers use to coordinate buying and selling are (1) improving buyers' appreciation for the store environment, (2) making store visits, and (3) assigning employees to coordinating roles.

Improving Appreciation for the Store Environment   Some retailers have management trainees who work in the stores before they become buyers. Others utilize a mixed career path in which managers are encouraged to float between store and corporate assignments. This store experience helps corporate managers and buyers gain an appreciation for the activities performed in the stores, the problems salespeople and department managers encounter, and the needs of customers.

Making Store Visits   Another approach to increasing customer contact and communication is to have buyers and other executives visit the stores. Every week, Terry Lundgren, Macy's CEO, goes into several stores, calls the store managers on their cell phones, and asks them to meet him on the selling floor. These unannounced visits don't give the stores or their managers time to prepare to answer questions or change anything on the selling floor, so he sees the stores just as the customers do.[17] The visits provide managers and buyers with a richer view of store and customer needs than they could get from reading impersonal sales reports or talking on the phone.

Assigning Employees to Coordinating Roles   Some retailers, like TJX, maintain people in both the merchandise division (planners and allocators who work with buyers) and stores who are responsible for coordinating buying and selling activities. Many national retail chains have regional and even district personnel to coordinate buying and selling activities.

Macy's CEO, Terry Lundgren, gets to know his customers and employees by visiting stores.

For example, Macy's has district planners that are in stores everyday working with store personnel and customers to keep a pulse on what customers want and the inventory needs of the stores. It is their responsibility to translate, consolidate, and communicate this information to the central buying organization. Zara store managers around the globe have biweekly meetings via telephone with the design team at the corporate headquarters in A Coruña, Galicia, Spain, to communicate new fashion trends and coordinate inventory issues. In addition to developing an organization structure, HR management undertakes a number of activities to improve employee performance, build commitment among employees, and reduce turnover. In the following section, we examine these human resource management activities.

WINNING THE EMPLOYEE TALENT WAR

As we indicated at the beginning of the chapter, the pool of potential employees is decreasing due to changing demographics. There is, however, a need for managers who can effectively deal with the increased complexities of retail jobs, such as the use of new technologies, increased global competition, and a diverse workforce. Thus, retailers are engaged in a "war" with their competitors for talent, that is, for effective employees and managers.[18] Corporate HR departments are the generals in the war for talent. They are responsible for developing programs that will attract, develop, motivate, and keep talent.

Attracting Talent: Employment Marketing

The HR departments for retailers such as Starbucks and Marriott develop marketing programs to attract the "best and brightest" potential employees. These programs, called **employment marketing** or **employment branding**, involve undertaking marketing research to understand what potential employees are seeking, as well as what they think about the retailer; developing a value proposition and an employment brand image; communicating that brand image to potential employees; and then fulfilling the brand promise by ensuring that the employee experience matches

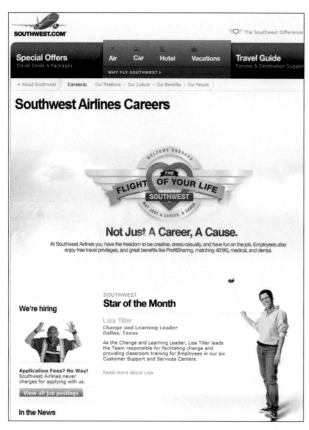

Southwest Airlines attracts talent with employment marketing programs.

that which was advertised. Retailers often use advertising agencies that specialize in employment marketing to develop creative approaches to attract employees.[19]

For example, Starbucks' research revealed that prospective and existing employees like their jobs. The rewards they receive from working at Starbucks go beyond pay and promotion opportunities. So Starbucks developed an employment marketing program based on the theme "Love What You Do." Southwest uses a similar tagline for its employment marketing program: "The Flight of Your Life, Not Just a Career, a Cause."

Starbucks uses the Love What You Do theme on its Internet site, in its printed material available to prospective employees in stores, and in videos designed to describe the Starbucks employee experience. In this collateral material, real employees describe why they love what they do.[20] Starbucks encourages all of its partners (employees) to get involved in recruiting potential employees. Employees in its stores are trained to respond to customer inquiries about job opportunities and questions about working in the stores.

Developing Talent: Selection and Training

Two activities that retailers undertake to develop knowledge, skills, and abilities in their human resources are selection and training. Retailers that build a competitive advantage through their human resources are very selective in hiring people and make significant investments in training.

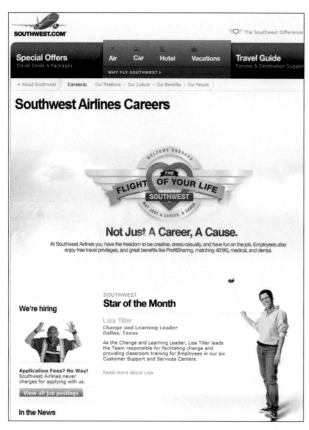

Pret A Manger believes it can teach people to make sandwiches, but not to be happy. So, they hire happy people.

Selective Hiring   The first step in building an effective workforce is to recruit the right people. At U.K.-based sandwich shop chain Pret A Manger, candidates applying for any position, including in the corporate offices, must work in a shop for a day. The team who works there gets a say on whether the candidate will fit in with the team. If not, the candidate isn't hired. Pret goes out of its way to hire happy people. Its philosophy is you can't hire someone who can make sandwiches and teach them to be happy. So it hires happy people and teaches them to make sandwiches.[21]

Zappos, the online shoe, apparel, and accessories retailer, also takes special care in the hiring process. It wants people who believe in what they are doing and love doing it. Hiring the right people is so important to Zappos that it offers new hires $2,000 to quit—although that might not be enough since only 1 percent of new hires take Zappos up on the offer.[22]

Electronics retailer Best Buy has refocused its selection process to include more women. After 20 years of focusing on selling to males between the ages of 18 and 25, Best Buy recognized that female spending represents a huge share of its sales. It also found that women preferred to buy from other women.[23]

Training   Training is particularly important in retailing because the overwhelming majority of retail employees have direct contact with customers, which means they are responsible for helping customers satisfy their needs and resolve their problems.

At the Zappos family of companies, each new hire, regardless of position, begins his or her job with five weeks of training, including time taking phone orders. This allows new employees to learn about the merchandise and the importance of satisfying customers. This experience also helps weed out employees who believe they are too important to spend time helping customers.[24]

An interesting challenge facing retailers is how to train younger employees. Retailers have recognized that Generation Y, the first generation to grow up with the Internet and Internet-based games, learns differently than previous generations do. So, for example, children's apparel retailer The Children's Place developed a series of training modules about loss prevention and store safety that are modeled after the television series *CSI: Crime Scene Investigation* and called "Place Scene Investigation" or PSI. These modules are much more interactive than the typical click-next modules typically found in retailing.[25] Retailing View 9.4 describes an approach that illustrates Peet's Coffee and Tea's commitment to training.

At Zappos, each new hire begins his or her job with five weeks of training, including time taking phone orders.

RETAILING VIEW   Careful Employee Selection = Low Employee Turnover at The Container Store   **9.3**

In the retail industry, annual employee turnover of more than 100 percent is not uncommon, particularly with part-time employees. How does The Container Store, with 48 stores and 4,000 employees, experience just 10 to 15 percent annual turnover?

It does a lot of things to help retain employees, and a careful selection process is integral to its success. Consider how it hires for a "transition team," which is a group of associates hired for less than a week to transition a store between selling seasons, such as after the back-to-school season. Hiring consists of two interviews: one in a group setting and one face-to-face lasting an hour and a half. Sometimes the candidate is taken for a walk around the store and asked "what if" questions that are largely oriented to how the person would interact with customers. This is a lot of trouble to go through to hire part-time associates who are going to change displays and fixtures and move merchandise but not sell merchandise.

The Container Store also wants to be sure the company is the right fit for the prospective employee. What better pool to choose from than its own customers. The company considers it symbolic that its first hire was one of its customers. Most current employees are former customers. Many were approached by sales associates or managers on the sales floor when they were shopping. The Container Store also finds a lot of employees through online applications to its Web site.

The Container Store uses a careful and extensive employee selection process. Its best talent pool is from its own customers.

Source: Gene Detroyer, "The Container Store: The Employee as an 'Extension of the Brand,'" *Retail Wire*, March 20, 2009.

Motivating Talent: Aligning Goals

The task of aligning the employees' and the firm's goals is often difficult, because employees' goals usually differ from those of the firm. For example, a sales associate might find it more personally rewarding to arrange a display creatively than to help a customer. Retailers generally use three methods to motivate their employees' activities: (1) written policies and supervision, (2) compensation-based incentives, and (3) organization culture.

Policies and Supervision   Perhaps the most fundamental method of coordination is to prepare written policies that indicate what employees should do and then to have supervisors enforce these policies. For example, retailers may set policies about when and how merchandise can be returned by customers. If employees use

9.4   RETAILING VIEW   Peet's Knows Its Tea

Why would someone pay $2 or more for a cup of tea when it costs only pennies to buy a Lipton tea bag and put it in a cup of hot water? Because companies like Peet's Coffee and Tea have learned to create value by training employees to provide great customer service. Peet's, known as the "grandfather of specialty coffee," was started by Alfred Peet in 1966 a few blocks from the University of California at Berkeley. Although its primary business is coffee, Peet's managers know that if everything they sell—including tea—isn't as good as it can be, business will suffer.

Peet's first priority is educating its staff. In addition to knowing how to brew tea, employees need to know about the beverage they're serving. How are green, black, and oolong teas grown and processed? How do they differ? How do they taste? What about their caffeine content?

Once the staff members know all there is to know about tea, they can educate their customers, who generally fall into two categories: those few who know a lot about tea and everyone else. Knowledgeable tea enthusiasts may ask very specific questions, whereas most neophyte tea buyers probably don't understand why tea is so expensive compared with coffee. (The answer? A single serving of coffee requires much less actual coffee than the actual tea a serving of tea requires.) Most customers also grew up with tea bags, so they need to be educated about how to brew the loose tea that Peet's sells.

At Peet's, the employees also have a "cheat sheet" for every tea container with information they can pass on to customers. The sheet illustrates how much tea should be used, how long it should brew for optimal taste, and how hot the water should be. If the employees don't know the answer to a customer's question, they find out by asking their manager or the home office.

Selling and consuming tea can be a very personal experience, so Peet's staff members are encouraged to interact with customers. For instance, they might ask drinkers to describe their favorite tea and how it tastes and then use those details to suggest new, alternative teas. But the best way to sell tea is to drink it. Having the employees test and taste different teas gives them the confidence and knowledge needed to be good

At Peet's Coffee and Tea, the employees are provided in-depth product knowledge that enables them to serve their customers better than the competition can.

tea emissaries. Peet's has figured out that the key to its success is not just good coffee and tea but excellent service delivered by knowledgeable employees.

Sources: Tara Fitzpatrick, "Hospitali-Tea," *Beverage Cart,* August 2008; www.peets.com (accessed December 2, 2009).

the written policies to make return decisions, their actions will be consistent with the retailer's strategy. But strict reliance on written policies also can reduce employee motivation, because employees have little opportunity to use their own initiative to improve performance in their areas of responsibility. As a result, they eventually might find their jobs uninteresting.

Relying on rules as a method of coordination leads to a lot of red tape. Situations will arise that aren't covered by a rule, in which case employees may need to talk to a supervisor. Alternatively, many retailers empower their employees to make decisions on their own. Empowerment is discussed later in this chapter and in Chapter 18.

Compensation-Based Incentives   The second method of motivating and coordinating employees involves the use of various forms of compensation to encourage them to perform activities consistent with the retailer's objectives.

A common type of compensation for retail salespeople is a **commission,** which is a type of incentive based on a percentage of their sales or margin. Many retailers base at least part of salespeople's compensation on commissions.

Another individual incentive is a **bonus,** which is additional compensation awarded periodically on the basis of an evaluation of the employee's performance. For example, store managers often receive bonuses at the end of the year based on their store's performance relative to its budgeted sales and profits. In addition to receiving compensation-based incentives based on individual performance, retail managers often receive income based on their firm's performance. Known as **profit sharing,** this type of incentive can be offered as a cash bonus based on the firm's profits or as a grant of stock options that link additional income to the performance of the firm's stock.

Some retailers use stock incentives to motivate and reward all employees, including sales associates. Employees are encouraged to buy shares in their companies at discounted prices through payroll deduction plans. These stock incentives align employees' interests with those of the company and can be very rewarding when the company does well. However, if growth in the company's stock price declines, employee morale declines too, corporate culture is threatened, and demands for higher wages and more benefits develop.

An increasingly important compensation-based incentive for retail employees is the provision of health care benefits. As health care costs continue to rise, some employees find this benefit as important as the basic compensation program, particularly if it includes other family members. For instance, Burgerville, a 39-restaurant chain in Vancouver, Washington, pays at least 90 percent of health care premiums for hourly employees who work at least 20 hours a week. Executives there believe this unusual benefit has saved money by cutting turnover, boosting sales, and improving productivity.[28]

Incentives are very effective at motivating employees to perform the activities on which the incentives are based. But incentives also may cause employees to ignore other activities. For example, salespeople whose compensation is based entirely on their sales may be reluctant to spend time restocking fixtures and shelves. Excessive use of incentives to motivate employees also can reduce employee commitment. Company loyalty falls because employees feel that the firm hasn't made a commitment to them (because it is unwilling to guarantee their compensation). Thus, if a competitor offers to pay a higher commission rate, they'll feel free to leave.

Organization Culture   The final method for motivating and coordinating employees is to develop a strong organization culture. An **organization culture** is the set of values, traditions, and customs of a firm that guides employee behavior. These guidelines aren't written down as a set of policies and procedures; they are traditions passed along by experienced employees to new employees.

Many retail firms have strong organization cultures that give employees a sense of what they ought to do on their jobs and how they should behave to be

REFACT

The late Mary Kay Ash, founder of Mary Kay Cosmetics, was fond of saying, "There are two things that people want more than sex and money—recognition and praise."[27]

REFACT

Sam Walton, Walmart's founder and one of the wealthiest people in the world when he passed away, flew first-class only once in his life, on a trip to Africa.[29]

Nordstrom has one rule in its policy manual, "Use your best judgment to do anything you can to provide service to our customers."

consistent with the firm's strategy. For example, Nordstrom's strong organization culture emphasizes customer service, whereas Walmart's focuses on reducing costs so that the firm can provide low prices to its customers.

An organization culture often has a much stronger effect on employees' actions than do rewards offered through compensation plans, directions provided by supervisors, or written company policies. Nordstrom emphasizes the strength of its organization culture in the policy manual given to new employees.[30] The manual has one rule: "Use your best judgment to do anything you can to provide service to our customers." Lack of written rules doesn't mean that Nordstrom employees have no guidelines or restrictions on their behavior; rather, the organization culture guides employees' behavior. New salespeople learn from other employees that they should always wear clothes sold at Nordstrom, that they should park their cars at the outskirts of the parking lot so that customers can park in more convenient locations, that they should approach customers who enter their department, that they should accept any merchandise returned by a customer even if the merchandise wasn't purchased at a Nordstrom store, and that they should offer to carry packages to the customer's car.

Organization cultures are developed and maintained through stories and symbols.[31] Values in an organization culture are often explained to new employees and reinforced to present employees through stories. For example, each day at every Ritz-Carlton around the world, employees from every department meet to review guest experiences, resolve issues, and discuss ways to improve service.[32] During the meeting, a "wow story" is read. The same story is told in every Ritz-Carlton, and it singles out a staff person who offers exemplary service. For instance, a family staying at the Ritz-Carlton in Bali had carried specialized eggs and milk for their son who suffered from food allergies. Upon arrival, they saw that the eggs had broken and the milk had soured. When the staff failed to find the special items locally, the executive chef contacted his mother-in-law in Singapore and asked that she buy the products and fly to Bali to deliver them, which she agreed to do.

Whole Foods strengthens its organization culture by working in teams and using its employees during the hiring process.[33] Each store is organized into approximately 10 teams, each responsible for a different category or aspect of store operations, such as customer service or checkout lines. Store operations are highly decentralized, so many purchasing and operational decisions are made by the teams. When hiring, team leaders screen candidates, but a two-thirds majority of the team must approve each hire.

Using symbols is another technique for managing organization culture and conveying its underlying values. Symbols are an effective means of communicating with employees because the values they represent can be remembered easily. Walmart makes extensive use of symbols and symbolic behavior to reinforce its emphasis on controlling costs and keeping in contact with its customers. Photocopy machines at corporate headquarters have cups on them for employees to use to pay for any personal copying. At the traditional Saturday morning executive meeting, employees present information on the cost-control measures they've recently undertaken. Managers who have been traveling in the field report on what they've seen, unique programs undertaken in the stores, and promising merchandise. Headquarters are spartan. Founder Sam Walton, one of the world's wealthiest people before he died, lived in a modest house and drove a pickup truck to work.

Keeping Talent: Building Employee Commitment

Having attracted and developed effective employees, an important challenge in retailing is to keep them, that is, to reduce turnover. High turnover reduces sales and increases costs. Sales are lost because inexperienced employees lack the skills and knowledge about company policies and merchandise to interact effectively with customers; costs increase due to the need to recruit and train new employees. Retailing View 9.5 illustrates how Walmart builds a committed workforce by investing in it.

Consider what happens when Bob Roberts, meat department manager in a supermarket chain, leaves the company. His employer promotes a meat manager from a smaller store to take Bob's position, promotes an assistant department manager to the position in the smaller store, promotes a meat department trainee to the assistant manager's position, and hires a new trainee. Now the supermarket chain needs to train two meat department managers and one assistant manager and hire and train one trainee. The estimated cost for replacing Bob Roberts is almost $10,000.

RETAILING VIEW   Walmart Cares about Its Employees   9.5

Is the corporation's commitment to environmentalism, personal fitness, and a healthy lifestyle why people work at Walmart? IBM, Microsoft, and other white-collar companies already sponsor fitness and lifestyle improvement programs for their employees. But now the world's largest retailer, which employs 1.3 million people who make an average of less than $20,000 per year, is launching a voluntary personal sustainability project.

Approximately 50 percent of its employees are participating in the program. Walmart is holding workshops to teach employees the benefits of carpooling to work with three colleagues, discontinuing cigarette smoking, and turning off the television. Employees are learning the importance of environmental sustainability, reducing carbon emissions, and consuming healthy and environmentally friendly food.

Walmart is helping its employees live better through its personal sustainability projects.

REFACT

Since 2006, 20,000 Walmart employees have quit smoking, lost a combined 184,000 pounds, recycled 3 million pounds of plastic, and swam, biked, or walked 1.1 million miles.

As a result of the seminars, employees have already taken the initiative to tailor environmental practices that fit with their new lifestyles. Employees have pledged to start recycling at home and improve their physical health with healthier food and more exercise. One employee created a "zero waste" break room, where the employees had to use mugs instead of Styrofoam cups and recycling bins were set up for aluminum cans and plastic bottles. Employees are also lobbying for healthier Subway restaurants, instead of McDonald's, in Walmart stores.

What was first thought to be a public relations stunt for Walmart is turning out to be a positive project that could improve the quality of life and the productivity of its employees, reduce health care costs for the company, improve its image among its customers, and help it become a corporate leader in environmentalism.

Sources: Matt Turner, "Walmart's Personal Sustainability Project," *NWA-homepage.com*, February 17, 2009; www.fastcompany.com/magazine/118/getting-personal.html (accessed December 2, 2009); http://walmartstores.com/sites/sustainabilityreport/2009/s_ao_psp.html (accessed December 2, 2009); http://walmartstores.com/sites/sustainabilityreport/2007/associatesPersonal.html (accessed December 2, 2009); Michael Barbaro, "At Wal-Mart, Lessons in Self-Help," *New York Times*, April 5, 2007; www.walmart.com (accessed December 2, 2009).

GET OUT AND DO IT!

1. **CONTINUING CASE ASSIGNMENT** Meet with the store manager of the retailer you have chosen for this Continuing Case Assignment. Ask the store manager which company HR policies he or she feels are very effective and which are not effective. Why? Also ask the manager about the store's policies concerning the legal and regulatory issues discussed in the chapter. Does the retailer have written policies that enable the manager to deal effectively with any situations that arise? Have situations arisen that were not covered by the policies? How were the situations addressed? To what degree does the manager feel that he or she is empowered to make decisions that affect the performance of the store? Would the manager like more or less decision-making authority? Why?

2. **INTERNET EXERCISE** Go to the Society of Human Resource Management's home page, www.shrm.org. An organization of human resource professionals, SHRM publishes *HR Magazine*, with articles available online at www.workforceonline.com. Find and summarize the conclusions of articles addressing the HR challenges that retailers are facing, such as the management of a diverse workforce, international expansion, and the use of technology to increase productivity.

3. **INTERNET EXERCISE** The Fair Measures Law Consulting Group provides training and legal services for employers. Go to its Web site, www.fairmeasures.com, and choose one of the legal areas to investigate (sexual harassment, wrongful termination, and so forth). Another source of information about legal issues regarding employees is www.law.cornell.edu/topics/employment.html. Read the most recent court opinions and articles about employment issues, and summarize the implications for human resource management in retailing.

4. **INTERNET EXERCISE** Go to the home page of Retail Human Resources PLC at www.retailhuman-resources.com/. How does this recruitment consultancy help U.K. retailers and job seekers to find the best employment matches?

5. **INTERNET EXERCISE** Go to the home page of the National Retail Federation Foundation (NRFF), at www.nrffoundation.com/CareersCenter/default.asp/, and click on "Experience Retail" to read about the different career paths in marketing/advertising, store operations, loss prevention, store management, finance, human resources, IT and e-commerce, sales and sales-related, distribution/logistics/supply chain management, merchandise buying/planning, and entrepreneurship. Which area appeals to you the most? Explain your preference for this career direction.

6. **LIBRARY EXERCISE** Go to one of your college's or university's library business databases, and find a recent newspaper or journal article that discusses human resource management in the retail industry. Briefly tie the concepts in the article back to the chapter or to your Continuing Case Assignment (question 1 above).

7. **WEB OLC EXERCISE**
   a. Go to the student side of this book's Web site, and review the student résumés. Which résumés do you think are effective? Ineffective? Why?
   b. Update your résumé, and prepare for an interview for a manager training program with a large lumber and building supply retailer. This full-time position promises rapid advancement upon completion of the training period. A college degree and experience in retail, sales, and marketing are preferred. The base pay is between $28,000 and $34,000 per year. This retailer promotes from within, and a new manager trainee can become a store manager within two to three years, with an earning potential of $100,000 or more. The benefits package is generous, including medical/hospitalization/dental/disability/life insurance, a 401(k) plan, profit sharing, awards and incentives, paid vacations, and holidays. Your résumé should include your contact information, education and training, skills, experience and accomplishments, and honors and awards.
   c. Role-play a practice interview for this position. Pair up with another student, and read each others' résumés; then spend 20 to 30 minutes on each side of the interview. One student should be the human resource manager screening applicants, and the other person should be the candidate for the manager training program. Here are some questions to use in the role-play scenario:
   - Why are you applying for this position?
   - What are your strengths and weaknesses for this position?
   - Why should this organization consider you for this position?
   - Why are you interested in working for this company?
   - What are your career goals for the next 5 to 10 years?
   - Describe your skills when working in a team setting.
   - What questions do you have about the company?

DISCUSSION QUESTIONS AND PROBLEMS

1. Why is human resource management more important in retailing firms than in manufacturing firms?

2. How can retailers use hiring, selecting, training, and motivating employees in their human resource management practices to gain competitive advantage?

3. Describe the similarities and differences between the organizations of small and large retail companies. Why do these similarities and differences exist?

4. Some retailers have specific employees (merchandise assistants) assigned to restock the shelves and maintain the appearance of the store. Other retailers have sales associates perform these tasks. What are the advantages and disadvantages of each approach?

5. How can national retailers like Best Buy and Victoria's Secret, which both use a centralized buying system, make sure that their buyers are aware of the local differences in consumer needs?

6. Reread Retailing View 9.3 on The Container Store. What are the positive and negative aspects of employee turnover? How is this retailer reducing the turnover of its sales associates? How can other retail firms learn from this example?

7. To motivate employees, several major department stores are experimenting with incentive compensation plans, although compensation plans with a lot of incentives often don't promote good customer service. How can retailers motivate employees to sell merchandise energetically and, at the same time, not jeopardize customer service?

8. Assume that you're starting a new restaurant that caters to college students and plans to use college students as servers. What human resource management problems would you expect to have? How could you build a strong organization culture in your restaurant to provide outstanding customer service?

9. Three approaches for motivating and coordinating employee activities are policies and supervision, incentives, and organization culture. What are the advantages and disadvantages of each?

10. Why should retailers be concerned about the needs of their employees? What can retailers do to satisfy those needs?

11. What HR trends are helping meet employees' needs, increase job satisfaction, and lower turnover?

SUGGESTED READINGS

Arndt, Aaron, Todd J. Arnold, and Timothy D. Landry. "The Effects of Polychronic-Orientation upon Retail Employee Satisfaction and Turnover." *Journal of Retailing* 82, no. 4 (2006).

Bhattacharya, C. B., Sankar Sen, and Daniel Korschun. "Using Corporate Social Responsibility to Win the War for Talent." *Sloan Management Review* 49, no. 2 (2008), pp. 37–44.

Booth, Simon, and Kristian Hamer. "Labour Turnover in the Retail Industry." *International Journal of Retail and Distribution Management* 35, no. 4 (2007), pp. 289–307.

Grippo, Robert M. *Macy's: The Store, the Star, the Story.* Garden City Park, NY: Square One, 2009.

Harvey, David Peterson, and Gloria Stevensen. *Sexual Harassment: Workplace Issues.* Scotts Valley, CA: CreateSpace, 2008.

Jackson, Susan E., Randall S. Schuler, and Steve Werner. *Managing Human Resources,* 10th ed. Mason, OH: South-Western College, 2008.

Lipman, Fredrick D., and Steven E. Hall. *Executive Compensation Best Practices.* Hoboken, NJ: Wiley, 2008.

Mujtaba, Ghulam Bahaudin. *Business Ethics of Retail Employees: How Ethical Are Modern Workers?* Fort Worth: ILEAD Academy, 2009.

Netemeyer, Richard G., J. G. Maxham, and D. Lichtenstein. "The Retail Value Chain: Linking Employee Perceptions to Employee Performance, Customer Evaluations, and Store Performance." *Marketing Science,* 2008.

"The 100 Best Companies to Work For 2009," *Fortune,* February 2, 2009.

Information Systems and Supply Chain Management

EXECUTIVE BRIEFING

Ramesh Murthy, Vice President for Supply Chain and Inventory Management, CVS

I'm a bioengineer by training, but my career moved into retail through a series of key opportunities. I took advantage of these opportunities and ultimately ended up in retail because I found it was a great place to take on complex challenges. It also gives me a chance to apply some of the theory I learned in engineering to large-scale issues where the outcome has to be achieved in a fairly short time. What's been consistent in my career path is that I've always looked for positions that demand a driving intellect and that combine analytical challenge with the need for a real-world, practical, fast-speed outcome.

CVS (Consumer Value Stores) was founded in 1963 and has been growing ever since through acquisitions, mergers, and service launches that have led us to a market niche that combines retail, pharmacies, and pharmacy benefit management services. We recently celebrated the opening of the 7,000th CVS/pharmacy; annual sales are in excess of $22 billion. The company's success rests on the fact that we are constantly looking for ways to get the leading edge for retail and health care. For example, in 2007 we merged with Caremark Rx, Inc., which made us the largest integrated provider of prescriptions and health-related services in the country. Our business model, which is a retailer with a pharmacy benefits manager, is one that no one else has today.

I am responsible for making sure that our customers have every single thing they need in every single one of our stores every day. I can't think of anything more important to us because if the item isn't there, we lose the sale. I rely on my scientific background, with its heavy emphasis on analysis, to avoid those losses. Understanding and interpreting data can help us predict and prepare for changes in the marketplace.

My key focus every day is improving our business. I ask myself what I can do to make sure my team members are growing, developing, and moving forward in their careers. I challenge myself regularly with questions like how we

CHAPTER 10

QUESTIONS

How do merchandise and information flow from the vendor to the retailer to consumers?

What activities are undertaken in a distribution center?

What information technology (IT) developments are facilitating vendor-retailer communications?

What are the benefits to vendors and retailers for collaborating on supply chain management?

How do retailers and vendors collaborate to make sure the right merchandise is available when customers are ready to buy it?

What is RFID, and how will it affect retailing?

can improve our customer service, what issues have emerged in the marketplace and how we can deal with them, and what initiatives are needed to add capability or improve our bottom line.

I enjoy retail because of the challenge. It has so many moving parts, it's very high velocity, it's analytically challenging, and it's relatively intensive. Then there is the satis-faction of seeing the results of your labor: No matter where you work in retail, you end up going into stores where you see a customer choosing and appreciating your merchandise. That's very satisfying. Bottom line, what keeps me coming back is that, in this business, you learn something new every day.

Joe Jackson wakes up in the morning, takes a shower, dresses, and goes to his kitchen to make a cup of coffee and toast a bagel. He slices the bagel and puts it in his toaster oven, but, to his dismay, the toaster oven is not working. As he reads the newspaper and eats his untoasted bagel with his coffee, he notices that Target is having a sale on Michael Graves toaster ovens. The toaster ovens look great. So, on his way home from work, he stops at a Target store to buy one. He finds the advertised Michael Graves model on the shelf and buys it.

Joe expected to find the Michael Graves toaster oven, as well as other models, available at Target, but he probably didn't realize that a lot of behind-the-scene activities were going on to get those toaster ovens to the store. Target uses sophisticated information and supply chain management systems to make sure that the Michael Graves toaster ovens and other brands are available in its stores whenever Joe and other customers want them. When Joe bought the toaster oven, the information about his transaction was automatically forwarded by the information systems to Target's regional distribution center, the home appliance planner at Target's corporate headquarters in Minneapolis, and the toaster oven manufacturer in China. A computer information system monitors all toaster oven sales and inventory levels in every Target store and indicates when to have toaster ovens shipped from the manufacturer in China to the regional distribution centers and then from the centers to the stores. Shipments to the distribution centers and stores are monitored using a satellite tracking system that locates the ships and trucks transporting the toaster ovens.

Of course, Target could ensure the availability of toaster ovens and other merchandise by simply keeping a large number of units in the stores at all times. But stocking a large number of each SKU would require much more space to store the items and a significant investment in additional inventory. So the challenge for Target is to limit its inventory and space investment but still make sure products are always available when customers want them.

This chapter begins by outlining how retailers can gain a strategic advantage through supply chain management and information systems. Then the chapter describes information and product flows in the supply chain and the activities undertaken in distribution centers. Next, it examines a set of decisions that retailers make to determine the structure of the supply chain, such as whether to use distribution centers or direct store deliveries and whether to outsource some supply chain functions. The chapter continues with a discussion of how vendors and retailers work together to efficiently manage the movement of merchandise from the vendor through the retailer's distribution centers to its stores and customers. The chapter concludes with a discussion of a new technology, radio frequency identification (RFID), being used to improve supply chain efficiency.

CREATING STRATEGIC ADVANTAGE THROUGH SUPPLY MANAGEMENT AND INFORMATION SYSTEMS

As discussed in Chapter 1, retailers are the connection between customers and product manufacturers. It is the retailers' responsibility to gauge customers' wants and needs and work with the other members of the supply chain—distributors, vendors, and transportation companies—to make sure the merchandise that customers want is available when they want it. A simplified supply chain is illustrated in Exhibit 10–1. Vendors ship merchandise either to a **distribution center** (as is the case for vendors V_1 and V_3) or directly to stores (as is the case for vendor V_2). The factors considered in deciding to ship directly to stores versus to distribution centers are discussed later in this chapter.

Supply chain management is a set of activities and techniques firms employ to efficiently and effectively manage the flow of merchandise from the vendors to the retailer's customers. These activities ensure that the customers are able to purchase merchandise in the desired quantities at a preferred location and appropriate time.[1]

Retailers are increasingly taking a leadership role in managing their supply chains. When retailers were predominantly small businesses, larger manufacturers and distributors dictated when, where, and how merchandise was delivered. But with the consolidation and emergence of large, international retail chains, retailers now play an active role in coordinating supply chain management activities. The size of these international retailers typically makes them more knowledgeable and powerful than their vendors and thus better able to control their supply chains. Retailers are in a unique position to collect information about customer shopping behavior and purchases. As we will discuss later in the chapter, this information is being shared with suppliers to plan production, promotions, deliveries, assortments, and inventory levels. Efficient supply chain management is important to retailers because it can provide a strategic advantage that increases product availability and an inventory turnover that produces a higher return on assets.

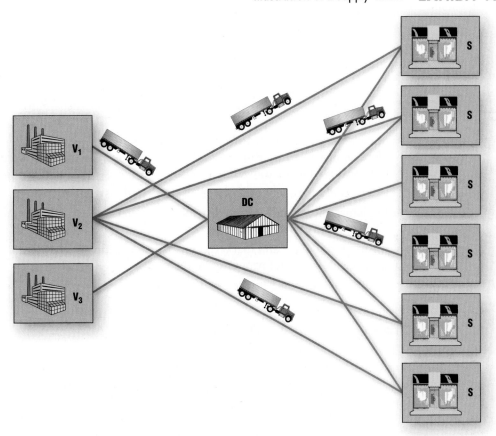

Strategic Advantage

As we discussed in Chapter 5, strategic advantage is the unique and sustainable advantage that enables retailers to realize a higher-than-average return on their assets. Of course, all retailers strive to develop a competitive advantage, but not all retailers can develop a competitive advantage from their information and supply chain systems. However, if they do develop such an advantage, the advantage is sustainable because it is difficult for competitors to duplicate it.

For example, a critical factor in Walmart's success is its information and supply chain management systems. Even though competitors recognize this advantage, they have difficulty achieving the same level of performance as Walmart's systems for four reasons. First, Walmart has made substantial initial and continuing investments in developing its systems over a long time period. Second, it has the scale economies to justify these investments. Third, the supply chain activities take place within the firm and are not easily known and copied by competitors. Its systems are not simply software packages that any firm can buy from a software supplier. Through its continuous learning process, Walmart is always refining its systems to improve its performance. Fourth, the effective use of these systems requires top management support and the coordinated effort of employees and functional areas throughout the company.

Walmart's systems are so well regarded that retailers in emerging economies are anxious to partner with Walmart in hopes of acquiring some of these skills. For example, Bharti Enterprises in India has a joint venture with Walmart to wholesale food and other products to small Indian retailers. With Walmart's supply chain management systems in place, farmers and small manufacturers are directly linked to retailers, thus streamlining the supply chain.[2]

To understand the complexity of the tasks performed by these systems and the need for coordinated efforts, consider the various activities that retailers undertake to keep merchandise in stock:

- Accurately forecast sales and needed inventory levels for each category and SKU.
- Monitor sales to detect derivations from the forecast.
- Transport the right amount of merchandise from the distribution centers to each store.
- Make sure that accurate information is available that indicates where the merchandise is—either in the vendor's warehouse, the distribution center, the store, sold to customer, or in transit.
- Place accurate, timely orders with vendors and distribution centers.
- Replenish merchandise from distribution centers with the right quantities when the stores need it.
- Ensure that buyers and marketing managers coordinate merchandise delivery with special sales and promotional materials.
- Collect and process returned merchandise.

Improved Product Availability

Efficient supply chain management provides two benefits to retailers and their customers: (1) fewer stockouts and (2) tailored assortments. These benefits translate into greater sales, lower costs, higher inventory turnover, and lower markdowns for retailers.

Fewer Stockouts   A **stockout** occurs when an SKU that a customer wants is not available. What would happen if Joe went to the Target store and the store did not have Michael Graves toaster ovens because the distribution center did not ship enough to the store? The store would give Joe a rain check so that he could come back and still pay the sale price when the store receives a new shipment. But Joe would not be pleased because he would have made a wasted trip to the store. As a result of the stockout, Joe might decide to buy another model, or he might go to a nearby Walmart to buy a toaster oven. While at Walmart, he could buy other items in addition to the toaster oven. He also might be reluctant to shop at Target in the future and might tell all of his friends about the negative experience he had. This bad experience could have been avoided if Target had done a better job of managing its supply chain.

In general, stockouts have significant short- and long-term effects on sales and profits. Data show that the first time customers experience a stockout, they will purchase a substitute item 70 percent of the time. With a second out-of-stock occurrence, that rate drops to 50 percent, with customers going to a competitor the other 50 percent of the time. By the third instance, there is a 70 percent chance that the retailer has lost the sale entirely and, most likely, the customers' loyalty as well. Customers may never come back.[4]

Tailored Assortments   Another benefit provided by information systems that support supply chain systems is making sure that the right merchandise is available at the right store. Most national retail chains adjust assortments in their stores on the basis of climate—stocking more wool sweaters in northern stores and cotton sweaters in southern stores during the winter. Some retailers are now using sophisticated statistical methods to analyze sales transaction data and adjust store assortments for a wide range of merchandise on the basis of the characteristics of customers in each store's local market.

Higher Return on Assets

From the retailer's perspective, an efficient supply chain and information system can improve its ROA because the system increases sales and net profit margins, without increasing inventory. Net sales increase because customers are offered more attractive, tailored assortments that are in stock. Consider Joe Jackson's toaster oven purchase. Target, with its information systems, could accurately estimate how many Michael Graves toaster ovens each store would sell during the special promotion. Using its supply chain management system, it would make sure sufficient stock was available at Joe's store so that all the customers who wanted to buy one could.

Net profit margin is improved by increasing the gross margin and lowering expenses. An information system that coordinates buyers and vendors allows retailers to take advantage of special buying opportunities and obtain the merchandise at a lower cost, thus improving their gross margins. Retailers also can lower their operating expenses by coordinating deliveries, thus reducing transportation expenses. With more efficient distribution centers, merchandise can be received, prepared for sale, and shipped to stores with minimum handling, further reducing expenses.

By efficiently managing their supply chains, retailers can carry less backup inventory yet still avoid stockouts. Thus, inventory levels are lower, and with a lower inventory investment, total assets are also lower, so the asset and inventory turnovers are both higher. Retailing View 10.1 describes how supply chain management is changing the way fashion comes to market.

THE FLOW OF INFORMATION AND PRODUCTS IN A SUPPLY CHAIN

The complexities of the merchandise and information flows in a typical multistore chain are illustrated in Exhibit 10–2. Although information and merchandise flows are intertwined, in the following sections we describe first how information about customer demand is captured at the store, which triggers a series of responses from buyers and planners, distribution centers, and vendors. This information is used to make sure that merchandise is available at the store when the customer

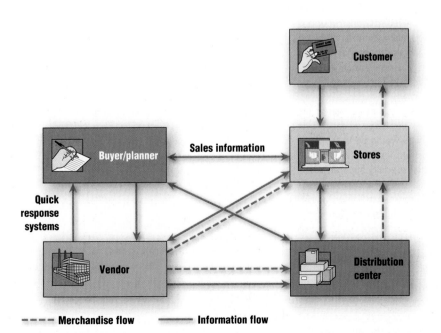

EXHIBIT 10–2
Information and Merchandise Flows

10.1   RETAILING VIEW   Zara Delivers Fast Fashion

 Fast fashion is a retail business strategy that involves using the supply chain management process to introduce fashionable merchandise rapidly and respond to customer demand for the merchandise quickly. This business strategy was pioneered by Zara, a global specialty apparel chain located in La Coruna, Spain, and adopted by other retailers such as H&M (headquartered in Sweden), TopShop (United Kingdom), and Forever 21 (United States).

The fast-fashion process starts with receiving timely information from store managers. At Zara, store managers are equipped with handheld devices linked directly to the company's corporate office in Spain. They report daily on what customers are

Zara's competitive advantage in specialty apparel retailing is based on its efficient supply chain that delivers fashionable merchandise to its stores frequently.

buying and not buying and what they are asking for but not finding. For instance, when buyers find that customers are requesting a purple shirt that is similar to one they are selling in pink, they pass this information on to the designers in Spain, who initiate a process that results in making and shipping purple shirts to its stores in a very short period of time.

Zara successfully reduces lead time by communicating electronically with the factory, using automated equipment, assemblers who are in close proximity to the factory, and premium transportation. Zara buys undyed fabric from Asia, but the bulk of its apparel manufacturing occurs in Spain and Portugal. On the basis of its new design concepts and the customer response in stores, fabric gets cut and dyed by robots in the company's 23 highly automated factories in Spain. The final construction is entrusted to a network of 300 or so small assemblers located near its factories in Galicia, Spain, and northern Portugal. To ensure that the apparel is delivered in a timely manner, merchandise is shipped by truck to stores in Europe and by air express to stores in the rest of the world.

Instead of shipping new products a few times a season (as many fashion retailers do), Zara makes deliveries to each of its stores every few days. The purple shirts would be in stores in two weeks—compared with the several months it would take for most department stores and other specialty apparel stores to accomplish the same feat. For instance, if a Zara store is running low on a medium Kelly green sweater, its fast-fashion system will ensure a shorter lead time than that of more traditional retailers. As a result, it's less likely that the Zara store will be out of stock before the next sweater shipment arrives. Limiting the stock in stores also creates a sense of scarcity among its customers. If they don't buy now, the item might not be available next time they visit the store. Finally, by producing and shipping small quantities, Zara can quickly recover from a fashion faux pas.

Due to the efficiency of its supply chain, Zara does not have to discount nonselling merchandise as much as do other specialty store apparel retailers. At Zara, the number of items that end up marked down is about half the industry average. Zara is able to achieve these results and still have 10,000 new designs and 40,000 new SKUs each year.

H&M and Forever 21 use a slightly different strategy. About one-quarter of their assortments are made up of fast-fashion items that are designed in-house and produced by independent, local factories. As at Zara, these items move quickly through the stores and are replaced frequently with fresh designs. But H&M also keeps a significant inventory of basic, everyday items sourced from low-cost Asian factories.

The fast-fashion approach is particularly effective for specialty apparel retailers targeting customers who are very fashion-conscious and always want to have a new look, not the same things their friends are wearing. And these customers want to achieve this fashion ability on a limited budget. Because more shoppers are loading up on fast fashion every few weeks instead of purchasing a few higher-priced basics once every few months, they are less sentimental about quickly unloading them to help finance the next round. Thus, sales of fast-fashion merchandise in second-hand stores are growing dramatically.

REFACT

Consumers in central London visit the average apparel store four times annually, but Zara's customers visit its shops an average of 17 times a year.[6]

Sources: Vertica Bhardwaj and Ann Fairhurst, "Fast Fashion: Response to Changes in the Fashion Industry," *International Review of Retail, Distribution and Consumer Research* 20 (February 2010), pp.165–173; Carmen Lopez and Ying Fan, "Case Study: Internationalisation of the Spanish Fashion Brand Zara," *Journal of Fashion Marketing and Management* 13, no. 2 (2009), pp. 279–296; Mark Mulligan, "Spanish Professor Who Uncovers the Detail in Retail: Constant Contact with Corporate Life Is a Valuable Teaching Tool," *Financial Times,* August 18, 2008, p. 12; Brian Dunn, "Inside the Zara Business Model," *DNR,* March 20, 2006, p. 11.

EXHIBIT 10–3
Information Flows

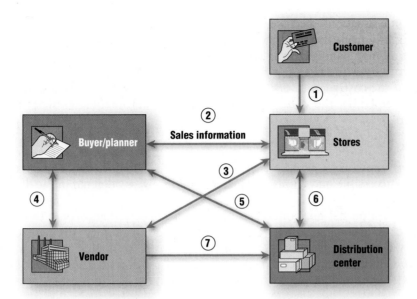

wants it. Then we discuss the physical movement of merchandise from vendors through distribution centers to the stores.

Information Flows

When Joe Jackson bought his toaster oven at Target, he initiated the information flows illustrated in Exhibit 10–3 (the numbers in parentheses refer to the path in the exhibit).

The Target cashier scans the **Universal Product Code (UPC)** tag on the toaster oven box (1), and a sales receipt is generated for Joe. The UPC tag is a black-and-white bar code containing a 13-digit code that indicates the manufacturer of the item, a description of the item, information about special packaging, and special promotions. The codes for all products are issued by GS1 US (gs1us.org), formerly the Uniform Code Council. In the future, RFID tags, discussed later in this chapter, may replace UPC tags.

The information about the transaction is captured at the point-of-sale (POS) terminal and sent to Target's information system, where it can be accessed by the planner for the toaster oven product category (2). The planner uses this information to monitor and analyze sales and decide when to reorder more toaster ovens or reduce their prices if sales are below expectations.

The sales transaction data also are sent to Target's distribution center (6). When the store inventory drops to a specified level, more toaster ovens are shipped to the store, and the shipment information is sent to the Target computer system (5) so that the planner knows the inventory level that remains in the distribution center.

When the inventory drops to a specified level in the distribution center (4), the planner negotiates terms and shipping dates and places an order with the manufacturer of the toaster ovens. The planner then informs the distribution center about the new order and when the store can expect delivery (5).

When the manufacturer ships the toaster ovens to the Target distribution center, it sends an advanced shipping notice to the distribution center (7). An **advance shipping notice (ASN)** is a document that tells the distribution center what specifically is being shipped and when it will be delivered. The distribution center then makes appointments for trucks to make the delivery at a specific time, date, and loading dock. When the shipment is received at the distribution center, the planner is notified (5) and then authorizes payment to the vendor.

REFACT

Shortly after 8 a.m. on June 26, 1974, the first UPC tag was scanned in Troy, Ohio, when Clyde Dawson bought a 10-pack of Wrigley's Juicy Fruit gum for 67 cents in a Marsh supermarket. Now, over 10 billion items are scanned each day.[7]

In some situations, discussed later in this chapter, the sales transaction data are sent directly from the store to the vendor (3), and the vendor decides when to ship more merchandise to the distribution center and stores. The fulfillment of sales from nonstore channels may involve the vendor shipping merchandise directly to the customer. In other situations, especially when merchandise is reordered frequently, the ordering process is done automatically, bypassing the planners.

Data Warehouse   Purchase data collected at the point of sale goes into a database known as a *data warehouse*. The information stored in the data warehouse is accessible on various dimensions and levels, as depicted in the data cube in Exhibit 10–4.

As shown on the horizontal axis, data can be accessed according to the level of merchandise aggregation—SKU (item), vendor, category (dresses), department (women's apparel), or all merchandise. Along the vertical axis, data can be accessed by level of the company—store, division, or total company. Finally, along the third dimension, data can be accessed by point in time—day, season, or year.

The CEO might be interested in how the corporation is generally doing and could look at the data aggregated by quarter for a merchandise division, a region of the country, or the total corporation. A buyer may be more interested in a particular vendor in a specific store on a particular day. Analysts from various levels of the retail operation extract information from the data warehouse to make a plethora of retailing decisions about developing and replenishing merchandise assortments.

Data warehouses also contain detailed information about customers, which is used to target promotions and group products together in stores. These applications are discussed in Chapter 11. To economically collect this information, most

EXHIBIT 10–4   Retail Data Warehouse

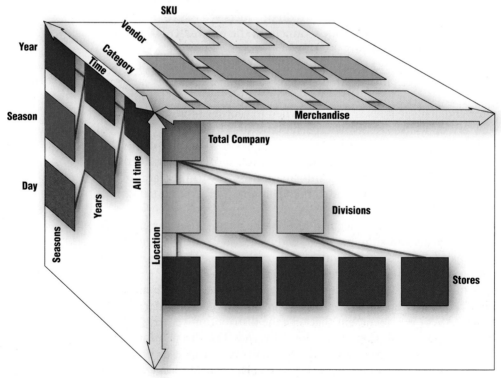

SOURCE: SAS Retail.

of the communication between vendors and retailers and within the retailer is done via electronic data interchange (EDI).

Electronic Data Interchange   In the past, retailer-vendor information flows were accomplished by sending handwritten or typed documents through the mail or by fax. Now most communications between vendors and retailers occur via electronic data interchange. **Electronic data interchange (EDI)** is the computer-to-computer exchange of business documents in a standardized format. To facilitate the adoption of EDI, the retail industry agreed to use specific symbols to delineate the purchase order number, the vendor's name, the address the merchandise is being shipped to, and so forth.

Retailers also have developed standards for exchanging information about purchase order changes, order status, transportation routings, advance shipping notices, on-hand inventory status, and vendor promotions, as well as information that enables vendors to put price tags on merchandise. The development and use of these standards is critical to the use of EDI because they enable all retailers to use the same format when transmitting data to their vendors.

EDI transmissions between retailers and vendors occur over the Internet. Because the Internet is a publicly accessible network, its use to communicate internally and externally with vendors and customers raises security issues. Some potential implications of security failures are the loss of business data essential to conducting business, disputes with vendors and customers, loss of public confidence and its effect on brand image, bad publicity, and loss of revenue from customers using an electronic channel.

To help secure information, retailers have incorporated security policies. A **security policy** is the set of rules that apply to activities involving computer and communication resources that belong to an organization. Retailers also train employees and add the necessary software and hardware to enforce the rules. The objectives of a security policy are:

- *Authentication.* The system ensures or verifies that the person or computer at the other end of the communication really is who or what it claims to be.
- *Authorization.* The system ensures that the person or computer at the other end of the comunication has permission to carry out the request.
- *Integrity.* The system ensures that the arriving information is the same as that sent, which means that the data have been protected from unauthorized changes or tampering through a data encryption process.

The Physical Flow of Merchandise—Logistics

Exhibit 10–5 illustrates the physical flow of merchandise within the supply chain.

1. Merchandise flows from vendor to distribution center.
2. Merchandise goes from distribution center to stores.
3. Alternatively, merchandise can go from vendor directly to stores or even the customer.

Logistics is the aspect of supply chain management that refers to the planning, implementation, and control of the efficient flow and storage of goods, services, and related information from the point of origin to the point of consumption to meet customers' needs.[10] In addition to managing inbound and outbound transportation, logistics involves the activities undertaken in the retailer's distribution center. For example, sometimes merchandise is temporarily stored at the distribution center; other times it just passes through the center from an inbound to an outbound truck. Merchandise shipments might be prepared for stores in the center. For example, the center might break down received shipping cartons into smaller quantities that can be more readily utilized by the individual stores and/or

EXHIBIT 10–5
Merchandise Flow

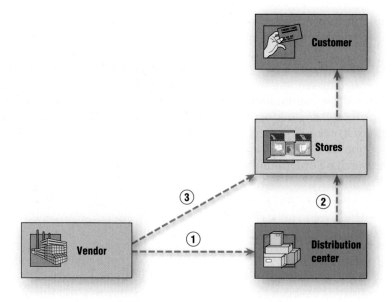

apply price tags and the retailer's labels. The following section describes activities undertaken in a distribution center.

THE DISTRIBUTION CENTER

The distribution center performs the following activities: coordinating inbound transportation; receiving, checking, storing, and cross-docking; getting merchandise "floor-ready"; and coordinating outbound transportation. To illustrate these activities, we shall follow a shipment of Sony PlayStation systems that is arriving at a Sears distribution center.

Management of Inbound Transportation

Traditionally, buyers focused their efforts, when working with vendors, on developing merchandise assortments, negotiating prices, and arranging joint promotions. Now, buyers and planners are much more involved in coordinating the physical flow of merchandise to the stores. The Sears game buyer has arranged for a truckload of systems to be delivered to its Houston, Texas, distribution center on Monday between 1 and 3 p.m. The buyer has also specified the particular way that the merchandise should be placed on pallets for easy unloading.

The truck must arrive within the specified time because the distribution center has all of its 100 receiving docks allocated throughout the day and much of the merchandise on this particular truck is going to be shipped to stores that evening. Unfortunately, the truck was delayed in a snowstorm. The **dispatcher**—the person who coordinates deliveries to the distribution center—reassigns the truck delivering the Sony game stations to a Wednesday morning delivery slot, notifies the planner, and charges the firm several hundred dollars for missing its delivery time. Although many manufacturers pay transportation expenses, some retailers negotiate with their vendors to absorb this expense.

Receiving and Checking

Receiving is the process of recording the receipt of merchandise as it arrives at a distribution center. **Checking** is the process of going through the goods on receipt to make sure that they arrived undamaged and that the merchandise ordered was the merchandise received.

Checking merchandise is a very labor-intensive and time-consuming task. When retailers have developed good relationships with vendors, they often do not check the number of items received compared to the number sent as indicated on the vendor's ASN for all merchandise received. They randomly check a sample of shipments to monitor the accuracy of the vendor's ASNs. In the future, retailers may be able to automatically check the contents of each carton by detecting signals sent from RFID chips placed on each item of merchandise in a carton.

Storing and Cross-Docking

After the PlayStations are received and checked, they are either stored or cross-docked. When PlayStations are stored, the cartons are transported by a conveyor system and forklift trucks to racks that go from the distribution center's floor to its ceiling. Then, when the Play Stations are needed in the stores, a forklift driver goes to the rack, picks up the carton, and places it on a conveyor system that routes the carton to the loading dock of a truck going to the stores.

Cross-Docking   PlayStation cartons that are **cross-docked** are prepackaged by Sony for a specific store. The UPC label on each carton indicates the store to which it is to be sent. Sony may also affix a price tag to each item in the carton. The PlayStation cartons are placed on a conveyor system that routes them from the unloading dock at which they were received to the loading dock for the truck going to the specific store—thus, the term *cross-docked*. The cartons are routed on the conveyor system automatically by sensors that read the UPC labels on the cartons. These cross-docked cartons are only in the distribution center for a few hours before they are shipped to the stores.

The size, sales rate, and vendor performance typically determine whether cartons are cross-docked or stored. Merchandise is cross-docked only if an entire carton can be shipped to a store. For example, it would be inefficient to cross-dock toothbrush cartons if a received carton contained 500 units but a store only sold 50 units a day. In this situation, the received toothbrush carton would be opened and a smaller number of units along with other merchandise would be put in a carton going to a store. Finally, when cross-docking cartons, retailers are assuming that the number and type of merchandise, and the store designation are correctly encoded in the vendor's UPC labels. Thus retailers are reluctant to cross-dock merchandise from unreliable vendors because it is very costly to correct errors that are not discovered until the cartons are first opened in stores.

Getting Merchandise Floor-Ready

For some merchandise, additional tasks are undertaken in the distribution center to make the merchandise floor-ready. **Floor-ready merchandise** is merchandise that is ready to be placed on the selling floor. Getting merchandise floor-ready entails ticketing, marking, and, in the case of some apparel, placing garments on hangers.

Ticketing and marking refer to affixing price and identification labels to the merchandise. It is more

Important activities undertaken in distribution centers are ticketing and marking merchandise so that it is floor-ready.

efficient for a retailer to perform these activities at a distribution center than in its stores. In a distribution center, an area can be set aside and a process implemented to efficiently add labels and put apparel on hangers. Conversely, getting merchandise floor-ready in stores can block aisles and divert salespeople's attention from their customers. An even better approach from the retailer's perspective is to get vendors to ship floor-ready merchandise, thus totally eliminating the expensive, time-consuming ticketing and marking process.

Preparing to Ship Merchandise to a Store

At the beginning of the day, the computer system in the distribution center generates a list of items to be shipped to each store on that day. For each item, a pick ticket and shipping label are generated. The **pick ticket** is a document or display on a screen in a forklift truck that indicates how much of each item to get from specific storage areas. The forklift driver goes to the storage area, picks up the number of cartons indicated on the pick ticket, places UPC shipping labels on the cartons that indicate the stores to which the items are to be shipped, and puts the cartons on the conveyor system, where they are automatically routed to the loading dock for the truck going to the stores.

An automated conveyor system moves most cartons to outbound trucks for delivery to stores.

Pick tickets and labels are also generated for the break pack area. In the break pack area, cartons with too many items to be shipped to a single store (like the toothbrushes discussed above) are packaged for the store. Employees, using the pick ticket, select items from open cartons and put them into a new carton. When all the items have been picked, a shipping label indicating the store's destination is attached to the carton, which is then placed on the conveyor system and routed to the appropriate loading dock.

So the conveyor system feeds cartons from three sources to the loading dock for a truck going to a specific store: (1) cross-docked cartons directly from the vendor's delivery trucks, (2) cartons stored in the distribution center, and (3) cartons from the break pack area. These cartons are then loaded onto the trucks by employees.

Management of Outbound Transportation

The management of outbound transportation from distribution center to stores is quite complex. Most distribution centers run 50 to 100 outbound truck routes each day. To handle this complex transportation problem, the centers use sophisticated routing and scheduling computer systems that consider the locations of the stores, road conditions, and transportation operating constraints to develop the most efficient routes possible. As a result, stores are provided with an accurate estimated time of arrival, and vehicle utilization is maximized.

Retailers also need to determine the mode of transportation—planes, ships, or trucks. Some retailers mix modes of transportation to reduce overall costs and time delays. For example, many Chinese vendors send Europe-bound cargo by ship to the U.S. West Coast. From there, the cargo is flown to its final destination in Europe. By combining the two modes of transport, sea and air, the entire trip takes about two weeks, as opposed to four or five weeks with an all-water route, and the cost is about half that of an all-air route.

Dollar General, an extreme-value, full-line discount store, developed an interesting, low-tech approach for dealing with a challenge it faced with outbound transportation to its stores. Controlling cost and distributing merchandise efficiently to its 8,000 stores is key to maintaining its low prices and still making a profit. Each week, more than 2,000 cartons are delivered to a typical store, and 12 person-hours are required to unload a delivery truck—time the employees could have spent helping customers. Labor scheduling is a real problem because store managers have to schedule additional staff on truck days and then, in some cases, the drivers cannot make deliveries at the preplanned time. In addition, many of the stores are located in urban areas that make it difficult to park delivery trucks at a convenient location for an extended time period.

To address these challenges, Dollar General invested $100 million in a delivery system called *EZ store*. The EZ store system involves packing merchandise for shipment to stores in easy-to-move containers called *roll-tainers*. Instead of having store staff unload the truck when it arrives, the truck drivers alone can unload the 25 roll-tainers for the typical store in about 90 minutes. Store employees no longer need to wait for the truck to arrive and then walk 3 to 8 miles, lifting 6,000 pounds of merchandise, on truck days. Instead, they can unpack merchandise from the roll-tainers and stock it on shelves during slow times in the day. The roll-tainers are also designed to protect the merchandise. When drivers make their next delivery, they offload the filled roll-tainers and pick up the empty ones. The system has led to significant reductions in employee injuries and turnover, reduced labor hours, and greater customer satisfaction.[11]

Retailing View 10.2 describes how Netflix automates many of these activities so that it can efficiently process and ship over 2 million DVDs a day and make sure the customers get the right ones.

SYSTEM DESIGN ISSUES

This section reviews the factors affecting the decisions made by retailers concerning their supply chains. These decisions involve determining what activities, if any, should be outsourced to independent firms; what merchandise, if any, should be delivered directly to the store, bypassing the distribution center; and how shipments directly to customers should be made.

Outsourcing Logistics

To streamline their operations and make more productive use of their assets and personnel, some retailers **outsource** supply chain functions. Many independent companies are very efficient at performing individual activities or all the supply chain activities. There are a large number of companies that can transport merchandise from the vendor to distribution centers or from the centers to the retailer's stores. Rather than owning warehouses to store merchandise, retailers can use **public warehouses** that are owned and operated by an independent company. Rather than outsource specific activities, retailers can use freight forwarders to arrange for the storage and shipping of their merchandise. **Freight forwarders** usually provide a full range of services including tracking inland transportation, preparing shipping and export documents, warehousing, booking cargo space, negotiating freight charges, consolidating freight, insuring cargo, and filing insurance claims.[12]

Advantages and Disadvantages of Outsourcing Supply Chain Activities
The primary benefit of outsourcing is that the independent firms can perform the activity at a lower cost or more efficiently than the retailer. Independent

firms typically have a lower cost because they perform the activity for many retailers and thus realize scale economies. For example, independent trucking firms have more opportunities to fill their trucks on the return trip (backhaul) with merchandise for other retailers after delivering merchandise to one retailer's stores. In addition, when there are many independent firms available to undertake the activity, retailers can have the firms bid against each other to undertake the activity and thus drive down the costs.

However, when retailers outsource a supply chain activity they can no longer develop a competitive advantage based on the performance of this activity. If the retailer's competitor discovers that the retailer is significantly reducing its costs or improving its efficiency by using an independent firm, the competitor can match the performance improvement by contracting with the same provider.[13]

10.2 RETAILING VIEW   How Netflix Makes Sure You Enjoy Your Movie

Netflix's semiautomated system for processing rented CDs gives it a competitive advantage.

Imagine the disappointment of inserting the DVD of *The Blind Side* and sitting back on your couch to enjoy the movie only to suddenly realize that the DVD is actually *Shrek 2*. Netflix, the California-based online movie subscription rental service, has a sophisticated system to ensure that customers get exactly what they want and don't have to wait more than a day or two to receive it.

In order to support its disc rental services, the company operates 58 distribution centers in the United States. The fulfillment process starts at 3 a.m., when employees seated at rows of desks start tearing open thousands of red envelopes. To get the envelopes to the facility that early, Netflix sends trucks to postal facilities at night to pick up the DVDs that have been returned by customers and bring them back to the hub.

For the next five hours, each employee repeats the same few steps over and over: Rip red envelope. Remove disc from white sleeve. Inspect disc for scratches and cracks. Make sure it's the correct disc. Clean disc. Return to sleeve. Place the disc in appropriate bin. An average employee can go through 650 discs in an hour, after receiving a month-long training.

Next, the envelopes are fed twice through a sorting machine—once to register the DVDs Netflix has received, a process which

automatically e-mails the customer who sent it and asks him or her to rate the movie, and a second time to determine if that DVD has been promised to another customer. If it has, the machine automatically places it in a bin marked with its destination.

Continuing on its journey, the bin with the envelope is brought over to "The Stuffer," a machine Netflix created to speed up the process of stuffing and sealing the red envelopes. At a rate of 3,200 an hour, the machine opens an envelope, stuffs the sleeve inside, removes the adhesive strip, seals the envelope, and places another seal on it.

The final stop is another trip to the mail sorter, where the sealed envelope gets scanned to determine its destination, has the address printed on it, and then gets sorted by zip code into a bin attached to the machine. Starting about 4 p.m., white trucks drive the bins to mail-processing and distribution centers. All the postal service has to do is load them on its trucks to send that little red envelope on its way to someone else's mailbox.

Sources: Etan Horowitz, "Netflix Distribution Centers: A Portrait of Speed and Efficiency," *Orlando Sentinel,* August 2009; Christopher Borrelli, "How Netflix Gets Your Movies to Your Mailbox So Fast," *Chicago Tribune,* August 4, 2009.

Pull and Push Supply Chains

Another supply chain decision retailers make is determining whether merchandise will be pushed from the distribution centers to the stores or pulled from the distribution centers to the stores. Information and merchandise flows such as those described in Exhibit 10–2 illustrate a **pull supply chain**—a supply chain in which requests for merchandise are generated at the store level on the basis of sales data captured by POS terminals. Basically, in this type of supply chain, the demand for an item pulls it through the supply chain. An alternative and less sophisticated approach is a **push supply chain,** in which merchandise is allocated to stores on the basis of forecasted demand. Once a forecast is developed, specified quantities of merchandise are shipped (pushed) to distribution centers and stores at predetermined time intervals.

In a pull supply chain, there is less likelihood of being overstocked or out of stock because the store requests for merchandise are based on customer demand. A pull approach increases inventory turnover and is more responsive to changes in customer demand, and it becomes even more efficient than a push approach when demand is uncertain and difficult to forecast.[14]

Although generally more desirable, a pull approach is not the most effective in all situations. First, a pull approach requires a more costly and sophisticated information system to support it. Second, for some merchandise, retailers do not have the flexibility to adjust inventory levels on the basis of demand. For example, commitments must be made months in advance for fashion and private-label apparel. Because these commitments cannot be easily changed, the merchandise has to be allocated to the stores at the time the orders are formulated. Third, push supply chains are efficient for merchandise that has steady, predictable demand, such as milk and eggs, basic men's underwear, and bath towels. Because both pull and push supply chains have their advantages, most retailers use a combination of these approaches.

Distribution Centers versus Direct Store Delivery

As indicated in Exhibit 10–5, retailers can have merchandise shipped directly to their stores—direct store delivery (path 3)—or to their distribution centers (paths 1 and 2). **Direct store delivery (DSD)** is a method of delivering merchandise to stores in which vendors distribute merchandise directly to the stores.[15]

The vendors offering DSD also undertake additional services such as merchandising (arranging merchandise on racks or shelves) and information gathering about inventory levels. As part of the DSD process, vendor employees visit the retailer's store several times a week. In those store visits, trained personnel assess stock levels and backroom inventory to determine the right order amount, replenish the order, and display products based on local preferences.

The decision to use DSD or distribution centers depends on the characteristics of the merchandise and the nature of demand. To determine which distribution system is more efficient, retailers balance the total cost of each alternative and the impact of the alternatives on customer satisfaction.

Distribution centers lower inventory levels because the amount of backup stock needed in a centralized distribution center is less than the amount of backup stock needed in all the stores served by the center. For example, to achieve the desired product availability with direct delivery, each store might need to stock 10 Michael Graves toasters for a total of 500 units in the 50 stores served by a distribution center. By delivering products to a distribution center and feeding the 50 stores from the center, the retailer could achieve the same level of product availability with only 350 toasters (5 in each store and 100 in the distribution center). Since the stores get frequent deliveries from the distribution center, they need to carry relatively less extra merchandise as backup stock. Thus, distribution centers

top suppliers put RFID tags on all pallets, cases, cartons, and high-margin items.[33] Metro (Germany's largest retailer), Target, Best Buy, and Albertson's are also experimenting with RFID programs.[34] To meet these demands, vendors have been forced to make significant investments to acquire the necessary technology and equipment. Retailing View 10.5 describes how American Apparel innovated use of RFID on individual items instead of cartons or pallets, which are the typical current application in retailing.

10.4 RETAILING VIEW   West Marine Uses CPFR to Build a Competitive Advantage

West Marine's founder and chairman, Randy Repass, channeled his passion for boating into a business that revolutionized the way people shop for boating supplies. Forty years ago, when Randy started selling nylon rope out of his garage, boat supply stores were dark, disorganized places staffed by a couple of salty but indifferent clerks who preferred swapping sea stories with one another to helping customers find what they came in to buy. Randy's vision was to provide a one-stop shopping experience with great customer service for boaters. Today, West Marine has more than 400 stores across the United States and Canada and sells supplies through catalog and Internet channels. The company offers more than 50,000 products, ranging from the rope that started it all to the latest in marine electronics.

The boating market is highly seasonal; more than 50 percent of sales occur between April and October. Whereas the holiday season and Christmas are the peak seasons for most retailers, West Marine's peak sales occur during the week before the 4th of July. In addition, boat supply retailers are very promotional, and this introduces more variation and uncertainty into sales forecasts. West Marine found that these wide variations in demand resulted in lost sales due to inefficiencies in its supply chain.

To address this issue, West Marine and its key suppliers implemented collaboration, planning, forecasting, and replenishment (CPFR) programs. The first step West Marine took was to meet with key suppliers to develop a better forecasting system. Now, every night, West Marine collects SKU-level sales and inventory information for each of its stores, and every day it generates a 52-week forecast for demand by store at the SKU level. The forecast factors in all marketing and promotional events. The forecast is shared with the suppliers so that they can order parts and schedule production.

West Marine has made CPFR an integral part of its merchandising and planning operations. Each West Marine category

West Marine ues CPFR to engage in collaborative planning and supply chain management with its vendors.

manager (CM) partners with a merchandise planner (MP). The CM is responsible for the vendor strategies and marketing relationships; the MP is responsible for directing the supply chain relationship. West Marine MPs and CMs conduct quarterly supply chain planning meetings with each CPFR supplier. These meetings involve teams from both companies and include the key marketing, forecasting, production planning, distribution, and transportation players. In addition, the planners from both sides engage in a monthly collaborative meeting that reviews results, manages current initiatives, and identifies and resolves any supply issues on the basis of the order forecast. Team members beyond the primary planners frequently attend and contribute to these monthly meetings as well.

Sources: www.westmarine.com (accessed June 14, 2010); T. Schoenherr and V. M. R. Tummala, "Best Practices for the Implementation of Supply Chain Management Initiatives," *International Journal of Logistics Systems and Management* 4, no. 4 (2008), pp. 391–410.

Types of RFID Tags

There are three types of RFID tags: active, semipassive, and passive tags. Active and semipassive RFID tags use internal batteries to power their circuitry. An active tag also uses its battery to broadcast radio waves to a reader, whereas a semipassive tag relies on the reader to supply its power for broadcasting. Because these tags involve more hardware than passive RFID tags, they are more expensive.

Active and semipassive tags are mostly used for costly items that require tracking from about 100 feet or more. When tags must be read from even farther away, additional batteries can increase a tag's range to over 300 feet.

Passive RFID tags can be read from up to 20 feet away, and they have lower production costs, ranging from 7 to 20 cents each. The RFID industry is aiming to get the cost of a passive RFID tag down to 5 cents each once more retailers adopt them. These tags can be applied to less expensive merchandise such as cosmetics and some clothes. These tags are manufactured to be disposable, along with the disposable consumer goods on which they are placed.

Benefits of RFID

Some of the benefits of RFID include:

* *Reduced warehouse and distribution labor costs.* Warehouse and distribution costs typically represent 2 to 4 percent of operating expenses for retailers. Replacing

RETAILING VIEW   RFID at American Apparel   10.5

Known for its "Made in Downtown LA" motto, American Apparel is accustomed to turning heads. The Los Angeles–based company's RFID push began with a pilot program at one of the firm's New York stores. Every one of the roughly 40,000 items from basic T-shirts to shiny gold lamé hot shorts in the store was RFID-tagged.

The objective of American Apparel's RFID system is to provide improved inventory accuracy and better-stocked sales floors. American Apparel has an unusual approach to merchandising. It puts only one of everything on the floor to give the appearance of selling unique merchandise—customers can buy something no one else will be wearing. But that means that once an item is sold, that particular SKU is out of stock on the sales floor. To restock the store, employees would periodically take a list of items sold from the POS system and make trips to the stockroom, where they'd search for each item.

American Apparel saw quick benefits from the technology. As an item leaves the sales floor—because it has been sold, accidentally returned to the stockroom, or stolen—its departure is displayed at stockroom workstations, enabling workers to quickly get

American Apparel is experimenting with placing RFID tags on each item to ensure that all items are on display on store fixtures.

the item restocked. Personnel can easily keep the sales floor fully stocked. The time required to do the weekly process of taking inventory of items in the store was reduced from 32 to 4 hours. This gives employees more time to assist customers directly and carry out other tasks.

Sources: Claire Swedberg, "American Apparel Adds RFID to Two More Stores, Switches RFID Software," *RFID Journal,* January 12, 2010; Mary Catherine O'Connor, "American Apparel Makes a Bold Fashion Statement with RFID," *RFID Journal,* August 14, 2008.

point-and-read, labor-intensive operations with sensors that track pallets, cases, cartons, and individual products anywhere in the facility can significantly reduce labor costs by as much as 30 percent.

- *Reduced point-of-sale labor costs.* Using RFID at the product level can help retailers reduce the labor costs needed for checking shelf inventory. In addition, RFID-enabled products will improve self-scan checkouts and increase the use of self-scans, thus shortening checkout times and reducing employee fraud.

- *Inventory savings.* RFID reduces inventory errors, ensuring that the inventory recorded is actually available. By tracking pieces more exactly, companies have more accurate information about what was sold and what inventory is actually needed.

- *Elimination of counterfeit merchandise.* Using RFID on individual items can help eliminate counterfeit merchandise.[37] For example, California planned for pharmaceutical manufacturers to utilize RFID technology starting in January 2009 for its mass serialization and e-pedigree requirements; however, the deal has now been delayed and is scheduled to go into effect in a phased manner between 2015 and 2017. A drug pedigree is a statement of origin that identifies each prior sale, purchase, or trade of a drug, including the date of the transactions and the names and addresses of all parties to them.[38] The primary purpose of an e-pedigree is to protect consumers from contaminated medicine or counterfeit drugs. As the product moves down the supply chain, each company is required to carry forward all previous e-pedigree information. In this way, the final point of sale has the complete lineage of every unit. Such a system would require fairly significant changes to the company's data interchange. The use of RFID forms the basis of such a secured supply chain system. Oregon and New York, as well as France, Japan, and Spain, are all making moves toward similar legislation.

- *Reduced theft.* With RFID, products can be tracked through the supply chain to pinpoint where a product is at all times; this helps reduce theft in transportation, at distribution centers, or in stores. RFID has already been successfully deployed in stores, particularly on costly items prone to theft, such as Gillette Mach 3 razor blades.

- *Reduced out-of-stock conditions.* Because RFID facilitates accurate product tracking, forecasts are more accurate and thus stockouts decrease. Using RFID, store managers can be automatically notified when specific SKUs are not on the shelves and need to be stocked, as noted in Retailing View 10.5.[39]

Impediments to the Adoption of RFID

A major obstacle to the widespread adoption of RFID has been the high costs, which make the present return on investment low. The cost of RFID tags is 15 cents per tag.[40] However, with demand increasing and tag production costs declining, the tags are expected to reach only 5 cents per tag, and they may be reusable in some applications.

Another reason RFID has not been adopted by more retailers is that it generates more data than can be efficiently processed and, therefore, retailers find it difficult to justify the implementation costs. Most retailers are not capable of transmitting, storing, and processing the data that would be available about the location of pallets, cases, cartons, totes, and individual products in the supply chain.

Vendors are pushing back as well. Some claim that instead of saving labor, RFID tagging actually increases it: Bar codes are printed on cases at the factory, but because most manufacturers have yet to adopt RFID, those tags have to be put on by hand at the warehouse.

Finally, consumers, particularly in the United States, are wary that once the tags are on individual items, they could be used to track individual buyers—an obvious invasion of privacy.[41] The problem is less acute in the European Union, where retailers have educated consumers on RFID use and changed procedures to accommodate consumers' fears by developing tag-removal policies. Germany's Metro and England's Marks & Spencer are both using item-level RFID on a limited basis.

SUMMARY

Supply chain management and information systems have become important tools for achieving a sustainable competitive advantage. Developing more efficient methods of distributing merchandise creates an opportunity to reduce costs and prices and ensure that the right merchandise is available when and where customers want it.

The systems used to control the flow of information to buyers and then on to vendors have become quite sophisticated. Retailers have developed data warehouses that provide them with intimate knowledge of who their customers are and what they like to buy. The data warehouses are being used to strengthen the relationships with their customers and improve the productivity of their marketing and inventory management efforts.

Most large retailers own and operate their own distribution centers. Some of the activities performed by the center are managing inbound and outbound transportation, receiving and checking merchandise shipments, storing and cross-docking, and getting merchandise floor-ready.

In designing their supply chain management systems, retailers make decisions about what activities to outsource, when to use a push and pull system for replenishing stores, what merchandise to cross-dock, and whether to ship merchandise to stores through a distribution center, use direct store delivery, or have products drop shipped to customers.

Retailers and vendors are collaborating to improve supply chain efficiency. Electronic data interchange enables retailers to communicate electronically with their vendors. The Internet has accelerated the adoption of EDI. Other, more involving and effective collaborative approaches include information sharing, VMI, and CPFR. These approaches represent the nexus of information systems and logistics management. They reduce lead time, increase product availability, lower inventory investments, and reduce overall logistics expenses.

Finally, RFID has the potential of further streamlining the supply chain. The small RFID devices are affixed to pallets, cartons, and individual items and can be used to track merchandise through the supply chain and store information, such as when an item was shipped to a distribution center. Although still relatively expensive to be placed on all items, RFID technology can reduce labor, theft, and inventory costs.

KEY TERMS

advance shipping notice (ASN), *253*

bullwhip effect, *264*

checking, *256*

collaborative planning, forecasting, and replenishment (CPFR), *267*

consignment, *267*

consumer direct fulfillment, *263*

cross-docked, *257*

direct store delivery (DSD), *261*

dispatcher, *256*

distribution center, *248*

drop shipping, *263*

electronic data interchange (EDI), *255*

floor-ready merchandise, *257*

freight forwarders, *259*

logistics, *255*

outsourcing, *259*

pick ticket, *258*

public warehouse, *259*

pull supply chain, *261*

push supply chain, *261*

radio frequency identification (RFID), *267*

receiving, *256*

reverse logistics, *262*

security policy, *255*

stockout, *250*

supply chain management, *248*

ticketing and marking, *257*

Universal Product Code (UPC), *253*

vendor-managed inventory (VMI), *266*

GET OUT AND DO IT!

1. **CONTINUING ASSIGNMENT** Interview the store manager working for the retailer you have selected for the Continuing Assignment. Write a report that describes and evaluates the retailer's information and supply chain systems. Use this chapter as a basis for developing a set of questions to ask the manager. Some of the questions might be these: Where is the store's distribution center? Does the retailer use direct store delivery from vendors? How frequently are deliveries made to the store? Does the merchandise come in ready for sale? What is the store's percentage of stockouts? Does the retailer use a push or pull system? Does the store get involved in determining what merchandise is in the store and in what quantities? Does the retailer use VMI, EDI, CPFR, or RFID?

2. **INTERNET EXERCISE** Go to Barcoding Incorporated's Web page at www.barcoding.com/, and search for *retail*, *warehouse management*, and *RFID*. How is this company using technology to support retailers with information systems and supply chain management?

3. **INTERNET EXERCISE** Go to the home page of *Stores Magazine* at www.stores.org/, and search for *supply chain* in the current issue. Summarize one of the recent articles, and explain how the key concept(s) described could make the shopping experience better for consumers and improve efficiency in the supply chain.

4. **INTERNET EXERCISE** Go to the home page of Vendor Managed Inventory at www.vendormanaged-inventory.com/index.php, and answer the following questions: What is vendor-managed inventory? What are the benefits and limitations of a vendor-managed inventory approach?

DISCUSSION QUESTIONS AND PROBLEMS

1. Retail system acronyms include DSD, VMI, EDI, CPFR, and RFID. How are these terms related to one another?

2. Explain how an efficient supply chain system can increase a retailer's level of product availability and decrease its inventory investment.

3. This chapter presents some trends in logistics and information systems that benefit retailers. How do vendors benefit from these trends?

4. What type of merchandise is most likely to be cross-docked at retailers' distribution centers? Why is this often the case?

5. Why haven't more fashion retailers adopted an integrated supply chain system similar to Zara's?

6. Explain the differences between pull and push supply chains.

7. Consumers have five key reactions to stockouts: buy the item at another store, substitute a different brand, substitute the same brand, delay the purchase, or do not purchase the item. Consider your own purchasing behavior, and describe how various categories of merchandise would result in different reactions to a stockout.

8. Abandoned purchases as a result of stockouts can mean millions of dollars a year in lost sales. How are retailers and manufacturers using technology to reduce stockouts and improve sales?

9. What is a Universal Product Code (UPC)? How does this code enable manufacturers, distributors, and retailers to track merchandise throughout the supply chain?

10. Reread Retail View 10.2 about Netflix. How is this online retailer using inventory management and distribution centers to deliver the correct movies requested by customers?

SUGGESTED READINGS

Ayers, James B., and Mary Ann Odegaard. *Retail Supply Chain Management*. Boca Raton, FL: Auerbach, 2007.

Bernon, Michael, and John Cullen. "An Integrated Approach to Managing Reverse Logistics." *International Journal of Logistics: Research & Applications* 10, no. 1 (2007), pp. 41–56.

Fernie, John, and Leigh Sparks. *Logistics and Retail Management: Emerging Issues and New Challenges in the Retail Supply Chain*, 3rd ed. London: Kogan, 2009.

Finne, Sami, and Hanna Sivonen. *The Retail Value Chain: How to Gain Competitive Advantage through Efficient Consumer Response (ECR) Strategies*. London: Kogan, 2009.

Fisher, Marshall, and Ananth Raman. *The New Science of Retailing: How Analytics Are Transforming the Supply Chain and Improving Performance*. Boston: Harvard Business Press, 2010.

Hsu, Hy Sonya, Christine A. Alexander, and Zhiwei Zhu. "Understanding the Reverse Logistics Operations of a Retailer: A Pilot Study." *Industrial Management & Data Systems* 109, no. 4 (2009), pp. 515–531.

Kauremaa, Jouni, Johanna Smaros, and Jan Holmstrom. "Patterns of Vendor-Managed Inventory: Findings from a Multiple-Case." *International Journal of Operations & Production Management* 29, no. 11 (2009), pp. 1109–1139.

Niederman, Fred, Richard G. Mathieu, Roger Morley, and Kwon Ik-Whan. "Examining RFID Applications in Supply Chain Management." *Communications of the ACM* 50, no. 7 (2007), pp. 93–101.

Reyes, Pedro. *RFID in the Supply Chain: Secure and Cost Effective Installation*. New York: McGraw-Hill, 2010.

Sari, Kazim. "On the Benefits of CPFR and VMI: A Comparative Simulation Study." *International Journal of Services and Operations Management* 6, no. 1 (2010), pp. 73–88.

Wong, Chien Yaw, and Duncan McFarlane. "Radio Frequency Identification Data Capture and Its Impact on Shelf Replenishment." *International Journal of Logistics: Research & Applications* 10, no. 1 (2007), pp. 71–93.

Customer Relationship Management

EXECUTIVE BRIEFING

Simon Hay, Managing Director of U.K. and Ireland, dunnhumby

Luck and good fortune played part in how I got where I am today. I am a geographer by training, with a degree from the University of Reading in the United Kingdom. My interest was in looking at humans in relation to their environment in a spatial/geographic way, such as the development of towns and urban areas, transportation systems, and so on. In my senior year, some of my professors who were interested in the geography of retailing got me interested in retailing.

In my first job, we used census data to determine where people lived, worked, and how they traveled. We used that data to map out car dealer and retail store networks. As computer power developed in the late 80s and early 90s, we realized that transactional data, that is, what people purchased, would give us a better idea of consumer behavior than would geographic data. That realization is the idea behind dunnhumby, where I was the first full-time employee and where I have been for the past 18 years.

Dunnhumby helps retailers and brands understand and connect with their customers by helping them to analyze and understand transactional data that they collect primarily through their loyalty (CRM) programs. It's just that simple. While computer power is generally a positive thing, it does lead to a superabundance of data. Understanding these data, communicating findings to executives in an easy-to-understand way, and formulating strategy from the data are actually pretty difficult. To further complicate the situation, the sheer speed at which customer needs and preferences change has increased exponentially in recent years. Understanding consumers' behaviors, developing an overarching strategy based on those behaviors, and retaining flexibility to respond to changing circumstances is what we at dunnhumby do best.

My job is essentially to run dunnhumby's home base in the United Kingdom and Ireland. Each day is a juggling act involving where we are externally with our clients and

CHAPTER 11

QUESTIONS

What is customer relationship management?

Why do retailers engage in customer relationship management?

What is customer lifetime value?

How do retailers determine who their best customers are?

What do retailers do to increase their share of wallet from their best customers?

What can retailers do to alleviate the privacy concerns of their customers?

How can retailers get rid of unprofitable customers?

---

internally with our organization. While no two days are ever the same, I may visit stores to find out what people are thinking and feeling in response to particular promotions. I might talk with manufacturers about trends in retailing environments and promotions and about how our services are resonating with them. I might also spend time developing strategies for major clients like Kroger. On the organizational front, I also work with staff training and development personnel and communicate regularly with senior staff to help problem-solve.

I love the journey of learning, and my job gives me the opportunity to learn something new every day. I like challenging myself, and I enjoy challenging others. I find it fascinating to suggest to retail clients that they do something completely different than they did in the past so that they do things better rather than just more and faster. Using data to help make organizations be more effective has always been a major interest of mine. Last, but not least, I enjoy working with bright, engaging people.

The business press and retailers are talking a lot about the importance of becoming more customer-centric and managing their customer relationships. Retailers are spending billions of dollars on computer systems to collect and analyze data about their customers. With all of this buzz, you'd think that the customer is a popular new kid in the neighborhood. However, the customer is more like an old friend who's been taken for granted—until now[1]

Consider the following example: Shari Ast is on her third business trip this month. She takes a cab from Boston Logan Airport to the Ritz-Carlton, her favorite hotel in Boston. As the doorman opens the car door for her, he greets her with, "Welcome back to the Ritz-Carlton, Ms. Ast." When she goes to the registration desk, the receptionist gives her a room key. Then she goes to her room and finds just what she prefers—a room with a view of the Boston Commons, a single queen-size bed, an extra pillow and blanket, a printer with a wireless connect to her laptop, and a basket with her favorite fruits and snacks.

Shari Ast's experience is an example of Ritz-Carlton's customer relationship management program. **Customer relationship management (CRM)** is a business philosophy and set of strategies, programs, and systems that focuses on identifying and building loyalty with a retailer's most valued customers. The retailer's goal of CRM

The Ritz-Carlton provides personalized service for its preferred customers. They are greeted by name when checking in, and their preferences for amenities are known on the basis of past visits.

is to develop a base of loyal customers and increase its **share of wallet**—the percentage of the customers' purchases made from the retailer.

Traditionally, retailers have focused their attention on encouraging more customers to visit their stores, look through their catalogs, and visit their Web sites. To accomplish this objective, they have used mass-media advertising and sales promotions to attract visits from customers. This approach treats all existing and potential customers the same. They all receive the same messages and the same promotions.

Now retailers are concentrating on developing customer loyalty and increasing share of wallet by providing more value to their best customers by using targeted, more personalized promotions and services. This change in perspective is supported by research indicating that retailers are more profitable when they focus on retaining and increasing sales to their best customers rather than attempting to generate sales from new customers or marginal existing customers.[2] In the following sections of this chapter, we discuss in more depth the objective of CRM programs and the elements of the CRM process.

THE CRM PROCESS

Based on the CRM philosophy that retailers can increase their profitability by building relationships with their better customers, the goal of CRM is to develop a base of loyal customers who patronize the retailer frequently. In this section, the concept of customer loyalty is defined and the process of building this loyalty is outlined.

What Is Loyalty?

The objective of the customer relationship management process is to develop customer loyalty and repeat-purchase behavior among a retailer's best customers. Customer loyalty is more than customers' simply being satisfied with a retailer and making repeat visits. **Customer loyalty** means that customers are committed to purchasing merchandise and services from the retailer and will resist the activities of competitors attempting to attract their patronage. Loyal customers have a bond with the retailer, and the bond is based on more than a positive feeling about the retailer.[3]

The bond that loyal customers have with a retailer is a personal connection. They feel that the retailer is a friend. Their goodwill toward the retailer encourages them to repeatedly patronize the retailer and recommend it to their friends and family. Programs that just encourage repeat buying by simply offering price discounts do not provide an enduring advantage because they can be easily copied by competitors. In addition, these types of price-promotion programs encourage customers to always look for the best deal rather than develop a relationship with one retailer. However, when a retailer develops a personal connection with a customer, it is difficult for a competitor to attract that customer.[4]

All the elements in the retail mix contribute to the development of customer loyalty and repeat-purchase behavior. Customer loyalty can be enhanced by creating an appealing brand image and providing convenient locations, attractive merchandise at compelling prices, and an engaging shopping experience. However, personal attention is one of the most effective methods for developing loyalty. For example, many small, independent restaurants build loyalty by functioning as neighborhood cafés, where waiters and waitresses recognize customers by name and know their preferences. Nordstrom has found that paying personal attention to customers by inviting them to grand-opening celebrations, pampering them during private shopping parties, and offering them concierge services, free alterations, and shipping is more important than giving them discounts.[5]

The CRM programs and activities discussed in this chapter focus on using information systems and customer data to personalize the retailer's offering and increase the value its best customers receive. Personalized value is also provided by employees in face-to-face interactions with customers (see Chapter 18).

Overview of the CRM Process

Exhibit 11–1 illustrates that CRM is an iterative process that turns customer data into customer loyalty through four activities: (1) collecting customer data, (2) analyzing the customer data and identifying target customers, (3) developing CRM programs, and (4) implementing CRM programs. The process begins with the collection and analysis of data about a retailer's customers and the identification of its best customers. The analysis translates the customer data into information and activities that offer value to these targeted customers. Then these activities are executed through communication programs undertaken by the marketing department and customer service programs implemented by customer contact employees, typically sales associates. Each of the four activities in the CRM process is discussed in the following sections. Retailing View 11.1 describes the development of the CRM program at Harrah's.

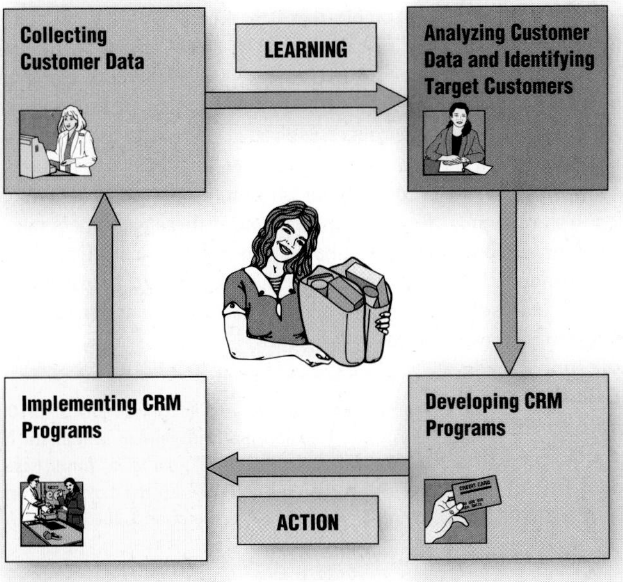

REFACT

The first CRM program began in 1981 with the launch of the American Airlines Advantage program.[6]

EXHIBIT 11–1
The CRM Process Cycle

COLLECTING CUSTOMER DATA

The first step in the CRM process is to construct a **customer database**. This database is part of the data warehouse described in Chapter 10. It contains all the data the firm has collected about its customers and is the foundation for subsequent CRM activities.

II.I   RETAILING VIEW   Harrah's Hits the Jackpot with CRM

Andrew, a 30-something New Yorker, planned to visit Harrah's Resort in Atlantic City for the day. When he arrived, he inquired about staying for the night and was told no rooms were available. After using his Harrah's Total Rewards card while playing blackjack, the pit boss told him to go to the front desk, where he was informed that a room had become available for a "special rate of $100 a night." When Andrew checked out two nights later, he was told all the room charges were on the house. This is one example of how Harrah's CRM program has enabled Harrah's to grow from its first casino in Reno, Nevada, opened over 70 years ago, into one of the largest casino entertainment retailers in the world. It now owns, operates, or manages over 60 facilities in seven countries.

In the 1990s, many of Harrah's competitors were making substantial investments to build the most opulent hotels and casinos on the Las Vegas Strip. Lacking the resources to compete in this building frenzy, Harrah's decided to bet on building customer value and loyalty with a CRM program. The company hired Gary Loveman, a Harvard Business School professor and now Harrah's CEO, and other employees who specialized in CRM but had no gaming experience.

In 1997, when Harrah's launched its Total Rewards program, most casinos provided special perks for "high rollers," customers who gambled extensively. But Harrah's CRM program expanded the breadth and depth of the customer data collected and used. The first step was to enroll customers in the program and give them encoded ID cards. Players collect points and rewards based on the amount they gamble. When "gamers"—casino lingo for *customers*—gamble, they swipe a card through the slot machine or a pit boss estimates their bets at a table. As the points accumulate, card holders earn new status titles: With 4,000 points, gamers earn Platinum status and a few privileges,

Harrah's best customers earn points toward benefits and upgrades on the basis of how much they spend through the Total Rewards loyalty card program. The program collects the data that enables Harrah's to provide more value by personalizing rewards.

such as shorter wait times in line. With 10,000 points, gamers earn the Diamond card, which entitles them to benefits such as free valet parking, room upgrades, and free weekend reservations.

Next Harrah's combined the gambling data with data from its other retail offerings, such as the company's hotels, restaurants, and entertainment reservation systems. Then Harrah's integrated the customer data warehouses from each casino to get a complete view of each customer's preference and value to Harrah's. Harrah's now knows which of its 40 million customers like golf, chardonnay, down pillows, and rooms close to the elevator and which properties they visit, what games they play, and which promotional offers they redeem.

Harrah's marketing managers can analyze that information to design and tweak Harrah's products. Customer service representatives can access the data in real time to reward valued customers, like Andrew, with promotions such as complimentary meals, hotel room upgrades, or tickets to events. Analysis of the database helped Harrah's identify a profitable segment of customers that it had been ignoring, such as the "low rollers," the so-called retail or small gamblers who spend less than $50 per visit but account for 40 percent of Harrah's business. Before Harrah's identified this segment, bonus points, targeted at high rollers, expired at the end of a visit. To reward the low rollers, who typically live in urban areas near a casino and visit frequently for short time periods, Harrah's changed the Total Rewards program to let these customers take up to six months to accrue bonus and regular points. Data from low rollers also convinced Harrah's to redesign its casino floors to include a higher percentage of lower-denomination slot machines and video poker games.

Sources: www.harrahs.com (accessed July 3, 2010); Christine A. Vogt, "Customer Relationship Management in Tourism: Management: Needs and Research Applications," *Journal of Travel Research,* August 2010, pp.1–9; Michael Bush, "Why Harrah's Loyalty Effort Is Industry's Gold Standard," *Advertising Age,* October 5, 2009, p. 8.

REFACT

Americans spend 10 times more money on gaming than on trips to movie theaters, and more money is lost during a typical casino visit than is spent on an average visit to a mall.[7]

Customer Database

Ideally, the database should contain the following information:

- *Transactions.* A complete history of the purchases made by the customer, including the purchase date, the SKUs purchased, the price paid, the amount of profit, and whether the merchandise was purchased in response to a special promotion or marketing activity.

- *Customer contacts.* A record of the interactions that the customer has had with the retailer, including visits to the retailer's Web site, inquiries made through in-store kiosks, and telephone calls made to the retailer's call center, plus information about contacts initiated by the retailer, such as catalogs and direct mail sent to the customer.

- *Customer preferences.* What the customer likes, such as favorite colors, brands, fabrics, and flavors, as well as apparel sizes. At a Brooks Brothers store in New York, a sales associate looked up a customer's recent purchases at its POS terminal. She saw that the customer purchased a navy pinstripe suit several months ago. Using this information, she knew exactly which dress shirts would go with the suit and took the opportunity to show him some coordinating ties, too. By the time she rang up the sale, it included three dress shirts, two ties, underwear, and socks.[8]

- *Descriptive information.* Demographic and psychographic data describing the customer that can be used in developing market segments.

- *Responses to marketing activities.* Analyses of transaction and contact data provide information about the customer's responsiveness to marketing activities.

Customer transaction data are collected by a **POS** terminal and stored in the customer database. Many retailers have Internet-enabled **POS** terminals from which sales associates can access information in the customer database.

Different members of the same household might also have interactions with a retailer. Thus, to get a complete view of the customer, retailers need to be able to combine individual customer data from each member of a household. For example, Richards is a family-owned apparel chain in Westport and Greenwich, Connecticut. Husbands and wives buy presents for each other at Richards. The chain's database keeps track of both household-level purchases and individual purchases so that sales associates can help one spouse buy a gift for the other. The database also keeps track of spending changes and habits. Anniversaries, birthdays, and even divorces and second marriages are tracked along with style, brand, size, and color preferences; hobbies; and sometimes pets' names and golf handicaps.[9]

Identifying Information

It is relatively easy to construct a database for catalog, Internet, and warehouse club customers. Customers buying merchandise through nonstore channels must provide their contact information, name, and address so that the purchases can be sent to them. It is also easy to keep track of purchases made by customers patronizing warehouse clubs because they need to present their membership cards when they make a purchase. In these cases, the identification of the customer is always linked to the transaction. When retailers issue their own credit cards, they also can collect the contact information for billing when customers apply for the card. However, identifying most customers who are making in-store transactions is more difficult because they often pay for the merchandise with a check, cash, or a third-party credit card such as Visa or MasterCard.

Four approaches that store-based retailers use to overcome this problem are (1) asking customers for their identifying information, (2) using biometrics to identify customers, (3) offering frequent shopper programs, and (4) connecting Internet and store purchasing data.

Asking for Identifying Information   Some retailers have their sales associates ask customers for identifying information, such as their phone number or name and address, when they process a sale.[10] This information is then used to link all the transactions for the customer. However, some customers may be reluctant to provide the information because they feel that the sales associates are violating their privacy.

Using Biometrics   Rather than asking for identifying information, some retailers use biometrics to identify customers and provide a cardless, cashless method of payment. For example, Dorothy Lane Market, based in Dayton, Ohio, uses pre-registered fingerprints so that its customers can pay efficiently and the company can accumulate the customer information quickly and accurately. Customers entering the store can have their finger scanned to receive a printout of their personalized product discounts. At checkout, customers can pay using the finger scan and automatically debit the amount from a checking account. This system eliminates all cards, completely and fully integrates customer data, and makes rewards easily available with the simple act of a fingerprint scan.[11]

Offering Frequent-Shopper Programs   **Frequent-shopper programs**, also called **loyalty programs**, are programs that identify and provide rewards to customers who patronize a retailer. Some retailers issue customers a frequent-shopper card, whereas others use a **private-label credit card**—a credit card that has the store's name on it. In both cases, customer transaction data are automatically captured when the card is scanned at the point-of-sale terminal. In addition, when customers enroll in one of these programs, they provide some descriptive information about themselves and their household. The customers then are offered an incentive to use the card when they make purchases from the retailer. Research has shown that customers generally prefer to get something extra—a reward—for their purchases, rather than lower prices.[12]

Research has shown that enrolling in frequent-shopper programs and showing cards when making purchases has a limited effect on increasing loyalty toward the retailers.[14] Most of the members of frequent-shopper programs patronized the retailers before they introduced the programs. A study of supermarket shoppers found that 88 percent of frequent-shopper card holders were clients of the store two years before joining the program.[15] In addition, the effects are limited because several retailers in the same geographic area typically offer similar programs and consumers enroll in multiple competing programs. The primary benefits of these programs for retailers are collecting the customer data and using the information to target communications and promotions.

Frequent shoppers have a limited effect in terms of increasing share of wallet because customers enroll in all the programs offered by retailers in their area.

Connecting Internet Purchasing Data with the Stores   When customers use third-party credit cards such as Visa or MasterCard to make a purchase in a store, the retailer cannot identify the purchase by the customer. However, if the customer used the same credit card while shopping at the retailer's Web site and provide shipping information, the retailer could connect the credit card purchases through its store and electronic channels.

Privacy and CRM Programs

The collection and analysis of information about customer attitudes, preferences, and shopping behaviors enable retailers to provide greater value to their customers. However, many customers are concerned that retailers are violating their privacy when they collect this detailed personal information. Even if customers trust a retailer, they are concerned that the data may not be secure and they may be susceptible to identity theft.

Privacy Concerns   There is no consensus about the definition of personal information. Some people feel that personal information is all information that is not publicly available; others include both public (e.g., driver's license, mortgage data) and private (hobbies, income) information. The degree to which consumers feel their privacy concerning personal information has been violated depends on:

- *Their control over their personal information when engaging in marketplace transactions.* Do they feel they can decide the amount and type of information that is collected by the retailer?
- *Their knowledge about the collection and use of personal information.* Do they know what information is being collected and how the retailer will be using it? Will the retailer be sharing the information with other parties?[17]

These concerns are particularly acute for customers using an electronic channel because many of them do not realize the extensive amount of information that can be collected without their knowledge. This information is easily collected using cookies. **Cookies** are text files that identify visitors when they return to a Web site. Because of the data in the cookies, customers do not have to identify themselves or use passwords every time they visit a site. However, the cookies also can collect information about other sites the people have visited and what pages they have downloaded.

Hackers can also use cookies to collect data about a person. When a person visits an infected Web page or reads an infected blog, the cookies on the person's computer are then sent back to the hacker unknowingly by the user. During a "live" session with a blog or Web site, the hacker can access the cookies without needing the log-in information. A user can also receive a scam e-mail that tempts the person to click on a link to a Web site. If the person then types in his or her user name and password, this information is sent directly to the hacker.

The data that can be collected through cookies includes e-mails that people send or receive, historical data on how they spend money online, their interactions on social networking sites, and other data used to create detailed profiles. Such tracking of information is particularly disturbing when people do not know who is tracking them. In the absence of clear privacy laws and security standards, such practices leave individuals vulnerable to warrantless searches, attacks from identity thieves, child predators, and other criminals.[19]

Protecting Customer Privacy   In the United States, existing legislation for consumer privacy is limited to the protection of information associated with government functions and with practices in credit reporting, video rentals, banking, and health care. Thus customers have to rely on retailers to take the necessary precautions to protect consumer privacy by incorporating privacy safety software such as firewalls and encrypting data every time it is transferred to prevent its being intercepted.[20]

However, the European Union (EU), Australia, New Zealand, and Canada have different and more stringent consumer privacy laws. Some of the provisions of the EU directive on consumer privacy are the following:

- Businesses can collect consumer information only if they have clearly defined the purpose, such as completing the transaction.
- The purpose must be disclosed to the consumer from whom the information is being collected.

- The information can be used only for that specific purpose.
- The business can keep the information only for the stated purpose. If the business wants to use the information for another purpose, it must initiate a new collection process.
- Businesses operating in Europe can export information from the 27 EU countries only to importing countries with similar privacy policies. Thus, U.S. retailers, hotel chains, airlines, and banks cannot transfer information from Europe to the United States because the United States does not have similar privacy policies.

Basically, the EU perspective is that consumers own their personal information, so retailers must get consumers to agree explicitly to share this personal information. This agreement is referred to as an **opt in**. In contrast, personal information in the United States is generally viewed as being in the public domain, and retailers can use it in any way they desire. American consumers must explicitly tell retailers not to use their personal information—they must **opt out**.[21]

The EU has delayed enforcement of its directive. The United States is currently negotiating a safe-harbor program that would enable U.S. companies abiding by the EU directives to export information. However, due to increasing concerns about consumer privacy, Congress is considering new legislation on consumer privacy. The Federal Trade Commission has developed the following set of principles for fair information practices:

- *Notice and awareness.* Covers the disclosure of information practices, including a comprehensive statement of information use, such as information storage, manipulation, and dissemination.
- *Choice/consent.* Includes both opt-out and opt-in options and allows consumers to have the opportunity to trade information for benefits.
- *Access/participation.* Allows for the confirmation of information accuracy by consumers.
- *Integrity/security.* Controls for the theft of and tampering with personal information.
- *Enforcement/redress.* Provides a mechanism to ensure compliance by participating companies.[22]

In summary, there is growing consensus that personal information must be fairly collected, that the collection must be purposeful, and that the data should be relevant, maintained as accurate, essential to the business, subject to the rights of the owning individual, kept reasonably secure, and transferred only with the permission of the consumer. To address these concerns, many retailers that collect customer information have privacy policies. The Electronic Privacy Information Center (www.epic.org) recommends that privacy policies clearly state what information is collected from each visitor and how it will be used, give consumers a choice as to whether they provide information, and allow them to view and correct any personal information held by an online retail site. Retailers need to assure their customers that information about them is held securely and not passed on to other companies without the customer's permission.

ANALYZING CUSTOMER DATA AND IDENTIFYING TARGET CUSTOMERS

The next step in the CRM process (see Exhibit 11–1) is to analyze the customer database and convert the data into information that will help retailers develop programs for increasing the value they offer to their best customers. Two objectives for analyzing the customer database are (1) identifying patterns in the data that can improve the effectiveness of retailing decisions such as forecasting sales and allocating merchandise to stores and (2) deciding where to place merchandise categories in a store.

Retail Analytics

Retail analytics are the application of statistical techniques and models to find patterns in customer purchase data and make recommendations for improving the effectiveness of retailers.[23]

Market basket analysis is a specific type of retail analytics that focuses on examining the composition of the basket, or bundle, of products purchased by a household during a single shopping occasion. This analysis is often useful for suggesting where to place merchandise in a store. An often-used example of market basket analysis is the discovery by a supermarket chain that on Friday evenings between 6 and 7 p.m. many market baskets, particularly those bought by men, contained both beer and baby diapers. This relationship between beer and baby diapers arises because diapers come in large packages, so wives, who do most of the household shopping, leave the diaper purchase to their husbands. When husbands bought diapers at the end of the workweek, they also wanted to get some beer for the weekend. When the supermarket discovered this shopping pattern, it put the premium beer display next to the diapers. Because the premium beer was so conveniently placed next to the diapers, men tended to be up-sold and bought the premium brands rather than spend time going to the beer aisle for lower-priced brands. Some other examples of market basket analysis used in determining product locations are:

- Because bananas are the most common item in Americans' grocery carts, supermarkets often place bananas in the cereal aisle, as well as in the produce section.

- Tissues are in the paper goods aisle and also mixed in with cold medicine.

- Measuring spoons appear in the housewares section and also hang next to baking supplies such as flour and shortening.

- Flashlights are placed in the hardware aisle and with a seasonal display of Halloween costumes.

- Snack cakes are found in the bread aisle and also next to the coffee.

- Bug spray is merchandised with hunting gear and household cleaning supplies.

Retailing View 11.2 examines how U.K.-based Tesco uses the information collected through its Clubcard program to target promotions and tailor assortments in its stores to preferences of customers in the store's trading area.

Identifying the Best Customers

One of the objectives of CRM is to identify and cater to the best, most profitable customers. For instance, Home Depot realized that 70 to 80 percent of its kitchen renovation sales were coming from 20 to 30 percent of the department's customers.[24] It speculated that these heavy spenders might spend even more if it organized the department around meeting their needs. It knew that heavy spenders want lots of choices and information. So it added more assortment, better-trained associates, a computer-aided design system, and suites of innovative kitchen layouts arranged so that customers could readily sense what their kitchens would look like after a renovation. The results: higher sales and profit per square foot than traditional departments designed to satisfy all customers.

Using information in the customer database, retailers can develop a score or number indicating how valuable customers are to the firm. A commonly used measure to score each customer is called customer lifetime value. **Customer lifetime value (CLV)** is the expected contribution from customers to the retailer's profits over their entire relationship with the retailer.

To estimate CLV, retailers use past behaviors to forecast future purchases, the gross margin from these purchases, and the costs including the cost of advertising, promotions used to acquire the customers, and processing merchandise that the customers have returned. Thus, customers who purchases $200 of groceries from a supermarket every month would probably have a lower CLV for that supermarket than a customer who buys $20 on each visit and shops at the store three times a week. Similarly, customers who buy apparel only when it is on sale in a department

---

II.2   RETAILING VIEW   Tesco Uses Data Collected from Its Frequent-Shopper Program

Tesco, the largest supermarket chain in the United Kingdom and the third largest in the world, has been very effective at analyzing and exploiting the data it collects through its Clubcard frequent-shopper program. To encourage customers to enroll in the program, Tesco gives them points for every pound they spend in its stores, on its Web site, and at its gas stations. Customers who spend 25 pounds a week for 10 weeks get double points. The points are redeemed by reducing the shopping bill when customers check out.

In addition, customers can get more benefits by joining one of Tesco's clubs. For example, members of the Baby and Toddler Club get expert advice and exclusive offers to help them through the stages of parenting from pregnancy to childhood (tesco.com/babyclub). Members get discount coupons on baby essentials, a permit allowing them to park nearer to the store, and a free Pampers Hamper filled with baby items and special treats for the mother.

Analysis of the sales transactions identified six customer segments such as the "Finer Foods" segment, which includes affluent, time-strapped shoppers who buy upscale products, and the "Traditional" segment, shoppers who are homemakers and have time to cook meals. Unique marketing programs are developed for each of the segments.

Tesco uses retail analytics to alter its merchandise selection in stores, develop new products, and target specific customer groups.

REFACT

Over 90 percent of Tesco's Clubcard holders feel that enrolling in the program has increased the value they receive.[25]

Tesco frequently sends personalized coupon packages to Clubcard members. Some coupons are for products the customer normally buys, and others are for products that the retailer believes the customer would like to try. More than 1 million unique sets of coupons are distributed for each promotion. Between 15 and 20 percent of the coupons are redeemed, compared with the industry average redemption rate of 1 to 2 percent.

Based on an analysis of the data, Tesco introduced "World Foods," which features Asian herbs and other ethnic food, into stores located in Indian and Pakistani neighborhoods. However, when Tesco looked at the locations from which the customers traveled to buy the unique merchandise in these stores, it found that more than 25 percent of customers were coming from other neighborhoods. This discovery led Tesco to add an assortment of World Foods to other stores.

Tesco also introduced a premium private-label brand, Tesco Finest, that includes duck pâté and premium wines and cheeses because it discovered, through retail analytics, that its affluent customers were not buying wine, cheese, fruit, and other higher-priced–higher-margin items from Tesco.

Sources: Yan Ma, Jianxun Ding, and Wenxia Hong, "Delivering Customer Value Based on Service Process: The Example of Tesco.Com," *International Business Research* 3, no. 2 (2010), pp. 131–135; Andrew Smith and Leigh Sparks, "Reward Redemption Behaviour in Retail Loyalty Schemes," *British Journal of Management* 20, no. 2 (2008), pp. 204–218; www.Tesco.com (accessed July 1, 2010).

store would have a lower CLV than customers who typically pay full price and buy the same amount of merchandise.

These measures of CLV are based on the assumption that the customer's future purchase behaviors will be the same as they have been in the past. Sophisticated statistical methods are typically used to estimate the future contributions from past purchases.[26] For example, these methods might consider how recent purchases have occurred. The expected CLV of a customer who purchased $600 of merchandise on one visit six months ago is probably less than the CLV of a customer who has been purchasing $100 of merchandise every month for the last six months, because the $600 purchase might have been a one-time purchase by a person visiting from out of town.

Customer Pyramid   For most retailers, a relatively small number of customers account for the majority of their profits. This condition is often called the **80-20 rule**—80 percent of the sales or profits come from 20 percent of the customers. Thus, retailers could group their customers into two categories on the basis of their CLV scores. One group would be the 20 percent of the customers with the highest CLV scores, and the other group would be the rest. However, this two-segment scheme, "best" and "rest," does not consider important differences among the 80 percent of customers in the "rest" segment.[27] A commonly used segmentation scheme divides customers into four segments, as illustrated in Exhibit 11–2, or even 10 deciles. This scheme allows retailers to develop more effective strategies for each of the segments. Each of the four segments is described next.

- *Platinum segment.* This segment is composed of the customers with the top 25 percent CLVs. Typically, these are the most profitable and loyal customers who, because of their loyalty, are typically not overly concerned about merchandise prices. Customers in this quartile buy a lot of the merchandise sold by the retailer and often place more value on customer service.

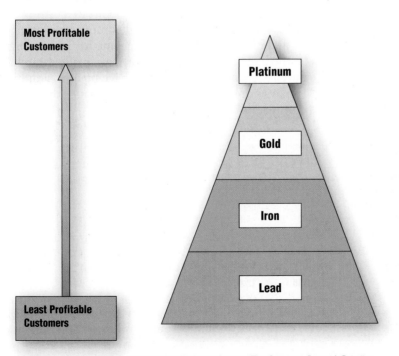

EXHIBIT 11–2
The Customer Pyramid

SOURCE: Valarie Zeithaml, Roland Rust, and Katherine Lemon, "The Customer Pyramid: Creating and Serving Profitable Customers," *California Management Review* 43 (Summer 2001), p. 125. Reprinted by permission.

Simply looking at how many miles these customers have flown may be a poor indicator of their lifetime values.

- *Gold segment.* The next quartile of customers, in terms of their CLVs, make up the gold segment. Even though they buy a significant amount of merchandise from the retailer, they are not as loyal as platinum customers and probably patronize some of the retailer's competitors. The profitability levels of the gold-tier customers are less than those of the platinum-tier customers because price plays a greater role in their decision making.

- *Iron segment.* The customers in this quartile purchase a modest amount of merchandise, but their spending levels, loyalty, and profitability are not substantial enough for special treatment.

- *Lead segment.* Customers with the lowest CLVs can make a negative contribution to the firm's income. They often demand a lot of attention but do not buy much from the retailer, or they buy a lot of merchandise on sale and abuse return privileges. They may even cause additional problems by complaining about the firm to others.

The use of customer lifetime values to classify customers into these segments is based on the profitability of the customers, not sales. The use of sales for identifying a retailer's better customers can be misleading. For example, airlines assign rewards in their frequent-flier programs on the basis of miles flown. These programs provide the same rewards to customers who take low-cost, less profitable flights as to those who make a larger contribution to the airline's profit by flying first class and paying nondiscounted prices. Some airlines, such as Lufthansa, have adopted a CLV measure based on the profitability of the miles flown instead of the number of miles.[28]

RFM Analysis   An **RFM analysis** (recency, frequency, monetary analysis), often used by catalog retailers and direct marketers, is a scheme for identifying the retailer's best prospects on the basis of how recently they have made a purchase, how frequently they make purchases, and how much they have bought. Exhibit 11–3 is an example of an RFM analysis done by a catalog apparel retailer that mails a catalog each month to its customers.

EXHIBIT 11–3
RFM Analysis for a Catalog Retailer

Frequency	Monetary	RECENCY			
		0–2 months	3–4 months	5–6 months	Over 6 months
1–2	<$50	5.0%*	3.5%	1.0%	0.1%
1–2	Over $50	5.0	3.6	1.1	0.1
3–4	<$150	8.0	5.0	1.5	0.6
3–4	Over $150	8.8	5.0	1.7	0.8
5–6	<$300	10.0	6.0	2.5	1.0
5–6	Over $300	12.0	8.0	2.7	1.2
Over 6	<$450	15.0	10.0	3.5	1.8
Over 6	Over $450	16.0	11.0	4.0	2.0

*Percentage of customers in the cell who made a purchase from the last catalog mailed to them.

SOURCE: Reprinted by permission of Harvard Business School Press. Adapted from Robert Blattberg, Gary Getz, and Jacquelyn Thomas, *Customer Equity: Building and Managing Relationships as Valuable Assets* (Boston: Harvard Business School Press, 2001), p. 18. Copyright © 2001 by the Harvard Business School Publishing Corporation; all rights reserved.

The catalog retailer divides its customers into 32 groups or segments on the basis of how many orders each customer has placed during the last year, how much merchandise the customer has purchased, and the last time the customer placed an order. Each segment is represented by one cell in Exhibit 11–3. For example, the customers in the upper-left cell have made one or two purchases in the last year, made a purchase within the last two months, and purchased less than $50 of merchandise.

Catalog retailers often use this type of analysis to determine which customer groups should receive catalogs. For each of the RFM groups, they will determine the percentage of customers in the group who made a purchase from the last catalog sent to them. For example, 5 percent of the customers in the upper-left cell of Exhibit 11–3 placed an order from the last catalog sent to them. With information about the response rate and the average gross margin from orders placed by customers in each cell, the catalog retailer can calculate the expected profit from sending catalogs to different customers. For example, if the average gross margin from orders placed by customers in the upper-left cell is $20 and the cost of sending a catalog to customers in the cell is $0.75, the catalog would make $0.25 per customer from each catalog mailed to those customers.

$20 contribution $\times$ .05 response
= $1.00 expected contribution $-$ $0.75 cost
= $0.25 per customer.

Thus, RFM analysis is basically a method of estimating the CLV using the recency, frequency, and monetary value of past purchases. Exhibit 11–4 illustrates how RFM can be used to develop customer target strategies. Retailing View 11.3 describes how CVS Caremark uses the data it collects and analyzes to target promotions.

RETAILING VIEW   CRM at CVS Caremark, Inc.   11.3

The market intelligence group at CVS Caremark is responsible for analyzing the purchasing data the retailer has on its customers and developing programs and promotions that increase CVS pharmacy's share of wallet. Customers in its ExtraCare frequent-shopper program earn ExtraBucks—2 percent on most in-store and online purchases and $1 for every two prescriptions purchased—that can be used when shopping in its stores or online. ExtraCare customers also receive e-mails and direct mailings with helpful health and beauty insights, new product information, and valuable coupons, in addition to free merchandise when CVS Caremark has special vendor promotions.

By analyzing the buying behavior of its ExtraCare customers, CVS discovered some interesting opportunities for cross-promotions. For example, about two-thirds of the customers buying toothpaste did not buy toothbrushes from CVS Caremark. To encourage its ExtraCare customers to buy toothbrushes as well as toothpaste, the retailer targets these customers for a special toothbrush promotion.

It also uses special promotions to increase the average size of its customers' market basket. For example, it offers a $4 coupon to customers with an average market basket of $15 who buy $25 of merchandise. Customers who normally purchase $25 of merchandise get a $10 coupon if they make a $50 purchase.

Each quarter CVS Caremark distributes over 5 million messages to its customers. These messages contain information and offers tailored to the customers' buying behaviors. Like most drugstore chains, over 20 percent of its sales involve some form of promotion. The promotions increase sales but can lower its gross margin. CVS Caremark experiments with different messages and offerings and then analyzes customer buying behavior to determine which promotions are more profitable.

CVS Caremark is very concerned about its customers' privacy. Its programs are opt-in, and therefore it sends mailings only to customers who give it permission to do so. At times, it uses outside processing companies as its agents to help print and send mailings, but these agents never receive any personal customer information beyond name and address. CVS Caremark values its customers' privacy and never gives or sells any specific information about them to any manufacturer or direct marketer.

Sources: Personal communication, February 6, 2010; Antoinette Alexander, "Consumers Put Extracare in Saving," *Drug Store News*, February 9, 2009, pp. 1–2; Mike Troy, "Consumer Insights Drive Success," *Retailing Today*, March 17, 2008, pp. 3–4.

EXHIBIT II–4
RFM Target Strategies

Frequency	Monetary	RECENCY			
		0–2 months	3–4 months	5–6 months	Over 6 months
1–2	<$50	First-time customers		Low-value customers	
1–2	Over $50				
3–4	<$150	Early repeat customers		Defectors	
3–4	Over $150				
5–6	<$300	High-value customers		Core defectors	
5–6	Over $300				
Over 6	<$450				
Over 6	Over $450				

SOURCE: Reprinted by permission of Harvard Business School Press. Adapted from Robert Blattberg, Gary Getz, and Jacquelyn Thomas, *Customer Equity: Building and Managing Relationships as Valuable Assets* (Boston: Harvard Business School Press, 2001), p. 18. Copyright © 2001 by the Harvard Business School Publishing Corporation; all rights reserved.

DEVELOPING CRM PROGRAMS

Having classified customers on the basis of a statistical model estimating CLV or an RFM set of rules, the next step in the CRM process is to develop CRM programs for the different customer segments (see Exhibit 11–1). For example, the CRM programs directed toward customers in the high-CLV segment (high-RFM value) attempt to maintain loyalty, increase retention, and gain a greater share of wallet by providing more value to them. Some customers that have a low-CLV and have made infrequent, small purchases might be first-time customers. The objective of CRM programs directed toward this segment of customers is to convert them into repeat customers and eventually high-value customers. However, customers who have a low lifetime value, have not purchased, or are committed to another retailer and may be difficult to capture are not worth pursuing. In the following sections, we discuss programs retailers use to (1) retain their best customers, (2) convert good customers into high-LTV customers, and (3) get rid of unprofitable customers.

Customer Retention

Four approaches that retailers use to retain and increase share of wallet from their best customers are (1) frequent-shopper programs, (2) special customer services, (3) personalization, and (4) community.

Frequent-Shopper Programs   As mentioned previously, frequent-shopper programs are used to both build a customer database by identifying customers by their transactions and encourage repeat purchase behavior and retailer loyalty. However, the effects of these programs on building loyalty are limited. Some suggestions for designing programs that build repeat purchases and loyalty are:

- *Use tiers.* Rewards should be tiered according to the volume of purchase to motivate customers to increase the level of their purchases. The tiers can be based on individual or cumulative transactions. Some programs combine both discounts and points for rewards. For example, a $5 discount on purchases between $100 and $149.99, $10 dollars off purchases from $150 to $249.99, and $15 off purchases of $250 or more. Beyond $250, customers accumulate points that can be redeemed for rewards, such as free merchandise. Customers generally accept the idea that people who spend more should receive greater rewards.

- *Offer choices.* Not all customers value the same rewards. Thus, the most effective frequent-shopper programs offer customers choices. For example, Coles Myer, a leading Australian retailer, originally offered customers air miles but shifted to a menu of rewards when it discovered that many customers did not value air miles. Sainsbury, a U.K. supermarket chain, allows customers to use their Nectar points for vouchers at a variety of retail partners, such as Blockbuster.

- *Incorporate charitable contributions.* Link the frequent-shopper program to charitable causes. For example, Target donates 1 percent of all purchases charged to Target's REDcard to a program that benefits local schools. Although these altruistic rewards can be an effective part of a frequent-shopper program, such incentives probably should not be the focal point of the program. Research indicates that the most effective incentives benefit the recipient directly, not indirectly, as is the case with charitable contributions.

- *Reward all transactions.* To ensure they collect all customer transaction data and encourage repeat purchases, programs need to reward all purchases, not just purchases of selected merchandise.

- *Feature transparency and simplicity.* Customers need to be able to understand quickly and easily when they will receive rewards, what the rewards are, how much they have earned, and how they can redeem the points they have accumulated. The ground rules need to be clearly stated. There should be no surprises or confusion. Some companies mail a separate catalog to customers that describes the reward levels and available prizes. Knowing exactly what the rewards are pushes customers to move to the next spending level to receive the desired prizes.

Limitations   Three factors limiting the effectiveness of frequent-shopper programs are cost, negative reactions to changes, and inability to develop strategic advantage. First, frequent-shopper programs can be expensive. For example, a 1 percent price discount can cost large retailers over $100 million a year. In addition, for a large retailer, the initial launch and maintenance investments (store training, marketing, fulfillment support, and information technology and systems costs) can be as high as $30 million. Annual maintenance costs can reach $5 million to $10 million when marketing, program support, offer fulfillment, customer service, and IT infrastructure costs are included. Then there are the marketing support costs needed to maintain awareness of the program.

Second, it is difficult to make corrections in programs when problems arise. Programs become part of the customer's shopping experience, so customers must be informed about even the smallest changes in programs. They react negatively to any perceived "take away" once a program is in place, even if they are not actively involved in it. Negative reactions can reduce customer trust in and loyalty toward the retailer.

Third, and perhaps most important, it is difficult to gain a competitive advantage based on a frequent-shopper program. Because the programs are visible, they can be easily duplicated by competitors. Between 50 and 70 percent of all grocery retailers offer a loyalty card to their customers, and 80 percent of households have at least one of these grocery stores' cards in their wallets. Yet the perceived value of the cards is low. Supermarkets' loyalty cards allow customers access to price discounts, which encourages the price-conscious shoppers but not necessarily the loyal customer who would shop at the store regardless of whether it offered discounts or points for prizes. In general, consumers see little difference between the programs when they all provide a minor discount on detergent.[29]

To avoid these problems, retailers are offering special customer services and more personalized benefits and are engaging customers in communities to build loyalty from their best customers rather than focusing on price discounts. These benefits are based on the retailer's unique knowledge of the customer and are more "invisible" to competitors. Retailing View 11.4 describes how the Neiman Marcus InCircle program goes beyond offering price discounts to build loyalty with its best customers.

Special Customer Services   Some retailers provide unusually high-quality customer service to build and maintain the loyalty of their best customers. Nordstrom holds complementary private parties for invitees to view new clothing lines. Saks Fifth Avenue offers free fur storage, complimentary tailoring, and dinner at the captain's table on a luxury cruise line. Neiman Marcus InCircle members receive exclusive offers and shopping events and earn Perk Cards good for in-store dining, alterations, parking, delivery, and more.

Personalization   An important limitation of CRM strategies developed for market segments, such as a platinum segment in the customer pyramid (Exhibit 11–2), is that each segment is composed of a large number of customers who are not identical. Thus, any offering will be most appealing for only the typical customer and not as appealing to the majority of customers in the segment. For example, customers in the platinum segment with the highest CLVs might include a 25-year-old single woman whose needs are quite different from those of a 49-year-old working mother with two children.

With the availability of customer-level data and analysis tools, retailers can now economically offer unique benefits and target messages to individual customers. They have the ability to develop programs for small groups of customers and even specific individuals. For example, at Harry Rosen, a Canadian men's apparel specialty retailer, customers are occasionally contacted by the salesperson with whom they

11.4   RETAILING VIEW   CRM at Neiman Marcus

All Neiman Marcus credit card customers are enrolled in the Neiman Marcus InCircle program and receive rewards, services, and special gifts. Customers whose higher spending levels place them in the President's or "Chairman's" category receive additional rewards and services. The median household income of the over 500,000 InCircle members is $877,000, and they spend an average of over $10,000 per year at Neiman Marcus.

Like other frequent-shopper programs, customers earn points for each dollar charged on their Neiman Marcus credit cards. However, these points are redeemed for truly unique rewards such as a limited-edition Emilio Pucci silk scarf, an eight-night excursion through India, or a complete Sony home movie theater. Reward options are refined and expanded annually, but the options are always designed to enhance Neiman's exclusive image and reputation for uniqueness.

InCircle members receive frequent communications from Neiman Marcus throughout the year, including emails and the quarterly InCircle *Entrée* magazine, a quality publication produced by Time, Inc. publishers.

Customer relationships are also nurtured at the store level. Neiman's sales associates can tap into information about customers' past purchases and shopping behaviors and are encouraged to contact these customers personally. Sales associates have the freedom to be creative in helping InCircle customers shop in multiple departments and use the various services from in-store gift wrapping to travel services through InCircle Access.

Neiman Marcus's InCircle program provides special benefits to build the retailer's share of wallet with its best customers.

Recognizing the value of these preferred customers, Neiman invites InCircle members to participate in various surveys and provide feedback and suggestions on how Neiman can improve its customers' shopping experience.

Sources: Vanessa O'Connell, "Posh Retailers Pile on Perks for Top Customers," *Wall Street Journal*, April 26, 2007; www.incircle.com (accessed August 29, 2007); www.neimanmarcus.com (accessed August 29, 2007).

REFACT

In 1984, Neiman Marcus launched the first frequent-shopper program sponsored by a retailer.[30]

have developed a personal relationship. If Harry Rosen receives a new shipment of Armani suits, the salesclerk will contact customers who have purchased Armani in the past. If a customer has been relatively inactive, the retailer might send him a $100 certificate on something he has not bought in a while.[31]

Developing retail programs for small groups or individual customers is referred to as **1-to-1 retailing.** Many small, local retailers have always practiced 1-to-1 retailing. They know each of their customers, greet them by name when they walk into the store, and then recommend merchandise they know the customers will like. These local store owners do not need customer databases and data-mining tools; they have the information in their heads. But most large retail chains and their employees do not have this intimate knowledge of their customers. Thus, the CRM process enables larger retailers to efficiently develop relationships similar to those that many small local retailers have with customers.

The Internet channel provides an opportunity for retailers to automate the practice of 1-to-1 retailing. Some use site registration to customize what shoppers see according to their demographic data and expressed interests.[32] Others have shoppers rate specific products they like the most so that they receive "similar item" recommendations.

Nearly every retailer using an electronic channel allows shoppers to search selectively for the items in which they are most interested. Some retailers attempt to match specialized promotions to the customer's search. If someone is searching for cell phones, for instance, the Web site can offer a "10 percent off" sale on cell phones. The retailer can also customize its home page so that the next time the customer logs on, he or she will see special promotions on items similar to those previously searched. Amazon.com, for instance, greets customers by name on its home page, and the products displayed are based on the company's analysis of past purchasing behavior.

The personalized rewards or benefits that customers receive are based on unique information possessed by the retailer and its sales associates. This information, in the retailer's customer database, cannot be accessed or used by competitors. Thus, it provides an opportunity to develop a sustainable competitive advantage.

The effective use of this information creates the positive-feedback cycle in the CRM process (see Exhibit 11–1). Increasing repeat purchases from a retailer increases the amount of data collected from the customer, which enables the retailer to provide more personalized benefits, which in turn increases the customer's purchases from the retailer.

Amazon customizes the landing page for each visitor on the basis of his or her past search behavior and purchases.

Community   A fourth approach for building customer retention and loyalty is to develop a sense of community among customers. A **retail brand community** is a group of customers who are bound together by their loyalty to a retailer and the activities in which the retailer engages. Community members identify themselves with other members and share a common interest and participation in activities related to the retailer. They also feel an obligation to attract new members of the community and help other members of the community by sharing their experiences and

---

11.5   RETAILING VIEW   REI's Retail Community Provides Value and Builds Customer Loyalty

REI is a category specialist targeting people who engage in active, outdoor activities. It operates more than 80 stores in 27 states that offer apparel, equipment, and services and also provide a variety of in-store facilities for testing equipment, including bike test trails, climbing pinnacles, and camp stove demonstration tables.

REI has developed a sense of community among its customers by providing a vast array of services that encourage outdoor enthusiasts to interact with one another and share their experiences. Frequent in-store clinics and REI-sponsored events provide opportunities for customers to learn about the outdoors and rugged sports. REI is committed to helping people enjoy outdoor activities ranging from weekend family camping trips to Mt. Everest expeditions.

REI annually arranges for more than 90 domestic and international small-group tours.

REI develops a sense of community associated with the retailer by offering outdoor adventures and volunteer activities.

These tours avoid the typical tourist destinations, focusing on bicycling, trekking, kayaking, hiking, camping, and mountaineering adventures. Get-away weekends that it sponsors include rock climbing in northern Virginia and New Hampshire; kayaking in the San Juan Islands, Charleston harbor, and Yellowstone lakes; and backpacking in the Shenandoah and Smokey Mountains. Each store organizes local volunteer stewardship projects dedicated to restoring and improving areas in which people can better enjoy outdoor recreation. The stores recruit local members and volunteers to perform hands-on, community-based conservation work.

REI emphasizes that one of the best parts of participating in the volunteer activities, adventure trips, and weekend activities is being with other REI members who share common values and a passion to explore the world around them.

Participants will make connections with new friends whom they will want to keep for life.

REI uses its Web site to foster the sense of community among its members. On the Web site, the members can find information about volunteer activities near where they live and special events in their local stores, as well as more detailed product information. The company communicates with its members through its blogs, Facebook, and Twitter. Members can share pictures of their experiences on the Web site.

REI's employees are involved in and contribute to building this sense of community among its customers. In 2005, REI was inducted into *Fortune* magazine's "Hall of Fame" and included in *Fortune's* "100 Greatest Places to Work." This recognition is based on REI's outdoor-focused culture that encourages outdoor activity as an extension of its business, its community involvement and support for outdoor-focused clubs and nonprofit organizations, and its Brand Challenge Grant program that provides equipment and clothing to employees for outdoor adventures.

REI's ownership structure also contributes to the sense of community members have toward the retailer. REI is the largest consumer cooperative (co-op) in the United States. Anyone can shop at REI, but co-op members, who pay $20 for a lifetime membership, own the company. The 3.5 million active members vote for REI's board of directors and receive the majority of the co-op's profits through annual refunds based on their purchases.

Sources: www.rei.com (accessed July 14, 2010); Christopher Tkaczyk, "100 Best Companies to Work For—REI," *Fortune,* June 14, 2010, p. 52; Kate Pickert, "Camping for the Hotel Set," *Time,* May 4, 2009, p. 48.

product knowledge. By participating in such a community, customers become more reluctant to leave the "family" of other people patronizing the retailer.[33]

The Nike stores create a sense of community by hosting running groups that meet two times a week, after which the runners meet at the store for refreshments. Members who have logged more than 100 miles earn special recognition, and the Nike Plus Web site communicates with runners' Apple iPods to track their running metrics. More than half of the runners involved in Nike's program use this system, visiting the Web site more than four times a week. In comparison, even Starbucks' core customers frequent its stores only about 15 times a month.[34] Retailing View 11.5 describes REI's community of outdoor enthusiasts.

Converting Good Customers into Best Customers

In the context of the customer pyramid (Exhibit 11–2), increasing the sales made to good customers is referred to as *customer alchemy*—converting iron and gold customers into platinum customers.[35] A way to achieve customer alchemy is through **add-on selling**, which involves offering and selling more products and services to existing customers to increase the retailer's share of wallet with these customers.

A retailer's customer database also reveals opportunities for add-on selling. Many retailers use their data on customers' shopping histories to suggest products to them. For example, if a supermarket discovers that customers are buying cat food and not kitty litter, it might distribute coupons for kitty litter to the customers. These coupons could be provided to the customers when they enter the store and swipe their frequent-shopper cards, when they log on to the retailer's Web site, or through messages sent to the customers' mobile phones.

Amazon.com is a master of generating add-on sales through its recommendations. Personalized recommendations, based on past purchases, are made when consumers first visit the Web site. If they scroll down to get more information about a book, the site recommends other books that have been bought by customers who purchased the book being examined. Then a bundle of two books, the one being examined and a complementary book, is offered at a discounted price.[36]

American Girl provides many add-on sales opportunities for its customers. In its seven retail stores, Web site, and catalog, American Girl offers a line of historical

18-inch dolls and accessories. The initial line of dolls, introduced in 1986, were 9-year-old fictional heroines that lived in important times in America's past These historical dolls and associated apparel and accessories provide "girl-sized" views of significant events that shaped the United States. The company added a contemporary line of dolls and accessories, called Just Like You, that represent the individuality and diversity of today's American girls. American Girl has earned the loyalty of millions of girls and the trust of their parents. For younger girls, ages 3 to 6, American Girl also introduced the Bitty Baby line of soft, huggable baby dolls and related toys. Since 1986, 18 million American Girl dolls have been sold through the company's retail stores, Web site, and catalogs.

American Girl offers its customers many opportunities for making more and continued purchases of products and services it offers.

Before bringing home a Kit Kittredge doll for Christmas, Pam Stolte wanted to make sure it was what her daughter Avery really wanted. This member of the American Girl doll collection was not cheap. Stolte made sure Avery would not let the $89 doll sit alone in a corner in her room. Three years later, Kit accompanies Avery to ballet and soccer (in appropriate athletic and dance outfits that her parents have bought) and goes on family trips. Avery took the doll to see herself in the movie *Kit Kittredge: An American Girl*, and her parents bought the DVD of the movie for Avery.

American Girl also offers Avery the opportunity to buy accessories for her doll and a six-book series about each of the dolls and to subscribe to an American Girl magazine. But the major opportunity for add-on sales comes when Avery takes a trip with her mother to an American Girl store. The store trip is likely to include a photo shoot of Avery with her doll, a salon visit to shape and style her doll's hair, a three-course lunch at the café with a seat provided for her doll, and the purchase of an outfit to match her doll's outfit. If repairs are needed, the store has a hospital. This outing can cost more than $300, but parents, after getting over the sticker shock, feel the experience is worth it.

Community activities have been developed around American Girl dolls. For example, local libraries host American Girl parties. The events attract 40 girls and their dolls and focus on the time period of specific dolls. Service organizations have developed American Girl fashion shows to support local charities.[37]

Dealing with Unprofitable Customers

In many cases, the bottom tier of customers actually has a negative CLV. Retailers lose money on every sale they make to these customers. For example, catalog retailers have customers who repeatedly buy three or four items and return all but one of them. The cost of processing two or three returned items is much greater than the profits coming from the one item that the customer kept. Customers in the bottom tier may also be there because they stopped buying from the store and then started again. For example, customers may vanish because a competitor is offering a more attractive offer or they are dissatisfied and then return months or years later as a new customer. The costs of their (re)acquisition make them unprofitable. The process of no longer selling to these unprofitable customers can be referred to as "getting the lead out," in terms of the customer pyramid.[38]

Approaches for getting the lead out are (1) offering less costly services to satisfy the needs of lead customers and (2) charging customers for the services they are abusing. For example, a retailer might get 50,000 Web site visits a day and 70,000 daily calls, about three-quarters of which go to automated systems that cost the company less than $1 each. The remaining calls are handled by call center agents, who cost $13 per call. The retailer could contact 25,000 lower-tier customers who placed a lot of calls to agents and tell them they must use the Web site or automated calls for simple account and price information. Each name could be flagged and routed to a special representative who would direct callers back to automated services and tell them how to use it.

Customers who make an excessive number of returns typically are unprofitable. Some examples of these costly returners include people who buy a large-screen television for their Super Bowl party and then return it after the game or who buy an expensive dress for a special occasion and return it after they wear it once. Professional thieves steal merchandise from stores and return it for cash refunds or credits that they can turn into cash by selling them at a discount on the Internet. Best Buy is undertaking a strategy to focus on gold and platinum customers and get rid of lead customers. To lure high spenders, it is providing more effective customer service. To discourage undesirable customers, it is reducing promotions that tend to draw them into the store and removing them from direct marketing lists. The challenge is to deter bad customers without turning off good ones. Best Buy cannot bar undesirable customers from its stores, but it is taking steps to put a stop to their most damaging practices. It's enforcing a restocking fee of 15 percent of the purchase price on returned merchandise.

Rejecting customers is a delicate business. Filene's Basement was criticized extensively by the press for asking two Massachusetts customers not to shop at its stores because of their frequent returns and complaints. Best Buy's CEO apologized in writing to students at a Washington, D.C., school after employees at one store barred a group of African-American students while admitting a group of white students.

IMPLEMENTING CRM PROGRAMS

As discussed throughout this chapter, increasing sales and profits through CRM programs is a challenge. Effective CRM strategies require more than appointing a CRM manager, installing a computer system to manage and analyze a customer database, and making speeches about the importance of customers. The effective implementation of CRM programs requires the close coordination of activities by different functions in a retailer's organization. The IT department needs to collect and analyze the relevant information and make it readily accessible to the employees implementing the programs—the frontline service providers and sales associates and the marketers responsible for communicating with customers through impersonal channels (mass advertising, direct mail, e-mail). Store operations and human resource management needs to hire, train, and motivate the employees who will be using the information to deliver personalized services.

Most retailers are product-centric, not customer-centric; as shown in Chapter 9, buyers in a retail firm are organized by type of product. Typically, there is no area of a retail firm organized by customer type and responsible for delivering products and services to different types of customers. Perhaps in the future, retailers will have market managers to perform this coordinating function.

SUMMARY

To develop a strategic advantage, retailers must effectively manage their critical resources—their finances (Chapter 6), human resources (Chapter 9), real estate and locations (Chapters 7 and 8), inventory and information (Chapter 10), and customers (Chapter 11). This chapter focuses on activities that retailers undertake to increase their sales and profits by providing more value to their better customers. Customer relationship management is a business philosophy and set of strategies, programs, and systems that focuses on identifying and building loyalty with a retailer's most valued customers. Loyal customers are committed to patronizing a retailer and are not prone to switch to a competitor. In addition to building loyalty through increasing customer value, CRM programs are designed to increase the share of wallet from the retailer's best customers.

Customer relationship management is an iterative process that turns customer data into customer loyalty through four activities: (1) collecting customer data, (2) analyzing the customer data and identifying target customers, (3) developing CRM programs, and (4) implementing CRM programs. The first step of the process is to collect and store data about customers. One of the challenges in collecting customer data is identifying the customer in connection with each transaction. Retailers use a variety of approaches to overcome this challenge.

The second step is to analyze the data to develop insights into shopping behaviors and identify the most profitable customers. An example of retail analytics is a market basket analysis that provides information for the location of merchandise categories. Two approaches used to rank customers according to their profitability are calculating the customer's lifetime value and categorizing customers on the basis of characteristics of their buying behavior—their recency, frequency, and monetary value.

Using this information about customers, retailers can develop programs to build loyalty in their best customers, increase their share of wallet with better customers (e.g., converting gold customers into platinum customers), and deal with unprofitable customers (getting the lead out). Four approaches that retailers use to build loyalty and retain their best customers are (1) launching frequent-shopper programs, (2) offering special customer services, (3) personalizing the services they provide, and (4) building a sense of community. Unprofitable customers are dealt with by developing lower-cost approaches for serving them. Effectively implementing CRM programs is difficult because doing so requires coordinating a number of different areas in a retailer's organization.

KEY TERMS

add-on selling, *293*	80-20 rule, *285*	opt out, *282*
cookies, *281*	frequent-shopper program, *280*	private-label credit card, *280*
customer database, *278*	loyalty program, *280*	retail brand community, *292*
customer lifetime value (CLV), *284*	market basket analysis, *283*	RFM analysis, *286*
customer loyalty, *276*	1-to-1 retailing, *291*	share of wallet, *276*
customer relationship management (CRM), *275*	opt in, *282*	

GET OUT AND DO IT!

1. **CONTINUING ASSIGNMENT** Interview the store manager working for the retailer you have selected for the Continuing Assignment. Ask the manager if the store offers a frequent-shopper/loyalty program and how effective it is in terms of increasing the store's sales and profits. Find out why the manager has these views and what could be done to increase the effectiveness of the program. Then talk to some customers in the store. Ask them why they are members or not. Find out how membership in the program affects their shopping behavior and relationship with the retailer.

2. **INTERNET EXERCISE** Go to the home page of a retailer that you frequent and review its privacy policy. How is this retailer protecting its customers' information? Which policies, or lack of policies, raise your concern? Why? Which policies give you comfort that your private information is being protected? Why?

3. **INTERNET EXERCISE** Go to the Web site of the Electronic Privacy Information Center (www.

epic.org), and review the issues raised by the organization. What does this watchdog organization feel are the most important retailers' consumer privacy issues? How will these issues evolve in the future?

4. **INTERNET EXERCISE** Go to Macy's credit card home page at www1.macys.com/service/credit/overview.ognc. Read about the different levels of membership for this customer rewards program. Describe how Macy's is using the customer pyramid (Exhibit 11–2) in its CRM program to target and classify customers. Does this loyalty program encourage good customers to become best customers? Explain why or why not.

5. **INTERNET EXERCISE** Go to the home page of 1-800-Flowers at www.1800flowers.com, and read about the Fresh Rewards program. How does this company's CRM program help it to track its best customers, grow its business, and increase customer loyalty?

DISCUSSION QUESTIONS AND PROBLEMS

1. What is a customer relationship management (CRM) program? Describe one CRM program that you have participated in as a customer.

2. Why do retailers want to determine the lifetime value of their customers? How does past customer behavior help retailers anticipate future customer retention?

3. Why do some customers have a low or negative CLV value? What approach can retailers take with these customers to minimize their impact on the bottom line?

4. Why do customers have privacy concerns about the frequent-shopper programs that supermarkets offer, and what can supermarkets do to minimize these concerns?

5. What are some examples of opportunities for add-on selling that might be pursued by (a) travel agents, (b) jewelry stores, and (c) dry cleaners?

6. Which of the following types of retailers do you think would benefit most from instituting a CRM program: (a) supermarkets, (b) banks, (c) automobile dealers, or (d) consumer electronics retailers? Why?

7. Develop a CRM program for a local store that sells apparel and gifts with your college's or university's logo. What type of information would you collect about your customers, and how would you use this information to increase the sales and profits of the store?

8. What are the different approaches retailers can use to identify customers by their transactions? What are the advantages and disadvantages of each approach?

9. A CRM program focuses on building relationships with a retailer's better customers. Some customers who do not receive the same benefits as the retailer's best customers may be upset because they are treated

differently. What can retailers do to minimize this negative reaction?

10. Think of one of your favorite places to shop. How does this retailer create customer loyalty and satisfaction, encourage repeat visits, establish an emotional bond between the customer and the retailer, know the

customer's preferences, and provide personal attention and memorable experiences to its best customers?

11. How would a retailer use transactions, customer contacts, customer preferences, descriptive information, and responses to marketing activities in its customer database?

SUGGESTED READINGS

Bell, Chip R., and John R. Patterson. *Customer Loyalty Guaranteed: Create, Lead, and Sustain Remarkable Customer Service.* Cincinnati, OH: Adams Media, 2007.

Blattberg, Robert C., Edward C. Malthouse, and Scott A. Neslin. "Customer Lifetime Value: Empirical Generalizations and Some Conceptual Questions." *Journal of Interactive Marketing* 23 (May 2009), pp. 157–168.

Buttle, Francis. *Customer Relationship Management,* 2nd ed. Newark, NJ: Butterworth-Heinemann, 2008.

Hochman, Larry. *The Relationship Revolution: Closing the Customer Promise Gap.* Hoboken, NJ: Wiley, 2010.

Newell, Frederick. *Why CRM Doesn't Work: How to Win by Letting Customers Manage the Relationship.* New York: Bloomberg Press, 2010.

Reimann, Martin, Oliver Schilke, and Jacquelyn S. Thomas. "Customer Relationship Management and Firm Performance: The Mediating Role of Business Strategy." *Journal of the Academy of Marketing Science* 38 (June 2010), pp. 326–346.

Sun, Zhiwei. "Customer Relationship Management and Privacy." *International Business Research* 2, no. 1 (2000).

Tsiptsis, Konstantinos, and Antonios Chorianopoulos. *Data Mining Techniques in CRM: Inside Customer Segmentation.* Hoboken, NJ: Wiley, 2010.

Merchandise Management

Section II reviewed the strategic decisions made by retailers— the development of their retail market strategy, their financial strategy associated with the market strategy, their store location opportunities and factors affecting the selection of a specific site, their development of human resources, the systems they use to control the flow of information and merchandise, and the approaches they take to manage relationships with their customers. These decisions are more strategic than tactical because they involve committing significant resources to develop long-term advantages over the competition in a target retail market segment.

This section, Section III, examines the more tactical merchandise management decisions undertaken to implement the retail strategy.

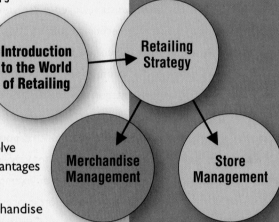

Chapter 12 provides an overview of how retailers manage their merchandise inventory—how they organize the merchandise planning process, evaluate their performance, forecast sales, establish an assortment plan, determine the appropriate service levels, allocate merchandise to stores, and monitor the performance of the merchandise inventory control activities.

Chapter 13 explores how retailers buy merchandise from vendors—their branding options, negotiating processes, and vendor relationship-building activities.

Chapter 14 addresses the question of how retailers set and adjust prices for the merchandise and services they offer.

Chapter 15 looks at the approaches that retailers take to build their brand image and communicate with their customers.

The following section, Section IV, focuses on store management decisions.

Managing the Merchandise Planning Process

EXECUTIVE BRIEFING

Darius Jackson, Buyer, Men's Outerwear and Swim JCPenney

After graduating from the University of Nebraska, I went to work for JCPenney as an assistant buyer in the young men's collections. During the preceding summer, I was an intern with the same team. Over the last seven years, I have received a number of promotions that exposed me to different merchandise categories and also different functions in the buying organization. Each promotion I have received at Penney's has involved more responsibility and provided the opportunity to further develop my merchandising and management skills. For example, one of my promotions to a planner position improved my financial analyst skills. I enjoy my job and continue to develop my career at JCPenney. I am given all the responsibility I can handle and the support I need to be successful.

I am currently the buyer and leader of the team that manages the men's outerwear and swim merchandise categories. Our team consists of a Planner who does the financial analyses, an Allocator who determines the assortments that stores will have, a Direct Inventory Analyst who creates the purchase orders and monitors our direct (Internet and catalog) business, an Assistant Buyer, and a Merchandise Assistant.

My team is responsible for identifying opportunities and developing a set of brands that our customers will find appealing. When I was on the boy's team, for example, we offered a traditional brand, US Polo, and a hip-hop, streetwear brand, Southpole, but didn't have a brand targeting the "stakeboarder" segment. We tested several brands targeting this segment and decided on Vans. Our customers in this segment felt Vans was more authentic and captured the spirit of skateboarding.

To be a successful you need to develop a good understanding of your customer and your competition. Retailing is a very dynamic industry. You need to quickly read and respond to what your competitors are doing. I continually monitor the merchandise, prices, and promotions at my principal competitors, Macy's and Kohl's, and check out the latest men's apparel fashions shown in trade publications and Web sites. I also go to five or six trade shows and markets each year to see the new merchandise.

One great thing about retailing is that you get immediate feedback on the quality of your decisions. I really look forward to reviewing my daily financial results, which is basically a report card that tracks the sales and gross margin generated in my merchandise categories. It's a great feeling to see strategies we implemented succeed.

QUESTIONS

What is the merchandise management process?

How are merchandise management processes different for staple and fashion merchandise?

How do retailers forecast sales for merchandise categories?

What trade-offs do buyers consider in developing merchandise assortments?

How do retailers plan their assortments and determine the appropriate inventory levels?

How do multistore retailers allocate merchandise to stores?

How do retailers evaluate the performance of their merchandise management process?

Even when sales are below expectations, I am excited about the challenge of turning things around.

Everyday I am doing something interesting and exciting in my retailing career. On any day, I might be with a national label vendor, working with our designers to develop private label merchandise, reviewing our financial projections with the planner, or analyzing our direct sales to see how we need to change the assortment to make it more appealing to direct customers. My job is challenging and rewarding, both personally and financially.

Merchandise management activities are undertaken primarily by buyers and their superiors, divisional merchandise managers (DMMs) and general merchandise managers (GMMs). Many people view these jobs as very exciting and glamorous. They think that buyers spend most of their time trying to identify the latest fashions and trends, attending designer shows replete with celebrities in Paris and Milan, and going to rock concerts and other glamorous events to see what the trendsetters are wearing. But, in reality, the lives of retail buyers are more like those of Wall Street investment analysts than globe-trotting trend spotters.

Investment analysts manage a portfolio of stocks. They buy stocks in companies they think will increase in value and sell stocks in companies they believe do not have a promising future. They continuously monitor the performance of the stocks they own to see which are increasing in value and which are decreasing. Sometimes they make mistakes and invest in companies that do not perform well. So they sell their stock in these companies and lose money, but they use the money from the sold stocks to buy more attractive stocks. Other times, the stocks they buy increase dramatically in price, and they wish they had bought more shares.

Rather than managing a portfolio of stocks, retail buyers manage a portfolio of merchandise inventory. They buy merchandise they think will be popular with their customers. Like investment analysts, they use an information system to monitor the performance of their merchandise portfolio—to see what is selling and what is not. Retail buyers also make mistakes. When the merchandise they bought is not selling well, they get rid of it by putting it on sale so that they can use the money to buy better-selling merchandise. However, they also might take a chance

Retail merchandise management is very similar to managing an investment portfolio. Retail buyers make and manage investments in inventory rather than stocks.

and buy a lot of a new product and be rewarded when it sells well, while competitors, who were more conservative, don't have enough of the product.

Chris Manning, a former swimwear buyer at Macy's, draws an analogy between surfing and buying merchandise:

> My job is like surfing. Sometimes you catch a big wave (trend) and it's exhilarating, and sometimes you think you've caught a good wave and brown turns out not to be the color this season. But the real fun is getting the most out of the wave you can. Let me give you an example of how I worked a big wave. Vendors started to show tankinis— women's bathing suits with bikini bottoms and tank tops. My customers were women in their 40s that had a couple of kids. I thought they would really go for this new style because it had the advantages of a two-piece bathing suit, but wasn't much more revealing than a one-piece suit. I bought a wide color assortment—bright reds, yellows, pink, and black—and put them in our fashion-forward stores in January for a test. The initial sales were good, but our customers thought they were a little too skimpy. Then I started to work the wave. I went back to the vendor and got them to recut the top so that the suit was less revealing, and I placed a big order for the colors that were selling best. Sales were so good that the other Macy's divisions picked up on it, but we rode the wave the longest and had the best swimwear sales of all of the divisions.[1]

Merchandise management is the process by which a retailer attempts to offer the right quantity of the right merchandise in the right place at the right time and meet the company's financial goals. Buyers need to be in touch with and anticipate what customers will want to buy, but this ability to sense market trends is just one skill needed to manage merchandise inventory effectively. Perhaps an even more important skill is the ability to analyze sales data continually and make appropriate adjustments in prices and inventory levels.

The first part of this chapter provides the background needed to understand the merchandise management process. In this introduction, we discuss how the process is organized, who makes the merchandise decisions, and how merchandise management performance is evaluated. The last part of the chapter examines the steps in the merchandise management process—forecasting sales, formulating an assortment plan, determining the appropriate inventory level, developing a merchandise management plan, allocating merchandise to stores, and monitoring performance. The two appendixes to this chapter provide more detailed discussions of the steps in developing a merchandise budget plan and the retail method of calculating inventory value. Other activities involved in merchandise management reviewed in subsequent chapters are buying merchandise (Chapter 13) and pricing (Chapter 14).

MERCHANDISE MANAGEMENT OVERVIEW

This section provides an overview of the merchandise management process, including the organization of a retailer's merchandise management activities, the objectives and measures used to evaluate merchandise management performance, the differences in the process for managing fashion and seasonal merchandise versus basic merchandise, and the steps in the merchandise management process. In the following section, we review each of the steps in the merchandise management process.

The Buying Organization

Every retailer has its own system for grouping categories of merchandise, but the basic structure of the buying organization is similar for most retailers. Exhibit 12–1 illustrates this basic structure by depicting the organization of the merchandise division for a department store chain such as Macy's, Belk, or Dillard's. Exhibit 12–1 shows the organization of buyers in the merchandise division. A similar structure for planners parallels the structure for buyers.

The highest classification level is the **merchandise group.** The organization chart shown in Exhibit 12–1 has four merchandise groups: (1) women's apparel; (2) men's, children's, and intimate apparel; (3) cosmetics, shoes, jewelry, and accessories; and (4) home and kitchen. Each of the four merchandise groups is managed by a general merchandise manager (GMM), who is often a senior vice president in the firm. Each of the GMMs is responsible for several departments. For example, the GMM for men's, children's, and intimate apparel makes decisions about how the merchandise inventory is managed in five departments: men's dress apparel, men's sportswear, young men's apparel, children's apparel, and intimate apparel.

The second level in the merchandise classification scheme is the **department.** Departments are managed by divisional merchandise managers (DMMs). For

Illustration of Merchandise Classifications and Organization   **EXHIBIT 12–1**

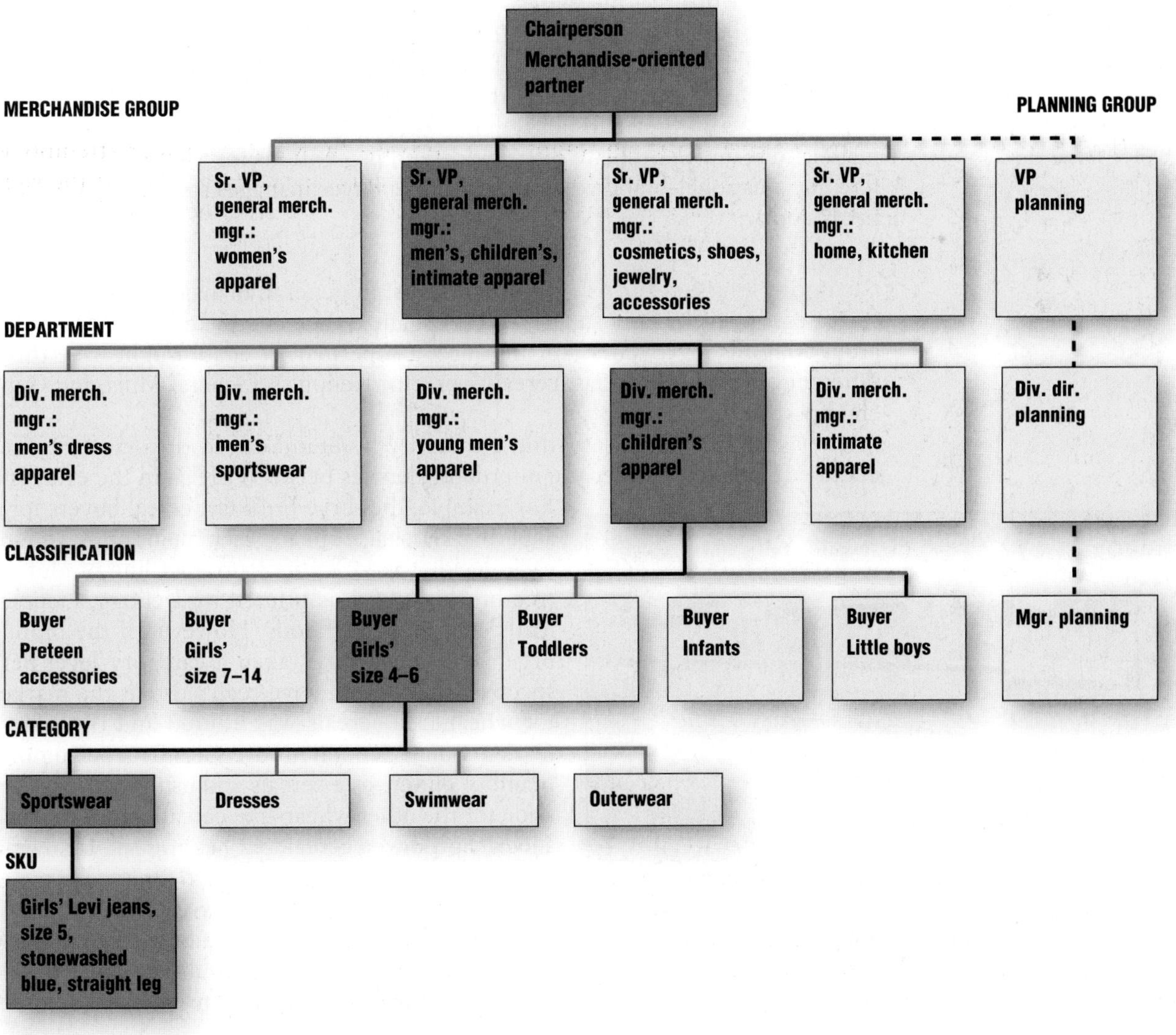

example, the DMM highlighted in Exhibit 12–1 is in charge of children's apparel and manages the buyers responsible for six merchandise departments.

The classification is the third level for categorizing merchandise and organizing merchandise management activities. A **classification** is a group of items targeting the same customer type, such as girls' sizes 4 to 6. Categories are the next lower level in the classification scheme. Each buyer manages several merchandise categories. For example, the girls' sizes 4 to 6 buyer manages the sportswear, dresses, swimwear, and outerwear categories for girls who wear sizes 4 to 6.

A **stock-keeping unit (SKU)** is the smallest unit available for inventory control. In soft-goods merchandise, for instance, an SKU usually means a particular size, color, and style. For example, a pair of size 5, stonewashed, blue, straight-legged Levi jeans is an SKU.

Merchandise Category—The Planning Unit

The merchandise category is the basic unit of analysis for making merchandising management decisions. A **merchandise category** is an assortment of items that customers see as substitutes for one another. For example, a department store might offer a wide variety of girls' dresses sizes 4 to 6 in different colors, styles, and brand names. A mother buying a dress for her daughter might consider the entire set of dresses when making her purchase decision. Lowering the price on one dress may increase the sales of that dress but also decrease the sales of other dresses. Thus, the buyers' decisions about pricing and promoting specific SKUs in the category will affect the sales of other SKUs in the same category.

Some retailers may define categories in terms of brands. For example, Tommy Hilfiger might be one category and Polo/Ralph Lauren another category because the retailer feels that the brands are not substitutes for each other. A "Tommy" customer buys Tommy and not Ralph. Also, it is easier for one buyer to purchase merchandise and coordinate distribution and promotions for the merchandise offered by a national-brand vendor. Typically, a buyer manages several categories of merchandise.

Category Management   While retailers, in general, manage merchandise at the category level, many supermarkets organize their merchandise management around brands or vendors. For instance, a supermarket chain might have three different buyers for breakfast cereals—one for Kellogg's, General Mills, and General Foods.[2]

Managing merchandise within a category by brand can lead to inefficiencies because it fails to consider the interdependencies between SKUs in the category.

The chilled-drinks department consists of a number of different categories each managed by a buyer.

For example, the three breakfast cereal buyers for a supermarket chain, one for each major brand, might each decide to stock a new product line of gluten-free breakfast cereals offered by Kellogg, General Mills, and General Foods. However, if the brand-organized buyers had taken a category-level perspective, they would have realized that the market for wheat-free cereals was limited and the supermarket would generate more sales by stocking one brand of gluten-free cereals and using the space set aside for the other wheat-free cereal brands to stock a locally produced cereal that has a strong following among some customers.

The **category management** approach to managing merchandise assigns one buyer or category manager to oversee all merchandising activities for the entire category. Managing by category can help ensure that the store's assortment includes the "best" combination of sizes and vendors—the one that will get the most profit from the allocated space.[3]

Category Captain Some retailers select a vendor to help them manage a particular category. The vendor, known as the **category captain,** works with the retailer to develop a better understanding of shopping behavior, create assortments that satisfy consumer needs, and improve the profitability of the merchandise category.[4]

Selecting vendors as category captains has its advantages for retailers. It makes merchandise management tasks easier and can increase profits. Vendors are often in a better position to manage a category than are retailers because they have superior information because of their focus on a specific category. In addition, they have acquired insights from managing the category for other retailers.

A potential problem with establishing a vendor as a category captain is that the vendor could take advantage of its position. It is somewhat like "letting the fox into the henhouse." Suppose, for example, that Frito-Lay chose to maximize its own sales, rather than the retailer's sales, in managing the salty snack category. It could suggest an assortment plan that included most of its SKUs and exclude SKUs that are more profitable to the retailer, such as high-margin, private-label SKUs. Thus retailers are becoming increasingly reluctant to turn over these important decisions to their vendors. They have found that working with their vendors and carefully evaluating their suggestions is a much more prudent approach.[6] There are also antitrust considerations. The vendor category captain could collude with the retailer to fix prices. It could also block other brands, particularly smaller ones, from access to shelf space.[7]

REFACT

Red Bull (energy drinks), Hershey (confectionary), Frito-Lay (salty snacks/cookies/crackers), and Pepsi-Cola (soft drinks) are considered the best category captains in convenience stores.[5]

Evaluating Merchandise Management Performance

As we discussed in Chapter 6, a good performance measure for evaluating a retail firm is ROA. Return on assets is composed of two components, asset turnover and net profit margin percentage. But ROA is not a good measure for evaluating the performance of merchandise managers because they do not have control over all of the retailer's assets or all the expenses that the retailer incurs. Merchandise managers have control only over the merchandise they buy (the retailer's merchandise inventory assets), the price at which the merchandise is sold, and the cost of the merchandise. Thus, buyers generally have control over the gross margin but not operating expenses, such as store operations, human resources, real estate, and logistics and information systems.

GMROI A financial ratio that assesses a buyer's contribution to ROA is gross margin return on inventory investment (GMROI, typically pronounced "jim-roy"). It measures how many gross margin dollars are earned on every dollar of inventory investment made by the buyer. GMROI combines gross margin percentage and the sales-to-stock ratio, which is related to inventory turnover.

$$\text{GMROI} = \text{Gross margin percentage} \times \text{Sales-to-stock ratio}$$

$$= \frac{\text{Gross margin}}{\text{Net sales}} \times \frac{\text{Net sales}}{\text{Average inventory at cost}}$$

$$= \frac{\text{Gross margin}}{\text{Average inventory at cost}}$$

The difference between the stock-to-sales ratio and inventory turnover is the numerator of the equation. When you are calculating the sales-to-stock ratio, the numerator is net sales. When you are calculating inventory turnover, the numerator is the cost of goods sold. To convert the sales-to-stock ratio to inventory turnover, simply multiply the sales-to-stock ratio by (1 − gross margin percentage).

EXHIBIT 12–2
Illustration of GMROI

			Fresh Bakery Bread	Gourmet Canned Food
		sales	$1,000,000	200,000
		gross margin	200,000	100,000
		average inventory	100,000	50,000

		Gross Margin / Net Sales	×	Net Sales / Average Inventory	=	Gross Margin / Average Inventory
	GMROI =	$\dfrac{\text{Gross Margin}}{\text{Net Sales}}$	×	$\dfrac{\text{Net Sales}}{\text{Average Inventory}}$	=	$\dfrac{\text{Gross Margin}}{\text{Average Inventory}}$
Fresh Bakery Bread	GMROI =	$\dfrac{200,000}{1,000,000}$	×	$\dfrac{1,000,000}{100,000}$	=	$\dfrac{200,000}{100,000}$
	=	20%	×	10	=	200%
Gourmet Canned Food	GMROI =	$\dfrac{100,000}{200,000}$	×	$\dfrac{200,000}{50,000}$	=	$\dfrac{50,000}{100,000}$
	=	50%	×	4	=	200%

Thus, if the sales-to-stock ratio is 9.0 and the gross margin percentage is .40, the inventory turnover for the category is 5.4:

Inventory turnover = (1 − Gross margin percentage) × Sales-to-stock ratio
5.4 = (1 − .4) × 9.0

Buyers have control over both components of GMROI. The gross margin component is affected by the prices they set and the prices they negotiate with vendors when buying merchandise. The sales-to-stock ratio is affected by the popularity of the merchandise they buy. If they buy merchandise that customers want, it sells quickly and the sales-to-stock ratio is high.

Like the profit and asset management paths to assess ROA paths, there are two paths to achieving high GMROI, margin and turnover. For instance, within a supermarket, some categories (e.g., wine) are high-margin–low-turnover, while other categories (e.g., milk) are low-margin–high-turnover. If the wine category's performance were compared with that of milk using inventory turnover alone, the contribution of wine to the supermarket's performance would be undervalued. In contrast, if only gross margin were used, wine's contribution would be overvalued.

Consider the situation in Exhibit 12–2, in which a supermarket wants to evaluate the performance of two categories: fresh bakery bread and gourmet canned food. If evaluated on gross margin percentage or sales alone, gourmet canned food is certainly the winner, with a 50 percent gross margin and sales of $300,000, compared with fresh bakery bread's gross margin of 1.33 percent and sales of $150,000. Yet gourmet canned food's sales-to-stock ratio is only 4, whereas fresh bakery bread has a sales-to-stock ratio of 150. Using GMROI, both categories achieve a GMROI of 200 percent and so are equal performers from an ROA perspective.

Exhibit 12–3 shows the GMROI percentages for selected departments in discount stores. Jewelry, apparel, and housewares have the highest gross margin percentages. Their sales-to-stock ratios range from 8.75 (food) to 3.24 (jewelry). We might expect food to have the highest sales-to-stock ratio because it is perishable. It is either sold quickly or spoils. However, jewelry has a relatively low sales-to-stock

The bakery in a supermarket typically has a low sales-to-stock ratio but high gross margin.

EXHIBIT 12–3
GMROI for Selected
Departments in Discount
Stores

Department	Gross Margin %	Sales-to-Stock Ratio	GMROI
Apparel	37	6.35	235
Housewares	35	4.63	162
Food	20	8.75	175
Jewelry	38	3.24	123
Furniture	31	4.09	90
Health and beauty supplies	22	5.14	113
Consumer electronics	21	5.05	106

ratio because the jewelry department needs to be stocked with many different items to satisfy customers who want to consider many different items before making a purchase decision. Furniture also has a low sales-to-stock ratio because a relatively large assortment of costly items is needed to support the sales level.

In this case, GMROI ranges from 235 (apparel) to 90 (furniture). Thus, it's not surprising that department stores currently are emphasizing apparel and have de-emphasized furniture. Full-line discount stores continue to carry consumer electronics and health and beauty products—both with low GMROIs—because these categories have traditionally attracted customers into the store. These retailers hope that while customers buying products from these categories are in the store, they will also purchase higher-GMROI items.

Measuring Sales-to-Stock Ratio   Retailers normally express sales-to-stock ratios (and inventory turnover) on an annual basis rather than for part of a year. If the sales-to-stock ratio for a three-month season equals 2.3, the annual sales-to-stock ratio will be four times that number (9.2). Thus, to convert a sales-to-stock ratio based on part of a year to an annual figure, multiply it by the number of such time periods in the year.

The most accurate way to measure average inventory is to measure the inventory level at the end of each day and divide the sum by 365. Most retailers can use their information systems to get accurate average inventory estimates by averaging the inventory in stores and distribution centers at the end of each day. Another method is to take the end-of-month (EOM) inventories for several months and divide by the number of months. For example,

Month	End-of-Month Inventory at Retail Prices
January	$22,000
February	33,000
March	38,000
Total inventory	93,000
Average inventory	31,000

Managing Inventory Turnover

Increasing inventory turnover can increase sales volume, improve sales associates' morale, and provide more resources to take advantage of new buying opportunities. Higher inventory turnover increases sales because new merchandise is continually available to customers. New merchandise attracts customers to visit the store more frequently because they know they will be seeing different merchandise each time they visit the store. When inventory turnover is low, the merchandise begins to look shopworn—slightly damaged from being displayed and handled by customers for a long time. Increasing the amount of new merchandise also improves sales associates' morale. Salespeople are excited about and more

Excessively high inventory turnover causes frequent stockouts.

motivated to sell the new merchandise, and thus sales increase, increasing inventory turnover even further. Finally, when inventory turnover increases, more money is available to buy new merchandise. Having money available to buy merchandise late in a fashion season can open up profit opportunities. For instance, buyers can take advantage of special prices offered by vendors that have too much inventory left over at the end of the season.

One approach for increasing turnover is to reduce the number of SKUs within a category. However, if customers can't find the size or color they seek—or even worse, if they can't find the brand or product line at all—due to the reduced assortment, patronage and sales can decrease. Customers who are disappointed on a regular basis will shop elsewhere and possibly urge their friends to do the same.

Another approach for increasing inventory turnover is to buy merchandise more often and in smaller quantities, as this reduces average inventory without reducing sales. But buying smaller quantities decreases the gross margin because buyers can't take advantage of quantity discounts and transportation economies of scale. Buying merchandise frequently in small quantities can also increase operating expenses, since buyers spend more time placing orders and monitoring deliveries.

Thus, buyers need to strike a balance while determining the level of inventory turnover. Some approaches for improving inventory turnover can lower GMROI by lowering sales volume, increasing the cost of goods sold, and increasing operating expenses.

Merchandise Management Process

Buyers forecast category sales, develop an assortment plan for merchandise in the category, and determine the amount of inventory needed to support the forecasted sales and assortment plan. Then buyers develop a plan outlining the sales expected for each month, the inventory needed to support the sales, and the money that can be spent on replenishing sold merchandise and buying new merchandise. Along with developing the plan, the buyer or planners decide what type and how much merchandise should be allocated to each store. Having developed the plan, the buyer negotiates with vendors and buys the merchandise. Merchandise buying activities are reviewed in Chapter 13.

Finally, buyers continually monitor the sales of merchandise in the category and make adjustments. For example, if category sales are less than the forecast in the plan and the projected GMROI for the category falls below the buyer's goal, the buyer may decide to dispose of some merchandise by putting it on sale and then use the money generated to buy merchandise with greater sales potential or to reduce the number of SKUs in the assortment to increase inventory turnover.

Although Exhibit 12–4 suggests that these decisions follow each other sequentially, in practice, some decisions may be made at the same time or in a different order. For example, a buyer might first decide on the amount of inventory to invest in the category, and this decision might determine the number of SKUs that can be offered in the category.

Types of Merchandise Management Planning Processes   Retailers use two different types of merchandise management planning systems for managing (1) staple and (2) fashion merchandise categories. **Staple merchandise categories,** also called **basic merchandise categories,** are categories that are in continuous demand over an extended time period. While consumer packaged goods companies introduce many line extensions each year, the number of really new

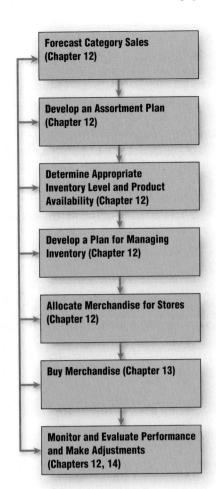

EXHIBIT 12–4
Merchandise Planning
Process

product introductions each year in these categories is limited. Some examples of staple merchandise categories include most categories sold in supermarkets and white paint, copy paper, basic casual apparel such as t-shirts, and men's underwear.

Because sales of staple merchandise are relatively steady from week to week, it is relatively easy to forecast demand, and the consequences of making mistakes in forecasting are not great. For example, if a buyer overestimates the demand for canned soup and buys too much, the retailer will have excess inventory for a short period of time. Eventually the canned soup will be sold without having to resort to discounts or special marketing efforts. Because the demand for staple merchandise is predictable, merchandise planning systems for staple categories often involve **continuous replenishment.** These systems involve continuously monitoring merchandise sales and generating replacement orders, often automatically, when inventory levels drop below predetermined levels.

Fashion merchandise categories are in demand only for a relatively short period of time. New products are continually introduced into these categories, making the existing products obsolete. In some cases, the basic product does not change, but the colors and styles change to reflect what is "hot" that season. Some examples of fashion merchandise categories are athletic shoes, mobile phones, and women's apparel. Retailing View 12.1 describes how Mango creates and manages its fashion merchandise assortments.

Forecasting the sales for fashion merchandise categories is much more challenging than doing so for staple categories. Buyers for fashion merchandise categories have much less flexibility in correcting forecasting errors. For example, if the notebook computer buyer for Best Buy buys too many units of a particular model, the excess inventory cannot be easily sold when a new upgraded model is introduced. Due to the short selling season for fashion merchandise, buyers often do not have a chance to reorder additional merchandise after an initial order is placed. So if buyers initially order too little fashion merchandise, the retailer may not be able to satisfy the demand for the merchandise and will develop a reputation for not having the most popular merchandise in stock. Thus, an important objective of merchandise planning systems for fashion merchandise categories is to be as close to out of stock as possible at the same time that the SKUs become out of fashion.

Seasonal merchandise categories consist of items whose sales fluctuate dramatically depending on the time of year. Some examples of seasonal merchandise are Halloween candy, Christmas ornaments, swimwear, and snow shovels. Both staple and fashion merchandise can be seasonal categories. For example, swimwear

12.1 RETAILING VIEW   Fast Fashion at Mango

"We know how to improvise," says David Egea, Mango's merchandising director and a top executive. "To react and have what people want, we have to break some rules." Mango/MNG Holding SL, with over 1,200 stores in 91 countries, typifies the new retail trend of "fast fashion," pioneered by Spain's Zara, Sweden's H&M, and the United States' Forever 21. These chains fill their racks with a steady stream of new, "gotta-have-it" merchandise. Their retail strategy combines stylistic and technological resources built on flexibility and speed, from design sketch to the store shelf.

Mango is famous for an eclectic mix of body-hugging styles; a black pinstriped jacket sells for $60 and a tight black mini-dress for $40. It maintains tight controls over the design and manufacturing of its private-label merchandise. Last-minute changes, like substituting a fabric or dropping a hemline, are a built-in part of the creative process. As long as the company has fabric in stock, it can move a design from sketchpad to store in four weeks.

Mango's merchandise planning cycle begins every three months when designers meet to discuss important new trends for each of its main collections, which contain five or six mini-collections. So shops receive a near-constant stream of merchandise, ranging from clingy short dresses to work wear and sparkly evening gowns. New items are sent to its stores once a week, roughly six times as often as the case at the typical apparel clothing chain.

To get ideas for each collection, designers attend the traditional fashion shows and trade fairs. But they also stay close to the customer. They take photos of stylish young women and note what people are wearing on the streets and in nightclubs. "To see what everyone's going to do for next season is very easy," says Egea. "But that doesn't mean this is the thing that is going to catch on." Hoping to stay *au courant*, design teams meet each week to adjust to ever-changing trends. Mango commissioned Penelope Cruz and her sister Monica to design a

25-piece collection to compete with the other fast-fashion companies that have used celebrities as designers.

Each of Mango's stores is also described by a set of traits such as trendy, dressy, or suitable for

Mango carefully plans and manages its inventory to provide new fashion apparel to stores frequently and consistently.

hot weather. When collection designs are set, Mango's product management and distribution team assigns them traits and then a proprietary computer program matches the new product's traits with compatible stores.

Mango stores display only a limited merchandise assortment. On each rack, only one size per item is hung. This policy encourages a sense of urgency by playing on customers' worst fear: Maybe your size is going to run out.

Sources: www.mangoshop.com (accessed April 15, 2010); Vertica Bhardwaj and Ann Fairhurst, "Fast Fashion: Response to Changes in the Fashion Industry," *International Review of Retail, Distribution and Consumer Research* 20 (February 2010), pp. 165–173; Joao Pedro Almeida Couto and Maria Teresa Borges Tiago, "The Internationalization Process of Fashion Retailers," *Business Review* 13 (Summer 2009), pp. 278–287.

is a fashion merchandise category; whereas snow shovels are a staple merchandise category. Thus seasonal merchandise has characteristics of both fashion and staple merchandise.

However, from a merchandise planning perspective, retailers buy seasonal merchandise in much the same way that they buy fashion merchandise. Retailers could store unsold snow shovels at the end of the winter season and sell them the next winter, but it is typically more profitable to sell the shovels at a steep discount near the end of the season rather than incur the cost of carrying this excess inventory until the beginning of the next season. Thus, plans for seasonal merchandise, like fashion merchandise, zero out merchandise at the end of the season.

These two different merchandise planning systems affect the nature of the approaches used to forecast and manage inventory. In the following section, each of the steps in the merchandise management process described in Exhibit 12–4 is examined.

FORECASTING SALES

As indicated in Exhibit 12–4, the first step in merchandise management planning is to develop a forecast for category sales. The methods and information used for forecasting staple and fashion merchandise categories are discussed in this section.

Forecasting Staple Merchandise

Use of Historical Sales   The sales of staple merchandise are relatively constant from year to year. Thus, forecasts are typically based on extrapolating historical sales. Because there are substantial sales data available, sophisticated statistical techniques can be used to forecast future sales for each SKU. However, these statistical forecasts are based on the assumption that the factors affecting item sales in the past will be the same and have the same effect in the future. Thus, even though sales for staple merchandise categories are relatively predictable, controllable and uncontrollable factors can have a significant impact on them.

Adjustments for Controllable Factors   Controllable factors include openings and closings of stores, the price set for the merchandise in the category, special promotions for the category, the pricing and promotion of complementary categories, and the placement of the merchandise categories in the stores. Some factors beyond the retailer's control are the weather, general economic conditions, special promotions or new product introductions by vendors, the availability of products, pricing, and promotional activities by competitors. Thus, buyers need to adjust the forecast on the basis of statistical projections to reflect the effects of these controllable and uncontrollable factors. Retailing View 12.2 illustrates how retailers use long-range weather forecasts to improve their forecasts.

Forecasting Fashion Merchandise Categories

Forecasting sales for fashion merchandise is challenging because buyers typically need to place orders and commit to buying specific quantities between three and six months before the merchandise will be delivered and made available for sales. In addition, for fashion items, there often is no opportunity to increase or decrease the quantity ordered before the selling season has ended. Suppliers of popular merchandise usually have orders for more merchandise than they can produce and excess inventory of unpopular items. Finally, forecasting fashion merchandise sales is particularly difficult because some or all of the items in the category are new and different from units offered in previous seasons or years. Some sources of information that retailers use to develop forecasts for fashion merchandise categories

REFACT

The "Lipstick Index," a term coined after an observation made by Estée Lauder chairman Leonard Lauder, suggests that lipstick sales increase as perceptions of economic conditions decline.[8]

are (1) previous sales data, (2) market research, (3) fashion and trend services, and (4) vendors.

Previous Sales Data   Although items in fashion merchandise categories might be new each season, many items in a fashion category are often similar to items sold in previous years. Thus, accurate forecasts might be generated by simply projecting past sales data. For example, football video games might change from season to season with new games and editions, but while the SKUs are different each season, the total number of football video games sold each year might be relatively constant and predictable.

Market Research   Buyers for fashion merchandise categories undertake a variety of market research activities to help them forecast sales. These activities range from informal, qualitative research about trends affecting the category to more formal experiments and surveys.

To find out what customers are going to want in the future, buyers immerse themselves in their customers' world. For example, buyers look for information about trends by going to Internet chat rooms and blogs, attending soccer games and rock concerts, and visiting hot spots around town like restaurants and nightclubs to see what people are talking about and wearing. Buyers are information junkies and read voraciously. What movies are hits at the box office, and what are the stars wearing? Who is going to see them? What books and albums are on the top-10 lists? What magazines are consumers purchasing? Are there themes that keep popping up?

12.2   RETAILING VIEW   Weather's Effect on Retail Sales

Retailers know that when hurricane season comes, they need to be ready with bottled water, batteries, flashlights, plywood, and generators. However, more subtle weather conditions, like a warmer-than-normal holiday season, can have a significant impact on retail sales.

To incorporate these weather effects in their forecasts, many retailers subscribe to long-range weather forecasting services. Merchandise managers use the information provided by these services to make decisions about the timing of merchandise deliveries, promotions, and price discounts. For example, if warmer weather is forecast this year than last for the preholiday season, full-line general merchandise retailers will plan to sell more electronics than winter apparel. Supermarkets that stock meat and other barbecue items in anticipation of sunshine are often left with unsold food if the weather is rainy and cold instead.

REFACT

A temperature increase of 18 degrees generally triples sales of barbecue meat and increases demand for lettuce by 50 percent.[9]

Sources: Julia Werdiger, "Tesco, British Grocer, Uses Weather to Predict Sales," *New York Times*, September 2, 2009; "Forecasting Retail Successes: Walmart Turns to Weather Info to Plan Inventory," *DSN Retailing Today*, October 2006, pp. 13–14; Pia Sarkar, "Retailers Use Weather to Forecast Their Sales," *San Francisco Chronicle*, December 4, 2006.

The first cold snap in the fall stimulates the sale of winter apparel.

Social media sites are important sources of information for buyers. Buyers learn a lot about their customers' likes, dislikes, and preferences by monitoring their past purchases and by monitoring their interactions with social network sites such as Facebook. Customers appear keen to submit their opinions about their friends' purchases, interests, polls, and blogs.

Retailers also use traditional forms of marketing research such as depth interviews and focus groups. The **depth interview** is an unstructured personal interview in which the interviewer uses extensive probing to get individual respondents to talk in detail about a subject. For example, one grocery store chain goes through the personal checks received each day to identify customers to interview. Representatives from the supermarket chain call these customers and interview them to find out what they like and don't like about the merchandise in the store.

Youths in Japan have become the world's trendsetters for new fashions.

A more informal method of interviewing customers is to require that buyers spend some time on the selling floor waiting on customers. Buying offices for Target and The Gap are in Minnesota and northern California, respectively, yet their stores are located throughout the United States. It has become increasingly hard for buyers in large chains to be attuned to local customer demand. Frequent store visits help resolve the situation. Some retailers require that their buyers spend a specified period of time, like one day a week, in a store.

A **focus group** is a small group of respondents interviewed by a moderator using a loosely structured format. Participants are encouraged to express their views and comment on the views of others in the group. To keep abreast of the teen market, for instance, some stores have teen boards consisting of opinion leaders who meet to discuss merchandising and other store issues. Abercrombie & Fitch brings in groups of teenagers and has them rate and trade off their preferences for different items.

Asda, a full-line U.K. supercenter owned by Walmart, regularly surveys its customers to forecast the sales of new products. It e-mails a group of 18,000 customers, which it has termed its "Pulse of the Nation" group, images and descriptions of new products. The Pulse group is asked to respond, positively or negatively, and indicate whether or not they think the new products should be carried in the stores.[10]

Finally, many retailers have a program for conducting merchandise experiments. For example, Claire's, an international specialty accessory retail chain targeting teens, continually runs experiments to determine whether new merchandise concepts will produce adequate sales. It introduces the new merchandise into a representative sample of stores and sees what sales are generated for the items. Multichannel retailers often run similar experiments by offering new items on their Web sites before making a decision to stock them in their stores

Fashion and Trend Services   There are many services that buyers, particularly buyers of apparel categories, can subscribe to that forecast the latest fashions, colors, and styles. For example, Doneger Creative Services offers a range of services related to trend and color forecasting and analysis for apparel, accessories, and lifestyle markets in the women's, men's, and youth merchandise categories through its print publications, online content, and live presentations. Its color forecast service provides color direction for each season using dyed-to-specification color standards plus suggested color combinations and applications for specific categories. Its online clipboard reports present actionable information and style news from the runways to the streets.

Vendors   Vendors have proprietary information about their marketing plans, such as new product launches and special promotions that can have a significant impact on retail sales for their products and the entire merchandise category. In addition, vendors tend to be very knowledgeable about market trends for merchandise categories because they typically specialize in fewer merchandise categories than do retailers. Thus, information from vendors about their plans and market research about merchandise categories is very useful to buyers as they develop category sales forecasts.

Sales Forecasting for Service Retailers

Due to the perishable nature of services, service retailers face an even more extreme problem than fashion retailers. Their offering perishes at the end of the day, not at the end of the season. If there are empty seats when a plane takes off or a rock concert ends, the revenue that might have been generated from these seats is lost forever. However, if more people are interested in dining at a restaurant than there are tables available, a revenue opportunity also is lost. So service retailers have devised approaches for managing demand for their offering so that it meets but does not exceed capacity.

Some service retailers attempt to match supply and demand by taking reservations or making appointments. Physicians often overbook their appointments, so many patients have to wait. They do this so that they will always fill their capacity and not have unproductive, non-revenue-generating time. Restaurants take reservations so that customers will not have to wait for a table. In addition, the reservations indicate the staffing levels needed for the meal. Another approach is selling advance tickets for a service.[11]

DEVELOPING AN ASSORTMENT PLAN

After forecasting sales for the category, the next step in the merchandise management planning process is to develop an assortment plan (see Exhibit 12-4). An **assortment plan** is the set of SKUs that a retailer will offer in a merchandise category in each of its stores. The assortment plan thus reflects the breadth and depth of merchandise that the retailer plans to offer in a merchandise category.

Category Variety and Assortment

In Section II, we discussed variety and assortment as an aspect of a retailer's strategy. **Variety,** or breadth, of a retailer's merchandise is the number of different merchandising categories offered, and the **assortment,** or depth, of merchandise is the number of SKUs within a category. In the context of merchandise planning, the concepts of variety and assortment are applied to a merchandise category rather than a retail firm or store. At the category level, variety reflects the number of different types of merchandise, and assortment is the number of SKUs per type. For example, the assortment plan for girls' jeans in Exhibit 12–5 includes 10 types or varieties (traditional or boot cut, regular denim or stonewashed, and three price points reflecting different brands). For each type, there are 81 SKUs (3 colors × 9 sizes × 3 lengths). Thus, this retailer plans to offer 810 SKUs in girls' jeans.

Assortment Plan for Girls' Jeans   **EXHIBIT 12–5**

Styles	Traditional	Traditional	Traditional	Traditional	Traditional	Traditional
Price levels	$20	$20	$35	$35	$45	$45
Fabric composition	Regular denim	Stonewashed	Regular denim	Stonewashed	Regular denim	Stonewashed
Colors	Light blue	Light blue	Light blue	Light blue	Light blue	Light blue
	Indigo	Indigo	Indigo	Indigo	Indigo	Indigo
	Black	Black	Black	Black	Black	Black

Styles	Boot-Cut	Boot-Cut	Boot-Cut	Boot-Cut
Price levels	$25	$25	$45	$45
Fabric composition	Regular denim	Stonewashed	Regular denim	Stonewashed
Colors	Light blue	Light blue	Light blue	Light blue
	Indigo	Indigo	Indigo	Indigo
	Black	Black	Black	Black

Determining Variety and Assortment

The process of determining the variety and assortment for a category is called **editing the assortment.** When editing the assortment for a category like jeans, the buyer considers the following factors: the firm's retail strategy, the effect of assortments on GMROI, the complementarities between categories, the effects of assortments on buying behavior, and the physical characteristics of the store.

Retail Strategy   The number of SKUs offered in a merchandise category is a strategic decision. For example, Costco focuses on customers who are looking for a few SKUs in a category. In contrast, Best Buy focuses on consumers interested in comparing many alternatives in specific consumer electronic categories and thus offers more SKUs in each category.

The breadth and depth of the assortment in a merchandise category can affect the retailer's brand image.[14] Retailers might increase the assortment in categories that are closely associated with their image. For example, Costco typically has few SKUs per category, but it has a broad and deep assortment of wines because its offering in this category reinforces its image of offering quality products with good value.

Assortments and GMROI   In developing the assortment plan, buyers need to be sensitive to the trade-off of increasing sales by offering greater breadth and depth but, at the same time potentially reducing inventory turnover and GMROI because of the increased inventory investment. Increasing assortment breadth and depth also can decrease gross margin. For example, the more SKUs offered, the greater the chance of **breaking sizes**—that is, stocking out of a specific size or color SKU. If a stockout occurs for a popular SKU in a fashion merchandise category and the buyer cannot reorder during the season, the buyer will typically discount the entire merchandise type, thus reducing gross margin. The buyer's objective is to remove the merchandise type from the assortment altogether so that customers will not be disappointed when they don't find the size and color they want.

Complementary Merchandise   When buyers develop assortment plans, they need to consider the degree to which categories in a department complement each other.[15] For instance, DVD players may have a low GMROI, suggesting that the buyer carry a limited assortment. But customers who buy a DVD player might also buy complementary products and services such as accessories, cables, and

REFACT

Supermarkets typically stock 30,000 to 40,000 SKUs in a store, with less than 5 percent accounting for more than half the store's sales. However, the typical household buys only about 400 SKUs in an entire year. Month after month, customers buy the same items.[13]

warranties that have a high GMROI. Thus, the buyer may decide to carry more DVD-player SKUs to increase the more profitable accessory sales.

Effects of Assortment Size on Buying Behavior   Offering large assortments provides a number of benefits to customer. First, increasing the number of SKUs that customers can consider increases the chance they will find the product that best satisfies their needs. Second, large assortments are valued by customers because they provide a more informative and stimulating shopping experience due to the complexity associated with numerous products and the novelty associated with unique items. Third, large assortments are particularly appealing to customers who seek variety—those who want to try new things.

However, offering a large assortment can make the purchase decision more complex and time-consuming.[16] Research has shown that customers actually buy more if there are modest reductions of redundant items in assortments, such as reductions in the number of different ketchup bottle sizes or low-share brands carried by a supermarket.[17]

Walmart, like many retailers, has initiated an SKU rationalization program—a program that increases inventory turnover by reducing the number of SKUs. The initiative was spurred by an industry study showing that shoppers thought Target had a larger assortment than Walmart. However, Walmart found just the opposite during its comparative shopping studies. Walmart thinks that the shoppers' perceptions of Target's assortment were influenced by Target's merchandise presentation rather than the number of SKUs it carries. So Walmart clarified its offering so that categories weren't diluted and fuzzy. Even with SKUs cut by 10 to 50 percent, Walmart has been able to achieve higher sales.[18] Other factors affecting how customers perceive assortments are discussed in Chapter 17.

Physical Characteristics of the Store   Buyers need to consider how much space to devote to a category. More space is needed to display categories with large assortments. In addition, a lot of space is needed to display individual items in some categories, and this limits the number of SKUs that can be offered in stores. For example, furniture takes up a lot of space, and thus furniture retailers typically display one model of a chair or sofa and then have photographs and cloth swatches or a virtual room on a computer to show how the furniture would look with different upholstery.

Multichannel retailers address the space limitations in stores by offering a greater assortment through their Internet and catalog channels than they do in stores. For example, Staples offers more types of laptop computers and printers on its Internet site than it stocks in its stores. If customers do not find the computer or printer they want in the store, sales associates direct them to the company's Internet site and can even order the merchandise for them from a POS terminal.

SETTING INVENTORY AND PRODUCT AVAILABILITY LEVELS

After developing the assortment plan, the third step in the merchandise planning process is to determine the model stock plan for the category.

Model Stock Plan

The **model stock plan,** illustrated in Exhibit 12–6, is the number of each SKU in the assortment plan that the buyer wants to have available for purchase in each store. For example, the model stock plan in Exhibit 12–6 includes nine units of size 1, short, which represent 2 percent of the 429 total units for girls' traditional $20 denim jeans in light blue. Note that there are more units for more popular sizes.

EXHIBIT 12–6
Model Stock Plans

LENGTH		SIZE								
		1	2	4	5	6	8	10	12	14
Short	%	2	4	7	6	8	5	7	4	2
	units	9	17	30	26	34	21	30	17	9
Medium	%	2	4	7	6	8	5	7	4	2
	units	9	17	30	26	34	21	30	17	9
Long	%	0	2	2	2	3	2	2	1	0
	units	0	9	9	9	12	9	9	4	0
Total 100% 429 units										

Retailers typically have model stock plans for the different store sizes in a chain. For example, retailers typically classify their stores as A, B, and C stores on the basis of their sales volume. The basic assortment in a category is stocked in C stores. For the larger stores, because more space is available, the number of SKUs increases. The larger A and B stores may have more brands, colors, styles, and sizes.

Product Availability

The number of units of **backup stock,** also called **buffer** or **safety stock,** in the model stock plan determines product availability. **Product availability** is defined as the percentage of the demand for a particular SKU that is satisfied. For instance, if 100 people go into a PetSmart store to purchase a small, Great Choice, portable kennel but only 90 people can make the purchase before the kennel stock is depleted, the product availability for that SKU is 90 percent. Product availability is also referred to as the **level of support** or **service level.**

The model stock plan needs more backup stock if the retailer wants to increase product availability, that is, increase the probability that customers will find the product they want when they visit the retailer's store. Choosing an appropriate amount of backup stock is critical to successful assortment planning. If the backup stock is too low, the retailer will lose sales and possibly customers too when they find that the products they want are not available from the retailer. If the level is too high, scarce financial resources will be wasted on needless inventory rather than being more profitably invested in increasing variety or assortment.

Exhibit 12–7 shows the trade-off between inventory investment and product availability. Although the actual inventory investment varies in different situations, the general relationship shows that extremely high level of product availability results in a prohibitively high inventory investment.

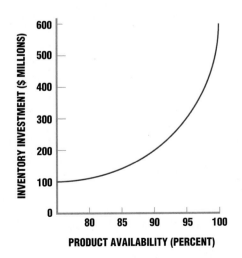

EXHIBIT 12–7
Inventory Investment and
Product Availability

Several factors need to be considered to determine the appropriate level of backup stock and thus the product availability for each SKU. Retailers often classify merchandise categories or individual SKUs as A, B, or C items, reflecting the product availability the retailer wants to offer. The A items are best-sellers bought by many customers. For example, white paint is an A item for Sherwin Williams, and copy paper is an A item for Office Depot. A retailer rarely wants to risk A-item stockouts because running out of these very popular SKUs would diminish the retailer's image and customer loyalty. On the other hand, lower product availability is acceptable for C items, which are purchased by a small number of customers and are not readily available from other retailers. Some other factors considered in determining backup stock levels and product availability are the fluctuations in demand, the lead time for delivery from the vendor, the fluctuations in vendor lead time, and the frequency of store deliveries. These factors are discussed in the next section.

The trade-off among variety, assortment, and product availability is a crucial issue in determining a retailer's merchandising strategy. Buyers have a limited budget for the inventory investments they can make in a category. Thus, they are forced to sacrifice breadth of merchandise if they opt to increase depth, or they must reduce both depth and breadth to increase product availability.

ESTABLISHING A CONTROL SYSTEM FOR MANAGING INVENTORY

The first three steps in the merchandise planning process—forecasting SKU and category sales, determining the assortment plan, and establishing the model stock plan (see Exhibit 12–4)—quantify the buyer's sales expectations and service level. The fourth step in the merchandise management process is to establish a control system for how the orders, deliveries, inventory levels, and merchandise sales will evolve over time. The objective of this control system is to manage the flow of merchandise into the stores so that the amount of inventory in a category is minimized but the merchandise will still be available when customers want to buy it. The differences between the control systems for staple and fashion merchandise are discussed in the following sections.

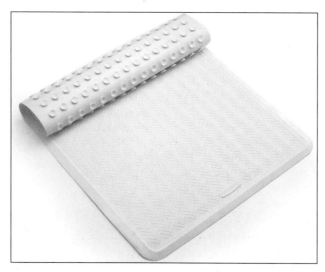

Staple merchandise management systems are used for items like this rubber bath mat.

Control System for Managing Inventory of Staple Merchandise

SKUs in a staple merchandise category are sold month after month, year after year. Lowe's sales of purple paint this month will be about the same as they were during the same month a year ago. If the sales of purple paint are below forecast this month, the excess inventory of purple paint can be sold during the following month. Thus an automated continuous replenishment control system is used to manage the flow of staple merchandise SKUs and categories. The continuous replenishment system monitors the inventory level of each SKU in a store and automatically triggers a reorder of an SKU when the inventory falls below a predetermined level.

Flow of Staple Merchandise   Exhibit 12–8 illustrates the merchandise flow in a staple merchandise management system. At the beginning of week 1, the retailer

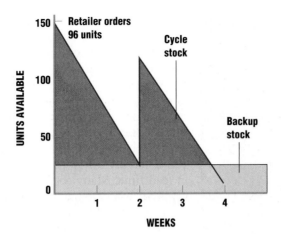

EXHIBIT 12–8
Merchandise Flow of a
Staple SKU

had 150 units of the SKU in inventory and the buyer or merchandise planner placed an order for 96 additional units. During the next two weeks, customers purchased 130 units, and the inventory level decreased to 20 units. At the end of week 2, the 96-unit order from the vendor arrived, and the inventory level jumped up to 116 units. The continuous replenishment system placed another order with the vendor that will arrive in two weeks, before customer sales decrease the inventory level to zero and the retailer stocks out.

Inventory for which the level goes up and down due to the replenishment process is called **cycle stock** or **base stock.** The retailer hopes to reduce the cycle-stock inventory to keep its inventory investment low. One approach for reducing the cycle stock is to reorder smaller quantities more frequently. But more frequent, smaller orders and shipments increase administrative and transportation costs.

Because sales of the SKU and receipts of orders from the vendor cannot be predicted with perfect accuracy, the retailer has to carry backup stock, as a cushion, so that it doesn't stock out before the next order arrives. Backup stock is shown in yellow in Exhibit 12–8. **Backup stock** is the level of inventory needed to ensure merchandise is available in light of these uncertainties.

Determining the Level of Backup Stock   Several factors determine the level of backup stock needed for a SKU. First, the level depends on the product availability the retailer wants to provide. As discussed previously, more backup stock is needed when the retailer wants to reduce the chances of a stockout and increase the availability of the SKU. Thus, if Lowe's views white paint as an A item and rarely wants to stock out of it, a higher level of backup stock is needed. However, if melon paint is a C item and 75 percent product availability is acceptable, the level of backup stock can be lowered.

Second, the greater the fluctuation in demand, the more backup stock is needed. Suppose a Lowe's store sells an average of 30 gallons of purple paint in two weeks. Yet in some weeks sales are 50 gallons, and in other weeks they are only 10 gallons. When sales are less than average, the store ends up carrying a little more merchandise than it needs. But when sales are much more than average, there must be more backup stock to ensure that the store does not stock out. Note in Exhibit 12–8 that during week 4, sales were greater than average, so the retailer had to dip into its backup stock to avoid a stockout.

Third, the amount of backup stock needed is affected by the lead time from the vendor. **Lead time** is the amount of time between the recognition that an order needs to be placed and the point at which the merchandise arrives in the store and is ready for sale. If it took two months to receive a shipment of purple paint, the possibility of running out of stock is greater than it would be if the lead time was only two weeks. The shorter lead times inherent in collaborative supply chain management systems like CPFR (described in Chapter 10) result in

When planning the amount of inventory to order for a staple merchandise category, such as paint, Lowe's buyers must consider current inventory, customer demand, lead time for replenishment, and backup stock needed to avoid stockouts in the department.

a lower level of backup stock required to maintain the same level of product availability.

Fourth, fluctuations in lead time also affect the amount of backup stock needed. If Lowe's knows that the lead time for purple paint is always two weeks, plus or minus one day, it can more accurately plan its inventory levels. But if the lead time is one day on one shipment and then ten days on the next shipment, the stores must carry additional backup stock to cover this uncertainty in lead time. Many retailers using collaborative supply chain management systems require that their vendors deliver merchandise within a very narrow window—sometimes two or three hours—to reduce the fluctuations in lead time and thus the amount of required backup stock.

Fifth, the vendor's fill rate also affects the retailer's backup stock requirements. For example, Lowe's can more easily plan its inventory requirements if the vendor normally ships every item that is ordered. If, however, the vendor ships only 75 percent of the ordered items, Lowe's must maintain more backup stock to be certain that the paint availability for its customers isn't adversely affected. The percentage of complete orders received from a vendor is called the **fill rate.**

Automated Continuous Replenishment   Once the buyer sets the desired product availability and determines the variation in demand and the vendor's lead time and fill rate, the continuous replenishment systems for staple SKUs can operate automatically. The retailer's information system determines the inventory level at each point in time, the **perpetual inventory,** by comparing the sales made through the POS terminals with the shipments received by the store. When the perpetual inventory level falls below the predetermined level, the system sends an EDI reorder to the retailer's distribution center and the vendor. When the reordered merchandise arrives at the store, the level of inventory is adjusted up.

However, it is difficult to achieve fully automated continuous replenishment of staple merchandise because of errors in determining the actual inventory. For example, the retailer's information system might indicate that 10 Gillette Fusion razors are in the store when, in fact, 10 razors were stolen by a shoplifter and there are actually zero razors in the store. Since there are no razors in the store, there are no sales and the automated continuous replenishment system will never reorder razors for the store. Such inaccuracies also can arise when an incorrect number of units is inputted into the information system about a shipment from the distribution center to the store. To address these problems, store employees need to periodically check the inventory recorded in the system with the actual inventory in the store.

Inventory Management Report   The inventory management report provides information about the inventory management for a staple category. The report indicates the decision variables set by the buyer, such as product availability, the backup stock needed to provide the product availability, the order points and quantities plus performance measures such as planned and actual inventory turnover, the current sales rate or velocity, sales forecasts, inventory availability, and the amount on order. Exhibit 12–9 is an inventory management report for Rubbermaid bath mats.

The first five columns of Exhibit 12–9 contain the descriptions of each item, how many items are on hand and on order, and sales for the past 4 and 12 weeks. The first-row SKU is a Rubbermaid bath mat in avocado green. There are 30 units

	Quantity On Hand	Quantity On Order	Sales Last 4 Wks	Sales Last 12 Wks	Forecast Next 4 Wks	Forecast Next 8 Wks	Product Availability	Backup Stock	Turnover Planned	Turnover Actual	Order Point	Order Quantity
RM- Bath												
RM Bath Mat - Avocado	30	60	72	215	152	229	99	18	12	11	132	42
RM Bath Mat - Blue	36	36	56	130	115	173	95	12	9	10	98	26
RM Bath Mat - Gold	41	72	117	325	243	355	99	35	12	13	217	104
RM Bath Mat - Pink	10	12	15	41	13	25	90	3	7	7	13	0

on hand and 60 on order. Thus, the quantity available of this SKU is 90. Sales for the past 4 and 12 weeks were 72 and 215 units, respectively.

Sales forecasts for the next 4 and 8 weeks are determined by the system using a statistical model that considers the trends in past sales and the seasonal pattern for the SKU. However, in this case, the buyer made an adjustment in the forecast for the next 4 weeks to reflect an upcoming special promotion on avocado, blue, and gold bath mats.

The product availability is a decision variable input by the buyer. For the avocado bath mat SKU, the buyer wants 99 out of every 100 customers to find it in stock. But the buyer is less concerned about stocking out of pink bath mats and thus sets its product availability at 90 percent. The system then calculates the necessary backup stock for the avocado bath mat based on a predetermined formula—18 units. This number is determined by the system on the basis of the specified product availability, the variability in demand, the vendor delivery lead time, and the variability in the lead time.

The planned inventory turnover for the SKU, 12 times, is a decision variable also set by the buyer on the basis of the retailer's overall financial goals; it drives the inventory management system. For this SKU, the system determined that the actual turnover, based on the cost of goods sold and average inventory, is 11.

Order Point   The **order point** is the amount of inventory below which the quantity available shouldn't go or the item will be out of stock before the next order arrives. This number tells the buyer that when the inventory level drops to this point, additional merchandise should be ordered. For this SKU, the buyer needs to place an order if the quantity in inventory falls to 132 or fewer units to produce the desired product availability.

Order Quantity   When inventory reaches the order point, the buyer, or system, needs to order enough units to ensure product availability before the next order arrives. Using the avocado bath mats in Exhibit 12–9 as an example, the order quantity is 42 units.

Control System for Managing Inventory of Fashion Merchandise

The control system for a fashion merchandise category is called a merchandise budget plan. The **merchandise budget plan** specifies the planned inventory investment in dollars in a fashion merchandise category on the basis of how much merchandise will be ordered, delivered, and sold each month during the selling season. It is a financial plan that specifies how many dollars will be spent each month to support sales and achieve the desired GMROI objectives. The merchandise budget plan also considers the effects on GMROI from the active intervention of the buyer to make adjustments if the actual sales differ from planned sales.

EXHIBIT 12–10   Six-Month Merchandise Budget Plan for Men's Casual Slacks

	Spring	April	May	June	July	August	September
1. Sales % Distribution to Season	100.00%	21.00%	12.00%	12.00%	19.00%	21.00%	15.00%
2. Monthly Sales	$130,000	$27,300	$15,600	$15,600	$24,700	$27,300	$19,500
3. Reduc % Distribution to Season	100.00%	40.00%	14.00%	16.00%	12.00%	10.00%	8.00%
4. Monthly Reductions	$16,500	$6,600	$2,310	$2,640	$1,980	$1,650	$1,320
5. BOM Stock to Sales Ratio	4.00	3.60	4.40	4.40	4.00	3.60	4.00
6. BOM Inventory	$98,280	$98,280	$68,640	$68,640	$98,800	$98,280	$78,000
7. EOM Inventory	$65,600	$68,640	$68,640	$98,800	$98,280	$78,000	$65,600
8. Monthly Additions to Stock	$113,820	$4,260	$17,910	$48,400	$26,160	$8,670	$8,420

Merchandise Budget Plan   Exhibit 12–10 shows a six-month merchandise budget plan for men's casual slacks at a national specialty store chain. The merchandise budget plan determines how much merchandise in dollars should be delivered in each month to achieve the GMROI goal for the period. The amount of merchandise that needs to be delivered during each month is based on the sales forecast, the planned discounts to employees and customers, and the level of inventory needed to support the sales. Appendix 12A describes in detail how the plan is developed. Most retailers use commercially available software packages to develop merchandise budget plans.

Evaluating the Merchandise Budget Plan   Inventory turnover, GMROI, and the sales forecast are used for both planning and control. Buyers negotiate GMROI, inventory turnover, and sales forecast goals with their superiors, the GMMs and DMMs. Then merchandise budgets are developed to meet these goals. Well before the season, buyers purchase the amount of merchandise specified in the last line of the merchandise budget plan to be delivered in those specific months—the monthly additions to stock.

After the selling season, the buyer must determine how the category actually performed compared with the plan. If the actual GMROI, turnover, and forecast are greater than those in the plan, performance is better than expected. However, performance evaluations should not be based solely on any one of these measures. Several additional questions should be answered to evaluate the buyer's performance: Why did the performance exceed or fall short of the plan? Was the deviation from the plan due to something under the buyer's control? (For instance, was too much merchandise purchased?) Did the buyer react quickly to changes in demand by either purchasing more or having a sale? Was the deviation instead due to some external factor, such as a change in competitive level or economic activity? Every attempt should be made to discover answers to these questions. Later in this chapter, several additional tools used to evaluate merchandise performance will be examined.

Open-to-Buy System

After the merchandise is purchased on the basis of the merchandise budget plan, the **open-to-buy** system is used to keep track of the actual merchandise flows— what the present inventory level is, when purchased merchandise is scheduled for delivery, and how much has been sold to customers. In the same way that you must keep track of the checks you write, buyers need to keep track of the merchandise they purchase and when it is to be delivered. Without the open-to-buy system keeping track of merchandise flows, merchandise could be delivered when it isn't needed and be unavailable when it is needed.

The open-to-buy system compares the planned end-of-month inventory to the actual end-of-month inventory. Differences between actual and plan may arise because an order was shipped late or sales deviated from the forecast. When sales are greater than planned, the system determines how much merchandise to buy, in terms of dollars the buyer has available, to satisfy the increased customer demand.

ALLOCATING MERCHANDISE TO STORES

After developing a plan for managing merchandise inventory in a category, the next step in the merchandise management process is to allocate the merchandise purchased and received to the retailer's stores (see Exhibit 12–4). Research indicates that these allocation decisions have a much bigger impact on profitability than does the decision about the quantity of merchandise to purchase.[19] In other words, buying too little or too much merchandise has less impact on a category's profitability than does making mistakes in allocating the right amount and type of merchandise to stores. Allocating merchandise to stores involves three decisions: (1) how much merchandise to allocate to each store, (2) what type of merchandise to allocate, and (3) when to allocate the merchandise to different stores.

Amount of Merchandise Allocated

Retail chains typically classify each of their stores on the basis of annual sales. Thus A stores would have the largest sales volume and typically receive the most inventory, while C stores would have the lowest sales volume and receive the least inventory for a category. In addition to the store's sales level, when making allocation decisions for a category, allocators consider the physical characteristics of the merchandise and the depth of assortment and level of product availability that the firm wants to portray for the specific store.

Type of Merchandise Allocated

The geodemographics of a store's trading area (discussed in Chapter 8) are considered in making allocation decisions. Consider the allocation decision of a national supermarket for its ready-to-eat cereal assortment. Some stores are located in areas dominated by segments called "Rustbelt Retirees," and other areas are dominated by the "Laptops and Lattes" segment, as described in Exhibit 12–11.

The ready-to-eat breakfast cereal planner would offer different assortments for stores in these two areas. Stores with a high proportion of Rustbelt Retirees in

Laptops and Lattes: The most eligible and unencumbered marketplace	Rustbelt Retirees
Laptops and Lattes are affluent, single, and still renting. They are educated, professional, and partial to city life, favoring major metropolitan areas such as New York, Boston, Chicago, Los Angeles, and San Francisco. Median household income is more than $87,000; median age is 38 years. Technologically savvy, the Laptops and Lattes segment is the top market for notebook PCs and PDAs. They use the Internet on a daily basis to trade stocks and make purchases and travel plans. They are health conscious and physically fit; they take vitamins, use organic products, and exercise in the gym. They embrace liberal philosophies and work for environmental causes.	Rustbelt Retirees can be found in older, industrial cities in the Northeast and Midwest, especially in Pennsylvania and other states surrounding the Great Lakes. Households are mainly occupied by married couples with no children and singles who live alone. The median age is 43.8 years. Although many residents are still working, labor force participation is below average. More than 40 percent of the households receive Social Security benefits. Most residents live in owned, single-family homes, with a median value of $118,500. Unlike many retirees, these residents are not inclined to move. They are proud of their homes and gardens and participate in community activities. Some are members of veterans' clubs. Leisure activities include playing bingo, gambling in Atlantic City, going to the horse races, working crossword puzzles, and playing golf.

EXHIBIT 12–11

Example of Different Geodemographic Segments

EXHIBIT 12–12

Apparel Size Differences for Store X and the Chain Average

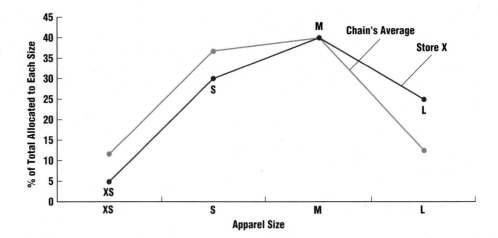

their trading areas would get an assortment of lower-price, well-known brands and more private-label cereals. Stores in areas dominated by the Laptops and Lattes geodemographic segment would get an assortment with higher-price brands that feature low sugar, organic ingredients, and whole wheat. Private-label cereals would be de-emphasized.

Even the sales of different apparel sizes can vary dramatically from store to store in the same chain. Exhibit 12–12 illustrates this point. Notice that store X sells significantly more large sizes and fewer small sizes than is average for the chain. If the planner allocated the same size distribution of merchandise to all stores in the chain, store X would stock out of large sizes, have an oversupply of small sizes, and be out of some sizes sooner than other stores in the chain. Retailing View 12.3 provides a glimpse of how Saks Fifth Avenue allocates merchandise to stores on the basis of customer characteristics.

12.3   RETAILING VIEW   Customer-Centric Merchandise Allocation at Saks Fifth Avenue

Having the right merchandise in the right stores is the key to merchandising success for fashion retailers like Saks Fifth Avenue. For instance, Saks considers its core shopper at its New York flagship store in Manhattan to be a woman, between 46 and 57 years of age, with a largely "classic" style, especially when it comes to work clothes, and a taste for slightly more modern looks when she goes out with friends on weekends. But it also recognizes that the merchandise selections for stores located elsewhere need to be less New York–centric. Even stores close to New York City attract different types of shoppers. A Greenwich, Connecticut, Saks caters to a slightly older shopper than does the Saks in Stamford, Connecticut, about 5 miles away. Stamford shoppers tend to be women who work in town, whereas Greenwich attracts a higher proportion of women who are at home full-time. Shoppers on the Saks Web site, now the chain's second-biggest revenue generator after its New York flagship store, are on average approximately seven years younger than the typical Saks customer and spend more per transaction.

To better match its assortments with its stores, Saks has developed a nine-box grid. On one side of the matrix are style categories: "Park Avenue" classic; "Uptown," or modern; and "Soho," meaning trendy or contemporary. On the other axis

are pricing levels, from "good" (brands such as Dana Buchman, Ellen Tracy, Real Clothes [Saks's private label], Eileen Fisher, Spanx, and Lafayette 148) to "better" (Piazza Sempione, Armani Collezioni, Carmen Marc Valvo, Diane von Furstenberg, Max-Mara, Moschino, and some Ralph Lauren) to "best" (Chanel, Gucci, Louis Vuitton, Oscar de la Renta, Valentino, Yves Saint Laurent, Zac Posen, Helmut Lang, Herve Lege, and Bill Blass). By cross-referencing the preferred styles and spending levels at each location, the grid charts the best mix of clothes, brands, and accessories to stock at the store.

Saks must take care, however, to balance its assortment planning by store with its goal to project a consistent personality through national marketing. In its "Want It" ad campaign, Saks promoted velour sweaters for men in the fall. But many men, especially older ones and those who live in the South, didn't especially go for this fabric. Saks therefore tweaked the campaign to include more classic items with broader appeal, such as navy blazers. At the same time, it is increasing its efforts to tailor its marketing to local markets.

Sources: Vanessa O'Connell, "Park Avenue Classic or Soho Trendy?" *Wall Street Journal,* April 20, 2007, p. B1; www.saks.com (accessed May 25, 2010).

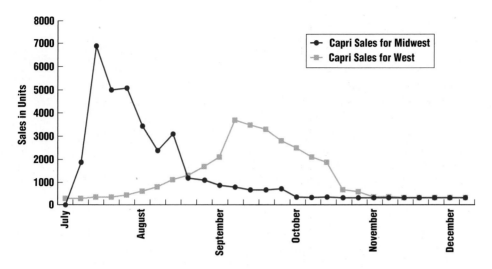

EXHIBIT 12–13
Sales of Capri Pants by
Region

Timing of Merchandise Allocation

In addition to the need to allocate different inventory levels and types of merchandise across stores, differences in the timing of category purchases across stores need to be considered. Exhibit 12–13 illustrates these differences by plotting sales data over time for capri pants in different regions of the United States. Comparing regions shows that capri sales peak in late July in the Midwest and at the beginning of September in the West, due to seasonality differences and differences in consumer demand. To increase inventory turnover in the category, buyers need to recognize these regional differences and arrange for merchandise to be shipped to the appropriate regions when customers are ready to buy.

Retailers are considering the "paycheck cycle" when making merchandise allocation and promotion decisions, particularly in difficult economic times. Cash-strapped consumers are showing a tendency to make their largest purchases when they get their paychecks at the beginning of the month and to cut back on purchases as that money runs out toward the end of the month. So some supermarket chains devote more shelf space and promote larger-package sizes at the beginning of the month and small sizes at the end of the month.[20]

The issues involved in allocating merchandise inventory to stores, as just described, are particularly important for both fashion merchandise and new staple items. If merchandise sells and evolves into staple merchandise, it gets replenished over time, either by the vendor or through distribution centers. As we discussed in Chapter 10, retailers use either a pull or a push distribution strategy to replenish merchandise. With a pull distribution strategy, orders for merchandise are generated at the store level on the basis of sales data captured by point-of-sale terminals. With a push distribution strategy, merchandise is allocated to the stores on the basis of historical demand, the inventory position at the distribution center, and the needs of the stores. As Chapter 10 noted, a pull strategy is more sophisticated and more responsive to customer demand and can correct initial misallocations.

ANALYZING MERCHANDISE MANAGEMENT PERFORMANCE

The next step in the merchandise planning process (see Exhibit 12–4) is to analyze the performance of the process and make adjustments, such as ordering more or less merchandise, lowering prices to increase sales, allocating different assortments to specific stores, or changing the assortment and model stock

EXHIBIT 12–14
Example of a Sell-Through
Analysis

Stock Number		Description	WEEK 1			WEEK 2		
			Plan	Actual-to-Plan		Plan	Actual-to-Plan	
				Actual	Percentage		Actual	Percentage
1011	Small	White silk V-neck	20	15	−25%	20	10	−50%
1011	Medium	White silk V-neck	30	25	−16.6	30	20	−33
1011	Large	White silk V-neck	20	16	−20	20	16	−20
1012	Small	Blue silk V-neck	25	26	4	25	27	8
1012	Medium	Blue silk V-neck	35	45	29	35	40	14
1012	Large	Blue silk V-neck	25	25	0	25	30	20

plans. Three types of analyses related to the monitoring and adjustment step are (1) sell-through analysis, (2) ABC analysis of assortments, and (3) multiattribute analysis of vendors. The first analysis provides an ongoing evaluation of the merchandise management plan compared with actual sales. The remaining two analyses offer approaches for evaluating and altering the assortment plan using the specific SKUs in the plan and the vendors that provide the merchandise to support the plan.

Sell-Through Analysis Evaluating Merchandise Plan

A **sell-through analysis** compares actual and planned sales to determine whether more merchandise is needed to satisfy demand or whether price reductions (markdowns) are required. Exhibit 12–14 shows a sell-through analysis for blouses for the first two weeks of the season.

These blouses are high-fashion items that experience significant uncertainty in sales. Thus, after two weeks in the stores, the buyer reviews sales and determines if adjustments are needed. The need to make adjustments depends on a variety of factors, including experience with the merchandise in the past, plans for featuring the merchandise in advertising, and the availability of **markdown money** from vendors (funds that a vendor gives a retailer to cover lost gross margin dollars that result from markdowns).

In this case, the white blouses are selling significantly less well than planned. Therefore, the buyer makes an early price reduction to ensure that the merchandise isn't left unsold at the end of the season. The decision regarding the blue blouses isn't as clear. The small blue blouses are selling slightly ahead of the plan, and the medium blue blouses are also selling well, but the large blue blouses start selling ahead of plan only in the second week. In this case, the buyer decides to wait another week or two before taking any action. If actual sales stay significantly ahead of planned sales, a reorder might be appropriate.

Evaluating the Assortment Plan and Vendors

ABC Analysis   An **ABC analysis** identifies the performance of individual SKUs in the assortment plan. It is used to determine which SKUs should be in the plan and how much backup stock and resulting product availability are provided for each SKU in the plan. In an ABC analysis, the SKUs in a merchandise category are rank-ordered by several performance measures, such as sales, gross margin, inventory turnover, and GMROI. Typically, this rank order reveals the general 80-20 principle; namely, approximately 80 percent of a retailer's sales or profits come from 20 percent of the products. This principle suggests that retailers should concentrate on the products that provide the biggest returns.

After rank-ordering the SKUs, the next step is to classify the items. On the basis of the classification, the buyer determines whether to maintain the items in the assortment plan and, if so, what level of product availability to offer. For example, a men's dress shirt buyer might identify the A, B, C, and D SKUs by rank-ordering them by sales volume. The A items account for only 5 percent of the SKUs in the category but represent 70 percent of sales. The buyer decides that these SKUs should never be out of stock and thus plans to maintain more backup stock for A items, such as keeping more sizes of long- and short-sleeved white and blue dress shirts than of the B and C items.

The B items represent 10 percent of the SKUs and 20 percent of sales. These items include some of the other better-selling colors and patterned shirts and contribute to the retailer's image of having fashionable merchandise. Occasionally, the retailer will run out of some SKUs in the B category because it does not carry the same amount of backup stock for B items as it does for A items.

The C items account for 65 percent of SKUs but contribute to only 10 percent of sales. The planner may plan to carry some C items only in very small or very large sizes of the most basic shirts, with special orders used to satisfy customer demand.

Finally, the buyer discovers that the remaining 20 percent of the SKUs, D items, have virtually no sales until they are marked down. Not only are these items excess merchandise and an unproductive investment, but they also distract from the rest of the inventory and clutter the store shelves. The buyer decides to eliminate most of these items from the assortment plan.

Multiattribute Method for Evaluating Vendors   The **multiattribute analysis** method for evaluating vendors uses a weighted-average score for each vendor. The score is based on the importance of various issues and the vendor's performance on those issues. This method is similar to the multiattribute approach that can be used to understand how customers evaluate stores and merchandise, as we discussed in Chapter 4. Retailing View 12.4 describes Home Depot's system for vendor evaluation.

To better understand the multiattribute method of evaluating vendors, either current or proposed, consider the example in Exhibit 12–15 for vendors of men's casual slacks.

EXHIBIT 12–15
Multiattribute Model for Evaluating Vendors

Issues (1)	Importance Evaluation of Issues (I) (2)	Brand A (P_a) (3)	Brand B (P_b) (4)	Brand C (P_c) (5)	Brand D (P_d) (6)
Vendor reputation	9	5	9	4	8
Service	8	6	6	4	6
Meets delivery dates	6	5	7	4	4
Merchandise quality	5	5	4	6	5
Markup opportunity	5	5	4	4	5
Country of origin	6	5	3	3	8
Product fashionability	7	6	6	3	8
Selling history	3	5	5	5	5
Promotional assistance	4	5	3	4	7
Overall evaluation a $\sum_{i=1}^{n} I_j \times P_{ij}$		280	298	212	341

$\sum_{i=1}^{n}$ = Sum of the expression.
I_i = Importance weight assigned to the ith dimension.
P_{ij} = Performance evaluation for jth brand alternative on the ith issue.
1 = Not important.
10 = Very important.

12.4   RETAILING VIEW   Home Depot Takes Vendor
Evaluations Seriously

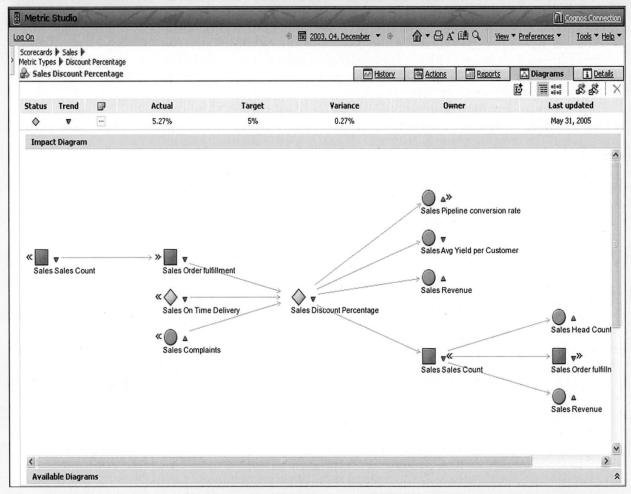

Home Depot's vendor analysis scorecard gives everyone a quick view of how the vendor is doing. Green is good, but red isn't.

Home Depot's vendor evaluation program focuses on three categories of excellence. The first, behavioral, helps it protect the reputation of its brand while instilling social and environmental responsibility into its vendor relationships. The second, manufacturing, is designed to improve product quality, cost, and innovation. The third, the supply chain category, is intended to reduce overall costs through process integration and standardization.

Home Depot has high expectations in terms of product quality, innovation, availability, on-time delivery, safety in production and shipping, compliance with laws and codes of conduct, and sensitivity to brand reputation. Its system measures service and ensures compliance specifically through the Vendor Center Web site. It features continuously updated information about how to do business with Home Depot, including the corporate performance policy, updates, news, information on events and training, and scorecards. Included in the laundry list of expectations is Home Depot's Social and Environmental Responsibility (SER) program, which addresses a wide range of issues related to vendors' proper treatment of their workers and the environment, including age requirements, wages, working conditions, emergency planning, health and safety, and prohibitions

against forced labor, fraud, and discrimination. The program combines regular audits of vendor factories with extensive education to help vendors understand the retailer's expectations.

Home Depot posts online vendor scorecards, providing graphical representations of their performance levels. Each participating vendor is rated on criteria such as compliance with shipping-platform standards and import on-time delivery. The vendors and Home Depot can observe trends over 13-month periods. Green, yellow, and red "lights" for each category let vendors know how they have been rated at a glance.

Although Home Depot's compliance program focuses on education instead of punishment, vendors pay a price if they fail to meet the company's strict requirements. Fines for noncompliance with its shipping standards amount to $10,000 for the first violation and $25,000 each time thereafter.

Sources: "Retail Supply Chains: 'Back End' or Business Value?" www.Cognos.com, November 29, 2006; Robert J. Bowman, "Home Depot Turns Its Attention to Vendor Performance Management," SupplyChainBrain.com, June 2006.

A buyer can evaluate vendors using the following five steps:

1. Develop a list of issues to consider in the evaluation (column 1).

2. In conjunction with the GMM, determine the importance weights for each issue in column 1 on a 1-to-10 scale (column 2), where 1 equals not important and 10 equals very important. For instance, the buyer and the merchandise manager believe that vendor reputation should receive a 9 because it's very important to the retailer's image. Merchandise quality receives a 5 because it's moderately important. Finally, a vendor's selling history is less important, so it could be rated 3.

3. Make judgments about each individual brand's performance on each issue (remaining columns). Note that some brands have high ratings on some issues but not on others.

4. Develop an overall score by multiplying the importance of each issue by the performance of each brand or its vendor. For instance, vendor reputation importance (9) multiplied by the performance rating for brand A (5) is 45. Promotional assistance importance (4) multiplied by the performance rating (7) for vendor D is 28. This type of analysis illustrates an important point: It doesn't pay to perform well on issues that retailers don't believe are very important. Although vendor D performed well on promotional assistance, the buyer didn't rate this issue highly in importance, so the resulting score was still low.

5. To determine a vendor's overall rating, add the products for each brand for all issues. In Exhibit 12–15, brand D has the highest overall rating (341), so D is the preferred vendor.

SUMMARY

This chapter provides an overview of the merchandise management planning process. Merchandise is broken down into categories for planning purposes. Buyers and planners manage these categories, often with the help of their major vendors.

The key performance measures used to assess merchandise management are GMROI and its components, sales-to-stock ratio, inventory turnover, and gross margin. High inventory turnover is important for a retailer's financial success. But if the retailer attempts to push inventory turnover to its limit, stockouts and increased costs may result.

The steps in the merchandise management process are (1) forecasting category sales, (2) developing an assortment plan, (3) determining appropriate inventory levels and product availability, (4) developing a plan for managing inventory, (5) allocating merchandise to stores, and (6) monitoring and evaluating performance and making adjustments.

Buying systems for staple merchandise are very different from those for fashion merchandise. Because staple merchandise is sold month after month and the sales levels are predictable, an automated continuous replenishment system is often used to manage staple merchandise categories.

The performance of buyers, vendors, and individual SKUs must be determined. Three different approaches can evaluate merchandise performance. The sell-through analysis is more useful for examining the performance of individual SKUs in the merchandise plan. The buyer compares actual with planned sales to determine whether more merchandise needs to be ordered or whether the merchandise should be put on sale. In an ABC analysis, merchandise is rank-ordered from highest to lowest. The merchandising team uses this information to set inventory management policies. For example, the most productive SKUs should carry sufficient backup stock to never be out of stock. Finally, the multiattribute method is most useful for evaluating vendors' performance.

Appendix 12A to this chapter presents a more detailed description of the development of a merchandise budget plan for fashion merchandise. Appendix 12B discusses the retail inventory method.

KEY TERMS

ABC analysis, *326*

assortment, *314*

assortment plan, *314*

backup stock, *317*

base stock, *319*

basic merchandise category, *308*

breaking sizes, *315*

buffer stock, *317*

category captain, *305*

GET OUT AND DO IT!

1. **CONTINUING EXERCISE** Go to a retailer's store, and audit the variety and assortment for a specific merchandise category. Record the breadth and depth of the assortment and the level of support (average number of items for the SKUs in each category). Compare the variety, assortment, and support for the same category in a competing retail store.

2. **INTERNET EXERCISE** Go to the home page of Merchandise Management Company (MMC), the exclusive merchandising service partner for Kohl's, at www.merchmanco.com/Default.aspx. Watch the three-minute video, and read the posted information and press releases at this Web site. How does this service provider support vendors to manage merchandise sold at this discount department store? What is the "Store Vision" system? How is it used to measure merchandise performance?

3. **IN-STORE OR INTERNET EXERCISE** Go to the store location or home page of a craft store such as Michaels Stores, Jo-Ann Fabric and Craft Stores, or A.C. Moore Arts & Crafts (www.michaels.com, www.joann.com, or www.acmoore.com). How does this retailer organize its merchandise in terms of merchandise group, department, category, and stock-keeping unit? Select two categories of merchandise: one that you would expect to have a high inventory turnover; the other, a low inventory turnover. Explain your reasoning for each selection.

4. **GO SHOPPING** Visit a big-box office supply store and then a discount store to shop for school supplies. Contrast the variety and assortment offered at each. What are the advantages and disadvantages of breadth versus depth for each retailer? What are the advantages and disadvantages from the consumer's perspective?

5. **INTERNET EXERCISE** Go to the home page of the following three retail trade publications: *WWD* at www.wwd.com/, *Chain Store Age* at www.chainstoreage.com/, and *Retailing Today* at www.retailingtoday.com/. Find an article in each that focuses on managing merchandise. How can these articles assist retailers with merchandise planning decisions?

6. **INTERNET EXERCISE** Go to www.sas.com/industry/retail/merchandise/index.html, the SAS Merchandise Intelligence Web site. How does the SAS Merchandise Intelligence product provide retailers with information to support merchandising planning, forecasting, and measurement?

7. **WEB OLC EXERCISE** The merchandise budget plan determines how much merchandise should be purchased in each month of a fashion buying season (in dollars), given the sales and reduction forecast, inventory turnover goals, and seasonal monthly fluctuations in sales. Go to the student side of the Online Learning Center, and click "Merchandise Budget Plan." The merchandise budget plan generally covers one fashion season for one merchandise category. This application presents both one-month and six-month examples. In addition, practice calculations are presented for the one-month example. Have your calculator ready! In the calculation section, you have access to an Excel-based six-month merchandise budget plan that can be used to complete Case 11 in the text.

8. **WEB OLC EXERCISE** The vendor evaluation model utilizes the multiattribute method to evaluate vendors. Go to the student side of the Online Learning Center, and click "Vendor Evaluation Model." There are two spreadsheets. Open the first spreadsheet, vendor evaluation 1.xls. This spreadsheet is the same as Exhibit 12–15. If you were selling brand A to the retailer, which numbers would change? Change the numbers in the matrix, and see the effect of that change on the overall evaluation. Go to the second spreadsheet, evaluation 2.xls. This spreadsheet can be used to evaluate brands or merchandise you might stock in your store. Assume you own a bicycle shop. List the brands you might consider stocking and the issues you would consider in selecting the brands to stock. Fill in the importance of the issues (10 = very important, 1 = not very important) and the evaluation of each brand on each characteristic (10 = excellent, 1 = poor). Determine which is the best brand for your store.

DISCUSSION QUESTIONS AND PROBLEMS

1. How and why would you expect variety and assortment to differ between a traditional bricks-and-mortar store and its Internet counterpart?

2. Simply speaking, increasing inventory turnover is an important goal for a retail manager. What are the consequences of turnover that's too slow? Too fast?

3. Assume you are the grocery buyer for canned fruits and vegetables at a five-store supermarket chain. Del Monte has told you and your boss that it would be responsible for making all inventory decisions for those merchandise categories. Del Monte will now determine how much to order and when shipments should be made. It promises a 10 percent increase in gross margin dollars in the coming year. Would you take Del Monte up on its offer? Justify your answer.

4. A buyer at Old Navy has received a number of customer complaints that he has been out of stock on some sizes of men's t-shirts. The buyer subsequently decides to increase this category's product availability from 80 percent to 90 percent. What will be the impact on backup stock and inventory turnover? Would your answer be the same if the product category were men's fleece sweatshirts?

5. Variety, assortment, and product availability are the cornerstones of the merchandise planning process. Provide examples of retailers that have done an outstanding job of positioning their stores on the basis of one or more of these issues.

6. The fine jewelry department in a department store has the same GMROI as the small appliances department, even though characteristics of the merchandise are quite different. Explain this situation.

7. Calculate the GMROI and inventory turnover given annual sales of $20,000, average inventory (at cost) of $4,000, and a gross margin of 45 percent.

8. As the athletic shoe buyer for Sports Authority, how would you go about forecasting sales for a new Nike running shoe?

9. Using the 80-20 principle, how can a retailer make certain that it has enough inventory of fast-selling merchandise and a minimal amount of slow-selling merchandise?

10. A buyer at a sporting goods store in Denver receives a shipment of 400 ski parkas on October 1 and expects to sell out by January 31. On November 1, the buyer still has 350 parkas left. What issues should the buyer consider in evaluating the selling season's progress?

11. A buyer is trying to decide from which vendor to buy a certain item. Using the information in the table below, determine from which vendor the buyer should buy.

	VENDOR PERFORMANCE		
	Importance Weight	Vendor A	Vendor B
Reputation for collaboration	8	9	8
Service	7	8	7
Meets delivery dates	9	7	8
Merchandise quality	7	8	4
Gross margin	6	4	8
Brand name recognition	5	7	5
Promotional assistance	3	8	8

SUGGESTED READINGS

Boyd, D. Eric, and Kenneth D Bahn. "When Do Large Product Assortments Benefit Consumers? An Information-Processing Perspective." *Journal of Retailing* 85 (September 2009), pp. 288–301.

Clodfelter, Richard. *Retail Buying: From Basics to Fashion,* 3rd ed. New York: Fairchild Publications, 2008.

Field, Clifton Coutard. *Retail Buying; Modern Principles and Practice.* General Books, 2010.

Jacbobsen, Maire Louise. *The Art of Retail Buying.* Hoboken, NJ: Wiley, 2008.

Kok, A. Gorhan, Marshall L. Fisher, and Ramnath Vaidyanathan. "Assortment Planning: Review of Literature and Industry Practice," in *Retail Supply Chain Management: Quantitative Models and Empirical Studies,* eds. Narendra Agrawal and Stephen A. Smith. New York: Springer, 2009, pp. 99–150.

Kurtulus, Mumin, and L. Berl Toktay. "Category Captaincy in the Retail Industry," in *Retail Supply Chain Management: Quantitative Models and Empirical Studies,* eds. Narendra Agrawal and Stephen A. Smith. New York: Springer, 2008, pp. 79–99.

Mantrala, Murali K., Michael Levy, Barbara E. Kahn, Edward J. Fox, Peter Gaidarev, Bill Dankworth, and Denish Shahg. "Why Is Assortment Planning So Difficult for Retailers? A Framework and Research Agenda." *Journal of Retailing* 85, no. 1, pp. 71–83.

Rabolt, Nancy, and Judy Miller. *Concepts and Cases in Retail and Merchandise Management*, 2nd ed. New York: Fairchild, 2008.

Reda, Susan. "America's Favorite Brands: With SKU Reductions Underway, Which Will Survive?" *Stores*, February 2010, pp. 12–15.

Tepper, Bette. *Mathematics for Retail Buying*. New York: Fairchild, 2008.

APPENDIX 12A   Merchandise Budget Report and Open-to-Buy System for a Fashion Merchandise Category

MERCHANDISE BUDGET PLAN

In this appendix, we describe the steps in developing the merchandise budget plan for a fashion merchandise category. These steps are taken to develop the bottom line—line 8, "Monthly Additions to Stock"—in Exhibit 12–16.

The figures on this line tell the buyer how much merchandise in retail dollars he or she needs to have, on average, at the beginning of each month for the retailer's financial goals to be met. Note that Exhibit 12–16 is the same as Exhibit 12–10 in the chapter.

EXHIBIT 12–16   Six-Month Merchandise Budget Plan for Men's Casual Slacks

	Spring	April	May	June	July	August	September
1. Sales % Distribution to Season	100.00%	21.00%	12.00%	12.00%	19.00%	21.00%	15.00%
2. Monthly Sales	$130,000	$27,300	$15,600	$15,600	$24,700	$27,300	$19,500
3. Reduc % Distribution to Season	100.00%	40.00%	14.00%	16.00%	12.00%	10.00%	8.00%
4. Monthly Reductions	$16,500	$6,600	$2,310	$2,640	$1,980	$1,650	$1,320
5. BOM Stock to Sales Ratio	4.00	3.60	4.40	4.40	4.00	3.60	4.00
6. BOM Inventory	$98,280	$98,280	$68,640	$68,640	$98,800	$98,280	$78,000
7. EOM Inventory	$65,600	$68,640	$68,640	$98,800	$98,280	$78,000	$65,600
8. Monthly Additions to Stock	$113,820	$4,260	$17,910	$48,400	$26,160	$8,670	$8,420

Monthly Sales Percentage Distribution to Season (Line 1)

Line 1 of the plan projects what percentage of the total sales is expected to be sold in each month. In Exhibit 12–16, 21 percent of the six-month sales are expected to occur in April.

	Six-Month Data	SPRING			SUMMER		
		April	May	June	July	August	September
Sales % Distribution to 1 Month	100.00%	21.00%	12.00%	12.00%	19.00%	21.00%	15.00%

Historical sales data provide the starting point for determining the percentage distribution of sales by month. The percentage of total category sales that occurs in a particular month doesn't vary much from year to year. However, the buyer might adjust the historical percentages to reflect changes in buying patterns and special promotions. For instance, the buyer might feel that the autumn selling season for men's casual slacks continues to be pushed further back into summer and thus increase the percentages for July and decrease the percentages for August and September. The buyer might also decide to hold a special Easter sale promotion, increasing the April percentage and decreasing the other percentages.

Monthly Sales (Line 2)

Monthly sales are the forecasted total sales for the six-month period in the first column ($130,000) multiplied by each monthly sales percentage (line 1). In Exhibit 12–16, monthly sales for April = $130,000 × 21 percent = $27,300.

	Six-Month Data	SPRING			SUMMER		
		April	May	June	July	August	September
Sales % Distribution to							
1 Month	100.00%	21.00%	12.00%	12.00%	19.00%	21.00%	15.00%
2 Monthly sales	$130,000	$27,300	$15,600	$15,600	$24,700	$27,300	$19,500

Monthly Reductions Percentage Distribution to Season (Line 3)

To have enough merchandise every month to support the monthly sales forecast, the buyer needs to consider other factors that reduce the inventory level in addition to sales made to customers. Although sales are the primary reduction, the value of the inventory is also reduced by markdowns (sales discounts), shrinkage, and discounts to employees. The merchandise budget planning process builds these additional reductions into the planned purchases. If these reductions were not considered, the category would always be understocked. Note that in Exhibit 12–16, 40 percent of the season's total reductions occur in April as a result of price discounts (markdowns) during end-of-season sales.

Markdowns also can be forecasted from historical records. However, changes in markdown strategies—or changes in the environment, such as competition or general economic activity—must be taken into consideration when forecasting markdowns.

Discounts to employees are like markdowns, except that they are given to employees rather than to customers. The level of the employee discount is tied fairly closely to the sales level and number of employees. Thus, employee discounts also can be forecasted from historical records.

Shrinkage refers to inventory losses caused by shoplifting, employee theft, merchandise being misplaced or damaged, and poor bookkeeping. Retailers measure shrinkage by taking the difference between (1) the inventory's recorded value based on merchandise bought and received and (2) the physical inventory actually in stores and distribution centers. Shrinkage varies by department and season, but typically it varies directly with sales as well. So if sales of men's casual pants increase by 10 percent, then the buyer can expect a 10 percent increase in shrinkage.

	Six-Month Data	SPRING			SUMMER		
		April	May	June	July	August	September
3 Reduction % Distribution to Season	100.00%	40.00%	14.00%	16.00%	12.00%	10.00%	8.00%

Monthly Reductions (Line 4)

Monthly reductions are calculated by multiplying the total reductions by each percentage in line 3. The total reductions for this example are based on historical data. In Exhibit 12–16, April reductions = $16,500 × 40 percent = $6,600.

	Six-Month Data	SPRING			SUMMER		
		April	May	June	July	August	September
3 Reduction % Distribution to Season	100.00%	40.00%	14.00%	16.00%	12.00%	10.00%	8.00%
4 Monthly reductions	$16,500	$6,600	$2,310	$2,640	$1,980	$1,650	$1,320

BOM (Beginning-of-Month) Stock-to-Sales Ratio (Line 5)

The **stock-to-sales ratio,** listed in line 5, specifies the amount of inventory that should be on hand at the beginning of the month to support the sales forecast and maintain the inventory turnover objective for the category.

Thus, a stock-to-sales ratio of 2 means that the retailer plans to have twice as much inventory on hand at the beginning of the month as there are forecasted sales for the month. Both the BOM stock and forecasted sales for the month are expressed in retail sales dollars.

	Six-Month Data	SPRING			SUMMER		
		April	May	June	July	August	September
5 BOM stock-to-sales ratio	4.0	3.6	4.4	4.4	4.0	3.6	4.0

Rather than specifying the stock-to-sales ratio, many retailers specify a related measure, weeks of inventory. A stock-to-sales ratio of 4 means there are 16 weeks of inventory, or approximately 112 days, on hand at the beginning of the month. A stock-to-sales ratio of 1/2 indicates a two-week supply of merchandise, or enough for approximately 14 days. The stock-to-sales ratio is determined so the merchandise category achieves its targeted performance—its planned GMROI and inventory turnover. The steps in determining the stock-to-sales ratio for the category are shown next.

Step 1: Calculate Sales-to-Stock Ratio

The GMROI is equal to the gross margin percentage times the sales-to-stock ratio. The sales-to-stock ratio is conceptually similar to inventory turnover except the denominator in the stock-to-sales ratio is expressed in retail sales dollars, whereas the denominator in inventory turnover is the cost of goods sold (sales at cost). The buyer's target GMROI for the category is 123 percent, and the buyer feels the category will produce a gross margin of 45 percent. Thus,

$$\text{GMROI} = \text{Gross margin percent} \times \text{Sales-to-stock ratio}$$
$$\text{Sales-to-stock ratio} = \text{GMROI/Gross margin percent}$$
$$= 123/45 = 2.73$$

Because this illustration of a merchandise budget plan is for a six-month period rather than a year, the sales-to-stock ratio is based on six months rather than annual sales. So for this six-month period, sales must be 2.73 times the inventory cost to meet the targeted GMROI.

Step 2: Convert the Sales-to-Stock Ratio to Inventory Turnover

Inventory turnover is

$$\text{Inventory turnover} = \text{Sales-to-stock ratio} \times (1.00 - \text{Gross margin \%}/100)$$
$$= 2.73 \times (1.00 - 45/100)$$
$$1.50 = 2.73 \times .55$$

This adjustment is necessary because the sales-to-stock ratio defines sales at retail and inventory at cost, whereas inventory turnover defines both sales and inventory at cost. Like the sales-to-stock ratio, this inventory turnover is based on a six-month period.

Step 3: Calculate Average Stock-to-Sales Ratio

The average stock-to-sales ratio is

$$\text{Average stock-to-sales ratio} = 6 \text{ months/Inventory turnover}$$
$$4 = 6/1.5$$

If preparing a 12-month plan, the buyer divides 12 by the annual inventory turnover. Because the merchandise budget plan in Exhibit 12–16 is based on retail dollars, it's easiest to think of the numerator as BOM retail inventory and the denominator as sales for that month. Thus, to achieve a six-month inventory turnover of 1.5, on average, the buyer must plan to have a BOM inventory that equals four times the amount of sales for a given month, which is equivalent to four months, or 16 weeks of supply.

One needs to be careful when thinking about the average *stock-to-sales ratio*, which can be easily confused with the *sales-to-stock ratio*. These ratios are not the inverse of each other. Sales are the same in both ratios, but stock in the sales-to-stock ratio is the average inventory at cost over all days in the period, whereas stock in the stock-to-sales ratio is the average BOM inventory at retail. Also, the BOM stock-to-sales ratio is an average for all months. Adjustments are made to this average in line 5 to account for seasonal variation in sales.

Step 4: Calculate Monthly Stock-to-Sales Ratios

The monthly stock-to-sales ratios in line 5 must average the stock-to-sales ratio calculated previously to achieve the planned inventory turnover. Generally, monthly stock-to-sales ratios vary in the opposite direction of sales. That is, in months when sales are larger, stock-to-sales ratios are smaller, and vice versa.

To make this adjustment, the buyer needs to consider the seasonal pattern for men's casual slacks in determining the monthly stock-to-sales ratios. In the ideal situation, men's casual slacks would arrive in the store the same day and in the same quantity that customers demand them. Unfortunately, the real-life retailing world isn't this simple. Note in Exhibit 12–16 (line 8) that men's casual slacks for the spring season start arriving slowly in April ($4,260 for the month), yet demand lags behind these arrivals until the weather starts getting warmer. Monthly sales then jump from 12 percent of annual sales in May and June to 19 percent in July (line 1). But the stock-to-sales ratio (line 5) decreased from 4.4 in May and June to 4.0 in July. Thus, in months when sales increase (e.g., July), the BOM inventory also increases (line 6) but at a slower rate, which causes the stock-to-sales ratios to decrease. Likewise, in months when sales decrease dramatically, like in May (line 2), inventory also decreases (line 6), again at a slower rate, causing the stock-to-sales ratios to increase (line 5).

When creating a merchandise budget plan for a category such as men's casual slacks with a sales history, the buyer also examines previous years' stock-to-sales ratios. To judge how adequate these past ratios were, the buyer determines if inventory levels were exceedingly high or low in any months. Then the buyer makes minor corrections to adjust for a previous imbalance in inventory levels, as well as for changes in the current environment. For instance, assume the buyer is planning a promotion for Memorial Day. This promotion has never been done before, so the stock-to-sales ratio for the month of May should be adjusted downward to allow for the expected increase in sales. Note that monthly stock-to-sales ratios don't change by the same percentage that the percentage distribution of sales by month is changing. In months when sales increase, stock-to-sales ratios decrease but at a slower rate. Because there is no exact method of making these adjustments, the buyer must make some subjective judgments.

BOM Stock (Line 6)

The amount of inventory planned for the beginning-of-the-month (BOM) inventory for April equals

$$\underset{\$98,280}{\text{BOM inventory}} = \underset{= \$27,300}{\underset{\text{(line 2)}}{\text{Monthly sales}}} \times \underset{\times 3.6}{\underset{\text{ratio (line 5)}}{\text{BOM stock-to-sales}}}$$

	Six-Month Data	SPRING			SUMMER		
		April	May	June	July	August	September
6 BOM inventory	$98,280	$98,280	$68,640	$68,640	$98,800	$98,280	$78,000

EOM (End-of-Month) Stock (Line 7)

The BOM stock for the current month is the same as the EOM (end-of-month) stock in the previous month. That is, BOM stock in line 6 is simply EOM inventory in line 7 from the previous month. Thus, in Exhibit 12–16, the EOM stock for April is the same as the BOM stock for May, $68,640. Forecasting the ending inventory for the last month in the plan is the next step in the merchandise budget plan. Note that EOM inventory for June is high, which indicates planning for a substantial sales increase in July.

	Six-Month Data	SPRING			SUMMER		
		April	May	June	July	August	September
7 EOM inventory	$65,600	$68,640	$68,640	$98,800	$98,280	$78,000	$65,600

Monthly Additions to Stock (Line 8)

The monthly additions to stock needed is the amount to be ordered for delivery in each month to meet the inventory turnover and sales objectives.

$$\text{Additions to stock} = \text{Sales (line 2)} + \text{Reductions (line 4)}$$
$$+ \text{EOM inventory (line 7)}$$
$$- \text{BOM inventory (line 6)}$$
$$\text{Additions to stock (April)} = \$27,300 + 6,600$$
$$+ 68,640 - 98,280$$
$$= \$4,260$$

At the beginning of the month, the inventory level equals BOM stock. During the month, merchandise is sold, and various inventory reductions affecting the retail sales level occur, such as markdowns and theft. So the BOM stock minus monthly sales minus reductions equals the EOM stock if nothing is purchased. But something must be purchased to get back up to the forecast EOM stock. The difference between EOM stock if nothing is purchased (BOM stock − sales − reductions) and the forecast EOM stock is the additions to stock.

	Six-Month Data	SPRING			SUMMER		
		April	May	June	July	August	September
8 Monthly additions to stock	$113,820	$4,260	$17,920	$48,400	$26,160	$8,670	$8,420

OPEN-TO-BUY SYSTEM

The open-to-buy system is used after the merchandise is purchased and is based on the merchandise budget plan or staple merchandise management system. The merchandise management systems discussed previously provide buyers with a plan for purchasing merchandise. The **open-to-buy** system keeps track of merchandise flows while they are occurring. It keeps a record of how much is actually spent purchasing merchandise each month and how much is left to spend.

In the same way that you must keep track of the checks you write, buyers need to keep track of the merchandise they purchase and when it is to be delivered. Without the open-to-buy system keeping track of merchandise flows, buyers might buy too much or too little. Merchandise could be delivered when it isn't needed and be unavailable when it is needed. Thus, sales and inventory turnover would suffer. For consistency, we will continue with our example of an open-to-buy system using the merchandise budget plan previously discussed. The open-to-buy system is also applicable to staple goods merchandise management systems.

To make the merchandise budget plan successful (i.e., meet the sales, inventory turnover, and GMROI goals for a category), the buyer attempts to buy merchandise in quantities with delivery dates such that the actual EOM stock for a month will be the same as the forecasted EOM stock. For example, at the end of September, which is the end of the spring/summer season, the buyer would like to be completely sold out of spring/summer men's casual slacks so there will be room for the fall styles. Thus, the

Buying Merchandise

EXECUTIVE BRIEFING
Tim Adams, Chief Private Brands Officer
at Macy's

After graduating from the University of Georgia, I went to work for the Merchandising Division at Macy's in Atlanta. I moved to San Francisco in 1980 and for the next 6 years held various merchandising positions from buyer to merchandise administrator to general merchandise manager, in the areas of home furnishings, women's apparel, and accessories and cosmetics. In 1997 I was named president of The Bon Marché in Seattle, which was a division of Federated Department Stores, which also owned Macy's. Three years later, I took on the position of chairman at the Macy's Florida division and, in 2005, relocated to New York to run the national Home Store, which had been founded the year before to extend Macy's leadership in home fashions. In February 2009, I assumed my current role of Chief Private Brands Officer at our corporate headquarters in New York.

Private brands are of strategic importance to Macy's. We design and source products that compete with all the famous and prestigious national brands. The process involves looking for areas within our assortment where we can either do better than our national-brand vendors or fill a void in the assortment that they aren't serving. We strive to be market leaders in every category in which we compete. Our customers have the same expectation of us as they would of any other vendor, and if our private-label products don't offer competitive value, we won't outperform the market.

It's my responsibility to make sure our private brands are market leaders, including recruiting and retaining the best talent. I work with the designers to find and develop the most current fashion ideas. These ideas are then transformed into products that are sourced from vendors around the world. Our sourcing team finds vendors who can transform our design ideas into high-quality products with the correct fit, and they must do it at a cost that allows us to provide our customers with an excellent value. Once the products are made, we work with our logistics team to make sure the merchandise is delivered at the right time to meet customer needs. We work side by side with our stores' organization to train our sales associates

CHAPTER 13

QUESTIONS

What branding options are available to retailers?

How do retailers buy national brands?

What issues do retailers consider when buying and sourcing private-label merchandise internationally?

How do retailers prepare for and conduct negotiations with their vendors?

Why are retailers building strategic relationships with their vendors?

What legal and ethical issues are involved in buying merchandise?

---

on the features and benefits of the product and with our buyers and allocators to ensure that we get our customers exactly what they want.

I really love this job! As with so many parts of retailing, it is exciting to come up with a product concept, watch its design develop, oversee its production, and ultimately watch our customers love it and buy it. Since the private-label component is such an important part of Macy's overall strategy, I feel that my team and I are really getting something important accomplished—every day.

The preceding chapter outlined the merchandise management process and the steps in the process that buyers go through to determine what and how much merchandise to buy. After creating an assortment plan for the category, forecasting sales, and developing a plan outlining the flow of merchandise (how much merchandise needs to be ordered and when it needs to be delivered), the next step in the merchandise management process is to acquire the merchandise. The process for acquiring merchandise differs for well-known national brands and private-label brands that are available exclusively from the retailer. Thus, the first strategic decision that needs to be made is to determine the type of brands to buy for the category.

When buying merchandise, buyers meet with vendors at wholesale markets or in their offices and negotiate many issues such as prices, delivery dates, payment terms, and financial support for advertising and markdowns. The buying process for private-label merchandise is often more complex. Some retailers have their own design and sourcing departments that work with buyers to specify the merchandise designs and then negotiate with manufacturers to produce the merchandise. Because merchandise is often manufactured outside the United States, these retailers need to deal with the complexities of international business transactions. In other cases, buyers might negotiate with national-brand vendors or manufacturers to buy merchandise designed by the supplier exclusively for the retailer.

Although buyers meet and negotiate with national-brand vendors and private-label manufacturers each season concerning new merchandise, there is a trend toward developing long-term strategic relationships with key suppliers. These partnerships enable the collaboration needed to develop the efficient supply chains discussed in Chapter 10, as well as joint merchandise and marketing programs.

This chapter begins with a description of the different merchandise branding alternatives. Then the issues involved in buying national brands and private-label merchandise, including negotiating with vendors, are reviewed. Next, the development of strategic partnering relationships between retailers and their suppliers is discussed. The chapter concludes with an examination of the legal, ethical, and social responsibility issues surrounding the buying of merchandise.

BRAND ALTERNATIVES

REFACT

Private-label sales in grocery stores, drugstores, and discount department stores in the United States have been growing at over 7 percent and amount to $86 billion annually, including sales by Walmart. In contrast, sales of branded merchandise have been declining by over 3 percent.[1]

Retailers and their buyers face a strategic decision about the mix of national brands and private-label brands sold exclusively by the retailer. The advantages and disadvantages of these branding alternatives are discussed in this section.

National Brands

National brands, also known as **manufacturer's brands,** are products designed, produced, and marketed by a vendor and sold to many different retailers. The vendor is responsible for developing the merchandise, producing it with consistent quality, and undertaking a marketing program to establish an appealing brand image. In some cases, vendors use an **umbrella** or **family brand** associated with their company and a **subbrand** associated with the product, such as Kellogg's (family brand) Frosted Flakes (subbrand) or Ford (family brand) F150 truck (subbrand). In other cases, vendors use individual brand names for different product categories and don't associate the brands with their companies. For example, most consumers probably don't know that Procter & Gamble makes Iams pet food, Crest toothpaste, Ivory soap, Vick's NyQuil, Folgers coffee, Hugo by Hugo Boss cologne, and Pringles potato chips.

By offering these national brands, retailers attract customers to their stores and Web sites and therefore do not have to incur the cost of developing and promoting the brand's image and associated merchandise.

Some retailers organize their buying activities around national-brand vendors that cut across merchandise categories. For instance, buyers in department stores may be responsible for all cosmetic brands offered by Estée Lauder (Estée Lauder, Origins, Clinique, and Prescriptives) rather than for a product category such as skin care or eye makeup. Managing merchandise by vendor, rather than by category, gives retailers more clout when dealing with vendors. However, as indicated in Chapter 12, there are inefficiencies associated with managing merchandise at the brand or vendor level rather than the category level.

Private-Label Brands

Private-label brands, also called **store brands, house brands,** or **own brands,** are products developed by retailers. In many cases, retailers develop the design and specifications for their private-label products and then contract with manufacturers to produce those products. In other cases, national-brand vendors work with a retailer to develop a special version of its standard merchandise offering to be sold exclusively by the retailer. In these cases, the national-brand vendor or manufacturer is responsible for the design and specification as well as the production of the merchandise. Retailing View 13.1 describes Asda's private-label strategy.

RETAILING VIEW   U.K.'s Asda Loves Private-Label Brands   13.1

The British supermarket retailer Asda, owned by Walmart, has a private-label portfolio that accounts for 45 percent of its grocery and 50 percent of its nonfood sales. Asda has extended its own label into such categories as healthy eating, organics, and food for kids and now is placing more emphasis on developing premium-price private labels.

Asda offers six private-label brands in the food, health and beauty, and household categories. In addition, it has its successful George private-label clothing brand and a selection of Asda-branded financial services, including home, motor, and life insurance. Some of its brands include:

- Smart Price—economy-value, no-frills food and general merchandise essentials.
- Best-in-market everyday food and general merchandise items at low prices.
- Good for you!—foods with lower fat content than standard Asda brand alternatives.
- Organic—best-value organic "everyday" products.
- Onn—midlevel eclectic brand with stylized designs.
- Extra Special—Asda's premium private-label food brand.
- More for Kids—healthier, fun products for kids across the food and health and beauty categories.

The Extra Special premium private-label brand has grown from 40 SKUs in 2000 to more than 750 across categories that include confectionery, soft drinks, snacks, trifles, specialty breads, prepared meat and fish meals, and a wide range of cheeses and sliced meats. The criteria for an Extra Special branded product include better taste and the finest ingredients, compared with standard alternatives or national premium equivalents, but affordable at a 10 to 15 percent lower price than competitors' premium private-label equivalents.

Asda, a U.K. chain owned by Walmart, developed George, a private-label apparel and footwear brand. Although very successful in the United Kingdom, the brand has not been as successful in Walmart stores in the United States.

Asda's private-label clothing and footwear brand, George, is the fourth-largest apparel brand in the United Kingdom. Created by George Davies, the former owner of a successful chain of British apparel stores, George merchandise comprises sleek but inexpensive clothing, accessories, and undergarments for women and men. Walmart is importing George merchandise and selling it in its U.S. stores as part of its effort to upgrade its apparel offering. But George merchandise has not been as successful in the United States.

Sources: www.asda.co.uk (accessed April 26, 2010); "Odin Drives ASDA 'Extra Special' Range onto Shelves," *Retail Bulletin,* August 30, 2007; Bill Condie, "Asda Plans to Spruce Up Tired George Label as Growth Slows Down," *Knight Ridder Tribune Business News,* September 14, 2007.

REFACT

Private labels are big business in Europe: At Aldi and Lidl's, private brands account for 94 percent of their merchandise; at Tesco, 50 percent; at Walmart, 39 percent; and at Carrefour, 34 percent.[4]

REFACT

Over the past few years, private-label brands have consistently made up about 16 percent of supermarket sales, and 41 percent of shoppers say they frequently buy private-label brands, up from 26 percent five years ago.[5]

REFACT

In one year, private-label organic food sales rose 34 percent, to $1.1 billion. In 2005, organic private-label sales totaled just $166 million.[8]

In the past, sales of private label brands were limited. National brands had the resources to develop loyalty toward their brands through aggressive marketing. It was difficult for smaller local and regional retailers to gain the economies of scale in design, production, and promotion that were needed to develop well-known brands.

In recent years, as the size of retail firms has increased, more retailers have the scale economies to develop private-label merchandise and use this merchandise to establish a distinctive identity. Buyers at these retailers look for holes in their assortment—individual SKUs or whole categories that they believe their suppliers aren't fulfilling or that they believe they can make and market better. In addition, manufacturers and national-brand suppliers are more willing to accommodate the needs of retailers and develop exclusive private labels for them.

Four categories of private brands—premium, copycat, exclusive, and generic—are discussed next.

Premium Private-Label Brands

Premium private-label brands offer the consumer a private label that is comparable to a manufacturer's brand quality, sometimes with modest price savings. Examples of premium private labels include Kroger's Private Selection, Tesco Finest (U.K.), "The Men's Collection" at Saks Fifth Avenue, and Bloomingdale's Aqua.[6] President's Choice is Canadian retailer Loblaw's premium private label. It competes on quality, not price. Kellogg has two scoops of raisins in its cereal, but President's Choice cereal has four and is cheaper. The Decadent chocolate-chip cookie under the President's Choice label has 39 percent chocolate chips by weight, compared with 19 percent in Chips Ahoy. In addition, it uses real butter instead of hydrogenated coconut oil and quality chocolate instead of artificial chips. The resulting product is Canada's market leader in chocolate-chip cookies, despite being sold in only 20 percent of the market held by Loblaw.[7]

A subcategory of premium private-label brands is environmentally sensitive or organic. Although Whole Foods Market has been the pioneer and leader in these products, Supervalu Inc., which owns Shaw's and Albertsons and is the fourth-largest U.S. food retailer by sales, doubled the number of SKUs in its Wild Harvest organic brand to over 300 in just a few months. At Safeway Inc., the third-largest U.S. food retailer, its organic brand (called O Organics) has proved so successful that it sells the products to other retailers.[9]

Consumers' increased interest in organic products has caused grocery retailers like Shaw's and Albertsons to increase their organic food offerings.

Copycat Brands

Copycat brands imitate the manufacturer's brand in appearance and packaging, generally are perceived as lower-quality, and are offered at lower prices. Copycat brands abound in drugstores and grocery stores. Many retailers monitor the introduction of new national brands and then modify them to meet the needs of their target customers. For instance, CVS or Walgreens brands are placed next to the manufacturer's brands and often look like them.

Exclusive Brands

An **exclusive brand** is a brand that is developed by a national-brand vendor, often in conjunction with a retailer, and is sold exclusively by the retailer. The simplest form of an exclusive brand occurs when a national-brand manufacturer assigns different model numbers and has different exterior features for the same basic product sold by different retailers but it is still marketed under the manufacturer's brand. For example, a Canon digital camera sold at Best Buy might have a different model number

EXHIBIT 13–1
Exclusive Brands

Retailer	Manufacturer/ Designer	Product Category	Product Name
Kohl's	Estée Lauder	Cosmetics	American Beauty, Flirt, and Good Skin
Walmart	Mary Kate and Ashley Olsen	Apparel and accessories	Mary Kate and Ashley
Walmart, Best Buy*	Hewlett-Packard	Computers	
Macy's†	Martha Stewart	Soft home (sheets, towels)	Martha Stewart Collection
Macy's	Jones Apparel Group (Rachel Roy)	Apparel and accessories	Rachel by Rachel Roy
McDonald's	Newman's Own Organic	Coffee	Newman's Own Organic
JCPenney‡	Ralph Lauren	Home goods, apparel, and accessories	American Living
JCPenney	Nicole Miller	Apparel and accessories	Nicole by Nicole Miller

*Christopher Lawton, "Tweaking the Standard-Issue PC," *Wall Street Journal*, June 14, 2007, p. D1.

†Lisa Biank Fasig, "Celebrities, Designers Court Macy's for Exclusive Lines," *Business Courier of Cincinnati*, August 31, 2009; Teresa F. Lindeman, "Brands Expand: Retailers Work to Create Exclusive Products to Set Themselves Apart," *Pittsburgh Post-Gazette*, August 24, 2007.

‡Ibid; Stuart Elliott, "No Polo Pony, but Penney's New Label Is Pure Ralph Lauren Americana," *New York Times*, February 19, 2009.

than a Canon digital camera with similar features available at Walmart. These exclusive models make it difficult for consumers to compare prices for virtually the same camera sold by different retailers.

A more sophisticated form of exclusive branding occurs when a manufacturer develops an exclusive product or product category for a retailer and it is marketed under a brand name that is exclusive to the retailer. For example, cosmetics powerhouse Estée Lauder sells three brands of cosmetics and skin care products—American Beauty, Flirt, and Good Skin—exclusively at Kohl's. The products are priced between mass-market brands such as Cover Girl or Maybelline (sold mainly in drugstores, discount stores, and supermarkets) and Lauder's higher-end brands (sold primarily in more fashion-forward department stores such as Macy's and Dillard's). Levi Strauss has also developed the Signature brand jeans for sale at Walmart. Examples of these and several other exclusive brands you might recognize are found in Exhibit 13–1.

Generic Brands   **Generic brands** target a price-sensitive segment by offering a no-frills product at a discount price. These products are used typically for commodities like milk or eggs in grocery stores and underwear in discount stores. Once the mainstay of private-label brands, the sales of generics have been declining. These products are labeled with the name of the commodity and thus actually have no brand name distinguishing them.

National Brands or Private Labels?   Exhibit 13–2 outlines the advantages and disadvantages of national versus private-label brands. Buying from vendors of national brands can help retailers build their image and traffic flow and reduce their selling/promotional expenses. Many customers have developed loyalty to specific national brands. They patronize retailers selling the national-brand merchandise and ask for it by name. This loyalty toward the brand develops because customers know what to expect from the products, like them, and trust them. If a retailer does not offer the national brands, customers might decide to patronize a retailer that does.

National-brand vendors devote considerable resources to creating images of their brands that build customer loyalty. As a result, retailers need to spend relatively less money selling and promoting national brands. For instance, Sony attempts to communicate a constant and focused message about the quality and

REFACT

Exclusive brands from Martha Stewart, Donald Trump, and Tommy Hilfiger account for more than 16 percent of Macy's sales. Its total private-label sales account for 35 percent of sales—about $25 billion annually.[10]

Estee Lauder sells three exclusive co-brands at Kohl's—American Beauty, Flirt, and Good Skin.

performance of its products to its customers by coordinating advertising with in-store promotions and displays. Thus, Best Buy and Walmart do not need to engage in image advertising for Sony products.

But because vendors of national brands assume the expenses of designing, manufacturing, distributing, and promoting the brand, retailers typically realize a lower gross margin percentage for them compared with the percentages for their private-label brands. Also, because national brands are sold by other retailers, competition can be intense. Customers compare prices for these brands across stores, which means retailers often have to offer significant discounts on some national brands to attract customers to their stores, further reducing their gross margins. Large retailers, however, can push some of the financial risk of buying the merchandise back onto the national-brand vendor. If, for instance, a product doesn't sell, the retailer can negotiate to either send the merchandise back to the vendor or have the vendor pay for the difference in lost gross margin if the merchandise has to be marked down.

Stocking national brands can increase or decrease store loyalty. If the national brand is available through a limited number of retail outlets (e.g., Kiehl's skin care products, Eureka vacuum cleaners), customers loyal to the brand will also become loyal to the limited number of stores selling the brand. If, however, manufacturer brands are readily available from many retailers in a market, store loyalty may decrease because the retailer can't differentiate itself from its competition.

Another problem with manufacturer's brands is that they can limit a retailer's flexibility. Vendors of strong brands can dictate how their products are displayed, advertised, and priced. Jockey, for instance, tells retailers exactly when and how its underwear products should be advertised.

EXHIBIT 13–2

Impact on Store	TYPE OF VENDOR	
	National Brands	Private-Label Brands
Store loyalty	?	+
Store image	+	+
Traffic flow	+	+
Selling and promotional expenses	+	−
Restrictions	−	+
Differential advantages	−	+
Margins	?	?

+ advantage to the retailer, − disadvantage to the retailer, ? depends on circumstances.

Exclusive models and brands make it difficult for consumers to compare prices for virtually the same item sold by different retailers. Since the retailers are less likely to compete on price when selling exclusive brands, their margin percentage for the products is higher, and they are motivated to devote more resources toward selling the exclusive brands than they would for similar national brands.[11]

The exclusivity of strong private labels boosts store loyalty. Well-known and highly desirable private labels and exclusive brands can enhance the retailer's image and draw customers to the store. For instance, Kohl's exclusive brands, as discussed in Retailing View 13.2, are not available from its competitors.

But there are drawbacks to private labels.[12] Although gross margin percentage may be higher for private-label brands than for national brands, the gross margin dollars might be lower if the unit price is lower. In addition, the retailer incurs other expenses. Retailers must make significant investments to design merchandise, manage global manufacturers, create customer awareness, and develop a favorable image for their private-label and exclusive brands. If the private-label or exclusive merchandise doesn't sell, retailers may not be able to negotiate to either return the merchandise or receive compensation from the manufacturer.

In the next two sections, we discuss the buying process for national-brand and private-label merchandise.

RETAILING VIEW   Only at Kohl's   13.2

Kohl's is a department store chain that offers fashionable merchandise in convenient, off-the-mall locations. Previously known as a discount apparel store, Kohl's is changing its image by offering trendy exclusive brands, such as Daisy Fuentes' intimate apparel, featuring the former MTV host; Candies, which uses several celebrity spokespeople; Ralph Lauren's Chaps; and an *ELLE Magazine* apparel line. Its exclusive brands currently make up 45 percent of its sales.

It is also building an entire marketing campaign around an exclusive arrangement with a single private-label vendor. Vera Wang, a famous designer best known for her luxury bridal gowns, has codesigned and is selling women's clothing, accessories, shoes, jewelry, and even bath and bedding under the brand Simply Vera exclusively at Kohl's.

The Wang collection is attracting slightly more hip, upscale customers to Kohl's. Wang is able to sell dresses and accessories at a fraction of the price of her regular collection. Wang is following in the footsteps of her former employer, Ralph Lauren. Lauren has brilliantly translated the fashion market from the upper echelons to the middle masses. Like Lauren, Wang's high-end line is made with the finest materials and workmanship; whereas the Kohl's line, although still fashionably designed, is made with less expensive materials and less labor-intensive details. Yet Simply Vera excites consumers! Customers recognize the Vera Wang brand name and are attracted to Kohl's as a result.

Simply Vera by Vera Wang is one of Kohl's exclusive brands. The Simply Vera brand sells at a fraction of Vera Wang's regular line.

Sources: Suzanne S. Brown, "Fashion's Look-Back Decade," *Manila Bulletin Publishing*, December 31, 2009; "Kohl's Expands Its New York Private Brand Design Office," *MyPrivateBrand*, January 5, 2010; Vanessa O'Connell, "Is Discount a Good Fit for Vera Wang?" *Wall Street Journal*, September 5, 2007; Kelly Nolan, "Striking a Balance between Mass & Fashion," *Retailing Today*, August 13, 2007; Kelly Nolan, "Kohl's Plans to Keep Shoppers Shopping—Across the Store," *Retailing Today*, June 18, 2007; www.kohls.com/VeraWang (accessed November 28, 2007).

BUYING NATIONAL-BRAND MERCHANDISE

In this section, we review how retail buyers of national brands meet with vendors, review the merchandise they have to offer at wholesale markets, and place orders.

Meeting National-Brand Vendors

A **wholesale market** for retail buyers is a concentration of vendors within a specific geographic location, perhaps even under one roof or over the Internet. Wholesale markets may be permanent wholesale market centers or annual trade shows or trade fairs. Retailers also interact with vendors at their corporate headquarters. A listing of more than 350,000 trade shows, designer showrooms, retailers, and global manufacturers for the fashion industry can be viewed at www.infomat.com.

Wholesale Market Centers   For many types of merchandise, particularly fashion apparel and accessories, buyers regularly visit with vendors in established market centers. Wholesale market centers have permanent vendor showrooms that retailers can visit throughout the year. At specific times during the year, these wholesale centers host **market weeks** during which buyers make appointments to visit the various vendor showrooms. Vendors that do not have permanent showrooms at the market center lease temporary space to participate in market weeks.

Probably the world's most well-known wholesale market center for many merchandise categories is in New York City. The Fashion Center, also known as the Garment District, is located from Fifth to Ninth avenues and from 34th to 41st streets. Thousands of apparel buyers visit every year for 5 market weeks and 65 annual trade shows. The Garment District hosts more than 5,000 showrooms and 4,500 factories.[13] There are also major wholesale market centers in London, Milan, Paris, and Tokyo. The United States also has various regional wholesale market centers, like the Dallas Market Center (the world's largest) or the Atlanta Merchandise Mart, that are used by smaller retailers to view and purchase merchandise.

Trade Shows   **Trade shows** provide another opportunity for buyers to see the latest products and styles and interact with vendors. Vendors display their merchandise in designated areas and have sales representatives, company executives, and sometime even celebrities available to talk with buyers as they walk through the exhibit area. For example, consumer electronics buyers attend the annual International Consumer Electronics Show (CES) in Las Vegas, the world's largest trade show for consumer technology.[15] The trade show, like most, is closed to the public, but vendors, developers, and suppliers of consumer technology hardware, content, delivery systems, and related products and services are among the more than 140,000 attendees from over 110 countries. Trade shows are typically staged at convention centers not associated with wholesale market centers. McCormick Place in Chicago (the nation's largest convention complex, with more than 2.7 million square feet) hosts over 65 meetings and trade shows a year, including the National Hardware Show and National Housewares Manufacturers Association International Exposition.[16] Other trade shows are The Super Show, sponsored by the Sporting Goods Manufacturers Association,[17] and the Frankfurt Book Fair.[18]

Vendors from outside the United States and private-brand manufacturers attend trade shows to learn about the market and pick up trend information. Some private-label manufacturers attend and display at trade shows, but most participants are national-brand vendors.

National-Brand Buying Process

When attending market weeks or trade shows, buyers and their supervisors typically make a series of appointments with key vendors. During these meetings, the buyers discuss the performance of the vendor's merchandise during the previous

REFACT

Wholesale transactions amounting to an estimated $8.5 billion are conducted within the Dallas Market Center complex annually.[14]

The International Consumer Electronics Show (CES) in Las Vegas is the world's largest trade show for consumer technology.

season, review the vendor's offering for the coming season, and possibly place orders for the coming season. These meetings take place in conference rooms in the vendors' showrooms at wholesale market centers. During trade shows, these meetings typically are less formal. The meetings during market weeks offer an opportunity for an in-depth discussion, whereas trade shows provide the opportunity for buyers to see a broader array of merchandise in one location and gauge reactions to the merchandise by observing the level of activity in the vendor's display area.

Often buyers do not negotiate with vendors and place orders during the market week or trade show. They typically want to see what merchandise and prices are available from all the potential vendors before deciding what items to buy. So, after attending a market week or trade show, buyers return to their offices, review requested samples of merchandise sent to them by vendors, meet with their supervisors to review the available merchandise, make decisions about which items are most attractive, and then negotiate with the vendors before placing an order. The issues involved in negotiating the purchase of national-brand merchandise are discussed later in this chapter.

DEVELOPING AND SOURCING PRIVATE-LABEL MERCHANDISE

Retailers use a variety of different processes to develop and buy private-label merchandise.

Developing Private-Label Merchandise

Larger retailers that offer a significant amount of private-label merchandise, such as JCPenney, Macy's, The Gap, and American Eagle Outfitters, have large divisions with people devoted to the development of their private-label merchandise. Employees in these divisions specialize in identifying trends, designing and specifying products, selecting manufacturers to make the products, maintaining a worldwide staff to monitor the conditions under which the products are made, and managing facilities to test the quality of the manufactured products. For example, MAST Industries, a subsidiary of Limited Brands, is one of the world's biggest contract manufacturers, importers, and distributors of apparel, with manufacturing operations and joint ventures in more than a dozen countries including China, Israel, Mexico, and Sri Lanka. In addition to being the major private-label supplier of Limited Brands (Victoria's Secret and Bath & Body Works), it provides private-label merchandise for Abercrombie & Fitch, Lane Bryant, New York & Company, White House Black Market, and Chico's. However, most retailers do not own and operate manufacturing facilities.

Smaller retail chains can offer private-label merchandise without making a significant investment in the supporting infrastructure. Smaller retailers often ask national-brand or private-label suppliers to make minor changes to products they offer and then provide the merchandise with the store's brand name or a special label copyrighted by the national brand. Alternatively, private-label manufacturers will sell to them from a predetermined stock selection. Hollander, for instance, makes 150,000 private-label pillows a day for companies like Laura Ashley and Simmons Beautyrest.[19] Retailing View 13.3 describes how Chinese manufacturers achieve low costs by developing economies of scale without exploiting workers.

13.3   RETAILING VIEW   Datang, China, Is Sock City

Datang, China, is called Sock City because 9 billion pairs of socks, more than one set for every person in the world, and 2.6 pairs for each American, are produced there each year. Its annual trade fair attracts 100,000 buyers from around the world. Southeast of Datang is Shenzhou, which is the world's necktie capital; to the west is Sweater City and Kids' Clothing City; and to the south is Underwear City.

As a result of government and private investment, China has become the leading manufacturer of private-label and national-brand merchandise.

socks at home. Now, she is the owner of Zhejiang Socks and a sock millionaire.

The Chinese government has also designated large areas for development, formed giant industrial parks, given tax benefits, and developed the infrastructure and transportation networks needed to move products quickly to market. It has created networks of support businesses located near one another, such as the button capital that furnishes most of the buttons on the world's shirts, pants, and jackets. Private companies, with the support of the government, have built huge textile factory complexes, complete with dormitories and hospitals, that provide food, shelter, and health care, along with close supervision.

This specialization creates the economies of scale that have made Chinese businesses the world's leading garment manufacturers. Buyers from New York to Tokyo can place orders for 500,000 pairs of socks all at once—or 300,000 neckties, 100,000 children's jackets, or 50,000 size 36B bras—in China's giant new specialty textile cities.

Textile production is a prime example of how the Chinese government guides development indirectly through local planning instead of state ownership. In the late 1970s, Datang was a rice-farming village with 1,000 people, who gathered in small groups and stitched socks together at home and then sold them in baskets along the highway. But the government designated Datang's sock makers as producers and ordered them to stop retailing socks. Now, they produce over one-third of the world's output. Due to the policy, there are many rags-to-riches tales in Datang, such as that of Dong Ying Hong, who in the 1970s gave up a $9-a-month job as an elementary school teacher to make

Huafang Group, one of China's largest textile companies, has over 100 factory buildings, 30,000 employees, and round-the-clock operations. More than 20,000 workers live free of charge in Huafang's dormitories. Conditions aren't great, but they are often better than the conditions in the inland provinces from which the workers come. Many women go there after high school, stay for a few years, and then return home to be married. As they return home, another 10,000 are bused in from the countryside.

Sources: Geoffrey Colvin, "Saving America's Socks—but Killing Free Trade," *Fortune*, August 22, 2005, p. 38; Evan Clark, "China's Foothold on Socks," *Women's Wear Daily*, December 5, 2005.

Retailers with private-label departments or divisions use different processes to develop merchandise. For some retailers, designers in the private-label division use their insight about market trends to develop a product line. They then present the designs to buyers. The buyers then make decisions about which items to buy from the merchandise developed by the division. In some firms, the buyers are instructed to buy specific items or a specific amount of private-label merchandise from the firm's division. In other retail firms, the private-label division operates somewhat independently, like a national-brand vendor, and the buyers are free to buy the private-label merchandise offered by the division or buy national brands. In retailing firms that only sell private-label merchandise, the buyers and designers typically work together closely to develop the merchandise.

Sourcing Merchandise

Once the decision has been made about which and how much private-label merchandise will be acquired, the designers develop a complete specification and work with the sourcing department to find a manufacturer for the merchandise. For example, JCPenney has sourcing and quality assurance offices in 18 countries. These offices take the specification developed by the designer, negotiate a contract to produce the item with manufacturers, and monitor the production process.[20] Since barriers to international trade are diminishing, retailers can consider sources for merchandise anywhere in the world. In this section, we examine factors affecting global sourcing costs; human rights, child-labor, and sustainability issues; resident buying offices; and reverse auctions.

Costs Associated with Global Sourcing Decisions

Retailers use production facilities located in developing economies for much of their private-label merchandise because of the very low labor costs in these countries. To counterbalance the lower acquisition costs, however, there are other expenses that can increase the costs of sourcing private-label merchandise from other countries. These costs include the relative value of foreign currencies, tariffs, longer lead times, and increased transportation costs.[21]

Retailers can hedge against short-term foreign currency fluctuations by buying contracts that lock the retailer into a set price regardless of how the currency fluctuates. But in the longer term, the relative value of foreign currencies can have a strong influence on the cost of imported merchandise. For example, if the Indian rupee has a sustained and significant increase relative to the U.S. dollar, the cost of private-label merchandise produced in India and imported for sale into the United States will increase. **Tariffs,** also known as **duties,** are taxes collected by a government on imports. Import tariffs have been used to shield domestic manufacturers from foreign competition. Inventory turnover also is likely to be lower when purchasing from foreign suppliers. Because lead times are longer and more uncertain, retailers using foreign sources must maintain larger inventories to ensure that the merchandise is available when the customer wants it. Larger inventories mean larger inventory carrying costs. Finally, transportation costs are higher when merchandise is produced in foreign countries.

The decline of the value of the U.S. dollar against the Euro and other important world currencies has made imports to the United States more expensive and exports from the United States less expensive.

Managerial Issues Associated with Global Sourcing Decisions

Whereas the cost factors associated with global sourcing are easy to quantify, some more subjective issues include quality control, time to market, and social/political risks. When sourcing globally, it's harder to maintain consistent quality standards than it is when sourcing domestically. Quality control problems can cause delays in shipment and adversely affect a retailer's image.

The collaborative supply chain management approaches described in Chapter 10 are more difficult to implement when sourcing globally. Collaborative systems are based on short and consistent lead times. Vendors provide frequent deliveries of smaller quantities. For a collaborative system to work properly there must be a strong alliance between the vendor and the retailer that is based on trust and sharing of information. These activities are more difficult to perform globally than domestically.

Another issue related to global sourcing is the problem of policing potential violations of human rights and child-labor laws. Many retailers have had to publicly defend themselves against allegations of human rights, child-labor, or other abuses involving the factories and countries in which their goods are made.[22] Due to the efforts of U.S. retailers and nonprofit organizations, fewer imported goods are produced in sweatshop conditions today. Some retailers are quite proactive in enforcing the labor practices of their suppliers. Limited Brands, for instance, was one of the first U.S. apparel manufacturers to develop and implement policies requiring that vendors and their subcontractors and suppliers observe core labor standards as a condition of doing business. Among other things, this requirement ensures that each supplier pays minimum wages and benefits; limits overtime to local industry standards; does not use prisoners, forced labor, or child labor; and provides a healthy and safe environment.[23] Many other companies that produce or sell goods made in low-wage countries conduct similar self-policing. Self-policing allows companies to avoid painful public revelations. Retailing View 13.4 examines how Walmart is pushing its vendors to be environmentally responsible.

Resident Buying Offices   Many retailers purchasing private-label merchandise use **resident buying offices,** which are organizations located in major market centers that provide services to help retailers buy merchandise. As retailers have become larger and more sophisticated, these third-party independent resident buying offices have become less important. Now many retailers have their own buying offices in other countries.

To illustrate how buying offices operate, consider how David Smith of Pockets Men's Store in Dallas utilizes his resident buying offices when he goes to market

13.4   RETAILING VIEW   It Isn't Easy to Sell to Walmart

Walmart is known for its low prices—and for driving its vendors to tears to get them. Now it is pressuring its vendors to also supply it with environmentally friendly merchandise with labels to prove it. In the future, merchandise sold at Walmart will have the environmental equivalent of nutritional labels, providing information on the product's carbon footprint, the amount of water and air pollution used to produce it, and other environmental issues. To measure how a vendor's products are doing, Walmart has developed a sustainability index that simultaneously takes several issues into consideration.

Walmart is also requiring that its top 200 factories become 20 percent more energy-efficient by 2012; a feat that many experts believe may be impossible, even with Walmart's help. Initial results are promising, however. For example, Jiangsu Redbud Dyeing Technology in China has cut coal consumption by one-tenth and is attempting to cut its toxic emissions to zero.

Walmart hasn't always been touted as a good corporate citizen. In the 1990s, it came to light that workers at some factories producing clothing for Walmart were subjected to inhumane conditions. More recently, two government organizations accused Walmart of buying from 15 factories that engage in abuse

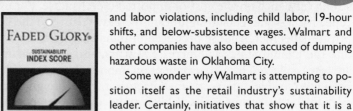

and labor violations, including child labor, 19-hour shifts, and below-subsistence wages. Walmart and other companies have also been accused of dumping hazardous waste in Oklahoma City.

Some wonder why Walmart is attempting to position itself as the retail industry's sustainability leader. Certainly, initiatives that show that it is a good corporate citizen enhance its image. But Walmart expects that these initiatives will be good for business as well. Its customers, especially those born between 1980 and 2000, are increasingly concerned about how the products they use impact the environment and the people that produce them. Also, Walmart believes that many of these initiatives will help streamline supply chain processes and therefore provide additional financial benefits to its suppliers and customers.

REFACT

Walmart buys some $9 billion worth of merchandise annually from about 20,000 vendors.

Sources: Stephanie Rosenbloom, "At Wal-Mart, Labeling to Reflect Green Intent," *New York Times*, July 16, 2009; Stephanie Rosenbloom, "Wal-Mart to Toughen Standards," *New York Times*, October 22, 2008; Adam Aston, "Wal-Mart: Making Its Suppliers Go Green," *BusinessWeek*, May 18, 2009.

in Milan. Smith meets with market representative Alain Bordat of the Doneger Group. Bordat, an English-speaking Italian, knows Smith's store and his upscale customers, so before Smith's visit, he set up appointments with Italian vendors that he believes will fit Pockets' image.

When Smith is in Italy, Bordat accompanies him to the appointments and acts as a translator, negotiator, and accountant. Bordat informs Smith of the cost of importing the merchandise into the United States, taking into account duty, freight, insurance, processing costs, and so forth.

Once the orders are placed, Bordat writes the contracts and follows up on delivery and quality control. The Doneger Group also acts as a home base for buyers like Smith, providing office space and services, travel advisers, and emergency aid. Bordat and his association continue to keep Smith abreast of what's happening on the Italian fashion scene through reports and constant communication. Without the help of a resident buying office, it would be difficult, if not impossible, for Smith to access the Italian wholesale market.

Reverse Auctions   Rather than negotiating with a specific manufacturer to produce the merchandise, some retailers use reverse auctions to get quality private-label merchandise at low prices.[24] In traditional auctions like those conducted on eBay, there is one seller and many buyers. Auctions conducted by retailer buyers of private-label merchandise are called **reverse auctions** because there is one buyer, the retailer, and many potential sellers, the manufacturing firms. In a reverse auction, the retail buyer provides a specification for what it wants to a group of potential vendors. The competing vendors then bid on the price at which they are willing to sell until the auction is over. However, the retailer is not required to place an order with the lowest bidder. The retailer can choose to place an order at the offered price from whichever vendor the retailer feels will provide the merchandise in a timely manner and with the specified quality.

The most common use of reverse auctions is to buy the products and services used in retail operations rather than merchandise for resale. Some operating materials that are frequently bought through reverse auctions are store carpeting, fixtures, and supplies. However, reverse auctions also are being used by several retailers to procure private-label merchandise, such as commodities and seasonal merchandise like lawn furniture.

Reverse auctions are not popular with vendors. Few vendors want to be anonymous contestants in bidding wars where price alone, not service or quality, seems to be the sole basis for winning the business. Strategic relationships are also difficult to nurture when the primary interactions with vendors are through electronic auctions.

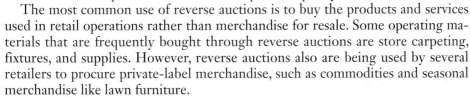

NEGOTIATING WITH VENDORS

When buying national brands or sourcing private-label merchandise, buyers and firm employees responsible for sourcing typically enter into negotiations with suppliers. To understand how buyers negotiate with vendors, consider a hypothetical situation in which Carolyn Swigler, women's jeans buyer at Bloomingdale's, is preparing to meet with Dario Carvel, the salesperson from Juicy Couture, in his office in New York City. Swigler, after reviewing the merchandise during the women's wear market week in New York, is ready to buy Juicy Couture's spring line, but she has some merchandising problems that have yet to be resolved from last season.

Knowledge Is Power

The more Carolyn Swigler knows about her situation and Juicy Couture's, as well as the trends in the marketplace, the more effective she will be during the negotiations. First, Swigler assesses the relationship she has with the vendor. Although

When negotiating with a vendor, the more knowledge that is available about the vendor, the market, and the products, the more successful the negotiation will be.

Swigler and Carvel have met only a few times in the past, their companies have had a long, profitable relationship. A sense of trust and mutual respect has been established, which Swigler feels will lead to a productive meeting.

Although Juicy Couture jeans have been profitable for Bloomingdale's in the past, three styles sold poorly last season. Swigler plans to ask Carvel to let her return some merchandise. Swigler knows from past experience that Juicy Couture normally doesn't allow merchandise to be returned but does provide **markdown money**—funds vendors give retailers to cover lost gross margin dollars due to the markdowns needed to sell unpopular merchandise.

Vendors and their representatives are excellent sources of market information. They generally know what is and isn't selling. Providing good, timely information about the market is an indispensable and inexpensive marketing research tool. So Swigler plans to spend at least part of the meeting talking to Carvel about market trends.

Just as Carvel can provide market information to Swigler, she can provide information to him. For example, on one of her buying trips to Japan, she found jeans in a great new wash made by a small Japanese firm on old selvage looms. She bought a pair and gave them to Carvel, who passed it along to Juicy Couture's designers. They used the jeans to develop a new wash that was a big success.

Swigler also knows that Carvel will want her to buy some of the newest and most avant-garde designs in Juicy Couture's spring product line. Carvel knows that many U.S. buyers go to market in New York and that most stop at Bloomingdale's to see what's new, what's selling, and how it's displayed. Thus, Carvel wants to make sure that Juicy Couture is well represented at Bloomingdale's.

Negotiation Issues

In addition to taking care of last season's leftover merchandise, Swigler is prepared to discuss six issues during the upcoming meeting: (1) prices and gross margin, (2) additional markup opportunities, (3) terms of purchase, (4) exclusivity, (5) advertising allowances, and (6) transportation.

Price and Gross Margin   Of course, Swigler wants to buy the merchandise at a low price so that she will have a high gross margin. In contrast, Carvel wants to sell the jeans at a higher price because he is concerned about Juicy Couture's profits. Two factors that affect the price and gross margin are margin guarantees and slotting allowances.

Margin Guarantees   Swigler, like most buyers, has a gross margin goal for each merchandise category that is quantified in her merchandise budget plans (Chapter 12). The wholesale price Swigler negotiates for the Juicy Couture merchandise might enable her to achieve her gross margin goal. However, if the merchandise does not sell as expected, Swigler might have to put the items on sale and she will not make her margin goal. Faced with this uncertainty, Swigler, and other buyers, may seek a commitment from Juicy Couture to "guarantee" that she will realize her gross margin goal on the merchandise. If she has to mark down the merchandise, she wants Juicy Couture to provide her with markdown money.

Carvel, like many vendors, might be willing to provide this gross margin guarantee. However, Carvel is concerned that Swigler might not aggressively promote Juicy Couture's merchandise if she knows that her gross margin is guaranteed. Thus, Carvel will offer the guarantee only in exchange for a commitment from Swigler that she will feature Juicy Couture merchandise in the store and advertise the product line.

Slotting Fees   In addition to negotiating the wholesale price, supermarket buyers often negotiate slotting fees. **Slotting fees,** or **slotting allowances,** are charges imposed by a retailer to stock a new item. When a vendor agrees to pay that fee, the retailer will stock the product for a period of time, assess its sales and margin, and, if it is successful, continue to offer the product after the trial period. For example, when Kraft wants to introduce a new product, supermarket chains might charge between $1 million and $2 million for a national rollout to stock the product. The fee varies depending on the nature of the product and the relative power of the retailer. Products with low brand loyalty pay the highest slotting allowances. Likewise, large supermarket chains can demand higher slotting allowances than can small, independent retailers.

Vendors may view slotting allowances as extortion, and small vendors believe these fees preclude their access to retail stores. However, retailers, and most economists, argue that slotting allowances are a useful method for retailers to determine which new products merit inclusion in their assortment. The vendor has more information than the retailer about the quality of its new product. Thus, the slotting fee is a method for getting the vendor to reveal this private information. If the new product is good, the vendor will be willing to pay the fee, because the vendor knows that the product will sell and generate adequate margins during the trial period. However, a vendor promoting a poor product will be reluctant to pay the fee.[25]

Additional Markup Opportunities   At times in the past, Juicy Couture has offered Swigler discounted prices to take excess merchandise. The excessive merchandise arises from order cancellations, returned merchandise from other retailers, or simply an overly optimistic sales forecast. Although Swigler can realize higher-than-normal gross margins on this merchandise or put the merchandise on sale and pass the savings on to customers, Bloomingdale's has to preserve its image as a fashion leader and thus Swigler is not very interested in any excess inventory that Juicy Couture has to offer.

Terms of Purchase   Swigler would like to negotiate for a long period in which to pay for merchandise. A long payment period improves Bloomingdale's cash flow, lowers its liabilities (accounts payable), and can reduce its interest expense if it's borrowing money from financial institutions to pay for its inventory. But Juicy Couture also has its own financial objectives it wants to accomplish and thus would like to be paid soon after it delivers the merchandise.

Exclusivity   Retailers often negotiate with vendors for an exclusive arrangement so that no other retailer can sell the same item or brand. Through an exclusive arrangement, the retailer can differentiate itself from competitors and realize higher margins due to reduced price competition. In some cases, vendors also benefit by making sure that the image of retailers selling their merchandise is consistent with their brand image. For example, Prada might want to give exclusive rights for its apparel to only one store in a major market, such as Neiman Marcus. In addition, an exclusive arrangement offers a monopoly to the retailer and thus a strong incentive to promote the item.

In fashion merchandise categories, being the first retailer in a market to carry certain products helps that retailer hold a fashion-leader image and achieve a differential advantage. Swigler wants her shipment of the new spring line to arrive as early in the season as possible and would like to have some jeans styles and washes that won't be sold to competing retailers. In contrast, Juicy Couture wants to have its products sold by many different retailers to maximize its sales.

Advertising Allowances   Retailers often share the cost of advertising through a cooperative arrangement with vendors known as **co-op (cooperative) advertising**—a program undertaken by a vendor in which the vendor agrees to pay for all or part of a pricing promotion. As a fashion leader, Bloomingdale's advertises heavily. Swigler would like Juicy Couture to support an advertising program with a generous advertising allowance.

Transportation   Transportation costs can be substantial, although this point isn't a big issue for the Juicy Couture jeans because the merchandise has a high unit price and low weight. Nonetheless, the question of who pays for shipping merchandise from the vendor to the retailer will be a significant negotiating point.

Now that some of the issues involved in the negotiation between Juicy Couture and Bloomingdale's are on the table, the next section presents some tips for effective negotiations.

Tips for Effective Negotiating[26]

Have at Least as Many Negotiators as the Vendor   Retailers have a psychological advantage at the negotiating table if the vendor is outnumbered. At the very least, retailers want the negotiating teams to be the same size. Swigler plans to invite her divisional merchandise manager (DMM) to the discussion if Carvel comes with his sales manager.

Choose a Good Place to Negotiate   Swigler may have an advantage in the upcoming meeting because it will be in her office. She'll have ready access to information, plus secretarial and supervisory assistance. From a psychological perspective, people generally feel more comfortable and confident in familiar surroundings. However, Swigler also might get more out of the negotiation if

In a negotiation, have at least as many negotiators as the vendor.

Carvel feels comfortable. In the end, selecting the location for a negotiation is an important decision.

Be Aware of Real Deadlines   Swigler recognizes that Carvel must go back to his office with an order in hand, because he has a quota to meet by the end of the month. She also knows that she must get markdown money or permission to return the unsold jeans by the end of the week or she won't have sufficient open-to-buy funds to cover the orders she wishes to place. Recognizing these deadlines will help Swigler come to closure quickly in the upcoming negotiation.

Separate the People from the Problem   Suppose Swigler starts the meeting with, "Dario, you know we've been friends for a long time. I have a personal favor to ask. Would you mind taking back $10,000 in shirts?" This personal plea puts Carvel in an uncomfortable situation. Swigler's personal relationship with Carvel isn't the issue here and shouldn't become part of the negotiation. An equally detrimental scenario would be for Swigler to say, "Dario, your line is terrible. I can hardly give the stuff away. I want you to take back $10,000 in jeans. After all, you're dealing with Bloomingdale's. If you don't take this junk back, you can forget about ever doing business with us again." Threats usually don't work in negotiations. They put the other party on the defensive. Threats may actually cause negotiations to break down, in which case no one wins.

Insist on Objective Information   The best way to separate the people from the business issues is to rely on objective information. Swigler must know exactly how many jeans need to be returned to Juicy Couture or how much markdown money is necessary to maintain her gross margin. If Carvel argues from an emotional perspective, Swigler will stick to the numbers. For instance, suppose that after Swigler presents her position, Carvel says that he'll get into trouble if he takes back the merchandise or provides markdown money. With the knowledge that Juicy Couture has provided relief in similar situations in the past, Swigler should ask what Juicy Couture's policy is regarding customer overstock problems. She should also show Carvel a summary of Bloomingdale's buying activity with Juicy Couture over the past few seasons. Using this approach, Swigler forces Carvel to acknowledge that providing assistance in this overstock situation—especially if it has been done in the past—is a small price to pay for a long-term profitable relationship.

Invent Options for Mutual Gain   Inventing multiple options is part of the planning process, but knowing when and how much to give, or give up, requires quick thinking at the bargaining table. Consider Swigler's overstock problem. Her objective is to get the merchandise out of her inventory without significantly hurting her gross margin. Carvel's objective is to maintain a healthy yet profitable relationship with Bloomingdale's. Thus, Swigler must invent options that could satisfy both parties, such as offering to buy some of Juicy Couture's most avant-garde jeans in return for markdown money for her excess inventory.

Let Them Do the Talking   There's a natural tendency for one person to continue to talk if the other person involved in the conversation doesn't respond. If used properly, this phenomenon can work to the negotiator's advantage. Suppose Swigler asks Carvel for special financial support for Bloomingdale's Christmas catalog. Carvel begins with a qualified no and cites all the reasons he can't cooperate. But Swigler doesn't say a word. Although Carvel appears nervous, he continues to talk. Eventually, he comes around to a yes. In negotiations, those who break the silence first lose.

Know How Far to Go   There's a fine line between negotiating too hard and walking away from the table without an agreement. If Swigler negotiates too aggressively for the markdown money, better terms of purchase, and a strong advertising allowance, the management of Juicy Couture may decide that other retailers are more worthy of early deliveries and the best styles. Carvel may not be afraid to say no if Swigler pushes him beyond a legal, ethical, profitable relationship.

Don't Burn Bridges   Even if Swigler gets few additional concessions from Carvel, she shouldn't be abusive or resort to threats. Bloomingdale's may not want to stop doing business with Juicy Couture on the basis of this one encounter. From a personal perspective, the world of retailing is relatively small. Swigler and Carvel may meet at the negotiating table again, possibly both working for different companies. Neither can afford to be known in the trade as unfair, rude, or worse.

Don't Assume   Many issues are raised and resolved in any negotiating session. To be certain there are no misunderstandings, participants should orally review the outcomes at the end of the session. Swigler and Carvel should both summarize the session in writing as soon as possible after the meeting.

STRATEGIC RELATIONSHIPS

Chapter 5 emphasized that maintaining strong vendor relationships is an important way to develop a sustainable competitive advantage. Chapters 10 and 12 discussed some of the ways partnering relations can improve information exchange, planning, and the management of supply chains. For example, a vendor-managed inventory system cannot operate effectively without the vendor and retailer making a commitment to work together and invest in the relationship.[27] In this section, we examine how retailers develop strategic relationships and the characteristics of successful long-term relationships.

Defining Strategic Relationships

Traditionally, relationships between retailers and vendors have focused on haggling over how to split up a profit pie.[28] The relationships were basically win-lose encounters because when one party got a larger portion of the pie, the other party got a smaller portion. Both parties were interested exclusively in their own profits and unconcerned about the other party's welfare. These relationships continue to be common, especially when the products being bought are commodities and have limited impact on the retailers' performance. In these situations there is no benefit to the retailer from entering into a strategic relationship.

A **strategic relationship,** also called a **partnering relationship,** emerges when a retailer and vendor are committed to maintaining the relationship over the long term and investing in opportunities that are mutually beneficial to both parties. In this relationship, it's important for the partners to take risks to expand the profit pie to give the relationship a strategic advantage over other companies. In addition, the parties have a long-term perspective. They are willing to make short-term sacrifices because they know that they will get their fair share in the long run.[29]

Strategic relationships are win-win relationships. Both parties benefit because the size of the profit pie increases. Both the retailer and the vendor increase their sales and profits because the parties in strategic relationships work together to develop and exploit joint opportunities. They depend on and trust each other heavily. They share goals and agree on how to accomplish those goals, and they thus reduce the risks of investing in the relationship and sharing confidential information. For example, when Kohl's and Vera Wang embarked on their exclusive branding strategy, they worked together to determine their customers' needs, likes, and dislikes. (See Retailing View 13.2.) Then they jointly developed an assortment and pricing strategy that has proved to be much more successful than would have been possible if they had worked separately and just negotiated a quantity and price. To sustain their successful momentum, they share trends in the market and agree to respond quickly when a change occurs or when a product should be produced in a short time.

A strategic relationship is like a marriage. When businesses enter strategic relationships, they're wedded to their partners for better or worse. For example, Spain-based fast-fashion retailer Zara manufactures about 40 percent of its finished garments.[30] Once the fabric is cut, it is sent to about 450 independently owned workshops located near the corporate headquarters for the labor-intensive activity of sewing the pieces into finished garments. Most of these relatively small workshops have had long-term relationships with Zara. Zara provides them with technology, logistics and financial support, and other types of assistance. In return, the workshops support Zara's mission of being able to quickly provide women and men in 73 countries with relatively inexpensive fashion apparel. Like any supplier, these small workshops sometimes miss a deadline or make a mistake on a garment. But as in a marriage, Zara doesn't dump them and move on to someone else. It works with them to make things work.

Maintaining Strategic Relationships

The four foundations of successful strategic relationships are mutual trust, open communication, common goals, and credible commitments.

Mutual Trust   The glue in a strategic relationship is trust. **Trust** is a belief that a partner is honest (reliable and stands by its word) and benevolent (concerned about the other party's welfare).[32] When vendors and buyers trust each other, they're more willing to share relevant ideas, clarify goals and problems, and communicate efficiently. Information shared between the parties becomes increasingly comprehensive, accurate, and timely. There's less need for the vendor and buyer to constantly monitor and check up on each other's actions, because each believes the other will not take advantage, even given the opportunity.[33] If Walmart's sustainability initiatives described in Retailing View 13.4 are to be achieved, it is important for Walmart to trust its vendors and vice versa.

Common Goals   Vendors and buyers must have common goals for a successful relationship to develop.[34] Shared goals give both members of the relationship an incentive to pool their strengths and abilities and exploit potential opportunities between them. They also create an assurance that the other partner will not do anything to hinder goal achievement within the relationship.

For example, Walmart and its vendors have recognized that it was in their common interest to develop and sell products that have a positive impact on the environment. Walmart can't demand that its vendors take on sustainability programs that are so expensive that they won't make money, and its vendors must try to accommodate the demands of its biggest customer. With a common goal, Walmart and its suppliers have an incentive to cooperate, because they know that by doing so, both can achieve their common sustainability goals and still make profits.

Common goals also help sustain the relationship when goals aren't realized according to plan. If, for instance, a vendor fails to reach an acceptable score on Walmart's sustainability index but has made significant progress, Walmart won't suddenly call off the whole arrangement. Instead, Walmart is likely to work harder to help the vendor raise its score and remain in the relationship, because Walmart knows that it and the vendor are committed to the same goals in the long run.

REFACT

Bentonville, Arkansas, the corporate headquarters for Walmart, has a population of 34,000. More than 450 companies that are suppliers to Walmart have opened offices in Bentonville, otherwise known as Vendorville, including Microsoft, Oracle, Rubbermaid, Disney, Dreamworks, and Procter & Gamble.[31]

Walmart builds strategic relationships with its vendors by fostering mutual trust; having open communications and common goals; and making credible commitments.

Open Communication   To share information, develop sales forecasts together, coordinate deliveries, and achieve their sustainability common goals, Walmart and its vendors must have open and honest communication. This requirement may sound easy in principle, but most businesses don't like to share information with their business partners. They believe it is none of the other's business. But open, honest communication is a key to developing successful relationships. Buyers and vendors in a relationship need to understand what is driving each other's business, their roles in the relationship, each firm's strategies, and any problems that arise over the course of the relationship.

Credible Commitments   Successful relationships develop because both parties make credible commitments. Credible commitments are tangible investments in the relationship. They go beyond just making the hollow statement, "I want to be your partner." Credible commitments involve spending money to improve products or services and, in the case of Walmart and its vendors, taking mutual steps to improve the sustainability index. For example, the goal of reducing Jiangsu Redbud Dyeing Technology's toxic emissions in China is a joint effort and investment by Walmart and Jiangsu.

Building Partnering Relationships

Although not all retailer-vendor relationships should or do become strategic partnerships, the development of strategic partnerships tends to go through a series of phases characterized by increasing levels of involvement: (1) awareness, (2) exploration, (3) expansion, and (4) commitment.

Awareness   In the awareness stage, no transactions have taken place. This phase might begin with the buyer seeing some interesting merchandise at a retail market or an ad in a trade magazine. The reputation and image of the vendor can play an important role in determining if the buyer moves to the next stage.

Exploration   During the exploration phase, the buyer and vendor begin to explore the potential benefits and costs of a partnership. At this point, the buyer may make a small purchase and try to test the demand for the merchandise in several stores. In addition, the buyer will get information about how easy it is to work with the vendor.

Expansion   Eventually, the buyer has collected enough information about the vendor to consider developing a longer-term relationship. The buyer and the vendor determine if there is the potential for a win-win relationship. They begin to work on joint promotional programs, and the amount of merchandise sold increases.

Commitment   If both parties continue to find the relationship mutually beneficial, it moves to the commitment stage and becomes a strategic relationship. The buyer and vendor then make significant investments in the relationship and develop a long-term perspective toward it.

It is difficult for retailer-vendor relationships to be as committed as some supplier-manufacturer relationships. Manufacturers can enter into monogamous (sole-source) relationships with other manufacturers. However, an important function of retailers is to provide an assortment of merchandise for their customers. Thus, they must always deal with multiple, sometimes competing suppliers.

Regardless of which partner-building phase a retailer is in with a supplier, the retailer is constantly involved in the give-and-take process of negotiations. The next section looks at some of the legal and ethical issues that arise when buying merchandise.

LEGAL, ETHICAL, AND SOCIAL RESPONSIBILITY ISSUES FOR BUYING MERCHANDISE

Legal and Ethical Issues

Given the many negotiations and interactions between retail buyers and vendors, ethical and legal issues are bound to arise. This section reviews some practices that arise in buyer-vendor negotiations that may have legal and/or ethical implications, and it looks at some ways that retailers are becoming more socially responsible in their buying practices.

Terms and Conditions of Purchase   The Robinson-Patman Act, passed by the U.S. Congress in 1936, potentially restricts the prices and terms that vendors can offer to retailers. The act makes it illegal for vendors to offer different terms and conditions to different retailers for the same merchandise and quantity. Sometimes called the "Anti-Chain-Store Act," it was passed to protect independent retailers from chain-store competition. Thus, if a vendor negotiates a good deal on the issues discussed in the previous section (price, advertising allowance, markdown money, transportation), the Robinson-Patman Act requires that the vendor offer the same terms and conditions to other retailers.

However, vendors can offer different terms to retailers for the same merchandise and quantities if the costs of manufacturing, selling, or delivery are different. The cost of manufacturing is usually the same, but selling and delivery could be more expensive for some retailers. For example, vendors may incur larger transportation expenses due to smaller shipments to independent retailers.

Different prices can also be offered if the retailers are providing different functions. For example, a large retailer can get a lower price if its distribution centers store the merchandise or its stores provide different services valued by customers.

In addition, lower prices can be offered to meet competition and dispose of perishable merchandise.[35]

Commercial Bribery   **Commercial bribery** occurs when a vendor or its agent offers or a buyer asks for "something of value" to influence purchase decisions. Say a salesperson for a ski manufacturer takes a sporting goods retail buyer to lunch at a fancy private club and then proposes a ski weekend in Vail. These gifts could be construed as bribes or kickbacks, which are illegal unless the buyer's manager is informed of them. To avoid such problems, many retailers forbid employees to accept any gifts from vendors. Because some Home Depot buyers allegedly accepted large cash kickbacks from suppliers, the retailer has tightened its ethics code to ban buyers from accepting any gifts or entertainment from vendors—a zero tolerance policy.[36] Other retailers have a policy that it is fine to accept limited entertainment or token gifts, such as flowers or wine for the holidays. In either case, they want their buyers to decide on purchases solely on the basis of what is best for the retailer.

Chargebacks   A **chargeback** is a practice used by retailers in which they deduct money from the amount they owe a vendor. Retailers often use a chargeback when a vendor did not meet the agreed-on terms, for example, when a vendor improperly applied labels to shipping containers or merchandise or sent shipments that had missing items or were late. Chargebacks are especially difficult for vendors because once the money is deducted from an invoice and the invoice is marked "paid," it is difficult to dispute the claim and get the amount back. Vendors sometimes feel that the chargebacks retailers take are not justifiable and thus are unethical.

Buybacks   Similar to slotting allowances, **buybacks,** also known as **stocklifts** or **lift-outs,** are activities engaged in by vendors and retailers to get products into retail stores. Specifically, in a buyback situation, either a retailer allows a vendor to create space for its merchandise by "buying back" a competitor's inventory and removing it from the retailer's system or the retailer forces a vendor to buy back slow-moving merchandise. A vendor with significant market power can violate federal antitrust laws if it stock lifts from a competitor so often that it shuts the competitor out of a market, but such cases are difficult to prove.

Counterfeit Merchandise   Selling counterfeit merchandise can negatively affect a retailer's image and its relationship with the vendor of the legitimate brand. **Counterfeit merchandise** includes goods made and sold without the permission of the owner of a trademark or copyright. Trademarks and copyrights are **intellectual property,** that is, intangible and created by intellectual (mental) effort as opposed to physical effort. A **trademark** is any mark, word, picture, device, or nonfunctional design associated with certain merchandise (e.g., the crown on a Rolex watch, the red Levi's tag on the back pocket of a pair of jeans). A **copyright** protects the original work of authors, painters, sculptors, musicians, and others who produce works of artistic or intellectual merit. This book is copyrighted, so these sentences cannot be used by anyone without the consent of the copyright owners.

The nature of counterfeiting has changed during the past decade. Counterfeit name-brand merchandise, such as women's handbags, have improved in quality, making them more expensive and difficult to distinguish from the real merchandise. Also, there is a thriving business in counterfeit information products such as software, CDs, and CD-ROMs. This type of merchandise is attractive to counter-

It is illegal for this "street retailer" to sell counterfeit watches because it violates the watch manufacturers' rights to control the use of their trademarks.

feiters because it has a high unit value, is relatively easy to duplicate and transport, and prompts high consumer demand. The ease of illegally downloading and distributing music means that neither the record label nor the artist receives any money for their investment, work, or talent, and thus both may be less motivated to develop and produce music.

Do Internet markets like eBay have the responsibility to police counterfeiting on their sites? It depends on where they are. In the United States, jeweler Tiffany & Company lost a case against eBay in which it was established that the online company does not have the legal responsibility to prevent its users from selling counterfeit items. It is up to the trademark holders, like Tiffany, to monitor the Web sites as long as eBay and others promptly remove material when complaints are filed.[37] In a similar case in France, however, luxury manufacturer and retailer Hermes won against eBay. The court found that eBay had "committed acts of counterfeit" and "prejudice" against Hermes by failing to monitor the authenticity of goods being sold on its Web site.[38]

Gray-Market, Diverted, and Black-Market Merchandise **Gray-market goods,** also known as **parallel imports,** involve the flow of merchandise through distribution channels, usually across international borders, other than those authorized or intended by the manufacturer or producer. For example, to increase its profits, McGraw-Hill, the publisher of this textbook, charges a higher wholesale price for this textbook in the United States than in other countries. An importer could buy textbooks at a low price in other countries, import them into the United States, and sell them at a price lower than that in U.S. bookstores.

Diverted merchandise is similar to gray-market merchandise except there need not be distribution across international borders. Suppose, for instance, that the fragrance manufacturer Givenchy grants an exclusive scent to Saks Fifth Avenue. The Saks buyer has excess inventory and sells it at a low price to a discount retailer in the United States, such as an off-price retailer. In this case, the merchandise has been diverted from its legitimate channel of distribution, and Saks would be referred to as the *diverter.* While Saks may benefit from this transaction, the vendor is concerned about gray markets and diversions. Making the product available at discount stores at low prices may reduce the vendor's brand image and the service normally provided with the brand. So, while such practices are usually legal, vendors generally oppose gray market and diverted merchandise. A **black market,** on the other hand, occurs when consumer goods are scarce, such as water or gasoline after a natural disaster; heavily taxed, such as cigarettes or alcohol; or illegal, such as drugs or arms. We rarely see black-market merchandise sold through legitimate channels in the United States.

Vendors engage in a number of activities to avoid gray-market/diversion problems. They require that all of their retail and wholesale customers sign a contract stipulating that they will not engage in gray marketing. If a retailer is found in violation of the agreement, the vendor will refuse to deal with it in the future. Another strategy is to produce different versions of products for different markets. For instance, McGraw-Hill sells a different version of this textbook in India than it sells in the United States. Retailing View 13.5 examines why it is hard to tell whether merchandise is gray-market or counterfeit.

13.5   RETAILING VIEW   Where Did T.J.Maxx Get Its Coach Handbags?

The national brands that off-price retailers like T.J.Maxx, Marshalls, Ross, and Loehmann's sell at lower prices than those at their department and specialty store competitors come from a variety of sources. Sometimes the merchandise comes directly from manufacturers like Coach, the luxury leather goods maker, because the item was last year's model, it didn't sell well at the retail store where it was originally offered and was returned by the luxury retail customer, or Coach overestimated demand and therefore had excess inventory left over. Coach sells a very small percentage of its bags to off-price stores. Although luxury manufacturers prefer not to have their merchandise sold in off-price stores, these stores provide an excellent opportunity for luxury manufacturers to rid themselves of excess inventory.

Another source of Coach bags for off-price retailers may be luxury retailers. These retailers may have bought too many bags or specific styles that did not sell and may need to dispose of them at the end of a season. One alternative is for the retailers to mark down the price and put the handbags on sale. But sales on luxury products like Coach bags might damage the retailer's image. Also, Coach may not want its bags sold at a discount at luxury stores. So the retailer might sell the excess inventory to off-price retailers like T.J.Maxx. This diverting of merchandise to an unauthorized retailer is creating a gray market for Coach bags. If Coach discovers that one of its luxury retailers is diverting its newer merchandise to off-price retailers, it might refuse to sell to that retailer in the future.

Luxury-brand vendors hope that their products don't end up in off-price outlets, but they definitely fight to make sure that counterfeit products are not sold anywhere. While it is relatively

Off-price stores like T.J.Maxx regularly sell gray-market goods but not counterfeit merchandise.

harmless for gray-market luxury-branded products to end up in an off-price store, it is quite harmful to the luxury brands if a counterfeit bag is sold at a retail store. As a result, some luxury-brand vendors have taken steps to ensure that counterfeit products under their name are not sold, as we discussed in the cases of Tiffany & Company and Hermes suing eBay.

REFACT

TJX, owner of T.J.Maxx and Marshalls, employs 600 buyers who purchase from more than 10,000 vendors in over 60 countries.[39]

Sources: "TJX Takes Off-Price Retail to the Maxx," *Dow Theory Forecasts,* October 26, 2009, pp. 1, 8; Jena McGregor, "TJX: Dressed to Kill for the Downturn," *BusinessWeek,* October 27, 2008, p. 60.

Exclusive Dealing Agreements   **Exclusive dealing agreements** occur when a vendor restricts a retailer to carrying only its products and nothing from competing vendors. For example, Ford may require that its dealers sell only Ford cars and no cars made by General Motors. The effect of such arrangements on competition is determined by the market power of the vendor. For example, it may be illegal for a market leader like Coca-Cola to sell its products to a small supermarket chain only if the chain agrees not to sell a less popular cola product like RC Cola.

Tying Contract   A **tying contract** exists when a vendor requires that a retailer take a product it doesn't necessarily desire (the tied product) to ensure that it can buy a product it does desire (the tying product). Tying contracts are illegal if they substantially lessen competition or tend to create a monopoly. But the complaining party has the burden of proof. Thus, it is typically legal for a vendor to require that a buyer buy all items in its product line. For example, if a gift store sued a postcard manufacturer for requiring that it purchase as many "local view" postcards (the tied product) as it did licensed Disney character postcards (the tying product), the court would probably dismiss the case because the retailer would be unable to prove a substantial lessening of competition.

Refusal to Deal   The practice of refusing to deal (buy or sell to) can be viewed from both vendors' and retailers' perspectives. Generally, both vendors and retailers have the right to deal or refuse to deal with anyone they choose. But there are exceptions to this general rule when there's evidence of anticompetitive conduct by one or more firms that wield market power. A vendor may refuse to sell to a particular retailer, but it can't do so for the sole purpose of benefiting a competing retailer. For example, Mattel decided not to offer certain popular Barbie packages to wholesale clubs. This action in itself would have been legal. However, it was determined that Mattel agreed to do so as part of a conspiracy among 10 toy manufacturers orchestrated by Toys "R" Us to prevent wholesale clubs from underselling the same toy packages that Toys "R" Us sold. The refusal to deal then became an illegal group boycott.[40]

Corporate Social Responsibility

Corporate social responsibility describes the voluntary actions taken by a company to address the ethical, social, and environmental impacts of its business operations. Retailers act socially responsible in many ways, from giving to charity to donating time to philanthropic community activities. Recently, however, retailers have been increasing their efforts to buy merchandise in a socially responsible way.

Whole Foods considers local to be anything produced within seven hours of one of its stores. The retailer says that most local producers are within 200 miles of a store. It requires that all its stores buy from at least four local farmers. It gives $10 million a year in low-interest loans to help small, local farmers and producers of grass-fed and humanely raised meat, poultry, and dairy animals.

Some retailers are getting involved in **fair trade,** a socially responsible movement that ensures that producers receive fair prices for their products. The coffee retailers Starbucks and Peet's offer some, but not all, blends that use fair trade coffee.[42] Walmart is investing heavily in fair trade coffee, partially in response to a new corporate philosophy that goes beyond "everyday low prices" to "doing well by doing good." Bono, the U2 lead singer and an activist, is selling his high-priced fair trade apparel line, Edun, to stores such as Saks Fifth Avenue and Nordstrom.

Home Depot is encouraging its suppliers to include their products in its Eco Options marketing campaign. Some products are obviously attractive to green

Whole Foods is increasing its efforts to provide locally grown produce to support the local economy and save the carbon emissions involved in transporting produce from distant producers.[43]

customers, such as organic gardening products and high-efficiency lightbulbs. But a number of less obvious products are also good for the environment. Electric chain saws are green because they are not gas-powered, and bug zappers reduce the use of poisonous sprays. Home Depot also has introduced some new environmentally sensitive products into its assortment, including solar-powered landscape lighting, biodegradable peat pots, and paints that discharge fewer pollutants. Home Depot encourages its vendors to use recyclable plastic or cardboard packaging. It estimates that a 5 percent reduction in packaging will prevent 667,000 metric tons of carbon dioxide from entering the atmosphere while also resulting in $3.4 billion in cost savings.[44]

Other retailers are demanding smaller, eco-friendly packages from their suppliers. Smaller packages save not only materials but also energy. Because more packages can be transported on a truck, the transportation cost per unit goes down. Walmart plans to reduce packaging by 5 percent by 2013, a move that could save $3.4 billion.

McDonald's Europe has helped persuade agribusiness giants to stop buying soybeans from newly deforested tracts in protected regions of the Amazon. Walmart is urging its suppliers to combat global warming by using less energy and incorporating alternative sources. Tiffany & Co. has been calling on gold miners to end waste dumping in pristine lakes and adhere to international labor standards.

These initiatives and many others suggest a complicated business model. Are socially responsible activities good for business? Some are more expensive than traditional products and initiatives. Are consumers interested in or willing to pay the higher prices? Are firms really interested in improving the environment, or are they **greenwashing** (doing a green whitewash) or practicing **green sheen,** which is the disingenuous practice of marketing products or services as being environmentally friendly with the purpose of gaining public approval and sales rather than actually improving the environment. Consumers should question whether a firm is spending significantly more money or time advertising that it's **green** or that it operates with consideration for the environment rather than spending resources on environmentally sound practices.[45]

SUMMARY

This chapter examines issues surrounding purchasing merchandise and vendor relations. Retailers can purchase either national brands or private-label brands. Each type has its own relative advantages. Choosing appropriate brands and a branding strategy is an integral component of a firm's merchandise and assortment planning process.

Buyers of manufacturer's brands attend trade shows and wholesale market centers to meet with vendors, view new merchandise, and place orders. Virtually every merchandise category has at least one annual trade show at which retailers and vendors meet.

The process for buying private-label merchandise can be more complicated than that for buying national brands because the retailer takes on some of the responsibilities that a national-brand manufacturer normally would have, such as designing and specifying products and selecting manufacturers to make the products. A large percentage of private-label merchandise is manufactured outside the United States. The cost, managerial, and ethical issues surrounding global sourcing decisions must be considered.

Buying merchandise sometimes is facilitated by resident buying offices. Market representatives of the resident buying offices facilitate merchandising purchases in foreign markets.

Buyers of both national brands and private labels engage in negotiating a series of issues with their vendors, including markdown money, slotting fees, advertising allowances, terms of purchase, exclusivity, and transportation costs. Successful vendor relationships depend on planning for and being adept at negotiations.

Retailers that can successfully team up with their vendors can achieve a sustainable competitive advantage. There needs to be more than just a promise to buy and sell on a regular basis. Strategic relationships require trust, shared goals, strong communications, and a financial commitment.

Buyers need to be aware of ethical and legal issues that can guide them in their negotiations and purchase decisions. There are also problems associated with counterfeit and gray-market merchandise and issues that vendors face when selling to retailers, such as exclusive territories and tying contracts. Care should be taken by vendors when placing restrictions on which retailers they will sell to, what merchandise, how much, and at what price. Some retailers are taking giant steps toward being more socially responsible.

KEY TERMS

black market, *363*

buybacks, *362*

chargeback, *362*

commercial bribery, *362*

co-op (cooperative) advertising, *356*

copycat brands, *344*

copyright, *362*

corporate social responsibility, *365*

counterfeit merchandise, *362*

diverted merchandise, *363*

duties, *351*

exclusive brands, *344*

exclusive dealing agreements, *365*

fair trade, *365*

family brand, *342*

generic brands, *345*

gray-market goods, *363*

green, *366*

green sheen, *366*

greenwashing, *366*

house brands, *343*

intellectual property, *362*

lift-outs, *362*

manufacturer's brands, *342*

markdown money, *354*

market weeks, *348*

national brands, *342*

own brands, *343*

parallel imports, *363*

partnering relationship, *358*

premium private-label brands, *344*

private-label brands, *343*

resident buying offices, *352*

reverse auctions, *353*

slotting allowances, *355*

slotting fees, *355*

stocklifts, *362*

store brands, *343*

strategic relationship, *358*

subbrand, *342*

tariffs, *351*

trademark, *362*

trade shows, *348*

trust, *359*

tying contract, *365*

umbrella brand, *342*

wholesale market, *348*

GET OUT AND DO IT!

1. **CONTINUING ASSIGNMENT** Go visit the retailer you have selected for the continuing assignment and perform an audit of its manufacturer's and private brands. Interview a manager to determine whether the percentage of private brands has increased or decreased during the past five years. Ask the manager to comment on the store's philosophy toward manufacturer's versus private brands. On the basis of what you see and hear, assess its branding strategy.

2. Read the article "NBA Warns Fans about Counterfeit Products" posted at http://cbs11tv.com/local/NBA.Counterfeit.Merchandise.2.1481903.html. Follow

the story's link to the home page for the Coalition to Advance the Protection of Sports Logos (CAPS) at www.capsinfo.com, and read "About CAPS." What are college and professional sports teams doing to prevent the sale of counterfeit merchandise? Will these measures be effective? Explain why or why not.

3. Go to the home page for the Private Label Manufacturers Assciation (PLMA), and read the "Market Profile," which can be found at www.plma.com/storeBrands/sbt05.html. What are store-brand products? Who purchases store brands? Who makes store brands? What store brands are you purchasing on a regular basis?

4. Read the "Recession, Recovery & Store Brands" report based on an exclusive survey of shopping attitudes by GfK Custom Research North America for the Private Label Manufacturers Association (www.plma.com/share/press/FOR_IMMEDIATE_RELEASE/PLMA_Recession_Recovery_and_Store_Brands.pdf). The findings in this report are based on a poll of nearly 800 main household grocery shoppers. How does a recession impact the demand for private-label merchandise? How would shoppers perceive store brands in an economic upturn? What can retailers do to maintain store-brand loyalty regardless of the external economic environment?

5. Go to your favorite food store, and look up the prices for the items in the following table. Be sure to select the same-size packages for this price comparison of manufacturer's brands and store brands. How much can consumers save by purchasing private-label brands of these products? How would you compare the percentage of savings on different categories of merchandise? How did the various grocery stores selected by the class compare in terms of price savings on their private-label brands versus the national brands?

	Raspberry Cereal Bars	Coffee	Macaroni & Cheese Mix	Tissues	Cola
National brand					
Private-label brand					

DISCUSSION QUESTIONS AND PROBLEMS

1. Assume you have been hired to consult with The Gap on sourcing decisions for sportswear. What issues would you consider when deciding whether you should buy from Mexico or China or find a source within the United States?

2. What is the difference between counterfeit, gray-market, and black-market merchandise? Is the selling of this type of merchandise legal? Do you believe that selling these types of merchandise should be allowed? Provide a rationale for your position. Would you purchase a counterfeit wallet? What about a counterfeit car part or prescription medication?

3. What are the advantages and disadvantages of manufacturer's brands versus private-label brands? Consider both the retailer's and customer's perspectives.

4. Does your favorite clothing store have a private-label brand strategy? If yes, how does it build store loyalty? If no, how could a private-label brand create loyalty?

5. Explain why a grocery store, such as Kroger, offers more than one tier of private-label brands within a particular product category.

6. Why have retailers found exclusive private labels to be an appealing branding option? Choose a department store, a discount store, and a grocery store. What exclusive private-label brands do they offer? How are they positioned in relation to their national brand counterparts?

7. When you go shopping, in which product categories do you prefer private labels or national brands? Explain your preference.

8. What are retailers doing to be more socially responsible in buying merchandise? Why are they becoming more socially responsible? Do you buy products that you believe were produced in a socially responsible manner, even if they cost more?

9. You have decided that you don't want to take the final in this class. Explain how you would negotiate this request with the instructor. Consider place, deadlines, past relationship, possible objections, options for mutual gain, and how to maintain a professional relationship.

SUGGESTED READINGS

Deepak, Malhotra, and Max Bazerman. *Negotiation Genius: How to Overcome Obstacles and Achieve Brilliant Results at the Bargaining Table and Beyond.* New York: Bantam, 2008.

Diamond, Jay. *Retail Buying*, 8th ed. Upper Saddle River, NJ: Pearson, 2007.

Donaldson, Bill, and Tom O'Toole. *Strategic Market Relationships: From Strategy to Implementation*, 2nd ed. Indianapolis: Wiley, 2007.

Foros, Oystein, Hans Jarle Kind, and Jan Yngve Sand. "Slotting Allowances and Manufacturers' Retail Sales Effort." *Southern Economic Journal* 76, no. 1 (2009), pp. 266–282.

Johnston, Robert, and Roy Staughton. "Establishing and Developing Strategic Relationships: The Role for Operations Managers." *International Journal of Operations & Production Management* 29, no. 6 (2009), pp. 564–590.

Kennedy, Gavin. *Negotiation: An A-Z Guide (Economist A-Z Guide).* London: Economist Books, 2009.

Kumar, Nirmalya, and Jan-Benedict E. M. Steenkamp. *Private Label Strategy: How to Meet the Store Brand Challenge.* Boston: Harvard Business Press, 2007.

Lincoln, Keith, and Lars Thomassen. *Private Label: Turning the Retail Brand Threat into Your Biggest Opportunity.* London: Kogan, 2009.

Quelch, John A. "Brands vs. Private Labels: Fighting to Win." *Harvard Business Review*, March 3, 2009.

Shell, Richard G. *Bargaining for Advantage: Negotiation Strategies for Reasonable People*, 2nd ed. New York: Penguin, 2006.

Sugden, David R. *Gray Markets: Prevention, Detection and Litigation.* New York: Oxford University Press, 2009.

Timmor, Yaron. "Manufacturing for Overseas Private Labels: A Win–Win Strategy for Retailers and Producers." *International Review of Retail, Distribution & Consumer Research* 17, no. 2 (2007), pp. 121–138.

Retail Pricing

EXECUTIVE BRIEFING
Donna Rosenberg, Senior Vice President,
Pricing—Staples, Inc.

After graduating from the University of Massachusetts–Amherst, I went to work at Grant Thornton as a certified public accountant (CPA). In 1991, I started with Staples as staff assistant to the CEO. The company had opened five years earlier and had under $1 billion in sales and 120 stores. During the time I've been with Staples, it's grown to become the world's largest office products company, with over 2,000 stores in 27 countries. We sell office supplies, technology, furniture, and business services in stores, on the Internet, through catalogs, and through our B2B contract sales force.

As the company has grown, I've moved up through the organization, holding positions including director of strategic planning, vice president of marketing strategy, and vice president of pricing. I've been in my current position as senior vice president of pricing for 12 years.

I am responsible for a key driver of sales and profitability: pricing. We sell between 7,000 and 8,000 products in our stores and over 30,000 items on our Web site. Having low prices is the "cost of entry" to compete in the office products space. Knowing what items matter most to our customers in forming positive price and value perception is critical. We do this by understanding price and promotional elasticity—this gives us the information we need to attract and retain customers in a dynamic market. Testing a variety of price points on the same item in a diverse group of stores allows us to build demand curves and better understand overall profitability.

Comparing prices has never been easier, with consumers able to access this information directly from their mobile devices. However, since price is the easiest strategic lever for the competition to copy, efforts to gain market share solely by lowering price can backfire. My team's role is to find the proper balance between delighting our customers and ensuring we meet our short-term and long-term sales and profit goals. It's a constant juggling act that involves developing an appropriate merchandise assortment strategy (e.g., good, better, best), developing a compelling everyday pricing strategy, developing compelling offers and promotions, and monitoring competitive activities.

QUESTIONS

Why do some retailers have frequent sales while others attempt to maintain an everyday low-price strategy?

What factors do retailers consider when pricing merchandise?

How do retailers set retail prices?

Why do retailers reduce their prices by taking markdowns?

What pricing techniques do retailers use for increasing sales and profits?

What legal and ethical issues should be considered when setting retail prices?

I enjoy working with the talented, smart and committed people who make up the Staples Leadership Team, and I derive a great deal of satisfaction from the work we do. I know my team and I are making a difference in driving performance for Staples. I also feel a great deal of pride in working for Staples, a Fortune 500 company that has experienced tremendous growth and success during the 18 years I have been with the organization.

The decisions examined in this textbook are directed toward facilitating exchanges between retailers and their customers. As discussed in Chapter 1, retailers offer a number of benefits to their customers, including making merchandise available to customers when they want it, at a convenient location, and in the quantities they want. In addition, retailers provide services such as the opportunity for customers to see and try out merchandise before buying it. In exchange for these benefits, customers pay money for the merchandise and services provided by retailers.

The importance of pricing decisions is growing because today's customers have more alternatives to choose from and are better informed about the alternatives available in the marketplace. Thus, they are in a better position to seek a good value when they buy merchandise and services. **Value** is the ratio of what customers receive (the perceived benefit of the products and services offered by the retailer) to what they have to pay for it:

$$\text{Value} = \frac{\text{Perceived benefits}}{\text{Price}}$$

Thus, retailers can increase value and stimulate more sales (exchanges) by either increasing the perceived benefits offered or reducing the price. To some customers, a good value means simply paying the lowest price because other benefits offered by retailers are not important to them. Others are willing to pay extra for additional benefits as long as they believe they're getting their money's worth in terms of product quality or service.

If retailers set prices higher than the benefits they provide, sales and profits will decrease. In contrast, if retailers set prices too low, their sales might increase but profits might decrease because of the lower profit margin. In addition to offering an attractive value to customers, retailers need to consider the value proposition offered by their competitors and legal restrictions related to pricing. Thus, setting the right price can be challenging.

The first section of this chapter examines two very different pricing strategies used by retailers. The factors retailers consider in setting retail prices are then reviewed. Then the actual process that retailers use to determine prices is described. The next section examines the reasons retailers reduce their prices when taking markdowns. The pricing techniques retailers use for increasing sales and profits are then examined. The chapter concludes with a discussion of the legal and ethical issues retailers should consider when making pricing decisions.

PRICING STRATEGIES

Retailers use two basic retail pricing strategies: high/low pricing and everyday low pricing. Each of these strategies and its advantages and disadvantages is discussed in this section.

High/Low Pricing

Retailers using a **high/low pricing** strategy frequently—often weekly—discount the initial prices for merchandise through sales promotions. However, some customers learn to expect frequent sales and simply wait until the merchandise they want goes on sale and then stock up at the low prices.

Everyday Low Pricing

Many retailers, particularly supermarkets, home improvement centers, and discount stores, have adopted an **everyday low-pricing (EDLP)** strategy. This strategy emphasizes the continuity of retail prices at a level somewhere between the regular nonsale price and the deep-discount sale price of high/low retailers. Although EDLP retailers embrace their consistent pricing strategy, they occasionally have sales, just not as frequently as their high/low competitors.

The term *everyday low pricing* is somewhat misleading, because *low* doesn't mean "lowest." Although retailers using EDLP strive for low prices, they aren't always the lowest prices in the market. At any given time, a sale price at a high/low retailer may be the lowest price available in a market.

To reinforce their EDLP strategy, many retailers have adopted a **low-price guarantee policy** that guarantees customers the retailer will have the lowest price in a market for products it sells. The guarantee usually promises to match or better any lower price found in the market and might include a provision to refund the difference between the seller's offer price and the lower price.

The retailer on the left is using a high/low pricing strategy; whereas the one on the right is using everyday low pricing.

Advantages of the Pricing Strategies

The high/low pricing strategy has the following advantages:

- *Increases profits.* High/low pricing allows retailers to charge higher prices to customers who are not price-sensitive and will pay the "high" price and to charge lower prices to price-sensitive customers who will wait for the "low" sale price.

- *Creates excitement.* A "get them while they last" atmosphere often occurs during a sale. Sales draw a lot of customers, and a lot of customers create excitement. Some retailers augment low prices and advertising with special in-store activities, such as product demonstrations, giveaways, and celebrity appearances.

- *Sells merchandise.* Sales allow retailers to get rid of slow-selling merchandise.

The EDLP approach has its own advantages, as follows:

- *Assures customers of low prices.* Many customers are skeptical about initial retail prices. They have become conditioned to buying only on sale—the main characteristic of a high/low pricing strategy. The EDLP strategy lets customers know that they will get the same low prices every time they patronize the EDLP retailer. Customers do not have to read the ads and wait for items they want to go on sale.

- *Reduces advertising and operating expenses.* The stable prices caused by EDLP limit the need for the weekly-sale advertising used in the high/low strategy. In addition, EDLP retailers do not have to incur the labor costs of changing price tags and signs and putting up sale signs.

- *Reduces stockouts and improves inventory management.* The EDLP approach reduces the large variations in demand caused by frequent sales with large markdowns. As a result, retailers can manage their inventories with more certainty. Fewer stockouts mean more satisfied customers, resulting in higher sales. In addition, a more predictable customer demand pattern enables the retailer to improve inventory turnover by reducing the average inventory needed for special promotions and backup stock.

CONSIDERATIONS IN SETTING RETAIL PRICES

Four factors retailers consider in setting retail prices are the price sensitivity of consumers, the cost of the merchandise, competition, and legal constraints. Legal constraints are discussed at the end of the chapter. Additional considerations occur when setting prices for services and are discussed in this section.

Customer Price Sensitivity and Cost

Generally, as the price of a product increases, the sales for the product will decrease because fewer and fewer customers feel the product is a good value. The price sensitivity of customers determines how many units will be sold at different price levels. If customers in the target market are very price-sensitive, sales will decrease significantly when prices increase. If customers are not very price-sensitive, sales will not decrease significantly if the prices are increased.

To determine the most profitable price for a riblet basket, a restaurant chain sets different prices at different locations.

One approach that can be used to measure the price sensitivity of customers is a price experiment. Consider the following situation: A restaurant chain wants to determine the best price for a new item, a riblet basket. It selects restaurants in the chain with very similar trading areas and sets prices at different levels in each

So, if the private-label DVD player described in the preceding example costs $50, the profit-maximizing price would be:

$$\text{Profit-maximizing price} = \frac{\text{Price elasticity} \times \text{Cost}}{\text{Price elasticity} + 1}$$

$$= \frac{-2.4005 \times \$50}{-2.4005 + 1} = \$85.70$$

Competition

Consumers have lots of choices for goods and services, and they typically search for the best value. Retailers therefore need to consider competitors' prices when setting their own. The previous discussion about setting price on the basis of customer price sensitivity (elasticity) ignores the effects of competitors' prices. For example, assume the restaurant chain that conducted the experiment had a $7.50 price for the riblet basket and, following the results of its experiment, dropped its price to $7 to increase sales and profits. If the increased sales occurred, other restaurant chains would see a decline in their sales and react by dropping their prices to $7, and the experimenting restaurant chain might not realize the sales and profit increases it anticipated. Retailing View 14.1 examines the impact of intense price competition in the United Kingdom.

Retailers can price above, below, or at parity with the competition. The chosen pricing policy must be consistent with the retailer's overall strategy and its relative market position. Consider, for instance, Walmart and Tiffany and Co. Walmart's overall strategy is to be the low-cost retailer for the merchandise it sells. It tries to price the products it sells below its competition. Tiffany, in contrast, offers significant benefits to its customers beyond just the merchandise. Its brand name and customer

14.1   RETAILING VIEW   U.K. Grocery Chains Battle It Out

In the United Kingdom, major grocery retailers Sainsbury, Tesco, Morrisons, and Asda are waging a price war. Walking into any of these stores, customers are confronted by a plethora of clearance signs, along with blaring advertising that compares prices against those offered by competitors. Grocers that have built their images and reputations on their high quality are functioning out of the fear that their customers will start flocking to their competitors.

Furthermore, comparison shopping is much easier in Britain, compared with in the United States, because U.K. grocers have sophisticated online businesses and uniform national prices. At 9 a.m., Asda receives an e-mail listing the prices of every item sold on different grocers' Web sites. If Asda finds it is more expensive on any product, it immediately alerts its stores to adjust their prices.

Sainsbury's slogan has long been "Taste the Difference," in reference to its

In the United Kingdom, Asda is in a price war with other major grocery retailers Sainsbury, Tesco, and Morrisons.

high-quality products. But during the course of the price wars, it has changed its slogan to "Spot the Difference," referring to its prices. Not to be outdone, Tesco proclaimed itself "Britain's Biggest Discounter"—although the company quickly pulled that slogan after the Advertising and Standards Authority ruled it was likely to mislead customers.

The corporate winner of this price war is far from certain. Clearly, however, consumers benefit from the lower prices.

Sources: Andrea Felsted and Elizabeth Rigby, "Battle for Supermarket Customers," *Financial Times*, April 3, 2010; Andrea Felsted, "Price War Gets Intense as Asda Takes on Tesco," *Financial Times*, January 6, 2010; Owen McAteer, "Now Its Price War in the Aisles as Tesco Makes the Finest Cuts of All," *Northern Echo*, December 8, 2009; Rupert Steiner, "Asda Declares Festive Price War on Tesco," *McClatchy-Tribune Business News*, November 13, 2009; Cecile Rohwedder, "U.K. in Price Fight, and It's Drawing Customers," *Wall Street Journal*, August 10, 2009.

EXHIBIT 14–2
Competitive Price Data

SKU	CVS	Winn-Dixie	Walmart
Centrum Vitamins (130 tablets)	$9.49	$9.99	$8.26
Tylenol Liquid	6.49	4.69	5.47
Emfamil Liquid Baby Food	3.29	2.99	3.13
VO5 Shampoo	0.99	1.19	0.97
Pedialyte (1 liter)	5.79	5.29	
Colgate Toothpaste (6 oz.)	2.99	2.99	2.84
Duracell AA Batteries (4 pack)	4.79	3.49	3.24
9 Lives Canned Cat Food	1.49	1.29	0.98
Advil (50 caps)	5.99	5.59	
Edge Shaving Gel (7 oz.)	2.39	2.39	2.14
Competitive Price Index*	100%	91%	85%

*Only common items are indexed.

service assure customers that they will be satisfied with the jewelry they purchase. Due to the unique nature of its offering, Tiffany is able to set its prices higher than those of competitors.

Collecting and Using Competitive Price Data   Most retailers routinely collect price data about their competitors to see if they need to adjust their prices to remain competitive. Competitive price data are typically collected using store personnel, but pricing data also are available from business service providers such as ACNielsen and IRI.

A hypothetical example of price comparison data appears in Exhibit 14–2. In this example, CVS, the national drugstore chain, sets its prices generally above Winn-Dixie and Walmart; however, pricing for shampoo, toothpaste, and shaving gel is very competitive. Similarly, Winn-Dixie, a grocery chain, is moderately priced with low prices on select items, like baby food. Walmart is generally priced below its competitors.

Pricing Services

Additional issues that need to be considered when pricing services are (1) the need to match supply and demand and (2) the difficulties customers have in determining service quality.[2]

Matching Supply and Demand   Services are intangible and thus cannot be inventoried. When retailers are selling products, if the products don't sell one day, they can be stored and sold the next day. However, when a plane departs with empty seats or a play is performed without a full house, the potential revenue from the unused capacity is lost forever. In addition, most services have limited capacity. For example, restaurants are limited in the number of customers that can be seated. Due to capacity constraints, services retailers might encounter situations in which they cannot realize as many sales as they could make.

To maximize sales and profits, many services retailers engage in yield management.[3] **Yield management** is the practice of adjusting prices up or down in response to demand to control the sales generated. Airlines are masters at yield management. Using sophisticated computer programs, they monitor the reservations and ticket sales for each flight and adjust prices according to capacity utilization. Prices are lowered on flights when sales are below forecasts and there is significant excess capacity. As ticket sales approach capacity, prices are increased.

Airlines use yield management to adjust prices in response to demand.

Other services retailers use less sophisticated approaches to match supply and demand. For example, more people want to go to a restaurant for dinner or see a movie at 7 p.m. than at 5 p.m. Restaurants and movie theaters thus might not be able to satisfy the demand for their services at 7 p.m. but have excess capacity at 5 p.m. Therefore, restaurants and movie theaters often price their services lower for customers who use them at 5 p.m. rather than 7 p.m. in an effort to shift demand from 7 p.m. to 5 p.m.

Theaters use a variety of strategies to try to ensure that the seats are sold and that they are sold at prices equivalent to what customers are willing to pay. Targeted direct mail coupons are often used when a play opens, and two-for-one tickets are introduced about halfway through the run. In some cities, like New York and Boston, theaters partner with half-price ticket brokers, which sell unsold tickets for 50 percent off the ticket price but only for performances that same day.

Determining Service Quality   Due to the intangibility of services, it is often difficult for customers to assess service quality, especially when other information is not available.[4] Thus, if consumers are unfamiliar with a service or service provider, they may use price to make quality judgments. For example, most consumers have limited information about lawyers and the quality of legal advice they offer. They may, therefore, base their assessment of the quality of legal services offered on the fees they charge. They may also use other nondiagnostic cues to assess quality, such as the size and décor of the lawyer's office.

Another factor that increases the dependence on price as a quality indicator is the risk associated with a service purchase. In high-risk situations, many of which involve credence services such as medical treatment or legal consulting, the customer will look to price as a surrogate for quality.

Because customers depend on price as a cue of quality and because price creates expectations of quality, service prices must be determined carefully. In addition to being chosen to manage capacity, prices must be set to convey the appropriate quality signal. Pricing too low can lead to inaccurate inferences about the quality of the service. Pricing too high can set expectations that may be difficult to match in service delivery.

SETTING RETAIL PRICES

As described in the previous section, theoretically, retailers maximize their profits by setting prices on the basis of the price sensitivity of customers and the cost of merchandise. One limitation of just using price sensitivity and cost for setting prices is that doing so fails to consider the prices being charged by competitors. Another problem is that implementing this approach requires knowledge of the price sensitivity (price elasticity) of each item. Many retailers have to set prices for more than 50,000 SKUs and make thousands of pricing decisions each month. From a practical perspective, they cannot conduct experiments or do statistical analyses to determine the price sensitivity for each item.

Setting Prices Based on Costs

Most retailers set price by marking up the item's cost to yield a profitable gross margin. Then this initial price is adjusted on the basis of insights about customer price sensitivity and competitive pricing. The following section describes how retailers typically set prices solely on the basis of merchandise cost.

Retail Price and Markup   When setting prices on the basis of merchandise cost, retailers start with the following equation:

Retail price = Cost of merchandise + Markup

The **markup** is the difference between the retail price and the cost of an item. Thus, if a sporting goods retailer buys a tennis racket for $75 and sets the retail price at $125, the markup is $50. The appropriate markup is the amount that covers all of the retailer's operating expenses (labor costs, rent, utilities, advertising, etc.) incurred to sell the merchandise and produces a profit for the retailer.

The **markup percentage** is the markup as a percentage of the retail price:

$$\text{Markup percentage} = \frac{\text{Retail price} - \text{Cost of merchandise}}{\text{Retail price}}$$

Thus, the markup percentage for the tennis racket is:

$$\text{Markup percentage} = \frac{\$125 - \$75}{\$125} = 40\%$$

The retail price based on the cost and markup percentage is:

Retail price = Cost of merchandise + Markup

Retail price = Cost of merchandise + Retail price × Markup percentage

$$\text{Retail price} = \frac{\text{Cost of merchandise}}{1 - \text{Markup percentage (as a fraction)}}$$

Thus, if a buyer for an office supply category specialist purchases calculators at $14 and needs a 30 percent markup to meet the financial goals for the category, the retail price needs to be:

$$\text{Retail price} = \frac{\text{Cost}}{1 - \text{Markup percentage}} = \frac{\$14.00}{1 - 0.30} = \$20$$

Traditionally, apparel retailers used a 50 percent markup, an approach referred to as **keystoning,** that sets the retail price by simply doubling the cost.

Initial Markup and Maintained Markup   The previous discussion is based on the assumption that the retailer sells all items at an initially set price. However, retailers rarely sell all items at the initial price. They frequently reduce the price of items for special promotions or to get rid of excess inventory at the end of a season. In addition, discounts are given to employees, and some merchandise is lost to theft and accounting errors (inventory shrinkage). These factors that reduce the actual selling price from the initial sales price are called **reductions.** Thus, there is a difference between the initial markup and the maintained markup. The **initial markup** is the retail selling price initially set for the merchandise minus the cost of the merchandise. The **maintained markup** is the actual sales realized for the merchandise minus its costs. Thus, the maintained markup is equivalent to the gross margin for the product.

The difference between the initial and maintained markups is illustrated in Exhibit 14–3. The item illustrated costs $0.60, and the initial price for the item is $1.00, so the initial markup is $0.40 and the initial markup percentage is 40 percent.

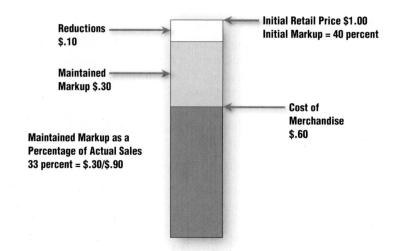

EXHIBIT 14–3
Difference between Initial Markup and Maintained Markup

Reductions $.10

Maintained Markup $.30

Maintained Markup as a Percentage of Actual Sales 33 percent = $.30/$.90

Initial Retail Price $1.00
Initial Markup = 40 percent

Cost of Merchandise $.60

However, the average actual sale price for the item is $0.90. The reductions are $0.10, so the maintained markup is $0.30 and the maintained markup percentage is 33 percent (0.30/0.90).

The relationship between the initial and maintained markup percentages is:

$$\text{Initial markup percentage} = \frac{\substack{\text{Maintained markup percentage} \\ \text{(as a percentage of planned} \\ \text{actual sales)}} + \substack{\text{Percent reductions} \\ \text{(as a percentage of planned} \\ \text{actual sales)}}}{100\% + \substack{\text{Percent reductions} \\ \text{(as a percentage of planned} \\ \text{actual sales)}}}$$

Thus, if the buyer setting the price for the item shown in Exhibit 14–3 planned on reductions of 10 percent of actual sales and wanted a maintained markup of 33 percent, the initial markup should be:

$$\text{Initial markup percentage} = \frac{33\% + (\$0.10/\$0.90 = 11.111\%)}{100\% + 11.111\%} = 40\%$$

and the initial retail price should be:

$$\text{Initial retail price} = \frac{\text{Cost}}{1 - \text{Initial markup percentage}} = \frac{\$0.60}{1 - 0.40} = \$1.00$$

Pricing Optimization Software

Setting prices by simply marking up the merchandise cost neglects a number of other factors that retailers need to consider, such as price sensitivities, competition, and the sales of complementary products. A relatively new approach to setting retail prices takes a more comprehensive approach that uses **pricing optimization software.** The software programs use a set of algorithms that analyze past and current merchandise sales and prices, estimate the relationship between prices and sales generated, and then determine the optimal (most profitable) initial price for the merchandise and the appropriate size and timing of markdowns. To set initial prices, the software uses historical sales data from its own and competitors' stores. It determines the price-sales relationship of complementary items—those that have a similar sales pattern, such as Pepsi and Lays Potato Chips. So not only can the software tell buyers the best price for Pepsi, but it also suggests a price for the chips. Buyers can also determine how much Pepsi they will sell at a given price if they lower the price of Coke or their private-label brand.

The software can incorporate other factors, such as whether a store has a cheap or premium price image, the proximity of the nearest rival, seasonal factors (e.g., soft drinks sell better in the summer than in the winter), or whether an item is featured in coupons.[5]

Merchandising optimization software can be expensive, but its use can have an impressive impact on bottom-line profitability. For instance, the Walgreens-owned and New York City–based Duane Reade pharmacy chain used merchandising optimization software to boost its sales of diapers.[6] The chain had tried discounts and coupons, but the category was losing ground to the competition. The software indicated that the markup should be a function of the child's age. Therefore, Duane Reade made newborn sizes more expensive and big-kid pull-ups cheaper. After a year, the increased diaper sales helped boost baby care revenues by 27 percent, and the category's gross margin rose 2 percent. A traditional analysis could not provide the insight that parents of newborns are far less price-sensitive than parents of toddlers.

Profit Impact of Setting a Retail Price: The Use of Break-Even Analysis

Retailers often want to know the number of units they need sell to begin making a profit. For example, a retailer might want to know:

- Break-even sales to generate a target profit.
- Break-even volume and dollars to justify introducing a new product, product line, or department.
- Break-even sales change needed to cover a price change.

A useful analytical tool for making these assessments is **break-even analysis,** which determines, on the basis of a consideration of fixed and variable costs, how much merchandise needs to be sold to achieve a break-even (zero) profit.

The **break-even point quantity** is the quantity at which total revenue equals total cost, and then profit occurs for additional sales.

The formula for calculating the sales quantity needed to break even is:

$$\text{Break-even quantity} = \frac{\text{Total fixed costs}}{\text{Actual unit sales price} - \text{Unit variable cost}}$$

The following examples illustrate the use of this formula in determining the break-even volume of a new private-label product and the break-even change in volume needed to cover a price change.

Calculating Breakeven for a New Product   Hypothetically, PetSmart is considering an introduction of a new private-label, dry dog food targeting owners of older dogs. The cost of developing this dog food is $700,000, including salaries for the design team and costs of testing the product. Because these costs do not change with the quantity of product produced and sold, they're known as **fixed costs.** PetSmart plans to sell the dog food for $12 a bag—the unit price. The **variable cost** is the retailer's expenses that vary directly with the quantity of product produced and sold. Variable costs often include direct labor and materials used in producing the product. PetSmart will be purchasing the product from a private-label manufacturer. Thus, the only variable cost is the dog food's cost, $5, from the private-label manufacturer.

$$\begin{aligned}
\text{Break-even quantity} &= \frac{\text{Fixed costs}}{\text{Actual unit sales price} - \text{Unit variable cost}} \\
&= \frac{\$700,000}{\$12 - \$5} = 100,000 \text{ bags}
\end{aligned}$$

Thus, PetSmart needs to sell 100,000 bags of dog food to break even, or make zero profit, and for every additional bag sold, it will make $7 profit.

Now assume that PetSmart wants to make $100,000 profit from the new product line. The break-even quantity now becomes:

$$\text{Break-even quantity} = \frac{\text{Fixed cost}}{\text{Actual unit sales price} - \text{Unit variable cost}}$$

$$= \frac{\$700,000 + \$100,000}{\$12 - \$5} = 114,286 \text{ bags}$$

Calculating Break-Even Sales   An issue closely related to the calculation of a break-even point is determining how much unit sales would have to increase to make a profit from a price cut or how much sales would have to decline to make a price increase unprofitable. Continuing with the PetSmart example, assume the break-even quantity is 114,286 units, based on the $700,000 fixed cost, the $100,000 profit, a selling price of $12, and a cost of $5. Now PetSmart is considering lowering the price of a bag of dog food to $10. How many units must it sell to break even if it lowers its selling price by 16.67 percent, to $10? Using the formula:

$$\text{Break-even quantity} = \frac{\text{Fixed cost}}{\text{Actual unit sales price} - \text{Unit variable cost}}$$

$$= \frac{\$700,000 + \$100,000}{\$10 - \$5} = 160,000 \text{ bags}$$

So, if PetSmart decreases its price by 16.67 percent, from $12 to $10, unit sales must increase by 40 percent: $(160,000 - 114,286) \div 114,286$.

MARKDOWNS

The preceding section reviewed how retailers initially set prices on the basis of the merchandise cost and desired maintained margin. However, retailers also take **markdowns** by reducing the initial retail price. This section examines why retailers take markdowns, how they optimize markdown decisions, how they reduce the amount of markdowns, and how they liquidate markdown merchandise.

Reasons for Taking Markdowns

Retailers' reasons for taking markdowns can be classified as either clearance (to dispose of merchandise) or promotional (to generate sales). Clearance markdowns are examined in this section, while promotional markdowns are discussed later in this chapter as a method of increasing sales and profits.

When merchandise is selling at a slower rate than planned, will become obsolete at the end of its season, or is priced higher than competitors' goods, buyers generally mark it down for clearance purposes. As discussed in Chapter 12, slow-selling merchandise decreases inventory turnover; prevents buyers from acquiring new, better-selling merchandise; and can diminish the retailer's image for selling the most current styles and trends.

Markdowns are part of the cost of doing business, and thus buyers plan for them. They tend to order more fashion merchandise than they forecast actually selling because they are more concerned about underordering and stocking out of a popular item before the end of the season than about overordering and having to discount excess merchandise at the end of the season. Stocking out of popular merchandise can have a detrimental effect on a fashion retailer's image, whereas discounting merchandise at the end of the season just reduces maintained markup.

Thus, a buyer's objective isn't to minimize markdowns. If markdowns are too low, the buyer is probably pricing the merchandise too low, not purchasing enough merchandise, or not taking enough risks with the merchandise being purchased. So buyers set the initial markup price high enough that, even after markdowns and other reductions have been taken, the planned maintained markup is still achieved.

Optimizing Markdown Decisions   Retailers have traditionally created a set of arbitrary rules for taking markdowns to dispose of unwanted merchandise. One retailer, for instance, identifies markdown candidates when its weekly sell-through percentages fall below a certain level. Another retailer cuts prices on the basis of how long the merchandise has been in the store—marking products down by 20 percent after 8 weeks, then by 30 percent after 12 weeks, and finally by 50 percent after 16 weeks. Such a rule-based approach, however, is limiting because it does not consider the demand for the merchandise at different price points or in different locations and thus produces less-than-optimal profits.

The optimization software described previously in this chapter, used to set initial retail prices, can also indicate when to take markdowns and how much they should be in different locations.[9] It works by continually updating its pricing forecasts on the basis of actual sales throughout the season and factoring in differences in price sensitivities. For example, the software recognizes that in early November, a winter item's sales are better than expected in Colorado, so it delays taking a markdown that had been planned, but takes the markdown in New England. Each week, as new sales data become available, it readjusts the forecasts to include the latest information. It computes literally thousands of scenarios for each item—a process that is too complicated and time-consuming for buyers to do on their own. It then evaluates the outcomes on the basis of expected profits and other factors and selects the action that produces the best results across all regions.

REFACT

Some vendors, such as Gucci, Cartier, and Christian Louboutin, have become so concerned with protecting their images that they require that some of their retailers exclude them from certain markdown sales events.[8]

What If	Number of Items 4	Outdate Range 12/31/04 - 12/31/04							
Columns represent data for week ending dates specified below. Assumes price was changed on first day of the week. An asterisk (*) indicates a partial month.									
Action (select action) ▾ Apply Recalculate									
	FCEOL	EOL	LTD	TTOOS	7/31/04	8/7/04	8/14/04	8/21/04	8/28/04
Fill Right/Left						< >	< >	< >	< >
Rec Ticket Price					$34.50	$18.95	$18.95	$18.95	$18.95
Orig. Price					$34.50	$34.50	$34.50	$34.50	$34.50
Price Ladder					PERM MD ▾	PERM MD ▾	PERM MD ▾	PERM MD ▾
Override Price		$32.37	$17.50	$34.50	$22.95 ▾	$22.95 ▾	$22.95 ▾	$15.95 ▾
Sales $	$247,577.92	$244,816.87	$11,622.42	$233,194.45	$15,801.00	$26,071.20	$29,926.80	$27,149.85	$32,091.40
Sales Units	13,791	13,688	359	13,329	458	1,136	1,304	1,183	2,012
GM $ (Retail)	$89,387.62	$83,736.62	$8,216.62	$75,520.00	$11,455.96	$(27,201.35)	$21,697.38	$19,684.04	$2,299.22
GM % (Retail)	36.1 %	34.2 %	70.7 %	32.4 %	72.5 %	-104.3 %	72.5 %	72.5 %	7.2 %
MD $	$266,043.13	$264,491.33	$763.08	$263,728.25	$.00	$167,648.25	$.00	$.00	$76,244.00
Sell Thru %	89.9 %	89.3 %	2.3 %	89.0 %	3.1 %	7.8 %	9.7 %	9.8 %	18.5 %
EOH Units	1,703	1,759	14,973	1,759	14,515	13,379	12,075	10,892	8,880
EOH $ (Retail)	$16,944.85	$21,020.05	$516,568.50	$21,020.05	$500,767.50	$307,048.05	$277,121.25	$249,971.40	$141,636.00
Promo Flag									

The output from the Oracle Retail markdown model indicates that the model's recommended markdown of $18.95 will result in more than $5,000 greater profit than the buyer's planned markdown of $22.95.

Pricing optimization software recognizes when sales for winter coats are slower than expected and suggests appropriate markdowns.

The Gap is testing different localized promotions, such as offering 10 percent discounts over three days to military families in southern California at its Old Navy chain.[10] The approach has worked so well that the company has set up a military discount day on the first day of each month throughout the discount chain. The Gap's Banana Republic division takes different markdowns across the country, and even within the same market, on the basis of localized demand and inventory levels. For instance, within New York City, a Banana Republic store in the World Financial Center may offer a skirt for $39.99, marked down from $69. At the SoHo store, just a few blocks away, the same skirt might be priced at $33.99.[11]

Reducing the Amount of Markdowns   Retailers work closely with their vendor partners to coordinate deliveries and help reduce the financial burden of taking markdowns. Supply chain management systems (discussed in Chapter 10) reduce the lead time for receiving merchandise so that retailers can monitor changes in trends and customer demand more closely, thus reducing markdowns.

Vendors have a partnering relationship with their retailers and thus a vested interest in their success. Vendors that are knowledgeable about the market and competition can help with stock selections. Of course, a retailer must also trust its own taste and intuition; otherwise, its store will have the same merchandise as all other stores. As discussed in Chapter 13, buyers can often obtain markdown money—funds a vendor gives the retailer to cover lost gross margin dollars that result from markdowns and other merchandising issues. Another method of reducing markdowns is to buy smaller quantities.[12] By adopting a just-in-time inventory policy, in which small amounts of merchandise arrive just in time to be sold, customers perceive a scarcity and purchase at full price. (See Chapter 13 for more on this strategy.)

Creating a feeling of scarcity among customers is an excellent method of reducing markdowns. Even if there are adequate quantities of merchandise available in the stockroom or in a distribution center, displaying just a few items on the sales floor sends a signal to the customer to "buy them now, while they last!" If retailers simply change their displays frequently, customers will perceive that the merchandise is new and available in limited quantities.

When customers believe that a particular retailer offers them a good value, they will be less likely to wait for markdowns. An everyday low-price strategy implies that a retailer's products are already at low prices and therefore will not be further discounted. Zara and H & M don't need to advertise their low prices. Loyal customers return time after time to look for low-priced treasures. A few retailers, like Apple, focus on quality and image and therefore simply don't have sales! It is an enviable position, to which most retailers can only aspire.

Liquidating Markdown Merchandise   Even with the best planning, some merchandise may remain unsold at the end of a season. Retailers use one of five strategies to liquidate this unsold merchandise.

Sell to Another Retailer   Selling the unsold merchandise to another retailer has been very popular among retailers. For instance, off-price retailers such as TJX Corporation (owners of T.J.Maxx and Marshalls) and Bluefly.com purchase end-of-season merchandise from other retailers and sell it at deep discounts. However, this approach for liquidating unsold merchandise only enables retailers to recoup a small percentage of the merchandise's cost—often a mere 10 percent.

Consolidate Unsold Merchandise   Markdown merchandise can be consolidated in a number of ways. First, the consolidation can be made into one or a few of the retailer's regular locations. Second, markdown merchandise can be consolidated into another retail chain or an outlet store under the same ownership. Saks Fifth Avenue OFF Fifth and Neiman Marcus Last Call Clearance Center use this approach. Third, unsold merchandise can be shipped to a distribution center or a rented space such as a convention center (Barney's New York and J.Crew) for final sale. However, consolidation sales can be complex and expensive due to the extra transportation and record keeping involved.

Sell at Internet Auction   The Internet is increasingly useful for liquidating unsold merchandise. For example, an electronics store might utilize eBay to sell goods it has received from trade-ins. Many retailers have separate areas of their Web sites for clearance merchandise.

Donate to Charity   Donating clearance merchandise to charities is a common practice. Charitable giving is always a good corporate practice. It is a way of giving back to the community and has strong public relations benefits. Also, the cost value of the merchandise can be deducted from income.

Carry the Merchandise Over to the Next Season   The final liquidation approach— to carry merchandise over to the next season—is used with relatively high-priced nonfashion merchandise, such as traditional men's clothing and furniture. Generally, however, it is not profitable to carry over merchandise because of excessive inventory carrying costs.

PRICING TECHNIQUES FOR INCREASING SALES AND PROFITS

This section reviews several techniques used by retailers to increase sales and profits. The first is variable pricing, in which retailers charge different prices to different customers. The other techniques—dealing with perceptions of fairness, leader pricing, price lining, and odd pricing—take advantage of the way customers process information. The section concludes with a discussion of how the Internet has changed the way retailers and their customers make pricing decisions.

Variable Pricing and Price Discrimination

Retailers use a variety of techniques to maximize profits by charging different prices to different customers.

Individualized Variable Pricing   Ideally, retailers could maximize their profits if they charged each customer as much as the customer was willing to pay. For instance, if a wealthy, price-insensitive customer wants to buy a new car battery, AutoZone would like to price the battery at $200 but then price the same battery at $125 to make a sale to a more price-sensitive, lower-income customer. Charging each individual customer a different price based on their willingness to pay is called **first-degree price discrimination**.[13] Retailing View 14.2 provides an example of how the Internet has facilitated individualized variable pricing for entertainment and sporting events.

Pricing merchandise through auction bidding is an example of first-degree price discrimination. A retailer offering a 1960 Porsche Speedster on eBay maximizes its profits because the customer with the highest willingness to pay bids and pays the highest price.

Priceline.com offers a unique pricing scheme for booking airline flights, hotel rooms, and rental cars that helps service providers match supply and demand and captures some profit through price discrimination. Customers can visit its Web site and specify the price they are prepared to pay and the acceptable range of times, days, and/or quality for a particular leisure travel service. For example, a customer can indicate she wants to fly from Miami to Chicago, anytime between 6 a.m. and 10 p.m. on September 14 or stay in any four-star hotel in Maui from January 15 to January 20. Thus, the service for which the customer is paying is opaque; the customer does not know the specific nature of the service that will be offered. Then Priceline.com accesses databases of participating suppliers to determine whether it can fulfill the customer's offer and whether it wants to accept the price designated by the consumer. Consumers agree to hold their offers open for a specified period of time (generally, not longer than a minute) to determine whether they want to accept the offer. Once fulfilled, offers generally cannot be canceled, making such purchases nonrefundable. The service that Priceline.com offers benefits both buyers and sellers. Price-sensitive buyers save money, and airlines generate incremental revenue by selling their services at below-retail prices but without disrupting their existing retail pricing structures.[15] Another example of retailers practicing first-degree price discrimination occurs when they allow customers to haggle over price, as described in Retailing View 14.3.

Although individualized variable pricing is legal and widely used in some retail sectors, such as automobile and antique dealers, it is impractical in most retail stores. First, it is difficult to assess each customer's willingness to pay; second, retailers cannot change the posted prices in stores as customers with different willingness to pay enter the store. In addition, customers might feel they are being treated unfairly if they realize that they are being charged a higher price than other customers.

However, individualized variable pricing is possible when selling merchandise on the Internet. Retailers can assess each customer's willingness to pay by analyzing past purchase behavior and then serve up Web pages with unique pricing based on the customer's willingness to pay.[16]

Self-Selected Variable Pricing   An alternative approach for variable pricing is to offer the same multiple-price schedule to all customers but require that customers do something to get the lower price—something that discourages customers with a high willingness to pay from taking advantage of the lower price. This approach is referred to as **second-degree price discrimination.** For example,

REFACT

R. H. Macy, founder of Macy's, did away with bargaining over price by initiating fixed prices when he opened his first dry goods store in 1858. He was the first to advertise these fixed prices in a newspaper.[17]

14.2   RETAILING VIEW   Hey, Wanna Buy a Ticket?

Typically, promoters of entertainment and sports events offer tickets for a specific seat and date at a fixed price. Individual brokers buy the tickets at the list price and then make a profit by reselling them at a premium to price-insensitive consumers. Software even allows brokers to buy tickets from Ticketmaster, the leading broker of sports, concerts, and theater events, in bulk and then resell them at three or four times the face-value price.

Before the Internet, these brokers or individuals, often called *scalpers*, would stand in front of the venue for the event and raise their hand with tickets for sale. However, StubHub, owned by eBay, and other online businesses have created a legitimate $2 billion-plus secondary market for seats at plays, concerts, and sports events. Brokers or individuals with tickets to events can list them on an Internet site that people around the world can access. In addition to providing a market by bringing buyers and sellers together, StubHub guarantees customers similar or better seats if anything goes wrong.

To prevent scalpers from making money in the secondary market, some sports teams are threatening to revoke season-ticket holders' rights to put their seats up for sale without authorization. However, major-league baseball teams are capturing the profits from this form of price discrimination by reselling their own tickets online and collecting a transaction fee.

Now sports teams are engaging in even more sophisticated forms of price discrimination, including increasing the prices of tickets for special games, such as those against important rivals or on special holidays.

Sources: Ethan Smith and Su Xuanming, "Optimal Pricing with Speculators and Strategic Consumers," *Management Science* 56, no. 1 (2010), pp. 25–40; Clark P. Kirkman, "Who Needs Tickets? Examining Problems in the Growing Online Ticket Resale Industry," *Federal Communications Law Journal*, June 2009; Phillip Leslie, and Alan Sorensen, "The Welfare Effects of Ticket Resale," *NBER*, November 2009; "Hannah Montana Battles the Bots," *Wall Street Journal*, October 5, 2007, p. B1; Amy Feldman, "Hot Tickets," *Fast Company*, September 2007, pp. 44–46.

sports teams alter ticket prices on the basis of the opponent, the day of the week, and the time of the year; but these prices are set before the season. The San Francisco Giants are actually varying ticket prices up until game day on the basis of ticket sales data, weather forecasts, and other variables.[18] Anyone can buy these tickets; however, price-sensitive consumers are more likely to be attracted to the less popular, lower-priced games.

Promotional Markdowns   Buyers employ promotional markdowns to promote merchandise and increase sales. Markdowns can increase customer traffic flow. Retailers plan promotions in which they take markdowns for holidays, for special events, and as part of their overall promotional program. In fact, small portable appliances (such as toasters) are called *traffic appliances* because they're often sold at promotional

RETAILING VIEW   Haggling for a Better Price   14.3

While out shopping a few weeks ago, Regina Ranonis was trying to decide between trendy low-heeled boots or a more conservative style. Then the sales associate spoke up: If she would spring for both pairs, he would knock $270 off the total price.

Does this sound like the local flea market? It wasn't. A number of retailers are hoping to reel in sales by allowing haggling, or some form of it. The practice isn't entirely new—and it remains officially denied by most companies— but good consumers say they're getting deals everywhere, from Home Depot to Best Buy. Big-name stores like Saks and Macy's say savvy shoppers who can cite competitors' prices may also find some wiggle room.

The Internet has given a real boost to haggling for bargains. Fashion sites such as RetailMeNot.com list promotional codes that can be used online at checkout. Because many retailers honor a lower price on the same item found at a competitor's store or Internet site, savvy customers use search engines to find the best deal.

Some retailers offer special prices to their best customers, either while in the store or through an e-mail alert. At Neiman Marcus, for instance, customers are regularly invited to "midday dash" sales that last for two hours. Customers receive an e-mail about the sale earlier the same day. They can purchase at 50 percent off by clicking on a link in the e-mail message.

Customers in most countries, except the United States, Canada, Australia, and parts of England, are expected to haggle. Chinese consumers even have taken haggling to a new level— group haggling! The practice, called *tuangou*, or team purchase, begins in Internet chat rooms, where consumers devise plans to buy items like appliances, food, or even cars in bulk. Next, they show up together at the stores and demand discounts.

Many of the biggest U.S. retailers, from The Gap to Pottery Barn, say they're sticking to firm no-haggling policies. Many retailers use cash registers that won't accept unauthorized discount

If you think you can't haggle for a better price at national chain stores, think again.

prices without managerial approval. Some even have video cameras not only to watch shoppers but also to make sure the employees aren't cutting sweetheart deals for their friends.

Some of the best negotiating territory is at franchises, where owners have the flexibility to operate more like mom-and-pop shops. But even at major department stores and small chains, a growing number of managers are now authorized to lower a price to meet the competition or throw in free alterations or delivery. Many stores take pains to insist that haggling is off-limits, even as customers and sales associates say it goes on all the time. The policy is, "Try not to come down in price too much, but don't let the business walk out."

Sources: Susan Reda, "Do You Haggle?" *Stores*, June 2009, p. 6; Marianne Rohrlich, "Adventures in Haggling the Retailers' View," *New York Times*, January 29, 2009, p. D7; Jeanine Poggi and Lily-Hayes Kaufman, "How to Find Secret Shopping Savings," *Forbes*, April 7, 2009; Stephanie Rosenbloom, "High-End Retailers Offering More Discounts," *New York Times*, August 1, 2009; Matt Richtel, "Even at Megastores, Hagglers Find No Price Is Set in Stone," *New York Times*, March 23, 2009, p. A1.

or reduced prices to generate in-store traffic. Retailers hope that customers will purchase other products at regular prices while they're in the store. Another opportunity created by promotional markdowns is to increase the sale of complementary products. For example, a supermarket's markdown on hot-dog buns may be offset by increased demand for hot dogs, mustard, and relish—all sold at regular prices.

Clearance Markdowns for Fashion Merchandise   While the discussion of clearance markdowns earlier in the chapter focused primarily on how retailers get rid of unwanted merchandise, this merchandise can also be used to attract different market segments based on their degree of price sensitivity. Fashion-conscious customers who have a high willingness to pay because they want to be the first to wear the latest fashions self-select to pay higher prices. More price-sensitive customers wait to buy the merchandise at the end of the season when prices are lower.

Coupons   **Coupons** offer a discount on the price of specific items when they're purchased. Coupons are issued by manufacturers and retailers in newspapers, on products, on the shelf, at the cash register, over the Internet, and through the mail. Retailers use coupons because they are thought to induce customers to try products for the first time, convert first-time users to regular users, encourage large purchases, increase usage, and protect market share against the competition. Coupons are considered a form of second-degree price discrimination because, in general, price-sensitive customers will expend the extra effort to collect and redeem coupons whereas price-insensitive customers will not. Considered a form of sales promotion, coupons are discussed further in Chapter 15.

McDonald's uses price bundling when it combines a sandwich, french fries, and a soft drink in a Value Meal.

Price Bundling   **Price bundling** is the practice of offering two or more different products or services for sale at one price.[19] For instance, McDonald's offers a bundle of a sandwich, french fries, and a soft drink in a Value Meal at a discount compared with buying the items individually. Price bundling increases both unit and dollar sales by increasing the amount of merchandise bought during a store visit. The practice is an example of second-degree price discrimination because it offers more price-sensitive customers a lower-priced alternative.

Multiple-Unit Pricing   The term **multiple-unit pricing,** or **quantity discounts,** refers to the practice of offering two or more similar products or services for sale at one lower total price. For example, a convenience store may sell 3 liters of soda for $2.39 when the price per unit is 99 cents—a saving of 58 cents. Like price bundling, this variable-pricing approach is used to increase sales volume. Depending on the type of product, however, customers may stockpile the items for use at a later time, thus having no impact on sales over time. Multiunit pricing is an example of second-degree price discrimination because customers who buy and consume more of a product are presumably more price-sensitive and thus attracted by the lower prices if they buy more units.

Variable Pricing by Market Segment   Retailers often charge different prices to different demographic market segments, a practice referred to as **third-degree price discrimination.** For example, movie theaters have lower ticket prices for seniors and college students, presumably because these segments are more price-sensitive than other customers. This practice is generally legal, although gender-based pricing, in which men and women are charged different prices for the same service, has come into question, as Retailing View 14.4 describes.

Another example of third-degree price discrimination is zone pricing. **Zone pricing** is the practice of charging different prices in different stores, markets, regions, or zones. Retailers generally use zone pricing to address different competitive situations in their various markets. For example, some multichannel retailers implement zone pricing by asking customers to enter their zip code before they are quoted a price. Food retailers often have up to four or five pricing zones in a single city. They'll have one zone if they're

Offering two or more similar products or services for sale at one lower price is called multiple-unit pricing.

next to a Walmart and another zone if they're next to a less price-competitive regional chain. Drugstores and supermarkets have been known to charge higher

RETAILING VIEW   Men Are Winning the Battle against Gender-Based Pricing   14.4

Despite the enduring popularity of Kool and the Gang's 1979 hit, it may not be ladies' night anymore in several states. New Jersey has outlawed ladies' nights in bars. Traditionally, bars have chosen one night a week and designated it "ladies' night," the night when women are admitted either for free or at a reduced rate and, once inside, are served drinks at reduced prices.

A New Jersey man sued under New Jersey's Law Against Discrimination and won. Because the bar offered public accommodation, it could not charge higher prices to men. The bar offered in its defense that the difference in prices had a legitimate business purpose and no intent of hostility toward men. It argued that the ladies' night discounts attracted more women and subsequently men, thus increasing sales and profits.

Women lost a different battle in Las Vegas. The Nevada Equal Rights Commission found that an athletic club's reduced rates to women were discriminatory. The club defended its position by saying that men cost the club more, in part because they are more likely to fail to pay their bills.

Women have always paid more to have their shirts laundered, and that tradition continues to endure. Dry cleaners argue that women's shirts don't fit properly on the industrial presses, so they have to be done by hand. Some dry cleaners have taken a rational and presumably fairer approach. Shirts that can be pressed on the shirt-pressing machines get one price, while hand-pressed shirts get another, higher price. All dry-cleaned shirts are charged the same price.

If price discrimination on the basis of gender is under attack, then what about age discrimination? Should children be able to see a movie at a reduced rate? Why should seniors get a discount on the ski slopes?

Should bars be allowed to have "ladies' night" when women are admitted either for free or at a reduced rate and, once inside, are served drinks at reduced prices?

Sources: "Frugal Dilemmas: Women's Drycleaning Costs More than Men's, but Why?" *Baltimore Sun,* June 4, 2009; Steve Friess, "Lower Rates for Women Are Ruled Unfair," *New York Times,* August 13, 2008; Berny Morson, "Ladies' Night Foe Aims Complaint at Rockies," *Rocky Mountain News,* October 16, 2007; Brittany Bacon, "'Ladies' Night' Lawsuit on the Rocks?" *ABC News,* July 25, 2007.

prices in poor urban areas and neighborhoods populated by elderly retirees, because customers in those areas have relatively few shopping choices and therefore tend to be relatively insensitive to price and the cost of operating businesses in those areas can be more expensive than others. Third-degree price discrimination, when used in this manner to discriminate on the basis of income and age, is considered an unethical practice by many.

How and why retailers engage in price discrimination is discussed later in the chapter. In many cases customers are not aware that they are being charged different prices. For example, retailers are able to target price promotions to customers on the basis of their zip codes, shopping time of day, speed of Internet connection, whether they are in the store or online, or even their Google browsing habits.[20] So a customer with a high-speed Internet connection in the South may get a free-shipping offer, while another customer in the West may be offered live customer service instead. If, however, customers become aware of this practice, they may feel they are being treated unfairly and be reluctant to patronize the retailer in the future.

Dealing with Perceptions of Fairness   Setting different prices for similar products or services, such as a shirt sold at the manufacturer's suggested retail price versus discounted at the end of the season or a seat on an airplane discounted on the day of the flight, may seem unfair to customers. To lessen this feeling, retailers can offer additional benefits with the higher-priced products or services or more restrictions on the less expensive items.[21] For instance, full-priced items may have an unlimited return policy, whereas sale items may be sold "as is" or as "final sale."

Another way to make such transactions seem more fair to customers is through customization.[22] A retailer, for instance, may be able to charge significantly more for a similar product by emblazing the purchaser's initials on the cuff of a shirt or making a pair of sneakers with the purchaser's college colors on it.

Provide as much information about the product or service as possible so that the customer can decide whether the price is fair. To help lessen the impact of a perceived unfair price, retailers can draw the customer's attention to particular attributes that add perceived value, such as hand-work on apparel or friendly cancellation policies at a hotel.

To the extent possible, make relevant cost and quality information available to customers. For instance, a retailer can allude to the high quality of materials and workmanship inherent in its products, indirectly referring to higher costs and therefore justifying its prices.[23]

Leader Pricing

Leader pricing is pricing certain items lower than normal to increase customers' traffic flow or boost sales of complementary products. Some retailers call these products **loss leaders.** In a strict sense, loss leaders are sold below cost. But a product doesn't have to be sold below cost for the retailer to use a leader-pricing strategy.

Walmart, Amazon, and Target are using leader pricing to sell top-selling books. Prices for the books are nearly 70 percent below cover prices.[24] Since publishers charge 50 percent of a hardcover book's cover price, these mega-retailers are losing money on these sales. The purpose of this leader-pricing structure is to attract customers to the company's online site, where they may then order additional items. The danger is that independent booksellers or eBay merchants would purchase multiple copies for resale. To prevent independent bookstores from buying the best-sellers for resale, Walmart, Amazon, and Target have set purchasing limits on these books.

The best items for leader pricing are frequently purchased products like white bread, milk, and eggs or well-known brand names like Coca-Cola and Kellogg's

Corn Flakes.[25] Customers take note of ads for these products because they're purchased weekly. The retailer hopes consumers will also purchase their entire weekly grocery list while buying the loss leaders.

One problem with leader pricing is that it might attract shoppers referred to as **cherry pickers,** who go from one store to another, buying only items that are on special. These shoppers are clearly unprofitable for retailers.[26]

Price Lining

Retailers frequently offer a limited number of predetermined price points within a merchandise category, a practice known as **price lining.** For instance, a grocery store like Jewel has three SKUs for strawberry preserves that reflect good, better, and best quality at three different price points. Both customers and retailers can benefit from such a strategy for several reasons:

- Confusion that often arises from multiple-price choices is essentially eliminated. The customer can choose the tire with the low, medium, or high price.
- From the retailer's perspective, the merchandising task is simplified. That is, all products within a certain price line are merchandised together. Furthermore, when going to market, the firm's buyers can select their purchases with the predetermined price lines in mind.
- Price lining can also give buyers greater flexibility. If a strict formula is used to establish the initial retail price (initial markup), there could be numerous price points. But with a price-lining strategy, some merchandise may be bought a little below or above the expected cost for a price line. Of course, price lining can also limit retail buyers' flexibility. They may be forced to pass up potentially profitable merchandise because it doesn't fit into a price line.

Although many manufacturers and retailers are simplifying their product offerings to save distribution and inventory costs and make the choice simpler for consumers, price lining can be used to get customers to "trade up" to a more expensive model. Research indicates a tendency for people to choose the product in the middle of a price line. For example, if a camera store starts carrying a "super deluxe" model, customers will be more likely to purchase the model that was previously the most expensive. Retailers must decide whether it's more profitable to sell more expensive merchandise or save money by paring down their stock selection.[27]

Odd Pricing

Odd pricing refers to the practice of using a price that ends in an odd number, typically a 9. Odd pricing has a long history in retailing. In the 19th and early 20th centuries, odd pricing was used to reduce losses due to employee theft. Because

When retailers like Jewel offer three SKUs for strawberry preserves that reflect good, better, and best quality at three different price points, they are using a price-lining technique.

REFACT

Each extra syllable in the price reduces the chances of its being recalled by 20 percent.[28] In other words, someone faced with a $77.51 camera (eight syllables) and a $62.30 bookshelf (five syllables) is about 60 percent more likely to forget the camera's price than the bookshelf's after half a minute.

REFACT

Apple Computer may have saved the music industry from oblivion by pricing iTunes at 99 cents in 2003. At the time, no one was sure that anyone would pay for online music when people could steal it from several peer-to-peer networks.[31]

merchandise had an odd price, salespeople typically had to go to the cash register to give the customer change and record the sale, making it more difficult for salespeople to keep the customer's money. Odd pricing was also used to keep track of how many times an item had been marked down. After an initial price of $20, the first markdown would be $17.99, the second markdown $15.98, and so on.

The results of empirical studies in this area are mixed;[29] however, many retailers believe that odd pricing can increase profits. For example, the computerized pricing system at CVS stores begins by applying the necessary markup to an item's cost. After that is completed, the program takes the pennies digit of the resulting price and raises it to the nearest 5 or 9. Walmart takes a different approach to this fine-tuning. The exact prices are determined by marking costs up by a fixed percent, thus producing a variety of price endings.[30]

The theory behind odd pricing is the assumption that shoppers don't notice the last digit or digits of a price, so that a price of $2.99 is perceived as $2. An alternative theory is that "9" endings signal low prices. Thus, for products that are believed to be sensitive to price, many retailers will round the price down to the nearest 9 to create a positive price image. If, for example, the price would normally be $3.09, many retailers will lower the price to $2.99.

Research results suggest the following guidelines for making price-ending decisions:

- When the price sensitivity of the market is high, it is likely to be advantageous to raise or lower prices so that they end in high numbers such as 9.

- When the price sensitivity of the market is not especially high, the risks to the retailer's image of using "9" endings are likely to outweigh the benefits. In such cases, the use of even dollar prices and round-number endings would be more appropriate.

- Many upscale retailers appeal to price-sensitive segments of the market through periodic discounting, which suggests the value of a combination strategy: Only break from a standard policy of round-number endings to use "9" endings when communicating discounts and special offers.[32]

The practice of offering odd prices—a price that ends in an odd number, typically a 9—is over 100 years old. Although empirical studies have mixed results, many retailers believe that the practice can increase profits.

Using the Internet to Make Pricing Decisions

The growth of the electronic channel has changed the way consumers get and use information to make purchasing decisions based on price. Traditionally, price competition between store-based retailers offering the same merchandise was reduced by geography because consumers typically shop at the stores and malls closest to where they live and work. However, Internet sites such as Shopzilla, RedLaser, TheFind, ShopStyle, and PriceGrabber.com allow customers to compare prices across a range of retailers.[33]

Although consumers shopping electronically can collect price information with little effort, they also can get a lot of other information about the quality and performance of products at a low cost. For instance, an Internet site that offers custom-made Oriental rugs can clearly show real differences in the patterns and materials used for construction. Electronic grocery services offered by Safeway and Albertson's allow customers to sort cereals by nutritional content, thus making it easier to use that attribute in their decision making. If a customer wants to make an egg dish for breakfast, the site can also recommend numerous recipes that include eggs, as well as providing the nutritional information. The additional information about product quality might lead customers to pay more for high-quality products, thus decreasing the importance of price.

Retailers using an electronic channel can reduce the emphasis on price by providing better services and information. Because of these services, customers might be willing to pay higher prices for the merchandise. For example, Amazon.com provides customers with the table of contents and synopsis of a book, as well as reviews and comments by the author or authors and people who have read the book. When the customer finds an interesting book, Amazon's system is programmed to suggest other books by the same author or of the same genre. Finally, customers can tell Amazon about their favorite authors and subjects and then receive e-mails about new books that might be of interest. The classic response to the question "What are the three most important things in retailing?" used to be "location, location, location." In the world of electronic retailing, the answer will be "information, information, information."

LEGAL AND ETHICAL PRICING ISSUES

Retailers need to consider legal and ethical issues when setting prices. For example, pricing has been particularly difficult for Carrefour hypermarkets in France, where regulation prohibits how much it can lower its prices on branded merchandise. Carrefour has been hurt by competitors, such as two German chains, ALDI and Lidl, both of which sell private-label merchandise that is not subject to the French rules and thus can be priced more cheaply than Carrefour's products. Both of these retailers aggressively entered the French market, winning over many Carrefour shoppers.[35]

Some of the legal and ethical pricing issues are predatory pricing, resale price maintenance, horizontal price fixing, bait-and-switch tactics, scanned versus posted prices, and deceptive reference prices.

Predatory Pricing

Predatory pricing arises when a dominant retailer sets prices below its costs to drive competitive retailers out of business. Eventually, the predator hopes to raise prices when the competition is eliminated and earn back enough profits to compensate for its losses. For instance, independent booksellers accuse Walmart, Target, and Amazon of selling best-selling books below their cost, such as Stephen King's *Under the Dome* for as low as $8.95 when the cover price is $35. The American Booksellers Association has complained to the Department of Justice,

Independent booksellers accuse Walmart, Target, and Amazon of predatory pricing when they sell best-selling books below their cost, such as Stephen King's *Under the Dome* for as low as $8.95 when the cover price is $35.

claiming that these retailers are engaging in illegal predatory pricing, which is damaging to the book industry and harmful to consumers.[36] Some states have old statutes that declare it illegal to sell goods at unreasonably low prices, usually below their cost. However, a retailer generally may sell merchandise at any price as long as the motive isn't to eliminate competition.

Resale Price Maintenance

As discussed in Chapter 13, vendors often encourage retailers to sell their merchandise at a specific price, known as the manufacturer's suggested retail price (MSRP). Vendors set MSRPs to reduce retail price competition among retailers, eliminate free riding, and stimulate retailers to provide complementary services. Vendors enforce MSRPs by withholding benefits such as cooperative advertising or even refusing to deliver merchandise to noncomplying retailers. The U.S. Supreme Court recently ruled that the ability of a vendor to require that retailers sell merchandise at MSRPs should be decided on a case-by-case basis, depending on the individual circumstances.[37]

Horizontal Price Fixing

Horizontal price fixing involves agreements between retailers that are in direct competition with each other to set the same prices. This practice clearly reduces competition and is illegal. As a general rule of thumb, retailers should refrain from discussing prices or terms and conditions of sale with competitors. If buyers or store managers want to know competitors' prices, they can look at a competitor's advertisements, its Web sites, or its stores.

Bait-and-Switch Tactics

A **bait and switch** is an unlawful, deceptive practice that lures customers into a store by advertising a product at a lower-than-normal price (the bait) and then, once they are in the store, induces them to purchase a higher-priced model (the switch). Bait and switch usually involves the store either having inadequate inventory for the advertised product or pushing salespeople to disparage the quality of the advertised model and emphasize the superior performance of a higher-priced model. To avoid disappointing customers and risking problems with the Federal Trade Commission (FTC), the retailer needs to have sufficient inventory of advertised items and offer customers rain checks if stockouts occur.

Scanned versus Posted Prices

Although customers and regulators are concerned about price-scanning accuracy, studies usually find a high level of accuracy. In general, retailers lose money from scanning errors because the scanned price is below the posted price.[38] However, consumer groups and state's attorney generals' offices do find and pursue price discrepancies in retailers' favor. Periodic price audits are an essential component of good pricing practices. Price audits of a random sample of items should be done periodically to identify the extent and cause of scanning errors and develop procedures to minimize errors.

Deceptive Reference Prices

A **reference price** is the price against which buyers compare the actual selling price of the product, and thus it facilitates their evaluation process. Typically, the retailer labels the reference price as the "regular price" or "original price." When consumers view the "sale price" and compare it with the provided reference price, their perceptions of the value of the product or service will likely increase.[39]

If the reference price is bona fide, the advertisement is informative. If the reference price has been inflated or is just plain fictitious, however, the advertisement is deceptive and may cause harm to consumers. But it is not easy to determine whether a reference price is bona fide. What standard should be used? If an advertisement specifies a "regular price," just what qualifies as regular? How many units must the store sell at this price for it to be a bona fide regular price—half the stock? A few? Just one? Finally, what if the store offers the item for sale at the regular price but customers do not buy any? Can it still be considered a regular price? In general, if a seller is going to label a price as a regular price, the Better Business Bureau suggests that at least 50 percent of the sales should have occurred at that price.[40]

SUMMARY

Setting prices is a critical decision in implementing a retail strategy because price is a critical component in customers' perceived value. Retailers use two basic retail pricing strategies: everyday low pricing (EDLP) and high/low pricing. Each of these strategies has its advantages and disadvantages. The high/low strategy increases profits through price discrimination, creates excitement, and provides an opportunity to sell slow-moving merchandise. The EDLP approach assures customers of low prices, reduces advertising and operating expenses, reduces stockouts, and improves supply chain management.

In setting prices, retailers consider the price sensitivity of customers in their target market, the cost of the merchandise and services offered, competitive prices, and legal and ethical restrictions. Theoretically, retailers maximize their profits by setting prices on the basis of the price sensitivity of customers and the cost of merchandise. However, this approach does not consider the prices being charged by competitors. Another problem with attempting to set prices on the basis of customer price sensitivity is the implementation challenges associated with the large number of pricing decisions a retailer must make. Additional challenges arise when pricing services, due to the need to match supply and demand and the difficulties customers have in determining service quality. Retailers use yield management techniques to match supply and demand for services.

Although some large retailers are using pricing optimization software to set prices, most retailers just mark up the item's cost to yield a profitable maintained margin. Then the cost-based initial price might be adjusted according to the retail buyer's insights about customer price sensitivity and competitive pricing.

Initial prices are adjusted over time using markdowns and for different market segments using variable-pricing strategies. Retailers take markdowns to either dispose of merchandise or generate sales. Markdowns are part of the cost of doing business, and thus buyers plan for them.

Retailers use a variety of techniques to maximize sales and profits by charging different prices to different customers. These techniques include setting different prices for individual customers, providing an offering that enables customers to self-select the price they are willing to pay, and setting different prices according to customer demographics. Retailers also use price lining, leader pricing, and odd pricing to stimulate sales.

Finally, there are several legal and ethical issues retailers consider when setting prices. These include predatory pricing, resale price maintenance, horizontal price fixing, bait-and-switch tactics, scanned versus posted prices, and deceptive reference prices.

KEY TERMS

bait and switch, *394*

break-even analysis, *381*

break-even point quantity, *381*

cherry picker, *391*

coupons, *388*

everyday low pricing (EDLP), *372*

first-degree price discrimination, *385*

fixed cost, *381*

GET OUT AND DO IT!

1. **CONTINUING ASSIGNMENT** Go shopping at the retailer you have selected for the Continuing Assignment. Does the retailer use high/low pricing or an EDLP strategy? Ask the store manager how markdown decisions are made and how the store decides how much a markdown should be. What rule-based approaches are used to make markdowns? Does the retailer use techniques for stimulating sales such as price lining, leader pricing, bundling, or multiunit and odd pricing? Are the prices on its Web site the same as those in the store? Evaluate your findings. Do you believe the retailer is using the best pricing strategies and tactics for its type of store? What, if anything, could it do to improve?

2. Go to the Web page of Overstock.com, and look at its top-selling merchandise. Select a few key items, and compare the price of each product at other online retail sites, such as Target.com, Amazon.com, Sears.com, and Macys.com. How do the prices at this Internet outlet compare to those at a discount store, online retailer, and department store? Are the results what you expected, or were you surprised? Explain your reaction.

3. Go to the Web site of Sandals (www.sandals.com), and see what you can get for an all-inclusive price. Describe how bundling services and products provides vacationers with value. Find an example of price bundling outside the travel industry. Which do you believe provides the customer with the best value? Which makes the retailer or service provider more profits?

4. Go to three different types of stores, and try to bargain your way down from the tagged price. Explain your experience. Was there any difference in your success rate as a result of the type of store or merchandise? Did you have better luck if you spoke to a manager rather than a salesperson?

5. Go to your favorite food store and your local Walmart to find their prices for the market basket of goods listed in the table below. What was the total cost of the market basket at each store? How did the prices compare? Did Walmart live up to its slogan of "Always lower prices"?

Competitive Pricing: Grocery Store vs. Walmart

Item	Size	Brand	Grocery	Walmart	Price Difference	Percent Savings
Grocery						
Ground coffee	11.5 oz can	Folgers				
Raisin Bran	25.5 oz box	Kellogg's				
Pet Supplies						
Puppy Chow	4.4 lb bag	Purina				
Cleaning						
Liquid laundry detergent	100 oz bottle	All				
Dryer sheets	80 count	Bounce				
Liquid dish detergent	25 oz bottle	Palmolive				
Health and Beauty						
Shampoo	12 oz bottle	Dove				
Toothpaste	4.2 oz tube	Colgate Total				
Total Cost of the Market Basket of Goods						

6. Go to the student side of the Online Learning Center. Click on "Pricing" and then on "Markdown model." Oracle Retail has provided you the opportunity to play buyer and test your analytical abilities for taking markdowns. You will be given the opportunity to make markdown decisions for several products over several weeks. You can play this simulation game either on your own or against your classmates.

DISCUSSION QUESTIONS AND PROBLEMS

1. What types of retailers often use a high/low pricing strategy? What types of retailers generally use an everyday low-pricing strategy? How would customers likely react if a retailer switched its pricing strategy from one to the other? Explain your response.

2. Why would sewing pattern manufacturers such as Simplicity, Butterick, and McCall's print a price of $12.95 (or more) on each pattern and then two times a year offer patterns for sale at $1.99 each? How could this markdown influence demand, sales, and profits?

3. Why would retailers risk violating any of the legal issues discussed in this chapter, such as predatory pricing, price fixing, deceptive pricing, bait and switch, or discriminatory pricing? Explain your answer.

4. Reread Retailing View 14.2, "Hey, Wanna Buy a Ticket?" Describe how supply and demand can impact the price of tickets for sporting events, concerts, and other entertainment. How does the secondary online ticket market impact consumers and the original ticket sellers?

5. What is the difference between bundled pricing and multiunit pricing?

Note: **For questions 6 to 10, you may use the Online Learning Center. Click on "pricing."**

6. A department store's maintained markup is 38 percent, reductions are $560, and net sales are $28,000. What's the initial markup percentage?

7. Maintained markup is 39 percent, net sales are $52,000, and reductions are $2,500. What are the gross margin in dollars and the initial markup as a percentage? Explain why initial markup is greater than maintained markup.

8. The cost of a product is $150, markup is 50 percent, and markdown is 30 percent. What's the final selling price?

9. Men's Wearhouse purchased black leather belts for $15.99 each and priced them to sell for $29.99 each. What was the markup on the belts?

10. Answer the following questions: (a) The Limited is planning a new line of jackets for fall. It plans to sell the jackets for $100. It is having the jackets produced in the Dominican Republic. Although The Limited does not own the factory, its product development and design costs are $400,000. The total cost of the jacket, including transportation to the stores, is $45. For this line to be successful, The Limited needs to make $900,000 profit. What is its break-even point in units and dollars? (b) The buyer has just found out that The Gap, one of The Limited's major competitors, is bringing out a similar jacket that will retail for $90. If The Limited wants to match The Gap's price, how many units will it have to sell?

SUGGESTED READINGS

Ailawadi, Kusum L., J. P. Beauchamp, Naveen Donthu, Dinesh K. Gauri, and Venkatesh Shankar. "Communication and Promotion Decisions in Retailing: A Review and Directions for Future Research." *Journal of Retailing* 85, no. 1 (2009), pp. 42–55.

Baker, Walter L., Michael V. Marn, and Craig Zawada. *The Price Advantage.* New York: Wiley, 2004.

Chiou-Wei, Song-Zan, and J. Jeffrey Inman, "Do Shoppers Like Electronic Coupons? A Panel Data Analysis." *Journal of Retailing* 84, no. 3 (2008), pp. 297–307.

Harvard Business Review on Pricing. Boston: Harvard Business Press, November 3, 2008.

Holden, Reed, and Mark Burton. *Pricing with Confidence: 10 Ways to Stop Leaving Money on the Table.* New York: Wiley, February 25, 2008.

Kopalle, Praveen, Dipayan Biswas, Pradeep K. Chintagunta, Jia Fan, Koen Pauwels, Brian T. Ratchford, James A. Sills.

"Retailer Pricing and Competitive Effects." *Journal of Retailing* 85, no. 1 (2009), pp. 56–70.

Maxwell, Sarah. *The Price Is Wrong: Understanding What Makes a Price Seem Fair and the True Cost of Unfair Pricing.* New York: Wiley, 2008.

Nagle, Thomas T., and John Hogan. *The Strategy and Tactics of Pricing: A Guide to Growing More Profitably.* Upper Saddle River, NJ: Wiley, 2005.

Popkowski, Peter T. L., Leszczyc Chun Qiu, and Yongfu Hec. "Empirical Testing of the Reference-Price Effect of Buy-Now Prices in Internet Auctions." *Journal of Retailing* 85, no. 2 (2009), pp. 211–221.

Zhang, Jie, and Michel Wedel. "The Effectiveness of Customized Promotions in Online and Offline Stores." *Journal of Marketing Research* 46, no. 2 (2009), pp. 190–206.

Retail Communication Mix

EXECUTIVE BRIEFING
Krista Gibson, Vice President, Marketing
Chili's Grill & Bar Restaurants

Chili's Grill & Bar, a division of Brinker International, is a leader in the casual dining segment of the restaurant industry. My team is responsible for building Chili's brand image and customer loyalty, designing special promotions and events, undertaking market and customer satisfaction research, and providing a customer's perspective on the nature of our offering from the ambience of our restaurants to the items on the menu.

Before the recession in 2008, the casual dining restaurants were thriving. The percent of meals eaten away from home was increasing each year and the industry responded by opening more restaurants anticipating this trend would continue. Excess capacity coupled with the recession has created an intensely competitive environment. When we don't fill the seats in our restaurants, those sales are lost forever. One of the challenges we face is walking the fine line between using price promotions to attract guests but not have our guest feel the price promotions are the only reason they are going to Chili's.

In addition to using the traditional media—television, radio, and billboards—to communicate with our customers, we are using a variety of Internet tools and social media. Our guests can go to our Web site, chillis.com, select their closest Chili's restaurant and place an order with the desired pick-up time. Chili's To Go orders are made Right and Right on Time™ providing meal solutions for hectic family schedules and business meetings.

We have a Facebook page with over 400,000 friends, a Chili's application for iPhones, and we Twitter. We also connect with our guests through Foursquare, a location-based social media platform for smartphones. Participating locations are identified on Foursquare with a "special offer" flag whenever a guest is within 200 yards of the restaurant. Guests checking in on Foursquare get an instant redemption coupon for Chili's chips and salsa free.

CHAPTER 15

QUESTIONS

How can retailers use communication programs to develop brand images and build customer loyalty?

How do retailers communicate with their customers?

What steps are involved in developing a communication program?

While we are experimenting with these social media tools, it is very hard to measure their effectiveness. For example, our experience with Facebook suggests that our guests like to have the opportunity to share their views and be treated specially through social media, but they do not want to be bombarded with ads and promotions. Our most effective Internet-based communication tool has been our opt-in e-mail list. Our guests get a free appetizer for joining our e-mail club and respond to the exclusive offers and information we send them.

I really like working in marketing. It gives me a chance to be creative, and develop and implement new marketing ideas ranging from new products to new communication approaches. Having multiple locations gives us the opportunity to test out these new ideas with a sample of stores and find out what works and what doesn't.

The preceding chapters in this section on merchandise management described how retailers develop an assortment and merchandise budget plan and then buy and price merchandise. The next step in the retail management decision-making process is to develop and implement a communication program to build appealing brand images, attract customers to stores and Internet sites, and encourage those customers to buy merchandise. The communication program informs customers about the retailer as well as the merchandise and services it offers and plays a role in developing repeat visits and customer loyalty.

Communication programs can have both long- and short-term effects on a retailer's business. From a long-term perspective, communication programs can be used to create and maintain a strong, differentiated image of the retailer and its private-label brands. This image develops customer loyalty and creates a strategic advantage. Thus, brand-image-building communication programs complement the objectives of a retailer's CRM program, as discussed in Chapter 11.

In addition, retailers frequently use communication programs to realize the short-term objective of increasing sales during a specified time period. For example, retailers often have sales, during which some or all merchandise is priced at a discount for a short time. Supermarkets usually place weekly ads with coupons that can be used to save money on purchases made during the week.

The first part of this chapter examines the role of communication programs in building brand images. The second part of the chapter focuses on developing and implementing communication programs.

USING COMMUNICATION PROGRAMS TO DEVELOP BRAND IMAGES AND BUILD CUSTOMER LOYALTY

A **brand** is a distinguishing name or symbol, such as a logo, that identifies the products or services offered by a seller and differentiates those products and services from the offerings of competitors.[1] In a retailing context, the name of the retailer is a brand that indicates to consumers the type of merchandise and services offered by that retailer. As we discussed in Chapter 13, some retailers develop private-label brands that are exclusively sold through their channels. In some cases, private-label merchandise bears the retailer's name, such as Walgreens aspirin and Victoria's Secret lingerie. In other cases, special brand names are used, such as Walmart's Ol' Roy dog food and Sears' Die Hard batteries.

Value of Brand Image

Brands provide value to both customers and retailers. Brands convey information to consumers about the nature of the shopping experience—the retailer's mix—they will encounter when patronizing a retailer. They also affect customers' confidence in their decisions to buy merchandise from a retailer. Finally, brands can enhance customers' satisfaction with the merchandise and services they buy. Consumers feel different when wearing jewelry bought from Tiffany rather than from Zales or when staying at a Ritz-Carlton hotel rather than a Fairfield Inn.

The value that a brand image offers retailers is referred to as **brand equity.** Strong brand names can affect the customer's decision-making process, motivate repeat visits and purchases, and build loyalty. In addition, strong brand names enable retailers to charge higher prices and lower their marketing costs.

Customer loyalty to brands arises from heightened awareness of the brand and emotional ties to it. For example, Chapter 4 discussed the need for retailers to be in a customer's consideration set. Some retail brands such as Walmart and Macy's are so well known by consumers that they typically appear in those consumers' consideration sets. In addition, customers identify and have strong emotional relationships with some brands. For example, going to Target has become a cool experience, because people think it is trendy to save money and buy fashionable merchandise in the same store. Customers affectionately use the faux French pronunciation of

The ad on the left focuses on a short-term objective—building sales during Mother's Day. The Abt ad on the right is directed toward building Abt's brand image—a long term objective.

"Tar-zhay" when referring to Target. High brand awareness and strong emotional connections reduce the incentive of customers to switch to competing retailers.

A strong brand image also enables retailers to increase their margins. When retailers have high customer loyalty, they can engage in premium pricing and reduce their reliance on price promotions to attract customers. Brands with weaker images are forced to offer low prices and frequent sales to maintain their market share.

Finally, retailers with strong brand names can leverage their brands to introduce new retail concepts with only a limited amount of marketing effort. For example, The Gap has efficiently extended its brand to GapKids, gapbody, GapMaternity, and babyGap, and Toys "R" Us has extended its brand name to Babies "R" Us.

As we discussed in Chapter 5, a strong brand name creates a strategic advantage that is very difficult for competitors to duplicate. Just think how hard it would be for Kmart to change its image to that of Walmart or Target, the more successful discount store chains.

Retailing View 15.1 outlines how J.Crew has managed to develop its own brand identity, distinct from those of its closest competitors.

RETAILING VIEW "Even If You Can't Afford It, You Respect It": J.Crew's Reputation for Quality 15.1

The brand has strong name recognition: Lots of shoppers have heard of J.Crew. But in the mid-2000s, many of those shoppers heard the name and thought only "boring and preppy." When CEO Millard "Mickey" Drexler took the reins in 2003, he decided that to change J. Crew's image, he had to appeal to customers' hearts through their fingers—that is, with the feel and look of quality clothing. By providing high-quality versions of classic clothing pieces at what it considers reasonable prices, J.Crew has been able to increase its profits, lower its debt, and expand the number of stores.

For its cashmere cardigans, for example, J.Crew doesn't use just any wool supplier. It turns to the well-known brand Loro Piana to ensure the quality. And then it makes sure the name "Loro Piana" is prominent in the clothing. As the company promises on its Web site, it "partners with the finest global fabric mills and craftsmen—as well as with iconic brands such as Jack Purcell, Timex, Thomas Mason and Red Wing (to name just a few)." Customers therefore come to associate the J.Crew name with high-end suppliers. But such quality comes at a price. Customers of J.Crew pay more for the promise of higher quality.

Other mall-based retailers operate at much lower price points. No one is likely to find leather boots made by Prada at The Gap, as customers can at J.Crew. Even for seemingly similar offerings, J.Crew sets itself apart in discernible ways, such as adding hand-stitched sequins to a basic T-shirt.

Mickey Drexler also believes in allowing customers to dictate the brand image. When he received feedback indicating that women were purchasing multiple J.Crew sundresses in different colors to use as bridesmaids' gowns, he launched J. Crew bridal. The line opened its first dedicated bridal store in May

J.Crew's CEO Mickey Drexler helped change the retailer's image by providing high-quality versions of classic clothing at what it considers to be reasonable prices.

2010. When European customers complained about their inability to have J.Crew merchandise shipped overseas, he entered a partnership with an online retailer to make items available nearly worldwide.

This positioning is part of what has earned Drexler the nickname "the merchant prince." Although J.Crew holds tight to its hard-earned preppy reputation, it has gained a position in customers' minds as a source of quality at reasonable prices. It also reveals a willingness to shift as needed to meet customers' changing and demanding expectations.

Sources: Tina Gaudoin, "Mickey Drexler: Retail Therapist," *Wall Street Journal,* June 10, 2010; Meryl Gordon, "Mickey Drexler's Redemption," *New York Magazine,* May 21, 2005; www.jcrew.com/AST/FooterNavigation/aboutus.jsp (accessed July 10, 2010).

Building Brand Equity

The activities that a retailer needs to undertake to build brand equity for its firm or its private-label merchandise are (1) create a high level of brand awareness, (2) develop favorable associations with the brand name, and (3) consistently reinforce the image of the brand.

Brand Awareness   **Brand awareness** refers to a potential customer's ability to recognize or recall that the brand name is a particular type of retailer or product/service. Thus, brand awareness is the strength of the link between the brand name and the type of merchandise or service in the minds of customers.

There is a range of awareness, from aided recall to top-of-mind awareness. **Aided recall** occurs when consumers indicate they know the brand when the name is presented to them. **Top-of-mind awareness,** the highest level of awareness, occurs when consumers mention a specific brand name first when they are asked about the type of retailer, a merchandise category, or a type of service. For example, Best Buy has a high top-of-mind awareness if most consumers respond "Best Buy" when asked about retailers that sell consumer electronics. High top-of-mind awareness means that a retailer probably will be in the consideration set when customers decide to shop for a type of product or service.

Retailers build top-of-mind awareness by having memorable names; repeatedly exposing their names to customers through advertising, locations, and sponsorships; and using memorable symbols. Some brand names are easy to remember, such as the name Home Depot. Because "Home" is in its brand name, it probably is more memorable and closely associated with home improvements than the name Lowe's.

Zara does very little advertising but has high awareness because of the large number of stores it has in great locations. Customers walk and drive by the stores, look at their artfully designed windows, and are drawn in. Customers know that if they don't purchase the high-fashioned, reasonably priced apparel when they see it in the store, it probably won't be there the next time.

Symbols involve visual images that typically are more easily recalled than words or phrases and thus are useful for building brand awareness. For example, the image of an apple and the golden arches enhance the ability of customers to recall the names Apple Store and McDonald's.

Sponsorships of well-publicized events also can provide considerable exposure to a retailer's name and increase awareness. For example, watching the Macy's Thanksgiving Parade in New York City has become a holiday tradition for many families. The Macy's brand name is exposed to tens of millions of television viewers for three hours. In addition, newspaper articles are devoted to previewing the parade and describing it afterward.

Associations   Building awareness is only one step in developing brand equity, but the value of the brand is largely based on the associations that customers make with the brand name. **Brand associations** are anything linked to or connected with the brand name in a consumer's memory. For example, some of the associations that consumers might have with Apple are its innovative products, such as the iPhone, iPod, and Mac computers, as well as its easy-to-use computer interface and innovative stores. These strong associations influence consumer buying behavior.

Macy's annual Thanksgiving Day Parade and the accompanying publicity builds top-of-mind awareness for the retailer.

Some common associations that retailers develop with their brand name are as follows:

1. *Merchandise category.* The most common association is to link the retailer to a category of merchandise. For example, Office Depot would like to have consumers associate its name with office supplies. Then when a need for office supplies arises, consumers immediately think of Office Depot.

2. *Price/quality.* Some retailers, such as Saks Fifth Avenue, want to be associated with offering unique, high-fashion merchandise. Other retailers, such as Walmart, want associations with low prices and good value.

3. *Specific attribute or benefit.* A retailer can link its stores to attributes, such as 7-Eleven's association with providing convenience or Nordstrom's connection with offering a high level of customer service.

4. *Lifestyle or activity.* Some retailers associate their name with a specific lifestyle or activity. For example, Patagonia, a retailer offering outdoor sports equipment, is linked to an active, environmentally friendly lifestyle. Pottery Barn is associated with comfortable living in the home.

When people think of Patagonia, they think about an active, environmentally friendly lifestyle.

The **brand image** consists of a set of associations that are usually organized around some meaningful themes. Thus, the associations that a consumer might have about McDonald's might be organized into groups such as kids, service, and type of food. Retailing View 15.2 illustrates how L.L.Bean nurtures its brand image of selling high-quality, functional products and providing helpful service for outdoor living.

Integrated Marketing Communication Program   Retailers need to develop an **integrated marketing communication program**—a program that integrates all the communication elements to deliver a comprehensive, consistent message to all customers over time, across all elements of their retail mix, and across all delivery channels. Without this coordination, the communication methods might work at cross-purposes. For example, the retailer's televised advertising campaign might attempt to build an image of exceptional customer service, but the firm's sales promotions might all emphasize low prices. If communication methods aren't used consistently, customers may become confused about the retailer's image and therefore not patronize the store.

JCPenney is engaging its customers online as well as in the store with its interactive virtual runway show on JCP.com.[3] Styles from Nicole Miller, Allen B. Schwartz, and Charlotte Ronson are on 360-degree-view models with music to make it seem like a live show. About 800,000 women visit JCP.com each week. Customers can see a realistic view of the clothes online as well as check their availability at their local bricks-and-mortar store. This JCPenney runway campaign is also being communicated in other ways, including direct mail and e-mail.

Talbots also provides its customers with an integrated marketing communication program. The company strives to give all of its outlets the residential feel of the company's first store, which was in a 17th-century Massachusetts home. Interiors

15.2   RETAILING VIEW   L.L.Bean Celebrates the Outdoors

Leon Leonwood Bean, an outdoorsman living in Freeport, Maine, founded L.L.Bean in 1912. The first product he sold through the mail was boots (the Maine hunting shoe) with waterproof rubber bottoms and lightweight leather tops. The boots provided significant benefits over heavyweight, all-leather boots in wet weather. However, the first pairs he sold had a stitching problem. Bean decided to refund each customer's money, which led to L.L.Bean's legendary "Guarantee of 100% Satisfaction." Some of the associations that L.L.Bean reinforces through its advertising and Web site, as well as other elements in its retail mix, are:

- *Friendly.* L.L.Bean is comfortable and familiar, easy to approach.

- *Honest.* L.L.Bean is straightforward and honest. It would never mislead its customers. It provides factual information about its products.

- *Expertise.* L.L.Bean's employees are experts about its products and the outdoors. They'll do anything they can to help customers choose which product is best for them or even help them find the best place to camp.

- *Practical and economical.* Building on its Yankee New England roots, L.L.Bean offers products that are functional, with no-nonsense features, at fair prices. As Bean once said, "I attribute our success to the fact that, to the best of my judgment, every article we offer for sale is practical for the purpose for which we recommend it."

As times change, however, so must L.L.Bean. Its association with New England heritage may lead some to associate it with old-fashioned, male-oriented merchandise. To help reposition its image and attract a new, younger clientele without alienating its core customers, Bean has introduced the Signature collection to compete directly with popular, preppy retailers such as J.Crew and Ralph Lauren. L.L.Bean needed some way to communicate that it was expanding beyond the outdoorsy image it had cultivated for so long. So when a college student volunteered to promote the new Signature collection at a local coffee shop, the company jumped at the chance.

In this case, L.L.Bean had a unique opportunity to recruit college students who already had expressed interest in the brand. These brand ambassadors now have input on design and

L.L.Bean has introduced the Signature collection to compete directly with popular preppy retailers such as J.Crew and Ralph Lauren.

Web site decisions. In exchange for free clothes (which cost the company virtually nothing), they talk up the new collection at campuses throughout the northeast United States while creating additional promotional networks on those campuses. The ambassadors also use Facebook and word of mouth to generate crowds at their gatherings, where they showcase samples from the collection and raffle off L.L.Bean gift cards and clothes.

Sources: Jenn Abelson, "With Student Help, L.L. Bean Tries Younger Look," *Boston Globe,* March 15, 2010; Leon Gorman and Aaron Pressman, "Want Some Pajamas with That Kayak?" *BusinessWeek,* November 20, 2006, p. 76; *L.L. Bean: The Making of an American Icon* (Boston: Harvard Business School Press, October 3, 2006); Edward Murphy, "Portland, Maine–Based L.L. Bean Ranks High in Customer Loyalty," *Knight Ridder Tribune Business News,* April 8, 2005, p. 1; www.llbean.com (accessed November 14, 2010).

Talbots utilizes an integrated communication strategy, which includes bright red doors on its stores, and is also featured in its catalogs and Web site.

are decorated with maple floors and wainscoting, and walls are hung with traditional botanical and equestrian prints to simulate the atmosphere of old New England. In addition, each store has a bright red door and, wherever possible, matching red awnings over the windows. The overall ambience and the red door in particular are ever present in its catalogs and Web site.[4]

Extending the Brand Name

Retailers can leverage their brand names to support the growth strategies discussed in Chapter 5. For example, IKEA used its strong brand image to enter the U.S. home furnishing retail market successfully; Pottery Barn launched its Pottery Barn Kids catalog to target families with children. In other cases, retailers have pursued growth opportunities using a new and unrelated brand name. For example, Abercrombie & Fitch uses the brand name Hollister for stores that target high school students and the name Gilly Hicks for its undergarment stores, and Sears named its home store concept The Great Indoors.

There are both pluses and minuses to extending a brand name to a new concept. An important benefit of extending the brand name is that minimal communication expenses are needed to create awareness and a brand image for the new concept. Customers will quickly transfer their awareness and associations about the original concept to the new concept. However, in some cases, the retailer might not want to have the original brand's associations connected with the new concept. For example, Abercrombie & Fitch decided to invest in building a new and different brand image for Gilly Hicks and Hollister & Co. rather than branding them with a similar name.

These issues also arise as a retailer expands internationally. Associations with the retailer's brands that are valued in one country may not be valued in another. For example, French consumers prefer to shop at supermarkets that offer good service and high-quality grocery products, whereas German shoppers prefer supermarkets that offer low prices and good value. Thus, a French supermarket retailer with a brand image of quality and service might not be able to leverage its image if it decides to enter the German market.

Retailers communicate with customers using a mix of methods, such as advertising, sales promotion, publicity, e-mail, blogs, and social media like Twitter, Facebook, and YouTube. This chapter focuses on these and other communication vehicles. Chapter 17 examines how retailers communicate with customers through their store layouts, design, and visual merchandising; and Chapter 18 touches on how they communicate through personal selling, as it relates to customer service.

In large retail firms, the communication mix elements examined in this chapter are managed by the firm's marketing or advertising department and the buying organization. The other elements, such as store atmosphere and salespeople, are managed by store personnel and are thus discussed in Section IV. The following sections of this chapter examine the methods that retailers use to communicate with their customers and how they plan and implement communication programs to build brand equity as well as short-term sales.

METHODS OF COMMUNICATING WITH CUSTOMERS[5]

For any communications campaign to succeed, the firm must deliver the right message to the right audience through the right media, with the ultimate goal of profiting from long-term customer relationships rather than just short-term transactions. Reaching the right audience is becoming more difficult, however, as the media environment grows more complicated.[6]

No single type of media is necessarily better than another. The goal of a retail communication strategy is to use the media in conjunction so that the sum exceeds the total of the individual media types. However, advances in technology have led to a variety of new, along with the traditional, media options for consumers, all of which vie for consumers' attention. Print media have also grown and become more specialized. This proliferation of media has led many retailers to shift their promotional dollars from advertising to direct marketing, use of Internet sites, and other forms of promotion in search of the best way to deliver messages to their target audiences.

We now examine the individual elements of a retail communication strategy and the way each contributes to a successful communication campaign (see Exhibit 15–1). The elements can be viewed on two axes: passive and interactive (from the consumer's perspective) and offline and online. Note that as the retailer's repertoire of communication elements has expanded, so too have the ways in which retailers can communicate with their customers. So, for instance, direct marketing appears in three of the four boxes. Firms have also expanded their use of traditional media (e.g., advertising, public relations, and sales promotions) from pure offline to a combination of offline and online.

EXHIBIT 15–1
Elements of an IMC Strategy

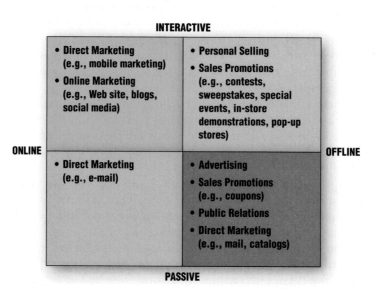

SOURCE: Dhruv Grewal and Michael Levy, *Marketing*, 3rd ed. (New York: McGraw-Hill/Irwin, 2012).

Direct Marketing

Direct marketing is marketing that communicates directly with target customers to generate a response or transaction. Direct marketing contains a variety of traditional and new forms of marketing communication initiatives and is represented in three of the four quadrants in Exhibit 15–1. Traditional direct marketing includes mail and catalogs sent through the mail; today it also includes Internet-enabled methods such as e-mail and mobile marketing.

The increased use of customer databases has enabled retailers to identify and track consumers over time and across purchase situations, and this has contributed to the growth of direct marketing. Retailers have been able to build these databases, thanks to consumers' increased use of credit and debit cards, store-specific credit and loyalty cards, and online shopping, all of which require the buyer to give the seller personal information that becomes part of its database. Because firms understand customers' purchases better when they possess such information, they can more easily focus their direct marketing efforts appropriately.

Direct marketing retailers try to carefully target their customers so that they will be more receptive to their messages. Omaha Steaks, for example, sends e-mail coupons for items that customers have purchased previously, mails slick pictures of gourmet steaks and meal packages to addresses that have received orders in the past, and calls customers personally during likely gift-giving occasions, such as the holidays, to offer to repeat a previous gift order. These different forms of direct marketing demonstrate how this communication method can vary on both the interactivity and online/offline dimensions of Exhibit 15–1.

Direct Mail   **Direct mail** includes any brochure, catalog, advertisement, or other printed marketing material delivered directly to the consumer through the mail or a private delivery company.[8] Retailers have communicated with their customers through the mail for as long as the mail has existed. The direct mail piece can go to all customers, to a subset of the customers according to their previous purchases, or even on a personalized basis to individual customers. Although relatively expensive on a per-customer basis (because of printing, mail costs, and a relatively low response rate), direct mail is still extensively used by many retailers because people respond favorably to personal messages.

E-mail   **E-mail** is a direct marketing communication vehicle that involves sending messages over the Internet. E-mail, like other forms of electronic communications (e.g., Web sites, m-commerce), can be personalized to the specific consumer and thus is similar to communications delivered by salespeople. However, when the same message is delivered electronically to all recipients, electronic communications more closely resemble advertising. Retailers use e-mail to inform customers of new merchandise and special promotions, confirm the receipt of an order, and indicate when an order has been shipped.

Mobile Marketing   **Mobile marketing** is marketing through wireless handheld devices, such as cellular telephones, and **m-commerce** or **mobile commerce** involves completing a transaction via the cell phone.[9] Smartphones have become far more than tools for placing calls; they offer a kind of mobile computer with the ability to obtain sports scores, weather, music, videos, and text messages, as well as to purchase merchandise. Many consumers conceive of their handheld devices as a way to stay in touch with friends, making them largely resistant to the idea of receiving marketing messages on them.[10] Retailers' success with mobile marketing rests on integrating marketing communications with fun, useful apps that are consistent with these consumer attitudes toward mobile devices. In response, firms are steadily improving customers' potential experience with their mobile interfaces by creating applications for consumers.

The RedLaser shopping comparison application for the iPhone takes a picture of a product's bar code and lists the prices for that item at various local retailers.

For example, the RedLaser shopping comparison application for the iPhone takes a picture of a product's bar code and lists the prices for that item at various local retailers. Google Shopper has the same capability for the Android. NearbyNow and Amazon's mobile applications allow users to buy products and complete their transactions through their cell phones.

Foursquare and WeReward target mobile phone users and send them marketing messages on the basis of GPS technology. Started by a video game aficionado,[11] Foursquare awards points to consumers who try local retailers, enabling them to unlock "badges" and earn titles, such as "Mayor" of a particular venue.[12] The badges and titles entitle the recipient to discounts or special offers. For example, Starbucks Mayors can unlock their offers to get a $1 discount on a Frappuccino.[13] The application is based on GPS locations, so users can recommend nearby retailers to friends in the area. Furthermore, the application's data analytics capabilities allow retailers to track the impact of mobile marketing campaigns. But despite the promise of mobile commerce, it continues to have its drawbacks. One recent study found that 90 percent of U.S. survey respondents had absolutely no interest in receiving mobile ads.[14] Combining geographic location services with social media could increase crime rates;[15] for example, burglars would know how far away home owners are, and kidnappers could learn the exact location of young children. Some disreputable companies have hacked into the system and distributed unwanted text messages, harming public perceptions of mobile commerce. Understanding and addressing these challenges would help marketers access a worldwide audience, in the form of more than 4.6 billion cell phone users.[16]

Online Marketing

We now examine in greater depth several online media vehicles with which customers can interact (Exhibit 15–1): Web sites, blogs, and social media.

Web Sites   Retailers are increasing their emphasis on communicating with customers through their Web sites. Retailers use their Web sites to build their brand images; inform customers of store locations, special events, and the availability of merchandise in local stores; and sell merchandise and services.

In addition, some retailers provide services that help garner customer loyalty and indirectly increase sales. Office Depot's Web site, for example, has a Business Resource Center that provides advice and product knowledge, as well as a list of links to other businesses. By providing this information, Office Depot reinforces its image as the essential source of products, services, and information for small businesses.

Foursquare encourages consumers to buy at participating retailers by offering discounts and special offers.

Other retailers devote areas of their Web sites to community building. These sites offer an opportunity for customers with similar interests to learn about products and services that support their hobbies and to share information with others. Visitors to these Web sites can also post questions seeking information and/or comments about issues, products, and services. For example, REI, an outdoor apparel and equipment retailer, offers adventure travel planning resources for hiking trips, bike tours, paddling, adventure cruises, and other trips. By doing so, REI creates a community of customers who engage in activities using the merchandise that REI sells. The community thus reinforces REI's brand image.

Many retailers also encourage customers to post reviews of products they have bought or used and even have visitors to their Web sites rate the quality of the reviews. Research has shown that these online product reviews increase customer loyalty and provide a competitive advantage for sites that offer them.[17]

Blogs   A blog (Weblog) contains periodic posts on a common Web page. A well-received blog can communicate trends, announce special events, and create **word-of-mouth**, which is communication between people about a retailer.[18] Blogs connect customers by forming a community, allow the company to respond directly to customers' comments, and facilitate long-term relationships between customers and the company. By their very nature, blogs are supposed to be transparent and contain authors' honest observations, which can help customers determine their trust and loyalty levels. Nowadays, blogs are becoming more interactive as the communication between bloggers and customers has increased.

Many retailers utilize blogs as part of the communication strategy. A top-ranked retailer blog is Omnivoracious, Amazon's blog, which is, naturally, about books. Dell, Apple, Sears, Best Buy, and QVC also have highly rated blogs.[19]

Social Media   **Social media** is media content distributed through social interactions. Three major online facilitators of social media are YouTube, Facebook, and Twitter. As another online vehicle for word-of-mouth communications, online social media enable consumers to review, communicate about, and aggregate information about products, prices, and promotions. This type of social media also allows users to interact among themselves (e.g., form a community). Such online communities enable users to provide other like-minded consumers and retailers with their thoughts and evaluations about a retailer's products or services.

Retailers are using social media to engage their customers in a proactive dialogue. When a retailer provides content in a social media Web site, people often begin sharing and commenting on it. The retailer then must monitor the feedback and respond if necessary—especially if the commentary is negative. When a retailer finds an unhappy customer, it should recognize the event as a prime customer service opportunity, engage the consumer, and attempt to remedy the situation. By proactively engaging with its customers, a retailer can build stronger relationships. Furthermore, retailers can help cultivate their images through social media that depict them in a certain way, adding a human element that otherwise might not exist.

The social networking site Shopstyle.com features clothing and accessories from hundreds of other Internet stores. Shoppers can browse different looks that feature items across several retailers, put together outfits on their own, and then share and discuss them with friends.

Not all social media have positive results though.[22] Social media eliminate boundaries, often exposing companies to customers' true (and sometimes mean) thoughts and behaviors. Consider the situation in which Kevin Smith, the popular director of films such as *Clerks* and *Dogma* and the actor who played Silent Bob in several of his movies, was removed from a Southwest flight because his large size required him to purchase two seats. Smith immediately tweeted about the situation to his more than 1.6 million Twitter followers. Then when he got onto another flight, he followed up with a picture of himself, proclaiming "SouthwestAir! Look how fat I am on your

REFACT

Of shoppers who buy from Web sites with product reviews, 40 percent said a review was the main reason they made the purchase. That group of product review users was also 21 percent more satisfied with their purchases than other buyers and 18 percent more likely than other buyers to buy from that site the next time they needed similar products.[20]

REFACT

A 2009 survey by Nielsen indicated that 90 percent of Internet users trust recommendations from their friends but only about 40 percent trust online advertisements.[21]

REFACT

Today, more than half the people in the United States trust their peers for information about a company or products more than they trust experts, such as doctors and academics.[23]

Home Depot fosters its identity with instructional do-it-yourself videos on YouTube.

plane! Quick! Throw me off!"[24] Southwest quickly responded on its blog, citing its long-standing rules and concern for other passengers. But the responses have been about equally split in support of the airline and Smith.[25]

The largest facilitators of online social media today are YouTube, Facebook, and Twitter, which we discuss next.

YouTube   On this video-sharing social media platform users upload, share, and view videos. This medium gives retailers a chance to express themselves in a different way than they have before. A retailer like television home shopping company HSN can broadcast its own channel, that is, a YouTube site that contains content relevant only to the company's own products.[26] (See Retailing View 15.3.)

YouTube also provides an effective medium for hosting contests and posting instructional videos. Home Depot attracts more than 4,400 viewers per day with an array of videos detailing new products available in stores, as well as instructional do-it-yourself videos, like "How-To Tips for Mowing Your Lawn" or

---

15.3   RETAILING VIEW   YouTube and HSN

Begun as a local cable channel in 1982, Home Shopping Network (HSN) offered consumers a central location from which to buy through their televisions. As competition in this field increased, HSN tailored its communication strategy to reach more shoppers. For example, HSN.com was one of the top-10 most visited e-commerce sites in 2009, and its Facebook and MySpace pages fill out HSN's marketing mix. But perhaps the most powerful tool HSN has added to its communication strategy is YouTube.

YouTube videos show up in Google searches, making it an appealing vehicle for retailers, and the site's demographics indicate visitors are affluent, of the age range most appealing to retailers, and racially reflective of the wider U.S. population. By reaching 40 to 50 percent of the company's target market, YouTube gives HSN a way to interact differently with customers and further increase its share of wallet with its current customers. The video format humanizes the connection and provides additional information about products.

For example, HSN has a dedicated channel on YouTube that enables it to control the content and look of its page. The site's tracking capabilities also facilitate a deeper understanding of HSN customers, including which other videos and programs attract their attention.

For consumers, YouTube offers a seamless experience. Products promoted on HSN, such as Tori Spelling's jewelry line, are available on YouTube almost immediately after they appear on television. Then HSN marketers can use the information gathered from YouTube to target its direct mail campaigns. For example, it could send jewelry promotions to households that viewed the YouTube video clip for a necklace from the Tori Spelling Collection. Consumer responses get monitored

YouTube allows customers to view Tori Spelling's (left) jewelry line almost immediately after it appears on HSN.

24/7 and measured against hourly sales goals. There's never a dull moment—its like the CNN of shopping.

Sources: www.gstatic.com/youtube/engagement/platform/autoplay/advertise/downloads/YouTube_InTheKnow.pdf; www.gstatic.com/youtube/engagement/platform/autoplay/advertise/downloads/YouTube_BrandChannels.pdf (accessed June 28, 2010); www.gstatic.com/youtube/engagement/platform/autoplay/advertise/downloads/YouTube_Insight.pdf (accessed June 28, 2010); http://mediacommons.futureofthebook.org/imr/2010/03/24/re-branding-dynasty-tori-spellings-hsn-clips-youtube (accessed March 25, 2010).

"How to Repair a Toilet."[27] These videos maintain the core identity of the Home Depot brand while also adding value for consumers, who learn useful ways to improve their homes.

Facebook This social media platform with more than 400 million active users gives companies a forum to interact with fans. Retailers have access to the same features that regular users do, including a "wall" where they can post company updates, photos, and videos or participate in a discussion board.

An excellent example of a fan page is that of the discount clothing retailer Forever 21.[28] When a fan clicks to indicate that he or she "likes" a certain post, the message gets relayed into a news feed, so every friend of that user sees what he or she likes, creating a huge multiplier effect.[29] Accordingly, marketers must consistently update and maintain their fan pages to exploit them as the tremendous assets they can be.

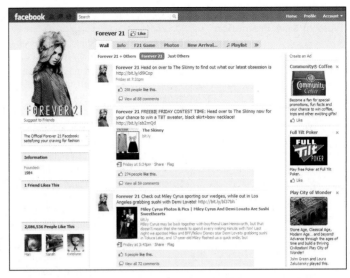

Retailers like Forever 21 are utilizing Facebook to communicate with its customers and create a sense of community.

Twitter This microblogging site, in which users are limited to 140-character messages, is also a platform to facilitate communication using social media. Twitter provides another option for retailers and their customers to communicate using social media.

Twitter is actively used by both small and large retailers. Small retailers with limited marketing budgets love the response they can induce by sending a promotional message immediately. A local bakery tweets, "Two new scones: Lemon Blueberry and Chorizo Cheddar!" and gets responses from 400 Twitter followers—a huge captive audience for a local entity. Large retailers that have enough funds to mass-market through national campaigns use Twitter as a way to stay in personal touch with their customers. For instance, Macy's gave away ¼-karat diamond rings each day for two weeks before Valentine's Day to the people who sent the "sweetest tweet," and a three-stone diamond ring on Valentine's Day to one grand-prize winner.[30] Whole Foods offers many Twitter options to its customers, such as updates on cheese and wine and news from metropolitan areas and individual stores.[31]

Macy's and other retailers use Twitter to create a more personal message than they could using mass media.

Sales Promotions

Sales promotions are special incentives or excitement-building programs that encourage consumers to purchase a particular product or service; they are typically used in conjunction with other advertising or personal selling programs. Like personal selling and telemarketing, sales promotions are a form of offline/interactive communication (Exhibit 15–1). Many sales promotions, like free samples or point-of-purchase (POP) displays, attempt to build short-term sales, whereas others, like loyalty programs, contests, and sweepstakes, have become integral components of retailers' long-term customer relationship management

EXHIBIT 15–2
Types of Sales Promotion

	Advantages	Disadvantages	Promotion
Coupons	Stimulate demand Allow for direct tracing of sales	Have low redemption rates Have high cost	
Rebates	Stimulate demand Increase value perception	Are easily copied by competitors May just advance future sales	
Premiums (prize or award)	Build goodwill Increase perception of value	Consumers buy for premium, not product Have to be carefully managed	
Samples	Encourage trial Offer direct involvement	Have high cost to the firm	
POP displays	Provide high visibility Encourage brand trial	Can be difficult to get a good location in the store Can be costly to the firm	
Special events	Generate excitement and traffic	Can be costly Can distract customers from purchasing during the event	
Pop-up stores	Generate customer interest Open up new markets and market segments	Have high cost Must hire store personnel May take sales away from other company-owned stores	

(CRM) programs, which they use to build customer loyalty. The tools used in sales promotions, along with their advantages and disadvantages, are presented in Exhibit 15–2 and discussed below.

Coupons Coupons offer a discount on the price of specific items when they're purchased. Coupons are issued by manufacturers and retailers in newspapers, on products, on the shelf, at the cash register, over the Internet, and through the mail. Retailers use coupons because they are thought to induce customers to try products for the first time, convert first-time users to regular users, encourage large purchases, increase usage, and protect market share against competition Some retailers have linked coupons directly to their loyalty programs. Drugstore giant CVS, for instance, tracks its customers' purchases from its Extra Care loyalty card and gives them coupons that are tailored just for them.[33]

Coupon promotions, like all temporary promotions, may be stealing sales from a future period without any net increase in sales. For instance, if a supermarket runs a coupon promotion on sugar, households may buy a large quantity of sugar and stockpile it for future use. Thus, unless the coupon is used mostly by new buyers, the net impact on sales is negligible, and there will be a negative impact on profits due to the amount of the redeemed coupons and cost of the coupon redemption procedures. Coupons may annoy, alienate, and confuse consumers and therefore do little to increase store loyalty. Customers see an ad for a supermarket with a headline reading "Double Coupons" but don't realize that there might be conditions, such as a minimum purchase required, or that the offer may apply only to manufacturers' paper coupons.

Some stores, like CVS, are making coupons more effective by customizing coupon content to alter customers' purchasing patterns. For instance, if a customer typically spends a small amount during each

CVS tracks its customers' purchases from its Extra Care loyalty card and gives them coupons that are tailored just for them.

shopping trip, the customer will receive coupons that encourage larger purchases, such as "buy one, get one free." If another customer spends a lot each time she shops but shops sporadically, that customer will get coupons that expire relatively quickly. Unique coupons will also encourage customers to try new brands within categories that they normally purchase, or products that complement their usual purchases, such as shampoo to customers that purchase hair color.[35]

Shopping bot sites, such as MyCoupons.com, provide customers with a large selection of coupons by bringing all the coupons available throughout the Web onto one Web site. For instance, a customer might go to Target and find a KitchenAid mixer for $199.99. A cell phone scan of the bar code through ShopSavvy.com might find the same item at a Walmart a mile away for $179.99. Then the customer might visit MyCoupons.com and see that Walmart is offering a $20 coupon, thus saving the customer $40 in a matter of minutes.

A new breed of coupon, printed from the Internet or sent to mobile phones, is packed with information about the customer who uses it. While the coupons look standard, their bar codes can be loaded with a startling amount of data, including identification about the customer, Internet address, Facebook page information, and even the search terms the customer used to find the coupon in the first place. For instance, if a customer came into a store with a coupon for T-shirts, the information on the coupon could reveal whether the customer was searching for "underwear" or "muscle shirts."

MyCoupons.com provides customers with a large selection of coupons by bringing all the coupons available throughout the Web onto one Web site.

Rebates   **Rebates** provide another form of discounts for consumers off the final selling price. In this case, however, the manufacturer, instead of the retailer, issues the refund as a portion of the purchase price returned to the buyer in the form of cash. Retailers generally welcome rebates from vendors because they generate sales in the same way that coupons do but the retailers incur no handling costs.

Many products, such as consumer electronics, offer rebates that may lower the price of the item significantly. Some vendors enjoy the added exposure of appearing on consumer Web sites like PriceGrabber.com and Nextag.com that sort products by price and then link the customer to the retailer's Web site. Vendors offer such generous rebates because the likelihood that consumers will actually apply for the rebate is low. Others firms, like Staples and Apple, have simplified the rebate redemption process with "Easy Rebates" and Apple.com/promo.[36]

REFACT

Twenty percent of shoppers say they plan to use cell phones to shop. Of those, 45 percent say they would use their phones to research prices, 32 percent say they would use them to find coupons or read reviews, and 25 percent say they would make purchases from their phones.[37]

Premiums   A **premium** offers an item for free or at a bargain price to reward some type of behavior, such as buying, sampling, or testing. Such rewards build goodwill among consumers, who often perceive high value in them. Premiums can be distributed in a variety of ways: They can be included in the product packaging, such as the toys inside cereal boxes; placed visibly on the package, such as a coupon for free milk on a box of Cheerios; handed out in the store; or delivered in the mail, such as the free-perfume offers Victoria's Secret mails to customers.

Samples   **Samples** offer potential customers the opportunity to try a product or service before they make a buying decision. Distributing samples is one of the most costly sales promotion tools but also one of the most effective. Quick-service restaurants and grocery stores frequently utilize sampling. For instance, Whole Foods provides samples of products to customers. Costco uses so many samples that customers can have an entire meal.

Point-of-purchase displays stimulate impulse purchases while customers are waiting to pay for their purchases.

Point-of-Purchase Displays   Point-of-purchase (POP) displays are merchandise displays located at the point of purchase, such as at the checkout counter in a supermarket. Retailers have long recognized that the most valuable real estate in the store is at the POP. Customers see products like a magazine or a candy bar while they are waiting to pay for their items and impulsively purchase them. In the Internet version of a point-of-purchase display, shoppers are stimulated by special merchandise, price reductions, or complementary products that Internet retailers feature on the checkout screen.

Special Events   A **special event** is a sales promotion program comprising a number of sales promotion techniques built around a seasonal, cultural, sporting, musical, or some other event.[38] Special events can generate excitement and traffic to the store. Apparel and department stores do trunk shows, made-to-measure events, and fashion shows. Sporting goods stores do demonstrations of equipment, while grocery stores might have cooking classes. Book stores do readings and book signings. Car dealerships can have rallies or shows of new or vintage models. Even if the sales registered during the event aren't significant, the long-term effect can be quite beneficial.

Pop-Up Stores   An extreme type of sales promotion is a pop-up store. **Pop-up stores** are temporary storefronts that exist for only a limited time and generally focus on a new product or limited group of products offered by a retailer. They are also used by some retailers during the holiday season to increase exposure and convenience shopping for their customers without having to invest in a long-term lease. Retailing View 15.4 describes an online version of a pop-up store, the temporary private Internet sale.

15.4   RETAILING VIEW   Pop-Ups Go Virtual

Whereas physical pop-up stores often serve to increase exposure, online pop-ups work on a different principle. The goal is to limit the exposure of extreme discounts to "members only" or best customers.

In a struggling economy, retailers often find themselves left with significantly more unsold inventory than they would like. They need to get rid of it somehow, and online pop-up stores are providing an apt opportunity. There are two types of such stores.

First, retailers such as Neiman Marcus and Saks send e-mail notifications of limited-time events to registered customers. These e-mailed messages promise, for example, a two-hour sale of Burberry handbags at half price. If the customer misses the two-hour window, he or she misses the sale. By offering massive discounts to select customers, these retailers avoid gaining a reputation for low prices or clearance sales—images incompatible with the concepts of wealth and luxury that these stores have worked so hard to build.

Second, the Internet's versions of off-price retailers, such as Hautelook.com, Ruelala.com, and Gilt.com, gather items from well-known brands or retailers and sell them at deep discounts.

The sales last only a day or two and then get replaced by sales of other designers' goods. They require customers to register to access the sales, and, again, if they miss an offer, they are out of luck. The sites continue to grow, attracting legions of consumers who willingly offer their contact information for the chance to grab a deal.

In either case, these pop-up sale sites influence customers in several ways. They feel special, as if they are members of a select club that receives notification of such special events. In addition, they are driven by the promise of massive markdowns. That is, $2,310 may seem like a lot to spend on a Marchesa Couture structured silk dress—until that price appears next to the original price of $6,600.

Sources: Stephanie Rosenbloom, "High-End Retailers Offering More Discounts," *New York Times,* July 31, 2009; Nieman Marcus, www.neiman-marcus.com/common/store/catalog/templates/ET1.jhtml?tv=lc&N=4294967291&Ns=MAX_RETAIL_PRICE%7c1&st=s (accessed July 10, 2010); Steven Dennis, "The Private Sales Flash Sites Jump the Shark," *GLG News,* July 3, 2010, www.glgroup.com/News/The-Private-Flash-Sales-Sites-Jump-The-Shark-49302.html (accessed July 10, 2010).

Gucci's pop-up stores, named Gucci-Icon Temporary, carry special items with classic Gucci design elements.

Italian leather retailer and manufacturer, Gucci, has opened pop-up stores named Gucci-Icon Temporary in New York's SoHo, Miami Beach, Tokyo, London, Berlin, Paris, and Hong Kong. The stores feature limited-edition sneakers retailing for $500 to $600, with classic Gucci design elements and some special features like a silver or gold dog tag.[39]

Although most sales promotions are effective at generating short-term interest among customers, they aren't very useful for building long-term loyalty. Customers who participate in a promotion might learn more about a store and return to it, but typically customers attracted by sales promotions are interested in the promoted merchandise, not the retailer. Unfortunately, when a specific promotion is effective for a retailer, competing retailers learn about it quickly and offer the same promotion, which prevents the innovating retailer from gaining any long-term advantage.

Personal Selling

Personal selling is a communication process in which sales associates help customers satisfy their needs through face-to-face exchanges of information. It is a form of offline/interactive communication (Exhibit 15–1). The cost of communicating directly with a potential customer is quite high compared with other forms of promotion, but it is simply the best and most efficient way to sell certain products and services. Customers can buy many products and services without the help of a salesperson, but salespeople simplify the buying process by providing information and services that save customers time and effort. In many cases, sales representatives add significant value, which makes the added expense of employing them worthwhile. The impact of personal selling on customer service is examined in Chapter 18.

Advertising

Advertising entails the placement of announcements and persuasive messages purchased by retailers and other organizations that seek to inform and/or persuade members of a particular target market or audience about their products, services, organizations, or ideas.[40] After automobile manufacturers, retailers are the second-largest group of national advertisers, spending over $20 billion annually. Walt Disney, McDonald's, Sears Holding, Macy's, JCPenney, Target, and Home Depot are among the 30 largest advertisers, each spending more than $1 billion a year.[41]

REFACT

France recently lifted a ban on television advertising by supermarkets, department stores, hypermarkets, and other retailers. On the first day after the ban was lifted, only minutes after midnight, merchants monopolized all 11 spots on TF1, the most-watched television channel in France.[42]

REFACT

In 2005, Macy's put 71 percent of its advertising budget in newspapers; by the end of 2008, it was down to 59 percent. During the same period, Macy's TV advertising budget grew from 17 percent of its budget to 27 percent.[44]

Mass advertising can entice consumers into a conversation with retailers, although it does not necessarily require much action by consumers, which places it on the passive end of the spectrum. Traditionally, advertising has been passive and offline (e.g., ads on TV, in magazines, and in newspapers) (Exhibit 15–1). However, recently there has been a growth in online advertising. This section reviews advertising's traditional media and examines a method of lowering the retailer's advertising cost through cooperative advertising with vendors.

Newspapers Retailing and newspaper advertising grew up together over the past century. But the growth in retail newspaper advertising has slowed recently as retailers have begun using other media. Still, 57 percent of newspapers' advertising dollars are generated by retailers.[43] In addition to displaying ads with their editorial content, newspapers distribute freestanding inserts. A **freestanding insert (FSI),** also called a **preprint,** is an advertisement printed at the retailer's expense and distributed as an insert in the newspaper. However, there are so many FSIs in some newspapers that readers can become overwhelmed. As a result, some retailers have reduced the number of FSIs they use because of the clutter and because younger readers, who may be their primary target markets, don't regularly read newspapers.

Because newspapers are distributed in well-defined local market areas, they're effective at targeting specific retail markets. Newspapers also offer a quick response. There's only a short time between the deadline for receiving the advertisement and the time that the advertisement will appear. Thus, newspapers are useful for delivering messages on short notice.

Newspapers, like magazines, effectively convey a lot of detailed information. Readers can go through an advertisement at their own pace and refer to part of the advertisement when they want. But newspaper ads aren't effective for showing merchandise, particularly when it's important to illustrate colors, because of the poor reproduction quality.

The life of a newspaper advertisement is short because the newspaper is usually discarded after it's read. In contrast, magazine advertising has a longer life because consumers tend to save magazines and read them several times during a week or month.

Finally, the cost of developing newspaper ads is relatively low. However, the cost of delivering the message may be high if the newspaper's circulation is broader than the retailer's target market, requiring the retailer to pay for exposure that won't generate sales.

Magazines Advertising in national magazines is mostly done by national retailers such as Target and The Gap. With the growth of local magazines, regional editions of national magazines, and specialized magazines, local retailers can take advantage of this medium. Retailers tend to use this medium for image advertising because the reproduction quality is high. Due to the lead time—the time between submitting the advertisement and publication—a major disadvantage of magazine advertising is that the timing is difficult to coordinate with special events and sales.

Television Television commercials can be placed on a national network or local station. A local television commercial is called a **spot.** Retailers typically use TV for image advertising, to take advantage of the high production quality and the opportunity to communicate through both visual images and sound. Television ads can also demonstrate product usage. For example, TV is an excellent medium for car, furniture, and consumer electronics dealers.

In addition to its high production costs, broadcast time for national TV advertising is expensive. Spots have relatively small audiences, but they may be economical for local retailers. To offset the high production costs, many vendors provide modular commercials, in which the retailer can insert its name or a "tag" after information about the vendor's merchandise.

Radio Many retailers use radio advertising because messages can be targeted to a specific segment of the market.[45] Some radio stations' audiences are highly loyal to their announcers. When these announcers promote a retailer, listeners are impressed. The cost of developing and broadcasting radio commercials is relatively low.

One disadvantage of radio advertising, however, is that listeners generally treat the radio broadcast as background, which limits the attention they give the message. Consumers must get the information from a radio commercial when it's broadcast, so they can't refer to the advertisement for information they didn't hear or remember.

Co-op Programs **Co-op (cooperative) advertising** is a promotional program undertaken by a vendor and a retailer working together. The vendor pays for part of the retailer's advertising but dictates some conditions. For example, Best Buy might pay for only half of its expenses for ads including Sony digital TVs. In addition to lowering costs, co-op advertising enables a retailer to associate its name with well-known national brands and use attractive artwork created by the national brands.

Co-op advertising has some drawbacks though. First, vendors want the ads to feature their products, whereas retailers are more interested in featuring their store's name, location, and assortment of merchandise and services offered. This conflict in goals can reduce the effectiveness of co-op advertising from the retailer's perspective. Second, ads developed by the vendor often are used by several competing retailers and may list the names and locations of all retailers offering their brands. Thus, co-op ads tend to blur distinctions between retailers. Third, restrictions the vendor places on the ads may further reduce their effectiveness for the retailer. For example, the vendor may restrict advertising to a period of time when the vendor's sales are depressed, but the retailer might not normally be advertising during that time frame.

Public Relations

Public relations (PR) involves managing communications and relationships to achieve various objectives, such as building and maintaining a positive image of the retailer, handling or heading off unfavorable stories or events, and maintaining positive relationships with the media. In many cases, public relations activities support other promotional efforts by generating "free" media attention and general goodwill.

For years, Walmart did little to promote itself as a positive social force, believing its low prices would speak for themselves. But it increasingly has been subjected to public criticism from labor unions and environmentalists, so Walmart hired its first public relations firm. The public relations firm set up a war room to respond quickly to attacks or adverse news. Internet blogs and grassroots initiatives were developed to stimulate popular support for Walmart. The firm also looked for proactive opportunities to demonstrate Walmart's social consciousness. For example, after the devastating earthquake in Haiti, Walmart contributed more than $1.5 million in direct

Designers like Marchesa benefit from positive public relations when celebrities like Sandra Bullock appear at media events like the Oscars wearing their gowns.

financial support as well as in-kind contributions, such as prepackaged food kits, blankets, and face masks. In addition, through various in-store and online fund-raising campaigns, Walmart associates and customers globally have contributed more than $3 million for the relief effort.[46] Retailing View 15.5 describes how Neiman Marcus annually creates newsworthy events by offering unusual gifts in its Christmas catalog and thus further builds its image of offering unique merchandise.

Retailers also benefit when celebrities wear their fashions. For instance, when photos were posted on the Internet of First Lady Michelle Obama wearing a J.Crew cream-colored cardigan and "dazzling dots" skirt on a visit to a cancer center in London, the retailer's Web site sold out almost immediately.[47] The placement of designer apparel at media events like the Oscars benefits the retailer, the designer, and the celebrity. And nothing happens by accident. Public relations people on both sides help orchestrate the events to get the maximum benefit for both parties.

Certainly the Chili's restaurant chain conducts plenty of media buys in traditional advertising spaces. But it also has partnered, since 2004, with St. Jude's Research Hospital in successful cause-related marketing (i.e., commercial activity

---

15.5   RETAILING VIEW   Neiman Marcus Fantasy Gifts

The Neiman Marcus Christmas book is perhaps the nation's best-known retail catalog. Its reputation is largely due to its annual tradition of ultra-extravagant his-and-hers gifts. The Christmas book was first distributed in 1915 as a Christmas card inviting Neiman Marcus customers to visit the store during the holiday season. In the late 1950s, customers were asking Neiman Marcus about unique gifts and merchandise not available in the store or from other catalogs.

In 1959, the gift of a black angus steer, delivered on the hoof or in steaks, generated a lot of publicity and elevated the catalog to national prominence. The most expensive gift was an unfinished Boeing business jet for more than $35 million. Most of these gifts do not sell. A highly publicized chocolate Monopoly set was purchased by Christie Hefner, president of Playboy Enterprises, for her father, Hugh Hefner, founder of *Playboy* magazine.

The 2007 Christmas book featured a $1.59 million private holiday concert for 500 people featuring piano virtuoso Lola Astanova. The evening, hosted by Regis Philbin, would be filmed as a party favor for guests. The Steinway Concert Grand piano on which the artist plays, and featuring her autograph, gets left for the host. One of the outstanding gifts of 2009 was a car that looks like a cupcake, travels up to seven miles per hour, and costs $25,000. The Neiman Marcus

The Neiman Marcus Christmas catalog featured a car that looks like a cupcake, travels up to seven miles per hour, and costs $25,000.

Christmas book is mailed to 1.8 million customers and is also available on its Web site.

Sources: "Neiman Marcus 2009 Christmas Book Released," *Dallas Business Journal*, October 6, 2009; Jennifer Paull, "Neiman Marcus Christmas Book—Inside the Holiday Fantasy," *Stylist.com*, November 15, 2009; Nathalie Atkinson "Who Wants Another Lexus?" *National Post*, November 8, 2007; Maria Halkias, "Marcus Unwraps Its Christmas Catalog," *Dallas Morning News*, October 3, 2007; www.neimanmarcus.com (accessed June 29, 2010).

in which businesses and charities form a partnership to market an image, product, or service for their mutual benefit).[48] For several years, the restaurant has offered customers the opportunity to purchase a paper icon, in the shape of a chili natch, that they may color and hang on restaurant walls. The cause marketing campaign runs in September, which is also National Childhood Cancer Awareness Month. On the last Monday of the month, the restaurant puts its money where its mouth is and donates all its profits on sales during the day to St. Jude. In addition to the retailer's sales of relatively common Create-a-Chili paper icons, its restaurant employees make and sell customized T-shirts and wristbands. Chili's also hosts a dedicated Web site, www.createapepper.com, where civic-minded consumers can purchase or donate more, as well as buy St. Jude–branded Chili's gift cards.[49]

Another very popular PR tool is event sponsorship. **Event sponsorship** occurs when corporations support various activities (financially or otherwise), usually in the cultural or sports and entertainment sectors. Some retailers sponsor sporting events such as the Little Caesar's Pizza Bowl in Detroit, while others buy naming rights to a sporting venue, such as the Staples Center, which is home to the NBA's Los Angeles Lakers, the Los Angeles Clippers, and the NHL's Los Angeles Kings.

When retailers and vendors use **product placement,** they pay to have their product included in nontraditional situations, such as in a scene in a movie or television program.[50] For instance, Elisa and Jack of *30 Rock* discuss whether McDonald's McFlurry is the best dessert in the world. On CBS's *The Big Bang Theory*, Sheldon says that he "needs access to the Cheesecake Factory walk-in freezer." In *The Biggest Loser*, the contestants have to run from one Subway restaurant to the next.[51]

Little Caesar's Pizza Bowl provides positive public relations for the restaurant chain.

Subway pays to have its products featured in nontraditional situations, like when contestants on *The Biggest Loser* run from one Subway restaurant to the next.

PLANNING THE RETAIL COMMUNICATION PROGRAM

Exhibit 15–3 illustrates the four steps involved in developing and implementing a retail communication program: Establish objectives, determine a budget, allocate the budget, and implement and evaluate the program. The following sections detail each of these steps.

Establish Objectives

Retailers establish objectives for their communication programs to provide (1) direction for people implementing the program and (2) a basis for evaluating its effectiveness. As discussed at the beginning of this chapter, some communication programs can have a long-term objective, such as creating or altering a retailer's brand image. Other communication programs focus on improving short-term performance, such as increasing store traffic on a specific weekend.

Communication Objectives   Although retailers' overall objective is to generate long- and short-term sales and profits, they often use communication objectives rather than sales objectives to plan and evaluate their communication programs. **Communication objectives** are specific goals related to the retail communication mix's effect on the customer's decision-making process.

Exhibit 15–4 shows some hypothetical information about customers in the target market for a Safeway supermarket. This information illustrates the goals related to the stages in the consumer decision-making process outlined in Chapter 4. Note that 95 percent of the customers are aware of the store (the first stage in the decision-making process) and 85 percent know the type of merchandise it sells. But only 45 percent of the customers in the target market have a favorable attitude toward the store. Thirty-two percent intend to visit the store during the next few weeks; 25 percent actually visit the store during the next two weeks; and 18 percent regularly shop at the store.

In this hypothetical example, most people know about the store and its offering. The major problem confronting the Safeway supermarket is the big drop between knowledge and favorable attitudes. Thus, the store should develop a communication program with the objective of increasing the percentage of customers with a favorable attitude toward it.

To effectively implement and evaluate a communication program, its objectives must be clearly stated in quantitative terms. The target audience for the communication mix needs to be defined, along with the degree of change expected and the time period during which the change will be realized.

For example, a communication objective for a Safeway program might be to increase from 45 to 55 percent within three months the percentage of customers within a 5-mile radius of the store who have a favorable attitude toward the store. This objective is clear and measurable. It indicates the task that the program should address. The people who implement the program thus know what they're supposed to accomplish.

EXHIBIT 15–3   Steps in Developing a Retail Communication Program

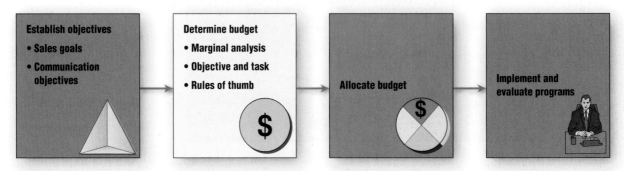

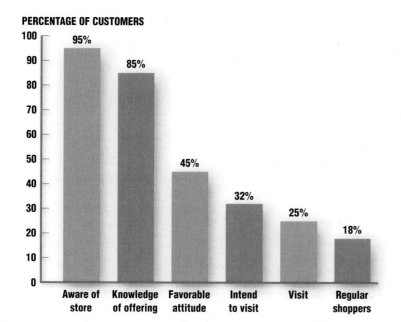

The communication objectives and approaches used by vendors and retailers differ, and the differences can lead to conflicts. Some of these points of conflict are as follows:

- *Long-term versus short-term goals.* Most communications by vendors are directed toward building a long-term image of their products. In contrast, retailer communications typically are used to announce promotions and special sales that generate short-term revenues.

- *Product versus location.* When vendors advertise their branded products, they aren't concerned about where customers buy them as long as they buy their brands. In contrast, retailers aren't concerned about what brands customers buy as long as they buy them in their stores.

- *Breadth of merchandise.* Typically, because vendors have a relatively small number of products to promote, they can devote a lot of attention to developing consistent communication programs for each brand they make. Retailers have to develop communication programs that promote a much wider range of products.

Determine the Communication Budget

The second step in developing a retail communication program is to determine a budget (see Exhibit 15–3). The economically correct method for setting the communication budget is marginal analysis. Even though retailers usually don't have enough information to perform a complete marginal analysis, the method shows managers how they should approach budget-setting programs. The marginal analysis method for setting a communication budget is the approach that retailers should use when making all of their resource allocation decisions, including the number of locations in a geographic area (Chapter 8), the allocation of merchandise to stores (Chapter 13), the staffing of stores (Chapter 16), and the floor and shelf space devoted to merchandise categories (Chapter 17).

Marginal Analysis Method   **Marginal analysis** is based on the economic principle that firms should increase communication expenditures as long as each additional dollar spent generates more than a dollar of additional contribution. To illustrate marginal analysis, consider Diane West, the owner and manager of a specialty store selling women's business clothing. Exhibit 15–5 shows her analysis to determine how much she should spend next year on her communication program.

EXHIBIT 15–5   Marginal Analysis for Setting Diane West's Communication Budget

Level	Communication Expenses (1)	Sales (2)	Gross Margin Realized (3)	Rental Expense (4)	Personnel Expense (5)	Contribution before Communication Expenses (6) = (3) − (4) − (5)	Profit after Communication Expenses (7) = (6) − (1)	
1	$ 0	$240,000	$ 96,000	$44,000	$52,200	$ (200)	$ (200)	
2	5,000	280,000	112,000	48,000	53,400	10,600	5,600	
3	10,000	330,000	132,000	53,000	54,900	24,100	14,100	
4	15,000	380,000	152,000	58,000	56,400	37,600	22,600	
5	20,000	420,000	168,000	62,000	57,600	48,400	28,400	
6	25,000	460,000	184,000	66,000	58,800	59,200	34,200	
7	30,000	500,000	200,000	70,000	60,000	70,000	40,000	Last year
8	35,000	540,000	216,000	74,000	61,200	80,800	45,800	
9	40,000	570,000	228,000	77,000	62,100	88,900	48,900	
10	45,000	600,000	240,000	80,000	63,000	97,000	52,000	
11	50,000	625,000	250,000	82,500	63,750	103,750	53,750	
12	55,000	650,000	260,000	85,000	64,500	110,500	55,500	Chosen budget
13	60,000	670,000	268,000	87,000	65,100	115,900	55,900	
14	65,000	690,000	276,000	89,000	65,700	121,300	56,300	Best profit
15	70,000	705,000	282,000	90,500	66,150	125,350	55,350	
16	75,000	715,000	286,000	91,500	66,450	128,050	53,050	
17	80,000	725,000	290,000	92,500	66,750	130,750	50,750	
18	85,000	735,000	294,000	93,500	67,050	133,450	48,450	
19	90,000	745,000	298,000	94,500	67,350	136,150	46,150	
20	95,000	750,000	300,000	95,000	67,500	137,500	42,500	
21	100,000	750,000	300,000	95,000	67,500	137,500	37,500	

For 21 different communication expense levels (column 1), she estimates her store sales (column 2), gross margin (column 3), and other expenses (columns 4 and 5). Then she calculates the contribution, excluding expenses on communications (column 6), and the profit when the communication expenses are considered (column 7). To estimate the sales generated by different levels of communications, West can simply rely on her judgment and experience, or she might analyze past data to determine the relationship between communication expenses and sales. Historical data also provide information about the gross margin and other expenses as a percentage of sales.

Notice that at low levels of communication expenses, an additional $5,000 in communication expenses generates more than a $5,000 incremental contribution. For example, increasing the communication expense from $15,000 to $20,000 increases the contribution by $10,800 (or $48,400 − $37,600). When the communication expense reaches $65,000, further increases of $5,000 generate less than $5,000 in additional contributions. For example, increasing the budget from $65,000 to $70,000 generates only an additional $4,050 in contribution ($125,350 − $121,300).

In this example, West determines that the maximum profit would be generated with a communication expense budget of $65,000. But she notices that expense levels between $55,000 and $70,000 all result in about the same level of profit. Thus, West makes a conservative decision and establishes a $55,000 budget for her communication expenses.

In most cases, it's very hard to perform a marginal analysis because managers don't know the relationship between communication expenses and sales. Note that the numbers in Exhibit 15–5 are simply West's estimates; they may not be accurate.

Sometimes retailers perform experiments to get a better idea of the relationship between communication expenses and sales. Say, for example, a catalog retailer

Objective: Increase the percentage of target market (working women) who know of our store's location and who purchase business attire from 25 percent to 50 percent over the next 12 months.	
Task: 480, 30–second radio spots during peak commuting hours	$12,000
Task: Sign with store name near entrance to mall	4,500
Task: Display ad in the Yellow Pages	500
Objective: Increase the percentage of target market who indicate that our store is their preferred store for buying their business wardrobe from 5 percent to 15 percent in 12 months.	
Task: Develop TV campaign to improve image and run 50, 30–second commercials	$24,000
Task: Hold four "Dress for Success" seminars followed by a wine-and-cheese party	8,000
Objective: Sell merchandise remaining at end of season.	
Task: Special event	$6,000
Total budget	$55,000

EXHIBIT 15–6
Illustration of Objective-and-Task Method for Setting a Communication Budget

selects several geographic areas in the United States with the same sales potential. The retailer then distributes 100,000 catalogs in the first area, 200,000 in the second area, and 300,000 in the third. Using the sales and costs for each distribution level, it could conduct an analysis like the one in Exhibit 15–5 to determine the most profitable distribution level. (Chapter 14 described the use of experiments to determine the relationship between price and sales.)

Some other methods that retailers use to set communication budgets are the objective-and-task and rules-of-thumb methods, which include the affordable, percentage-of-sales, and competitive parity methods. These methods are less sophisticated than marginal analysis but easier to use.

Objective-and-Task Method   The **objective-and-task method** determines the budget required to undertake specific tasks to accomplish communication objectives. To use this method, the retailer first establishes a set of communication objectives and then determines the necessary tasks and their costs. The total of all costs incurred to undertake the tasks is the communication budget.

Exhibit 15–6 illustrates how Diane West could use the objective-and-task method to complement her marginal analysis. West establishes three objectives: to increase awareness of her store, to create a greater preference for her store among customers in her target market, and to promote the sale of merchandise remaining at the end of each season. The estimated communication budget she requires to achieve these objectives is $55,000.

In addition to defining her objectives and tasks, West rechecks the financial implications of the communication mix by projecting the income statement for next year using the communication budget (see Exhibit 15–7). This income statement includes an increase of $25,000 in communication expenses compared with last year. But West believes this increase in the communication budget will boost annual sales from $500,000 to $650,000. According to West's projections, the increase in communication expenses will raise store profits. The results of both the marginal analysis and the objective-and-task methods suggest a communication budget between $55,000 and $65,000.

	Last Year	Next Year
Sales	$500,000	$ 650,000
Gross margin (realized)	200,000	260,000
Rental, maintenance, etc.	−70,000	−85,000
Personnel	−60,000	−64,500
Communications	−30,000	−55,000
Profit	$ 40,000	$ 55,500

EXHIBIT 15–7
Financial Implications of Increasing the Communication Budget

Rule-of-Thumb Methods   The previous two methods set the communication budget by estimating communication activities' effects on the firm's future sales or communication objectives. The **rule-of-thumb methods** discussed in this section use the opposite logic. They use past sales and communication activities to determine the present communication budget.[52]

Affordable Budgeting Method   When using the **affordable budgeting method,** retailers first forecast their sales and expenses, excluding communication expenses, during the budgeting period. The difference between the forecast sales and expenses plus the desired profit is then budgeted for the communication mix. In other words, the affordable method sets the communication budget by determining what money is available after operating costs and profits are subtracted.

The major problem with the affordable method is that it assumes that communication expenses don't stimulate sales and profit. Communication expenses are just a cost of business, like the cost of merchandise. When retailers use the affordable method, they typically cut "unnecessary" communication expenses if sales fall below the forecast rather than increasing communication expenses to increase sales.

Percentage-of-Sales Method   The **percentage-of-sales method** sets the communication budget as a fixed percentage of forecast sales. Retailers use this method to determine the communication budget by forecasting sales during the budget period and then applying a predetermined percentage to set the budget. The percentage may be the retailer's historical percentage or the average percentage used by similar retailers.

The problem with the percentage-of-sales method is that it assumes that the same percentage used in the past, or used by competitors, is appropriate for the future. Consider a retailer that hasn't opened new stores in the past but plans to open many new stores in the current year. It must create customer awareness for these new stores, so the communication budget should be much larger in the current year than in the past.

Using the same percentage as competitors also may be inappropriate. For example, a retailer might have better locations than its competitors. Due to these locations, customers may already have a high awareness of the retailer's stores. Thus, the retailer may not need to spend as much on communication as competitors with poorer locations.

One advantage of both the percentage-of-sales method and the affordable method for determining a communication budget is that the retailer won't spend beyond its means. Because the level of spending is determined by sales, the budget will go up only when sales go up and as the retailer generates more sales to pay for the additional communication expenses. When times are good, these methods work well because they allow the retailer to communicate more aggressively with customers. But when sales fall, communication expenses are cut, which may accelerate the sales decline.

Competitive Parity Method   Under the **competitive parity method,** the communication budget is set so that the retailer's share of its communication expenses equals its share of the market. For example, consider a sporting goods store in a small town. To use the competitive parity method, the owner manager would first estimate the total amount spent on communication by all sporting goods retailers in town. Then the owner-manager would estimate his or her store's market share for sporting goods and multiply that market share percentage by the sporting goods stores' total advertising expenses to set the budget. Assume that the owner-manager's estimate of advertising for sporting goods by all stores is $5,000 and the estimate of his or her store's market share is 45 percent. On the basis of these estimates, the owner-manager would set the store's communication budget at $2,250 to maintain competitive parity.

Similar to the other rule-of-thumb methods, the competitive parity method doesn't allow retailers to exploit the unique opportunities or problems they confront in a market. If all competitors used this method to set communication budgets, their market shares would stay about the same over time (assuming that the retailers develop equally effective campaigns and other retail mix activities).

Allocate the Promotional Budget

After determining the size of the communication budget, the third step in the communication planning process is to allocate the budget (see Exhibit 15–3). In this step, the retailer decides how much of its budget to allocate to specific communication elements, merchandise categories, geographic regions, or long- and short-term objectives. For example, Dillard's must decide how much of its communication budget to spend in each area it has stores: Southeast, Mid-Atlantic, Southwest, Midwest, and West Coast. Michaels decides how much to allocate to merchandise associated with different crafts. The sporting goods store owner-manager must decide how much of the store's $2,250 communication budget to spend on promoting the store's image versus generating sales during the year and how much to spend on advertising and special promotions.

Research indicates that allocation decisions are more important than the decision about the amount to spend on communications.[53] In other words, retailers often can realize the same objectives by reducing the size of the communication budget but allocating it more effectively.

An easy way to make such allocation decisions is to spend about the same in each geographic region or for each merchandise category. But this allocation rule probably won't maximize profits because it ignores the possibility that communication programs might be more effective for some merchandise categories or for some regions than for others. Another approach is to use rules of thumb, such as basing allocations on the sales level or contributions for the merchandise category.

Allocation decisions, like budget-setting decisions, should use the principles of marginal analysis. The retailer should allocate the budget to areas that will yield the greatest return. This approach for allocating a budget is sometimes referred to as the **high-assay principle.** Consider a miner who can spend his time digging on two claims. The value of the gold on one claim is assayed at $20,000 per ton, whereas the assay value on the other claim is $10,000 per ton. Should the miner spend two-thirds of his time at the first mine and one-third of his time at the other mine? Of course not! The miner should spend all of his time mining the first claim until the assay value of the ore mined drops to $10,000 a ton, at which time he can divide his time equally between the claims.

Similarly, a retailer may find that its customers have a high awareness and very favorable attitude toward its women's clothing but do not know much about its men's clothing. In this situation, a dollar spent on advertising men's clothing might generate more sales than a dollar spent on women's clothing, even though the sales of women's clothing are greater than the sales of men's clothing.

Plan, Implement, and Evaluate Communication Programs—Two Illustrations

The final stage in developing a retail communication program is its implementation and evaluation (see Exhibit 15–3). This final section of the chapter illustrates the planning and evaluation process for two communication programs: an advertising campaign by a small specialty retailer and a sales promotion opportunity confronting a supermarket chain.

Advertising Campaign   Hypothetically, imagine South Gate West is one of several specialty import home furnishing stores competing for upscale shoppers in Charleston, South Carolina. The store has the appearance of both a fine antique store and a traditional home furnishing shop, but most of its merchandise is new Asian imports.

Harry Owens, the owner, realized his communication budget was considerably less than the budget of the local Pier 1 store. (Pier 1 is a national chain that sells imported home furnishings.) He decides to concentrate his limited budget on a specific segment and use very creative copy and distinctive artwork in his advertising. His target market is knowledgeable, sophisticated consumers of housewares and home decorative items. His experience indicates the importance of personal selling for more seasoned shoppers because they (1) make large purchases and (2) seek considerable information before making a decision. Thus, Owens spends part of his communication budget on training his sales associates.

The advertising program Owens develops emphasizes his store's distinctive image. He uses the newspaper as his major vehicle. Competitive ads contain line drawings of furniture with prices. His ads emphasize imagery associated with Asian furniture by featuring off-the-beaten-path scenes of Asian countries with unusual art objects. This theme is also reflected in the store's atmosphere.

To evaluate his communication program, Owens needs to compare the results of his program with the objectives he has developed during the first part of the planning process. To measure his campaign's effectiveness, he conducts an inexpensive tracking study. Telephone interviews are performed periodically with a representative sample of furniture customers in his store's trading area. Communication objectives are assessed using the following questions:

Communication Objectives	Questions
Awareness	What stores sell East Asian furniture?
Knowledge	Which stores would you rate outstanding on the following characteristics?
Attitude	On your next shopping trip for East Asian furniture, which store would you visit first?
Visit	Which of the following stores have you been to?

Here are the survey results for one year:

Communication Objective	Before Campaign	6 Months After	One Year After
Awareness (% mentioning store)	38%	46%	52%
Knowledge (% giving outstanding rating for sales assistance)	9	17	24
Attitude (% first choice)	13	15	19
Visit (% visited store)	8	15	19

The results show a steady increase in awareness, knowledge of the store, and choice of the store as a primary source of East Asian furniture. This research provides evidence that the advertising is conveying the intended message to the target audience.

Sales Promotion Opportunity

Many sales promotion opportunities undertaken by retailers are initiated by vendors. For example, Colgate-Palmolive might offer the following special promotion to Kroger: During a one-week period, Kroger can order Fab laundry detergent in the 48-ounce size at 15 cents below the standard wholesale price.

However, if Kroger elects to buy Fab at the discounted price, the grocery chain must feature the 48-ounce container of Fab in its Thursday newspaper advertisement at $1.59 (20 cents off the typical retail price). In addition, Kroger must have an end-aisle display of Fab.

Before Kroger decides whether to accept such a trade promotion and then promote Fab to its customers, it needs to assess the promotion's impact on its own profitability. Such a promotion may be effective for the vendor but not for the retailer.

To evaluate a trade promotion, the retailer considers:

- The realized margin from the promotion.
- The cost of the additional inventory carried due to buying more than the normal amount.
- The potential increase in sales from the promoted merchandise.
- The potential loss suffered when customers switch to the promoted merchandise from more profitable private-label brands.
- The additional sales made to customers attracted to the store by the promotion.[54]

When Fab's price is reduced to $1.59, Kroger will sell more Fab than it normally does. But Kroger's margin on Fab will be less because the required retail discount of 20 cents isn't offset by the wholesale discount of 15 cents. In addition, Kroger might suffer losses because the promotion encourages customers to buy Fab, which has a lower margin than Kroger's private-label detergent that those customers might have bought. Customers may even stockpile Fab, buying several boxes, which will reduce sales of Kroger's private-label detergent for some time after the special promotion ends. In contrast, the promotion may attract customers who don't normally shop at Kroger but who will visit to buy Fab at the discounted price. These customers might buy additional merchandise, providing a sales gain to the store that it wouldn't have realized if it hadn't promoted Fab.

The end-aisle display of Fab is part of a special Colgate-Palmolive promotion in which the supermarket bought Fab at a discount in exchange for the prominent display.

SUMMARY

A communication program can be designed to achieve a variety of objectives for the retailer, such as building a brand image of the retailer in the customer's mind, increasing sales and store traffic, providing information about the retailer's location and offering, and announcing special activities.

Retailers communicate with customers both online and offline and interactively and passively. Direct marketing has received the greatest increase in attention by retailers and can occur using telemarketing (offline/interactive), mobile marketing (online/interactive), direct mail and catalogs (offline/passive), and e-mail (online/passive). These elements in the communication mix must be coordinated so that customers have a clear, distinct image of the retailer and are not confused by conflicting information.

Retailers go through four steps to develop and implement their communication program: Establish objectives, determine a budget, allocate the budget, and implement and evaluate the program. Marginal analysis is the most appropriate method for determining how much should be spent to accomplish the retailer's objectives because it maximizes the profits that could be generated by the communication mix. Since marginal analysis is difficult to implement, however, many retailers use rule-of-thumb methods to determine the size of the promotion budget.

KEY TERMS

advertising, *415*

affordable budgeting method, *424*

aided recall, *402*

brand, *400*

brand associations, *402*

brand awareness, *402*

brand equity, *400*

brand image, *403*

communication objectives, *420*

competitive parity method, *424*

cooperative (co-op) advertising, *417*

coupons, *412*

direct mail, *407*

direct marketing, *407*

e-mail, *407*

event sponsorship, *419*

freestanding insert (FSI), *416*

high-assay principle, *425*

integrated marketing
   communication program, *403*

marginal analysis, *421*

m-commerce, *407*

mobile commerce, *407*

mobile marketing, *407*

objective-and-task method, *423*

percentage-of-sales method, *424*

personal selling, *415*

pop-up store, *414*

premium, *413*

preprint, *416*

product placement, *419*

public relations (PR), *417*

rebates, *413*

rule-of-thumb methods, *424*

sales promotion, *411*

samples, *413*

social media, *409*

special event, *414*

spot, *416*

top-of-mind awareness, *402*

word of mouth, *409*

GET OUT AND DO IT!

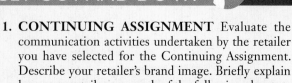

1. **CONTINUING ASSIGNMENT** Evaluate the communication activities undertaken by the retailer you have selected for the Continuing Assignment. Describe your retailer's brand image. Briefly explain how your retailer uses each of the following elements of its communication program: direct marketing, online marketing, personal selling, sales promotions, direct mail and e-mail, mobile marketing, advertising (media used?), social media, public relations, Web site, and events. Do all of these elements send a consistent brand-image message to customers? Why, or why not?

2. Go to the home page for BrandZ at www.brandz. com/output/, and click on "Retail Report." On the basis of the report, list the top-20 global retail brands. In two or three paragraphs, describe what makes a strong retail brand. How were brand equity and financial performance used to measure brand value for these retailers?

3. Retailers and manufacturers deliver coupons through the Internet in addition to delivering them by mail or as inserts. Go to www.coolsavings.com for coupons offered over the Internet. How does this coupon distribution system compare with the other two distribution systems?

4. Trader Joe's is a gourmet grocery store offering items such as health foods, organic produce, and nutritional supplements. The company has about 325 stores in 25 states at which it offers more than 2,000 private-label products. Go to www.traderjoes.com, and see how the firm uses its Internet site to promote its retail stores and merchandise. Why does this retailer include recipes and a seasonal guide on its Web site? Does the information provided on the Web page reinforce the store's upscale grocery image? Explain why or why not.

5. Go to the social media site for a retailer that you have shopped at during the last few weeks. How was social media used as an element in the retailer's communication program? What audience is being reached with social media? Is the social media message consistent or inconsistent with other communication elements? Is this a strong or weak strategy? Please explain.

6. Go to the home page for Target's Pressroom at http:// pressroom.target.com/pr/news/news.aspx. How does this retailer use public relations to communicate with investors and customers? Is this an effective communication tool for this retailer? Provide support for your response.

DISCUSSION QUESTIONS AND PROBLEMS

1. How do brands benefit consumers? Retailers?

2. How can brand strategy, advertising, personal selling, public relations, direct marketing, and sales promotion complement one another in an integrated marketing communication program? How can a retailer's customer relationship management program support these activities?

3. What are the positive and negative aspects of direct marketing from the customer's perspective?

4. Review Exhibit 15–2, "Kinds of Sales Promotion," and describe which of these consumer promotions have been successful with you as a consumer. Which ones have not been successful? Explain your responses.

5. What factors should be considered in dividing up the advertising budget among a store's different merchandise areas? Which of the following should receive the highest advertising budget: staple, fashion, or seasonal merchandise? Why?

6. Outline some elements in a communication program that can be used to achieve the following objectives: (a) Increase store loyalty by 20 percent. (b) Build awareness of the store by 10 percent. (c) Develop an image as a low-price retailer. How would you determine whether the communication program met each of these objectives?

7. Retailers use television advertising to build brand image. Television advertisers have identified many types of markets on the basis of the day, time, and type of show during which their ads may appear. During which days, times, and types of shows should retailers advertise the following categories of merchandise: grocery, paint, beer, cars, and health club memberships? Why?

8. A retailer plans to open a new store near a university. It will specialize in collegiate merchandise such as apparel, accessories, and school supplies. Consider the pros and cons of each of the following media: TV, radio, city newspaper, university newspaper, local magazine, Web site, blog, and event sponsorship for this retailer to capture the university market.

9. Why do some online retailers include editorials and customer reviews along with product information on their Web sites? Explain how this may influence the consumer's buying behavior.

10. Where do you think pop-up stores would be most successful? Why? What type of merchandise would sell well from this format? Explain.

SUGGESTED READINGS

Aaker, David, and Erich Joachimsthaler. *Brand Leadership: Building Assets in an Information Economy*. New York: Free Press, 2009.

Belch, George, and Michael Belch. *Advertising and Promotion: An Integrated Marketing Communications Perspective*, 8th ed. New York: McGraw-Hill, 2009.

Bradlow, Eric T., Andres Musalem, and Jagmohan S. Raju. "Who's Got the Coupon? Estimating Consumer Preferences and Coupon Usage from Aggregate Information." *Journal of Marketing Research* 45, no. 6 (2008), pp. 715–730.

Grewal, Dhruv, and Michael Levy. "Retailing Research: Past, Present, and Future." *Journal of Retailing* 83, no. 4 (2007), pp. 447–464.

Halligan, Brian, and Dharmesh Shah. *Inbound Marketing: Get Found Using Google, Social Media, and Blogs*. New York: Wiley, 2009.

Orth, Ulrich R., Harold F. Koenig, and Zuzana Firbasova. "Cross-National Differences in Consumer Response to the Framing of Advertising Messages." *European Journal of Marketing* 41, no. 3–4 (2007), pp. 327–348.

Prins, Remco, and Peter C. Verhoef. "Marketing Communication Drivers of Adoption Timing of a New E-Service among Existing Customers." *Journal of Marketing* 71, no. 2 (2007), pp. 169–183.

Scott, David Meerman. *The New Rules of Marketing and PR: How to Use Social Media, Blogs, News Releases, Online Video, and Viral Marketing to Reach Buyers Directly*. New York: Wiley, 2010.

Sernovitz, Andy. *Word of Mouth Marketing: How Smart Companies Get People Talking*. New York: Kaplan Press, 2009.

Tsiros, Michael, and David M. Hardesty. "Ending a Price Promotion: Retracting It in One Step or Phasing It Out Gradually." *Journal of Marketing* 74, no. 1 (2010), pp. 49–64.

Store Management

Section IV focuses on the implementation issues associated with store management, including managing store employees and controlling costs (Chapter 16), presenting merchandise (Chapter 17), and providing customer service (Chapter 18).

Traditionally, the issues pertaining to merchandise management were considered the most important retail decisions, and buying merchandise was considered the best career path for achieving senior retail management positions. Now, developing a strategic advantage through merchandise management is becoming more and more difficult because competing stores often have similar assortments of national-brand merchandise.

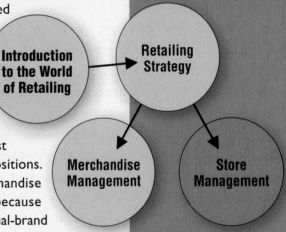

Because customers can find the same assortments in a number of conveniently located retail outlets and through the Internet, store management issues have become a critical basis for developing strategic advantage. Retailers are increasing their emphasis on differentiating their offering from competitive offerings on the basis of the experience that customers have in the stores, including the service they get from store employees and the quality of the shopping environment.

Managing the Store

EXECUTIVE BRIEFING
Heather Graham, Store Manager,
Walgreens

Between my junior and senior year, I took an internship with Walgreens in the summer. Based on this experience, I accepted an offer to enter the Walgreens management training program when I graduated. One of the challenges I faced was winning the respect of employees I supervised who were much older than I was. I found that if I respected them and valued their experience and suggestions, they would respect me.

After three years, I was promoted to store manager. When I was a student at the University of Florida, I thought about starting my own business. However, I now realize that I am running my own business as a Walgreens store manager. The sign outside my store might say Walgreens, but it is Heather Graham's store. I am responsible and rewarded for my store's performance. Of course, Walgreens provides the tools needed to manage the store, but my team is involved in selecting the promotional and seasonal merchandise sold in my store. I also hire, train, evaluate, and manage the 50 people working in my store.

I really like working in a store, particularly one that is the size of a Walgreens store. My store is small enough that I know most of the customers and all of the employees. I would be bored if I had to sit behind a desk all day.

I need to walk around and talk with people. As a store manager, I interact with a lot of people—customers, store employees, people in our district office—and I do a variety of different things. In a single day, I will handle some personnel issues, help customers find what they need, decide on how to display some new merchandise, and review reports summarizing the financial performance of my store.

I am a very results-oriented person. Another thing I like about retailing is that you get a scorecard everyday. When I come to work in the morning I can see what the sales were the day before and how they compared to last year's sales. I really feel a sense of accomplishment when I try something out and sales go up.

Walgreens is a great place to work because it shares my values. The company cares about its customers and employees just like I do. As the manager of this business, I try to create an environment in which my store employees feel they are all part of a team working

CHAPTER 16

QUESTIONS

What are the responsibilities of store managers?

How do store managers recruit, select, motivate, train, and evaluate their employees?

How do store managers compensate their salespeople?

What legal and ethical issues must store managers consider in managing their employees?

What can store managers do to increase productivity and reduce costs?

How can store managers reduce inventory losses due to employee theft and shoplifting?

What are retailers doing to reduce energy costs?

---

together to provide an attractive offering for our customers. I want all of my team members to learn more about how our store and company operates, develop their skills, and realize their potential. By working together and helping each other, we can all achieve our goals.

Store managers play a critical role in retail companies. Due to their daily contact with customers, they have the best knowledge of customer needs and competitive activity.[1] From this unique vantage point, store managers play an important role in formulating and executing retail strategies. Buyers can develop exciting merchandise assortments and procure them at low cost, but the retailer realizes the benefits of the buyers' efforts only when the merchandise is sold. Good merchandise doesn't sell itself. Store managers must make sure that the merchandise is presented effectively and sales associates offer services that stimulate and facilitate customer buying decisions. Some store managers are responsible for $150 million in annual sales and manage more than 1,000 employees.

Even in national chains, store managers are treated as relatively independent managers of a business within the corporation. For example, James Nordstrom, former CEO of Nordstrom, told his store managers, "This is your business. Do your own thing. Don't listen to us in Seattle, listen to your customers. We give you permission to take care of your customers."

The first portion of this chapter focuses on the management of store employees and complements the strategic human resource management issues discussed in Chapter 9. Chapter 9 examined the organization of the tasks performed by retailers and the general approaches for motivating retail employees and building their commitment to the firm. This chapter discusses how store managers implement the retailer's human resource strategy.

STORE MANAGEMENT RESPONSIBILITIES

The responsibilities of store managers are shown in Exhibit 16–1. These functions are divided into four major categories: managing employees, controlling costs, managing merchandise presentation, and providing customer service. Issues pertaining to the management of store employees and controlling costs are discussed in this chapter. Subsequent chapters examine the store manager's responsibilities in presenting and managing merchandise and providing customer service.

Store managers are responsible for increasing the productivity of two of the retailer's most important assets: the firm's investments in its employees and its real estate. Most of this chapter is devoted to increasing labor productivity—the sales generated by each store employee. Labor productivity is improved by effectively recruiting, selecting, training, and managing store employees so that they perform at high levels.

In addition to increasing labor productivity, store managers affect their stores' profits by controlling costs. The major costs are compensation and benefits for employees. Store managers are responsible for controlling these costs by efficiently scheduling labor. But store managers are also responsible for costs associated with operating and maintaining their buildings. Retailers are engaging in innovative cost-cutting initiatives that are also environmentally friendly. Another important retail cost-controlling activity is reducing inventory shrinkage resulting from shoplifting and employee theft. These cost-control issues are discussed at the end of the chapter.

Exhibit 16–2 outlines the steps in the management process that affect store employees' productivity: (1) recruiting and selecting effective employees, (2) improving their skills through socialization and training, (3) motivating them to perform at higher levels, (4) evaluating them, and finally (5) compensating and rewarding them.[2] Store managers also need to develop employees who can assume more responsibility and be promoted to higher-level management positions. By developing subordinates, managers help both their firms and themselves. Effective subordinates increase the retailer's sales and reduce its cost. Store managers benefit because the firm is confident that there will be an effective replacement when the manager is considered for promotion.

EXHIBIT 16–1

Responsibilities of Store Managers

MANAGING STORE EMPLOYEES (Chapter 16)

Recruiting and selecting
Socializing and training
Motivating
Evaluating and providing constructive feedback
Rewarding and compensating

CONTROLLING COSTS (Chapter 16)

Increasing labor productivity
Reducing maintenance and energy costs
Reducing inventory losses

MANAGING MERCHANDISE

Displaying merchandise and maintaining visual standards (Chapter 17)
Working with buyers
    Suggesting new merchandise
    Buying merchandise
    Planning and managing special events
    Marking down merchandise

PROVIDING CUSTOMER SERVICE (Chapter 18)

Steps in the Process of Managing Store Employees   **EXHIBIT 16–2**

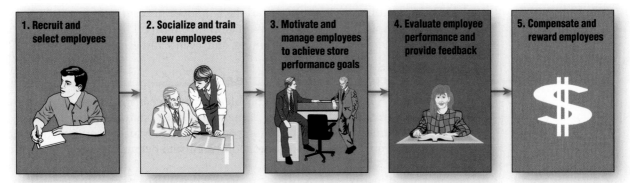

RECRUITING AND SELECTING STORE EMPLOYEES

The first step in the employee management process is recruiting and selecting employees. To recruit employees effectively, store managers need to undertake a job analysis, prepare a job description, find potential applicants with the desired capabilities, and screen the best candidates to interview. (Appendix 1A to Chapter 1 describes the recruiting and selection process from the perspective of people interested in pursuing retail careers and applying for management trainee positions.)

Job Analysis

The **job analysis** identifies essential activities and is used to determine the qualifications of potential employees. For example, retail salespeople's responsibilities vary from company to company and department to department within a store. Retail employees in self-service stores such as supermarkets and full-line discount stores typically help customers find merchandise, bring out and display merchandise, and ring up sales. In contrast, employees who work in jewelry stores, high-end apparel departments, or furniture stores get involved in a selling process that begins with finding out what customers want and then proposing solutions. The skill level required for employees involved in selling high-involvement merchandise such as jewelry or a home entertainment system is much greater than that for employees who have limited interactions with customers.

Managers can obtain the information needed for a job analysis by observing employees presently doing the job and determining the characteristics of exceptional performers. Exhibit 16–3 lists some questions that managers use when undertaking a job analysis of store employees. Information collected in the job analysis is then used to prepare a job description.

EXHIBIT 16–3

Questions for Undertaking a Job Analysis

- How many salespeople will be working in the department at the same time?
- Do the salespeople have to work together in dealing with customers?
- How many customers will the salesperson have to work with at one time?
- Will the salesperson be selling on an open floor or working behind the counter?
- How much and what type of product knowledge does the salesperson need?
- Does the salesperson need to sell the merchandise or just ring up the orders and provide information?
- Is the salesperson required to make appointments with customers and develop a loyal customer base?
- Does the salesperson have the authority to negotiate price or terms of the sale?
- Does the salesperson need to demonstrate the merchandise?
- Will the salesperson be expected to make add-on sales?
- Is the salesperson's appearance important? How should an effective salesperson look?
- Will the salesperson be required to perform merchandising activities such as stocking shelves and setting up displays?
- Whom will the salesperson report to?
- What compensation plan will the salesperson be working under?

Job Description

A **job description** includes (1) activities the employee needs to perform and (2) the performance expectations expressed in quantitative terms. The job description is a guideline for recruiting, selecting, training, and, eventually, evaluating employees.

Locating Prospective Employees

Staffing stores is becoming a critical problem because changing demographics are reducing the size of the labor pool. Some approaches being used by retailers to recruit applicants, in addition to placing ads in local newspapers and posting job openings on Web sites such as monster.com, are listed below.

Recruiting Minorities, Immigrants, and Older Workers   To increase the pool of potential applicants, retailers are aggressively pursuing minorities and older workers. Applications are being printed in Spanish as well as English. Some retailers are working with the American Association of Retired Persons (AARP) to match seniors with job openings at their companies. Retailing often is attractive to seniors because its flexibility in scheduling fits seniors' lifestyle. In addition, some retailers pay health care benefits to part-time workers, an important consideration for seniors.[3]

Partnering with Government Agencies   CVS and other retailers are partnering with the government to help it recruit the unemployed and former welfare recipients.[5] CVS also has developed partnerships around the country to improve recruiting, training, and retention. The company established seven Regional Learning Centers, colocated with local government employment offices. For example, when the Washington, D.C., Department of Employment Services interviews people who match CVS's qualifications, it sends them to the company for further talks. Selected people may be sent back to the one-stop center for training in a mock CVS store. After the store has completed a hire, the government still stays involved by helping connect new CVS employees with services such as transportation and child care that enable them to transition to work. The partnership among CVS and the government benefits all the parties: CVS staffs its stores, and the public sector moves people off the unemployment rolls.

Using Employees as Talent Scouts   Retailers often ask their own employees if they know someone the company could hire. For example, an employee might identify a particularly good sales associate when shopping at another store or might know a customer who he or she believes would make a good employee. The women's specialty store chain Chico's, for instance, often hires its best customers because they already know and love the store's merchandise and can relate to other customers like them.

Many retailers provide incentives for such referrals by employees. For example, at The Container Store, recruiting is part of everyone's job. Employees get $500 for every full-time hire and $200 for every part-timer. All employees, from stockers to managers, carry recruiting cards to pull out when chatting with customers. The program is so successful that the company often goes six to eight months without placing a single classified advertisement.[6]

Screening Applicants to Interview

The screening process matches applicants' qualifications with the job description. Many retailers use automated prescreening programs as a low-cost method of identifying qualified candidates. Applicants initially interact with a Web-enabled store kiosk or call a toll-free telephone number.[7]

Home Depot and other retailers find that the productivity and commitment of older employees are higher than those of younger employees.

For example, Finish Line, the athletic footware and apparel retailer, asks a series of questions of applicants in a prescreening process. The company has set up online applications for the initial interview through kiosks in its stores and on its Web site. By automating a portion of the application process, the retailer can select from a larger pool of applicants and allow managers to focus more on managing the store, not just interviewing new applicants. More than 75 percent of applicants apply online, and 30 percent are eliminated in the automated portion of the interview. After implementing this automated application tool, Front Line's average sales per hour for associates have increased from $112 to $135, and employee retention has increased by 9 percent.[8]

Application Forms **Job application forms** contain information about the applicant's employment history, previous compensation, reasons for leaving his or her previous employment, education and training, personal health, and references. This information enables the manager to determine whether the applicant has the minimum qualifications, and it also provides information that is useful when the manager interviews the applicant.

References and Online Checks A good way to verify the information given on an application form is to contact the applicant's references or do an online check. Contacting references is helpful for collecting additional information from people who have worked with the applicant. In addition, store managers should check with former supervisors not listed as references and should not rely solely on references from colleagues or friends. Because people are more likely to be frank in conversation, managers should always talk to the references, rather than relying on written opinions. Due to potential legal problems, however, many companies have a policy of not commenting on prior employees.

Store managers generally expect to hear favorable comments from an applicant's references or previous supervisors, even if they may not have thought highly of the applicant. One approach for reducing this positive bias is to ask the reference to rank the applicant relative to others in the same position. For example, the manager might ask, "How would you rate Pat's customer service skill in relation to other retail sales associates you have worked with?" Another approach is to ask specific questions, rather than yes-or-no questions or vague "tell me about John" types of questions.

The Internet has become an excellent source of information on prospective employees. A quick look at someone's Facebook entry can often reveal more about the person than a face-to-face interview. A Google search can also be useful for finding out information that may not appear on the job application or emerge through contacts with references.[10] For instance, a search could reveal that an applicant was once involved in illegal or otherwise undesirable activities.

Testing Intelligence, ability, personality, and interest tests can provide insights about potential employees. For example, intelligence tests yield data about the applicant's innate abilities and can be used to match applicants with job openings and to develop training programs. However, tests must be scientifically and legally valid. They can be used only when the scores have been shown to be related to job performance. It is illegal to use tests that assess factors that are not job-related or that discriminate against specific groups.

Due to potential losses from theft, many retailers require that applicants take drug tests. Some retailers also use tests to assess applicants' honesty and ethics. Paper-and-pencil honesty tests include questions designed to find out if an applicant

Retailers are automating applicant screening by using kiosks in stores and on the Web.

REFACT

Over 44 percent of the résumés employers receive come from unqualified candidates.[9]

REFACT

Of retailers, 71 percent check references as part of the selection process, 54 percent do drug screening, and 43 percent use paper-and-pencil honesty tests.[11]

REFACT

Drug use in the workplace costs U.S. companies more than $81 billion a year in turnover and lost productivity.[12]

has ever thought about stealing and if he or she believes other people steal ("What percentage of people take more than $1 from their employer?").

Realistic Job Preview   Turnover declines when applicants understand both the attractive and unattractive aspects of the job.[13] Many retailers want their new hires to have previous retail experience. They have found that experience, even if the previous job was significantly different from the new opportunity, gives the applicant an appreciation for what a life in retailing is all about. Thus, retailing internships are mutually beneficial—the employee gains experience and gets a realistic view of what a more permanent job might entail, and the retailer gets access to good talent that it may be able to hire in the future.

PetSmart, a pet supply category specialist, shows each applicant a 10-minute video that begins with the advantages of being a company employee and continues with scenes of employees dealing with irate customers and cleaning up animal droppings. This type of job preview typically screens out many applicants who would most likely quit within three months if they were hired.

Selecting Applicants

After screening applicants, the selection process typically involves a personal interview. Because the interview is usually the critical factor in the hiring decision, the store manager needs to be well prepared and have complete control over the interview.

Preparation for the Interview   The objective of the interview is to gather relevant information, not simply to ask a lot of questions. The most widely used interview technique, called the *behavioral interview*, asks candidates how they have handled actual situations they have encountered in the past, especially situations requiring the skills outlined in the job description. For example, applicants applying for a job requiring that they handle customer complaints would be asked to describe a situation in which they were confronted by someone who was angry about something they had done. Candidates might be asked to describe the situation, what they did, and the outcomes of their actions. These situations also can be used to interview references for the applicants.[14]

An effective approach to interviewing involves some predetermined questions but also allows some flexibility in question selections. Managers need to develop objectives for what they want to learn about the candidate. Each topic area covered in the interview starts with a broad question, such as "Tell me about your last job," which is designed to elicit a lengthy response. The broad opening questions are followed by a sequence of more specific questions, such as "What did you learn from that job?" or "How many subordinates did you have?" Managers need to avoid asking questions that are discriminatory.

Managing the Interview   Exhibit 16–4 lists some questions the manager might ask. Here are some suggestions for questioning the applicant during the interview:

- Encourage long responses by asking questions like "What do you know about our company?" rather than "How familiar are you with our company?"
- Avoid asking questions that have multiple parts.
- Avoid asking leading questions like "Are you prepared to provide good customer service?"
- Be an active listener. Evaluate the information being presented and sort out the important comments from the unimportant ones. Some techniques for active listening include repeating or rephrasing information, summarizing the conversation, and tolerating silences.

EDUCATION

What were your most and least favorite subjects in college? Why?

What types of extracurricular activities did you participate in? Why did you select those activities?

If you had the opportunity to attend school all over again, what, if anything, would you do differently? Why?

How did you spend the summers during college?

Did you have any part-time jobs? Which of your part-time jobs did you find most interesting? What did you find most difficult about working and attending college at the same time? What advice would you give to someone who wanted to work and attend college at the same time?

What accomplishments are you most proud of?

PREVIOUS EXPERIENCE

What's your description of the ideal manager? Subordinate? Coworker?

What did you like most/least about your last job?

What kind of people do you find it difficult/easy to work with? Why?

What has been your greatest accomplishment during your career to date?

Describe a situation at your last job involving pressure. How did you handle it?

What were some duties on your last job that you found difficult?

Of all the jobs you've had, which did you find the most/least rewarding?

What is the most frustrating situation you've encountered in your career?

Why do you want to leave your present job?

What would you do if . . . ?

How would you handle . . . ?

What would you like to avoid in future jobs?

What do you consider your greatest strength/weakness?

What are your responsibilities in your present job?

Tell me about the people you hired on your last job. How did they work out? What about the people you fired?

What risks did you take in your last job, and what were the results of those risks?

Where do you see yourself in three years?

What kind of references will your previous employer give?

What do you do when you have trouble solving a problem?

QUESTIONS THAT SHOULD NOT BE ASKED PER EQUAL EMPLOYMENT OPPORTUNITY GUIDELINES

Do you have plans for having children/a family?

What are your marriage plans?

What does your husband/wife do?

What happens if your husband/wife gets transferred or needs to relocate?

Who will take care of your children while you're at work?

(Asked of men) How would you feel about working for a woman?

How old are you?

What is your date of birth?

How would you feel working for a person younger than you?

Where were you born?

Where were your parents born?

Do you have any handicaps?

As a handicapped person, what help are you going to need to do your work?

How severe is your handicap?

What's your religion?

What church do you attend?

Do you hold religious beliefs that would prevent you from working on certain days of the week?

Do you feel that your race/color will be a problem in your performing the job?

Are you of _____ heritage/race?

Legal Considerations in Selecting and Hiring Store Employees

Heightened social awareness and government regulations emphasize the need to avoid discriminating against hiring people with disabilities, women, minorities, and older workers. Title VII of the Civil Rights Act prohibits discrimination on the basis of race, national origin, gender, or religion in company personnel practices. Discrimination is specifically prohibited in the following human resource decisions: recruitment, hiring, discharge, layoff, discipline, promotion, compensation, and access to training. In 1972, the act was expanded by the **Equal Employment Opportunity Commission (EEOC)** to allow employees to sue employers that violate the law. Several major retailers have been successfully sued because they discriminated in hiring and promoting minorities and women.

Discrimination arises when a member of a protected class (women, minorities, etc.) is treated differently from nonmembers of that class (**disparate treatment**) or when an apparently neutral rule has an unjustified discriminatory effect (**disparate impact**). An example of disparate treatment occurs when a qualified woman does not receive a promotion given to a less qualified man. Disparate impact occurs, for instance, when a retailer requires high school graduation for all its employees, thereby excluding a larger proportion of disadvantaged minorities, when at least some of the jobs (e.g., custodian) could be performed just as well by people who did not graduate from high school. In such cases, the retailer is required to prove that the imposed qualification is actually needed to be able to perform the job. The **Age Discrimination in Employment Act** makes it illegal to discriminate in hiring and terminating people over the age of 40 years.

Finally, the **Americans with Disabilities Act (ADA)** opens up job opportunities for disabled individuals by requiring that employers provide accommodating work environments. A **disability** is any physical or mental impairment that substantially limits one or more of an individual's major life activities or any condition that is regarded as being such an impairment. Although being HIV-positive does not limit any life activities, it may be perceived as doing so and is therefore protected as a disability. Similarly, extreme obesity may be either actually limiting or perceived as such and be protected as long as the obese person can perform the duties of the job.

ORIENTATION AND TRAINING PROGRAMS FOR NEW STORE EMPLOYEES

REFACT

It costs retailers more than $4,000 to replace a store employee.[15]

After hiring employees, the next step in developing effective employees (as Exhibit 16–2 shows) is introducing them to the firm and its policies. Retailers want the people they hire to become involved, committed contributors to the firm's successful performance. Moreover, newly hired employees want to learn about their job responsibilities and the company they've decided to join.

Orientation Programs

Orientation programs are critical in socializing new employees and overcoming the differences in the employee's previous and new roles.[16] For example, overcoming entry shock can be a problem for even the most knowledgeable and mature new employees. College students who accept management trainee positions often find significant differences between their student and their employee roles. Retailing View 16.1 describes some of these differences.

Orientation programs can last from a few hours to several weeks. The orientation and training program for new store employees might be limited to several hours

16.1 RETAILING VIEW Transition from Student to Management Trainee

Many students have some difficulty adjusting to the demands of their first full-time job because student life and professional life are very different. Students typically "report" to three or four supervisors (professors), but the student selects new "supervisors" every four months. In contrast, management trainees have limited involvement, if any, in selecting the one supervisor they'll report to, often for several years.

Student life has fixed time cycles—one- to two-hour classes with a well-defined beginning and end. Retail managers, however, are involved in a variety of activities with varied time horizons, ranging from having a five-minute interaction with a customer to implementing a plan to develop a sales associate into an assistant manager.

The decisions students encounter differ dramatically from the decisions retail managers encounter. For example, business students might make several major decisions in a day when they discuss cases in class. These decisions are made and implemented in one class period, and then a new set of decisions is made and implemented in the next class. In a retail environment, strategic decisions evolve over a long time period. Most decisions, such as those regarding merchandise buying and pricing, are made with incomplete information. Store managers in real life often lack the extensive information provided in many business cases studied in class. Finally, there are long periods of time when store managers undertake mundane tasks associated with implementing decisions and no major issues are being considered. Students typically don't have these mundane tasks to perform.

Source: Professor Daniel Feldman, University of Georgia.

during which the new employee learns the retailer's policies and procedures and how to use the POS terminal. Other retailers, like The Container Store, have a much more intensive training program. Selected by *Fortune* magazine as one of the best places to work, new Container Store employees go through a program called Foundation Week.[17] First, they receive a handbook and assignment before employment even begins. The first day of Foundation Week begins with the company philosophy and a visit from the store manager. Employees immediately see this introduction as different from the traditional first day, which typically entails completing forms and learning where to park. Days 2 through 5 continue with hands-on, on-the-floor training, including interaction with and instruction from various positions in the store. The culmination of Foundation Week is a ceremony during which the new employees finally receive their aprons, signifying their membership in this elite organization. The orientation process also continues past Foundation Week. Customer service is the company's core competency, so every first-year, full-time salesperson receives about 241 hours of training, compared with 8 hours in the retail industry on average. Training continues throughout an employee's career.

Disney overhauled its orientation program to build emotional bonds rather than learn company policies and procedures. The program begins with current employees, referred to as *cast members*, discussing their earliest memories of Disney, their visions of great service, and their understanding of teamwork. Then trainers relate "magic moments" they have witnessed to emphasize that insignificant actions can have a big impact on a guest. For example, a four-year-old trips and falls, spilling his box of popcorn. The boy cries, the mother is concerned, and a costumed cast member, barely breaking stride, picks up the empty box, takes it to the popcorn stand for a refill, presents it to the child, and goes on his way.

The orientation program is just one element in the overall training program. It needs to be accompanied by a systematic follow-up to ensure that any problems and concerns arising after the initial period also are considered.

Training Store Employees

Effective training for new store employees includes both structured and on-the-job learning experiences.

Structured Program   During a **structured training program,** new employees acquire the basic skills and knowledge they'll need to do their job. For example, sales associates learn what the company policies are, how to use the point-of-sale terminal, and how to perform basic selling skills. Stockroom employees learn procedures for receiving merchandise. This initial training might be done in virtual or real classrooms or with manuals and correspondence distributed to the new employees.

Some larger firms are finding that structured programs using e-training over the Internet have some benefits over on-the-job training. For example, there is greater consistency, because the training takes place with one rather than several supervisors. Costs are lower; once the system is

In this structured training program, newly hired Men's Wearhouse salespeople learn about merchandise they will be selling.

The manager of this Sandy Hill, Utah, Shopko store is a democratic leader who holds meetings to keep employees informed about company and store activities. He encourages them to make suggestions about improving store performance.

employees what to do. For example, an autocratic store manager determines who will work in each area of the store, when they'll take breaks, and what days they'll have off.

In contrast, a **democratic leader** seeks information and opinions from employees and bases his or her decisions on this information. Democratic store managers share their power and information with their employees. The democratic store manager asks employees where and when they want to work and makes schedules to accommodate those employee desires.

Leadership Styles   There is no one best leadership style. Effective store managers use all styles, selecting the style most appropriate for each situation. For example, a store manager might be autocratic and relations-oriented with an insecure new trainee but democratic and task-oriented with an effective, experienced employee.

The previous discussion and most of this chapter describe specific behaviors, activities, and programs that store managers use to influence their employees. But the greatest leaders and store managers go beyond influencing employee behaviors. **Transformational leaders** get people to transcend their personal needs for the sake of the group or organization. They generate excitement and revitalize organizations.

Transformational store managers create this enthusiasm in their employees through their personal charisma. They are self-confident, have a clear vision that grabs employees' attention, and communicate this vision through words and symbols. Finally, transformational leaders delegate challenging work to subordinates, have free and open communication with them, and provide personal mentoring to develop subordinates.

Retailing View 16.2 examines the inherent difficulties of leading employees with diverse values.

Motivating Employees

Motivating employees to perform up to their potential may be store managers' most important and challenging task. The following hypothetical situation illustrates some issues pertaining to employee motivation and evaluation.

After getting an associate's degree at a local community college, Jim Taylor was hired for a sales position at a department store in San Jose's Eastridge Mall. The position offered firsthand knowledge of the firm's customers, managers, and policies. Taylor was told that if he did well in this assignment, he could become a management trainee.

His performance as a sales associate was average. After observing Taylor on the sales floor, his manager, Jennifer Chen, felt that he was effective only when working with customers like himself: young, career-oriented men and women. To encourage Taylor to sell to other types of customers, Chen reduced his fixed salary and increased his commission rate. She also reviewed Taylor's performance goals with him.

The Sears manager builds morale and motivates her sales associates by holding "ready meetings" before the store opens. At this meeting, the manager is discussing approaches for improving customer service.

Taylor now feels a lot of pressure to increase his sales level. He's beginning to dread coming to work in the morning and is thinking about getting out of retailing and working for a bank.

In this hypothetical situation, Chen focused on increasing Taylor's motivation by providing more incentive compensation. In discussing this illustration, we'll examine the appropriateness of this approach versus other approaches for improving Taylor's performance.

Setting Goals or Quotas

Employee performance improves when employees feel that (1) their efforts will enable them to achieve the goals set for them by their managers and (2) they'll receive rewards they value if they achieve their goals. Thus, managers can motivate employees by setting realistic goals and offering rewards that employees want.[23]

For example, Jennifer Chen set specific selling goals for Jim Taylor when he started to work in her department. Taylor, like other store sales associates, has goals in five selling areas: sales per hour, average size of each sale, number of multiple-item (add-on) sales, number of preferred clients, and number of appointments made with preferred clients. (**Preferred clients** are customers whom salespeople communicate regularly with, send notes or e-mails to about new merchandise and sales in the department, and make appointments with for special presentations of

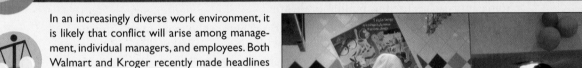

RETAILING VIEW   Should Managers Make Them Do It?   16.2

In an increasingly diverse work environment, it is likely that conflict will arise among management, individual managers, and employees. Both Walmart and Kroger recently made headlines because a staff pharmacist refused to dispense the Plan B "morning after" contraceptive pill, which he said ran counter to his religious beliefs. In another situation, Muslims who work at grocery checkouts in a Target supercenter said their strict interpretation of the Koran prohibited their handling of pork products or even packaged pork products. So they refused to touch, scan, or bag products that contained any pork.

Do managers have the right or the corporate responsibility to force employees to take actions that are contrary to their beliefs, even if they are within the law? Should the pharmacist or the checkout clerks cast aside their personal beliefs to do the job they have otherwise voluntarily been hired to do?

These questions have no clear answer, but it is the retailers' responsibility to attempt to foster the values of their employees and, at the same time, be able to conduct normal business and satisfy their customers. The U.S. Food and Drug Administration (FDA) has helped solve the contraceptives conflict by ruling that the Plan B pill can be dispensed without a prescription to women over the age of 18 years but requiring that it be kept behind the counter to prevent underage girls from gaining access to it without a parent's permission. Retailers therefore have more flexibility in handling the situation, because an employee who is not morally opposed to the product can conduct the transaction. Although the practicality of the solution is not as clear, Target could also have other employees step in and

Store managers often have to resolve conflicts between company policies and the cultural and ethical vales of store employees.

help in situations in which Muslim checkout clerks cannot handle pork.

What would you do if you were faced with these or similar ethically sensitive situations?

Sources: Lolita Mancheno-Smoak, Grace M. Endres, Rhonda Potak, and Yvonne Athanasaw, "The Individual Cultural Values and Job Satisfaction of the Transformational Leader," *Organization Development Journal* 27 (Fall 2009), pp. 9–22; Curt Woodward, "Court: Druggists May Deny Emergency Pill," *Associated Press*, November 12, 2007; Kevin Coupe, "We Are the World," *Chain Store Age*, May 2007; Chris Serres and Matt McKinney, "Customer Service and Faith Clash at Registers," *Star Tribune*, March 12, 2007.

merchandise—the upper-tier customer discussed in Chapter 11.) In addition to being evaluated on their selling goals, salespeople are evaluated on the overall department shrinkage due to stolen merchandise, the errors they make in using the POS terminal, and their contribution to maintaining the department's appearance.

Chen also designed a program for Taylor's development as a sales associate. The activities she outlined over the next six months required Taylor to attend classes to improve his selling skills. Chen needs to be careful in setting goals for Taylor though. If she sets the goals too high, he might become discouraged, feel the goals are unattainable, and thus not be motivated to work harder. However, if she sets the goals too low, Taylor can achieve them easily and won't be motivated to work to his full potential.

Rather than setting specific goals for each salesperson, this retailer uses the average performance for all salespeople as its goal. However, goals are most effective at motivating employees when they're based on the employee's experience and confidence. Experienced salespeople have confidence in their abilities and should have "stretch" goals (high goals that will make them work hard). New salespeople need lower goals that they have a good chance of achieving. The initial good experience of achieving and surpassing goals builds new salespeople's confidence and motivates them to improve their skills. The use of rewards to motivate employees is discussed later in this chapter.

Maintaining Morale

Store morale is important in motivating employees. Typically, morale goes up when things are going well and employees are highly motivated. But when sales aren't going well, morale tends to decrease and employee motivation declines. Some approaches used to build morale are:

- Holding storewide or department meetings before the store opens, during which managers pass along information about new merchandise and programs and solicit opinions and suggestions from employees.
- Educating employees about the firm's finances, setting achievable goals, and throwing a party when the goals are met.
- Dividing the charity budget by the number of employees and inviting employees to suggest how their "share" should be used.
- Creating stickers that tell customers that this sandwich was "wrapped by Roger" or this dress was "dry cleaned by Sarah."
- Giving every employee a business card with the company mission printed on its back.

For example, one store manager used real-time sales data collected in her firm's information system (see Chapter 10) to build excitement among her employees. On the first day of the Christmas season, she wrote $3,159 on a blackboard in the store. That was the store's sales during the first day of the Christmas season last year. She told her sales associates that beating that number was not enough; she wanted to see a 36 percent increase, the same sales increase the store achieved over the previous Christmas season.

By setting financial objectives and keeping sales associates informed of up-to-the-minute results, managers can convert an eight-hour shift of clock watchers into an excited team of racers. All day, as customers come and go, sales associates take turns consulting the backroom computer that records sales from the store's POS terminals. Retailing View 16.3 describes the distinct efforts that may be required to motivate various generational cohorts.

Sexual Harassment

Sexual harassment is an important issue in terms of the productivity of the work environment. Managers must avoid, and make sure that store employees avoid, any actions that are, or can be interpreted as, sexual harassment. Otherwise, the retailer and the manager may be held liable for the harassment. The EEOC guidelines define **sexual harassment** as a form of gender discrimination, as follows:

> Unwelcome sexual advances, requests for sexual favors, and other verbal or physical conduct of a sexual nature constitutes sexual harassment when . . . submission to or rejection of such conduct by an individual is used as a basis for employment decisions affecting such individual, or . . . such conduct has the purpose or effect of unreasonably interfering with an individual's work performance or creating an intimidating, hostile, or offensive working environment.

RETAILING VIEW   Motivating Different Generational Cohorts   16.3

The major generational cohorts working in retail stores include baby boomers (born between 1946 and 1960), Generation X (born 1961–1979), and Generation Y (1980–present). Because employees in each of these age cohorts grew up in different environments, they need to be managed and motivated differently.

Baby boomers grew up during a period of economic growth, which has given them great expectations of success. Thus, they typically are optimistic and self-motivated. They feel that they will earn rewards if they work hard enough. Baby boomers tend to recognize the authority and expertise of their superiors and undertake tasks they are asked to do without questioning their superiors.

Generation X employees generally perceive corporations as less supportive, largely because of the experiences of their parents when economic problems arose. They often are skeptical about the firms they work for, and their loyalty to their employer is limited. Instead, they are more concerned about job security and being treated fairly. In turn, they typically desire a more informal and flexible work environment instead of one that embraces a hierarchical authority. Generation Y is the first in history to have lived their entire lives with information technology. It is not easy for them to even understand a world without it. Their childhood was comfortable and prosperous, making them more individualistic than earlier generations. Although they demand autonomy in their opinions and behavior, they also remain very interested in social relationships with their managers and coworkers.

Employees in this age cohort generally are not motivated by an inherent loyalty to their employer but, rather, develop high expectations for themselves and want to work for managers who will help them grow and develop their professional skills. These younger workers thus are transforming the workplace from the "get rich quick" attitude of the 1990s to a culture of empowerment and contribution. At the end of the day, they want to feel as though they are part of something essential and that they have contributed to its achievement. A key to managing this generation, therefore, is to create excitement about the company's achievements and, even more important, to help them recognize their role in accomplishing that mission.

Generation Y employees want a role in the decision-making process. Meetings shouldn't be just a method of broadcasting

These Generation Y store employees want to feel they are involved in making decisions that affect their store's and their personal performance.

decisions that already have been made. Rather, meetings should be considered two-way communication opportunities, forums for asking other employees to contribute their ideas and letting them know that their contribution is not only welcome but valued and carefully considered.

Generation Y employees also want their managers to be mentors, not taskmasters. Unlike their parents, who may have found fulfillment in a steady paycheck, the new-generation employees want a relationship with someone they feel understands them and their goals. Young people don't want to show up every day to just do the same thing. They look for meaning—in their work, in their lives, and in their interactions with their bosses. An important component of mentoring requires that managers know their employees and understand their goals. One person's goal might be to express herself creatively in her job, whereas another person might aspire to a specific position in the organization or industry.

Sources: Brude Tugan, *Not Everyone Gets a Trophy: How to Manage Generation Y* (San Francisco: Jossey-Bass, 2009); Haejung Kim, Dee K. Knight, and Christy Crutsinger, "Generation Y Employees' Retail Work Experience: The Mediating Effect of Job Characteristics," *Journal of Business Research* 62 (May 2009), pp. 548–556; "Dueling Age Groups in Today's Workforce: From Baby Boomers to Generations X and Y," *Knowledge@Wharton,* April 22, 2007.

Tolerating sexual harassment can significantly decrease labor productivity and employee morale.

An appropriate procedure for dealing with a sexual harassment allegation is outlined below:

Step 1: Establish and post an anti-sexual harassment policy, including a complaint procedure outside the normal supervisory channels. Supervisors are often accused of sexual harassment.

Step 2: If a complaint is made, always treat it seriously.

Step 3: Get information from the alleged victim. Ask questions like these:

- Tell me what happened. Who was involved?
- What did the harasser do and say?
- When did this happen? If this wasn't the first time, when has it happened before?
- Where did it happen?
- Were there any witnesses?
- Have you told anyone else about this or these instances?
- Has anyone else been the object of harassment?
- How did you react to the harasser's behavior?
- Would you care to speak with someone else: another member of management, the personnel department, or the company employment assistance plan person?

Step 4: Document the meeting with the alleged victim.

Step 5: Inform the human resource department or the next-higher level of company management of the complaint and of the meeting with the alleged victim.[24]

EVALUATING STORE EMPLOYEES AND PROVIDING FEEDBACK

The fourth step in the management process (Exhibit 16–2) is evaluating and providing feedback to employees. The objective of the evaluation process is to identify the employees who are performing well and those who aren't. On the basis of the evaluation, high-performing employees should be rewarded and considered for positions with greater responsibility. Plans need to be developed to increase the productivity of employees performing below expectations. Should poor performers be terminated? Do they need additional training? What kind of training do they need?[25]

Who Should Do the Evaluation?

In large retail firms, the evaluation system is usually designed by the human resource department. But the evaluation itself is done by the employee's immediate supervisor—the manager who works most closely with the employee. For example, in a discount store, the department manager is in the best position to observe a sales associate in action and understand the reasons for the sales associate's performance. The department manager also oversees the recommendations that come out of the evaluation process. Inexperienced supervisors are often assisted by a senior manager in evaluating employees.

How Often Should Evaluations Be Made?

Most retailers evaluate employees annually or semiannually. Feedback from evaluations is the most effective method for improving employee skills. Thus, evaluations should be done more frequently when managers are developing inexperienced employees' skills. However, frequent formal evaluations are time-consuming for managers and may not give employees enough time to respond to suggestions before the next evaluation. Effective managers supplement formal evaluations with frequent informal ones. For example, Jennifer Chen should work with Jim Taylor informally and not wait for the formal six-month evaluation. The best time for Chen to provide this informal feedback is immediately after she has obtained, through observations or reports, positive or negative information about Taylor's performance.

Format for Evaluations

Evaluations are only meaningful if employees know what they're required to do, the expected level of performance, and how they'll be evaluated. Exhibit 16–5 shows a specialty retailer's criteria for evaluating sales associates.

In this case, the employee's overall evaluation is based on subjective evaluations made by the store manager and assistant managers. It places equal weight on individual sales/customer relations activities and activities associated with overall store performance. By emphasizing overall store operations and performance, the assessment criteria motivate sales associates to work together as a team.

The criteria used at the department store to evaluate Jim Taylor are objective sales measures based on point-of-sale data, not subjective measures like those used by the specialty store. Exhibit 16–6 summarizes Taylor's formal six-month evaluation. The

Factors Used to Evaluate Sales Associates at a Specialty Store   **EXHIBIT 16–5**

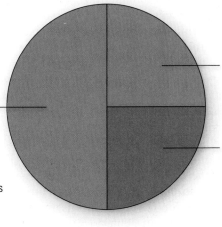

50%
SALES/CUSTOMER RELATIONS

1. Greeting. Approaches customers within 1 to 2 minutes with a smile and friendly manner. Uses open-ended questions.

2. Product knowledge. Demonstrates knowledge of product, fit, shrinkage, and price and can relay this information to the customer.

3. Suggests additional merchandise. Approaches customers at fitting room and cash/wrap areas.

4. Asks customers to buy and reinforces decisions. Lets customers know they've made a wise choice and thanks them.

25%
OPERATIONS

1. Store appearance. Demonstrates an eye for detail (color and finesse) in the areas of display, coordination of merchandise on tables, floor fixtures, and wall faceouts. Takes initiative in maintaining store presentation standards.

2. Loss prevention. Actively follows all loss prevention procedures.

3. Merchandise control and handling. Consistently achieves established requirements in price change activity, shipment processing, and inventory control.

4. Cash/wrap procedures. Accurately and efficiently follows all register policies and cash/wrap procedures.

25%
COMPLIANCE

1. Dress code and appearance. Complies with dress code. Appears neat and well groomed. Projects current fashionable store image.

2. Flexibility. Able to switch from one assignment to another, open to schedule adjustments. Shows initiative, awareness of store priorities and needs.

3. Working relations. Cooperates with other employees, willingly accepts direction and guidance from management. Communicates to management.

EXHIBIT 16–6
Summary of Jim Taylor's
Six-Month Evaluation

	Average Performance for Sales Associates in Department	Actual Performance for Jim Taylor
Sales per hour	$75	$65
Average amount per transaction	$45	$35
Percentage multiple transactions	55%	55%
Number of preferred customers	115	125
Number of preferred customer appointments	95	120
Departmental shrinkage	2.00%	1.80%
Systems errors	10	2
Merchandise presentation (10-point scale)	5	8

evaluation form lists results for various factors in terms of both what's considered average performance for company salespeople and Taylor's actual performance. His department has done better than average on shrinkage control, and he has done well on system errors and merchandise presentation. However, his sales performance is below average, even though he made more than the average number of presentations to preferred customers. These results suggest that Taylor's effort is good but his selling skills may need improvement.

Evaluation Errors

Managers can make evaluation errors when they first form an overall opinion of the employee's performance and then allow this opinion to influence their ratings of each performance factor. For example, a store manager might feel that a salesperson's overall performance is below average and then rate the salesperson as below average on selling skills, punctuality, appearance, and stocking. When an overall evaluation casts such a halo on multiple aspects of a salesperson's performance, the evaluation is no longer useful for identifying specific areas that need improvement.

In making evaluations, managers are often unduly influenced by recent events and their evaluations of other salespeople. For example, a manager might remember a salesperson's poor performance with a customer the day before and forget the salesperson's outstanding performance over the past three months. Similarly, a manager might be unduly harsh in evaluating an average salesperson just after completing an evaluation of an outstanding salesperson. Finally, managers have a natural tendency to attribute performance (particularly poor performance) to the salesperson and not to the environment in which the salesperson is working. When making evaluations, managers tend to underemphasize effects of external factors on the department, such as merchandise and competitors' actions.

The department store's evaluation of sales associates (Exhibit 16–6) avoids many of these potential biases because most of its ratings are based on objective data. In contrast, the specialty store evaluation (Exhibit 16–5) considers a wider range of activities but uses more subjective measures of performance. Because subjective information about specific skills, attitudes about the store and customers, interactions with coworkers, enthusiasm, and appearance aren't used in the department store's evaluation, performance on these factors might not have been explicitly communicated to Jim Taylor. The subjective characteristics in the specialty store evaluation are more prone to bias, but they also might be more helpful to salespeople as they try to improve their performance. To avoid bias when making subjective ratings, managers need to observe performance regularly, record their observations, avoid evaluating many salespeople at one time, and remain conscious of the various potential biases.

COMPENSATING AND REWARDING STORE EMPLOYEES

The fifth and final step in improving employee productivity (Exhibit 16–2) is compensating and rewarding employees. Store employees receive two types of rewards from their work: extrinsic and intrinsic. **Extrinsic rewards** are rewards provided by either the employee's manager or the firm, such as compensation, promotion, and recognition. **Intrinsic rewards** are rewards employees get personally from doing their job well. For example, salespeople often like to sell because they think it's challenging and fun. Of course, they want to be paid, but they also find it rewarding to help customers and make sales.[26]

Extrinsic Rewards

Managers can offer a variety of extrinsic rewards to motivate employees.[27] However, store employees don't all seek the same rewards. For example, some salespeople want more compensation; others strive for a promotion in the company or public recognition of their performance. Jim Taylor wants a favorable evaluation from his manager so that he can enter the management training program. Part-time salespeople often take a sales job to get out of the house and meet people. Their primary work objective isn't to make money.

Because of these different needs, managers may not be able to use the same rewards to motivate all employees. Large retailers, however, find it hard to develop unique reward programs for each individual. One response is to offer **à la carte plans** that give effective employees a choice of rewards for their good performance. For example, salespeople who achieve their goals could choose a cash bonus, extra days off, or a better discount on merchandise sold in the store. This type of compensation plan enables employees to select the rewards they want. Recognition is another important nonmonetary extrinsic reward for many employees. Although telling employees they've done a job well is appreciated, it's typically more rewarding for them when their good performance is recognized publicly. In addition, public recognition can motivate all store employees, not just the star performers, because it demonstrates management's interest in rewarding employees.

Most managers focus on extrinsic rewards to motivate employees. For example, a store manager might provide additional compensation if a salesperson achieves a sales goal. However, an emphasis on extrinsic rewards can make employees lose sight of their job's intrinsic rewards. Employees can begin to feel that their only reason for working is to earn money and that the job isn't fun.

Benefits   Benefits are often more important to employees than financial compensation. For example, an employee survey conducted by Burgerville, a quick-service restaurant chain headquartered in Vancouver, Washington, revealed that the number-one concern of the chain's employees was affordable health care. So Burgerville made a sizable bet, approximately $1.5 million, that it could increase employee retention and commitment by offering affordable health care. And the bet paid off. Under Burgerville's plan, employees who have been with the company for at least six months and worked 20 hours a week are eligible for health insurance. It costs each employee $15 per month, or $90 monthly for family coverage. Before Burgerville implemented the plan, turnover rates hovered around 125 percent. One year after the new initiative went into effect, turnover dropped to 54 percent and held steady at that level. Productivity and employee confidence are up, absenteeism is down, and, by reducing turnover, Burgerville has saved more than $500,000 that it would have had to invest in recruiting and training.[28]

Intrinsic Rewards

Note that Jennifer Chen tried to motivate Jim Taylor by using extrinsic rewards when she linked his compensation to how much he sold. This increased emphasis

Public recognition programs make employees feel they are appreciated and motivate them to improve their performance. Marshalls stores that deliver exceptional customer service are recognized by the "All-Star Award," which includes a plaque to hang in the store.

on financial rewards may be one reason Taylor now dreads coming to work in the morning. He might not think his job is fun anymore.

When employees find their jobs intrinsically rewarding, they're motivated to learn how to do them better. They act like a person playing a video game: The game itself is so interesting that the player gets rewards from just trying to master it. For example, at a high-fashion, music-inspired apparel store, employees are intrinsically rewarded by getting involved. Because trends change so quickly, the company encourages store associates to call the buyers after they come back from a club or a concert to tell them what everyone is wearing. The associates thus feel appreciated and involved.

Contests   Another approach to making work fun is to hold contests with relatively small prizes. Contests are most effective when everyone has a chance to win. Contests in which the best salespeople always win aren't exciting and may even be demoralizing.

For example, consider a contest in which a playing card is given to salespeople for each men's suit they sell during a two-week period. At the end of two weeks, the best poker hand wins. This contest motivates all salespeople during the entire period of the contest. A salesperson who sells only four suits can win with four aces. Contests should be used to create excitement and make selling challenging for everyone, not to pay the best salespeople more money.

Job Enrichment   Experienced employees often lose interest in their jobs. Extrinsic rewards, such as pay or promotion, may not be particularly motivating because the employees might be satisfied with their present income and job responsibilities. But these employees can be motivated by intrinsic rewards presented as job enrichment. **Job enrichment** is the redesign of a job to include a greater range of tasks and responsibilities. For example, an experienced sales associate who has lost some interest in his or her job could be given responsibility for merchandising a particular area, training new salespeople, or planning and managing a special event.

Compensation Programs

The objectives of a compensation program are to attract and keep good employees, motivate them to undertake activities consistent with the retailer's objectives, and reward them for their effort. In developing a compensation program, the store manager must strike a balance between controlling labor costs and providing enough compensation to keep high-quality employees.

A compensation plan is most effective for motivating and retaining employees when the employees feel that the plan is fair and that their compensation is related to their efforts. In general, simple plans are preferred to complex plans. Simple plans are easier to administer, and employees have no trouble understanding them.

Types of Compensation Plans   Retail firms typically use one or more of the following compensation plans: straight salary, straight commission, salary plus commission, and quota-bonus.

With **straight salary compensation,** salespeople or managers receive a fixed amount of compensation for each hour or week they work. For example, a salesperson might be paid $12 an hour or a department manager $1,000 a week. This plan is easy for the employee to understand and for the store to administer. Under a straight salary plan, the retailer has flexibility in assigning salespeople to different activities and sales areas. For example, salaried salespeople will undertake nonselling activities, such as stocking shelves, and won't be upset if they're transferred from a high-sales-volume department to a low-sales-volume department.

The major disadvantage of the straight salary plan is employees' lack of immediate incentives to improve their productivity. They know their compensation won't change in the short run, whether they work hard or slack off. Another disadvantage for the retailer is that a straight salary becomes a fixed cost that the firm incurs even if sales decline.

Incentive compensation plans reward employees on the basis of their productivity. Many retailers now use incentives to motivate greater sales productivity by their employees.[29] With some incentive plans, a salesperson's income is based entirely on commission—called a **straight commission.** For example, a salesperson might be paid a commission based on a percentage of sales made minus merchandise returned. Normally, the percentage is the same for all merchandise sold (such as 7 percent of sales). But some retailers use different percentages for different categories of merchandise (such as 4 percent for low-margin items and 10 percent for high-margin items). Different percentages provide additional incentives for salespeople to sell specific items. Typically, the compensation of salespeople selling high-priced items such as men's suits, cars, furniture, and appliances is based largely on their commissions.

Incentive plans also may include a fixed salary plus a commission on total sales or a commission on sales over quota. For example, a salesperson might receive a salary of $200 per week plus a commission of 2 percent on all sales over a quota of $50 per hour.

Incentive compensation plans are a powerful motivator for salespeople to sell merchandise, but they have a number of disadvantages. For example, it's hard to get salespeople who are compensated totally by commission to perform nonselling activities. Understandably, they're reluctant to spend time stocking shelves when they could be making money by selling. Also, salespeople will concentrate on the more expensive, fast-moving merchandise and neglect other merchandise. Sales incentives can also discourage salespeople from providing services to customers. Finally, salespeople compensated primarily by incentives don't develop loyalty to their employer. The employer doesn't guarantee them an income, so they feel no obligation to the firm.

Under a straight commission plan, salespeople's incomes can fluctuate from week to week, depending on their sales. Because retail sales are seasonal, salespeople might earn most of their income during the Christmas season but much less during the summer months. To provide a more steady income for salespeople who are paid by high-incentive plans, some retailers offer a **drawing account.** With a drawing account, salespeople receive a weekly check based on their estimated annual income, and commissions earned are credited against the weekly payments. Periodically, the weekly draw is compared with the commissions earned. If the draw exceeds the earned commissions, the salespeople return the excess money they've been paid and their weekly draw is reduced. If the earned commissions exceed the draw, salespeople are paid the difference.

Quotas are often used with compensation plans. A **quota** is a target level used to motivate and evaluate performance. Examples might include sales per hour for salespeople or maintained margin and inventory turnover for buyers. For department store salespeople, selling quotas vary across departments due to differences in sales productivity levels.

A **quota-bonus plan** provides sales associates with a bonus when their performance exceeds their quota. A quota-bonus plan's effectiveness depends on setting reasonable, fair quotas, but this can be hard to do. Usually, quotas are set at the same level for everyone in a department, yet salespeople in the same department may have different abilities or face different selling environments. For example, in the men's department, salespeople in the suit area have much greater sales potential than salespeople in the accessories area. Newly hired salespeople might have a harder time achieving a quota than more experienced salespeople. Thus, a quota based on average productivity may be too high to motivate the new salesperson and too low to motivate the experienced salesperson effectively. Quotas should be developed for each salesperson on the basis of his or her experience and the nature of the store area in which he or she works.[30]

To encourage employees in a department or store to work together, some retailers provide additional incentives based on the performance of the department or store as a whole. For example, salespeople might be paid a commission based on their individual sales and then receive additional compensation according to the amount of sales over plan, or quota, generated by all salespeople in the store. The group incentive encourages salespeople to work together in their nonselling activities and while handling customers so that the department sales target will be achieved.[31]

Designing the Compensation Program

A compensation program's two elements are the amount of compensation and the percentage of compensation based on incentives. Typically, market conditions determine the amount of compensation. When economic conditions are good and labor is scarce, retailers pay higher wages. Retailers that hire inexperienced salespeople pay lower wages than those that recruit experienced salespeople with good skills and abilities.

Incentive compensation is most effective when a salesperson's performance can be measured easily and precisely. It's difficult to measure individual performance when salespeople work in teams or must perform a lot of nonselling activities. Retailers can easily measure a salesperson's actual sales, but it's hard to measure her or his customer service or merchandising performance.

When the salesperson's activities have a great impact on sales, incentives can provide additional motivation. For example, salespeople who are simply cashiers have little effect on sales and thus shouldn't be compensated with sales incentives. However, incentives are appropriate for salespeople who provide a lot of information and assistance about complex products, such as designer dresses or stereo systems. Incentives are less effective with inexperienced salespeople, who are less confident in their skills, because they inhibit learning and thereby can cause excessive stress.

Finally, compensation plans in which too much of the incentive is based on sales may not promote good customer service. Salespeople on commission become interested in selling anything they can to customers, but they aren't willing to spend time helping customers buy the merchandise they need. They tend to stay close to the cash register or the dressing room exits so that they can ring up a sale for a customer who's ready to buy.

Setting the Commission Percentage

Assume that a specialty store manager wants to hire experienced salespeople. To get the type of person she wants, she feels she must pay $12 an hour, and her selling costs are budgeted at 8 percent of sales. With compensation of $12 an hour, salespeople need to sell $150 worth of merchandise every hour ($12 divided by 8 percent) for the store to keep within its sales cost budget. The manager believes the best compensation would be one-third salary and two-thirds commission, so she decides to offer a compensation plan consisting of a $4-an-hour salary (33 percent of $12) and a 5.33 percent commission on sales. If salespeople sell $150 worth of merchandise an hour, they'll earn $12 an hour ($4 an hour in salary plus $150 multiplied by 5.33 percent, which equals $8 an hour in commission).

Legal Issues in Compensation

The **Fair Labor Standards Act** of 1938 set minimum wages, maximum hours, child labor standards, and overtime-pay provisions. Enforcement of this law is particularly important to retailers because they hire many low-wage employees and teenagers and ask their employees to work long hours.

The **Equal Pay Act,** now enforced by the EEOC, prohibits unequal pay for men and women who perform equal work or work of comparable worth. *Equal work* means that the jobs require the same skills, effort, and responsibility and are performed in the same working environment. *Comparable worth* implies that men and women who perform different jobs of equal worth should be compensated the same. Differences in compensation are legal when compensation is determined by a seniority system, an incentive compensation plan, or market demand.

CONTROLLING COSTS

Labor scheduling, making stores "green" and more energy-efficient, and store maintenance offer three opportunities to reduce store operating expenses. Retailing View 16.4 describes how a convenience store chain reengineered its operations to reduce costs and increase customer service.

Labor Scheduling

Using store employees efficiently is an important and challenging problem. Although store employees provide important customer service and merchandising functions that can increase sales, they also are the store's largest operating expense. **Labor scheduling** (determining the number of employees assigned to each area of the store) is difficult because of the multiple shifts and part-time workers needed to staff stores up to 24 hours a day, seven days a week. In addition, customer traffic varies greatly during the day and the week. Bad weather, holidays, and sales can dramatically alter normal shopping patterns and staffing needs.

Managers can spot obvious inefficiencies like long checkout lines and sales associates with nothing to do. But some inefficiencies are more subtle. For example, if 6 percent of a store's sales volume and 9 percent of the total labor-hours occur between 2 and 3 p.m., the store might be overstaffed during this time period. Many retailers utilize computer software to deal with the complexities of labor scheduling.[32] The software tracks individual store sales, transactions, units sold, and customer traffic in 15-minute increments over seven weeks, and then compares the data to the previous year's, before scheduling workers. It also considers factors like how much time it takes to sell particular merchandise or unload a truck to predict how many workers will be needed at certain times. For example, a women's apparel specialty store retailer established standards for how long it should take for employees to complete certain tasks: three seconds to greet a shopper; two minutes to help someone trying on clothing; 32 seconds to fold a sweater; and, most important, five minutes to clinch a sale. Its goal was to figure out how many employees it needed in a store at any given time, on the basis of customer traffic.[33]

Although these scheduling systems benefit both retailers and customers, they can have an adverse impact on employees. Sales associates can be burdened with unpredictable schedules; they may be asked to be "on call" to meet customer surges or may be sent home because of a lull. Some systems assigned the most productive sales associates to the key selling times. However, when retailers provide this extrinsic reward on the basis of sales, associates may engage in practices, such as high-pressure selling, that have positive short-term effects but decrease customer satisfaction and have negative long-term effects.[34]

Retailers also consider the mix of full-time and part-time employees when scheduling labor.[35] Although full-time employees provide stability in the workforce, part-time workers typically receive lower per-hour wages and no benefits. Retailers trying to control labor costs often shift to more part-time employees. Some employees prefer part-time work because it fits in with their lifestyle, whereas others are concerned that a shift toward more part-time work will reduce their incomes and benefits.

Labor scheduling is even more difficult in some European countries. For example, in France, a store manager works only 35 hours a week, rarely works at night or on weekends, and has six weeks of annual paid vacation. A store manager in the United States with similar responsibilities works 44 hours a week, including evening and weekend shifts; frequently brings work home at night; spends some off-time shopping the competitors; and has two weeks of paid vacation. Workers in France are guaranteed five weeks' paid vacation by law. Most stores other than discount stores are closed during lunch and after 7 p.m. Few stores are open on Sunday. Store hours are even more restricted in Germany and Italy.

16.4   RETAILING VIEW   Increasing Operating Efficiency

Sheetz, a convenience store chain with 310 stores based in Altoona, Pennsylvania, started a series of detailed studies to determine how store-level tasks could be performed more efficiently. It looked at everything from how the store managers closed out the day to how the staff emptied the trash. Two years after the company implemented the recommendations from the study, it had saved $5.1 million in payroll costs alone.

Sheetz found that store managers were taking three to four hours to close out their sales day. Each day, they had to fill out 40 computer screens of information and would spend an hour looking for a $5 error. Furthermore, the time spent on closing was affecting customer service. Managers would do the paperwork during the morning of the following day, the busiest traffic time, when they should have been out in the stores managing. When Sheetz

Sheetz, a Pennsylvania-based convenience store chain, reengineered its operations to reduce costs and increase customer service.

reexamined these practices, it eliminated over 160,000 hours annually of time the store managers were spending on nonproductive administrative tasks.

Sheetz also found that a lot of the information being sent to store managers was of questionable value. There were too many redundant reports. Thus, the 204 reports that had been available on the store managers' computers were reduced to 23.

Sheetz saved 55 employee-hours per week per store by reexamining its labor scheduling. Before the study, staffing for stores was based on sales. However, this approach did not consider that some stores generate a lot of sales from labor-intensive activities such as food service, while others derive

sales from labor-free, pay-at-the-pump transactions (called *outside sales* by convenience store operators). Some tasks performed in the store were eliminated, and the company stopped tracking newspapers at the SKU level. On some newspapers, Sheetz makes only a two-cent margin. If store employees spend time receiving and tracking them by SKU, the firm loses money on each paper it sells.

Sources: "Sheetz Hits the Mark," *Retail Merchandiser*, September–October 2007, pp. 28–31; Neil Stern, "Convenience REBORN," *Chain Store Age*, May 2007, pp. 34–39; Rick Romel, "Convenience Stores with a Little Extra," *Knight Ridder Tribune Business*, May 9, 2005, p. 1.

Green and Energy-Efficient Stores

Increasing energy costs, coupled with a greater awareness of businesses' and society's impact on the environment, have caused retailers to make their buildings more energy-efficient and **green**—made or maintained in an environmentally and ecologically friendly way, such as by using renewable resources. For example, the Maine-based grocery chain Hannaford Bros. Co. is building a new, state-of-the-art, green supermarket.[36] Plants growing on part of the store's roof add insulation and control storm water. On another part of the roof, photovoltaic panels generate solar energy. The store also relies on geothermal heating and cooling, high-efficiency refrigeration, energy-efficient lighting, and an advanced recycling program.

Going green increases profits as well as being socially responsible. For example, Peter DiPasqua, a Subway franchisee with 89 stores in central Florida, originally thought his green store in Kissimmee was largely a "feel-good thing." The store cost about 20 percent more to build, but now he is impressed with the benefits of LEED-certified construction. He saves 20 percent a month on electricity even though the store is selling 43 percent more than a store down the street. "I underestimated it all," he said. "What's amazing is 43 percent more bakes in the oven, and doors opening and toilets flushing. And to have 20 percent less energy consumption?"[37]

Walmart is controlling energy consumption by all its stores with a team of 100 specialists at its corporate headquarters.[38] If a store manager wants the temperature lowered, the corporate energy team asks a series of questions, such as the exact spot in the store that feels too warm, and then possibly approves the request. Walmart is also reducing its energy costs by buying more produce closer to its stores, which minimizes food-delivery trips; building "high-efficiency" stores that employ wind power and "waterless" urinals; and installing state-of-the-art air-conditioning/heating, refrigeration, and lighting systems.

Walmart also is implementing a strategy to ensure that it has a positive impact on the environment by reducing packaging across its global supply chain by 5 percent by 2013.[39] In addition to preventing millions of pounds of trash from reaching landfills, it is saving energy and reducing emissions. Walmart and its suppliers have developed a packaging scorecard to evaluate their performance, using metrics known as the "7Rs of Packaging": remove, reduce, reuse, recycle, renew, revenue, and read.

Store Maintenance

Store maintenance entails the activities involved with managing the exterior and interior physical facilities associated with the store. The exterior facilities include the parking lot, entrances to the store, and signs on the outside of the

Hannaford supermarket is being socially responsible in protecting the environment and also reducing energy costs.

store. The interior facilities include the walls, flooring, ceiling, and displays and signs. Store maintenance affects both the sales generated in the store and the cost of running the store. A store's cleanliness and neatness affect consumer perceptions of the quality of its merchandise, but maintenance is costly. For instance, floor maintenance for a 40,000-square-foot home center runs about $10,000 a year. Poor maintenance shortens the useful life of air-conditioning units, floors, and fixtures.

REDUCING INVENTORY SHRINKAGE

An important issue facing store management is reducing inventory losses due to employee theft, shoplifting, mistakes, inaccurate records, and vendor errors. Examples of employee mistakes are failing to ring up an item when it's sold and miscounting merchandise when it's received or during physical inventories. Inventory shrinkage due to vendor mistakes arises when vendor shipments contain less than the amount indicated on the packing slip.

Although shoplifting receives the most publicity, employee theft accounts for more inventory loss. A recent survey attributes 47 percent of inventory shrinkage to employee theft, 32 percent to shoplifting, 14 percent to mistakes and inaccurate records, and 4 percent to vendor fraud, with an unaccounted for 3 percent.[40]

In developing a loss prevention program, retailers confront a trade-off between providing shopping convenience and a pleasant work environment, on the one hand, and preventing losses due to shoplifting and employee theft, on the other. The key to an effective loss prevention program is determining the most effective way to protect merchandise while preserving an open, attractive store atmosphere and a feeling among employees that they are trusted. Loss prevention requires coordination among store management, visual merchandising, and store design.

REFACT

Total shrinkage in the United States is estimated at $45.5 billion a year.[41]

Calculating Shrinkage

Shrinkage is the difference between the recorded value of inventory (at retail prices) based on merchandise bought and received and the value of the actual inventory (at retail prices) in stores and distribution centers, divided by retail sales during the period. For example, if accounting records indicate that inventory should be $1,500,000, the actual count of the inventory reveals $1,236,000, and sales were $4,225,000, the shrinkage is 6.2 percent [($1,500,000 − $1,236,000)/ $4,225,000]. Reducing shrinkage is an important store management issue. Retailers' annual loss from shrinkage averages about 1.6 percent of sales.[42] Every dollar of inventory shrinkage translates into a dollar of lost profit.

Organized and High-Tech Retail Theft

Although more than 70 percent of shoplifting is performed by amateurs, professional shoplifters now account for an estimated $15 billion to $30 billion in losses annually, representing almost 25 percent of reported shoplifting cases. These gangs of professional thieves concentrate in over-the-counter medications, infant formula, health and beauty aids, electronics, and specialty clothing. Internet sales, especially through auctions, have provided a ready outlet for this merchandise.

One popular scam is to create counterfeit bar codes at lower prices.[43] For example, a thief created $19 bar codes for $100 Lego sets and got away with sets worth approximately $600,000. Bar-code thieves are hard to catch, because when an alert cashier notices the mispriced item, the thief can either pay the difference or just walk out the door.

REFACT

Target Corp. estimates that more than 50 percent of theft at the Target chain involves some high-tech twist—whether in how the goods are stolen or how they are unloaded.[44]

Another technology-based scam is tampering with gift cards by professional and amateur shoplifters and employees. The thieves may create duplicate gift cards that can be used by the thief or resold online, or they may use active gift card account information to create duplicate cards or make Web purchases. Thieves also have been known to steal merchandise and then return it to the store for credit in the form of gift cards. An excellent market for gift cards is eBay. It is estimated that 70 percent of the gift cards sold on eBay were fraudulently obtained.[45]

Some gangs are using store credits to steal.[46] In one case, a valid $500 store credit receipt was scanned and digitally altered to $1,200. Then gang members printed copies and presented them in 16 stores across 12 states within an hour of one another.

Detecting and Preventing Shoplifting

Losses due to shoplifting can be reduced by store design, merchandise policies, special security measures, personnel policies, and prosecution of shoplifters.[47]

Store Design   The following store design issues should be used to reduce inventory shrinkage:

* Do not place expensive or small merchandise near an entrance.
* Keep the height of fixtures low and arranged with no "blind spots" so that the store maintains open sight lines to store entrances and dressing rooms and employees can see customers in the store and watch for shoplifters while providing better service.
* Use mirrors. Strategically placed one-way observation mirrors and hanging mirrors can help store employees observe customers.
* Because cash wraps are always staffed, they should be near areas where theft is likely to occur. (**Cash wraps** are the places in a store where customers can buy their purchases and have them "wrapped"—placed in a bag.)
* Alternate clothing hanger directions. Professional shoplifters can steal a tremendous amount of clothing by grabbing it off the rack. If the hangers are alternated, it is difficult for thieves to steal a lot at once.

Merchandise Policies   The following merchandise policies should be utilized to reduce inventory shrinkage:

* Require a receipt for all returns, because many shoplifters steal with the intent of returning the merchandise for a cash refund.
* Lock up small, expensive items. Expensive apparel items can be chained. Legitimate customers will understand, and shoplifters will be deterred.

Security Measures   The following security measures help reduce inventory shrinkage:

* Use closed-circuit TV cameras that can be monitored from a central location. Because purchasing the equipment and hiring people to monitor the system can be expensive, some retailers install nonoperating equipment that looks like a TV camera to provide a psychological deterrent to shoplifters but save costs.
* Use **electronic article surveillance (EAS) systems.** These special tags are placed on merchandise. When the merchandise is purchased, the tags are deactivated by the point-of-sale (POS) scanner. If a shoplifter tries to steal the merchandise, the active tags are sensed when the shoplifter passes a detection device at the store exit and an alarm is triggered. If the store cannot afford an EAS system, it can still use the EAS tags to deter

Retailers use **EAS** tags to reduce shoplifting. The tags contain a device that is deactivated when the merchandise is purchased. If a customer has not purchased the merchandise, an alarm is triggered when the stolen merchandise passes through sensor gates at the store's exit.

prospective thieves. The EAS tags do not affect shopping behavior, because most customers do not realize they're on the merchandise. Due to the effectiveness of tags in reducing shoplifting, retailers using them can increase sales by displaying theft-prone, expensive merchandise openly rather than locking or chaining it up. Historically, supermarkets have attached EAS tags to small, valuable items targeted by thieves, such as perfume, DVDs, and razor blades—the most commonly stolen items. Now they are tagging joints of lamb, organic chickens, and even pecorino cheese.[49]

Personnel Policies   The following personnel policies may help deter shoplifting:

- Use mystery and honesty shoppers—people posing as real shoppers—to watch for employee and customer theft.
- Have store employees monitor fitting rooms. Fitting rooms provide a good environment for stealing.
- Store employees should be trained to be aware, visible, and alert to potential shoplifting situations. Exhibit 16–7 outlines some rules for spotting shoplifters. Perhaps the best deterrent to shoplifting is an alert employee who is very visible.
- Provide excellent customer service. If employees know the customers and offer assistance, shoplifters will be deterred.

Prosecution   Many retailers have a policy of prosecuting all shoplifters. They feel a strictly enforced prosecution policy deters shoplifters. Some retailers also

EXHIBIT 16–7
Spotting Shoplifters

DON'T ASSUME THAT ALL SHOPLIFTERS ARE POORLY DRESSED
To avoid detection, professional shoplifters dress in the same manner as customers patronizing the store. Over 90 percent of all amateur shoplifters arrested have the cash, checks, or credit to purchase the merchandise they stole.

SPOT LOITERERS
Amateur shoplifters frequently loiter in areas as they build up the nerve to steal something. Professionals also spend time waiting for the right opportunity but less conspicuously than amateurs.

LOOK FOR GROUPS
Teenagers planning to shoplift often travel in groups. Some members of the group divert employees' attention while others take the merchandise. Professional shoplifters often work in pairs. One person takes the merchandise and passes it to a partner in the store's restroom, phone booths, or restaurant.

LOOK FOR PEOPLE WITH LOOSE CLOTHING
Shoplifters frequently hide stolen merchandise under loose-fitting clothing or in large shopping bags. People wearing a winter coat in the summer or a raincoat on a sunny day may be potential shoplifters.

WATCH THE EYES, HANDS, AND BODY
Professional shoplifters avoid looking at merchandise and concentrate on searching for store employees who might observe their activities. Shoplifters' movements might be unusual as they try to conceal merchandise.

sue shoplifters in civil proceedings for restitution of the stolen merchandise and the time spent in the prosecution.

Although many of these measures reduce shoplifting, they can also make the shopping experience more unpleasant for honest customers. The atmosphere of an apparel store is diminished when guards, mirrors, and TV cameras are highly visible. Customers may find it hard to try on clothing secured with a lock and chain or an electronic tag. They can also be uncomfortable trying on clothing if they think they're secretly being watched via a surveillance monitor. Thus, when evaluating security measures, retailers need to balance the benefits of reducing shoplifting with the potential losses in sales.

Reducing Employee Theft

The most effective approach for reducing employee theft and shoplifting is to create a trusting, supportive work environment. When employees feel they're respected members of a team, they identify their goals with the retailer's goals. Stealing from their employer thus becomes equivalent to stealing from themselves or their family, and they go out of their way to prevent others from stealing from the "family." Thus, retailers with a highly committed workforce and low turnover typically have low inventory shrinkage. Additional approaches for reducing employee theft are carefully screening employees, creating an atmosphere that encourages honesty and integrity, and establishing security policies and control systems.

The increasing use of gift cards has created a new opportunity for employee theft. At the Saks flagship store in Manhattan, a 23-year-old sales clerk was caught ringing up $130,000 in false merchandise returns and siphoning the money onto a gift card. The sales associate entered a fake refund for merchandise and then used a POS terminal to electronically fill a gift card for the amount refunded and took the card. Walking out of the store with a card in the wallet is a lot easier than lugging a big-screen TV out the back of a store.

Online marketplaces like eBay provide a convenient place for thieves to convert fraudulently acquired gifts and other merchandise into cash. It is one thing for a shopper to return a $300 power drill, refund it for a $300 gift card, and auction the card on eBay, but it is far more suspicious when someone auctions 20 gift cards. Many retailers have loss prevention specialists who monitor online auctions of gift cards to identify thieves. Bowing to retailers' concerns, eBay now bars sellers from auctioning cards over $500 in value or more than one gift card a week. Other approaches for reducing employee theft are discussed in the following sections.[52]

Screening Prospective Employees   As mentioned previously, many retailers use paper-and-pencil honesty tests and undertake extensive reference checks to screen out potential employees with theft problems. A major problem related to employee theft is drug use. Some retailers now require that prospective employees submit to drug tests as a condition of employment. Employees with documented performance problems, an unusual number of accidents, or erratic time and attendance records are also tested. Unless they're involved in selling drugs, employees who test positive are often offered an opportunity to complete a company-paid drug program, submit to random testing in the future, and remain with the firm.

Establishing Security Policies and Control Systems   To control employee theft, retailers need to adopt policies related to certain activities that may facilitate theft. Some of the most prevalent policies are:

- Randomly search containers, such as trash bins, where stolen merchandise can be stored.

- Require that store employees enter and leave the store through designated entrances.

- Assign salespeople to specific POS terminals, and require that all transactions be handled through those terminals.
- Restrict employee purchases to working hours.
- Provide customer receipts for all transactions.
- Have all refunds, returns, and discounts cosigned by a department or store manager.
- Change locks periodically, and issue keys to authorized personnel only.
- Provide a locker room where all employees' handbags, purses, packages, and coats must be checked before the employees leave.
- Maintain rotating employee assignments. Team different employees together.

In the end, it is important that employees do not feel that management is overly suspicious of their actions or that they are treated with disrespect, as this sense will erode morale.

Using Technology   Retailers are turning to technology to help stop shoplifting. Some stores have installed systems that use computer software to analyze shoppers' movements captured by TV cameras. When the system recognizes unusual activity, such as a customer removing 10 items from a shelf at once or opening a case that's normally kept closed and locked, the system alerts guards via alarms or handheld devices. If someone opens a back door at 2 a.m., the system records who entered and links the alert with snapshots of the previous and next persons to use the door.[54]

A favorite trick of professional shoplifters is to load up carts and simply run out of the store. To thwart this activity, some retailers use carts equipped with radio frequency identification (RFID) chips on the cartwheels and antennas around the periphery of the store that broadcast signals to the chips. When a cart approaches the store boundary, its wheels lock up so that thieves cannot walk out with it.

Shoplifters also may use the rungs underneath the cart to sneak out items. In response, stores are mounting cameras in the cashiers' stands to scrutinize the bottom racks of carts. If an item matches an image in a database, the system computes the price of the product and adds it to the customer's bill.

Although stores already are using RFID tags to keep track of inventory in the supply chain, as the price of the tags continues to decrease, they likely will replace EAS tags altogether, because they are a more precise and inconspicuous way of tracking items on a sales floor. The tags, which come in different shapes, many smaller than postage stamps, can communicate with a handheld device, telling workers when a large number of items is being moved or leaving the store.

Because almost half of inventory shrinkage is due to employee theft, new transaction-monitoring software also pulls information from registers into a central database and looks for unusual patterns. An excess of manually entered credit card numbers could be a signal that employees are stealing customers' information. Returns of the same type of sweater 10 times in a row at one register, for instance, could indicate that an employee is processing fake returns for a friend or being conned into making fraudulent returns.

Data-mining programs combined with video technology permit a more comprehensive look at cash register activity. Managers can highlight irregular register transactions on their computers and pull up corresponding videos. This function could enable managers to catch cashiers who cut deals for their friends or pocket cash refunds. It could also curtail fraudulent returns by tracking the route customers take to the customer service desk; do they head straight there, or do they meander through the store, picking up their "return" merchandise along the way?[55]

SUMMARY

Effective store management can have a significant impact on a retail firm's financial performance. Store managers increase profits by increasing labor productivity, decrease costs through labor deployment decisions, and reduce inventory loss by developing a dedicated workforce.

Increasing store employees' productivity is challenging because of the difficulties in recruiting, selecting, and motivating store employees.

Employees typically have a range of skills and seek a spectrum of rewards. Effective store managers need to motivate their employees to work hard and develop skills so that they improve their productivity. To motivate employees, store managers need to understand what rewards each employee is seeking and then provide an opportunity for the employee to realize those rewards. Store managers must establish realistic goals for employees that are consistent with the store's goals and motivate each employee to achieve them.

Store managers also must control inventory losses due to employee theft, shoplifting, and clerical errors. Managers use a wide variety of methods to develop loss prevention programs, including security devices and employee screening during the selection process. However, the critical element of any loss prevention program is building employee loyalty to reduce employee interest in stealing and increase attention to shoplifting.

KEY TERMS

Age Discrimination in Employment Act, *440*

à la carte plan, *451*

Americans with Disabilities Act (ADA), *440*

autocratic leader, *443*

cash wraps, *459*

democratic leader, *444*

disability, *440*

discrimination, *439*

disparate impact, *439*

disparate treatment, *439*

drawing account, *453*

electronic article surveillance (EAS) system, *459*

Equal Employment Opportunity Commission (EEOC), *439*

Equal Pay Act, *455*

extrinsic reward, *451*

Fair Labor Standards Act, *455*

green, *457*

group maintenance behavior, *443*

incentive compensation plan, *453*

intrinsic reward, *451*

job analysis, *435*

job application form, *437*

job description, *436*

job enrichment, *452*

labor scheduling, *455*

leadership, *443*

on-the-job training, *442*

preferred clients, *445*

quota, *453*

quota-bonus plan, *454*

sexual harassment, *447*

shrinkage, *458*

store maintenance, *457*

straight commission, *453*

straight salary compensation, *453*

structured training program, *441*

task performance behavior, *443*

transformational leader, *444*

GET OUT AND DO IT!

1. **CONTINUING CASE ASSIGNMENT** Go to the store you have selected for the Continuing Case Assignment, and meet with the person responsible for personnel scheduling. Report on the following:
   - Who is responsible for employee scheduling?
   - How far in advance is the schedule made?
   - How are breaks and lunch periods planned?
   - How are overtime hours determined?
   - On what is the total number of budgeted employee hours for each department based?
   - How is flexibility introduced into the schedule?
   - How are special requests for days off handled?
   - How are peak periods (hours, days, or seasons) planned for?
   - What happens when an employee calls in sick at the last minute?
   - What are the strengths and weaknesses of the personnel scheduling system from the manager's and employees' perspectives?

2. **CONTINUING CASE ASSIGNMENT** Go to the store you have selected for the Continuing Case Assignment, and talk to the person responsible for human resource management to find out how sales associates are compensated and evaluated for job performance.
   - How are sales associates trained? What are the criteria for evaluation?
   - How often are they evaluated?
   - Do salespeople have quotas? If they do, how are they set? What are the rewards of exceeding quotas? What are the consequences of not meeting these objectives?

- Can sales associates make a commission? If yes, how does the commission system work? What are the advantages of a commission system? What are the disadvantages?
- If there is no commission system, are any incentive programs offered? Give an example of a specific program or project used by the store to boost employee morale and productivity.

Evaluate each of the answers to these questions, and make recommendations for improvement where appropriate.

3. **GO SHOPPING** Go to a store, observe the security measures in the store, and talk with a manager about the store's loss prevention program.
   - Are there surveillance cameras? Where are they located? Are the cameras monitored, or are they just there to thwart shoplifting?
   - What is the store's policy against shoplifters?
   - What are the procedures for approaching a suspected shoplifter?
   - What roles do sales associates and executives play in the security programs?
   - Is employee theft a problem? Elaborate.
   - How is employee theft prevented in the store?
   - How is customer service related to loss prevention in the store?
   - What is this retailer doing well in terms of security and loss prevention, and in which areas should it improve its policies and procedures?

4. **INTERNET EXERCISE** Go online and research the shoplifting laws implemented by the state where you live or attend school. What are the fines, jail time, community service, or punishments for perpetrators in your local jurisdiction? What factors are weighed and evaluated in shoplifting cases? Are the laws in your state a deterrent to shoplifting? Please explain.

5. **INTERNET EXERCISE** Read the description of IntelliVid video intelligence software for the retail industry at www.americandynamics.net/products/IntelliVid_Video_Intelligence.aspx. How does this high-tech system help retailers reduce shrinkage, track suspicious behavior, and support loss prevention staff?

6. **LIBRARY EXERCISE** Go to one of your library's business databases and find an article that describes a case of a retailer violating Title VII in either its hiring or promotion practices. Summarize the case and court decision. What should this retailer do differently in the future to improve its employment policies?

7. **INTERNET EXERCISE** Go to the home page for Greening Retail (www.greeningretail.ca), and examine the company's research and programs that help retailers implement environmental best practices. Select a company in the "Featured Retailer Archive" (www.greeningretail.ca/featured/archive.dot) as a case example, and briefly descibe what this retailer is doing to be a more sustainable company.

DISCUSSION QUESTIONS AND PROBLEMS

1. How do on-the-job training, Internet training, and classroom training differ? What are the benefits and limitations of each approach?

2. Give examples of a situation in which a manager of a McDonald's fast-food restaurant should utilize different leadership styles.

3. Using the interview questions in Exhibit 16–4, role-play with another student in the class as both the interviewer and the applicant for an assistant store manager position at a store of your choice.

4. Name some laws and regulations that affect the employee management process. Which do you believe are the easiest for retailers to adhere to? Which are violated the most often?

5. What's the difference between extrinsic and intrinsic rewards? What are the effects of these rewards on the behavior of retail employees? Under what conditions would you recommend that a retailer emphasize intrinsic rewards over extrinsic rewards?

6. Many large department stores, such as JCPenney, Sears, and Macy's, are changing their salespeople's reward system from a traditional salary to a commission-based system. What problems can incentive compensation systems cause? How can department managers avoid these problems?

7. When evaluating retail employees, some stores use a quantitative approach that relies on checklists and numerical scores similar to the form in Exhibit 16–6. Other stores use a more qualitative approach, whereby less time is spent checking and adding and more time is devoted to discussing strengths and weaknesses in written form. Which is the best evaluation approach? Why?

8. Explain how changing demographics of the workforce are affecting staffing and recruiting efforts for retail sales and management positions.

9. List the skills, knowledge, and abilities that can be successfully taught to new retail employees through an orientation program, a formal training program, and on-the-job training.

10. Discuss how retailers can reduce shrinkage from shoplifting and employee theft.

11. Drugstore retailers, such as CVS, place diabetic test strips and perfume behind locked glass cabinets and nearly all over-the-counter medicines behind Plexiglas panels. These efforts are designed to deter theft. Describe how these security measures influence honest customers.

SUGGESTED READINGS

Aberson, Christopher L. "Diversity, Merit, Fairness, and Discrimination Beliefs as Predictors of Support for Affirmative-Action Policy Actions." *Journal of Applied Social Psychology* 37, no. 10 (2007), pp. 2451–2474.

Ackfeldt, Anna-Lena, and Leonard Coote. "A Study of Organizational Citizenship Behaviors in a Retail Setting." *Journal of Business Research* 58 (February 2005), pp. 151–163.

Beck, Adrian, and Colin Peacock. *New Loss Prevention: Redefining Shrinkage Management*. New York: Palgrave Macmillan, 2009.

Bernardin, H. John. *Human Resource Management: An Experiential Approach*, 5th ed. Burr Ridge, IL: McGraw-Hill, 2010.

Cascio, Wayne, and Herman Aguinis. *Applied Psychology in Human Resource Management*, 8th ed. Upper Saddle River, NJ: Pearson/Prentice Hall, 2010.

Chadwick, Clint, and Aadina Dabu. "Human Resources, Human Resource Management and the Competitive Advantage of Firms: Toward a More Comprehensive Model of Causal Linkages." *Organization Science* 20 (January 2009), pp. 253–272.

Davis, Elizabeth, Matthew Freedman, Julia Lane, and Brian McCall. "Product Market Competition and Human Resource Practices in the Retail Food Sector." *Industrial Relations* 46 (April 2009), pp. 350–372.

Esbjerg, Lars, Nuka Bucka, and Klaus G. Grunerta. "Making Working in Retailing Interesting: A Study of Human Resource Management Practices in Danish Grocery Retail Chains." *Journal of Retailing and Consumer Services* 17 (March 2010), pp. 97–108.

Grossman, Gary, and J. Robert Parkinson. *Becoming a Successful Manager*, 2nd ed. New York: McGraw-Hill, 2010.

Hollinger, Richard, and Amanda Adams. *2009 National Retail Security Survey Final Report*. Gainesville, FL: Security Research Project, University of Florida, 2010.

Ivancevich, John. *Human Resource Management*. New York: McGraw-Hill, 2009.

Lessons Learned: Hiring and Firing. Boston: Harvard Business School Press, 2008.

Mondy, R. Wayne. *Human Resource Management*, 11th ed. New York: McGraw-Hill, 2009.

Rothstein, Mark, and Lance Leibman. *Employment Law*, 6th ed. St. Paul, MN: Thomson/West, 2007.

Sennewald, Charles A., and John H. Christman. *Retail Crime, Security, and Loss Prevention: An Encyclopedic Reference*. Woburn, MA: Butterworth-Heinemann, 2008.

Store Layout, Design, and Visual Merchandising

EXECUTIVE BRIEFING

Jens Nordfält
Dean, Nordic School of Retail Management,
Stockholm School of Economics and CEO,
Hakon Swenson Research Foundation

Prior to founding the School of Retail Management and the Hakon Swenson Research Foundation, I was the CFO of an ICA AB subsidiary. ICA is the largest retailer in Scandinavia. Its convenience stores, supermarkets, and hypermarkets account for 50 percent of the food sales in Sweden.

As CFO, I analyzed the company's sales data and I was struck by how relatively minor changes in the location of products in the stores had substantial changes in the product sales. I became so interested in these effects of store design and visual merchandising that I completed a Ph.D. program in the Stockholm School of Economics on consumer behavior and established a retail research center to study in-store shopping behavior. Over the last ten years, we have conducted hundreds of field experiments with ICA and other retailers like H&M and IKEA to learn more about how the store environment affects shopping behavior.

Marketers propose the consumers go through a rational, multistage process when making a purchase decision—a process that begins with the recognition of a need and then progresses through information collection and evaluation and selection stages. However, our research, and research by others, suggests that consumers do not devote the time or effort to engage in such a thoughtful process when shopping in retail stores. In supermarkets, they are confronted with over 10,000 different products to choose from. They typically look at only one product in a category and select products in seconds. They process the vast amount of information in the store unconsciously.

CHAPTER 17

QUESTIONS

What are the critical issues retailers consider in designing a store?

What are the advantages and disadvantages of alternative store layouts?

How is store floor space assigned to merchandise departments and categories?

What are the considerations in where to display products in a category?

What are the best techniques for merchandise presentation?

How can retailers create a more appealing shopping experience?

How exciting should a store environment be?

Simply attracting the attention of shoppers has a big effect on what they buy. We find that attracting the attention of shoppers using special displays has a much bigger impact on sales than reducing price or increasing advertising. But we also find that there are a few general principles that can be used to design stores. For example, some types of special displays are more effective for specific types of products and specific types of retailers.

We have also done a number of studies of the effectiveness of digital signs. We have varied the size of signs from small 12-inch flat-panel screens to large 80-inch screens, the content displayed, and the number of screens in the store. We have found some interesting results concerning the impact of digital signage on overall store sales. The use of digital signs in hypermarkets can increase store sales by as much as 10 percent. However, sales actually decrease when digital signs are used in smaller supermarkets. It appears that the use of digital signage in smaller format distracts the attention from the products offered and reduces sales.

The environment in a store, the design of the store, and the presentation and location of merchandise in the store have a significant impact on shopping behavior. The design of a store or Web site can attract customers to visit the location, increase the time they spend in the store or at the site, and increase the amount of merchandise they purchase. Store design can also have long-term effects on building customer loyalty toward the retailer by enhancing the retailer's brand image and providing rewarding shopping experiences that encourage repeat visits.

This chapter is part of the Store Management section because store managers are responsible for implementing the design and visual merchandising developed by specialists at the retailer's corporate headquarters. They adapt the prototype plans to the unique characteristics of their stores and then make sure the image and experience provided by the design are consistent over time. However, as discussed in this chapter, store design and visual merchandising are also elements of a retailer's communication mix and play an important role in creating and reinforcing a retailer's brand image.

The chapter begins with a discussion of store design objectives. Next, the elements of store design are discussed. Then the decisions about how much space to allocate to different merchandise categories and departments and where they should be located in the store are reviewed. The chapter concludes with an examination of how retailers use store design elements, such as color, lighting, and music, to enhance the customer's shopping experience.

STORE DESIGN OBJECTIVES

REFACT

Retailers remodel their stores every eight years on average.[1]

Some store design objectives are to (1) implement the retailer's strategy, (2) build loyalty by providing a rewarding shopping experience, (3) increase sales on a visit, (4) control costs, and (5) meet legal requirements.

Implement Retail Strategy

The primary store design objective is to implement the retailer's strategy. The design must be consistent with and reinforce the retailer's strategy by meeting the needs of the target market and building a sustainable competitive advantage. For example, to develop a more upscale brand image that appeals to its European target market, McDonald's remodeled its stores with lime-green designer chairs and dark leather upholstery to create a more relaxed, sophisticated atmosphere.[2] It also implemented nine different designs for different location types and target markets, ranging from "purely simple," with minimalist decor in neutral colors, to "Qualité," featuring large pictures of lettuces and tomatoes and gleaming stainless-steel kitchen utensils such as meat grinders. In developing these redesigns, McDonald's had to make sure that the new designs projected a more appealing image but still enabled customers to recognize the store as a McDonald's and continue to have favorable associations with the McDonald's brand.

The Apple Store on Fifth Avenue in Manhattan reinforces the company's image of developing products with innovative design features.[3] Its most striking feature is a transparent glass cube, 32 feet on each side, marking the entrance to the store. The cube houses a cylindrical glass elevator and a spiral glass staircase leading to a 10,000-square-foot subterranean retail space.

Build Loyalty

When customers consistently have rewarding experiences when patronizing a retailer's store and/or Web site, they are motivated to visit the store or Web site repeatedly and develop loyalty toward the retailer. Store design plays an important role in making shopping experiences rewarding. Customers seek two types of

McDonald's restaurants in Europe feature a design that complements its strategy of targeting a more upscale market.

benefits when shopping—utilitarian and hedonic benefits.[4] Store design provides **utilitarian benefits** when it enables customers to locate and purchase products in an efficient and timely manner with minimum hassle.

Utilitarian benefits are becoming increasingly important with the rise in two-income and single head-of-household families. Due to the limited time these families have, they are spending less time shopping. They want to get their shopping done as quickly as possible. To accommodate these utilitarian-oriented shoppers, some Whole Foods stores have redesigned their checkout areas so that customers form a serpentine single line that feeds into multiple cash registers.[5] Although banks and amusement parks have used a similar checkout system for decades, supermarkets and other retailers have generally favored the one-line-per-register system, because they are concerned that a long line will scare off shoppers. However when customers stand in one line that feeds multiple checkout stations, there are no "slow" lines, delayed by a coupon-counting customer or slow cashier. Using this system, the wait can be reduced 50 to 75 percent compared with using a traditional system.

Store design provides **hedonic benefits** by offering customers an entertaining and enjoyable shopping experience. This shopping experience encourages customers to spend more time in a store because the visit itself is rewarding. For example, Cabela's, a chain of stores catering to outdoor enthusiasts, provides an educational and entertaining experience with a mix of museum-quality animal displays in colorful dioramas, huge aquariums stocked with native fish, a restaurant featuring wild-game sandwiches, and a shooting gallery providing fun along with the opportunity to learn basic shooting skills in a safe environment. Its stores are known as shopping and tourism destinations, drawing customers not only from the local area but also from hundreds of miles away.[7]

The Apple Store in New York City reinforces the company's image of developing and retailing products with innovative design features.

Increase Sales on Visits

A third design objective is to increase sales made to customers on a visit. Store design has a substantial effect on which products customers buy, how long they stay in the store, and how much they spend during a visit. Since so little time and thought is spent shopping and selecting items in supermarkets, the purchase decisions are greatly influenced by what products customers see during their visit and what they see is affected by the store layout and how the merchandise is presented. Thus retailers attempt to design their stores in a manner that motivates unplanned purchases. The substantial effects of the customer's experience in stores also is causing consumer packaged goods companies such as Proctor & Gamble to shift their attention and marketing communications to influencing customers when they are in stores rather than at home watching television.[8]

Control Cost

The fourth design objective is to control the cost of implementing the store design and maintaining the store's appearance. For instance, Cabela's stores, described above, are very expensive to build and maintain. Certain types of lighting that Neiman Marcus uses to effectively highlight expensive jewelry and crystal use

Cabela's store design offers hedonic benefits to its customers. The rewarding shopping experience attracts customers and motivates them to spend more time in its stores.

more electricity and are less ecologically friendly than rows of bare fluorescent bulbs.

The store design can also affect labor costs and inventory shrinkage. Some stores are organized into departments that are isolated from one another. This design provides an intimate and comfortable shopping experience that can result in more sales. However, the design prevents sales associates from observing and covering adjacent departments, which makes it necessary to have at least one sales associate permanently stationed in each department to provide customer service and prevent shoplifting.

Retailing View 17.1 describes how Walmart is building environmentally sensitive stores that reduce energy costs, help build Walmart's image as a socially responsible retailer, and enable it to provide low prices to its customers.

Another design consideration related to controlling cost is flexibility. Retailing is a very dynamic business. Competitors enter a market and cause existing retailers to change the mix of merchandise offered. As the merchandise mix changes, so must the space allocated to merchandise categories and the layout of the store change. Thus store designers attempt to design stores with maximum flexibility. Flexibility affects the ability to physically modify, move, and store components and the costs of doing so.[9]

Flexibility is an important design consideration for college bookstores because they need to expand and contract their spaces to accommodate the large seasonal fluctuations inherent in the college-bookstore business. At the beginning of a semester, considerable space needs to be allocated to textbooks. But, after the first week of the semester, the demand for textbooks decreases quickly and space allocated to textbooks needs to be reallocated to apparel and consumer electronics. The key to providing this flexibility lies in an innovative fixture and wall system that portions off the textbook area. **Fixtures** are the equipment used to display merchandise.

Legal Considerations—Americans with Disabilities Act

Store design or redesign decisions must comply with the 1990 Americans with Disabilities Act (ADA).[10] This law protects people with disabilities from discrimination in employment, transportation, public accommodations, telecommunications, and activities of state and local governments. It affects store design because the act calls for "reasonable access" to merchandise and services in retail stores that were built before 1993. Stores built after 1993 must be fully accessible.

← ramps, wide enough aisles, elevator, etc

The act also states that retailers should not have to incur "undue burdens" to comply with ADA requirements. Although retailers are concerned about the needs of their disabled customers, they are also worried that making merchandise completely accessible to people in a wheelchair or a motorized cart will result in less space available to display merchandise and thus will reduce sales. However, providing for wider aisles and more space around fixtures can result in a more pleasant shopping experience for able-bodied as well as disabled customers.

ADA does not clearly define critical terms such as "reasonable access," "fully accessible," or "undue burden." So the actual ADA requirements are being defined through a series of court cases in which disabled plaintiffs have filed class action suits against retailers.[11] On the basis of these court cases, retailers are typically required to (1) provide 32-inch-wide pathways in the main aisle, to bathrooms,

RETAILING VIEW   Walmart Goes Green and Lowers Its Energy Costs   17.1

Walmart is designing new stores and retrofitting older stores to be more energy-efficient. These stores are among the "greenest" in the world. The three main design objectives for these stores are to (1) reduce the amount of energy and natural resources required to operate and maintain a store, (2) reduce the amount of raw materials needed to construct a facility, and (3) use, when appropriate, renewable materials to construct and maintain a facility. Although many of the design features reduce the stores' impact on the environment, these stores are expensive to build, and some of their elements make economic sense only if energy costs significantly increase. Initial projections call for the energy used at these stores to be 30 to 50 percent less than at the older stores that have not been retrofitted, reducing a store's energy costs by $500,000 annually.

Some of the sustainable features are as follows:

- A wind turbine on top of a store produces enough energy to reduce a store's electricity consumption by 5 percent.

- A rainwater harvesting and treatment system provides 95 percent of the water needed for on-site irrigation and reduces demand on the local storm-water system.

- Grass for landscaping should be of varieties that do not need irrigation or mowing.

- Stores are lower in height than a typical Supercenter. The height reduction means fewer building materials are needed, plus it reduces heating and cooling needs.

- Instead of fluorescent lighting, refrigerated cases use LEDs (GE's Lumination Refrigerated Lighting system). Unlike fluorescent lights, LEDs can be switched on and off in cold temperatures without any loss of life expectancy. So the lights stay off until the customer opens the case. In addition to saving energy, the lights add a theatrical appeal for customers.

- The main store area lighting uses high-output linear fluorescent lamps that, in combination with natural daylight and dimming controls, are expected to generate a lighting savings of 300,000 kilowatt-hours a year.

- Heat generated by the building's refrigeration system is captured and redirected to heat the water used in the restroom sinks and help heat the water used in the radiant floor-heating system beneath the entries and other areas.

- Cooking oil from the fryers and waste engine oil are burned in a biofuel boiler to generate heat that is directed into the heating, ventilation, and radiant floor-heating systems, conserving energy. The boiler generates heat for the building, reducing the demand for natural gas to operate mechanical equipment.

Sources: www.walmart.com (accessed July 23, 2010); Michelle Moran, "Seeing Green," *Progressive Grocer*, March 2010, pp. 16–31; Cathy Jett, "New Design's Goal: To Cut the Clutter," *McClatchy-Tribune Business News*, October 14, 2009; Aaron Besecker, "Walmart Store Gets Green Light," *McClatchy-Tribune Business News*, August 31, 2009.

dressing rooms, and elevators, and around most fixtures, (2) lower most cash wraps (checkout stations) and fixtures so that they can be reached by a person in a wheelchair, and (3) make bathrooms and dressing rooms fully accessible. These accessibility requirements are somewhat relaxed for retailers in very small spaces and during peak sales periods such as the Christmas holidays.[12]

Design Trade-Offs

Typically, a store design cannot achieve all of these objectives, so any store design involves trade-offs among the objectives. Home Depot's traditional warehouse design can efficiently store and display a lot of merchandise with long rows of floor-to-ceiling racks, but this design is not conducive for a pleasant shopping experience, particularly for the female customers who account for more than half of the sales in home improvement centers. Women preferred to shop in Lowe's stores. So Home Depot lowered the ceilings, increased the lighting, widened the aisles, and provided better signage—design aspects that tend to appeal to women.[13]

Retailers often make trade-offs between stimulating impulse purchases and making it easy to buy products. For example, supermarkets place milk, a commonly purchased item, at the back of the store to make customers walk through the entire store, thus stimulating more impulse purchases. Realizing that some customers may want to buy only milk, Walgreen's places its milk at the front of the store, enabling it to compete head-to-head with convenience stores.

The trade-off between making it easy to find merchandise and providing an interesting shopping experience is determined by the customer's shopping needs. For example, supermarket and drugstore shoppers typically focus on utilitarian benefits and want to minimize the time they spend shopping, so the design of supermarkets emphasizes the ease of locating merchandise. In contrast, customers shopping for specialty goods like a computer, a home entertainment center, or furniture are more likely to spend time in the store browsing, comparing, and talking with the salesperson. Thus specialty store retailers that offer this type of merchandise place more emphasis on providing hedonic benefits and encouraging exploration than on making it easy to find merchandise.

Another trade-off is the balance between giving customers adequate space in which to shop and productively using this scarce resource for merchandise. For example, customers are attracted to stores with wide aisles and fixtures whose primary purpose is to display rather than hold the merchandise. However, this type of design reduces the amount of merchandise that can be available to buy and thus may also reduce impulse purchases and the customers' chances of finding what they are looking for. But too many racks and displays in a store can cause customers to feel uncomfortable and even confused. In addition, shoppers do not like it when a store is so cramped that they touch one another. This is referred to as the "butt-brush effect."[14] However, the preference for shopping in less crowded environments is not universal, as illustrated in Retailing View 17.2.

STORE DESIGN ELEMENTS

Three elements in the design of stores are the (1) layout, (2) signage, and (3) feature areas. Each of these elements is discussed in this section.

Layouts

Retailers use three general types of store layout design: grid, racetrack, and free form. Each of these layouts has advantages and disadvantages that are discussed in this section.

Grid Layout   The **grid layout,** illustrated in Exhibit 17–1, has parallel aisles with merchandise on shelves on both sides of the aisles. Cash registers are located at the entrances/exits of the stores.

The grid layout is well suited for customers who are primarily interested in the utilitarian benefits offered by the store. They are not interested in the hedonic benefits provided by a visually exciting design. They want to easily locate products they want to buy, and they make their purchases as quickly as possible. Most supermarkets and full-line discount stores use the grid layout because this design enables their customers to easily find the product they are looking for and minimize the time spent on a shopping task that most don't enjoy.

The grid layout is also cost-efficient. There's less wasted space with the grid layout than with other layouts because the aisles are all the same width and designed to be just wide enough to accommodate shoppers and their carts. The use of high shelves for merchandise enables more merchandise to be on the sales floor compared with other layouts. Finally, because the fixtures are generally standardized, the cost of the fixtures is low.

RETAILING VIEW   Western Store Designs Are Not Appealing to Indian Shoppers   **17.2**

Kishore Biyani's supermarkets in Mubai, India, were initially designed like most Western-style supermarkets. But customers walked down the wide aisles, past neatly stocked shelves, and out the door without buying. Biyani soon recognized that part of his target market, lower-middle-income customers, did not like the sterile environment. His other target market segment, wealthier families, generally employed servants to do the grocery shopping. These servants were accustomed to shopping in small, cramped stores filled with haggling customers. Most Indians buy fresh produce from street vendors or small stores, and the merchandise is kept under burlap sacks.

Biyani therefore redesigned his stores to make them messier, noisier, and more cramped, much like a public market. He spent about $50,000 to replace the long wide aisles with narrow crooked ones. The stores have floors of gray granite tiling, common in markets and train stations, so that his customers will feel at home. Instead of having long aisles and tall shelves, the stores feature bins on low shelves, an arrangement that allows customers to handle the products from all different sides. Indian customers are used to buying commodities like wheat, rice, and lentils in bulk. Although bulk displays can be messy, store employees are instructed not to clean up because customers are less likely to check out the merchandise if it is in neat stacks.

Because Indian markets are noisy and full of bartering, Biyani's stores employ people to walk around using megaphones to announce promotions, adding to the din of music

Consumers in India prefer to shop in stores that are more crowded.

and commercials playing in the background. Many of the stores aren't air-conditioned, not in an effort to save money but, rather, because the heat adds to the ambience. There is no quiet, relaxed atmosphere here.

Biyani's approach to store design has worked. His company, Panaloon Retail (India), Ltd., is now the country's largest retailer, with annual sales of approximately $900 million.

Sources: Eric Bellman, "In India, a Retailer Finds Key to Success Is Clutter," *Wall Street Journal,* August 8, 2007, p. A1; Curt Hazletter, "Controlled Explosion," *Shopping Centers Today* 28, no. 3 (2007), pp. 63–67; Ritu Upadhyay, "Retailing's Rapid Rise in India," *WWD: Women's Wear Daily,* February 20, 2007.

EXHIBIT 17–1
Grid Store Layout

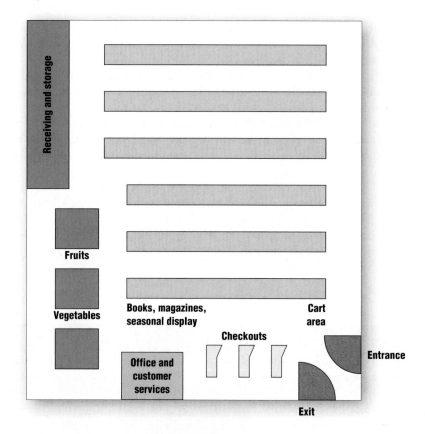

One limitation of the grid layout, from the retailer's perspective, is that customers typically aren't exposed to all the merchandise in the store because, due to the height of the shelves, they see only products displayed in the aisle they are in. Thus the layout does not encourage unplanned purchases. Supermarket retailers overcome this limitation, to some extent, by complementing the packaged goods in the center-store grid with a racetrack of fresh, perishable merchandise categories (meat, seafood, dairy, poultry, baked goods, and produce) around the periphery of the store. Unplanned purchases are also stimulated by special displays and adjacencies which are discussed later in the chapter.

In the past, supermarket retailers and consumer packaged goods manufacturers did not feel this limitation was very important. They felt that customers would be exposed to all the merchandise in the store because they would walk up and down each aisle pushing their shopping carts. However, researchers have equipped carts with GPS locators and found that most supermarket customers enter a supermarket, turn right, go along the racetrack on the periphery of the store looking down the aisles, and occasionally walk down an aisle with their carts or leave the cart at the end of the aisle and walk down the aisle to select a specific item and return to the cart. A path taken by a typical customer is shown in Exhibit 17–2.[15]

Supermarket retailers and consumer packaged goods companies now recognize this problem of decreased traffic in the center core of supermarkets. The real estate along the outer rim of supermarkets has been buzzing with improvement and excitement for several years. "Store perimeters have become warm, inviting, exciting, genuine and diverse," says David Milka, director of consumer insight for S.C. Johnson. But the center store, where S.C. Johnson brands reside, has remained "cold, obscure, boring and non-differentiated," he adds.[16]

To expose customers to more merchandise and increase their unplanned purchases in the core, supermarket retailers need to get customers to walk down more aisles. One approach for increasing traffic in the core that some

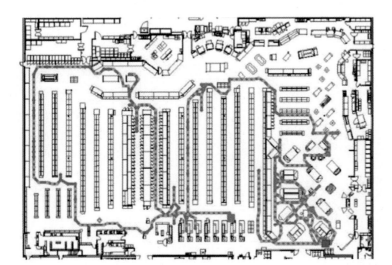

EXHIBIT 17–2
Example of a Traffic
Pattern in a Grid Layout
Supermarket

supermarket chains are considering is a layout that alters the straight aisles to form a zig-zag pattern. Products are merchandised more clearly in highly related categories by using pods and interactive kiosks and creating many aisle adjacencies to tangential products and categories. Another approach is locating power brands, brands with high awareness and market share such as Coca-Cola and Tide, and eye-attracting displays in the middle of the aisle rather than at the end of the aisle. The power brands are displayed from the top to the bottom shelves, creating a swath of color that captures the attention of customers as they peek down the aisle.

Racetrack Layout   The **racetrack layout,** also known as a **loop,** is a store layout that provides a major aisle that loops around the store to guide customer traffic around different departments within the store. Cash register stations are typically located in each department bordering the racetrack.

The racetrack layout facilitates the goal of getting customers to see the merchandise available in multiple departments and thus encourages unplanned purchasing. As customers go around the racetrack, their eyes are forced to take different viewing angles rather than looking down one aisle, as in the grid design. Low fixtures are used so that customers can see merchandise beyond the products displayed on the racetrack.

Exhibit 17–3 shows the layout of the JCPenney store in the NorthPark Center in Dallas, Texas. Because the store has multiple entrances, the racetrack layout places all departments on the main aisle by drawing customers through the store in a series of major and minor loops. To entice customers through the various departments, the design places some of the more popular departments, like juniors, toward the rear of the store. The newest items are featured on the aisles to draw customers into departments and around the loop.

To lead customers along the racetrack, the racetrack is wider than other aisles and defined by a change in flooring surface or color. For instance, the aisle flooring in the store is marblelike tile, whereas the department floors vary in material, texture, and color, depending on the desired ambience.

Since many department store customers seek hedonic benefits, they typically spend more time shopping at department stores, and the more time they spend, the more they buy.[17] Kohl's has modified the racetrack layout to increase shopper convenience and provide more utilitarian benefits to time-poor customers. Kohl's stores, in convenient, off-mall locations, are about half the size of most mall-based department stores. A middle aisle that divides the track is provided to serve as a

EXHIBIT 17–3   JCPenney Racetrack Layout at NorthPark Center in Dallas

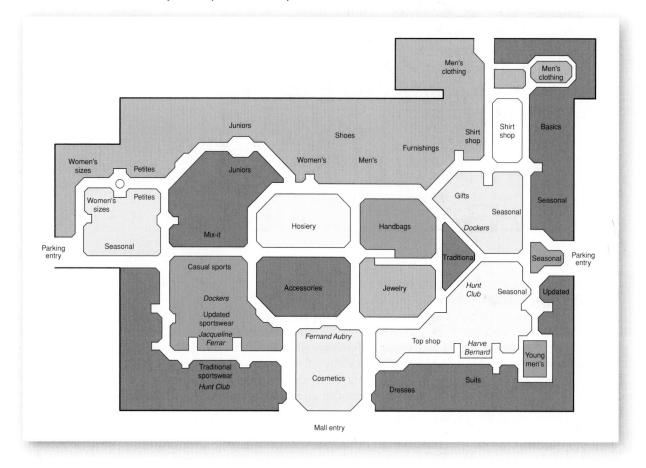

shortcut for shoppers who don't want to finish the whole circuit. Cash register stations are located at several points along the racetrack.[18]

Free-Form Layout   A **free-form layout,** also known as **boutique layout,** arranges fixtures and aisles in an asymmetric pattern (Exhibit 17–4). It provides an intimate, relaxing environment that facilitates shopping and browsing.

However, creating this pleasing shopping environment is costly. Because there is no well-defined traffic pattern, as there is in the racetrack and grid layouts, customers aren't naturally drawn around the store, and personal selling becomes more important to encourage customers to explore merchandise offered in the store. In addition, the layout reduces the amount of merchandise than can be displayed.

Signage and Graphics

Signage and graphics help customers locate specific products and departments, provide product information, and suggest items or special purchases. Graphics, such as photo panels, can reinforce a store's image.

Signage is used to identify the location of merchandise categories within a store and the types of products offered in the category. The signs are hung typically from the ceiling to enhance their visibility. Frequently, icons rather than words are used to facilitate communication with customers speaking different languages. For example, a red and yellow circus tent icon identifies the area for children's toys more effectively than a black and white, worded rectangular sign. Smaller signs are used to identify sale items and provide more information about

EXHIBIT 17–4
Free-Form Store Layout

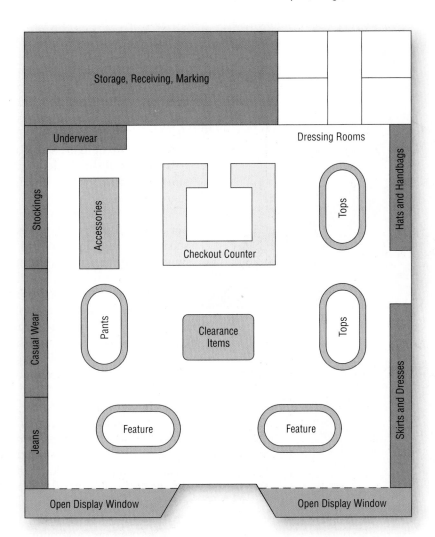

specific products. Finally, retailers may use images, such as pictures of people and places, to create moods that encourage customers to buy products. Some different types of signs are:

- **Category signage.** Used within a particular department or sector of the store, category signs are usually smaller than directional signs. Their purpose is to identify types of products offered; they are usually located near the goods to which they refer.

- **Promotional signage.** This signage describes special offers and may be displayed in windows to entice the customer into the store. For instance, value apparel stores for young women often display large posters in their windows of models wearing the items on special offer.

- **Point-of-sale signage.** Point-of-sale signs are placed near the merchandise they refer to so that customers know its price and other detailed information. Some of this information may already be on product labels or packaging. However, point-of-sale signage can quickly identify for the customer those aspects likely to be of greater interest, such as whether the product is on special offer.

Digital Signage   Traditional print signage is typically developed and produced at corporate headquarters, distributed to stores, and installed by store employees or contractors.[19] Many retailers are beginning to replace traditional

H&M effectively uses graphic photo panels to enhance its store image.

Digital signs are more effective at attracting the attention of shoppers than are traditional static signs.

signage with digital signage systems. **Digital signage** includes signs whose visual content is delivered digitally through a centrally managed and controlled network, distributed to servers in stores, and displayed on a flat-panel screen. The content delivered can range from entertaining video clips to simple displays of the price of merchandise.

Digital signage provides a number of benefits over traditional static-print signage. Due to their dynamic nature, digital signs are more effective in attracting the attention of customers and helping them recall the messages displayed. Digital signage also offers the opportunity to enhance a store's environment by displaying complex graphics and videos to provide an atmosphere that customers find appealing.[20]

Digital signage overcomes the time-to-message hurdle associated with traditional print signage. Changing market developments or events can immediately be incorporated into the digital sign. The ease and speed (flexibility) of content development and deployment of digital signage enables the content to be varied within and across stores at different times of the day or days of the week. For example, the weather could lead to automatic adjustments to digital in-store signage such as automatically advertising cold drinks like Coca-Cola when the temperature rises above 80 degrees Fahrenheit or advertising sunscreen three days before a weekend that's forecast to be sunny and warm.

Because the content is delivered digitally, it can easily be tailored to a store's market and changed during the week or even the day and hour. For instance, one retailer experimented with changing the content of its storefront digital signage. In the morning, the signage emphasized merchandise with lower price points and sale items. The merchandise at higher price points and more consistent with the retailer's brand image was displayed later in the day.

The ability to control digital signage content centrally ensures that the retailer's strategy for communicating with its customers is properly executed systemwide. Digital signage thus eliminates the challenge facing retailers that send out static signage to stores announcing a special promotion or a new marketing initiative and then find the signage stacked in the storage area, never put on the selling floor, during the promotion. Digital signage ensures that the signage is installed in the right place at the right time.

Finally, digital signage eliminates the costs associated with printing, distributing, and installing static signage. In addition, it may decrease store labor costs while improving labor productivity. However, the drawback to using digital signage is the initial cost of the display devices and the system that supports the delivery of the signage.

Feature Areas

In addition to using layout and signage, retailers can guide customers through stores and influence buying behavior through the placement of feature areas. **Feature areas** are the areas within a store that are designed to get customers' attention. They include windows, entrances, freestanding displays, end caps, promotional aisles or areas, walls, dressing rooms, and cash wraps.

Windows   Window displays draw customers into the store and provide a visual message about the type of merchandise offered in the store and the type of image the store wants to portray. Research suggests that storefront window displays are an effective tool for building the store image, particularly with new customers who are unfamiliar with the store.[21]

Entrances   The first impression caused by the entry area affects the customer's image of the store. Department stores typically have the cosmetics and fragrance categories at the main entrance because these categories are visually appealing and create a sense of excitement. While the entry area plays a prominent role in creating an image, the first 10 feet of the store are often referred to as the "decompression zone," because customers are making an adjustment to the new environment: escaping from the noisy street or mall, taking off their sunglasses, closing their umbrellas, and developing a visual impression of the entire store. Customers are not prepared to evaluate merchandise or make purchase decisions in the decompression zone, so retailers try to keep this area free of merchandise, displays, and signage.[22]

Freestanding Displays   **Freestanding displays** are fixtures or mannequins that are located on aisles and designed primarily to attract customers' attention and bring them into a department in stores using a racetrack or free-form layout. These fixtures often display and store the newest, most exciting merchandise in the particular department.

End Caps   **End caps** are displays located at the end of an aisle in stores using a grid layout. Due to the high visibility of end caps, sales of a product increase dramatically when that merchandise is featured on an end cap. Thus retailers use end caps for higher-margin, impulse merchandise. In the supermarket industry, vendors often negotiate for their products to be on end-cap displays when they are offering special promotional prices.

Promotional Aisle or Area   A **promotional aisle** or **promotional area** is a space used to display merchandise that is being promoted. Drugstores, for instance, use promotional aisles to sell seasonal merchandise, such as lawn and garden

End caps at Whole Foods are used to merchandise seasonal, temporary, promotional, and/or high-margin items.

products in the summer and Christmas decorations in the fall. Shaw's supermarkets contain a "10 for $10" aisle. From this promotional aisle, customers can purchase 10 selected items for $10. The products change each week and are highlighted in weekly grocery ads. Products can also be mixed, so customers do not have to buy 10 of the same item. Apparel stores, like The Gap, often place their sale merchandise at the back of the store so that customers must pass through the full-price merchandise to get to the sale merchandise.

Walls   Because retail floor space is often limited, many retailers increase their ability to store extra stock, display merchandise, and creatively present a message by utilizing wall space. Merchandise can be stored on shelving and racks and coordinated with displays, photographs, or graphics featuring the merchandise. At the French clothier Lacoste, for instance, merchandise is displayed in bold color swaths relatively high on the wall. Not only does this allow the merchandise to "tell a story," but it also helps customers feel more comfortable because they aren't crowded by racks or other people and they can get a perspective on the merchandise by viewing it from a distance.

Dressing Rooms   Dressing rooms are critical space in which customers decide whether or not to purchase an item. Large, clean, and comfortable dressing rooms put customers in the mood to buy merchandise. Women's dressing rooms often have photographs of local communities hung on the walls, fresh flowers, and natural light. Men's dressing rooms, in contrast, are decorated in dark wood, leather furniture, and linen wall coverings.

Retailers are using technologies in their dressing rooms to enhance the buying experience. Interactive mirrors, 3-D scanners, and holographic sales assistants may sound like they belong in a sci-fi movie, but they'll likely be part of the shopping experience in the near future. Currently, customers bring five or six items into the dressing room and try to narrow down their selection. Often they cannot remember how they looked in each outfit as they try the items on. By putting an interactive mirror in a dressing room, customers can simultaneously see pictures of themselves in all the items they try on.[25]

By using interactive mirrors and Web cams, customers can include friends or parents in their shopping experience. Through RFID tagging, the dressing-room registers the items shoppers take in to try on and produces video and images of the merchandise. A touch screen gives shoppers the option to invite friends

New technologies are making it easier for shoppers to try on merchandise and involve friends and family in their decision-making process.

to participate in the buying process. Through their personal cell phones or key pads, they can then send an e-mail or text message to friends. By clicking on a URL and logging on to a Web site, the friends can see the items being tried on and make comments. The Web site could also suggest other, complementary merchandise available from the retailer. Customers can then click on one of the recommendations, and it will appear in the mirror superimposed over their image, as though they were trying on the garment.[26]

Although technology and decor can enhance the experience of trying on clothing, some retailers are cautious about the extent to which they will use technology. The personal attention provided by sales associates remains the most effective agent for providing customer service.

Cash Wraps   **Cash wraps,** also known as **point-of-purchase (POP) counters** or **checkout areas,** are places in the store where customers can purchase merchandise. Because many customers go to these areas and may wait in line to make a purchase, retailers often use these areas to display impulse items. For example, in supermarkets, batteries, candy, razors, and magazines are often shelved at the checkout counter.

Discount and extreme-value retailers and category specialists use centralized checkouts at the front of their stores. But department stores have traditionally placed cash wraps off the main aisle within each department. Several department store chains are now switching to centralized cash wraps. By centralizing the checkout areas, these stores increase customer convenience and reduce staff.[27]

SPACE MANAGEMENT

The space within stores and on the stores' shelves and fixtures is a scarce resource. Space management involves two resource decisions: (1) the allocation of store space to merchandise categories and brands[28] and (2) the location of departments or merchandise categories in the store.

Space Allocated to Merchandise Categories

Some factors that retailers consider when deciding how much floor or shelf space to allocate to merchandise categories and brands are (1) the productivity of the allocated space, (2) the merchandise's inventory turnover, (3) the impact on overall store sales, and (4) the display needs for the merchandise.

Space Productivity   A simple rule of thumb for allocating space is to allocate on the basis of the merchandise's sales. For example, if artificial plants represent 15 percent of the total expected sales for a hobby and craft retailer such as Michaels, then 15 percent of the store's space is allocated to artificial plants.

But, as the discussion of marginal analysis for advertising allocations in Chapter 15 indicates, retailers should allocate space to a merchandise category on the basis of its effect on the profitability of the entire store. In practice, this recommendation means that Michaels should add more space to the artificial plant section as long as the profitability of the additional space is greater that the profitability of the category from which space was taken away. In this condition, the additional space for artificial plants will increase the profitability of the entire store. However, at some point, it will be more profitable to not take away space from other categories.

Two commonly used measures of space productivity are **sales per square foot** and **sales per linear foot.** Apparel retailers that display most of their merchandise on freestanding fixtures typically measure space productivity as sales per square foot. In supermarkets, most merchandise is displayed on shelves. Because the shelves have approximately the same width, only the length, or the linear dimension sales per linear foot, is used to assess space productivity.

A more appropriate productivity measure, such as gross margin per square foot, would consider the contribution generated by the merchandise, not just the sales. Thus, if salty snacks generate $400 in gross margin per linear foot and canned soup generates only $300 per linear foot, more space should be allocated to salty snacks. However, factors other than marginal productivity need to be considered when making space allocation decisions. These factors are discussed in the next section.

In addition, retailers need to allocate space to maximize the profitability of the store, not just a particular merchandise category or department. For instance, supermarkets "overallocate" space to some low-profitability categories such as milk because an extensive assortment in these categories attracts customers to the store and positively affects the sales of other categories. Retailers might also overallocate space to categories purchased by their platinum customers, the customers with the highest lifetime value.

Inventory Turnover   Inventory turnover affects space allocations in two ways. First, as discussed in Chapter 12, both inventory turnover and gross margin contribute to GMROI—a measure of the retailer's return on its merchandise inventory investment. Thus, merchandise categories with higher inventory turnover merit more space than merchandise categories with lower inventory turnover.

Second, the merchandise displayed on the shelf is depleted quicker for fast-selling items with high inventory turnover. Thus, more space needs to be allocated to fast-selling merchandise to minimize the need to restock the shelf frequently to reduce stockouts.

Display Considerations   The physical limitations of the store and its fixtures affect space allocation. For example, the store planner needs to provide enough merchandise to fill an entire fixture dedicated to a particular item.

A retailer might decide that it wants to use a merchandise display to build its image. For example, JCPenney has a very appealing offering of its private-label bath towels. To emphasize this offering, it might overallocate space for bath towels and present a wide range of colors.

Location of Merchandise Categories and Design Elements

As discussed previously, the store layout, signage, and feature areas can guide customers through the store. The location of merchandise categories also plays a role in how customers navigate through the store.[29] By strategically placing impulse and demand/destination merchandise throughout the store, retailers increase the chances that customers will shop the entire store and that their attention will be focused on the merchandise that the retailer is most interested in selling—merchandise with a high GMROI. **Demand/destination merchandise** is products that customers have decided to buy before entering the store.

As customers enter the store and pass through the decompression zone, they are welcomed with introductory displays, including graphics. Once through the decompression zone, they often turn right (in Western cultures) and observe the prices and quality of the first items they encounter. This area, referred to as the "strike zone," is critical because it creates the customer's first impression of the store's offering. Thus, retailers display some of their most compelling merchandise in the strike zone.

After passing through the strike zone, the most heavily trafficked and viewed area is the right-hand side of the store. By this point in their journey through the store, customers have become accustomed to the environment, have developed a first impression, and are ready to make purchase decisions. Thus the right-hand side is a prime area for displaying high GMROI merchandise. For example, supermarkets typically locate the produce section in this area because produce appeals to the shoppers' senses. The smell of fresh fruits and vegetables gets a shopper's mouth watering, and the best grocery store customer is a hungry one.

Impulse Merchandise   The prime store locations for selling merchandise are heavily trafficked areas such as 10 feet beyond the entrance on the right side of the store, the right-hand side of the store, and areas near escalators and cash wraps. In multilevel stores, a space's value decreases the farther it is from the entry-level floor. Thus, **impulse products,** or products that are purchased without planning, such as fragrances and cosmetics in department stores and magazines in supermarkets, are almost always located near the front of the store, where they're seen by everyone and may actually draw people into the store.

Demand Merchandise   Demand merchandise and promotional merchandise are often placed in the back left-hand corner of the store. Placing high-demand merchandise in this location pulls customers through the store, increasing the visibility of other products along the way. So supermarkets typically put items almost everyone buys—milk, eggs, butter, and bread—in the back left-hand corner. In department stores, children's merchandise and furniture, as well as customer service areas like beauty salons, credit offices, and photography studios, are demand or destination areas and thus located in lightly trafficked areas of the store.

The checkout counter at a supermarket is an ideal place to display merchandise typically bought on impulse.

Special Merchandise   Some merchandise categories involve a buying process that is best accomplished in a lightly trafficked area. For example, Steuben glass sculptures are unique, expensive art pieces that require thought and concentration for their purchase decision. Thus Neiman Marcus locates this merchandise in a lightly trafficked area to minimize distractions to customers contemplating a purchase. Similarly, women's lingerie is typically located in a remote area to offer a more private shopping experience.

Categories that require large amounts of floor space, like furniture, are often located in less desirable locations. Some categories, like curtains, need significant wall space, whereas others, like shoes, require easily accessible storage rooms.

The lingerie department is typically located in a low-traffic area in a department store to give customers some privacy as they look through the merchandise.

Category Adjacencies   Retailers often put complementary categories next to each other to encourage unplanned purchases. For example, men's dress shirts and ties are located next to each other between men's and boy's apparel. Sporting goods retailers often locate exercise equipment next to sporting goods and apparel for children so that mothers can see children while the mothers are shopping for treadmills.

Location of Merchandise within a Category

Retailers use a variety of rules to locate specific SKUs within a category.[30] For instance, supermarkets and drugstores typically place private-label brands to the right of national brands. Because Western consumers read from left to right, they will see the higher-priced national brand first and then see and possibly purchase the lower-priced, higher-margin private-label item on the right that looks similar to the national brand. Produce departments in grocery stores are arranged so that apples are the first item most customers see, because apples are a very popular produce item and thus can best initiate a buying pattern.

Supermarkets typically display merchandise on four shelves, with the most profitable merchandise on the third shelf from the floor. The third shelf attracts the most attention because it is at eye level for adults. Merchandise that appeals to a smaller group of customers is often displayed on the top shelf because reaching for the items requires significant effort. Heavy, bulky items are stocked on the bottom shelf for safety reasons.

However, when purchase decisions are influenced by shorter consumers, positioning merchandise on the lower shelves might be more effective. For example, children may influence breakfast cereal purchases when accompanying their parents to the supermarket. Thus the second shelf from the floor might be a prime location for the most profitable cereal brands. The most appealing and profitable placement for pet treats might be on the bottom shelf to appeal to pets accompanying their pet parents on visits to a pet supply supercenter.

Some tools, discussed in the following section, which retailers use to make decisions on the positioning of items in a category are planograms, videotapes of consumers as they move through the store, and virtual-store software. Retailing View 17.3 outlines suggestions that a vendor, Nestlé Purina, has for merchandising the pet food category.

Planograms   A **planogram** is a diagram that shows how and where specific SKUs should be placed on retail shelves or displays to increase customer purchases. The locations can be illustrated using photographs, computer output, or artists' renderings. In developing the planogram, retailers need to make the category visually appealing, consider the manner in which customers shop (or the manner in which the retailer would like customers to shop), and achieve the retailer's strategic and financial objectives. The technology for computer-generated planograms is quite sophisticated.

Planograms are also useful for merchandise that doesn't fit nicely on shelves in supermarkets or discount stores. Most specialty apparel retailers provide their managers with photographs and diagrams of how merchandise should be displayed. Retailing View 17.4 describes how the SAS planogramming system automated Marks & Spencer's food business.

Virtual-Store Simulation   Virtual-store simulations are another tool used to determine the effects of placing merchandise in different areas of a store and evaluating the profit potential for new items.[31] In these simulations, customers stand in front of computer screens that depict a store aisle. Retina-tracking devices record the eye movements of the customers. When the customers push forward on a handle, similar to the handle on a shopping cart, they progress down the simulated aisle. Customers

RETAILING VIEW   Suggestions for Merchandising a Pet Food Category   17.3

On the basis of an audit of many major retailers across multiple retail formats, Nestlé Purina offers the following suggestions on how to best allocate space within the pet category.

Space Allocation

The typical supermarket dedicates about 100 feet of gondola run to the pet category. The allocation varies widely, however, from a low of about 60 feet to a high of nearly 150 feet. Supermarkets with larger **sets** (space devoted to the pet category) have roughly a 60-40 split between foods (traffic drivers) and nonfoods (higher margin). Supercenters and pet category specialties have about one-third of the space for foods and two-thirds for higher-margin supplies. Supermarkets with smaller sets have about three-quarters of the space dedicated to foods and one-quarter to supplies. Retailers tend to dedicate about 60 percent of available food space to dog items and about 40 percent to cat items. Space allocated across food types (wet, dry, treats) differs widely between species and also by region of the country. The typical retailer across all formats allocates about half or more of total dog food space to dry foods. The remaining space is nearly evenly split between dog treats and wet dog foods. On the cat side, however, the dry-wet division is much more evenly split. Dry cat foods represent half of the cat category space, while the other half is occupied mostly by wet foods except for about 5 to 10 percent that is filled by cat treats. In the eastern region of the United States, however, wet cat food has approximately 50 to 60 percent of the cat food space dedicated to canned and pouch cat food items.

Merchandising Tips

To best align the category with the in-store traffic flow, the most popular product segments should be at the main entrance to the aisle. Since customers entering the store generally circle in a counterclockwise pattern, the predominant traffic flow in center-store aisles tends to be from the back of the store toward the front checkouts. In the pet aisle:

- Dog products should be across the aisle from cat products.
- Place the pet category as close to the back of the store as possible in stores with less than a full aisle for pet products.

This is a pet food category set consistent with recommendations developed by Nestlé Purina, a leading manufacturer of pet foods, using category and consumer research.

- Face in-aisle shippers toward the back of the store.
- Establish back-of-store dedicated end caps—this is the gateway to the aisle.
- Place shippers and clip strips on the left side of the aisle, since shoppers with carts buy 2-to-1 from items on their left in center-store aisles.
- Place treats, supplies, premium products, and signature items in the hot zone (the first 8 feet that can be seen as customers circle the core) to attract the "aisle skippers," those shoppers who tend to skip the pet aisle completely.
- Put planned purchase items, dog food and cat food, closer to the center of the aisle to increase total aisle exposure.

Vertical blocking (displaying the same merchandise vertically on the shelves) is consistent with the way customers buy the dry and wet pet food categories. Each segment, dry and wet, is seen as a separate purchase decision, and shoppers view these product categories differently. They begin with an initial scan of a product category, seeing only about 50 percent of the brands on the shelf. Then they return to a more manageable "consideration set" from which they make their final decision. Vertical blocking allows shoppers to easily and quickly make "like-product" comparisons. Shoppers need to be able to compare products, price, ingredients, and package size on similar items.

Source: Nestlé Purina PetCare, "Creating Your Most Effective Pet Aisle," www.retailwire.com/objects/objects.ctm. 851.

Kimberly-Clark is using virtual-store software that uses a retina-tracking device to record a customer's glances. The information obtained from the software enables the retailer to get a fast read on new product designs and displays without having to conduct real-life tests in the early stages of product development.

can virtually reach forward, pick an item off the shelf, look at the packaging, and then place the item in the virtual cart. These virtual shopping trips allow retailers and their suppliers to develop a better understanding of how customers will respond to different planograms.

Videotaping Consumers Another research method used to assess customer reactions to planograms involves tracking customers in actual store environments. GPS tracking devices are placed in customer shopping carts and on shoppers to determine where customers and carts go in a store. Small video cameras are strapped on the shoppers' foreheads

17.4 RETAILING VIEW   Marks & Spencer Automates with Planograms

Marks & Spencer is a large retailer of clothing, home goods, and high-quality food products in the United Kingdom. Its food business, specializing in high-quality convenience and fresh foods, such as sandwiches and take-home dinners, occupies a prominent position in the U.K. food retailing sector.

The retailer is continuously updating its product range with new products developed in conjunction with leading manufacturers of short-life food products. Until recently, this process had been labor-intensive. For example, the adjustment of 50 displays in 50 stores requires 2,500 new individual planograms, unless some stores are exactly the same, which is not likely. It would take between 80 and 100 full-time planogrammers to implement weekly changes in its 310 stores.

The $8.6 billion retailer began looking for a planogramming system for its fresh-food products. Store-specific space plans were necessary to reflect each store's individual needs.

Working with SAS, the retailer was able to develop an automated planogramming system that could optimize weekly fresh-food assortments to individual stores, as well as improve product layout and customer satisfaction.

The Marks & Spencer SAS system calculates an optimal layout by determining how many shelf facings are needed for each SKU in each store. At the same time, the system maintains a consistent look but considers specific fixtures and store layouts.

By implementing automated space planning, Marks & Spencer has greatly increased the productivity of its centralized space-planning team and gained control over store layout and product presentation. It can now do weekly plans with 20 planogrammers— and it does a much better job than before. Product placement is now more efficient and uniform throughout the chain, and customers can more easily find specific products. This ease is of particular importance to Marks & Spencer, as many of its customers shop in more than one of its stores.

Source: Communication with SAS.

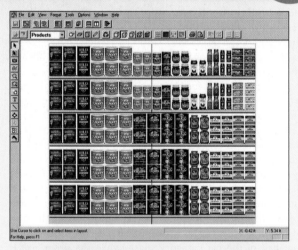

Marks & Spencer in the United Kingdom uses a planogram system developed by Marketmax to develop a layout that maximizes space productivity.

to provide information on their eye movements. These videos can be used to improve layouts and planograms by identifying the causes of slow-selling merchandise, such as poor shelf placement. By studying customers' movements, retailers can also learn where customers pause or move quickly or where there is congestion. This information can help retailers decide, for instance, if the layout and merchandise placement is operating as expected or if new or promoted merchandise is getting the attention it deserves.

VISUAL MERCHANDISING

Visual merchandising is the presentation of a store and its merchandise in ways that will attract the attention of potential customers. This section examines issues related to the presentation of merchandise, and the following section explores more sensory aspects of the store's environment. This section begins with a review of the fixtures used to display merchandise and then discusses some merchandise presentation techniques.

Fixtures

The primary purposes of fixtures are to efficiently hold and display merchandise. At the same time, they define areas of a store and direct traffic flow. Fixtures work in concert with other design elements, such as floor coverings and lighting, as well as the overall image of the store. For instance, in stores designed to convey a sense of tradition or history, customers automatically expect to see lots of wood rather than plastic or metal fixtures. Wood mixed with metal, acrylic, or stone changes the traditional orientation. Apparel retailers utilize the straight-rack, rounder, and four-way fixtures, while the principle fixture for most other retailers is the gondola.

The **straight rack** consists of a long pipe balanced between supports in the floor or attached to a wall (Exhibit 17–5A). Although the straight rack can hold a lot of apparel, it cannot effectively feature specific styles or colors. All the customer can see is a sleeve or a pant leg. As a result, straight racks are often found in discount and off-price apparel stores.

A **rounder,** also known as a **bulk fixture** or **capacity fixture,** is a round fixture that sits on a pedestal (Exhibit 17–5B). Although smaller than the straight rack, it's designed to hold a maximum amount of merchandise. Because they are easy to move and efficiently store apparel, rounders are found in most types of apparel stores. But, as with the straight rack, customers can't get a frontal view of the merchandise.

A **four-way fixture,** also known as a **feature fixture,** has two crossbars that sit perpendicular on a pedestal (Exhibit 17–5C). This fixture holds a large amount of merchandise and allows the customer to view the entire garment. The four-way is harder to maintain properly than is the rounder or straight rack, however. All merchandise on an arm must be of a similar style and color, or the customer may become confused. Due to their superior display properties, four-way fixtures are commonly utilized by fashion-oriented apparel retailers.

Shirts face out

Gondolas are extremely versatile (Exhibit 17–5D). They're used extensively, but not exclusively, in grocery and discount stores to display everything from canned foods to baseball gloves. Gondolas are also found displaying towels, sheets, and housewares in department stores. Folded apparel too can be efficiently displayed on gondolas, but because the items are folded, it's even harder for customers to view apparel on gondolas than it is on straight racks.

Presentation Techniques

Some presentation techniques are idea-oriented, item and size, color, price lining, vertical merchandising, tonnage merchandising, and frontage presentation.

EXHIBIT 17–5
Types of Fixtures

(A) Straight rack

(B) Rounder

(C) Four-way

(D) Gondola

Idea-Oriented Presentation   Some retailers use an **idea-oriented presentation**—a method of presenting merchandise based on a specific idea or the image of the store. Individual items are grouped to show customers how the items could be used and combined. Women's blouses are often displayed with skirts and accessories to present an overall image or idea. Also, furniture stores display a combination of furniture in room settings to give customers an idea of how it would look in their homes. At Sony Style, mini-living rooms showcase what a particular flat-panel TV might look like over a fireplace or a dresser. This approach encourages the customer to make multiple complementary purchases.

Item and Size Presentation   Probably the most common technique of organizing stock is by style or item. Discount stores, grocery stores, hardware stores, and drugstores employ this method for nearly every category of merchandise, as do many apparel retailers. When customers look for a particular type of merchandise, such as breakfast cereals, they expect to find all items in the same location.

Arranging items by size is a common method of organizing many types of merchandise, from nuts and bolts to apparel. Because the customer usually knows the desired size, it's easy to locate items organized in this manner.

Color Presentation   A bold merchandising technique is organizing by color. For instance, in winter months, women's apparel stores may display all white cruise wear together to let customers know that the store is "the place" to purchase clothing for their winter vacations.

Price Lining **Price lining** occurs when retailers offer a limited number of predetermined price points and/or price categories within another classification. This approach helps customers easily find merchandise at the price they wish to pay. For instance, men's dress shirts may be organized into three groups selling for $49, $69, and $99. (Also see Chapter 14.)

Vertical Merchandising Another common way of organizing merchandise is **vertical merchandising.** In this approach, merchandise is presented vertically using walls and high gondolas. Customers shop much as they read a newspaper—from left to right, going down each column, top to bottom. Stores can effectively organize merchandise to follow the eye's natural movement. Retailers take advantage of this tendency in several ways. Many grocery stores put national brands at eye level and store brands on lower shelves because customers scan from eye level down. In addition, retailers often display merchandise in bold vertical bands of an item. For instance, you might see vertical columns of towels of the same color displayed in a department store or a vertical band of yellow and orange boxes of Tide detergent followed by a band of blue Cheer boxes in a supermarket.

The towel display is an example of vertical merchandising.

Tonnage Merchandising As the name implies, **tonnage merchandising** is a display technique in which large quantities of merchandise are displayed together. Customers have come to equate tonnage with low price, following the retail adage "Stock it high and let it fly." Tonnage merchandising is therefore used to enhance and reinforce a store's price image. Using this display concept, the merchandise itself is the display. The retailer hopes customers will notice the merchandise and be drawn to it. For instance, before many holidays, grocery stores use an entire end of a gondola (i.e., an end cap) to display six-packs of Pepsi.

Frontal Presentation Often, it's not possible to create effective displays and efficiently store items at the same time. But it's important to show as much of the merchandise as possible. One solution to this dilemma is the **frontal presentation,** a method of displaying merchandise in which the retailer exposes as much of the product as possible to catch the customer's eye. Book manufacturers, for instance, make great efforts to create eye-catching covers. But bookstores usually display books exposing only the spine. To create an effective display and break the monotony, book retailers often face an occasional cover out like a billboard to catch the customer's attention. A similar frontal presentation can be achieved on a rack of apparel by simply turning one item out to show the merchandise.

CREATING AN APPEALING STORE ATMOSPHERE

To provide a rewarding shopping experience, retailers go beyond presenting appealing merchandise. For example, Disney plans to spend about $1 million a store to create a highly entertaining and rewarding experience for its customers using interactive technology. The chain's traditional approach of displaying row after row of toys and apparel geared to Disney franchises will be given a high-tech makeover. Children will be able to watch film clips of their own selections in a theater, participate in karaoke contests, or chat live with Disney Channel stars via satellite. Computer chips embedded in packaging will activate hidden features. When children walk by a "magic mirror" while holding a Princess tiara, Cinderella will appear and say something to them.

Pike Place Fish Markets' employees play a major role in creating an entertaining and rewarding shopping experience.

Disney will adopt Apple touches like mobile checkout (employees will carry miniature receipt printers in their aprons) and the emphasis on community (Disney's theater idea is an extension of Apple's lecture spaces). The focus will be on interactivity—parents will be able to book a Disney Cruise on touch-screen kiosks while their children play.[32]

Employees also play a major role in creating an appealing store environment. For example, atmosphere at Pike Place is unusual. Employees, known as fishmongers, throw fish over the counter to coworkers for wrapping. The fishmongers also invite customers to get in on the action and try to catch fish. What could be a dull store is transformed into a place where customers and employees are smiling, laughing, and connecting with one another, while keeping an eye out for flying fish.[33]

Amy's Ice Cream (a 13-store chain of premium ice-cream shops in Austin, San Antonio, and Houston, Texas) has similarly transformed what could be a boring transaction into a fun experience. Visit an Amy's store, and you'll see employees performing in a manner you won't forget. They juggle with their serving spades, toss scoops of ice cream to one another behind the counter, and break-dance on the freezer top. If there's a line out the door, they might pass out samples or offer free ice cream to any customer who'll sing or dance, recite a poem, mimic a barnyard animal, or win a 60-second cone-eating contest.[34]

In addition to these interactive technologies, retailers use lighting, colors, music, and scent to stimulate customers' perceptual and emotional responses and ultimately affect their purchase behavior. **Atmospherics** refers to the design of an environment by stimulation of the five senses.[35] Many retailers have discovered the subtle benefits of developing atmospherics that complement other aspects of the store design and the merchandise. Research has shown that it is important for the atmospheric elements to work together—for example, the right music with the right scent.[36]

Lighting

Good lighting in a store involves more than simply illuminating space. Lighting can highlight merchandise, sculpt space, and capture a mood or feeling that enhances the store's image. Retailers are exploring ways to save energy with technologically advanced lighting. Having the appropriate lighting has been shown to positively influence customer shopping behavior.[37]

Highlighting Merchandise   A good lighting system helps create a sense of excitement in the store. At the same time, lighting must provide an accurate color rendition of the merchandise. For instance, Walmart has been putting skylights into the roofs of its stores. This addition cuts energy costs and creates more natural light, which is excellent for hardware and home goods. However, it is best to use artificial light for apparel so that customers can clearly see details.

Another key use of lighting is called **popping the merchandise**—focusing spotlights on special feature areas and items. Using lighting to focus on strategic pockets of merchandise trains shoppers' eyes on the merchandise and draws customers strategically through the store. Nike, for example, uses a lot of contrast and shadows, highlighting the merchandise but not necessarily the architecture.

Mood Creation   Traditionally, U.S. specialty and department stores have employed incandescent lighting sources to promote a warm and cozy ambience. Overall lighting sources were reduced, and accent lighting was pronounced to call attention to merchandise and displays. It was meant to feel like someone's home—dim lighting overall, with artwork and other areas of interest highlighted. Ralph Lauren stores and boutiques in department stores use low levels of light to coordinate with their overall ambience of resembling a townhouse. Department and mass-market retailers, in contrast, tend to be more brightly lit overall.

Energy-Efficient Lighting   As the price of energy soars and retailers and their customers become more energy-conscious, retailers are looking for ways to cut their energy costs and be more ecologically friendly. One obvious source of energy consumption is the lighting in a store. Stores are switching from incandescent lighting to more energy-efficient fluorescent lights.

Color

The creative use of color can enhance a retailer's image and help create a mood. Warm colors (red, gold, and yellow) produce emotional, vibrant, hot, and active responses, whereas cool colors (white, blue, and green) have a peaceful, gentle, calming effect. Colors may have a different impact depending on the culture of the customers. For instance, research suggests that French-Canadians respond more to warm-color decors, whereas Anglo-Canadians respond more positively to cool colors.[38]

Music

Like color and lighting, music can either add to or detract from a retailer's total atmospheric package.[39] Unlike other atmospheric elements, however, music can be easily changed. For example, one retailer has a system that allows certain music to be played at certain times of the day. It can play jazzy music in the morning and adult contemporary in the afternoon, although only in stores on the East Coast. These selections mirror the findings that most of its morning shoppers are older, whereas afternoon shoppers tend to be in the 35-to-40-year age range. For its West Coast stores, it wants modern rock in the morning and Caribbean beats in the afternoon. And in Texas, it's country music all day, every day. The retailer also can "zone" music by demographics, playing more Latin music in stores that attract a higher Hispanic population.

Retailers also can use music to affect customers' behavior. Music can control the pace of store traffic, create an image, and attract or direct consumers' attention. For instance, one U.K. toy store switched from children's songs like "Baa Baa Black Sheep" to relaxed classical music and watched sales jump by 10 percent.[40] Managers realized that although children are the consumers of their products, adults are the customers. In general, though, slow is good. A mix of classical or otherwise soothing music encourages shoppers to slow down, relax, and take a good look at the merchandise.

Scent

Smell has a large impact on customer's mood and emotions. Scent, in conjunction with music, has a positive impact on the customer's level of excitement and satisfaction with the shopping experience.[42] Scents that are neutral produce more positive feelings toward the store than no scent. Customers in scented stores think they spent less time in the store than do those in unscented stores. Stores using scents thus may improve customers' subjective shopping experience by making

REFACT
The U.S. firm Muzak supplies 400,000 shops, restaurants, and hotels around the world—including The Gap, McDonald's, and Burger King—with songs tailored to reflect their identities.[41]

them feel that they are spending less time examining merchandise or waiting for sales help or to check out.

Retailers use different essences in different departments: baby powder in the baby store; suntan lotion in the bathing suit area; lilacs in lingerie; and cinnamon and pine scents during the holiday season.[43] Upscale shirt retailer Thomas Pink pipes the smell of clean, pressed shirts into its stores. The essence of lavender wafts out of L'Occitane skin care stores. The scents from frequent cooking demonstrations at Williams-Sonoma kitchen stores help get customers in the cooking and buying mood. Even Sony Style stores have adopted the scent of cinnamon sticks simmering on a wood-burning stove during the holiday season and a mandarin orange and vanilla fragrance year-round. KB Toys has experimented with scents of Creamsicle, cotton candy, and Play-Doh. Some customers, however, find the scents annoying, and for some, it even aggravates their allergies and asthma.

How Exciting Should a Store Be?

Retailers such as REI, The Sharper Image, Bass Pro Shops, and Barnes & Noble attempt to create an entertaining shopping environment by viewing their stores as theatrical scenes: The floor and walls constitute the stage and scenery; the lighting, fixtures, and displays are the props; and the merchandise represents the performance. This creation of a theatrical experience in stores has resulted in the combination of retailing and entertainment. In contrast, retail chains such as Costco and Home Depot successfully use minimalist, warehouse-style shopping environments.

Does providing an exciting, entertaining store environment lead customers to patronize a store more frequently and spend more time and money during each visit? The answer to this question is: It depends.[45]

The impact of the store's environment depends on the customer's shopping goals. The two basic shopping goals are task completion (utilitarian), such as buying a new suit for a job interview, and recreation (hedonic, such as spending a Saturday afternoon with a friend wandering through a mall). When customers are shopping to complete a task that they view as inherently unrewarding, they prefer to be in a soothing, calming environment—a simple atmosphere with slow music, dimmer lighting, and blue-green colors. However, when customers go shopping for fun, an inherently rewarding activity, they want to be in an exciting atmosphere—a complex environment with fast music, bright lighting, and red-yellow colors.

What does this mean for retailers? They must consider the typical shopping goals for their customers when designing their store environments. For example, grocery shopping is typically viewed as an unpleasant task, and thus supermarkets should be designed in soothing colors and use slow background music. In contrast, shopping for fashion apparel is typically viewed as fun, so an arousing environment in apparel retail outlets will have a positive impact on the shopping behavior of their customers.

The level of excitement caused by the environment might vary across the store. For example, a consumer electronics retailer might create a low-arousal environment in the accessories area to accommodate customers who typically are task-oriented when shopping for print cartridges and batteries, and it might create a high-arousal environment in the home-entertainment centers that are typically visited by more pleasure-seeking shopping customers.

Finally, retailers might vary the nature of their Web sites for customers depending on their shopping goals. For example, research suggests that Amazon should serve up complex, high-arousal Web sites with rich media to customers who indicate they are browsing but provide simpler, low-arousal sites to customers looking for a specific book.[46] Some similar parallels between store and Web site designs are drawn in the following section.

WEB SITE DESIGN

In many, but not all, cases, good design principles that apply to a physical store can also be applied to a Web site.[47] Consider the following examples.

Simplicity Matters

A good store design allows shoppers to move freely, unencumbered by clutter. There is a fine line between providing customers with a good assortment and confusing them with too much merchandise.

Similarly, at a Web site it is not necessary to mention all the merchandise available at the site on each page. It is better to present a limited selection tailored to the customer's needs and then provide a few links to related merchandise and alternative assortments. It is also important to include a search engine feature on each page in case a customer gets lost. The search feature in the virtual world is similar to having sales associates readily available in the physical world. Also, less is more. Having a small number of standard links on every page makes it more likely that users can learn the navigation scheme for the site.

Getting Around

When a store is properly designed, customers should be able to find what they are looking for easily. The products that customers frequently purchase together are often displayed together. For example, umbrellas are displayed with raincoats, soft drinks with snack foods, and tomato sauce with pasta. One way to help customers get around a Web site is by using local links internal to the site. When establishing local links, Web sites should connect:

- Products that are similar in price.
- Complementary products.
- Products that differ from the product shown on some important dimension (e.g., a link to a color printer if the user is looking at a black-and-white printer).
- Different versions of the shown product (e.g., the same blouse in yellow if the customer is viewing a red blouse).

Let Them See It

Stores are designed so that customers can easily view the merchandise and read the signs. But in a store, if the lighting isn't good or a sign is too small to read, the customer can always move around to get a better view. Customers don't have this flexibility on the Internet. Web designers should assume that all potential viewers lack perfect vision. They should strive for realistic colors and sharpness. Some retailers that use the Internet channel have developed interesting ways of viewing merchandise in multiple dimensions (see, for instance, landsend.com).

Blend the Web Site with the Store

It is important to visually reassure customers that they're going to have the same satisfactory experience on the Web site that they have in stores. Even if the electronic store is designed for navigation efficiency, there should still be some design elements that are common to both channels. For instance, although very different store types, tiffany.com and officedepot.com both have looks and feels similar to those of their stores.

Prioritize

Stores become annoying if everything jumps out at you as if to say, "Buy me! No buy me!" Other stores are so bland that the merchandise appears boring. Setting priorities for merchandise displays and locations is just as important on a Web site as it is in a physical store. A common mistake on many Internet sites is that everything is too prominent, resulting from an overuse of colors, animation, blinking, and graphics. If everything is equally prominent, then *nothing* is prominent. Being too bland is equally troublesome. The site should be designed to advise customers and guide them to the most important or most promising choices, while also ensuring their freedom to go anywhere they please. Like a newspaper, the most important items or categories should be given the bigger headlines and more prominent placement.

Type of Layout

Some stores are laid out to be functional, like supermarkets and discount stores. They use a grid design to make it easy to locate merchandise. Other stores, like department stores or bookstores, use a more relaxed layout to encourage browsing. The trick is to pick the appropriate layout that matches the typical motives of the shopper.

Here is where store layout and Web site layout differ. Although many higher-end multichannel retailers experimented with fancy and complex designs in their early years on the Internet, most have become much more simple and utilitarian than their bricks-and-mortar counterparts (see, for instance, polo.com, neimanmarcus.com, and bloomingdales.com). When shopping on the Web, customers are interested in speed, convenience, and ease of navigation, not necessarily fancy graphics.

Store designers also strive to make their stores seem different, to stand out in the crowd. A Web site, however, must strike a balance between keeping customers' interest and providing them with a basic comfort level based on convention. Users spend most of their time at *other* sites, so that's where they form their expectations about how most sites work.

When trying to make a decision about Web site design, good designers look at the most visited sites on the Internet to see how those sites organize their information. If 90 percent or more of the big sites do things in a single way, then that way is the de facto standard.

Checkout

Physical stores recognize the perils of long lines at checkout, and some have taken steps to alleviate the problem, as we discussed earlier in this chapter. The problem of abandoned carts at checkout is even more acute with Internet stores. Approximately half of all online customers abandon their purchases during the checkout process—one of the greatest causes of lost revenue for online retailers.[48]

Some tips for lessening the abandoned-online-cart problem are as follows:[49]

- *Make the process seem clear and simple.* Make sure the customer knows what to expect from the checkout process, how long it will take, and what details he or she must provide. Because customers hate hidden charges and delivery costs, make this information clear at the beginning of the process. Giving some visible signs of progress through the checkout stages also helps.

- *Close off the checkout process.* Remove links to any parts of the site other than the specific stages of the checkout process to focus the customer's mind. Once in the checkout area, there should be only one place customers can go: purchase confirmation.

- *Make the process navigable without threatening the loss of information.* Customers may need to make changes at different stages, so making it possible for them to go back and forth through the process without losing any of the details they have already entered is vital to minimize frustration. Back buttons on the form, which save data when clicked, are a good way to achieve this functionality and offer an alternative to hitting the back button on a browser, which causes customers to lose information. Enabling them to use the browser to navigate through checkout and still not lose their data would be even better.

- *Reinforce trust in the checkout process.* Display clear signs of server security and third-party verification logos. The company's full address and phone number should also be provided, as well as links to information about the terms and conditions, delivery, and payment rules.

SUMMARY

Some objectives for a store design are to (1) implement the retailer's strategy, (2) influence customer buying behavior, (3) provide flexibility, (4) control design and maintenance costs, and (5) meet legal requirements. Typically, a store design cannot achieve all of these objectives, so managers make trade-offs among objectives, such as providing convenience versus encouraging exploration.

The basic elements in a design that guides customers through the store are the layout, signage, and feature areas. A good store layout helps customers find and purchase merchandise. Several types of layouts commonly used by retailers are the grid, racetrack, and free form. The grid design is best for stores in which customers are expected to explore the entire store, such as grocery stores and drugstores. Racetrack designs are more common in large upscale stores like department stores. Free-form designs are usually found in small specialty stores and within large stores' departments.

Signage and graphics help customers locate specific products and departments, provide product information, and suggest items or special purchases. In addition, graphics, such as photo panels, can enhance the store environment and the store's image. Digital signage has several advantages over traditional printed signage, but the initial fixed costs have made the adoption of this technology slow. Feature areas are areas within a store designed to get the customer's attention. They include freestanding displays, end caps, promotional aisles or areas, windows, cash wraps or point-of-sale areas, and walls.

Space management involves two decisions: (1) the allocation of store space to merchandise categories and brands and (2) the location of departments or merchandise categories in the store. Some factors that retailers consider when deciding how much floor or shelf space to allocate to merchandise categories and brands are (1) the productivity of the allocated space, (2) the merchandise's inventory turnover, (3) the impact on store sales, and (4) the display needs for the merchandise. When evaluating the productivity of retail space, retailers generally use sales per square foot or sales per linear foot.

The location of merchandise categories also plays a role in how customers navigate through the store. By strategically placing impulse and demand/destination merchandise throughout the store, retailers can increase the chances that customers will shop the entire store and that their attention will be focused on the merchandise that the retailer is most interested in selling. In locating merchandise categories, retailers need to consider typical consumer shopping patterns.

Retailers utilize various forms of atmospherics—lighting, colors, music, and scent—to influence shopping behavior. The use of these atmospherics can create a calming environment for task-oriented shoppers or an exciting environment for recreational shoppers.

Although a retailer's Web site is different from its physical store, in many but not all cases good design principles that apply to a physical store space can also be applied to a Web site.

KEY TERMS

atmospherics, *490*
boutique layout, *476*
bulk fixture, *487*
capacity fixture, *487*
cash wrap, *481*
category signage, *477*
checkout area, *481*
demand/destination merchandise, *482*
digital signage, *478*
end cap, *479*
feature area, *479*
feature fixture, *487*
fixture, *471*
four-way fixture, *487*

free-form layout, *476*
freestanding display, *479*
frontal presentation, *489*
gondola, *487*
grid layout, *473*
hedonic benefit, *469*
idea-oriented presentation, *488*
impulse product, *483*
loop, *475*
planogram, *484*
point-of-purchase (POP) counter, *481*
point-of-sale signage, *477*
popping the merchandise, *490*
price lining, *489*

promotional aisle, *479*
promotional area, *479*
promotional signage, *477*
racetrack layout, *475*
rounder, *487*
sales per linear foot, *481*
sales per square foot, *481*
set, *485*
straight rack, *487*
tonnage merchandising, *489*
utilitarian benefit, *469*
vertical blocking, *485*
vertical merchandising, *489*
visual merchandising, *487*

GET OUT AND DO IT!

1. **CONTINUING ASSIGNMENT** Go into the physical store location of the retailer you have chosen for the Continuing Assignment, and evaluate the store layout, design, and visual merchandising techniques employed. Explain your answers to the following questions:
   (a) In general, are the store layout, design, and visual merchandising techniques consistent with the exterior of the store and its location?
   (b) Is the store's ambience consistent with the merchandise presented and the customer's expectations?
   (c) How does the store's layout, design, and visual merchandising support the following objectives: (1) implements the retailer's strategy, (2) builds loyalty, (3) increases sales, (4) controls costs, and (5) meets legal requirements?
   (d) To what extent are the store's layout, design, and merchandising techniques flexible?
   (e) How does the store utilize atmospheric elements such as color, lighting, music, and scent? Are these uses appropriate given the store's merchandise and target market?
   (f) Is the store's design environmentally friendly? If yes, please describe. If no, how could it become more "green"?
   (g) Are the fixtures consistent with the merchandise and the overall ambience of the store? Are they flexible?
   (h) Evaluate the store's signage. Does it do an effective job of selling merchandise?
   (i) Has the retailer used any theatrical effects to help sell merchandise?
   (j) Does the store layout help draw people through the store?
   (k) Has the retailer taken advantage of the opportunity to sell merchandise in feature areas?
   (l) Does the store make creative use of wall space?
   (m) What type of layout does the store use? Is it appropriate for the type of store? Would another type of layout be better?
   (n) Ask the store manager how the profitability of space is evaluated (e.g., profit per square foot). Is there a better approach?
   (o) Ask the store manager how space is assigned to merchandise. Critically evaluate the answer.
   (p) Ask the store manager if planograms are used. If so, try to determine what factors are considered when putting together a planogram.
   (q) Are departments in the most appropriate locations? Would you move any departments?
   (r) What method(s) has the retailer used to organize merchandise? Is this the best way? Suggest any appropriate changes.

2. **INTERNET EXERCISE** Go to your favorite multichannel retailer's Internet site. Evaluate its degree of simplicity, ease of navigation, readability, use of color, consistency with the brand image, and similarity of pricing and merchandise offered with those at its bricks-and-mortar stores.

3. **INTERNET EXERCISE** Go to the home page of ACNielsen to read about the Nielsen retail measurement products Shelfbuilder and Spaceman (http://en-us.nielsen.com/content/nielsen/en_us/product_families/nielsen_retail_measurement/fact_sheet_library.html). How can retailers use these tools to optimize assortment planning and improve planograms to enhance visual impact, match consumers' shopping patterns, and strengthen financial earnings?

4. **INTERNET EXERCISE** *VMSD* is the leading resource for retail designers and store display professionals, serving the retail industry since 1869 (then called *Display World*). Go to its Web page at http://vmsd.com, and develop a list of three or four items that describe the latest trends in visual merchandising.

5. **INTERNET EXERCISE** Go to the home page of Envirosell (www.envirosell.com). How does this marketing research consulting firm support retailers by collecting consumer information to assist with store layout, design, and visual merchandising?

DISCUSSION QUESTIONS AND PROBLEMS

1. One of the fastest-growing sectors of the population is the over-60 age group. Customers in this group may have limitations in their vision, hearing, and movement. How can retailers develop store designs with this population's needs in mind?

2. Assume you have been hired as a consultant to assess a local discount store's floor plan and space productivity. Look back at Chapter 6 and decide which analytical tools and ratios you would use to assess the situation.

3. What are the different types of design that can be used in a store layout? How does the layout impact the types of fixtures used to display merchandise? Describe why some stores are more suited for a particular type of layout than others.

4. A department store is building an addition. The merchandise manager for furniture is trying to convince the vice president to allot this new space to the furniture department. The merchandise manager for men's clothing is also trying to gain the space. What points should each manager use when presenting his or her rationale?

5. As an architect for retail space, you are responsible for Americans with Disabilities Act compliance. How

would you make sure that a store's retail layout both meets accessibility requirements and enables the company to reach profitability objectives?

6. Describe the ways in which designing a Web site is similar to and different from designing a physical store layout.

7. What are the pros and cons for both centralized cash wraps and departmental cash wraps for stores such as JCPenney and Kohl's?

8. Complete the table below by briefly describing how the different retail formats could use each of areas listed to enhance the store's image and atmosphere.

Area	Drugstore	Clothing Store	Music Store	Restaurant
Entrance				
Walls				
Windows				
Merchandise displays				
Cash wrap				

9. Reread Retailing View 17.1, "Walmart Goes Green and Lowers Its Energy Costs." Which of the environmental practices discussed do you think will be implemented by other retailers? Explain your response.

10. How can signage and graphics help both customers and retailers? Consider the following types of retail formats that you likely have visited in the past: discount store, department store, office superstore, and card and gift store. Describe which retail formats have implemented the best practices for coordinating signs and graphics with each store's image and which formats should improve this aspect of their store layout, design, and visual merchandising.

SUGGESTED READINGS

Davis, Lenita, Sijun Wang, and Andrew Lindridge. "Culture Influences on Emotional Responses to On-Line Store Atmospheric Cues." *Journal of Business Research* 61 (August 2008), pp. 806–812.

Dean, Corrina. *Inspired Retail Space: Attract Customers, Build Branding, Increase Volume.* Rockport, ME: Rockport, 2005.

Diamond, Jay, and Ellen Diamond. *Contemporary Visual Merchandising and Environmental Design*, 5th ed. Upper Saddle River, NJ: Prentice Hall, 2010.

Kent, A. M., and A. E. Kirby, "The Design of the Store Environment and Its Implications for Retail Image." *International Review of Retail, Distribution and Consumer Research* 19 (September 2009), pp. 457–477.

Kretschme, Robert. *Window and Interior Display: The Principles of Visual Merchandising.* Scotts Valley, CA: CreateSpace, 2009.

Manganari, Emmanouela E., George J. Siomkos, and Adam P. Vrechopoulos. "Store Atmosphere in Web Retailing." *European Journal of Marketing* 43 (September 2010), pp. 1140–1153.

Pegler, Martin. *Store Presentation and Design*, 3rd ed. New York: RSD, 2010.

Retail Design Institute and VSD. *Stores and Retail Spaces*, 10th ed. Cincinnati, OH: ST Media Group International, 2009.

Sorensen, Herb. *Inside the Mind of the Shoppper.* Upper Saddle River, NJ: Pearson Education, 2009.

Underhill, Paco. *What Women Want: The Global Marketplace Turns Female Friendly.* New York: Simon & Schuster, 2010

Underhill, Paco. *Why We Buy: The Science of Shopping.* New York: Simon and Schuster, 2000.

Customer Service

EXECUTIVE BRIEFING

Mike Millares, Recruiting Development &
Retention Management, Tires Plus Total Car Care

I graduated from the University of Miami, with a degree in biology. I continue to be interested in the sciences, but fell in love with a career in retail. I worked part time at Tires Plus to support myself while in college and discovered that I really liked interacting with customers and the staff in my store. I had planned to go to graduate school after getting my undergraduate degree, but, as graduation approached, Tires Plus made me an offer I couldn't refuse. The company offered me a job as a store manager and I took the opportunity.

Tires Plus is a division of Bridgestone Retail Operations, LLC. We have over 500 stores and 5,000 employees in 23 states. In addition to selling, installing, and maintaining tires, our technicians are qualified to provide a wide range of automobile maintenance and repair services. Some people have this image of an auto repair shop as a gloomy, dirty place that offers unreliable service. At Tires Plus, we provide an alternative to this stereotype. When you walk into one of our stores, you immediately notice the brightly lit, colorfully merchandised showroom. You are greeted by a clean, well-dressed, well-trained service professional. Our philosophy is "We won't sell you tires, we'll help you buy them." Our customers can be confident that we will provide honest and timely service and treat them and their vehicles as if they were one of our own.

Cars are a very important element in a person's life and people can get very upset when they have problems with their cars. We want our teammates to view these situations as opportunities to solve customer concerns. Simply satisfying their needs is not enough. We want our customers to have such a great experience and be so pleased, that they will come back and tell their friends about us.

In college, I was really excited about biology, but I have found that it is even more challenging and rewarding to interact with customers and employees in a retail environment. When I was a store manager, one of my unforgettable customers was a single parent with two small children. He owned an Acura Integra and was very demanding when he came in to have his car serviced. I decided to treat this situation as a challenge. I wanted to provide the perfect service experience for him. I knew

CHAPTER 18

QUESTIONS

What services do retailers offer customers?

How can retailers build a competitive advantage through customer service?

How do customers evaluate a retailer's customer service?

What activities can a retailer undertake to provide high-quality customer service?

How can retailers recover from a service failure?

---

that to earn his business, I would have to listen to his needs and prove that I represented a company that would care for him, his car, and his well being. He became one of my best customers.

After working as a store manager for a couple of years, I was promoted to assistant district manager and then to my present position in human resource management in the headquarters' office. When I interview job candidates, I often ask them to describe a difficult customer and how they handled the situation. The response of candidates to these challenging customer service situations provides some insight into how they will fit into our culture.

Suppose you are surfing the Internet for a digital camera. At www.RealCheap Cameras.com, a hypothetical site, you are asked to type in the name of the specific brand and model number you want. Then you are quoted a price with shipping charges and asked for your credit card number and a shipping address. Now suppose you go to Best Buy's Web site, www.bestbuy.com. You can go through the same steps to get prices and place an order for a digital camera, but you can also review the specifications for different cameras or look through reviews of different cameras by experts and other consumers. You can then go to a store to see the cameras, get additional information about them from a sales associate, and look at accessories, such as a carrying case and additional memory units. Thus, Best Buy's multichannel offering is providing some valuable services to you—services that you cannot get from RealCheapCameras.com.

Customer service is the set of activities and programs undertaken by retailers to make the shopping experience more rewarding for their customers. These activities increase the value customers receive from the merchandise and services they purchase. Some of these services are provided by store and call center employees interacting directly with customers, while others are provided by the design of the retailer's store and/or Web site.

The next sections discuss retailers' opportunities to develop strategic advantages through customer service, the nature and types of customer service provided, and how customers evaluate a retailer's customer service. Then we outline how retailers exploit these opportunities to build a competitive advantage by providing high-quality customer service.

REFACT

The word *service* comes from the Latin term *servus*, meaning "slave."[1]

Improving Internal Communications   When providing customer service, service providers often must manage the conflict between the customers' and the retail firm's needs.[48] For example, while retailers expect their sales associates to encourage customers to make multiple purchases and buy more expensive items, customers are looking for the best-value choices to fit their needs. The sales associates therefore may be conflicted between meeting corporate and customers' goals.

Retailers can reduce such conflicts by issuing clear guidelines and policies concerning service and explaining the rationale for these policies. For instance, employees may be taught to apologize for a service failure even if the failure was caused by someone else in the organization or was a result of something the customer did. It is difficult for many people to apologize for something that was not their fault. But if employees are taught that an apology for a service failure can help retain the customer, they should understand it as a necessity and apologize when necessary.

Conflicts can also arise when retailers set goals that are inconsistent with the other behaviors expected from store employees. For example, as discussed in Chapter 16, if salespeople are expected to provide customer service, they should be evaluated and compensated on the service they provide, not just the sales they make.

Finally, conflicts can arise between different areas of the firm. A men's specialty store known for its high levels of customer service has salespeople who promise rapid alterations and deliveries to please their customers. Unfortunately, the alterations department includes two elderly tailors who work at their own speed, regardless of the workload. From time to time, management must step in to temper the salespeople's promises and reallocate priorities for the tailors.

REFACT

Ritz-Carlton personnel at the front desks of its hotels are empowered to issue unhappy customers up to $2,000 credit without asking a supervisor's approval.[50]

Empowering Store Employees   **Empowerment** means allowing employees at the firm's lowest levels to make important decisions regarding how service will be provided to customers. When the employees responsible for providing service are authorized to make important decisions, service quality improves.[49]

Nordstrom provides an overall objective—satisfy customer needs—and then encourages employees to do whatever is necessary to achieve the objective. For example, a Nordstrom department manager bought 12 dozen pairs of hosiery from a competitor in the mall when her stock was depleted because the new shipment was delayed. Even though Nordstrom lost money on this hosiery, management applauded her actions to make sure customers found hosiery when they came to the store looking for it. Empowering service providers with only a rule like "Use your best judgment" can cause chaos. At Nordstrom, department managers avoid abuses by coaching and training salespeople. They help salespeople understand what "Use your best judgment" means.

However, empowering service providers can be difficult. Some employees prefer to have the appropriate behaviors clearly defined for them. They don't want to spend the time learning how to make decisions or assume the risks of making mistakes. For example, a bank found that when it empowered its tellers, the tellers were afraid to make decisions about large sums of money. The bank had to develop decision guideposts and rules until tellers felt more comfortable.

In some cases, the benefits of empowering service providers may not justify the costs. For example, if a retailer uses a standardized service delivery approach like McDonald's, the cost of hiring, training, and supporting empowerment may not lead to consistent and superior service delivery. Also, studies have found that empowerment is not embraced by employees in different cultures. For example, employees in Latin America expect their managers to possess all the information needed to make good business decisions. The role of employees is not to make business decisions; their job is to carry out the decisions of managers.[51]

Providing Incentives   As discussed in Chapter 16, many retailers use incentives, like paying commissions on sales, to motivate employees. But retailers have found that commissions on sales can decrease customer service and job satisfaction and motivate high-pressure selling, which leads to customer dissatisfaction. However, incentives can also be used effectively to improve customer service.

Home Depot launched a customer service initiative that earmarks as much as $25,000 per quarter to stores that provide the best customer service.[52] Individual employees can receive bonuses of as much as $2,000 per month or $10,000 per quarter. Home Depot determines which store is rewarded by looking at several factors: reviews by peers and managers, focus groups, and "voice of the customer" surveys. Between 150,000 and 250,000 customers call the company's 800 number each week or visit its Internet site—the URL is printed at the bottom of receipts—to rate their customer service experience.

Developing Solutions to Service Problems   The previously discussed approaches for closing the service gap rely on informing, empowering, and motivating store personnel to provide better service. Retailers also use systems and technology to close the delivery gap.

Finding ways to overcome service problems can improve customer satisfaction and, in some cases, reduce costs. For example, Massachusetts-based Zoots dry cleaners doesn't want to be like its competitors, which are open from 8 a.m. to 6 p.m.—when most customers are at work. So it devised an automated system for 24/7 pickup and drop-off. When customers swipe their credit cards, the machine automatically identifies their garments and brings the order from the clothes rack to a small window or accepts a new dry-cleaning order.[53]

Using Technology   Many retailers are installing kiosks with broadband Internet access in their stores. In addition to offering customers the opportunity to order merchandise not available in the store, kiosks can provide routine customer service, freeing employees to deal with more demanding customer requests and problems.[55] For example, customers can use kiosks to locate merchandise in the store and determine whether specific products, brands, and sizes are available. Kiosks can also be used to automate existing store services, such as gift registry management, rain checks, film drop-off, credit applications, and preordering services for bakeries and delicatessens.

Customers can use kiosks to find more information about products and how they are used. For example, an hh-gregg customer might use a kiosk to look at side-by-side comparisons of two DVRs and find more detailed information than is available from the shelf tags or a sales associate. The information provided by the kiosk could be tailored to the specific customer, on the basis of the retailer's customer database. For example, a customer who is considering a new set of speakers might not remember the preamplifier he or she purchased previously from hhgregg. This customer might not know whether the speakers are compatible with the preamplifier or what cables are needed to connect the new speakers. These concerns could be

REFACT

Self-service technology for gas pumps originated in 1947, when two Californians simultaneously hit on the idea. About 90 percent of gasoline purchases now are made at self-serve stations.[54]

This salesperson is using an Internet-enabled terminal to locate merchandise for a customer.

This retail store assistant helps shopping and reduces the delivery gap by providing customers with information and services.

addressed by accessing the retailer's customer database through the kiosk. Such applications can complement the efforts of salespeople and improve the service they can offer to customers.

Sephora introduced a touchscreen system to help customers find a new fragrance or an old favorite. The interactive wall-mounted screen is a tool not only for Sephora's fragrance experts but also for customers who want to "play." By tapping a finger on the display, customers can find detailed information on the latest fragrances, discover fragrances from the same fragrance family, view images, run videos, or find thousands of worldwide reviews on a time-honored favorite.[56]

At some retailers, instead of taking a shopping list to the store, a customer can swipe a loyalty card or enter a phone number at a kiosk[57] or use a similar device called a retail store assistant (RSA) attached to a shopping cart.[58] Any information the customer has entered online from home will show up on the associated profile. On the basis of the customer's shopping habits, which are stored in the retailer's database, the RSA provides special offers that match the customer's purchase record. On the back of the coupons that the RSA provides is a map of the store and the location of each item, eliminating the need to explore every aisle. If a printed piece of paper is too cumbersome, this list and information also could be transferred via Bluetooth technology to a mobile device, such as a phone.

 Some retailers use hand-held scanners to provide customer service. Customers can register a credit card number at the front counter and get a wireless hand-held scanner. As they walk the aisles, they scan in the bar codes of their desired items and then pay for the purchases when they are finished shopping. The items scanned are then delivered to their homes the same day. The use of hand-held scanners eliminates the need for customers to carry around bulky items in the store and transport them home. The physical and psychological limits on how much is purchased in a single trip are reduced, so the average customer purchase using this service is 10 times greater than that of customers not using the service.[59]

Communicating the Service Promise: The Communications Gap

The fourth factor leading to a customer service gap is the difference between the service promised by the retailer and the service actually delivered. Overstating the service offered raises customer expectations. Then, if the retailer doesn't follow through by improving actual customer service, expectations exceed perceived service and customers are dissatisfied. For example, if an Internet site store offers free shipping but the free alterations are available only for purchases greater than $200, the customer may be disappointed. Raising expectations too high might bring in more customers initially, but it can also create dissatisfaction and reduce repeat business. The communications gap can be reduced by making realistic commitments and managing customer expectations.

Realistic Commitments   Promotion programs are typically developed by the marketing department, whereas the store operations division delivers the service. Poor communication between these areas can result in a mismatch between an ad campaign's promises and the service the store can actually offer. This problem is illustrated by Holiday Inn's "No Surprises" ad campaign. Market research indicated that hotel customers wanted greater reliability in lodging, so Holiday Inn's agency developed a campaign promising no unpleasant surprises. Even though hotel managers didn't feel they could meet the claims promised in the ads, top management accepted the campaign. The campaign raised customer expectations to an unrealistic level and gave customers who did confront an unpleasant surprise an additional reason to be angry. The campaign was discontinued soon after it started.

Managing Customer Expectations   How can a retailer communicate realistic service expectations without losing business to a competitor that makes inflated service claims? American Airlines' "Why Does It Seem Every Airline Flight Is Late?" ad campaign is an example of a communication program that addresses this issue. In print ads, American recognized its customers' frustration and explained some uncontrollable factors causing the problem: overcrowded airports, scheduling problems, and intense price competition. Then the ads described how American was improving the situation.

Information presented at the point of sale can be used to manage expectations. For example, theme parks and restaurants indicate the waiting time for an attraction or a table. Electronic retailers tell their customers whether merchandise is in stock and when customers can expect to receive it. Providing accurate information can increase customer satisfaction even when customers must wait longer than desired.

Sometimes service problems are caused by customers. Customers may use an invalid credit card to pay for merchandise, not take time to try on a suit and have it altered properly, or use a product incorrectly because they fail to read the instructions. Communication programs can inform customers about their role and responsibility in getting good service and give tips on how to get better service, such as the best times of the day to shop and the retailer's policies and procedures for handling problems.

SERVICE RECOVERY

The delivery of customer service is inherently inconsistent, so service failures are bound to arise. Rather than dwelling on negative aspects of customer problems, retailers should focus on the positive opportunities the problems generate. Service problems and complaints are an excellent source of information about the retailer's offering (its merchandise and service). Armed with this information, retailers can make changes to increase their customers' satisfaction.[60]

Service problems also enable a retailer to demonstrate its commitment to providing high-quality customer service. By encouraging complaints and handling problems, a retailer has an opportunity to strengthen its relationship with its customers. Effective service recovery efforts significantly increase customer satisfaction, purchase intentions, and positive word of mouth. However, postrecovery satisfaction generally is less than the satisfaction level before the service failure.

Most retailers have standard policies for handling problems. If a correctable problem is identified, such as defective merchandise, many retailers will make restitution on the spot and apologize for inconveniencing the customer. The retailer

When resolving customers' problems, service representatives should listen to customers, provide a fair solution, and resolve the problems quickly.

will offer replacement merchandise, a credit toward future purchases, or a cash refund.

In many cases, the cause of the problem may be hard to identify (did the salesperson really insult the customer?), uncorrectable (the store had to close due to bad weather), or a result of the customer's unusual expectations (the customer didn't like his haircut). In these cases, service recovery might be more difficult. The steps in effective service recovery are (1) listen to the customer, (2) provide a fair solution, and (3) resolve the problem quickly.[61]

Listening to Customers

Customers can become very emotional about their real or imaginary problems with a retailer. Often this emotional reaction can be reduced by simply giving customers a chance to get their complaints off their chests.

Store employees should allow customers to air their complaints without interruption. Interruptions can further irritate customers who may already be emotionally upset. It's very hard to reason with or satisfy an angry customer.

Customers want a sympathetic response to their complaints. Thus, store employees need to make it clear that they're happy the problem has been brought to their attention. Satisfactory solutions rarely arise when store employees have an antagonistic attitude or assume that the customer is trying to cheat the store.

Employees also need to listen carefully to determine what the customer perceives to be a fair solution. For example, a hotel employee might assume that a customer who's irritated about a long wait to check in will be satisfied with an apology. But the customer might be expecting to receive a free drink as compensation for the wait. A supermarket employee may brusquely offer a refund for spoiled fruit when the customer is also seeking an apology for the inconvenience of having to return to the store. Store employees shouldn't assume they know what the customer is complaining about or what solution the customer is seeking.[62]

Providing a Fair Solution

Customers like to feel that they are being treated fairly. They base their perception of fairness on how they think others were treated in similar situations and with other retailers. Customers' evaluations of complaint resolutions thus are based on distributive fairness and procedural fairness.[63]

Distributive Fairness   **Distributive fairness** is a customer's perception of the benefits received compared with his or her costs in terms of inconvenience or monetary loss. What seems to be fair compensation for a service failure for one customer may not be adequate for another. For example, one customer might be satisfied with a rain check for a food processor that was advertised at a discounted price but sold out. This customer feels the low price for the food processor offsets the inconvenience of returning to the store. But another customer may need the food processor immediately, so a rain check won't be adequate compensation for him. To satisfy this customer, the salesperson must locate a store that has the food processor and have it delivered to the customer's house.

Customers typically prefer tangible rather than intangible resolutions to their complaints. A low-cost reward, such as a free soft drink or a $1 discount, communicates more concern to the customer than a verbal apology.

Procedural Fairness   **Procedural fairness** is the perceived fairness of the process used to resolve complaints. Customers consider three questions when evaluating procedural fairness:

1. Did the employee collect information about the situation?
2. Was this information used to resolve the complaint?
3. Did the customer have some influence over the outcome?

Customers typically feel they have been dealt with fairly when store employees follow company guidelines. Guidelines reduce variability in handling complaints and lead customers to believe they're being treated like everyone else. But rigid adherence to guidelines can have negative effects. Store employees need some flexibility in resolving complaints, or customers may feel they had no influence on the resolution.

Resolving Problems Quickly   Customer satisfaction is affected by the time it takes to get an issue resolved. As a general rule, store employees who deal with customers should be made as self-sufficient as possible to handle problems. Customers are more satisfied when the first person they contact can resolve a problem. When customers are referred to several different employees, they waste a lot of time repeating their story. Also, the chance of conflicting responses by store employees increases. Retailers can minimize the time needed to resolve complaints by reducing the number of people customers must contact and providing clear instructions.

Resolving customer complaints increases satisfaction. But when complaints are resolved too abruptly, customers might feel dissatisfied because they haven't received enough personal attention. Retailers must recognize the trade-off between resolving the problem quickly and taking time to listen to and show concern for the customer.[64]

SUMMARY

Due to the inherent intangibility and inconsistency of services, providing high-quality customer service is challenging. However, customer service also provides an opportunity for retailers to develop a strategic advantage. Retailers use two basic strategies for providing customer service: personalized service and standardized service. The personalized approach relies primarily on sales associates. The standardized approach places more emphasis on developing appropriate rules, consistent procedures, and optimum store designs.

Customers evaluate customer service by comparing their perceptions of the service delivered with their expectations. Thus, to improve service, retailers need to close the gaps between the service delivered and the customer's expectations. This gap may be reduced by knowing what customers expect, setting standards to provide the expected service, providing support so that store employees can meet the standards, and realistically communicating the service offered to customers.

Due to inherent inconsistency, service failures are bound to arise. These lapses in service provide an opportunity for retailers to build even stronger relationships with their customers.

KEY TERMS

assurance, *505*
communication gap, *509*
customer service, *499*
delivery gap, *509*
distributive fairness, *520*
emotional support, *515*
empathy, *506*

empowerment, *516*
instrumental support, *515*
knowledge gap, *508*
mystery shopper, *514*
personalized service, *501*
procedural fairness, *521*
reliability, *505*

responsiveness, *506*
service gap, *508*
standardized service, *501*
standards gap, *509*
tangibility, *506*

GET OUT AND DO IT!

1. **CONTINUING ASSIGNMENT** Go to a local store outlet of the retailer you selected for the Continuing Assignment, and describe and evaluate the service it offers. What service is offered? Is the service personalized or standardized? Ask the store manager if you can talk to some customers and employees. Choose customers who have made a purchase, customers who have not made a purchase, and customers with a problem (refund, exchange, or complaint). Talk with them about their experiences, write a report describing your conversations, and make suggestions for improving the store's customer service. Ask employees what the retailer does to assist and motivate them to provide good service.

2. **INTERNET EXERCISE** Bizrate (www.bizrate.com) is a company that collects information about consumer shopping experiences with electronic retailers. Go to Bizrate's Web site, and review the evaluations of different retailers that sell products electronically. How useful is this information to you? What could Bizrate do to make the information more useful?

3. **INTERNET EXERCISE** Visit Amazon.com and shop for a best-selling book. How does the Web site help you locate best-sellers? How does the customer service offered by this Web site compare to the service you would get at another book retailer's Web site or in a bricks-and-mortar bookstore?

4. **GO SHOPPING** Go to a discount store such as Walmart, a department store, and a specialty store to buy a pair of jeans. After visiting all three, compare and contrast the level of customer service you received in each of the stores. Which store made it easiest to find the pair of jeans you would be interested in buying? Evaluate the perceived service experience in terms of reliability, assurance, tangibility, empathy, and responsiveness. Does the service quality match the store format? Explain your response.

DISCUSSION QUESTIONS AND PROBLEMS

1. For each of the following services, give an example of a retailer for which providing the service is critical to its success and an example of a retailer for which providing the service is not critical: (a) personal shoppers, (b) home delivery, (c) money-back guarantees, and (d) credit.

2. Both Nordstrom and McDonald's are noted for their high-quality customer service, but their approaches to providing quality service are different. Describe this difference. Why has each of these retailers elected to use its particular approach?

3. Have you ever worked in a job that required you to provide customer service? If yes, describe the skills you needed and tasks you performed on this job. If no, what skills and abilities would you highlight to a potential employer that was interviewing you for a position that included customer service in the job description?

4. Review Retailing View 18.2, about customer service at IKEA. How does this retailer utilize a self-service model as a competitive advantage strategy, compared to traditional furniture stores?

5. Assume you're the department manager for menswear in a local department store that emphasizes empowering its managers. A customer returns a dress shirt that's no longer in the package in which it was sold. The customer has no receipt, says that when he opened the package he found that the shirt was torn, and wants cash for the price at which the shirt is now being sold. The shirt was on sale last week when the customer claims to have bought it. What would you do?

6. Consider a situation in which you received poor customer service in a retail store or from a service provider. Did you make the store's management aware of your experience? Whom did you relay this experience to? Have you returned to this retailer or provider? For each of these questions, explain your reasons.

7. Gaps analysis provides a systematic method for examining a customer service program's effectiveness. Top management has told an information systems manager that customers are complaining about the long wait to pay for merchandise at the checkout station. Taking the role of the systems manager, use the gap analysis table below to evaluate this problem and suggest possible strategies for reducing the wait time.

	Problem Encountered	Strategies to Close this Gap
Knowledge Gap		
Standards Gap		
Delivery Gap		
Communication Gap		

8. How could an effective customer service strategy lower a retailer's costs?

9. How can retailers provide high-quality personalized service? Use an ophthalmologist's office that also sells eyeglass frames and fills prescriptions for contact lenses as your example. How does this retailer's service compare with the service provided by 1-800 CONTACTS online or in-store at its bricks-and-mortar partner, Walmart?

10. Consider a recent retail service experience you have had, such as a haircut, doctor's appointment, dinner in a restaurant, bank transaction, or product repair (not an exhaustive list), and answer the questions below:
  a. Describe an excellent service delivery experience.
  b. What made this quality experience possible?

c. Describe a service delivery experience in which you did not receive the performance that you expected.
d. What were the problems encountered, and how could they have been resolved?

SUGGESTED READINGS

Berry, Leonard L. *Management Lessons from Mayo Clinic: Inside One of the World's Most Admired Service Organizations.* New York: McGraw-Hill, 2010.

Bettencourt, Lance. *Service Innovation: How to Go from Customer Needs to Breakthrough Services.* New York: McGraw-Hill, 2010.

Bolton, Ruth N., Dhruv Grewal, and Michael Levy. "Six Strategies for Competing through Service: An Agenda for Future Research." *Journal of Retailing* 83, no. 1 (2007), pp. 1–4.

Gerson, Richard F. *Beyond Customer Service: Keep Your Customers. And Keep Them Satisfied*, 3rd ed. Mississauga, Ontario, Canada: Crisp Learning, 2010.

Hess, Ronald L., Jr., Shankar Ganesan, and Noreen M. Klein. "Interactional Service Failures in a Pseudorelationship: The Role of Organizational Attributions." *Journal of Retailing* 83, no. 1 (2007), pp. 79–95.

Lusch, Robert F., Stephen L. Vargo, and Matthew O'Brien. "Competing through Service: Insights from Service-Dominant Logic." *Journal of Retailing* 83, no. 1 (2007), pp. 5–18.

Spector, Robert, and Patrick McCarthy. *The Nordstrom Way to Customer Service Excellence.* Hoboken, NJ: Wiley, 2005.

Zeithaml, Valarie. *Delivering Quality Service.* New York: Free Press, 2010.

Zeithaml, Valarie, Mary Jo Bitner, and Dwayne D. Gremler. *Services Marketing*, 5th ed. New York: McGraw-Hill/Irwin, 2008.

APPENDIX A
Starting Your Own Retail Business

Starting a retail business can be an enticing and daunting prospect. On the one hand, you can be your own boss, enjoy complete creative control, and reap the full rewards of your hard work. On the other hand, retail business owners must assume large amounts of responsibility, bear the consequences of poor decisions, and ultimately shoulder the blame for the success or failure of the business. Owning your own business involves a great deal of effort, sacrifice, and patience. It is inherently risky, and consequently, fewer than 20 percent of new retail businesses survive to the five-year mark. Yet the rewards of successfully navigating the unpredictable landscape of business ownership can be enormous, both personally and financially. You might grow your business and become the next Sam Walton (Walmart), Maxine Clark (Build-A-Bear Workshop), or John Mackey (Whole Food Markets).

The sense of accomplishment garnered from creating and sustaining a thriving enterprise of one's own is immense. Retail owners have the uniquely satisfying opportunity to craft a tangible expression of their own professional visions, talents, and hard work. In addition, they can contribute value to their communities by creating jobs, strengthening the economy, and providing excellent service to customers. Those who join the successful 20 percent of retail entrepreneurs often earn sufficient financial rewards to live securely and comfortably according to their own standards.

The purpose of this appendix is to demonstrate broadly how to achieve these goals by starting a retail business. A wealth of information discusses entrepreneurship, retailing, and business start-ups—and all of it could not possibly be contained within the confines of an appendix. Instead, this appendix provides an overview of the process and offers some further resources that anyone with serious aspirations for starting his or her own retail business can use to take the first step.

DO YOU HAVE WHAT IT TAKES TO BE A SUCCESSFUL ENTREPRENEUR?

Before starting a business, it is important to take an inventory of skills. Debate continues about the inherent nature of entrepreneurial success. Can someone acquire entrepreneurial skills, or are successful entrepreneurs just people with an innate ability to see and seize an opportunity? It seems that the answer lies somewhere in between.

The skills needed to be a successful entrepreneur can by divided into two broad skill categories: technical training and personal characteristics. To start a retail business, it is very important that the owner possess business skills. Do you understand how to read a financial statement and evaluate your performance and viability? Can you make an effective presentation to potential investors? Do you have an understanding of what customers want? Can you manage the people who work for you? Do you have an understanding of how to launch an electronic channel for your retail business?

For those lacking these business skills, many major universities offer online degrees in a wide variety of disciplines, including business, as well as the option of full-time enrollment. It may be difficult to balance family, work, and school, but owning a business will be just as time consuming. This process can be a litmus test for a person's entrepreneurial work ethic.

A work ethic is a quality that cannot be taught, and for entrepreneurs it is vital. Passion for a chosen business is another quality that cannot be taught. No one will be looking over a retail business owner's shoulder to ensure he or she is doing everything possible to guarantee

---

*This appendix was prepared by Christian Tassin MSE 2008, University of Florida, under the supervision of Professor Barton Weitz.

the success of the venture. Can you maintain the level of energy required to sustain a business? Can you handle rejection from investors and still have the confidence to keep going? Seeing opportunity is another skill that is difficult to acquire, but it can be learned through practice. A person can train his or her mind to look for ways to improve the things that need improvement. Visit a retail store to evaluate its practices. What works? What does not? Where is the opportunity to improve on the qualities that do not work? How can value be created from improving on the shortcomings of current business practices?

DEVELOPING A CONCEPT FOR THE RETAIL VENTURE

The genesis of any business venture starts with an idea. A retail store concept should satisfy three objectives. First, the pursuit should be something that the retailer is passionate about. With the intense effort required for successful entrepreneurship, why would a person want to be involved in something that he or she does not enjoy? Sustainability in a retail business becomes virtually impossible if the owner does not have a burning desire to see it succeed. Second, the concept must provide sufficient value to its customers. The purpose of a business is to make a profit, and if people are not willing to pay for the products or services offered, then failure is ensured. Third, the concept must provide an offering that is differentiated—not available from competitors and not something that competitors can easily copy.

An important issue to consider is the application of intellectual property to the retail concept. Do you have a patentable concept? Do you have a trademark for your brand name and logo? If an entrepreneur crafts a business venture on company time at his or her day job, it is considered that company's property. Working in an industry related to the retail concept can make this ownership even easier to prove. Will the concept compete with an existing employer? Many companies require that employees sign noncompete clauses. If an idea violates one of those agreements, the business could be over before it even gets started. If you believe your concept or business process is unique, or are not sure if you can legally execute your retail concept, an attorney who deals in intellectual property can be a great resource.

THE "QUICK SCREEN"

The first step in deciding whether to start a retail business is to examine the retail concept in detail. Essentially, the prospective retailer wants to determine whether he or she merely has an interesting idea or a viable opportunity. Four questions that help determine the viability of an opportunity are as follows:

1. Does it create or add significant value for customers?
2. Does it solve a significant problem or meet a significant demand or need in the marketplace for which someone is willing to pay a premium?
3. Is there a large enough market and sufficient margins to generate profits?
4. Is there a good fit between the skills of the management team and the skills required to operate the business?

If an idea does not fulfill these four requirements, the potential retailer needs to revise it, or else create a new one. For example, if you love the beach and want to start a retail store that sells bathing suits and beach accessories, but you also live in Colorado, the concept lacks the key elements of success. The market for beach goods will not be significant enough, no financially realizable value is being created for the people in the community, and even with a competent team, the idea would be unattractive. Answers to these questions may not be as readily apparent for different concepts, but this simplified example illustrates the effectiveness that the "Quick Screen" can have in testing an idea for true value. Revising an idea is much more efficient in the planning stages than it would be midexecution.

A potential revision of the beachwear retail concept in Colorado would be to open a sporting goods store named, say, "Mountain Sporting Goods," that caters to people who participate in mountain sports such as skiing, hiking, climbing, and rafting. This concept passes the "Quick Screen," in that it creates value for customers, fulfills a need, has good market potential, and has a suitable risk/reward balance. If a potential venture passes this quick test, it is time to become immersed in the details of its potential by preparing a business plan.

PREPARING A BUSINESS PLAN

The preparation of a business plan is an excellent way to take a hard look at the concept in a structured, practical way. A well-done business plan can help mitigate or address the potential risks involved in starting a business before they actually occur. By thoroughly considering both the merit and the execution strategy of a vision, a prospective retailer can significantly improve its chances of success. A good business plan should concisely and effectively demonstrate the value of the concept to others—especially potential investors. The more prepared the retailer is to demonstrate and execute the value of the proposition, the less risk it poses, and the better investment opportunity the retail concept presents.

Business plans are dynamic and should evolve with the business. There is no set formula for a business plan, but there are some elements that every good business plan should include. First and foremost, a business plan should be well written, concise, and professional. No one will ever invest in a new venture if the business plan is verbose, boring, sloppy, or unprofessional. Nowhere is this more important than in the executive summary. Investors often see hundreds of business plans, and many of them read no further than the executive summary. If a plan does not grab their attention, or inadvertently casts a negative light, the venture proposal will not make it past a cursory reading at best. Structurally, a business plan should include at least the following content:

1. Executive summary.
2. Environmental analysis (trends, customers, competitors, economy).
3. Description of the retail concept and strategy (target market, retail format, competitive advantage).
4. Implementation plan, including the approach for attracting customers.
5. Team, or the other people involved in business.
6. Funding request.
7. Financial plan.

The key points of writing a retail business plan are illustrated below with the creation of a fictitious retail business. The examples include less detail than an actual business plan would require, but they are designed as a starting point from which the entrepreneur can initiate further research. The overarching themes also can be applied to a wide variety of retail businesses.

Environmental Analysis

The scope of the environmental analysis depends on the long-term objective. If the retailer's objective is simply to operate one or two outlets, the environmental analysis should focus on the local environment, such as the trade area of the store, as discussed in Chapter 8. However, if the long-term objective is to open and operate multiple retail outlets, the retailer needs to examine all the elements in the macroenvironment, such as industry size and trends and the competition and profitability of the industry, as discussed in Chapter 5. The elements in the environmental analysis detailed next apply to supporting a venture that starts in Colorado Springs, with ambitions to expand regionally and potentially nationally.

Industry Size and Trends   Various databases can provide detailed information about industrywide figures. For example, Hoover's Online and IBISWorld US Industry reports both provide detailed industry data, analyses of publicly traded companies, and customer demographics. Many libraries subscribe to these types of services, and a local librarian can be helpful in providing guidance on accessing them. Many publicly traded companies offer information on their Web sites, and they are required to publish financial data with the Securities and Exchange Commission. Trade organizations and publications such as the Sporting Goods Manufacturers Association (sgma.com), the National Sporting Goods Association (nsga.com), and *Sporting Goods Dealer* often provide detailed information about specific retail sectors. Census data, available at census.gov, give great insight into the population of the focal community in terms of companies and people. For example, there are 625 specialty-line sporting goods establishments in Colorado, according to the Census Bureau.

For smaller local businesses, it can more difficult to find information. Knowledge of the local area therefore can be a great asset. Also, gathering information from the customers and suppliers of competitors in the industry can provide valuable information. Resourcefulness and persistence are a key to discovering certain information, and it can be very beneficial to take the time to do so. Visit similar retailers and look at what they have to offer. Where is the unmet need? How can a new retailer rise to meet it?

Market size also is critical. How much money is being generated in the specific retail area? How is the money distributed within the industry? For example, the sporting goods industry in the United States generates about $55 billion in sales annually. This number is a significant starting point, in that it illustrates the overall monetary potential of the industry, but more focused data also are necessary.

Research shows that the sporting goods industry is highly fragmented, with many small retailers rather than dominant control by larger players. Therefore, opportunity appears to exist for the growth and expansion of a smaller retailer. Information like this is important to investors, because it can be used to illustrate that the industry is ready for a new retail business concept. For example, the implementation plan for the new store could demonstrate the growth potential that would enable it to consolidate smaller businesses and gain a significant market share in the sporting goods industry. The correlation of industry data to real opportunity makes for a compelling narrative that entices financiers to invest in the company. In other words, an implementation plan should demonstrate how an interesting opportunity can provide a high return on investment.

To find where the specific opportunity lies, you must whittle industry data down to the niche level. In the United States, sporting goods sales derive from retailers such as Sports Authority, Walmart, and a multitude of smaller retailers. These stores sell equipment, apparel, and shoes for every sporting need imaginable all across the country. For simplicity, Mountain Sporting Goods might focus only on sporting equipment, which makes up 46 percent of the sporting goods industry. It can further narrow its focus by defining what mountain sports mean for Mountain Sporting Goods. What mountain sports segments will be targeted?

Examination of the sports equipment data makes it apparent that camping, fishing tackle, hunting, and firearms account for 6.9, 9.0, and 12.1 percent (hunting and firearms combined) of the sports equipment market, respectively. Should the concept therefore be expanded to include these segments, in addition to skiing, hiking, rafting, and climbing? A moral disagreement with hunting might be a factor to consider as well. Does the significant financial opportunity outweigh the ethical uncertainty that selling hunting equipment might cause? What are the federal and local licenses required to sell firearms? Will the store sell tags for hunting certain animals? The reconciliation of these types of conflicting issues will help refine the concept.

Target Customers   Another critical element is defining the target market. What age demographic is the typical customer? What is his or her socioeconomic status and gender? Where do customers live in relation to the proposed store location? Where do they work? Will the store provide goods for the whole family or focus on individuals? How will the retail concept provide them with value? Will it compete on the basis of low prices or differentiated, higher-quality products? Finding the right balance of these factors is key. An overly narrow focus can be problematic, because it implies insufficient demand for the offering. A focus that is too broad also can hinder the retailer's ability to forge its own identity. Research findings might narrow these options. For example, if Mountain Sporting Goods opened in Aspen, Colorado, it would be reasonable for it to deal in specialty, high-quality, high-price goods because of the affluent customer base that resides there.

Competitors   The final step in analyzing the retail environment is to study potential competitors. How does the retail concept compare with those of others that offer similar merchandise? How do these competitors reach their customers? What kind of advertising strategy do they use? How long have they been in business? Do they have an e-commerce component to their business? How similar are the products they sell? How high are their goods priced? How well do their employees know their product? What is their store layout like?

Many larger sporting goods retailers carry a broad array of sporting products, so naturally there will be some overlap in what Walmart sells and what Mountain Sporting Goods offers. How important is this overlap? Walmart may take a small portion of customers, but it offers only a general sampling of what Mountain Sporting Goods specializes in providing. Sports Authority would be a bigger threat though, because it offers only sporting goods, spanning the spectrum of equipment, shoes, apparel, camping equipment, and more. Walmart and Sports Authority also can leverage their sizes to compete on price more easily than can a small retail business. Factors such as these must be considered when establishing the new retailer's strategic position. Initially, Mountain Sporting Goods would have to compete on the basis of its ability to offer more differentiated specialty products than some of the bigger chains, and create an environment that draws customers to the store. After a good deal of growth, it might achieve economies of scale by purchasing high volumes of products, as this lowers costs and increases its ability to compete on price.

The other segment of sporting goods retailers, which makes up the majority of the industry, is local businesses. Local research will be very important in determining local competitors' strengths and weaknesses. Do some reconnaissance work to see how competitors operate, and put yourself in the role of the customer to browse their shops. How big is the store? Does it feel cramped? Were you treated well by employees? How knowledgeable were they about the products they sell? Did they have the range of goods that you desire? Were the hours of operation adequate to meet local needs? How can a new store create a more pleasurable shopping experience?

Other issues to consider are the location of competitors, their proximity to the desired demographic, parking lot layout, building condition, and so forth. If Mountain Sporting Goods sells almost the same goods for the same price as a competitor but customers do not have to drive as far, can park more easily, and can enjoy a nicer facility, Mountain Sporting Goods gains a distinct competitive advantage.

Retail Concept

After completing the industry analysis, it is time to combine the original conceptual idea with the data uncovered through industry research in the form of a company description. Who is Mountain Sporting Goods? To whom will it sell its products? How does it do so better than others? How can it exploit competitive advantages to make the company grow?

Mountain Sporting Goods has decided to include the following information in its company description: It will locate in Colorado Springs, Colorado, to exploit the rapid growth of the community and the prevalence of a young, ecocentric population. Colorado Springs has an unmet need for ecofriendly stores and a large enough population of people who are willing to pay a premium for that attribute. Therefore, the store will sell the best-quality, most environmentally friendly skiing, hiking, whitewater rafting, mountain climbing, and camping equipment available. Customers will range in age from 23 to 35 years, and they will place environmental friendliness at the top of their priority list. These young single or coupled professionals without children have a fair amount of disposable income.

In turn, the management for the company must have an extensive background in sustainability and a passion for outdoor activities. As Mountain Sporting Goods gains customers and increases sales revenue, it might begin to acquire other, similarly sized firms to gain market share. These firms must be geographically accessible so that the company can pool resources and increase its purchasing power, as well as reduce costs through the consolidation of tasks such as distribution, purchasing, and accounting. In this way, the firm will be able to achieve the benefits of size and develop economies of scale.

A business plan must present these facets of the business in such a way that they draw the reader into the concept. The company description segment therefore should illustrate the founder's passion for the concept. It should also emphasize the opportunities that it creates and explain the competitive advantages that enable those opportunities to reach fruition.

The research and brainstorming accomplished thus far are detailed in the remainder of the business plan, so the following portions are the most finely detailed. The potential investor should have been able to recognize the value of the potential business already; the remainder of the plan provides proof of that value. The marketing, operations, management, and financial segments of the business plan thus tell the investor how the concept will be executed, what the retailer intends to sell, who will execute the process, how much money will be required to make it happen, and the money that can be earned as a result.

THE IMPLEMENTATION PLAN

The main goal of an implementation plan is to determine how the retail business will attract consumers in the target market and convert them into loyal customers. This essential portion of a retail business plan not only describes how the company will position itself in the market but also outlines the components required to make it a reality. The plan should describe the following elements in detail:

1. *Merchandise offered.* Number and breadth of lines to be carried, styles of merchandise and accessories, names of suppliers, supplier credit terms, quality of merchandise, opening stock, inventory levels, and expected turnover rate (see Chapters 12 and 13).

2. *Customer services offered.* Customer service levels and contact provided, credit policies, exchange and return policies, alterations, and gift wrapping (Chapter 18).

3. *Facilities.* Store appearance, any renovation required, interior decor, storefront, layout, lighting, window displays, wall displays, and overall atmosphere (Chapter 17).

4. *Location.* Buy, lease, or rent; terms of contract; local ordinances; zoning regulations; parking; accessibility; local demographics; and conditions for remodeling (Chapters 7 and 8).

5. *Pricing.* Price ranges to offer, competitive pricing, profitable pricing, margins, markdowns, and discount prices (Chapter 14).

6. *Promotion.* One-year promotional plan, advertising budgets, selection of media, cost of local media options, promotional displays, cooperative advertising efforts, and public relations (Chapter 15).

7. *Employees.* Compensational plan and wage scale to be offered, job specifications, employee training program, career and promotion schedule, employee benefits, social security taxes, sources and types of employees to hire (e.g., age, gender, appearance, education level), and policy on family employees (Chapters 9 and 16).

8. *Security.* Security guards, fire and theft alarms, computer security system, windows, locks, merchandise protection services, liability insurance, and other insurance (Chapter 16).

9. *Equipment.* Cash registers, sales desk, computer systems, display racks, office equipment, office supplies, telephone systems, management information system, software, security, and personal computer requirements (Chapter 10).

10. *Controls.* Inventory control and replenishment methods and financial performance analysis. (Chapters 6 and 12).

Team

Who will help to execute the vision? One of the most important factors in starting a business is finding a group of people whose skill sets complement those of the founder. It is virtually impossible for one person to possess all of the requisite skills for creating and growing a business. For example, if Mountain Sporting Goods intends to follow through with its plans to acquire other businesses, it would be beneficial to bring someone into the group with experience in the area of mergers and acquisitions. Also, the owner/manager of Mountain Sporting Goods has a background in sustainability, which represents a great asset in setting up a business whose cornerstone is environmental awareness.

The team section showcases the talent of the people who will run the retail start-up. It is both a "who's who" of the business venture and a way to assure investors that their money will be handled by people of quality. This assurance is especially effective if someone with experience in starting retail stores joins the team. Such a person lends significant credibility to the business endeavor, as well as a great deal of sage advice. Experienced people do not necessarily have to be paid employees or managers but instead could serve on a board of advisors or board of directors. Each person should be listed, with his or her credentials outlined and role within the company clarified.

Funding Request

One of the objectives of a business plan is to seek financing and show how the firm might use investors' money, whether debt or equity financing. For a small retailer, a loan request (debt financing) is more common. If Mountain Sporting Goods' aspiration is to be a local lifestyle business, it still needs to show where the money is going and how the lender will receive a return on its investment through the company's ability to generate enough revenue to repay the loan, as well as the timing of the repayments.

A company with higher aims might seek venture capital support for its major growth. The owner/manager of this company would negotiate with venture capitalists about what portion of their equity should be provided for the desired financial support. Investors would receive shares (equity) in the company in exchange for the financing that they provide.

At a certain point, probably within a few years, venture capitalists typically can monitize those shares after the company is bought by another company, has its initial public offering (IPO), or buys the investors' share of the company back. For example, Mountain Sporting Goods might explain how it will execute its growth plans and generate a return on investment for its financiers. At a specified time, Mountain Sporting Goods will have enough revenue growth and profits to go public, represent a significant enough threat to larger competitors that they buy it out, or pay back the investors at the desired rate of return. Investors base their evaluation of the venture on how much they predict the company will be worth at the designated time of sale, IPO, or buyback. If they believe the company can generate the intended value that they seek, they will invest.

Financial Plan

The financial plan can be one of the more intimidating aspects of business plan writing, but it also is essential to determine the value of the retail business. The financial plan provides investors with information that enables them to decide whether the business concept is worth their risk. Taking the time to learn how to create the financial plan therefore has great value. Moreover, the financial plan offers the prospective retailer a detailed understanding of the major contributing factors that might result in success or failure. With this knowledge, the retailer can safeguard the business and deal with accomplished businesspeople and investors with greater confidence. Financial projections vary depending on the degree of complexity sought for the financing, but the following discussion provides a simple overview of the process. The only way to learn, though, is to roll up your sleeves and do it.

Financial projections for a completely new business are especially difficult, in that they must be based solely on assumptions because there are no historical data. No one has uncovered the secret to predicting the future, but it is possible to make educated estimates. The key is finding where to start. What are the initial elements that an entrepreneur requires to build a financial model of a potential venture?

The income statement, cash flow, balance sheet, financing, and break-even analysis constitute the basics that must be included. The purpose of these projections is to tell investors when the business will actually become profitable and how fast it will grow. The groundwork laid by the implementation plan is a good place to start.

The elements required to reach target customers indicate both start-up and fixed costs, which represent the basis of the financial projections. For example, if Mountain Sporting Goods has done enough research, it will have narrowed down how much the location lease or mortgage will cost and, from merchandise sources, learned how much the inventory will cost. These and many other factors will be "known" entities, from which the fixed start-up and operating costs can be established. Other miscellaneous start-up elements, such as legal fees, also should be included.

After the costs have been established, sales figures must be projected. There are two methods for estimating financial statements: the comparable method and the build-up method. The retailer should employ both methods and compare their results to come up with the final projection. The comparable method uses financial data from a similar company or ratios from the industry and then compares them to the projected data for the concept company. The build-up method examines sales and builds expected revenues and expenses by determining what they might be on an average day, such as the products sold on an average day, the types of products, the buyers and how many people buy, and the amount each would spend. By establishing an average day's sales, the retailer can extrapolate these data to months, years, and so on. The data also can be adjusted for seasonal variances, which are important for any retail business. After reconciling any differences between the estimates produced by the two different methods, all that remains is to construct the financial statements for inclusion in the business plan.

The business plan requires perpetual refining and updating as new information, such as opportunities and threats in the environment that prompt a change in the retail concept, becomes available. The business plan also should be referred to and used at all stages of growth. Just as in a business's infancy, it remains important to evaluate who it is, what it does, and how it will do so on a continuing basis.

GETTING STARTED

Now that the business plan has been completed, there are a few other miscellaneous costs and issues that must be considered. With a strong retail concept, the business must address certain procedural processes. One of the most important is to set up its legal structure. Will the company be a sole proprietorship, a partnership, or an incorporated firm? These structures all incur unique costsal though the least expensive is a sole proprietorship. A sole proprietorship, however, does not remove any personal assets from the responsibility owed to creditors for the failure or success of the business. If an entrepreneur elects to sell shares of the company to investors, he or she will need to have the appropriate structure in place, and this often requires the assistance of an attorney, who can help file for the appropriate business structure that shields personal assets from certain risks and that has the most advantageous tax implications. Another necessary regulatory step is to file for an employer identification number (EIN) or federal tax identification number, which is required by law to operate a business.

Assuming that the company finds the financing required to launch the retail concept, the entrepreneur is now staring at the precipice of opportunity. The groundwork laid by the business plan now can be put to excellent use. It is a time of mixed emotions. The plan that the retailer has toiled so long and hard to craft will soon be battle tested. Theory will be put into practice, and the owner will determine its true value according to the response of the market. Will you achieve the fulfilling personal and financial success to which you aspire? The only way to know is to take that first step off the edge.

ADDITIONAL SOURCES OF INFORMATION

Bond, Ronald L. *Retail in Detail: How to Start and Manage a Small Retail Business.* Irvine, CA: Entrepreneur Press, 2005.

Davis, Charlene. *Start Your Own Clothing Store and More.* Irvine, CA: Entrepreneur Press, 2007.

Dion, Jim, and Ted Topping. *Start & Run a Retail Business,* 2nd ed. Bellingham, WA: Self-Counsel Press, 2007.

Mikaelsen, Debbra, and Pamela Skillings. *FabJob Guide to Become a Boutique Owner.* Calgary, Alberta, Canada: FabJob Guides, 2007.

Schroeder, Carol L. *Specialty Shop Retailing: Everything You Need to Know to Run Your Own Store,* 3rd ed. Indianapolis, IN: Wiley, 2007.

Start Your Own Successful Retail Business. Irvine, CA: Entrepreneur Press, 2003.

APPENDIX B
Starting a Franchise Business

Like hot dogs, baseball, and apple pie, franchising is an American institution. A proven means to realize the entrepreneurial dream, franchising also is taking over much of the retail trade in the United States. The 14 highest-performing franchises are listed in Exhibit B–1. This appendix explores franchising options in terms of their merits and drawbacks. With more than 2,900 franchises to choose from, finding the best one can be almost as hard as starting a business.

Franchises are popular largely because of their historical success. In the late 1980s the U.S. Chamber of Commerce published a study revealing that 97 percent of new franchises remained in business after five years.[1] That sounds terrific, especially since 80 percent of independent businesses fail within five years. But not all franchises are secure investments. Arthur Treacher's Fish and Chips, Jerry Lewis Theaters, and Chicken Delight all have one thing in common: They failed. As a result, thousands of dreams were shattered, and millions of dollars were lost. Buying a franchise can be a dream come true, or it can be a nightmare. The key is buying smart, which requires planning and investigating before signing a contract. Franchising can be a very satisfactory method of starting a business. It also can be extremely rewarding, both personally and financially, and it offers ownership and decision-making privileges not afforded by working for someone else.

Some interesting franchise facts to consider:

- The franchise concept began in the 1850s when Singer Sewing Machine Company (franchisor) sold sales rights to independent entrepreneurs (franchisees) in an effort to raise business capital.
- Today, franchised businesses account for nearly 50 percent of all retail sales in the United States.
- McDonald's was one of the first companies to sell franchises internationally in the 1970s.

EXHIBIT B–1
The 14 Highest-Performing Franchises

1.	Edible Arrangements
2.	Firehouse Subs
3.	Massage Envy
4.	Microtel
5.	Primrose School, Daycare
6.	Pump It Up
7.	Comfort Inn
8.	Comfort Suites
9.	Holiday Inn Express
10.	Culver's Frozen Custard
11.	Hampton Inns
12.	Bruster's
13.	Little Caesar's Pizza
14.	FastSigns

Source: www.nuwireinvestor.com/articles/
the-14-best-performing-franchises-in-the-
us-52499.aspx (accessed June 14, 2010).

*This appendix was prepared by Professor Tracy Meyer, University of North Carolina–Wilmington.

- Fast food is the top franchise industry.
- Subway has the most franchised stores in the world, with more than 32,900 units.
- Subway's international growth initiatives include the addition of 500 stores in China by 2015.
- The service industry has the fastest-growing U.S. franchises (health and fitness, security, and senior care).

THE BASICS OF FRANCHISING

So how does franchising work? Basically, the franchisor (the company) sells the rights to use its business trademark, service mark, or trade name, or another commercial symbol of the company, to the franchisee for a one-time franchise fee, which might range anywhere from $0 to $225,000 (the franchise fee for Subway is approximately $15,000). In addition, the franchisor charges an ongoing royalty fee, typically expressed as a percentage of gross monthly sales. Ongoing royalty fees typically range from 2 to 10 percent (the royalty fee for Subway is 12.5 percent and includes 8 percent toward franchise royalties and 4.5 percent toward advertising). For example, if a Subway shop generates $20,000 in sales in a given month, the franchisee must pay the franchisor $2,500 (12.5 percent of $20,000). Some franchisors instead calculate the ongoing royalty fee on a sliding scale, with the percentage fee decreasing as sales increase beyond preestablished thresholds. Suppose the monthly sales threshold for a hypothetical franchise is $50,000. For the first $50,000 of sales, the ongoing royalty fee charged is 6 percent, or $3,000, but for sales of more than $50,000, the franchisor collects a 3 percent royalty fee. Therefore, if sales for a one-month period total $80,000, the royalty fee equals $3,900, rather than the $4,800 that would have been due if the sliding scale were not in place. The sliding scale thus encourages franchisees to continue to find ways to increase sales volume.

Attractions of Franchise Ownership

When considering the franchise option, potential franchisees must understand the attractions and drawbacks of buying a franchise versus starting a retail business from scratch. There are many reasons to consider franchise ownership, including the success rate, which results partially from the proven business model that the franchisor offers. Success also results from the unique relationship between the franchisor and the franchisee, in which both parties benefit from the success of the franchisee. To get franchisees off to a good start, most franchisors provide off- and on-site training, location analysis assistance, advertising, and sometimes a protected territory (i.e., no other franchise may open a store within a certain radius of the first store). Some franchisors even provide financing or offer third-party financing opportunities.

Drawbacks to Franchise Ownership

There are also several drawbacks to franchise ownership. In addition to having to pay money to the franchisor, the franchisee needs financing for start-up costs, including rent or purchase price of office/retail space, modification of the space according to the guidelines of the franchisor (e.g., paint colors, flooring, lighting, layout), signage, opening inventory, and equipment. For example, a traditional Subway restaurant in the United States creates up-front costs ranging from $114,800 to $258,300, including the $15,000 franchise fee. The variation in the cost estimates is primarily due to the cost of leasehold improvements, which can range from $59,500 to $134,500.[2]

In addition to incurring the capital costs, the franchisee must adhere to the franchisor's rules and operating guidelines. In many cases, the franchisee is required to purchase operating materials from the franchisor, especially in fast-food franchises that rely on standardized products across franchises for the success of the brand. The franchisor also might require the franchisee to purchase the equipment needed to offer a new product, such as fryers at a Burger King or beds at a Holiday Inn. The hours of operation and days of the year that the business is allowed to close also may be dictated by the franchisor.

Finally, sales and profits can be hurt by events outside the control of the franchisee. For example, in 2005, a scam artist reported she had found a severed finger in her Wendy's chili; in response, franchise sales dropped significantly in the subsequent weeks.[3] In another case, a Jackson-Hewitt franchisee actually was caught falsifying tax returns to get larger refunds for its clients, which enabled it to collect higher fees.[4] Whether true or false, such incidents harm the image of the entire franchise system and materially influence consumers' future purchase decisions.

FRANCHISE EVALUATION PROCESS

The key to making a smart purchase of a franchise is taking the necessary time to research franchise opportunities thoroughly. The five steps outlined below offer a methodical approach to the decision process:

Step 1: Initial investigation.

Step 2: Formal request for information from franchisors.

Step 3: Interviews.

Step 4: Evaluation of fit.

Step 5: Choice of franchise.

Step 1: Initial Investigation

For a potential franchisee, the best way to begin a search for franchise opportunities is to consider franchise businesses that seem fundamentally appealing. To determine if a business operates as a franchise, look through *The Franchise Handbook*, a quarterly magazine (franchisehandbook.com) or simply visit the Web site of the firm you're interested in pursuing. Also consider attending franchise trade shows, such as the National Franchise & Business Opportunities Show. Shows travel throughout cities all over the world and offer an excellent way to gain a closer look at what the industry has to offer (franchiseshowinfo.com). Potential franchisees should pick five to ten franchises that look interesting and affordable. The due-diligence process starts with collecting all information available about each business.

Step 2: Formal Request for Information from Franchisors

After completing the initial information review, if the franchise is still of interest, the potential franchisee should formally request information directly from the franchisor. Most franchisors provide a link on their Web sites (usually at the very bottom of the page) that allows potential franchisees to fill out an online form requesting information. The forms vary dramatically in the amount of information they require. Beyond asking for the basics of name and address, the form may require information relative to education, work experience, personal financial status, and references.

Franchising is governed by the Federal Trade Commission's Franchise Opportunity Rule,[5] which requires franchisors to provide full disclosure of the information that a prospective franchisee needs to make a rational decision about whether to invest in the franchise. The information appears in the form of the Uniform Franchise Offering Circular (UFOC). All 50 states use the same UFOC, although each state retains the right to impose stricter provisions if it so desires. The UFOC lists lawsuits against the company and provides revenue and earnings figures. Franchisors must provide a copy of the UFOC at least 10 days before the signing of any contract or the exchange of any money. A side-by-side comparison of the UFOCs of several franchisors can reveal crucial differences in costs and corporate support.

Step 3: Interviews

Potential Franchisee Interviews Franchisor   The interview process goes both ways. The potential franchisee interviews the franchisor, and at the same time the franchisor is interviewing the potential franchisee. From the perspective of the potential franchisee, the historical success rate of franchisees, the territories that are available, the extent of training and ongoing support provided, and the advertising support offered are key issues. The financial strength of the franchisor is also of great consequence, because it is important for the franchisee to be confident that the franchisor will be successful for many years ahead.

Franchisor Interviews Potential Franchisee   The franchisor will want to interview the prospective franchisee to determine whether he or she possesses the desire and skill set needed to succeed, such as the prospective franchisee's management and people skills and willingness to learn. Does the applicant possess basic business skills? Does the prospective franchisee have access to sufficient capital? These factors are important to the successful operation of a franchise. The franchisor also wants to be sure that the applicant understands what owning a franchise will require, in terms of both time and money.

Potential Franchisee Interviews Other Franchisees   Assuming the process is proceeding satisfactorily, the prospective franchisee should interview existing franchisees to gain information about any issues or problems that they have experienced with the franchisor. The prospective franchisee should ask tough questions, such as the following: Do you have any complaints about the business? How many hours a week do you devote to the business? Is it hard to find staffing? If you had to do it over again, would you purchase the same franchise? The existing franchisee also might have advice to offer. At this point, it may become apparent that some aspects of operating the franchise business had not been previously considered, good and bad!

Step 4: Evaluation of Fit

The gathered information can now be used to determine whether the franchise represents a good opportunity. An evaluation of fit requires the prospective franchisee to sift through the information he or she has obtained and outline both the positives and the negatives associated with owning the business. Assuming the financial commitment is plausible and the amount of time required to run the business sounds reasonable, the potential franchisee also should consider if this work is what he or she wants to do. The purchase also may require the move to a new city. These are all things to consider before narrowing the search too much.

Step 5: Choice of a Franchise

This is it! Having completed the information-gathering and evaluation process, the time is right to choose a franchise. Recall that the most important element is making sure that the basic idea of the business sounds appealing. At this point, the potential franchisee should solicit the advice of an accountant to review the financials, a lawyer to review the franchise agreement, and potentially a banker to assist with the financing. The potential franchisee also should know exactly what he or she is getting into before committing.

Diligence in following these five steps improves the odds that the potential franchisee will transform into a proud owner of a *successful* franchise.

ADDITIONAL READING

Federal Trade Commission Facts for Consumers: Buying a Franchise
http://www.ftc.gov/bcp/edu/pubs/consumer/invest/inv05.shtm

International Franchise Association
www.franchise.org/defaultindustry.aspx

The American Franchisee Association
www.franchisee.org/

Entrepreneur magazine
www.entrepreneur.com/franchiseopportunities/index.html

U.S. Chamber of Commerce Small Business Center,
www.uschamber.com/sb/business/tools/franch_m.asp

1. www.the-franchise-guy.com/facts.htm (accessed June 8, 2010).

2. www.subway.com/subwayroot/Development/becoming/docs/Capital_Req_US_Canada.pdf (accessed June 8, 2010).

3. www.snopes.com/horrors/food/chili.asp (accessed June 8, 2010).

4. www.ftc.gov/bcp/edu/pubs/consumer/invest/inv05.shtm (accessed June 8, 2010).

5. http://money.cnn.com/2007/04/16/smbusiness/jackson_hewitt/index.htm?section5money_topstories (accessed June 8, 2010).

Cases

Cases	CHAPTER																		
	1	2	3	4	5	6	7	8	9	10	11	12	13	14	15	16	17	18	C
1 Tractor Supply Company Targets the Part-Time Rancher	P	P			P		S											S	
2 Build-A-Bear Workshop—Where Best Friends are Made	P	P			S														P
3 Walmart's Sustainability 360	P								S				S						
4 Netflix Personalizes the Customer's Experience			P															S	
5 The Decision-Making Process for Buying a Bicycle				P															
6 Retailing in India: The Impact of Hypermarkets	P	S		S	P														
7 Diamonds from Mine to Market				S	P					P			P						
8 Save-A-Lot: An Extreme-Value Retailer		P			P	S										S			P
9 Royal Ahold: The Biggest Supermarket Retailer You Have Never Heard Of					P				S										
10 Abercrombie & Fitch and American Eagle Compete for 18- to 22-Year-Olds	S	S			P									P					
11 Merchandise Strategy: Process for Success					P							P	S						
12 Tiffany's and Walmart: Comparing Financial Performance					S	P													
13 Choosing a Store Location for a Boutique							P												
14 Hutch: Locating a New Store								P											
15 Avon Embraces Diversity			S		S				P										
16 Attracting Generation Y to a Retail Career									P						S				
17 Nordstrom Rewards Its Customers											P							S	
18 Active Endeavors Analyzes Its Customer Database											P								
19 Developing an Assortment Plan for Hughes											P								
20 Preparing a Merchandise Budget Plan												P							
21 PenAgain Sells to Walmart													P						
22 American Furniture Warehouse Sources Globally													P						
23 Merchandise Exclusively for JCPenney													P						
24 How Much for a Good Smell?														P					
25 Promoting a Sale														S	P				
26 Target Marketing with Google AdWords			S													P			
27 Enterprise Rent-A-Car Focuses on Its People					S											P		S	
28 Diamond in the Rough																P			

countinued

Cases	CHAPTER																		C
	1	2	3	4	5	6	7	8	9	10	11	12	13	14	15	16	17	18	
29 "Touch and Feel at Sephora"			S		S												P	S	
30 A Stockout at Discmart																S	P	P	
31 Customer Service and Relationship Management at Nordstrom							S		S									P	
32 Building the Apple Store																	P	S	
33 Generating Advertising Revenue from a Digital Screen Network at Harrods of London																S	P		
34 Starbucks' Retail Strategy					P										S	S			P
35 Yankee Candle: New Product Innovation													S						P
36 PetSmart: Where Pets Are Family					S				S									S	P
37 Lindy's Bridal Shop						S	S					S				S			P
38 Interviewing for a Management Trainee Position	P								S							S			

P Primary Use
S Secondary Use
C Comprehensive

CASE 1   Tractor Supply Company Targets the Part-Time Rancher

Tractor Supply Company (TSC), a large and fast-growing retailer with over $3 billion in annual sales and over 900 stores in 44 states, was the inventor of the "do-it-yourself" (DIY) trend. Its origins date to 1938, when Charles E. Schmidt Sr. established a mail-order tractor parts business. After the success of his first retail store in Minot, North Dakota, he opened additional stores to serve the needs of local farmers. But eventually TSC's sales stagnated because small farms and ranches were being acquired by large farming and ranching corporations. These large agricultural firms buy supplies and equipment directly from manufacturers rather than through local farm supply stores like TSC.

TARGET MARKET

Since the early 1990s, TSC has targeted a growing group of people interested in recreational farming and ranching. Called "sundowners," "U-turners," "hobby farmers," "ruralpolitans," "micropolitans," "gentlemen farmers," and "X-urbanites," these people have turned to farming to escape the hubbub of urban and suburban life. They are drawn to what they believe is a more private, simple, and stress-free lifestyle. They typically live on 5 to 20 acres in a rural community outside a metropolitan area, where they work at a full-time profession, and use some of their earnings to keep their farms in operation. Many of them are the sons and daughters of traditional production farmers and inherited the family farm and decided to keep it running. Today less than 10 percent of TSC's customers classify themselves as full-time farmers or ranchers, and many of its customers do not farm at all.

RETAIL OFFERING

The typical TSC store has 15,000 to 24,000 square feet of inside selling space and a similar amount of outside space used to display agricultural fencing, livestock equipment, and horse stalls. The company tries to locate stores in the prime retail corridor of rural communities, two or three counties away from major metropolitan areas. Fifty percent of its stores are in previously occupied buildings.

The typical store stocks about 15,000 SKUs, using a combination of national and private-label brands. TSC constantly tests new merchandise programs in its stores. For instance, based on a successful test of expanded clothing and footwear categories, TSC doubled the size of these areas of the store and added more lifestyle clothes and workwear for both men and women.

TSC stores are designed to make shopping an enjoyable experience and, at the same time, maximize sales and operating efficiencies. Their environment allows plenty of space for individual departments and visual displays. Informative signs assist customers with purchasing decisions by delineating "good, better, best" qualities, pointing out their "everyday low-pricing" policy, and providing useful information regarding product benefits and suggestions for appropriate accessories.

TSC emphasizes customer service. The company tries to hire store employees who have farming and

EXHIBIT 1
TSC's Value and Mission
Statements

ranching backgrounds. Its training programs include (1) a full management training program, which covers all aspects of its operations, (2) product knowledge modules produced in conjunction with key vendors, (3) frequent management skills training classes, (4) semi-annual store managers' meetings, with vendor product presentations, (5) vendor-sponsored in-store training programs, and (6) ongoing product information updates at its management headquarters. This extensive training, coupled with a management philosophy that stresses empowerment, enables store employees to assist customers in making their purchase decisions and solve customer problems as they arise. Store employees wear highly visible red vests, aprons, or smocks and nametags. TSC uses a variety of incentive programs that provide the opportunity for store employees to receive additional compensation based on their team, store, and/or company performance.

While TSC creates a "hometown farmer" shopping experience for customers, there is nothing "small-town" or "laid back" about its operations and use of technology. Its management information and control systems include a point-of-sale system, a supply chain management and replenishment system, a radio frequency picking system in the distribution centers, a vendor purchase order control system, and a merchandise presentation system. These systems work together to track merchandise from the initial order through to the ultimate sale.

TSC has a centralized supply chain management team that focuses on replenishment and forecasting and a buying team that selects merchandise, develops assortments, and evaluates new products and programs. Almost all purchase orders and vendor invoices are transmitted through an electronic data interchange (EDI) system.

VALUES AND MISSION

Despite changes to TSC's retail strategy in the past 70 years, its values and mission have remained constant. The company's value and mission statements appear on its Web site (Exhibit 1), on cards handed out to all employees, and on the walls of every store. According to TSC management, the first discussion with new employees centers on the firm's values and mission because the firm steadfastly maintains that "being a great place to work enables the company to be a great place to shop and invest."

DISCUSSION QUESTIONS

1. What is Tractor Supply Company's growth strategy? What retail mix does TSC provide?

2. Why and how has TSC's target customer changed over time?

3. How does TSC's retail mix provide the benefits sought by its target market?

4. How vulnerable is TSC to competition? Why is this the case?

5. Why does TSC place so much emphasis on training employees?

Sources: Tractor Supply Co., Annual Report 2009; www.tractorsupply.com (accessed July 7, 2010).

This case was written by Barton Weitz, University of Florida.

CASE 2   Build-A-Bear Workshop: Where Best Friends Are Made

Modern consumers want good value, low prices, and convenience, but they also appreciate a great shopping experience. Build-A-Bear Workshop usually locates its more than 400 stores in malls worldwide. It generates over $450 million in annual sales by offering customers the opportunity to make their own stuffed animals, complete with clothing and accessories.

In 1997, Maxine Clark came up with the idea for Build-A-Bear Workshop and opened a storefront in St. Louis. She had plenty of experience in the corporate side of retailing, having worked for Payless ShoeSource and May Department Stores. Clark left corporate America on a mission to bring the fun back to retailing. Currently, the company has sold more than 70 million furry friends.

The bear-making process consists of eight steps, Choose Me, Hear Me, Stuff Me, Stitch Me, Fluff Me, Dress Me, Name Me, and Take Me Home. The stores mirror the chain's name: Customers, or builders, choose an unstuffed animal and, working with the retailer's staff, move through eight "creation stations" to build their own bear (or other animal). At the first station, the Stuffiteria, children can pick fluff from bins marked "Love," "Hugs and Kisses," "Friendship," and "Kindness." The stuffing is sent through a long, clear tube and into a stuffing machine. A sales associate holds the bear to a small tube while the builder pumps a foot peddle. In seconds, the bear takes its form. Before the stitching, builders must insert a heart. The builders follow the sales associates' instructions and rub the heart between their hands to make it warm. They then close their eyes, make a wish, and kiss the heart before putting it inside the bear. After selecting a name and having it stitched on their animal, builders take their bears to the Fluff Me station, where they brush their bears on a "bathtub" that features spigots blowing air. Finally, they move to a computer station to create a birth certificate.

Bears go home in Cub Condo carrying cases, which act as mini-houses complete with windows and doors. In addition to serving as playhouses, the boxes advertise Build-A-Bear Workshop to the child's friends. "[You] could buy a bear anywhere," says Clark, Chief Executive Bear. "It's the experience that customers are looking for." The experience isn't limited to the stores themselves. The retailer's Web site, buildabear.com, embraces the same theme.

Build-a-Bearville (buildabearville.com) is its online virtual world where users can play with each other and play games. The bears that they bought at the store have a unique code that allows the user to redeem gifts while playing games in Build-a-Bearville.

Customers pay about $25 for the basic bear, but they can also buy music, clothing, and accessories. To keep the experience fresh, Build-A-Bear Workshop regularly introduces new and limited-edition animals. Clothes and accessories are also updated to reflect current fashion trends. Outfits for the bears complement the owner's interests and personalities with themes such as sports, colleges, hobbies, and careers. Some children and their parents hold in-store birthday parties, with music playing from the store's official CD. To ensure customers enjoy a great experience every time they visit, all sales associates attend a three-week training program at "Bear University," and the firm offers incentive programs and bonuses. The inventory in the stores changes frequently, with different bear styles arriving weekly. Build-A-Bear Workshops also feature limited-edition and seasonal merchandise, such as a Beary Businesslike Curly Teddy for Father's Day; mummy, wizard, and witch bears for Halloween; and a Sweet Hugs & Kisses Teddy for Valentine's Day.

REFACT

The teddy bear came into being in 1903, when President Teddy Roosevelt refused to shoot a cub while bear hunting. The spared animal was thereafter referred to as the Teddy Bear.

DISCUSSION QUESTIONS

1. Is the Build-A-Bear Workshop concept a fad, or does it have staying power?
2. Describe the target customer for this retailer.
3. What can Build-A-Bear Workshop do to generate repeat visits to the store?

Sources: www.buildabear.com (accessed July 7, 2010); www.buildabearville.com (accessed July 7, 2010);

This case was written by Barton Weitz, University of Florida.

CASE 3   Walmart's Sustainability 360

Walmart's reach is vast. *Fortune* magazine named it the "most admired company in America," and the *Financial Times* included it on its "Most Respected in the World" list. The retail giant has received various honors and accolades, such as being selected as among the "Top 50 Companies for Executive Women" by the National Association for Female Executives and "Top 50 Companies for African American MBAs" by *Black MBAs Magazine*. As the world's largest retailer, Walmart operates more than 8,400 retail units in 15 countries around the world, works with more than 100,000 suppliers, and employs more than

2 million people across the globe. Customer visits total more than 200 million each week, and the company posted sales of $405 billion for fiscal year 2010.

These statistics add up to a company capable of exerting massive pressure on its suppliers and employees and capable of making substantial differences in the lives of its customers. With this power comes choice. Walmart could offer low prices and eek out every penny of profits for its shareholders without regard to factors like employee working conditions or environmental impact. In fact, this was Walmart's approach until it came under fire from critics of the company's sourcing policies, employee wages and benefits, adverse effects on small businesses, and contributions to urban sprawl. Many communities took legal steps to keep Walmart and other big-box retailers out of town. Local governments claimed that Walmart stores increased traffic, drove local retailers out of business, transformed middle-class retail jobs into lower-paying jobs that lacked health care and other benefits, shrunk the tax base, and increased welfare. Some economists estimate that Walmart business practices annually caused a $4.7 billion loss of wages for workers in the retail sector.

With its reputation in jeopardy, Walmart faced a quandary: continue with existing practices, or use its position to effect meaningful changes in retail practices, beginning with its own business. On the surface, the latter approach appears to drive up costs and reduce profits, since organic products or those produced sustainably have traditionally carried a higher price tag. Walmart would then face tremendous difficulty in fulfilling both aspects of its mission, to help people live better by saving them money, since improving living conditions would result in price hikes, but low prices would mean less responsible business practices.

However, Walmart CEO Mike Duke views offering low prices and responsibly produced products as a both/and concept, not an either/or one. He launched an across-the-board sustainability effort known as "Sustainability 360," which is based on the belief that a companywide commitment to economic, environmental, and social sustainability can help Walmart uncover and remedy unsustainable practices. These efforts will save the company—and the consumer—money by reducing waste, increasing productivity, improving communities, and inspiring innovation. Only by saving customers money, decreasing its environmental footprint, and bettering working conditions can the company fulfill its mission of saving people money so that they can live better.

SAVING MONEY AND IMPROVING LIVES

A recessionary economy with high unemployment means Walmart's traditional customers need to make their dollars stretch even further when they visit the store. It also means more customers may shop Walmart's shelves as they try to make a diminished household income cover all of life's necessities. According to Walmart's 2010 sustainability report, ensuring that these individuals receive value, convenience, and quality for their dollar is integral to the company's mission, but these goals cannot be achieved at the expense of the environment or the lives of workers throughout the supply chain. Walmart is working internally and with partners and stakeholders to minimize waste, which saves money. The company is also working to improve economic conditions for individuals, families, and communities by requiring that partners adhere to the labor and environmental regulations of their area, creating new jobs, and generating tax revenue that supports key priorities like education and transportation projects. The retail giant claims to provide new markets for small businesses—including

local farmers—and to support small and medium-size suppliers to drive production chains.

Initiatives helping shoppers maximize their earnings go beyond low prices on prescriptions and consumer goods; Walmart's Financial Services division provides low-cost options such as check cashing, money orders, money transfers, bill payment, and prepaid credit cards. In addition, Walmart makes charitable contributions and in-kind donations to organizations in the United States and abroad, and its employees, known as associates, volunteer at charitable organizations within their communities. These programs, Walmart believes, contribute to its ability to do well as a business and as a neighbor.

DECREASING ENVIRONMENTAL IMPACT

In 2005, Walmart set three core goals for environmental sustainability: to be supplied 100 percent by renewable energy, to create zero waste, and to sell products that sustain resources and the environment. Since then, the company has defined baselines for its effort, identified metrics to help measure progress toward key initiatives and goals, and implemented new programs both in the United States and abroad. Initiatives span the supply chain and include increasing fleet efficiency, improving efficiency of and lowering greenhouse gas emissions from existing stores, retrofitting refrigerated display cases in U.S. stores with energy-saving LED lighting, minimizing waste due to overstocking of perishables, and reducing the amount of waste going to landfills through recycling efforts or packaging changes. In its annual sustainability report, Walmart updates stakeholders on improvements, such as a 16.1 percent reduction in plastic bag waste over a two-year period. Other waste reduction programs have directed excess food to food banks throughout the United States; increased recycling of aluminum, plastic, paper, and cardboard; and increased use of packaging that has been created using less energy and fewer natural resources and/or that has been transported using less fuel.

SELLING SUSTAINABLE PRODUCTS

Selling sustainable products at competitive prices helps consumers reduce their own energy consumption, thus saving them money while they help protect the environment. For example, Walmart stocks compact fluorescent (CFL) lightbulbs and has sold more than 350 million of these bulbs in the United States alone. Consumers using these bulbs will save $13 billion over the life of the bulbs. Energy-efficient air conditioners and flat-screen televisions will likewise help consumers lower their electricity costs while ensuring that televisions, personal computers, MP3 players, video games, and cameras are compliant with the Reduction of Hazardous Substances (RoHS) directive.

Walmart's Sam's Club was the first mass-market retailer in the United States to offer Fair Trade Certified bananas. These bananas support sustainable communities, since profits return to the community in the form of funding for education and development projects. They also help Walmart's environmental sustainability efforts by reducing the amount of herbicides needed to ensure a healthy crop. In its apparel line, Walmart has developed best-practices guidelines and a toolkit to help suppliers in cut-and-sew factories and dye houses reduce waste scrap and energy use, use water more efficiently, and conform to acceptable social and ethical practices. Driving wastes out of the supply chain makes business more efficient, helping keep prices down.

In 2009, Walmart announced discussions of the development of a Sustainable Product Index to rate products on the basis of their sustainability. The ratings, which will be based on use of energy and natural resources, production efficiency, and contributions to individuals and community, will appear on product labels and are intended to evolve into a tool that will help improve sustainable practices throughout the supply chain and empower customers to make environmentally friendly purchasing decisions. Data collection also helps Walmart identify suppliers whose practices fall below sustainability standards so that these suppliers can receive additional training and support. Walmart expects the first stage of the project—collecting data on the life cycle of products from raw-material use to disposal—to be completed within five years.

MAINTAINING A SUSTAINABLE WORKFORCE

A sustainable company requires streamlined business practices and innovative technology, and it also requires a healthy and motivated workforce. Sickness, injury, lack of motivation, stress, family concerns, and minimal education can all affect a company's performance, so Walmart has committed to social sustainability along with its environmental sustainability goals. Under this initiative, Walmart has set goals and requirements for its suppliers. These parameters cover adherence to local social and environmental regulations and ethical standards, quality and safety of manufactured products, and energy use. Within different geographic areas of the world, Walmart has identified specific challenges, ranging from excessive overtime and unsafe work conditions to discrimination, poor production planning, and undeclared subcontracting. Regular auditing helps identify suppliers in need of further investigation or support. Efforts aren't confined to suppliers: Walmart is reviewing its buying practices to see how they affect factory conditions and is ensuring that its own workforce is fairly and equitably compensated, that women and minorities have opportunities to progress to management positions,

and that health care coverage is broadly available. Providing this combination of pay, benefits, and opportunities helps reduce turnover, keep staff healthy and at work, and build loyalty to the company. The company further ensures a strong future workforce through contributions to workforce development programs, community efforts to reduce poverty, and improved access to education or clean, safe drinking water and food.

DISCUSSION QUESTIONS

1. Is Walmart good for society? Would society be better off with or without Walmart?

2. Walmart says that it creates new markets for small- and medium-size businesses and that it supports growth and innovation for these businesses. For some of these suppliers, Walmart is their primary customer and thus the business owners have little choice about adopting Walmart's standards. Do you think this is fair? Do you think Walmart's powerful position helps these business owners or hinders them?

3. Walmart's sustainability program addresses each of the criticisms leveled against it. If a company is forced to launch an initiative to prevent falling sales or public relations problems, do you think the company is fully committed to those efforts? How could you tell if the company was making progress toward its stated goal?

4. Walmart's Sustainable Product Index is intended to provide consumers with a ranking of a product's sustainability across its life cycle. Would this ranking influence your buying decisions? Why or why not?

Sources: Walmart 2009 Sustainability Report (accessed June 25, 2010); Walmart 2010 Sustainability Report (accessed June 25, 2010); Arindrajit Dube, T. William Lester, and Barry Eidlin, "Firm Entry and Wages: Impact of Wal-Mart Growth on Earnings throughout the Retail Sector," Institute for Research on Labor and Employment Working Paper Series, No. iirwps-126-05, August 6, 2007; Wayne F. Cascio, "The High Cost of Low Wages," *Harvard Business Review* 84, no. 12 (December 2006), p. 23; Joshua Green, "The New War over Wal-Mart," *Atlantic Monthly*, June 2006.

This case was prepared by Barton Weitz, University of Florida, and Kate Woodworth.

CASE 4   Netflix Personalizes the Customer's Experience

The landscape of the video rental business altered when a small company named Netflix began operations in 1999. Utilizing the far-reaching scope of Internet-based commerce and an advanced inventory control system, Netflix was able to compete directly with the large bricks-and-mortar companies of the day, such as Blockbuster. For years Blockbuster had offered fixed-time rentals that incurred a fee for late returns. Netflix saw the customer dissatisfaction with this system and developed its core focus

on customer service. The company introduced a system through which subscribers could have a predetermined number of discs out at one time, based on membership levels and monthly fees. When a customer returned a disc, Netflix mailed the next selection from a customer-created list. This approach eliminated the penalty of late fees.

In further support of its customer focus, Netflix was able to offer extremely competitive pricing structures by utilizing proprietary inventory management software.

This system effectively keeps 98 percent of the inventory in active circulation at any given point, thus reducing costs associated with warehousing excess inventory. Netflix has continued to streamline inventory systems to the point that the company was able to reduce staff by more than half while expanding its subscription base from 75,000 in 1999 to 14 million and growing.

While customers were initially drawn to Netflix in large part because of the elimination of late fees and ease of use, Netflix competitor Blockbuster was not blind to the market share Netflix began to gain. Blockbuster introduced its own video-by-mail distribution channel, with the added perk of also being able to return and exchange videos in its stores. With such a direct threat, Netflix needed to ensure that it maintained its customer service edge. The online video rental company focused on two main areas within this vision.

First, Netflix made deals with major movie studios to begin streaming movies and television shows. The company recognized the need to embrace new technology and enhance its overall offering. This service offering became a significant differentiator between Netflix and Blockbuster and also helped differentiate Netflix from cable satellite providers, since the company can also provide physical media and a vast library of titles. The company has positioned itself to move toward a streaming distribution platform as more homes across America get high-speed Internet connections. With the success of its streaming platform to PCs, Netflix has aggressively made deals with television, set-top box, and game system manufacturers to bundle its software. These forward-thinking deals have led to Netflix's streaming movies and TV shows to millions of new households.

For its second area of focus, Netflix realized early on that the lack of a bricks-and-mortar presence means its software has to fulfill the role of a store salesperson. The company must offer online recommendations that rival those of human counterparts, all in a user-friendly interface. To this end, in 2006 Netflix offered a $1 million prize to any team of programmers who could improve its internal movie recommendation software. Several teams began creating complex algorithms to interpret the massive database of user movie ratings Netflix had compiled since its inception. While teams had relative success on their own, the biggest take-away from the contest was the power of collaboration between the groups. Ultimately several algorithms were combined to form the predictive recommendation engine that currently aids subscribers in their choices.

Armed with complex recommendation software, proprietary inventory management, and an ever-growing library of videos streamed directly to its subscriber base, Netflix seems poised to dominate the video rental environment. However, major hurdles still confront the company. Blockbuster has sought to copy Netflix in the past and still has major market share potential. Video on demand from cable and satellite companies offers higher picture quality than Netflix's current streaming content. And as computing power continues to evolve, more new players are likely to emerge in the digital e-commerce field.

DISCUSSION QUESTIONS

1. In exchange for greater amounts of streaming content, Netflix has begun making deals with major movie studios that delay the release of DVDs and blu-rays by 28 days. This gives bricks-and-mortar stores, e-commerce sites, and cable and satellite companies a window of time when they carry movies that Netflix cannot. Are these types of deals beneficial to Netflix? Why or why not?

2. Should Netflix charge for streaming content or continue to provide it without limit as part of its physical media offerings? Why or why not?

3. What are some of the potential problems Netflix will face in the near future as the company continues its reliance on DVD and blu-ray offerings by mail?

Sources: Beth Snyder Bulik, "How Netflix Stays Ahead of Shifting Consumer Behavior," *New York Times*, February 22, 2010; www.retailtouchpoints.com/solutions-spotlight/281-atg-recommendations.html (accessed July 13, 2010); Brock Webb, "Netflix Movie Recommendations: Secret to the Value of Social Networking?" www.govloop.com, March 16, 2010; Steve Lohr, "Netflix Competitors Learn the Power of Teamwork," *New York Times*, July 28, 2009; Stephen Baker, "The Web Knows What You Want," *BusinessWeek*, July 16, 2009; www.netflix.com, accessed July 13, 2010.

This case was written by Kate Woodworth.

CASE 5   The Decision-Making Process for Buying a Bicycle

The Sanchez family lives in Corona, California, west of Los Angeles. Jorge is a physics professor at the University of California–Riverside. His wife Anna is a volunteer, working 10 hours a week at the Crisis Center. They have two children: Nadia, age 10, and Miguel, age 8.

In February, Anna's parents sent her $100 to buy a bicycle for Nadia's birthday. They bought Nadia her first bike when she was five. Now they wanted to buy her a full-size bike for her 11th birthday. Even though Anna's parents felt every child should have a bike, Anna didn't think Nadia really wanted one. Nadia and most of her friends didn't ride their bikes often, and she was afraid to ride to school because of the traffic. So Anna decided to buy her the cheapest full-size bicycle she could find.

Since most of Nadia's friends didn't have full-size bikes, she didn't know much about them and had no preferences for a brand or type. To learn more about the types available and their prices, Anna and Nadia checked the catalog for Performance Bicycle, a large mail-order bicycling equipment retailer. The catalog was given to them by a friend of Anna's, who was an avid biker. After looking through the catalog, Nadia said the only thing she cared about was the color. She wanted a blue bike, blue being her favorite color.

Using the Internet, Anna located and called several local retail outlets selling bikes. To her surprise, she found that the local Kmart store actually had the best price for a 26-inch bicycle, even lower than Toys "R" Us and Walmart.

Anna drove to Kmart, went straight to the sporting goods department, and selected a blue bicycle before a salesperson approached her. She took the bike to the cash register and paid for it. After making the purchase, the Sanchezes found out that the bike was cheap in all senses. The chrome plating on the wheels was very thin and rusted away in six months. Both tires split and had to be replaced.

A year later, Anna's grandparents sent $200 for a bike for Miguel. From their experience with Nadia's bike, the Sanchezes realized that the lowest-priced bike might not be the least expensive option in the long run. Miguel is very active and somewhat careless, so they want to buy a sturdy bike. Miguel said he wanted a red, 21-speed, light-weight mountain bike with a full-suspension aluminum frame and cross-country tires.

The Sanchezes were concerned that Miguel wouldn't maintain an expensive bike with full suspension. When they saw an ad for a bicycle sale at Target, Anna and Jorge went to the store with Miguel. A salesperson approached them at an outdoor display of bikes and directed them to the sporting goods department inside the store. There they found row after row of red, single-speed BMX bikes with no suspension and minimal accessories to maintain—just the type of bike Anna and Jorge felt was ideal for Miguel.

Another salesperson approached them and tried to interest them in a more expensive bike. Jorge dislikes sales-people trying to push something on him and interrupted her in mid-sentence. He said he wanted to look at the bikes on his own. With a little suggestion, Miguel decided he wanted one of these bikes. His desire for accessories was satisfied when they bought a multifunction cyclocomputer for the bike. After buying a bike for Miguel, Jorge decided he'd like a bike for himself to ride on weekends. Jorge had ridden bikes since he was five. In graduate school, before he was married, he'd owned a 10-speed road bike. He frequently took 50-mile rides with friends, but he hadn't owned a bike since moving to Riverside 15 years ago.

Jorge didn't know much about current types of bicycles. He bought a copy of *Bicycling* at a newsstand to see what was available. He also went online to read *Consumer Reports*' evaluation of road, mountain, and hybrid bikes.

On the basis of this information, he decided he wanted a Cannondale. It had all the features he wanted: a light-weight frame, durable construction, and a comfort sports saddle. When Jorge called the discount stores and bicycle shops, he found they didn't carry the Cannondale brand. He thought about buying the bicycle from an Internet site but was concerned about making such a large purchase without a test ride. He then decided he might not really need a bike. After all, he'd been without one for 15 years.

One day, after lunch, he was walking back to his office and saw a small bicycle shop. The shop was run down, with bicycle parts scattered across the floor. The owner, a young man in grease-covered shorts, was fixing a bike. As Jorge was looking around, the owner approached him and asked him if he liked to bicycle. Jorge said he used to but had given it up when he moved to Riverside. The owner said that was a shame because there were a lot of nice places to tour around Riverside.

As their conversation continued, Jorge mentioned his interest in a Cannondale and his disappointment in not finding a store in Riverside that sold them. The owner said that he could order a Cannondale for Jorge but that they weren't in inventory and delivery took between six and eight weeks. He suggested a Trek and showed Jorge one he currently had in stock. Jorge thought the $700 price was too high, but the owner convinced him to try it next weekend. They would ride together in the country. The owner and some of his friends took a 60-mile tour with Jorge. Jorge enjoyed the experience, recalling his college days. After the tour, Jorge bought the Trek.

DISCUSSION QUESTIONS

1. Outline the decision-making process for each of the Sanchezes' bicycle purchases.

2. Compare the different purchase processes for the three bikes. What stimulated each of them? What factors were considered in making the store choice decisions and purchase decisions?

3. Go to the student site of the Online Learning Center (OLC), and click on the multiattribute model. Construct a multiattribute model for each purchase decision. How do the attributes considered and importance weights vary for each decision?

This case was written by Dan Rice and Barton Weitz, University of Florida.

CASE 6   Retailing in India: The Impact of Hypermarkets

The history of India contains a wealth of change and alteration, and the modern era is no different as the country blossoms into a major player in the global economy. Sizable economic growth during the past decade, particularly in the retail sector, has changed the way consumers behave. Although the size of the current Indian retail sector is impressive, its potential really speaks to what retailing will mean in the future. The retail market in India was approximately $353 billion in 2010, and by 2014 it will reach $543 billion in total sales, of which modern retailing accounts for 27 percent.

International retailers are slowly making their way into India. India's government allows foreign companies to open only single-brand stores. Large retailers with more than one brand are required to engage in a joint venture with an Indian company. Walmart, Tesco, and Carrefour have opened hypermarkets in India, but doing so was not an easy process. Carrefour waited 10 years to open its first store as a result of the restrictions. Hypermarkets, large retail outlets, combine the products found in a department store and supermarket, with the goal of turning shopping into an experience. The large store layouts and variety of merchandise force customers to spend more time in the stores, which in turn leads to more sales. The potential for hypermarkets in India sheds light on the country's changing retail landscape and the shopping habits of its consumers.

Before 2000, Indian consumers generally purchased many of their retail goods from local mom-and-pop stores called *kiranas*, which sold mainly provisions and groceries. Shopping at *kiranas* is easy and convenient, because the small stores serve specific neighborhoods and establish personal relationships with their customers. The new infusion of hypermarkets threatens to rob local store owners of their customer base—approximately a 23 percent decrease in sales in one year.

There are over 300 hypermarkets and 6,800 supermarkets in India. India has been experiencing 20 percent annual growth in retail markets. Hypermarket sales are expected to increase fivefold from 2009 to 2013, and supermarket sales are expected to increase 150 percent during the same period. Each new store opening may draw customers from 20 to 25 *kiranas* and fruit and vegetable stands, affecting over 100,000 vendors.

Most *kiranas* cannot compete with hypermarkets, because these larger retail outlets create more efficiency within the supply chain. Much local produce in India currently gets wasted, because the country lacks sufficient infrastructure. Even as it progresses through rapid development, India still lacks some amenities that Westerners take for granted, like refrigeration in retail operations. If a large retailer wants to open a hypermarket in India, it will have to invest capital to ensure freshness throughout the supply chain and help reduce waste. The Indian government is expected to spend $500 billion (U.S.) over the next few years to develop a world-class infrastructure, which should spur growth in the retail sector.

The lack of infrastructure underlies a related issue facing hypermarkets. Unlike in Western nations, India's rather poor roads and transportation systems do not allow retailers to locate on large plots of land on the outskirts of town, since fewer consumers can reach them. Therefore, hypermarkets must look for retail space in more urban areas, which provide little available real estate. Buying up space from existing stores means displacing local corner shops already inhabiting that space, and this may prompt protests from Indian consumers and store owners who value the Indian tradition that the *kiranas* represent. Yet larger retail outlets in India could have a dramatic impact on the economy, possibly creating millions of jobs in the next 10 years. Although many Indians may not appreciate the notion of hypermarkets immediately, their presence is likely inevitable.

Much of the impetus for the emergence of hypermarkets in India also comes from changes among Indian consumers. The country's younger generations are exposed to a host of innovative products that were unknown to their parents. They are far more receptive to new products and ideas. In addition, this segment of the population reflects the shifting age demographics; more than half of India's current population is younger than 25 years of age. With such a large percentage of younger consumers, it seems inevitable that India's cultural tastes will evolve. The strength and abundance of local *kiranas* have been a cultural mainstay, but they cannot efficiently offer Indians access to new and technologically advanced products. Because hypermarkets combine department stores and supermarkets, they carry product lines that local vendors cannot. They sell brand-name products at affordable prices, thereby enabling Indians to purchase a wide assortment of goods that they otherwise could not have.

This shift, from local mom-and-pop stores to more organized retail outlets, is happening very quickly in India. It is embraced by many consumers despite the cultural and legal considerations associated with hypermarkets. Furthermore, because hypermarkets offer potential benefits for both the economy and the national infrastructure, local governments generally support the arrival of a hypermarket. The ultimate target market, however, is not the government but the consumers, and just as in any country at any time, the challenge lies in understanding what those consumers want and how to get it to them.

DISCUSSION QUESTIONS

1. How might a hypermarket located in India appeal to consumers and orient them to shopping in larger stores?

2. Is the Indian government's willingness to spend $500 billion to improve the nation's infrastructure good news for international retailers? Why or why not?

3. Identify the main changes that mark Indian consumers. How can international retailers learn more about India's youthful demographic?

Sources: "Infra Red—India's Ambitious Development Plans Hinge on Attracting Private Capital," *Economist*, July 8, 2010; "A Wholesale Invasion—a French Supermarket Chain Takes a Bet on India," *Economist*, May 20, 2010; Armina Ligaya, "India Puts Squeeze on Hypermarkets," *National*, September 16, 2009; "India—Tier I & II Cities May Have 300 Hypermarkets by 2011," *RNCOS*, August 13, 2009; www.ibef.org/industry/retail.aspx (accessed July 15, 2010); "Coming to Market—Retailing in India," *Economist*, April 15, 2006, p. 69; "Despite Growing Debt, the Indian Consumer Banks on Tomorrow," *India Knowledge@Wharton*, October 31, 2006; Ranjan Biswas, "India's Changing Consumers," *Chain Store Age*, May 2006; John Elliott, "Retail Revolution," *Fortune*, August 9, 2007, pp. 14–16; Amelia Gentleman, "Indians Protest Wal-Mart's Wholesale Entry," *New York Times*, August 10, 2007.

This case was written by Todd Nicolini, while an MBA student at Loyola College in Maryland, under the supervision of Professor Hope Corrigan, and Britt Hackmann, Babson College.

CASE 7   Diamonds from Mine to Market

According to the American Museum of Natural History, a diamond is carbon in its most concentrated form. Because of their chemical makeup and crystalline structure, diamonds possess unique characteristics, including transparency. They are the hardest-known natural substance. These traits determine their status as the "king of gems," a reference to their vast popularity as jewelry and decoration.

To provide diamonds to the millions of consumers who demand them, the supply chain consists of six steps: exploration, mining, sorting, cutting and polishing, jewelry design and production, and retail display. According to the Web site for De Beers, the producer of approximately 40 percent of the world's supply of rough or uncut diamonds, members of this extensive supply chain include geologists, engineers, environmentalists, miners, sorters, distributors, cutters, polishers, traders, manufacturers, exporters, and salespeople, who in turn employ vast technological, artistic, and skill-related resources to discover, produce, and distribute jewelry-quality diamonds.

The jewelry-quality designation refers to a particular rating according to four key elements of a diamond, better known as the Four Cs: cut, carat, color, and clarity. The De Beers Corporation introduced these criteria in 1939 to provide consumers with a reference for evaluating diamonds, as Exhibit 1 summarizes.

Before they reach showrooms to be evaluated on these criteria, diamonds endure approximately 3 billion years of hot temperatures and intense pressures under the Earth's surface. Production estimates from the World Diamond Council indicate diamond mining operations are in more than 20 countries, including Russia, Botswana, the Democratic Republic of the Congo, Australia, South Africa, Canada, Angola, Namibia, Ghana, Brazil, and Sierra Leone.

The world diamond supply is dominated by African countries, which generate between 60 and 65 percent (by weight) of current diamond production. Other key sources for diamonds span the globe; for example, the remote northern regions of western Australia produce roughly 30 million carats (20 percent of global production) each year from both open-pit and underground operations. These diamonds are known for their range of colors, especially pink stones.

Diamonds prompt significant competition, as depicted in the movie *Blood Diamond*, which portrays the gruesome conflict and violence in Sierra Leone over diamonds. In many countries, profits from diamonds go to fund civil wars that take millions of lives. To prevent such abuses, the Kimberley Process, an international diamond certification scheme, was established to abolish trade in diamonds that fund conflict. Since its launch in 2003, the Kimberley Process has become law in 75 countries and received backing from the United Nations. It requires that governments of diamond-producing nations certify that shipments of rough diamonds are not funding violence.

EXHIBIT I

De Beers' Description of the Four Cs for Diamond Quality

Cut	Cut refers to the angles and proportions a skilled craftsperson creates in transforming a rough diamond into a polished diamond.
	A well-cut diamond will reflect light internally from one mirrorlike facet to another, dispersing it through the top of the stone.
	To cut a diamond perfectly, a craftsperson will often need to cut away more than 50 percent of the rough diamond.
	Cut also refers to the shape of a diamond: round, emerald, heart, marquise, or pear.
Carat weight	Carat is often confused with size, even though it is actually a measure of weight. The cut of a diamond can make it appear much larger or smaller than its actual weight.
	One carat is the equivalent of 200 milligrams. One carat can also be divided into 100 "points." A .75-carat diamond is the same as a 75-point- or a three-quarter-carat diamond.
Color	Most diamonds appear icy white, but many have tiny hints of color. Diamonds are graded on a color scale established by the Gemological Institute of America (GIA), ranging from D (colorless) to Z.
	Colorless diamonds are extremely rare and therefore very valuable.
	Diamonds are also sometimes found in "fancy" colors: pink, blue, green, yellow, brown, orange, and, very rarely, red. These diamonds, called "fancies," are incredibly rare and valuable. These colors extend beyond the GIA color grading system.
Clarity	Diamonds, like people, have natural blemishes in their makeup. Minerals or fractures form these tiny faults, or inclusions, while the diamond is forming in the earth.
	When light enters a diamond, it is reflected and refracted. If anything disrupts the flow of light in the diamond, such as an inclusion, a proportion of the light reflected will be lost.
	Most inclusions are not visible to the naked eye unless magnified.
	To view inclusions, trained gemologists use a magnifying loupe. This tool allows experts to see a diamond at 10 times its actual size. Even with a loupe, the birthmarks in the VVS (Very, Very Slightly Included) to VS (Very Slightly Included) range can be extremely difficult to find. It is only when a diamond is graded "I" that it is possible to see the birthmarks with the naked eye.

Even with a certification process, though, some diamonds continue to be smuggled out of African countries and support rebel armies. Violent groups find ways to exploit the Kimberley Process to traffic in illicit diamonds. "Conflict diamonds continue to be certified in countries that are members of the Kimberley Process, legitimized by the very scheme which was designed to eradicate them." However, a contrasting report from the World Diamond Council claims that "because of the Kimberley Process, more than 99% of the world's diamond supply is from sources free from conflict."

When the international diamond industry agreed to implement a voluntary system of warranties, it promised consumers it could track diamond jewelry up to the point of sale. Invoices for the sale of conflict-free diamond jewelry must include a written guarantee of that status. To ensure the diamonds they purchase for their spouses, fiancées, or themselves are indeed sourced appropriately, consumers are expected to take some responsibility, such as asking a series of questions of the jeweler from which they are purchasing:

- What is the country of origin for the diamonds in your jewelry?
- Can I see a copy of your company's policy on conflict-free diamonds?
- Can you show me a copy of the written warranty from your diamond supplier stating that your diamonds are conflict-free?

DISCUSSION QUESTIONS

1. How important is it for consumers to buy conflict-free diamonds? Why?
2. What should the jewelry industry do to inform diamond customers about buying conflict-free gems and about the Kimberley Process?
3. Select a retail jewelry store in your area to visit. Is its policy on conflict diamonds posted anywhere, such as in the store or on the company's Web site? Ask store personnel the three questions posed at the end of the case. What did you learn from the Web page and store visit?

Sources: "Blood Diamonds Are Still a Reality," Amnesty International, http://web.amnesty.org/pages/ec-230107-feature-eng; "Combating Conflict Diamonds," Global Witness, www.globalwitness.org/pages/en/conflict_diamonds.html; "Conflict Free Diamond Jewelry," Brilliant Earth, www.brilliantearth.com/conflict-free-diamond-definition; "Diamond Pipe," Antwerp Diamond Centre, www.awdc.be/diamond-pipeline; "Forever Diamonds," Gemnation, www.gemnation.com/base?processor=getPage'pageName=forever_diamonds_1; "Kimberley Process," www.kimberleyprocess.com/home/index_en.html; "The Argyle Diamond Mine," Argyle Diamonds, www.argylediamonds.com.au/index_whoweare.html; "The Four Cs," DeBeers, www.debeers.com/page/guidance&layout=popups#author2.

This case was written by Hope Bober Corrigan, Loyola University, Maryland.

CASE 8   Save-A-Lot: An Extreme-Value Retailer

In 1977, Bill Moran was the vice president of sales for a food wholesaler in St. Louis. His customers, independent grocers, were facing a weak economy and stiff competition from the growth of regional supermarket chains. He developed an extreme-value, limited-assortment concept to give small grocery stores a way to compete. He then tested the concept in several stores. Even though the concept worked in the test stores, the wholesaler believed the concept would not work when the economy improved.

Today, Save-A-Lot has 1,200 stores across the United States. Seventy-five percent of the stores are operated by licensees, and the remainder are operated by the company.

Save-A-Lot targets a value- and convenience-oriented psychographic segment. The consumers in this segment are looking for a good value, namely, quality merchandise at low prices. Its stores average about 14,000 to 18,000 square feet, less than half the size of a conventional supermarket. These smaller stores appeal to shoppers who don't want to search for merchandise in a 30,000-square-foot grocery store.

Stores stock approximately 2,100 SKUs of the most popular items, compared with over 30,000 SKUs in a traditional supermarket. Save-A-Lot's large customer base and edited-assortment format equate to high sales volume and lower costs. For example, a traditional supermarket may carry 35 SKUs of ketchup—different brands, sizes,

and flavors. Save-A-Lot carries just one, made to the same specifications as the leading national brand. Eighty-five percent of its 2,100 SKUs are exclusive to Save-A-Lot. The chain has buying power with its vendors by purchasing one size and variety of an item for more than 4 million weekly shoppers. In addition, vendors give Save-A-Lot low prices because Save-A-Lot doesn't ask for an advertising allowance, fees for stocking items, merchandise return privileges, or charge-backs.

To offer quality merchandise at low prices and remain profitable, Save-A-Lot tightly controls its operating costs. Stores are located on inexpensive real estate, and staff in the stores is limited. Merchandise is displayed on shelves in cut-off shipping boxes to reduce the labor costs incurred by taking cans and bottles out of the boxes and placing them on the shelves. Save-A-Lot customers typically bag their own groceries. Some stores charge extra for bags, such as 3 cents for plastic bags, 5 cents for paper grocery bags, and 10 cents for reusable polyurethane bags. Due to these cost-cutting approaches, Save-A-Lot can offer quality merchandise to its customers at prices 20 to 40 percent lower than those of traditional supermarkets.

When Save-A-Lot started, it focused simply on providing value to customers by selling the basics: bread, eggs, milk, flour, sugar, and canned goods. It charged low prices in a bare-bones atmosphere. Over time, as its market research revealed that customers' concept of value was changing, Save-A-Lot began adding more unique items to its assortment. The stores' customers, regardless of their income levels, sometimes want to treat themselves to something special, so Save-A-Lot included frozen shrimp, now one of its best-selling items. By buying at half the price charged by traditional supermarkets, its customers can still have a special meal at a reasonable price.

Save-A-Lot's success has attracted competitors, such as the extreme-value general merchandise chains (e.g., Dollar General, Family Dollar) that are now offering more food items. But Save-A-Lot's efficient food distribution system might be difficult to duplicate. At the same time, Save-A-Lot faces more competition in the United States from ALDI, the German company that originated the extreme-value business model in food retailing. ALDI now operates more than 8,000 stores worldwide, including approximately 1,000 in the United States.

DISCUSSION QUESTIONS

1. What is Save-A-Lot's retail strategy—its target market, format, and bases of competitive advantage?
2. How do the elements in the strategic profit model for Save-A-Lot differ from those of a traditional supermarket?
3. What are the pluses and minuses of offering a limited assortment from the perspective of the consumer and the perspective of the retailer?
4. What are the advantages and disadvantages of stores operated by licensees rather than by the company directly?

Sources: www.save-a-lot.com (accessed July 12, 2010); "Aldi, Save-A-Lot Make the Most Out of Private Label," *Refrigerated & Frozen Foods Retailer*, May 2010.

This case was written by Barton Weitz, University of Florida.

CASE 9   Royal Ahold: The Biggest Supermarket Retailer You Have Never Heard Of

The name Royal Ahold does not appear on a single store, yet the company has been in business for more than 100 years and is one of the world's largest food retailers. Royal Ahold began in 1887, when 22-year-old Albert Heijn took over his father's small grocery store in west Holland. Over the next century, Ahold (an abbreviation of Albert Heijn Holding) grew within the Netherlands and launched an acquisition strategy that remains fundamental to its growth plans today. By 2003, Royal Ahold was the world's second-largest food retailer, operating 1,600 stores in 27 countries with sales of more than 72 billion euros (89 billion U.S. dollars).

In addition to acquiring supermarket chains, the company bought U.S. Foodservice, America's second-largest supplier of ready-made meals, prepared foods, and ingredients sold to restaurants, hotels, hospitals, and other institutions. At the tail end of the 90s, Ahold USA's retail operations consisted of Stop & Shop, Giant-Landover, Giant-Carlisle, Tops, Bi-Lo, and Bruno's. Royal Ahold also operated under 26 different names in Europe, America, Asia, and Latin America. Claiming to provide group efficiencies while answering local needs, the company has used a variety of formats for its stores, ranging from tiny gas station outlets in the Netherlands to 150,000-square-foot hypermarkets in northern Brazil. Ahold refers to its strategy as "multilocal, multiformat, multichannel," employing new products, services, and store formats to make shopping for healthy and comparably priced food more convenient.

Ahold USA also owns Peapod, an Internet grocer that attracts 1.5 million visits per month and brings in upward of $375,000 million annually. Now over 20 years old, Peapod allows busy shoppers to select fresh fruits and vegetables, seafood, meat, dairy products, home and office needs, private-label and national brands, and ready-to-eat foods from their computers. These products are delivered to the customers' doorsteps as soon as the next day. Peapod maximizes technology across its business, using a proprietary system to build efficiencies into delivery routes and tools that allow shoppers to sort and compare items by price and nutritional information and to create personal shopping lists. Site enhancements, both current and future, include personalized online coupons and social network recommendations.

Royal Ahold's growth strategy focuses on food sales, which account for a vast majority of its revenues. During the economic boom years, the company attempted to increase its share of the wallet through acquisitions of food service companies. Now that purse strings are tighter, the company is focused more closely on retail food stores and carefully controlled expansion. Nevertheless, strategic objectives vary by market. On the East Coast, for example, where Ahold operates retail stores, Peapod serves as an alternative to a Stop & Shop or Giant visit that still brings the dollars to the parent company. Customers using both shopping channels further increase Ahold's income. A current goal is to bring Peapod services to all locations that have a Stop & Shop or Giant in the trade area. Although, in keeping with its "slow but steady" growth strategy, Ahold adds only small groupings of zip codes at a time to serve via Peapod. Within the stores, Ahold continues to increase customer convenience through technology additions such as personal shopper scanners that scan groceries and deliver targeted offers to loyalty customers.

In Chicago, where Peapod has no retail partner, the company is expanding its delivery range and adding local specialty goods and prepared meals. Advertising stresses

Peapod's local products to attract customers wanting to "shop local." Like other retailers, Ahold USA and Ahold Europe have increased value messaging and promotions to help minimize the effects of a challenging economy.

Ahold has hit some bumps along the way. In 2002, the company lost money for the first time. Fallout led to an investigation that resulted in both the company's CEO and CFO being charged with fraud. Four years later, Royal Ahold sold a number of its holdings, retaining only Stop & Shop, Giant-Landover, Giant-Carlisle, Martin's, and Peapod in the United States and six brands in Europe. The move shifted the company from second-largest global food retailer to twelfth, and in 2009 Ahold announced further restructuring on both sides of the Atlantic. Changes in leadership positions are intended to provide a firm foundation for profitable growth. Despite these bumps and a sluggish economy, however, some business areas—such as Peapod—are growing.

Walmart and Carrefour, the two largest food retailers, use a different approach. From Paris to Shanghai, all Carrefour stores look the same and have identical layouts (to reach the deli counter, for example, you always turn left at the entrance). Walmart uses its name on most of its stores across the world. Several years ago, it acquired the Asada chain in the United Kingdom and still operates the stores under the Asada name. But when it bought the Wertkauf chain and some Spar stores in Germany, it converted the stores to Walmarts. Poor profits forced the company to sell its German chain soon thereafter.

In contrast to Royal Ahold's approach, Walmart and Carrefour focus on operating larger supercenters or hypermarkets that offer general merchandise as well as food. Other than Royal Ahold, no European retailer has been successful in entering the U.S. market. Over two-thirds of

Royal Ahold's sales now come from U.S. acquisitions. Carrefour tried opening two stores in suburban Philadelphia in the late 1980s but gave up quickly when it faced labor problems and the enduring loyalty customers had to their local supermarket chains.

DISCUSSION QUESTIONS

1. What are the advantages and disadvantages of the growth strategies pursued by Royal Ahold, Carrefour, and Walmart?

2. Should Royal Ahold use its name on all of its stores, as Walmart and Carrefour do? Why or why not?

3. What are the advantages and disadvantages of Walmart's and Carrefour's more centralized decision making compared with Royal Ahold's decentralized decision making?

4. Do you think Royal Ahold should have divested its food service divisions? Why or why not?

Sources: www.ahold.com (accessed June 23, 2010); Steward Hamilton and Alicia Micklethwait, "Too Much Too Fast?" *European Business Forum,* Spring 2007, pp. 47–50; Jim Frederick, "Ahold Trims Down and Focuses on Profit Message," *Drug Store News,* April 23, 2007, pp. 110–111; Jon Springer, "Staying Power: Peapod Turns 20," *Supermarket News,* November 2, 2009; Michael Garry, "Stop & Shop/Giant: Personal Scanners Account for 13% of Sales," *Supermarket News,* June 17, 2010.

This case was written by Barton Weitz, University of Florida; Michael Levy, Babson College; and Kate Woodworth.

CASE 10   Abercrombie & Fitch and American Eagle Compete for 18- to 22-Year-Olds

Jennifer Shaffer, a 19-year-old college student living in Cupertino, California, used to shop at Abercrombie & Fitch (A&F) once a month. She thought the prices were high, but the brand name and image appealed to her. As she says, "It's like I really had to have Abercrombie." Then an American Eagle (AE) store opened about 15 minutes from her home. "They look the same, and they're both really cute," she says. "But American Eagle's prices are a little cheaper."

Both A&F and AE are still growing into their present strategy of selling casual apparel to the teen/college market. When A&F was established as an outdoor sporting goods retailer over 100 years ago, it sold the highest-quality hunting, fishing, and camping goods. It also outfitted some of the greatest explorations in the early part of the 20th century, including Robert Perry's expedition to the North Pole and Theodore Roosevelt's trips to the Amazon and Africa.

Over time, its safari image became less attractive to consumers. The chain experienced a significant decline in

sales and profits, and in 1977 it was forced to declare bankruptcy. The company, initially acquired by Oshman's Sporting Goods, did not experience a turnaround until The Limited Inc. acquired it in 1988. Initially, The Limited positioned A&F as a tailored clothing store for men. In 1995, The Limited repositioned A&F to target both men and women in the teen and college market, with an emphasis on casual American style and youth.

In 1999, The Limited (now Limited Brands) sold A&F. Now A&F operates 340 Abercrombie & Fitch stores, 205 Abercrombie kids stores, 507 Hollister Co. stores, and 16 Gilly Hicks (personal care products and intimate apparel) stores in the United States, as well as four Abercrombie & Fitch, eight Hollister Co., and two Abercrombie kids stores internationally. Furthermore, A&F offers its merchandise online at abercrombie.com, abercrombiekids.com, hollisterco.com, and gillyhicks.com.

American Eagle, although lacking the rich tradition of A&F, also was positioned as an outfitter when it started in

CASE 12   Tiffany's and Walmart: Comparing Financial Performance

Of all the great American brands, Tiffany & Co., which has been around for over 160 years and is more than a luxury jewelry retailer, is an American icon that has worked its way into movies and songs. The company's flagship location on Fifth Avenue in New York City has become a tourist attraction. Even the company's trademarked robin's-egg-blue boxes have become known as "Tiffany blue" and symbolize the brand's quality and craftsmanship. Such reputations can be profitable. The company has grown aggressively—from $456 million in sales in 1990 to $2.7 billion in 2009.

With the mission to be the world's most respected jewelry retailer, Tiffany's plans to continue this growth. In an attempt to appeal to a wider variety of customers, the company advertises items ranging from $200 to $100,000 in daily ads in the *New York Times* as well as in upscale fashion and lifestyle magazines. The variety in the ads is designed to attract both mall habitués in Guess Jeans as well as ladies who lunch in Chanel suits.

Walmart is the largest retailer in the world and is constantly expanding its store count—the company operates close to 4,300 stores in the United States, including over 2,600 Supercenters, 900 discount stores, 600 Sam's Clubs, and about 150 Neighborhood Markets. Even as discount retailers face intense competition from category specialists, like Best Buy and Home Depot, and increasingly compete against grocery and pharmacy retailers, Walmart continues to improve its value to its customers. Some hundreds of millions of people a week buy into its "Save More, Live Better" message.

To ensure continued growth and success, Walmart continues to innovate its retail format. In addition to its traditional merchandise categories, Walmart is the third-largest pharmacy retailer in the United States and has plans to start offering products and services as diverse as household appliances and Internet access. Walmart has become the world's largest food retailer through its Supercenters—huge stores that carry groceries in addition to the usual general merchandise.

Sources: Walmart Annual Report, 2009; Tiffany & Co. Annual Report, 2009; www.walmart.com; www.tiffany.com.

DISCUSSION QUESTIONS

1. Using Exhibit 2, construct strategic profit models for Tiffany and Walmart using data from the abbreviated income statements and balance sheets in Exhibit 1. You can do these calculations by hand or go to the student side of the Online Learning Center (OLC) and use the Strategic Profit Model Excel spreadsheet that is available.

2. Calculate the gross margin percentage, expenses-to-sales ratio, net profit margin (after taxes), inventory turnover, asset turnover, and return on asset ratio for Tiffany and Walmart using the financial data in Exhibit 1.

3. Explain, from a marketing perspective, why the ratios calculated from question 2 (gross margin percentage, expenses-to-sales ratio, net profit margin, inventory turnover, and asset turnover) are different for Tiffany and Walmart.

4. Assess which chain has better overall financial performance using ROA. Why is ROA a good measure of each of the retailers' financial performance?

This case was prepared by Britt Hackmann, Babson College.

EXHIBIT 1

2009 Financial Data for Walmart and Tiffany's ($ millions)

	Walmart's Income statement	Tiffany's Income statement
Net sales	$401,244	$2,709
Less: Cost of goods sold	$306,158	$1,179
Gross margin	$ 95,086	$1,530
Less: SG&A expenses	$ 76,561	$1,089
Less: Interest expense	$ 1,900	$ 55
Net income before taxes	$ 16,625	$ 386
Less: Taxes	$ 5,686	$ 124
Net income after taxes	$ 10,939	$ 262
	Walmart's Balance sheet	**Tiffany's Balance sheet**
Cash	$ 7,275	$ 785
Accounts receivable	$ 3,905	$ 158
Inventory	$ 34,511	$1,427
Other current assets	$ 3,258	$ 75
Total current assets	$ 48,949	$2,445
Fixed assets	$114,480	$1,041
Current liabilities	$ 55,390	$ 600
Long-term liabilities	$ 98,144	$1,603
Stockholders' equity	$ 65,285	$1,883

EXHIBIT 2   Strategic Profit Model

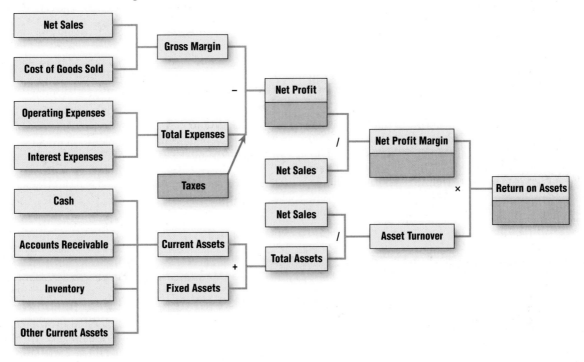

CASE 13   Choosing a Store Location for a Boutique

Stephanie Wilson must decide where to open a ready-to-wear boutique she's been contemplating for several years. Now in her late 30s, she's been working in municipal government ever since leaving college, where she majored in fine arts. She's divorced with two children (ages five and eight) and wants her own business, at least partly to be able to spend more time with her children. She loves fashion, feels she has a flair for it, and has taken evening courses in fashion design and retail management. Recently, she heard about a plan to rehabilitate an old arcade building in the downtown section of her midwestern city. This news crystallized her resolve to move now. She's considering three locations.

THE DOWNTOWN ARCADE

The city's central business district has been ailing for some time. The proposed arcade renovation is part of a master redevelopment plan, with a new department store and several office buildings already operating. Completion of the entire master plan is expected to take another six years.

Dating from 1912, the arcade building was once the center of downtown trade, but it's been vacant for the past 15 years. The proposed renovation includes a three-level shopping facility, low-rate garage with validated parking, and convention center complex. Forty shops are planned for the first (ground) floor, 28 more on the second, and a series of restaurants on the third.

The location Stephanie is considering is 900 square feet and situated near the main ground-floor entrance.

Rent is $20 per square foot, for an annual total of $18,000. If sales exceed $225,000, rent will be calculated at 8 percent of sales. She'll have to sign a three-year lease.

TENDERLOIN VILLAGE

The gentrified urban area of the city where Stephanie lives is called Tenderloin Village because of its lurid past. Today, however, the neat, well-kept brownstones and comfortable neighborhood make it feel like a trendy enclave. Many residents have done the remodeling work themselves and take great pride in their neighborhood.

About 20 small retailers are now in an area of the village adjacent to the convention center complex, along with some vegetarian and nouveau cuisine restaurants. There are also three small women's specialty clothing stores.

The site available to Stephanie is on the village's main street on the ground floor of an old house. Its space is also about 900 square feet. Rent is $15,000 annually, with no extra charge based on the level of sales. The landlord knows Stephanie and will require a two-year lease.

APPLETREE MALL

This suburban mall has been open for eight years. A successful regional center, it has three department stores and 100 smaller shops just off a major interstate highway about 8 miles from downtown. Of its nine women's clothing retailers, three are in a price category considerably higher than what Stephanie has in mind.

Appletree has captured the retail business in the city's southwest quadrant, although growth in that sector has slowed in the past year. Nevertheless, mall sales are still running 12 percent ahead of the previous year. Stephanie learned of plans to develop a second shopping center east of town, which would be about the same size and character as Appletree Mall. But groundbreaking is still 18 months away, and no renting agent has begun to enlist tenants.

The location available to Stephanie in Appletree is two doors from the local department store chain. At 1,200 square feet, it's slightly larger than the other two possibilities. But it's long and narrow—24 feet in front by 50 feet deep. Rent is $24 per square foot ($28,800 annually). In addition, on sales that exceed $411,500, rent is 8 percent of sales. There's an additional charge of 1 percent of sales to cover common-area maintenance and mall promotions. The mall's five-year lease includes an escape clause if sales don't reach $411,500 after two years.

DISCUSSION QUESTIONS

1. List the pluses and minuses of each location.
2. What type of store would be most appropriate for each location?
3. If you were Stephanie, which location would you choose? Why?

This case was prepared by Professor David Ehrlich, Marymount University.

CASE 14   Hutch: Locating a New Store

In June, after returning from a trip to the Bahamas, Dale Abell, vice president of new business development for the Hutch Corporation, began a search for a good location to open a new store. After a preliminary search, Abell narrowed the choice to two locations, both in Georgia. He now faces the difficult task of thoroughly analyzing each location and determining which will be the site of the next store.

COMPANY BACKGROUND

The Hutch store chain was founded in 1952 by John Henry Hutchison, a musician and extremely successful insurance salesman. Hutchison established the headquarters in Richmond, Virginia, where both the executive offices and one of two warehouse distribution centers are located. Hutch currently operates 350 popularly priced women's clothing stores throughout the Southeast and Midwest. Manufacturers ship all goods to these distribution centers. They are delivered floor-ready, in that the vendor has attached price labels, UPC identifying codes, and source tags for security purposes and placed appropriate merchandise on hangers. Once at the distribution centers, the merchandise is consolidated for reshipment to the stores. Some staple merchandise, such as hosiery, is stored at these distribution centers. All Hutch stores are located within 400 miles of a distribution center. This way, as Abell explains, "A truck driver can deliver to every location in two days."

HUTCH FASHIONS

Hutch Fashions is considered one of the leading popularly priced women's fashion apparel chains in the Southeast. The stores carry trendy apparel selections in juniors', misses', and women's sizes, all at popular prices. The chain offers a complementary array of accessories in addition to its main features of dresses, coats, and sportswear. Located mainly in strip centers and malls, these shops typically require 4,000 to 5,000 square feet.

HUTCH EXTRA

Hutch Extra stores are primarily located in strip centers and malls. They bear a strong resemblance to Hutch Fashions. The difference is that Hutch Extra stores require less space (2,000–3,000 square feet) and cater to women requiring large and half-size apparel. (Women who wear half-sizes require a larger size but are not tall enough to wear a standard large size. In other words, a size 18½ is the same as size 18 except that it is cut for a shorter woman.)

HUTCH FASHIONS* HUTCH EXTRA

Although Hutch Fashions and Hutch Extra stores selectively appear as separate entries, the corporate goal is to position both as a single entity. The combination store emerged in 1986 and is now used for all new stores. The Hutch Fashions* Hutch Extra combination occupies a combined space of 6,000–7,000 square feet, with separate entrances for each entity. A partial wall separates the two frontal areas of the store but allows for a combined checkout/customer service area in the rear. These stores are primarily located in strip centers and can occasionally be found in malls. (Exhibit 1 shows a typical layout.)

MARKETING STRATEGY

Customers
Hutch's target market is women between the ages of 18 and 40 years who are in the lower–middle to middle-income range. Abell explains, "We don't cater to any specific ethnic group, only to women who like to wear the latest fashions."

Product/Price
Hutch positions merchandise and price levels between the mass merchandisers and the department stores. You won't find any bluelight specials or designer boutiques in a

EXHIBIT 1
Layout of Hutch Fashions* Hutch Extra Store

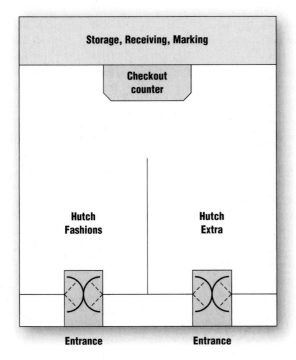

Hutch store. By avoiding direct competition for customers with the large discounters (Target, Walmart) and the high-fashion department stores and specialty shops, Hutch has secured a comfortable niche for itself. "Our products must be priced at a level where our customers perceive our products to be elegant and fashionable but not too expensive," notes Abell.

Location
Hutch stores are located throughout the Southeast and Midwest and must be within a 400-mile radius of a Hutch distribution center. Within this geographic area, Hutch stores are located in communities with a population range of 10,000 to 50,000 and a trade area of 50,000 to 150,000. These locations are characterized by a large concentration of people in the low- to middle-income brackets who work in agriculture and industry.

Hutch stores are primarily located in strip malls or strip centers—generally ones anchored by either a regional or national discount store (Walmart or Target). In addition, these centers contain a mix of several nationally recognized and popular local tenants. Hutch stores are primarily located adjacent to the center's anchor. Mall locations must be on the main corridor, as close to "center court," as economics (rent) will allow. Abell remarked, "We don't care if it's the only center in the region. If the only space available is at the end of the mall, we won't go in there. Our plan is to be a complement to the anchor and to feed off the traffic coming to it. We may have a reputation for being picky and having one of the toughest

lease agreements in the business, but it's one of the main reasons for our continued success."

DATA SOURCES
Abell is using several reports generated by Claritas to help him decide which location to choose for the next Hutch store. He has chosen reports that describe the 10-mile ring around each of the proposed locations. Exhibits 2 and 3 summarize these reports. They contain detailed population, household, race, income, education, and employment data, plus figures on retail sales and number of establishments. The reports also provide information about women's apparel sales and give a market index that estimates the annual per-person spending potential for the trade area divided by the national average (see Exhibit 3). Dalton's 99 index means that the spending potential for women's clothing is slightly lower than the national average of 100. Finally, Abell is using Claritas/UDS's PRIZM lifestyle reports. These reports contain numeric figures and percentages on the population, households, families, sex, age, household size, and ownership of housing. An excerpt from the report is given in Exhibit 4. Some of the cluster group names are described in Exhibit 5.

THE POTENTIAL LOCATIONS
Dalton
Dalton produces most of the carpeting in the United States. Consequently, carpet mills are the major employers in Dalton. Stain Master carpeting has been putting a strain on the city's water supply. Stain Master is said to require seven times the amount of water as regular carpeting and is rapidly becoming the largest proportion of carpeting produced. Expressing concern over market viability, Abell said, "If the Dalton area were ever to experience a severe drought, the carpet mills would be forced to drastically reduce production. The ensuing layoffs could put half the population on unemployment."

The proposed site for the new store is the Whitfield Square shopping center located off the main highway, approximately two miles from the center of town (see Exhibit 6). After meeting with the developer, Abell was pleased with several aspects of the strip center. He learned that the center has good visibility from the highway, will be anchored by both Walmart and Kroger (a large grocery chain), and has ample parking. Abell is also reasonably pleased with the available location within the center, which is one spot away from Walmart. However, he is concerned about the presence of two large outparcels in front of the center that would reduce the number of parking spaces and direct visibility of the center. (An outparcel is a freestanding structure at the front of a mall, commonly a fast-food outlet, a bank, or a gas station.) Other tenants in the center include a nationally recognized shoe store, a beauty salon, two popular restaurants (Chinese and Mexican), and McSpeedy's Pizza at the end of the center, as well as a Century 21 real estate training school in the middle.

EXHIBIT 2

Population and Competitive Profile, 10-Mile Ring from Centers of Dalton and Hinesville, Georgia

		Dalton	Hinesville
Population	2015 projection	93,182	64,195
	2010 estimate	87,293	57,945
	1999 Census	79,420	49,853
	1990 Census	71,373	34,125
	% change, 1999–2008	9.9%	16.2%
	% change, 1990–1999	11.3%	46.1%
	In group quarters (military base) 2008	.9%	11.2%
Household	2015 projection	35,570	20,010
	2010 estimate	33,140	17,541
	1999 Census	29,340	14,061
	1990 Census	24,302	8,557
	% change, 1999–2008	12.9%	24.7%
	% change, 1990–1999	20.7%	64.3%
Families	2010 estimate	24,347	14,277
Race	White	92.0%	54.1%
	Black	4.9%	38.3%
	American Indian	0.2%	0.5%
	Asian or Pacific Islander	0.6%	3.1%
	Other	2.3%	4.0%
Age	0–20	31.2%	40.2%
	21–44	37.1%	47.0%
	45–64	21.7%	9.2%
	65+	9.9%	3.4%
	Median age	33.7	23.9
	Male	32.5	23.6
	Female	35.0	24.6
Household size	1 person	21.0%	15.2%
	2 persons	32.3%	26.6%
	3–4 persons	38.1%	45.7%
	5+ persons	8.7%	12.6%
Income	Median household income	$30,516	$23,686
	Average household income	$40,397	$28,677
Sex (% male)		49.1%	55.8%
Education	Population age 25+	49,298	22,455
	No high school diploma	41.0%	15.5%
	High school only	28.6%	41.2%
	College, 1–3 years	19.1%	29.7%
	College, 4+ years	11.3%	13.5%
Industry	Manufacturing: nondurable goods	42.3%	7.2%
	Retail trade	12.6%	23.3%
	Professional and related services	13.3%	21.4%
	Public administration	2.2%	20.0%
Retail sales ($ thousands)	Total	$706,209	$172,802
	General merchandise stores Apparel stores	$26,634	$9,339
Retail establishments	General merchandise stores	12	3
	Women's apparel stores	21	8

EXHIBIT 3

Sales Potential Index for Women's Apparel

	Area Sales ($ mil.)	Area Sales per Capita	U.S. Sales per Capita	Index (area sales ÷ U.S. sales)
Dalton	$18.01	$206.26	$207.65	99
Hinesville	$8.97	$154.74	$207.65	75

PRIZM Neighborhood Clusters **EXHIBIT 4**

Prizm Cluster	Population, 2008	Percentage of Population	Prizm Cluster	Population, 2008	Percentage of Population
Dalton			**Mines & mills**	7,694	8.8
Big fish, small pond	4,727	5.4%	Back country folks	4,293	4.9
New homesteaders	6,030	6.9			
Red, white, & blues	31,123	35.7	**Hinesville**		
Shotguns & pickups	8,881	10.2	Military quarters	45,127	77.9
Rural industrial	12,757	14.6	Scrub pine flats	3,476	6.0

PRIZM Lifestyle Clusters **EXHIBIT 5**

Big Fish, Small Pond

Small-town executive families; upper-middle incomes; age groups 35–44, 45–54; predominantly white. This group is married, family-oriented, and conservative. Their neighborhoods are older. Best described as captains of local industry, they invest in their homes and clubs and vacation by car in the United States.

Rural Industrial

Low-income, blue-collar families; lower-middle incomes; age groups <24, 25–34; predominantly white, high Hispanic. Nonunion labor found in this cluster, which is comprised of hundreds of blue-collar mill towns on American's rural backroads.

Mines & Mills

Older families; mine and mill towns; poor; age groups 55–64, 65+; predominantly white. Down the Appalachians, across the Ozarks to Arizona, and up the Missouri, this cluster is exactly as its name implies. This older, mostly single population with a few children lives in the midst of scenic splendor.

Shotguns & Pickups

Rural blue-collar workers and families; middle income; age groups 35–44, 45–54; predominantly white. This cluster is found in the Northeast, the Southeast, and the Great Lakes and Piedmont industrial regions. They are in blue-collar jobs; most are married with school-age kids. They are churchgoers who also enjoy bowling, hunting, sewing, and attending car races.

Back Country Folks

Older farm families; lower-middle income; age groups 55–64, 65+; predominantly white. This cluster is centered in the eastern uplands along a wide path from the Pennsylvania Poconos to the Arkansas Ozarks. Anyone who visits their playground in Branson, Missouri, or Gatlinburg, Tennessee, can attest that these are the most blue-collar neighborhoods in America. Centered in the Bible Belt, many back country folks are hooked on Christianity and country music.

Scrub Pine Flats

Older African-American farm families; poor; age groups 55–64, 65+; predominantly black. This cluster is found mainly in the coastal flatlands of the Atlantic and Gulf states from the James to the Mississippi rivers. These humid, sleepy rural communities, with a mix of blacks and whites, live in a seemingly timeless, agrarian rhythm.

New Homesteaders

Young middle-class families; middle income; age groups 35–44, 45–54; predominantly white. This cluster is above-average for college education. Executives and professionals work in local service fields such as administration, communications, health, and retail. Most are married; the young have children, the elders do not. Life is homespun with a focus on crafts, camping, and sports.

Red, White, & Blues

Small-town blue-collar families; middle income; age groups 35–54, 55–64; predominantly white, with skilled workers primarily employed in mining, milling, manufacturing, and construction. Geocentered in the Appalachians, Great Lakes industrial region, and western highlands, these folks love the outdoors.

Military Quarters

GIs and surrounding off-base families; lower-middle income; age groups under 24, 25–34; ethnically diverse. Since this cluster depicts military life with personnel living in group quarters, its demographics are wholly atypical because they are located on or near military bases. Racially integrated and with the highest index for adults under 35, "Military Quarters" like fast cars, bars, and action sports.

Hinesville

Like Dalton, Hinesville has one major employer, the Fort Stuart army base. Abell recalls that popularly priced stores generally do very well in military towns. In addition, Fort Stuart is a rapid-deployment force base. Because the United States currently is involved in a number of international activities, Abell is concerned with a comment by a Hinesville native: "If these guys have to ship out, this place will be a ghost town." The location under consideration is the Target Plaza at the junction of State Route 119 and U.S. Highway 82 (see Exhibit 7). The center is anchored by Target and a grocery store that is part of a popular Eastern U.S. chain. The two anchors are located side by side in the middle of the center. The spot available in the center is a 6,800-square-foot combination of three smaller units immediately adjacent to Target. Other tenants in the center include a bookstore, a waterbed store, a shoe store, an electronics retailer, a yogurt store, a video store, and a movie theater.

DISCUSSION QUESTIONS

1. How do the people living in the trade areas compare with Hutch's target customer?
2. How do the proposed locations, including the cities, tenant mix, and the locations within the malls, fit with Hutch's location requirements?
3. Which location would you select? Why?

This case was written by Michael Levy, Babson College.

EXHIBIT 6
Whitfield Square Shopping
Center, Dalton, Georgia

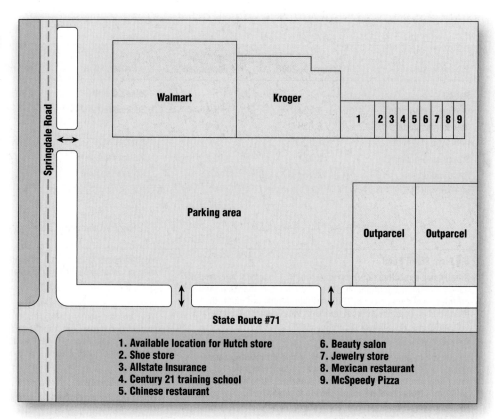

State Route #71

1. **Available location for Hutch store**
2. **Shoe store**
3. **Allstate Insurance**
4. **Century 21 training school**
5. **Chinese restaurant**
6. **Beauty salon**
7. **Jewelry store**
8. **Mexican restaurant**
9. **McSpeedy Pizza**

EXHIBIT 7
Target Plaza, Hinesville,
Georgia

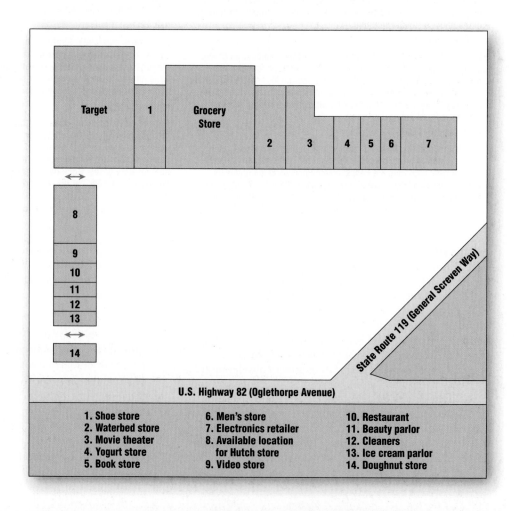

U.S. Highway 82 (Oglethorpe Avenue)

1. **Shoe store**
2. **Waterbed store**
3. **Movie theater**
4. **Yogurt store**
5. **Book store**
6. **Men's store**
7. **Electronics retailer**
8. **Available location for Hutch store**
9. **Video store**
10. **Restaurant**
11. **Beauty parlor**
12. **Cleaners**
13. **Ice cream parlor**
14. **Doughnut store**

CASE 15   Avon Embraces Diversity

Women have always played an important role at Avon, a leading global beauty firm that has $10 billion in annual revenue and is 125 years old. Mrs. P. F. Albee of Winchester, New Hampshire, pioneered the company's now-famous direct-selling method. Women have been selling Avon products since 1886—34 years before women in the United States won the right to vote! As the world's largest direct seller, Avon markets to women in over 100 countries through the efforts of more than 6 million independent Avon sales representatives. Avon's merchandise includes beauty products, fashion jewelry, and apparel.

Although most of Avon's employees and customers are women, until recently the company was run by men. However, a series of poor strategic decisions in the 1980s led the company to increase aggressively the number of women and minorities in its executive ranks. This decision to increase diversity among its managers was a major factor in Avon's improved financial performance.

Today, Avon is recognized as a leader in management diversity. Fifty-five percent of Avon's management positions are filled by women, and half of the members of its board of directors are women. The company also has undertaken various programs to ensure that women and minorities have opportunities for development and advancement. In the United States and elsewhere, Avon has internal networks of associates, including a parents' network, a Hispanic network, a black professional association, an Asian network, and a gay and lesbian network. The networks act as liaisons between associates and management to bring their voices to bear on critical issues that affect both the workplace and the marketplace. Avon is committed to social responsibility. The Avon Foundation, founded in 1955, is the largest corporate philanthropic organization dedicated to women's causes globally and focuses on breast cancer and domestic violence.

In the 1970s, Avon's top management team was composed solely of men. Avon essentially ignored its own marketing research that indicated more women were entering the workforce and seeking professional careers. It also failed to realize that cosmetic needs were changing and new approaches for selling products to its customers were needed. Sales growth slowed, and the company reacted by seeking growth through unrelated diversifications. Finally, as the firm was on the brink of bankruptcy, a new top management team entered. Led by CEO Jim Preston, Avon refocused itself on its roots and developed strategies to reach women in a changing marketplace.

Preston realized that Avon's customers needed to be represented in the senior management team. He enacted policies to promote more women into higher-level positions. In addition, Preston shifted the firm's organizational culture to being more accommodating of all its employees.

The current management team launched several growth initiatives to build on Avon's strong brand name and distribution channel through its customer representative network. Avon product lines include private-label brands such as Avon Color, Anew, Skin-So-Soft, Advance Techniques Hair Care, Avon Naturals, and Mark. Avon also markets an extensive line of fashion jewelry and apparel.

Avon sells more than 125 million lipsticks per year or 4 lipsticks every second of the day, making Avon the top seller of lipstick in the mass market. Its Anew brand is the number-one line of anti-aging skin care products in the world. The Advance Techniques hair care line offers high-performance hair products for every hair type, age group, and ethnic background to accommodate a diverse, worldwide consumer base.

Avon Wellness promotes a balanced, healthy lifestyle for women and their families and includes nutritional supplements, a weight management line, and therapeutic products. Avon partnered with the fitness phenomenon Curves, an international fitness franchise, to help women look and feel their best. Through this partnership, Avon Wellness offers an array of Curves-branded exercise videos and DVDs, fitness apparel, accessories, and comfortable footwear that support an active lifestyle.

Finally, Avon is using technology to support the efforts of its 6 million independent sales representatives. An electronic ordering system allows the representatives to run their businesses more efficiently and improve order-processing accuracy. Avon representatives use the Internet to manage their business electronically. In the United States, Avon representatives use an online marketing tool called youravon.com, which helps them build their own Avon business by selling through personalized Web pages developed in partnership with Avon. Avon e-representatives can promote special products, target specific groups of customers, place and track orders online, and capitalize on e-mail to share product information, selling tips, and marketing incentives.

DISCUSSION QUESTIONS

1. Why is Avon so committed to diversity?
2. Select another retailer that also values diversity. How does this commitment affect its financial results?
3. What values have helped Avon to be a successful company even after 125 years?

Sources: www.avoncompany.com (accessed July 13, 2010); Avon Annual Report, 2009; www.avonfoundation.org (accessed July 13, 2010).

This case was written by Barton Weitz, University of Florida, and Hope Bober Corrigan, Loyola College in Maryland.

CASE 16   Attracting Generation Y to a Retail Career

THE DIVA BRAND

Diva is a specialty retail store focused on fast-fashion jewelry and accessories. The brand's origins are in Australia, but recent years have seen rapid international expansion and the brand now has stores in America, Russia, and Europe. Diva is predominantly located in shopping centers, with some stores in high-street locations, and is always positioned in/around apparel fashion clusters. The stores are clean, simplistic, and brightly lit, reflecting their fast-moving, funky, and vibrant product range targeted at the youth market (predominantly 15- to 25-year-old females). Diva's positioning sees it as the only fashion jewelry/hair accessory specialist retailer in Australia.

Due to Diva's recent expansion, staff numbers have grown significantly. However, Diva is confronted with the problem of attracting and retaining experienced and talented people, particularly from Generation Y. In an attempt to counteract this problem, Diva has implemented several internal talent policies to provide a point of difference and be an employer of choice, including:

- Training plans/workshops to fill skill gaps.
- Career development program for top store managers.
- Leadership development program for top regional managers.
- Increased salary package offers for certain roles to attract talent/skill.
- Global expansion, with new offers of career progression.

GENERATIONAL DIFFERENCES IN THE WORKFORCE

As a result of key demographic and lifestyle issues such as aging populations, declining fertility, delayed retirements, rising labor participation rates, and higher life expectancies, there is a demographic trough in the Asia Pacific workforce, in which there is soon to be smaller proportions of younger-aged members and larger cohorts of mature-aged workers. This is further compounded by a shrinking talent pool and the fact that retail is not perceived as a career of choice by the adult population, who have limited sight of career path opportunities "beyond the shop floor."

Although research acknowledges the pertinence of this issue in retailing today, it remains unclear how to effectively manage generational diversity in the workplace. This is not a new issue; however, wider age groups are culminating in less segregated work arrangements. In the past, older staff undertook senior managerial positions, while younger workers assumed front-desk or field positions. However, today it is common to see staff members from all age groups working together on projects, with senior employees managing across several generations or younger employees managing older generations. It is important to note that, if managed poorly, intergenerational impacts can cause conflict for employers and among employees, hampering workplace productivity and morale.

Retailers, as well as organizations from many other industries, therefore need to identify and adopt the best approaches in attracting and retaining staff across all retail functions, optimizing the experiences of mature-aged workers while capitalizing on the potential of young employees. This involves understanding each generation and its unique perspectives, communication styles, and working styles in order to provide tailored support. Each generation holds different perspectives of work, including the definition of an attractive working environment, leadership qualities, and preferred team playing approaches, and has an individual information processing style. For example, Generation Y believes in having fluid work patterns and influencing job terms and conditions. Conversely, the baby-boomer generation regards work as a primary security in life, while Generation X values a balance between work and life.

GENERATION Y

Born between 1981 and 2000, members of Generation Y were one of the key segments of focus in *Shopfloor to Boardroom* given their sheer numbers and prospective employment in retail as recent or upcoming workforce entrants. While organizations have had time to understand baby boomers and Generation X-ers, determining the needs of Generation Y-ers has been challenging, especially given their vastly different values. This is particularly important given the significant career opportunities that exist for Generation Y in retailing. In better understanding the unique career motivations, perceptions, and aspirations of Generation Y, a number of focus groups were conducted with university students who were studying a business major and currently working in retail and high school students who were studying retail-related subjects and currently working in retail or interested in doing so.

In terms of perceptions of working in retail, our research found that retail is simply not viewed as a career of choice by Generation Y. This is primarily due to the feeling that retail involves "just being a checkout chick," has limited or no career paths "beyond the shop floor" and is therefore a short-term employment solution, and has difficult conditions at times (e.g., long hours, repetitive tasks, low salaries). A related concern was that the retail industry is not generally perceived as prestigious in the eyes of the general public.

Despite such issues, there were a number of motivators (other than financial) for working in retail for Generation Y, such as improving one's social life and extending friendship circles, gaining work experience while studying, and following a particular passion (i.e., fashion). Generation Y-ers also reported a variety of career aspirations that were generally consistent with the courses or subjects they were studying. Despite the fact that few listed retail as their number-one career option, a strong desire was found for a career that could be facilitated by the retail industry, such as marketing, HR, or buying.

Focused on self-improvement, Generation Y-ers also expressed enjoyment in working for organizations that provide constant learning environments; they want to be involved in the organization's vision and mission, desire mobility and flexibility in the workplace, and seek instant gratification. Members of Generation Y also thrive on systematic feedback and value positive reinforcement at accelerated rates, as compared to previous generations. This is the primary reason that Generation Y questions starting at the bottom of the organizational ladder, having developed a strong desire for rapid career progression from years of high-level education.

DISCUSSION QUESTIONS

1. How can Diva demystify what happens behind the scenes and make potential Generation Y employees aware of the opportunities available to them beyond the shop floor?

2. Diva has implemented a learning organizational culture in an attempt to attract and retain staff.

Discuss the possible pros and cons of this strategy for Generation Y.

3. Give examples of how other organizations (perhaps even nonretailers) attract a Generation Y workforce. What could Diva learn from other organizations?

This case was written by Sean Sands, Monash University, and Carla Ferraro, Monash University.

CASE 17   Nordstrom Rewards Its Customers

From consultants ready to solve fashion crises to personal concierge services and spa treatments at Le Couvent des Minimes Spa by L'Occitane in Provence, France, Nordstrom is using its varied loyalty programs to retain and increase its share of wallet among key customers. The retailer's research indicates that customers who have relationships with Nordstrom through either the rewards program or a salesperson spend more at Nordstrom than those who do not.

Nordstrom shoppers automatically become members of Nordstrom's Fashion Rewards program when they sign up for the store's credit card. They earn points, or Nordstrom Notes, whenever they use the card—including on purchases made from other vendors—although Nordstrom purchases result in twice the points. Each time a customer accumulates 2,000 points, he or she receives a $20 Nordstrom Note, a gift certificate redeemable for Nordstrom merchandise or services. The program's different levels are based on annual net purchases; the higher the customer's annual spending, the more rewards earned. Nordstrom Notes encourage shoppers to move up to the higher levels by shopping at Nordstrom and by using the store's credit card no matter where they shop. Benefits available at different levels include free standard shipping, free trial-size beauty products, invitations to private shopping events, Nordstrom On Call (a 24-hour fashion emergency hotline), early access to Nordstrom's Anniversary Sale (the biggest sale of the year), and complimentary tickets to Nordstrom designer runway shows and a private shopping party hosted by Nordstrom.

Nordstrom is not alone in its efforts. Its competitors have also ramped up their loyalty programs. Saks Fifth Avenue's SaksFirst program allows shoppers to accrue points from in-store purchases made using a Saks credit card or another form of payment and from credit card purchases made outside the store with the Saks' "little black card." Points earned vary depending on tier and whether the purchase was made at Saks or at an outside vendor. Diamond Plus customers, who spend at least $25,000 a year at the store, receive free local delivery, complimentary valet parking, storage of one fur item at no cost, advance notice of sales, invitations to special events, and complimentary shipping on online and catalog orders. Saks also partners with exclusive vendors such as Mercedes, The Palm restaurant, and The Yachts of Seabourn on exclusive offerings, and it rewards its top shoppers with elite travel services.

Of the various programs, though, Neiman Marcus's InCircle, launched nearly 30 years ago, remains the granddaddy of them all. Customers at different spending levels earn points by using their Neiman Marcus credit card. Customers usually get 1 point for each dollar they spend, although at the highest tiers the point-earning formulas become more generous and members may choose one day each year on which to receive double points. Points are redeemable for gift certificates, in-store dining, alterations, fur storage, store delivery, or airline miles. The program's five tiers include the President's Circle, achieved by spending between $75,000 and $599,999 annually. Neiman's President's Circle members receive custom-designed travel, entertainment, or gifts. For example, members might take in a Broadway preview and dine with the cast, savor a private cooking class in a Tuscan villa with an Italian chef and sommelier, or enjoy the Kentucky Derby from Millionaire's Row seating and relax at the Barnstable Brown party.

DISCUSSION QUESTIONS

1. What are the design characteristics of an effective loyalty program?

2. How effective is Nordstrom's program in terms of developing customer loyalty?

3. Whom should Nordstrom target for its loyalty program?

4. Is the Nordstrom program worth what it spends to reward customers? Why or why not? Explain.

5. Are luxury consumers more drawn to reward/loyalty programs than are those in other economic groups? Are they drawn to different types of programs?

6. What do you see as the strengths or weaknesses of loyalty programs such as Nordstrom's Fashion Rewards or InCircle at Neiman Marcus?

Sources: Bill Brohaugh, "Neiman Marcus Sweet Rewards Target Loyalty," *Colloquy*, March 23, 2007, p. 2; "Nordstrom Launches 'Fashion Rewards,'" *PR Newswire–First Call* (accessed April 26, 2007); Vanessa O'Connell, "Posh Retailers Pile on Perks for Top Customers," *Wall Street Journal*, April 26, 2007, p. D1; InCircle Web site, www.incircle.com/store/catalog/templates/Entry.jhtml?itemId=cat103411&parentId=cat103410&parentId=cat000001&icid=points1 (accessed June 23, 2010); SaksFirst Web site, www.saksfifthavenue.com/SaksFirst/rewards.jsp?bmUID=1277232322125 (accessed June 23, 2010); Nordstrom Fashion Rewards Web site, http://about.nordstrom.com/nordstromfashionrewards/#rewards_1 (accessed June 3, 2010).

This case was written by Barton Weitz, University of Florida; Michael Levy, Babson College; and Kate Woodworth.

Planning Data

SALES FORECAST $ _____

Planned GMROI = (Gross Margin / Net Sales) × (Net Sales / Inventory Costs)

[ ] = ($ / $) × ($ / $)

(Sales / Inventory Costs) × (100% – GM%) = Inventory Turnover

[X] × [%] = [X]

12 ÷ Inventory Turnover = B.O.M. Stock/Sales

÷ [X] = [X]

Forecasted Ending Inventory [$]

The Plan

		%	$
Markdowns		%	$
Discounts +		%	$
Shortages +		%	$
Total Reductions		%	$

		Jan	Feb	Mar	Apr	May	Jun	Jul	Aug	Sept	Oct	Nov	Dec	Total (Average)	Remarks
% Distribution of Sales by Month	1													100.0%	History/Projection
Monthly Sales	2														Step (1) × Net Sales
% Distribution of Reductions/Mo	3													100.0%	History/Projection
Monthly Reductions	4														Step (3) × Total Reductions
B.O.M. Stock/Sales Ratios	5														Adjusted by Mo. Sales Fluctuations
B.O.M. Stock ($000)	6													(Forecasted End Inventory)	Step (2) × Step (5)
E.O.M. Stock ($000)	7														EOM Jan = BOM Feb
Monthly Additions to Stock ($000)	8														Steps 2 + 4 + 7–6 Sales + Reductions + EOM–BOM

CASE 21 PenAgain Sells to Walmart

Wednesday was one of the most important days in Colin Roche's and Bobby Ronsse's careers. The pair had an appointment with a Walmart buyer in Bentonville, Arkansas, to present their ergonomic pen, the PenAgain, to the world's largest retailer. Getting into Walmart is an entrepreneur's equivalent of playing in the Super Bowl. A favorable response from Walmart would transform their invention from a niche product into a household name. But getting Walmart to stock a new product in the mature writing instrument market was a real challenge.

Roche's path to Bentonville, Arkansas, began during a Saturday detention at his Palo Alto, California, high school. Roche was playing with a toy robot that doubled as a pen and discovered that when he wrote with one index finger between the robot's legs, he didn't need to grip the pen as tightly and he no longer experienced writer's cramp. He refined the design while in college, and after graduation he teamed with his fraternity brother Ronsse to launch Pacific Writing Instruments. They filed for a patent, launched a Web site (penagain.com), and set up production in the San Francisco Bay area. The aging pop-

ulation of baby boomers dealing with carpal-tunnel syndrome and arthritis created a vast need for ergonomic pens, but their design was truly radical. Traditional pen manufacturers had been attempting to satisfy the market's need by adjusting a pen's length or width or the texture of the grip—never by varying its basic stick design.

Initially, PenAgain focused on small retailers and eventually produced $2 million in annual revenue from 5,000 independent stationery and office supply stores, 200 Staples in Canada, and various other chain outlets, including Fred Meyer and Hobby Lobby. To provide an attractive offering to large retailers like Walmart, PenAgain needed to lower its prices and obtain high-volume manufacturing capability, which meant moving production overseas. It lowered its manufacturing costs so that it could offer a $3.99 pen, and it expanded its product line to 10 items, including a pencil, highlighter, hobby knife, whiteboard marker, and children's writing instrument, all in a wide variety of colors and textures.

After talking to local Walmart store managers and attending a trade show hosted by the School, Home, &

"co-brand" with an outside designer
the area of fashion and whose telev
huge success throughout the Unite
several years. This designer was hi
teen market and offered products wi
in the current JCPenney assortmen
and considered all of the potential ri
ing this product line. He didn't wan
cial investment in an unproven proc
department store retailer. Howeve
was a "once-in-a-lifetime" opportu
highly recognized name in fashion
could help him gain additional mai
lieved that success of this co-brand
fast track within the organization.

JCPenney had continued to pu
key designers and manufacturers as
pany strategy to differentiate itself
The "Exclusive to JCPenney" co-b
a number of different departments s
pany; they included brands such a
Ralph Lauren's Global Brand Conce
en's, and baby areas, along with t
Cindy Crawford's Style in the home
sories area. Other exclusive co-bra
the apparel lines with Liz Claiborne
increased the level of fashion for th
believed that this was an important s
include, at least in part, for his future
ing the positives and negatives of de
sive brand in the juniors' area, he no

Positives

1. The ability to add market share l
   visibility and name-brand awarer
2. Added advertising benefits from
   the co-branding partner.
3. Increase of fashion level for both
   and overall assortment.
4. Continue to stay in line with con
   utilizing exclusive brands.
5. Point of differentiation from con
   not carry the product line.

Negatives

1. High level of risk involved for int
   product line.
2. Product development issues conc
   opment, and delivery standards.
3. Contract terms more complex tha
   or national-branded products.
4. Possible negative effect on sales f
   product assortment.

After listing these positives and
cided to meet with his boss and dis
During the meeting, he inquired ab
mitment that he would have to make
ing this exclusive co-brand. He was
would be at least a three-year com
the designer on this product line if th

Office Products Association, the partners landed an appointment with a Walmart buyer. The meeting opened with some bad news: "I've seen this design before and passed," the buyer said, mentioning a competitor's product manufactured in Korea with a similar shape. Roche quickly responded, "The difference is that we are building a brand. Rather than going to you first, we've got a base of independent retailers and distributors worldwide who have already picked us up." (Walmart doesn't like to account for more than 30 percent of a supplier's total business.) He showed her the testimonials, media write-ups, and product extensions. Finally, as their time allotment came to a close, the buyer closed her notebook and said simply, "Okay. We'll give you a trial period."

But that acceptance was just the beginning. Over the next 10 months, PenAgain's founders completed the intensive paperwork required to become an official Walmart vendor. Walmart placed an order for 48,000 pens and located them on end caps in 500 stores. To earn a more permanent shelf position throughout the entire chain, PenAgain had to sell 85 percent of the pens during the one-month trial period. The PenAgain model sold for $3.76, compared with a nearly identical pen priced at $6.49 on www.amazon.com and more than $12 elsewhere.

Walmart did not provide any marketing support for the pens, and PenAgain was too small to afford traditional print or television advertising. So the partners developed a viral marketing program, reaching out to their national fraternity headquarters and consumer groups that had already shown interest in the PenAgain. The company also marketed through its general e-mail list of some 10,000 customers who regularly bought the pens.

The Walmart buyer did not have time to monitor pen sales, so the partners tracked daily sales over the Internet, using Walmart's Retail Link software system. The PenAgain founders also produced an extra 100 displays for use in Walmart stores and kept them in their own ware-house. PenAgain then hired a merchant service organization, a third-party group that sends representatives into stores to check out display placement and consumer traffic and then report back electronically to the supplier.

In providing its products, PenAgain had to adhere to Walmart's detailed packaging and shipping requirements, which specified the thickness of the cardboard used for display cartons; the placement of a reddish stripe around the shipping container to help Walmart employees know where to place the merchandise in the stores; and shipping labels that included purchase order numbers, distribution center details, and other information.

As the PenAgain partners prepare for what may be the most crucial 30 days of their business careers, they seem realistic about the challenges ahead. "There are things that could go tremendously well, and things that could sink," Roche says. "We have a lot on the line, and honestly, we are nervous as hell."

> **REFACT**
>
> Each year, about 10,000 new products are presented to Walmart buyers. Only 200 are stocked in its stores.

DISCUSSION QUESTIONS

1. What are the key steps that PenAgain took to get Walmart to stock its products?
2. If you were one of PenAgain's small retail customers, how would you react to the company's selling its products through Walmart?
3. Forecast sales for PenAgain in the 30-day trial.

Sources: www.penagain.com (accessed July 15, 2010); Gwendolyn Bounds, "The Long Road to Walmart," *Wall Street Journal*, September 19, 2005, p. R1; Gwendolyn Bounds, "One Mount to Make It," *Wall Street Journal*, May 30, 2006, p. B1

This case was written by Barton Weitz, University of Florida.

CASE 22 American Furniture Warehouse Sources Globally

The year 1975 saw the tail end of a recession that came on the heels of the 1973 Arab oil embargo, the fall of Saigon, and the resignation of Richard Nixon. That same year, Jake Jabs took over the American Furniture Company in Denver, Colorado, renamed it American Furniture Warehouse (AFW), and started turning it into a high-volume discount home furnishings retailer. Jabs responded to concerns that resonated with consumers in a tough economy: tighter pocketbooks, job insecurity, rising energy costs, a growing number of households as baby boomers branched out, and greater receptivity to generic products. Jabs was an experienced furniture retailer and had operated his own furniture manufacturing concern. Unbeknown to Jabs at the time, global sourcing would become a more prominent way for his company to stock its showrooms.

Fast-forward to the present. Consumers' tastes change at a faster clip. They have higher standards than ever, and they demand bargains. As an inherently frugal man, Jake Jabs loves to give the public good value while keeping overhead low

Jabs is the CEO, but he employs no executives. No titles of vice president or executive vice president are anywhere in sight. The company is family-owned and is not beholden to stockholders demanding that high profit margins or quarterly objectives be met. Without pressure from such entities, AFW has continued to grow and thrive. Jake Jabs obsessively trolls for ideas on how to keep prices low, quality high, and merchandise current.

People from all over the western United States visit AFW's megastores. They are intrigued with the values and constantly ask that AFW open a showroom near them. To date, AFW has preferred to remain a regional player. Its buys are based on the preferences and trends of Colorado customers.

Some of the many tenets to which AFW subscribes include striving to offer the lowest prices and the best guarantee, employing a no-pressure sales staff, having the best displays and selection, employing a careful delivery staff that works seven days a week, providing outstanding product information and customer service, and repairing merchandise on-site rather than shipping anything back to the manufacturer.

In the 35 years AFW has been oper
strong vendor relationships worldwi
sources goods from 30 different countrie
partners include Malaysia, Indonesia, C
Mexico. It has a buying office in Asia. Its
tured to the point where vendors travel
bring samples to a foreign AFW buying
buying staff maximizes its time by havir
buyers at specified dates and times; buyer
make arduous trips through countries
stead, they spend their time efficiently
wholesale market centers and trade shov
of the AFW buying offices the majority

One of the dilemmas AFW has be
centers around setting guidelines under
time to see a new vendor. AFW's reputa
and vendors clamor to get appointment
team on their limited market and trade

Many factories in developing countri
structures than those closer to home,
stringent government regulations, low
benefits for workers. Foreign factories
manufacturing one or two items well
stantly changing what product is on th
is often the case in the United States.
line process is less flexible but more cos

Since AFW sells so much, it is able to
directly imports full containers of merch
staff travels the world looking for the bes
buyers are often able to negotiate prices
less than competitors' prices for compar
This is due in part to the size of the orde
in which it is shipped. AFW sometimes
get a better price, and it has a policy of
time—a value factories respect and rev
exploring other ways in which AFW can
in the buying process.

An example of how AFW has applied
solving to reduce cost unfolds throug
build its own chairs, saving dramatically
garden-variety hardwood dinette chair
tured abroad and the pieces assembled a
less than the cost if it were shipped al
Typically, 1,000 assembled dinette chairs
size container. AFW buys 4,000 identica
and fits them in that same container. It
workers roughly $2 per chair to assemb
sell each chair at retail for less than wh
pay for the same chair at wholesale.

Yet another manifestation of its crea
cost-reduction: AFW takes delivery on
merchandise rather than carton-wrappe
the blankets reusable, but not putting th
cartons in the first place can save as much

CASE 23   Merchandise Exclu

Jason Miller had just returned from a c
meeting and began to consider how to str
chandise assortment. He was a new buyer
apparel area, having been with the com

CASE 24   How Much for a Good Smell?

For the past two Christmas seasons, Courtney's, an up-scale gift store, has carried a sweet-smelling potpourri in a plastic bag with an attractive ribbon. Heavily scented with cloves, the mixture gives a pleasant holiday aroma to any room, including the store.

Two years ago, the mixture cost $4.50 a bag. Courtney's (the only store in town that carried it) sold 300 pieces for $9.50. Courtney's supply ran out 10 days before Christmas, and it was too late to get any more.

Last year, the manufacturer raised the price to $5.00, so Courtney's raised its retail price to $9.95. Even though the markup was lower than that in the previous year, the store owner felt there was "magic" in the $10 ($9.95) price. As before, the store had a complete sellout, this time five days before Christmas. Sales last year were 600 units.

This year, the wholesale price has gone up to $5.50, and store personnel are trying to determine the correct retail price. The owner once again wants to hold the price at $10 ($9.95), but the buyer disagrees: "It's my job to push for the highest possible markup wherever I can. This item is a sure seller, as we're still the only store around with it, and we had some unsatisfied demand last year. I think we should mark it $12.50, which will improve the markup to 56 percent. Staying at $10 will penalize us unnecessarily, especially considering the markup would be even lower than last year. Even if we run into price resistance, we'll only have to sell 480 to maintain the same dollar volume."

The owner demurs, saying, "This scent is part of our store's ambience. It acts as a draw to get people into the store, and its pleasant smell keeps them in a free-spending state of mind. I think we should keep the price at $9.95, despite the poorer markup. And if we can sell many more at this price, we'll realize the same dollar gross margin as last year. I think we should buy 1,000. Furthermore, if people see us raising a familiar item's price 25 percent, they might wonder whether our other prices are fair."

DISCUSSION QUESTIONS

1. What prices caused Courtney's new charges?
2. Which price would result in the highest profit?
3. What other factors should Courtney's consider?
4. What price would you charge, and how many units would you order?

This case was written by Professor David Ehrlich, Marymount University.

CASE 25   Promoting a Sale

A consumer electronics chain in the Washington, D.C., area is planning a big sale in its suburban Virginia warehouse over the three-day President's Day weekend (Saturday through Monday). On sale will be nearly $2 million worth of consumer electronics products—50 percent of the merchandise sold in the store. The company hopes to realize at least $900,000 in sales during the three days. In the retailer's past experience, the first day's sales were 50 percent of the total. The second day's were 35 percent, and the last day's, 15 percent. One of every two customers who came made a purchase.

Furthermore, the retailer knows that large numbers of people always flock to such sales, some driving as far as 50 miles. They come from all economic levels, but all are confirmed bargain hunters. You're the assistant to the general merchandise manager, who has asked you to plan the event's marketing campaign. You have the following information:

1. A full-page *Washington Post* ad costs $10,000, a half-page ad costs $6,000, and a quarter-page ad costs $3,500. To get the maximum value from a newspaper campaign, it is company policy to run two ads (not necessarily the same size) for such events.
2. The local northern Virginia paper is printed weekly and distributed free to some 15,000 households. Ads cost $700 for a full page and $400 for a half page.
3. To get adequate TV coverage, at least three channels must be used, with a minimum of eight 30-second spots on each at $500 per spot, spread over three or more days. Producing a television advertisement costs $3,000.
4. The store has contracts with three radio stations. One appeals to a broad, general audience aged 25 to 34 years. One is popular with the 18-to-25 age group. The third, a classical music station, has a small but wealthy audience. Minimum costs for a saturation radio campaign, including production, on all three stations are $8,000, $5,000, and $3,000, respectively.
5. Producing and mailing a full-color flyer to the store's 80,000 charge customers costs $10,000. When the company used such a mailing piece before, about 3 percent of recipients responded.

DISCUSSION QUESTIONS

1. Knowing that the company wants a mixed-media ad campaign to support this event, prepare an ad plan for the general merchandise manager that costs no more than $40,000.
2. Work out the daily scheduling of all advertising.
3. Work out the dollars to be devoted to each medium.
4. Justify your plan.

This case was prepared by David Ehrlich, Marymount University.

CASE 26   Target Marketing with Google AdWords

Australia's oldest retailer evolved from Appleton and Jones in 1835 to David Jones in 1838. Today, David Jones, or simply DJs, has dozens of department stores, predominantly in Australia's capital cities. Similar to many retailers, and despite having a mail-order business since the late 1800s, DJs suffered a few missteps with its online presence in the early 2000s. Now however, the David Jones Web site, davidjones.com.au, is integral to DJs' daily operations.

Chris Taylor, a recent university graduate, manages DJs' online presence. Thanks to its successful Web site and changing media habits, David Jones is considering online advertising to drive targeted traffic to the Web site. Given the prominence of Google and sponsored search, Chris would like to test Google AdWords.

Starting late last century, search engines began to develop interactive advertising models based on user interests, such as keywords typed into a search engine. The concept, *sponsored search*, aligns online advertisements with search engine queries. In sponsored search—also known as paid search, keyword advertising, pay-per-click (PPC) advertising, and search advertising—advertisers pay for search engine traffic to their Web sites via link-based ads that search engines display in response to user queries. Thus, if a user searches Google using the keyword *retailers*, AdWords ads that mention retailing would appear. If the user clicks on an ad, the user then goes to a specific Web page—the landing page—on the advertiser's Web site.

As the leading search engine, Google has driven developments in sponsored search beyond search engine results. In addition to placing advertisements on Google and affiliated search engine results, such as AOL.com and Ask.com, advertisers can place AdWords on other Web sites. Via its content network, Google dynamically matches ads to a Web page's content and pays the Web site owner if a visitor clicks on the ad. Google's content network includes millions of Web sites in over 100 countries and 20 languages, such as the British travel site Lonely Planet and the French television channel M6. In the United States, for example, the *New York Times* earns revenue by placing AdWords on its Web pages. Thus, advertisers can place AdWords on search engine results and on the millions of Web sites in Google's content network.

AdWords are simple text-based ads with four lines of copy predominantly in the right-hand column and at the top of Google search results. The first line, or headline, has a maximum of 25 characters. The next two lines and the final line with the Web site address have a maximum of 35 characters each. Two sample AdWords advertisements for David Jones are shown in Exhibit 1. The copy is identical except for the first half of the third line, "Great holiday specials" versus "Expanded holiday hours." The ad on the left should interest value-conscious market segments, while the one on the right should attract consumers seeking after-hours shopping.

In addition to their simple and nonintrusive nature, AdWords' advantages over traditional advertising such as print or television include better segmentation and more direct targeting. Advertisers select the keywords and the

EXHIBIT 1
Sample AdWords

Christmas at David Jones	Christmas at David Jones
Convenient major city locations	Convenient major city locations
Great holiday specials; visit now	Expanded holiday hours; visit now
DavidJones.com.au	DavidJones.com.au

geographic location of the person doing the search. For geographic segmentation, David Jones might want its ads to appear only for people in a key source market such as Sydney or Melbourne.

To target consumer interests, David Jones could use keywords such as *Christmas, holidays, shopping,* and *retailers.* But these keywords could be too expensive because they are so generic. Although generic terms may attract clicks on an AdWords advertisement, many of these clicks may be from random rather than targeted David Jones Web shoppers. Unlike a cost-per-thousand model based on impressions, this contextual advertising based on keywords charges advertisers on a cost-per-click basis. Chris and her team want to pay for targeted clicks.

To minimize paying for unwanted clicks, online advertisers also include negative keywords such as *cheap* or *free.* Including the negative keyword *cheap* alongside the keywords *Christmas* and *shopping* means that no AdWords ads will show on search results for users keying in the three keywords *cheap, Christmas,* and *shopping.*

Furthermore, advertisers bid on the cost per click in a dynamic auction. When many advertisers bid on generic terms such as *Christmas* and *shopping,* this drives the cost up for these keywords. Thus clever advertisers bid on specific phrases such as *Christmas shopping* rather than on *Christmas* and *shopping.*

Chris and her team use four Google Web sites to understand and determine applicable content network Web sites, keywords, and estimated keyword costs:

- Google AdWords Glossary (https://adwords.google.com/support/bin/topic.py?topic=29)
- Google Content Network (http://www.google.com/adwords/contentnetwork/)
- Google Keyword Tool (https://adwords.google.com/select/KeywordToolExternal)
- Google Traffic Estimator (https://adwords.google.com/select/TrafficEstimatorSandbox)

As AdWords accounts are easy to set up and manage, the testing possibilities are many. Major considerations that Chris and her team would like to test include:

- Appropriate keywords, keyword phrases, and negative keywords
- Geographic segmentation
- Advertising copy and appeals
- Keyword pricing

- Google's content network
- Aligning the landing page with the AdWords copy

The final point above—the landing page—leads to a key aspect of David Jones' online presence, its Web site. As davidjones.com.au illustrates, the Web site serves many target markets and offers many products. For example, online visitors may find information on store events, employment, publicly traded stock shares, and registration for e-mail alerts and bridal registries, as well as traditional department store products such as clothing. Effective AdWords align the advertising copy with the landing page. That is, the advertisement directs consumers to a relevant Web page rather than to the David Jones home page at davidjones.com.au. The left-column ad in Exhibit 1, which focuses on holiday specials, would take visitors to a landing page with holiday specials. Similarly, the right-column ad in Table 1 would take visitors to a landing page featuring expanded holiday hours.

DISCUSSION QUESTIONS

1. On the basis of your review of the David Jones Web site davidjones.com.au, use examples to explain how different sections of the home page serve different audiences. What other audiences would you suggest David Jones serve via its Web site? Why?
2. On the basis of your review of the David Jones Web site, davidjones.com.au, design three separate AdWords advertisements.

This case was written by Jamie Murphy, Murdoch Business School; Meghan O'Farrell, Google; and Alex Gibelalde, Google.

CASE 27   Enterprise Rent-A-Car Focuses on Its People

Enterprise, with annual sales of more than $13 billion, is the largest and most profitable car-rental business in North America. The company runs more than 6,000 locations that fall within 15 miles of 90 percent of the U.S. population. Enterprise also operates in Canada, Germany, Ireland, and the United Kingdom.

When Jack Taylor started Enterprise in 1957, he adopted a unique strategy. Most car-rental firms targeted business and leisure travel customers who arrived at an airport and needed to rent a car for local transportation. Taylor decided to target a different segment—drivers whose own cars were being repaired or who were driving on vacation, hauling home improvement materials, in need of an extra vehicle for an out-of-town guest, or for some other reason simply needed an extra car for a few days.

Traditional car rental companies must charge relatively high daily rates because their locations in or near airports are expensive. In addition, their business customers are price-insensitive, because their companies pay for the rental expenses. While the airport locations are convenient for business customers, these locations are inconvenient for people seeking a replacement car while their car is in the shop. Although Enterprise has airport locations, it also maintains rental offices in downtown and suburban areas, near where its target market lives and works. The firm provides local pickup and delivery service in most areas.

Enterprise also rewards entrepreneurship at a local level. The company fosters a sense of ownership among its employees. For example, its management training program starts by defining a clear career path for each management trainee. Then it teaches employees how to build their own business. Their compensation is tied directly to the financial results of the local operation. Employees from the rental branch offices often advance to the highest levels of operating management.

The firm hires college graduates—8,000 each year from 1,000 campuses—for its management trainee positions because it believes a college degree demonstrates intelligence and motivation. Rather than recruiting students with the highest GPA, it focuses on hiring people who were athletes or officers of social organizations, such as fraternities, sororities, and clubs, because they typically have the good interpersonal skills needed to deal effectively with Enterprise's varied customers.

Jack Taylor's growth strategy is based on providing high-quality, personalized service so that customers will return to Enterprise when they need to rent a car again. One of his often-quoted sayings summarizes his philosophy: "If you take care of your customers and employees, the bottom line will take care of itself." But because operating managers initially were compensated on the basis of sales growth, not customer satisfaction, service quality declined.

The first step Enterprise took to improve customer service was to develop a customer satisfaction measure, called the Enterprise Service Quality Index. The questionnaire that customers complete to assess ESQI was developed on the basis of input from operating managers, which in turn gave those managers a sense of ownership of the measurement tool. As ESQI gained legitimacy, Enterprise made a bigger deal of it. It posted the scores for each location prominently in its monthly operating reports—right next to the net profit numbers that determined managers' pay. The operating managers were able to track how they were doing and how all their peers were doing because all of the locations were ranked.

Feedback is also provided to service providers. If a customer mentions in the questionnaire that "I really liked Jill behind the counter; she just was terrific," that comment gets sent the very next morning to the local branch so that Jill knows that she did a great job and that a customer said something nice about her. Likewise, if somebody said that a car was dirty, the next day the local manager knows it and can determine why it happened.

To increase motivation among managers and improve service at their locations, Enterprise also announced that managers could be promoted only if their customer satisfaction scores were above the company average. Then it demonstrated that it would abide by this policy by failing to promote some star performers who had achieved good growth and profit numbers but had below-average satisfaction scores.

To provide a high level of service, new employees generally work long, grueling hours for what many see as relatively low pay. Before they are put in a branch and learn how to rent a car, Enterprise tells new hires about what the company means, what is important to customers, and what it deems important in terms of being a good team member. The company operates like a confederation of small businesses. New employees, like all Enterprise managers, are expected to jump in and help wash or vacuum cars when the location gets backed up. But all this hard work can pay off. The firm does not hire outsiders for other than entry-level jobs. At Enterprise, every position is filled by promoting someone already inside the company. Thus, Enterprise employees know that if they work hard and do their best, they may very well succeed in moving up the corporate ladder and earn a significant income.

DISCUSSION QUESTIONS

1. What are the pros and cons of Enterprise's human resource management strategy?
2. Would you want to work for Enterprise? Why or why not?
3. How does its human resource strategy complement the quality of customer service delivered by its representatives?

Sources: Fay Hansen, "Enterprises's Recruiting Model Transforms Interns into Managers," *Workforce Management Online*, May 2009; www.erac.com (accessed July 14, 2010); www.enterprise.com (accessed July 14, 2010); http://images.businessweek.com/ss/10/02/0218_customer_service_champs/1.htm (accessed July 14, 2010).

This case was written by Barton Weitz, University of Florida.

CASE 28 Diamond in the Rough

Ruth Diamond, president of Diamond Furriers, was concerned that sales in her store appeared to have flattened out. She was considering establishing a different method for compensating her salespeople.

Diamond was located in an affluent suburb of Nashville, Tennessee. Ruth's father had founded the company 40 years earlier, and she had grown up working in the business. After his retirement in 1980, she moved the store into an upscale shopping mall not far from its previous location and sales boomed almost immediately, rising to just over $1 million in five years. However, once it reached that sales volume, it remained there for the next three years, making Ruth wonder whether her salespeople had sufficient incentive to sell more aggressively.

Diamond's staff was all women, ranging in age from 27 to 58 years. There were four full-timers and four part-timers (20 hours a week), all of whom had at least three years of experience in the store. All of them were paid at the same hourly rate, $10, with liberal health benefits. Employee morale was excellent, and the entire staff displayed strong personal loyalty to Diamond.

The store was open 78 hours a week, which meant that there was nearly always a minimum staff of three on the floor, rising to six at peak periods. Diamond's merchandise consisted exclusively of fur coats and jackets, ranging in price from $750 to more than $5,000. The average unit sale was about $2,000. Full-timers' annual sales averaged about $160,000, and the part-timers' were a little over half of that.

Diamond's concern about sales transcended her appreciation for her loyalty toward her employees. She asked them, for example, to maintain customer files and call their customers when new styles came in. Although some of them were more diligent about this than others, none of them appeared to want to be especially aggressive about promoting sales.

She began to investigate commission systems and discussed them with some of her contacts in the trade. All suggested lowering the salespeople's base pay and installing either a fixed or a variable commission rate system.

One idea was to lower the base hourly rate from $10 to $7 and let them make up the difference through a 4 percent commission on all sales, to be paid monthly. Such an arrangement would allow them all to earn the same as they currently do.

However, she also realized that such a system would provide no incentive to sell the higher-priced furs, which she recognized might be a way to improve overall sales. So she also considered offering to pay 3 percent on items priced below $2,000 and 5 percent on all those above.

Either of these systems would require considerable extra bookkeeping. Returns would have to be deducted from commissions. And she was also concerned that disputes might arise among her people from time to time over who had actually made the sale. So she conceived of a third alternative, which was to leave the hourly rates the same but pay a flat bonus of 4 percent of all sales over $1 million and then divide it among the salespeople on the basis of the proportion of hours each had actually worked. This "commission" would be paid annually, in the form of a Christmas bonus.

DISCUSSION QUESTIONS

1. What are the advantages and disadvantages of the various alternatives Ruth Diamond is considering?
2. Do you have any other suggestions for improving the store's sales?
3. What would you recommend? Why?

This case was prepared by Professor David Ehrlich, Marymount University.

CASE 29   "Touch and Feel" at Sephora

Sephora, a division of Moet Hennessy Louis Vuitton SA (LVMH), the world's largest luxury goods company, is an innovative retail concept from France that is changing the way cosmetics are sold. The store first arrived in the United States in mid-1998 with two store locations, in New York and Miami. Its flagship store, encompassing 21,000 square feet, opened in Rockefeller Center in New York City in October 1999. Now Sephora operates approximately 1,000 stores in 14 countries worldwide, including 250 stand-alone stores in the United States and another 150 locations inside JCPenney department stores. In addition to its strong presence throughout the United States, it also runs stores in Canada, China, the Czech Republic, France, Greece, Italy, Luxembourg, the Middle East, Monaco, Netherlands, Poland, Portugal, Romania, Russia, Spain, and Turkey. The company continues to expand both in the United States and globally.

Most fashion-oriented cosmetics are still sold in department stores. The scent and cosmetics areas in these stores consist of counters devoted to products made by each manufacturer. Salespeople specializing in a specific line stand behind the counter and assist customers in selecting merchandise. Services include applying products to the customer's face and showing her how to use products and how the colors will look with her skin and hair color, in addition to making suggestions. Although customers are not required to make a purchase in return for makeup lessons or full makeovers, many feel compelled to buy at least a lipstick or mascara in return for the services.

In contrast, Sephora uses an open-sell approach and offers customers over 200 brands of beauty products, including cosmetics, skin and hair care, and bath and body items and covering natural and organic products as well as gifts, personal care products, and shaving necessities for men. Brands cover new lines, best-sellers, classics, and an exclusive Sephora collection that accounts for about 10 percent of sales. The impressive store inventory totals over 13,000 different products—a collection that can be overwhelming for some shoppers. Customers can choose their own level of service, touching, feeling, and trying products on their own or soliciting advice from product consultants. Sephora takes great pride in training its employees about the history and use of the products in its stores, as well as in skills for customer interactions, to provide appropriate service to its shoppers.

Recently cosmetic and skin care companies recognized that women need higher-than-expected levels of help navigating the dizzying array of beauty products and tools that regularly change in response to trends and celebrity endorsements. Previous estimates put the percentage of shoppers needing help at the makeup counter at about 20 percent, but recent research indicates the number may be over 50 percent. The economic downturn has also motivated women to replace a lipstick or gloss that works with the rest of their beauty arsenal rather than replacing their entire repertoire to reflect a new season or trend. These women need more assistance than they did in the past.

To meet the needs of these customers, Sephora provides all of its consultants with a four-day course that teaches them the science and uses of the products sold in stores. Consultants desirous of more education can enroll in advanced classes. Successful completion of these classes results in an "expert" pin for skin care, color, and fragrance. Consultants wear their pins in stores so that customers know whom to go to for more information.

Classes are taught at Sephora University, the company's San Francisco–based training facility that opened in 2007. Using skills gained at the university, consultants answer customer questions, help women find the best solution to their skin care and beauty needs, and provide free, 10-minute in-store "express services" on a one-on-one basis to customers, covering specific topics such as matching foundation and skin type or transitioning makeup from day to night. Unlike department stores, where these learning sessions occur at the counter, Sephora express services occur in a salonlike setting on the store floor. Learning opportunities are directed to both consultants and managers so that all employees have the full range of knowledge they need to provide an optimal shopping experience for customers and the skills and insights necessary to run a successful and innovative cosmetic and skin care company.

This multichannel retailer also reaches customers through its highly interactive Web site (sephora.com). Shoppers using the Web site can search by hundreds of class and prestige brands, product category, editor's picks, hot new items, and Sephora favorites. Many retailers have been unsuccessful selling cosmetics online because customers cannot "touch and feel" products, because beauty products cannot be displayed properly in a two-dimensional format, or for reasons not yet understood. Yet Sephora has, once again, managed to set itself apart from competitors by making its Web site work while still yielding a profit. Some of the brands offered online are difficult to find in department stores, so the convenience of the Sephora site has tremendous appeal. For women who use a variety of brands, Sephora's one-stop shopping is also a significant asset. Women know they can find the brands they love at a reasonable price with no hassles.

Sephora also uses direct mail to market its products and services. Catalogs mailed several times each year include beauty tips and trends and showcase a variety of brands and products.

In October 2006, Sephora began expanding its reach even further by opening stores inside JCPenney stores. At about 1,500 square feet, these stores within stores are smaller than their stand-alone counterparts and are the only beauty offering inside JCPenney. The assortment comprises nearly 50 brands; additional offerings include the Beauty Studio, with its 10-minute express services. In 2007, Sephora launched Beauty Insider, the company's loyalty program. Members accumulate points for purchases, and these points can be redeemed for perks like free samples or limited-edition products.

DISCUSSION QUESTIONS

1. Describe Sephora's target market.
2. Why would women prefer a choice between Sephora's combined self-service and service-oriented environment rather than the traditional model offered in department store cosmetic areas?
3. What training opportunities are available to Sephora employees? How does this training help set Sephora apart from its competitors?

4. How can a beauty retailer make multichannel retailing work? What makes Sephora's online site so successful?
5. What value do the Sephora stores within JCPenney offer to customers? To Sephora? To JCPenney?

Sources: www.sephora.com (accessed July 13, 2010); Susan Carpenter, "Brush Up at the Counter," *Los Angeles Times*, June 13, 2010; www.sephora.com/university/index.jhtml (accessed July 13, 2010); www.sephora.com/help/about_sephora.jhtml (accessed July 13, 2010).

This case was prepared by Barton Weitz, University of Florida, and Kate Woodworth.

CASE 30 A Stockout at Discmart

Robert Honda, the manager of a Discmart store (a discount retailer similar to Target and Walmart) in Cupertino, California, was surveying the Sunday morning activity at his store. Shoppers were bustling around with carts; some had children in tow. On the front side of the store, a steady stream of shoppers was heading through the checkout counters. Almost all the cash registers that he could see from his vantage point were open and active. The line in front of register 7 was longer than the other lines, but other than that, things seemed to be going quite smoothly.

The intercom beeped and interrupted his thoughts. A delivery truck had just arrived at the rear of the store. The driver wanted to know which loading dock to use to unload merchandise. Honda decided to inspect the available space before directing the driver to a specific loading dock. As he passed the cash registers on his way to the rear of the store, he noticed that the line at register 7 had gotten a little bit longer. The light over the register was flashing, indicating that the customer service associate (CSA) requested assistance. (At Discmart, all frontline personnel who interact with customers are called CSAs.) As he passed by the register, he could not help overhearing the exchange between what seemed to be a somewhat irate customer and the CSA. The customer was demanding that another item should be substituted for an item that was on sale but currently out of stock, and the CSA was explaining the store policy to the customer. Normally, during a busy time like this, Honda would have tried to help the CSA resolve the situation, but he knew that the truck driver was waiting to unload merchandise that was needed right away on the floor. Hence, he quickly walked to the rear of the store.

After assigning the truck to a docking bay for unloading, Honda headed back toward the front of the store. On the way back, he ducked into the break room to get a Coke and noticed that Sally Johnson, the CSA who had been at register 7, was on a break. Sally had been on the Discmart team for about a year and was considered a very capable employee who always kept the store's interests at heart.

Robert: Hi Sally, I noticed that you had quite a line in front of your register earlier today.

Sally: Hi Robert. Yes, I had a very irate customer, and it took us a while to resolve the issue.

Robert: Oh really! What was he irate about?

Sally: We are out of stock on the 100-ounce Tide Liquid Detergent that was advertised in our flyer and was on sale at 20 percent off. I offered the customer a rain check or the same discount on the same size of another brand, but he kept insisting that he wanted us to substitute a 200-ounce container of Tide Liquid Detergent at the same discount. Apparently, Joe Chang [the assistant manager] had told the customer that we would substitute the 200-ounce size.

Robert: Did you point out to the customer that our sale prices are valid only while supplies last?

Sally: I did mention this to him, but he thought it was strange that we ran out of stock on the morning of the first day of the sale.

Robert: Well, I guess you should have gone ahead and given him what he wanted.

Sally: As you know, our point-of-sale systems allow me to make adjustments only on designated items. Since the 200-ounce sizes were not designated as substitutes, I had to request a supervisor to help me.

Robert: I am glad that you got it resolved.

Sally: Well, the customer got tired of waiting for the supervisor, who was busy helping another customer, so he decided to take a rain check instead. He seemed quite dissatisfied with the whole episode and mentioned that we should stop running these TV ads claiming that we are always in stock and that we guarantee satisfaction.

Robert: I do hate it when they run these ad campaigns and we have to take the heat on the floor, trying to figure out what those cowboys in marketing promised the customer.

Sally: Well, my break is nearly over. I have to get back.

Honda pondered the encounter that Johnson had with the customer. He wondered whether to discuss this issue with Joe Chang. He remembered talking to him about inventory policies a couple of days ago. Chang had indicated that their current inventory levels were fairly high and that any further increases would be hard to justify from a financial perspective. He mentioned some market research that had surveyed a random sample of customers who had redeemed rain checks. The results of the survey indicated that customers by and large were satisfied with Discmart's rain check procedures. On the basis of this finding, Chang had argued that current inventory levels, supplemented with a rain check policy, would keep customers satisfied.

DISCUSSION QUESTIONS

1. Why did this service breakdown occur?
2. How was this service gap related to the other gaps (standards, knowledge, delivery, and communications) described in the Gaps model in Chapter 18?

This case was prepared by Kirthi Kalyanam, Retail Management Institute, Santa Clara University. © Dr. Kirthi Kalyanam.

CASE 31   Customer Service and Relationship Management at Nordstrom

Nordstrom's unwavering customer-focused philosophy traces its roots to founder Johan Nordstrom's values. Johan Nordstrom believed in people and realized that consistently exceeding their expectations would lead to success and a good conscience. He built his organization around a customer-oriented philosophy. The organization focuses on people, and its policies and selections are designed to satisfy people. As simple as this philosophy sounds, few of Nordstrom's competitors have truly been able to grasp it.

A FOCUS ON PEOPLE

Nordstrom employees treat customers like royalty. Employees are instructed to do whatever is in the customer's best interest. Customer delight drives the values of the company. Customers are taken seriously and are at the heart of the business. Customers are even at the top of Nordstrom's so-called organization chart, which is an inverted pyramid. Moving down from the customers at the top of the inverted pyramid are the salespeople, department managers, and general managers. Finally, at the bottom is the board of directors. All lower levels work toward supporting the salespeople, who in turn work to serve the customers.

Employee incentives are tied to customer service. Salespeople are given personalized business cards to help them build relationships with customers. Uniquely, salespeople are not tied to their respective departments but to the customer. Salespeople can travel from department to department within the store to assist their customer, if that is needed. For example, a Nordstrom salesperson assisting a woman shopping for business apparel helps her shop for suits, blouses, shoes, hosiery, and accessories. The salesperson becomes the "personal shopper" of the customer to show her merchandise and provide fashion expertise. This approach is also conducive to building long-term relationships with customers, as over time the salesperson comes to understand each customer's fashion sense and personality.

The opportunity to sell across departments enables salespeople to maximize sales and commissions while providing superior customer service. As noted on a *60 Minutes* segment, "[Nordstrom's service is] not service like it used to be, but service that never was."

Despite the obsession with customer service at Nordstrom, ironically, the customer actually comes second. Nordstrom understands that customers will be treated well by its employees only if the employees themselves are treated well by the company. Nordstrom employees are treated almost like the extended Nordstrom family, and employee satisfaction is a closely watched business variable.

Nordstrom is known for promoting employees from within its ranks. The fundamental traits of a successful Nordstrom salesperson (e.g., commitment to excellence, customer service) are the same traits emphasized in successful Nordstrom executives.

Nordstrom hires people with a positive attitude, a sense of ownership, initiative, heroism, and the ability to handle high expectations. This sense of ownership is reflected in Nordstrom's low rate of shrinkage. Shrinkage, or loss due to theft and record-keeping errors, at Nordstrom is under 1.5 percent of sales, roughly half the industry average. The low shrinkage can be attributed in large part to the diligence of salespeople caring for the merchandise as if it were their own.

Employees at all levels are treated like businesspeople and empowered to make independent decisions. They are given the latitude to do whatever they believe is the right thing, with the customers' best interests at heart. All employees are given the tools and authority to do whatever is necessary to satisfy customers, and management almost always backs subordinates' decisions.

In summary, Nordstrom's product is its people. The loyal Nordstrom shopper goes to Nordstrom for the service received—not necessarily the products. Of course, Nordstrom does offer quality merchandise, but that is secondary for many customers.

CUSTOMER-FOCUSED POLICIES

One of the most famous examples of Nordstrom's customer service occurred in 1975 when a Nordstrom salesperson gladly took back a set of used automobile tires and gave the customer a refund, even though Nordstrom had never sold tires! The customer had purchased the tires from a Northern Commercial Company store, whose retail space Nordstrom had since acquired. Not wanting the customer to leave the Nordstrom store unhappy, the salesperson refunded the price of the tires.

Nordstrom's policies focus on the concept of the "Lifetime Value of the Customer." Although little money is made on the first sale, when the lifetime value of a customer is calculated, the positive dollar amount of a loyal customer is staggering. The lifetime value of a customer is the sum of all sales and profits generated from that customer, directly or indirectly. To keep its customers for a "lifetime," Nordstrom employees go to incredible lengths. In a Nordstrom store in Seattle, a customer wanted to buy a pair of brand-name slacks that had gone on sale. The store was out of her size, and the salesperson was unable to locate a pair at other Nordstrom stores. Knowing that the same slacks were available at a competitor nearby, the sales clerk went to the rival, purchased the slacks at full price using petty cash from her department, and sold the slacks to the customer at Nordstrom's sale price. Although this sale resulted in an immediate loss for the store, the investment in promoting the loyalty of the happy customer went a long way.

Nordstrom's employees try to "Never Say No" to the customer. Nordstrom has an unconditional return policy. If a customer is not completely satisfied, he or she can return the new and generally even heavily used merchandise at any time for a full refund. Ironically, this is not a company policy; rather, it is implemented at the discretion of the salesperson to maximize customer satisfaction. Nordstrom's advice to its employees is simply, "Use good judgment in all situations." Employees are given the freedom, support, and resources to make the best decisions to enhance customer satisfaction. The cost of Nordstrom's high service, such as its return policy, coupled with its competitive pricing would, on the surface, seem to cut into profit margins. This cost, however, is recouped through increased sales from repeat customers, limited markdowns, and, if necessary, the "squeezing" of suppliers.

Nordstrom's vendor relationships also focus on maximizing customer satisfaction. According to former CEO Bruce Nordstrom, "[Vendors] know that we are liberal with our customers. And if you're going to do business with us, then there should be a liberal influence on their return policies. If somebody has worn a shoe and it doesn't wear satisfactorily

for them, and we think that person is being honest about it, then we will send it back." Nordstrom realizes some customers will abuse the unconditional return policy, but it refuses to impose that abuse back onto the vendors. Here again, the rule of "doing what is right" comes into play.

Nordstrom's merchandising and purchasing policies are also extremely customer-focused. A full selection of merchandise in a wide variety of sizes is seen as a measure of customer service. An average Nordstrom store carries roughly 150,000 pairs of shoes with a variety of sizes, widths, colors, and models. Typical shoe sizes for women range from 2½ to 14, in widths of A to EEE. Nordstrom is fanatical about stocking only high-quality merchandise. Once when the upper parts of some women's shoes were separating from the soles, *every* shoe from that delivery was shipped back to the manufacturer.

DISCUSSION QUESTIONS

1. What steps does Nordstrom take to implement its strategy of providing outstanding customer service?

2. How do these activities enable Nordstrom to reduce the gaps between perceived service and customer expectations, as described in Chapter 18?

3. What are the pros and cons of Nordstrom's approach to developing a competitive advantage through customer service?

This case was written by Alicia Lueddemann, the Management Mind Group, and Sunil Erevelles, University of North Carolina, Charlotte.

CASE 32 Building the Apple Store

Founded in 1976 by Steve Jobs and Steve Wozniak, Apple has become an innovative leader in the consumer electronics industry. In addition to offering traditional desktop and laptop computers, all of which feature Apple's OS X operating system, Apple essentially founded the digital music player when it introduced the iPod and online music store markets with iTunes; launched easy to use iPhones and iPads with increasingly more features; and introduced online movie/TV services through AppleTV and publishing and multimedia software.

BEFORE APPLE RETAIL STORES

During the early 1990s, Apple struggled as computer sales began shifting from specialized computer stores to mainstream retail stores. Big-box retailers such as Best Buy and Circuit City could offer a wider selection of computers at lower prices, although they lacked adequate customer service and support. These big-box retailers and specialized stores faced even more competition in the form of mail-order outlets, including CompuAdd, Gateway, and Dell.

Beginning in 1990, Dell shifted from selling its computers in warehouse and specialized computer stores to operating as an online direct mail-order company. Dell facilitated its online operations with an efficient online store that could handle high-volume sales. The online

Dell store (dell.com) represented a new strategy for manufacturing: Computers were built as they were ordered. In turn, Dell could reduce inventory, because it no longer produced computers in mass quantities and then pushed inventory through the channel to resellers.

While establishing its online store, Apple needed to balance its direct orders with the sales initiated by its channel partners, mail-order resellers, independent dealers, and CompUSA, with which it initiated a "stores within stores" strategy to focus on Apple's products. Apple's partnership with CompUSA paid off. When the San Francisco Comp USA store was equipped with Macs, Apple's sales jumped from 15 to 35 percent of overall store sales.

Apple also put its own employees to work in various retail outlets to help inform and educate customers, as well as ensure its products were being displayed in working order. The company estimated it spent between $25,000 and $75,000 per month on this initiative. Apple executives soon realized they could not compete with PC brands by selling just laptops and desktops in big-box retail stores, because retailers could earn greater profits by selling lower-quality PC models. They had little to no incentive to sell Macs. Without its own retail store, Apple would always be at the mercy of the independent dealers and partners that operated with different strategic goals.

DESIGNING THE APPLE STORE

To compete with the PCs sold by big-box retailers, Apple needed to shift from selling its electronics through intermediaries to offering products directly through Apple stores. This shift would not come easily. Steve Jobs, Apple's dynamic founder, first looked to bring in new executives. Mickey Drexler, former CEO of The Gap and now CEO of J.Crew, was hired in 1999 as part of Apple's board of directors. Next, Jobs brought in Ron Johnson, who had been a merchandising executive with Target, to run Apple's retail division as vice president of retail operations.

Instead of launching stores from the start, Drexler suggested that Jobs rent a warehouse and build a prototype store, coined Apple Store Version 0.0. Apple executives then continuously redesigned the store until they achieved a layout that would entice shoppers to not only enter but make purchases. The first store prototype was configured by product category, with hardware laid out according to the internal organization of the company rather than by how customers logically shop. Executives quickly decided to redesign the store to match customer interests better. Although the redesign cost Apple more than six months, the executives believed this time investment was necessary to achieve a successful store that could compete with well-established electronics retailers and remain consistent with the Apple brand. Its first store opened in Tyson's Corner, Virginia, in May 2001.

THE APPLE STORE LAYOUT

When considering a site for a retail store, Apple uses its customer base to forecast visitor volume and revenues. Most Apple stores locate within existing shopping malls or lifestyle centers, where retail traffic is already present. There are two types of full-size stores, a street-facing building or an in-mall store. The stores range from 3,600 to 20,000 square feet, although most fall in the 3,000- to 6,000-square-feet range. Storefronts are typically all glass with a backlit Apple logo, and the front display windows change occasionally to focus on the newest marketing campaign. Apple's internal team designs the window displays, often using slot and cable systems to suspend design elements within the window. In some cases, the swinging entrance doors are in the middle, but in other stores, a logo wall appears in the middle with two doors located on either side. Store interiors feature only three materials: glass, stainless steel, and wood.

In addition to the retail floor, Apple stores have backroom areas that sometimes include a public restroom, offices, and the inventory area. At some sites that lack sufficient space, inventory storage is located at a separate facility, always within walking distance.

The store layout changes multiple times throughout the year. Apple executives organize planograms to coincide with the introduction of new products or heavily marketed merchandise. The layouts depend on the size of the store. A typical in-mall store locates merchandise in the front half of the store and customer service and support areas in the rear. Apple stores carry fewer than 20 products, and every display piece is available for hands-on use so that customers can get an accurate feel for the available hardware and software.

On tables along the right wall, iPhones and iPods take up the front half of the store. Along the left wall, tables hold various models of general and high-end desktop and laptop computers. These displays give way to The Studio, a newer section hosted by experts who will answer application-oriented, creative questions. Two to three island tables in the front center display software on Apple computers; additional island tables exhibit peripherals such as iPod docking stations and printers. A small children's area houses Apple computers running children's software. The Genius Bar takes up the back wall, with stools before a counter staffed with Apple experts for repairs and consultations. Larger stores also have a theater area in the back, featuring a rear-projection screen with an audience area of either U-shaped wooden benches or full theater seats in rows. This store layout is typical for a store located in a super-regional mall.

Apple stores thus follow a free-form layout, which allows customers to browse the store according to their own interests. Signage hanging from the ceiling, for greater visibility, directs customers to specific areas within the store. Bright lighting draws attention to merchandise and creates a sense of excitement. Highlighted merchandise also helps draw customers strategically through the store. As customers browse the products, employees wearing Apple T-shirts and lanyards make themselves available to answer any questions.

Through its intensive development efforts, Apple has created a unique, customer service–oriented shopping experience. Customers can schedule face-to-face appointments at an Apple store to test-drive products. One-to-one personal training sessions help customers become familiar with the array of Apple products. The company also offers free one-hour instructional or informational workshops every day for iPod, iPhone, and Mac owners. It also offers support for business customers by providing insight and advice about how to create a presentation from start to finish using Apple products.

DISCUSSION QUESTIONS

1. Have you ever visited an Apple store? If yes, did you make a purchase? Why or why not?
2. Why are Apple's store layout and atmosphere important?
3. Is Apple America's best retailer?
4. Visit your local Apple store. Does the layout of the store help to provide you with an excellent customer experience? Explain.

Sources: Philip Elmer-Dewitt, "Apple Ranks No. 4 in E-Retailing Survey," *Fortune*, May 5, 2010; www.apple.com/retail (accessed July 14, 2010); Daniel Eran, "Apple's Retail Challenge," 2006, www.roughlydrafted.com/RD/Q4.06/1DDD598A-7CE0-479E-A6F9-912777CAB484.html (accessed July 14, 2010); www.ifoapplestore.com/the_stores.html (accessed July 14, 2010); Jerry Useem, "Apple: America's Best Retailer," *Fortune*, March 8, 2007.

This case was written by Brienne Curley, while an MBA student at Loyola College in Maryland, under the supervision of Hope Corrigan.

CASE 33 Generating Advertising Revenue from a Digital Screen Network at Harrods of London

Retailers have slowly been implementing digital screen networks. In most instances the messages are focused on branding and impacting the customer shopping experience. Very few networks, like Walmart's SMART Network and, to a lesser extent, Target's Channel Red, have also been able to generate a stream of advertising revenue. In the department store category, Harrods is the only high-end luxury store to successfully sell advertising on its in-store digital signage network. Factors such as a solid and consistent customer base and the store's unique environment have contributed to the success of the signage.

It is difficult to imagine any retail environment as unique as Harrods. It is a key destination for millions of visitors who come to the United Kingdom every year (it is the U.K.'s third-largest tourist attraction). It houses the world's finest luxury brands across a million square feet of retail space. It has a history dating back to 1849 and can count the rich and famous from all corners of the globe as its customers. The brand is synonymous with luxury, the "finer things in life," and a range of merchandise unequaled under one roof. Average daily traffic is 45,000 customers (occasionally rising to 100,000 on special days). Many of them are high-net-worth individuals, including royalty from around the world, as well as celebrities and billionaires.

Advertisements on the network are sold to premium brands, such as Armani and Cartier. The medium is often sold as part of an integrated marketing campaign, which often includes other media like posters, lift-wraps (signage on elevator doors), windows, and even pages in the Harrods magazine. Combined with other in-store media, screens are an integral part of the campaign providing impact, awareness, and, often, directional signage leading customers to the "heart of the promotion"—the place where the product and the customer meet.

The specific location of each screen was carefully considered so that each customer would have a multiscreen sight line. In most cases, customers see more than one screen within their view. The same content appears simultaneously on each screen in the network, so the advertisers have high impact with their ads appearing several times at once.

In most cases, screens are positioned on the sides of escalators in the store. Unlike the case at many transport hubs, most customers in Harrods stand still on the moving steps. As they glide up to the next floor, they take in the view, which includes the digital screens. Each advertiser has a 15-second slot.

Harrods' digital screen network is managed all in-house. There is a dedicated ad sales team, operations team, and technical and creative team who are all committed Harrods employees who live and breathe the brand. These employees believe in and are included in how and what is being marketed. They sit in the building and pass by the media that they are selling and marketing 20 times a day. They also see with their own eyes the audience that they are selling to the advertisers. They see the clothes they are wearing, the limos that deliver them to the store, and the number of Harrods' famous green bags they are carrying. They can see the impact that the screens can have on a consumer purchasing decision, or even simply see customers watching content through their Dior sunglasses as they glide up an escalator.

Network staff also have relationships with the brands and the advertisers. They have a relationship which has been nurtured and developed so that they are working "alongside" a brand to find marketing solutions to drive brand sales and awareness, which in turn benefits not only the brand but also Harrods as a store.

The store is continuously changing, and as part of that development, additional digital screens are introduced as part of new departments and remodels. When Harrods first introduced its digital signage network, it realized that it had to do something special to integrate the screens into the environment. It didn't want screens hanging from ceilings above walkways that look tacky, amateur, and cheap. It invested heavily in each screen installation, with customized reinforced glass, polished steel bezels, additional cooling fans, and color schemes that are consistent with the store's decor. This gave the screens a look of luxury. A lot of care, thought, and attention has been invested in each location to give the advertiser the optimum in presentation.

Harrods monitors the effectiveness of a campaign via sales data. It has some impressive results from advertisers who have enjoyed double-digit sales increases during and following a digital campaign in the store. You'd naturally be asking the question, "Well, why isn't everyone advertising on the screens?" The answer to this question involves many factors including, among other things, the following:

- The medium is new and many vendors are unfamiliar with its benefits.
- Vendors are not always sure about where the funding of digital screen ads should come from. That is, is it a marketing/advertising expenditure or an in-store promotional expenditure?
- There are creative challenges associated with messages. For instance, is the message capturing the attention of the customers? Does it have a call to action or an offer?

If there is one way to deter advertisers, then it's to have blank, malfunctioning screens. It seems obvious, but so many networks in retail lumber on with as many as 25 percent of the screens nonoperational. No wonder they find selling ads a struggle! Harrods has a "zero tolerance" strategy within the operations team, resulting in the team's touring the store every morning before the store opens checking that all is as it should be. As well, it has invested heavily in preventive maintenance contracts, and has a backup stock of spare screens available, should a screen die and require replacement.

Digital networks can make money for a retailer. Harrods has realized both ad sales revenue and increased sales of advertised products. However, such results take significant investments in time, resources, and money. The future success for generating advertising sales is dependent on improvements in technical reliability of the hardware and software, combined with more investment in content and creativity. Interactivity via mobile/cell phones is clearly part of the future. Harrods is investing in the latest technology, implementing new and unique content that captures people's imagination, and working alongside brands that are prepared to invest to realize the benefits.

DISCUSSION QUESTIONS

1. What are the reasons that Harrods has been successful at selling advertising on its digital signage network and other retailers have not? Why would consumer product manufacturers be interested in advertising on Harrods' network?
2. What are the pluses and minuses for a retailer offering a digital network in its stores?

This case was written by Steven Keith Platt, Platt Retail Institute, and Guy Cheston, Director of Advertising Sales & Sponsorship, Harrods.

CASE 34   Starbucks' Retail Strategy

Since its early days in the 1980s, Starbucks has been the leading retailer of specialty coffee and beans and related food and merchandise. Its most recent annual revenues were $9.8 billion from 8,832 company-owned stores and 7,803 licensed stores in airports and shopping centers in the United States and in 50 countries across the world. Worldwide, the company employs 142,000 people. Designed to provide a community gathering place and social experience as well as a premium cup of coffee or hot or cold beverage, the brand intentionally mimics the cafés of Italy.

In addition to its direct retailing activities, Starbucks has formed strategic alliances with Unilever, Kraft Foods, and PepsiCo to expand its product and distribution portfolios. Starbucks coffee beans, ice cream, and ready-to-drink (RTD) beverages appear on supermarket and warehouse club shelves. The company promotes sustainable best practices for quality and yield among its suppliers, boasts relatively low staff turnover, and encourages customer loyalty through its Starbucks Card program.

Starbucks' licensed retail store operations include the Starbucks and Seattle's Best Coffee brands. In addition to having store locations in more than 50 countries, Starbucks licenses the right to produce its products both in the United States and abroad through several partnerships. These include the North American Coffee Partnership, a joint venture with PepsiCo, Inc., to manufacture and market RTD beverages, such as bottled Frappuccino, in the United States and Canada; a licensing agreement with Unilever for Starbucks' superpremium ice-cream products in the United States; a licensing agreement with a partnership formed by Unilever and Tazo Tea RTD beverages in the United States; and licensing agreements for the manufacturing, marketing, and distribution of Starbucks Discoveries and Starbucks DoubleShot in Japan and Korea. Starbucks sells its branded coffee beans in 39,000 supermarkets and mass-merchandise stores domestically and abroad through an agreement with Kraft and has a partnership with Jim Beam through which it developed a coffee liqueur.

Several alternative channels include the sale of whole beans through Nordstrom department stores and coffee by the cup in cafés in Barnes & Noble bookstores. Additional channels include distribution through service providers like Holland America Cruise Lines, United Airlines, and Sheraton and Westin Hotels.

Starbucks was nearly synonymous with premium coffee beverages and seemed to be on an unstoppable growth trajectory until Howard Schultz, the company's founder, chairperson, and CEO, left his daily leadership role to become owner of the Seattle Supersonics. Schultz soon realized his move was a mistake for both himself and Starbucks. Store traffic was falling for the first time in U.S. stores, and competition from premium brands and mass-market coffee vendors gnawed at Starbucks' market share. In addition, the economy had soured. In 2008, Schultz returned to the company's helm, reawakening the vision of the Starbucks brand and initiating a transformation process that involved cost reductions, quality improvements in every aspect of the company's operations, and a renewed commitment to providing a unique customer experience. Two years later, despite the still-sluggish economy, Starbucks is once again on a profitable path.

THE COFFEE MARKET

The commercial market for coffee began in AD 1000 when Arab traders brought the coffee tree from its native Ethiopia to the Middle East. Over the next 200 years, coffee drinking spread throughout the Arab world and was eventually introduced in Europe in the 1500s by Italian traders. By 1650, coffeehouses emerged as popular meeting places in England and France. Well-known public figures frequented London coffeehouses to discuss political and literary issues.

Coffee consumption flourished in the mid-20th century, aided by developments in manufacturing and cultivation. By 1940, large coffee processors such as Nestlé (Hills Bros. brand), Kraft General Foods (Maxwell House), and Procter & Gamble (Folgers) developed instant and decaffeinated coffee varieties in addition to their staple regular ground. Supermarkets emerged as the primary distribution channel for traditional coffee sales.

In the late 1980s, per-capita coffee consumption fell slowly and steadily as consumers turned to soft drinks, bottled water, juices, and iced teas. The three major manufacturers—Procter & Gamble, Nestlé, and Kraft— fought for market share in a stagnant market. All the major coffee brands were unprofitable. In an effort to regain profitability, the majors decreased their historically high expenditures on image advertising, increased the use of robusta coffee beans (as opposed to high-quality Arabica beans) to reduce costs, and converted from 16-ounce to 13-ounce cans, claiming that the contents produced the same amount of coffee. Coupons and in-store promotions dominated manufacturer marketing plans as the price war continued.

THE STARBUCKS COFFEE COMPANY: BACKGROUND

Inspiration for the present Starbucks concept came to Howard Schultz when he went to Italy on a buying trip in 1983. While wandering through the ancient piazzas of Milan, Schultz took particular note of the many cheerful espresso bars and cafés he passed. Italians, he felt, had captured the true romance of the beverage. Coffee drinking was an integral part of the Italian culture, but Americans lacked the opportunity to savor a good cup of coffee while engaging in good conversation in a relaxed atmosphere. He returned to the United States convinced that Americans would find the Italian coffeehouse culture attractive. In 1987, Schultz bought Starbucks.

RETAIL OFFERING

Starbucks offers more than a cup of coffee; it offers an experience that includes the beverage, the store, the service, and an opportunity to take a break from life's hectic pace to relax with friends or mull over a thorny problem. In short, Starbucks offers the coffee experience Schultz imported from abroad.

Although designs vary in any particular store to match the local market, the typical Starbucks store works around a planned mix of organic and manufactured components: light wood tones at the counters and signage areas; brown bags; polished dark marble countertops; glass shelves; thin, modern, white track lighting; and pure white cups. Even the logo delivers the double organic/modern message: The Starbucks icon is earthy-looking yet rendered in a modern abstract form, in black and white with a band of color around the center only. The colors of the lamps, walls, and tables mimic coffee tones, from green (raw beans) to light and darker browns. Special package and cup designs are coordinated to create livelier, more colorful tones around holidays. Starbucks also keeps its look lively with rotating in-store variations based on timely themes.

Starbucks stores are spacious so that customers can read in overstuffed chairs, gather around tables, or wander around the store while drinking their coffee. Stores sell pastries, breakfast sandwiches, and lunch offerings as well as coffee paraphernalia ranging from coffee beans and mugs to French presses and home cappuccino machines. Although coffee beverages are standardized across outlets, food offerings vary from store to store.

Starbucks also has strict quality standards. For example, espresso is brewed precisely 18 to 23 seconds and thrown away if not served within 10 seconds of brewing. Coffee beans are donated to charities if they are still in the store seven days after coming out of their vacuum-sealed packs. Drip coffee is thrown away if it is not served within

an hour of making it. Throughout the store, there exists a keen attention to aroma: Employees are not allowed to wear colognes, stores use no scented cleaning products, and smoking is *verboten*.

HUMAN RESOURCE MANAGEMENT

The company, recognizing that its frontline employees are critical to providing "the perfect cup," has built an organizational culture based on two principles: (1) strict standards for how coffee should be prepared and delivered to customers and (2) a laid-back, supportive, and empowering attitude toward its employees. As part of his recovery strategy, Schultz shared his vision with the entire workforce through memos designed to both lead and inspire. He also rolled out new training to encourage store partners, or employees, to improve service, beverage quality, and store appearance.

All new hires go through an initial 24-hour training program that instills a sense of purpose, commitment, and enthusiasm for the job. New employees are treated with the dignity and respect that goes along with their title as *baristas* (Italian for bartenders). To emphasize their responsibility in pleasing customers, baristas are presented with scenarios describing customers complaining about beans that were ground incorrectly. The preferred response, baristas learn, is to replace the beans on the spot without checking with the manager or questioning the complaint. Baristas learn to customize each espresso drink, explain the origins of different coffees, and distinguish Sumatran from Ethiopian coffees.

Holding on to its motivated, well-trained employees is important, so all partners are eligible for health benefits and a stock option plan called Bean Stock. Baristas know about and are encouraged to apply for promotions to store management positions. Every quarter, the company has open meetings at which company news, corporate values, and financial performance data are presented and discussed.

Due to the training, empowerment, benefits, and growth opportunities, Starbucks' turnover is only 70 percent. This total is considerably less than the 150 to 200 percent turnover at other firms in the food service business.

LOCATION STRATEGY

Traffic is the major determinant in selecting cities and locations for retail stores. Because Starbucks can tailor the size and format of its stores to the surrounding community, stores can be located in nearly any high-traffic, high-visibility location, including college campuses, office buildings, downtown or suburban settings, and rural or off-highway locations. The company operates approximately 2,650 drive-thru locations and continues to expand development of these businesses.

Starbucks' retail expansion strategy has historically been based on conquering one area of a city or region at a time. Centralized cities served as hubs or regional centers for rollout expansions into nearby markets (e.g., Chicago as a hub for the Midwest). "Clustering" was also key to its location strategy. Major markets were saturated with stores before new markets were entered. For example, there were over 100 Starbucks in the Seattle area before the company expanded to a new region. Having many stores in close proximity to one another generally increased overall revenues. However, comparable store sales growth eventually slowed due to cannibalization.

In response to the increasing competition and dropping traffic, Schultz and his management team elected to close 800 underperforming stores in the United States and 100 international stores. However the fundamental strategy for new store openings remains the same.

SUPPLY CHAIN

In the 1990s, the specialty coffee market experienced substantial growth, driven largely by the coffee-drinking habits of college graduates and young professionals. While retailers like Starbucks benefited from this growth, coffee growers and suppliers did not, due to the worldwide oversupply of lower-grade coffee beans. Although Starbucks promised the highest-quality Arabica beans and paid premium prices, all growers suffered from the oversupply. Even though Starbucks dominated the specialty coffee industry, it did not use its purchasing power to negotiate lower prices from growers and suppliers and squeeze their profits. Instead, the company decided to use its market power to implement social change within its supply chain. It partnered with Conservation International, an environmental nonprofit organization, to develop CAFE (Coffee and Farmer Equity) practices. These practices are designed to build relationships beneficial to growers and suppliers; increase economic, social, and environmental sustainability; and promote transparency and economic fairness within the supply chain. Economic incentives encourage suppliers to adhere to these standards.

The CAFE practices further encouraged farmers to ensure their workers' wages and safety standards met or exceeded the minimum requirements established under local and national laws. Suppliers that scored well on the independently assessed CAFE practices received a price premium and the largest orders. Starbucks' ultimate goal is to buy the majority of its beans from suppliers that meet CAFE standards.

The company also operates Farmer Support Centers in Costa Rica and Rwanda. These centers, staffed by agronomists and sustainability experts, provide information and implementation support for sustainable best practices for quality and yield to coffee farmers.

GROWTH STRATEGIES

With the company back on solid footing, executives are planning controlled growth internationally of both retail and licensed stores and selective development of new distribution channels. The company will focus initially on growth in markets where the brand already has a strong presence, but it is also viewing China as potentially the largest market for Starbucks outside the United States.

Innovative products that improve the customer experience will fuel growth, as will new products introduced in the grocery channel. Among recent in-store innovations are new food and beverage pairings and discount offerings, healthier food choices, and the launch of VIA Ready

Brew, an instant coffee that meets Starbucks standards. Executives describe VIA as an important new growth platform and a significant innovation in instant coffee, a market worth $21 billion globally.

To ensure strategies appeal to its target market, Starbucks engages consumers through social media and the company's My Starbucks Idea Web sites. New iPhone applications launched by the company help customers locate stores, search for nutrition information, and reload Starbucks Cards.

CHANGING CUSTOMER BASE

As Starbucks grew, its customer base evolved. Starbucks' historical customer profile—affluent, well-educated, white-collar women between the ages of 24 and 44 years—expanded. For example, about half of the stores in southern California welcome large numbers of Hispanic customers. Newer customers tended to be younger, less well educated, and in a lower income bracket than Starbucks' more established customers. These newer customers were more interested in convenience than the experience, so Starbucks installed automatic espresso machines in its stores. But as mass-market vendors like McDonald's and Dunkin' Donuts improved their coffee offerings and touted their lower prices and premium brands like Peet's threatened Starbucks' dominance, the company realized that its drive toward convenience was commoditizing the Starbucks experience. Returning to the company core values and guiding principles, including quality beverages and customer service, has been fundamental to reversing the company's slide.

THE TRANSFORMATION JOURNEY

Schultz's campaign to restore Starbucks to preeminence involved a rigorous and disciplined review of all aspects of the business, with special attention paid to operational efficiency from the beginning of the supply chain to the barista at the counter. One result was trimming $580 million in costs from the business. But another was investing in the company's core values, including a significant sum spent to bring Starbucks employees to a city hit by hurricane Katrina. The staff spent their time there as volunteers, fixing up houses and cleaning roads. The project, says Schultz, reminded staff of the company's commitment to being an important part of the community and helped reinstall company values. The company also invested in technology and tools that increase the speed and lower the cost of bringing new products and strategies to market and better staff training to improve the customer experience.

While the recession lingers and no retailer can afford to be complacent, Starbucks has managed an impressive recovery that solidifies its unique image in a competitive market. Schultz insists on taking responsibility for past errors and on remembering the lessons learned. Nevertheless, Starbucks' resurrection acts as an illustration of how a corporation can be turned around by aligning employees behind a provocative vision that is backed by careful strategy.

DISCUSSION QUESTIONS

1. What is Starbucks' retail strategy? What is its target market, and how does it try to develop an advantage over its competitors?

2. Describe Starbucks' retail mix: location, merchandise assortment, pricing, advertising and promotion, store design and visual merchandising, customer service, and personal selling. How does its retail mix support its strategy?

3. What factors in the environment provided the opportunity for Starbucks to develop a new, successful retail chain? What demand and supply conditions prevailed in the U.S. coffee market when Howard Schultz purchased Starbucks in 1987? What insight did Schultz have that other players in the coffee market did not possess?

4. What have been the principal drivers behind Starbucks' success in the marketplace? What does the Starbucks brand mean to consumers? How have the growth opportunities that Starbucks has pursued affected the value of its brand name?

5. What are the major challenges facing Starbucks as it goes forward? Is the brand advantage sustainable going forward? Can Starbucks defend its position against other specialty coffee retailers?

Sources: Starbucks Annual Report, 2009; Greg Farrell, "Return of the Barista-in-Chief," *Financial Times*, March 21, 2010; www.starbucks. com (accessed July 13, 2010); www.starbucksstore.com/products/ shprodli.asp?DeptNo=8100&ClassNo=0351&SubClassNo=0069 (accessed July 13, 2010).

This case was written by Barton Weitz, University of Florida, and Kate Woodworth.

CASE 35 Yankee Candle: New Product Innovation

Yankee Candle Company (YCC) is a leading designer, manufacturer, wholesaler, and retailer of premium scented candles in the giftware industry. The core product lines for YCC are scented candles and candle accessories. The premium-quality scented candles are offered in over 150 fragrances. Almost all candles are produced on-site at the advanced manufacturing facility in Whately, Massachusetts. Candles are made by master chandlers (candlemaking experts) who oversee a complex manufacturing process with strict quality control standards. As well as creating the candles themselves, YCC builds competitive advantage through expertise in formulating the scents that make up "the fragrance experience." According to information on the YCC Web site, master perfumers develop the fragrances, which are then rigorously screened, reviewed, and tested. The scents are unique compared to competitive products in that they maintain intensity through the life of the candle. In short, quality control of the candles and fragrances ensures premium products that provide high value to customers in the form of a true scent, long burn time, and consistency of fragrance over the life of the candle.

Candles are available in clear or frosted glass House-warmer jars, Sampler votive candles, wax potpourri Tarts, pillars, tapers, and tea lights. Related products are air fragrance products (sprays, electric air fresheners), car fresheners, odor control and insect repellant items, and candle accessories (decorative lids for the jar candles); taper holders; pillar and jar bases; matching jar shades, plates, and sleeves; votive holders; and tea light holders.

INNOVATION AT YANKEE CANDLE

Success at YCC over time is due, in large part, to the ability of the management team to implement innovative strategies at two levels—in product development (new fragrances and extensions to the product line) and in selling/distribution strategies.

First, innovation in product development is an ongoing cross-functional effort to keep merchandise offerings new and fresh for consumers. For example, in 2007 YCC introduced the World Collection, which used indigenous extracts and oils from exotic sources. The initial fragrances included Tahitian Tiare Flower, Brazilian Passion Fruit, New Zealand Wild Berry, and five others. Marketing and innovation vice president Rick Ruffolo said the World Collection line "was consistent with the Yankee Candle brand positioning—a passion for fragrance; it played to our core competencies as the world leader in candles and home fragrances; it connected with consumers on an emotional level; and it was clearly aspirational and 'trend-right'" (Newman, 2007).

As well as developing new fragrances and product lines in-house, YCC parent Yankee Holding Company acquires small firms whose products fit within the brand portfolio. Aroma Naturals is one such company, founded in California by a noted aromatherapist with a commitment to using natural ingredients. Aroma Naturals, bought in 2005, appeals to consumers interested in wellness and environmentally authentic products. Similarly, the purchase of the Illuminations Company in 2006 gave the Yankee Candle organization a new set of candle and accessory products that appeal to a more upscale demographic. Both of these acquisitions kept their original brand identities in the marketplace to preserve existing brand equity and to avoid consumer confusion with YCC-branded goods.

A second source of success through innovation is the strategy of multichannel distribution. To date, YCC operates 498 company-owned retail (bricks-and-mortar) stores in 43 states. YCC sells direct to consumers via its online store (yankeecandle.com) and by direct mail catalog orders. In 2001, top management at YCC began cultivating partnerships with mass retailers to carry limited product selections. Past partners include Bed Bath & Beyond, T.J.Maxx, and Linens 'n Things, to name a few. The wholesale distribution channel is equally important in the multichannel mix. This is a network of approximately 20,800 independent stores that sell YCC products across the United States. Many of these stores are small businesses with Hallmark and other gift-related franchises. For all of these retail and wholesale channels, products are YCC-branded goods.

Again, through the acquisition of Aroma Naturals, Yankee Holdings Company was able to generate revenue in new outlets such as mass grocery store chains (e.g., Whole Foods) and others with natural/wellness product areas (e.g., Shaw's, Wegmans). The revenues from the additional channels (supermarkets) and new target markets (health/wellness-conscious consumers) are beneficial for growth. Also, they do not cannibalize the existing YCC lines in traditional distribution channels. The same strategy was used for the Illuminations candle products sold in 28 stores, mostly located on the West Coast of the United States, and direct to consumers via catalog and Internet.

HISTORICAL SUMMARY AND PRESENT-DAY SITUATION

During its 40-year history, the company grew from an entrepreneurial family business started by Mike Kittredge to a publicly traded company in 1999. Craig Rydin joined YCC in 2001 as CEO. Under his leadership the company flourished; sales climbed higher than ever in company-owned stores and through the wholesale channel. Rydin was instrumental in establishing the partnerships with mass retailers including Bed Bath & Beyond and Linens 'n Things.

In 2006, YCC purchased Illuminations, the California-based multichannel retailer of high-quality candles and home accessories. The logic behind this decision was sound; acquisition of a similar product in the giftware industry allowed YCC to leverage its position and to target a new, more upscale demographic. In February 2007, YCC went from a publicly traded firm to a private corporation. Madison Dearborn Partners LLC acquired YCC for $1.6 billion, and it was delisted from the New York Stock Exchange.

The major financial crisis in September 2007 caused a dramatic decrease in demand across all consumer sectors of the economy. The giftware industry was hit hard; items such as premium candles are nonessentials for most consumers. YCC and all of its partners were affected. Some partners, such as Linens 'n Things, went completely out of business. Others managed to survive while enduring significant financial losses. YCC was restructured in 2009; this resulted in closure of all 28 Illuminations retail stores, shutting the Aroma Naturals operation, closing one company-owned store, and laying off 330 employees (*Retailer Daily*, 2009).

In 2010, the financial statements and investor information indicate the company is relatively stable while riding some challenging waves due to the lingering effects of the financial crisis. Illuminations-branded products are continuing to be sold through the wholesale network. As of early 2010, 498 company-owned stores in 43 states are in operation. Other channels include the direct mail catalog and Web site (yankeecandle.com). Aroma Naturals is reported as owned by parent company YCC and a subsidiary of Madison Dearborn Partners. It operates primary as an online retailer at present. Internationally, YCC sells products through a subsidiary, Yankee Candle Company (Europe), Ltd. This subsidiary has an international wholesale customer network of approximately 4,000 stores and distributors across 46 countries.

The latest annual report, for the 2009 calendar year, shows sales revenue of $681 million, gross profits of $404.3 million, and net income of $16.4 million. This represents an improvement over performance in calendar-year 2008 (net income loss of $409.3 million), according to the 2009 10-K filing (Morningstar, 2010). An overview of sales in the first quarter of 2010 compared to the first quarter of 2009 is shown below.

Sales by Category	1st Quarter 2010 (in millions)	1st Quarter 2010 vs. 2009 Percentage Change
Total sales	$141.0	+18
Wholesale	67.3	+23
Retail	73.7	+14
Stores		+ 9.4
Direct		+ 9.1

DISCUSSION QUESTIONS

1. What is next for Yankee Holding Company, in general? Consider the three distinct brands under the ownership of Yankee Holding Company—YCC, Illuminations, and Aroma Naturals. Examine the Web sites of each (yankeecandle.com, illuminations.com, and aromanaturals.com). For this set of offerings, develop a SWOT analysis for Yankee Holding Company.

2. It is helpful for a company to periodically assess its core target market in terms of demographics and lifestyles. The investor-owners of YCC, Madison Dearborn Partners LLC, don't want to do an expensive market research study. Using the business and management databases in your university library, research this question: Who is the scented-candle customer?

   a. On the basis of secondary data findings, describe the target market that buys premium scented candles.

   b. What are the advantages and disadvantages of using secondary data to answer this research question?

Sources: Faye Brookman, "Natural Products Rekindle Candle Sales," *Women's Wear Daily* 193, no. 117 (June 2007), p. 9; Morningstar Document Research, Yankee Holding Corporation, Form 10-K, April 1, 2010, http://yankeecandle.investorroom.com/index.php?s=127 (accessed June 25, 2010); Karen Newman, "A Mandate to Innovate," *Global Cosmetics Industry*, May 2007, pp. 36–39; "Yankee Candle to Restructure—Lay Off 330, Close 29 Stores," *Retailer Daily*, January 21, 2009, http://www.retailerdaily.com/entry/10793/yankee-candle-to-restructure-lay-off-330-close-29-stores/; www.yankeecandle.com (accessed June 24, 2010).

This case was written by Elizabeth J. Wilson, Suffolk University.

CASE 36   PetSmart: Where Pets Are Family

In the animal-loving society of the United States, 62 percent of households, or 71.4 million homes, have pets. The resulting pet retail industry has benefited from pet owners' tendency to humanize their pets and treat them like family members, which has increased industry revenues rapidly. As depicted in Exhibit 1, pet industry expenditures have almost tripled since 1994, making pet care the second-fastest-growing retail category, with an average annual growth rate of 9 percent. By 2010, U.S. pet industry expenditures are forecast to exceed $47 billion and are projected to continue to grow.

An industry once dominated by bland pet food and basic supplies has transformed into a highly differentiated market with diverse and creative offerings including pet fashions and accessories, gourmet pet cuisine, and even pet massages. Exhibit 2 depicts the ever-expanding composition of pet industry spending, including the sale of pet food, supplies, veterinary care, medicine, animal purchases, and pet services such as grooming and boarding.

PETSMART CAPITALIZES ON INDUSTRY TRENDS

A survey conducted by the Washington-based Pew Research Center found that 85 percent of pet owners call their dogs members of the family, as do 78 percent of those with cats. The study also noted that 80 percent of the owners buy holiday and birthday gifts for their pets, and nearly half of the female respondents said that they relied more on their pet's affection than on their spouse's or children's. Pet owners have become emotionally tied to their pets and, in turn, treat their pets like humans by

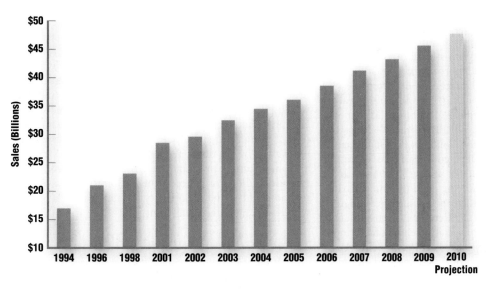

EXHIBIT 1

U.S. Pet Industry Expenditures

Source: American Pet Products Association, Inc., http://americanpet products.org/press_industrytrends.asp.

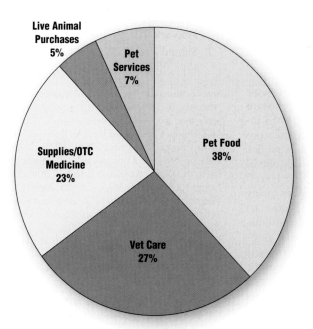

EXHIBIT 2

Estimated 2010 U.S. Pet Expenditures by Category

Source: American Pet Products Association, Inc., http://americanpetproducts. org/press_industrytrends.asp.

dressing them in the latest fashions, prolonging their lives through expensive medical treatments, and buckling them into specially designed car seats.

PetSmart has taken advantage of pet humanization trends and increased revenues and profitability. Three key features mark the expanded pet retail industry: (1) increased merchandise offerings, (2) more licensing agreements for pet products, and (3) innovative pet services.

Pet ownership drives demand, and profitability for retailers depends on the ability to generate store traffic effectively. To meet growing demand, PetSmart has expanded its store offerings to include a wider range of merchandise and services. A typical PetSmart store stocks 10,000 in-store products and offers an even larger variety of products online. In addition, this retailer has increased its assortment within each product category. PetSmart presently stocks a deep selection of pet foods from a large array of suppliers, including low-cost, all-natural, breed-specific, preservative-free, diet, organic, and premium foods with real meats and vegetables. To provide total solutions for its customers, the company introduced a wide range of private-label brands, positioned as low-cost alternatives to national brands. According to the Private Label Manufacturers Association, store brands account for 11 percent of cat food, 12 percent of dog food, 13 percent of pet supplies, and 21 percent of cat litter sales.

Consumers interested in spoiling their pets often walk into a pet store to buy and coordinate outfits for their cat or dog, with choices ranging from personalized T-shirts to dresses to water-activated cooling bandanas. Through partnerships with PetSmart, renowned companies are leveraging their own brands within the pet sector. Store aisles are lined with toys, clothing, accessories, bedding, and aquariums displaying popular cartoon characters such as Sponge-Bob SquarePants, Clifford the Big Red Dog, Barbie, Blues Clues, Disney, and Peanuts. In an exclusive manufacturing and marketing deal with Martha Stewart Pets, PetSmart is now offering a new line of pet apparel, bedding, and grooming and bath supplies. In addition, companies from a diverse collection of industries, such as Paul Mitchell, Polo Ralph Lauren, Harley-Davidson, and Old Navy, have developed their own pet product lines. Even Jeep has released its own line of branded strollers and pet ramps for cars and trucks to attempt to profit from the endless licensing opportunities within the pet retailing industry.

In the past, pet retailers provided just the most basic products. Today, they aim to create lasting relationships with customers. The service sector of the pet retail industry has higher profit margins, so PetSmart is incorporating various service offerings into its business model, including in-store grooming, six- to eight-week obedience training sessions, doggie day care, and "Pet Hotel" boarding facilities with cozy beds and televisions airing Animal Planet programming. As a result, PetSmart earned more than $575 million from its service businesses, representing 11 percent of its annual sales revenue in 2010. Pet service industry competitors similarly attempt to position themselves to reach a portion of the market. Doggie spas, for example, offer high-end services such as massage therapy and pedicures, while pet walking and waste pick-up services enjoy greater success within the industry.

HUMAN RESOURCES AS A BRAND STRATEGY

Through various employee development programs, PetSmart trains its employees to reinforce the firm's brand image. It hires people who love pets and thus helps provide customers with value, quality, and service. PetSmart administers a 120-hour educational program for its trainers, a 6-month instructional program for its groomers, and 16 hours of role-play training before any store opens to the public. As a result, the cheerful demeanor of PetSmart employees remains consistent across the country. PetSmart's staff passionately converses with customers, asks pet-related questions, and gives recommendations. This sense of helpfulness and friendliness aligns the service staff with the company's overall brand strategy and creates an emotional connection to the brand. Well-behaved pets are allowed to shop with their owners, which creates a pleasant, comfortable, animal-loving store atmosphere that furthers supports brand equity.

PetSmart regularly displays highly visible corporate charity and donation-related signs for animal-related causes (spay/neuter initiatives, pet adoption programs, food for pet shelters, etc.) at its checkout counters to reinforce the company's animal-loving culture. The business made a conscious decision to encourage adoption from shelters instead of selling cats and dogs, even though sales of cats and dogs would generate higher annual revenues. The decision to encourage and facilitate adoptions is decreasing euthanization of abandoned animals. PetSmart CEO Philip Francis notes that "by the time you factor in the bed, food, a collar, a leash, a training program, a bath, and a vet appointment, this adopted dog or cat could be a $300 to $400 event for us, and could be the opportunity for a lifetime relationship with that pet and that pet parent."

DISCUSSION QUESTIONS

1. What else could PetSmart do to increase its store traffic, revenues, and profitability?
2. Consider other retailers that might begin to sell a larger assortment of pet products and services. How will this competition affect PetSmart?
3. Should PetSmart expand its operations internationally? Why or why not?

Sources: American Pet Products Manufacturers Association, Inc., "Industry Statistics and Trends," http://americanpetproducts.org/press_industrytrends.asp (accessed June 27, 2010); Catherine M. Dalton, "A Passion for Pets: An Interview with Philip L. Francis, Chairperson and CEO of PETsMART, Inc.," *Business Horizons*, 2005, pp. 469–475; Constantine Von Hoffman, "Upscale Amenities Go to the Dogs," *Brandweek*, January 8, 2007; Diane Brady, Paula Lehman, Christopher Megerian, Christopher Palmeri, and Arlene Weintraub, "The Pet Economy; Americans Spend an Astonishing $41 Billion a Year on their Furry Friends," *BusinessWeek*, August 6, 2007; Doug Desjardins, "Off and Running: Pet Products Lure Licensed Brands," *Retailing Today*, June 18, 2007; Joseph Tarnowski, "Pet Care: Furry Forecast," *Progressive Grocer*, January 1, 2006; Mike Troy, "Global Pet Expo: Booming Pet Industry Fetches Strong Returns," *Retailing Today*, March 5, 2007.

This case was written by James Pope, while an MBA student at Loyola University Maryland, under the supervision of Professor Hope Corrigan.

CASE 37   Lindy's Bridal Shop

Located in Lake City (population 80,000), Lindy's Bridal Shop, a small bridal store, sells bridal gowns, prom gowns, accessories, and silk flowers. It also rents men's formal wear and performs various alteration services.

Lindy Armstrong, age 33, has owned the store since its founding in March 2007. She is married to a high school teacher and is the mother of three young children. A former nurse, she found the demands of hospital schedules left too little time for her young family. An energetic, active woman with many interests, she wanted to continue to work but also have time with her children.

The silk flowers market initially enabled Lindy to combine an in-home career with child rearing. She started Lindy's Silk Flowers with $75 of flower inventory in Vernon, a small town of about 10,000 people 10 miles from Lake City. Working out of her home, she depended on word-of-mouth communication among her customers, mainly brides, to bring in business. As Lindy's Silk Flowers prospered, a room was added onto the house to provide more space for the business. Lindy was still making all the flowers herself. Her flower-making schedule kept her extremely busy. Long hours were the norm.

Lindy was approached by a young photographer named Dan Morgan, who proposed establishing a one-stop bridal shop. In this new business, Dan would provide photography, Lindy would provide silk flowers, and another partner, Karen Ross (who had expertise in the bridal market), would provide gowns and accessories. The new store would be located in Vernon in a rented structure. Shortly before the store was to open, Dan and Karen decided not to become partners, and Lindy became the sole owner. She knew nothing about the bridal business. Having no merchandise or equipment, Lindy was drawn to an ad announcing that a bridal store in a major city was going out of business. She immediately called and arranged to meet the owner. Subsequently, she bought all his stock (mannequins, racks, and carpet) for $10,000. The owner also gave her a crash course in the bridal business.

The location in Vernon was chosen primarily because it was close to her home. While Vernon is a very small town, Lindy felt that location was not a critical factor in her store's success. She maintained that people would travel some distance to make a purchase as important as a bridal gown. Rent was $1,500 per month plus utilities. Parking was a problem.

Lindy's Bridal Shop has continued to grow. Bridal gowns and accessories as well as prom dresses have sold well. As the time approached for Lindy to renew her lease, she wondered about the importance of location. She decided to move to a much larger town, Lake City, which is the site of a state university.

RETAIL FORMAT

Certain times of the year see more formal events than others. Many school proms are held during late April and May, and June, July, and August are big months for weddings. Since traditional dates for weddings are followed less and less closely, Lindy believes that the business is becoming less seasonal, although January and February are quite slow. Lindy's Bridal Shop's major product lines are new wedding, prom, and party gowns. No used gowns are sold. Discontinued styles or gowns that have been on the rack for a year are sold at reduced prices, primarily because discoloration is a major problem. Gowns tend to yellow after hanging on the racks for a year. A wide variety of accessories are provided. Lindy believes it's important that her customers do not have to go anywhere else for them. These accessories include shoes, veils, headpieces, jewelry, and foundations. Slips may be rented instead of purchased. One room of Lindy's Bridal Shop is used only to prepare silk flowers.

Lindy's Bridal Shop's major service offering is fitting and alteration. Most gowns must be altered, for which there's a nominal charge. Lindy feels that personal attention and personal service set her apart from her competitors. Emphasizing customer satisfaction, she works hard to please each customer. This isn't always easy. Customers can be picky, and it takes time to deal with unhappy people.

Lindy's Bridal Shop engages in various promotional activities but is constrained by limited finances. The firm has no formal operating budget and thus no formal appropriation for advertising expenses. Newspaper ads constitute the primary promotional medium, although radio is occasionally used. Ads for prom dresses are run only during prom season. These ads usually feature a photograph of a local high school student in a Lindy's Bridal Shop gown plus a brief description of the student's activities. Other promotional activities include bridal shows at a local mall. Lindy feels they have been very successful, although they're a lot of work. A recent prom show in a local high school used students as models, which proved to be an excellent way to stimulate sales. Lindy hopes to go into several other area high schools during the next prom season, although this expansion will demand much planning.

Lindy's Bridal Shop is located at the end of Lake City's main through-street. Initially Lindy didn't think location was important to her bridal store's success, but she's changed her mind. Whereas business was good in Vernon, it's booming in Lake City. Vehicular traffic is high, and there's adequate, if not excess, parking.

Lindy's Bridal Shop has a 12-year lease. Rent ($2,000 per month) includes heat and water, but Lindy's Bridal Shop must pay for interior decoration. The physical facility is generally attractive, with open and inviting interior display areas. But some areas both inside and outside the store have an unfinished look.

Some storage areas require doors or screens to enhance the interior's appearance. The fitting room ceilings are unfinished, and the carpeting inside the front door needs replacing. One other interior problem is insufficient space; there seems to be inadequate space for supporting activities such as flower preparation, customer fittings, and merchandise storage, which gives the store a cluttered look.

Several external problems exist. The signs are ineffective, and there's a strong glare on the front windows, which detracts from the effectiveness of the overall appearance and interior window displays. The parking lot needs minor maintenance: Parking lines should be painted, and curbs must be repaired. Much should be done to add color and atmosphere through basic landscaping.

STORE OPERATIONS

The majority of Lindy's Bridal Shop's current sales are made to individuals who order bridal gowns from the rack or from the catalogs of three major suppliers. At the time of the order, the customer pays a deposit, usually half of the purchase price. The balance is due in 30 days. Lindy would like payment in full at the time of ordering, regardless of the delivery date, but payment is often delayed until delivery. Once ordered, a gown must be taken and the bill paid when delivered. No tuxedos are carried in the store, so customers must order from catalogs. Fitting jackets and shoes are provided to help patrons size their purchases. Lindy's Bridal Shop rents its men's formal wear from suppliers. Payment from the customer is due on delivery.

Lindy, the sole owner and also the manager of the firm, finds it hard to maintain a capable workforce. A small company, Lindy's Bridal Shop can't offer premium salaries for its few positions. There's one full-time salesperson. The part-time staff includes a salesperson, alterations person, bookkeeper, and custodian. Lindy handles all the paperwork. Her responsibilities include paying bills, ordering merchandise and supplies, hiring and firing personnel, fitting customers, and selling various items. She makes all the major decisions that directly affect the firm's operations. She also makes all the silk flowers herself. This is time-consuming, but she isn't satisfied with how anyone else makes them.

COMPETITION

Lindy's Bridal Shop is the only bridal shop in Lake City. Lindy believes she has four main competitors. Whitney's Bridal Shop is 30 miles from Lake City; Ender's Brides, a new shop with a good operation, is in Spartan City, 50 miles away; Carole's is a large, established bridal shop in Smithtown, 70 miles distant; and Gowns-n-Such is in Andersonville, 75 miles away. A new store in Yorktown (15 miles away) is selling used gowns and discontinued styles at very reduced prices. Lindy watches this new- and used-gown store closely.

Some of her potential customers are buying wedding gowns from electronic retailers such as The Knot (theknot.com) and the Wedding Channel (weddingchannel.com). Lindy is concerned that some of the services offered by these electronic retailers (such as gift registries, e-mail notices, wedding planning, and wedding picture displays) will attract more of her customers.

THE FUTURE

Lindy Armstrong is uncertain about the future. She enjoys the business but feels that she's working very hard and not making much money. During all the years of Lindy's Bridal Shop's operation, she hasn't taken a salary. She works 60 hours or more a week. Business is excellent and growing, but she's tired. She has even discussed selling the business and returning to nursing.

DISCUSSION QUESTIONS

1. Should Lindy change the emphasis of her merchandise mix to increase her sales?
2. Which products should have more emphasis? Which should have less?
3. What personnel decisions must Lindy face to improve her business?
4. How could someone like Lindy Armstrong balance the demands of her family and her business?

This case was prepared by Linda F. Felicetti and Joseph P. Grunewald, Clarion University of Pennsylvania.

CASE 38   Interviewing for a Management Trainee Position

1. Assume the role of the college recruiter for a national retail chain that is reviewing résumés to select candidates to interview for a management trainee position. Which of the three résumés on the following pages do you find effective? Ineffective? Why? Which applicant would you select to interview? Why?

2. Update your résumé and prepare for an interview for a manager training program with a large lumber and building supply retailer. This full-time position promises rapid advancement on completion of the training period. A college degree and experience in retail, sales, and marketing are preferred. The base pay is between $35,000 and $45,000 per year, plus a bonus of up to $7,000. This retailer promotes from within, and a new manager trainee can become a store manager within two to three years, with earnings potential of $100,000 or more. The benefits package is generous, including medical, hospitalization, dental, disability, and life insurance; a 401(k) plan; profit sharing; awards and incentives; and paid vacations and holidays. Your résumé should include your contact information, education and training, skills, experience and accomplishments, and honors and awards.

3. Role-play a practice interview for this position. In pairs, read each other's résumés, and then spend 20 to 30 minutes representing each side of the interview. One student should be the human resource manager screening applicants, and the other should be the candidate for the manager training program. As the human resource manager, ask appropriate questions of the applicant, such as the following:

- Why are you applying for this position?
- What are your strengths and weaknesses for this position?

- Why should this organization consider you for this position?
- Why are you interested in working for this company?
- What are your career goals for the next 5 to 10 years?

- Describe your skills when working in a team setting.
- What questions do you have about the company?

This case was written by Cecelia Schulz, University of Florida.

Martin L. Cox

xxxx@ufl.edu, (xxx) 3xx-xxxx
123 Your Street, Apt. 301
Gainesville, Florida 32605

OBJECTIVE
Seeking a marketing internship utilizing leadership experience, strong work ethic, and interpersonal skills with a focus in product planning.

EDUCATION
Bachelor of Science in Business Administration   May 2009
University of Florida, Gainesville, Florida   GPA 3.69
Major in Marketing

LEADERSHIP
Student Government
    Theatre Nights Chair   Jan. 2008-Present
    Emerging Leaders Conference Executive Assistant   Sept. 2007-Present
    Student Integrity Court Justice   May 2007-Present
    Banquet Cabinet Assistant Director   May 2007-Present
    Innovate Party House Representative   Jan. 2007-April 2007
    Homecoming Supper Staff   Oct. 2006, 2007 Pan-Hellenic Council
    Assistant Director of Jr. Pan-Hellenic   Dec. 2006-Present
    Jr. Pan-Hellenic Executive VP Int. Relations   Sept. 2006-Jan. 2007 Tri-Delta
Philanthropy   Triple Play
    Intramural Soccer-Captain   Oct. 2006, 2007
    Intramural Basketball-Captain   Sept. 2007-Present
    Member since Aug. 2003   Jan. 2007-Present

HONORS
Savant UF Leadership Honorary   Oct. 2007-Present
Sandra Day O'Connor Pre-Law Society   Sept. 2007-Present
Alpha Lambda Delta Honor Society   Inducted March 2007
Phi Eta Sigma Honor Society   Inducted March 2007

COMMUNITY SERVICE
Mentor to Freshmen Students for SG Mentor/Mentee   Sept. 2007-Present
Basketball On Wheels Volunteer   Sept. 2007-Present
Dance Marathon Dancer   Jan. 2007-March 2007
After School Gators Volunteer   Jan. 2007-April 2007
Pillows for Patriots Service Project Volunteer   Sept. 2006-Dec. 2006

WORK EXPERIENCE
Senior Customer Service Associate, Video-R-Us, Tampa, FL   Jan. 2005-Aug. 2006
Secretarial Assistant, Law Firm, Mount Dora, FL   June-Aug. 2005

References available upon request.

Tina Acosta
123 Your Street #335
Gainesville, FL 32608
(727) xxx-xxxx
lxxx@ufl.edu

OBJECTIVE

To integrate my financial and business background with my creative and artistic skills in a fast-paced industry

EDUCATION

University of Florida
Warrington College of Business
Bachelor of Science in Finance
Minor in Spanish
Graduation: May 2009
GPA: 3.73

International Baccalaureate Program
St. Petersburg High School
Focus in Theatre, English, and History
Graduation 2005
GPA: 4.0

RELEVANT CLASSES

Retail Management, Study Abroad in Spain, Business Finance, Managerial Accounting, Problem Solving Using Computer Software, Debt and Money Markets

EXPERIENCE

Abercrombie & Fitch—Gainesville, FL   Brand Representative (October 2007-Present)
- Oversaw customer service on the sales floor
- Maintained and updated the sales floor design
- Handled purchases and returns at the register
- Prepared shipments and the floor for an internal audit
- Promoted the brand name for the women's fashion line

Olive Garden—St. Petersburg, FL   Server (April 2006-August 2006)
- Used a computerized food and beverage ordering system
- Maintained the management's expectations through customer service
- Interacted with customers
- Memorized an extensive menu and recommended foods satisfying customer's needs while maximizing the restaurant's profits

Sacino's Formalwear—St. Petersburg, FL   Sales Representative (August 2004-August 2005)
- Managed incoming and outgoing shipment responsibilities
- Organized financial paperwork
- Oversaw customer service on the sales floor
- Headed the formal wear department for young women

SKILLS

Proficient in Spanish
Office XP: Word-Document Formatting, Letters, Tables, Flyers, and Macros
          Excel-Spreadsheets, Formulas, and Graph Database Analysis, Functions, and Simples Macros
          PowerPoint-Professional Presentations

HONORS

Third place in the preliminary competition for the University of Florida's Center for Entrepreneurship and Innovation
Florida's Bright Futures Scholar
University of Florida Dean's List Student 2006

Richard Kates
xxxxxx@ufl.edu

123 Your Street. #164	123 8th Ave N
Gainesville, Florida 32608	Tampa, Florida 33713
(352) xxx-xxxx	(813) xxx-xxxx

Objective	Seeking a position utilizing marketing, management, and organizational abilities, as well as interpersonal skills.

Education	**Marketing Major**	May 2009
	University of Florida	Gainesville, Florida
	Minor in Mass Communications and Minor in	
	Entrepreneurship GPA 3.7	

Experience	**Entrepreneur/CEO,** Long River PC, LLC	August 2005 to
	Tampa, FL	Present
	-Helped create and manage a new software company based in South Florida.	
	-Helped develop revolutionary program that will aid the visually impaired. Researched and developed multiple original non-disclosure as well as non-compete agreements.	
	-Responsible for hiring, funding, managing, and controlling progress of almost a dozen private software engineers. Reported to and allocated funds of angel investors.	
	Server, Carraba's	April 2007 to
	Gainesville, Florida	Present
	-Help train new employees through shadowing and demonstration.	
	-Serve over 70 guests per day, and ensure customer satisfaction and attentiveness.	
	-Multiple top sales, as well as winner of "Perfect Check" contest.	
	Usher/Security/Technician, Ben Hill Griffin Stadium	August 2005 to
	Gainesville, Florida	August 2007
	Pool/Health Club Attendant, Don Cesar Resort	May 2004 to
	St. Petersburg, Florida	August 2006

Leadership	**Executive Board Member, Varsity Tennis Team. Social Chair**
	University of Florida August 2006 to Present
	Organized, planned, and financed all Tennis Team social events. In charge of planning large events, gatherings at home and away meets, coordinating the activities of over 60 members.
	Executive Board Member, Fisher School of Accounting
	University of Florida January 2007 to May 2007
	Aided in revision and draft of new official Fisher School of Accounting Council's by-laws.
	Drafted a new 5 year program for the expansion and direction of the new Fisher School including member growth, activities, graduate prerequisites, and facility uses.
	CHAMPS Mentoring Volunteer Program
	Gainesville Florida January 2007 to Present
	Met with an "at risk" elementary school student 2 hours per week each semester to spend quality time encouraging the child's healthy growth and development.

Affiliations	**Phi Eta Sigma Honor Society,** Member active 2005 to present
	Florida Tennis Team, Fall 2005 to Spring 2007. Varsity Fall 2006 to Spring 2007
	Team Florida Cycling, Spring 2007 to present
	Student Alumni Association Member, Fall 2006 to present
	American Marketing Association, Member Fall 2007
	International Business Society, Fall 2007
	Business Administration College Council, Fall 2007 Member-at-Large
	The Entrepreneurs Club, Fall 2007

Skills	Computer-Fluent in Microsoft Word, Excel, PowerPoint, Explorer, and Media Player, Fluent-Spanish

References	Available upon request.

ABC analysis An analysis that rank orders SKUs by a profitability measure to determine which items should never be out of stock, which should be allowed to be out of stock occasionally, and which should be deleted from the stock selection.

accessibility (1) The degree to which customers can easily get into and out of a shopping center; (2) ability of the retailer to deliver the appropriate retail mix to customers in the segment.

accessories Merchandise in apparel, department, and specialty stores used to complement apparel outfits. Examples include gloves, hosiery, handbags, jewelry, handkerchiefs, and scarves.

accordion theory A cyclical theory of retailer evolution suggesting that changes in retail institutions are explained in terms of depth versus breadth of assortment. Retail institutions cycle from high-depth/low-breadth to low-depth/high-breadth stores and back again.

account opener A premium or special promotion item offered to induce the opening of a new account, especially in financial institutions and stores operating on an installment credit basis.

accounts payable The amount of money owed to vendors, primarily for merchandise inventory.

accounts receivable The amount of money due to the retailer from selling merchandise on credit.

actionability Criteria for evaluating a market segment scheme indicating what the retailer should do to satisfy its needs.

activity-based costing (ABC) A financial management tool in which all major activities within a cost center are identified, calculated, and then charged to cost objects, such as stores, product categories, product lines, specific products, customers, and suppliers.

additional markup An increase in retail price after and in addition to an original markup.

additional markup cancellation The percentage by which the retail price is lowered after a markup is taken.

additional markup percentage The addition of a further markup to the original markup as a percentage of net sales.

add-on selling Selling additional new products and services to existing customers, such as a bank encouraging a customer with a checking account to apply for a home improvement loan from the bank.

administered vertical marketing system A form of vertical marketing system designed to control a line or classification of merchandise as opposed to an entire store's operation. Such systems involve the development of comprehensive programs for specified lines of merchandise. Vertically aligned companies—manufacturers or wholesalers—even though in non-ownership positions, may work together to reduce the total systems cost of such activities as advertising, transportation, and data processing. See also *contractual vertical marketing system* and *corporate vertical marketing system*.

advance shipping notice (ASN) An electronic document received by the retailer's computer from a supplier in advance of a shipment.

advertising Paid communications delivered to customers through nonpersonal mass media such as newspapers, television, radio, direct mail, and the Internet.

advertising manager A retail manager who manages advertising activities such as determining the advertising budget, allocating the budget, developing ads, selecting media, and monitoring advertising effectiveness.

advertising reach The percentage of customers in the target market exposed to an ad at least once.

affinity marketing Marketing activities that enable consumers to express their identification with an organization. An example is offering credit cards tied to reference groups like the consumer's university or an NFL team.

affordable budgeting method A budgeting method in which a retailer first sets a budget for every element of the retail mix except promotion and then allocates the leftover funds to a promotional budget.

Age Discrimination and Employment Act A federal act that makes it illegal to discriminate in hiring and termination decisions concerning people between the ages of 40 and 70 years.

agent (1) A business unit that negotiates purchases, sales, or both but does not take title to the goods in which it deals; (2) a person who represents the principal (who, in the case of retailing, is the store or merchant) and acts under authority, whether in buying or in bringing the principal into business relations with third parties.

aging The length of time merchandise has been in stock.

aided recall When consumers indicate they know the brand when the name is presented to them.

à la carte plans An employee reward program giving employees a choice of rewards and thus tailoring the rewards to the desires of individual employees.

allocator Position in merchandise management responsible for allocating merchandise and tailoring the assortment in several categories for specific stores in a geographic area.

alteration costs Expenses incurred to change the appearance or fit, to assemble, or to repair merchandise.

Americans with Disabilities Act (ADA) A federal civil rights law that protects people with disabilities from discrimination in employment, transportation, public accommodations, telecommunications, and the activities of state and local government.

analog approach A method of trade area analysis also known as the *similar store* or *mapping* approach. The analysis is divided into four steps: (1) describing the current trade areas through the technique of customer spotting; (2) plotting the customers on a map; (3) defining the primary, secondary, and tertiary area zones; and (4) matching the characteristics of stores in the trade areas with the potential new store to estimate its sales potential.

anchor store A large, well-known retail operation located in a shopping center or Internet mall and serving as an attracting force for consumers to the center.

ancillary services Services such as layaway, gift wrap, and credit that are not directly related to the actual sale of a specific product within the store.

anticipation discount A discount offered by a vendor to a retailer in addition to the cash discount or dating, if the retailer pays the invoice before the end of the cash discount period.

anticompetitive leasing arrangement A lease that limits the type and amount of competition a particular retailer faces within a trading area.

antitrust legislation A set of laws directed at preventing unreasonable restraint of trade or unfair trade practices. Aim is to foster a competitive environment. See also *restraint of trade.*

application form A form used to collect information on a job applicant's education, employment experience, hobbies, and references.

artificial barriers In site evaluations for accessibility, barriers such as railroad tracks, major highways, or parks.

asset management path One of the two paths in the strategic profit model affecting a retailer's return on assets.

assets Economic resources, such as inventory or store fixtures, owned or controlled by an enterprise as a result of past transactions or events.

asset turnover Net sales divided by total assets.

assortment The number of SKUs within a merchandise category. Also called *depth of merchandise.*

assortment plan A list of merchandise that indicates in very general terms what should be carried in a particular merchandise category.

assurance A customer service characteristic that customers use to evaluate service quality; the knowledge and courtesy of the employees performing the service and their ability to convey trust and confidence.

atmospherics The design of an environment through visual communications, lighting, colors, music, and scent to stimulate customers' perceptual and emotional responses and ultimately to affect their purchase behavior.

auction A market in which goods are sold to the highest bidder; usually well publicized in advance or held at specific times that are well known in the trade. Auctions are becoming very popular over the Internet.

autocratic leader A manager who makes all decisions on his or her own and then announces them to employees.

automatic reordering system A system for ordering staple merchandise in which an automatic reorder is generated by a computer on the basis of a perpetual inventory system and reorder point calculations.

average BOM stock-to-sales ratio The number of months in the period divided by planned inventory turnover for the period.

average inventory The sum of inventory on hand at several periods in time divided by the number of periods.

Baby Boomer The generational cohort of people born between 1946 and 1964.

back order A part of an order that the vendor has not filled completely and that the vendor intends to ship as soon as the goods in question are available.

backup stock The inventory used to guard against going out of stock when demand exceeds forecasts or merchandise is delayed. Also called *safety stock* or *buffer stock.*

backward integration A form of vertical integration in which a retailer owns some or all of its suppliers.

bait and switch An unlawful deceptive practice that lures customers into a store by advertising a product at lower than usual prices (the bait), then inducing the customers to switch to a higher-price model (the switch).

balance sheet The summary of a retailer's financial resources and claims against the resources at a particular date; indicates the relationship between assets, liabilities, and owners' equity.

bank card Credit card issued by a bank, such as Visa and MasterCard.

bar code See *Universal Product Code (UPC).*

bargain branding A branding strategy that targets a price-sensitive segment by offering a no-frills product at a discount price.

bargaining power of vendors A characteristic of a market in which retailers are so dependent on large, important vendors that their profits are adversely affected.

barriers to entry Conditions in a retail market that make it difficult for firms to enter the market.

base stock See *cycle stock.*

basic merchandise See *staple merchandise.*

basic stock list The descriptive and record-keeping function of an inventory control system; includes the stock number, item description, number of units on hand and on order, and sales for the previous periods.

basic stock method An inventory management method used to determine the beginning-of-month (BOM) inventory by considering both the forecast sales for the month and the safety stock.

benchmarking The practice of evaluating performance by comparing one retailer's performance with that of other retailers using a similar retail strategy.

benefits The customer's specific needs that are satisfied when the customer buys a product.

benefit segmentation A method of segmenting a retail market on the basis of similar benefits sought in merchandise or services.

big box stores Large, limited service retailers.

black market The availability of merchandise at a high price when it is difficult or impossible to purchase under normal market circumstances; commonly involves illegal transactions.

block group A collection of adjacent census blocks that contain between 300 and 3,000 people that is the smallest unit for the sample data.

blog A public Web site where users post informal journals of their thoughts, comments, and philosophies.

blue laws Laws prohibiting retailers from being open two consecutive days of the weekend—ostensibly to allow employees a day of rest or religious observance. Most states no longer have blue laws.

bonus Additional compensation awarded periodically, based on a subjective evaluation of the employee's performance.

book inventory system See *retail inventory method.*

bottom-up planning When goals are set at the bottom of the organization and filter up through the operating levels.

boutique (1) Departments in a store designed to resemble small, self-contained stores; (2) a relatively small specialty store.

boutique layout See *free-form layout.*

brand A distinguishing name or symbol (such as a logo, design, symbol, or trademark) that identifies the products or services offered by a seller and differentiates those products and services from the offerings of competitors.

brand association Anything linked to or connected with the brand name in a consumer's memory.

brand awareness The ability of a potential customer to recognize or recall that a particular brand name belongs to a retailer or product/service.

brand building The design and implementation of a retail communication program to create an image in the customer's mind of the retailer relative to its competitors. Also called *positioning.*

brand equity The value that brand image offers retailers.

brand image Set of associations consumers have about a brand that are usually organized around some meaningful themes.

brand loyalty Indicates customers like and consistently buy a specific brand in a product category. They are reluctant to switch to other brands if their favorite brand isn't available.

breadth of merchandise See *variety.*

break-even analysis A technique that evaluates the relationship between total revenue and total cost to determine profitability at various sales levels.

break-even point quantity The quantity at which total revenue equals total cost and beyond which profit occurs.

breaking bulk A function performed by retailers or wholesalers in which they receive large quantities of merchandise and sell them in smaller quantities.

breaking sizes Running out of stock on particular sizes.

broker A middleman that serves as a go-between for the buyer or seller; assumes no title risks, does not usually have physical custody of products, and is not looked upon as a permanent representative of either the buyer or seller.

buffer stock Merchandise inventory used as a safety cushion for cycle stock so the retailer won't run out of stock if demand exceeds the sales forecast. Also called *safety stock.*

building codes Legal restrictions describing the size and type of building, signs, type of parking lot, and so on that can be used at a particular location.

bulk fixture See *rounder.*

bullwhip effect The buildup of inventory in an uncoordinated channel.

buyback A strategy vendors and retailers use to get products into retail stores, either when a retailer allows a vendor to create space for goods by "buying back" a competitor's inventory and removing it from a retailer's system or when the retailer forces a vendor to buy back slow-moving merchandise.

buyer Person in a retailing organization responsible for the purchase and profitability of a merchandise category. Similar to *category manager.*

buyer's market Market occurring in economic conditions that favor the position of the retail buyer (or merchandiser) rather than the vendor; in other words, economic conditions are such that the retailer can demand and usually get concessions from suppliers in terms of price, delivery, and other market advantages. Opposite of a *seller's market.*

buyer's report Information on the velocity of sales, availability of inventory, amount of order, inventory turnover, forecast sales, and, most important, the quantity that should be ordered for each SKU.

buying behavior The activities customers undertake when purchasing a good or service.

buying calendar A plan of a store buyer's market activities, generally covering a six-month merchandising season based on a selling calendar that indicates planned promotional events.

buying committee A committee that has the authority for final judgment and decision making on such matters as adding or eliminating new products.

buying power The customer's financial resources available for making purchases.

buying process The stages customers go through to purchase merchandise or services.

buying situation A method of segmenting a retail market based on customer needs in a specific buying situation, such as a fill-in shopping trip versus a weekly shopping trip.

buzz Genuine, street-level excitement about a hot new product.

capacity fixture See *rounder.*

career path The set of positions to which management employees are promoted within a particular organization as their careers progress.

cash Money on hand.

cash discounts Reductions in the invoice cost that the vendor allows the retailer for paying the invoice prior to the end of the discount period.

cash wraps The places in a store where customers can purchase merchandise and have it "wrapped"—placed in a bag.

catalog retailer A nonstore retailer that communicates directly with customers using catalogs sent through the mail.

catalog retailing Nonstore retail format in which the retail offering is communicated to a customer through a catalog.

category An assortment of items (SKUs) the customer sees as reasonable substitutes for one another.

category captain A supplier that forms an alliance with a retailer to help gain consumer insight, satisfy consumer needs, and improve the performance and profit potential across the entire category.

category killer A discount retailer that offers a narrow but deep assortment of merchandise in a category and thus dominates the category from the customers' perspective. Also called a *category specialist.*

category life cycle A merchandise category's sales pattern over time.

category management The process of managing a retail business with the objective of maximizing the sales and profits of a category.

category manager See *buyer.*

category signage Signage within a particular department or sector of the store, category signs are usually smaller than directional signs. Their purpose is to identify types of products offered; they are usually located near the goods to which they refer.

category specialist See *category killer.*

caveat emptor Latin term for "let the buyer beware."

census A count of the population of a country as of a specified date.

census block An area bounded on all sides by visible (roads, rivers, etc.) and/or invisible (county, state boundaries) features that is the smallest geographic entity for which census data are available.

census tracts Subdivisions of a Metropolitan Statistical Area (MSA), with an average population of 4,000.

central business district (CBD) The traditional downtown business area of a city or town.

centralization The degree to which authority for making retail decisions is delegated to corporate managers rather than to geographically dispersed regional, district, and store management.

centralized buying A situation in which a retailer makes all purchase decisions at one location, typically the firm's headquarters.

central market See *market.*

central place A center of retailing activity such as a town or city.

central place theory Christaller's theory of retail location suggesting that retailers tend to locate in a central place. As more retailers locate together, more customers are attracted to the central place. See also *central place.*

chain discount A number of different discounts taken sequentially from the suggested retail price.

chargeback A practice used by retailers in which they deduct money from the amount they owe a vendor.

chat room Location in an Internet site at which customers can engage in interactive, real-time, text-based discussions.

checking The process of going through goods upon receipt to make sure that they arrived undamaged and that the merchandise received matches the merchandise ordered.

checkout areas See *cash wraps.*

cherry picking Customers visiting a store and buying only merchandise sold at big discounts or buying only the best styles or colors.

chief financial officer (CFO) An executive that works with the CEO on financial issues such as equity-debt structure and credit card operations.

chief marketing officer (CMO) An executive that works with staff to develop marketing, advertising and other promotional programs.

chief operations officer (COO) An executive that oversees managers in charge of management information systems (MIS), supply chain, human resources, and visual merchandising.

classification A group of items or SKUs for the same type of merchandise, such as pants (as opposed to jackets or suits), supplied by different vendors.

classification dominance An assortment so broad that customers should be able to satisfy all of their consumption needs for a particular category by visiting one retailer.

classification merchandising Divisions of departments into related types of merchandise for reporting and control purposes.

Clayton Act (1914) An act passed as a response to the deficiencies of the Sherman Act; it specifically prohibits price discrimination, tying arrangements, and exclusive dealing contracts that have the effect of limiting free trade, and it provides for damages to parties injured as a result of violations of the act.

clearance sale An end-of-season sale to make room for new goods; also pushing the sale of slow-moving, shopworn, and demonstration model goods.

closeout (1) An offer at a reduced price to sell a group of slow-moving or incomplete stock; (2) an incomplete assortment, the remainder of a line of merchandise that is to be discontinued and so is offered at a low price to ensure immediate sale.

closeout retailer Off-price retailer that sells a broad but inconsistent assortment of general merchandise as well as apparel and soft home goods, obtained through retail liquidations and bankruptcy proceedings.

COD (cash on delivery) Purchase terms in which payment for a product is collected at the time of delivery.

collaborative planning, forecasting, and replenishment (CPFR) A collaborative inventory management system in which a retailer shares information with vendors. CPFR software uses data to construct a computer-generated replenishment forecast that is shared by the retailer and vendor before it's executed.

commercial bribery A vendor's offer of money or gifts to a retailer's employee for the purpose of influencing purchasing decisions.

commission Compensation based on a fixed formula, such as percentage of sales.

committee buying The situation whenever the buying decision is made by a group of people rather than by a single buyer. A multiunit operation is usually the type of firm that uses this procedure.

common area maintenance (CAM) The common facilities maintenance that a shopping center management is responsible for, such as the parking area, providing security, parking lot lighting, outdoor signage for the center, advertising, and special events to attract consumers.

common stock The type of stock most frequently issued by corporations. Owners of common stock usually have voting rights in the retail corporation.

communication gap The difference between the actual service provided to customers and the service promised in the retailer's promotion program. This factor is one of the four factors identified by the Gaps model for improving service quality.

communication objectives Specific goals for a communication program related to the effects of the communication program on the customer's decision-making process.

community strip shopping centers See *neighborhood strip shopping centers.*

comparable store sales growth See *same store sales growth.*

comparative price advertising A common retailing practice that compares the price of merchandise offered for sale with a higher "regular" price or a manufacturer's list price.

comparison shopping A market research method in which retailers shop at competitive stores, comparing the merchandise, pricing, visual display, and service to their own offering.

comparison shopping situation A type of shopping situation whereby consumers have a general idea about the type of product or service they want, but they do not have a well-developed preference for a brand or model.

compatibility The degree to which the fashion is consistent with existing norms, values, and behaviors.

compensation Monetary payments including salary, commission, and bonuses; also, paid vacations, health and insurance benefits, and a retirement plan.

competition-oriented pricing A pricing method in which a retailer uses competitors' prices, rather than demand or cost considerations, as guides.

competitive parity method An approach for setting a promotion budget so that the retailer's share of promotion expenses is equal to its market share.

competitive rivalry The frequency and intensity of reactions to actions undertaken by competitors.

competitor analysis An examination of the strategic direction that competitors are likely to pursue and their ability to successfully implement their strategy.

complexity The ease with which consumers can understand and use a new fashion.

composite segmentation A method of segmenting a retail market using multiple variables, including benefits sought, lifestyles, and demographics.

computerized checkout See *point-of-sale (POS) terminal.*

conditions of sale See *terms of sale.*

conflict of interest A situation in which a decision maker's personal interest influences or has the potential to influence his or her professional decision.

congestion The amount of crowding of either cars or people.

consideration set The set of alternatives the customer evaluates when making a merchandise selection.

consignment Items not paid for by the retailer until they are sold. The retailer can return unsold merchandise; however, the retailer does not take title until final sale is made.

consortium exchange A retail exchange that is owned by several firms within one industry.

consumer cooperative Customers own and operate this type of retail establishment. Customers have ownership shares and share in the store's profits through price reductions or dividends.

consumer direct fulfillment See *drop shipping (Chapter 10).*

Consumer Goods Pricing Act (1975) The statute that repealed all resale price maintenance laws and made it possible for retailers to sell products below suggested retail prices.

consumerism The activities of government, business, and independent organizations designed to protect individuals from practices that infringe on their rights as consumers.

contest Promotional activity in which customers compete for rewards through games of chance. Contests can also be used to motivate retail employees.

continuous replenishment

contract distribution service company Firm that performs all of the distribution functions for retailers or vendors, including transportation to the contract company's distribution center, merchandise processing, storage, and transportation to retailers.

contractual vertical marketing system A form of vertical marketing system in which independent firms at different levels in the channel operate contractually to obtain the economies and market impacts that could not be obtained by unilateral action. Under this system, the identity of the individual firm and its autonomy of operations remain intact. See also *administered vertical marketing system* and *corporate vertical marketing system.*

contribution margin Gross margin less any expense that can be directly assigned to the merchandise.

convenience center A shopping center that typically includes such stores as a convenience market, a dry cleaner, or a liquor store.

convenience goods Products that the consumer is not willing to spend the effort to evaluate prior to purchase, such as milk or bread.

convenience shopping situation When consumers are primarily concerned with minimizing their effort to get the product or service they want.

convenience store A store that provides a limited variety and assortment of merchandise at a convenient location in a 2,000- to 3,000-square-foot store with speedy checkout.

conventional supermarket A self-service food store that offers groceries, meat, and produce with limited sales of non-food items, such as health and beauty aids and general merchandise.

conversion rates Percentage of consumers who buy the product after viewing it.

cookies Computer text files that identify visitors when they return to a Web site.

coop advertising Enables a retailer to associate its name with well-known national brands and use attractive art work created by the national brand. Also a method a retailer uses to share the cost of advertising with a vendor.

co-op (cooperative) advertising A program undertaken by a vendor in which the vendor agrees to pay all or part of a promotion for its products.

cooperative buying When a group of independent retailers work together to make large purchases from a single supplier.

copy The text in an advertisement.

copycat branding A branding strategy that imitates the manufacturer brand in appearance and trade dress but generally is perceived as lower quality and is offered at a lower price.

copyright A regulation that protects original works of authors, painters, sculptors, musicians, and others who produce works of artistic or intellectual merit.

core assortment A relatively large proportion of the total assortment that is carried by each store in the chain, regardless of size.

corporate social responsibility Voluntary actions taken by a company to address the ethical, social, and environmental impacts of its business operations and the concerns of its stakeholders.

corporate vertical marketing system A form of vertical marketing system in which all of the functions from production to distribution are at least partially owned and controlled by a single enterprise. Corporate systems typically operate manufacturing plants, warehouse facilities, and retail outlets. See also *administered vertical marketing system* and *contractual vertical marketing system*.

cost The financial expenditure required to obtain something in return.

cost code The item cost information indicated on price tickets in code. A common method of coding is the use of letters from an easily remembered word or expression with nonrepeating letters corresponding to numerals. For example, y o u n g b l a d e 1 2 3 4 5 6 7 8 9 0.

cost complement Used in the cost method of accounting, the percentage of net sales represented by the cost of goods sold.

cost method of accounting A method in which retailers record the cost of every item on an accounting sheet or include a cost code on the price tag or merchandise container. When a physical inventory is conducted, the cost of each item must be determined, the quantity in stock is counted, and the total inventory value at cost is calculated. See *retail inventory method*.

cost multiplier Used in the cost method of accounting, the cumulative markup multiplied by 100 percent minus cumulative markup percentage.

cost-oriented method A method for determining the retail price by adding a fixed percentage to the cost of the merchandise; also known as *cost-plus pricing*.

cost per thousand (CPM) A measure that is often used to compare media. CPM is calculated by dividing an ad's cost by its reach.

cotenancy clause A clause in a leasing contract that requires a certain percentage of a shopping center be leased, while others name specific retailers or types of retailers that are to remain open.

counterfeit merchandise Goods that are made and sold without permission of the owner of a trademark, a copyright, or a patented invention that is legally protected in the country where it is marketed.

coupons Documents that entitle the holder to a reduced price or X cents off the actual price of a product or service.

courtesy days The days on which stores extend to loyalty club customers the privilege of making purchases at sale prices in advance of public sale.

coverage The theoretical number of potential customers in the retailer's target market that could be exposed to an ad in a given medium.

credit Money placed at a consumer's disposal by a retailer, financial or other institution. For purchases made on credit, payment is due in the future.

credit limit The quantitative limit that indicates the maximum amount of credit that may be allowed to be outstanding on each individual customer account.

cross-docked Items that are unloaded from the shippers' truck and within a few hours reloaded onto trucks going to stores. These items are prepackaged by the vendor for a specific store, such that the UPC labels on a carton indicate the store to which it is to be sent.

cross-docking distribution area An area in a distribution center in which merchandise is delivered to one side of the facility by vendors, is unloaded, and is immediately reloaded onto trucks that deliver merchandise to the stores. With cross-docking, merchandise spends very little time in the warehouse.

cross-selling When sales associates in one department attempt to sell complementary merchandise from other departments to their customers.

cross-shopping A pattern of buying both premium and low-priced merchandise or patronizing expensive, status-oriented retailers and price-oriented retailers.

culture The meaning and values shared by most members of a society.

cumulative attraction The principle that a cluster of similar and complementary retailing activities will generally have greater drawing power than isolated stores that engage in the same retailing activities.

cumulative markup Used in the cost method of accounting, the average percentage markup for the period; the total retail price minus cost divided by retail price.

cumulative quantity discounts Discounts earned by retailers when purchasing certain quantities over a specified period of time.

cumulative reach The cumulative number of potential customers that would see an ad that runs several times.

current assets Cash or any assets that can normally be converted into cash within one year.

current liabilities Debts that are expected to be paid in less than one year.

customer allowance An additional price reduction given to the customer.

customer buying process The stages a customer goes through in purchasing a good or service. Stages include need recognition, information search, evaluation and choice of alternatives, purchase, and postpurchase evaluation.

customer database See *data warehouse*.

customer delight A high level of customer satisfaction created by retailers providing greatly unexpected services.

customer lifetime value (CLV) The expected contribution from the customer to the retailer's profits over his or her entire relationship with the retailer.

customer loyalty Customers' commitment to shopping at a store.

customer relationship management (CRM) A business philosophy and set of strategies, programs, and systems that focuses on identifying and building loyalty with a retailer's most valued customers.

customer returns The value of merchandise that customers return because it is damaged, doesn't fit, and so forth.

customer service The set of retail activities that increase the value customers receive when they shop and purchase merchandise.

customer service department The department in a retail organization that handles customer inquiries and complaints.

customer spotting A technique used in trade area analysis that "spots" (locates) residences of customers for a store or shopping center.

customization approach An approach used by retailers to provide customer service that is tailored to meet each customer's personal needs.

cycle stock The inventory that goes up and down due to the replenishment process. Also known as *base stock*.

cycle time The time between the decision to place an order and the receipt of merchandise and placement in the store.

cyclical theories Theories of institutional change based on the premise that retail institutions change on the basis of cycles. See also *wheel of retailing* and *accordion theory*.

data mining Technique used to identify patterns in data found in data warehouses, typically patterns that the analyst is unaware of prior to searching through the data.

data warehouse The coordinated and periodic copying of data from various sources, both inside and outside the enterprise, into an environment ready for analytical and informational processing. It contains all of the data the firm has collected about its customers and is the foundation for subsequent CRM activities.

dating A series of options that tells retailers when discounts can be taken from vendors and when the full invoice amount is due.

deal period A limited time period allowed by manufacturers for retailers to purchase merchandise at a special price.

decentralization When authority for retail decisions is made at lower levels in the organization.

deceptive advertising Any advertisement that contains a false statement or misrepresents a product or service.

decile analysis A method of identifying customers in a CRM program that breaks customers into ten deciles based on their LTV (lifetime value). When using decile analysis, the top 10 percent of the customers would be the most valued group.

deferred billing An arrangement that enables customers to buy merchandise and not pay for it for several months, with no interest charge.

delivery gap The difference between the retailer's service standards and the actual service provided to customers. This factor is one of the four factors identified by the Gaps model for improving service quality.

demalling The activity of revitalizing a mall by demolishing a mall's small shops, scrapping its common space and food courts, enlarging the sites once occupied by department stores, and adding more entrances into the parking lot.

demand/destination area Department or area in a store in which demand for the products or services offered is created before customers get to their destination.

demand/destination merchandise Products that customers have decided to buy before entering the store.

demand-oriented method A method of setting prices based on what the customers would expect or be willing to pay.

democratic leader A store manager who seeks information and opinions from employees and bases decisions on this information.

demographics Vital statistics about populations such as age, sex, and income.

demographic segmentation A method of segmenting a retail market that groups consumers on the basis of easily measured, objective characteristics such as age, gender, income, and education.

department A segment of a store with merchandise that represents a group of classifications the consumer views as being complementary.

department store A retailer that carries a wide variety and deep assortment, offers considerable customer services, and is organized into separate departments for displaying merchandise.

depth interview An unstructured personal interview in which the interviewer uses extensive probing to get individual respondents to talk in detail about a subject.

depth of merchandise See *assortment*.

deseasonalized demand The forecast demand without the influence of seasonality.

destination store A retail store in which the merchandise, selection, presentation, pricing, or other unique feature acts as a magnet for customers.

dialectic theory An evolutionary theory based on the premise that retail institutions evolve. The theory suggests that new retail formats emerge by adopting characteristics from other forms of retailers in much the same way that a child is the product of the pooled genes of two very different parents.

digital signage Signs whose visual content is delivered digitally through a centrally managed and controlled network and displayed on a television monitor or flat panel screen.

direct investment The investment and ownership by a retail firm of a division or subsidiary that builds and operates stores in a foreign country.

direct mail Any brochure, catalog, advertisement, or other printed marketing material delivered directly to the consumer through the mail or a private delivery company.

direct-mail catalog retailer A retailer offering merchandise or services through catalogs mailed directly to customers.

direct-mail retailer A nonstore retailer that communicates directly with customers using mail brochures and pamphlets to sell a specific product or service to customers at one point in time.

direct marketing A form of nonstore retailing in which customers are exposed to merchandise through print or electronic media and then purchase the merchandise by telephone, mail, or over the Internet.

direct product profitability (DPP) The profit associated with each category or unit of merchandise. DPP is equal to the per-unit gross margin less all variable costs associated with the merchandise such as procurement, distribution, sales, and the cost of carrying the assets.

direct-response advertising Advertisements on TV and radio that describe products and provide an opportunity for customers to order them.

direct retailing See *nonstore retailing.*

direct selling A retail format in which a salesperson, frequently an independent distributor, contacts a customer directly in a convenient location (either at a customer's home or at work), demonstrates merchandise benefits, takes an order, and delivers the merchandise to the customer.

direct store delivery (DSD) A method of delivering merchandise to stores in which vendors distribute merchandise directly to the stores rather than going through distribution centers.

disability Any physical or mental impairment that substantially limits one or more of an individual's major life activities or any condition that is regarded as being such an impairment.

disclosure of confidential information An unethical situation in which a retail employee discloses proprietary or confidential information about the firm's business to anyone outside the firm.

discount A reduction in the original retail price granted to store employees as a special benefit or to customers under certain circumstances.

discount-oriented center See *promotional center.*

discount store A general merchandise retailer that offers a wide variety of merchandise, limited service, and low prices.

discrimination An illegal action of a company or its managers when a member of a protected class (women, minorities, etc.) is treated differently from nonmembers of that class (see *disparate treatment*) or when an apparently neutral rule has an unjustified discriminatory effect (see *disparate impact*).

disintermediation When a manufacturer sells directly to consumers, thus competing directly with its retailers.

disparate impact The case of discrimination when an apparently neutral rule has an unjustified discriminatory effect, such as if a retailer requires high school graduation for all its employees, thereby excluding a larger proportion of disadvantaged minorities, when at least some of the jobs (e.g., custodian) could be performed just as well by people who did not graduate from high school.

disparate treatment The case of discrimination when members of a protected class are treated differently from nonmembers of that class—if a qualified woman (protected class), for example, does not receive a promotion given to a lesser qualified man.

dispatcher A person who coordinates deliveries from the vendor to the distribution center or stores or from the distribution center to stores.

distribution See *logistics.*

distribution center A warehouse that receives merchandise from multiple vendors and distributes it to multiple stores.

distribution channel A set of firms that facilitate the movement of products from the point of production to the point of sale to the ultimate consumer. Similar to a supply chain.

distribution intensity The number of retailers carrying a particular category.

distributive fairness A customer's perception of the benefits received compared to their costs (inconvenience or loss) when resolving a complaint.

distributive justice Arises when outcomes received are viewed as fair with respect to outcomes received by others.

diversification growth opportunity A strategic investment opportunity that involves an entirely new retail format directed toward a market segment not presently being served.

diversionary pricing A practice sometimes used by retailers in which low price is stated for one or a few goods or services (emphasized in promotion) to give the illusion that the retailer's prices are all low.

diverted merchandise Merchandise that is diverted from its legitimate channel of distribution; similar to *gray-market merchandise* except there need not be distribution across international boundaries.

diverter A firm that buys diverted merchandise from retailers and manufacturers and then resells the merchandise to other retailers. See *diverted merchandise.*

double coupon A retail promotion that allows the customer to double the face value of a coupon.

drawing account A method of sales compensation in which salespeople receive a weekly check based on their estimated annual income.

drop shipping A supply chain system in which retailers receive orders from customers and relay these orders to a vendor and then the vendor ships the merchandise ordered directly to the customer.

drugstore Specialty retail store that concentrates on pharmaceuticals and health and personal grooming merchandise.

duty See *tariff.*

economic order quantity (EOQ) The order quantity that minimizes the total cost of processing orders and holding inventory.

editing the assortment Selecting the right assortment of merchandise.

efficient customer response (ECR) The set of programs supermarket chains have undertaken to manage inventory and increase inventory turnover.

80–20 rule A general management principle where 80 percent of the sales or profits come from 20 percent of the customers.

electronic agent Computer program that locates and selects alternatives based on some predetermined characteristics.

electronic article surveillance (EAS) system A loss prevention system in which special tags placed on merchandise in retail stores are deactivated when the merchandise is purchased. The tags are used to discourage shoplifting.

electronic data interchange (EDI) The computer-to-computer exchange of business documents from retailer to vendor and back.

electronic retailing A retail format in which the retailers communicate with customers and offer products and services for sale over the Internet.

e-mail A paid personal communication vehicle that involves sending messages over the Internet.

emotional support Supporting retail service providers with the understanding and positive regard to enable them to deal with the emotional stress created by disgruntled customers.

empathy A customer service characteristic that customers use to evaluate service quality; refers to the caring, individualized attention provided to customers, such as personalized service, sending of notes and e-mails, or recognition by name.

employee discount A discount from retail price offered by most retailers to employees.

employee productivity Output generated by employee activities. One measure of employee productivity is the retailer's sales or profit divided by its employee costs.

employee turnover The number of employees occupying a set of positions during a period (usually a year) divided by the number of positions.

employment branding Programs undertaken by employers to understand what potential employees are seeking, as well as what they think about the retailer; developing a value proposition and an employment brand image; communicating that brand image to potential employees; and then fulfilling the brand promise by ensuring the employee experience matches that which was advertised.

employment marketing See *employment branding.*

empowerment The process of managers sharing power and decision-making authority with employees.

empty nest A stage in a family life cycle where children have grown up and left home.

empty nester Household where all children are grown and have left home.

end cap Display fixture located at the end of an aisle.

end-of-month (EOM) dating A method of dating in which the discount period starts at the end of the month in which the invoice is dated (except when the invoice is dated the 25th or later).

energy management The coordination of heating, air conditioning, and lighting to improve efficiencies and reduce energy costs.

environmental apparel Merchandise produced with few or no harmful effects on the environment. Part of a green marketing program.

Equal Employment Opportunity Commission (EEOC) A federal commission that was established for the purpose of taking legal action against employers that violate Title VII of the Civil Rights Act. Title VII prohibits discrimination in company personnel practices.

Equal Pay Act A federal act enforced by the Equal Employment Opportunity Commission that prohibits unequal pay for men and women who perform equal work or work of comparable worth.

escape clause A clause in a lease that allows the retailer to terminate its lease if sales don't reach a certain level after a specified number of years or if a specific cotenant in the center terminates its lease.

e-tailing See *electronic retailing.*

ethics A system or code of conduct based on universal moral duties and obligations that indicate how one should behave.

evaluation of alternatives The stage in the buying process in which the customer compares the benefits offered by various retailers.

event sponsorship A type of marketing communication for which corporations support various activities usually in the cultural or sports and entertainment sectors.

everyday low pricing (EDLP) A pricing strategy that stresses continuity of retail prices at a level somewhere between the regular nonsale price and the deep-discount sale price of the retailer's competitors.

evolutionary theories Theories of institutional change based on the premise that retail institutions evolve. See *dialectic theory* and *natural selection.*

exclusive brand A brand developed by a national brand vendor, often in conjunction with a retailer, and sold exclusively by the retailer.

exclusive dealing agreement Restriction a manufacturer or wholesaler places on a retailer to carry only its products and no competing vendors' products.

exclusive geographical territory A policy in which only one retailer in a certain territory is allowed to sell a particular brand.

exclusive use clause A clause in a lease that prohibits the landlord from leasing to retailers selling competing products.

executive training program (ETP) A training program for retail supervisors, managers, and executives.

expenses Costs incurred in the normal course of doing business to generate revenues.

express warranty A guarantee supplied by either the retailer or the manufacturer that details the terms of the warranty in simple, easily understood language so customers know what is and what is not covered by the warranty.

extended problem solving A buying process in which customers spend considerable time at each stage of the decision-making process because the decision is important and they have limited knowledge of alternatives.

external sources of information Information provided by the media and other people.

extra dating A discount offered by a vendor in which the retailer receives extra time to pay the invoice and still take the cash discount.

extranet A collaborative network that uses Internet technology to link businesses with their suppliers, customers, or other businesses.

extreme-value food retailers See *limited assortment supermarkets.*

extreme-value retailers Small, full-line discount stores that offer a limited merchandise assortment at very low prices.

extrinsic reward Reward (such as money, promotion, or recognition) given to employees by their manager or the firm.

factoring A specialized financial function whereby manufacturers, wholesalers, or retailers sell accounts receivable to financial institutions, including factors or banks.

factory outlet Outlet store owned by a manufacturer.

fad A merchandise category that generates a lot of sales for a relatively short time—often less than a season.

Fair Labor Standards Act A federal law, enacted in 1938, that sets minimum wages, maximum hours, child labor standards, and overtime pay provisions.

fair trade Purchasing practices that require producers to pay workers a living wage, well more than the prevailing minimum wage, and offer other benefits, like onsite medical treatment.

fair trade laws See *resale price maintenance laws.*

family brand A product's brand name associated with the company's name

fashion A type of product or a way of behaving that is temporarily adopted by a large number of consumers because the product, service, or behavior is considered to be socially appropriate for the time and place.

fashion merchandise Category of merchandise that typically lasts several seasons, and sales can vary dramatically from one season to the next.

fashion/specialty center A shopping center that is composed mainly of upscale apparel shops, boutiques, and gift shops carrying selected fashions or unique merchandise of high quality and price.

feature area Area designed to get the customer's attention that includes end caps, promotional aisles or areas, freestanding fixtures and mannequins that introduce a soft goods department, windows, and point-of-sale areas.

feature fixture See *four-way fixture.*

features The qualities or characteristics of a product that provide benefits to customers.

Federal Trade Commission Act (1914) The congressional act that created the Federal Trade Commission (FTC) and gave it the power to enforce federal trade laws.

fill rate The percentage of an order that is shipped by the vendor.

financial leverage A financial measure based on the relationship between the retailer's liabilities and owners' equity that indicates financial stability of the firm.

first-degree price discrimination Charging customers different prices on the basis of their willingness to pay.

fixed assets Assets that require more than a year to convert to cash.

fixed costs Costs that are stable and don't change with the quantity of product produced and sold.

fixed expenses Expenses that remain constant for a given period of time regardless of the sales volume.

fixed-rate lease A lease that requires the retailer to pay a fixed amount per month over the life of the lease.

fixtures The equipment used to display merchandise.

flexible pricing A pricing strategy that allows consumers to bargain over selling prices.

flextime A job scheduling system that enables employees to choose the times they work.

floor-ready merchandise Merchandise received at the store ready to be sold, without the need for any additional preparation by retail employees.

FOB (free-on-board) destination A term of sale designating that the shipper owns the merchandise until it is delivered to the retailer and is therefore responsible for transportation and any damage claims.

FOB (free-on-board) origin A term of sale designating that the retailer takes ownership of the merchandise at the point of origin and is therefore responsible for transportation and any damage claims.

focus group A marketing research technique in which a small group of respondents is interviewed by a moderator using a loosely structured format.

forward buy An opportunity to purchase at an extra discount more merchandise than the retailer normally needs to fill demand.

forward integration A form of vertical integration in which a manufacturer owns wholesalers or retailers.

four-way fixture A fixture with two cross-bars that sit perpendicular to each other on a pedestal.

franchisee The owner of an individual store in a franchise agreement.

franchising A contractual agreement between a franchisor and a franchisee that allows the franchisee to operate a retail outlet using a name and format developed and supported by the franchisor.

franchisor The owner of a franchise in a franchise agreement.

free-form layout A store design, used primarily in small specialty stores or within the boutiques of large stores, that arranges fixtures and aisles asymmetrically. Also called *boutique layout.*

free riding A situation in which a retailer, such as a discount store, takes more than its fair share of the benefits derived by another retailer's promotional or service efforts but does not incur its fair share of the costs and is thus able to sell the merchandise at a lower price.

freestanding display Fixtures or mannequins that are located on aisles and designed primarily to attract customers' attention and bring customers into a department in stores using a racetrack or free-form layout.

freestanding fixture Fixtures and mannequins located on aisles that are designed primarily to get customers' attention and bring them into a department.

freestanding insert (FSI) An ad printed at a retailer's expense and distributed as a freestanding insert in the newspaper. Also called a *preprint.*

freestanding site A retail location that is not connected to other retailers.

free trade zone A special area within a country that can be used for warehousing, packaging, inspection, labeling, exhibition, assembly, fabrication, or transshipment of imports without being subject to that country's tariffs.

freight collect When the retailer pays the freight from the vendor.

freight forwarders Companies that purchase transport services. They then consolidate small shipments from a number of shippers into large shipments that move at a lower freight rate.

freight prepaid When the freight is paid by the vendor to the retailer.

frequency The number of times a potential customer is exposed to an ad.

frequent-shopper program A reward and communication program used by a retailer to encourage continued purchases from the retailer's best customers. See *loyalty program.*

fresh supermarket A supermarket that is smaller than a traditional supermarket (30,000 versus 40,000 square feet), is more convenient, has less space devoted to packaged goods, but more space devoted to fresh produce, meat, and other fresh items.

fringe trade area See *tertiary trade area.*

frontal presentation A method of displaying merchandise in which the retailer exposes as much of the product as possible to catch the customer's eye.

full-line discount store Retailers that offer a broad variety of merchandise, limited service, and low prices.

full-line forcing When a supplier requires a retailer to carry the supplier's full line of products if the retailer wants to carry any part of that line.

full warranty A guarantee provided by either the retailer or manufacturer to repair or replace merchandise without charge and within a reasonable amount of time in the event of a defect.

functional discount See *trade discount.*

functional needs The needs satisfied by a product or service that are directly related to its performance.

functional product grouping Categorizing and displaying merchandise by common end uses.

functional relationships A series of one-time market exchanges linked together over time.

future dating A method of dating that allows the buyer additional time to take advantage of the cash discount or to pay the net amount of the invoice.

Gaps model A conceptual model that indicates what retailers need to do to provide high-quality customer service. When customers' expectations are greater than their perceptions of the delivered service, customers are dissatisfied and feel the quality of the retailer's service is poor. Thus, retailers need to reduce the service gap—the difference between customers' expectations and perceptions of customer service to improve customers' satisfaction with their service.

general merchandise catalog retailers Nonstore retailers that offer a broad variety of merchandise in catalogs that are periodically mailed to their customers.

generational cohort People within the same generation who have similar purchase behaviors because they have shared experiences and are in the same stage of life.

Generation X The generational cohort of people born between 1965 and 1976.

Generation Y The generational cohort of people born between 1977 and 1995.

generic brand Unbranded, unadvertised merchandise found mainly in drug, grocery, and discount stores.

gentrification A process in which old buildings are torn down or restored to create new offices, housing developments, and retailers.

geodemographic segmentation A market segmentation system that uses both geographic and demographic characteristics to classify consumers.

geographic information system (GIS) A computerized system that enables analysts to visualize information about their customers' demographics, buying behavior, and other data in a map format.

geographic segmentation Segmentation of potential customers by where they live. A retail market can be segmented by countries, states, cities, and neighborhoods.

glass ceiling An invisible barrier that makes it difficult for minorities and women to be promoted beyond a certain level.

global operations president An executive that oversees retailing operations outside the home country.

gondola An island type of self-service counter with tiers of shelves, bins, or pegs.

graduated lease A lease that requires rent to increase by a fixed amount over a specified period of time.

gray-market goods Merchandise that possesses a valid U.S. registered trademark and is made by a foreign manufacturer but is imported into the United States without permission of the U.S. trademark owner.

green A marketing strategy that promotes environmentally safe or beneficial products or services.

green marketing A strategic focus by retailers and their vendors to supply customers with environmentally friendly merchandise.

green product A product that is environmentally safe or beneficial.

green sheen The disingenuous practice of marketing products or services as being environmentally friendly with the purpose of gaining public approval and sales rather than actually improving the environment.

greenwashing See *green sheen.*

greeter A retail employee who greets customers as they enter a store and who provides information or assistance.

grid layout A store design, typically used by grocery stores, in which merchandise is displayed on long gondolas in aisles with a repetitive pattern.

gross margin The difference between the price the customer pays for merchandise and the cost of the merchandise (the price the retailer paid the supplier of the merchandise). More specifically, gross margin is net sales minus cost of goods sold.

gross margin return on investment (GMROI) Gross margin dollars divided by average (cost) inventory.

gross profit See *gross margin.*

gross sales The total dollar revenues received from the sales of merchandise and services.

group maintenance behaviors Activities store managers undertake to make sure that employees are satisfied and work well together.

habitual decision making A purchase decision involving little or no conscious effort.

hedonic benefit Shopping for pleasure, entertainment, and/or to achieve an emotional or recreational experience.

hedonic needs Needs motivating consumers to go shopping for pleasure.

high-assay principle A resource allocation principle emphasizing allocating marketing expenditures on the basis of marginal return.

high/low pricing A strategy in which retailers offer prices that are sometimes above their competition's everyday low price, but they use advertising to promote frequent sales.

holding inventory A major value-providing activity performed by retailers whereby products will be available when consumers want them.

home improvement center A category specialist offering equipment and material used by do-it-yourselfers and construction contractors to make home improvements.

horizontal price fixing An agreement between retailers in direct competition with each other to charge the same prices.

house brand See *generic brand.*

Huff's gravity model A trade area analysis model used to determine the probability that a customer residing in a particular area will shop at a particular store or shopping center.

human resource management Management of a retailer's employees.

hype Artificially generated word of mouth, manufactured by public relations people.

hypermarket Large (100,000–300,000 square feet) combination food (60–70 percent) and general merchandise (30–40 percent) retailer.

idea-oriented presentation A method of presenting merchandise based on a specific idea or the image of the store.

identifiability A criteria for evaluating market segments in which retailers must be able to identify the customers in a target segment for the segmentation scheme to be effective. By identifying the segment, it allows retailers to determine (1) the segment's size and (2) with whom the retailer should communicate when promoting its retail offering.

illegal discrimination The actions of a company or its managers that result in a number of a protected class being treated unfairly and differently than others.

impact An ad's effect on the audience.

implied warranty of merchantability A guarantee that accompanies all merchandise sold by a retailer, assuring customers that the merchandise is up to standards for the ordinary purposes for which such goods are used.

impulse buying A buying decision made by customers on the spot after seeing the merchandise.

impulse merchandise See *impulse products.*

impulse products Products that are purchased by customers without prior plans. These products are almost always located near the front of the store, where they're seen by everyone and may actually draw people into the store.

impulse purchase An unplanned purchase by a customer.

incentive compensation plan A compensation plan that rewards employees on the basis of their productivity.

income statement A summary of the financial performance of a firm for a certain period of time.

independent exchange A retail exchange owned by a third party that provides the electronic platform to perform the exchange functions.

infomercials TV programs, typically 30 minutes long, that mix entertainment with product demonstrations and solicit orders placed by telephone from consumers.

information search The stage in the buying process in which a customer seeks additional information to satisfy a need.

infringement Unauthorized use of a registered trademark.

ingress/egress The means of entering/exiting the parking lot of a retail site.

in-house credit system See *proprietary store credit card system.*

initial markup The retail selling price initially placed on the merchandise less the cost of goods sold.

inner city Typically a high-density urban area consisting of apartment buildings populated primarily by ethnic groups.

input measure A performance measure used to assess the amount of resources or money used by the retailer to achieve outputs.

installment credit plan A plan that enables consumers to pay their total purchase price (less down payment) in equal installment payments over a specified time period.

institutional advertisement An advertisement that emphasizes the retailer's name and positioning rather than specific merchandise or prices.

in-store kiosk Spaces located within stores containing a computer connected to the store's central offices or the Internet.

instrumental support Support for retail service providers such as appropriate systems and equipment to deliver the service desired by customers.

integrated marketing communication (IMC) program The strategic integration of multiple communication methods to form a comprehensive, consistent message.

intellectual property Property that is intangible and created by intellectual (mental) effort as opposed to physical effort.

intelligent agent A computer program that locates and selects alternatives based on some predetermined characteristics.

interactive electronic retailing A system in which a retailer transmits data and graphics over cable or telephone lines to a consumer's TV or computer terminal.

interest The amount charged by a financial institution to borrow money.

interest income The income a retailer can generate through proprietary credit cards, bank deposits, bonds, treasury bills, fixed income investments, and other investments.

internal sources of information Information in a customer's memory such as names, images, and past experiences with different stores.

Internet retailing See *electronic retailing.*

intertype competition Competition between retailers that sell similar merchandise using different formats, such as discount and department stores.

intranet A secure communication system that takes place within one company.

intratype competition Competition between the same type of retailers (e.g., Kroger versus Safeway).

intrinsic rewards Nonmonetary rewards employees get from doing their jobs.

inventory Goods or merchandise available for resale.

inventory management The process of acquiring and maintaining a proper assortment of merchandise while keeping ordering, shipping, handling, and other related costs in check.

inventory shrinkage See *shrinkage.*

inventory turnover Net sales divided by average retail inventory; used to evaluate how effectively managers utilize their investment in inventory.

invoice cost The actual amount due for the merchandise after both trade and quantity discounts are taken.

irregulars Merchandise that has minor mistakes in construction.

job analysis Identifying essential activities and determining the qualifications employees need to perform them effectively.

job application form A form a job applicant completes that contains information about the applicant's employment history, previous compensation, reasons for leaving previous employment, education and training, personal health, and references.

job description A description of the activities the employee needs to perform and the firm's performance expectations.

job enrichment The redesign of a job to include a greater range of tasks and responsibilities.

job sharing When two or more employees voluntarily are responsible for a job that was previously held by one person.

joint venture In the case of global expansion, an entity formed when the entering retailer pools its resources with a local retailer to form a new company in which ownership, control, and profits are shared. More generally, any business venture in which two or more firms pool resources to form a new business entity.

key items The items that are in greatest demand. Also referred to as best sellers or "A" items (in the case of an ABC analysis).

keystone method A method of setting retail prices in which retailers simply double the cost of the merchandise to obtain the original retail selling price.

kickback See *commercial bribery.*

kiosk See *merchandise kiosk.*

knockoff A copy of the latest styles displayed at designer fashion shows and sold in exclusive specialty stores. These copies are sold at lower prices through retailers targeting a broader market.

knowledge gap The difference between customer expectations and the retailer's perception of customer expectations. This factor is one of four identified by the Gaps model for improving service quality.

labor scheduling The process of determining the number of employees assigned to each area of the store at each hour the store is open.

layaway A method of deferred payment in which merchandise is held by the store for the customer until it is completely paid for.

leader pricing A pricing strategy in which certain items are priced lower than normal to increase the traffic flow of customers or to increase the sale of complementary products.

leadership The process by which a person attempts to influence another to accomplish some goal or goals.

lead time The amount of time between recognition that an order needs to be placed and the point at which the merchandise arrives in the store and is ready for sale.

leased department An area in a retail store leased or rented to an independent company. The leaseholder is typically responsible for all retail mix decisions involved in operating the department and pays the store a percentage of its sales as rent.

lessee The party signing the lease.

lessor The party owning a property that is for rent.

less-than-carload (LCL) The transportation rate that applies to less-than-full carload shipments.

level of support See *service level.*

liabilities Obligations of a retail enterprise to pay cash or other economic resources in return for past, present, or future benefits.

licensed brand Brand for which the licensor (owner of a well-known name) enters a contractual arrangement with a licensee (a retailer or third party). The licensee either manufactures or contracts with a manufacturer to produce the licensed product and pays a royalty to the licensor.

lifestyle Refers to how people live, how they spend their time and money, what activities they pursue, and their attitudes and opinions about the world they live in.

lifestyle center A shopping center with an outdoor traditional streetscape layout with sit-down restaurants and a conglomeration of specialty retailers.

lifestyle segmentation A method of segmenting a retail market based on how consumers live, how they spend their time and money, what activities they pursue, and their attitudes and opinions about the world they live in.

lift-out See *buyback.*

limited-assortment supermarkets A supermarket offering a limited number of SKUs.

limited problem solving A purchase decision process involving a moderate amount of effort and time. Customers engage in this type of buying process when they have some prior experience with the product or service and their risk is moderate.

limited warranty A type of guarantee in which any limitations must be stated conspicuously so that customers are not misled.

local links A way to help customers get around a Web site on the Internet by using links that are internal to the Web site.

locavore movement

logistics Part of the supply chain process that plans, implements, and controls the efficient, effective flow and storage of goods, services, and related information from the point of origin to the point of consumption to meet customers' requirements.

long-term liabilities Debts that will be paid after one year.

loop layout See *racetrack layout.*

loss leader An item priced near or below cost to attract customer traffic into the store.

low-price guarantee policy A policy that guarantees that the retailer will have the lowest possible price for a product or group of products and usually promises to match or better any lower price found in the local market.

loyalty program A program set up to reward customers with incentives such as discounts on purchases, free food, gifts, or even cruises or trips in return for their repeated business.

magalog Combination of magazine and catalog.

mail-order retailer See *direct-mail catalog retailer.*

Main Street The central business district located in the traditional shopping area of smaller towns, or a secondary business district in a suburb or within a larger city.

maintained markup The amount of markup the retailer wishes to maintain on a particular category of merchandise; net sales minus cost of goods sold.

maintenance-increase-recoupment lease A provision of a lease that can be used with either a percentage or straight lease. This type of lease allows the landlord to increase the rent if insurance, property taxes, or utility bills increase beyond a certain point.

mall A shopping center with a pedestrian focus where customers park in outlying areas and walk to the stores.

management by objectives A popular method for linking the goals of a firm to goals for each employee and providing information to employees about their role.

managing diversity A set of human resource management programs designed to realize the benefits of a diverse workforce.

manufacturer brand A line of products designed, produced, and marketed by a vendor. Also called a *national brand.*

manufacturer's agent An agent who generally operates on an extended contractual basis, often sells within an exclusive territory, handles noncompeting but related lines of goods, and possesses limited authority with regard to prices and terms of sale.

manufacturer's outlet store A discount retail store owned and operated by a manufacturer.

manufacturer's suggested retail price (MSRP) The lowest price specified by a manufacturer at which a retailer can sell the manufacturer's product.

maquiladoras An assembly plant in Mexico, especially one along the border between the United States and Mexico, to which foreign materials and parts are shipped and from which the finished product is returned to the original market.

marginal analysis A method of analysis used in setting a promotional budget or allocating retail space, based on the economic principle that firms should increase expenditures as long as each additional dollar spent generates more than a dollar of additional contribution.

markdown The percentage reduction in the initial retail price.

markdown cancellation The percentage increase in the retail price after a markdown is taken.

markdown money Funds provided by a vendor to a retailer to cover decreased gross margin from markdowns and other merchandising issues.

market A group of vendors in a concentrated geographic location or even under one roof or over the Internet; also known as a *central market.*

market attractiveness/competitive position matrix A method for analyzing opportunities that explicitly considers the capabilities of the retailer and the attractiveness of retail markets.

market basket analysis Specific type of data analysis that focuses on the composition of the basket (or bundle) of products purchased by a household during a single shopping occasion.

market development See *market penetration growth opportunity.*

market expansion growth opportunity A strategic investment opportunity that employs the existing retailing format in new market segments.

marketing segmentation The process of dividing a retail market into homogeneous groups. See *retail market segment.*

market penetration growth opportunity An investment opportunity strategy that focuses on increasing sales to present customers using the present retailing format.

market research The systematic collection and analysis of information about a retail market.

market share A retailer's sales divided by the sales of all competitors within the same market.

market week See *trade show.*

markup The increase in the retail price of an item after the initial markup percentage has been applied but before the item is placed on the selling floor.

markup percentage The markup as a percent of retail price.

marquee A sign used to display a store's name or logo.

mass customization The production of individually customized products at costs similar to mass-produced products.

mass-market theory A theory of how fashion spreads that suggests that each social class has its own fashion leaders who play a key role in their own social networks. Fashion information trickles across social classes rather than down from the upper classes to the lower classes.

Mazur plan A method of retail organization in which all retail activities fall into four functional areas: merchandising, marketing communications, store management, and accounting and control.

m-commerce (mobile commerce) Communicating with and even selling to customers through wireless handheld devices, such as cellular telephones and personal digital assistants.

media coverage The theoretical number of potential customers in a retailer's market who could be exposed to an ad.

memorandum purchases Items not paid for by a retailer until they are sold. The retailer can return unsold merchandise; however, the retailer takes title on delivery and is responsible for damages. See *consignment goods.*

mentoring program The assigning of higher-level managers to help lower-level managers learn the firm's values and meet other senior executives.

merchandise budget plan A plan used by buyers to determine how much money to spend in each month on a particular fashion merchandise category, given the firm's sales forecast, inventory turnover, and profit goals.

merchandise category See *category.*

merchandise classification See *classification.*

merchandise group A group within an organization managed by the senior vice presidents of merchandise and responsible for several departments.

merchandise kiosks Small, temporary selling spaces typically located in the walkways of enclosed malls, airports, train stations, or office building lobbies.

merchandise management The process by which a retailer attempts to offer the right quantity of the right merchandise in the right place at the right time while meeting the company's financial goal.

merchandise show See *trade show*.

merchandising See *merchandise management*.

merchandising optimization software Set of algorithms (computer programs) that monitors merchandise sales, promotions, competitors' actions, and other factors to determine the optimal (most profitable) price and timing for merchandising activities, especially markdowns.

merchandising planner A retail employee responsible for allocating merchandise and tailoring the assortment in several categories for specific stores in a geographic area.

message board Location in an Internet site at which customers can post comments.

metropolitan statistical area (MSA) A city with 50,000 or more inhabitants or an urbanized area of at least 50,000 inhabitants and a total MSA population of at least 100,000 (75,000 in New England).

Metro Renters One of ESRI's Community Tapestry segmentation scheme clusters. Young, well-educated singles beginning their professional careers in the largest cities, such as New York, Chicago, and Los Angeles.

micropolitan statistical area (MiSA) A city with only 10,000 inhabitants in its core urban area.

mission statement A broad description of the scope of activities a business plans to undertake.

mixed-use development (MXD) Development that combines several uses in one complex—for example, shopping center, office tower, hotel, residential complex, civic center, and convention center.

mobile commerce See *m-commerce*.

mobile marketing See *m-commerce*.

model stock list A list of fashion merchandise that indicates in very general terms (product lines, colors, and size distributions) what should be carried in a particular merchandise category; also known as a model stock plan.

model stock plan A summary of the desired inventory levels of each SKU stocked in a store for a merchandise category.

monthly additions to stock The amount to be ordered for delivery in each month, given the firm's turnover and sales objectives.

months of supply The amount of inventory on hand at the beginning of the month expressed in terms of the time it will take to sell. A six-month supply means it will take six months for the merchandise to sell. A six-month supply is equivalent to an inventory turnover of two.

multiattribute analysis A method for evaluating vendors that uses a weighted average score for each vendor, which is based on the importance of various issues and the vendor's performance on those issues.

multiattribute attitude model A model of customer decision making based on the notion that customers see a retailer or a product as a collection of attributes or characteristics. The model can also be used for evaluating a retailer, product, or vendor. The model uses a weighted average score based on the importance of various issues and performance on those issues.

multichannel retailer Retailer that sells merchandise or services through more than one channel.

multilevel network A retail format in which people serve as master distributors, recruiting other people to become distributors in their network.

multiple-unit pricing Practice of offering two or more similar products or services for sale at one price. Also known as *quantity discounts*.

mystery shopper Professional shopper who "shops" a store to assess the service provided by store employees.

national brand See *manufacturer brand*.

natural barrier A barrier, such as a river or mountain, that impacts accessibility to a site.

natural selection A theory of retail evolution that argues that those institutions best able to adapt to changes in customers, technology, competition, and legal environments have the greatest chance for success.

needs The basic psychological forces that motivate customers to act.

negligence A product liability suit that occurs if a retailer or a retail employee fails to exercise the care that a prudent person usually would.

negotiation An interaction between two or more parties to reach an agreement.

neighborhood strip shopping center A shopping center that includes a supermarket, drugstore, home improvement center, or variety store. Neighborhood centers often include small stores, such as apparel, shoe, camera, and other shopping goods stores.

net invoice price The net value of the invoice or the total invoice minus all other discounts.

net lease A lease that requires all maintenance expenses such as heat, insurance, and interior repairs to be paid by the retailer.

net profit A measure of the overall performance of a firm; revenues (sales) minus expenses and losses for the period.

net profit margin Profit a firm makes divided by its net sales.

net sales The total number of dollars received by a retailer after all refunds have been paid to customers for returned merchandise.

network direct selling See *multilevel direct selling*.

net worth See *owners' equity*.

never-out list A list of key items or best sellers that are separately planned and controlled. These items account for large sales volume and are stocked in a manner so they are always available. These are "A" items in an ABC analysis.

noncumulative quantity discount Discount offered to retailers as an incentive to purchase more merchandise on a single order.

nondurable Perishable product consumed in one or a few uses.

nonstore retailing A form of retailing to ultimate consumers that is not store-based. Nonstore retailing is conducted through the Internet, vending machines, mail, direct selling, and direct marketing.

North American Industry Classification System (NAICS) Classification of retail firms into a hierarchical set of six-digit codes based on the types of products and services they produce and sell.

notes payable Current liabilities representing principal and interest the retailer owes to financial institutions (banks) that are due and payable in less than a year.

objective-and-task method A method for setting a promotion budget in which the retailer first establishes a set of communication objectives and then determines the necessary tasks and their costs.

observability The degree to which a new fashion is visible and easily communicated to others in a social group.

observation A type of market research in which customer behavior is observed and recorded.

odd pricing The practice of ending prices with an odd number (such as 69 cents) or just under a round number (such as $98 instead of $100).

off-price retailer A retailer that offers an inconsistent assortment of brand-name, fashion-oriented soft goods at low prices.

off-the-job training Training conducted in centralized classrooms away from the employee's work environment.

omnicenter A combination of mall, lifestyle, and power center components in a unified, open-air layout.

one hundred percent location The retail site in a major business district or mall that has the greatest exposure to a retail store's target market customers.

one-price policy A policy that, at a given time, all customers pay the same price for any given item of merchandise.

one-price retailer A store that offers all merchandise at a single fixed price.

1-to-1 retailing Developing retail programs for small groups or individual customers.

online chat A customer service offering that provides customers with an opportunity to click a button at anytime and have an instant messaging, e-mail, or voice conversation with a customer service representative.

online retailing See *electronic retailing*.

on-the-job training A decentralized approach in which job training occurs in the work environment where employees perform their jobs.

open-to-buy The plan that keeps track of how much is spent in each month and how much is left to spend.

operating expenses Costs, other than the cost of merchandise, incurred in the normal course of doing business, such as salaries for sales associates and managers, advertising, utilities, office supplies, and rent.

opinion leader Person whose attitudes, opinions, preferences, and actions influence those of others.

opportunity cost of capital The rate available on the next best use of the capital invested in the project at hand. The opportunity cost should be no lower than the rate at which a firm borrows funds, since one alternative is to pay back borrowed money. It can be higher, however, depending on the range of other opportunities available. Typically, the opportunity cost rises with investment risk.

optical character recognition (OCR) An industrywide classification system for coding information onto merchandise; enables retailers to record information on each SKU when it is sold and transmit the information to a computer.

opt in A customer privacy issue prevalent in the European Union. Takes the perspective that consumers "own" their personal information. Retailers must get consumers to explicitly agree to share this personal information.

option credit account A revolving account that allows partial payments without interest charges if a bill is paid in full when due.

option-term revolving credit A credit arrangement that offers customers two payment options: (1) pay the full amount within a specified number of days and avoid any finance charges or (2) make a minimum payment and be assessed finance charges on the unpaid balance.

opt out A customer privacy issue prevalent in the United States. Takes the perspective that personal information is generally viewed as being in the public domain and retailers can use it in any way they desire. Consumers must explicitly tell retailers not to use their personal information.

order form When signed by both parties, a legally binding contract specifying the terms and conditions under which a purchase transaction is to be conducted.

order point The amount of inventory below which the quantity available shouldn't go or the item will be out of stock before the next order arrives.

organization chart A graphic that displays the reporting relationships within a firm.

organization culture A firm's set of values, traditions, and customs that guide employee behavior.

organization structure A plan that identifies the activities to be performed by specific employees and determines the lines of authority and responsibility in the firm.

outlet center Typically stores owned by retail chains or manufacturers that sell excess and out-of-season merchandise at reduced prices.

outlet store Off-price retailer owned by a manufacturer or a department or specialty store chain.

outparcel A building or kiosk that is in the parking lot of a shopping center but isn't physically attached to a shopping center.

output measure Measure that assesses the results of retailers' investment decisions.

outshopping Customers shopping in other areas because their needs are not being met locally.

outsourcing Obtaining a service from outside the company that had previously been done by the firm itself.

overstored trade area An area having so many stores selling a specific good or service that some stores will fail.

own brand See *private-label brand*.

owners' equity The amount of assets belonging to the owners of the retail firm after all obligations (liabilities) have been met; also known as *net worth* and *stockholders' equity*.

pallet A platform, usually made of wood, that provides stable support for several cartons. Pallets are used to help move and store merchandise.

parallel branding A branding strategy that represents a private label that closely imitates the trade dress (packaging) and product attributes of leading manufacturer brands but with a clearly articulated "invitation to compare" in its merchandising approach and on its product label.

parallel import See *gray-market goods.*

parasite store A store that does not create its own traffic and whose trade area is determined by the dominant retailer in the shopping center or retail area.

partnering relationship See *strategic relationship.*

party plan system Salespeople encourage people to act as hosts and invite friends or coworkers to a "party" at which the merchandise is demonstrated. The host or hostess receives a gift or commission for arranging the meeting.

patent A law that gives the owner of a patent control over the right to make, sell, and use a product for a period of 17 years (14 years for a design).

penetration A low-pricing strategy for newly introduced products or categories.

percentage lease A lease in which rent is based on a percentage of sales.

percentage lease with specified maximum A lease that pays the lessor, or landlord, a percentage of sales up to a maximum amount.

percentage lease with specified minimum The retailer must pay a minimum rent no matter how low sales are.

percentage-of-sales method A method for setting a promotion budget based on a fixed percentage of forecast sales.

periodic reordering system An inventory management system in which the review time is a fixed period (e.g., two weeks), but the order quantity can vary.

perpetual inventory See *retail inventory method.*

perpetual ordering system The stock level is monitored perpetually and a fixed quantity is purchased when the inventory available reaches a prescribed level.

personalized approach A customer service strategy that encourages service providers to tailor their service to meet each customer's personal needs.

personalized service A customer service strategy that requires service providers to tailor their services to meet each customer's personal needs.

personal selling A communication process in which salespeople assist customers in satisfying their needs through face-to-face exchange of information.

physical inventory A method of gathering stock information by using an actual physical count and inspection of the merchandise items.

pick ticket A document that tells the order filler how much of each item to get from the storage area.

pilferage The stealing of a store's merchandise. See also *shoplifting.*

planners Employees in merchandise management responsible for the financial planning and analysis of the merchandise category and, in some cases, the allocation of merchandise to stores.

planogram A diagram created from photographs, computer output, or artists' renderings that illustrates exactly where every SKU should be placed.

point-of-purchase (POP) area See *point-of-sale area.*

point-of-sale area An area where the customer waits at checkout. This area can be the most valuable piece of real estate in the store, because the customer is almost held captive in that spot.

point-of-sale signage Signs placed near the merchandise they refer to so that customers know the price and other detailed information.

point-of-sale (POS) terminal A cash register that can electronically scan a UPC code with a laser and electronically record a sale; also known as *computerized checkout.*

polygon Trade area whose boundaries conform to streets and other map features rather than being concentric circles.

popping the merchandise Focusing spotlights on special feature areas and items.

population density The number of people per unit area (usually square mile) who live within a geographic area.

pop-up store Stores in temporary locations that focus on new products or a limited group of products.

positioning The design and implementation of a retail mix to create in the customer's mind an image of the retailer relative to its competitors. Also called *brand building.*

postpurchase evaluation The evaluation of merchandise or services after the customer has purchased and consumed them.

poverty of time A condition in which greater affluence results in less, rather than more, free time because the alternatives competing for customers' time increase.

power center Shopping center that is dominated by several large anchors, including discount stores (Target), off-price stores (Marshalls), warehouse clubs (Costco), or category specialists such as Home Depot, Office Depot, Circuit City, Sports Authority, Best Buy, and Toys "R" Us.

power perimeter The areas around the outside walls of supermarket that have fresh merchandise categories.

power retailer See *category killer* or *category specialist.*

power shopping center An open-air shopping center with the majority of space leased to several well-known anchor retail tenants—category specialists.

predatory pricing A method for establishing merchandise prices for the purpose of driving competition from the marketplace.

preferred client High-purchasing customers salespeople communicate with regularly, send notes to about new merchandise and sales in the department, and make appointments with for special presentations of merchandise.

premarking Marking of the price by the manufacturer or other supplier before goods are shipped to a retail store. Also called *prepricing.*

premium A type of sales promotion whereby an item is offered free of charge or at a bargain price to reward some type of behavior, such as buying, sampling, or testing.

premium branding A branding strategy that offers the consumer a private label at a comparable manufacturer-brand quality, usually with a modest price savings.

premium merchandise Offered at a reduced price, or free, as an incentive for a customer to make a purchase.

premium private-label brands A private label product that is comparable to a manufacturer's brand quality, sometimes with modest price savings. Examples of premium private labels include Kroger's Private Selection, Tesco Finest (U.K.), "The Men's Collection" at Saks Fifth Avenue, and Bloomingdale's Aqua.

prepricing See *premarking.*

preprint An advertisement printed at the retailer's expense and distributed as a freestanding insert in a newspaper. Also called a *freestanding insert (FSI).*

president of direct channels An executive responsible for the selection and pricing of the merchandise assortment offered through the catalog and Internet channels, the maintenance and design of the retailer's Web site, customer call centers, and the fulfillment centers that fill orders for individual customers.

press conference A meeting with representatives of the news media that is called by a retailer.

press release A statement of facts or opinions that the retailer would like to see published by the news media.

prestige pricing A system of pricing based on the assumption that consumers will not buy goods and services at prices they feel are too low.

price bundling The practice of offering two or more different products or services for sale at one price.

price comparison A comparison of the price of merchandise offered for sale with a higher "regular" price or a manufacturer's list price.

price discrimination An illegal practice in which a vendor sells the same product to two or more customers at different prices. See *first-degree price discrimination* and *second-degree price discrimination.*

price elasticity of demand A measure of the effect a price change has on consumer demand; percentage change in demand divided by percentage change in price.

price fixing An illegal pricing activity in which several marketing channel members establish a fixed retail selling price for a product line within a market area. See *vertical price fixing* and *horizontal price fixing.*

price lining A pricing policy in which a retailer offers a limited number of predetermined price points within a classification.

pricing experiment An experiment in which a retailer actually changes the price of an item in a systematic manner to observe changes in customers' purchases or purchase intentions.

pricing optimization software A type of software program that uses a set of algorithms that analyzes past and current merchandise sales and prices, estimates the relationship between prices and sales generated, and then determines the optimal (most profitable) initial price for the merchandise and the appropriate size and timing of markdowns.

primary data Marketing research information collected through surveys, observations, and experiments to address a problem confronting a retailer.

primary trading area The geographic area from which a store or shopping center derives 50 to 70 percent of its customers.

private exchanges Exchanges that are operated for the exclusive use of a single firm.

private-label brands Products developed and marketed by a retailer and only available for sale by that retailer. Also called *store brands.*

private-label president An executive responsible for the conceptualization, design, sourcing, quality control, and marketing of private-label and exclusive merchandise.

private-label credit card A system in which credit cards have the store's name on them, but the accounts receivable are sold to a financial institution.

PRIZM (potential rating index for zip markets) A database combining census data, nationwide consumer surveys, and interviews with hundreds of people across the country into a geodemographic segmentation system.

procedural fairness The perceived fairness of the process used to resolve customer complaints.

procedural justice An employee's perception of fairness (how he or she is treated) that is based on the process used to determine the outcome.

product attributes Characteristics of a product that affect customer evaluations.

product availability A measurement of the percentage of demand for a particular SKU that is satisfied.

productivity measure The ratio of an output to an input determining how effectively a firm uses a resource.

product liability A tort (or wrong) that occurs when an injury results from the use of a product.

product line A group of related products.

product placement A type of retail communication whereby retailers and vendors pay to have their product included in nontraditional situations, such as in a scene in a movie or television program.

profitability A company's ability to generate revenues in excess of the costs incurred in producing those revenues.

profit margin Net profit divided by net sales.

profit margin management path One of two paths in the strategic profit model to increasing return on assets.

profit sharing A type of compensation incentive offered to a retail manager as a cash bonus based on the firm's profits or as a grant of stock options that link additional income to the performance of the firm's stock.

prohibited-use clause A clause in a lease that keeps a landlord from leasing to certain kinds of tenants.

promotion Activities undertaken by a retailer to provide consumers with information about a retailer's store, its image, and its retail mix.

promotional aisle Area aisle or area of a store designed to get the customer's attention. An example might be a special "trim-the-tree" department that seems to magically appear right after Thanksgiving every year for the Christmas holidays.

promotional allowance An allowance given by vendors to retailers to compensate the latter for money spent in advertising a particular item.

promotional area A feature area in a store in which merchandise on sale is displayed.

promotional center A type of specialty shopping center that contains one or more discount stores plus smaller retail tenants. Also called *discount-oriented center.*

promotional department store A department store that concentrates on apparel and sells a substantial portion of its merchandise on weekly promotion.

promotional signage This signage describes special offers and may be displayed in windows to entice the customer into the store.

promotional stock A retailer's stock of goods offered at an unusually attractive price in order to obtain sales volume; it often represents special purchases from vendors.

promotion from within A staffing policy that involves hiring new employees only for positions at the lowest level in the job hierarchy and then promoting employees for openings at higher levels in the hierarchy.

promotion mix A communication program made up of advertising, sales promotions, Web sites, store atmosphere, publicity, personal selling, and word of mouth.

proprietary EDI systems Data exchange systems that are developed and used primarily by large retailers for the purpose of exchanging data with their vendors.

proprietary store credit card system A system in which credit cards have the store's name on them and the accounts receivable are administered by the retailer; also known as *in-house credit system*.

protected class A group of people, such as women or minorities, that are treated differently or discriminated against, such as when a qualified woman does not receive a promotion given to a less qualified man.

providing assortments A function performed by retailers that enables customers to choose from a selection of brands, designs, sizes, and prices at one location.

psychographics Refers to how people live, how they spend their time and money, what activities they pursue, and their attitudes and opinions about the world they live in.

publicity Communications through significant unpaid presentations about the retailer (usually a news story) in impersonal media.

public relations (PR) A retail communication tool for managing communications and relationships to achieve various objectives, such as building and maintaining a positive image of the retailer, handling or heading off unfavorable stories or events, and maintaining positive relationships with the media.

public warehouse Warehouse that is owned and operated by a third party.

puffing An advertising or personal selling practice in which the seller exaggerates the benefits or quality of a product in very broad terms.

pull supply chain Strategy in which orders for merchandise are generated at the store level on the basis of demand data captured by point-of-sale terminals.

push money (PM) An incentive for retail salespeople provided by a vendor to promote, or push, a particular product; also known as *spiff*.

push supply chain Strategy in which merchandise is allocated to stores on the basis of historical demand, the inventory position at the distribution center, and the stores' needs.

pyramid scheme When the firm and its program are designed to sell merchandise and services to other distributors rather than to end users.

quantity discount The policy of granting lower prices for higher quantities. Also known as *multiple-unit pricing*.

quick response (QR) delivery system System designed to reduce the lead time for receiving merchandise, thereby lowering inventory investment, improving customer service levels, and reducing distribution expenses; also known as a just-in-time inventory management system.

quota Target level used to motivate and evaluate performance.

quota–bonus plan Compensation plan that has a performance goal or objective established to evaluate employee performance, such as sales per hour for salespeople and maintained margin and turnover for buyers.

racetrack layout A type of store layout that provides a major aisle to facilitate customer traffic that has access to the store's multiple entrances. Also known as a *loop layout*.

radio frequency identification (RFID) A technology that allows an object or person to be identified at a distance using radio waves.

rain check When sale merchandise is out of stock, a written promise to customers to sell them that merchandise at the sale price when it arrives.

reach The actual number of customers in the target market exposed to an advertising medium. See *advertising reach*.

reachable A requirement of a viable market segment that the retailer can target promotions and other elements of the retail mix to the consumers in that segment.

rebate Money returned to the buyer in the form of cash based on a portion of the purchase price.

receipt of goods (ROG) dating A dating policy in which the cash discount period starts on the day the merchandise is received.

receiving The process of filling out paperwork to record the receipt of merchandise that arrives at a store or distribution center.

recruitment Activity performed by a retailer to generate job applicants.

reductions Includes three things: markdowns, discounts to employees and customers, and inventory shrinkage due to shoplifting, breakage, or loss.

reference group One or more people whom a person uses as a basis of comparison for his or her beliefs, feelings, and behaviors.

reference price A price point in the consumer's memory for a good or service that can consist of the price last paid, the price most frequently paid, or the average of all prices customers have paid for similar offerings. A benchmark for what consumers believe the "real" price of the merchandise should be.

refusal to deal A legal issue in which either a vendor or a retailer reserves the right to deal or refuse to deal with anyone it chooses.

region In retail location analysis, refers to part of the country, a particular city, or Metropolitan Statistical Area (MSA).

regional mall Shopping malls less than 1 million square feet.

regression analysis A statistical approach for evaluating retail locations based on the assumption that factors that affect the sales of existing stores in a chain will have the same impact on stores located at new sites being considered.

Reilly's law A model used in trade area analysis to define the relative ability of two cities to attract customers from the area between them.

related diversification growth opportunity A diversification opportunity strategy in which the retailer's present offering and market share something in common with the market and format being considered.

relational partnership Long-term business relationship in which the buyer and vendor have a close, trusting interpersonal relationship.

reliability A customer service characteristic that customers use to evaluate service quality; the ability to perform the service dependably and accurately, such as performing the service as promised or contracted or meeting promised delivery dates.

reorder point The stock level at which a new order is placed.

resale price maintenance laws Laws enacted in the early 1900s to curb vertical price fixing. These laws were designed to help protect small retailers by prohibiting retailers from selling below manufacturer's suggested retail price. Also called *fair trade laws*. In 1975, these laws were repealed by the Consumer Goods Pricing Act.

resale price management (RPM) A requirement imposed by a vendor that a retailer cannot sell an item for less than the specific price (the manufacturer's suggested retail price).

resident buying office An organization located in a major buying center that provides services to help retailers buy merchandise.

responsiveness A customer service characteristic that customers use to evaluate service quality; the willingness to help customers and provide prompt service, such as returning calls and e-mails immediately.

restraint of trade Any contract that tends to eliminate or stifle competition, create a monopoly, artificially maintain prices, or otherwise hamper or obstruct the course of trade and commerce as it would be carried on if left to the control of natural forces; also known as unfair trade practices.

retail audit See *situation audit*.

retail brand community A group of customers who are bound together by their loyalty to a retailer and the activities in which the retailer engages.

retail chain A firm that consists of multiple retail units under common ownership and usually has some centralization of decision making in defining and implementing its strategy.

retailer A business that sells products and services to consumers for their personal or family use.

retail exchanges Electronic marketplaces operated by organizations that facilitate the buying and selling of merchandise using the Internet.

retail format The retailers' type of retail mix (nature of merchandise and services offered, pricing policy, advertising and promotion program, approach to store design and visual merchandising, and typical location).

retail format development growth opportunity An investment opportunity strategy in which a retailer offers a new retail format—a format involving a different retail mix—to the same target market.

retail information system System that provides the information needed by retail managers by collecting, organizing, and storing relevant data continuously and directing the information to the appropriate managers.

retailing A set of business activities that adds value to the products and services sold to consumers for their personal or family use.

retailing concept A management orientation that holds that the key task of a retailer is to determine the needs and wants of its target markets and direct the firm toward satisfying those needs and wants more effectively and efficiently than competitors do.

retail inventory method (RIM) An accounting procedure whose objectives are to maintain a perpetual or book inventory in retail dollar amounts and to maintain records that make it possible to determine the cost value of the inventory at any time without taking a physical inventory; also known as *book inventory system* or *perpetual book inventory*.

retailer loyalty

retail market A group of consumers with similar needs (a market segment) and a group of retailers using a similar retail format to satisfy those consumer needs.

retail market segment A group of customers whose needs will be satisfied by the same retail offering because they have similar needs and go through similar buying processes.

retail mix The combination of factors used by a retailer to satisfy customer needs and influence their purchase decisions; includes merchandise and services offered, pricing, advertising and promotions, store design and location, and visual merchandising.

retail-sponsored cooperative An organization owned and operated by small, independent retailers to improve operating efficiency and buying power. Typically, the retail-sponsored cooperative operates a wholesale buying and distribution system and requires its members to concentrate their purchases from the cooperative wholesale operation.

retail strategy A statement that indicates (1) the target market toward which a retailer plans to commit its resources, (2) the nature of the retail offering that the retailer plans to use to satisfy the needs of the target market, and (3) the bases upon which the retailer will attempt to build a sustainable competitive advantage over competitors.

retained earnings The portion of owners' equity that has accumulated over time through profits but has not been paid out in dividends to owners.

return on assets Net profit after taxes divided by total assets.

return on owners' equity Net profit after taxes divided by owners' equity; also known as return on net worth.

reverse auction Auction conducted by retailer buyers. Known as a *reverse auction* because there is one buyer and many potential sellers. In reverse auctions, retail buyers provide a specification for what they want to a group of potential vendors. The competing vendors then bid down the price at which they are willing to sell until the buyer accepts a bid.

reverse logistics The process of moving returned goods back through the supply chain from the customer, to the stores, distribution centers, and vendors.

review time The period of time between reviews of a line for purchase decisions.

revolving credit A consumer credit plan that combines the convenience of a continuous charge account and the privileges of installment payment.

RFM (recency, frequency, monetary) analysis Often used by catalog retailers and direct marketers, a scheme for segmenting customers on the basis of how recently they have made a purchase, how frequently they make purchases, and how much they have bought.

ribbon center See *strip shopping center.*

road condition Includes the age, number of lanes, number of stoplights, congestion, and general state of repair of roads in a trade area.

road pattern A consideration used in measuring the accessibility of a retail location from major arteries, freeways, or roads.

Robinson-Patman Act (1946) The Congressional act that revised Section 2 of the Clayton Act and specifically prohibits certain types of price discrimination.

rounder A round fixture that sits on a pedestal. Smaller than the straight rack, it is designed to hold a maximum amount of merchandise. Also known as a *bulk* or *capacity fixture.*

routine decision making See *habitual decision making.*

rule-of-thumb method A type of approach for setting a promotion budget that uses past sales and communication activity to determine the present communications budget.

safety stock See *buffer stock.*

sale-leaseback The practice in which retailers build new stores and sell them to real estate investors who then lease the buildings back to the retailers on a long-term basis.

sales associate The same as a salesperson. The term is used to recognize the importance and professional nature of the sales function and avoids the negative image sometimes linked with the term "salesperson."

sales consultant See *sales associate.*

sales per cubic foot A measure of space productivity appropriate for stores such as wholesale clubs that use multiple layers of merchandise.

sales per linear foot A measure of space productivity used when most merchandise is displayed on multiple shelves of long gondolas, such as in grocery stores.

sales per square foot A measure of space productivity used by most retailers since rent and land purchases are assessed on a per-square-foot basis.

sales promotions Paid impersonal communication activities that offer extra value and incentives to customers to visit a store or purchase merchandise during a specific period of time.

sales-to-stock ratio The net sales divided by average inventory at cost. It is one component of GMROI and is similar in concept to inventory turnover except the numerator is expressed at retail (net sales) rather than at cost (cost of good sold)

same store sales growth The sales growth in stores that have been open for over one year.

samples A type of sales promotion; a small amount or size of a product given to potential customers as an inducement to purchase.

satisfaction A postconsumption evaluation of the degree to which a store or product meets or exceeds customer expectations.

saturated trade area A trade area that offers customers a good selection of goods and services, while allowing competing retailers to make good profits.

scale economies Cost advantages due to the size of a retailer.

scanning The process in point-of-sale systems wherein the input into the terminal is accomplished by passing a coded ticket over a reader or having a hand-held wand pass over the ticket.

scrambled merchandising An offering of merchandise not typically associated with the store type, such as clothing in a drugstore.

search engines Computer programs that search for and provide a listing of all Internet sites selling a product category or brand with the price of the merchandise offered. Also called *shopping bots.*

seasonal discount Discount offered as an incentive to retailers to place orders for merchandise in advance of the normal buying season.

seasonal merchandise Inventory whose sales fluctuate dramatically according to the time of the year.

secondary data Market research information previously gathered for purposes other than solving the current problem under investigation.

secondary trading area The geographic area of secondary importance in terms of customer sales, generating about 20 percent of a store's sales.

second-degree price discrimination Charging different prices to different people on the basis of the nature of the offering.

security An operating unit within a retail organization that is responsible for protecting merchandise and other assets from pilferage (internal or external). Those working in security may be employees or outside agency people.

security policy Set of rules that apply to activities in the computer and communications resources that belong to an organization.

self-analysis An internally focused examination of a business's strengths and weaknesses.

self-service retailer A retailer that offers minimal customer service.

selling agent An agent (sales organization) that operates on an extended contractual basis; the agent sells all of a specified line of merchandise or the entire output of the principal (manufacturer) and usually has full authority with regard to prices, terms, and other conditions of sale. The agent occasionally renders financial aid to the principal.

selling, general, and administrative expenses (SG&A) Operating expenses, plus the depreciation and amortization of assets.

selling process A set of activities that salespeople undertake to facilitate the customer's buying decision.

selling space The area set aside for displays of merchandise, interactions between sales personnel and customers, demonstrations, and so on.

sell-through analysis A comparison of actual and planned sales to determine whether early markdowns are required or more merchandise is needed to satisfy demand.

seniors The generational cohort of people born before 1946.

senior vice president (SVP) of merchandising An executive who works with buyers and planners to develop and coordinate the management of the retailer's merchandise offering and ensures that it is consistent with the firm's strategy.

senior vice president (SVP) of stores An executive who supervises all activities related to stores, including working with the regional managers, who supervise district managers, who supervise the individual store managers.

service gap The difference between customers' expectations and perceptions of customer service to improve customers' satisfaction with their service.

service level A measure used in inventory management to define the level of support or level of product availability; the number of items sold divided by the number of items demanded. Service level should not be confused with customer service. Compare *customer service*.

services retailer Organization that offers consumers services rather than merchandise. Examples include banks, hospital, health spas, doctors, legal clinics, entertainment firms, and universities.

set

sexual harassment Unwelcome sexual advances, requests for sexual favors, or other verbal or physical conduct with sexual elements.

share of wallet The percentage of total purchases made by a customer in a store.

shelf talkers Signs on the shelf providing information about the merchandise and its price.

Sherman Antitrust Act (1890) An act protecting small businesses and consumers from large corporations by outlawing any person, corporation, or association from engaging in activities that restrain trade or commerce.

shoplifting The act of stealing merchandise from a store by employees, customers, or people posing as customers.

shopping bots See *search engines*.

shopping center A group of retail and other commercial establishments that is planned, developed, owned, and managed as a single property.

shopping goods Products for which consumers will spend time comparing alternatives.

shopping guide Free paper delivered to all residents in a specific area.

shopping mall Enclosed, climate-controlled, lighted shopping centers with retail stores on one or both sides of an enclosed walkway.

shortage See *shrinkage*.

shrinkage An inventory reduction that is caused by shoplifting by employees or customers, by merchandise being misplaced or damaged, or by poor bookkeeping.

situation audit An analysis of the opportunities and threats in the retail environment and the strengths and weaknesses of the retail business relative to its competitors.

skimming A high-pricing strategy for newly introduced categories or products.

SKU See *stockkeeping unit*.

sliding scale lease A part of some leases that stipulates how much the percentage of sales paid as rent will decrease as sales go up.

slotting allowance Fee paid by a vendor for space in a retail store. Also called *slotting fee*.

slotting fee See *slotting allowance*.

socialization The steps taken to transform new employees into effective, committed members of the firm.

social media Media content distributed through social interactions. Three major online facilitators of social media are YouTube, Facebook, and Twitter (see Chapter 15).

social shoppers People who participate in virtual communities to obtain not just information for future use but also an enhanced emotional connection to other participants in the shopping experience.

sole proprietorship An arrangement in which an unincorporated retail firm is owned by one person.

span of control The number of subordinates reporting to a manager.

special event Sales promotion program comprising a number of sales promotion techniques built around a seasonal, cultural, sporting, musical, or other event.

specialization The organizational structure in which employees are typically responsible for only one or two tasks rather than performing all tasks. This approach enables employees to develop expertise and increase productivity.

specialty catalog retailer A nonstore retailer that focuses on specific categories of merchandise, such as fruit (Harry and David), gardening tools (Smith & Hawken), or seeds and plants (Burpee).

specialty department store A store with a department store format that focuses primarily on apparel and soft home goods (such as Neiman Marcus or Saks Fifth Avenue).

specialty product A product which the customer will expend considerable effort to buy.

specialty shopping Shopping experiences when consumers know what they want and will not accept a substitute.

specialty store A type of store concentrating on a limited number of complementary merchandise categories and providing a high level of service.

spending potential index (SPI) Compares the average expenditure in a particular area for a product to the amount spent on that product nationally.

spiff See *push money*.

split shipment A vendor ships part of a shipment to a retailer and back orders the remainder because the entire shipment could not be shipped at the same time.

spot A local television commercial.

spot check Used particularly in receiving operations when goods come in for reshipping to branch stores in packing cartons. Certain cartons are opened in the receiving area of the central distribution point and spot-checked for quality and quantity.

spotting technique See *analog approach*.

staging area Area in which merchandise is accumulated from different parts of the distribution center and prepared for shipment to stores.

standardized service A customer service strategy that is based on establishing a set of rules and procedures for providing high-quality service and ensuring that they get implemented consistently by service providers (see Chapter 18).

standards gap The difference between the retailer's perceptions of customers' expectations and the customer service standards it sets. This factor is one of four factors identified by the Gaps model for improving service quality.

staple merchandise Inventory that has continuous demand by customers over an extended period of time. Also known as *basic merchandise*.

stockholders' equity See *owners' equity*.

stock-keeping unit (SKU) The smallest unit available for keeping inventory control. In soft goods merchandise, an SKU usually means a size, color, and style.

stocklift See *buyback*.

stockout A situation occurring when an SKU that a customer wants is not available.

stock overage The amount by which a retail book inventory figure exceeds a physical count of the ending inventory.

stock-to-sales ratio Specifies the amount of inventory that should be on hand at the beginning of the month to support the sales forecast and maintain the inventory turnover objective. The beginning-of-month (BOM) inventory divided by sales for the month. The average stock-to-sales ratio is 12 divided by planned inventory turnover. This ratio is an integral component of the merchandise budget plan.

store advocates Customers who like a store so much that they actively share their positive experiences with friends and family.

store atmosphere The combination of the store's physical characteristics (such as architecture, layout, signs and displays, colors, lighting, temperature, sounds, and smells), which together create an image in the customers' mind. See *atmospherics*.

store brand See *private-label brand*.

store image The way a store is defined in a shopper's mind. The store image is based on the store's physical characteristics, its retail mix, and a set of psychological attributes.

store maintenance The activities involved with managing the exterior and interior physical facilities associated with the store.

straight commission A form of salesperson's compensation in which the amount paid is based on a percentage of sales made minus merchandise returned.

straight lease A type of lease in which the retailer pays a fixed amount per month over the life of the lease.

straight rack A type of fixture that consists of a long pipe suspended with supports going to the floor or attached to a wall.

straight salary compensation A compensation plan in which salespeople or managers receive a fixed amount of compensation for each hour or week they work.

strategic alliance Collaborative relationship between independent firms. For example, a foreign retailer might enter an international market through direct investment but develop an alliance with a local firm to perform logistical and warehousing activities.

strategic profit model (SPM) A tool used for planning a retailer's financial strategy based on both margin management (net profit margin) and asset management (asset turnover). Using the SPM, a retailer's objective is to achieve a target return on assets.

strategic relationship Long-term relationship in which partners make significant investments to improve both parties' profitability.

strategic retail planning process The steps a retailer goes through to develop a strategic retail plan. It describes how retailers select target market segments, determine the appropriate retail format, and build sustainable competitive advantages.

strengths and weaknesses analysis A critical aspect of the situation audit in which a retailer determines its unique capabilities—its strengths and weaknesses relative to its competition.

strip shopping center A shopping center that usually has parking directly in front of the stores and does not have enclosed walkways linking the stores.

structured training program Training that teaches new employees the basic skills and knowledge they will need to do their job.

style The characteristic or distinctive form, outline, or shape of a product.

subbrand Part of a branding strategy in which a product's brand name is associated with the description of the product, such as Frosted Flakes, where the family brand is Kellogg's.

subculture A distinctive group of people within a culture. Members of a subculture share some customs and norms with the overall society but also have some unique perspectives.

subculture theory A theory of how fashion spreads that suggests that subcultures of mostly young and less affluent consumers, such as motorcycle riders and urban rappers, have started fashions for such things as colorful fabrics, t-shirts, sneakers, jeans, black leather jackets, and surplus military clothing.

supercenter Large store (150,000 to 220,000 square feet) combining a discount store with a supermarket.

superregional mall Shopping center that is similar to a regional center, but because of its larger size, it has more anchors and a deeper selection of merchandise, and it draws from a larger population base.

superstore A large supermarket between 20,000 and 50,000 square feet in size.

supply chain A set of firms that make and deliver a given set of goods and services to the ultimate consumer.

supply chain management The set of approaches and techniques firms employ to efficiently and effectively integrate their suppliers, manufacturers, warehouses, stores, and transportation intermediaries to efficiently have the right quantities at the right locations, and at the right time.

support groups A group of employees with common interests, goals or characteristics, such as minority or female executives, that are put together by a retailer to exchange information and provide emotional and career support for members who traditionally haven't been included in the majority's networks.

survey A method of data collection, using telephone, personal interview, mail, or any combination thereof.

sustainable competitive advantage A distinct competency of a retailer relative to its competitors that can be maintained over a considerable time period.

sweepstakes A promotion in which customers win prizes based on chance.

tangibility A customer service characteristic that customers use to evaluate service quality; it is associated with the appearance of physical facilities, equipment, personnel, and communication materials when a service is being performed.

target market The market segment(s) toward which the retailer plans to focus its resources and retail mix.

tariff A tax placed by a government upon imports. Also known as *duty*.

task performance behaviors Planning, organizing, motivating, evaluating, and coordinating store employees' activities.

teleshopping See *television home shopping*.

television home shopping A retail format in which customers watch a TV program demonstrating merchandise and then place orders for the merchandise by phone.

terms of purchase Conditions in a purchase agreement between a retailer and a vendor that include the type(s) of discounts available and responsibility for transportation costs.

terms of sale Conditions in a sales contract with customers including such issues as charges for alterations, delivery, or gift wrapping or the store's exchange policies.

tertiary trading area The outermost ring of a trade area; includes customers who occasionally shop at the store or shopping center.

theme/festival center A shopping center that typically employs a unifying theme that is carried out by the individual shops in their architectural design and, to an extent, their merchandise.

third-degree price discrimination Charging different prices to different demographic market segments.

third-party logistics company Firm that facilitates the movement of merchandise from manufacturer to retailer but is independently owned.

thrift store A retail format offering used merchandise.

ticketing and marking Procedures for making price labels and placing them on the merchandise.

tie-in An approach used to attract attention to a store's offering by associating the offering with an event.

timing The determination of when and how often an ad should run.

tonnage merchandising A display technique in which large quantities of merchandise are displayed together.

top-down planning One side of the process of developing an overall retail strategy where goals are set at the top of the organization and filter down through the operating levels.

top-of-mind awareness The highest level of brand awareness; arises when consumers mention a brand name first when they are asked about a type of retailer, a merchandise category, or a type of service.

trade area A geographic sector that contains potential customers for a particular retailer or shopping center.

trade discount Reduction in a retailer's suggested retail price granted to wholesalers and retailers; also known as a *functional discount*.

trade dress A product's physical appearance, including its size, shape, color, design, and texture. For instance, the shape and color of a Coca-Cola bottle is its trade dress.

trademark Any mark, work, picture, or design associated with a particular line of merchandise or product.

trade show A temporary concentration of vendors that provides retailers opportunities to place orders and view what is available in the marketplace; also known as a *merchandise show* or *market week*.

traditional distribution center Warehouse in which merchandise is unloaded from trucks and placed on racks or shelves for storage.

traffic appliance Small portable appliance.

traffic flow The balance between a substantial number of cars and not so many that congestion impedes access to the store.

transformational leader A leader who gets people to transcend their personal needs for the sake of realizing the group goal.

travel time contours Used in trade area analysis to define the rings around a particular site based on travel time instead of distances.

trialability The costs and commitment required to initially adopt a fashion.

trickle-down theory A theory of how fashion spreads that suggests that the fashion leaders are consumers with the highest social status—wealthy, well-educated consumers. After they adopt a fashion, the fashion trickles down to consumers in lower social classes. When the fashion is accepted in the lowest social class, it is no longer acceptable to the fashion leaders in the highest social class.

triple-coupon promotion A retail promotion that allows the customer triple the face value of the coupon.

trust A belief that a partner is honest (reliable, stands by its word, sincere, fulfills obligations) and benevolent (concerned about the other party's welfare).

tying contract An agreement between a vendor and a retailer requiring the retailer to take a product it does not necessarily desire (the tied product) to ensure that it can buy a product it does desire (the tying product).

umbrella brand see *family brand (Chapter 13)*.

understored trade area An area that has too few stores selling a specific good or service to satisfy the needs of the population.

unit pricing The practice of expressing price in terms of both the total price of an item and the price per unit of measure.

Universal Product Code (UPC) The black-and-white bar code found on most merchandise; used to collect sales information at the point of sale using computer terminals that read the code. This information is transmitted computer to computer to buyers, distribution centers, and then to vendors, who in turn quickly ship replenishment merchandise.

unrelated diversification growth opportunity Diversification in which there is no commonality between the present business and the new business.

UPC See *Universal Product Code*.

URL (uniform resource locator) The standard for a page on the World Wide Web (e.g., www.nrf.org).

utilitarian benefit A motivation for shopping in which consumers accomplish a specific task, such as buying a suit for a job interview.

utilitarian needs Needs motivating consumers to go shopping to accomplish a specific task.

value Relationship of what a customer gets (goods/services) to what he or she has to pay for it.

values of lifestyle survey (VALS2) A tool used to categorize customers into eight lifestyle segments. Based on responses to surveys conducted by SRI Consulting Business Intelligence.

variable costs Costs that vary with the level of sales and can be applied directly to the decision in question.

variable pricing Charging different prices in different stores, markets, or zones.

variety The number of different merchandise categories within a store or department.

vending machine retailing A nonstore format in which merchandise or services are stored in a machine and dispensed to customers when they deposit cash or use a credit card.

vendor Any firm from which a retailer obtains merchandise.

vendor-managed inventory (VMI) An approach for improving supply chain efficiency in which the vendor is responsible for maintaining the retailer's inventory levels in each of its stores.

vertical blocking

vertical integration An example of diversification by retailers involving investments by retailers in wholesaling or manufacturing merchandise.

vertical merchandising A method whereby merchandise is organized to follow the eye's natural up-and-down movement.

vertical price fixing Agreements to fix prices between parties at different levels of the same marketing channel (for example, retailers and their vendors).

virtual community A network of people who seek information, products, and services and communicate with one another about specific issues.

virtual mall A group of retailers and service providers that can be accessed over the Internet at one location.

visibility Customers' ability to see the store and enter the parking lot safely.

visual communications The act of providing information to customers through graphics, signs, and theatrical effects—both in the store and in windows—to help boost sales by providing information on products and suggesting items or special purchases.

visual merchandising The presentation of a store and its merchandise in ways that will attract the attention of potential customers.

want book Information collected by retail salespeople to record out-of-stock or requested merchandise.

warehouse club A retailer that offers a limited assortment of food and general merchandise with little service and low prices to ultimate consumers and small businesses.

weeks of supply An inventory management method most similar to the stock-to-sales method. The difference is that everything is expressed in weeks rather than months.

wheel of retailing A cyclical theory of retail evolution whose premise is that retailing institutions evolve from low-price/service to higher-price/service operations.

wholesale market A concentration of vendors within a specific geographic location, perhaps even under one roof or over the Internet.

wholesaler A merchant establishment operated by a concern that is primarily engaged in buying, taking title to, usually storing, and physically handling goods in large quantities, and reselling the goods (usually in smaller quantities) to retailers or industrial or business users.

wholesale-sponsored voluntary cooperative group An organization operated by a wholesaler offering a merchandising program to small, independent retailers on a voluntary basis.

word of mouth Communications among people about a retailer.

yield management The practice of adjusting prices up or down in response to demand to control sales generated.

zone pricing Charging different prices for the same merchandise in different geographic locations to be competitive in local markets.

zoning The regulation of the construction and use of buildings in certain areas of a municipality.

Chapter 1

1. Target Corporate Responsibility Report 2007 (accessed January 5, 2010).

2. Luciano Barin Cruz and Eugênio Avila Pedrozo, "Corporate Social Responsibility and Green Management: Relation between Headquarters and Subsidiary in Multinational Corporations," *Management Decision* 47, no. 7 (2009), pp. 1174–1199.

3. Claire Adler, "Clean Campaign Gathers Traction," *Financial Times* (UK), November 8, 2008, p. 14.

4. Sarah Butler, "Would You Like a Bag with That, Madam?" *London Times*, October 7, 2006.

5. *Retail Industry Indicators* (Washington, DC: National Retail Foundation, August 2008).

6. *Retail Industry Indicators* (Washington, DC: National Retail Foundation, August 2008).

7. *2009 Global Powers in Retailing* (New York: Deloitte Touche Tohmatsu, January 2010).

8. Ibid.

9. Ibid.

10. Martin Baily and Diana Farrell, "How Europe's Regulations Hold It Back," *Financial Times* (UK): October 18, 2005, p. 13.

11. Marcus Walker, "Longer Store Hours in Germany; Scrapping of Restrictions Is Designed to Boost a Laggard Economy," *Wall Street Journal*, January 8, 2007, p. A5.

12. *2009 NRF Retail Compensation and Benefits* (Washington, DC: National Retail Federation, 2009).

13. Tom Robinson, *Jeff Bezos: Amazon.com Architect (Publishing Pioneers)* (Edina, MN: Abdo Publishing, 2009).

14. "Jeff Bezos: The Wizard of Web Retailing," *BusinessWeek*, December 2004, p. 13.

15. Yvon Dufour and Lise Lamothe, "Revisiting a Classic Case Study; Anita Roddick and the Body Shop International," *Journal of Strategy and Management* 2, no. 1 (2009), pp. 97–109.

16. http://www.ikea.com/ms/en_GB/about_ikea/the_ikea_way/history/index.html (accessed January 23, 2010).

17. "The World's Billionaires 2007," *Forbes*, March 8, 2003.

18. "Rating the Stores," *Consumer Reports*, November 1994, p. 714

19. Dan Scheraga, "Penney's Net Advantage," *Chain Store Age*, September 2000, pp. 114–118

20. http://www.wholefoodsmarket.com/company (accessed January 25, 2010); Nick Paumgarten, "Food Fighter," *New Yorker*, January 14, 2010, pp. 36–47; and Angela Cortez, "Whole Foods Holds On to Its Roots," *Natural Foods Merchandise*, October 2009, p. 46.

21. Marcus Leroux, "Recession Fails to Dent Shoppers' Ethical Beliefs," *The Times*, October 13, 2009.

Chapter 2

1. http://factfinder.census.gov/servlet/IBQTable?_bm=y&-geo_id=01000US&-filter=&-ds_name=NS0700A2&-dataitem=GEO_ID$|NAICS2007|NAICS2007$|ESTAB|RCPTOT&-NAICS2007=44-45 (accessed October 11, 2009).

2. http://www.economicindicators.gov/.

3. *Industry Outlook: Food Channel* (Columbus, OH: Retail Forward, April 2007).

4. http://supermarketnews.com/profiles/top25-2009/top-25/ (accessed October 12, 2009).

5. *Industry Outlook: Food Channel* (Columbus, OH: Retail Forward, July 2008), p. 23.

6. http://www.fmi.org/glossary/?search=Yes&letter=C.

7. http://www.fmi.org/docs/facts_figs/grocerydept.pdf.

8. http://www.tmcnet.com/usubmit/2007/10/13/3012485.htm.

9. "Roaring 20's Ends in Depression," *Chain Store Age Executive*, June 1994, p. 49.

10. http://www.tmcnet.com/usubmit/2007/10/13/3012485.htm.

11. "More Are Eating Out at the Grocery Store," Associated Press, September 9, 2008.

12. Julie Schmit, "Organic Food Sales Feel the Bite from Sluggish Economy," *USA Today*, August 19, 2008.

13. http://www.infoplease.com/spot/hhmcensus1.html.

14. www.northgatemarkets.com; http://www.northgatemarkets.com/news/LA_VOZ_NORTHGATE.pdf.

15. Jenalia Moreno, "Walmart Gives Its Supermercado Concept a Tryout," *Houston Chronicle*, April 30, 2009.

16. Cecilie Rohwedder and David Kesmodel, "ALDI Looks to U.S. for Growth," *Wall Street Journal*, January 13, 2009.

17. *Industry Outlook: Mass Channel* (Columbus, OH: Retail Forward, June 2009).

18. *Industry Outlook: Convenience Stores* (Columbus, OH: Retail Forward, March 2009).

19. http://www.gianteagle.com/Article.aspx?cntid=199069.

20. *Industry Outlook: Convenience Stores.*

21. Charlotte Ferrell Smith, "Hurricane Sheetz Readies for Opening," *Charlestown Daily Mail*, September 4, 2009.

22. http://www.7-eleven.com/AboutUs/FunFacts/tabid/77/Default.aspx; http://www1.mcdonalds.com/annualreport/index.html.

23. *Industry Outlook: Department Stores* (Columbus, OH: Retail Forward, June 2009).

24. David Moin, "Department Stores: The Issues," *WWD Infotracs*, June 1997, pp. 4–6.

25. Maria Halkias, "Shoppers Departing Department Stores—and May Not Be Back," *Dallas Morning News*, February 19, 2009.

26. Ibid.; Sarah Mahoney, "Department-Store Decline: It's *Not* the Economy," *AM Marketing Daily*, January 2, 2009.

27. http://www.walletpop.com/blog/2009/05/14/love-amidst-the-layoffs-macys-parades-its-new-fashion-label/.

28. http://industry.bnet.com/retail/10001935/kohls-pursues-exclusive-route-to-better-results/.

29. Halkias, "Shoppers Departing Department Stores."

30. http://industry.bnet.com/retail/10001935/kohls-pursues-exclusive-route-to-better-results/; http://www.wikinvest.com/stock/J.C._Penney_(JCP).

31. http://walmartstores.com/AboutUs/7606.aspx; *Industry Outlook: Mass Channel.*

32. *Industry Outlook: Mass Channel.*

33. http://www.hbc.com/hbc/about/abouthbtc/.

34. http://www.thestockmasters.com/node/1714.

35. http://www.scribd.com/doc/19488507/Supply-Chain-Practices-at-Zara.

36. *Industry Outlook: Drug Channel* (Columbus, OH: Retail Forward, December 2008).

37. Ibid.; Jennifer Halterman, *Industry Outlook: Drug Channel*, (Columbus OH: Retail Forward, November 2006), p. 3; "TNS Retail Forward ShopperScrape," June 2006, August 2007, and August 2008.

38. Joseph Pereira and Ann Zimmerman, "Newcomers Challenge Office-Supply Stalwarts," *Wall Street Journal*, April 29, 2009.

39. Ibid.

40. Susan Reda, "Dollar General Grows by Helping Shoppers Stretch Food Budgets," *Stores*, July 2008.

41. *Industry Outlook: Dollar Stores* (Columbus, OH: Retail Forward, October 2008).

42. Stephanie Rosenbloom, "Don't Ask. You Can Afford It," *New York Times*, May 2, 2009; http://money.cnn.com/magazines/fortune/fortune500/2007/snapshots/497.html.

43. Ibid.

44. Jean E. Palmieri, "Loehmann's in High Gear; Legendary Off-Pricer Plans to Add 10 Stores This Year as Men's Catalogs Become Richer and More Upscale," *DNR*, February 5, 2007, p. 44.

45. http://www.wikinvest.com/industry/Off-price_Retail.

46. "Back to the Future," *New York Times Magazine*, April 6, 1997, pp. 48–49.

47. Pallavi Gogoi, "Bargain Hunting: Luxury Retailers Find an Outlet," *BusinessWeek*, September 24, 2008.

48. Vanessa O'Connell, "Luxury Retailers Pin Hopes on Outlets," *Wall Street Journal*, April 30, 2008, p. B1.

49. http://www.zoots.com (accessed November 2, 2009).

50. Dhruv Grewal, Gopalkrishnan R. Iyer, Jerry Gotlieb, and Michael Levy, "Developing a Deeper Understanding of Post-Purchase Perceived Risk and Behavioral Intentions in a Service Setting," *Journal of the Academy of Marketing Science* 35 (2007), pp. 250–258; Margy P. Conchar, George M. Zinkhan, Cara Peters, and Sergio Olavarrieta, "An Integrated Framework for the Conceptualization of Consumers' Perceived-Risk Processing," *Journal of the Academy of Marketing Science*, Winter 2004, pp. 418–436; Dhruv Grewal, Jerry Gotlieb, and Howard Marmorstein, "The Moderating Effects of Message Framing and Source Credibility on the Price-Perceived Risk Relationship," *Journal of Consumer Research* 21 (June 1994), pp. 145–153.

51. Karen Robinson-Jacobs, "Labor-Starved Restaurant Industry Turns to Automation for Help," *Dallas Morning News*, August 30, 2006.

52. http://www.aaronsfranchise.com/Default.aspx?tabid=170.

Chapter 3

1. Brian Kilcourse and Steve Rowen, *Finding the Integrated Multi-Channel Retailer* (Miami: Retail Systems Research, 2008).

2. Stacy Gilliam, "Sweet Delivery," *Black Enterprise*, November 2006.

3. *Forrester Research Online Retail Forecast, 12/09 (US)* (Cambridge, MA.: Forrester Research, February 4, 2010).

4. Kelly Tackett, "Participation in Multi-Channel Shopping Activities Stagnates," Retail Forward (Columbus, OH), March 2008.

5. http://www.catalogs.com/info/b2b/catalog-merchandise.htmll, data from U.S. Census Bureau (accessed October 19, 2009).

6. Jeffrey Ball, "In Digital Era, Marketers Still Prefer a Paper Trail," *Wall Street Journal*, October 16, 2009.

7. Ibid.

8. Ibid.

9. http://dsa.org/pubs/numbers/.

10. http://dsa.org/pubs/numbers/.

11. Alex Tarquinio, "Selling Beauty on a Global Scale, *New York Times*, November 1, 2008.

12. Personal communication, Mindy Grossman, CEO of HSN.

13. http://www.qvc.com/qic/qvcapp.aspx/app.html/params.file.%7Ccp%7Cmainhqfact,html/left.html.file.%7Cnav%7Cnavhqabout,html/walk.html.%7Cnav%7Cnavhqwel,html.

14. http://www.hsn.com/hsn-shop-by-remote_at-3803_xa.aspx.

15. http://inventors.about.com/library/inventors/blvendingmachine.htm (accessed November 2, 2009).

16. David Lieberman, "DVD Kiosks Like Redbox Have Rivals Seeing Red," *USA Today*, August, 13, 2009.

17. "A Narrative History of Sears." www.searsarchives.com/history (accessed July 10, 2010).

18. Dirk Perrefort and Susan Silvers, "Inside the Mall, a Class of Cultures," *McClatchy-Tribune Business News*, January 7, 2010.

19. Susan Kuchinskas, "A Decade of E-Commerce," *Internetnews.com*, October 18, 2004.

20. Stephen Baker, "The Web Knows What You Want," *BusinessWeek Online*, July 16, 2009.

21. Alan Wolf, "Sears Deploys Live iPhone 'Personal Shopper' App," *TWICE*, January 7, 2010, p. 65.

22. Riccardo Mangiaracina and Alessandro Perego, "Payment Systems in the B2C eCommerce: Are They a Barrier for the Online Customer?" *Journal of Internet Banking and Commerce* 14 (December 2009), pp. 1–17.

23. James W. Peltier, George R. Milne, and Joseph E. Phelps, "Information Privacy Research: Framework for Integrating Multiple Publics, Information Channels, and Responses," *Journal of Interactive Marketing*, May 2009, pp. 191–205; Yue Payn, and George M. Zinkhan, "Exploring the Impact of Online Privacy Disclosures on Consumer Trust," *Journal of Retailing* 82, no. 4 (2006), pp. 331–338; Nam, Changi, Chanhoo Song, Euehun Lee, and Chan Ik Park, "Consumers' Privacy Concerns and Willingness to Provide Marketing-Related Personal Information Online," *Advances in Consumer Research*, vol. 33 (2006), pp. 213–217.

24. Stephanie Clifford, "Many See Privacy on Web as Big Issue, Survey Says," *New York Times*, March 16, 2009.

25. Tomas Falk, Jeroen Schepers, Maik Hammerschmidt, and Hans Bauer, "Identifying Cross-Channel Dissynergies for Multichannel Service Providers," *Journal of Service Research* 10, no. 2 (2007), pp. 143–155; David W. Wallace, Joan L. Giese, and Jean L. Johnson, "Customer Retailer Loyalty in the Context of Multiple Channel Strategies," *Journal of Retailing* 80, no. 4 (2004), pp. 249–263.

26. Maria Halkias, "Catalogs Make Paper Trails to Retailers," *Dallas Morning News*, October 9, 2006.

27. Scott A. Neslin, Dhruv Grewal, Robert Leghorn, Venkatesh Shankar, Marije L. Teerling, Jacquelyn S. Thomas, and Peter C. Verhoef, "Challenges and Opportunities in Multichannel Customer Management," *Journal of Service Research* 9, no. 2 (2006), pp. 95–112.

28. Randolph E. Bucklin and Catarina Sismeiro, "Click Here for Internet Insight: Advances in Clickstream Data Analysis in Marketing," *Journal of Interactive Marketing*, February 2009, pp. 35–48.

29. Nanda Kumar and Ranran Ruan, "On Manufacturers Complementing the Traditional Retail Channel with a Direct Online Channel," *Quantitative Marketing & Economics* 4, no. 3 (2006), pp. 289–323.

30. Jie Zhang, Paul Farris, John Irvin, Tarun Kushwaha, Thomas Steenburgh, and Barton Weitz, "Crafting Integrated Multichannel Retailing Strategies," *Journal of Interactive Marketing*, Spring, 2010.

31. "Study: Most Retailers Failing at Channel Integration," *retailcustomerexperience.com*, February 15, 2010.

32. "Retailers Don't Fully Coordinate Marketing across Channels, Study Says," *Internet Retailer*, September 21, 2006.

33. Karl Greenberg, "People Use Mobile Web Nearly 3 Hours/ Day," *Marketing Daily*, February 14, 2010.

34. James Bickers, "Mobile Monday: Macy's iShop," *retailcustomerexperience.com* (accessed February 15, 2010).

35. Aaron Baar, "Firms Point to E-tail, Mobile Internet 'Collision,'" *Marketing Daily*, February 15, 2010.

36. Zhang et al., "Crafting Integrated Multichannel Retailing Strategies"; Avery, Jill, Thomas J. Steenburgh, John Deighton, and Mary Caravella (2009), "Adding Bricks to Clicks: The Contingencies Driving Cannibalization and Complementarity in Multichannel Retailing," SSRN working paper, available at http:\\ssrn.com\abstract=961567.

37. "Organizing for Cross-Channel Retailing," white paper, J. C. Williams Group, Toronto, January 2008; "Customer Centricity Drives Retail's Multichannel Imperative," white paper, IBM Global Business Services, Armonk, NY, 2008.

38. "Customer Centricity Drives Retail's Multichannel Imperative."

39. Ibid.

40. Van Baal, Sebastian, and Christian Dach, "Free Riding and Customer Retention across Retailers' Channels," *Journal of Interactive Marketing*, 19 (Spring 2005), pp. 75–85.

Chapter 4

1. For a detailed discussion of customer behavior, see J. Paul Peter and Jerry C. Olson, *Consumer Behavior and Marketing Strategy*, 9th ed. (New York: McGraw-Hill, 2009); Michael R. Solomon, *Consumer Behavior: Buying, Having, and Being*, 8th ed. (Upper Saddle River, NJ: Prentice Hall, 2009).

2. Jason M. Carpenter and Marguerite Moore, "Utilitarian and Hedonic Shopping Value in the US Discount Sector," *Journal of Retailing and Consumer Services* 16 (January 2009), pp. 68–74; Ugur Yavas and Emin Babakus, "Modeling Patronage Behavior: A Tri-partite Conceptualization," *Journal of Consumer Marketing* 26, no. 7 (2009), pp. 516–526; Liz C. Wang, Julie Baker, Judy A. Wagner, and Kirk Wakefield "Can a Retail Website Be Social?" *Journal of Marketing* 71, no. 3 (2007), pp. 143–157; Gianluigi Guido, Mauro Capestro, and Alessandro M. Peluso, "Experimental Analysis of Consumer Stimulation and Motivational States in Shopping Experiences," *International Journal of Market Research* 49, no. 3 (2007), pp. 365–386.

3. Melody Vargas, "Frequent Leisure Time Shoppers Spend More per Trip," *About Retailing*, July 11, 2006.

4. Sylvie Morin, Laurette Dube, and Jean-Charles Chebat, "The Role of Pleasant Music in Servicescapes: A Test of the Dual Model of Environmental Perception," *Journal of Retailing* 83, no. 1 (2007), pp. 115–130; Nicole Bailey and Charles S. Areni, "When a Few Minutes Sound Like a Lifetime: Does Atmospheric Music Expand or Contract Perceived Time?" *Journal of Retailing* 82, no. 3 (2006), pp. 189–202; Michael A. Jones and Kristy E. Reynolds,

"The Role of Retailer Interest on Shopping Behavior," *Journal of Retailing* 82, no. 2 (2006), pp. 115–126.

5. Sangwoo Seo and Yuri Lee, "Shopping Values of Clothing Retailers Perceived by Consumers of Different Social Classes," *Journal of Retailing and Consumer Services*, 15 (November 2008), pp. 491–499; Kåre Skallerud, Tor Korneliussen, and Svein Ottar Olsen, "An Examination of Consumers' Cross-Shopping Behaviour," *Journal of Retailing and Consumer Services* 16 (May 2009), pp. 181–189.

6. Jihyun Kim and Hyun-Hwa Lee, "Consumer Product Search and Purchase Behaviour Using Various Retail Channels: The Role of Perceived Retail Usefulness," *International Journal of Consumer Studies* 32 (May 2008), pp. 619–627; Brian T. Ratchford, Debabrata Talukdar, and Myung-Soo Lee, "The Impact of the Internet on Consumers' Use of Information Sources for Automobiles: A Re-inquiry," *Journal of Consumer Research* 34, no. 1 (2007), pp. 111–119; Glenn J. Browne, Mitzi G. Pitts, and James C. Wetherbe, "Cognitive Shopping Rules for Terminating Information Search in Online Tasks," *MIS Quarterly* 31, no. 1 (2007), pp. 89–104.

7. Katie Weisman, "Fifth Avenue Outdoes Itself for the Holidays," *New York Times*, November 20, 2008.

8. Julie Nicholson, "Retail Shopping Communities Attract Shoppers, Influence Purchasing, and Retain Consumers," *ProQuest: PR Newswire*, September 9, 2009.

9. Thomas Pack, "Kicking the Virtual Tires: Car Research on the Web," *Information Today*, January 2009, p. 44.

10. Sridhar Moorthy, Brian T. Ratchford, and Debabrata Talukdar, "Consumer Information Search Revisited: Theory and Empirical Analysis," *Journal of Consumer Research* 23 (March 1997), pp. 263–287; Tilottama G. Chowdhury, S. Ratneshwar, and Praggyan Mohanty, "The Time-Harried Shopper: Exploring the Differences between Maximizers and Satisficers," *Marketing Letters* 20, no. 2, pp. 155–167; Peng Huang, Nicholas H. Lurie, and Sabyasachi Mitra, "Searching for Experience on the Web: An Empirical Examination of Consumer Behavior for Search and Experience Goods," *Journal of Marketing* 73, no. 2 (2009), pp. 55–69; and Anna Lund Jepsen, "Factors Affecting Consumer Use of the Internet for Information Search," *Journal of Interactive Marketing* 21, no. 3 (2008), pp. 21–34.

11. "Nielsen Names Sites with Highest Conversion Rates," *Nielsenwire*, January 7, 2009.

12. Spencer E. Ante, "How Amazon Is Turning Opinions into Gold," *BusinessWeek*, October 26, 2009, p. 47; Tim Sander, "Business Venues Find User Reviews Have a Growing Impact on Guests," *New Media Age*, October 22, 2009, p. 9

13. Teresa Lindeman, "Retailers Try to Convince Customers to Stick Around," *Miami Herald*, April 26, 2007.

14. Geoffrey A. Fowler and Yukari Iwatani Kane, "Price Check: Finding Deals with a Phone," *Wall Street Journal*, December 16, 2009; Philipp Broeckelmann and Andrea Groeppel-Klein, "Usage of Mobile Price Comparison Sites at the Point of Sale and Its Influence on Consumers' Shopping Behaviour," *International Review of Retail, Distribution and Consumer Research* 18 (May 2008), pp. 149–158.

15. John Lynch and Dan Ariely, "Wine Online: Search Costs Affect Competition on Price, Quality, and Distribution," *Marketing Science* 19 (Winter 2008), pp. 83–104.

16. Brian T. Ratchford, "Consumer Search and Pricing," in *Handbook of Pricing Research in Marketing*, ed. Vithala R. Rao (North Hampton, MA: Edward Elgar, 2009), pp. 93–108.

17. Richard J. Lutz and James R. Bettman, "Multi-Attribute Models in Marketing: A Bicentennial Review," *in Consumer and Industrial Buying Behavior*, eds. A.G. Woodside, J.N. Sheth, and P.D. Bennett (New York: Elsevier-North Holland, 1977), pp. 13–50; William L. Wilkie and Edgar D. Pessimier, "Issues in Marketing's Use of Multi-Attribute Attitude Models," *Journal of Marketing Research*, November 1973, pp. 428–441.

18. Jayne O'Donnell, "Electronics Retailers Find Service Sells," *USA Today*, July 23, 2008.

19. Donna Myers, "Cater to Women Shoppers, Ask What They Want," *Casual Living*, August 2009.

20. Peter N. Child, Suzanne Heywood, and Michael Kliger, "Do Retail Brands Travel?" *McKinsey Quarterly*, no. 1 (2002), pp. 25–34.

21. Sandro Castaldo, Francesco Perrini, Nicola Misani, and Antonio Tencati, "The Missing Link between Corporate Social Responsibility and Consumer Trust: The Case of Fair Trade Products," *Journal of Business Ethics* 84 (January 2009), pp. 1–15; Iain A. Davies, Bob Doherty, and Simon Knox, "The Rise and Stall of a Fair Trade Pioneer: The Cafédirect Story," *Journal of Business Ethics* 92 (March 2010), pp. 127–147; Shih-Mei Chen and Patricia Huddleston, "A Comparison of Four Strategies to Promote Fair Trade Products," *International Journal of Retail & Distribution Management* 37, no. 4 (2009), pp. 336–345.

22. Ruby Roy Dholakia and Miao Zhao, "Retail Web Site Interactivity: How Does It Influence Customer Satisfaction and Behavioral Intentions?" *International Journal of Retail & Distribution Management* 37 (2009), pp. 821–838.

23. Claire Cain Miller, "Closing the Deal at the Virtual Checkout Counter," *New York Times*, October 12, 2009.

24. Jason M. Carpenter, "Consumer Shopping Value, Satisfaction and Loyalty in Discount Retailing," *Journal of Retailing and Consumer Services* 15 (September 2008), pp. 358–363; Kerrie Bridsona, Jody Evans, and Melissa Hickmanc, "Assessing the Relationship between Loyalty Program Attributes, Store Satisfaction and Store Loyalty," *Journal of Retailing and Consumer Services* 15 (September 2008), pp. 364–374; Dhruv Grewal, Ram Krishnan, and Joan Lindsey-Mullikin, "Building Store Loyalty through Service Strategies," *Journal of Relationship Marketing* 7, no. 4 (2008), pp. 341–358.

25. "Beware of Dissatisfied Consumers: They Like to Blab," *Knowledge@Wharton*, March 8, 2006.

26. Piyush Sharma, Bharadhwaj Sivakumaran, and Roger Marshall, "Impulse Buying and Variety Seeking: A Trait-Correlates Perspective," *Journal of Business Research* 63 (March 2010), pp. 276–283; David H. Silvera, Anne M. Lavack, and Fredric Kropp, "Impulse Buying: The Role of Affect, Social Influence, and Subjective Wellbeing," *Journal of Consumer Marketing* 25, no. 1 (2008), pp. 23–33; Ronan De Kervenoael, D. Selcen, O. Aykac, and Mark Palmer, "Online Social Capital: Understanding E-Impulse Buying in Practice," *Journal of Retailing and Consumer Services* 16 (July 2009), pp. 320–328.

27. Moniek Buijzen and Patti M Valkenburg, "Human Observing Purchase-Related Parent-Child Communication in Retail Environments: A Developmental and Socialization Perspective," *Communication Research* 34 (January 2008), pp. 50–69; Julie Tinson, Clive Nancarrow, and Ian Brace, "Purchase Decision Making and the Increasing Significance of Family Types," *Journal of Consumer Marketing* 25, no. 1 (2008), pp. 45–56; R. K. Srivastava and Beverlee B. Anderson, "Gender Roles and Family Decision Making: A Study

of Indian Automobile Purchases," *International Journal of Services, Economics and Management* 2, no. 2 (2010), pp. 109–120.

28. Susan Reda, "What Are Shoppers Saying about You?" *Stores*, February 2007.

29. Sharon Jayson, "It's Cooler than Ever to Be a Tween," *USA Today*, September 2, 2009.

30. David Ackerman and Gerald Tellis, "Can Culture Affect Prices? A Cross-Cultural Study of Shopping and Retail Prices," *Journal of Retailing* 77 (Spring 2001), pp. 57–63; Aaron Ahuvia and Nancy Wong, "The Effect of Cultural Orientation in Luxury Consumption," in *Advances in Consumer Research*, Vol. 25, eds. Eric J. Arnould and Linda M. Scott (Ann Arbor, MI: Association for Consumer Research, 1998), pp. 29–32.

31. James Areddy, "Chinese Consumers Overwhelm Retailers with Team Tactics," *Wall Street Journal*, February 28, 2006, p. A1.

32. Cyndee Miller, "Top Marketers Take a Bolder Approach in Targeting Gays," *Marketing News*, July 4, 1994, pp. 1–2.

33. Yoo-Kyoung Seock and Lauren Bailey, "Fashion Promotions in the Hispanic Market: Hispanic Consumers' Use of Information Sources in Apparel Shopping," *International Journal of Retail & Distribution Management* 37, no. 2 (2009), pp. 161–181; Yoo-Kyoung Seock, "Influence of Retail Store Environmental Cues on Consumer Patronage Behavior across Different Retail Store Formats: An Empirical Analysis of US Hispanic Consumers," *Journal of Retailing and Consumer Services* 16 (September 2009), pp. 329–339.

34. Ann Zimmerman, "To Boost Sales, Wal-Mart Drops One-Size-Fits-All Approach," *Wall Street Journal*, September 7, 2006, p. A1.

35. Óscar González-Benito, César A. Bustos-Reyes, and Pablo A. Muñoz-Gallego, "Isolating the Geodemographic Characterisation of Retail Format Choice from the Effects of Spatial Convenience," *Marketing Letters* 18, no. 1–2 (2007), pp. 45–59; Richard Harris, Peter Sleight, and Richard Webber, *Geodemographics, GIS and Neighbourhood Targeting* (Hoboken, NJ: Wiley, 2005); Michael J. Weiss, *The Clustered World* (Boston: Little, Brown, 2000).

36. ESRI, "Tapestry Segmentation Reference Guide" and "Tapestry Segmentation: The Fabric of America's Neighborhood," www.esri.com (both accessed March 31, 2010).

37. Suzanne Kapner, "How to Beat Wal-Mart," *Fortune*, December 7, 2009, p. 98; Deena M. Amato-McCoy, "A Point of Differentiation," *Chain Store Age*, January 2007, pp. 26–27; Jeff Zabin, "The Importance of Being Analytical," *Brandweek*, July 24, 2006, p. 21; Mindy Fetterman, "Best Buy Gets in Touch with its Feminine Side," *USA Today*, December 20, 2006.

38. Patrik Asper, *Orderly Fashion* (Princeton, NJ: Princeton University Press, 2010); Grace I. Kunz, *Merchandising: Theory, Principles, and Practice* (New York: Fairchild, 2010); Roman Espejo, *The Fashion Industry* (Farmington Hills, MI: Greenhaven Press, 2010); Jennifer Craik, *Fashion: The Key Concepts* (Gordonsville, VA: Berg, 2009).

39. Adam Sage, "Happy Birthday: The 'Shocking and Immoral' Bikini Hits 60," *The Times*, April 16, 2006.

40. Vanessa O'Connell, "How Fashion Makes Its Way from the Runway to the Rack," *Wall Street Journal*, February 8, 2007, p. D1. For additional information about fashion and the fashion industry, see Giannino Malossi, ed., *The Style Engine: Spectacle, Identity, Design, and Business: How the Fashion Industry Uses Style to Create Wealth* (New York: Monacelli Press, 1998).

Chapter 5

1. See David Aaker, *Strategic Market Management*, 6th ed. (New York: Wiley, 2009).

2. Roger Evered, "So What Is Strategy?" *Long Range Planning* 16 (Fall 1983), p. 120.

3. Michael E. Porter and Mark R. Kramer, "Strategy and Society: The Link between Competitive Advantage and Corporate Social Responsibility," *Harvard Business Review*, December 2006; Michael Porter, *On Competition* (Boston: Harvard Business School Press, 1998); Michael Porter, "What is Strategy?" *Harvard Business Review*, November–December 1996, pp. 61–78.

4. Mike Albo, "O Chant after Them: Super . . . ," *Wall Street Journal*, October 15, 2009; Bryant Urstadt, "Lust for Lulu: How the Yoga Nr and Lululemon Turned Fitness into a Spectator Sport," *New York Times*, July 26, 2009; and Danielle Sacks, "Lululemon's Cult of Selling," *Fast Company*, March 18, 2009.

5. www.magazineluiza.com.br (accessed April 4, 2010); Guillermo D'Andrea, "Latin American Retail: Where Modernity Blends with Tradition," *International Review Of Retail, Distribution and Consumer Research* 20 (February 2010), pp. 85–101; Rob Katz, "How Magazine Luiza Courts the Poor," *HBS Working Knowledge*, April 18, 2007.

6. www.curves.com (accessed March 20, 2010); Laura O'Toole, "McDonald's at the Gym? A Tale of Two Curves®," *Qualitative Sociology* 32 (March 2009), pp. 75–91; Shelley Widhalm, "Women Weigh Need for Exercise; More Are Drawn to Benefits of Regular Workouts at the Gym," *Washington Times*, June 19, 2007, p. B01.

7. www.savealot.com (accessed March 25, 2010).

8. Anthony Boardman and Aidan Vining, "Defining Your Business Using Product-Customer Matrices," *Long Range Planning* 29 (February 1996), pp. 38–48.

9. Morten Hansen and Nitin Nohria, "How to Build Collaborative Advantage," *MIT Sloan Management Review* 46 (Fall 2004), pp. 22–28; Jeffrey Dyer and Harbir Singh, "The Relational View: Cooperative Strategy and Sources of Interorganizational Competitive Advantage," *Academy of Management Review* 23 (October 1998), pp. 660–680; Cynthia Montgomery, "Creating Corporate Advantage," *Harvard Business Review*, May–June 1998, pp. 71–80; Shelby Hunt and Robert Morgan, "The Comparative Advantage Theory of Competition," *Journal of Marketing* 59 (April 1995), pp. 1–15; Kathleen Conner and C. K. Prahalad, "A Resource-Based Theory of the Firm: Knowledge versus Opportunism," *Organizational Science* 7 (September–October 1996), pp. 477–501.

10. Jeffrey H. Dyer and Harbir Singh, "The Relational View: Cooperative Strategy and Sources of Interorganizational Competitive Advantage," *Academy of Management Review* 23 (October 1998), pp. 660–679; Robert M. Morgan and Shelby Hunt, "Relationship-Based Competitive Advantage: The Role of Relationship Marketing in Marketing Strategy," *Journal of Business Research* 46 (November 1999), pp. 281–290; Shelby D. Hunt and Robert M. Morgan," The Comparative Advantage Theory of Competition," *Journal of Marketing* 59 (April 1995), pp. 1–15.

11. Kelly Hlavinka, "What Price Loyalty? The 2010 COLLOQUY Retail Loyalty Index," *COLLOQUY Talk*, March 2010.

13. www.llbean.com (accessed April 12, 2010).

14. Karlene Lukovitz, "GMA Study: Shopper Marketing Still Siloed," *Marketing Daily*, November 3, 2009.

15. Nawel Amrouche and Georges Zaccour, "Shelf-Space Allocation of National and Private Brands," *European Journal of* *Operational Research* 180, no. 2 (2007), pp. 648–663; Miguel Gomez, Vithala Rao, and Edward W. McLaughlin, "Empirical Analysis of Budget and Allocation of Trade Promotions in the U.S. Supermarket Industry," *Journal of Marketing Research* 44, no. 3 (2007), pp. 410–424.

16. Frances X. Frei and Amy C. Edmondson, "Influencing Customer Behavior in Service Operations," Harvard Business School Publications, Case 9-606-061, March 10, 2006; Rajnish Jain and Sangeeta Jain, "Towards Relational Exchange in Services Marketing: Insights from Hospitality Industry," *Journal of Services Research* 5, no. 2 (2006), pp. 139–150; Tim Matanovich, "Know Your Service Strategy," *Marketing Management*, July-August 2004, pp. 14–16.

17. Carmine Gallo, "Employee Motivation the Ritz-Carlton Way," *BusinessWeek*, February 29, 2008.

18. www.nist.gov/public_affairs/releases/baldrige_recipients2009.html (accessed March 30, 2010).

19. Lars Meyer-Waarden1 and Christophe Benavent, "Grocery Retail Loyalty Program Effects: Self-Selection or Purchase Behavior Change?" *Journal of the Academy of Marketing Science* 37 (September 2009), pp. 345–335; Russell Lacey, "Limited Influence of Loyalty Program Membership on Relational Outcomes," *Journal of Consumer Marketing*, 26, no. 6 (2009), pp. 392–402.

20. Hollie Shaw, "Harry Rosen Dons New Look for Expansion; CEO's Pragmatic View," *National Post's Financial Post & FP Investing*, September 3, 2008; Shaun Proulx, "Harry Goes Lofty, Large and Luxe," *Toronto Globe and Mail*, September 13, 2008; Denise Power, "Harry Rosen Embracing Technology," *Daily News Record*, February 12, 2007, p. 16.

21. Murali Mantrala, Suman Basuroy, and Shailendra Gajanan, "Do Style-Goods Retailer's Demands for Guaranteed Profit Margins Unfairly Exploit Vendors?" *Marketing Letters* 16, no. 1 (2005), pp. 53–66.

22. David Lei and John Slocum Jr., "Strategic and Organizational Requirements for Competitive Advantage," *Academy of Management Executive*, February 2005, pp. 31–46.

23. Maria Halkias, "Penney Remakes Culture to Remake Image," *Dallas Morning News*, February 12, 2007.

24. Richard Cuthbertson, Gerd Islei, Peter Franke, and Balkan Cetinkaya, "What Will the Best Retail Supply Chains Look Like in the Future?" *European Retail Digest*, Summer 2006, pp. 7–15; "Competitive Advantage through Supply-Chain Innovation," *Logistics & Transport Focus*, December 2004, pp. 56–59.

25. Vaidyanathan Jayaraman and Luo Yadong, "Creating Competitive Advantages through New Value Creation: A Reverse Logistics Perspective," *Academy of Management Perspectives* 21, no. 2 (2007), pp. 56–73; David Bryce and Jeffrey H. Dyer, "Strategies to Crack: Well-Guarded Markets," *Harvard Business Review* 85, no. 5 (2007), pp. 84–92.

26. Igor Ansoff, "Strategies for Diversification," *Harvard Business Review*, 35 (September–October 1957), pp.113–124.

27. Janet Adamy, "Dunkin' Donuts Whips Up a Recipe for Expansion," *Wall Street Journal*, May 3, 2007, p. B1.

28. www.tescocorporate.com/ (accessed April 15, 2010).

29. Andrew Sorkin and Michael De La Merced, "Home Depot Sells a Unit That Never Fit," *New York Times*, June 20, 2007, p. C1; Andrew Sorkin and Michael De La Merced, "Home Depot Supply Unit May Be Sold," *New York Times*, February 13, 2007, p. C1.

30. "2010 Global Powers of Retailing," *Stores*, January 2010, pp. G17–G21.

31. Frank Badillo, "Global Retail Outlook," *Retail Forward*, May 2009; *2009 Global Retail Development Index* (New York: Kearney, 2009).

32. "Chain Stores in India," *The Economist*, May 29, 2008.

33. Hana Ben-Shjabat, Mike Moriarty, and Deepa Bahgara, *Windows of Hope for Global Retailing* (Chicago: Kearney, 2009); Ken Schepy, "Retailing in India: Challenges and Opportunities," *Chain Store Age*, July 2008; Mehul Srivastava, "Big Retailers Still Struggle in India," *BusinessWeek India*, October 16, 2009.

34. "China's Retail Revolution: An Interview with Wal-Mart's Ed Chan," *BusinessWeek*, October 2009.

35. Matthew Boyle, "Wal-Mart's Painful Lessons," *BusinessWeek*, October 13, 2009.

36. Ben-Shjabat, Moriarty, and Bahgara, *Windows of Hope for Global Retailing*.

37. Daniel Nilsson, "A Cross-Cultural Comparison of Self-Service Technology Use," *European Journal of Marketing* 41, no. 3-4 (2007), pp. 367–381; Lisa Penaloza and Mary Gilly, "Marketer Acculturation: The Changer and the Changed," *Journal of Marketing* 63 (Summer 1999), pp. 84–95.

38. Don Lee, "A Chinese Lesson for Big Retailers," *Los Angeles Times*, July 2, 2006; Peter N. Child, "Lessons from a Global Retailer: An Interview with the President of Carrefour China," *McKinsey Quarterly*, 2006; "Company Spotlight: Carrefour," *MarketWatch: Global Round-Up* 6, no. 4 (2007), pp. 67–72.

39. "India Retail: Foreign Chains Eye the Potential, but Will They Succeed?" *Knowledge at INSTEAD*, May 28, 2007, quotation from Paddy Padmanabhan.

40. www.carrefour.com (accessed September 14, 2010).

41. Michael R. Czinkota and Ilkka A. Ronkainen, *International Marketing*, 9th ed. (Mason, OH: Thomson South-Western, 2009).

42. www.marksandspencer.com (accessed April 17, 2010).

43. Donald Lehman and Russell Winer, *Analysis for Marketing Planning*, 7th ed. (Burr Ridge, IL: McGraw-Hill/Irwin, 2007).

44. Linda Stallworth Williams, "The Mission Statement," *Journal of Business Communication* 45, no. 2 (2008), pp. 94–119.

45. Personal communications.

46. Tony Grundy, "Rethinking and Reinventing Michael Porter's Five Forces Model," *Strategic Change* 15, no. 5 (2006), pp. 213–229; Michael Porter, "Strategy and the Internet," *Harvard Business Review*, March 2001, pp. 63–78; Michael Porter, *Competitive Strategy* (New York: The Free Press, 1980).

47. Susan Reda, "Sights Set on the Subcontinent," *Stores*, September 2006.

48. Linda Matchan, "The Sleek, Smooth Design of Apple's iPod Is Not Mirrored in the Architecture of Some of the Company's High-Profile Stores," Boston Globe, June 29, 2006; Stephanie Kang, "Questions For . . . Wendy Clark," Wall Street Journal, June 20, 2007.

Chapter 6

1. Robert Kaplan and David Norton, "How Strategy Maps Frame an Organization's Objectives," *Financial Executive*, March–April 2004, pp. 40–46.

2. www.Target.com (accessed April 21, 2010).

3. www.familydollar.com (accessed April 21, 2010).

4. John W. Mullins, "Why Business Plans Don't Deliver," *Wall Street Journal*, June 22, 2009, p. R3.

5. Jane O'Donnel, "Retailers Want a Place in Your Wallet," *USA Today*, July 10, 2006.

6. Sandra Skrovan, "Industry Outlook: Dollar Stores," *Retail Forward*, December 2009.

Chapter 7

1. Kris Hudson and Ann Zimmerman, "Mall Glut to Clog Market for Years," *Wall Street Journal*, September 10, 2008, p. B1.

2. Judy Weil, "Mall REITs: JCPenney Is Warning You," *SeekingAlpha.com*, November 17, 2008.

3. Terry Pristin, "Squeezing Big-Box Retailing into Small City Spaces," *New York Times*, June 11, 2008.

4. Matt Woolsey, "World's Most Expensive Addresses," *Forbes*, July 17, 2008.

5. Ryan, Chittum, "Where Angels Fear to Tread," *Shopping Centers Today*, April 2008.

6. Nancy Kaffer, "Downtowns Become Boomertowns," *Metromode*, October 25, 2007.

7. http://www.icic.org/site/c.fnJNKPNhFiG/b.3476157/k.BE44/SICE.htm (accessed July 26, 2010).

8. Terry Pristin, "With a Little Help, Greens Come to Low-Income Neighborhoods," *New York Times*, June 17, 2009, p. B6.

9. http://www.simon.com/about_simon/index.aspx (accessed July 26, 2010).

10. http://history.sandiego.edu/gen/soc/shoppingcenter.html (accessed October 8, 2009); http://www.icsc.org/srch/sct/sct0707/center_stage_art_deco.php (accessed October 8, 2009).

11. http://www.kingofprussiamall.com/upload/264.pdf (accessed July 26, 2010).

12. Brandon Rogoff, "The Performance of U.S. Shopping Centers," *ICSC Research Review* 16, no. 1 (2009), pp. 8–10.

13. Ibid.

14. Michael Donohue, "Mall of Misfortune," *The National*, June 12, 2008.

15. Husna Hag, "Ethnic Malls Are Buzzing," *Christian Science Monitor*, August 31, 2009, based on research by the economic and demographic forecasting group at the University of Georgia in Athens.

16. Elaine Misonzhnik, "Full Speed Ahead," *Retail Traffic*, February 1, 2009.

17. Maria Matzer Rose, "Easton Shuffle," *Columbus Dispatch*, January 31, 2010; Tim Feran, "Easton Town Center Has Become Such a Popular Fixture, It's Hard to Remember That Its Concept Was a Risky Decision," *Columbus Dispatch*, July 5, 2009.

18. http://www.icsc.org/srch/lib/Mixed-use_Definition.pdf (accessed October 31, 2009).

19. http://www.miznerpark.com/ (accessed July 26, 2010).

20. Sascha M. Pardy, "Outlet Centers Rise to the Top during Recession," *COStar Group News*, September 30, 2009.

21. Ibid.

22. Jane L. Levere, "Come for the Prices. Stay for the Movie," *New York Times*, October 22, 2008.

23. Riccardo A. Davis, "Outlets Grow Upscale," *Retail Traffic*, January 2008.

24. Linda Humphers, "European Outlet Sector Grew 5 Percent in 2008," *International Outlet Journal*, Spring 2009.

25. http://www.simon.com/mall/default.aspx?id=857 (accessed July 26, 2010).

26. Natalie Zmuda, "Pop-Up Stores Pop Up as Inexpensive Way to Build Buzz," *AdAge.com*, August 31, 2009.

27. Jennifer Saranow, "Retailers Give It the Old College Try," *Wall Street Journal*, August 28, 2008.

28. Elizabeth Holmes, "View from the Market Booth," *Wall Street Journal*, December 8, 2006, p. B1.

29. Jane L. Levere, "At Kennedy, Shopping and Dining, Followed by a Takeoff," *New York Times*, July 30, 2008.

30. Ibid.

31. Misonzhnik, "Full Speed Ahead."

32. Jon Entine, "Wal-Mart: Ethical Retailing—From Evil Empire to Jolly Green Giant," *Ethicalcorporation.com*, June 7, 2008; Kerri Linden, "Wal-Mart Pressures Suppliers to Get Greener," *Retailing Today*, November 2007; Claudia H. Deutsch, "Wal-Mart's Environmental Report Card," *New York Times*, November 16, 2007.

33. http://walmartstores.com/FactsNews/NewsRoom/9333.aspx (accessed July 26, 2010).

Chapter 8

1. U.S. Bureau of the Census, http://www.census.gov/population/www/estimates/metroarea.html; http://www.census.gov/geo/www/maps/msa_maps2008/msa2008_previews_html/cbsa_us_wall_1108.html (accessed July 26, 2010).

2. http://www.census.gov/popest/metro/CBSA-est2008-annual.html (accessed July 26, 2010).

3. "Company Profile," *Hoovers Online* (www.hoovers.com), July 2007.

4. Michael Hartnett, "MapInfo Helps LaCuracao Find Its Target Customers," *Stores*, August 2008.

5. http://www.rhddlaw.com/PracticeAreas/Wage-Claims-Overtime.asp (accessed November 30, 2009).

6. Jenn Abelson, "Doughnuts the Old-Fashioned Way," *Boston Globe*, October 6, 2009.

7. "Publix Pushes Forward with Reopening of New and Ex-Albertson's Units," *Progressive Grocer*, October 28, 2008,

8. Bray, Hiawatha, "Microsoft Takes Page from Apple Retail Plan," *Boston Globe*, July 18, 2009.

9. http://www.partycity.com (accessed November 10, 2009); John Beaney, "A Growing Party," *Chain Store Age*, December 2005.

10. http://www.census.gov/mso/www/c2000basics/chapter1.htm (accessed November 10, 2009).

11. http://www.census.gov/popest/states/NST-ann-est.html (accessed November 10, 2009).

12. http://www.census.gov/geo/www/GARM/Ch11GARM.pdf (accessed July 26, 2010).

13. http://www.esri.com/library/fliers/pdfs/tapestry_segmentation.pdf; http://www.ci.rocky-hill.ct.us/EconomicDev/LifestyleTapestryReport.pdf (accessed July 26, 2010).

14. David L. Huff, "Defining and Estimating a Trade Area," *Journal of Marketing* 28 (1964), pp. 34–38; David L. Huff and William Black, "The Huff Model in Retrospect," *Applied Geographic Studies* 1, no. 2 (1997), pp. 22–34.

15. Giuseppe Bruno and Gennaro Improta, "Using Gravity Models for the Evaluation of New University Site Locations: A Case Study," *Computers & Operations Research* 35, no. 2 (2008), pp. 436–444; Tammy Drezner and Zvi Drezner, "Validating the Gravity-Based Competitive Location Model Using Inferred Attractiveness," *Annals of Operations Research* 111 (March 2002), pp. 227–241.

16. Andrea Chang, "Tiffany Sues to Keep H&M Away in Century City," *latimes.com*, September 10, 2009.

Chapter 9

1. Susan Jackson and Randall Schuler, *Managing Human Resources through Strategic Relationships*, 10th ed. (Mason, OH: Southwestern, 2008), p. 12.

2. Personal communication.

3. Susan Reda, "Retailers Take Different Approaches to Keeping Associates in the Fold," *Stores*, October 2008, statistics taken from National Retail Federation.

4. Jeffrey Pfeffer, *What Were They Thinking? Unconventional Wisdom about Management* (Boston: Harvard Business School Press, 2007).

5. "Out of Stock? It Might Be Your Employee Payroll—Not Your Supply Chain—That's to Blame," *Knowledge@Wharton*, April 4, 2007, based on research by Marshall L. Fisher, Serguei Netessine, and Jayanth Krishnan.

6. Kris Maher, "More People Pushed into Part-Time Work Force," *Wall Street Journal*, March 8, 2008.

7. Ibid.

8. Matthew Guthridge, Asmus B. Komm, and Emily Lawson, " Making Talent a Strategic Priority," *McKinsey Quarterly*, January 2008.

9. *Retail Industry Indicators* (Washington, DC: National Retail Foundation, August 2006), p. 25.

10. *Retail Industry Indicators*, p. 25.

11. David M. Walker, "Older Workers: Some Best Practices and Strategies for Engaging and Retaining Older Workers" *GAO Reports* (GAO-07-433T), February 28, 2007; Amy Joyce, "Retired, and Rehired to Sell," *Washington Post*, July 27, 2006.

12. Chi-yue Chiu, LeeAnn Mallorie, Hean Tat Keh, and Wilbert Law, "Perceptions of Culture in Multicultural Space: Joint Presentation of Images from Two Cultures Increases In-Group Attribution of Culture-Typical Characteristics," *Journal of Cross-Cultural Psychology* 40 (March 2009), pp. 282–300; Shali Wu and Boaz Keysar, "The Effect of Culture on Perspective Taking," *Psychological Science* 18, no. 7 (2007), pp. 600–606; Fred O. Walumbwa, John J. Lawler, and Bruce J. Avolio, "Leadership, Individual Differences, and Work-Related Attitudes: A Cross-Culture Investigation," *Applied Psychology: An International Review* 56, no. 2 (2007), pp. 212–230.

13. David Jolly, "Steel Maker Plans Deep Layoffs in Spain," *New York Times*, June 3, 2009.

14. Donald C. Dowling, "How to Conduct a Layoff outside the U.S.," *CIO.com*, March 16, 2009.

15. *Retail Industry Indicators*, p. 35.

16. www.mellerio.fr/ (accessed December 2, 2009); "Business Antiquities," *Wall Street Journal*, November 17, 1999.

17. Adam Bryant, "Knock-Knock: It's the C.E.O.," *New York Times*, April 12, 2009.

18. Sylvia Ann Hewlett, *Top Talent: Keeping Performance Up When Business Is Down* (Boston: Harvard Business School Press, 2009).

19. Stewart Black, "The Employee Value Proposition: How to Be the Employer of Choice," *Knowledge@INSEAD* (accessed October 9, 2007); Dina Berta, "Chains Build Employment Brands to Compete for Workers," *Nation's Restaurant News*, December 18, 2006, pp. 10–18; " 'Brand' Your Company to Get—and Keep—Top Employees," *HR Focus*, October 2006, pp. 7–10.

20. www.starbucks.com/aboutus/.

21. http://www-theinsider.blogspot.com/2008_08_01_archive.html (accessed December 4, 2009).

22. Ellen Davis, "Building a Brand That Matters, One Employee at a Time: The Zappos Story," *shop.org*, February 3, 2009.

23. Christine McConville, "Women May Become Chain's Best Buyers," *Bostonherald.com*, August 22, 2008.

24. Jackson and Schuler, *Managing Human Resources*; www.containerstore.com/about/index.html (accessed December 5, 2009).

25. Davis, "Building a Brand That Matters."

26. www.rootlearning.com/www/tcpCaseStudy.htm (accessed December 16, 2009); www.watercoolernewsletter.com/downloads/Q4%202006.pdf (accessed December 16, 2009).

27. www.edwardlowe.org/index.elf?page=sserc&storyid=8660&function=story (accessed December 3, 2009).

28. Sarah E. Needleman, "Burger Chain's Health-Care Recipe," *Wall Street Journal*, August 31, 2009.

29. Jackson and Schuler, *Managing Human Resources*; www.businessheroes.org/sam_walton.htm (accessed December 2, 2009).

30. Robert Spector and Patrick D. McCarthy, *The Nordstrom Way to Customer Service Excellence: A Handbook for Implementing Great Service in Your Organization* (New York: Wiley, 2005).

31. Bronwen Bartley, Gomibuchi Seishi, and Robin Mann, "Best Practices in Achieving a Customer-Focused Culture," *Benchmarking: An International Journal* 14, no. 4 (2007), pp. 482–496; Donna McAleese and Owen Hargie, "Five Guiding Principles of Culture Management: A Synthesis of Best Practice," *Journal of Communication Management* 9 (2004), pp. 155–165.

32. http://corporate.ritzcarlton.com/en/About/Default.htm (accessed December 2, 2009); Carmine Gallo, "How Ritz-Carlton Maintains Its Mystique," *BusinessWeek Online*, February 14, 2007.

33. Gary Hamel, and Bill Green, "Creating a Community of Purpose: Whole Foods Market: Management Innovation in Action," *Future of Management*, October 9, 2007; Tamara J. Erickson and Lynda Gratton, "What It Means to Work Here," *Harvard Business Review* 85, no. 3 (March 2007), pp. 104–112; John R. Wells and Travis Haglock, "Whole Foods Market, Inc.," Harvard Business School Publications (9-705-476), June 1, 2005.

34. Yahya Melhem, "The Antecedents of Customer-Contact Employees' Empowerment," *Employee Relations* 26 (2004), pp. 72–78.

35. Personal communication with Chet Cadieux, president and CEO of Quik Trip; John Lofstock, "Applauding the QT Culture," *Convenience Store Decisions*, April 2007, pp. 20–24.

36. Personal communication with authors, June 2010.

37. Maria Halkias, "Penney Remakes Culture to Remake Image," *Dallas Morning News*, February 12, 2007.

38. David Larcker and Brian Tayan, "Attention Shoppers: Executive Compensation at Kroger, Safeway, Costco, and Whole Foods," Stanford Graduate School of Business, February 15, 2008.

39. Personal communication, September 2009.

40. "Job-less: Steve Jobs's Succession Plan Should Be a Top Priority for Apple," *Knowledge@Wharton*, January 7, 2009; George W. Bohlander and Scott A. Snell, *Managing Human Resources*, 15th ed. (Mason, OH: South-Western College, 2009).

41. Sue Shellenbarger, "Perking Up: Some Companies Offer Surprising New Benefits," *Wall Street Journal*, March 18, 2009.

42. Suzanne C. De Janasz and Scott J. Behson, "Cognitive Capacity for Processing Work-Family Conflict: An Initial Examination," *Career Development International* 12, no. 4 (2007), pp. 397–411; Cath Sullivan and Janet Smithson, "Perspectives of Homeworkers and Their Partners on Working Flexibility and Gender Equity," *International Journal of Human Resource Management* 18, no. 3 (2007), pp. 448–461.

43. http://investormation.com/?p=60 (accessed December 2, 2009); Charlotte Huff, "With Flextime, Less Can Be More," *Workforce Management*, May 2005, pp. 65–69; Joe Mullich, "Giving Employees Something They Can't Buy with a Bonus Check," *Workforce Management*, July 2004, pp. 66–68; John Brandon, "Best Buy Rethinks the Time Clock," *Business 2.0*, March 15, 2007.

44. Michelle Conlin, "Gap to Employees: Work Wherever, Whenever You Want," *Businessweek.com*, September 17, 2009.

45. Aldred H. Neufeldt, James Watzke, Gary Birch, and Denise Buchner, "Engaging the Business/Industrial Sector in Accessibility Research: Lessons in Bridge Building," *Information Society* 23, no. 3 (2007), pp. 169–181.

46. "80 Most Influential People in Sales and Marketing," *Sales & Marketing Management*, October 1998, p. 78.

47. Ann Zimmerman, "Big Retailers Face Overtime Suits as Bosses Do More 'Hourly' Work," *Wall Street Journal*, May 26, 2004, p. B1.

48. "Report: OSHA Should Improve Safety Checks," *Wall Street Journal*, November 16, 2009; David Twomey, *Labor and Employment Law: Text & Cases*, 14th ed. (Mason, OH: South-Western College/West, 2009); William Atkinson, "Safety, Service Equals Satisfaction," *Beverage World* 126, no. 7 (2007); Tahira M. Probst and Ty L. Brubaker, "Organizational Safety Climate and Supervisory Layoff Decisions: Preferences versus Predictions," *Journal of Applied Social Psychology* 37, no. 7 (2007), pp. 1630–1648; Daniel Corcoran and Joshua D. Shackman, "A Theoretical and Empirical Analysis of the Strategic Value of Beyond Compliance Occupational Health and Safety Programs," *Journal of Business Strategies* 24, no. 1 (2007), pp. 49–68; www.osca.com/ (accessed August 20, 2007).

49. Steve Rosen, "Shopper Safety: OSHA Urging Retailers to Step Up Black Friday Precaution," *Bloomberg News*, November 19, 2009.

50. Jill S. Levenson, "Sexual Harassment or Consensual Sexual Relations? Implications for Social Work Education," *Journal of Social Work Values and Ethics* 3, no. 2 (2006); Bonnie G. Mani, "The Employer's Advantage in Sexual Harassment Cases: How the Courts Have Discouraged the Victims of Sexual Harassment," *Review of Public Personnel Administration* 24, no. 1 (2004), pp. 41–69; Lesle P. Francis, *Sexual Harassment as an Ethical Issue in Academic Life* (Lanham, MD: Rowman & Littlefield, 2001); Linda Wirth, *Breaking through the Glass Ceiling: Women in Management* (Washington, DC: International Labor Office, 2001).

51. Paul Dolan, Richard Edlin, Aki Tsuchiya, and Allan Wailoo, "It Ain't What You Do, It's the Way That You Do It: Characteristics of Procedural Justice and Their Importance in Social Decision-Making," *Journal of Economic Behavior and Organization* 64, no. 1 (2007), pp. 157–170.

Chapter 10

1. David Simchi-Levi, Philip Karminsky, and Edith Simchi-Levi, *Designing and Managing the Supply Chain: Concepts, Strategies, and Case Studies*, 4th ed. (New York: McGraw-Hill/Irwin, 2010); Roberta S. Russell, *Operations Management: Creating Value along the Supply Chain*, 7th ed. (Hoboken, NJ: Wiley, 2010); Barbara Flynn, Michiya Morita, and Jose Machuca, *Managing Global Supply Chain Relationships: Operations, Strategies and Practices* (Hauppauge, NY: Nova Science, 2010); Faustino Taderera, *Logistics and Supply Chain Management: Warehousing, Distribution* (Saarbrücken, Germany: Lap Lambert Academic, 2010);

Jayaraman Vaidyanathan, "Creating Competitive Advantages through New Value Creation: A Reverse Logistics Perspective," *Academy of Management Perspectives* 21, no. 2 (2007), pp. 56–73.

2. "Bharti Enterprises and Walmart Join Hands in Wholesale Cash-and-Carry to Serve Small Retailers, Manufacturers and Farmers," *PR Newswire*, August 6, 2007.

3. Lee Holman and Greg Buzek, "What's the Deal with Out-of-Stocks?" *IHL Group*, December 2008.

4. Jesper Aastrup and Herbert Kotzab, "Forty Years of Out-of-Stock Research—and Shelves Are Still Empty," *International Review of Retail, Distribution and Consumer Research*, February 20, 2010, pp. 147–164; Jesper Aastrup and Herbert Kotzab, "Analyzing Out-of-Stock in Independent Grocery Stores: An Empirical Study," *International Journal of Retail & Distribution Management* 37, no. 9 (2009), pp. 765–789; Mike Griswold, "Out of Stock," *Forbes*, December 14, 2006.

5. Holman and Buzek, "What's the Deal with Out-of-Stocks?"

6. Kristine Miller, "Fashion's New Fast Lane," *Forbes*, September 12, 2006.

7. "Bar Codes Change the Way Retailers Stocked, Priced Products," *Boston Globe*, June 29, 2004, p. C1.

8. Pradeep Gopalakrishna and Ram Subramanian, "Understanding Virtual Value Chains in a Retail Environment: A Case Study of Wal-Mart," *International Journal of Productivity and Quality Management* 3 (November 2008), pp. 263–274.

9. Constance Hays, "What Walmart Knows about Customers' Habits," *New York Times*, November 14, 2004, p. C1.

10. Council of Supply Chain Management Professionals, http://cscmp.org/ (accessed August 18, 2007).

11. Susan Elzey, "Location Part of Store Closing," *Knight Ridder Tribune Business News*, July 19, 2007; Dollar General Corporation, 10-K form, filed with the SEC on February 2, 2007; Amy Sung, "Dollar General Cites Progress with Store Receiving System," *Supermarket News*, October 10, 2005, p. 49.

12. www.businessdictionary.com/definition/freight-forwarder.html (accessed June 19, 2010).

13. Oliver E. Williamson, "Outsourcing: Transaction Cost Economics and Supply Chain Management," *Journal of Supply Chain Management* 44, no. 2, pp. 5–16; Salla Lutza and Thomas Ritter, "Outsourcing, Supply Chain Upgrading and Connectedness of a Firm's Competencies," *Industrial Marketing Management* 38 (May 2009), pp. 387–393; Erin Anderson and Barton Weitz, "Make or Buy Decisions: Vertical Integration and Marketing Productivity," *Sloan Management Review* 27 (Spring 1986), pp. 3–19.

14. Huaqin Zhang and Guojie Zhao, "Strategic Selection of Push-Pull Supply," *Modern Applied Science* 2, no. 1 (2008).

15. Andreas Otto, Franz Josef Schoppengerd, and Ramin Shariatmadari, *Direct Store Delivery: Concepts, Applications and Instruments* (New York: Springer, 2009).

16. Eric P. Jack, Thomas L. Powers, and Lauren Skinner, "Reverse Logistics Capabilities: Antecedents and Cost Savings," *International Journal of Physical Distribution & Logistics Management* 40, no. 3 (2010), pp. 228–246; S. Dowlatshahia, "A Cost-Benefit Analysis for the Design and Implementation of Reverse Logistics Systems: Case Studies Approach," *International Journal of Production Research* 48, no. 5 (January 2010), pp. 1361–1380; James Stock and J. P. Mulki, "Product Returns Processing: An Examination of Practices of Manufacturers, Wholesalers/Distributors, and

Retailers," *Journal of Business Logistics* 30, no. 1 (2009), pp. 33–63; Michael Bernon and John Cullen, "An Integrated Approach to Managing Reverse Logistics," *International Journal of Logistics: Research & Applications* 10, no. 1 (2007), pp. 41–56.

17. David Blanchard, "Supply Chains Also Work in Reverse," *Industry Weekly*, May 1, 2007 (accessed January 8, 2008).

18. Sherry Chiger, "Reverse Logistics: Every Department's Challenge," *Multichannel Merchant* 3, no. 6 (2007).

19. Keith Regan, "Toys 'R' Us Wins Right to End Amazon Partnership," *E-Commerce Times*, March 3, 2006.

20. "Top 12 Drop-Shipping Best Practices," *Multichannel Merchant*, October 27, 2009; Karen E. Klein, "How Drop-Shipping Works for Retailers and Manufacturers," *BusinessWeek*, September 23, 2009; and Elliot Rabinovich, Manus Rungtusanatham, Timothy M. Laseter, "Physical Distribution Service Performance and Internet Retailer Margins: The Drop-Shipping Context," *Journal of Operations Management* 26 (November 2008), pp. 767–781.

21. M. V. Greene, "Subway Taking a Fresh Approach to Greening Its Supply Chain," *Stores*, September 2009.

22. Huynh Trung Luong and Nguyen Huu Phien, "Measure of Bullwhip Effect in Supply Chains: The Case of High Order Autoregressive Demand Process," *European Journal of Operational Research* 183, no. 1 (2007), pp. 197–209; Hau Lee, V. Padmanabhan, and Seungjin Whang, "The Bullwhip Effect in Supply Chains," *Sloan Management Review*, Spring 1997, pp. 93–102.

23. Seung-Kuk, Paik, and Prabir K. Bachi, "Understanding the Causes of the Bullwhip Effect in a Supply Chain," *International Journal of Retail & Distribution Management* 35, no. 4 (2007), pp. 308–324.

24. www.ecrnet.org (accessed June 4, 2009).

25. Mattias Holweg, Stephen Disney, Jan Holmstrom, and Johanna Smaros, "Supply Chain Collaboration: Making Sense of the Strategy Continuum," *European Management Journal* 23 (April 2005), pp. 170–181.

26. Mohsen Attaran and Sharmin Attaran, "Collaborative Supply Chain Management: The Most Promising Practice for Building Efficient and Sustainable Supply Chains," *Business Process Management Journal* 13, no. 3 (2007), pp. 390–404.

27. V. G. Narayanan and Ananth Raman, "Aligning Incentives in Supply Chains," *Harvard Business Review*, November 2004, pp. 94–102.

29. Lisa Harrington, "The Consumer Products Supply Chain: Shopping for Solutions," http://inboundlogistics.com, August 2006; Jamie Swedberg, "Collaboration Can Speed Fashion Cycle," *Apparel Magazine*, June 2004, p. 33.

30. www.i2.com/industries/consumer_industries/vmi/vendor_managed_inventory.cfm (accessed June 15, 2010).

31. Chang, Tien-Hsiang, Hsin-Pin Fu, Wan-I Lee, Yichen Lin, and Hsu-Chih Hsueh, "A Study of an Augmented CPFR Model for the 3C Retail Industry," *Supply Chain Management* 12, no. 3 (2007), pp. 200–209; Attaran and Attaran, "Collaborative Supply Chain Management."

32. S. P. Singh, M. McCartney, J. Singh, and R. Clarke, "RFID Research and Testing for Packages for Apparel, Consumer Goods, and Fresh Produce in the Retail Distribution Environment," *Packaging Technology and Science* 21 (2008), pp. 91–102.

33. Gary McWilliams, "Walmart's Radio-Tracked Inventory Hits Static," *Wall Street Journal*, February 15, 2007, p. B1.

34. Ibid.; Zeynep Ton, Vincent Dessain, and Monika Stachow-iak-Joulain, "RFID at the Metro Group," *Harvard Business School Publications* (9-606-053), November 9, 2005.

35. B. C. Hardgrave, S. Langford, M. Waller, and R. Miller, "Measuring the Impact of RFID on Out of Stocks at Wal-Mart," *MIS Quarterly Executive* 7, no. 4 (2008).

36. Rebecca Logan, "American Apparel Tries Item-Level Tagging On for Size," *Stores*, July 2008.

37. Rhonda Ascierto, "IBM Updates Web Sphere RFID with Drug ePedigree," *CBR*, August 9, 2007.

38. FDA 2006 Compliance Policy Guide for the Prescription Drug Marketing Act.

39. B. Hardgrave, Matthew Waller, and R. Miller, "Does RFID Reduce Out of Stocks? A Preliminary Analysis," Sam M. Walton College of Business, University of Arkansas, Information Technology Research Institute, November 2005, http://itri.uark.edu/research/display.asp?articles=ITRI-WP058-1105.

40. Michael Mecham, "RFID in Dollars and Sense," *Aviation Week & Space Technology*, June 15, 2009.

41. Lynn A. Fish and Wayne C. Forrest, "A Worldwise Look at RFID," *Supply Chain Management Review*, April 2007, pp. 48–55.

Chapter 11

1. Marianne Wilson, "Delighting the Customer," *Chain Store Age*, January 2010, pp. 28-29; Brian Jones, "Customer-Centric Retailing Returns," *Canadian Grocer*, May 2009, p. 80; Arnie Capitanelli III, "Win the Retail Street Fight with Customer Centric Tactics," *Casual Living*, September 2009, p. 126; Francey Smith, "Four Degrees of Customer Centricity," *Multichannel Merchant*, October 2009, p. 46.

2. Chris Zook and James Allen, *Profit from the Core: A Return to Growth in Turbulent Times*, updated ed. (Boston: Harvard Business Press, 2010); Neil Morgan, Rebecca Slotegraaf, and Douglas Vorhies, "Linking Marketing Capabilities with Profit Growth," *International Journal of Research in Marketing* 26 (December 2009), pp. 284–293; Lerzan Aksoy, Timothy L. Keiningham, and David Bejou, "Objectives of Customer Centric Approaches in Relationship Marketing," *Journal of Relationship Marketing* 6 (January 2008), pp. 1–8; Bart Larivière, "Linking Perceptual and Behavioral Customer Metrics to Multiperiod Customers," *Journal of Service Research* 11, no. 1 (2008), pp. 3–21; Werner Reinartz and V. Kumar, "The Mismanagement of Customer Loyalty," *Harvard Business Review*, July 2002, pp. 86–94.

3. Alan S. Dick and Kunal Basu, "Customer Loyalty: Toward an Integrated Conceptual Framework," *Journal of the Academy of Marketing Science* 22 (March 1994), pp. 99–113.

4. Dr. Rajagopal, "Stimulating Retail Sales and Upholding Customer Value," *Journal of Retail & Leisure Property* 6, no. 2 (2007), pp. 117–135; Timothy L. Keiningham, Bruce Cooil, Lerzan Aksoy, Tor W. Andreassen, and Jay Weiner, "The Value of Different Customer Satisfaction and Loyalty Metrics in Predicting Customer Retention, Recommendation, and Share-of-Wallet," *Managing Service Quality* 17, no. 4 (2007), pp. 361–384; Deborah Brown McCabe, Mark S. Rosenbaum, and Jennifer Yurchisin, "Perceived Service Quality and Shopping Motivations: A Dynamic Relationship," *Services Marketing Quarterly* 29, no. 1 (2007), pp. 1–21.

5. Vanessa O'Connell, "Posh Retailers Pile on Perks for Top Customers," *Wall Street Journal*, April 26, 2007, p. D1.

6. Lauren Freedman, "Delivering the Added Value Consumers Expect from Personalized Product Recommendations: A Practical Guide for E-Tailors," *The E-Tailing Group*, June 2009; Kelly Hlavinka and Rick Ferguson, *Quo Vadis: Sizing Up the U.S. Loyalty Marketing Industry* (Milford, OH: Colloquy, April 2007).

7. "How Casinos Can Find and Target Their Favorite Customers: The Biggest Losers," *Knowledge@Wharton*, May 13, 2009.

8. Susan Reda, "Service That Stacks Up," *Stores*, March 2007.

9. Marcelle S. Fischler and Abby Gruen, "Shopping: A Cappuccino with That $5,000 Suit?" *New York Times*, November, 19, 2006, p. 2.

10. Personal communication with stores, August 23, 2007.

11. "Grocer Launches Biometric Service for Shoppers," *Business Courier of Cincinnati*, July 10, 2007.

12. www.cmbinfo.com/pdf/WSJ_Nordstrom.pdf (accessed September 8, 2007).

13. "Best Buy Reward Zone Program: Innovations in Driving Retail Loyalty," *mallnetworks.com*, 2009.

14. Lars Meyer-Waarden and Christophe Benavent, "Grocery Retail Loyalty Program Effects: Self-Selection or Purchase Behavior Change?" *Academy of Marketing Science Journal* 37 (September 2009), pp. 345–351; Yuping Liu and Rong Yan, "Competing Loyalty Programs: Impact of Market Saturation, Market Share, and Category Expandability," *Journal of Marketing* 73 (January 2009), pp. 93–108; Siddharth S. Singh, Dipak C. Jain, and Trichy V. Krishnan, "Research Note—Customer Loyalty Programs: Are They Profitable?" *Management Science* 54 (June 2008), pp. 1205–1211; Donghoon Kim, Seung-Yon Lee, Kyunghee Bu, and Seho Lee, "Do VIP Programs Always Work Well? The Moderating Role of Loyalty," *Psychology and Marketing* 26, no. 6 (2009), pp. 590–609.

15. Lars Meyer-Waarden and Christophe Benavent, "Rewards That Reward," *Wall Street Journal*, September 17, 2008.

16. Freedman, "Delivering the Added Value Consumers Expect."

17. Natalie Petouhoff, "How Much Is Your Customers' Trust Worth?" *Customer Relationship Management*, September 2006.

18. Sara Dolnicar and Yolanda Jordaan, "A Market-Oriented Approach to Responsibly Managing Information Privacy Concerns in Direct Marketing," *Journal of Advertising* 36, no. 2 (2007), pp. 123–149; William E. Spangler, Kathleen S. Hartzel, and Mordechai Gal-Or, "Exploring the Privacy Implications of Addressable Advertising and Viewer Profiling," *Communications of the ACM* 49, no. 5 (2006), pp. 119–123.

19. "Online Behavioral Tracking and Targeting, Legislative Primer," Center for Digital Democracy, September 2009.

20. Junko Yoshida, "Sounding the Alarm as Big Brother Goes Digital," *Electronic Engineering Times*, April 4, 2005, pp. 1–2; Orin S. Kerr, "The Fourth Amendment and New Technologies: Constitutional Myths and the Case for Caution," *Michigan Law Review* 102, no. 5 (March 2004), pp. 801–889; Mary Culnan, "Protecting Privacy Online: Is Self-Regulation Working?" *Journal of Public Policy & Marketing* 19 (Spring 2000), pp. 20–26.

21. www.ftc.gov/bcp/conline/pubs/alerts/privprotalrt.shtm (accessed September 6, 2007).

22. www.ftc.gov/reports/privacy3/fairinfo.shtm (accessed September 6, 2007).

23. Thomas H. Davenport, "Realizing the Potential of Retail Analytics: Plenty of Food for Those with Appetite," Babson Working Knowledge Research Center, June 2009.

24. Yan Ma, Jianxun Ding, and Wenxia Hong, "Delivering Customer Value Based on Service Process: The Example of Tesco.com," *International Business Research* 3, no. 2 (2010), pp. 131–135.

25. George Stalk Jr., "In Praise of the Heavy Spender," *Toronto Global and Mail*, May 21, 2007.

26. Sharad Borle, Siddharth S. Singh, and Dipak C. Jain, "Customer Lifetime Value Measurement," *Management Science* 54 (January 2008), pp. 100–112; Robert C. Blattberg, Edward C. Malthouse, and Scott A. Neslin, "Customer Lifetime Value: Empirical Generalizations and Some Conceptual Questions," *Journal of Interactive Marketing* 23 (May 2009), pp. 157–168.

27. Dennis Pitta, Frank Franzak, and Danielle Fowler, "A Strategic Approach to Building Online Customer Loyalty: Integrating Customer Profitability Tiers," *Journal of Consumer Marketing* 23, no. 7 (2006), pp. 421–429; Werner Reinartz and V. Kumar, "The Mismanagement of Customer Loyalty," *Harvard Business Review*, July 2002; Valarie Zeithaml, Roland Rust, and Katherine Lemon, "The Customer Pyramid: Creating and Serving Profitable Customers," *California Management Review* 43 (Summer 2001), p. 124.

28. V. Kumar and Denish Shah, "Building and Sustaining Profitable Customer Loyalty for the 21st Century," *Journal of Retailing* 80, no. 4 (2004), pp. 317–329.

29. Kate Fitzgerald, "Grocery Cards Get an Extra Scan," *Credit Card Management* 16, no. 13 (March 2004), p. 34.

30. Mark Albright, "Peddling Prestige," *St. Petersburg Times*, August 22, 2001, p. 8E.

31. Ed McKinley, "Custom-Fit Solutions," *Stores*, June 2005, p. 23.

32. Joe Lichtman, "Is 'Personalized Merchandising' Becoming an E-Commerce Reality?" *E-Commerce Times*, August 20, 2007.

33. Susan Fournier and Lara Lee, "Getting Brand Communities Right," *Harvard Business Review*, July 2009, pp. 106–113; Hope Jensen Schau, Albert M. Muñiz Jr., and Eric Arnould, "How Brand Community Practices Create Value," *Journal of Marketing* 73 (September 2009), pp. 30–51; John W. Schouten, James H. McAlexander, and Harold F. Koenig, "Transcendent Customer Experience and Brand Community," *Journal of the Academy of Marketing Science* 35 (September 2007), pp. 357–368.

34. Jonathan Birchall, "Just Do It, Marketers Say," *Financial Times*, April 30, 2007.

35. Roland Rust, Valerie Zeithaml, and Katherine Lemon, *Driving Customer Equity* (New York: Free Press, 2002), chap. 13; Zeithaml, Rust, and Lemon, "The Customer Pyramid."

36. Tobias Kowatsch and Wolfgang Maass, "In-Store Consumer Behavior: How Mobile Recommendation Agents Influence Usage Intentions, Product Purchases, and Store Preferences," *Computers in Human Behavior* 26 (July 2010), pp. 697–704; Daniel Fleder and Artik Hosanagar, "Blockbuster Culture's Next Rise or Fall: The Impact of Recommender Systems on Sales Diversity," *Management Science* 35 (May 2009); Robert Garfinkel, Ram Gopal, Bhavik Pathak, and Fang Yin, "Shopbot 2.0: Integrating Recommendations and Promotions with Comparison Shopping," *Decision Support Systems* 46 (December 2008), pp. 61–70.

37. www.americangirl.com (accessed July 15, 2010); Judy Newman, "American Girl Invites Girls to Give, Customize Dolls—and Return to the Company's Website," *McClatchy-Tribune Business News*, June 30, 2010; Erinn Hutkin, "Dolled Up for 'American Girls' Debut," *McClatchy-Tribune Business News*, July 2, 2008; Patrice Stewart, "Dolls, Trips to Stores a Sensation with Local Girls," *McClatchy-Tribune Business News*, April 12, 2009.

38. Vikas Mittal, Matthew Sarkees, and Feisal Murshed, "The Right Way to Manage Unprofitable Customers," *Harvard Business Review*, April 2008; Rust, Zeithaml, and Lemon, *Driving Customer Equity*, chap. 13.

Chapter 12

1. Personal communication.

2. Jesper Aastrup, David B. Grant, and Mogens Bjerr, "Value Creation and Category Management through Retailer-Supplier Relationships," *International Review of Retail, Distribution and Consumer Research*, December 2007, pp. 523–545.

3. Jonathan O'Brien, *Category Management in Purchasing: A Strategic Approach to Maximize Business Profitability* (London: Kogan Page, 2009).

4. Dal-Young Chun and Jack M. Cadeaux, "How Supplier Category Management Policy Influences Category Sales Performance," *Asia Pacific Journal of Marketing and Logistics* 22, no. 2 (2010), pp. 222–231; Arto Lindblom and Rami Olkkonenb, "An Analysis of Suppliers' Roles in Category Management Collaboration," *Journal of Retailing and Consumer Services* 15 (January 2008), pp. 1–8.

5. "Captains of Excellence," *Convenience Store News*, March 4, 2007.

6. Subir Bandyopadhyay, Anna Rominger, and Savitri Basaviaha, "Developing a Framework to Improve Retail Category Management through Category Captain Arrangements," *Journal of Retailing and Consumer Services* 16 (July 2009), pp. 315–319.

7. Joshua D. Wright, "Antitrust Analysis of Category Management: Conwood v United Tobacco," *Supreme Court Economic Review* 17, no. 1 (2009), pp. 27–35.

8. Elisa Anniss, "Innovative Retail Ideas Go on the Net," *Financial Times*, June 15, 2009, p. 5.

9. Julia Werdiger, "Tesco, British Grocer, Uses Weather to Predict Sales," *New York Times*, September 2, 2009.

10. Joel Warady, "Asda Takes the 'Pulse of the Nation,'" *Retail Wire*, July 16, 2009.

11. Jinhong Xie and Steven Shugan, "Advance Selling," in *Handbook of Pricing Research in Marketing*, ed. V. Rao (North Hampton, MA: Edward Elgar, 2009), pp. 451–477.

12. Lian Bratt and Ann Zimmerman, "Retailers Cut Back on Variety, Once the Spice of Marketing," *Wall Street Journal*, June 26, 2009.

13. Herb Sorensen, "How Should Supermarkets Manage the 'Long Tail' of In-Store Media?" *Retail Wire*, November 5, 2008.

14. Stephan Hamilton and Timothy Richards, "Product Differentiation, Store Differentiation, and Assortment Depth Management," *Management Science* 55 (August 2009), pp. 1368–1376.

15. Ram Bezawada, S. Balachander, P. K. Kannan, and Venkatesh Shankar, "Cross-Category Effects of Aisle and Display Placements: A Spatial Modeling Approach and Insights," *Journal of Marketing* 73 (May 2009), pp. 99–110.

16. Tammy Worth, "Too Many Choices Can Tax the Brain, Research Shows Having a Wealth of Options Can Lead to Poor Decision-Making, Experts Say," *Los Angeles Times*, March 16, 2009.

17. Susan Broniarczyk, "Product Assortment," in *Handbook of Consumer Psychology*, eds. Curtis Haugtvedt, Paul Herr, and Frank Kardes (New York: Psychology Press, 2008), pp. 755–708.

18. Warren Thayer, "Changes in the Wind at Wal-Mart," *RFF Retailer*, February 17, 2009.

19. Murali Mantrala, P. Sinha, and A. Zoltners, "Impact of Resource Allocation Rules on Marketing Investment-Level Decisions and Profitability," *Journal of Marketing Research* 29, no. 2 (May 1992), pp. 162–175.

20. Anjali Cordeiro, "Consumer-Goods Makers Heed 'Paycheck Cycle,'" *Wall Street Journal*, February 23, 2009.

Chapter 13

1. Stacy Straczynski, "Nielsen: U.S. Private Label Sales Up 7.4%," Brandweek.com, August 13, 2009; "Consumers Cut Back: Retail Sales Change as Value Trumps All," *Neilsen-Wire*, January 29, 2009.

2. www.federated-fds.com/AboutUs/History/MacysAHistory.aspx (accessed January 13, 2010).

3. "Best Global Brands 2009," www.interbrand.com/best_global_brands.aspx (accessed January 13, 2010).

4. www.privatelabelmag.com/issues/pl-nov-2009/global-analysis.cfm (accessed January 13, 2010). Nirmalya Kumar and Jan-Benedict E.M. Steenkamp, *Private Label Strategy: How to Meet the Store Brand Challenge* (Boston: Harvard Business Press, 2007).

5. Nichole Monroe Bell, "Store Brands Have Come a Long Way," *Charlotte Observer*, February 4, 2008, based on information and a survey from the Private Label Manufacturers Association.

6. Christina Binkley, "House-Brand Menswear That Aims to Be a Cut Above," *Wall Street Journal*, July 30, 2009; www.privatelabelmag.com/pdf/pli_fall2004/13.cfm (accessed October 22, 2007); Kumar and Steenkamp, *Private Label Strategy*.

7. Kumar and Steenkamp, *Private Label Strategy*.

8. Timothy W. Martin, "Organic Foods Get on Private-Label Wagon," *Wall Street Journal*, July 27, 2009.

9. Ibid. (Data from Nielsen.)

10. Lisa Biank Fasig, "Celebrities, Designers Court Macy's for Exclusive Lines," *Business Courier of Cincinnati*, August 31, 2009.

11. Mark Bergen, Shantanu Dutta, and Steven Shugan, "Branded Variants: A Retail Perspective," *Journal of Marketing Research*, February 1996, pp. 9–20.

12. Vanessa O'Connell and Cheryl Lu-Lien Tan, "Exclusive Lines May Prove Risky in Cool Economy," *Wall Street Journal*, April 11, 2008, p. B1.

13. www.nycfashioninfo.com/getdoc/8dc193de-9b7d-48fc-9d45-edf9aada3379/NYC-Fashion-Wholesale-Report_081209.aspx.

14. www.dallasmarketcenter.com/documents/oview_impact.pdf (accessed January 13, 2010).

15. www.cesweb.org/.

16. www.mccormickplace.com (accessed October 11, 2007).

17. www.thesupershow.com (accessed December 19, 2009).

18. www.frankfurter-buchmesse.de (accessed December 19, 2009).

19. www.hollander.com/index-designer.html (accessed January 25, 2010).

20. Masaaki Kotabe and Ram Mudamba, "Global Sourcing and Value Creation: Opportunities and Challenges," *Journal of International Management* 15, no. 1 (2009), pp. 121–125;

J.C. Penney 2007 10-K Report, filed with the Securities and Exchange Commission, February 3, 2007, p. 2.

21. Bernice Hurst, "Turning Points 2008: Global Sourcing Not Always a Sure Winner," *Retail Wire*, December 16, 2008.

22. "In Brief: Retailers Sever Ties over Child Labor," *Spokesman-Review*, October 31, 2009; George Anderson, "Wal-Mart Says 'No' to Uzbek Cotton over Child Labor," *Retail Wire*, October 1, 2008; Dan McDougall, "Child Sweatshop Shame Threatens Gap's Ethical Image," *Observer*, October 28, 2007.

23. www.limitedbrands.com/social_responsibility/labor/labor.jsp (accessed January 25, 2010); www.greenamericatoday.org/ (accessed January 25, 2010).

24. Cigdem A. Gumussoy and Fethi Calisir, "Understanding Factors Affecting E-Reverse Auction Use: An Integrative Approach," *Computers in Human Behavior* 25, no. 4 (2009), pp. 975–988; Elisa Martinelli and Gianluca Marchi, "Enabling and Inhibiting Factors in Adoption of Electronic-Reverse Auctions: A Longitudinal Case Study in Grocery Retailing," *International Review of Retail, Distribution and Consumer Research* 17, no. 3 (2007), pp. 203–218; Liz Parks, "See It, Move It, Sell It," Stores, 89, no. 6 (2007), p. 52.

25. Oystein Foros, Hans Jarle Kind, and Jan Yngve Sand, "Slotting Allowances and Manufacturers Retail Sales Effort," *Southern Economic Journal* (Southern Economic Association) 76 no. 1 (2009), pp. 266–282; David Hoffman, "Vendor Allowances in Retail Industry, Not Cut and Dry," *Chain Store Age*, July 29, 2009; Dmitr Kuksov and Amit Pazgal, "The Effects of Costs and Competition on Slotting Allowances," *Marketing Science* 26 (March–April 2007), pp. 259–267; Paula Bone, France Fitzgerald, Karen Russo, and Richard Riley, "A Multifirm Analysis of Slotting Fees," *Journal of Public Policy & Marketing* 25 (Fall 2006), pp. 224–237; K. Sudhir and Vithala Rao, "Do Slotting Allowances Enhance Efficiency or Hinder Competition?" *Journal of Marketing Research* 43 (May 2006), pp. 137–155.

26. Gavin Kennedy, *Negotiation: An A-Z Guide (Economist A-Z Guide)* (London: Economist Books, May 2009); Deepak Malhotra and Max Bazerman, *Negotiation Genius: How to Overcome Obstacles and Achieve Brilliant Results at the Bargaining Table and Beyond* (New York: Bantam, August 2008); Richard G. Shell, *Bargaining for Advantage: Negotiation Strategies for Reasonable People*, 2nd ed. (New York: Penguin, 2006). These guidelines are based on Roger Fisher and William Ury, *Getting to Yes* (New York: Penguin, 1981).

27. Manus Rungtusanatham, Elliot Rabinovich, Bryan Ashenbaum, and Cynthia Wallin, "Vendor-Owned Inventory Management Arrangements in Retail: An Agency Theory Perspective," *Journal of Business Logistics* 28, no. 1 (2007).

28. Robert Johnston and Roy Staughton, "Establishing and Developing Strategic Relationships: The Role for Operations Managers," *International Journal of Operations & Production Management* 29, no. 6 (2009), pp. 564–590; Thomas Powers and William Reagan, "Factors Influencing Successful Buyer–Seller Relationships," *Journal of Business Research* 60 (December 2007), pp. 1234–1242; Kevin Celuch, John Bantham, and Chickery Kasouf, "An Extension of the Marriage Metaphor in Buyer–Seller Relationships: An Exploration of Individual–Level Process Dynamics," *Journal of Business Research* 59 (May 2006), pp. 573–581; Olaf Ploetner and Michael Ehret, "From Relationships to Partnerships—New Forms of Cooperation between Buyer and Seller," *Industrial Marketing Management* 35 (January 2006), pp. 4–9; Erin Anderson and Anne Coughlan, "Structure, Governance, and Relationship Management," in *Handbook of Marketing*, eds.

B. Weitz and R. Wensley (London: Sage, 2002), pp. 223–247; Barton Weitz and Sandy Jap, "Relationship Marketing and Distribution Channels," *Journal of the Academy of Marketing Sciences* 23 (Fall 1995), pp. 305–320; F. Robert Dwyer, Paul Shurr, and Sejo Oh, "Developing Buyer-Seller Relationships," *Journal of Marketing* 51 (April 1987), pp. 11–27.

29. Bill Donaldson and Tom O'Toole, *Strategic Market Relationships: From Strategy to Implementation*, 2nd ed. (Indianapolis: Wiley, 2007); Robert Handfield, *Supply Market Intelligence: A Managerial Handbook for Building Sourcing Strategies* (Boca Raton: Auerbach, January 2006).

30. Felipe Caro and Jérémie Gallien, "Zara Uses Operations Research to Reengineer Its Global Distribution Process," *MIT*, August 3, 2009; Cecilie Rohwedder and Keith Johnson, "Pace-Setting Zara Seeks More Speed to Fight Its Rising Cheap-Chic Rivals," *Wall Street Journal*, February 20, 2008; Personal communication with Jose Martinez, Chief Merchandising and Supply Chain Officer, Zara, July 2009; Pankaj Ghemawat and Jose Luis Nueno, "Zara: Fast Fashion," Harvard Business School Publications No. 90703-497, 2006.

31. www.bentonville-ar-relocation.com/ (accessed January 13, 2010); http://money.cnn.com/magazines/moneymag/bplive/2009/snapshots/PL0505320.html (accessed January 13, 2010); Jim Yardley, "Vendorville," *New York Times Magazine*, March 8, 1998, p. 62.

32. Anne Coughlan, Erin Anderson, Louis W. Stern, and Adel El-Ansary, *Marketing Channels*, 7th ed. (New York: Prentice Hall, 2005).

33. Plexus Consulting Group, *The Power of Partnership: Principles and Practices for Creating Strategic Relationships among Nonprofit Groups, For-Profit Organizations, and Government Entities* (Washington, D.C.: ASAE & The Center for Association Leadership and U.S. Chamber of Commerce, June 25, 2008).

34. "Strategic Relationships between Boundary-Spanning Functions: Aligning Customer Relationship Management with Supplier Relationship Management," *Industrial Marketing Management* 38, no. 8 (2009), pp. 857–864.

35. William H. Kitchens, "Is It Legal?" *Refrigerated & Frozen Foods Retailer* 5, no. 5 (June 2007); Paul Stancil, "Still Crazy after All These Years: Understanding the Robinson-Patman Act Today," *Business Law Today*, September–October 2004, pp. 34–44.

36. Rachel Tobin Ramos, "Kickbacks a Hazard for Home Depot, Other Big Retailers," *Atlanta Journal-Constitution*, March 23, 2008.

37. Brad Stone, "Court Clears eBay in Suit over Sale of Counterfeit Goods," *New York Times*, July 15, 2008.

38. Katya Foreman, "Court Rules for Hermes in eBay Counterfeit Suit," *WWD*, June 5, 2008.

39. TJX annual 10K report, 2008.

40. *In re Toys R Us AntiTrust Litigation*, 191 F.R.D. 347 (E.D.N.Y. 2000).

41. Laura Vozzella, "Grocers Jump on 'Local' Produce Bandwagon," *Baltimore Sun Reporter*, July 9, 2009; Len Lewis, "Eating Locally," *Stores*, April 2008; Len Lewis, "Growing Trend Has Consumers—and Retailers—Seeking Products Sourced Closer to Home, Stores, April 2008; Remi Trudeland and June Cotte, "Does Being Ethical Pay?" *Wall Street Journal*, May 12, 2008, p. R1; Julie Schmit, "'Locally Grown' Food Sounds Great, but What Does It Mean?" *USA Today*, October 27, 2008; Carol Ness, "Whole Foods, Taking Flak, Thinks

Local," *San Francisco Chronicle*, July 26, 2006; "Retailers Push Packagers to Think 'Green,'" *Reuters*, September 4, 2007.

42. Lewis, "Eating Locally." The term was coined by four San Francisco women in proposing that people eat foods grown within 100 miles of their homes. In 2007, it was named "Word of the Year" by the *New Oxford American Dictionary*.

43. www.globalexchange.org/campaigns/fairtrade/coffee/starbucks.html (accessed January 25, 2010); www.bsi.org (accessed January 25, 2010); G. Jeffrey MacDonald, "Stopping the Outcry before It Starts," *Christian Science Monitor*, August 28, 2006; Ylan Q. Mui, "For Walmart, Fair Trade May Be More than a Hill of Beans," *Washington Post*, June 12, 2006, p. A01.

44. Clifford Krauss, "At Home Depot, How Green Is That Chainsaw?" *New York Times*, June 25, 2007.

45. Michelle Moran, "Green Is the New Black," *Gourmet Retailer*, August 2007.

Chapter 14

1. Roger Kerin, Steven Hartley, Eric Berkowitz, and William Rudelius, *Marketing*, 10th ed. (New York: McGraw-Hill, 2010).

2. Valarie A. Zeithaml and Mary Jo Bitner, *Service Marketing: Integrating Customer Focus across the Firm*, 4th ed. (New York: McGraw-Hill, 2005).

3. William G. Brunger, "The Impact of the Internet on Airline Fares: The 'Internet Price Effect,'" *Journal of Revenue & Pricing Management* 9, no. 1–2 (2010), pp. 66–93; Leo MacDonald and Henning Rasmussen, "Revenue Management with Dynamic Pricing and Advertising," *Journal of Revenue & Pricing Management* 9, no. 1–2 (2010), pp. 126–136.

4. N. Janakiraman, R. J. Meyer, and A. C. Morales, "Spillover Effects: How Consumers Respond to Unexpected Changes in Prices and Quality," *Journal of Consumer Research* 33, no. 3 (2006), pp. 361–372; A. R. Rao, "The Quality of Price as a Quality Cue," *Journal of Marketing Research* 42, no. 4 (2005), pp. 401–409; Thomas T. Nagle and Reed K. Holden, *The Strategy and Tactics of Pricing*, 3rd ed. (Upper Saddle River, NJ: Pearson, 2002); Glenn Voss, A. Parasuraman, and Dhruv Grewal, "The Roles of Price, Performance and Expectations in Determining Satisfaction in Services Exchanges," *Journal of Marketing* 62, no. 4 (October 1998), pp. 46–61.

5. John D. Quillinan, "Introduction to Normalization of Demand Data—The First Step in Isolating the Effects of Price on Demand," *Journal of Revenue & Pricing Management* 9, no. 1–2 (2010), pp. 4–22; Brian Bergstein, "Pricing Software Could Reshape Retail," *Associated Press*, April 27, 2007.

6. Bergstein, "Pricing Software Could Reshape Retail."

7. Tom Ryan, "The High Cost of Discounting," *Retail Wire*, March 20, 2009, based on a Yankelovich survey.

8. Christina Binkley, "Death to Discounts? The Designers Rebel," *Wall Street Journal*, April 16, 2009.

9. Michael Levy, Dhruv Grewal, Praveen K. Kopalle, and James D. Hess, "Emerging Trends in Retail Pricing Practice: Implications for Research," *Journal of Retailing* 80, no. 3 (2004), pp. xiii–xxi; Scott Friend and Patricia Walker, "Welcome to the New World of Merchandising," *Harvard Business Review*, November 2001, pp. 133–141; Murali Mantrala and Surya Rao, "A Decision-Support System That Helps Retailers Decide Order Quantities and Markdowns for Fashion Goods," *Interfaces*, May–June 2001, part 2, pp. S146–163.

10. Andrea Cheng, "US Retailers Find New Ways to Fine-Tune Discounts," *Wall Street Journal*, July 3, 2009.

11. Ibid.; Tanya Batallas, "The Price Is Right: Retailers Are Thinking Local," *New Jersey Business News*, July 21, 2009.

12. Steve McKee, "How to Discount (If You Insist)," *BusinessWeek*, August 14, 2009; Teri Evans, "An Expert's Guide to Discounting," *BusinessWeek Online*, April 3, 2009.

13. Dimitris Bertsimas, Jeffrey Hawkins, and Georgia Perakis, "Optimal Bidding in Online Auctions," *Journal of Revenue and Pricing Management* 8 (2009), pp. 21–41.

14. "Levi Strauss Reacquires a Pair of Jeans, at Markup," *Wall Street Journal*, May 29, 2001, p. B13A.

15. Scott Fay and Juliano Laran, "Implications of Expected Changes in the Seller's Price in Name-Your-Own-Price," *Management Science* 55, no. 11 (2009), pp. 1783–1796; Chris K. Anderson, "Setting Prices on Priceline," *Interfaces* 39, no. 4 (2009), pp. 307–315; Tuo Wang, Ester Gal-Or, and Rabikar Chatteriee, "The Name-Your-Own-Price Channel in the Travel Industry: An Analytical Exploration," *Management Science* 55, no. 6 (2009), pp. 968–979; John G. Wilson and Guoren Zhang, "Optimal Design of a Name-Your-Own Price Channel," *Journal of Revenue & Pricing Management* 7, no. 3 (2008), pp. 281–290; Priceline.com 10-K report.

16. Bertsimas, Hawkins, and Perakis, "Optimal Bidding in Online Auctions."

17. "80 Most Influential People in Sales and Marketing," *Sales & Marketing Management*, October 1998, p. 78.

18. Ken Belson, "Baseball Tickets Too Much? Check Back Tomorrow," *New York Times*, May 18, 2009.

19. Raj Arora, "Price Bundling and Framing Strategies for Complementary Products," *Journal of Product & Brand Management* 17, no. 7 (2008), pp. 475–484.

20. Amy Schatz, "FTC Takes on Online Privacy," *Wall Street Journal*, December 7, 2009.

21. Lan Xia, Kent B. Monroe, and Jennifer L. Cox, "The Price Is Unfair! A Conceptual Framework of Price Fairness Perceptions," *Journal of Marketing* 68 (October 2004), pp. 1–15.

22. Lisa E. Bolton, Luk Warlop, and Joseph W. Alba, "Consumer Perceptions of Price (Un)Fairness," *Journal of Consumer Research* 29 (2003), pp. 474–491.

23. Amna Kirmani and Akshay R. Rao, "No Pain, No Gain: A Critical Review of the Literature on Signaling Unobservable Product Quality," *Journal of Marketing* 64 (April 2000), pp. 66–79.

24. Jeffrey A. Trachtenberg and Miguel Bustillo, "Amid Price War, Three Retailers Begin Rationing Books," *Wall Street Journal*, October 30, 2009.

25. Y. Jackie Luan and K. Sudhir, "Forecasting Marketing-Mix Responsiveness for New Products," *Journal of Marketing Research* 47, no. 3 (2010), pp. 444–457; Kusum L. Ailawadi, J. P. Beauchamp, Naveen Donthu, Dinesh Gauri, and Venkatesh Shankar, "Communication and Promotion Decisions in Retailing: A Review and Directions for Future Research," *Journal of Retailing* 85, no.1 (2009), pp. 42–55.

26. Leigh McAlister, Edward I. George, and Yung-Hsin Chien, "A Basket-Mix Model to Identify Cherry-Picked Brands," *Journal of Retailing* 85, no. 4 (2009), pp. 425–436; Dinesh Gauri, J. Gabor Pauler, and M. Trivedi, "Benchmarking Performance in Retail Chains: An Integrated Approach," *Marketing Science* 28, no.3 (May–June 2009), pp. 502–515; Dinesh Gauri, K. Ailawadi, J. P. Beauchamp, N. Donthu, and V. Shankar, "Customer Experience Management in Retailing: Communication Media and Promotions," *Journal of Retailing* 85, no. 1 (2009), pp. 42–55; Dinesh Gauri, K. Sudhir, and Debabrata Talukdar, "The Temporal and Spatial Dimensions of Price Search: Insights from Matching Household Survey and Purchase Data," *Journal of Marketing Research* 45, no. 2 (2008), pp. 226–240.

27. Itamar Simonson, "Shoppers Easily Influenced Choices," *New York Times*, November 6, 1994, p. 311, based on research by Itamar Simonson and Amos Tversky.

28. Marc Vanhuele, Gilles Laurent, and Xavier Dreze, "Consumers' Immediate Memory for Prices," *Journal of Consumer Research* 33, no. 2 (2006), pp. 163–172.

29. R. M. Schindler, "Patterns of Price Endings Used in U.S. and Japanese Price Advertising," *International Marketing Review* 26, no. 1 (2009), pp. 17–29; R. M. Schindler, "The 99-Price Ending as a Signal of a Low-Price Appeal," *Journal of Retailing* 82, no. 1 (2006), pp. 71–77; R. M. Schindler and R. Chandrashekaran, "Influence of Price Endings on Price Recall: A By-Digit Analysis," *Journal of Product and Brand Management* 13, no. 7 (2004), pp. 514–524.

30. Robert Schindler, "Fine Tuning a Retail Price," *Retail Navigator* (Gainesville, FL: Miller Center for Retailing Education and Research, April 2004).

31. Tim Arango, "Bet Your Bottom Dollar on 99 Cents," *New York Times*, February 8, 2009.

32. Schindler, "Fine Tuning a Retail Price".

33. Claire Cain Miller, "Mobile Phones Become Essential Tool for Holiday Shopping," *New York Times*, December 18, 2009; Geoffrey A. Fowler and Yukari Iwatani Kane, "New Mobile Applications Use Bar-Code Scanners," *Wall Street Journal*, December 16, 2009.

34. Andrew Gaffney, "Walmart Price Drops, Channel Transparency Accentuate Impact of Promo Optimization," *Retail TouchPoints*, December 3, 2009.

35. "Focus French Retailers Pin Hopes on Liberalisation of Price Negotiations," *AFX News*, October 16, 2007.

36. Steven W. Beattie, "Stephen King's New Face of Evil: Predatory Pricing," *Quill & Quire*, October 26, 2009.

37. Daniel M. Garrett, Michelle Burtis, and Vandy Howell, "Economics of Antitrust: An Economic Analysis of Resale Price Maintenance," www.GlobalCompetitionReview.com, 2008; Stephen Labaton, "Century-Old Ban Lifted on Minimum Retail Pricing," *New York Times*, June 29, 2007.

38. Jenn Abelson, "CVS Called a Leader in Pricing Violations," *Boston Globe*, May 7, 2009; www.ftc.gov/bcp/edu/pubs/consumer/products/pro01.shtm (accessed January 28, 2010); Richard Clodfelter, "Price Strategy and Practice: An Examination of Pricing Accuracy at Retail Stores That Use Scanners," *Journal of Product and Brand Management* 13 (2004), pp. 269–283.

39. Kevin M. Lemley, "Resolving the Circuit Split on Standing in False Advertising Claims and Incorporation of Prudential Standing in State Deceptive Trade Practices Law: The Quest for Optimal Levels of Accurate Information in the Marketplace," *University of Arkansas, Little Rock Law Review* 29 (2007), pp. 283, 285; Dhruv Grewal, Kent B. Monroe, and R. Krishnan, "The Effects of Price Comparison Advertising on Buyers' Perceptions of Acquisition Value and Transaction Value," *Journal of Marketing* 62 (April 1998), pp. 46–60.

40. Martin Eichenbaum, Nir Jaimovich, and Sergio Rebelo, "Reference Prices and Nominal Rigidities," *NBER*, March 5, 2008; Larry Compeau, Joan Lindsey-Mullikin, Dhruv Grewal, and Ross Petty, "An Analysis of Consumers' Interpretations of the Semantic Phrases Found in Comparative Price Advertisements," *Journal of Consumer Affairs* 38 (Summer 2004), pp. 178–187; Larry D. Compeau, Dhruv Grewal, and Diana S. Grewal, "Adjudicating Claims of Deceptive Advertised Reference Prices: The Use of Empirical Evidence," *Journal of Public Policy & Marketing* 14 (Fall 1994), pp. 52–62.

Chapter 15

1. David A. Aaker, *Brand Portfolio Strategy: Creating Relevance, Differentiation, Energy, Leverage, and Clarity* (New York: Free Press, 2004).

2. "History in the Making: A Look at 16 Campaigns That Helped Redefine Promotion Marketing," *Promo*, March 2002, p. 23.

3. Karl Greenberg, "Penney Debuts Interactive, Virtual Runway Show," *Marketing Daily*, February 25, 2009.

4. www.fundinguniverse.com/company-histories/The-Talbots-Inc-Company-History.html (accessed July 4, 2010).

5. This section draws from Dhruv Grewal and Michael Levy, *Marketing*, 3rd ed. (New York: McGraw-Hill), 2012.

6. Chris Barrows, "Unauthorized Verses," *Journal of Integrated Marketing Communications*, (Evanston: Northwestern University), 2009.

7. www.frederiksamuel.com/blog/ad-dictionary (accessed June 28, 2010).

8. Akihisa Fujita, "Mobile Marketing in Japan: The Acceleration of Integrated Marketing Communications," *Journal of Integrated Marketing Communications*, 2008, pp. 41–46; mobile update: www.businessinsider.com/henry-blodget-enough-empty-headed-puffery-about-mobile-ads-time-for-analysts-to-stop-jawboning-and-think-2009-10; www.informationweek.com/news/security/privacy/showArticle.jhtml?articleID=222300256 & subSection=News; www.nearbynow.com/info/iphone_platform.html (accessed May 26, 2010).

9. Fareena Sulta and Andrew J. Rohm, "How to Market to Generation M(obile)," *MIT Sloan Management Review*, Summer 2008.

10. Shane Snow, "Inside Foursquare: Checking In before the Party Started (Part 1)," *Wired*, May 24, 2010, www.wired.com/epicenter/2010/05/inside-foursquare-checking-in-before-the-party-started-part-i/3/.

11. Foursquare Web site, http://foursquare.com/ (accessed May 27, 2010).

12. Ludovic Privat, "When Cliché Becomes Reality: Starbucks Coupons for Foursquare Mayors," www.gpsbusinessnews.com/When-Cliche-Becomes-Reality-Starbucks-Coupons-for-Foursquare-Mayors_a2265.html, May 26, 2010.

13. Harris Interactive Inc., "Mobile Advertising."

14. "New Trend in Social Networking Could Be Open Invitation to Criminals," www.prnewswire.com/news-releases/geolocation-apps-and-social-networks-can-be-a-dangerous-combo-94918019.html, May 26, 2010.

15. "Number of Cell Phones Worldwide Hits 4.6 Billion," *CBS News*, February 15, 2010, www.cbsnews.com/stories/2010/02/15/business/main6209772.shtml.

16. Bonnie Rochman, "Sweet Spot," *Time*, November 2009.

17. Joan Voight, "Getting a Handle on Customer Reviews," *Adweek*, July 5, 2007, based on research by Top 40 Online Retail from Foresee Results and the University of Michigan.

18. Greet Van Hoye and Filip Lievens, "Social Influences on Organizational Attractiveness: Investigating If and When Word of Mouth Matters," *Journal of Applied Social Psychology* 37, no. 9 (2007), pp. 2024-2047; Robert East, Kathy Hammond, and Malcolm Wright, "The Relative Incidence of Positive and Negative Word of Mouth: A Multi-Category Study," *International Journal of Research in Marketing* 24, no. 2 (2007), pp. 175–184; Tom Brown, Thomas Barry, Peter Dacin, and Richard Gunst, "Spreading the Word: Investigating Antecedents of Consumers' Positive Word-of-Mouth Intentions and Behaviors in a Retailing Context," *Journal of the Academy of Marketing Science* 33 (Spring 2005), pp. 123–139.

19. Erin Jo Richey, "15 Top Internet Retailers Who Blog," *flatfrogblog.com*, January 7, 2010.

20. "Global Advertising: Consumers Trust Real Friends and Virtual Strangers the Most," *Nielsenwire.com*, July 7, 2009.

21. Ibid.

22. Chrysanthos Dellarocas, "Strategic Manipulation of Internet Opinion Forums: Implications for Consumers and Firms," *Management Science* 52 (October 2006), pp. 1577–1593; Liyun Jin, "Business Using Twitter, Facebook to Market Goods," *Pittsburgh Post-Gazette*, June 21, 2009.

23. Chris Lee, "Kevin Smith's Southwest Incident Sets Web All A-Twitter," *Los Angeles Times*, February 16, 2010 (http://articles.latimes.com/2010/feb/16/entertainment/la-et-kevin-smith16-2010feb16).

24. Christi Day, "Not So Silent Bob," February 14, 2010, www.blogsouthwest.com/blog/not-so-silent-bob.

25. "Brand Channels," *YouTube*, www.gstatic.com/youtube/engagement/platform/autoplay/advertise/downloads/YouTube_BrandChannels.pdf (accessed April 2010).

26. The Home Depot Branded Channel, www.youtube.com/user/homedepot?blend=2&ob=4#p/a (accessed April 2010).

27. Forever 21 Facebook Fan Page, www.facebook.com/#!/Forever21?ref=ts (accessed April 2010).

28. Ibid.

29. Tim Parry, "Macy's Looking for the Sweetest Tweet," Multichannel/Merchant.com, February 2, 2010.

30. www.wholefoodsmarket.com/twitter/ (accessed July 4, 2010).

31. "The Man Who Created Rudolph from an Idea That Almost Didn't Fly," *Chicago Tribune*, December 13, 1990, p. 1C.

32. Personal communication with Rob Price, VP of Retail Marketing, CVS, June 16, 2009; Carol Angrisani, "CVS Moves to Personalization," *SN: Supermarket News* 56, no. 2 (March 24, 2008), p. 29.

33. "The Man Who Created Rudolph."

34. Sarah Mahoney, "Study: Coupons Make Consumers Blush," *Marketing Daily*, February 17, 2009; personal communication with Rob Price, VP of Retail Marketing, CVS, June 16, 2009.

35. Claire Cain Miller, "Mobile Phones Become Essential Tool for Holiday Shopping," *The New York Times*, December 17, 2009, based on research by accounting and consulting firm Deloitte.

36. www.stapleseasyrebates.com/img/staples/paperless/pages/Landing.html (accessed April 7, 2010).

37. www.marketingpower.com/_layouts/Dictionary.aspx?dLetter=S (accessed June 28, 2010).

38. www.freshnessmag.com/2009/08/06/gucci-sneakers-pop-up-shop-gucci-icon-temporary/ (accessed July 2, 2010).

39. American Marketing Association, *Dictionary of Marketing Terms* (Chicago: American Marketing Association, 2008).

40. *100 Leading National Advertisers* (New York: Advertising Age, 2010).

41. Eric Pfanner, "Reins Off, French Retailers Rush to Buy TV Time," *New York Times*, January 9, 2007.

42. Newspaper Association of America, www.naa.org (accessed July 6, 2010).

43. David Kaplan, "As Macy's Stores Went Away, So Did Its Newspaper Ads," *www.paidcontent.org*, July 6, 2009.

44. Kim T. Gordon, "4 Keys to Radio Advertising," *Entrepreneur*, April 13, 2007.

45. www.walmartstores.com/haiti (accessed July 3, 2010).

46. Nicole Carter, "Michelle Obama J.Crew Outfits in London Prompt Shopping Frenzy Stateside," *Daily News*, April 3, 2009.

47. Jackie Huba, "A Just Cause Creating Emotional Connections with Customers," 2003, www.inc.com/articles/2003/05/25537.html.

48. www.createapepper.com (accessed March 14, 2010); http://causerelatedmarketing.blogspot.com/2008/03/how-chilis-used-cause-related-marketing.html (accessed March 14, 2010).

49. Eva A. van Reijmersdal, Peter C. Neijens, and Edith G. Smit, "A New Branch of Advertising: Reviewing Factors That Influence Reactions to Product Placement," *Journal of Advertising Research* 49, no. 4 (December 2009), pp. 429–449; Pamela Mills Homer, "Product Placement: The Impact of Placement Type and Repetition on Attitude," *Journal of Advertising*, Fall 2009; Elizabeth Cowley and Chris Barron, "When Product Placement Goes Wrong: The Effects of Program Liking and Placement Prominence," *Journal of Advertising*, Spring 2008.

50. Tom Lowry and Burt Helm, "Blasting Away at Product Placement," *BusinessWeek*, October 15, 2009.

51. Leonard Lodish, *Advertisers and Promotion Challenge Vaguely Right or Precisely Wrong* (New York: Oxford University Press, 1986).

52. Murali Mantrala, "Allocating Marketing Resources," in *Handbook of Marketing*, eds. Barton Weitz and Robin Wensley (London: Sage, 2002), pp. 409–435.

53. Ronald Curhan and Robert Kopp, "Obtaining Retailer Support for Trade Deals: Key Success Factors," *Journal of Advertising Research* 27 (December 1987–January 1988), pp. 51–60.

Chapter 16

1. James G. Maxham, III, Richard G. Netemeyer, and Donald R. Lichtenstein, "The Retail Value Chain: Linking Employee Perceptions to Employee Performance, Customer Evaluations, and Store Performance," *Marketing Science* 27 (March–April 2008), pp. 147–167.

2. H. John Bernardin, *Human Resource Management: An Experiential Approach*, 5th ed. (New York: McGraw-Hill, 2010); Raymond Noe, John Hollenbeck, Barry Gerhart, and Patrick Wright, *Fundamentals of Human Resource Management*, 7th ed. (New York: McGraw-Hill, 2010).

3. Denise Tanner, *Managing the Ageing Experience: Learning from Older People* (Bristol, UK: Policy Press, 2010).

4. James Thornton, "All Ages Welcome," *Human Resources*, March 2010, p. 23.

5. Mark Schoeff Jr., "CVS Optimas Award Winner for Partnership," *Workforce Management*, March 26, 2007, p. 30.

6. Justin Fox, "Employees First," *Time*, July 7, 2008; Vicki Powers, "Finding Workers Who Fit the Container Store Built a Booming Business for Neatniks Who Turned Out to Be Their Best Employees," *Business 2.0*, November 2004, p. 74.

7. D. Gail Fleenor, "Employ Automated Hiring," *Progressive Grocer*, May 2009, pp. 102–105.

8. Katherine Field, "High-Speed Hiring," *Chain Store Age*, June 2006.

9. Kirsten Valle, "Right Workers Still Hard to Find," *McClatchy-Tribune Business News*, January 30, 2010.

10. Diane Couatu, "We Googled You," *Harvard Business Review*, June 2007, pp. 37–47.

11. Richard C. Hollinger and Amanda Adams, *2010 National Retail Security Survey* (Gainesville: University of Florida, 2007), p. 16.

12. Jonathan Katz, "Rethinking Drug Test," *Industry Week*, March 2010, p. 16

13. W. Stanley Siebert and Nikolay Zubanov, "Searching for the Optimal Level of Employee Turnover: A Study of a Large U.K. Retail Organization," *Academy of Management Journal* 52 (April 2009), pp. 94–106; Shari L. Peterson, "Managerial Turnover in US Retail Organizations," *Journal of Management Development* 26, no. 7/8 (2007), pp. 770–789; Aaron Arndt, Todd J. Arnold, and Timothy D. Landry, "The Effects of Polychronic-Orientation upon Retail Employee Satisfaction and Turnover," *Journal of Retailing* 82, no. 4 (2006), pp. 319–330; Hiram Barksdale Jr., Danny Bellender, James Boles, and Thomas Brashear, "The Impact of Realistic Job Previews and Perceptions of Training on Sales Force Performance and Continuance Commitment: A Longitudinal Test," *Journal of Personal Selling and Sales Management* 23 (Spring 2003), pp. 125–140.

14. John Kador, *The Manager's Book of Questions: 1001 Great Interview Questions for Hiring the Best Person*, 2nd ed. (Burr Ridge, IL: McGraw-Hill, 2006); Robin Kessler, *Competency-Based Interviews: Master the Tough New Interview Style and Give Them the Answers That Will Win You the Job* (Franklin Lakes, NJ: Career Press, 2006); Deborah Walker, "Behavioral Interviews: 3 Steps to Great Answers," *PA Times*, 30, no. 9 (2007), p. 22; John Sullican, "Be Correctly Prepared," *PM Network*, 20, no. 4 (2006), p. 24.

15. Mya Frazier, "Help Wanted," *Chain Store Age*, April 2005, pp. 37–40.

16. Robert J. Taormina, "Organizational Socialization: The Missing Link between Employee Needs and Organizational Culture," *Journal of Managerial Psychology* 24 (2009), pp. 650–665; Jen-Te Yang, "Facilitating or Inhibiting Newcomer Socialisation Outcomes in International Hotels," *Tourism and Hospitality Research* 9 (2009), pp. 325–350; Keith Rollag, "Defining the Term 'New' in New Employee Research," *Journal of Occupational & Organizational Psychology* 80, no. 1 (2007), pp. 63–75; Keith Rollag, "The Impact of Relative Tenure on Newcomer Socialization Dynamics," *Journal of Organizational Behavior* 25 (November 2004), pp. 853–873.

17. Elly Valas, "Training Doesn't Cost, It Pays," *Dealerscope*, April 2008, p. 24; M. V. Greene, "Train and Retain," *Stores*, November 2007, p. 89.

18. Kathryn Tyler, "Training on a Shoestring," *HRMagazine*, January 2009, pp. 66-70; Jessica Marquez, "Faced with High Turnover, Retailers Boot Up E-Learning Programs for Quick Training," *Workforce Management*, August 2005, pp. 74–75.

19. Ibid.

20. George Anders, "Companies Find Online Training Has Its Limits," *Wall Street Journal*, March 26, 2007, p. B3.

21. Lorri Freifeld, "Focus on Retail: Best Buy Connects with Customers," *Sales and Marketing Management*, August 1, 2007.

22. Annie McKee, Richard Boyatzis, and Fran Johnston, *Becoming a Resonant Leader: Develop Your Emotional Intelligence, Renew Your Relationships, Sustain Your Effectiveness* (Boston: Harvard Business School Press, 2008); James B. Deconinck, "The Effect of Leader-Member Exchange on Turnover among Retail Buyers," *Journal of Business Research*, 62 (November 2009), pp. 1081–1095.

23. Frank Q. Fu, Keith A. Richards, and Eli Jones, "The Motivation Hub: Effects of Goal Setting and Self-Efficacy on Effort and New Product Sales," *Journal of Personal Selling*

and Sales Management, 29 (Summer 2009), pp. 277–292; C. Fred Miao and Kenneth R. Evans, "The Impact of Salesperson Motivation on Role Perceptions and Job Performance—A Cognitive and Affective Perspective," *Journal of Personal Selling & Sales Management* 27, no. 1 (2007), pp. 89–101.

24. Elissa L. Perry, Carol T. Kulik, and Marina P. Field, "Sexual Harassment Training: Recommendations to Address Gaps between the Practitioner and Research Literatures," *Human Resource Management*, 48 (September–October 2009), pp. 817–834; "What Constitutes 'Harassment,' and What HR Can Do about It," *HR Focus*, December 2008, pp. 4–6.

25. Vincent Onyemah, "The Effects of Coaching on Salespeople's Attitudes and Behaviors," *European Journal of Marketing* 43 (2009), pp. 938–960.

26. Jo En Yap, Liliana L. Bove, and Michael B. Beverland, "Exploring the Effects of Different Reward Programs on In-Role and Extra-Role Performance of Retail Sales Associates," *Qualitative Market Research* 12, no. 3 (2009), pp. 279–296; Arthur C. Brooks, "I Love My Work," *American: A Magazine of Ideas* 1, no. 6 (2007), pp. 20–28; John H. Fleming and Jim Asplund, *Human Sigma: Managing the Employee–Customer Encounter* (New York: Gallup Press, 2007).

27. Tará Burnthorne Lopez, Christopher D. Hopkins, and Mary Anne Raymond, "Reward Preferences of Salespeople: How Do Commissions Rate?" *Journal of Personal Selling & Sales Management* 26, no. 4 (2006), pp. 381–390; Richard G. McFarland and Blair Kidwell, "An Examination of Instrumental and Expressive Traits on Performance: The Mediating Role of Learning, Prove, and Avoid Goal Orientations," *Journal of Personal Selling & Sales Management* 26, no. 2 (2006), pp. 143–159.

28. Susan Reda, "Sticky Strategies for Retention," *Stores*, October 2008.

29. Rachel Dodes and Dana Mattioli, "Theory & Practice: Retailers Try On New Sales Tactics," *Wall Street Journal*, April 19, 2010.

30. Karolin Fellner, Royce Kallesen, Antonio Ruggiero, and Benson Yuen, "Improving Revenue through Fare Rationalization and a New Business Process between Revenue Management and Sales," *Journal of Revenue & Pricing Management* 5, no. 2 (2006), pp. 118–127.

31. James P. Guthrie and Elaine C. Hollensbe, "Group Incentives and Performance: A Study of Spontaneous Goal Setting, Goal Choice and Commitment," *Journal of Management* 30, no. 2 (2004), pp. 263–285.

32. Kris Maher, "Wal-Mart Seeks New Flexibility in Worker Shifts," *Wall Street Journal*, January 3, 2007, p. A1.

33. Vanessa O'Connell, "Retailers Reprogram Workers in Efficiency Push," *Wall Street Journal*, September 10, 2008.

34. "On the Clock: Are Retail Sales People Getting a Raw Deal?" *Knowledge@Wharton*, October 1, 2008.

35. Steven Greenhouse and Michael Barbaro, "Wal-Mart to Add Wage Caps and Part-Timers," *New York Times*, October 2, 2006.

36. Glenn Adams, "Grocer Pushes Earth-Friendly Store Design," *Los Angeles Times*, October 22, 2007.

37. Andrew Martin, "Green Plans in Blueprints of Retailers," *New York Times*, November 8, 2008.

38. Leila Abboud and John Biers, "Business Goes on an Energy Diet," *Wall Street Journal*, August 24, 2007.

39. www.walmartfacts.com/articles/4564.aspx (accessed November 30, 2007).

40. Hollinger and Adams, *2010 National Retail Security Survey*.

41. Ibid.

42. Ibid.

43. Ann Zimmerman, "As Shoplifters Use High-Tech Scams, Retail Losses Rise," *Wall Street Journal*, October 25, 2006, p. A1.

44. Ibid., estimate by Brad Brekke, vice president of assets protection at Target Corp.

45. Ibid., based on a study by the National Retail Federation.

46. Ylan Q. Mui, "Not-So-Happy Returns," *Washington Post*, December 25, 2006, p. D01.

47. Mike Delaney, "How to Beat Shoplifting," *about.com*, April 26, 2006; Ronald Bond, "Preventing Retail Theft," *entrepreneur.com*, July 18, 2007.

48. Delaney, "How to Beat Shoplifting."

49. Roger Waite Stores, "Tag Food to Stop Deli Thieves," *Sunday Times*, March 15, 2009.

50. Hollinger and Adams, *2010 National Retail Security Survey*, p. 28.

51. Ibid.

52. Steven Greenhouse, "Shoplifters? Studies Say Keep an Eye on Workers," *New York Times*, December 30, 2009.

53. Ibid.

54. Jennifer Davies, "Retailers Use Technology to Thwart Would-Be Thieves," *San Diego Union Tribune*, June 13, 2007; "Attention, Shoplifters," *BusinessWeek*, September 11, 2006.

Chapter 17

1. "Growing Pains," *Chain Store Age*, August 2005, p. 31A.

2. Karen Matthews, "Upscale McDonald's Brings European Style to America," *Associated Press*, November 21, 2009; Julia Werdigier, "To Woo Europeans, McDonald's Goes Upscale," *New York Times*, August 25, 2007.

3. Linda Matchan, "The Sleek, Smooth Design of Apple's iPod Is Now Mirrored in the Architecture of Some of the Company's High-Profile Stores," *Boston Globe*, June 29, 2006.

4. Eileen Bridges and Renée Florsheim, "Hedonic and Utilitarian Shopping Goals: The Online Experience," *Journal of Business Research* 61 (April 2008), pp. 309–314; Ravindra Chitturi, Rajagopal Raghunathan, and Vijay Mahajan, "Delight by Design: The Role of Hedonic versus Utilitarian Benefits," *Journal of Marketing* 72 (May 2008), pp. 48–63; Andrew Smitha and Leigh Sparks "It's Nice to Get a Wee Treat If You've Had a Bad Week," *Journal of Business Research* 62 (May 2009), pp. 542–547.

5. Michael Barbaro, "A Long Line for a Shorter Wait at the Supermarket," *New York Times*, June 23, 2007.

6. Carl Biakik, "Justice—Wait for It—on the Checkout Line," *Wall Street Journal*, August 19, 2009.

7. www.cabelas.com (accessed July 10, 2010).

8. Matthew Egol and Christopher Vollmer, "Major Media in the Shopping Aisle," *s+b*, Winter 2008.

9. Jonathan Reynolds, Elizabeth Howard, Christine Cuthbertson, and Latchezar Hristov, "Perspectives on Retail Format Innovation: Relating Theory and Practice," *International Journal of Retail & Distribution Management* 35, no. 8 (2007), pp. 647–660.

10. Stacey Menzel Baker, Jonna Holland, and Carol Kaufman-Scarborough, "How Consumers with Disabilities Perceive 'Welcome' in Retail Servicescapes: A Critical Incident Study," *Journal of Services Marketing* 21, no. 3 (2007), pp. 160–173; Robert Pear, "Plan Seeks More Access for Disabled," *New York Times*, July 16, 2008, p. 11: Rosemary

D. F. Bromley and David L. Matthew, "Reducing Consumer Disadvantage: Reassessing Access in the Retail Environment," *International Review of Retail, Distribution & Consumer Research* 17, no. 5 (2007), pp. 483–501; Marianne Wilson, "Accessible Fixtures," *Chain Store Age* 83, no. 2 (February 2007).

11. See, for example, *Disabled in Action of Metropolitan New York, Inc. et al. v. Duane Reade, Inc.*, U.S. District Court, Southern District of New York, Civil Action No. 01 Civ. 4692 (WHP), 2004; *Californians for Disability Rights v. Mervyn's*, Superior Court of California, No. 2002-051738 (RMS), 2003; *Shimozono, et al. v. May Department Stores Co. d/b/a Robinsons-May*, Federal Court, Central District of California, Case No. 00-04261 (WJR), 2001; *Access Now, et al., v. Burdines, Inc.*, Federal Court, Southern District of Florida, Case No. 99-3214 (CIV), 2000.

12. Michael Barbaro, "Department Stores Settle Disability Lawsuit," *Washington Post*, February 9, 2005, p. E02.

13. Lisa Eckelbecker, "Female Persuasion; Lowe's, Others Learn How to Design Stores with Women Shoppers in Mind," *Worcester Telegram & Gazette*, February 13, 2005, p. E1.

14. Paco Underhill, *Why We Buy: The Science of Shopping* (New York: Simon and Schuster, 2000).

15. Herb Sorensen, *Inside the Mind of the Shoppper* (Upper Saddle River, NJ: Pearson Education, 2009).

16. "Dale Buss, S. C. Johnson Promotes 'Reinventing' Center Store of Supermarkets," *CPG Matters*, January 5, 2009.

17. Ivan-Damir Anic, Sonja Radas, and Lewis K. S. Lim, "Relative Effects of Store Traffic and Customer Traffic Flow on Shopper Spending," *International Review of Retail, Distribution & Consumer Research* 20 (May 2010), pp. 237–243.

18. Willard N. Ander Jr. and Neil Z. Stern, *Winning at Retail: Developing a Sustained Model for Retail Success* (New York: Wiley, 2004).

19. Fiona Soltes, "It's the Message, Not the Medium," *Stores*, October 2007, p. 26; Michael Curran, "Now Playing: Interactive Retail Marketing *2.0*," *Stores*, August 2007, p. 92; Katherine Field, "Digital Signage: A Powerful New Medium," *Chain Store Age*, May 2006, p. 204; Steven Keith Platt, Kingshuck Sinha, and Barton Weitz, *Implications for Retail Adoption of Digital Signage Systems* (Chicago, IL: Platt Retail Institute, 2004).

20. Raymond R. Burke, "Behavioral Effects of Digital Signage," *Journal of Advertising Research* 49 (June 2009), pp, 180–186.

21. Britta Cornelius, Martin Natter, and Corinne Faure, "How Storefront Displays Influence Retail Store Image," *Journal of Retailing and Consumer Services* 17, no. 2 (March 2010), pp. 143–151; Shuo-Fang Liu, Wen-Cheng Wang, and Ying-Hsiu Chen, "Applying Store Image and Consumer Behavior to Window Display Analysis," *Journal of American Academy of Busines*, 3 (2009), pp. 70-75.

22. Mindy Fetterman and Jayne O'Donnell, "Just Browsing at the Mall? That's What You Think," *USA Today*, September 1, 2006: Paco Underhill, *Why We Buy: The Science of Shopping* (New York: Simon and Schuster, 2000).

23. Michael Applebaum, "More Eyeballs at Checkout," *Brandweek*, June 27–July 4, 2005, p. 54.

24. Jeanine Poggi, "Dressing Rooms of the Future," *Forbes*, July 22, 2008.

25. Sara Bauknecht, "Smart.Mirror Matches Fashion Rather than Reflect," *Pittsburgh Post-Gazette*, December 14, 2009.

26. Bo Begole, Takashi Matsumoto, Wei Zhang, Nicholas Yee, Juan Liu, and Maurice Chu, "Designed to Fit: Challenges of Interaction Design for Clothes Dressing Room Technologies,"

in *Human-Computer Interaction. Interacting in Various Application Domains* (Berlin/Heidelberg: Springer, 2009); Poggi, "Dressing Rooms of The Future."

27. Doris Hajewski, "JCPenney Now Hot on Kohl's Heels, Retail Industry Watchers Say," *Knight Ridder Tribune Business News*, November 7, 2004, p. 1.

28. Chase C. Murray, Debabrata Talukdar, and Abhijit Gosavi, "Joint Optimization of Product Price, Display Orientation and Shelf-Space Allocation in Retail Category Management," *Journal of Retailing* 86 (June 2010), pp. 125–136; Jared M. Hansen, Sumit Raut, and Sanjeev Swami, "Retail Shelf Allocation: A Comparative Analysis of Heuristic and Meta-Heuristic Approaches," *Journal of Retailing* 86 , no.1 (March 2010), pp. 94–105; B. Ramaseshan, N. R. Achuthan, and R. Collinson, "Decision Support Tool for Retail Shelf Space Optimization," *International Journal of Information Technology & Decision Making* 7, no. 3 (2008), pp. 547–565.

29. The concept of atmospherics was introduced by Philip Kotler, "Atmosphere as a Marketing Tool," *Journal of Retailing* 49 (Winter 1973), pp. 48-64. The definition is adapted from Richard Yalch and Eric Spangenberg, "Effects of Store Music on Shopping Behavior," *Journal of Service Marketing* 4, no. 1 (Winter 1990), pp. 31–39.

30. Pierre Chandon, J. Wesley Hutchinson, Eric T Bradlow, and Scott H Young, "Does In-Store Marketing Work? Effects of the Number and Position of Shelf Facings on Brand Attention and Evaluation at the Point of Purchase," *Journal of Marketing* 73 (November 2009), pp. 1–17.

31. Eric R. Spangenberg, David E. Sprott, Bianca Grohmann, and Daniel L. Tracy, "Gender-Congruent Ambient Scent Influences on Approach and Avoidance Behaviors in a Retail Store," *Journal of Business Research* 59, no. 12 (2006), pp. 1281–1287; Anna S. Mattila and Jochen Wirtz, "Congruency of Scent and Music as a Driver of In-Store Evaluations and Behavior," *Journal of Retailing* 77, no. 2 (Summer 2001), pp. 273–289.

32 Brooks Barnes, "Disney's Retail Plan Is a Theme Park in Its Stores," *New York Times*, October 13, 2009.

33. www.charthouse.com (accessed July 1, 2010).

34. www.amysicecrean.com (accessed July 10, 2010).

35. Julie Baker, Dhruv Grewal, Michael Levy, and Glenn Voss, "Wait Expectations, Store Atmosphere and Store Patronage Intentions." *Journal of Retailing* 79, no. 4 (2003), pp. 259–268.

36. Ibid.

37. Ibid.

38. Jean-Charles Chebat and Maureen Morrin, "Colors and Cultures: Exploring the Effects of Mall Décor on Consumer Perceptions," *Journal of Business Research* 60, no. 3 (2007), pp. 189–196; Malaika Brengman and Maggie Geuens, "The Four Dimensional Impact of Color on Shopper's Emotions," *Advances in Consumer Research* 31 (2003), pp. 122–125; Barry Babin, David Hardesty, and Tracy Suter, "Color and Shopping Intentions: The Intervening Effect of Price Fairness and Perceived Affect," *Journal of Business Research* 56 (July 2003), pp. 541–555.

39. Theunis Bates, "Volume Control," *Time*, August 2, 2007.

40. Ibid.

41.

42. Ylan Q. Mui, "Dollars and Scents," *Washington Post*, December 19, 2006, p. D01; Keith McArthur, "Marketers Next Hit? Right at Your Nose," *Toronto Globe and Mail*, January 26, 2006; Earl Print, "Euro Lighting," *VM&SD*, May 1999, pp. 38, 40.

43. Jung-Hwan Kim, Minjeong Kim, and Jay Kandampully, "The Impact of Buying Environment Characteristics of Retail Websites," *Service Industries Journal* 27, no. 7 (2007), pp. 865–880; David Cunningham, Liz Thach, and Karen Thompson, "Innovative E-Commerce Site Design: A Conceptual Model to Match Consumer MBTI Dimensions to Website Design," *Journal of Internet Commerce* 6, no. 3 (2007), pp. 1–27.

44. James J. Cappel and Zhenyu Huang, "A Usability Analysis of Company Websites," *Journal of Computer Information Systems* 48, no. 1 (2007), pp. 117–123.

45. Velitchka Kalcheva and Barton Weitz, "How Exciting Should a Store Be?" *Journal of Marketing*, Winter 2006, pp. 34–62; Benjamin Yen and P. C. Yen, "The Design and Evaluation of Accessibility on Web Navigation," *Decision Support Systems* 42, no. 4 (2007), pp. 2219–2235.

46. "Tips on Improving the Checkout Process," www.e-consultancy.com, July 1, 2010.

47. Ibid.

Chapter 18

1. Murray Raphael, "Tell Me What You Want and the Answer Is Yes," *Direct Marketing*, October 1996, p. 22.

2. Robert Cooperman, "Value over Profit," *T+D*, May 2010, pp. 58–62; Dhruv Grewal, Ram Krishnan, and Joan Lindsey-Mullikin, Building Store Loyalty through Service Strategies *Journal of Relationship Marketing* 7, no. 4 (2008), pp. 341–358; Jayne O'Donnell, "Electronics Retailers Find Service Sells," *USA Today*, July 23, 2008; Valarie Zeithaml, Leonard Berry, and A. Parasuraman, "The Behavioral Consequences of Service Quality," *Journal of Marketing* 60 (April 1996), pp. 31–46.

3. Clay M. Voorhees, Michael K. Brady, and David M. Horowitz, "A Voice from the Silent Masses: An Exploratory and Comparative Analysis of Noncomplainers," *Journal of the Academy of Marketing Science* 34 (October 2006), pp. 514–527; Sijun Wang and Lenard C. Huff, "Explaining Buyers' Responses to Sellers' Violation of Trust," *European Journal of Marketing* 41 (September 2007), pp. 1033–1052.

4. Laura Baverman, "In Bruising Times, Companies Use Secret Weapon: Customer Service," *Cincinnati Inquirer*, September 20, 2009.

5. "Retailers Join the War Effort," *Chain Store Age*, June 1994, p. 15.

6. Robert Spector and Patrick McCarthy, *The Nordstrom Way: The Inside Story of America's #1 Customer Service Company*, 3rd ed. (New York: Wiley, 2005).

7. Connie Robbins Gentry, "Zappos: Returns with a Smile," *Chain Store Age*, December 2008, p. 53.

8. Tara Siegel Bernard, "Nice Gift, but Ask If You Can Return It," *New York Times*, December 19, 2009.

9. Lloyd C. Harris, "Fraudulent Consumer Returns: Exploiting Retailers' Return Policies," *European Journal of Marketing* 44, no. 6 (2010), pp. 730–742.

10. Dwayne Ball, Pedro S. Coelho, and Manuel J. Vilares, "Service Personalization and Loyalty," *Journal of Services Marketing* 20 (September 2006), pp. 391–403; Carol F. Suprenant and Michael R. Solomon, "Predictability and Personalization in the Service Encounter," *Journal of Marketing* 51 (April 1987), p. 86.

11. Kwiseok Kwon, Jinhyung Cho, and Yongtae Park, "How to Best Characterize the Personalization Construct for E-Services," *Expert Systems with Applications* 37 (March 2010), pp. 2232–2240.

12. Lev Grossman, "If You Liked This . . . ," *Time*, June 7, 2010, p. 44.

13. Ibid.

14. Anne Eisenberg, "Thinking of Going Blond? Consult the Kiosk First," *New York Times*, March 29, 2009.

15. "Are the Days of the Checkout Worker Numbered?" *Daily Mail*, October 22, 2009.

16. Deena M. Amato-McCoy, "Putting the Best Foot Forward," *Retail Technology Quarterly*, October 2007, pp. 4A–6A.

17. Stephen L. Vargo, Kaori Nagao, Yi He, and Fred W. Morgan, "Satisfiers, Dissatisfiers, Criticals, and Neutrals: A Review of Their Relative Effects on Customer (Dis)Satisfaction," *Academy of Marketing Science Review*, January 2007, p. 1; Chezy Ofir and Itamar Simonson, "The Effect of Stating Expectations on Customer Satisfaction and Shopping Experience," *Journal of Marketing Research* 44 (February 2007), p. 37; Torsten Ringberg, Gaby Odekerken-Schröder, and Glenn L Christensen, "A Cultural Models Approach to Service Recovery," *Journal of Marketing* 71 (July 2007), p. 194; A. Parasuraman and Valarie Zeithaml, "Understanding and Improving Service Quality: A Literature Review and Research Agenda," in *Handbook of Marketing*, eds. B. Weitz and R. Wensley (London: Sage, 2002).

18. A. Parasuraman and V. Zeithaml, "Understanding and Improving Service Quality"; Michael A. Wiles, "The Effect of Customer Service on Retailers' Shareholder Wealth: The Role of Availability and Reputation Cues," *Journal of Retailing* 83, no. 1 (2007), pp. 19–31.

19. Bill Radford, "Broadmoor's Penrose Room Dons a 5th Gem," *Colorado Springs Gazette*, November 7, 2007; "Grand Plans for a Grande Dame," *Lodging Hospitality*, September 1, 2007, pp. 17–18; Andrew J. Czaplewski, Eric M. Olson, and Stanley F. Slater, "Applying the RATER Model for Service Success: Five Service Attributes Can Help Maintain Five-Star Ratings," *Marketing Management*, January–February 2002, pp. 14–20; www.broadmoor.com (accessed June 15, 2010).

20. Valerie Seckler, "The Shopping Experience: Service Is Key," *WWD*, August 10, 2005, p. 10.

21. Todd Beck, "Want Loyal Customers? Don't Stop at Satisfaction," *Customer Inter@ction Solutions*, February 2005, pp. 36–49.

22. Adrian Palmer, "Customer Experience Management: A Critical Review of an Emerging Idea," *Journal of Services Marketing* 24, no. 3 (2010), pp, 196–208; Tomas Falk, Maik Hammerschmidt, and Jeroen J. L. Schepers, "The Service Quality-Satisfaction Link Revisited: Exploring Asymmetries and Dynamics," *Journal of the Academy of Marketing Science* 38 (June, 2010), pp. 288–302; Timothy Keiningham and Terry Vavra, *The Customer Delight Principle* (Chicago: American Marketing Association, 2002); Roland T. Rust and Richard L. Oliver, "Should We Delight the Customer?" *Journal of the Academy of Marketing Science* 28 (January 2000), pp. 86–94.

23. Jingyun Zhanga, Sharon E. Beatty, and Gianfranco Walsh, "Review and Future Directions of Cross-Cultural Consumer Services Research," *Journal of Business Research* 61 (March 2008), pp. 211–224; M. Sajid Khan, Earl Naumann, Rob Bateman, Matti Haverila, "Cross-Cultural Comparison of Customer Satisfaction Research: USA vs Japan," *Asia Pacific Journal of Marketing and Logistics* 21, no. 3 (2009), pp. 376–396.

24. Mary Jo Bitner, "Self-Service Technologies: What Do Customers Expect? In This High-Tech World, Customers

Haven't Changed—They Still Want Good Service," *Marketing Management*, Spring 2001, pp. 10–15; Ofir and Simonson, "The Effect of Stating Expectations"; Jackie L. M. Tam, "Managing Customer Expectations in Financial Services: Opportunities and Challenges," *Journal of Financial Services Marketing* 11 (May 2007), pp. 281–289; Deirdre O'Loughlin and Isabelle Szmigin, "External and Internal Accountability of Financial Services Suppliers: Current Paradoxes in Managing Expectations and Experience," *Journal of Strategic Marketing* 13 (June 2005), pp. 133–147.

25. Linda Abu-Shalback Zid, "Another Satisfied Customer," *Marketing Management*, March–April 2005, p. 5.

26. The discussion of the gaps model and its implications is based on Valerie Zeithaml, Leonard Berry, and A. Parasuraman, "Communication and Control Processes in the Delivery of Service Quality," *Journal of Marketing* 52 (April 1988), pp. 35–48; Valerie Zeithaml, A. Parasuraman, and Leonard Berry, *Delivering Quality Customer Service* (New York: Free Press, 1990); Doen Nel and Leyland Pitt, "Service Quality in a Retail Environment: Closing the Gaps," *Journal of General Management* 18 (Spring 1993), pp. 37–57.

27. Ann Thomas and Jill Applegate, *Pay Attention! How to Listen, Respond, and Profit from Customer Feedback* (Hoboken, NJ: Wiley, 2010).

28. Kemba J. Dunham, "Beyond Satisfaction," *Wall Street Journal*, October 30, 2006, p. R4.

29. Devendra Mishra, "How Best Buy Uses Customer Input to Develop Private Label Line," *Dealerscope*, June 2007.

30. Pete Blackshaw, "Marketers Love Conversation, Unless the Consumer Starts It," *Ad Age*, August 11, 2008; ; James C. Ward and Amy L. Ostrom, "Complaining to the Masses: The Role of Protest Framing in Customer-Created Complaint Web Sites," *Journal of Consumer Research* 33 (September 2006), pp. 220–230; Simon J. Bell and James A. Luddington, "Coping with Customer Complaints," *Journal of Service Research* 8 (February 2006), pp. 221–233; Thorsten Gruber, Isabelle Szmigin, and Roediger Voss, "The Desired Qualities of Customer Contact Employees in Complaint Handling Encounters," *Journal of Marketing Management* 22 (June 2006), p. 619. Christian Homburg and Andrea Furst, "How Organizational Complaint Handling Drives Customer Loyalty: An Analysis of the Mechanistic and the Organic Approach," *Journal of Marketing* 69 (July 2005), pp. 95–107.

31. Jennifer Alsever, "Even Bad Reviews Boost Sales," *Fortune Small Business*, September 28, 2009; Andrea James, "More Online Shoppers Take the Word of Anonymous Product Reviewers," *Seattle Pilot*, December 21, 2008; James Covert, "Online Clothes Reviews Give 'Love That Dress' New Clout," *Wall Street Journal*, December 7, 2006, p. B1.

32. Spencer E. Ante, "Amazon: Turning Consumer Opinions into Gold," *BusinessWeek*, October 15, 2009.

33. Ryan Schuster, "Frustrated with Poor Service?" *Bakersfield Californian*, April 14, 2007.

34. Jonathan Birchall, "Home Depot Targets Customer Service," *Financial Times*, March 16, 2009.

35. Staci Kusterbeck, "Clienteling: Retailers Get Up Close and Personal with Customers," *Apparel*, May 2005, pp. 38–42.

36. Kemba J. Dunham, "Beyond Satisfaction," *Wall Street Journal*, October 30, 2006, p. R4.

37. Carmine Gallo, "How Ritz-Carlton Maintains Its Mystique," *BusinessWeek*, February 13, 2007; Peter Sanders, "Takin' Off the Ritz—a Tad," *Wall Street Journal*, June 23, 2006, p. B1; Jagdip Singh, "Performance Productivity and Quality of Frontline Employees in Service Organizations," *Journal*

of Marketing 64 (April 2000), pp. 15–34; Benjamin Schneider, William H. Macey, and Scott A Young, "The Climate for Service: A Review of the Construct with Implications for Achieving CLV Goals," *Journal of Relationship Marketing*, January 2006, p. 111; Mark Wickham and Melissa Parker, "Reconceptualising Organisational Role Theory for Contemporary Organisational Contexts," *Journal of Managerial Psychology* 22 (July 2007), pp. 440–464.

38. "Customers Seek Self-Service Alternatives," *nacsonline.com*, January 25, 2007.

39. A. Parasuraman, Valarie A. Zeithaml, and Leonard L. Berry, "Alternative Scales for Measuring Service Quality: A Comparative Assessment Based on Psychometric and Diagnostic Criteria," *Journal of Retailing* 70 (Autumn 1994), pp. 201–230; Evangelos Grigoroudis and Yannis Siskos, *Customer Satisfaction Evaluation: Methods for Measuring and Implementing Service Quality* (New York: Springer, 2009); Samar I. Swaid and Rolf T. Wigand, "Measuring the Quality of E-Service: Scale Development and Initial Validation," *Journal of Electronic Commerce Research* 10, no. 1 (2009), pp. 13–24.

40. Emily Le Coz, "Mystery Shoppers Help Businesses Improve Customer Service," *Knight Ridder Tribune Business News*, April 25, 2005, p. 1; Adam Finn, "Mystery Shopper Benchmarking of Durable-Goods Chains and Stores," *Journal of Service Research* 3 (May 2001), pp. 310–320.

41. James R. Detert and Ethan R. Burris, "Leadership Behavior and Employee Voice: Is the Door Really Open?" *Academy of Management Journal* 50 (August 2007), pp. 869–884; Gilad Chen, Bradley L. Kirkman, Ruth Kanfer, Don Allen, and Benson Rosen, "A Multilevel Study of Leadership, Empowerment, and Performance in Teams," *Journal of Applied Psychology* 92 (March 2007), p. 331; Adam Rapp, Michael Ahearne, John Mathieu, and Niels Schillewaert, "The Impact of Knowledge and Empowerment on Working Smart and Working Hard: The Moderating Role of Experience," *International Journal of Research in Marketing* 23 (September 2006), pp. 279–293.

42. Jonathan Birchall, "Home Depot Targets Customer Service," *Financial Times*, March 16, 2009.

43. Margery Weinstein, "Satellite Success," *Training*, January–February 2007; Barbara Allan and Dina Lewis, "Virtual Learning Communities as a Vehicle for Workforce Development: A Case Study," *Journal of Workplace Learning* 18 (August 2006), pp. 367–383.

44. Disney Institute and Michael Eisner, *Be Our Guest: Perfecting the Art of Customer Service* (New York: Disney, 2001); Lance A. Bettencourt and Stephen W. Brown, "Role Stressors and Customer-Oriented Boundary-Spanning Behaviors in Service Organizations," *Journal of the Academy of Marketing Science* 31 (Fall 2003), pp. 394–408; Linda L. Price, Eric J. Arnould, and Patrick Tierney, "Going to Extremes: Managing Service Encounters and Assessing Provider Performance," *Journal of Marketing* 59 (April 1995), pp. 83–97; Charles H. Schwepker Jr. and Michael D. Hartline, "Managing the Ethical Climate of Customer-Contact Service Employees," *Journal of Service Research* 7 (May 2005), pp. 377–397.

45. Sheryl Jean, "Seeking the 'Seamless' Shopping Experience," *Star-Telegram*, October 16, 2007.

46. Mark S. Rosenbaum, "Exploring Commercial Friendships from Employees' Perspectives," *Journal of Services Marketing* 23, no. 1 (2009), pp. 57–66; J. Craig Wallace, Bryan D. Edwards, Todd Arnold, M. Lance Frazier, and David M. Finch, "Work Stressors, Role-Based Performance, and the Moderating Influence of Organizational Support," *Journal of Applied Psychology* 94 (January 2009), pp. 254–262; Alison M.

Dean and Al Rainnie, "Frontline Employees' Views on Organizational Factors That Affect the Delivery of Service Quality in Call Centers," *Journal of Services Marketing* 23 (2009), pp. 326–337.

47. Hazel-Anne Johnson and Paul Spector, "Service with a Smile: Do Emotional Intelligence, Gender, and Autonomy Moderate the Emotional Labor Process?" *Journal of Occupational Health Psychology*, October 2007, pp. 319–333; Merran Toerien and Celia Kitzinger, "Emotional Labour in Action: Navigating Multiple Involvements in the Beauty Salon," *Sociology*, August 2007, pp. 645–662.

48. Todd Arnold, Karen E. Flaherty, Kevin E. Voss, and John C. Mowen, "Role Stressors and Retail Performance: The Role of Perceived Competitive Climate," *Journal of Retailing* 85 (June 2009), pp. 194–205.

49. Josh Bernoff and Ted Schadler, *Empowered: Unleash Your Employees, Energize Your Customers, and Transform Your Business* (Boston: Harvard Business Press, 2010).

50. Stefan Michel, David Bowen, Robert Johnston, "Making the Most of Customer Complaints," *Wall Street Journal*, September 22, 2008.

51. Jyh-Shen Chiou and Tung-Zong Chang, "The Effect of Management Leadership Style on Marketing Orientation, Service Quality, and Financial Results: A Cross-Cultural Study," *Journal of Global Marketing* '22 (April 2009), pp. 95–107; Graham Bradley and Beverly Sparks, "Customer Reactions to Staff Empowerment: Mediators and Moderators," *Group and Organization Management* 26 (March 2001), pp. 53–68.

52. Joyce Smith, "Positive Customer Service Pays Off Consumer, Loyalty May Take Financial Investment," *Myrtle Beach Sun News*, November 5, 2006.

53. JennAbelson, "Bar-Code Tags, ATM-Style Machines Drive High-Tech Laundry Business," *Boston Globe*, July 3, 2006; www.zoots.com (accessed November 5, 2007).

54. Tammy Joyner, "More Businesses Telling Customers: Do It Yourself," *Atlanta Journal-Constitution*, August 10, 2003, p. B2.

55. Hyun-Joo Lee, Ann E. Fairhurst, and Min-Young Lee, "The Importance of Self-Service Kiosks in Developing Consumers' Retail Patronage Intentions," *Managing Service Quality* 19, no. 6 (2009), pp. 687–701.

56. Antoinette Alexander, "Sephora Debuts Touch-Screen Scentsa Fragrance Locator," *Drugstore News*, June 20, 2008.

57. Erica Ogg, "HP Developing Shopping Kiosks of the Future," *silicon.com*, May 30, 2007.

58. www.stopandshop.com/stores/shopping_buddy.htm (accessed November 7, 2009); Shia Kapos, "High-Tech Shopping Lists Guide Grocery Shoppers," *Chicago Tribune*, June 20, 2005, p. C1.

59. Bert Weijters, Devarajan Rangarajan, Tomas Falk, and Niels Schillewaert, "Determinants and Outcomes of Customers' Use of Self-Service Technology in a Retail Setting," *Journal of Service Research* 10 (August 2007), pp. 3–21; Daniel Nilsson,

"A Cross-Cultural Comparison of Self-Service Technology Use," *European Journal of Marketing* 41 (March 2007), pp. 367–381; Alex Kuczynski, "A Weapon of Self-Destruction for Buyers," *New York Times*, March 23, 2006.

60. Stefan Michel, David Bowen, and Robert Johnston, "Making the Most of Customer Complaints," *Wall Street Journal*, September 22, 2008.

61. Chihyung Ok, Ki-Joon Back, and Carol W Shanklin, "Mixed Findings on the Service Recovery Paradox," *Service Industries Journal* 27 (September 2007), p. 671; Celso Augusto de Matos, Jorge Luiz Henrique, and Carlos Alberto Vargas Rossi, "Service Recovery Paradox: A Meta-Analysis," *Journal of Service Research* 10 (August 2007), pp. 60–77; Ringberg, Odekerken-Schröder, and Christensen, "A Cultural Models Approach to Service Recovery"; Mahesh S. Bhandari, Yelena Tsarenko, and Michael Jay Polonsky, "A Proposed Multi-Dimensional Approach to Evaluating Service Recovery," *Journal of Services Marketing* 21 (April 2007), pp. 174–185; James G. Maxham III and Richard G. Netemeyer, "A Longitudinal Study of Complaining Customers' Evaluations of Multiple Service Failures and Recovery Efforts," *Journal of Marketing* 66 (October 2002), pp. 57–71.

62. Hui Liao, "Do It Right This Time: The Role of Employee Service Recovery Performance in Customer-Perceived Justice and Customer Loyalty after Service Failures," *Journal of Applied Psychology* 92 (March 2007), p. 475; Kate L. Reynolds and Lloyd C. Harris, "When Service Failure Is Not Service Failure: An Exploration of the Forms and Motives of 'Illegitimate' Customer Complaining," *Journal of Services Marketing* 19 (July 2005), pp. 321–335; Gillian Naylor, "The Complaining Customer: A Service Provider's Best Friend?" *Journal of Consumer Satisfaction, Dissatisfaction and Complaining Behavior* 16 (January 2003), pp. 241–248.

63. Anthony W. Ulwick and Lance A. Bettencourt, "Giving Customers a Fair Hearing," *Sloan Management Review*, Spring 2008, pp. 14–22; Betsy Bugg Holloway, Sijun Wang, and Janet Turner Parish, "The Role of Cumulative Online Purchasing Experience in Service Recovery Management," *Journal of Interactive Marketing* 19 (July 2005), pp. 54–66; Anna S. Mattila and Paul G. Patterson, "Service Recovery and Fairness Perceptions in Collectivist and Individualist Contexts," *Journal of Service Research* 6 (May 2004), pp. 336–346.

64. Seokhwa Yun, Riki Takeuchi, and Wei Liu, "Employee Self-Enhancement Motives and Job Performance Behaviors: Investigating the Moderating Effects of Employee Role Ambiguity and Managerial Perceptions of Employee Commitment," *Journal of Applied Psychology* 92 (May 2007), p. 745; Ringberg, Odekerken-Schröder, and Christensen, "A Cultural Models Approach to Service Recovery"; Amy K. Smith, Ruth N. Bolton, and Janet Wagner, "A Model of Customer Satisfaction with Service Encounters Involving Failure and Recover," *Journal of Marketing Research* 36 (August 1999), pp. 356–372.

PHOTO CREDITS

Want an online, **searchable version** of your textbook?

Wish your textbook could be **available online** while you're doing your assignments?

Connect™ Plus Marketing eBook

If you choose to use *Connect™ Plus Marketing*, you have an affordable and searchable online version of your book integrated with your other online tools.

Connect™ Plus Marketing eBook offers features like:

- Topic search
- Direct links from assignments
- Adjustable text size
- Jump to page number
- Print by section

Want to get more **value** from your textbook purchase?

Think learning marketing should be a bit more **interesting**?

Check out the STUDENT RESOURCES section under the *Connect™* Library tab.

Here you'll find a wealth of resources designed to help you achieve your goals in the course. You'll find things like **quizzes, PowerPoints, and Internet activities** to help you study. Every student has different needs, so explore the STUDENT RESOURCES to find the materials best suited to you.

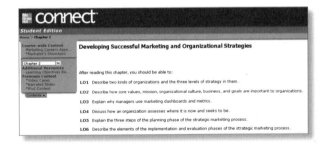

STUDENTS...

Want to get **better grades?** *(Who doesn't?)*

Ready to do **online interactive assignments** that help you apply what you've learned? *(You need to know how to use this stuff in the real world...)*

Need **new ways** to study before the big test? *(A little peace of mind is a good thing...)*

With **McGraw-Hill's *Connect*™ *Plus Marketing*,**

STUDENTS GET:

- **Interactive, engaging** content.

- Interactive Applications – chapter assignments that help you **APPLY** what you've learned in the course.

- **Immediate feedback** on how you're doing. (No more wishing you could call your instructor at 1 a.m.)

- **Quick access** to lectures, practice materials, eBook, and more. (All the material you need to be successful is right at your fingertips.)

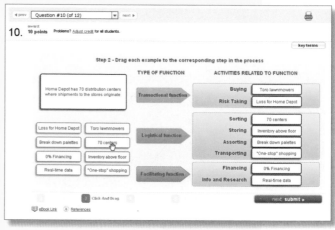